Karl Baedeker

The Eastern Alps

Karl Baedeker

The Eastern Alps

ISBN/EAN: 9783741149283

Manufactured in Europe, USA, Canada, Australia, Japa

Cover: Foto ©Andreas Hilbeck / pixelio.de

Manufactured and distributed by brebook publishing software (www.brebook.com)

Karl Baedeker

The Eastern Alps

THE
EASTERN ALPS.

MONEY-TABLE.
(Comp. p. xi.)

Approximate Equivalents.

American Money		English Money.			French Money		German Money		Austrian Money. *(comp. p. xi)*	
Doll.	Cts.	L.	S.	D.	Fr.	Cts.	ℳ	Pf.	Fl.	Kr.
—	1	—	—	½	—	5	—	4	—	2½
—	2½	—	—	1¼	—	12½	—	10	—	6
—	5	—	—	2½	—	25	—	20	—	12
—	10	—	—	5	—	50	—	40	—	24
—	12½	—	—	6¼	—	62½	—	50	—	30
—	20	—	—	9¾	1	—	—	80	—	48
—	25	—	1	—	1	25	1	—	—	60
—	50	—	2	—	2	50	2	—	1	20
—	75	—	3	—	3	75	3	—	1	80
1	—	—	4	—	5	—	4	—	2	40
1	25	—	5	—	6	25	5	—	3	—
1	50	—	6	—	7	50	6	—	3	60
1	75	—	7	—	8	75	7	—	4	20
2	—	—	8	—	10	—	8	—	4	80
2	25	—	9	—	11	25	9	—	5	40
2	50	—	10	—	12	50	10	—	6	—
3	—	—	12	—	15	—	12	—	7	20
4	—	—	16	—	20	—	16	—	9	60
5	—	1	—	—	25	—	20	—	12	—
25	—	5	—	—	125	—	100	—	60	—
125	—	25	—	—	625	—	500	—	300	—

THE
EASTERN ALPS,

INCLUDING

THE BAVARIAN HIGHLANDS, TYROL, SALZKAMMERGUT,

STYRIA, CARINTHIA, CARNIOLA, AND ISTRIA.

HANDBOOK FOR TRAVELLERS

BY

K. BAEDEKER.

WITH 31 MAPS, 9 PLANS, AND 7 PANORAMAS.

SIXTH EDITION, REMODELLED AND AUGMENTED.

LEIPSIC: KARL BAEDEKER, PUBLISHER.
LONDON: DULAU AND CO., 37 SOHO SQUARE, W.

1888.

All rights reserved.

"Go, little book, God send thee good passage,
And specially let this be thy prayere
Unto them all that thee will read or hear,
Where thou art wrong, after their help to call,
Thee to correct in any part or all."

PREFACE.

The object of the Handbook to the Eastern Alps is to describe all that is best worth seeing, to assist the traveller in planning his tour and disposing of his time to the best advantage, and thus to enable him the more thoroughly to enjoy the magnificent scenery of one of the most interesting regions in Europe.

The districts described in this Handbook were formerly embraced in the Handbook for Southern Germany and Austria, which is now for the third time published in two separate volumes. The information in the present volume, which corresponds with the twenty-third German edition, is, however, much fuller than that contained in the corresponding part of the older Handbook. The Eastern Alps have been repeatedly visited by the Editor within the last few years for the purpose of obtaining the most recent and trustworthy information; but, as many of the data in the Handbook relate to matters which are constantly undergoing alteration, he will highly appreciate any corrections or suggestions with which travellers may favour him. Those already received, which in many instances have proved most useful, he gratefully acknowledges.

The contents of the Handbook are divided into EIGHT SECTIONS (1. S. Bavaria; 2. Salzburg and Salzkammergut; 3. Gisela Railway and Hohe Tauern; 4. N.E. Tyrol and Zillerthal; 5. N.W. Tyrol, the Brenner Railway, and the Oetzthal; 6. S.W. Tyrol; 7. S.E. Tyrol, Pusterthal, and the Dolomites; 8. Alps of Upper and Lower Austria, Styria, Carinthia, Carniola, and Küstenland), each of which may be separately removed from the book by the mountaineer or pedestrian who desires to minimise the bulk of his luggage. To each section is prefixed a list of the routes it contains, so that each forms an approximately complete volume apart from the general table of contents.

The MAPS and PLANS, on which the utmost care has been bestowed, will, it is hoped, render the traveller hardly less material service than the letter-press.

The TIME TABLES contained in 'Hendschel's Telegraph', published at Frankfort on the Main, and issued monthly in summer, and in the '*Reichs-Kursbuch*', published at Berlin, and issued eight times a year, will be found satisfactory. The best Austrian publications of the kind are '*Waldheim's Conducteur*' and *Jacob's Eisenbahnführer*, which appear at Vienna monthly (price 50 kr.).

DISTANCES by railway and road are given approximately in English miles, and in the case of mountain-excursions they are expressed by the time in which they are usually walked. HEIGHTS are given in accordance with the new Austrian Ordnance Survey, or from other recent authorities (reduced to Engl. feet; 1 Engl. ft. = 0.3048 mètre). The POPULATIONS are those ascertained by the latest census.

HOTELS. The Editor has endeavoured to enumerate, not only the first-class hotels, but others of a less pretending kind, which may be safely selected by the 'voyageur en garçon', with little sacrifice of comfort, and great saving of expenditure. Hotel-charges, as well as carriage-fares and fees to guides, are stated in the Handbook, either in accordance with the personal experience of the Editor, or from information furnished by numerous travellers. They are of course liable to frequent variation, and generally have an upward tendency; but those mentioned in the following pages will at least afford the traveller an idea of his probable expenditure.

To hotel-keepers, tradesmen, and others, the Editor begs to intimate that a character for fair dealing towards travellers forms the sole passport to his commendation, and that advertisements of every kind are strictly excluded from his Handbooks.

CONTENTS.

	Page
I. Language. Money	xi
II. Passports. Custom Houses	xi
III. Plan of Tour. Season of the Year. Companions. Scenery. Headquarters	xii
IV. Walking Tours. Guides	xiv
V. Conveyances	xvii
VI. Maps	xix
VII. Hotels	xix
VIII. Vocabulary of Alpine Terms	xx
Abbreviations	xxii

I. S. Bavaria.

Route
1. From Munich to Lindau 3
2. From Immenstadt to Oberstdorf. The Algäu Alps 7
3. From Augsburg to Füssen (Hohenschwangau) and to Imst viâ Lermoos 14
4. From Immenstadt to Reutte and Partenkirchen 20
5. The Starnberger See and Ammersee. The Hohe Peissenberg 24
6. From Munich to Partenkirchen and to Zirl viâ Mittenwald 27
7. From Munich to Mittenwald viâ Benediktbenern. Kochel-see and Walchensee 37
8. From Munich to Tölz and Mittenwald 40
9. From Munich to Innsbruck viâ Tegernsee, Wildbad Krent, and the Achensee 43
10. From Munich to Kufstein viâ Schliersee and Bairisch-Zell 49
11. From Munich to Salzburg. Chiemsee 52
12. From Munich to Reit im Winkel and Kössen 56

II. Salzburg and Salzkammergut.

13. Salzburg and Environs 60
14. From Salzburg to Berchtesgaden. Königs-See. From Berchtesgaden to Reichenhall and Saalfelden 68
15. From Salzburg to Reichenhall 79
16. From Salzburg to Hallein and Golling 83
17. From Linz to Salzburg 86
18. From Salzburg to Ischl and Aussee. Salzkammergut 88
19. From Ischl to Hallstatt, and to Abtenau and Golling viâ Gosau 98

CONTENTS.

Route | Page
20. From Ischl to Salzburg viâ St. Gilgen. Schafberg 103
21. The Attersee and Mondsee 108

III. The Gisela Railway. The Hohe Tauern.

22. From Salzburg to Wörgl. 112
23. The Gastein Valley 120
24. The Rauris 126
25. The Fuscher Thal. From Ferleiten to Heiligenblut. . . 128
26. The Kaprun Valley 132
27. From Zell am See to Krimml. Upper Pinzgau . . . 134
28. From Lienz to Windisch-Matrei and Prägraten. The Iselthal 138
29. From Windisch-Matrei to Kals and Heiligenblut . . . 145
30. From Lienz to Heiligenblut 148

IV. North-Eastern Tyrol. The Zillerthal Alps.

31. From Munich to Innsbruck viâ Rosenheim and Kufstein 156
32. Innsbruck and Environs 161
33. From Wörgl to Mittersill. Hohe Salve 171
34. From Wörgl to Reichenhall viâ Lofer 175
35. The Zillerthal 178
36. The Ahrnthal 188

V. North-Western Tyrol. Brenner Railway. The Oetzthal Alps.

37. From Bregenz to Landeck. The Arlberg Railway . . . 195
38. From Bregenz to the Schrecken. The Bregenzer Wald . 206
39. From Reutte to the Arlberg through the Upper Lechthal 210
40. The Montavon and Patznaun Valleys 212
41. From Innsbruck to Botzen by the Brenner 219
42. The Stubaithal 227
43. From Innsbruck to Landeck 231
44. The Oetzthal 235
45. The Pitzthal 245
46. From Landeck to Meran. Finstermünz 246
47. The Passeierthal 253

VI. South-Western Tyrol.

48. Botzen and Environs 256
49. From Botzen to Meran 268
50. From Eyrs (Landeck, Meran) to Colico on the Lake of Como. Stelvio Pass 276
51. The Martellthal 286
52. The Suldenthal 287
53. From Botzen to Verona 293
54. From Trent to Riva, Lago di Garda 296

Route	Page
55. The Val Sacra. Giudicaria	303
56. From S. Michele to Tirano in the Val Tellina. Val di Non. Val di Sole. Tonale Pass. Passo d'Aprica. Val Camonica	309

VII. South-Eastern Tyrol. Pusterthal and the Dolomites.

57. From Trent to Bassano (and Venice) through the Val Sugana	316
58. The Valley of the Avisio (Fiemme and Fassa Valleys)	320
59. From Predazzo to Primiero	324
60. From Franzensfeste to Villach. Pusterthal	327
61. From Bruneck to Taufers. Reinthal	337
62. The Enneberg Valley or Gaderthal	340
63. From Toblach to Belluno. Val Ampezzo	344
64. From Cortina to Belluno viâ Agordo. Cordevole Valley	355

VIII. Alps of Upper and Lower Austria. Styria. Carinthia. Carniola. Küstenland.

65. From Vienna to Gratz	361
66. From Mürzzuschlag to Mariazell and Bruck on the Mur	370
67. From Mariazell to Gross-Reifling viâ Weichselboden and Wildalpen	376
68. From Vienna to Linz	379
69. From Linz to St. Michael viâ Steyr	383
70. From Linz to Lietzen viâ Kirchdorf and Windisch-Garsten. Stoder	389
71. From Selzthal to Aussee and Bischofshofen	392
72. From Radstadt to Spital over the Radstädter Tauern	397
73. Gratz and Environs	400
74. From Gratz to Trieste	405
75. From Marburg to Villach	414
76. From Bruck to Villach	424
77. From Laibach to Villach	429
78. From Villach to Udine. Pontebba Railway	433
79. Trieste and Environs	437
80. From Trieste to Villach viâ the Predil	441
81. From Trieste to Pola and Fiume	444
Index	447

Maps.

1. S. BAVARIA AND THE EASTERN ALPS, from the Splügen to Vienna: before the Title-page.
2. The ALGÄU ALPS AND BREGENZER WALD: between pp. 8, 9.
3. The ENVIRONS OF FÜSSEN, REUTTE, NASSEREIT, TELFS, MITTENWALD, PARTENKIRCHEN, AND WALCHENSEE: between pp. 14, 15.
4. The STARNBERGER SEE AND THE AMMERSEE: between pp. 24, 25.
5. The ENVIRONS OF TÖLZ, TEGERNSEE, AND SCHLIERSEE (from the STARNBERGER-SEE and WALCHENSEE to the INNTHAL): between pp. 40, 41.

MAPS AND PLANS.

6. The Environs of the Achensee, the Valley of the Inn from Innsbruck to Wörgl, and the Lower Zillerthal: between pp. 46, 47.
7. The Environs of Rosenheim, Kufstein, Traunstein, and Lofer (the Chiemsee and Achenthal): between pp. 52, 53.
8. The Environs of Salzburg, Reichenhall, Berchtesgaden and the Königssee, Hallein and Golling, the Schafberg and the St. Wolfgang-See between pp. 68, 69.
9. The N. Salzkammergut (Gmunden, Ischl, Hallstatt): between pp. 88, 89.
10. The S. Salzkammergut (Environs of Aussee and the Dachstein) between pp. 96, 97.
11. The Königssee and its Environs, Salzachthal, and Saalachthal (Pongau and Pinzgau): between pp. 112, 113.
12. The Gastein and Rauris Valleys: between pp. 120, 121.
13. The Gross-Venediger District: between pp. 140, 141.
14. The Gross-Glockner District: between pp. 144, 145.
15. The Environs of Innsbruck: between pp. 160, 161.
16. The Environs of Wörgl and Kitzbühel: between pp. 172, 173.
17. The Zillerthal: between pp. 178, 179.
18. The Vorarlberg: between pp. 194, 195.
19. The Montavon and Prättigau between pp. 212, 213.
20. The Stanzerthal and the Patznaunthal, from the Arlberg to Finstermünz between pp. 216, 217.
21. The Stubaithal, Selrainthal, Lower Oetzthal, and Pitzthal: between pp. 226, 227.
22. The Inner Oetzthal: between pp. 238, 239.
23. The Upper Innthal, the Oetzthal Alps, and the Vintschgau: between pp. 246, 247.
24. The Ortler District: between pp. 288, 289.
25. The Lago di Garda: between pp. 300, 301.
26. The Adamello, Presanella, and Brenta Alps, the Val di Non, Val di Sole, and the Valley of the Adige, from Botzen to Rovereto: between pp. 304, 305.
27. The Dolomite Alps, from Botzen to Auronzo and Belluno: between pp. 320, 321.
28. The Carinthian Alps, from Lienz to the Wörther See: between pp. 334, 335.
29. The Ampezzo Valley: between pp. 348, 349.
30. The Styrian and Austrian Alps, from Aussee to the Hochschwab: between pp. 384, 385.
31. The Karawanken and Sannthal Alps: between pp. 408, 409.
32. The Styrian and Carinthian Alps, from Murau to Gratz: between pp. 424, 425.
33. The Environs of Trieste: between pp. 436, 437.
34. Key Map of the Eastern Alps, after the Index.

Panoramas.

1. From the Gaisberg, near Salzburg, between pp. 66, 67.
2. " - Schafberg, near Ischl, pp. 104, 105.
3. " - Schmittenhöhe, between pp. 118, 119.
4. " - Kals-Matreier Thörl, p. 145.
5. " - Hohe Salve, between pp. 170, 171.
6. " - Kitzbühler Horn, p. 173.
7. " - Hintere Schöntaufspitze, p. 290.

Plans of Towns.

Botzen (p. 256), Gastein (p. 121), Gmunden (p. 88), Gratz (p. 400), Innsbruck (p. 160), Ischl (p. 89), Meran (p. 271), Salzburg (p. 60), Trieste (p. 436).

INTRODUCTION.

I. Language. Money.

LANGUAGE. For travellers purposing to explore the remoter parts of the Eastern Alps, a slight acquaintance with German is very desirable; but those who do not deviate from the beaten track will generally find that English or French is spoken at the principal hotels and the usual public resorts.

MONEY. The Austrian monetary unit is the *Florin* = 100 *Kreuzers;* and the paper florin, silver pieces of 10 and 20 kr., and copper pieces of 1 and 4 kr. are in most common circulation. Nominally the florin is the equivalent of 2*s*. (50 cents), and the gold coins (8 fl. and 4 fl.), which are rare, approximately attain this value. In all ordinary reckoning, however, the traveller will only have to deal with the paper or silver currency, in which the average value of a florin is about 1*s*. 8*d*. (2 francs). Thus the average rate of exchange for a sovereign (or a German gold piece of 20 marks) is 12-13 fl., and for a Napoleon 10 fl. Those who desire to convert considerable sums into Austrian notes should be careful to employ respectable bankers or money-changers; and they will effect the exchange to better advantage in the principal towns of Austria itself than at Munich or other towns in Southern Germany. Those who travel with large sums should be provided with circular notes (of 10*l*. each, issued by the London and other bankers), in preference to banknotes or gold, the value of the former being recoverable in case of loss.

The cost of a tour among the Alps of Bavaria and Tyrol depends of course on a great variety of circumstances; but, as a rule, travelling in S. Germany and among the Austrian mountains is less expensive than in most other parts of Europe. The pedestrian of moderate requirements, and tolerably proficient in the language, may, by avoiding the beaten track as much as possible, succeed in limiting his expenditure to 6-8*s*. per diem; but the traveller who prefers driving to walking, frequents hotels of the highest class, and requires the services of guides and commissionnaires, must be prepared to expend at least 25-30*s*. daily.

II. Passports and Custom Houses.

PASSPORTS are not absolutely necessary in Austria or in Germany; but they are sometimes called for in order to prove the identity of the traveller, they are not unfrequently serviceable in procuring admission to collections, and they must be presented at the post-office before the traveller can obtain delivery of registered letters. Travellers who expect to enter Germany from France through Alsace should have their passports visé'd by the German ambassador in London or Paris (fee 10s.). The following are the principal passport-agents in London: Lee and Carter, 440 West Strand; Dorrel and Son, 15 Charing Cross; E. Stanford, 55 Charing Cross; W. J. Adams, 59 Fleet Street.

CUSTOM-HOUSE formalities are now almost everywhere lenient. As a rule, however, articles purchased during the journey, which are not destined for personal use, should be declared at the frontier. At the Austrian frontier playing-cards, almanacks, and sealed letters are liable to confiscation. Tobacco and cigars, the sale of which in Austria is a monopoly of government, are liable to a duty of about 6 fl. per pound. According to the strict rule, one ounce of tobacco and 10 cigars only are exempt from duty. The keys should be sent along with all luggage forwarded in advance.

III. Plan of Tour.
Season of the Year. Companions. Scenery. Headquarters.

PLAN. The traveller will effect a considerable saving of time and money by carefully preparing his plan for a tour before starting. The following pages will enable him to ascertain how each day and even hour may be most advantageously employed, provided of course the weather be favourable.

SEASON. The best season for a visit to the mountains of S. Germany and Austria is from the middle of July to the middle of September; for excursions among the higher Alps, the month of August. In these lofty regions snow occasionally falls in the height of summer, rendering the paths impassable, but such an occurrence is exceptional. The lower Alps and the lakes may, however, be visited as early as the end of May, when the waterfalls moreover are seen in perfection. The southern districts of Tyrol should not be explored until late in autumn, as the heat in summer is unfavourable for walking excursions. Autumn is, moreover, the season for grapes, peaches, figs, and other fruits, which are plentiful in S. Tyrol.

COMPANIONS. A party of two travellers can always be accommodated in a light conveyance, or in the same room at an inn, while a third would often be found 'de trop'. The larger the party, the greater, as a rule, is the inconvenience, as well as the certainty that many of the true objects of travel will be sacrificed. The single traveller, on the other hand, who has attained some proficiency in the language of the country, will of course more speedily become acquainted with the people and their characteristics, and more readily derive instruction from his tour.

SCENERY. The following places in S. Bavaria and the Austrian Alps are recommended to lovers of the picturesque: —

PLAN OF TOUR. xiii

IN THE BAVARIAN OBERLAND: The Starnberger See (p. 24), the Hohe Peissenberg (p. 26), the Walchensee (p. 38), the Herzogstand (p. 38), Hinterriss (p. 48), the Tegernsee (p. 44), the Schliersee (p. 50), the Wendelstein (p. 51), the Chiemsee (p. 53), Reichenhall (p. 79), Berchtesgaden (p. 69), the Königssee (p. 73), Partenkirchen (p. 29), Hohenschwangau (p. 15), Linderhof (p. 23), and Oberstdorf (p. 8).

SALZBURG AND THE SALZKAMMERGUT: Salzburg (p. 60), the Gaisberg (p. 66), Golling (Schwarzbach Fall, p. 84; Aubach Fall, p. 86; Salzachöfen p. 85; Lammeröfen p. 103), the Liechtensteinklamm (p. 114), the Kitzlochklamm (p. 118), Gastein (p. 121), Ferleiten (p. 129), Zell am See (p. 116), the Schmittenhöhe (p. 117), Kaprun (Mooserboden, p. 132), Krimml (p. 137), the Seisenbergklamm (p. 78), the Vorderkaserklamm (p. 177), the Schwarzbergklamm (p. 177), Gmunden (p. 88) and the Traunsee (p. 90), Ischl (p. 92), the Schafberg (103), Hallstatt (p. 98), Gosau (p. 100), and the Zwiesel Alp (p. 101).

NORTH TYROL AND THE VORARLBERG: Kufstein (p. 157; Thierberg, Kaiserthal), the Hohe Salve (p. 177), the Kitzbühler Horn (p. 174), the Zillerthal (Dornaubergklamm, p. 184; Schwarzensteingrund, p. 185), the Achensee (p. 47), Innsbruck (p. 161), the Stubaithal (Bildstöckljoch, p. 230), the Oetzthal (Stuiben Fall, p. 236; Gurgl, p. 213; Ramoljoch. p. 214), Mittelberg in the Pitzthal (p. 245), the Fern Pass (p. 19), Landeck (p. 234), Finstermünz (p. 249), the Arlberg Railway (p. 195), Schruns (p. 213), the Lünersee and Seesaplana (p. 201), Bregenz (p. 195), and the Pfänder (p. 196).

CENTRAL AND SOUTH TYROL: The Brenner Railway (p. 219), Bozen (p. 256) and its environs (Klobenstein, p. 259; Schlern, p. 265; Mendel, p. 267), Meran (p. 269), the Stelvio Pass (Trafoi, p. 277; Piz Umbrail, p. 280; Bormio, p. 282), Sulden (Schöntaufspitze, p. 289; Cevedale, p. 289; Ortler p. 291), Martell (Zufall Hut, p. 286), Riva (p. 298), the Lago di Garda (p. 300), the Val di Genova (p. 306), Madonna di Campiglio (p. 305), the Val Fassa (Vigo, p. 322; Sella Pass, p. 264; Fedaja Pass, p. 323), the Primiero Valley (p. 326), Agordo (p. 358), Caprile (p. 356), Buncck (p. 328), Taufers (p. 338), the valley of Prags (p. 330), Schluderbach (p. 345), Cortina (p. 348), Pieve di Cadore (p 352), Sexten (Fischeleinboden, p. 333), Lienz (p. 334), Windisch-Matrei (Gschlöss, p. 140; Venediger, p. 140), the Kaiser Thörl (p. 145), and Kals (Gross-Glockner, p. 146).

LOWER AND UPPER AUSTRIA AND STYRIA: The Semmering Railway (p. 364), the Höllenthal (p. 365), the Schneeberg (p. 365), the Raxalp (p. 366), Mürzzuschlag (p. 368), Mariazell (p. 372), Weichselboden (p. 376), Wildalpen (p. 377), the Hochschwab (p. 376), the Oetscher (p. 384), Linz (p. 382), Waidhofen an der Ybbs (p. 381), Steyr (p. 383), Eisenerz (p. 385), the Gesäuse (Gstatterboden, p. 386), Johnsbachthal, p. 387), Admont (p. 387), Windisch-Garsten (p. 391), Stoder (p. 391), the Aussee (Grundlsee, Toplitzsee, p. 97), Schladming (Ramsau, p. 395), and Gratz (p. 400).

CARINTHIA AND CARNIOLA: Villach (Dobratsch p. 422), the Wörther See (p. 421), Eisenkappel (p. 417), Sulzbach (p. 408), Adelsberg (p. 411), St. Canzian (p. 413), Veldes (p. 429), Wochein (p. 430), Tarvis (p. 433), Raibl (p. 413), the Pontebba Railway (p. 435), Millstatt (p. 386), the Maltathal (p. 399), and Heiligenblut (p. 150).

HEADQUARTERS. The selection of convenient and comfortable headquarters, from which excursions and rambles may be made, is a matter of considerable importance to those who desire to make more than a merely superficial acquaintance with the country. Among the spots adapted for this purpose, the following may be specially mentioned: —

IN SOUTH BAVARIA: Tegernsee (2400'; p. 44); Schliersee (2588'; p. 50); Partenkirchen and Garmisch (2300'; p. 29); Barmsee (3070'; p. 35); Mittenwald (3000'; p. 34); Hohenschwangau (2930'; p. 15); Oberstdorf (2666', p. 8); Hinterstein (2825'; p. 21); Braunenburg (1660'; p. 156); Prien (1745'; p. 53); Niederaschau (2020'; p. 54); Reit im Winkel (2240'; p. 56); Berchtesgaden (1890'; p. 69).

SALZBURG AND THE SALZKAMMERGUT: Gmunden (1305'; p. 88); Ischl (1535'; p. 92); Goisern (1640'; p. 95); Hallstatt (1620'; p. 98); St. Wolfgang

(1800'; p. 105); Mondsee (1570'; p. 110); Kammer, Attersee, Weissenbach, Unterach on the Attersee (1525'; p. 109); Golling (1440'; p. 84); St. Johann im Pongau (1345'; p. 114); Zell am See (2475'; p. 116); Lofer (2093'; p. 176); Unken (1880'; p. 177); Bad Fusch (3750'; p. 129).

VORARLBERG AND NORTH TYROL: Bregenz (1290'; p. 195); Schwarzenberg (2275'; p. 207); Schruns (2250'; p. 213); Gaschurn (3120'; p. 215); Kitzbühel (2420'; p. 174); Waidring (2560'; p. 176); Kufstein (1800'; p. 157); Brixlegg (1680'; p. 159); Jenbach (2325'; p. 159); Achensee-Pertisau (3050'; p. 47); Mairhofen in the Zillerthal (3095'; p. 181); Igls (2900'; p. 170); Kühtai (6460'; p. 231); Seefeld (3860'; p. 37); Telfs (2045'; p. 233); Imst (2345'; p. 234); Oetz (2690'; p. 236); Landeck (2670'; p. 234).

CENTRAL AND SOUTH TYROL: Steinach (3430'; p. 220), Gries (1100'; p. 221), Brennerbad (4350'; p. 227), Gossensass (3480'; p. 222), and Sterzing (3105'; p. 222), on the Brenner Railway; Mühlbach (2540'; p. 323), Brunek (2670'; p. 328), Taufers (2830'; p. 338), St. Vigil (3900'; p. 310), Alt-Prags (4520'; p. 330), Niederdorf (3800'; p. 331), Toblach (3950'; p. 331), Höhlenstein (4615'; p. 344), Schluderbach (4750'; p. 345), Cortina (3970'; p. 348), Innichen (3825'; p. 332), Innicher Wildbad (4370'; p. 332), Sexten St. Veit (4300'; p. 332), Lienz (2190'; p. 334), in the Pusterthal; Sarnthein (3200'; p. 260); Klobenstein on the Ritten (3765'; p. 259); St. Ulrich in Gröden (3345'; p. 263); Bad Ratzes (3930'; p. 265); Trafoi (5080'; p. 277); Franzensböhe (7160'; p. 279); Sulden (6055'; p. 288); Bormio Bad (1395'; p. 284); S. Caterina (5700'; p. 2 2); Pinzolo (2475'; p. 305); Madonna di Campiglio (2550'; p. 305); S. Martino di Castrozza (4800'; p. 325).

LOWER AND UPPER AUSTRIA, STYRIA, etc.: Reichenau (1600'; p. 364), Semmering Hotel (3255'; p. 367), Mürzzuschlag (2200'; p. 368), on the Semmering Railway; Waidhofen an der Ybbs (1170'; p. 381); Steyr (990'; p. 3 3); Weichselboden (2220'; p. 376); Wildalpen (2000'; p. 377); Gstatterboden (1850'; p. 386); Admont (2100'; p. 387); Eisenerz (2145'; p. 385); Trofajach (p. 385); Windisch-Garsten (1970'; p. 391); Spital am Pyhrn (2120'; p. 392); Stoder (1920'; p. 391); Aussee (2145'; p. 391); Alt-Aussee (2325'; p. 97) and Grundlsee (2290'; p. 97); Schladming (2400'; p. 394); Gmünd (2400'; p. 398); Millstatt (1900'; p. 330); Eisenkappel (1830'; p. 417); Cilli (700'; p. 407); Veldes (1640'; p. 429); Weissenfels (2690'; p. 432); Tarvis (2110'; p. 438), and Raibl (2925'; p. 442).

IV. Walking Tours. Guides.

The Pedestrian, the most independent of travellers, is generally in the most favourable position for the enjoyment of beautiful scenery.

EQUIPMENT. The greatest drawback to the pleasure of travelling is a superabundance of baggage. To be provided with an actual sufficiency and no more, may be regarded as one of the golden rules for travellers. Who has not experienced a sense of freedom in shouldering his knapsack or wielding his own carpet-bag on quitting a steamboat or railway-station? And who at other times has not felt the misery of being surrounded by his 'impedimenta', and almost distracted by the importunities of porters, touters, and commissionnaires? A light 'gibecière' or 'Reisetasche', such as may be procured in every town, amply suffices to contain all that is necessary for a fortnight's excursion. A change of flannel shirts and worsted stockings, a few pocket-handkerchiefs, a pair of slippers, and a small dressing-case may, after the first few days, be carried with hardly a perceptible increase of fatigue. A piece of brown gauze or coloured spectacles to protect the eyes from the glare of the snow, a pair of stout leather or doeskin gloves, and a leather drinking-cup will also be found useful. For the pedestrian a light Scotch plaid is better than a waterproof. The traveller should of course have a more extensive reserve of clothing, especially if he purposes visiting towns of importance; but it should be contained in a valise of moderate size, which he can easily wield when necessary, and which he may forward from town to town by post.

The traveller who intends to ascend any of the loftier peaks should be provided with a well-tried *Alpenstock*, consisting of a pole of seasoned ash, 5-6 ft. long, shod with a steel point, and strong enough, when placed horizontally, with the ends supported, to bear the whole weight of the body. For the more difficult ascents an *Ice-Axe* and *Rope* are also necessary. These articles can generally be obtained from the guides, but in that case their quality is not so trustworthy as when the climber has selected them for himself. The best rope, light and at the same time strong, is made of silk or Manilla hemp. In crossing a glacier the precaution of using the rope should never be neglected. It should be securely tied round the waist of each member of the party, leaving a length of about 10′ between each one and his follower. Ice-axes are made in various forms, and are usually furnished with a spike at the end of the handle, so that they can in some measure be used like an Alpenstock. — Requisites for Alpine travelling may be obtained in London from *Carter*, 295 Oxford Street, or from *Adams & Sons*, 59 Fleet Street.

Rules. The enthusiastic traveller should curb his ardour at the outset of his excursion, and begin by moderate performances, as the overtaxing of his strength on a single occasion will sometimes incapacitate him altogether for several days. It often requires discrimination to determine what degree of fatigue can be borne with impunity, and when walking should be abandoned for the ease of a carriage; but all these experiences will be acquired without the aid of a guide-book. The first golden rule for the pedestrian is to start on his way betimes in the morning. If strength permits, and a suitable halting-place is to be met with, a two hours' walk may be accomplished before breakfast. At noon a moderate luncheon is preferable to a regular table-d'hôte dinner. Repose should be taken during the hottest hours, and the journey then continued till 5 or 6 p. m., when a substantial meal (evening table-d'hôte at the principal hotels) may be partaken of. When a mountain has to be breasted, the prudent pedestrian will pursue the 'even tenor of his way' with regular and steady steps (*'chi va piano va sano; chi va sano va lontano'*); the novice alone indulges in 'spurts'. If the traveller desires a further maxim for his guidance, it may be, 'When fatigue begins, enjoyment ceases'.

To prevent the feet from blistering during a protracted walking tour, they may be rubbed morning and evening with brandy and tallow. A warm foot-bath with bran will be found soothing after a long day's march. Soaping the inside of the stocking is another well-known safeguard against abrasion of the skin.

Excursions among the higher Alps should not be undertaken before July, nor at any period after a long continuance of rain or snow. Glaciers should, if possible, be traversed before 10 a. m., after which hour the rays of the sun soften the crust of ice formed over the fissures and crevasses during the night. It is hardly necessary to state that *experienced guides* are absolutely indispensable for such excursions.

The cold glacier-water of the higher regions should not be drunk except in small quantities, mixed with wine, cognac, or Kirschwasser. Cold milk is also prejudicial. Experienced mountaineers recommend cold tea as a safe remedy for thirst. Good old wine in small quantities is preferred by others.

Over all the movements of the pedestrian the *Weather* holds despotic sway. Those who claim acquaintance with the elements and their signs will tell him of numberless indications by which either foul or favourable weather may be predicted, and their advice will often be found valuable. The barometer, too, should be consulted when an opportunity offers. Mountain views are generally clearest in the morning or towards evening.

GUIDES. Within the last few years the guides among the S. German and Austrian Alps have greatly improved, chiefly owing to the exertions of the German and Austrian Alpine Club, and a tariff of fixed charges has been introduced at most of their headquarters. Competent guides can now be obtained in almost every part of Tyrol; and some of the Tyrolese guides rank with the best in Switzerland, having occasionally been employed by the most eminent English and German mountaineers for extensive tours beyond the limits of their native districts. The best centres for procuring guides are Sulden, Vent and Gurgl in the Oetzthal, Kals, Prägraten, Heiligenblut, and Cortina. The names of the best-known guides at each place are given in the Handbook, and the charges fixed by tariff for the principal excursions are also mentioned. Each guide is usually bound to carry 15 lbs. weight of luggage. Glacier-expeditions should never be attempted without a guide, except perhaps by a party of adepts. When a glacier is entirely free from snow ('aper') it may generally be traversed in safety by a party of two persons; otherwise the party should consist of three persons at least, all securely roped together. It need hardly be added that the relations between the traveller and his guide should always be pleasant and cordial.

CLUB HUTS. The numerous *Club Huts* erected within the last few years by the German-Austrian Alpine Club and the Austrian Tourist Club have done much to increase the pleasures and decrease the discomforts of the higher ascents. These huts are generally well fitted up, and contain mattresses or hay-beds, woollen coverlets, a small cooking-stove, cooking utensils, plates, and glasses. A small sum, fixed by tariff, is charged for the accommodation afforded. When the traveller purposes spending the night in one of these huts and starting thence for the ascent, he should take a good supply of portable provisions with him (tinned meats, 'Erbswurst', beef-extract, condensed milk, tea and coffee, etc.). The public-spirited German-Austrian Alpine Club, by which most of these huts have been erected, now numbers upwards of 21,000 members, who belong to 160 different Sections, about two-thirds of these being German and the other third Austrian. The usual annual subscription is 10 m., which entitles the subscriber to 24 numbers of the 'Mittheilungen' and to one volume of the 'Zeitschrift', with maps and illustrations. The Austrian Tourist Club (founded in 1869; 14,000 members) and the Austrian Alpine Club (founded in 1878; 800 members) have also done good work in building refuge-huts, improving paths, etc.

The accommodation afforded by the *chalets* of the Alpine herdsmen is generally very inferior to that of the club-huts. Whatever poetry there may be theoretically in a bed of hay, the traveller will find that the cold night-air piercing abundant apertures, the jangling of the cow-bells, and the grunting of the pigs are little conducive to refreshing slumber.

HEALTH. Tincture of arnica is a good remedy for *bruises*, and moreover has a bracing and invigorating effect if rubbed on the limbs after much fatigue; but it should never be applied to broken skin, as it is apt to produce erysipelas. Saturnine ointment or oxide of zinc ointment is beneficial in cases of inflammation of the skin, an inconvenience frequently caused by exposure to the glare of the sun on the snow. Cold cream, and, for the lips especially, vaseline or glycerine, are also recommended.

For *diarrhoea* 15 drops of a mixture of equal parts of tincture of opium and aromatic tincture may be safely taken every two hours until relief is afforded. The homœopathic tincture of camphor (5 drops on a lump of sugar every half-hour or so) is also a good remedy. The homœopathic camphor-globules are convenient, but are more apt to lose their strength.

V. Conveyances.

RAILWAY TRAVELLING in Germany is less expensive than in most other parts of Europe, and the carriages are generally clean and comfortably fitted up; but in Austria the fares are somewhat higher, and the carriages inferior. The second-class carriages, provided with spring-seats, are often better than those of the first class in England. The first-class carriages, lined with velvet, are comparatively little used, but are recommended to the lover of scenery and of fresh air, as he will be more likely to secure a seat next the win-

dow. The third-class travelling community are generally quiet and respectable, and the carriages tolerably clean. On a few railways there is even a fourth class, unprovided with seats. Smoking is allowed in all the carriages, except those 'Für Nichtraucher' and the coupés for ladies. The average fares for the different classes in S. Germany are $1^3/_5d.$, $1^1/_5d.$ and $^4/_5d.$ per Engl. M. respectively, but in Austria they are rather higher. The speed seldom exceeds 25 M. per hour, and as the railways are generally well organised and under the supervision of government, accidents are happily rare. On some lines 20–50 lbs. of luggage are free, in addition to smaller articles carried in the hand. Over-weight is charged for at moderate rates. In all cases the heavier luggage must be booked, and a ticket procured for it; and this being done, the traveller need be under no apprehension, as it will be kept in safe custody at its destination until he presents his ticket. When a frontier has to be crossed the traveller is strongly recommended to keep his luggage with him, and to superintend the custom-house examination in person. If luggage be sent across a frontier by goods-train or diligence the keys must be sent along with it, as otherwise it will be detained at the custom-house; but the pecuniary saving effected by such a course is far outweighed by the risk of vexatious delays, pilferage, and damage, for which it is difficult or impossible to obtain redress.
— Travellers in the Eastern Alps will in many cases be able to avail themselves of the CIRCULAR TICKETS for special tours, issued at all the chief towns of Germany and Austria.

DILIGENCES, called '*Eilwagen*' or '*Mallepostes*' in Austria, generally carry three passengers only, two in the inside, and one in the *coupé*. The latter alone affords a tolerable survey of the scenery, and should if possible be secured. In much-frequented districts it is frequently engaged several days beforehand. The guards, who are often retired non-commissioned officers, are generally well-informed and obliging. The usual quantity of luggage allowed to each passenger by the Eilwagen does not exceed 20lbs., over-weight being charged for by tariff. Passengers are sometimes required to book their luggage two hours before the time of starting, or even on the previous evening. — The old '*Stellwagen*', formerly the chief means of transit in Tyrol, has now been superseded by the more comfortable OMNIBUS. On nearly all the chief routes *Post-Omnibuses* now run, with relays of horses at the different stages. The best places are the cabriolet and the coupé; and travellers should secure their seats in good time.

EXTRA-POST. The usual tariff in Austria for a carriage and pair for four persons with moderate luggage is about 5 fl. per stage of 15 kilomètres ($9^3/_5$ Engl. M.). For a party of four persons posting is cheaper than travelling by diligence, and of course pleasanter. — In engaging PRIVATE CARRIAGES, the stipulation should always be made that the fare includes all tolls.

VI. Maps.

The maps contained in the Handbook will meet the requirements of all ordinary travellers, but the mountaineer and the pedestrian may occasionally desire to consult others on a larger scale.

The best maps on a large scale for the districts treated in the Handbook are the new *Austrian Ordnance Maps* (1 : 75,000; 50 kr. per sheet), of which the sheets issued comprise most of the Bavarian as well as the Austrian Alps. Special sheets of different groups of mountains (such as the Dolomites and the Ortler Alps), prepared from these maps, and printed in colours, will also be found very useful. Other first-class special maps are the following, published by the German-Austrian Alpine Club (scale 1 : 50,000): *Oetzthaler und Stubaier Alpen* (9 sheets, 50 pf. each), *Zillerthaler Alpen* (2 sheets, 2 m. each), *Venediger-Gruppe* (2 m.), *Rieserferner* (50 pf.), *Kaisergebirge* (1 m.), *Berchtesgadener Land* (4 sheets, 2 m. each). — Other useful publications are *Sonklar's Oetzthaler Alpen* (1 : 144,000; pub. by Perthes, Gotha; 4 m.), *Karte der Hohen Tauern* (1 : 144,000; pub. by Hölder, Vienna; 4 m.), and *Karte der Zillerthaler Alpen* (1 : 144,000; 3½ m.); *Payer's Specialkarten der Ortler- und Adamello-Alpen* (1 : 56,000), published in Petermann's 'Ergänzungshefte', Nos. 17, 18, 23, 27, and 31; *Grohmann's Karte der nördtichen Dolomit-Alpen* (1 : 100,000; pub. by the editor, Vienna; 8 m.); *Freytag's Specialkarte der Grossglockner Gruppe* (1 : 40,000; 1 m. 80 pf.); *Meurer & Freytag's Ortleralpen* (1 : 50,000; Vienna, 1 m. 80 pf.); *Pogliaghi, Carta del Gruppo Ortler-Cevedale* (1 : 40,000; Milan, 5 m.); *Freytag's Special Touristenkarten (Schneeberg-Raxalpe, Schneealpe-Veitsch, Hochschwab, Gesäuse* ; 1 : 50,000; Vienna, each 1 fl. 40 kr.); *Reisekarte des Salzkammerguts* (1 : 100,000; 8 m.).

Among maps on a small scale are: *Maschek's Touristenkarte der Oesterreichischen Alpen* (1 : 129,600; 11 sheets, 1 fl. each); *Ravenstein's Karte der Oesterreichisch-Deutschen Alpen* (1 : 250,000; 9 sheets, of which 6 have been published; 5 m. each, mounted 6 m.); *Mayr's Atlas der Alpenländer*, published by Perthes of Gotha (8 sheets, 1 : 450,000; 8 m.); and *Mayr's Karte von Tirol*, sold at Munich (1 : 500,000; mounted, 8 m.; also obtainable in two sheets, N. Tyrol 4 m., S. Tyrol 4 m. 40 pf.).

VII. Hotels.

Little variation occurs in the accommodation and charges of first-class hotels in the principal towns and watering-places throughout Germany and Austria; but it frequently happens that in old-fashioned hotels of unassuming exterior the traveller finds as much real comfort as in the modern establishments, while the charges are much lower. The best houses of both descriptions are therefore enumerated in the Handbook.

Where the traveller remains for a week or more at an hotel, it is advisable to pay, or at least call for his account every two or three days, in order to obviate the risk of erroneous insertions. Verbal reckonings are objectionable. A waiter's mental arithmetic is apt to be faulty, and his mistakes are seldom in favour of the traveller. A habit too often prevails of presenting the bill at the last moment, when no time is left for the detection of errors or wilful impositions. Those who purpose starting early in the morning will do well to ask for their bills on the previous evening.

A peculiarity of many of the Austrian inns is that they have a '*Gastzimmer*' for the humbler classes on the ground-floor, while the '*Salle à Manger*' for more distinguished visitors is on the first floor. The viands and liquors supplied in these apartments are generally the same, while the charges differ considerably. Pedestrians and travellers of moderate requirements will find the country inns in S. Germany and the German parts of Tyrol very reasonable, 5-6s. a day being generally sufficient to include every item. In the Italian districts, however, the charges are higher by about one-half, and larger gratuities are expected by the attendants. Travellers about to explore very remote districts are recommended to take a supply of tea, coffee, or chocolate with them. Where there are no inns, accommodation may generally be obtained at the curé's on reasonable terms.

The *Post Inns* are generally good. Those patronised by the 'Stellwagen' are very inferior, although convenient for persons travelling by those vehicles, especially when encumbered with luggage.

English travellers often impose considerable trouble by ordering things almost unknown in German usage, and are apt to become involved in disputes owing to their ignorance of the language. They should therefore endeavour to learn enough of the language to render them intelligible to the servants, and as far as possible to conform to the habits of the country. For this purpose *Baedeker's* 'Traveller's Manual of Conversation' will be found useful.

Valets-de-place generally charge 1 florin for half a day, and 2 fl. for a whole day.

VIII. Vocabulary of Alpine Terms.

Ach (Ger.), brook, torrent.

Alp (Ger.), a mountain-pasture, usually with a 'Sennhütte' or chalet.

Alpenglühen (Ger.), sunset glow on the mountains.

Arête (Fr.; Ger. *Grat*), a sharp and precipitous ridge, especially that which generally forms the final approach to the summit of a mountain.

Bauer (Ger.), peasant; often applied to a small mountain-farm, as well as to its owner.

Bergschrund (Ger.), a chasm or gulf between the névé, or snow at the head of a glacier, and

VOCABULARY OF ALPINE TERMS.

the snow that remains attached to the rock itself.
Boden (Ger.), the floor or level part of a valley.
Chaise-à-porteurs (Fr.; Ger. *Tragsessel*, Ital. *portantina*), an armchair resting on two poles, and carried like a sedan-chair.
Cheminée (Fr.; Ger. *Kamin*), a narrow and precipitous gully.
Cima (Ital.), summit, peak.
Col (Fr.), a depression in a mountain-ridge, the culminating point of a pass.
Couloir (Fr.), a gully filled with snow.
Crampons (Fr.; Ger. *Steigeisen*), climbing-irons, attached to the feet to facilitate an ascent over hardened snow.
Crevasse (Fr.), a rift or fissure in a glacier.
Ferner (Ger.), glacier, snow-mountain.
Firn (Ger.; Fr. *névé*), the frozen snow on the upper part of a glacier.
Fórcella (Ital., 'little fork'; Fr. *col*), the highest part of a mountain-pass.
Glacier Tables, slabs of rock on a glacier, which protect the ice below them from the influence of the sun, while the surrounding ice dissolves.
Gletscher (Ger.), glacier.
Gletscherschliff (Ger.), glacier-action, striation; also applied to rock striated, polished, or furrowed by glacier-action.
Grat, see *Arête*.
Hof (Ger.), farm-house, hamlet.
Horn (Ger.), peak, sharp summit.
Hütte (Ger.), hut, chalet.
Ice-fall, the extensive fracture in a glacier occasioned by a sudden change of level in its bed.

Joch (Ger., 'yoke'), see *Col*, *Forcella*.
Kamin, see *Cheminée*.
Kees (Ger.), glacier.
Kessel (Ger., 'kettle', 'cauldron'), a mountain-basin.
Klamm (Ger.), a cleft, a gorge.
Klause (Ger.), a defile.
Kofel, *Kogel*, *Kopf* (Ger.), mountain-summit.
Lawine (Ger.), avalanche. The *Staub-Lawine* ('dust-avalanche') is formed of loose, fresh-fallen snow; the *Grund-Lawine*, which occurs in spring, is more compact and consequently more destructive.
Loch (Ger., 'hole'), a cavern, a gorge.
Malga (Ital.), see *Alp*.
Massif (Fr.), a mountain-mass, the solid rock or foundation of a mountain.
Moraine (Fr.), heaps of rock and rubble or detritus at the margin of a glacier. *Lateral Moraines*, those on each side of the ice-stream. *Medial Moraines*, those in the middle of large glaciers formed by the junction of two smaller ones. *Terminal Moraines*, the deposits of rubbish at the foot a glacier.
Moulin (Fr.), a vertical opening in a glacier, with a stream, formed by the melting of the ice on the surface, falling into it.
Mulde (Ger., 'trough'), a hollow or basin in the side of a mountain.
Névé, see *Firn*.
Sasso (Ital.), rock, rocky mountain.
Sattel (Ger.), saddle, depression in a ridge (comp. *Col* and *Joch*).
Scharte (Ger.), gap, pass.

ABBREVIATIONS.

Schrund (Ger.), same as *Crevasse*.
Senner (Ger.), Alpine herdsman.
Sennhütte (Ger.), chalet.
Sérac (Fr.), a mass of snow or ice, particularly a huge square block in a glacier, formed by transverse crevasses.
Spitze (Ger.), a peak, pointed summit.
Stock, Gebirgsstock (Ger.), same as *Massif*.

Tauern (Ger.), the name of the principal chain of the E. Alps, also applied in Tyrol and Styria to the passes over it.
Thor, Thörl (Ger.), the culminating point of a pass; similar to *Joch*.
Tobel (Ger.), a gorge.
Tragsessel (Ger.), see *Chaise-à-porteurs*.
Vedretta (Ital.), a glacier.
Wand (Ger., 'wall'), mountain-slope, precipice.

Abbreviations.

R. = Room.
B. = Breakfast.
D. = Dinner.
A. = Attendance.
L. = Light.

M. = English mile.
N. = North, northern, etc.
S. = South, etc.
E. = East, etc.
W. = West, etc.

HEIGHT in feet is indicated by ' after the figures (2050' = 2050 feet).

DISTANCES. The number placed before the name of a place on a high road, when at the *beginning of a paragraph*, indicates its distance in English miles from the starting-point of the route or sub-route. The distances within the body of the text are reckoned from place to place. In railway-routes the distances invariably refer to the starting-point.

ASTERISKS. Objects of special interest, and hotels which are believed worthy of special commendation, are denoted by asterisks.

I. SOUTHERN BAVARIA.

1. **From Munich to Lindau** 3
   From Kaufering to Landsberg and Schongau, 3. — From Augsburg to Buchloe, 3. — From Kempten to Ulm, 4. — Excursions from Immenstadt, 4. — The Stuiben. Excursions from Oberstaufen, 5. — From Röthenbach to Bregenz viâ Weiler; to the Pfänder viâ Scheidegg, 6. — Excursions from Lindau. Schachenbad, Wasserburg, Hoierberg, 7.

2. **From Immenstadt to Oberstdorf. The Algäu Alps** . 7
   The Grünten, 8. — Excursions from Oberstdorf. Faltenbach Waterfall. Hofmann's Ruhe. Wasach. Tiefenbach. Freibergsee. Zwingsteg and Walser Schänzle. Spielmannsau. Hölltobel. Geisalpsee. Oythal. Birgsau, 8-11. — Mountain Ascents from Oberstdorf. Nebelhorn. Fellhorn. Rauheck. Kreuzeck. Gr. Krottenkopf. Mädelegabel. Biberkopf. Hohe Licht. Linkerskopf. Hohe Ifen, 11, 12. — From Oberstdorf to Holzgau by the Ober-Mädelejoch, and to Elmen over the Hornbachjoch, 12. — Schrofen Pass, 13. — Grosse Steinscharte. Gentscheljoch. Haldenwangereck. From Oberstdorf to Hittisau viâ Rohrmoos, 13.

3. **From Augsburg to Füssen (Hohenschwangau) and to Imst viâ Lermoos** 14
   From Kempten to Füssen, 14. — From Peissenberg to Füssen, 14. — Environs of Hohenschwangau. Neu-Schwanstein, 16. — From Neu-Schwanstein to Linderhof, 17. The Säuling, 17. — The Heiterwang-See, 18. — Seebensee and Drachensee. Grünsteinscharte. Upsberg. Wannig. Zugspitze, 19. — From Nassereit to Telfs, 20.

4. **From Immenstadt to Reutte and Partenkirchen** ... 20
   The Daumen, 20. — Hintersteiner Thal. Eisenbreche. Geishorn. Hochvogel. From Hinterstein to Oberstdorf over the Zeiger or the Himmeleck; to Tannheim over the Schafwanne or the Kirchdacharte, 21. — Vilsalpsee. Traualpsee, 22. — From the Plansee to Ober-Ammergau or to Hohenschwangau by the Graswangthal, 23.

5. **The Starnberger See and Ammersee. The Hohe Peissenberg** 24
   From Peissenberg to Ober-Ammergau, 26. — From Diessen to the Starnberger See or to Grafrath viâ Andechs, 27.

6. **From Munich to Partenkirchen and to Zirl viâ Mittenwald** 27
   Kohlgrub, 28. — From Eschenlohe to the Walchensee through the Eschenthal, 28. — Ober-Ammergau, 28. — Excursions from Partenkirchen. Partnachklamm. Graseck. Eckbauer. Schlattanbauer. Badersee. Eibsee. Höllenthalklamm. Kramer. Krottenkopf. Hochalpe. Alpspitze. Schachenalp. Hintere Rainthal and Blaue Gumpen. Zugspitze. Schneefernerkopf. Dreithorspitze. Hochwanner, 29. — From Partenkirchen to the Walchensee, 33. — From Partenkirchen to Lermoos; over the Thörlen to Ehrwald, 31. — Excursions from Mittenwald. Lautersee. Ferchensee. Kranz-

berg. Barmsee. Leutaschthal. Vereinsalpe. Karwendelspitze, 34. — Karwendelthal. Hinterauthal. Gleirschthal. To Innsbruck over the Lavatscher Joch or the Stempeljoch; to Zirl over the Erlsattel, 36. — The Reitherspitze. From Seefeld to Leutasch and Telfs, 37.

7. **From Munich to Mittenwald viâ Benediktbeuern. Kochelsee and Walchensee** 37
From Staltach to Murnau over the Aidlinger Höhe, 37. — The Benediktenwand, 38. — Herzogstand, 38. — Heimgarten. Jochberg, 39. — The Barmsee. From Krün to the Soiern Lakes, 40.

8. **From Munich to Tölz and Mittenwald** 40
From Starnberg to Tölz by Wolfratshausen, 41. — Excursions from Tölz. Blomberg. Zwiesel. Viâ Heilbrunn to Kochel. From Tölz to the Walchensee by Lenggries and Jachenau, 41. — Excursions from Lenggries. Benediktenwand. Brauneck, etc., 41, 42. — From Fall to Achenwald. Dürrachklamm. The Scharfreiter, 42. — The Riss. Schönalpelkopf. Ladiz and Laliders. Over the Plumser Joch to the Achensee, 43. — From Vorder-Riss by the Soiern to Mittenwald. The Schöttlkarspitze, 43.

9. **From Munich to Innsbruck viâ Tegernsee, Wildbad Kreut, and the Achensee** 43
Excursions from Tegernsee. Parapluie. Westerhof. Kaltenbrunn. Bauer in der Au. Freihof. Marble Quarries. Falls of the Rottach. Neureut. Riedererstein. Baumgartenschneid. Hirschberg, Risserkogl, 44. — Excursions from Kreut. Wolfsschlucht. Gaisalp. Königsalp. Schildenstein. Schinder, 46. — The Juifen. From Achenkirch to Steinberg, 47. — The Unnutz. Spieljoch. Bärenkopf. Sonnenjoch. From Pertisau to Hinter-Riss over the Gramai-Joch, 48. — The Sonnwendgebirge, 49.

10. **From Munich to Kufstein viâ Schliersee and Bairisch-Zell** 49
From Miesbach to Tegernsee, 49. — From Miesbach to Birkenstein, 50. — From Schliersee to Tegernsee, 50. — From Neuhaus to Falepp. Spitzingsee, 50. — From Falepp to Landl by the Elend-Alp, 51. — Excursions from Neuhaus. Brecherspitze. Jägerkamp. Rothwand. Miesing, etc., 51. — The Wendelstein. Traithen, 51. — From Bairisch-Zell to Oberaudorf. From Landl to Falepp over the Ackern-Alp, 52.

11. **From Munich to Salzburg. Chiemsee** 52
Ebersberg. From Munich to Rosenheim viâ Holzkirchen and Aibling, 53. — Niederaschau. The Kampenwand. To Kufstein viâ Sachrang, 54. — Wildbad Adelholzen. The Maxhütte. Hochfellen. Hochgern, 55.

12. **From Munich to Reit im Winkel and Kössen** . . . 56
Excursions from Marquartstein. Hochgern. Hochplatte. From Marquartstein to Kössen by Schleching. Pass Klobenstein, 56. — Excursions from Reit im Winkel. Möseralpe, Fellhorn, etc., 57. — From Reit im Winkel to Traunstein viâ Ruhpolding, 57. — Excursions from Kössen and Walchsee. The Habberg, 58.

1. From Munich to Lindau.

Comp. Map, p. 194.

138 M. RAILWAY *(Bairische Staatsbahn)* in 5¼-8 hrs. Views to the left. Munich, see *Baedeker's S. Germany*. Soon after leaving the station we observe on the right the park and château of *Nymphenburg*. 4½ M. *Pasing* is the junction for the lines to Augsburg and Starnberg (R. 5). After crossing the *Würm* (p. 24) and passing (7 M.) *Aubing*, the train enters the boggy *Dachauer Moos*. 15 M. Bruck (1735'; *Marthabräu; Post*), or *Fürstenfeldbruck*, pleasantly situated in the *Amperthal*, is frequented for its river-baths. In the neighbourhood is the suppressed Cistercian abbey of *Fürstenfeld*. The train traverses the *Schöngeisinger Wald* and reaches (20 M.) *Grafrath*, with its pilgrimage-church. To the left a pleasing glimpse is obtained of the Ammersee (steamboat on the Amper to *Stegen*, see p. 27). 24 M. *Türkenfeld;* 28½ M. *Schwabhausen;* 32 M. *Epfenhausen*. The train crosses the *Lech*. — 35 M. *Kaufering* (1940').

FROM KAUFERING TO SCHONGAU, branch-railway in 1¾ hr. — 5 M. Landsberg *(Glocke; Hahn)*, an ancient town on the Lech, with 5200 inhabitants. The late-Gothic *Liebfrauenkirche* was founded in 1458. The *Rathhaus*, which has been recently restored, is embellished with frescoes by Piloty. — Beyond Landsberg we proceed by a new local railway (tickets obtained in the carriages), traversing an uninteresting district and passing several unimportant stations, to (21 M.) Schongau (2250'; *Post; Stern*), a small and ancient town, picturesquely situated on a hill rising above the Lech. It possesses a well-equipped bathing-establishment, the *Johannisbad* (Restaurant). — An omnibus runs daily from Schongau to *Füssen* (*Hohenschwangau;* see p. 14).

Near (38 M.) *Iyting* the château of that name rises on the left. — 42¼ M. **Buchloe** *(Hôtel Ensslin*, near the station; *Rail. Restaurant)*, the junction of the lines to Augsburg and Memmingen.

FROM AUGSBURG TO BUCHLOE (25 M.), railway in 50-70 min. (from Augsburg to Lindau in 5-8 hrs.). The line traverses the *Lechfeld*, the plain between the Wertach and Lech, where Otho I. defeated the Hungarians in 955. Near the station of *Inningen*, to the right, beyond the Wertach, rises the *Wellenburg*, a château of Prince Fugger. Stations *Bobingen* (branch-line to Kaufering and Landsberg, see above), *Grossaitingen, Schwabmünchen* (a manufacturing place), *Westerringen*. The line then crosses the *Gennach*, and reaches *Buchloe*.

The train now enters the broad valley of the *Wertach*. 46½ M. *Beckstetten;* 50 M. *Pforzen*. Beyond the river is the monastery of *Irrsee*, now a lunatic asylum. The background of the landscape is formed by imposing mountains, among which the Zugspitze (9760'), the Hochplatte (6835'), and the Säuling (6680') are conspicuous.

At (54½ M.) **Kaufbeuren** (2240'; *Sonne; Hirsch*), an ancient town, the line crosses the river, and threads its way between densely wooded hills. 58 M. *Biessenhofen* (Post; branch-line to Oberdorf, see p. 14); 61 M. *Ruderatshofen;* 63½ M. *Aitrang*. — 69½ M. *Günzach*, with an old monastery converted into a brewery, the highest place (2770') on the line, lies on the watershed between the Wertach and the Iller. Fine view of the Günzthal; to the right *Obergünzburg*. The *Mittelberg*, ¾ M. to the S. W. of the station, commands a view of the Alps as far as the Säntis.

The line descends, at first through wood, and then through a broad grassy valley with peat-cuttings. 76 M. *Wildpoldsried*; 77½ M. *Betzigau*. The *Iller* is crossed.

81½ M. **Kempten** (2285'; **Algäuer Hof*, *Kronprinz*, at the station; **Krone*, *Post*, in the new town; *Deutscher Kaiser*, *Haase*, in the old town; *Frommlet's Old German Wine-Room*, near the station; **Railway Restaurant*), the capital of the *Algäu*, prettily situated on the Iller, which here becomes navigable for rafts, was a free town of the empire down to 1803. It contains 14,350 inhab., and consists of the *Neustadt*, on the higher ground, and the *Altstadt*, on the Iller. In the Residenz-Platz in the Neustadt, which is adorned with a tasteful fountain (statue of Empress Hildegarde), stands the old *Palace* of the once powerful Prince-Abbots of Kempten, built in the 18th cent.; the 'Fürstensaal' contains portraits of the abbots. Adjoining is the handsome *Abbey Church*, with a dome in the Italian style (1652). In the Altstadt are the *Rathhaus*, lately restored, and the *Protestant Church* (in the St. Mang-Platz). In front of the Realschule rises a monument in memory of the war of 1870-71.

To the S. of the town, between the station and the Iller, rises the *Burghalde*, a hill with remains of ancient fortifications (reached from the station in 10 min.; restaurant and grounds), once the site of the Roman fort *Campodunum*, subsequently the seat of the Prince-Abbots of Kempten, garrisoned by Imperial troops in 1633, by Swedes in 1616, fortified by the French in 1703, and finally destroyed by the Imperial army in 1705. Fine view hence of the Alps — the Mädelegabel, Grünten, Hochvogel, Wertachhorn, Sorgschrofen, Einstein, Aggenstein, Zugspitze, Säuling, etc. — A more extensive view is obtained from the **Marienberg*, 1 hr. to the W. (a pleasant walk viâ *Feilberg* and *Eggen*, or still better by the *Reichelsberg*; Inn at the top, adjoining the church), which looks down into the Illerthal, with Oberstdorf and Fischen, closed by the imposing Mädelegabel group.

FROM KEMPTEN TO ULM, railway viâ *Memmingen* in 4 hrs., being the direct route from Stuttgart to the Algäu, Hohenschwangau, etc. — From Kempten to *Füssen* and *Reutte*, see R. 3.

Beyond Kempten (from which the train backs out in the opposite direction; finest views now to the left) the line follows the left bank of the Iller. The valley gradually contracts. To the right, beyond (85 M.) *Waltenhofen* (2360'), at the foot of the *Stoffelsberg* (3900'), lies the *Nieder-Sonthofer See* (2240'). 88 M. *Oberdorf*. The line approaches the Iller. On the left rises the green and sharp-edged Grünten (p. 8), adjoined by the Daumen (p. 20).

95 M. **Immenstadt** (2360'; **Kreuz* or *Post*; **Hirsch*; *Engel*; *Traube*, with beer-garden; baths in the Ach, 5 min. above the town), a busy little town of 3000 inhab., lies picturesquely on both banks of the *Steigbach*, at the foot of the *Immenstadter Horn* (5050') and the *Mittag* (4690'), near the junction of the *Konstanzer Ach* with the Iller. To the E. rises the isolated and picturesque Grünten (p. 8); the background is formed by the *Daumen*, the *Geishorn*, and other Hinterstein Mts. (p. 21).

ENVIRONS. Fine views from the *Calvarienberg* (¼ hr.) and the *Schiessstätte* (¼ hr.; Restaurant). Opposite, at the foot of the *Horn* (¼ hr.), are shady pleasure-grounds (turn to the right at the entrance to the Steigbachthal; finger-post). — Pleasant walk to (1½ M.) *Rothenfels*. We follow the road on the right bank of the Ach, past the château of Count Rechberg, and after ½ M. cross to the *Königsqul* (Baron von Kicsen), on the left bank. Here we ascend by the path to the right (way-post) to the two farms on the crest of the hill, and then follow the new path to the left. The ruin commands an admirable view of the Alpsee and the mountains. We may descend through the gateway between the farms, and in 20 min. reach *Bühl* (Inn; pretty view from the garden), at the S.E. end of the Alpsee (see below). Thence back to (1½ M.) Immenstadt by the road.

The ascent of the *Stuiben (5780'; 3-3½ hrs.; guide unnecessary) is recommended. The route crosses the railway just above the 'Post', and follows the left bank of the *Steigbach*, past the twine-factory, into the *Steigbachthal*, a picturesque ravine between the Mittag and the Immenstadter Horn, through which the brook dashes over its rocky bed (observe the skilfully-constructed bulwarks and artificial channel). As far as the (³/₄ hr.) wooden *Chapel*, the path is rather steep (the path to the left here ascends the *Mittag*, see below). Beyond the (5 min.) finger-post, where we turn to the left, the path is almost level; 10 min., we cross the brook; ¼ hr., we turn to the right (the path to the left ascends the *Steinsberg*, see below), and again follow the left bank to the (½ hr.) *Almagmach Inn* (rustic). Hence we may ascend either by the cart-track to the right, viâ the (½ hr.) *Ehrenschwang Alp* (*Mittelberg*), or by a shady path to the left through wood, to (1¼ hr.) the *Stuiben-Hütte* (5445'; Inn, bed 1 m., hay-bed 50 pf.) and (20 min. farther on) the summit (pavilion and a mountain-indicator). The view is very striking, and is more picturesque and more extensive than that from the Grünten. To the S. is the chief group of the Algäu Alps, culminating in the Krottenkopf and the Mädelgabel; to the left of these are the mountains of Hinterstein and Tannheim, terminated by the Grünten on the E.; to the right (S. W.), beyond the long Gottesackerwände, rise the heights of the Bregenzer Wald, and more to the right are the Rhætikon Chain with the Scesaplana, the mountains of the Grisons and Glarus, and the Sentis; in the immediate foreground is the Rindalphorn with its conglomerate strata; to the W. stretches the Lake of Constance, on which Friedrichshafen may be descried in clear weather. — From the Almagmach Inn (see above) a new path ascends to (1 hr.) the top of the **Steineberg** (5510'), the view from which is scarcely inferior to that from the Stuiben.

From Immenstadt to *Sonthofen* and *Oberstdorf*, see R. 2; to the *Grünten*, see p. 8. — To *Reutte* viâ *Hindelang* and *Tannheim*, see R. 4.

The train now turns to the W., by the base of the Immenstadter Horn, into the valley of the Ach (to the right the *Kleinsee*), reaches the village of *Bühl*, on the *Alpsee* (2355'; 2 M. long), and skirts the N. bank of the lake. We next traverse the pleasant *Konstanzer Thal*, flanked with green hills, to (102 M.) *Thalkirchdorf*, and ascend a steep gradient to (103½ M.) **Oberstaufen** (2600'; *Büttner; Rail. Restaurant*, with rooms; *Adler; Ochs*), a market-town, frequented as a summer-resort, on the watershed between the Rhine and the Danube. At the end of a short tunnel, just before Oberstaufen is reached, and at several points beyond it, we obtain striking views of the profound Weissachthal, the wooded mountains of Bregenz, and the snow-clad peaks of Appenzell.

From Oberstaufen through the *Weissachthal* to *Hittisau* in the Bregenzer Wald (diligence daily in 3 hrs. 20 min.), see p. 206. — Pleasant excursions may be made viâ *Oberreute* to (6 M.) *Weiler* (p. 6); viâ the *Gschwendmühle* to (9 M.) *Sulzberg* (8300'; *Löwe; Bär*), a village in a commanding situation; or viâ *Steibis* in 4 hrs. (comp. p. 207) to the top of the *Hochgrat* (6170') and thence to the *Rindalphorn* (6070') in 1 hr.; etc.

LINDAU.

Beyond *Harbatzhofen* is the *Rentershofer Damm*, a viaduct 574 yds. long and 174' high. — 114 M. *Röthenbach* (2320'; Kolb).
A picturesque route for pedestrians leads hence to (18½ M.) Bregenz via Weiler. We follow the carriage-road past the small church of the 'Drei Heiligen' to (1½ M.) Weiler (1970; *Post; Wagus*), a pleasant village in the *Rotha-hthal*, frequented as a summer-resort (diligence from Röthenbach thrice daily in 1 hr.). Beyond Weiler we ascend the right side of the Rothachthal to (4½ M.) the customs-station of *Neuhaus*, then skirt the slope of the *Hirschberg* (p. 196) to (3 M.) *Langen* (Inn), and proceed past the lignite-mines and pretty waterfalls of the *Wirtatobel* to (3½ M.) *Fluh* and (3 M.) *Bregenz* (p. 195). — Another highly interesting route leads from Röthenbach direct to the Pfänder (6 hrs.). The road (diligence to Scheidegg thrice daily in 1½ hr.) leads past the church of the 'Drei Heiligen' (see above) to (3½ M.) *Gossholz*, with its neat mountain-houses, and reaches (1½ M.) the thriving market-town of *Lindenberg* (Krone), with large manufactories of straw-hats. At (3 M.) Scheidegg (2195'; *Post*), a large and picturesquely situated village, a good path diverges from the road to the left, and ascends to (1 hr.) *Möggers* (3280; Adler). Thence it proceeds along the hills, passing *Trögen* and commanding fine views of the Lake of Constance and the Bregenzer Wald, to (2 hrs.) the *Pfänder Hotel* (p. 196).

The line now winds through a partly-wooded district. Before reaching (123 M.) *Hergatz* (with peat-cuttings), we obtain another view of the Appenzell mountains. 128 M. *Schlachters*; 132 M. *Oberreitnau*. The line skirts the *Hoierberg* (see below), and then turns towards the S.E. A beautiful view of the Lake of Constance is now obtained: on the left Bregenz, in the foreground Lindau, and beyond it the green mountains of St. Gallen and Appenzell, and in the background the Kamor, Hohe Kasten, Altmann, and Sentis. A long embankment then carries the train across an arm of the lake to an island on which lies —

138 M. **Lindau**. — *Bayrischer Hof*, on the lake, near the station, R., L., & A. 3-4 m., D. 3 m.; *Krone or Post, R. 2 m.; *Hotel Reutemann; Helvetia, moderate; *Lindauer Hof; all these are on the quay. Sonne; Pension Gärtchen auf der Mauer, on the mainland. — *Garden-Restaurant* near the Bayrischer Hof; *Schützengarten*, with view; *Rupflin's* wine-house; *Rail. Restaurant*; also at the *Krone* (see above). — *Lake Baths* on the N.W. side of the town.

Lindau (1305'), once a free imperial town and fortress, and in the middle ages an important commercial place, lies on an island in the Lake of Constance, 350 yds. from the mainland, with which it is connected by the railway-embankment and a wooden bridge. It has recently come into notice as a summer-resort and bathing-place. Pop. 5337. The Romans under Tiberius defeated the Vindelici, a Celtic tribe, in a naval battle on the lake, and founded a fort on this island, of which a tower by the bridge (the so-called Heidenmauer) is a remnant. On the quay is a bronze statue of King Max II., erected in 1856. At the end of the S. pier is a large lion in marble; on that opposite rises a handsome lighthouse (100'; view: tickets at the custom-house, 40 pf. each). In the adjacent Reichs-Platz rises the handsome *Reichsbrunnen*, with a statue of 'Lindania' and other allegorical figures, cast in bronze in 1884 after designs by Thiersch and Rümann. The *Insel* is embellished with pleasure-grounds and a monument in memory of the war of 1870-71.

SONTHOFEN. *I. Route 2.* 7

EXCURSIONS. Pleasant walk on the bank of the lake to the W. (crossing the railway-embankment and turning to the left), passing the villas of *Lotzbeck* (with a fine park), *Giebelbach*, and *Lingg* (*Frescoes by Naue), to the (1½ M.) **Schachenbad** (*Restaurant & Pension*, 22-30 m. per week), with mineral and lake-baths, and the (¾ M.) **Lindenhof**, with a beautiful park, hothouses, etc. (admission on Frid. gratis, on other days 1 m.; closed on Sun.). Farther along the bank of the lake, beyond *Tegelstein* (to the right *Schloss Altwind*) and *Mitten*, lies (2½ M.) **Wasserburg** (*Hôtel-Pension Hornstein*, with terrace and fine view), a small village with a château and church, on a peninsula in the lake. We may return by steamboat. — Admirable view from the (¾ hr.) *Hoierberg (1496 ft.), reached either by the path parallel with the railway, or by the road from the Landthor through *Aeschach* (Schlatter) to the hamlet of *Hoiren*, at the foot of the vine-clad hill, and then by a path ascending at the back. On the summit are two inns and a belvedere with a good mountain-indicator. We may return by *Enzisweiler* (*Restaurant Schmid) and *Schachen* (Zum Schlössle).

The **Lake of Constance** (1305') is about 43 M. in length, 8 M. in width, and at the deepest place (between Friedrichshafen and Arbon) 912' in depth. Its principal feeder is the Rhine, the deposits of which have formed a broad delta at the influx of the river between Bregenz and Rorschach. The river emerges from the lake at Constance. This vast sheet of water, with its picturesque and well-peopled banks, its green and wooded hills on the S. side, and the view it commands of the distant snow-mountains, presents a very striking scene to the traveller approaching the Alps for the first time.

The principal places on the lake are *Friedrichshafen, Lindau, Bregenz, Rorschach, Romanshorn, Constance, Meersburg, Ueberlingen*, and *Ludwigshafen*, between which steamboats run at least once a day. On the more important routes the communication is more frequent. Thus between Lindau and Rorschach (1¼ hr.), Lindau and Romanshorn (1½ hr.), Friedrichshafen and Rorschach (1¼ hr.), Friedrichshafen and Romanshorn (1 hr.), and Friedrichshafen and Constance (1½ hr.) there are 4-6 trips daily. The lake being neutral, passengers' luggage is liable to examination at the custom-house wherever they land; but those proceeding from one German port to another may avoid the formality by obtaining a ticket for their luggage. The banks of the lake belong to three different states: Germany (Bavaria, Wurtemberg, and Baden), Switzerland, and Austria. (See also *Baedeker's Switzerland*.)

FROM LINDAU TO BREGENZ. Steamboat 6-7 times daily in 25 minutes. Railway in ¼-½ hr. (fares 54, 40, 27 kr.; view to the right). Intermediate station, *Lochau. — Bregenz*, see p. 195.

2. From Immenstadt to Oberstdorf.
The Algäu Alps.
Comp. Map, p. 14.

RAILWAY to (5½ M.) *Sonthofen* in 25 minutes. POST-OMNIBUS from Sonthofen to (8¾ M.) *Oberstdorf* at 8.10 and 11.50 a.m., and 3 and 6 p.m., in 2 hrs.; fare 1 m. 15 pf. (from Oberstdorf at 4.30 and 9.30 a.m. and 1 and 4.35 p.m.). One-horse carr. 6 m., two-horse carr. 9 m.

Immenstadt, see p. 4. The Sonthofen line skirts the left bank of the Iller (on the right bank the church-tower of *Rauhenzell*, see p. 8), passes (3 M.) *Blaichach*, a manufacturing place, and crosses the Iller and then the *Ostrach*. — 5½ M. **Sonthofen** (2420'; *Deutsches Haus*, at the station; *Engel; Adler; Ochs; Hirsch*), a thriving market-town, pleasantly situated in the broad green Illerthal. Fine view from the *Calvarienberg*, 5 min. from the 'Engel', embracing the Mädelegabel, which rises above the dark Himmelschroffen, the Kratzer (left), Biberkopf and Widderstein (right), Schlappolt and Fellhorn (in the foreground). — Route to *Hindelang*, see p. 20.

The "Grünten (5710') is frequently ascended from Sonthofen. Carriage-road to (3 M.) *Burgberg* (2460'; Löwe), at the S.W. base of the mountain, 1½ M. from Bleichach (see above). (From Immenstadt the direct route is by the *Untere Zollsteg* and *Rauhenzell* to Burgberg, 3½ M.) The new path from Burgberg to the summit of the Grünten (3½-4 hrs.; guide, unnecessary, 4 m.; mule 8 m.) is easy and easily found. We follow the road through the village to the chapel above it, then turn to the right and ascend through wood. After 5 min. we diverge to the left and ascend a ravine descending from the Grünten, and enclosed by huge precipices, to the (2 hrs.) *Gund-Alp* (4180'), a large basin, in which *Hirnbein's Inn* is situated (R. 1½-2 m.). In 25 min. more the summit is attained. From the *Hochwart* (5570'), on which a pavilion has been erected, a narrow ridge leads in 10 min. to the *Uebelhorn* (5710'), the central and highest of the peaks. "View of the mountains from the Zugspitze to the Sentis; in the foreground the Illerthal with Sonthofen and Oberstdorf; above them the Algäu Alps; to the extreme right, part of the Lake of Constance; to the N. the hills of Upper Swabia and the Bavarian plain as far as Peissenberg. The ascent on the N. side, viâ *Rettenberg*, is not recommended.

The OBERSTDORF ROAD crosses the Iller to (¾ M.) *Sigishofen*, and then ascends through wood, reaching a level high above the river and commanding a wide view. It then descends through *Weiler* to (3½ M.) the large village of *Fischen* (2490': *Löwe; Kreuz; road hence by *Maiselstein* and through the *Hirschsprung* to *Tiefenbach*, 4 M., see p. 9); then through (1½ M.) *Langenwang* and across the *Breitach* (before the bridge, a path to the right leads to Wasach and Tiefenbach) and the *Stillach* to (3 M.) Oberstdorf.

The OLD ROAD from Sonthofen to Oberstdorf ascends the right bank of the Iller viâ (1½ M.) *Altstetten* to (2½ M.) **Schöllang** (2715'; *Inn*), prettily situated on a height above the Iller; view from the (¼ hr.) cemetery on the '*Schöllanger Burg*'. Below Schöllang, on the Iller, lie the small sulphur-baths of *Au*. The road then descends by *Reichenbach* and *Rubi*, crossing the *Trettach*, to (4½ M.) *Oberstdorf*.

14½ M. **Oberstdorf** (2665 ft.; *Mohr*, R. 2 m., D. 1 m. 70 pf.; *Hirsch*, D. 1 m. 40 pf.; *Sonne; Löwe*, moderate; *Traube;* apartments at *Schwartzkopf's*, the *Walserhaus*, the *Rubihaus*, etc.), a thriving village and favourite summer-resort, is beautifully situated in a broad valley in the midst of the Algäu Alps. In front of the handsome church is a war-monument, consisting of a lion couchant in bronze. Behind the church, on the Loretto road, is the *Gesellschaftshaus*, with a restaurant, veranda, and garden. — About 1½ M. below the village the *Trettach*, *Stillach*, and *Breitach* unite to form the *Iller*. The ramifications of the valleys from which they descend afford a great variety of excursions.

Walks (contribution to the 'Verschönerungs-Verein' for a stay of 3 days, 1 pers. 1 m., a family 2 m.). On the banks of the Trettach, at the upper end of the village, are the shady promenades of the 'Verein'. Beyond the bridge (¼ hr. from the church) we ascend to the right, turn to the left at the sign-post and proceed through wood to (8 min.) the *Stern*, a space provided with benches. Here we may either take the path to the left, leading down to (¼ hr.) the *Trettachsteg* (path to Spielmannsau, see p. 10); or ascend a little and turn either to the right to the *Hofmann's Ruhe* (see p. 9), or to the left '*über den Rauhen*' to the (¼ hr.) *Baths* (open-air swimming-bath and separate baths, moderate;

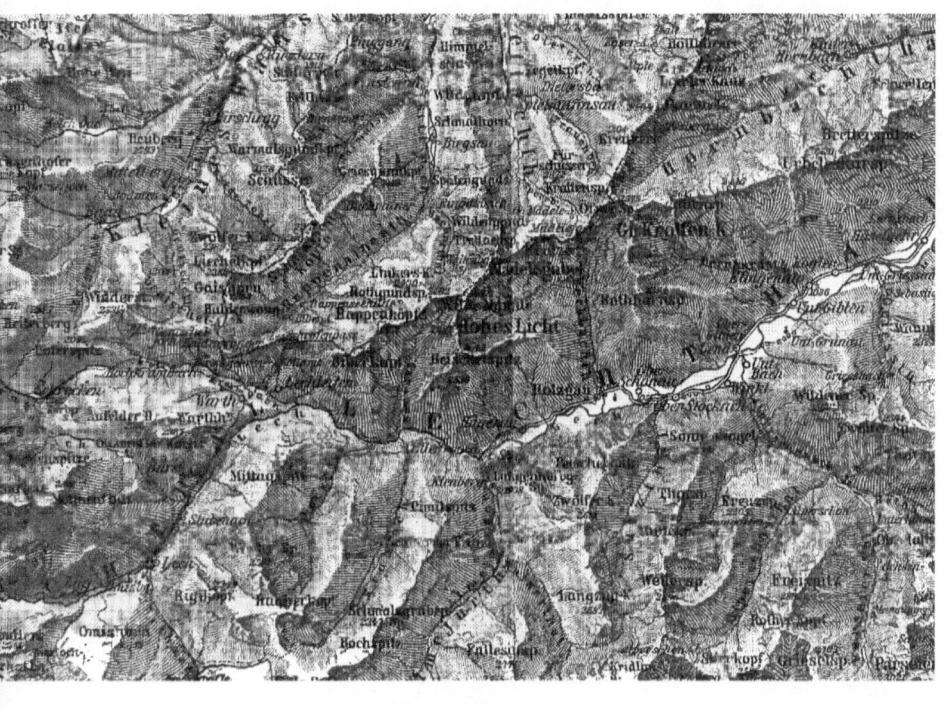

pleasant water). We may return to the *Alpenrose Inn* (see below) and thence viâ *Loretto* to (1/2 hr.) Oberstdorf.

Fallbach, or **Faltenbach Waterfall**, in the gorge between the Rubihorn and Schattenberg (1/2 hr.). Beyond the bridge over the Trettach (see p. 8) we pass some lime-kilns on the left, cross the brook at the end of the ravine, and ascend to a platform above the foaming cascade.

Hofmann's Ruhe (1/2 hr.). Pilgrimage-road from the church to (1 M.) the two chapels of *St. Loretto*, with a fine old lime-tree; then to the left up the hill, on the (1/4 hr.) top of which are two benches, shaded by trees and commanding a fine panorama. On the S. summit, 10 min. from St. Loretto, stands the inn "*Zur Alpenrose* (footpath to the *Baths* in 5 min., see p. 8). The descent may be made on the N. side to the (1/4 hr.) bridge over the Trettach at the upper end of Oberstdorf. — Similar view from the (3/4 hr.) *Burgstall*, at the foot of the Himmelschroffen (path to Spielmannsau, see p. 10).

°**Wasach**, a beautiful walk (1 hr.). We follow the Fischen road, cross the bridge over the Breitach, and ascend to the left, soon gaining a fine view of the Walser-Thal, to the °*Wasach Inn*, commanding a beautiful view (best by evening-light), which is still more extensive from the *Kapf*, 10 min. higher. The following are the most conspicuous mountains from left to right: the Rubihorn, Schattenberg, Höfatsspitze (7415'), Rauheck, Kreuzeck, Krottenköpfe (8710'), Kratzer, Himmelschroffen, Mädelegabel (8670'), Wilde Mannle, Linkerskopf, Rappenköpfe, Schlappolt, Widderstein, and the sharp crest of the Hohe Ifer, all upwards of 8000' in height. Below lies Oberstdorf. — From the Kapf in 10 min. (turning to the left beyond the house) to the *Judenkirche*, a natural archway in the rock, through which we obtain a fine view of the Rubihorn, etc. From Wasach to Oberstdorf, returning by *Tiefenbach* (11/4 hr.), see below.

Tiefenbach (1 hr.). At (25 min.) the inn *Zur Gebirgsaussicht* (see below) a path, diverging to the right from the carriage-road, descends through meadows and wood to the *Breitach-Thal*. Crossing the Breitach, it ascends to the right through wood to the sulphur-baths of *Tiefenbach* (2740'; Badhaus, rebuilt since a fire in 1878), situated in a narrow valley on the right bank of the *Lochbach*. We now follow the carriage-road, which ascends among the scattered houses of the village of *Tiefenbach*. From the point (5 min.) where the road divides, the branch to the right ascends past the church (2740') to (1/4 hr.) *Wasach* (see above); that to the left leads past the precipitous *Nase* (*Nasseand*; fine view, ascent by the direction-post to the left, 3/4 hr.) to the (1 M.) *Hirschsprung*, a cutting in the rock which affords a striking view of the lower Illerthal and the Grünten (the road goes on to Maiselstein and Fischen, p. 8).

°**Freiberg-See** (3060'; 1 hr.). To *St. Loretto*, see above; 4 min. farther on, by the direction-post, the path leads to the right, traversing the meadows and crossing the Stillach, and ascends to the saddle of the Freiberg, beyond which the dark green lake lies in a beautiful wooded basin. Fine view of the Linkerskopf (to the left), the Wilde Mannle), Griesgundkopf, Warmatsgundkopf, etc.; to the right, the Schlappolt. The log-hut (key at Dr. Itch's in Oberstdorf, 1 m.) contains a boat for excursions on the lake. — Shortly before reaching the lake we observe a finger-post on the right, pointing to the *Freibergshöhe*; from the point where the path ends we ascend to the right to a small hut with a table and benches, commanding a view of the valley of Oberstdorf.

°**Zwingsteg** and **Walser Schänzle** (11/2 hr.). Carriage-road from the N.W. end of the village viâ *Kornau*; pedestrians take the path leading due W. from the church to the foot-bridge over the Stillach, and then ascend and join the carriage-road. The inn *Zur Gebirgsaussicht* on the (25 min.) top of the hill commands an extensive view (footpath to the right to Tiefenbach, see above). Hence the road ascends the hill to the left (pretty views), and finally descends through wood into the *Kleine Walser-Thal*, watered by the Breitach. On the Austrian frontier is the *Walser Schänzle* (3260'; Inn, good wine). About 8 min. before it is reached, a path descends through the meadows and woods to the right to the °*Zwingsteg* (3005'), a bridge over a deep and narrow gorge, through which

10 *1. Route 2.*   OBERSTDORF.   *The Algäu Alps.*

the Breitach dashes, 230 ft. below. Beyond the bridge the path ascends in zigzags to (¼ hr.) a direction-post by a hut, and then descends past the mouth of the *Rohrmooser Thal* (p. 13) and by *Oib* to (1 hr.) Tiefenbach (see p. 9), or to (1½ hr.) Oberstdorf. — The next places in the Kleine Walser, or Mittelberger Thal, are (3 M.) *Riezlern* (*Engel; ascent of the *Hohe Ifer*, see p. 12), *Hirschegg* (2¼ M.), and (1½ M.) *Mittelberg* (3980'; Krone; Traube), the picturesquely situated capital of the valley. (From Mittelberg to Krumbach over the *Gentscheljoch*, see p. 209.) The road ends 3 M. farther on, at *Baad* (3925'; Inn), whence an easy path leads to the S., through the *Bergunter Thal* and across the saddle (6260') between the Widderstein and Hoferspitz, to (3½ hrs.) *Hochkrumbach* (p. 209). Another, but fatiguing and uninteresting pass crosses the *Starzeljoch* (6130') to (4 hrs.) *Schoppernau* (p. 209).

Spielmannsau (Trettachthal; carriage-road, 2½ hrs.). recommended for a morning-excursion. Road viâ (1 M.) Loretto, see p. 9; ¾ M. farther on is a finger-post, where the road leads to the left across the *Burgstall* (the N. spur of the *Himmelschroffen*, see p. 9) to a (1 M.) finger-post, showing the way to the left to Gerstruben (see below), and to the right to Spielmannsau. [Pedestrians are recommended to follow the path which crosses the bridge over the Trettach at the upper end of Oberstdorf, and to proceed to the right (sign-post) along the generally shady footpath which skirts the right bank of the Trettach viâ *Gruben* (or from the bridge proceed to the right through the promenades of the 'Verschönerungs-Verein' to the foot-bridge over the Trettach, see p. 8), and finally to cross the Gerstruben bridge to the good carriage-road which follows the left side of the finely-wooded Trettachthal.] On the left lies the small blue *Christles-See* (3015'). The Trettach and the *Trauchbach* are next crossed; (3 M.) *Spielmannsau* (3085'; *Inn), a small hamlet amid grand scenery. Fine view of the huge Trettachspitze to the S.; on the left the Kratzer. From this point it is interesting to explore the *Trauchthal*, from which a fatiguing route crosses the *Märste* (between the Kreuzeck and the Krottenspitze) to the Hornbachthal (p. 13). — A path, bad at places, leads from Spielmannsau through the wild ravine, and at length high on its right side, to the (1 hr.) *Sperrbachsteg* (4060'), in the midst of a grand rocky wilderness. Thence to the *Obermädele-Alp*, see p. 12.

Hölltobel (1½ hr.), at the end of the *Dietersbachthal*, a side-valley of the Spielmannsau. Either by the shady promenade on the right bank of the Trettach (see above), or by the road to Spielmannsau as far as (2½ M.) a direction-post indicating the road to Gerstruben, which descends to the left and crosses the Trettach, affording a fine view of the picturesque valley. At (12 min.) a finger-post our path diverges to the right, and after ¼ hr. more we ascend to the left along the *Dietersbach* to the deep rocky gully of the *Hölltobel*, in which the brook forms three waterfalls. The path first leads to a bridge over the lowest fall, then to a platform above the middle fall, and lastly to the (10 min.) *Upper Fall*, which takes a clear leap into a funnel-like basin. We ascend hence to (20 min.) **Gerstruben** (3770'; *Inn*, rustic), a hamlet in the upper part of the valley, at the base of the imposing *Höfatsspitze* (7415'; ascent from Gerstruben in 4-5 hrs., difficult, and suitable only for practised climbers with steady heads). About 1 hr. farther up the valley is the *Dietersbach-Alpe*, in the midst of imposing scenery (Höfatsspitze, Rauheck, Kreuzeck). A steep path (guide) leads from this point across the *Aelpele* (3825') between the Höfatsspitze and Rauheck, to the (3 hrs.) Käseralpe in the Oythal (p. 11). — A new and easy road, with picturesque views, has been constructed from Gerstruben, descending the slopes to the right in windings to (½ hr.) the bridge over the Trettach (see above; from the bridge to Oberstdorf 1 hr.).

Geisalpsee (3 hrs.; guide, advisable, 5 m.). Road to Schöllang (see p. 8) as far as (2½ M.) *Rubi*; then up to the right to (¾ hr.) the *Geisalp*, and past a fine waterfall formed by the Reichenbach to (1 hr.) the *Untere Geisalpsee* (4880'), picturesquely situated in a basin between the *Rubihorn* (*Geisalphorn*), on the right, and the *Entschenkopf* on the left. The small *Obere Geisalpsee* (5540') lies ½ hr. farther up; thence to the *Vordere Seealp* (p. 11) across the *Geisfuss* (6510') in 2 hrs., somewhat fatiguing.

Oythal (to the Stuiben 2½ hrs.), between the Schattenberg and Riffenkopf, carriage-road one-third of the way. By the lime-kilns beyond the Trettach bridge, at the upper end of the village, the road ascends to the right, rounding the base of the *Schattenberg*. [A footpath (to Spielmannsau, see p. 10) along the right bank of the Trettach to (25 min.) the bridge over the *Oybach*, and then uphill to the left, offers an alternative route.] The valley is at first monotonous and affords no view. After 1 hr. the road crosses the *Oybach* and enters an open grassy dale; on the left are the *Adlerwand* and the *Seewände*, with waterfalls, on the right the wooded *Riffenkopf*. After 20 min. a second bridge. The valley suddenly turns to the S., and a fine survey of the head of the valley, with the *Grosse Wilde* (7980'), *Höllenhörner* (7096'), and *Höfatsspitze* (7415'), is disclosed. At the (40 min.) *Gutenalpe* (3720') the path returns to the left bank and ascends steeply to (1/2 hr.) the *Stuiben Fall*, the beautiful fall of the copious Oybach, with picturesque surroundings. About ¼ hr. farther up is the solitary *Käseralpe* (4500'); thence across the *Aelpele* to *Gerstruben*, see p. 10; over the *Hornbachjoch* to' the *Hornbachthal*, see p. 13; across the *Himmeleck* to *Hinterstein*, see p. 21. A new path runs from the Himmeleck into the *Berggündele*, turning to the right at the first huts and leading round the precipitous slopes of the *Wilde* and *Wiedemer* direct to (5½ hrs. from Oberstdorf) the *Prinz Luitpold-Haus* on the *Hochvogel* (p. 24).

Birgsau (*Stillachthal*), by road 7 M. (one-horse carr. in 1 hr.), there and back 6 m.; two-horse carr. 10 m.); footpath thence to Einödsbach (½ hr.). The route is viâ Loretto; by a direction-post the road leads to the right, between the Himmelschroffen on the left, and the Freiberg and Schlappolt, and farther on, the Griesgundkopf and Warmatsgundkopf on the right. 7 M. *Birgsau* (3180'; Adler), a solitary hamlet commanding a beautiful view: in the centre the pyramidal Linkerskopf, on the right the two Rappenköpfe, over a depression to the left the Wilde Mannle, and to the extreme left the three peaks of the Mädelegabel. A good path now leads at the same level for 10 min., and then ascends the right side of the wild ravine of the Stillach; 20 min., a platform on the right, with a good view of the gorge (the *Bachergwänd*); 5 min. **Einödsbach** (3740'; *Schraudolph's Inn*, unpretending), a hamlet near the head of the valley (called beyond this the *Rappenalpenthal*). The *Bacher Loch*, a huge gully, ascends hence to the Mädelegabel. After 10 min., by a finger-post, the path turns to the left, leads round a stable, and ascends a little. It then follows the right side of the gorge. In 20 min. we reach a waterfall at the foot of the Mädelegabel, a little below which we pass the finest point in the valley. From a projecting point beyond the brook a second fall is observed in the gorge higher up. The beautiful 'Edelweiss' may be found (by good climbers) on the slopes above. — Pedestrians should return by the *Freibergsee* (see above); the route crosses the Stillach, 10 min. below Birgsau, and leads chiefly through wood, passing several isolated houses (*Faistenau*, *Ringgang*, *Schwanden*).

Mountain Ascents (guides: *Karl Brutscher*, *A. Köchler*, *Tim. Kappeler*, *Ign. Zobel*, *Moritz Mall*, all at Oberstdorf; *J. B. Schraudolf* at Einödsbach).

Nebelhorn (7385'), an easy ascent of 4-4½ hrs. (guide, unnecessary for adepts, 5 m.). The path ascends to the Fallbach (see above); beyond the second bridge it turns to the left, and ascends in zigzags, across meadows and through wood, to (1½ hr.) the *Vordere Seealp* (4225'), whence a second chalet (*Hintere Seealp*) is visible high above us, just below the *Zeiger* (see p. 21). — The route ascends gradually to (20 min.) the end of the valley, turns to the left, and for 1 hr. mounts the slope, which is stony at places; about 10 min. before reaching the chalet we ascend the grassy slopes to the left (N.), and farther on skirt a hollow inhabited by marmots. A beaten path leads thence to (1 hr.) the summit, a narrow ridge, descending almost perpendicularly towards the Retterschwangthal (p. 21). Magnificent view. The descent from the Nebelhorn or from the Hintere Seealp by the *Geisfuss* to the *Geisalp Lakes* (p. 10) is interesting but somewhat laborious (guide advisable). — An interesting pass leads from the upper Alp across the *Zeiger* (6520') and the *Wengenalp* to *Hinterstein* (p. 21; 7 hrs. from Oberstdorf, guide 10 m.).

12   *I. Route 2.*   OBERSTDORF.   *The Algäu Alps.*

Fellhorn (6600'), interesting and not difficult, 4½ hrs., with guide (6 m.). The route leads from *Faistenau* (see p. 11) to the *Birwanghütte*, and up steep grassy slopes. Easy descent to *Riezlern* in the Walserthal (p. 10; 2½ hrs.). — **Rauheck** (7885'; guide 8 m.) and Kreuzeck (7851'; guide 9 m.), ascent in each case 5 hrs., not difficult for mountaineers (across the *Dieterabachalpe*, see p. 10). Steep descent into the *Hornbachthal* (p. 13). — **Grosse Krottenkopf** (8710'), the second highest of the Algäu Alps; ascent across the *Mädelejoch* (see below) in 8 hrs. (guide 12 m.), fatiguing, but unattended with danger. Superb view. — **Hochvogel** (8450'), ascended in 9 hrs. viâ the *Himmeleck* (night spent in the Prinz Luitpold Haus), see pp. 11, 21 (guide 14 m., returning by Hinterstein 16 m.)

°**Mädelegabel** (8670'), the third highest summit in the Algäu Alps (Hohe Licht, 8816'; Grosse Krottenkopf, 8710'), ascent laborious, but for practised mountaineers unattended with danger (guide 10 m., from Einödsbach 7 m.). The path (lately improved) from *Einödsbach* (guide, Schraudolf) ascends the steep Bacherthal to (3-3½ hrs.) the *Waltenbergerhaus* (6710'), a club-hut in the *Bockkar*; it then crosses rocks and stones to the gap between the *Hochfrottspitze* and the *Bockkarkopf*, and traverses the small *Schneeferner*, which presents no difficulty, to the (1½ hr.) central peak. Magnificent °Panorama. — The ascent from the N. side is longer and more fatiguing. The route is through the Spielmannsau to the (5 hrs.) *Obermädele Alp* (see below), where the night should be spent. A fatiguing ascent thence of 3 hrs. to the summit. — The *Hochfrottspitze*, or W. peak of the Mädelegabel (8680'), may also be ascended from the N.E. without difficulty; the ascent of the *Trettachspitze* (N. peak, 8480') is more difficult, and should be attempted by none but experts.

Biberkopf (*Hundskopf*, 8515), a laborious ascent, should be attempted only by experts (8 hrs. from Oberstdorf; guide 14 m.). The route leads from (7 M.) *Birgsau* (p. 11) to (3/4 hr.) the *Buchrainer Alpe* at the end of the *Rappenalpenthal* (p. 13), and thence ascends to the left viâ the *Peters-Alpe*, *Linkers-Alpe*, and *Rappen-Alpe* to (2½ hrs.) the *Rappensee Club-hut* (6920'), amid grand scenery. The night is spent here. Hence to the top (fine view) by the W. side, in 2 hrs. — **Hohe Licht** (*Hochalpenspitze*, 8816'), the highest summit of the Algäu Alps, from the Rappensee hut in 2½-3 hrs. (guide 12 m.), another laborious ascent. We traverse the *Grosse Steinscharte* (p. 13) between the *Rothgundspitze* and the *Grosse Rappenkopf*, enter the upper Tyrolese *Hochalpenthal*, and reach the summit over debris and rocks. — **Linkerskopf** (7970'), an easy and interesting ascent of 1½ hr. from the Rappensee Club-hut (guide, 7 m.).

Hohe Ifer (7806'), an interesting ascent (guide 10 m.), facilitated by the recent improvement of the path. The route leads from *Riezlern* (see p. 10; guide, Karl Wüstner), across the *Breitach*, to *Egg*, and through the *Schwarzwasserthal* to (1½ hr.) *Auen* (4400'; night-quarters). Hence we continue to the right to the *Obere Auenalp*, and ascend the *Iferwand* by a new path to (3½ hrs.) the summit, which affords a splendid view. We descend across the fissured and undulating *Ifer Plateau*, from which rise the gigantic cliffs of the *Gottesackerwände* (the route is indicated by stone pyramids and red marks, but a guide is advisable), and passing the *Gottesacker-Alpe*, reach (2½ hr.) the *Scharte* (6575'). Thence the descent leads viâ the *Hochalpe* and *Kessleralpe* to (3 hrs.) the *Schrine* and (1½ hr.) *Rohrmoos* (p. 13).

Passes. FROM OBERSTDORF TO HOLZGAU on the Lech, over the *Ober-Mädelejoch* (7½ hrs.; guide 11 m.), an interesting route. Through the *Spielmannsau* (Trettachthal) as far as (3 hrs.) the *Sperrbachsteg*, see p. 10. Beyond the bridge the new path winds up steep grassy slopes, crossing the Sperrbach (on the right bank the *Sperrbachhütte*) at the *Obere Knie* (4386'), and traversing the *Sperrbachtobel*; then over grass and loose stones to (2 hrs.) the *Obermädele-Alp* (6020'; poor quarters). From this point the **Ober-Mädelejoch** (6470'), between the Kratzer and Krottenköpfe, is reached in ½ hr.; fine view, to the S., of the heights of the Lechthal, and to the E., of the *Grosse Krottenkopf* (see above). We now descend abruptly into the *Heckbachthal* past a waterfall, and follow the 'Gesprengte Weg' through the striking ravine of the Heckbach, to (2 hrs.) *Holzgau* (p. 214).

FROM OBERSTDORF TO ELMEN in the Lechthal over the *Hornbachjoch*

(10 hrs.), fatiguing, but on the whole repaying (guide to Hinter-Hornbach 10 m.). The route (shady in the early morning) first leads through the *Oythal* (p. 11), past the *Stuiben Fall*, to the (2¹/₂-3 hrs.) *Käseralpe* (p. 11); it then ascends steeply (the path soon becoming indistinct) to the highest pastures, and mounts fatiguing stony slopes to the (2 hrs.) Hornbachjoch (6700'), between the *Höllenhörner* and the *Lechler Kanz*. Splendid survey of the Lechthal Mts.; view towards the W. limited. We now descend rapidly (with the huge *Hochvogel* facing us; p. 21) into the *Jochthal* to the (1¹/₄ hr.) highest *Joch-Alpe*, and then by a tolerable path to (1 hr.) *Hinter-Hornbach* (3600'; Adler, by the church, rustic; good wine), a village charmingly situated at the opening of the Jochthal into the *Hornbachthal*. The ascent of the *Hochvogel* (8495'), which may be made hence in 5¹/₂ hrs. (with guide), viâ the *Schwabeck-Alpe* and the *Fuchsensattel*, is difficult and fatiguing (comp. p. 21). The *Urbeleskarspitze* (8500'), the highest summit of the Hornthal chain, ascended viâ the *Urbeleskar* in 5-6 hrs., is also difficult. — A good path now leads, chiefly through wood. to (¹/₂ hr.) *Vorder-Hornbach* (poor inn) in the broad *Lechthal*. Below the village we turn to the right and cross the Hornbach to the hamlet of *Mortenau*, then traverse the floor of the valley to the left, and cross the Lech to the road which leads to (1 hr.) *Elmen* (p. 210).

To the Upper Lechthal over the Schrofen Pass, 6¹/₂ hrs. to Lechleiten (guide advisable), the shortest way to the Arlberg. The route crosses the Stillach at (2¹/₂ hrs.) *Birgsau* (see above), and ascends the left bank to (³/₄ hr.) the *Buchrainer Alp* (Einödsbach remaining on the left); to the right, on the flank of the Griesgundkopf, is a shooting-box of Prince Luitpold of Bavaria. The upper Stillachthal (*Rappenalpenthal*) is monotonous and enclosed by wooded heights; towards the E. towers the Trettachspitze; farther up, on the left, the Biberkopf, on the right, the Rossgundkopf and Liechlkopf. The path crosses the Stillach thrice before reaching (1³/₄ hr.) the *Biberalp*, on a hill formed by stony deposits. Beyond it (20 min.) we again cross the brook and ascend the abrupt slope by a rough, stony path to (¹/₂ hr.) the Schrofen Pass (5570'), which commands a fine survey of the Gaishorn, Liechlkopf, Schafalpenköpfe, and (S.) Biberkopf. A good path now descends to (¹/₂ hr.) the Austrian custom-house of *Lechleiten* (p. 211), a few minutes above which, to the left, stands Felder's Inn. (The village lies on the hill to the left, 10 min. farther on.) From the custom-house we descend to the right into the *Krumbachthal*, cross the stream at the mill, and then re-ascend to (35 min.) *Warth* (4905'; Rössle); thence to (1¹/₂ hr.) *Lech* and across the *Flexensattel* to (2¹/₂ hrs.) *Stuben*, on the Arlberg, see p. 212. — Over the Grosse Steinscharte to Lechleiten, 9-10 hrs. with guide, a fatiguing but interesting pass. To the Scharte viâ the *Rappensee Club-hut*, see p. 12. Thence we descend into the *Hochalpenthal* and follow the right bank of the brook through the *Hochalpenwald* to the *Lechthal* (p. 211), where a bridle-path ascends to the right to Lechleiten.

From Oberstdorf to the Schrecken, a highly interesting route through the *Kleine Walser-Thal* and over the *Gentscheljoch* (8¹/₂ hrs. to the Schrecken; guide, 12 m., unnecessary; comp. p. 200). — Over the Haldenwangereck to Hochkrumbach, 7¹/₂ hrs. (guide to the Schrecken, not indispensable, 12 m.). Through the *Rappenalpenthal* to the (5 hrs.) *Biberalp*, see above; then on the left bank of the Stillach (the bridge and route to the Schrofen Pass remaining on the left) to the *Haidenwanger Alp* at the head of the Rappenalpenthal, and to the (1¹/₂ hr.) Haldenwangereck (6235'; fine view). The descent is by the *Hirschgehren-Alp* to (1 hr.) *Hochkrumbach* (p. 200).

From Oberstdorf to Hittisau viâ Rohrmoos, 8 hrs., a route somewhat deficient in interest. Cart-road from Tiefenbach on the left bank of the *Starzlach* to (2 hrs.) Rohrmoos (3525'), a large dairy-farm belonging to Prince Waldburg (inn kept by the manager). On the S. are the *Gottesackerwände* (p. 12). Then through the *Hirschgunder Thal*, by a bad and often marshy path to (1¹/₂ hr.) the *In der Schrine Inn* (on the left the fine cascade of the *Kesselbach*), and, crossing the small gorge of the *Feigenbach* (Austrian frontier), to (1¹/₂ hr.) *Sibratsgfäll* (3040'), whence a better

14   *I. Route 3.*   OBERDORF.   *From Augsburg*

road leads to (2 hrs.) *Hittisau* (p. 206). — A much more interesting route leads from Tiefenbach through the *Lochbachthal* viâ the *Freiburger Alp*, the *Gauchenwände*, and *Balderschwang* to (9 hrs.) *Hittisau*.

3. From Augsburg to Füssen (Hohenschwangau) and to Imst viâ Lermoos.

110½ M. RAILWAY viâ Biessenhofen to Oberdorf (45 M.) in 2½ hrs. DILIGENCE from Oberdorf to Füssen (20 M.) twice daily in 4½ hrs.; from Füssen to Reutte (9½ M.) twice daily in 3¾ hrs.; from Reutte viâ Lermoos to Imst (36 M.) twice daily in 8½ hrs. An OMNIBUS also plies from Reutte to Imst daily in 10 hrs. — Carriages for Hohenschwangau and Linderhof may be obtained at the railway-station and at the post-office in Oberdorf. Fare to Hohenschwangau, with one horse 18, with two horses 25 m.; from Hohenschwangau to Reutte 8 or 12, to Linderhof 20 or 36, to Murnau or Partenkirchen 45 or 60m. (comp. R. 6).

FROM KEMPTEN (p. 4) TO FÜSSEN (25 M.) diligence daily at 9 a. m. in 6½ hrs.; carr. to Hohenschwangau, with one horse 20, with two horses 36 m. We cross the railway-bridge (fine view) and in 12 min. reach the road to (3½ M.) *Durach* (3 M. to the S. of which, near *Sulzberg*, lie the small iodine baths of *Sulzbrunn*). Thence we ascend through wood, pass *Zollhaus*, and reach (7½ M.) *Oy*, a lofty village with a fine view, beyond which we descend to cross the *Wertach*, remounting again to (3¾ M.) *Nesselwang* (2345'; *Bär). The road now leads through *Kappel* and (3¾ M.) *Weissbach*, and past the *Weissensee*, enclosed with wood, to (7½ M.) *Füssen*. To the right, near the Weissensee, rises the ruined *Falkenstein* (fine view), reached by a new road in 1½ hr. This is a fine route, particularly the latter half, with a view of the pyramidal Säuling (p. 17). — TO REUTTE, a direct road diverges to the right at *Weissbach* (see above), which with the following villages of *Kirchdorf* and *Steinach* belongs to the parish of *Pfronten (Frons Raetiae)*, consisting of thirteen villages. We enter the broad valley of the *Vils*, which descends from the Tannheimer Thal and falls into the Lech 2 M. below the small town of *Vils*, and at the (13 M.) *Ulrichsbrücke* (p. 17) reach the Lech and the road from Füssen.

From *Sonthofen* (p. 7) to *Reutte* viâ *Hindelang*, *Tannheim*, and the *Gacht Pass*, see R. 4.

FROM PEISSENBERG (p. 26) TO FÜSSEN (34½ M.) post-omnibus once daily in 10 hrs., (carr. and pair to Hohenschwangau, 1-2 pers. 20 m., 3-4 pers. 40 m.), viâ *Hätten*, *Peiting* (Inn; ¾ M. to the N. the *Maierberg*, with a charming view), *Steingaden* (18 M.: Post), once a monastery with a Romanesque church, *Trauchgau*, *Buching* (*Löwe), and the *Bannwaldsee*. A little on this side of *Schwangau*, and 3¾ M. from Füssen, a bye-road to the left leads to (3 M.) *Hohenschwangau* (p. 15).

FROM SCHONGAU (p. 3) TO FÜSSEN (18 M.) omnibus every afternoon in 6 hrs.; carr. and pair to Hohenschwangau 40 m. The road descends to the Lech and then ascends its right bank to (2 M.) *Peiting*, on the road from Peissenberg to (16 M.) Füssen (see above).

Railway from Augsburg to (41 M.) *Biessenhofen*, see p. 9; branch-line from this point, through the *Wertach-Thal* to (4 M.) **Oberdorf** (2395'; *Post*), a market-town with a château.

The high-road from Oberdorf to Rosshaupten is monotonous. The most conspicuous mountains in the background are the *Säuling* (p. 17) and the *Aggenstein* (p. 22). To the E. of *Stötten* (Post) rises the isolated *Auerberg* (3445'), with a church and inn at the top, often ascended for the view (1 hr.).

Then by *Steinbach* to (12½ M., from Oberdorf) *Rosshaupten* (2590'; Bräuhaus), across the *Rosshauptner Höhe* (fine mountain-view), and down into the broad *Lechthal*. On the left, beyond the river, rise the *Trauchberg*, and, farther on, the *Tegelberg* and the castle of *Neuschwanstein*. We next reach (7½ M.) —

65 M. (from Augsburg) **Füssen** (2615'; *Post*; **Mohr; Löwe; Schiff; Rose; *Hecht*, unpretending), a small town on the Lech, on a hill crowned with a handsome castle which the bishops of Augsburg erected in 1322. The Rittersaal, with finely-painted ceiling, and the chapel were restored by Lewis I. Adjoining the castle are the suppressed Benedictine abbey of *St. Mang*, founded in 629 (present building, 18th cent.), and the *Church of St. Magnus*, erected in 1701, a good rococo edifice, decorated with marble, frescoes, gilding, and a few reliefs. To the left in the choir is a very early portrait of Charlemagne; on the right that of St. Leopold. In the Romanesque crypt is the Chapel of St. Magnus, with the drinking-cup, stole, and staff of the saint (d. 654), and four marble statues. On the left by the church-door is the entrance to the *Chapel of St. Anna*, adorned with a Dance of Death in 20 sections (beginning of 17th cent.), and a fine crucifix carved in wood.

On the right bank of the Lech, a few hundred paces above the bridge, a path with pilgrimage-stations ascends from the church to the **Calvarienberg* (¼ hr.), surmounted by three crosses, and commanding a beautiful view: N. the valley of the Lech and Füssen, S.W. the Schwansee, Hohenschwangau, and Neuschwanstein. A footpath leads hence, skirting the Schwansee, direct to (1 hr.) Hohenschwangau.

The ROAD from Füssen to Hohenschwangau ascends the right bank of the Lech from the bridge at Füssen, and turning to the right beyond a large cordage-factory, skirts the Calvarienberg and Schlossberg and reaches (3 M.) the village of *Hohenschwangau* (2735'; Alpenrose; Zur Liesl, well spoken of; Pens. Schwansee; lodgings in the village, usually full in summer). An easy footpath ascends from the village to the castle in 10 minutes. — The longer, but more attractive ROYAL ROAD, open to pedestrians only, follows the Reutte road past the *Mang Fall* (p. 17), diverges to the left at the *Schwarzbrücke*, just on this side of the Bavarian frontier-post, and crosses a beautifully wooded ridge to the *Schwansee*, where the park begins (3 M. to the castle). — The **ALPENROSENWEG*, a generally shady footpath, diverges to the right from the royal road about 3 min. beyond the Schwarzbrücke (see above), ascends the (10 min.) *Schwarzenberg*, and keeping high above the level of the Schwansee and commanding beautiful views, leads to the left through the park direct to the castle (3 M.; last turnings always to the left).

*Schloss Hohenschwangau (2930'), formerly called *Schwanstein*, situated on a wooded rock 3½ M. to the S.E. of Füssen, is said to have been once a Roman fort, and was subsequently a baronial castle. It was destroyed by the Tyrolese in 1809, sold for the trifling sum of 200 fl. in 1820, and in 1832 purchased by King Max II. of Bavaria (d. 1864), then crown-prince, who caused it to be entirely re-constructed by *Quaglio, Ohlmüller*, and *Ziebland*, and decorated with frescoes by Munich artists. Visitors admitted at any

16 *I. Route 3.* NEU-SCHWANSTEIN. *From Augsburg*

hour after 8 a. m. (in the afternoon only, if the Queen Dowager is in the castle); attendant 1 m.

We enter by the E. gate (ring). To the left, in the court is the *Marienbrunnen*, with a Madonna painted by Glink. The small garden (gardener 50 pf.) contains the *Marmorbad*, hewn in the rock, with two nymphs by Schwanthaler, and the *Lion-Fountain*, an imitation of the fountain of the lions in the Alhambra. The castle itself is now entered. The colonnade contains armour and weapons.

Frescoes on the FIRST FLOOR. In the *Schwan-Rittersaal* are 4 pictures, illustrating the legend of Lohengrin or the Knight of the Swan; in the *Schyrensaal* 8 pictures by Lindenschmitt from Bavarian history; in the *Oriental Room* reminiscences of King Max II.'s travels in the East; *Schwangau Room*, 7 scenes from the history of the castle, by Lindenschmitt; *Bertha Room*, history of the parents of Charlemagne, 5 paintings designed by Schwind; *Ladies' Room*, 'scenes from the life of a lady of the middle ages', from the history of the Countess Palatine Agnes, wife of Otho of Wittelsbach. — UPPER FLOOR: *Room of the Heroes*, representations from the Wilkina legend, a myth connected with the Nibelungenlied, commemorating the exploits of Dietrich of Bern, designed by Schwind; *Room of the Hohenstaufen*, 6 paintings by Lindenschmitt; *Room of the Guelphs*, 7 scenes from the history of Henry the Lion by Lindenschmitt; *Autharis Room*, 4 pictures representing the wooing of the Bajuvar princess Theudelinda by the Lombard king Autharis, designed by Schwind; *Room of the Knights*, scenes of mediæval chivalry, 9 paintings by Schwind; armorial bearings in silver, a wedding-gift from the Bavarian nobility; *Armida Room*, the bedchamber of King Lewis II., with a large bed; *Private Chapel*, stained-glass windows.

Delightful views are obtained from the windows of the different rooms, especially from the oriel-window of the king's study, whence the plain is also visible. Charming survey of the Alpsee from a temple on a rocky height, 5 min. to the E. of the castle.

A broad new road ascends from the Alpenrose in 40 min. to the castle of *Neu-Schwanstein, erected by King Lewis II. (d. 1886) on the site of the old castle of *Vorder-Schwangau*, and beautifully situated on a precipitous rock above the profound ravine of the *Pöllat* (adm. daily in summer, 9-12 and 2-5, 3 m ; closed on Frid.; tickets at the entrance).

The castle, built in the Romanesque style by Riedel, Dollmann, and Hofmann, consists of the *Palas* or m. in building, on the W., the *Ritterbau*, the unfinished *Kemenate* (women's apartments), and *Chapel* in the middle of the rocky ridge, and the *Thorbau* (or *Gatehouse*) on the E. The imposing PALAS has four stories: the ground-floor contains the offices, the first floor is occupied by the attendants, the second is unfinished, and the royal apartments are on the third. Entering by the Gatehouse, visitors are conducted to the extensive *Kitchen*, and then ascend to the third floor by a staircase of 96 steps in the massive N. tower, 195' high. The landing at the top of the staircase is adorned with frescoes by Aigner, illustrating the legend of Sigurd. To the right is the *Throne Room*, fitted up in the Byzantine taste, with pictures by Hauschild, representing the relations of monarchy to religion. The antechamber to the left leads to the *Dining Hall*, with pictures from the Contest of Minstrels at the Wartburg by F. Piloty, and commanding charming views from the windows. Next follow the royal *Bedchamber*, with an antique Byzantine altar, and illustrations of the story of Tristan and Isolde by Spiess; the *Chapel*, with paintings by Hauschild; the *Dressing Room*, with scenes from the life of Walter von der Vogelweide by Ille; the *Sitting Room*, with scenes from the Lohengrin legend by Hauschild, the *Study*, with scenes from the story of Tannhäuser by Aigner; and the '*Stalactite Grotto*', with its ivy-clad arbour, affording a fine view of the plain. Aigner has also adorned the landing at the top of the staircase on the fourth floor with a series of 12 pictures from the story of Gudrun. On this floor is the *Festsaal* or *Sängersaal* (Minstrels' Hall), 90' long, an imitation of the Minstrels' Hall in the Wartburg, with the 'Sängerlaube' and pictures from Parzival by Spiess, Munsch, and Piloty. The windows of this hall, like all the windows in the S. façade, command charming views of the deep gorge of the Pöllat; and an interesting panorama may be enjoyed from the uppermost gallery of the N. tower.

A footpath, running immediately under the W. façade of the castle, brings us to the S. side and to the bridle-path ascending to the left to the Marienbrücke. After 4 min., a few paces to the right, is the *Jugend* (about 3280'), a clearing in the wood commanding a fine view, whence a steep path to the left descends to the road (see p. 15). If we continue to follow the bridle-path we come (3 min.) to the height where it joins the carriage-road, which ascends from the right. [From this point to the Alpenrose Inn 40 min., in the reverse direction 50 min.; the route may be continued through the *Blöckenau* to Linderhof (see below).] We now ascend by the footpath to the left to (5 min.) the *Marienbrücke*, a handsome iron bridge 138' long, which boldly spans the rocky gorge of the Pöllat at a height of 295 ft. above the waterfall. A few paces beyond the bridge there opens a grand view of the Säuling, the highest of the neighbouring mountains.

Returning from the bridge, we take the footpath immediately to the right, and in 5 min. reach the path into the *Ravine of the Pöllat* (near the castle, to the right), which we descend in 2-3 min. to the *Fall of the Pöllat* (fine view of the castle of Neu-Schwanstein from below). We then retrace our steps to the Alpenrose Inn in ¹/₂ hr. (the path leading on through the valley is impracticable).

From Neu-Schwanstein a direct and interesting footpath leads to Linderhof (p. 23) in 5¹/₂ hrs. through the *Blöckenau* and across the Schützensteig or *Jägersteig* (guide to the Ammerwald-Alp advisable; K. Left in Hohenschwangau recommended).

The Säuling (6800'; guide 7 m.) may be ascended from Hohenschwangau viâ the *Aelpele* and the *Gemswiese* in 5 hrs., and commands an extensive view. The last part of the route, along the arête, is fatiguing. The ascent is better made from *Pflach* (see below) by the new path constructed by the German Alpine Club through the *Lehnbachthal* (3¹/₂ hrs., with guide).

PEDESTRIANS proceeding to Reutte (8 M.) need not return to Füssen. A good road ('*Fürstenstrasse*'), which walkers only may use, leads to the W., passing through the beautiful grounds and woods which enclose the *Alpsee*. About ¹/₂ M. from the inn a path leads to the left to the *Pindarplatz*, a height with a good echo, high above the beautiful blue lake. Opposite is the Pilgerschroffen, concealing the Säuling. From the end of the lake we return to the road. Just before reaching the (1³/₄ M.) Austrian frontier-station, we diverge to the left, and after a few paces take a path to the right, which finally crosses meadows and joins the public road (³/₄ M.). The *Kniepass* (3030'), a rocky barrier confining the Lech within narrow limits, is now crossed to (3 M.) *Pflach* (see below) and (2¹/₂ M.) Reutte.

The ROAD from Füssen to (9¹/₄ M.) Reutte leads past the *Mang Fall*, a picturesque fall of the Lech, and through a narrow ravine (on the left bank a monument to King Max II., and a war-monument) to (1 M.) the Austrian frontier (*Weisses Haus*, good wine), crosses the Lech by the (1¹/₂ M.) *Ulrichsbrücke*, above the influx of the *Vits* (p. 14), and near (5 M.) *Pflach*, at the S.W. base of the Säuling (see above), recrosses to the right bank. Pedestrians will find it pleasanter to diverge to the left before reaching the Ulrichsbrücke, and proceed by *Pinswang* and the *Kniepass* (p. 17) to (4½ M.) Pflach. Beyond Pflach the *Plansee-Ache* is crossed (p. 23). Then (1¾ M.) —

7¼/₄ M. **Reutte** (2770'; *Post; Krone; *Adler*, moderate; *Glocke; Hirsch*), a small town with picturesque houses, in the bed of an ancient lake, intersected by the Lech, and surrounded by lofty mountains: N. the *Säuling* (p. 17) and *Dürreberg*, E. the *Zwieselberg* and *Tauern*, S. the *Axljoch*, *Thaneller*, and *Schlossberg*, S.W. the *Schwarzhanskurkopf* and other Lechthal peaks, W. the *Gachtspitz*, *Gernspitz*, and *Gimpelspitz*.

The parish-church is at **Breitenwang**, ½ M. to the E. of Reutte. Emp. Lothaire died here in 1137, on his return from Italy. The mortuary chapel contains a Dance of Death in relief. — About ½ M. farther to the E. are the baths of *Mühl*, with a swimming-basin, well fitted up (pleasant water). In a hollow on the slope of the *Dürreberg*, about ½ hr. higher, lies the small green *Uri-See*.

The *Stuiben Fall* and *Plansee*, see p. 23. From Reutte to *Linderhof* and *Partenkirchen*, see p. 22. *Upper Lechthal*, see p. 210. *Pass Gacht*, and viâ *Tannheim* to *Immenstadt*, see p. 22. *Thaneller*, see below. — The ascent of the **Tauern** (6030') may be made from Reutte, with a guide, in 3½ hrs. The pleasant path, which is provided with finger-posts, diverges to the right from the road to the Plansee on this side of the Kleine Plansee (p. 23).

The considerable ruins of *Ehrenberg*, to the W., above the pass of that name (see below), crown the isolated, pine-clad *Schlossberg* (3280'). In the background (S.) rises the *Thaneller* (see below). The castle, destroyed by the French in 1800, was stormed in 1552 by Elector Maurice of Saxony, who with 22,000 men had forced his way through the pass, and would have surprised the Emp. Charles V. at Innsbruck, had not a mutiny broken out in one of his regiments at Reutte owing to their pay being in arrears. Charles thus gained a day, and was conveyed in a litter by a fatiguing and dangerous route across the Brenner to Bruneck. During the Thirty Years' War, Ehrenberg twice resisted the attacks of the Swedes under Bernhard of Weimar and Wrangel, but was taken by the Duke of Bavaria in the War of Succession in 1703.

The road skirts the Schlossberg, passes above the (2 M.) *Ehrenberger Klause* (Inn), a defile still entered by a gateway (through which pedestrians should pass by the old road, leaving the new road at the last houses of Reutte), and descends into the green valley of (2¾ M.) *Heiterwang* (3250'; Hirsch).

About 1 M. to the N.E. is the small **Heiterwang See** (3200'), well-stocked with trout, and connected with the *Plansee* (p. 23) by a narrow channel ¼ M. long. Boats may be hired from the fisherman; to the Plansee ½ hr's. row, Gschwend ¾ hr., Inn zur Forelle 1¼ hr. (comp. p. 23).

Farther on is (3 M.) *Bichlbach* (Hirsch), whence the *Thaneller* (7674'), a fine point of view, may be ascended in 4 hrs. (night-quarters in the loftily situated village of *Berwang*; comp. p. 210). At (2½ M.) *Lähn* the road reaches the infant river *Loisach*, and gradually descends into the extensive green basin of (3 M.) —

87½ M. **Lermoos** (3245'; *Drei Mohren*, with garden, affording a good view; *Post*, also with garden), from which on the E. rise the barren rocks of the imposing *Wetterstein-Gebirge*. To the N. rises the snowy summit of the *Zugspitze* (9710'), adjoining it on the S. are the *Schneefernerkopf* (9460') and *Wetterschroffen* (8880'), and opposite them, to the S., are the *Mieminger Mts.*, with the *Sonnenspitze* (7905') and the *Silberleiten*. A private house opposite the Post contains an interesting collection of arms and armour. — At the base of the Wetterstein, 1½ M. to the E., lies the village of Ehrwald (*Adler; Sonnenspitze; Grüner Baum), a little to the S. of the road to Partenkirchen (15 M, viâ *Griesen*, see pp. 34, 23 ; omn. daily at 4 p.m. in 3½ hrs.; one-horse carr. 12 m.).

EXCURSIONS (guides, *Joh. Guem, Jos. Paulweber*, and *R. Bader* at Ehrwald, *Tob. Posch* at Lermoos). To the **Seebensee** and **Drachensee**, 3½ hrs., a very interesting excursion (with guide). The route from Ehrwald ascends the *Gaisbach-Thal* to the E., past the picturesque *Seebenbach Fall*, to (1¼ hr.) the *Ehrwalder Alp*; here it turns to the right, and leads to the (1¼ br.) *Seebenalp* and (¼ hr.) the *Seebensee* (5360'), which lies in a depression between the *Sonnenspitze* (7905') and the *Tajakopf* (8018'). To the N. a fine view of the Wetterschroffen. (The shorter way by the *Hohe* or *Steile Gang* is a very steep and giddy route.) About ½ hr. higher, at the foot of the *Grünstein*, lies the small *Drachensee* (6155'). A trying pass leads from this point across the *Thörl* or *Grünsteinscharte* (7450'), between the Grünstein and Hochplatte, to (5 hrs.) *Obsteig* (p. 20).

The **Upsberg** or **Daniel** (7664'), to the N. of Lermoos, ascended viâ the *Duftelalp* in 4½ hrs., with guide, and the **Wannig** or *Wanneck* (8180'), ascended from Bieberwier viâ the *Marienbergjoch* (6876') in 5 hrs., with guide, are interesting and not difficult. — Another pleasant ascent is that of the **Schneefernerkopf** (9410'), which is accomplished by a good new path, with a guide, in 5½ hrs. (comp. p. 33). — The **Zugspitze** (9710'), viâ the *Schneekar* in 6 hrs. with guide, is difficult and should be attempted only by adepts. The night is passed in the *Wiener-Neustädter Hütte* (p. 33). An easier ascent leads past the *Pestkapelle* and the *Gatterl* to the *Knorrhütte* (p. 33; 6½ hrs.); thence to the top, 3½ hrs. — From Ehrwald by the *Ehrwalder-Alp* and the *Pestkapelle* to the (3¾ hrs.) *Tillfuss-Alp* in the *Gaisthal* and to (1¼ hr.) *Leutasch-Platzl*, see p. 35. From Tillfuss across the *Niedermünde-Sattel* (6770') to *Telfs* (p. 233) 5 hrs.; from Leutasch Platzl to *Telfs* 3 hrs., to *Seefeld* (p. 37) 2 hrs.

From Ehrwald viâ the *Thörlen* to the *Eibsee*, 3 hrs., see p. 34; guide advisable.

The road to Nassereit, the finest mountain-pass between Bavaria and Tyrol, should be traversed on foot (4 hrs.) or in an open carriage (from Lermoos to Nassereit 4½, with two horses 7½ fl.).

About 1½ M. to the S. of Lermoos lies *Bieberwier* (Inn), from which the road ascends, with a fine retrospect of the Wetterstein Mts., past the (2 M.) *Weissensee* (left) and (1½ M.) the *Blindsee* (to the right, below the road), to the (1½ M.) **Fern Pass** (3970'), 5½ M. from Lermoos and 5½ M. from Nassereit. About ¾ M. beyond the Pass is the inn *Zum Fern*, and ¾ M. farther, by the telegraph-post No. 172, the old road diverges to the right (about 1 M. shorter, damaged by floods, but good for pedestrians). The old road rapidly descends the W. slope of the mountain, at the foot of which it could formerly be closed by the rock-hewn gate of the castle of Fernstein (see below). The new road winds round to the E. side of the valley (a path descending to the right, by a cross 1 M. from the inn, is a short-cut), and then turns back and descends the W. side of the valley, below the old road. The strikingly picturesque castle of *Fernstein* rises above the road to the right. The *Fernstein Inn*, at its base, 3 M. from the pass, contains two

2*

rococo rooms, fitted up for King Lewis II. (adm. 50 kr.). To the left, in the deep pine-clad valley, on a rock rising from the small, dark-green *Fernstein Lake*, are the ruins of the *Sigmundsburg*, once a hunting-seat of Archduke Sigismund. The road crosses the outlet of the lake by a stone bridge and leads past the mouth of the *Tegesthal* (p. 210), on the right, and the slopes of the *Wannig* (8180'), on the left, to (2¼ M.) —

99 M. **Nassereit** (2740'; *Post, R. 40-80 kr.; *Platzwirth).

FROM NASSEREIT TO TELFS, 17½ M., diligence daily in 3 hrs. (fare 2 fl. 24 kr.). The road (to the right, at *Dormitz*, diverges a shorter but steeper route) ascends to the E., over the pine-clad *Holzleiten*, a saddle between the Wanneck and the Tschürgant, to (5½ M.) *Obsteig* (3274'; Löwe), and then descends. To the right in the valley a fragment of the castle of *Klamm* rises from the pine-forest. In descending we enjoy an extensive view of the Innthal; far below flows the river; in the background to the E. rises the *Solstein* (p. 232). — At (9½ M.) *Obermiemingen* (2840'; °Speckbacher) the road to (4½ M.) *Mötz* (p. 233) diverges to the right; walkers to Mötz, however, should leave the road at Obsteig (see above) or at the cross 1 M. before it, turn to the right, and proceed viâ *Wald* and the ravine of the *Klammbach*. The road to Telfs finally leads through a cutting in the rock, and passes a cotton-mill. 16 M. Village of *Telfs*. Then across the Inn to (17½ M.) the station of Telfs (p. 233).

The road to Imst (one-horse carr. 2½-3 fl.; extra-post with two horses 5½ fl.) passes a spinning-factory and traverses the broad, shadeless *Gurgl-Thal*; on the left the wooded *Tschürgunt* (p. 234). 8 M. *Dollinger Inn*. At *Tarrenz* (Inn), 2 M. farther on, the old castle of *Neu-Starkenberg*, now a brewery, stands on the slope to the right. A magnificent view of the Pitzthal and Oetzthal mountains now opens to the S. — Then (2 M.) —

109 M. **Imst** (p. 234). Then past *Brennbichl* and across the *Inn* to (110½ M.) the railway-station of Imst (p. 234).

4. From Immenstadt to Reutte and Partenkirchen.

Comp. Maps, pp. 194, 14.

55 M. RAILWAY to (5½ M.) Sonthofen in 25 minutes. POST-OMNIBUS from Sonthofen to (5 M.) Hindelang twice daily in 1¼ hr. (fare 60 pf.). DILIGENCE daily in summer in the afternoon from Hindelang to (5 M.) Schattwald in 1½ hr. (fare 2 m.), and from Schattwald to (19 M.) Reutte every forenoon in 4 hrs. (fare 1 fl. 50 kr.). ONE-HORSE CARRIAGE from Sonthofen to Hindelang in ¾ hr., 4 m., two-horse 6 m.; to Schattwald 10 and 16 m.; to Reutte 20 and 36 m.; from Reutte to Linderhof 12 m., with two horses 24 m. and gratuity, to Murnau or Partenkirchen 36 and 48 m.

To (5½ M.) *Sonthofen*, p. 7. The road to Hindelang leads to the E. by *Binswang* through the broad *Ostrach-Thal*. On the left, the *Grünten* (p. 8); at its base, the ruin of *Fluhenstein*. To the right, the *Imberger Horn* (5410'). The road crosses (2½ M.) the Ostrach, and follows the right bank by *Vorder-Hindelang* to (2½ M.) —

10½ M. **Hindelang** (2690'; *Adler*, moderate; *Hase*), prettily situated at the foot of the *Hirschberg*. At the base of the *Iseler* (6170'), ¾ M. to the E., lie the sulphur-baths of *Oberdorf*.

EXCURSIONS (guide, *Xaver Mühlegg* of Sonthofen). Ascent of the *Daumen* (7480') from Hindelang or Sonthofen in 5 hrs. (guide 6 m., including descent to Hinterstein 7 m.), interesting and not difficult. The route ascends to

VORDERJOCH. *I. Route 4.*

(2½ hrs.) the *Mitterhaus* chalet in the *Retterschwangthal* and thence leads viâ the *Huseneck-Alpe*, by a new club-path over the *Daumenscharte* and the *Kleine Daumen*, to (2½ hrs.) the summit. Fine view, with the *Erzgunder See* (6070') far below to the E. — The ascent from *Hinterstein* (see below) may be made in 4-4½ hrs. (guide 6 m.), either viâ the *Mösle-Alpe* and the *Nicken-Alpe* to the (3 hrs.) *Thür* (below us, to the left, the *Erzgunder See*), and thence by a well-marked path to (1 hr.) the top; or from the *Oberthal* (see below) past the *Laufbühler See* (4½ hrs.). Descent viâ the *Wengenalp* (p. 11) to *Oberstdorf*, 3½ hrs.

To the S.E. of Hindelang, between the *Iseler* and *Imberger Horn*, opens the *Hintersteiner Thal*, 10 M. in length. The road ascends the right bank of the Ostrach (passing the hamlet of *Bruck* at the mouth of the *Retterschwangthal* on the right) to (3½ M.) **Hinterstein** (2825'; *Fügenschuh; *Thannheimer; Brutscher*), a village 1¼ M. in length, picturesquely situated among lofty mountains (E. the Geishorn, Rauhhorn, Kugelhorn, Falken; W. the Breitenberg and the steeps of the Daumen). (Guides at Hinterstein: Joh. Besler, Ant. Kaufmann, and Jos. Wechs.) The road next passes the *Aueleswände* and ascends through forest to the (4 M.) *Eisenbreche*, a magnificent gorge. (A finger-post points to the right to a platform overhanging the abyss.) At the foot of the *Giebel*, 2½ M. farther on, the valley divides into the *Oberthal* on the right and the *Berggündele* on the left. The former is traversed by an attractive route, which crosses the *Wengenalp* and the **Zeiger** (6520') to *Oberstdorf* (5 hrs., guide 10 m.; the ascent of the *Nebelhorn* may easily be combined with this route, comp. p. 11). The pass from the *Berggündeletha l* across the *Himmeleck* to Oberstdorf is more fatiguing, but also interesting (9 hrs.; guide 10 m.). From the bifurcation of the valley (see above) to the lower *Berggündelehütte* (poor), 1 hr.; thence over steep grass slopes to (2 hrs.) the Himmeleck (6500'), between the Grosse Wilde and the Schnecken, affording a fine view of the wild Höfatsspitze (p. 10). We then descend to (1 hr.) the *Käseralpe* in the upper Oythal (p. 11), and (2½ hrs.) Oberstdorf.

From Hinterstein to the top of the *Daumen*, see p. 20. Another easy and interesting ascent is that of the *Geishorn* (7380'), accomplished viâ the *Willersalpe* (4725'; beds) in 4½ hrs. (guide 6, with descent to Schattwald 8 m.). Splendid view.

The ascent of the **Hochvogel** (8495'; 8-9 hrs.; guide 10 m.) is laborious and requires strength and endurance, but has been greatly facilitated by the erection of the *Prinz-Luitpold-Haus*, situated above a little lake in a basin (about 6230') at the foot of the *Fuchskarspitze* (7574'), and surrounded by huge precipices. The hut, which contains mattresses and beds, is reached from Hinterstein by the *Berggündele-Alp* in 4½-5 hrs.; thence to the summit about 3 hrs. more. The path ascends steeply to the *Balken* (a ridge overlooking the Schwarzwasserthal; 6375'), to the right of the *Fuchskarspitze*. Turning to the right we traverse the E. side of the arête to the steep slope of névé (snow-irons useful), and clamber up fatiguing rocky ledges to the cross on the top. . Abrupt descent over the *Fuchsensattel* into the *Hornbachthal* (p. 13; guide 12 m.). From the Prinz Luitpold Haus across the *Himmeleck* to Oberstdorf, see above and p. 11.

From Hinterstein to *Tannheim* (p. 22) viâ the *Willersalpe* (see above) and the *Geiseck* (about 6235'), between the *Rauhhorn* and *Geishorn*, and past the *Vilsalper See* (see below), 6 hrs. (guide). Another route, shorter but more tiring and less interesting, leads from the Willersalpe over the *Koltersattel* and the *Aelpete* (4 hrs.; guide). A third way leads past the *Wildsee* (5910') and across the *Kirchdachscharte* (6560'), to the S. of the Kugelhorn, and then descends to the left to the Vilsalpsee. A shorter route crosses the *Zipfelsalp*, between the Iseler and Bschcisser, to (3 hrs.) *Schattwald* (p. 22).

The road now ascends the Jochberg in windings, with a pleasant retrospect of the Ostrachthal (short-cuts for pedestrians). 2 M. *Oberjoch* (3700'); ¼ M. farther the road leads to the right (that to the left to *Unterjoch* and *Wertach*) and, before reaching (¼ M.) the **Vorderjoch** (3770'), passes the Bavarian custom-house on the right. We next cross a monotonous mossy plateau; on the right rises the *Iseler*. Beyond the (1½ M.) *Hinter-Joch* we descend across the Tyrolese frontier into the pine-clad *Obere Vilsthal*, pass the Austrian custom-house of *Vilsrein*, and reach (1 M.) —

15½ M. **Schattwald** (3480'; *Traube; Sonne), with a small sulphur-bath, at the W. end of the picturesque *Tannheimer-Thal*. The *Vils*, the discharge of the *Vilsalpsee*, descends hence to the N., and then to the E. by *Pfronten* (p. 14), and falls into the Lech at *Vils*, above Füssen (p. 14). — Farther on, the road is good but shadeless, and driving is preferable to walking. On the left rise the *Einstein* (6110') and *Aggenstein* (see below); in front, the *Gimpelspitze* (7340') and *Köllespitze* (7336'). — 3½ M. **Tannheim**, or *Höfen* (3590'; *Ochs, moderate ; *Kreuz*), the principal place in the valley.

To the (1 hr.) *Vilsalpsee (3700') a good path ascends through the *Vilsthal*, which opens on the S. We then follow the E. bank to the (½ hr.) chalet at the head of the valley, which is bounded by the *Geishorn*, *Rauhhorn*, and *Kugelhorn*. About 1½ hr. to the S., and higher up. lies the pretty *Traualpsee* (5345'), whence a route leads across the saddle between the *Rothspitze* and the *Lachenspitze* to the *Schwarzwasserthal* and to *Forchach* in the Lechthal (see p. 210). — To *Hinterstein* viâ the *Geiseck* or the *Kirchdachschurte*, see p. 21.

To the left lies the village of *Grähn* (ascent of the *Aggenstein*, 6506', 2½ hrs., with guide, interesting), whence a road leads to the N. through the *Enge* to (9 M.) *Pfronten* (p. 14). At the village of (2 M.) *Haldensee* we reach the picturesque green lake of that name (1¼ M. long), overshadowed by the precipitous, pine-clad *Grünspitz* (4555'). 3 M. *Nesselwängle* (3720'; Kreuz), at the base of the *Köllespitze* (7336'). On the left (S.) is the *Gachtspitze* (6595'); opposite us the *Schwarzhanskarkopf* (7296'). The Tannheimer-Thal terminates here. The road descends, passes between the hamlets of *Raut* and *Gacht* (with the wooded *Birkenthal*, the *Lachenspitze*, and the *Leilachspitze* on the right), enters the **Gacht Pass,** the profound and beautifully-wooded ravine of the *Weissenbach*, and winds down its left side. At (4½ M.) *Weissenbach* (2895'; Löwe) the road enters the broad and unattractive *Lechthal* (one-horse carr. to Reutte 3 fl., but not always to be had). We follow the left bank of the Lech (to the right is the *Thaneller*, p. 210) to (6 M.) **Reutte** (p. 18).

FROM REUTTE TO PARTENKIRCHEN, 20½ M., by a picturesque route passing the Plansee. At (½ M.) *Breitenwang* (p. 18), the road turns to the left at the well, and a few paces beyond it to the right, and ascends towards the double-peaked *Tauern*, on the pine-clothed N. slopes of which *(Rossrücken)* it gradually mounts. The small sulphur-baths of *Krekelmoos* are passed on the right. Fine retrospect (the Glimmspitze and Hochvogel, two peaks of the Lechthal, in the background). About 2 M. from Breitenwang, 80 paces beyond the second bridge by which the road crosses a torrent, is a stone (on the left) marking the steep descent through wood to the (8 min.) lower *Stuiben Fall, a broad cascade 100 ft. in height, formed by the *Ache*, the discharge of the Plansee, and finely framed with trees.

A good new footpath, with finger-posts, beginning at (20 min.) *Bad Mühl* (p. 18), ascends along the Lech direct to the ($1/2$ hr.) lower fall. Abundance of Alpine roses.

The path ascends the left bank of the Ache to the ($1/4$ hr.) smaller *Upper Fall*, and turning to the right soon regains the road near (10 min.) a small chapel, close to which is an excellent spring. Crossing the Ache, and passing the *Little Plansee*, we then reach the ($3/4$ M.) **Great Plansee** (3190'; *Seespitz Inn*, R. 50 kr.), a fine sheet of water, $2^3/4$ M. long by $1/4$–$1/2$ M. broad and 250 ft. deep, enclosed by wooded mountains. The shadeless road skirts the lake and passes the *Kaiserbrunnen*. At the ($3^3/4$ M.) *Austrian Frontier Station* there is a monument to King Max II. of Bavaria (*Zur Forelle*, a good inn; *Zum Linderhof*, a few minutes farther on, plain).

A road (omnibus from Reutte viâ Linderhof to Ober-Ammergau and Murnau, and vice versâ, twice daily) ascends from this point past the *Ammerwald-Alp* to the (10 M.) forester's house of *Linderhof* (quarters) in the upper *Ammer-Thal* or **Graswang-Thal**. Opposite, on the left bank of the Ammer, is the royal *Schloss Linderhof (adm. daily except Frid., 9-12 and 2-5, 3 m.; grotto and kiosk 2 m.; adm. to the Hundinghütte 1 m.), erected and splendidly decorated in the rococo style by King Lewis II. (d. 1886). The extensive grounds are embellished with fountains, statuary, etc., and contain the *Monopteros*, a small temple with a figure of Venus, and the *Blue Grotto*, with a subterranean lake, which can be illuminated with electric light (adm. every $1/2$ hr. from 9 to 11.30 and from 2.30 to 5 for parties of at least 12 pers.). Near the grotto is the *Moorish Kiosk*, richly gilded and decorated, with stalactite vaulting, enamelled peacocks, etc. About $4^1/2$ M. to the N. of the château, near the boundary, is the *Hundinghütte*, a blockhouse in the old German style (comp. Wagner's opera of the 'Walkyrie'). To the left of the entrance to the Linderhof is an *Inn* (R. 2-$2^1/2$ m.; early application advisable). — From Linderhof by ($4^1/2$ M.) *Graswang* (2895'; Inn) to (3 M.) *Ettal* or ($4^1/2$ M.) *Ober-Ammergau*, see p. 29.

A picturesque route to (15 M.) *Hohenschwangau* diverges to the left from the Graswang road, $4^1/4$ M. from the Plansee, and ascends by the 'Schützensteig' among fine woods to ($1^1/2$ hr.) the hunting-lodge at the summit of the pass. We descend to the (1 hr.) *Blöckenau*, and follow the carriage-road through the Pöllatthal (view of the Säuling, and farther down of the Marienbrücke, Schloss Neu-Schwanstein, and the Bavarian plain) to ($1^1/4$ hr.) *Hohenschwangau* (p. 15).

Across the Plansee to the *Heiterwanger See* (boats at the Forelle), see p. 18. A footpath, beginning at the Seespitz Inn (see above) and skirting first the W. bank of the Plansee and then the Heiterwanger See, also leads to ($4^1/2$ M.) Heiterwang.

The Plansee terminates $1/2$ M. farther, and the road enters the wood. It crosses ($3/4$ M.) a rocky barrier to the '*Drei Wassern*', where a bridge marks the Austrian frontier. The wooded *Naiderachthal* is now traversed. On the right is ($1^1/4$ M.) a broad mud-stream, with huge masses of detritus. $1^1/4$ M. farther on, we enjoy a fine view of the *Zugspitze*, the highest mountain in Bavaria. The road now quits the wood, and reaches ($1^1/4$ M.) the high-road and the Austrian and Bavarian custom-house at Griessen (2750'; *Inn*). Hence to *Lermoos*, see p. 18; through the *Elmauer Gries* to *Graswang* (see above), with guide, in 3 hrs.

24   *I. Route 5.*   STARNBERG.   *Lake of*

The Partenkirchen road descends the wooded *Loisachthal;* on the right is the Zugspitze, in front the distant Seinsgebirge. The road crosses the Loisach (3 M.) and follows its right bank; $^3/_4$ M. farther on the wood terminates. On the right rises the Waxenstein, beyond it the Zugspitze. The road to the *Badersee* (p. 31) diverges to the right a little on this side of ($1^3/_4$ M.) the *Schmelz* (Inn), at the mouth of the *Hammersbach* (p. 31). In the foreground lies Partenkirchen, and near it the domed tower of Garmisch; on the left the Kramer. $2^1/_2$ M. *Garmisch;* 1 M. *Partenkirchen,* see p. 29.

5. The Starnberger See and Ammersee. The Hohe Peissenberg.

RAILWAY from Munich to Starnberg ($17^1/_2$ M.) in 1 hr. 5 min.; to Peissenberg ($38^1/_2$ M.) in $2^1/_4$ hrs. — STEAMBOAT from Starnberg to Seeshaupt and back (round the whole lake) 4-5 times daily in summer (oftener on Sundays) in 3 hrs. Steamboat-tickets may be purchased at the railway-station in Munich. A circular ticket entitles the holder to break the journey twice, but a fee of 60 pf. must be paid for each additional halt.

The train quits the Lindau line (p. 3) at ($4^1/_2$ M.) *Pasing.* 9 M. *Planegg;* 12 M. *Gauting,* with a sulphur spring. Near ($14^1/_2$ M.) *Mühlthal* we have a glimpse of the pretty, wooded *Würmthal* to the left.

$7^1/_2$ M. **Starnberg** (**Bayrischer Hof,* R. & L. $2^1/_2$-3, B. 1 m.; **Wittelsbacher Hof,* both on the lake; **Pellet; Tutzinger Hof; Zur Eisenbahn; Pension Schmidt,* 4-5 m. per day), a considerable place at the N. end of the lake, is generally crowded in summer. The old château on a height now contains public offices. Bath in the lake 20 pf.; rowing-boat 80 pf. per hour.

The **Lake of Starnberg,* or **Würm-See** (1945'), $12^1/_2$ M. long, and 2-3 M. in width, is enclosed by banks of moderate height, which are covered with villas and parks, especially at the N. end. The principal charm of the scenery is the view of the distant mountains in clear weather. The following are the conspicuous peaks, from E. to W.: Wendelstein, Brecherspitze, Kirchstein, Benediktenwand, Karwendelgebirge, Jochberg, Herzogstand, Heimgarten, Krottenkopf, Wetterstein range with the Zugspitze, and Ettaler Mandl.

STEAMBOAT JOURNEY. On the hill to the right, immediately beyond Starnberg, rises the villa of the late Prince Charles of Bavaria (d. 1875). On the bank, farther on, are a number of other villas. Stat. *Niederpöcking. Possenhofen* (Zum Fischmeister) lies about $^1/_2$ M. from the railway-station of that name (p. 25). Duke Max of Bavaria has a château here. The garden, enclosed by a high wall, is not shown; but the park, about 2 M. in length, is open to the public. Pleasant walk through wood, keeping to the right (way-posts), to (1 M.) **Feldafing** (**Strauch's Hotel,* $^1/_4$ M. from the rail. stat., beautiful view from the terrace; **Hôtel-Pens. Neuschwanstein*). In the lake below lies the *Roseninsel* (shown by order obtained from the 'Obersthofmeister' at Munich, or from the 'Rentamt' at Starnberg), near which a lake-village was discovered by Desor.

Opposite Possenhofen (boat in 1/4 hr., 1 m.) lies **Leoni** (*Leoni Inn*, pens. 5 m. per day). On the hill above it rises the church of *Aufkirchen*.

About 1 M. to the N. of the pier is situated the royal château of **Berg** (adm. 50 pf.), with a beautiful park, where King Lewis II. of Bavaria perished in the lake in June, 1886. The road to it passes through the neat little village of Leoni and then enters the park and skirts the lake. The spot where the bodies of the King and Dr. von Gudden were found in the lake is indicated by a wooden cross. The château is plainly fitted up, and contains paintings and statuettes of scenes and characters from Wagner's operas. — Berg is a steamboat-station, but is not always stopped at.

*Rottmannshöhe (20 min.). The path ascends opposite the landing-place, and at the top of the hill turns to the right to the large *Hotel*, the veranda of which commands a beautiful survey of the lake and Alps, now somewhat interfered with by the trees. On a platform in front of the hotel stands a simple monument erected to Karl Rottmann (d. 1850), the famous landscape-painter, by the artists of Munich.

On the W. bank a number of parks and gardens extend from Possenhofen to (2 1/4 M.) *Garatshausen*, with a château of King Francis II. of Naples. Next stat. **Tutzing** (*Gasthaus am See*, with a garden; *Zur Eisenbahn*, at the rail. station, 1/3 M. from the lake, with *View from the veranda; *Sommerkeller*, a restaurant with groups of fine trees, 1/4 M. to the S. of the station), with Hr. Hallberger's château, the pleasant grounds of which are open from 1 to 3 p.m. — The *Johannesberg*, a grassy hill on the bank of the lake, 3/4 M. to the S. of the railway-station, commands a charming view (still finer from the*Ilkahöhe*, near *Oberzeismering*, 1 hr.). The lake, which forms a bay here towards the W., called the *Karpfenwinkel*, has now attained its greatest width (3 M.).

Stat. *Bernried* (Altwirth; Neuwirth), with a château of Hr. v. Wendland and fine clumps of trees. The banks become flatter, and the mountains more conspicuous. Stat. *Seeshaupt* (Inn) lies at the S. end of the lake. The steamer now steers along the wooded E. bank, passing the pilgrimage-church of *St. Heinrich* on the right, to *Ambach*, *Ammerland* (Inn), with a château of Count Pocci, *Allmannshausen* (Inn; all summer-resorts), *Leoni*, and *Starnberg*.

DILIGENCE from *Seeshaupt* daily to (2 1/4 M.) *St. Heinrich* and (6 M.) **Beuerberg** (2030'; *Post*), with a nunnery and girls' school, prettily situated on the Loisach. To the right of the road lies the *Oederbauer* (Restaurant; 2 M. there and back), which commands an admirable view of the mountains as far as the Kochelsee. — On the hill above Ambach lies the (3/4 hr.) church of *Holzhausen*, another charming point of view (descent to Ammerland 1 hr.). About 6 M. to the E. of Ambach (road by *Weidenkamp*) rises the château of **Eurasburg** (2180'), high above the Loisach, commanding a fine view of the Alps (thence to Beuerberg 1 hr.).

RAILWAY JOURNEY. Little is seen of the lake at first. 20 1/2 M. (from Munich) *Possenhofen*. Beyond (22 M.) *Feldafing* several pleasing glimpses are obtained. At (25 M.) *Tutzing* passengers for *Penzberg* (p. 37) change carriages. The Weilheim line turns towards the W. (view of the Zugspitze, etc., to the left). 27 1/2 M. *Diemendorf*, where the Hohe Peissenberg comes in view. The line ascends through deep cuttings and then traverses grassy dales. To the right, in the distance, rises the Hochschloss (p. 26). 30 1/2 M. *Wilzhofen* (to the right the Ammersee, see below). — At (33½ M.) **Weilheim** (1845'; *Post; *Traube; Luckerbräu), a small town on the *Ammer*, we change carriages for Peissenberg. (Route to Murnau and Partenkirchen, see p. 27.) Passing *Unter-Peissenberg* (Post), the train stops at (38½ M.) **Peissenberg** (1930'), where the railway ends. About ¼ M. from the station is *Bad Sulz* (*Inn, moderate), with shady walks. In the vicinity are extensive coal-mines.

The ROAD TO THE HOHE PEISSENBERG (guide unnecessary) leads from the station across the railway, turns to the left beyond the restaurant (finger-post), and ascends the pine-clad hill, passing the *Weinbauer* (Inn). In 1½ hr. we reach the summit. A footpath ascending to the right beyond Bad Sulz is shorter, but steeper.

The *Hohe Peissenberg (3240'), the Rigi of Bavaria, affords a remarkably extensive panorama owing to its isolated position opposite the centre of the Bavarian Alps. On the summit are a pilgrimage-church, a school (with an observatory on the roof; adm. 20 pf.), and a rustic *Inn*.

VIEW. The principal mountains visible are, from E. to W., the Wendelstein, Benediktenwand, Jochberg (beyond which in the extreme distance peeps the snowy Venediger), Herzogstand, Heimgarten (in front of which lies the Staffelsee), Karwendelgebirge, Kistenkopf, Krottenkopf, Dreithorspitze, Wetterstein range (with the Zugspitze), Daniel, Hochplatte, Hohe Bleiche, Gabelschroffen, Säuling, the mountains of the Loisach district, Grünten, and Stuiben. To the N. an extensive survey of the plain, embracing the Ammersee, Starnberger See, and innumerable towns and villages as far as Munich and Augsburg.

FROM THE STATION OF PEISSENBERG TO OBER-AMMERGAU. A carriage-road (diligence to Rottenbuch daily in 2¼ hrs.) leads round the E. flank of the Hohe Peissenberg to *Böbing* and (9 M.) *Rottenbuch* (*Post), with its ancient convent, picturesquely situated on the left bank of the deep *Ammerthal*. Thence past (4½ M.) *Bayersoyen* (Inn), near the little *Soyen Lake*, to (3 M.) *Saulgrub* (p. 28) and (7½ M.) *Ober-Ammergau*.

The **Ammersee** (1770'), 10 M. long, and 3-4 M. broad, situated 7 M. to the W. of the Starnberger See, is a less attractive lake. It commands a view of the distant Alpine range to the S., while the Hohe Peissenberg rises in the foreground. The banks are flat and wooded. A small steamboat plies on the lake (3-4 times a day between Diessen and Stegen in 1½ hr.; fares 1½ or 1 m.).

From stat. *Witzhofen* (p. 25) to (7½ M.) Diessen a diligence runs thrice daily in 2 hours. 1¾ M. *Pähl* (*Gattinger), a pleasant village. On the wooded hill above rises the **Hochschloss*, commanding a fine view (still finer from the *Sonnenhügel*; at the foot of the hill is a pretty ravine with a waterfall). The road next passes (1¾ M.) *Fischen* (road to the right to *Andechs*, 4 M., p. 27), traverses an extensive marsh, formerly the bed of a lake, crosses the sluggish *Ammer*, and reaches (4 M.) —

Diessen, or *Bayerdiessen* (*Post; Gattinger), an important-looking, straggling market-town and summer-resort at the S.W. end of the lake, with the extensive buildings of an old monastery. A little inland lies the hamlet of *St. Georgen*, the chapel of which afffords a fine view. Baths in the lake at the N. end of the town (20 pf.), and at *St. Alban*, ½ M. farther on.

The steamboat crosses the lake to *Fischen* (p. 26), and then skirts the E. bank to *Mühlfeld* and *Hersching* in the 'Herschinger Winkel' (the broadest part of the lake), the station for Andechs.

A road leads through the picturesque ravine of the *Kienthal* to (3 M.) **Andechs** (2570'), once the seat of the powerful counts of that name, and now a Benedictine monastery, with a favourite pilgrimage-church. The space in front of the church commands a survey of the mountains (more extensive from the tower, but the ascent is unpleasant). A flight of steps by the parsonage leads to the garden of the *°Inn. Erling* (Glocke), adjoins Andechs, forming a single large village (*Erling-Andechs*).

FROM ERLING TO THE STARNBERGER SEE, at first uninteresting, by (3 M.) *Machtlfing* and (1½ M.) *Traubing*. Thence to the left to (3 M.) *Feldafing* (p. 24), or to the right to (3½ M.) *Tutzing* (p. 25). Fine views in descending to the lake. — From Erling to *Starnberg* (9 M.) omnibus daily viâ *Perchting* in 2 hrs.

FROM ERLING TO INNING AND GRAFRATH. To the N. of Andechs a good road leads viâ *Hersching* to (6 M.) *Seefeld* (Inn), on the small *Pilsensee*, with a château of Count Törring (chapel and armoury interesting; fine view from the terrace), and past the lonely *Wörthsee* to (6 M.) *Inning* (Post) and (3½ M.) *Grafrath* (see below and p. 3).

The next stations are *Ried* on the E. and *Utting* on the W. bank. From stat. *Breitenbrunn* (Braun), on the E. bank, a road leads to *Seefeld* on the *Pilsensee* (see above). Then, on the W. bank, *Schondorf*, above which, to the left, are the village and château of *Greifenberg*; at the foot of the hill are the baths of that name with springs containing sulphur and arsenic (diligence daily in ½ hr. to *Türkenfeld*, p. 3). The *Amper* emerges from the lake near stat. *Stegen* (Inn), at the N. end. A small steamboat plies on the Amper (½ hr.; fares, 90, 60 pf.) to *Grafrath* (Inn), 1 M. from the railway-station of the same name (p. 3; omnibus from the landing-place to the station, or vice versâ, 20 pf.).

6. From Munich to Partenkirchen and to Zirl viâ Mittenwald.

Comp. Map, p. 14.

87 M. RAILWAY to (47 M.) Murnau in 2½ hrs. From the Murnau station POST-OMNIBUS twice daily in 3½ hrs. to (15 M.) Partenkirchen (to Oberau in 2½ hrs.). Another omnibus starts at 5.45 p.m. for Garmisch (2 m.) and Partenkirchen (2 m. 60 pf.). DILIGENCE from Partenkirchen to (10 M.) Mittenwald twice daily in 3 hrs. (1 m. 80 pf.); POST-OMNIBUS from Mittenwald to (15 M.) Zirl twice daily in 5½ hrs. (4 m.). One-horse carriage from Murnau to Partenkirchen 9 m.; from Partenkirchen to Mittenwald 8 m. and gratuity; two-horse carr. from Zirl to Partenkirchen (7¼ hrs.) 30 fl., to Garmisch 34 fl.

Beyond (33½ M.) *Weilheim* (p. 26) the train diverges to the left from the Peissenberg line, and ascends the right (E.) bank of the *Ammer*. 36 M. *Polling*; 39 M. *Huglfing*. The train ascends through the side-valleys of the *Hungerbach* and *Zeilbach*, commanding fine views of the mountains on the right, to (43½ M.) *Uffing*, which lies about ¾ M. from the N. end of the *Staffelsee* (2100'). The line runs at some distance from the E. bank of the lake, passing the villages of *Rieden* and *Seehausen*, to —

47 M. **Murnau** (2285'; *Tafelmair's Restaurant*), at the S.E.

end of the Staffelsee, and 140' above it. (*Hôtel Murnau, with chalybeate springs on the lake, 3/4 M. from the railway-station; *Fuchs, moderate; good baths in the lake.) About 3/4 M. from the station and the lake is the prettily-situated village of Murnau (Post; *Pantlbräu; *Griesbräu; Zacherlbräu; Angerbräu). The hill to the E. commands a good view of the mountains: to the left the Heimgarten, Kistenkopf, and Krottenkopf; to the right the Ammergau Mts.; in the background of the Loisachthal the Wetterstein Mts.

From *Ohlstadt*, 4 M. to the S.E., the *Heimgarten* (5860') may be ascended by a path indicated by marks (3½ hrs.; comp. p. 39). On the *Ochsenalpe*, 1 hr. from the top, is the *Heimgartenhütte*, a club-hut (4265'). — To the W. of Murnau a road crosses the hills between the Staffelsee and the Murnauer Moos to (9 M.) **Kohlgrub** (2690'; *Adler*); ½ M. to the S.W. is the chalybeate bath and health-resort of the same name (*Bad-Hôtel*, with dépendance, the *Linderschlösschen*, high charges), at the N. base of the *Hörnle* (5135'), which is easily ascended in 2 hrs. (extensive view, stretching as far as Munich). To the W. lies (1½ M.) *Saulgrub* on the Ammergau road (to *Ober-Ammergau*, see below, 6½ M., by carr. in 1 hr.). Walkers to Ammergau diverge from the road before reaching Kohlgrub by a path to the left, which strikes the Ammergau road at *Wurmesau*.

Passing *Höhendorf* the PARTENKIRCHEN ROAD traverses a broad marshy tract, crosses the *Ramsau* (navigable for rafts) near its confluence with the *Loisach*, and follows the left bank of the latter. At (6½ M.) **Eschenloh** (2095 ft.; *Altwirth*) the mountains are reached; to the left beyond the Loisach rise the roof-shaped Kistenkopf and the Hochriesskopf; in the background the imposing Wetterstein range with the Zugspitze; on the right the Ettaler Mandl. The best point of view is a chapel on the *Festbühel*, to the right of the road.

To THE WALCHENSEE (p. 39) through the Eschenthal (4 hrs.; cart-track; guide, advisable, 4 m.). We cross the *Loisach*, and then the *Eschenlahne*, the right bank of which we ascend; to the right lies a large gully of the *Kistenkopf*. A bridge (1 hr.) is crossed, and the left bank followed; 20 min., a view of the profound *Eschenklamm* (called the '*Gache Tod*') is obtained from the bridges across the abyss. The brook is again twice crossed. Descent to the Walchensee by a footpath to the left (the stony track to the right leads to *Obernach*, near the S. end of the lake).

To OBER-AMMERGAU, footpath over the moors and across the saddle between the *Aufacker* and the *Ettaler Mandl* (3 hrs., guide desirable). — Ascent of the *Krottenkopf* (6880'), in 5½-6 hrs., see p. 31.

At (4 M.) **Oberau** (2180'; *Post*) the Ober-Ammergau road diverges to the right.

This road ascends rapidly to (2½ M.) *Ettal* (2880'; Landes), a monastery dissolved in 1803, with extensive buildings, now the property of Count Pappenheim. The church contains a ceiling-painting by Knoller and a famous organ. On the N. side is a brewery of local repute. The village lies at the base of the *Ettaler Mandl* (5384'), a rocky peak, the ascent of which is laborious (3 hrs., with guide). The road then descends into the Ammerthal to (3 M.) Ober-Ammergau (2760'; *Wittelsbacher Hof*; *Schwabenwirth* or *Post*; *Stern*; *Diemer*; *Preisinger*, and others), celebrated for the passion plays performed here every ten years (1880, 1890, etc.). The theatre has seats for 5000 spectators. Wood and ivory carving is the chief occupation of the inhabitants (Lang's Depôt). About ¼ hr. to the W., at the base of the Sonnenberg, stands the *Crucifixion*, a colossal group in Kelheim marble, executed by Halbig, and presented by King Lewis II. in 1875.

The road next leads by (2 M.) *Unter-Ammergau* (2655'; Schuhwirth;

to Innsbruck.   PARTENKIRCHEN.   *I. Route 6.*   29

Rabe) and *Wurmesau* to (5 M.) *Saulgrub*. Thence (by the Schongau road) either to the N. viâ *Rottenbuch* to (13 M.) *Peiting* (p. 14), or to the E. viâ *Kohlgrub* (see p. 28) to (8¹/₂ M.) *Murnau* (p. 27).

To REUTTE. Road from Ober-Ammergau through the sequestered *Graswang-Thal*, past the château of *Linderhof*, the *Ammerwaldalpe*, and the *Plansee*, 24 M. (comp. p. 23; omnibus daily in 10 hrs., stopping 1¹/₂ hr. at *Linderhof* and ¹/₂ hr. at the *Hundinghütte*). For a visit to Linderhof, it is better to hire carriages at Murnau than at Oberau. — To HOHENSCHWANGAU (p. 15), 8 hrs.; the bridle-path diverges to the right by the Ammerwald-Alp, 6 M. beyond Linderhof.

Beyond (2¹/₂ M.) *Farchant* the broad basin of Partenkirchen becomes visible. On the left is the *Kuhflucht* (p. 30), descending from the Hohe Fricken. Fine view of the Wettersteingebirge from the Dreithorspitze to the Zugspitze. The road to Garmisch diverges to the right before the (¹/₄ M.) Loisach bridge is reached (pedestrians bound for Garmisch leave the road at Farchant). Then (1³/₄ M.) —

62 M. (from Munich) **Partenkirchen** (2370'; *Stern; *Post; *Pension Schweizerhaus, 5 m. per day; Villa Resch, with baths; Drei Mohren, moderate; Zum Rassen; Melber, well spoken of), the *Partanum* of the Romans, a favourite summer-resort, beautifully situated at the base of the *Eckenberg*, a spur of the Krottenkopf. The small town owes its modern appearance to serious fires which occurred in 1860, 1863, and 1865. Handsome modern Gothic church. A visit may be paid to the school of carving and design.

Garmisch (2270'; *Westermeier zum Husaren; *Lamm, 3¹/₂ m. per day; *Reiser zur Zugspitze; *Traube & Villa Buchwieser; *Drei Mohren, moderate; Kainzenfranz; Tutzinger Hof; Villa Sophia; Restaurant Russhütte, prettily situated on the Loisach), a thriving village 1 M. to the W. of Partenkirchen, with picturesque old houses, the seat of the district-court, is another favourite resort. The well-defined Alpspitze is conspicuous, but of the Zugspitze a small part only is seen to the left of the Waxenstein; to the E., between the Eckenberg and the Wetterwand, appear the Seinsgebirge. On the E. side of the village is the new *Wittelsbach Park*, with a bust of Prince-Regent Luitpold.

CARRIAGES are to be obtained at both Garmisch and Partenkirchen. Two-horse carr. to the Badersee 10 m., Walchensee (3³/₄ hrs.) 20, Ober-Ammergau 20, Murnau 14, Lermoos 20, Plansee and Reutte 30, Linderhof (3 hrs.) 30 m. (The driver expects a fee of 10 pf. for each mark of the fare. No other extras.)

EXCURSIONS (guides: *Jos. Reindl*, nicknamed *Spadill*, *Leon. Reindl*, alias *Bäuerle*, *Andr.* and *Joh. Witting*, alias *Gschwandner*, at Partenkirchen; *Joh. Ostler*, nicknamed *Keser*, *Jos. Ostler*, *Joh.* and *Jos. Dengg*, nicknamed *Zeisler*, and *Joh. Polz* at Garmisch). Finest view from the pilgrimage-church of **St. Anton**, to which a shady path ascends in 10 min. from Partenkirchen. The peaks, from left to right, are the Wetterwand, Dreithorspitze, Alpspitze, Waxenstein (behind it the Zugspitze), the pointed Upsberg (in the distance, beyond the Eibsee-Thörlen); to the right the Kramer, in the foreground Garmisch.

Faukenschlucht. Beyond Partenkirchen a zigzag path ascends to it to the right, and then leads on the right side of the ravine to the (20 min.) waterfall of the *Faukenbach*. A path also leads from *St. Anton* (see above) on the hill-side through wood to (20 min.) the entrance of the gorge.

The ruin of **Werdenfels** (2550') is reached in ¹/₄ hr. by a path leading to the left from the *Schwaige Wang*, 1 M. from Garmisch. View of the Loisachthal, the Krottenkopf, etc.; from the S. terrace, view of the Wetterstein.

The Kuhflucht (1½ hr.), entered from *Farchant* (p. 29; by the inn turn to the right, cross the Loisach, and ascend to the left through pine-wood), is a ravine descending from the *Hohe Fricken*, with pretty waterfalls. A path leads to (1 hr.) the highest fall (3755'; ascent uninteresting).

The Riesserbauer is a good point of view, ½ hr. from Garmisch. From the post-office we cross the meadows towards the S.W., in the direction of the *Riesserkopf*, a wooded height immediately below the Alpspitze. The farm (Rfmts. in summer) lies at the back of the hill, in a hollow containing a small lake (bathing-establishment). Fine view from a point a little higher up.

*Partnachklamm and Vorder Graseck (1¼ hr.; guide unnecessary). After following the Kainzenbad road (p. 34), to the S. of Partenkirchen (see below) for a few paces, we turn to the right at a finger-post, and in ½ hr. reach the first bridge, at the mouth of the *Partnach* valley. (From Garmisch a good, and in part shady footpath leads to the right from the Partenkirchen road beyond the bridge, crosses the Partnach and the island, and follows the right bank of the Partnach, joining the route from Partenkirchen about 10 min. before the above-mentioned bridge is reached.) Beyond the bridge a finger-post indicates our path to the left ('nach Graseck'; that to the right leads to the Rainthaler Bauer. p. 33); after ¼ hr. we cross the stream by a second bridge, beyond which the road to Graseck ascends abruptly to the left, while the path to the 'Klamm', or gorge, leads to the right; 6 min., third bridge. The (10 min.) fourth (iron) bridge is the finest point. The Partnach, which dashes through the rocky gorge 230' below, descends from the Rainthal (see below). Beyond the bridge the path ascends in 8 min. to the forester's house of Vorder-Graseck (2850'; *Restaurant*), where a fine view is enjoyed. From this point to the *Rainthal* and the *Schachen*, see p. 32. A narrow path, constructed for the use of the 'lumberers', leads along the bottom of the gorge, close to the water; but though it shortens the walk to the Schachen and the Rainthal by about ½ hr., no one who is at all subject to giddiness should attempt it. — FROM GRASECK TO MITTENWALD direct, through the *Ferchen-Thal*, 3 hrs. (guide unnecessary). From the forester's house we ascend the pastures for a short distance, and then turn to the right. After 20 min. we go straight on (not to the right to *Mittel-Graseck*) to (10 min.) *Hinter-Graseck*; ¾ hr., bridge over the Ferchenbach; then for ¼ hr. straight through the wood, and down to (7 min.) *Elmau* (3345'; Inn). (Walkers from Elmau to Graseck should avoid the bridle-path to the left, which leads to the Schachenalp, p. 32.) From this point a road ascends slowly, at first through wood but afterwards shadeless, to (3½ M.) the *Ferchensee*; it then descends, past the *Lautersee*, to (2¼ M.) *Mittenwald* (p. 34). From Elmau to the *Schachenalp*, see p. 32 (bridle-path, 2½-3 hrs.); to *Klais*, on the Mittenwald post-road (p. 34), 4½ M., by a carriage-road.

The *Eckbauer (3450'; 2 hrs.; guide 2 m., desirable). The road, which passes the *Kainzen-Bad* (p. 34), is tolerable. This excursion may also be thus combined with the preceding. After following the cart-road to Elmau (see above) for 10 min., we diverge by a narrow path to the left at a barn, ascend the grassy slopes in windings, pass through wood, and reach the Eckbauer in ½ hr. (*Inn*, with 6 rooms). The top of the hill, 2 min. beyond the house, commands an admirable panorama of the mountains: Karwendelgebirge, Wettersteinwand, Dreithorspitze with the Schachenalp and Frauenalpe, Alpspitze, Zugspitze, Kramer, and Krottenkopf; below lies the deep, wooded valley of the Ferchenbach.

Schlattanbauer (1-1¼ hr.). After about 1 hr. beyond the highest part of the Mittenwald road (p. 34), a path diverges to the left at a finger-post and leads to (5 min.) the *Schlattan Restaurant*, which affords a fine view of the Wetterstein and the Karwendel ranges. From the Schlattan a path, indicated by blue and white marks, leads to the (1 hr.) *Esterberg-Alp* (p. 31), forming the most direct route from Mittenwald to the top of the *Krottenkopf*.

*Badersee (6 M.; omnibus daily in 1¼ hr., starting at 8 a.m. and 2 p.m., returning at 11 a.m. and 7 p.m.; fare 1 m., return 1½ m.). The road diverges to the left from that to Lermoos, a few hundred yards beyond the *Schmelz* (p. 24), and leads viâ *Unter-Grainau*. The small, emerald-green lake, framed with trees, is overshadowed by the huge precipices of the Zugspitze. "*Hôtel Badersee* (pens. from 6½ m.), on its bank, pleasant for a prolonged stay. — Road hence to the (2¼ M.) Eibsee (see below).

The "Eibsee (3210'), 7 M. from Partenkirchen, at the base of the Zugspitze, is reached by the road viâ *Unter-Grainau* (omnibus from the Post at Partenkirchen daily in 2 hrs., starting at 8.30 a.m., returning in 1½ hr. at 6 p.m.; fare each way 1½ m.); or, from Garmisch, by the path to the left at the W. end of the village, which leads across meadows to (1¼ hr.) *Ober-Grainau* (small "Inn kept by the forester), and thence to (1 hr.) the lake. The Eibsee is enclosed by dark-wooded hills, above which tower the enormous rocky walls of the Zugspitze ("*Terne's Inn*, with veranda, boats, and baths, R. 1-1½ m., 'pens.' with R. 5 m.). Travellers are rowed (50 pf. each) to the *Schöne* or *Maximilian's Insel* in the middle of the lake, where the echoes are awakened by a shot (50 pf.). The huge Zugspitze is seen to great advantage from this lake, but on summer afternoons it is often shrouded in clouds. The picturesque little *Frittensee*, to the S.E. of the Eibsee, may be reached from the inn in 5 min. by boat, or in ¼ hr. by a stony path constructed along the bank of the Eibsee. — From the Eibsee over the *Thörlen* (5225') to *Ehrwald* (3 hrs.; with guide), see p. 34.

Hollenthal-Klamm (3½-4 hrs.; guide 3½ hr.). The best route is by *Ober-Grainau* (see above). A good new path (no risk of mistake; finger-posts) ascends thence, soon becoming steeper, through the *Stangenwald* to the (1¼ hr.) perpendicular rocks of the *Waxenstein*. The 'Stangensteig' (3' broad, steady head necessary) then skirts the precipice, commanding a fine view towards the plain, and leads to (¾ hr.) the bridge (3840') over the *Höllenthal-Klamm*, a narrow ravine through which the Hammersbach dashes, 250' below. A bad path (hazardous without a guide) ascends hence to (1¼ hr.) a deserted lead-mine (4720'), from which a fatiguing path leads to the (2½ hrs.) *Hochalpe* (p. 32). — Another but inferior route (also well marked) to the Höllenthal-Klamm diverges to the left at a guide-post, about 1½ M. on this side of Ober-Grainau (see above), ascends the left bank of the *Hammersbach*, passing the village of the same name, and mounts steeply through the Stangenwald to (1½ hr.) the Waxensteinwand (see above). [About 1½ M. beyond the village of Hammersbach, a path crosses the brook to the *Marklamm*, a pleasant digression requiring about ½ hr.] — From the *Höttenthalänger*, or innermost recess of the Höllenthal, in which is situated a forester's house (closed), a fatiguing but highly picturesque path leads over the *Riffetscharte*, between the Waxenstein and the Riffelspitze, to (7 hrs.) the *Eibsee* (see above). At the upper end of the Höllenthal is the *Höllenthal Glacier*. The ascent of the Zugspitze (9710') from this side is very difficult and fatiguing (guide 20 m.; comp. p. 38).

The Kramer (6510'), on the left bank of the Loisach, above Garmisch, affords an excellent survey of the Wetterstein range. Bridle-path to the (2½ hrs.) *Königsstand*; a narrow path, suitable for good climbers only, with guide, leads thence to the top in 2 hrs. more (guide to the Königsstand 3, to the top 4½ m.). — The Hirschbichlkopf (6510'), ascended without difficulty from Garmisch viâ the *Steppberg-Alpe* in 4½ hrs. (guide), commands a fine view.

The "Krottenkopf (6880'; 5 hrs.; guide 4½, if a night is spent, 7 m.), an easy and interesting ascent, affords a distant view of innumerable peaks (Gross-Glockner, Gross-Venediger, Stubai and Oetzthal Alps) and of the plain (Munich, Starnberg Lake, etc.). A cart-road leads from Partenkirchen viâ St. Anton, passing the parsonage, to the (2 hrs.) *Esterberg-See* (generally dry in summer) and the (10 min.) *Esterberg-Alp* (very poor inn). Bridle-path, steep, and stony at places, thence through the hollow between the Bischof and the Krottenkopf to the (2¼ hrs.) *Krottenkopf Club-Hut* (5560'; Inn in summer), on the saddle between the Krottenkopf and the Oberrisskopf, and to (20 min.) the top (pavilion; fine view). — The descent on the E. to the *Walchensee* is fatiguing (4½ hrs.; guide necessary). The descent on the N. to *Eschenloh* leads round the *Hohe Kistenkopf*, past the *Pusterthal-Alpe*, and through the *Eschenthal* (p. 28; 4½ hrs.; guide advisable).

Hochalpe (5555'; 4 hrs.; guide, 4½ m., hardly necessary). The route from Partenkirchen crosses the Partnach at the upper mill and leads towards the wooded Riesserkopf (p. 30), on the E. side of which it ascends (cart-track) to (3 hrs.) the *Kreuzalpe* (5220'), whence a fine view of the Eibsee is obtained. It then ascends on the E. slopes of the *Langenfeld*, and round the basin of the *Bodenlahnthal*, to (1 hr.) the *Hochalpe*, which commands an admirable view of the Wetterstein, Dreithorspitze, Alpspitze (see below; due S.), and other peaks. Far grander is the prospect from (1 hr.) the *Langenfeld*, which affords a striking view of the Höllenthal, with the Waxenstein, Höllenthalferner, and Zugspitze. The steep descent into the *Höllenthal* should be attempted by experts only, with a guide (see p. 29). By the *Bernardinalp* and *Gassenalp* into the *Bodenlahnthal* and to (2 hrs.) the *Rainthaler Bauer*, see below.

Alpspitze (8648'; 7-8 hrs.; guide 8 m.), fatiguing. From (2½ hrs.) the *Rainthaler Bauer* (see below) we ascend the *Bodenlahnthal* to (2 hrs.) the *Gassenalp*, pass the small *Stuibensee* (6235'; on the left), and reach the (2½-3 hrs.) summit by the S.E. slope. Survey of the Wetterstein, Zugspitze, Höllenthal, etc.; distant view limited.

"**Königshaus am Schachen** (5825'; 5½ hrs.; guide, 4½/2 m., unnecessary). From (1¼ hr.) Graseek the path descends and crosses the *Ferchenbach*, the left bank of which it then skirts to (¾ hr.) the *Steilenfälle* (sometimes dry). It then ascends rapidly to the right through the Wettersteinwald to a small shrine, turns to the left, and crosses a clearing after a few minutes, from which a broad path through the wood leads to the (1½ hr.) royal bridle-path. The latter ascends to the right above the (1½ hr.) *Schachenalp*, with the small *Schachensee*, and leads to (¾ hr.) the *Königshaus*, built by King Lewis II. (adm. 1 m.; Rfmts.). A pavilion, a few hundred paces to the W., on the brink of the abyss, commands a magnificent *View of the Rainthal below us, with the Plattach-Ferner and (to the S.) the Dreithorspitze and Wetterstein. To the N. stretches the vast Bavarian plain. The views from the *Teufelsgesass* (7005'; reached in 1½ hr. more, viâ the *Schachenplatte*) and from the (1 hr.) **Frauenalpe** (7765') are still more extensive, but the ascent of the latter requires a perfectly steady head and good guides (7 m.). — A laborious path crosses the *Wettersteingatterl* (7755'), to the E. of the *Dreithorspitze* (p. 33), whence the descent may be made either to the left through the *Berglenthal* to *Unter-Leutasch*, or to the right over the *Leutascher Platt* and through the *Puitenthal* to (3 hrs.) *Ober-Leutasch* (p. 35). — From *Elmau* (p. 34) a good bridle-path ascends to the Schachenalp in 2½-3 hrs., passing the finely-situated *Wetterstein-Alp* on the left.

Hintere Rainthal and "**Blaue Gumpen** (1½-5 hrs.; guide, unnecessary, 5 m.). The path descends from (1¼ hr.) Graseek and crosses the *Ferchenbach* (p. 30); at the finger-post it ascends to the right into the *Rainthal* and crosses the Partnach three times; 1 hr., finger-post pointing to the right 'Zum Rainthaler Bauern' (see below); 2 min. farther on, the path crosses the *Bodenlahne* (the Alpspitze rises at the end of the valley on the right), and then ascends to the right through the monotonous *Stuibenwald* (the *Mitter-Klamm* remaining on the left). After ¾ hr., at a point where the path again approaches the Partnach, we obtain a fine view of the wild *Hintere Klamm*. We now descend to the Partnach, and follow its left bank to (¾ hr.) the *Bocklhütte*, a forester's hut, where the magnificent Hintere Rainthal is disclosed to view. Then past the *Sieben Sprünge* (a copious spring) to (¾ hr.) the *Untere Blaue Gumpe* (3670'), beautifully situated. A hut (closed) on a rocky height at the lower end of the lake commands a splendid view both up and down the valley. The path now ascends the *Hintere Rainthal*, between huge fragments of rock, the remains of an old landslip; ½ hr., on the left, below us lies the grey-green *Obere Blaue Gumpe* (3830'). Thence to the (1½ hr.) *Angerhütte*, the *Knorrhütte*, and to the top of the *Zugspitze*, see p 33. — To the Rainthaler Bauer (3090'; 2½ hrs.). Path either by Graseck and through the Rainthal, ascending to the right from (2¼ hrs.) the finger-post (p. 32) to (25 min.) the summit; or, diverging to the right from the Graseck road at the opening of the Partnachthal (½ hr. from Partenkirchen) and crossing the *Hohe Steg*. View similar to that from Graseck, but less extensive. The farm belongs to Court-Chaplain Stöcker of Berlin, the Christian Socialist.

The *Zugspitze (9710'), the highest summit of the Bavarian Alps, requires two days (guide for 1 pers. 12, for 2 pers. 15 m., with descent to the Eibsee 15 and 18 m.). Ascent laborious, but very interesting and free from danger for climbers with steady heads. To (5 hrs.) the *Obere Blaue Gumpe*, see p. 32; farther up, the path deteriorates and ascends across an extensive avalanche-track (on the left the imposing *Fall of the Partnach*) to the *Anger*, the upper part of the valley. The (³/₄ hr.) top of the hill commands a fine view of the imposing head of the valley, and, in the opposite direction, of the Blaue Gumpen with the shooting-lodge on the Schachen high above. In the wood, just beyond this point, is the poor *Angeralp* (3970'), from which we mount in ³/₄ hr. to the *Upper Anger* (4430'; refuge-hut). In the neighbourhood (5 min. above the hut, reached by a path diverging to the left, at the last bridge over the Partnach, from the way to the Knorrhütte) is the *Partnach-Ursprung*, a gorge filled with the debris of avalanches, from which a copious brook bursts forth. Thence the path ascends to the right through creeping pines, and then through the *Brunnthal*, past a refuge-hut and the *Vettl-Brünnl*, to (2 hrs.) the **Knorrhütte** (6710'; */*nn* of the German Alpine Club; good spring). From the club-hut we ascend a rocky basin (the '*Weisse Thal*'), past a refuge-hut at the *Schneefernereck*, to the *Schnee-Ferner* or *Plattach Glacier*, which is easily crossed to the base of the Zugspitze. We next mount a stony slope (the '*Grosse Reissen*') to the arête (³/₄ hr. in length; wire-rope) and thus reach (3-3½ hrs. from the hut) the W. peak, on which is a refuge-hut. The *Panorama is superb. A new path (requiring a steady head) connects the W. with the E. summit (8-10 min.), which is said to be about 3 ft. higher, and is marked by a cross 16' in height. Extensive view to the E., and into the Höllenthal. — The ascent from *Ehrwald* (p. 18) is shorter and is recommended to experts. We may proceed from the (2 hrs.) *Pestkapelle* (p. 19) by the *Gatterl* (6670') and the *Plattsteig* to (4½ hrs.) the *Knorrhütte*, and then, as above described, to (3 hrs.) the summit. Or (if experts) we may go from Ehrwald direct, viâ the 'Georg-Jäger-Steig', passing the *Wieswaldhütten* and the *Ehrwalder Köpfe*, to the (3½ hrs.) **Wiener-Neustädter Hütte** in the *Oesterreichische Schneekar* (6940'; Inn in summer), and thence to the (2½ hrs.) W. summit. The descent may be made, but only by experts, to *Ehrwald* in 4 hrs.; a new path leads from the Ehrwalder Köpfe over the *Thörlrücken* to the *Eibsee* (4½ hrs.). The descent to the *Höllenthal Glacier* (p. 31) or through the *Ludergrube* to the Eibsee is very steep and difficult. — The shortest ROUTE TO INNSBRUCK from the Knorrhütte crosses the *Gatterl* and the *Trauchlet* and descends to the left to the (3½ hrs.) *Tillfuss-Alpe* in the *Gaisthal* (p. 35); thence either over the *Niedermunde-Sattel* (6770') in 5 hrs. (with guide) or viâ *Leutasch-Platzl* (p. 35) in 4¼ hrs. to *Telfs* (p. 233).

The ***Schneefernerkopf** (9410') may be ascended without difficulty from the Knorrhütte (see above), in 3 hrs. (with guide), viâ the *Weisse Thal* and the *Plattach-Ferner*. The view from the top is little inferior to that from the Zugspitze. Descent to Ehrwald, see p. 19. — The **Dreithorspitze** (*Partenkirchener Dreithorspitze*, 8485'; *Leutascher Dreithorspitze* or *Karlspitze*, 8766'), a more arduous undertaking (guide 18 m.), is most conveniently ascended from *Leutasch* across the *Leutascher Platt* (p. 32). — The **Hochwanner** (*Kothbachspitze*, 8990') is an interesting ascent of no great difficulty (4½ hrs. from the Knorrhütte; with guide). We ascend across the *Gattert* (see above) and over the *Kothbachsattel* to (2 hrs.) the *Stone Huts* (6830') in the *Kothbach Thal*, whither also a bridle-path ascends from the *Tillfuss-Alp* (p. 35); thence to the ridge above the *Leithenthal*, and across rocks and debris to the (2½-3 hrs.) summit (fine view).

The WALCHENSEE (p. 36) is 18 M. from Partenkirchen (carriage, p. 29, in 3½ hrs.). The Mittenwald road is quitted to the left at (6 M.) *Klais* (see below); 3 M. *Krün*, 9 M. the village of *Walchensee*. View of the Wetterstein and Karwendel-Gebirge almost the whole way. — By *Eschenloh* to the Walchensee, see p. 28.

To LERMOOS (p. 18), 15 M., by a good road through the wooded Loisachthal (omn. every forenoon in 3½ hrs.; carr. 10-12 m.). The frontier-inn at *Griesen* (p. 23) is 9 M. from Partenkirchen and 6 M. from Lermoos. — FROM THE EIBSEE OVER THE THÖRLEN TO EHRWALD (p. 19), 3 hrs., uninteresting (guide, advisable, 2½ m.). About ¼ M. beyond the Eibsee inn we diverge to the right from the road, cross a meadow, and pass through an enclosure by the wood. The stony cart-road, very steep at places, now ascends for ¾ hr. By the finger-post which indicates the way to the Zugspitze, to the left, we take the path to the right, and after 10 min. cross a small meadow. In 10 min. more the path to the left brings us to the frontier. From the (10 min.) crucifix which marks the summit of the Thörlen (5230') we obtain a view of Lermoos. In descending we incline to the right and reach the road from Griesen to Lermoos near the Schanze (p. 19); to Ehrwald (p. 19), 1½ hr.

The ROAD ascends from Partenkirchen to (10 M.) Mittenwald. To the right in the valley, 1 M. from Partenkirchen, lies the *Kainzen-Bad* (*Inn, pension 6 m.), with an alkaline spring (containing iodine, natron, and sulphur), used as a remedy for gout and cutaneous diseases. Farther up, a guide-post points to the left to the Schlattan (p. 30). The road traverses undulating pastures; on the right rises the Wetterstein, and in front are the bold peaks of the Karwendel range. 2½ M. *Kaltenbrunn*; 1½ M. *Gerold* (on the left the small *Wagenbrech See*); 1 M. *Klais* (to the *Barmsee* and *Krün*, see p. 40; to *Elmau*, see p. 30). The road passes the small and marshy *Schmalsee*, and descends abruptly into the *Isarthal*, where it unites with the road from Benedictbeuern and Walchensee (see R. 7). Then (4 M.) —

72 M. (from Munich) **Mittenwald** (3000'; *Post, with clever animal-paintings by Paul Meyerheim in the veranda; *Strodl, at the N. end of the village), the last Bavarian village, overshadowed by the precipitous *Karwendelgebirge*, the W. peak of which rises to a height of 7815'. The manufacture of violins and guitars, which are chiefly exported to England and America, forms the principal occupation of the inhabitants.

EXCURSIONS (guides, *Seb. Bittl* and *Georg Fütterer*.). The *Lautersee (3200'; ¾ hr.). We follow the road to the W. from the Post Inn, and then turn to the left (finger-post) into the *Lainthal*, in which a good path ascends, passing a swimming-bath and several small waterfalls of the Lainbach. On the plateau the path leads through wood to the lake, prettily situated among trees, and reflecting the jagged cliffs of the Karwendelgebirge on the E. — About ½ hr. farther up (rough cart-track) lies the lonely *Ferchensee* (3380'), close to the base of the Wetterstein and Grünkopf; thence to (1 hr.) *Elmau*, and to *Partenkirchen* viâ *Graseck*, see p. 30. — From the *Ferchensee* over the *Franzosensteig* (4185'), between the Grünkopf and Wetterstein, into the *Leutasch Valley*, 2 hrs., with guide; fatiguing descent.

*Leutaschklamm. Beyond the Mittenwald custom-house, by the last house on this side of the Isar bridge, we diverge to the right from the Scharnitz road. (Key of the 'Klamm Grotto' at the inn 'Zur Brücke'; 30 pf.) In 20 min. we reach the fine ravine, which was rendered accessible in 1880. The path is not continued beyond the waterfall (4 min.).

The *Hohe Kranzberg (4521'; 1½ hr.). We proceed to the W. from the church to the three crosses on the *Calvarienberg*, whence a distinct path, with red marks, leads to the summit (refuge-hut), which commands a fine view of the Zugspitze, Wetterstein, and Karwendelgebirge.

Barmsee (1½ hr.). We follow the Partenkirchen road for about 2 M., and at the telegraph-post No. 300 turn to the right and proceed across meadows to the lake, embosomed in wood. Remains of lake-dwellings have been discovered here. Fine view from *Zapf's Inn*, on a hill on the E. side. The lake affords boating and bathing, and there are pleasant walks on its banks. The Barmsee may be reached from Partenkirchen or Walchensee in 2½ hrs. (good halting-place on the route between these places, comp. pp. 31, 40; omnibus from the Rassen at Partenkirchen).

Leutaschthal (to Leutasch Mill, 1 hr.). We ascend to the right by the custom-house, before reaching the Isar bridge (road to the Lautersee, see p. 34), to the shooting-range, and proceed thence through wood, across the Austrian frontier, and past (25 min.) a chapel. We then descend gradually into the Leutaschthal, which at its mouth is a narrow gorge, but soon expands into a grassy valley, bounded on the N. by the enormous precipices of the Wetterstein. In the background are the Göhrenspitze and the Hohe Munde. After crossing the (¼ hr.) brook, we reach (8 min.) the Austrian custom-house (once forming a fortified barrier across the road) and (10 min.) the *Leutaschmühl* (3340'; Inn, rustic). Before reaching *Unterleutasch* ("Brückenwirth', also pension) the road crosses to the left bank of the Ache (to the right is the *Franzosensteig*, descending from the *Grünkopf*, see p. 34). Thence it continues past *Untere-Gasse* and *Obere-Gasse* to (1¾ hr.) *Leutasch-Widum* (3715'; *Xanderwirth*, plain; guides, *Draxl, Rauth*). From this point a road leads to the E. viâ the *Leutascher Mühder* to (2 hrs.) *Seefeld* (p. 37), while a fatiguing path ascends to the N., viâ the *Wettersteingatterl*, to the *Frauenalpte* (p. 32). — A cart-road, passing (20 min.) *Leutasch-Platzl* (4180'), at the mouth of the *Gaisthal*, and the base of the *Hohe Munde* (see below), leads through wood to the (¾ hr.) ridge dividing this valley from the Innthal (4185') and descends (steep and fatiguing) viâ *Buchen* (Restaurant) to (1¾ hr.) *Telfs* (p. 283). — The fatiguing but interesting ascent of the **Hohe Munde** (6495') may be made from Ober-Leutasch viâ the *Moos-Alp* in 4½-5 hrs. (with guide; comp. p. 283). — The *Tillfuss-Alpe* (4560'), with a shooting-box of the Duke of Altenburg, is situated in the Gaisthal, 1½ hr. above Leutasch-Platzl. Path hence viâ the *Pestkapelle* to (3 hrs.) *Ehrwald*, see p. 19; viâ the *Gatterl* to (4 hrs.) the *Knorrhütte*, see p. 33; across the *Niedermunde-Sattel* to (5 hrs.) *Telfs*, see p. 283.

Vereinsalpe (4460'; 3½ hrs.). At the *Hasselmühle*, 20 min. below Mittenwald, the path crosses the Isar and ascends to the left; by (1 hr.) the *Aschauer Chapel* it crosses the *Seinsbach*, and mounts steeply to the right, after which it reaches a tolerable road, running high up on the right side of the profound *Seinsgraben*, which is joined on the left by the wild ravines of the *Lausberg Lahne* and the *Reissende Lahne*. Opposite tower the imposing peaks of the Wörner, and behind us the Wetterstein. On the (2 hrs.) *Vereinsalpe* stands a shooting-box of the Duke of Nassau (Inn). — A bridle-path (comp. p. 43) leads hence to the right round the *Soiernspitze* and past the *Jägersruhe* to (3 hrs.) the royal shooting-box at the *Soiern* (p. 43); then through the *Fischbachthal* (at the bottom of which we cross the bridge to the left, and reach a finger-post in 10 min.), either to the right to (3 hrs.) *Vorder-Riss*, or to the left over the *Fischbachalp* to (3 hrs.) *Krün* (p. 40). — From the Vereinsalpe to the Riss there are two routes. The longer leads through the densely-wooded *Fermersbach-Thal* to (1 hr.) the *Prantl-Alp*. Thence a good path, high up on the left side of the valley, passing a point in the *Dreiergraben* where a steady head is necessary, leads to the *Peintl-Alp*, where it descends to the right, and, after crossing the *Rissbach*, reaches (2 hrs.) the *Oswaldhütte*, halfway between *Vorder-Riss* and *Hinter-Riss* (p. 42). The other route (with blue marks) descends to the right before reaching the Prantl-Alp, crosses the Fermersbach, and ascends the opposite slope through swampy wood to *Au* and (3½ hrs.) *Hinter-Riss* (guide necessary for this route).

The W. **Karwendelspitze** (7815'; 4½ hrs., with guide; fatiguing, but free from danger), ascended by a new path constructed by the German

Alpine Club, commands an imposing view. — The ascent of the **Wörner** (*Fahnenwörner* 8105', *Hochkarspitze* 8250') should not be attempted except by experts; the easiest route leads from the *Karwendelthal* (see below), taking 4½-5 hrs. from the *Larchet-Alp* (viâ the *Grosskar*), but the ascent is also sometimes made from the *Vereinsalpe*. — The *Schöttlkarspitze* (6400'). From the *Seinsbach* valley (p. 35) we ascend the *Felderkopf* to (3 hrs.) the *Felderrnkreuz*, and thence cross the pass to (1 hr.) the pavilion on the summit (descent to the *Soiern Lakes*, see p. 43).

Beyond Mittenwald the road crosses the Isar (before the bridge, on the right, the path to the Leutasch Klamm, p. 34) and traverses the level valley of the river as far as the (1 hr.) *Defile of Scharnitz*, the boundary between Bavaria and the Tyrol. During the Thirty Years' War, Claudia de' Medici, widow of Archduke Leopold V., constructed here the strongly fortified *Porta Claudia*, which resisted the attacks both of the French and the Swedes. In the Spanish War of Succession the stronghold came into the possession of the Bavarians, by whom it was destroyed. In 1805 it fell into the hands of the French (13,000 under Ney against 600 Austrians), and was completely destroyed by them and the Bavarians; traces of it still remain in some walls on the hill-side beyond the Isar. The defenders were commanded by Baron Swinburne, an English officer in the Austrian service, and a member of the same family as the poet. — Beyond the adjacent village of —

74½ M. **Scharnitz** (3160'; *Traube*), on the W., is the mouth of the united *Hinterau* and *Karwendel* valleys, from which the river *Isar* issues.

Through the **Karwendelthal** to (8 hrs.) Hinter-Riss, interesting (guide 4 fl., not indispensable; Thom. Fischer of Scharnitz may be recommended). Road viâ the (6 M.) *Larchet-Alp*, with a shooting-box of the Duke of Coburg (ascent of the Wörner, see above), to (3 M.) the *Angerhütte* (4245'; no accommodation in the shooting-season), grandly situated; about ¾ M. farther on, the road terminates, and a good bridle-path ascends in windings to (1 hr.) the *Hochalpe* (refreshments and bed of hay) and to (1½ hr.) the cross at the summit of the pass (5910'), which affords a fine view of the limestone rocks of the Hinterau range. We descend through wood, avoiding side-paths, to the (1 hr.) *Ahornboden* (p. 43) and then through the *Johannesthal* (p. 43) to (2½ hrs.) *Hinter-Riss* (p. 43).

Hinterauthal. A road leads past (3 M.) the opening of the *Gleirschthal* (see below) and (6 M.) the so-called *Source of the Isar*, two brooks descending from the Heissenkopf on the left, to (1½ M.) the *Hunting Lodge* of Prince Hohenlohe on the *Kasten-Alp* (3950'). We then ascend the *Lavatsch-Thal* to the right to the *Lavatscher Alp* and the (7½ M.) *Köhler Alp* (leaving the *Haller Anger-Alp* to the left at the top of the hill), and thence to the right to the (8 M.) **Lavatscher Joch** (6815'), which affords a view of the Zillerthaler and Stubaier Ferner. The road descends hence, turning to the right by the *Issenanger* and crossing the hill, to the (3½ M.) *Hall Salt Mine* (refreshments), and through the *Haller Thal* to (6 M.) *Hall* (p. 160). — The Innthal is also reached by several passes leading through the **Gleirschthal** (see above). We follow the Hinterauthal for 3 M. and diverge from it by a road to the right, cross the Isar, and ascend the right bank of the Gleirschbach in windings to the (6 M.) shooting-box by the (disused) *Amtssäge* (3960'), in a wild and grand situation. An interesting pass leads hence to ZIRL: it ascends on the bank of the *Kristenbach* to the S. to the (½ hr.) *Zirler Kristenalp* (4390') and the (1½ hr.) **Erlsattel** (6080'), whence the *Grosse Solstein* (8390') may be ascended without difficulty in 2 hrs. (comp. p. 232); it then descends to

the *Erlalp* and leads high up on the right side of the *Ebbachthal* to (3 hrs.) *Zirl*. — In the E. prolongation of the Gleirschthal (the head of which is called the *Samerthal* or *Pfeisthal*) a cart-road leads from the Amtssäge to the Stempeljoch (7190'; view limited); it then descends steeply over loose stones to the (1½ hr.) *Haller Berghaus* (p. 161) and (2 hrs.) *Hall* (p. 160). — Other passes (guides necessary) cross the *Frauhitt-Sattel* (7360'; *View), the *Mandlscharte* (ca. 7200'), and the *Arzlerscharte* (7050') to *Innsbruck*.
The road quits the Isar and ascends (to the right a view of the rounded cone of the *Hohe Munde* and of the bare limestone peaks of the Wetterstein) to (6 M.) —

80½ M. **Seefeld** (3860'; *Post; Bräuhaus*), with a Gothic church of the 14th cent., prettily situated on the watershed between the Isar and Inn and adapted for a stay of some time.

EXCURSIONS (guides, *Franz* and *Josef Heigl* of Seefeld, and *Jos. Haselwanter* of Reith). The *Reitherspitze (7780'; 3-3½ hrs.; guide 2 fl., not necessary for adepts; path marked) affords an admirable view of the N. and Central Alps. — From Seefeld to *Leutasch* by the *Leutascher Mähder* (6 M.), see p. 35; to *Telfs* (p. 293) via **Mösern** (4250'; *Inn*), with an imposing view of the valley of the Inn and the Selrain peaks, 3 hrs. (guide, advisable, 2½ fl.).

The road leads past the small and marshy *Wildsee* (fine retrospect of the Wettersteingebirge as far as the Plattach-Ferner; to the N., the Reitherspitze) and the village of *Auland* to (3 M.) *Reith* (3690'), beyond which it descends, via *Leiten*, in wide curves, which afford magnificent views of the Innthal and the Mts. to the S. of the Inn (Alps of Selrain and Stubai). On the last height above the road is the ruin of *Fragenstein*. (Those subject to giddiness should avoid the 'Schlossbergsteig', a path leading close by the castle, and cutting off the last curve of the road.)

87 M. **Zirl** (2035'; *Stern; *Löwe*), and thence across the Inn to (20 min.) the railway-station, see p. 232 (railway to Innsbruck, 9½ M., in 25 min.).

7. From Munich to Mittenwald viâ Benediktbeuern.
Kochelsee and Walchensee.
Comp. Maps, pp. 24, 14.

67½ M. RAILWAY to *Penzberg* (35½ M.) in 2¾ hrs. POST-OMNIBUS twice daily from Penzberg to *Benediktbeuern* in 1 hr. 10 min., and to *Kochel* in 2¼ hrs. OMNIBUS (1887) twice daily from Penzberg to *Mittenwald* in 7 hrs. (the night, on one of the trips, being spent at the Inn zum Kesselberg). — Pedestrians may reach the Kochelsee and Walchensee from *Murnau* (p. 27): from Murnau viâ Grent to *Schlehdorf* (p. 38) 2¼ hrs.

Route to (25 M.) *Tutzing*, see p. 25. The railway now skirts the Starnberger See. 28½ M. *Bernried*; 31½ M. *Seeshaupt* (*Inn), both (p. 25) ¾ M. from the railway. Farther on, the country is uninteresting. On the right the pretty *Ostersee*. 35½ M. *Staltach* (Brewery), with a model-farm belonging to Count Maffei.

FROM STALTACH TO MURNAU (3 hrs.). This pleasant route leads by *Iffeldorf* and *Antorf* to (1½ hr.) *Habach* (Inn); then over the *Aidlinger Höhe (2610'), which affords a beautiful view of the Wetterstein and the lakes, to *Aidling*; and finally past the marshy *Riedsee* (on the right) to (1½ hr.) *Murnau* (p. 27).

38½ M. **Penzberg** (2080'; *Inn*;), the terminus of the railway. — The road to Kochel crosses the *Loisach* and traverses a flat district to (4¼ M.) *Bichl* (*Löwe), with baths, and is there joined on the left by the road coming from Tölz viâ *Heilbrunn* (p. 41). Then (³/₄ M.) —

43½ M. **Benediktbeuern** (2055'; **Post*; **Zur Benediktenwand*), with a once wealthy and celebrated monastery, founded in 740, and consecrated by St. Boniface, now a military hospital and 'remonte depôt' (a few bedrooms at the tavern). To the left rises the Benediktenwand; to the S. the Jochberg, Herzogstand, and Heimgarten.

The **Benediktenwand** (5910') is ascended hence viâ the *Hausstatt-Alpe* in 4½ hrs. (with guide); the route is steep at places, but repays the fatigue. At the top is a cross. Magnificent view as far as the Gross-Glockner and Venediger; to the N. the extensive plain and six lakes. From *Kochel* (see below) to the top of the Benediktenwand viâ the *Mairalpe* and *Staffelalpe*, 4 hrs. (with guide). From *Lenggries*, see p. 41.

Beyond Benediktbeuern the road skirts the E. side of an extensive marsh, which bounds the Kochelsee on the N., and leads by *Ried* and *Besenbach* to (48 M.) *Kochel* (Abenthum, moderate), which is separated by a hill from (³/₄ M.) the lake (*Bad Kochel, nearer the lake, R. 1½ m.). The emerald-green **Kochelsee** (1970'), 3³/₄ M. long and 2½ M. broad, is fed by the Loisach, and is bounded on the S. by the Jochberg, Herzogstand, and Heimgarten. To the N. is the *Rohrsee*, beyond which lies a large marshy tract. The pavilion near Bad Kochel affords a good view.

On the opposite bank of the lake lies **Schlehdorf** (**Herzogenstand*, moderate), 2¼ hrs. from stat. Murnau (p. 27). From Schlehdorf ferry in ½ hr., passing the *Nasen*, which rise perpendicularly from the lake, to the *Müller am Joch* (Inn), at the foot of the Kesselberg. Footpath thence to the falls of the Kesselbach and the high-road (20 min.).

About 1¼ M. beyond Kochel, at the *Inn Zum Grauen Bären*, the road approaches the lake, but quits it again by the **Inn zum Kesselberg*, ³/₄ M. farther on (ferry to Bad Kochel 40 pf.; good echo on the lake). It then ascends gradually, and afterwards rapidly, between the Jochberg and the Herzogstand, to the pass of the *Kesselberg* (2760'). Higher up, a little to the right of the road, are the falls of the Kesselbach, to which a path cutting off an angle of the road ascends. On the road-side near the top of the hill, to the left, is a crucifix with the Bavarian and Hapsburg arms, commemorating the construction of the road by Duke Albert IV. of Bavaria in 1492. From the culminating point we obtain a view of the Karwendel and Wetterstein ranges in the distance, and, below us, of the beautiful, deep-blue ***Walchensee** (2630'), 4¼ M. long and 3 M. broad, surrounded by forests and mountains, the finest of the Bavarian lakes after the Königs-See. At the N. end are the two houses of (4 M.) *Urfeld* (Zum Jäger, on the lake, R. 1½ m.; new Inn at the fisherman's).

The "**Herzogstand** (5760'), a remarkably fine point of view, is ascended hence in 2½-3 hrs. (carriage-road to the old shooting-lodge; guide unnecessary). A narrow road diverges to the right from the road coming from the Kesselberg, about 8 min. from Urfeld (or a steep path leading from Urfeld direct to this road in 10 min. may be taken). In 1/2 hr. a pavilion, commanding a beautiful view of the lake, is reached. On the opposite side of the path is a bench affording a survey of the Kochelsee and the plain. A spring in a ravine is next passed (1 hr.), where a short-cut to the summit strikes off to the right. On the saddle, 1/4 hr. farther on, is the *Jagdhaus*, formerly a royal shooting-lodge, now belonging to the German Alpine Club (Inn). Beyond the lodge the path is nearly level to the foot (10 min.) of the highest peak, which is attained by zigzags in 1/2 hr. more. On the summit is a closed pavilion, and a little lower is an open hut. Admirable view of the mountains as far as the Oezthal glaciers, and of the plain with its numerous lakes. A narrow ridge, practicable only for travellers with steady heads, connects the Herzogstand with the (3/4 hr.) *Heimgarten* (5860'), to the W., from which we may descend (with guide) by the *Käseralpe* to *Schlehdorf* (p. 38), by the *Ochsenalpe* to *Ohlstadt* (p. 28), or by the *Ohlstädter Alpe* to *Walchensee* — Beyond the lodge, a narrow but good path to the right, affording at first a fine view of the Walchensee and mountains, and then leading through wood, descends to the hamlet of Walchensee in 1 1/2 hr. (Ascent of the Herzogstand from Walchensee 3 1/2 hrs., fatiguing.)

Jochberg (5060'; 2 1/2 hrs.; a fine point of view; guide not indispensable). By the 'brake' ('Radschuh') notice-board on the Kesselberg (p. 38) we ascend to the right to the (2 hrs.) *Jocher Alpe* and the (1/4 hr.) summit, which commands a beautiful view, particularly of the Walchensee and of the Tauern to the E. — Descent to Kochel, 2 1/2 hrs., with guide.

From Urfeld to *Jachenau* and *Tölz*, see p. 42. — *Boat* across the lake: to Walchensee (for 1, 2, 3, or 4 pers.) 1 m. 20, 1 m. 80, 2 m. 10, 2 m. 40 pf.; to Altlach 2, 3, 4, 4 1/2 m.; Zwerger 1 m. 30, 2 m., 2 m. 50, 2 m. 80 pf.; Obernach 2 1/2 m., 3 1/2 m., 4 m. 80, 5 m. 30 pf. — *Carriage* from Walchensee to Wallgau 5, with two horses 8 m.; to Kochel and Krün 6 and 9, to Barmsee 7 and 11, to Benediktbeuern and Mittenwald 9 and 15, to Vorder-Riss 11 and 18, to Partenkirchen 12 and 20, to Lenggries and Penzberg 13 and 22, to Murnau 15 and 24, to Tölz 16 and 28, to Tegernsee 30 and 50, to Achensee 33 and 56 m.

From Urfeld the road leads on the W. bank of the lake to (2 M.) the hamlet of —

56 M. **Walchensee** (*Post, pens. 4 m.), charmingly situated on a bay of the lake, and surrounded with beautiful woods. On the opposite bank are the church and parsonage of *Klösterl*. It is preferable to proceed from Urfeld to Walchensee by boat (1 hr.). From the middle of the lake (the 'Weitsee') a fine view is enjoyed. On the S. bank are the houses of *Altlach*, whence a good bridle-path ascends the *Hochkopf* (4010'; 1 1/2 hr.; comp. p. 43). Travellers bound for Mittenwald row from Walchensee in 3/4 hr. to the *Zwerger* (1/2 M. from the road) or in 1 hr. to the mouth of the *Obernach*, at the S. end of the lake ('Inn zum Paulus dem Einsiedler', see below). Thence to Wallgau by the high-road 4 M.

Boat from Obernach to Urfeld, 1 pers. 2, 2 pers. 3, 3 pers. 4 m., each person additional 1/2 m. more. Carr. with one horse to Mittenwald 7, to Partenkirchen 10 (two-horse carr. 20), to Lenggries 14, to Tölz 18 m. — From the Walchensee through the *Eschenthal* to *Eschenloh*, see p. 28 (4 hrs.; guide convenient).

Beyond the hamlet of Walchensee the road is carried over the steep *Katzenkopf* to the (2 M.) *Inn zum Paulus* (see above), where the *Obernach*, the principal feeder of the lake, is crossed. We now gradually ascend the pine-clad valley of the Obernach. At (5 M.) *Wallgau* (2840'; *Altwirth), the broad valley of the *Isar* is reached.

(Road to Vorder-Riss and Tölz, see p. 43.) — 1½ M. Krün (2835'; *Inn*, indifferent).

From Krün a road leads to the W., past the picturesquely situated **Barmsee** (*Inn*, see p. 35), to (2½ M.) *Klais*, on the high-road from Mittenwald to Partenkirchen (p. 34). — To the Soiern Lakes (3½ hrs.). A road ascends to the left to (2 hrs.) the *Fischbach-Alps*, with a shooting-lodge of Count Holnstein; thence we descend into the *Fischbachthal*, joining the path from Vorder-Riss, and ascend again to the right to (1½ hr.) the *Royal Shooting-Box* at the *Soiern* (ascent of the *Schöttlkarspitze*, etc., see p. 43).

On the S. the precipitous *Karwendelgebirge* is conspicuous; to the W. rises the *Wettersteingebirge*. At the mouth of the *Seinsbach* (p. 35) the road crosses the Isar twice within a short distance. Then past the *Husselmühle* to (3 M.) —

67½ M. *Mittenwald* (p. 34).

8. From Munich to Tölz and Mittenwald.

Comp. Maps, pp. 40, 46.

74 M. Railway to (36 M.) *Tölz* in 2¼ hrs. Post-Omnibus from Tölz to (5½ M.) *Lenggries* twice daily, in 1¼ hr.; to (9¼ M.) *Benediktbeuern* viâ *Bichel* daily in 2¼ hrs.; to (10½ M.) *Penzberg* daily, in 2½ hrs., also viâ *Bichel*. Post-Omnibus from Lenggries to *Vorder-Riss* thrice weekly (Mon., Wed., & Sat.), in 3 hrs. One-horse carriage from Tölz to the Walchensee 10, to Mittenwald 20 m.

The train soon turns towards the S.; to the left are seen the Bavaria and Ruhmeshalle, to the right the distant Alps. The direct line to Rosenheim diverges to the left (R. 11). — 3½ M. *Mittersendling*. At (6½ M.) *Grosshessellohe* the *Isar* is crossed by a fine iron bridge; to the left we obtain a view of the deep and gravelly bed of the river, with Munich in the distance. Then through wood. 11 M. *Deisenhofen*; 16 M. *Sauerlach* (2025'). The *Teufelsgraben* ('devil's ditch'), a deep, dry hollow, is crossed, and the train reaches (23 M.) **Holzkirchen** (2245'; *Rail. Restaurant*). the junction of the lines to Rosenheim (p. 53) and Schliersee (p. 49). View of the Alps, with the Wendelstein, beyond the station. The small town *(Post; Oberbräu)* lies ½ M. from the railway.

The line skirts the E. side of the town, and diverges to the right from the line to Schliersee. 26 M. *Ober-Warngau*. 30 M. **Schaftlach** (2480'; *Rail. Restaurant;* branch-line to Gmund, see p. 44). The mountains become grander; on the left rises the Benediktenwand. 32 M. *Reigersbeuern*, with a handsome château. The Tölz station (**Bellevue*, with fine view, adjacent) lies to the N. of the town, ½ M. from the Isar bridge (omnibus 20 pf.).

36 M. **Tölz** (2200'; **Post*; *Bürgerbräu*, *Bruckbräu*), with gardens; **Kolberbräu; Lechner*), a small town prettily situated on a hill on the *Isar*, with breweries and a trade in timber. Many of the houses are frescoed with Biblical subjects. The garden of the Bürgerbräu and the **Calvarienberg* command a fine survey of the Isarthal, stretching far into the distance; in the background, to the S.W., the long *Benediktenwand* (p. 41) and the cone of the *Kirchstein* (p. 42), to the S. the *Juifen* (p 47). On the left bank of the Isar are the baths

of **Krankenheil** (*Kurhôtel*, with baths; *Sedlmair*, with baths, R. 2, B. 1 m.; *Blomberg; Pension Spenger*, 5-7 m.; furnished rooms at the *Villa Bellevue, Daxenberger, Krinner*, etc.), with a *Conversations-Saal, Trinkhalle*, and *Bath House* (bath 2 m.). The water is conducted in leaden pipes from the springs, 4 M. distant, and contains natron and iodine. About ½ M. to the W. is the *Zollhaus* (*Inn, with baths). The left bank of the Isar, close to the town, is laid out with extensive woods and promenades. Visitors' tax, 1 pers. 7, 2 pers. 10, a family 12 m.

PEDESTRIANS may take the following pleasant route from Munich to Tölz. Railway to *Starnberg* (p. 24); walk along the E. bank of the lake to (3½ M.) *Berg* (p. 25) and (6 M.) **Wolfratshausen** (1895'; **Haderbräu; Post*), at the confluence of the *Loisach* and *Isar*. The lofty slope above the village commands a fine view of the mountains towards the S., and down the valley of the Isar. Then by the high-road to (8 M.) *Königsdorf* (Post), whence a footpath, easily followed, leads in 2 hrs. to *Tölz*.

EXCURSIONS FROM TÖLZ. To (½ hr.) *Gaisach* (Inn), with fine view; through the woods to (½ hr.) *Sigmundsruhe* and (1 hr.) the *Schweizer* (Inn), with fine view; by (1 hr.) *Wackersberg* (Altwirth) and the (¾ hr.) *Pestkapelle* to (¾ hr.) the *Baun-Alp* (refreshments). — Beyond the *Zollhaus* (see above) to the left, before the first bridge, viâ the (20 min.) *Sauersberg* and the (¾ hr.) *Sudhaus* (refreshments), to (8 min.) the *Krankenheil Springs*, and thence to (1¼ hr.) the top of the **Blomberg** (4060'; view), near the summit of which is the *Gustav-Quelle*. Turning to the right we skirt the fence for 5 min., then pass through it to the right, and reach (¾ hr.) the *Sauerberger Alpe*. Two paths lead hence to the **Zwiesel** (4800'), one direct in ½ hr., the other diverging to the left to (25 min.) the *Schnaitacher Alpe*, about 10 min. from the summit, on which there is a refuge-hut. Extensive view. The descent may be made from the Schnaitacher Alpe at a somewhat steep angle, crossing several grassy expanses, to a footpath, which leads to the left through wood and finally loses itself in the stony channel of the *Steinbach*. We descend the channel until we come to a path ascending to the left, which leads past (1 hr.) the *Baun-Alp* and the *Pestkapelle* to the (¾ hr.) *Wackersberg* (see above). Thence either direct to (1 hr.) Tölz, or viâ the *Dachshöhle* to the (40 min.) Zollhaus. — The *Benediktenwand* (5910') is better ascended from Lenggries (see below).

[FROM TÖLZ TO THE WALCHENSEE there are two roads: by *Kochel* (21 M.), or through the *Jachenau* (25 M.). The KOCHEL ROAD (one-horse carr. 12, two-horse 18 m.) leads to the W., past the *Zollhaus* (p. 41) and the *Stallauer Weiher*, to *Vorder-Stallau* and (6 M.) the baths of *Heilbrunn* (to the right), with the *Adelheidsquelle*, containing bromine and iodine. The road then passes *Enzenau* and *Unter-Steinbach*, and reaches (3 M.) *Bichel*, on the road from Penzberg to Kochel and Mittenwald (p. 38).

The LENGGRIES AND JACHENAU ROAD (one-horse carr. to Urfeld 18, two-horse 28 m.) follows the E. side of the broad Isarthal to (6½ M.) **Lenggries** (2220'; **Post; Altwirth*). [The footpath over the *Wackersberg* (see above) is recommended to pedestrians.] The Calvarienberg commands a pretty view; and about ¾ M. to the S. is the Duke of Nassau's château of *Hohenburg* (brewery and inn).

MOUNTAIN ASCENTS (guides, *J. Lebender, L. Mayr,* and *J. Oettl* in Tölz; *M. Greil* and *J. Bocksberger* in Lenggries). The ***Benediktenwand** (5910') may be ascended in 5½ hrs., with guide, by the *Längenthal-Alp* and *Probsten-Alp*. This ascent is longer but more interesting than that from Benediktbeuern (p. 38). — The **Brauneck** (5105') is easily ascended viâ the

Garland Alp in 2½ hrs., with guide. From the top we may descend to the *Brauneck Alp* and thence ascend (1 hr.) the *Kirchstein* (5600), which commands a view similar to that from the Benediktenwand. — The **Geigerstein** (4890'; 3 hrs., with guide) offers no very great attraction. — The **Fockenstein** (5130') and the **Kampen** (5505'), both of which may be ascended in 3-3½ hrs. viâ the *Hirschbachthal* and the *Hirschthal-Alp* (4000'), are two interesting points. (From the Hirschthal-Alp to the *Bauer in der Au* and to *Tegernsee*, see p. 45.) — A very attractive ascent is that of the ***Rossstein** (5550'), made from *Fleck* (see below) through the *Alpenbachthal* and viâ *Schönberg* and the *Rosssteinhütten* in 4½ hrs. (with guide); beautiful and extensive view from the top.

The road crosses the Isar (on the opposite bank, the château of Hohenburg, p. 41), and reaches (2½ M.) *Wegscheid* (Zum Pfaffensteffl, rustic). The narrow road now quits the valley of the Isar, skirts the wooded flanks of the *Langenberg*, and enters the **Jachenau**, a secluded valley, 10 M. in length, watered by the *Jachen*, and containing a few farm-houses. 8 M. *Zum Bäck Inn* (dear). About 2 M. farther on is the village of *Jachenau* (2620'; Neuwirth: Pfund), whence a road to the left leads past the *Jachenklamm* to *Niedernach* and along the S. bank of the Walchensee to *Altlach* and *Obernach* (see p. 39). The road to Urfeld (preferable) continues to ascend over the *Fieberberg* and then descends through wood to (4 M.) *Sachenbach*, at the E. end of the *Walchensee*, and (2 M.) *Urfeld* (p. 38).]

FROM TÖLZ TO MITTENWALD (38 M.; carr. with one horse to Vorder-Riss 18, with two horses 30 m.). To (6½ M.) **Lenggries**, see above. The road then follows the right bank of the Isar, passing *Anger* (on the left *Schloss Hohenburg*, see above), to (3 M.) *Fleck* (*Inn), with large saw-mills. Beyond (1 M.) *Winkel* the Isarthal turns to the S.W.; in the background rises the *Scharfreiter* (see below). The valley narrows; on the left are abrupt, wooded slopes, on the right flows the river in its wide and gravelly bed. The road rounds a jutting rock, crosses the *Walchen* or *Achen* and the *Dürrach*, and reaches (6 M.) the **Fall** (2365'; *Rieschenwirth; Fallerhof*). On the right a rapid of the Isar, here hemmed in by a rocky barrier.

On the right bank of the *Walchen* or *Achen*, which flows out of the Achensee, a narrow road leads to (9 M.) *Achenwald* on the Kreuth postroad (p. 47). — To the S. of the Fall is the *Dürrachklamm*, a gorge which deserves a visit (2 hrs. there and back, with guide). — The very interesting ascent of the *Juifen* (6520'; see p. 47) may be made hence in 4½ hrs., with guide. — A very fine point of view is the **Scharfreiter** (6680'; 6½ hrs., with guide). To the royal shooting-box on the *Krametseck* (view) 3 hrs.; thence by the *Wiesalpe* and *Mosenalpe* to the top in 3½ hrs. more. The descent may be made by the *Baumgartenjoch* (bridle-path thence) to (2½ hrs.) *Hinter-Riss* (p. 43); or from the Mosenalpe to the (2½ hrs.) *Oswaldhütte* (see below).

The valley expands. 6 M. **Vorder-Riss** (2570'), a royal shooting-lodge in a pine-clad dale *(Krametis-Au)*, at the confluence of the *Riss* with the Isar (*Inn* at the forester's; guide, Kaspar Krinner). In the distance are seen the Zugspitze and Karwendelgebirge.

THROUGH THE RISS TO THE ACHENSEE (9½-10 hrs.). The valley contracts at (3½ M.) the *Oswaldhütte*, at the mouth of the deep *Fermersbach-Thal*. (To *Mittenwald* by the *Vereinsalpe*, see p. 35.) The *Scharfreiter*

(6680') may be ascended hence in 5½ hrs. (easier from the Fall, p. 42). 5 M. **Hinter-Riss** (3105'), a shooting-lodge of the Duke of Coburg, in a finely-wooded valley. At the foot of the small Gothic château are the low buildings of a Franciscan monastery (*Inn*, adjoining the monastery; *Alpenhof*, ¼ hr. farther on).

EXCURSIONS. To the grand rocky amphitheatre in the *Rohnthal*, 1½ hr. (guide not indispensable). — To the top of the *Schönalpelkopf* (6520'), an agreeable and easy expedition (3 hrs.). — To **Ladiz** and **Laliders**, an attractive excursion for a whole day (10-11 hrs.). A bridle-path leads to the S. through the *Johannesthal* (see below) to the (2½ hrs.) *Ahornboden*, with a shooting-box; thence to the left to the (1 hr.) *Ladiz Alp* (5155'), which commands a striking view of the wild rocky masses of the Birkkarspitze, Kaltwasserkarspitze, etc.; then over the *Ladizer Jöchl* (5680'), between the Ladizkopf and the **Mahnkopf**, to the shooting-lodge of *Laliders* (4980'), the (2 hrs.) *Alp Laliders-Niederleger*, grandly situated, and through the *Laliderer-Thal* back to (3¼ hrs.) Hinter-Riss. Or we may again ascend from Laliders to the (1 hr.) *Hohljoch* (5870'), between the *Gamsjöchl* and the *Kühkarspitze* (*Laliderer Wand*), which may also be reached in 1½-2 hrs. direct from Ladiz, viâ the *Spielistjoch* (5830'), at the back of the *Falken*; thence we descend to (1 hr.) the *Eng-Alp* (3930'; Inn), in a fine situation at the base of the huge *Spritzkarspitze*, and return to (3¼ hrs.) *Hinter-Riss* through the *Eng-Thal* (see below). From the Eng over the *Gramaiser-Joch* to *Pertisau*, see p. 49; over the *Lamsen-Joch* to *Schwaz*, see p. 160. — From Hinter-Riss to the *Vereins-Alpe* and to *Mittenwald*, see p. 35. — Across the *Hochalpe* to the *Karwendelthal* and to *Scharnitz*, see p. 36.

From Hinter-Riss (provisions should be taken; guide unnecessary) the road ascends gently, past the mouths of the *Johannesthal* and *Laliderer-thal*, to the (2 hrs.) *Hagelhütte* (3340'), where the *Rissthal* (route over the *Gramais-Joch* to *Pertisau*, see p. 49). We then ascend by a new road, passing the *Plumser-Alp*, to the (2½ hrs.) **Plumser Joch** (5420'), which commands a fine view: behind us the Karwendelgebirge, to the E. the Seekarspitze and Rabenspitze, near the Achensee. We now descend in zigzags to the (1¼ hr.) *Gernalp* and through the wooded *Gernthal* to (1 hr.) *Pertisau* (p. 48).

FROM VORDER-RISS TO ALTLACH on the Walchensee (p. 39) over the *Hochkopf* (4010'), with a royal shooting-lodge, and fine view (good horse-track, 4 hrs.; direct footpath, 3½ hrs.).

The road crosses the Isar, and follows the left side of the secluded valley to (8 M.) *Wallgau* (p. 39), on the high-road from the Walchensee to (7½ M.) *Mittenwald* (p. 34).

FROM VORDER-RISS BY THE SOIERN TO MITTENWALD, a very attractive walk (bridle-path, 10 hrs.). After crossing the Rissbach, the path ascends the *Fischbachthal* to the left to (4 hrs.) the royal shooting-box at the *Soiern*, with the *Soiern Lakes* (5160'), in a wild valley (to the W. the Schöttl-karspitze, to the S. the Soiernspitze, to the E. the Krapfenkarspitze). [A new path leads from this point in 1½ hr. to the top of the *Schöttlkarspitze* (6400'), with a pavilion affording a fine view.] A bridle-path now ascends to the left to (1½ hr.) the saddle of the *Jägersruh*, between the Krapfenkar and the Soiernspitze. We descend into the *Steinkar*, then proceed to the right along the cliffs through the *Fritzenkar* (fine views of the Achensee and Karwendel mountains) to the saddle to the S. of the Soiernspitze. Thence a winding path leads down to (1½ hr.) the *Vereins-Alp* and (3 hrs.) *Mittenwald* (p. 34).

9. From Munich to Innsbruck,
viâ Tegernsee, Wildbad Kreut, and the Achensee.
Comp. Maps, pp. 40, 46.

94 M. RAILWAY to (34 M.) *Gmund* in 2½ hrs. DILIGENCE from Gmund at 8.45 a.m., 1.35 p.m., and 6.25 p.m. to Tegernsee (½ hr.) and Kreut

44   *I. Route 9.*   TEGERNSEE.   *From Munich*

(2½ hrs.; fare 1 m. 80 pf.). POST-OMNIBUS from Tegernsee to the Achensee daily (fare 4 m., coupé 5 m., from Kreut 1 m. less) starting at 9.15 a.m., and reaching Kreut at 11 a.m. and the Scholastika at 4.5 p.m.; returning at 9 a.m., reaching Kreut at 1 and leaving at 4 p.m., arriving at Tegernsee at 6 p.m. Another omnibus leaves Bad Kreut daily at 5.30 p.m. for Achenkirch (arriving at 8.30 p.m.), proceeding next morning at 5.15 a.m. to Jenbach in 2¼ hrs. In the reverse direction the omnibus leaves Jenbach at 9.30 a.m., reaching Achenkirch at 12.30, and Bad Kreut at 4.30 p.m. — One-horse carriage from *Gmund* to Tegernsee 4 m., two-horse 7 m.; from *Tegernsee* to Kreut one-horse 7, two-horse 12 m., to the Scholastika 16 or 24, to Jenbach 26 or 42 m. Two-horse carriage from *Bad Kreut* to the Scholastika 20 m. From the *Scholastika* to Jenbach 5 or 8, to Kreut 6 or 10½, to Tegernsee 8 or 14, to Gmund 10 or 17 fl. From *Jenbach* to Pertisau or the Scholastika, with extra horse for the hill, 7 or 12 fl.; to Kreut 16 or 21, Tegernsee 17 or 25 fl. (driver's fee and tolls included in each case).

Railway to (30 M.) *Schaftlach*, p. 40. The branch-line to Tegernsee diverges to the left from the line to Tölz (on the right, the Benediktenwand) and reaches the *Tegernsee* (3¾ M. long, 1¼ M. broad) at (34 M.) **Gmund** *(Herzog Max; Bellevue;* *Obermayer's Restaurant*, at the station, with view), where the *Mangfall* emerges from the lake.

Kaltenbrunn (Inn), a farm of Duke Charles Theodore, at the N.W. end of the lake, 1 M. from Gmund and 4½ M. from Tegernsee by land, or reached by boat in 1 hr. (1 m. 40 pf.), commands the best survey of the lake. Pleasant walk thence by the road on the W. bank to (6 M.) *Egern* (p. 45), viâ *Am Bach* and *Wiessee*. — A new path (distinguished by blue and white marks) ascends from Gmund to (2 hrs.) the *Neureut* (p. 45).

From Gmund a road leads along the E. bank, viâ *St. Quirin*, to —

37 M. **Tegernsee.** — Hotels. POST, R. 3½ m.; *GUGGEMOS, R., L., &* A. 2, D. 2 m.; *TEGERNSEER HOF*; *STEINMETZ*, pens. from 3 m.; PENSION VILLA HELENE, on the Lehberg. Lodgings may also be procured. — At *Rottach:* SCHEURER, R. from 1½, D. 2 m. — At *Egern*, at the S.E. end of the lake. on the road to Kreut: BACHMAIR, moderate; GASTHOF ZUR UEBERFAHRT; VILLA KORN. — Beer at the *Bräustübl*. — **Boat**, with rower, for 2 pers. 1 m. per hr., 3 pers. 1 m. 20, 4 pers. 1 m. 40 pf. — **Omnibus** from the Gmund station to the hotels in Tegernsee ½ m. — **Carriage** to Gmund, with one horse 4, with two horses 7 m.; to Kaltenbrunn 6 or 8, to the Rottach Falls 8 or 10, to Bauer in der Au 9 or 15 m.; to Kreut and the Achensee, see p. 43.

Tegernsee (2400'), a large and charmingly situated village, attracts numerous visitors in summer. Beautiful walks in the environs. The S. wing of the imposing *Schloss*, formerly a Benedictine abbey, said to have been founded in 719, and suppressed in 1804, now belongs to Duke Charles Theodore of Bavaria; the N. wing contains a brewery. Above the portal of the *Church* is an ancient relief in marble representing the princely founders of the abbey. In the churchyard is a monument to *Karl Stieler* (d. 1885), the poet.

ENVIRONS. A favourite point is the (½ hr.) **Grosse Parapluie**, an open summer-house. The path ascends the right bank of the Alphach about 100 yds. to the S. of the Guggemos Inn, and in a few minutes crosses a bridge (to the right) at the edge of the wood. Or the steps ascending to the left, about ½ M. from the S.E. angle of the Schloss, may be followed to the summer-house, which affords an admirable view of the lake and the encircling mountains (from left to right: Riedererstein, Wallberg, Setsberg, Ringberg, Hirschberg, Kampen). A good path leads hence to the *Lehberger* ('Inn); fine view of the head of the lake. Pleasant way back past the *Pfliegthof* (refreshments), 10 min. to the E. and through the

to Innsbruck. TEGERNSEE. *I. Route 9.* 45

Alpbachthal (1/2 hr.). — The **Westerhof**, 1/2 hr. above Tegernsee on the N.E., also commands a fine view. The path (shady in the early morning) ascends the Albachthal as far as (5 min.) the bridge, beyond which it ascends to the left, partly by wooden steps (thence to the *Neureut*, etc., see below). Good views also from the *Hochfeld*, on the slope of the Alpbachthal, and from the finely situated *Sängerschloss*, a sanitary establishment.

Bauer in der Au. We cross by boat (in 1/4 hr., 50 pf.) to *Abwinkel*, and then proceed past a saw-mill to the Egern road, which we follow to the right for about 8 min., till, immediately after crossing the bridge, we reach a pleasant forest-path ascending the *Söllbach* to (1 hr.) the farm (Rfmts.); fine view of the Kampen and Fockenstein. A cart-road leads hence viâ (1 1/2 hr.) the *Schwarzentenn-Alp* (3375') to (1 1/2 hr.) *Bad Kreut* (p. 46). A pleasant expedition may be made to LENGGRIES (4 hrs.) by a route diverging to the right from the above-mentioned road about 3 M. from the farm, crossing the brook, and ascending the *Stinkergraben* (sulphur-springs) to the (1 hr.) *Hirschthal-Alpe*, between the *Kampen* and the *Fockenstein* (each of which may be ascended from the Alp in 1 hr.; comp. p. 42), and thence by a good bridle-path down the picturesque *Hirschbach-Thal* to (1 1/2 hr.) *Schloss Hohenburg*, 1/4 hr. from *Lenggries* (p. 41). — From the Bauer in der Au we may return by a road to the right, on the slope of the *Ringberg*; where it emerges from the wood (1 M.) a footpath descends to the right to (1 hr.) *Egern*, at the S. end of the lake: thence by boat or by the ferry to Tegernsee (p. 44).

Freihof. Boat in 25 min. (75 pf.) to *Wiessee*, then up the *Zeiselbach* valley to the *Freihof* (Rfmts.), a charming route, with fine views.

Marble Quarries (1 1/4 hr.). The Kreut road is followed to (3 1/2 M.) a finger-post, which indicates the way (right) to (1/4 hr.) the interesting *Quarries*. Another finger-post, a few hundred paces farther on, points to (1/4 hr.) the *Lohbach Fall*, which is generally inconsiderable.

The *Falls of the **Rottach** are situated in a picturesque ravine, 5 1/2 M. from Tegernsee. The road leads from *Rottach* (p. 46) on the left bank of the stream of that name, passing *Elmau*, to the inn of *Enter-Rottach*; 1/2 M. farther on a finger-post shows where the path descends to the falls to the right; the path rejoins the road higher up. The road ascends hence to the *Wechselalp* (3490'), and descends through the picturesque wooded valley of the *Weisse Falepp* to (2 1/2 hrs.) the forester's house of *Falepp* (p. 50). Thence by the *Spitzingsee* to *Schliersee* 12 M., and from Schliersee to Tegernsee 10 M. — The whole round forms a pleasant drive of 10 hrs. (carr. and pair 30 m., carr. with one horse 20 m.).

The *Neureut* (3950'; shelter-hut at the top), to the N.E., is ascended from Tegernsee in 1 1/2 hr. by a path passing the *Westerhof* (see above). Splendid view (to the S. the Venediger). We may then either descend to *Gmund* (p. 44), or, keep along the ridge to the E., without descending, to the (3 3/4 hr.) *Gindelalpschneid* (4350') with fine views of the Schliersee, the Kaisergebirge, etc., and by the *Gindelalpe* to (2 hrs.) *Schliersee* (see p. 50).

Riedererstein (3960'), 2 hrs. to the S.E. At the edge of the wood we take the path parallel with that to the Parapluie, but lower down, which leads to (3/4 hr.) the *Lehberger* (p. 44). Hence we ascend by a somewhat rough path, and then by a 'chemin de la croix' with 14 stations, to (1 hr.) the conspicuous chapel, on a precipitous rock. — A path which can hardly be missed ascends to the E. along the crest of the hill to the (3/4 hr.) *Baumgarten-Alp* and the (1/4 hr.) **Baumgartenschneid** (5140'), whence a fine panorama is obtained. For the steep descent through the *Alpbachthal* to (1 1/2 hr.) Tegernsee a guide is advisable (to be procured at the chalets).

The *Hirschberg* (5635'; 4 1/2 hrs.) is an admirable point of view. We follow the Kreut road to (1 1/2 hr.) the *Lohbach Fall* (see above), cross the brook near the fall, and ascend a narrow forest-path, which afterwards widens, to (1 hr.) the *Holzpoint Alp*; then by a club-path past the *Ranhrck Alp* to the (3/4 hr.) summit (club-hut; fine panorama). Descent to Dorf Kreut, see p. 47.

The *Risserkogl* (5934'; 5 1/2 hrs., with guide; somewhat fatiguing) also affords a splendid view, embracing the Tauern and Zillerthal Ferner, and extending to the Zugspitze on the W.; to the N. rises the *Plankenstein*

(5800'; ascent difficult), at the foot of which are the Röthenstein and Plankenstein lakes. From Egern or Rottach we ascend viâ the (2½ hrs.) *Wallberger Alp* to the (⅔ hr.) top of the *Setzberg* (5800'), which commands a fine view. We then descend to the saddle above the *Setzberg-Alp* and follow the arête to the *Grubereck*, where our route is joined on the left by the path ascending from Dorf Kreut. A somewhat steep climb takes us to the summit in 2 hrs. more. The descent to the S.W. by the *Ableithen*, *Scheyrer*, and *Pletzerer Alps*, and that to the S. by the *Ries* and *Vorderlochberg Alps* to the *Langenauthal* and (2 hrs.) *Kreut*, are steep at first, and not advisable for inexperienced walkers.

FROM TEGERNSEE TO TÖLZ (18 M.). Road viâ *Gmund* and *Reichersbeuern* (one-horse carr. 6 m.; railway from Gmund viâ Schaftlach, see p. 44). — To *Schliersee*, see p. 50; to *Neuhaus*, see p. 51.

The high-road from Tegernsee to Kreut passes *Schweighof* (sulphur-spring), crosses the Rottach, and leads through (1¾ M.) *Rottach* (Scheuer), with its pretty country-houses. About 1 M. farther on (to the right is Egern, p. 44) it crosses the *Weissach* (*Bachmair's Inn, by the bridge).

Pedestrians save 1½ M. by taking the ferry across the S.E. arm of the lake from Lehberg to *Egern* (ferry 10 pf.; Gasthof zur Ueberfahrt, with lake-baths); the road on the other side leads straight from the ferry to the high-road, which it reaches at (1 M.) the Weissach bridge.

About 1 M. farther on the path to the *Marble Quarries* (p. 45) diverges to the right, and a few minutes afterwards, that to the *Lohbach Fall* (p. 45). Near (½ M.) *Scharling* (*Hoegg) a footpath diverges to the right, leading to the *Point* and rejoining the road farther on. The valley contracts near the village of (1½ M.) *Kreut* (2680'; *Obermayer), to the right of which rises the conical *Leonhardstein* (4760'). On the left is (¾ M.) the prettily-situated *Restaurant zur Rainer Alpe* (also pension), about ¾ M. beyond which a road to the left diverges to the (½ M.) —

44½ M. **Wildbad Kreut** (2720'), a large bath-house and hotel (R. 2½-3, D. 3 m.), the property of Duke Charles Theodore of Bavaria, situated on a broad green plateau. The springs, containing iron and sulphur, are generally used in combination with salt-baths.

WALKS in the grounds of the Curhaus. In a marble niche above a spring on the slope, ½ M. to the E. of the Curhaus, is a bust of King Max I. — The *Hohlenstein*, opposite the baths, to the E., commands a fine view of Tegernsee, etc. (to the cross, 1 hr.).

Wolfsschlucht (1¼ hr.), a ravine with two waterfalls. The path ascends the *Felsenweissach-Thal* to the *Pförner* and *Oberhofer Alps* and turns to the left into the gorge. A giddy path ascends from the Oberhofer Alp, 'über den Fels', to the *Schildenstein-Alp* (see below).

Gaisalpe (1 hr.). Descending at the back of the Bad and crossing the Felsenweissach, we follow a good path through wood, which is at first level, and afterwards ascends to the left on the hill-side to the pleasantly situated Alp (3700'). About 20 min. farther on is the Königsalpe or Kaltenbrunner-Alpe (3810'; Inn), which may also be reached in 2 hrs. by a good road, diverging to the left from the Achenthal road above the *Klammbach Fall* (p. 47), and ascending in zigzags. — The Schildenstein (5345') a good point of view, is ascended from the Gaisalpe or the Königsalpe in 1¾ hr.; last part of the ascent steep. The track descending from the *Schildenstein-Alpe* to the Achenthal road on the S.W., though marked, is marshy and bad (guide advisable).

The **Schinder** (5990'; 4½ hrs.) is a magnificent point of view. A road leads to the E. through the *Langenauthal* to the *Langenau-Alp* and

to *Innsbruck*.   ACHENSEE.   *I. Route 9.*   47

(8 M.) the *Baierbach-Alp*, from which a bridle-path ascends to the left by the (1 hr.) *Riesstsberg-Alp* to (½ hr.) the summit. Descent to *Falepp*, see p. 50.
The *Risserkopf* (5994'), 4 hrs., see p. 45. — The *Hirschberg* (p. 45) is easily ascended from Scharling (p. 46; path marked), or from Dorf Kreut viâ the *Weidberg-Alpe*, in 4 hrs.

The road from Bad Kreut to the Achensee crosses the Weissach and joins the main road. The latter gradually ascends the narrow Weissachthal, passing (2 M.) the small *Klammbach Fall* on the left, to (5 M.) **Glashütte** (3060'; rustic *Inn*), with the Bavarian custom-house of *Stuben*. At the *Stubenalp*, about 1 M. farther on, the road reaches its culminating point (3150'), then descends rapidly through profound ravines, and at the *Kaiserwacht*, in the once strongly-fortified defile of *Achen* (2860'), crosses the Tyrolese frontier. (Below, to the right, diverges the road through the Achenthal to *Fall* in the Isarthal, p. 42.) The Austrian custom-house is near the village of (2½ M.) **Achenwald** (2695'; *Hageninwald*).

The interesting and not difficult ascent of the Juifen (6510') may be made from Achenwald viâ the *Schulterberg-Alp* in 4½ hrs. (with guide). Fine view from the summit. Descent either by the *Rothwand Alpe* to *Fall* (p. 42), or by the *Joch-Alpe* to Achensee.

The road gradually ascends along the *Achen*, or *Walchen*, the outlet of the Achensee. At (2½ M.) **Leiten** (Hinterer's Inn) the *Ampelsbach-Thal* opens on the left; in the background rise the rocky horn of the *Guffert* (7190') and the long ridge of the *Unnutz* (p. 48).

A road on the left side of the Ampelsbach-Thal leads over the *Oberberg* (3435'), between the Guffert and the Unnutz, to (8 M.) **Steinberg** (3300'; *Adler*), a village prettily situated in a green Alpine valley. Ascent hence of the *Guffert* (or *Steinberger Spitze*, 7190'; 4 hrs., with guide), somewhat fatiguing, but repaying. Ascent of the *Unnutz* (6790'; 3 hrs.), viâ the *Kögljoch* (4080'), not difficult (see p. 48). Route to the Innthal viâ *Aschau* (to *Brixlegg* 6 hrs.; guide desirable), see p. 159.

59 M. (1 M. from Leiten) **Achenkirch** (3085'; *Post*, with baths; *Kern*, ½ M. on this side of the Post; *Adler*, good wine), a village 2½ M. long, the scattered houses of which extend almost to the Achensee. (In the height of summer passing travellers are more likely to find accommodation at Achenkirch than at the Achensee hotels, which are often full.)

The *Achensee (3050'), 5½ M. long, about ½ M. broad, and 430' deep, a dark-blue lake, the finest in N. Tyrol, lies 1250' above the valley of the Inn. At the N. end of the lake, 2½ M. from the Post at Achenkirch, is *Maier's Inn*, a little beyond which is the *Scholastika Inn* (so called after the former landlady; R. & B. 90 kr., D. 1 fl.), with a veranda. About ¾ M. farther to the S., on a green promontory, is the *Hôtel Seehof*, the property of L. Rainer, a well-known Tyrolese singer, with a café on the lake (music and singing in the evenings; R., L., & A. 1 fl. 20, D. 1 fl. 30 kr.). The road, hewn in the rock at some places, and built out into the lake at others, leads on the E. bank, commanding fine views, to (6 M.) *Buchau* (*Prantl), at the S.W. end of the lake (a drive of 1 hr.). In fine weather it is preferable to perform the journey by the lake. STEAMER six times daily to Seespitz (and back) in ¾ hr., calling at the Scholastika, Seehof, Fürstenhaus, and Buchau. Small boat from the Scholastika to Pertisau in 1½ hr. (1 pers. 70, 2 pers. 80 kr.); to Seespitz in 2 hrs. (1 fl. and 1 fl. 20 kr.).

Pleasant walks in the woods from the Scholastika to the *Aschbacher Höhe* and *Luisenruhe* (½ hr.), and from the Seehof to the *Kraxel Fall*, the *Eremitage*, and (¾ hr.) the *Gamspavillon*, commanding a pretty survey of the lake. Boating-expeditions may be made across the lake to *Theresenruh* on the W. bank, and to the *Gaisalpe* (Rfmts.), a green slope on the W. base of the abrupt Seekarspitze. The new *Mariensteig* (quite safe for those not subject to giddiness) leads round the *Seewinkel*, or N. end of the lake, to the (1½ br.) Gaisalpe (path from the Gaisalp to the Pertisau, 1¼ hr., for experts only).

EXCURSION (guides, *Bart.* and *Jos. Edenhauser*). The "Unnutz (6790'; 3 hrs.; guide, unnecessary for experts, 3 fl.; provisions and strong shoes with nails necessary), which commands a magnificent view, presents no serious difficulty. Good paths (marked with red) lead from the Scholastika, from Maier's Inn, and from the Seehof through wood (fine glimpses of the Achensee), and lastly up steep pastures to the (1¼ hr.) *Köglalp*. From the highest hut we cross the depression lying in front of us, then (20 min.) turn to the left, and (¼ hr.), where the path divides, follow the steep (marked) path to the right. Beyond a rocky hollow we ascend rapidly through creeping pines, and afterwards over easy grassy slopes, to the (1 hr.) summit (*Vorder-Unnutz*, 6790'). At all doubtful points during the last hour of the ascent, we keep to the right. The view embraces on the E. the Steinbergerspitze, and more in the background the Kaisergebirge, the Loferer Steinberge, and the Steinerne Meer; S.E. the Kitzbühler range, and the Tauern from the Hochtenn to the Dreiherrnspitze; S. the Sonnwendjoch, Zillerthaler Ferner, Duxer Ferner, Solstein, Oetzthaler Ferner, Karwendelgebirge, and Wettersteingebirge; far below lies the Achensee.

The **Spieljoch** (*Kothalpjoch*, 7065'), the N.W. summit of the *Sonnwendgebirge* (p. 49), another interesting point, may also be ascended with no great difficulty in 3 hrs. (guide 3 fl. 50 kr.). From the Seehof, a good path (marked with red), to the left of the waterfall, ascends rapidly through wood to the *Lower*, *Middle*, and (2 hrs.) *Upper Kothalp*; then to the left at a spring (38° Fahr.) across grass to the (1 hr.) summit. The beautiful Edelweiss grows in profusion on this mountain. Fine views of the Achensee, the Steinberger Thal, Innthal, and the chief range of the Zillerthal.

On the S.W. bank of the lake is the *Pertisau, a green pasture enclosed by precipitous mountains and frequented as a summer-resort (*Fürstenhaus*, on the lake, the property of the Benedictine abbey of Viecht, often full in summer, good cuisine, 'diner maigre' on Fridays; *Hotel Stephanie*, kept by Rainer jr., R. & A. 80 kr.; *Pfandler* and *Karl*, in the village. ¼ M. from the lake, unpretending; *Post & Telegraph Office; Lake-Baths*). Charming view of the lake, particularly by evening-light; to the S. the mountains of the Innthal and of the lower Zillerthal.

The **Bärenkopf** (6500'; 3 hrs.; guide 2½ fl.), ascended by the *Bärenbad-Alpe* (or from Maurach through the *Weissenbachthal*), affords an admirable survey of the lake and the environs. — The ascent of the **Sonnenjoch** (8050'; 6½ hrs.; guide 4 fl.) is fatiguing. The *Falzthurnthal* is followed to the (4½ hrs.) *Obere Gramais-Alp* (see below). Then a steep and stony ascent of 2 hrs. to the summit. Extensive panorama: E. the Tauern, S. the Oetzthaler Ferner rising behind the Lamsengebirge, N. the plains of Bavaria.

FROM PERTISAU TO HINTER-RISS over the *Plumser-Joch* (6 hrs.), see p. 43. The route viâ *Gramais* (8½-9 hrs.; guide 5 fl.) is preferable. The path (marked with red) ascends the *Falzthurnthal* to the S.W.; 1½ hr. *Falzthurnalpe* (4635'); ¾ hr. *Untere Gramais-Alp* (4135'); then a steep ascent to the right to the (1½ hr.) *Obere Gramais-Alp* (5600'), to the S. or the *Sonnenjoch* (see above). Then across the (1½ hr.) **Gramaiser Joch** (6210'), with view of the Gamsjoch to the W., and the Hochglück and Lamsenspitze to the S., to the (¾ hr.) *Lower Binsalpe*, the (½ hr.) *Eng* (3930'; Inn), and (3¼ hrs.) *Hinter-Riss* (p. 43). — Over the *Stanser Joch* to *Schwaz* (7 hrs.; guide 4½ fl.), see p. 160.

The road from Pertisau leads past the (1½ M.) *Seespitz* (Inn and boat-station at the S. end of the lake) to (1 M.) *Maurach* (3100'; Neuwirth), on the Achenkirch and Jenbach road, 1¼ M. to the S. of *Buchau* (see p. 47).

Maurach is the best starting-point for the ascent of the peaks of the **Sonnwendgebirge**, which afford many fine views (guide, Alois Brugger at Maurach). The route first leads through the valley ascending to the N.E. to the *Lower* and (2½ hrs.) the *Upper Maurits-Alpe* (6035'; poor quarters), finely situated. From this point we may ascend the *Hochiss*, or *Gamsspitze* (7590'), a splendid point of view, in 2 hrs. (The ascent is also made from Buchau by the *Dalfas-Alpe*, or from the Seehof by the *Koth-Alpe* in 4½ hrs.) The *Rofan* (7405') takes 1½ hr.; the *Vordere Sonnwendjoch* (7800'), 1½-2 hrs. — *Spieljoch*, see p. 48.

Farther on, the road passes *Eben*, on the hill to the left, the burial-place of St. Nothburga (d. 1313), with a chapel which attracts numerous pilgrims. It then descends rapidly through the picturesque valley of the *Kasbach* (railway in progress) to (3½ M.) —

71 M. **Jenbach** (1835'), see p. 159. Railway thence to (94 M.) *Innsbruck*, see R. 31.

PEDESTRIANS should row from Pertisau to the Seespitz (tariff, see p. 48), where they take a shady footpath to the right. At the bifurcation we follow the path to the left, which leads through the fence and across the meadows, and joins the road above the mill opposite the telegraph-post 108/82 (to Jenbach 1-1¼ hr., uphill 1½ hr.).

10. From Munich to Kufstein viâ Schliersee and Bairisch-Zell.

Comp. Map, p. 40.

65 M. RAILWAY to *Holzkirchen* and (38 M.) Schliersee in 2½ hrs. From Schliersee to (10 M.) Bairisch-Zell POST-OMNIBUS daily in 2 hrs.; thence to (17 M.) Kufstein carriage-road, but no public conveyance. Carriages to be had at Schliersee and Neuhaus.

Railway to (23 M.) *Holzkirchen* (change carriages), see p. 40. On the E. side of the village the line diverges to the left from the Tölz line (to the left the château of *Valley*, the property of Count Arco), and at (27 M.) *Darching* it enters the picturesque *Mangfall-Thal*. Opposite is *Weyarn*, formerly a monastery, now a school. Pleasant excursion to (1 hr.) the *Weyrer Lindl* (2370'; view).

30½ M. *Thalham* (2060'); on the right rises the *Taubenberg* (3015'), a fine point of view (1¼ hr.; Inn, 10 min. from the top). The train crosses the Mangfall, and traverses the wooded *Schlierach-thal*. — 33½ M. **Miesbach** (2285'; *Waizinger; *Post; Kreiterer; Alpenrose; Wendelstein*), a thriving village and summer-resort, prettily situated. In the vicinity are several coal-mines.

To TEGERNSEE (10 M.). The road (diligence every afternoon in 2½ hrs.) leads viâ *Schweinthal* to (3 M.) the *Wirth am Baum* (Inn), crosses the Mangfall, and then proceeds by *Festenbach* and *Dürrenbach* to (4 M.) *Gmund* (p. 44) and (3 M.) *Tegernsee*.

BAEDEKER's Eastern Alps. 6th Edit. 4

To BIRKENSTEIN (12 M.). Diligence from Miesbach daily in summer, in 2½ hrs., viâ *Parsberg*, the *Leitzachthal*, *Wörnsmühl*, and *Hundham* to (8¾ M.) *Ellbach* (2570'; ascent of the *Schwarzenberg*, 3925', 1½ hr., interesting). Then by (1¼ M.) the *Murbach Inn* and (¾ M.) *Fischbachau* to (1¼ M.) **Birkenstein** (*Krämerwirth; Birkenstein*), with a frequented pilgrimage-chapel, at the W. base of the *Wendelstein (6035'; p. 51), which may be ascended hence, viâ the *Spitzing-Alpe*, in 3¼ hrs. (best route, marked with red and green). — Beyond Birkenstein the road crosses the Leitzach and leads to (8 M.) *Aurach* (p. 51) and (2 M.) *Neuhaus* (shorter route viâ the *Fischeralpe*, marked with blue). Omnibus between Birkenstein and *Schliersee* twice daily.

The train crosses the Schlierach twice, passes *Agatharied* and *Hausham* (with coal-mines), and reaches —

38 M. **Schliersee** (*Post*, formerly *Fischerliesl*; *Seehaus; Wagner*, well spoken of; *Seerose; Hôtel-Pension Freudenberg*, on the peninsula; lodgings obtainable; baths in the lake), prettily situated on the *Schliersee* (2550'), and much frequented in summer. The (5 min.) *Weinbergkapelle* affords the best view of the environs (from E. to W., the Schliersberg, Rohnberg, Eipelspitz. Jägerkamp, Brecherspitze, Baumgartenberg, and Kreuzberg). Pleasant walk to (¾ M.) the *Oberleitner* (refreshments).

To TEGERNSEE (p. 44). The shortest route (3½ hrs.) leads from the peninsula of Freudenberg on the N.W. bank of the lake (reached by boat), or from the railway-station viâ the Seeklause, then to the right to the road, past the glass-works (on the left), and up the wooded *Breitenbach-Thal*. 3 M. *Breitenbach Inn* in the *Au* (2790'), whence a bridle-path ('*Prinzenweg*') follows the *Breitenbach*, crosses (left) the second bridge, ascends to the (1¼ hr.) saddle of the *Sagtleckt* (3745'), between the *Baumgartenschneide* (p. 45) and *Kreuzberg*, and descends through the pretty *Alpbachthal* to (1½ hr.) Tegernsee. — A more attractive route ascends from Breitenbach to the right to the (1½ hr.) *Gindelalpe* (4165') and the (¼ hr.) *Gindelalpschneid* (4385'), where a survey of the plain is enjoyed. The path then runs almost on the crest of the hill (paths descending to the left to be avoided) to the (¾ hr.) *Neureut* (p. 46; view of the mountains); to the S.E., beyond the Rothachthal, the Venediger), and descends rapidly to the *Westerhof* and (1 hr.) Tegernsee (4 hrs. in all; guide advisable). — Over the *Kühzackl* (4-4½ hrs. to Egern; see p. 51); ascent from the Au to the left through the *Dufthal*.

The road skirts the E. side of the lake. 2 M. *Fischhausen* (Niederwaldeck) lies at the S. end of the lake; high up to the left the ruin of *Hohenwaldeck*. At (¾ M.) **Neuhaus** (2655'; *Eham*), a favourite summer-resort, the road divides. To the E. rises the finely shaped Wendelstein; to the S. the Brecherspitze and Jägerkamp.

The road to the right leads through the *Max-Josephsthal*, past a paper-mill, and ascends the slope of the *Jägerkamp* (p. 51) in numerous windings, which the pedestrian may cut off. On the right the precipitous *Brecherspitze*; pleasing retrospect of the Schliersee. Beyond the (4¼ M.) pass (3740') between the *Stocker-Alp* and *Spitzing-Alp*, the road descends to the (¾ M.) lonely **Spitzing-See** (3524'). The lake is drained by a stream flowing into the *Rothe Falepp*, which the road follows. At the S. end of the lake is the *Wurzhütte*, a rustic inn; to the right, ½ M. from the lake, is the fall of the Falepp. 1½ M. *Waitzinger Alp* (beer); 2 M. the forester's house of **Falepp** (2850'; *Inn*), prettily situated in the midst of wood, below the union of the Rothe and Weisse Falepp. In the vicinity is the disused *Kaiserklause*. A path (lately improved) leads from Falepp by the *Erzherzog-Johannis-Klause* and through the *Brandenberger Thal* to *Brixlegg* (p. 159; 9-10 hrs., with guide). — Through the *Rottachthal* to Tegernsee, see p. 45.

— The *Schinder* (6010'; p. 46) is ascended from Falepp in 2½ hrs. by a new

to Kufstein. BAIRISCH-ZELL. *I. Route 10.* 51

path. — To LANDL ACROSS THE ELENDALP (4½ hrs.; with guide). This route may conveniently be combined with the ascent of the Rothwand (see below; provisions should be taken). We leave the Schliersee road at the guide-post (½ M.; to the right) marked 'Rothe Wand', and in 1 hr. more reach a second guide-post, from which the path to the left leads to the top of the *Rothwand (see below) in 2 hrs. (down again in 1½ hrs.). Keeping to the right from the guide-post, we reach (¼ hr.) the Elendalp (3730'), and continue through the *Elendgraben* to (1 hr.) the *Kloascheralp* and in ¾ hr. more to the road from Bairisch-Zell to Landl (to *Urspring*, 1½ M., see p. 52).

ASCENTS (routes in most cases indicated by coloured marks). **Brecherspitze** (5530'), 3 hrs. from Neuhaus viâ the *Angerl-Alp* (fatiguing; guide necessary). — **Bodenschneid** (5976'), 3 hrs., with guide, viâ the *Rainer Alp* and the *Rettenbäck Alp*, not difficult; admirable view. — **Jägerkamp** (5690'), 3 hrs., viâ the *Jägerbauern-Alp*, another excellent point of view. — *Rothwand (6200'), 4½ hrs., not difficult. We ascend from the Spitzing-See to the (1 hr.) *Lower* and (½ hr.) *Upper Wallenburger-Alp* (5365'; Rfmts.), whence a path constructed by the German Alpine Club leads up to the (1 hr.) summit. Magnificent *View (tower). Below the summit is a shelterhut. The Rothwand may also be ascended from Geitau (see below) viâ the *Steilenberg Alp* and the *Grosstiefenthal Alp* (between which lies the *Soinsee*, 5030'), and the *Kimpflscharte*, in 4 hrs., or from the *Walzinger Hütte* (p. 50) through the *Pfandlgraben*, over the *Kimpflalpe* and the *Kimpflscharte*, in 3 hrs., or from Falepp (p. 50) in 3½ hrs. — **Miesing** (6145'), from Geitau (see below) by *Kleintiefenthal* in 3 hrs., or (better) by *Grosstiefenthal* and the saddle between the Rothwand and the Miesing in 4 hrs. (view similar to that from the Rothwand). — **Auerspitze** (5968'), another fine point, ascended from Geitau by the *Obere Soinalp* in 4 hrs.

From NEUHAUS TO TEGERNSEE by the **Kühzackl** (3796'), 3½ hrs. (guide hardly necessary; several finger-posts). Bridle-path through the *Angelgraben* to (1¼ hr.) the saddle to the S. of the *Kühzackl alp*; we descend along the *Kühzackl bach* to (½ hr.) the farm of that name, then into the *Rottachthal* to the road from Falepp to (1½ hr.) *Tegernsee* (p. 44).

The road to Bairisch-Zell next passes (2 M.) *Aurach* (to the left the road to *Birkenstein*, see p. 50). Between (2¼ M.) *Geitau* (Inn) and (1¼ M.) *Osterhofen* the wide *Leitzachthal* is entered. — 2 M. **Bairisch-Zell** (2820'; *Zum Wendelstein; Post* or *Altwirth*), a small village with several handsome houses, prettily situated in a basin enclosed by the Wendelstein, Seeberg, and Traithen.

*Wendelstein (6035'; 3 hrs.; guide unnecessary; horse to the Wendelsteinhaus 8 m., if kept over night 12 m.), a very fine point of view and not difficult. We may either proceed to the N. through meadows to the foot of the mountain, and ascend by a path (marked with white and red) past the *Tanner Mühle* to the *Kreuther Bauer*, where we turn to the right to the *Lower* and (1¾ hr.) *Upper Wendelstein* or *Zeller Alp* (4980'); or we may follow the bridle-path, beginning behind the Wendelstein Inn and also marked with red and white, which ascends viâ the *Mitterberg-Alm* to the *Zeller-Alm*, where it joins the above footpath. From the Upper Wendelstein Alp we proceed to the left, skirting the *Schwaigerwand* and the *Gache Blick*, joining the path from Birkenstein above the spring, and crossing the *Baierlahner*, to the (1 hr.) *Wendelsteinhaus* (5655'; *Inn, with beds and mattresses for 120 people), at the foot of the cone. From this point we traverse the saddle (p. 156) and ascend to the left through an easy 'Cheminée' to the Wendelsteinwand and then by the 'Stangensteig', provided with a wirerope, to the (½ hr.) summit, a plateau 6-12 yds. broad and about 25 yds. in length, on which stand a small wooden chapel and a cross. The *View embraces (left to right) the Untersberg, Watzmann, Kaisergebirge, Tauern Mts. (with the Venediger and Gross-Glockner), and the Karwendel and Wetterstein ranges (with the Zugspitze); to the N. the extensive plain with the Chiemsee, Simmsee, and Starnberger See. — On the E. side of the peak, in the 'Kessel', is a limestone cavern, the entrance to which is covered with ice. A visit to it (there and back 3 hrs.) is fa-

4*

tiguing and should not be attempted without a guide. Descent to *Birkenstein*, see p. 50; to *Brannenburg*, see p. 156. From the upper Alp a marked path leads viâ the *Lacher-Alp* and the *Schweinsteiger-Alp* to the (3 hrs.) *Tatzelwurm* (thence to *Oberaudorf*, see p. 156). — The Traithen (6100'; easy and interesting) may be ascended from Bairisch-Zell in 3½-4 hrs. (with guide) by the *Urspring-Thal* and the *Vordere Wennebrand-Alp*. The descent may be made by the *Unterberg-Alp*, or (less convenient) by the *Fell-Alp* and the *Himmelmoos-Alp* to (3 hrs.) *Oberaudorf* (p. 156).

FROM BAIRISCH-ZELL TO OBERAUDORF OR BRANNENBURG, 4½-5 hrs. The road, steep at first, leads by the *Tannen-Alp* and the *Grafenherberg-Alp* to the *Auer-Brücke*, and through the *Aubachthal* to the (2½ hrs.) **Tatzelwurm** (2510'; *Inn*), near a fine fall of the Aubach (best viewed from the lower bridge). Then down the left bank of the deep Aubachthal past *Rechenau* to (2 hrs.) *Oberaudorf* (p. 156); or to the left from the Tatzelwurm to the saddle between the *Greater* and *Lesser Mühlberg*, descending past the *Kohlstatt-Alpe* and through the *Förchenbachthal* to (2½ hrs.) *Brannenburg* (p. 156).

The road to Kufstein follows the *Urspring-Thal*, enclosed by finely-wooded mountains; to the left is the *Traithen* (see above). We pass a small waterfall of the *Sillbach* on the right (2½ M.), and the small *Stocker Lakes* at the mouth of the *Kloascher-Thal* (over the *Elend-Alp* to *Falepp*, see p. 51). The valley expands for a short distance. On the right rises the *Hintere Sonnwendjoch* (see below). We reach the Austrian frontier at the (2 M.) *Bäckeralp* (2770'), and the *Inn Zur Urspring* ½ M. farther on. The road descends a beautiful wooded valley. Several fine glimpses of the Kaisergebirge. At the (2½ M.) pleasant village of **Landl** (2195'; *Inn*), in the *Thiersee-Thal*, is a shooting-lodge of Archduke Ludwig Victor.

TO FALEPP OVER THE ACKERNALP, 5 hrs., fatiguing and lacking interest. A cart-road, between the *Veitsberg* on the left and the *Hinter-Sonnwendjoch* (6555'; ascended without danger from Landl or from Falepp in 4-4½ hrs.) on the right, with picturesque retrospects of the Thiersee-Thal and Kaiser range, ascends to the (2½ hrs.) **Ackernalp** (4570'). Descent by a rough path through wood, high on the right side of the valley, past the (1½ hr.) *Reichstein-Alp*, and (steep) down into the *Ensengraben*; then under a wooden conduit, after passing which we re-ascend, and finally turn to the left to the forester's house of *Falepp* (p. 50).

The road forks here. The branch to the left leads through the valley of the *Thierseer Ache (Kieferthal)*, and after passing (2½ M.) an *Inn*, crosses to the right bank at *Wieshäusle*, and ascends rapidly to (2 M.) the *Thier-See* or *Schreck-See* (2040'; *Inn* at the Neuschmied's). Thence it crosses the *Marblinger Höhe* (fine view of the Kaisergebirge; to the S. the *Pendling*, p. 157), and descends through wood, passing the dark *Längsee* and the *Ed*, to (5 M.) **Kufstein** (p. 157).

The longer but more attractive road to the right from Landl ascends to (2 M.) **Hinter-Thiersee** or **Inner-Thiersee** (2800'; *Grasshammer*), where the peasants perform plays nearly every Sunday in summer (passion-play every tenth year, the next in 1895). Then by (2 M.) *Vorder-Thiersee* (Kirchenjackl) to the (¾ M.) *Thiersee*. — A pleasant route leads from Thiersee (diverging to the left from the road before the culminating point is reached) viâ the *Wachtl* (good wine) and through the *Kieferthal* to (5 M.) *Kiefersfelden* (p. 156).

11. From Munich to Salzburg. Chiemsee.
Comp. Maps, pp. 40, 68.

95 M. RAILWAY. Express in 3¼ hrs.; ordinary trains in 5-8 hrs. Travellers in the reverse direction should be provided with German money.

Munich, see *Baedeker's S. Germany*. The direct railway to Rosenheim viâ Grafing diverges to the left from the Holzkirchen line (see below) and skirts the town. Beyond the (3 M.) *Munich S. Station (Thalkirchen)* the train crosses the Isar canal and ascends through deep cuttings to the (6 M.) *Munich E. Station (Haidhausen)*, where the Simbach-Braunau line diverges to the left. Stations *Trudering, Haar, Zorneding, Kirchseeon*. — 23½ M. **Grafing** *(Railway Inn; Kaspersbräu)*, a considerable place, 1½ M. from the railway.

About 2 M. to the N. is the finely-situated town of **Ebersberg** *(Hölzerbräu*, and several other inns); the 'Keller', or summer garden of the Schloss brewery commands a magnificent view of the Alps (still more extensive from the belvedere on the *Ludwigshöhe*, 1 M. to the N.). The church contains a fine marble monument of the counts of Ebersberg.

Between *Assling* and *Ostermünchen* the broad dale of the *Attel* is traversed. To the right, opposite the traveller, rises the Wendelstein, to the left the Kaisergebirge. 37 M. *Gross-Karolinenfeld*.

40 M. **Rosenheim** (1465'; **Bayrischer Hof & Greiderer; *König Otto; Alte Post; Deutsches Haus; Stockhammerbräu; Rail. Restaurant)*, the junction of the Innsbruck, Holzkirchen, and Mühldorf lines, a town of 10,000 inhab., with salt-works, lies at the influx of the Mangfall into the Inn. The salt-water is conveyed hither from Reichenhall, upwards of 50 M. distant. About ¾ M. from the station are the **Badhôtel Marienbad* and the *Kaiserbad*, both 'hôtel-pensions', with salt and other baths. About 2 M. from the station, on the right bank of the Inn, is the *Schlossberg* (Restaurant), which affords a pretty view of the Innthal and the Alps.

FROM MUNICH TO ROSENHEIM VIÂ HOLZKIRCHEN, 46½ M., in 3 hrs. To (23 M.) *Holzkirchen*, see p. 40. We here diverge from the line to Sehliersee and enter the *Teufelsgraben* (p. 40), which ends at the valley of the *Mangfall*. The train runs at first high along the left slope of the valley and then descends to stat. *Westerham*. The valley expands. Stations *Bruckmühl, Heufeld* (with a chemical manufactory), and (40 M.) **Aibling** (1580'; **Ludwigsbad*, with garden; **Hôtel Duschl zur Post*, with garden and baths; *Villa Pentenrieder; Schuhbräu*, with veranda), a small town with salt and mudbaths. The Kaisergebirge, and beyond (43½ M.) *Kolbermoor*, with a large cotton-factory, the Gross-Venediger, become visible on the right.

The train crosses the *Inn*, and passes (44 M.) *Stephanskirchen*, the *Simmsee* (3¾ M. long), and (50 M.) *Endorf* (Post).

The line now runs to the S. through a hilly district to (56 M.) **Prien** (1745'; **Hôtel Chiemsee*, at the station, R., L., & A. 2½ m.; *Zur Kampenwand; Kronprinz; Ostermaier; Villa Rauch*, R. 1½ m.), a favourite summer-resort, in the smiling *Prienthal*.

From Prien a STEAM TRAMWAY runs in 10 min. to *Stock* (Hôtel Dampfschiff), the landing-place of the steamer on the Chiemsee, which plies eight times daily in ¼ hr. to the *Herreninsel* and six times daily in ½ hr. to the *Fraueninsel* (return-ticket, 2nd class in the steam-tramway, 1st class on the steamer, 1 m. 80 pf.). — The **Chiemsee** (1680'), 11 M. long and 7 M. broad, contains three islands: the large *Herreninsel*, now the property of the King of Bavaria; the *Fraueninsel*, with a nunnery, and the *Krautinsel* ('vegetable island'), formerly a kitchen-garden for the monks and nuns. The Fraueninsel is also the site of a fishing-village and an "*Inn*, a favourite resort of artists, as an album kept in the house will testify. On the extensive Herreninsel (9 M. in circumference) rises the large *Schloss Herrenchiemsee*, begun in the style of Louis XIV. by King Lewis II. after the model of Versailles, but not completed (adm. daily except Frid.; Thurs. 6, other days 3 m.; closed on 13th June). The *Old Castle* of Herrenwörth, a few min. walk from the pier, is now an *Inn. with a brewery and garden (suited for a stay of some time). About 1/2 M. farther on is the *New Palace*, built on three sides of a square (open on the E.), adjoined on the N. by a wing (unfinished) 480' long, and connected with the lake by a channel 3/4 M. long. In front of the W. façade, 345' long, are ornamental *Water Works* (without water at present), resembling those at Versailles, with basins of Fortune, Fame, *Latona, etc., surrounded by a lofty fence. The pillared *Vestibule*, adorned with an enamelled group of peacocks, opens on a *Court*, paved with black and white marble, on the right side of which is the magnificent *Staircase*, richly adorned with imitation marble and painting. On the first floor, turning to the right, we enter successively the *Salle des Gardes du Roi* (blue and gold), the *Première Antichambre* (lilac), the *Salle de l'Oeil du Boeuf* (green; with an equestrian statue of Louis XIV., by Perron), and the magnificent *Chambre de Parade*. This last apartment, an imitation of Louis XIV.'s Bed Chamber at Versailles, adorned in pure gold, with a lavishly gilded bed, is said to have cost alone over 125.000l. Of the remaining rooms the chief are the *Galerie des Glaces* or *Spiegelgallerie*, 245' long and illuminated with 33 lustres and 2000 candles, the *Salon de la Guerre* and the *Salon de la Paix*, opening on the right and left of the Galerie, the royal *Bed Chamber* and *Study*, the *Dining-Room* (with the table descending and ascending through the floor), the *Small Gallery*, the *Oval Saloon*, and the *Bath Room*. In all the rooms are costly furniture, clocks, etc. — The woods clothing the S. part of the island contain many picturesque points. The long chain of the Bavarian and Tyrolese Alps forms the background of the landscape on the S.; to the E. in the distance is the *Gaisberg* (p. 66) near Salzburg, then the conspicuous *Staufen* (6030'); S.E. the *Sonntagshorn* (6425'); in the foreground, rising abruptly from the valley, the *Hochgern* (5732'); S. the *Hochplatte* (6030'), the long, indented *Kampenwand* (5505'), and the *Mühlhorn*; S.W. the cone of the *Kranzhorn*, the pinnacles of the *Heuberg*, the *Wendelstein* (6006'), and the broad outline of the *Breitenstein* (5476').

From *Seebruck* ('Inn), at the N. end of the lake, a road leads to (2 1/2 M.) *Seeon*, an old monastery on a small lake, with a good bath-establishment. At *Stein* ('Inn), 4 M. to the E. of Seeon, is the old mountain-castle of the robber-knight Heinz v. Stein. — From *Chieming* ('Inn), on the E. bank of the lake, a pleasant footpath leads to (2 hrs.) *Traunstein* (p. 55).

A BRANCH LINE runs from *Prien* to the S. through the richly-wooded *Prienthal*, in 35 min., to the charmingly-situated village of (6 M.) Niederaschau (2020'; *Rest and other inns), another summer-resort. About 1 M to the S., in the middle of the valley, is the château of *Hohenaschau*, picturesquely situated on a rock, 100 ft. in height (at the foot a brewery and the *Inn zur Burg, R. 3m., generally crowded in summer). Pleasant excursions to the *Hofalpe*, an ascent of 1 1/2 hr. to the W., and to the *Aschauerkopf*, 1/2 hr. to the N., with fine view. The *Hochriss* (5115'), 3 1/2 hrs. from Niederaschau, viâ the *Hofalpe* and *Riesenalpe*, affords a more extensive view. — The *Kampenhöhe* (5120'), on the E. side of the valley, is another very fine point (3 1/2 hrs.; good bridle-path, with benches). Charming view of the lake and Hohenaschau from the chapel-hill beside the 19th bench. About 3/4 hr. below the top (on which is a refuge-hut) we pass the *Schlechtenberger Alp* (refreshments). The Kampenhöhe forms the W. prolongation of the *Kampenwandgrat*, where the *Sattel* (5330'), 2 1/2-3 hrs. from Niederaschau, affords a similar view. The jagged summit of the *Kampenwand* (5505') can be attained by active climbers only (path to the *Hochplatte*, see p. 56). The route across the *Möslern-Alp* (5155') and the *Steinberger-Alp* to (4 hrs.) *Schleching* in the Achenthal (p. 56) is attractive.

to Salzburg. TRAUNSTEIN. *I. Route 11.* 55

— The road in the Prienthal next leads by (2¹/₂ M.) *Hainbach* (to Schleching across the *Thalsen-Alp*, 3¹/₂ hrs.) and *Huben*, between the *Spitzstein* (5230') and the *Geigelstein* (5988'; ascent by marked path, 3¹/₂-4 hrs.), to (3¹/₂ M.) Sachrang (2370'; *Neumaier*), crosses the Tyrolese frontier at (1¹/₂ M.) *Wildbichl* ("Inn, good wine), and descends abruptly through the '*Stein*' pass to (3¹/₂ M.) *Sebi*, on the road from Waidsee to Kufstein (p. 58; the footpath from Wildbichl to *Niederndorf* viâ *Maierhof*, 1¹/₂ hr., is preferable).

The line skirts the S. bank of the Chiemsee. 59¹/₂ M. *Bernau.* From (64 M.) *Uebersee* (Heindl) a branch-railway runs to *Marquartstein* (p. 56). The train crosses the *Grosse Ache.* — 69 M. *Bergen*; the village (*Niederhauser) is prettily situated 1¹/₂ M. to the S.

Carriage-road (path by *Bernhaupten* preferable) from the railway-station to the baths of **Adelholzen** (2100'; rooms should be ordered beforehand; quarters also at *Atzing*, ¹/₂ M. to the E.), charmingly situated 1¹/₂ M. to the S.E., well fitted up, and possessing three different springs (saltpetre, sulphur, and alum). The hilly neighbourhood affords many pleasant walks. Carriage-road to (1¹/₄ M.) *Siegsdorf* (p. 57) and (4 M.) *Traunstein.*
— The foundries and blast-furnaces at the **Maxhütte** (2030'; Inn), in the *Weissachen-Thal*, 2 M. to the S.W. of Adelholzen (1 M. from the village of Bergen), are worthy of inspection. The ascent of the **Hochfellen** (5500'; 3 hrs.) is recommended (guide, A. Brandl of Bergen, 4 m.). — 6 M. The path traverses the *Schwarzachen-Thal*, the *Gleichenberg-Alpe*, and the *Bründling-Alpe* (refreshments). The **Hochgern** (5732'), another fine point, is ascended through the *Weissachen-Thal* and across the *Hinteralpe* (accommodation) in 4-4¹/₂ hrs., with guide (better from Marquartstein or Wessen, p. 56).

73 M. **Traunstein** (1930'; *Wiespauer; *Post; Prantl; Traube; Auwirth; Weisses Bräuhaus*, with garden; *Höllbräukeller*, at the station; *Kollerkeller*, ¹/₄ M. from the station, both with views), a thriving place with 4500 inhab., lies on a slope above the *Traun*. In the upper Platz stands a handsome marble fountain of 1526. The *Salt, Mineral,* and *Mud Baths* are well fitted up (large garden; pens., incl. R., 3¹/₂-7 m.). The extensive salt-works are situated in the suburb of *Au*, on the Traun; the brine evaporated here is conducted in pipes from Reichenhall (p. 80), a distance of 22¹/₂ M.

EXCURSIONS. *Empfing,* a well-appointed bath-house, on the left bank of the Traun, 1 M. to the N. — The *Weinleite* (¹/₂ hr. to the N.W.) affords a fine view of the town and mountains; more extensive from the (1 hr.) *Hochberg* (2536'; Inn), or from the *Hochhorn* (2546'), 3¹/₂ hrs. to the E., at the foot of the *Stoisser Alpe* (p. 82), beyond *Surberg.* — To *Siegsdorf, Adelholzen, Maria Eck,* etc., see above, and p. 58.

FROM TRAUNSTEIN TO REICHENHALL viâ *Inzell* (post-omnibus to Inzell daily in 3 hrs.; carr. and pair to Reichenhall 26 m.). The road, which will also repay the pedestrian, leads through the Traunthal to (4 M.) *Ober-Siegsdorf* (p. 57), at the confluence of the *Weisse* and *Rothe Traun,* and through the broad valley of the latter, by *Molberding, Hachau,* and *Wagenau,* to (11 M.) *Inzell* (2225'; *Post), a village in the bed of an ancient lake, where a succession of grand mountain-landscapes begins. Two wooded rocks guard the entrance to this part of the road: on the right the *Kienberg,* the E. spur of the *Rauschberg* (remarkable for mineral wealth); on the left the *Falkenstein,* beyond which is the abrupt *Stauffeneand.* An Alpine valley is now entered, in which, amid green pastures, lies the small village of *Weissbach* (1995'). Farther on, the valley contracts. The road is carried along the rocky slope on the left, adjoining the salt-water conduit; far below rushes the *Weissbach,* the bed of which becomes a deep gorge as the valley is ascended (on the opposite side rises the *Ristfeichthorn,* p. 82). At one of the finest points in this ravine is situated the *Mauthhäusel* (2075'), a solitary inn about 7 M. from Reichenhall, and 11¹/₄ M. from the Lofer road (p 82). 22¹/₂ M. *Reichenhall,* see p. 79.

The Salzburg train next skirts wooded and grassy hills. To the S., above the lower heights, towers the Stauffen, and farther on, the Untersberg (p. 67). Stations *Lauter*, (83 M.) *Teisendorf* (with the ruined castle of *Raschenberg*), and (89½ M.) **Freilassing** (1380'; *Föckerer's Inn* at the station, adapted for a short stay), the Bavarian frontier, and the junction of the Reichenhall line (p. 79). The train crosses the *Saalach*; to the right is *Schloss Klesheim*; among trees to the left, as Salzburg is approached, are seen the white walls of *Maria-Plain* (p. 67). The *Salzach* is then crossed.
95 M. **Salzburg**, see p. 60.

12. From Munich to Reit im Winkel and Kössen.
Comp. Map, p. 52.

RAILWAY to (64 M.) *Uebersee* in 2½-3½ hrs.; and thence by branch railway to (5 M.) *Marquartstein* in ½ hr. (tickets obtained from the guard). OMNIBUS from Marquartstein to (10 M.) *Reit im Winkel*, daily in summer in 2½ hrs. — *Kössen* is best reached from *Kufstein* (p. 157; diligence daily at 6 a.m., in 4¼ hrs.) or from *St. Johann in Tirol* (p. 120).

To (64 M.) *Uebersee*, see R. 11. The railway to Marquartstein leads to the S. through the broad valley of the *Ache*, past the stations of *Mietenkam* and *Staudach* (Zum Hochgern), near the latter of which is a cement-quarry. — 5 M. **Marquartstein** (1820'; *Hofwirth*), picturesquely situated on the right bank of the Ache, with a château of Baron Tautphœus.

The *Schnappen Kapelle* (1½ hr. from Staudach or Marquartstein), loftily situated on the *Schnappen*, a spur of the Hochgern, commands a fine view of the Chiemsee. — The Hochgern (5732'), an excellent point of view, is ascended from Marquartstein, Staudach, or Unter-Wessen (the best route) in 3½-4 hrs., with guide. — The **Hochplatte** (5285'; 3½ hrs., with guide) is also a fine point. (Path from the Hochplatte over the *Piesenhauser Hochalpe* to the *Kampenwand*, 1½ hr., p. 54.)

FROM MARQUARTSTEIN TO KÖSSEN. The road (beyond Schleching scarcely suitable for carriages) follows the left bank of the Ache, passing *Reuten* and *Mettenham*, to (4 M.) **Schleching** (1800'; *Niederhäuser*), pleasantly situated in a broad and smiling valley. On the N. rise the Hochplatte and Kampenwand, W. the Geigelstein, S.W. the Breitenstein and Rudersburg, all of which may be ascended without difficulty. [The most interesting point is the *Geigelstein* (5938'), ascended by the *Baumgartenalp* in 4 hrs., guide 7 m.; immediately to the N. is the *Tauron* (*Aschenthaler Wände*, 5895'), with rich flora.] The road now crosses the Ache, passes the Bavarian custom-station of *Streichen* (1¼ M.), and enters *Pass Klobenstein* (2040'), a magnificent gorge of the Ache (2 M. in length), in which it crosses the Tyrolese frontier (finest view from the forest-chapel). The road then descends to (3½ M.) *Kössen* (p. 58).

The road to Reit im Winkel runs on the right bank of the Ache to (2¼ M.) *Unter-Wessen* (1870'; Kellerer; Bräuhaus; ascent of the *Hochgern*, see above; guide, G. Klausner). It then follows the Wessener Bach, to the S.E., to (2¼ M.) *Ober-Wessen*, and (5½ M.) **Reit im Winkel** (2240'; *Oberwirth Hamberger*; *Unterwirth*), a Bavarian frontier-village, in a broad, picturesque valley, and an inexpensive summer-resort. To the S.W. rises the Kaisergebirge.

EXCURSIONS (guide, *Adv. Hörmann*) To the (1 M.) *Eck-Kapelle*, which affords a fine view of the valley, and thence to the right to (20 min.) the top of the *Walenberg* (view of the Chiemsee). Or we may turn to the

to Kössen. RUHPOLDING. *I. Route 12.* 57

left at the chapel, cross the hill through wood to the *Klapf-Alp*, and return by *Birnbach* (1½ hr. to Reit). — The '*Glocknerschau*', ¾ hr. to the W., on the way to the Möser-Alp, beyond the farms of *Klapf* and *Birnbach*, commands a view of the Gross-Glockner. — The °**Möser-Alpe** (2 hrs., guide) affords a fine view of the Tauern (Venediger, Glockner); easy descent to Kössen (see p. 58). — The ascent of the °**Fellhorn** (5784'; 3½-4 hrs.; not difficult; guide 4½ m.) is recommended The route leads viâ *Blindau*, the *Klausenberg-Alp*, and the (2¼ hrs.) *Neue-Alp* (4780') to (¾ hr.) the *Ecken-Alp* (5555'; Inn), in an open situation on the crest of the mountain (fine view). The broad summit of the *Fellhorn*, carpeted with Alpine roses, and commanding a superb panorama, is easily reached from the inn in ½ hr.; far below lies the Tyrolese Achenthal. The Ecken-Alp belongs to Kössen (see p. 58); descent to *Waidring* steep and fatiguing (p. 176). — Pleasant route (guide advisable) over the *Winkelmoos-Alp* (3710'; Rfmts. in the second hut) to (7½ hrs.) *Unken* (p. 177). From the (1½ hr.) *Seegatterl* (see below) we ascend to the right to the Alp, whence the route to the Fischbachthal leads to the left, and that to the Kammerköhr-Alp to the right (p. 177). We continue in a straight direction (marshy at places) and then descend to the left to (1¼ hr.) *Schwarzberg* and (10 min.) the *Schwarzbergklamm* (p. 177). Thence to Unken 2½ hrs.

[To TRAUNSTEIN (22 M.). The road, monotonous at first, leads through the wooded *Weissloferthal* to (2¾ M.) *Leitstuben*. At the saw-mill it turns to the left, ascends gradually to the (1¼ M.) *Seegatterl* (Inn), and leads through wood on the hill-side, past the *Weit-See, Mitter-See*, and *Löden-See*, to the (5½ M.) **Seehaus** (2455'; Inn), on the beautiful little *Förchensee*. It then follows the *See-Traun* to (1¼ M.) the hamlet of *Labau*, at the confluence of the *Fischbach* and the Traun.

A path to the right by a finger-post, fatiguing at places, ascends the narrow *Fischbachthal* to (1½ hr.) the °**Staubfall**, precipitated from the Sonntagshorn on the left, from a height of 590'. This fall is on the Austrian and Bavarian frontier. The path, which is rendered safe by an iron balustrade, leads behind the fall, and past several other fine cascades of the Fischbach, into (½ hr.) the *Unkener Heuthal* (3100'), whence a fine view of the Reitalpgebirge is obtained on the E. Thence to *Unken*, 2½ hrs.; to the °*Schwarzbergklamm* (guide necessary), 1½ hr. — Ascent of the °*Sonntagshorn* (6425') from the Heuthal, see p. 177. — The **Seehauser Kienberg** (5564') is ascended from the Seehaus by the *Brand-Alp* in 3-4 hrs., with guide; admirable view towards the S. and W. The ascent may also be made from the *Urschlau* viâ the *Röthelmoos-Alp*.

The road crosses the Traun (below this point called the *Weisse Traun*), and leads past the hamlets of *Fritz, Fuchsau*, and *Nieder-Vachenau* to (2¾ M.) **Ruhpolding** (2180'; *Post*), a large village, prettily situated at the influx of the *Urschlauer Ache* into the Traun. The church-hill, to the W., affords a good survey of the environs (to the S.E. the Rauschberg and Sonntagshorn).

EXCURSIONS. Through the **Urschlau** to Reit im Winkel, a pleasant walk of 4 hrs. (guide). The road leads by *Brand* (Inn) to the *Klause*, whence a footpath crosses the *Röthelmoos-Alpe* (2780'). — A road leads from Ruhpolding to the E., by *Zell, Aschenau*, and the small *Froschsee*, to (5½ M.) *Inzell* (p. 55). — Ascent of the **Rauschberg** (5512'), a fine point of view, 3½ hrs. (guide necessary, but no difficulty). — Ascent of the **Hochfellen** (2220'), viâ the *Thorau-Alpe*, 4 hrs. (better viâ *Hocherb* to the *Bründling-Alpe*, where we join the path ascending from the Maxhütte; thence to the top, from the N. side, comp. p. 55).

Passing (2¾ M.) *Eisenärzt*, with a government-foundry, we next reach (2 M.) **Ober-Siegsdorf** (1950'; *Oberwirth; *Unterwirth*). at the confluence of the *Weisse* and *Rothe Traun*, frequented as a summer-resort. A road leads to the E. to *Inzell* and *Reichenhall* (see p. 55). — To the W. (1¼ M.) are the baths of *Adelholzen* (p. 55).

EXCURSIONS. Pleasant walk to (2½ M.) Maria-Eck (2600'), a pilgrimage-church and inn, with a fine view of the Chiemgau. — Another fine point is the Stoisser Alpe (4875') on the *Teisenberg*, reached by *Neukirchen* (3 hrs.; guide); descent to stat. *Teisendorf* (p. 56) or to *Piding* (p. 79).

The road now follows the left bank of the Traun, passing *Haslach*, to (4 M.) *Traunstein* (p. 55; the 'Salinenstrasse' on the right bank is shorter). Omnibus from the railway-station of Traunstein to Ruhpolding, daily at 1 p.m., in 2¼ hrs.; to Siegsdorf three times daily.]

From Reit im Winkel a good road leads across the Tyrolese frontier and through the *Weisslofer-Thal* to (4 M.) Kössen (1930'; *Post, *Stadler), a large village, prettily situated in the broad valley of the *Grosse Ache*. The best view of the valley is obtained from (10 min.) the Calvarienberg (S. the Unterberg; S.W. the Kaisergebirge).

EXCURSIONS. Ascent of the *Möseralpe* (1¾ hr., a very fine point), see p. 57. — The *Eckenalpe* and *Fellhorn* (4 hrs.), rather arduous (better from Reit im Winkel, see p. 57). — Through *Pass Klobenstein* to *Schleching* and *Marquartstein*, see p. 56. — A road leads to the S. from Kössen through the monotonous *Gross-Achenthal*, between the *Unterberg* on the right and the *Fellhorn* on the left, to (8 M.) *Erpfendorf*, on the high-road from St. Johann to Lofer (p. 175). A pleasanter route is the rather longer road to (13 M.) *St. Johann* viâ *Schwendt* and the *Kohlnthal* (*Inn).

FROM KÖSSEN TO THE INNTHAL (to Kufstein, 16½ M., diligence daily in 5¼ hrs.; one-horse carr. from Reit im Winkel 10 m.). The road leads past *Kapell* (Bräuhaus) and through the *Weissenbach-Thal* to (6 M.) Walchsee (2190'; *Fischerwirth; Kramerwirth), a summer-resort prettily situated on the lake of that name (abounding in fish). On the S. rise the fissured rocks of the *Hintere Kaiser*.

The Habberg, or *Heuberg* (5162'), the extreme N.E. spur of the Kaisergebirge, ascended by *Durchholzen* and the *Jöchlalp* in 3 hrs. (no serious difficulty, but guide necessary), commands a magnificent view of the Kaisergebirge, Loferer Steinberge, and Tauern. — From Walchsee to *Kufstein* over the *Feldalpe* or the *Hochalpe* (8 hrs., guide), see p. 158.

The road then descends by (1¼ M.) *Durchholzen* (Inn; where a path, more attractive and 1¼ M. shorter, diverges to the left, following the hill-side to *St. Nikolaus* and *Ebbs*, see below) and (2½ M.) *Primau* (*Weinwirth), in the narrow wooded valley of the *Jenbach*, to (1 M.) *Sebi* (Inn), where it is joined on the right by the rough road descending from the *Prienthal* through the *Stein* (p. 55). About ¾ M. farther on the road divides: the branch to the right leads by *Niederndorf* (Gradl, rustic; Bräuhaus), to (3 M.) the custom-house (ferry), and then to the left to (1½ M.) *Oberaudorf*; that to the left leads by *Ebbs* (1540'; Oberwirth; Post), *Oberndorf*, and *Sparchen* (at the entrance of the *Kaiserthal*, p. 157), to (5¼ M.) *Kufstein* (p. 157).

II. SALZBURG AND THE SALZKAMMERGUT.

13. Salzburg and Environs 60
    Aigen. St. Jakob am Thurn, 65. — Gaisberg. Nockstein. Hellbrunn, 66. — Glanegg, etc. The Untersberg, 67.
14. From Salzburg to Berchtesgaden. Königs-See. From Berchtesgaden to Reichenhall and Saalfelden. . . . 68
    Excursions from Berchtesgaden. Lockstein. Brine Conduit. Aschauer Weiher, 70. — Tristramweg. Etzerschlössl. Gern. Theresienklause. Laroswacht. Au. Schönau, 71. — Almbach-Klamm. Vordereck and Upper Salzberg. Vorderbrand. Scharitzkehl-Alp. Kneifelspitze. Todte Mann. Jenner. Hochbrett, 72. — Kehlstein. Hohe Göll. Schneibstein. Kahlersberg, 73. — Gotzenalp, 74. — From the Königs-See to Golling across the Torrener Joch. The Steinerne Meer, 75. — The Upper Wimbach-Thal. Hundstod, 76. — Watzmann, 77. — Blaueis Glacier. Mühlsturzhorn. Hochkalter, 78. — Kammerlinghorn, 78. — Seisenbergklamm. Lamprechts-Ofenloch, 78.
15. From Salzburg to Reichenhall 79
    Excursions from Reichenhall. St. Zeno. Gross-Gmain. Padinger Alpe. Thumsee. Zwiesel, etc. 80-83.
16. From Salzburg to Hallein and Golling. 83
    The Dürnberg. The Kleine Barmstein, 83. — Rossfeld. Hohe Göll. Schlenken. From Hallein viâ Zill to Berchtesgaden, 84. — Almbachstrub. Faistenau, 84. — From Golling to Berchtesgaden over the Eckersattel, the Rossfeld, or the Ahornbüchsen, 85. — The Schwarzberg, 86.
17. From Linz to Salzburg 86
    From Lambach to Gmunden. The Traun Fall, 86. — From Attnang to Schärding. Wolfsegg. Tannberg, 87. — Mattsee, 88.
18. From Salzburg to Ischl and Aussee. Salzkammergut 88
    Excursions from Gmunden, 89. — Laudachsee. Traunstein. Almsee, 90. — Excursions from Langbath. The Langbath Lakes. The Kranabetsattel, 91. — Erlakogel. Offensee, 92. — Excursions from Ischl,93. — Ischl Salt Mine. Hutteneck-Alpe. Hohe Schrott. Zimitz. Hainzen. Predigtstuhl. Hohe Kalmberg, 94. — From Ischl to Alt-Aussee direct, 94. — The Chorinsky Klause. Excursions from Goisern, 95. — From Obertraun to Aussee over the Koppen, 96. — Excursions from Aussee. Alt-Aussee. Grundlsee. The Todte Gebirge, etc., 97.
19. From Ischl to Hallstatt, and to Abtenau and Golling viâ Gosau 98
    Excursions from Hallstatt. Steingrabenschneid. Plassen. Hirlatz. Zwölferkogel. Sarstein, 99. — Krippenstein. Hohe Gjaidstein. Dachstein, 100. — Excursions from Gosau. Dachstein. Thorstein. To Filzmoos over the Steigl, The Zwieselalp, 101. — From the Zwieselalp to Filzmoos and Bischofshofen. The Donnerkogl, 102.
20. From Ischl to Salzburg viâ St. Gilgen. Schafberg . 103
    From St. Wolfgang to the Schwarze See, 105. — From St. Gilgen to Scharfling. The Faistenauer Schafberg, 103.
21. The Attersee and Mondsee 108
    From Steinbach to the Langbath Lakes, 109. — Excursions from Mondsee. Kollmannsberg. Schober, etc., 110. — From Mondsee to Strasswalchen and Salzburg, 110.

13. Salzburg and Environs.

Hotels. °HÔTEL DE L'EUROPE (Pl. D, 1), opposite the station, with a large garden and fine view, R. 1 fl. 20-1 fl. 50, L. & A. 60 kr., pens. 4-5 fl. (lift); °HÔTEL D'AUTRICHE (Pl. a; D, 3), Schwarz-Str., R. from 1 fl., L. 25, B. 50, A. 80 kr.; °HÔTEL NELBÖCK (Pl. b; D, 1), near the station, R. 1½-2 fl., L. & A. 50, B. 60 kr., pens from 4 fl. In the town, on the left bank: °ERZHERZOG CARL (Pl. c; E, 4), Mozart-Platz; °GOLDNES SCHIFF (Pl. d; E, 4), Residenz-Platz, R. 1 fl., L. & A. 50 kr.; °SALZBURGER HOF (Pl. e; E, 4), Ludwig-Victor-Platz, moderate; °GOLDENE KRONE (Pl. f; D, 3), HIRSCH, MÖDLHAMMERBRÄU, °GOLDNES HORN, all in the Getreidegasse; MOHR (Pl. g; E, 3, 4), ZUR HÖLLE, Judengasse. On the right bank: ZUM STEIN (Pl. h; D, E, 5), by the bridge, with view; °GABLERBRÄU (Pl. i; D, 3), R. 80 kr.; °TRAUBE (Pl. k; D, 5), REGENBOGEN, TIGER, unpretending; STEIN-LECHNER'S GASTHAUS, Aigner-Str., moderate; PITTER, Westbahn-Str., well spoken of; STIEGLBRÄU (see below), R. from 50 kr.; SCHWARZES RÖSSL, Berg-Str. 5. — PENSION JUNG, near the station; KOLLER'S HÔTEL-GARNI (see below), Linzergasse, R. 80 kr.

Cafés. On the left bank of the Salzach: °*Tomaselli*, Ludwig-Victor-Platz; *Lobmayr*, Universitäts-Platz and Hafnergasse; *Wiesenberger*, Judengasse. On the right bank: *Café Bazar*, Schwarz-Str.; °*Koller*, Linzergasse, near the bridge (also rooms); *Edlmayr*, Theatergasse.

Restaurants. °*Curhaus* (see p. 64; concerts five or six times weekly in summer, 20-30 kr.). — WINE in °*St. Peter's Stiftskeller* (Pl. D, 4; p. 62; also a good restaurant); at *Glocker's* and *Keller's*, in the Getreidegasse; at the *Tiger*, *Mohren*, etc.; *Stehle's Restaurant*, Bahn-Str. — BEER at the *Stieglbräu*, Gstättengasse 8, in summer at the *Stieglkeller* (Pl. E, 4), on the way to the fortress, with view; °*Sternbräugarten*, Getreidegasse; °*Mirabellgarten*, Makart-Platz (concerts in summer); *Hofmann's Bierhalle*, near the station; *Schanzlkeller*, outside the Kajetaner-Thor, with view; *Mödlhammerkeller*, outside the Klausen-Thor, also with view; *Augustinerbräu*, at Mülln (quaint rooms; not open till 3 p.m.).

Baths. °*Curhaus*, Bahn-Str., admirably fitted up, with baths of every kind. °*Swimming Baths*, near Schloss Leopoldskron, 1¼ M. to the S.W. (p. 67; omnibus from the Stadt-Platz at 9.30 and 11.30 a.m., 4.15 and 7 p.m., 15 kr.; steam-tramway, see below). *Mud-, Pine-Cone-, and Peat*-baths at the *Ludwigsbad* and the *Marienbad*, 1¼ M. from the town (omnibus from the Goldene Hirsch and Goldene Horn at 7, 10, 2, and 6 o'clock).

Cabs. From the station into the town, with luggage, 60 kr. or (two horses) 1 fl.; at night, 90 kr. or 1 fl. 60 kr. — By time: half-a-day 3 fl. 20 kr. or 5 fl.; whole day 6 or 9 fl. — To *Berchtesgaden*, see p. 88. — Excursions with stay of 1 hr.: *Aigen*, *Marienbad*, *Hellbrunn*, or *Klesheim*, 2 or 3 fl. — Tolls and fees included in all cases

Steam Tramway (*Localbahn*) from the railway-station through the town to Nonnthal hourly (in 23 min.), and on to Hellbrunn and the Drachenloch several times a day (in 1 hr. 5 min.). The stations within the town are: *Fünfhaus*, *Ausweiche*, *Curhaus*, *Bazar*, *Innerer Stein*, and *Aeusserer Stein*, beyond which the line crosses the Carolinen-Brücke to (2 M.) *Nonnthal*. The next part of the line affords a succession of pretty views. Stations: *Leopoldskron*, *Cemetery*, *Kleingmain*, *Morzg*, (4¼ M.) *Hellbrunn* (p. 66), *Anif* (p. 66), *Grödig*, *St. Leonhard*, and (8 M.) the *Drachenloch*, on the Austrian frontier (p. 68).

Omnibus to *Hellbrunn* and *Aigen* thrice daily in good weather, starting from the Café Koller at 9.30 a.m. and 2.30 p.m. and from the Café Tomaselli at 3 p.m. (there and back 75 kr.; 1 hr. allowed at both places). To the *Fürstenbrunn*, starting from the Goldne Horn at 2 p.m.; returning at 6 p.m. (50 kr.; there and back 80 kr.) To *Berchtesgaden*, see p. 68; to *Mondsee*, see p. 110.

'**Dienstmann**' (commissionaire). 5 kr. per ¼ hr.; to carry luggage not exceeding 22 lbs. in weight to the station, 20 kr. — **Town Guides**, 25 kr. per hr.; 2 fl. per day. The following are good guides for mountain ascents: *Joh. Hodes*, *Ant. Karl*, *Jos. Klener*, *Jos. Langer*, *Joh. Wimmer*.

Post and Telegraph Office (Pl. 32; E, 4) in the Government Buildings,

Residenz-Platz, entrance to the right, by the guard-house. — *Telephone* to the Zistel-Alp and Gaisberg, in the Makart-Platz, next the Mirabellgarten.
English Church Service in the German Protestant Church at 11 a.m. and 4 p.m.

Salzburg (1350′), the ancient *Juvavum*, was once the capital of the wealthiest and most powerful ecclesiastical principality in S. Germany, which was secularised in 1802 and converted into a temporal Electorate. It afterwards became Austrian, then Bavarian, and finally, in 1816, Austrian again, and since 1849 has formed an independent domain of the crown. The town (25,000 inhab.; 350 Prot.) is now the seat of an archbishop and of the government and law-courts of the district. Few German towns can compare with Salzburg for beauty of situation. The town lies on both banks of the *Salzach*, bounded by the abrupt castle-hill and the *Mönchsberg* on the left bank, and by the *Capuzinerberg* on the right bank. Frequent fires have left few mediæval buildings here. Most of the principal edifices were built by the splendour-loving archbishops in the 17th and 18th centuries. The houses with their flat roofs, the numerous fountains, and the marble façades remind the traveller of Italy, whence the archbishops generally procured their architects. The shady promenades on the broad quays afford charming walks on both banks of the Salzach, from the railway-embankment to the Carolinen-Brücke. On the right bank, near the railway-station, a new and handsome quarter has sprung up since the demolition of the fortifications. The Stadtpark and Curhaus (p. 64) here form a favourite resort.

The older part of the town is on the left bank of the Salzach, its central point being the *Residenz-Platz* (Pl. E, 4), in the middle of which is the handsome **Hofbrunnen* (Pl. 3), 46 ft. in height, executed in 1664 by *Ant. Dario*. Each of the hippopotami and figures of Atlas is hewn out of a single block of marble. At the summit a Triton spouts water out of a horn. On the W. side of the Platz rises the spacious **Residenz-Schloss**, or Palace, erected in 1592-1724, and now occupied by the Grand-Duke of Tuscany. Opposite to it is the **Neubau**, including the *Government Buildings*, *Law Courts* (Pl. 34), and *Post* and *Telegraph* offices (Pl. 32), with a small tower containing a set of chimes, which play at 7, 11, and 6 o'clock. In front of it is the *Hauptwache* (Pl. 2), or Guard House. On the S. side is the handsome **Cathedral**, erected in 1614-28 by *Santino Solari* in the Italian style, in imitation of St. Peter's at Rome. A chapel to the left of the entrance contains a *Font in bronze, dating from 1321. In the Domplatz, on the W. side of the cathedral, rises a *Mariensäule* in lead by Hagenauer (1772).

***Mozart's Statue** (Pl. 28), in bronze, by *Schwanthaler*, erected in 1842, adorns the Mozart-Platz (to the E.). The house in which the great composer was born (b. 1756, d. 1791), No. 7 Getreidegasse (Pl. 27), contains the interesting *Mozart Museum* on the third floor (MSS., portraits, piano, etc.; open daily 8-11 and 1-4; Sun.

10-12; admission 50 kr.). — *Mozart's House* (Pl. 29; D, 3) is in the Makart-Platz (formerly Hannibal-Platz).

On the S. side of the cathedral lies the *Kapitel-Platz*, with its handsome marble horse-trough (1732; Pl. 4). On the left side of the Platz is the *Archiepiscopal Palace* (Pl. 1).

Nearly opposite, in the S.W. corner of the Platz, is the entrance to the *Burial Ground of St. Peter (Pl. 24), the oldest in Salzburg. The vaults hewn in the rock and the chapels attached, dating from the period of the consecration by St. Rupert about 696, are interesting. The late-Gothic *Church of St. Margaret* (Pl. 16) in the burial-ground, erected in 1481, restored in 1864, contains tombstones of the 15th century. One of the modern monuments in the cemetery (that of the Polish countess *Lanckoronska*, d. 1839) is by Schwanthaler. In the last vault of the arcades on the N. is interred the composer *Michael Haydn* (d. 1806), brother of the more celebrated Joseph Haydn. The **Church of St. Peter** (Pl. 18), a Romanesque edifice of 1131, badly restored in 1754, contains a poor monument to Michael Haydn (N. aisle, 5th chapel). In the right aisle is the tombstone of St. Rupert. — The *Benedictine Abbey of St. Peter* (Pl. 6) contains a library of 40,000 vols., with a collection of incunabula and ancient MSS., a very interesting treasury, and extensive archives (visitors admitted, generally at 1 p. m., by permission obtained at the Stiftspforte, to the left of the church-door). — At the N. entrance to the burial-ground is the *Stiftskeller* (p. 60; good wine).

In the vicinity is the **Franciscan Church** (Pl.9), of the 13th cent., with a fine Romanesque S. portal, and an elegant Gothic tower, restored in 1866. The interior is in the transition style, disfigured with modern additions. The hexagonal choir borne by columns, with its net-work vaulting and its series of chapels, dates from the 15th century. On the high-altar a *Madonna, in wood, by M. Pacher (1480). In the *Franciscan Monastery* opposite a performance is given daily (10.30. a.m.; ladies not admitted) on the 'Pansymphonicon', an instrument invented by Father Singer, one of the monks (d.1882).

Adjoining are the stables of the former prince-bishops, now a cavalry-barrack, with the **Summer Riding School** (Pl. 35; adm. 10 kr.), an amphitheatre hewn in the rocks of the Mönchsberg in 1693, and the *Winter Riding School*, with a ceiling-painting of a tournament (date 1690). To the left of the riding-school are the steps ascending to the Mönchsberg (p. 63).

On the N. side of the barracks, in the Universitäts-Platz, is a horse-trough with marble enclosure and a group of horse-tamers by *Mandl* (1670). Thence to the W. runs the *Neuthor, a tunnel 150 yds. long, hewn in 1767 through the conglomerate rock (breccia) of the Mönchsberg, leading out of the town. Beyond it rises a statue of St. Sigismund, by *Hagenauer*, in memory of Archb. Sigismund, the constructor of the tunnel, a medallion of whom has been placed at the end of the tunnel next the town.

Near the Convent of St. Ursula (Pl. 20) is the extensive and valuable *Museum Carolino-Augusteum (Pl. D, 3), entered from the Franz-Joseph-Quai (adm. 30 kr.; daily in summer, 8-1 and 2-6, Sun. and Thurs. in winter, 1-4; good light necessary).

Hall of Antiquities: Celtic and Roman antiquities from Salzburg, the Pinzgau, etc. *Music Room*, with a [fine collection of the musical instruments of the last three centuries. *Costume Saloon:* ladies' and gentlemen's costumes of the last three centuries. *Weapon Saloon:* weapons of the last three centuries. Romanesque *Chapel* and *Sacristy*, fitted up in the Gothic style. Also a number of rooms in the mediæval and rococo styles: *Dining-hall, Bed-chamber, Hunting Room, Sitting-room, Kitchen*, etc. Then a room containing miscellaneous antiquarian objects. Lastly an ichthyological and ornithological collection and a collection illustrating the flora of Salzburg. The *Second Floor* contains collections of prehistoric and natural history objects from the neighbourhood, paintings by local artists, a large relief-map by Keil, a planetarium, a library of 50,000 vols., a collection of Salzburg coins, a miners' guild-room of 1606, etc.

The houses of the adjacent *Gstättengasse* (Pl. C, 3) cling to the side of the Mönchsberg like swallows' nests, with rooms and cellars hewn in the conglomerate rock. Frequent landslips have taken place here, burying houses and their inhabitants. The *Klausenthor* was formerly the termination of this part of the town, lying between the hill and the river. The latter is now bordered by the broad *Franz-Joseph-Quai*, planted with trees. Beyond the gate is the new iron *Franz-Karl-Brücke* (foot-bridge; 1 kr.). Farther down, below the suburb of *Mülln* (Pl. B, C, 2), the river is crossed by the *Railway Bridge*.

Above the town, on the S.E. point of the Mönchsberg, rises the fortress of *Hohen-Salzburg (1780'; ticket for the interior and the tower 20 kr.), the pinnacled towers of which are 400 ft. above the Kapitel-Platz. The *Folter-Thurm* (80' high) commands a remarkably fine *Panorama. The direct route from the town to the fortress (1/4 hr.), indicated by notice-boards, leads from the Kapitel-Platz (Pl. E, 4) through the Festungsgasse (short-cuts by flights of steps), passing the restaurant *Zur Katz*, at the entrance to the fortress (fine view). The fortifications, founded in the 9th cent., were extended at different periods; the greater part of the present imposing pile dates from 1496-1519. The *Church of St. George* in the castle-yard, erected in 1502, contains statues of the Twelve Apostles in red marble. On the exterior is a relief, representing the founder Archb. Leonhard (d. 1519). The *Fürstenzimmer*, restored in the old style, are worth inspection. The *Rittersaal* contains a fine Gothic stove of 1501.

The *Mönchsberg (1646'), a wooded hill about 1½ M. in length, bounding the town on the W., affords charming walks with beautiful views. The finest points are the *Franz-Josef-Elisabeth-Höhe*, the *Carolinen-Höhe*, and *Achleitner's Thurm* (adm. 10kr.): to the left rises the fortress of Hohen-Salzburg, beyond it the Gaisberg, at the foot of which is the Aignerthal; beyond Schloss Hellbrunn are seen the long Tennengebirge, the narrow defile of

Pass Lueg, and the Hohe Göll adjoining it; above Schloss Leopoldskron the dark Untersberg; then the Lattengebirge, Müllnerhorn, Ristfeichthorn, Sonntagshorn, and Hochstauffen; in the plain Schloss Klesheim. In the foreground rises the rocky Reinberg (Ofenlochberg), with quarries of conglomerate. To the W. the Bavarian plain; N. Maria-Plain, with the village of Bergheim at its foot; N.E., adjoining the Gaisberg, is the Capuzinerberg, at the base of which lies the town, on the Salzach. The *Bürgerwehrsöller* (restaurant) affords a good survey of the town.

The direct route from the town to the Mönchsberg is by a flight of 283 steps near the Summer Riding School (p. 62); another leads from the suburb of *Mülln*, past the *Augustine Church* (Pl. 5; C, 2) and through the *Monica-Pforte*; a third from the suburb of *Nonnthal* (Zum Rothen Hahn), through the *Scharten-Thor* (Pl. D, 5). The road from the fortress (p. 63) to the Mönchsberg leads through a gateway under the Katz, and passes the *Ludwigs-Fernsicht* and the castellated *Villa Freyburg*.

The E. spur of the hill, below the fortress, is the **Nonnberg** (Pl. E, F, 4), so called from an Ursuline convent situated here. The Gothic *Convent Church* (founded 1009, restored in the 15th cent.), with a Romanesque portal, possesses a fine winged altarpiece, a crypt with handsome columns, and in the tower ancient frescoes. Charming view from the parapet. — Outside the adjacent Kajetaner-Thor, on the bank of the Salzach, is the **Künstlerhaus** (Pl. F, 4), an institution opened in 1885 for exhibitions of pictures and industrial art.

The Salzach is crossed in the middle of the town by the iron *Stadtbrücke*, 300 ft. long and 36 ft. broad. In the 'Platzl', near the bridge, on the right bank of the Salzach, is the *House of Paracelsus* (Pl. 30), indicated by his effigy.

The monument of this celebrated physician and empiric (d. 1541), erected in 1752 over the original tombstone, is in the vestibule of the church which adjoins the **Cemetery of St. Sebastian** (Pl. 25) at the end of the Linzergasse. The inscription describes him as the '*insignis medicinae doctor, qui dira illa vulnera lepram podagram hydroposim aliaque insanabilia corporis contagia mirifica arte sustulit*'. To the left of the path leading to the *Chapel* in the centre of the cemetery (erected 1597, recently restored; walls in mosaic by Castello), is the grave of *Mozart's Widow* (d. 1842).

To the N. of the Platzl the Dreifaltigkeitsgasse leads to the long *Mirabell-Platz*. Here, to the right, stands the *Custom House* (formerly *Stables*), and on the left **Schloss Mirabell** (Pl. D, 2), rebuilt after a fire in 1818, formerly the archiepiscopal palace, and now the property of the town. Behind it lies the *Mirabell Garden*, laid out in the old French fashion, embellished with marble statues, and containing an aviary (adm. 10 kr.).

Adjoining Schloss Mirabell on the N. is the well-kept **Stadtpark**, containing a handsome *Curhaus* and *Bath-House* (concerts, see p. 60). A building in the park contains *Sattler's Cosmorama* and a panorama of Salzburg (adm. 30 kr.).

An outlet on the W. side of the park leads to the Schwarz-Strasse and the Franz-Karl Bridge over the Salzach (p. 63). To the left, on the Elisabeth-Quai, is the *Protestant Church* (Pl. 14), a Romanesque edifice by *Götz* (1867). — The (1¹/₄ M.) garden of the *Villa Schwarz*, near the railway-station, contains an excellent bronze statue of *Schiller*, by Meixner.

In the Linzergasse on the right bank, about 200 paces from the Stadtbrücke, opposite the Gablerbräu Inn, and recognisable by its large stone portal, is the entrance to the *Capuzinerberg (2130')*. The *Capuchin Monastery* (Pl. 11) is reached by means of 225 stone steps. At the top visitors ring at the gate (3 kr.) and enter the park. On the left stands the '*Mozart-Häuschen*', brought from Vienna to its present site, in which Mozart completed his 'Zauberflöte' in 1791 (adm. 10 kr.). In front is a bronze bust of Mozart by E. Helmer. About 3 min. to the right is the 'Erste Stadt-Ansicht' (view-tower with coloured windows). Returning to the Mozart-Häuschen, we ascend through the wood by about 500 steps more. After 10 min. a finger-post on the left indicates the way to the '*Aussicht nach Bayern*', whence we survey the new town on the right bank and the railway-station in the foreground, to the right Maria-Plain, to the left Mülln, in the centre the Salzach stretching far into the plains of Bavaria. About 2 min. farther on another direction-post shows the way (diverging from the straight path to the restaurant) to the (5 min.) '*Stadt-Aussicht*', the finest point on the Capuzinerberg: admirable *View of the town and fortress, the Hochstauffen, Reichenhall Mts., Lattengebirge, Untersberg, Schönfeldspitze, Hohe Göll, Pass Lueg, and Tennengebirge. In 5 min. more we reach the *Francisci-Schlössl* (or *Capuziner Schlössl*), an old bastion on the E. side of the hill, 680 ft. above the Salzach, and commanding a very extensive prospect (restaurant). A shady path (pretty views) leads hence down the hill on the side farthest from the town, which we regain through the Linzer Thor.

Aigen, a château and park of Prince Schwarzenberg, at the foot of the Gaisberg, 3 M. to the S.E. of Salzburg, merits a visit (railway-station, see p. 83). Morning-light the best. At the entrance to the grounds (³/₄ M. from the station) is a *Restaurant, where a guide (30 kr.) may be procured. The *Kanzel* is the finest point.

An easy bridle-path leads from Aigen to the (1¹/₂ hr.) *Zistel-Alp* (p. 66), passing through the park, and then, by the waterfall, to the left, through the woods, to the *Steinwandtner Farms*, where it merges in a carriage-road. Another route leads from the *Kanzel* (see above) through fine woods to the hamlet of *Gaisberg*, whence a path ascends to the left.

About 1¹/₄ hr. above Aigen is Count Platz's château of **St. Jakob am Thurn**, an excellent point of view (¹/₂ hr. from stat. *Elsbethen*, p. 83). The château is occupied by the curé ("Restaurant, with fine view). From the 'Aussicht', 5 min. from the château, we enjoy a view of the mountains and the plain of the Salzach, most picturesquely grouped. The Tennengebirge, the Hohe Göll, Watzmann, Hochkalter, Untersberg, and Hochstauffen are especially conspicuous. In the background of the Salzachthal lies Salzburg.

The *Gaisberg (4220') is the finest point of view near Salzburg. A ZAHNRADBAHN, or rack-and-pinion railway, on the same principle as the Rigi railway, opened in May, 1887, ascends to the summit from *Parsch* (p. 83; 1420'), a station 6 min. by rail from Salzburg, or about 20 min. walk from the *Carolinen-Brücke* (Pl. F, 4) by the Aigen and Gaisberg road (omn. from the station in 20 min., 30 kr.). The ascent of the railway, which is $2^3/_4$ M. in length, with a maximum gradient of 25:100, takes 40 min. (fares, up 2, down $1^1/_2$, return-ticket 3, for holders of circular tickets $2^1/_2$ fl.). The line ascends on the S.W. side of the hill, passing the station of *Judenberg-Alpe* (2415'; Restaurant, with view), to ($1^3/_4$ M.) the *Zistel-Alp* (3270'; Restaurant), and then mounts in a wide curve towards the E., through cuttings in the rock, to the summit (4190'). A little to the W. of the terminal station is the *Hôtel Gaisbergspitze* (R., L., & A. from $1^1/_2$ fl.), with a view-tower (15 kr.). The *View embraces the Salzburg Alps and the plain, in which seven lakes may be descried (comp. the annexed Panorama). The E. and S. heights should also be visited.

For pedestrians the best route is by the 'Alpenvereinsweg', constructed by the German Alpine Club, and provided with finger-posts and benches (shade in the morning). From *Parsch* (see above) we proceed to (10 min.) the *Apothekerhöfe*, at the foot of the hill. The path then ascends to the left to the ($3/_4$ hr.) *Gersberg* (or *Zeisberg*) *Alpe* (2615'; °Inn), and thence in zigzags through wood on the N. side to the ($1^1/_4$ hr.) summit. [A new path leads from Gersberg to the Judenberg-Alpe in $1/_2$ hr.] — From the Apothekerhöfe to the *Zistel-Alp* (see above), on foot, $1^1/_2$ hr. ; thence to the top, $3/_4$ hr. Route from *Aigen* to the Zistel-Alp, see p. 65.

The **Nockstein** (3412') a rocky excrescence on the N. side of the Gaisberg, also repays a visit ($1^3/_4$ hr.; guide unnecessary). We follow the Ischl road, past the Capuzinerberg, to (3 M.) *Guggenthal* (see p. 103), whence the *Lamberg-Steig*, diverging to the right immediately behind the brewery, ascends in easy windings to the ($3/_4$ hr.) summit (magnificent view).

The imperial château of **Hellbrunn**, 3 M. to the S. of Salzburg (steam-tramway, see p. 60), with gardens and fountains in the style of the 17th and 18th cent., is adorned with frescoes by Mascagni and others (1615). [*Restaurant. The fountains play on Sundays gratis; fee on other days 50 kr.] To the left on entering the grounds is an iron gate (when closed, fee of 20 kr.) leading into the *Park*. Leaving the carriage-drive after 200 paces, and ascending the wooded hill to the right, we pass the *Monatsschlösschen* and arrive at ($1/_4$ hr.) the *Stadt-Aussicht*, commanding a fine view of Salzburg. Then through wood to (10 min.) the *Watzmann-Aussicht* on the other side of the hill, from which the Watzmann is seen to great advantage. On our way back we descend to the right, after 5 min., to the '*Steinerne Theater*', hewn in the rock, where pastorals and operas used to be performed before the archbishops. We then return by the drive. — About $1^1/_2$ M. to the S. of Hellbrunn, on the road to Hallein, is the Gothic château of *Anif* (Count Arco), situated on an island in a small lake. — From Hellbrunn to *Aigen* (p. 65) is a walk of about $3/_4$ hr. (steam-tramway, see p. 60).

To the S.W. of Salzburg (1¼ M.; steam-tramway, see p. 60) is the château of **Leopoldskron**, with a large fish-pond and *Swimming Bath* (p. 60; Restaurant). From this point the extensive *Leopoldskroner Moos* stretches southwards to the base of the Untersberg. On the 'Moos-Strasse', which traverses the moor to Glanegg, are a group of 200 houses inhabited by peat-cutters, and the 'Moos-Bäder' or peat-baths (omnibus, see p. 60). The *Ludwigsbad* is ¾ M. from Leopoldskron, and the *Marienbad* 1¼ M. From (4 M.) **Glanegg** (1460'; *Inn*), with its old château, a road ascending by the falls of the *Glan* leads to (2 M.) the source of the stream, called the *"Fürstenbrunnen* (1950'), the excellent water of which (42° Fahr.) is now conducted to Salzburg. On the road are several marble-cutting works and bullet-mills (omnibus, see p. 60). In the vicinity are the *Quarries* which yield the beautiful Untersberg marble (Restaurant zur Schönen Aussicht).

To the N. (3½ M.), on the right bank of the Salzach, rises the conspicuous and handsome pilgrimage-church of **Maria-Plain** (1720'), erected in 1674. The very extensive *View is partly obstructed by the trees. Evening-light most advantageous. A path diverging at Froschheim (Pl. F, 1) is shorter and pleasanter than the road (finger-post). Restaurant at the foot of the hill.

The **Untersberg**, the most conspicuous mountain in the environs of Salzburg, culminates in the *Geiereck* (5910'), the *Salzburger Hochthron* (8070'), and the *Berchtesgadener Hochthron* (8480'). The mountain is usually ascended from Glanegg (see above; provisions necessary). The paths have been recently improved by the German Alpine Club, and indicated by red marks, so that experienced mountaineers do not require a guide in good weather (see p. 60; *Ebner*, at the Fürstenbrunnen Inn, is recommended).

— For the *Geiereck* and *Salzburger Hochthron* an easy path leads from Glanegg through the *Rositlenthal* to (1½ hr.) the *Lower Rositten-Alp* (2650'), which we may also reach from *Grödig* (p. 68) by a new path over the *Grödiger Thörl* (3190'; also 1½ hr.). We then ascend to (1½ hr.) the *Upper Rositten-Alp* (4220'; Rfmts.). A few minutes farther on is a finger-post pointing to the left to the *Schellenberger-Sattel* (4700') and *Schellenberg*. We here follow the path to the right till we reach a second way-post, pointing (right) to the (10 min.) *°Kolowratshöhle*, a cavern containing fantastic ice-formations; a flight of steps in the rock, protected by railings, descends to the bottom of the cavern, which is 200 ft. deep. Proceeding to the left ('Nach den Gamslöchern und Geiereck') we reach (5 min.) a third finger-post indicating the position of the *"Gamslöcher*, a curious series of grottoes (fine view from two openings in the largest, the 'Halle'), which lie a few paces from the path. We now ascend to the right by the *Doppelsteig*, boldly hewn in the rocks of the Geiereck (345 yds. long; provided with a railing and free from danger), to the (1½ hr.) **Untersberg-Haus** (5410'; Inn), situated on the plateau of the Untersberg, whence the *Geiereck* (5910') may be reached in 40 minutes. The route hence to the (1½ hr.) *°Salzburger Hochthron* (8070'), the finest point of view, leads mostly over grass, and passes the *Jungfernbrunnen*. — The old path (improved) to the top of the Geiereck leads from Glanegg (turning, after ½ hr., to the right) to (2 hrs.) the *Firmian-Alp* (3120'); then through wood, up the steep and toilsome *Steinerne Stiege* and past the *Schafleck*, to (1¾ hr.) the plateau and (¾ hr.) the *Geiereck*. — In descending from the Salzburger Hochthron, we may choose the interesting route by the *Schweigmüller-Alpe* (4895') to Glanegg (3½ hrs.); the descent through the *Brunnthal* to the Fürstenbrunnen (3 hrs.) is fatiguing. — The *Berchtesgadener Hochthron* (8480') is best ascended from the W. side (Pass Hallthurm, p. 76) by the *Zehn-Kaser-Alp* (4975'; 3½-4 hrs.) or from Berchtesgaden by *Gern* (5-6 hrs.; way indicated by red marks, but a guide is advisable, 6 m.). The route from the Salzburger Hochthron by the *Mittagsscharte* takes about 3½ hrs., but is very trying. — Beneath the Untersberg, according to ancient lore, sleeps the Emperor Charlemagne, ready to arise when Germany is restored to her ancient glory.

14. From Salzburg to Berchtesgaden. Königs-See.
From Berchtesgaden to Reichenhall and Saalfelden.
Comp. *Map*, p. *112*.

16 M. STEAM TRAMWAY to the Austrian frontier at the *Drachenloch* (8 M.) in 1 hr. 5 min. (80 or 40 kr.); OMNIBUS thence to *Berchtesgaden* twice daily in 1½ hr. (50 kr., there and back 80 kr.), and to *Königs-See* thrice daily in 2 hrs. (70 kr., 1 fl. 20 kr.). Through-ticket from Salzburg to Berchtesgaden 90 kr., return 1 fl. 60 kr.; to Königs-See 1 fl. 10 kr., 2 fl. For a day's excursion the best plan is to leave Salzburg at 6 a.m. for Drachenloch and Königs-See, leave the latter at 9 a.m., and row to the Obersee and back (3 hrs.); then from Königs-See at 1.45 p.m. to the Salt Mines (2.30 p.m.) and thence back to Salzburg, which will be reached about 6.15 p.m. Luggage is charged for at the rate of 32½ kr. per cwt. from Salzburg to the Drachenloch, and 20 kr. from the Drachenloch to Berchtesgaden. — In summer (June-Oct.) several OMNIBUSES ply direct from Salzburg to the *Königs-See*, starting at 6 or 6.30 a.m., reaching the Königs-See at 9.30 or 10 a.m., leaving for the return-journey at 4 p.m., passing the Salt Mines at 5 p.m. (halt of 1 hr.), and regaining Salzburg at 9 p.m. (fare 1 fl. 10, there and back 2 fl. 20 kr.; from the Königs-See to Salzburg 2 m.). — CARRIAGE from Salzburg to Berchtesgaden 5 or 8 fl., there and back 6 or 10 fl.; to the Königs-See and back 8 or 12 fl. (visit to the salt-mines included in each case; the drive from Salzburg and back, with a visit to the salt-works, occupies 8 hrs.). The salt-mine is generally visited on the return-journey, but the coachman may be ordered to drive from Salzburg direct to the (2 hrs.) mining-offices. The usual halting-place on the way to Berchtesgaden is the Inn Zur Almbach-Klamm.

The STEAM TRAMWAY ('Salzburger Localbahn'; p. 60) leads through the suburb of *Nonnthal* (p. 64), passes the stations named at p. 60, and near (6¾ M.) *Grödig* (*Feichtner's Brewery) crosses the *Alm Canal*, conducted to Salzburg from the *Alm*, which drains the Königs-See. On the hill to the right is the old château of *Glanegg* (p. 67), behind which towers the pointed *Hochstauffen* (p. 82); on the left is the *Schmidtenstein* (5555'), with a summit resembling a castle. The road skirts the base of the Untersberg, passing (7½ M.) *St. Leonhard*, and reaches its present terminus at the station of (8 M.) *Drachenloch* (Restaurant). On the right, high up in the side of the Untersberg. is the curious opening called the *Drachenloch*. On the hill to the left is *Schloss Gartenau*.

A narrow defile, traversed by the Alm, between the Untersberg and the N. spur of the *Hohe Göll*, now leads to the district of Berchtesgaden. The boundary is formed by the *Hangende Stein* (1490'), a cliff rising above the Alm. The Austrian custom-station is on this side of the cliff; the Bavarian station is 1 M. farther on, near an old tower. Two reliefs on the rock mark the frontier between the two states. The first, the Austrian, represents St. Leopold, the patron-saint of the Archduchy (date 1818); the second, the Bavarian, is a crucifix with the inscription: *Pax Intrantibus et Inhabitantibus* (date 1514).

2½ M. **Schellenberg** (1555'; *Forelle*, near the church, with good trout; *Untersberg*), with a monument to the memory of natives who fell in 1870-71. The road follows the right bank of the Alm, and reaches the (2½ M.) *Inn Zur Almbach-Klamm* (p. 72), ½ M. beyond which the road from Hallein (p. 84) joins our road on the left. On the right rises the precipitous *Graue Wand*. The valley expands, and the *Grosse* and *Kleine Watzmann*, with the *Watzmann Glacier* between them, suddenly become visible. Crossing the *Larosbach*, and then the Alm by the (½ M.) *Freimannbrücke*, we ascend the slope on the left bank. (Path on the bank of the Alm, see p. 71.) We soon obtain (½ M.) the first glimpse of Berchtesgaden, with its well-built houses, delightfully situated on the slope of the mountain, and surrounded by meadows and trees. About ½ M. farther on, at a finger-post, 1 M. from Berchtesgaden, indicating the way to the 'Salzberg and Königs-See', a road (the direct route to the Königs-See) leads across the *Goldenbach-Brücke* to (¼ M.) the *Salt Mine*; on the right are the new mining-buildings, opposite which are the old entrance to the salt-mine (date 1628) and the new shaft.

*VISIT TO THE SALT MINE (easier, more expeditious, and less expensive than a visit to the Dürnberg mine at Hallein). Ticket for the regular trips at 10.30-11 a.m. and 5-5.30 p.m., 1½ m. each; at other hours, from 7 a.m. to 6.30 p.m., admission for one person 3½ m., for each additional person 1½ m. (tickets at the mining-office, opposite the entrance-shaft). Visitors of each sex are provided with appropriate miners' costumes and with lanterns. The mine is entered on foot, numerous flights of steps ascended, and an occasional descent accomplished by means of wooden slides inclined at an angle of 45° or more. These present no difficulty. Ladies are preceded by a miner, who acts as a drag and prevents the risk of a concussion at the bottom of the slide. Gentlemen are supplied with leathern gloves, and regulate their pace by allowing the rope at the side to slip more or less rapidly through their hands. The 'Salz-See', illuminated somewhat feebly by miners' lamps, is traversed in a boat. The party then passes through several other chambers and galleries, the most interesting of which is the huge Kaiser-Franz chamber, now deserted, and reaches the tramway by which the mine is quitted. Ladies are seated in rude cars, gentlemen on a long wooden horse on wheels. The miniature train descends on an inclined plane, its speed being regulated by a brakesman, and finally shoots out into the open air. The unwonted apparel having been discarded, specimens of the rock-salt and photographs may be purchased, and a trifling gratuity given to the attendant. Visitors may also be photographed on the spot in their mining costume.

The mine lies about ¾ M. from Berchtesgaden, to which the *Bergwerks-Allee* leads. — The road from Salzburg, leading straight on from the Goldenbach bridge (see above), crosses the *Gernbach* (on the left is the *Malerhügel*, a massive rock commanding a beautiful view), and ascends through the straggling suburb of *Nonnthal* to (1 M.) Berchtesgaden. Travellers bound for the Königs-See do not go through Berchtesgaden, but drive past the salt-works, round the base of the hill.

Berchtesgaden. — **Hotels.** BELLEVUE, with baths, R. 1¼-2, B. 1, pension 7-8 m.; *LEUTHAUS or POST, R. 1½-2 m., B. 70 pf., pension 6 m.; VIER JAHRESZEITEN, at the upper end of the village, near

11. Route 14. BERCHTESGADEN. *From Salzburg*

the royal villa, with garden and view, R., L., & A. 2½, D, 3, B. 1 m.; °WATZMANN, R. 1½-2 m.; NEUHAUS; SALZBURGER HOF; NONNTHALER WIRTHSHAUS; BÄR; LÖWE; TRIEMBACHER, R. 1 m. — Pensions (3-7 m. per day): °VILLA GEIGER; SCHWARZENBECK; °GRÖSSWANG; °BERGHOF; FEDERMANN; °SCHWABENWIRTH; GÖHLSTEIN; °MALTERLEHEN, °OBERHOFREIT, and °SCHWEIZER PENSION, in Schönau (see p. 71); °MORITZ, STEINER, and REGINA, on the upper Salzberg (p. 71). — *Apartments* to let are advertised on a column at the fountain in front of the Neuhaus. — °*Café Forstner*, near the Post; °*Knauer*, confectioner, with restaurant. — Money may be changed at *M. Grundner's*, next door to Knauer's Café.

Baths. Fresh and salt-water baths at the Bellevue and most of the other hotels and pensions, and at the salt-baths by the Salt Mine (see p. 69). *River Baths* ½ M. from the town, to the left of the Salzburg road, and at the *Aschauer Weiher*, 2 M. from the town, to the right of the old Reichenhall road. — The Carved Wares in wood, bone, and ivory, for which Berchtesgaden has been famous for centuries, are kept in great variety by *S.* and *P. Zechmeister, Kaserer, Walch, Wenig, Huber*, and others.

Carriages. To the *Königs-See* and back, with stay of 3 hrs., one-horse carriage 8 m., two-horse 11 m. 70 pf. (for each additional hour 1 m. 20 pf. or 2 m. more); to *Ramsau* 8 m. or 11 m. 70, there and back (1½ a day) 11 m. or 15 m. 70 pf.; *Hintersee* 11 m. 20 or 17 m., there and back 13 m. 40 or 20 m. 40 pf.; to *Aimbach-Klamm Inn* 7 m. and 11 m. 70 pf.; to *Steinhaus* two-horse carr. 11 m. 70 pf.; *Reichenhall* via Hallthurm 11 m. 20 pf. or 17 m.; *Reichenhall* via Schwarzbachwacht 15m. 40 or 22 m. 90 pf. — Fees included, but tolls extra.

English Church Service in summer at the Hôtel Bellevue.

Berchtesgaden (1885'), a small Bavarian town with 1900 inhab., was down to 1803 the seat of an independent provostry, or ecclesiastical principality, the dominions of which were so mountainous and so limited in extent (165 sq. M.), that it was jestingly said to be as high as it was broad. One-sixth part only was cultivated, the remainder consisting of rock, forest, and water. The handsome old abbey is now a royal château. The *Abbey Church* possesses Romanesque cloisters and carved stalls. The royal villa on the S. side of the small town commands a fine view: to the left the Schwarzort, Hohe Göll, and Hochbrett, in the background the Stuhlgebirge and Schönfeldspitze, to the right the Kleine and Grosse Watzmann. In the valley, on the Alm, are situated extensive *Salt Works*. Berchtesgaden is a very favourite summer-resort, and the environs afford an almost inexhaustible variety of beautiful walks and excursions.

WALKS. The °**Lockstein** (2235'; ½ hr.) commands an admirable view of the valley of Berchtesgaden, particularly by evening-light. We turn to the right by the abbey-church and ascend the *Doctorberg* by the old Reichenhall road; before reaching the hospital we turn to the right, again keeping to the right where the path divides at the *Weinfeld* farm, and proceeding through the wood to the restaurant (poor). — A few hundred paces before the path to the Lockstein diverges to the right, a charming path to the left skirts the precipitous *Kälberstein* (p. 71) by the '**Soolenleitung**,' or salt-water conduit, passes the *Fürstenstein* (formerly a summer-resort of the abbots) and the *Belvedere*, and returns via the *Calvarienberg* to (½ hr.) Berchtesgaden. — Another pleasant excursion may be made by following the old Reichenhall road past the hospital (see above) as far as the (½ hr.) *Rosthäusl* (2185'), and then proceeding to the right through the *Rostwald* to (½ hr.) the Aschauer Weiher (2135'), with swimming and other baths (¼ M. to the N.E. the *Restaurant Distfeldkaser*, picturesquely situated). We may return, at first through wood and then through meadows, to (40 min.) the *Weinfeld Farm* (see above), or to the left via the *Hilgerberg* to (3 M.) Berchtesgaden. — A pleasant return-route from the Rosthäusl to Berchtesgaden is offered by the **Königsweg**, extending for 1½ M. along the wooded slopes of the Kälberstein, as far as the beginning of the salt-water conduit, mentioned above; or we may follow the *Hermannsweg* (to the right the *Vogellhenn Inn*), passing the *Villa Ascania* and crossing the *Hienleithöhe* (view), to the new Reichenhall road and (1 hr.) Berchtesgaden. — The *Tristramweg, recently constructed, diverges to the right from the Ramsau road, on this side of the *Gmund* bridge (p. 76), and gradually ascends along the *Bischofswieser Ache*; it then forks, the left branch crossing the Ache to (1 hr.) the *Böcklweiher* in the *Strub*, and the right branch joining the new Reichenhall road beyond the *Urbanlehen*. — The **Etzerschlössl** (½ hr.; 2075'), a villa belonging to Prince Urusoff, is reached from the Nonnthal by the *Hilgerberg*, or from the Weinfeld farm by the *Pfannhausmaier*; in the vicinity are the *Elzermühle*, with a waterfall, and the '*Schlössibicht*' inn. A pleasant forest-path leads hence to (20 min.) the hamlet of **Gern** (2390'; *Inn*), with the pilgrimage-church of *Maria-Gern* (Inn), whence we may return by the *Metzenteiten* (1¼ hr.), or by *Hinter-Gern*, 20 min. farther up the Gern valley, whence a dizzy descent leads to the right, viâ the *Braunlehen*, on the N. slope of the *Kneifelspitze* (p. 72), to the Almbach-Klamm (p. 72). To the left a route (guide for inexperienced mountaineers advisable) leads viâ the *Dürrlehen* and the *Steinbühl* to the (1 hr.) **Theresienklause** (2300'), in the picturesque *Almbachthal*, at the foot of the Untersberg. Hence we may either ascend the left bank of the Almbach to (½ hr.) the pilgrimage-church of *Etlenberg* (2720'; Inn, unpretending), and descend to the *Krautschneider-Brücke* over the Königsseer Alm (2½ hrs. from Berchtesgaden); or we may return to the (½ hr.) way-post and follow the new path (for experts only) to the (1½ hr.) Almbach-Klamm.

Laroswacht (¾-1 hr.). We follow the level Salzburg road. By the Goldenbach-Brücke (p. 69) we diverge to the right by the *Königsallee* on the left bank of the Ache, cross to the right bank at the *Kilianlehen*, and regain the road below the Freimann-Brücke (p. 69). — The **Laros Water Conduit** may also be visited. From the salt-mine we proceed viâ the *Mausbichl* (¾ hr.) and skirt the slope of the Salzberg, passing through two tunnels; then from the end of the conduit we ascend the ravine of the Larosbach, to the left, to (1¼ hr.) *Au*. — **Au** (1½ hr.). To the (50 min.) *Laroswachl*, see above. Thence we ascend to the right, passing (20 min.) a chapel, in a commanding position, to (20 min.) the *Inn* of *Unterau*, which occupies a magnificent situation, affording views of the Hochbrett, Watzmann, Hochkalter, Untersberg, and other mountains. Thence to the *Dürnberg* (p. 83), 1 hr.; to *Zill* (p. 84), 1 hr.; to *Vordereck* (see below), 1½ hr. — The *Mehlweg* and the *Kleine Barmstein*, see p. 84.

The **Kalte Keller**, a deep rocky cleft above the *Herzogberg* (p. 72), is reached by a path ascending to the left beside the shooting-range (¾ hr.). The return may be made viâ the *Ollenlehen* (fine view) to the Königs-See road (¾ hr. to Berchtesgaden).

Schönau is a scattered village with numerous villas, on the plateau between the *Königsseeer Ache* and the *Ramsauer Ache* (pensions, see p. 70). A picturesque walk may be taken from the Berchtesgaden salt-works, past the château of *Luslheim* (p. 73), to the (1 hr.) *Kohlhiesl* (Café), returning by the Unterstein road (1½ hr.), or viâ *Ilsank* (p. 76; 2¼ hrs.). Charming views of the Hohe Göll, Brett, Kahlersberg, etc.

*Steinhaus and **Vordereck** on the *Upper Salzberg* (1½ hr.; donkey with attendant, 6 m.) may be reached by crossing the Ache at the rifle-range, and proceeding by a road, shaded the greater part of the way, past (1¼ hr.) the *Pension Steiner*. Beyond this point the road divides, the left branch leading to (¼ hr.) *Pension Vordereck* (3180'; below, *Pension Regina*), the right to (¼ hr.) **Steinhaus** (*Zum Hohen Göll*, with a terrace commanding a fine view) and to *Pension Moritz* (3135'), in a sheltered situation 2 min. farther on ('pens'. with R. 8 m.). The pensions on the Upper Salzberg (besides those already mentioned: *Villa Bergler; Amort*; in the cottages of the peasants *Holzl* and *Brandner*) are steadily growing in reputation as resorts for the mountain air cure. — An interesting path (indicated by red marks) leads from Pension Moritz to the (1½ hr.)

Scharitzkehlalp and (³/₄ hr.) *Vorderbrand* (see below), running all the way through wood. — Another path leads from Pension Moritz viâ *Hintereck* to *Vordereck* in 10 minutes. — Routes from Vordereck across the *Eckersattel* or the *Rossfeld* to *Golling*, see p. 85; ascent of the *Kehlstein* and *Hohe Göll*, see p. 73. — Beyond Hintereck the carriage-road leads in a straight direction through fine woods to the valley of the *Larosbach*, then ascends and again descends to (1¹/₄ hr.) *Au* (p. 71). This picturesque route, as far as the top of the Salzberg, is shaded from the morning sun.

The *Almbach-Klamm*, a picturesque gorge through which the *Almbach* descends in cascades from the Untersberg, is an interesting object for an excursion (1¹/₂ hr.; donkey with driver 6¹/₂ m.). We follow the Salzburg road to (3¹/₄ M.) the *Inn zur Almbach-Klamm* (p. 69), turn to the left through the yard and walk across fields to (5 min.) a bridge over the Ache, descend the left bank for 5 min., and near the *Almbach-Mühle* ascend to the left to the gorge. The path crosses the brook several times (railings at hazardous places). The finest point is the *Gumpe*, a rocky basin with a cascade 33′ high falling into a dark green pool, about ¹/₄ hr. from the entrance of the gorge. We may return by a path ascending among bushes on the left bank of the Ache (a few marshy places), and in ¹/₂ hr. cross a bridge without railings, to the high-road, ¹/₄ M. below the *Freimannbrücke* (p. 69).

*Vorderbrand (2 hrs.; donkey with attendant 7¹/₂ m.). About ¹/₂ M. beyond the Johannisbrücke (p. 73), on the Königs-See road, we diverge to the left by a route practicable for carriages, and cross the *Foselsberg* to (1¹/₂ hr.) *Vorderbrand* (3485′; Hallinger's Inn). Thence in 20 min. to the *Hinter-Brandkopf* (3795′) which affords a magnificent view of the Watzmann and the Königs-See. From this point to the *Scharitzkehlalp* ³/₄ hr.; to *Vordereck* (see above), 2¹/₄ hrs.; ascent of the *Jenner* (see below), 2 hrs.

*Scharitzkehl-Alp (3360′; 2 hrs.; guide, unnecessary, 3, donkey and attendant 10 m.). From the rifle-range we ascend the *Herzogberg* to the right, or (less advisable) diverge to the left from the Königs-See road opposite the salt-works, and pass the *Waldhäusl*. Both routes unite near the *Schiedlehen*. Or we may follow the road to Vorderbrand (see above) as far as (3 M.) the *Spinnerlehen*, where we ascend to the left. The Alp (Rfmts.) lies in an extensive meadow, surrounded by trees, between the Kehlstein and the Dürreck. About ³/₄ hr. farther up is the *Endsthal*, a desolate valley at the W. base of the Hohe Göll, containing rocky debris and patches of snow. Hence to *Vorderbrand* ³/₄ hr., to *Vordereck* 2 hrs. (see above).

MOUNTAIN EXCURSIONS (guides, *Jos. Hausmann*, nicknamed *Bindersepp*, *Franz Pfnür*, *Mich. Schwaiger*, and *Nep. Walch* at Berchtesgaden; *Mich. Brandner* at Königs-See; *Joh. Grill Sen.*, nicknamed *Köderbacher*, *Jakob Gruber*, and *Joh. Punz* at Ramsau). The *Kneifelspitze* (3900′; 2¹/₄ hrs.), the highest peak of the *Metzenleiten* (p. 71), commands an excellent view. The path is indicated by red marks (guide, unnecessary, 3 m.; donkey with attendant 6¹/₂ m.). We follow the Salzburg road, and beyond the river-baths ascend to the left, passing the villas Alpenruhe and Aldefeld; at the latter we either go to the left by *Kropfleiten* and *Murren* (better path), or to the right by *Freilehen*, to the (1¹/₂ hr.) *Gasperl Inn* (2970′), and to (1 hr.) the top, with a small refuge-hut (view of Salzburg, 3 min. to the E.). — The *Todte Mann* (4550′), a spur of the *Lattengebirge*, may be ascended by *Bischofswies* (p. 76; turn to the left ¹/₂ M. to the N. of the Brennerbascht) or by *Ilsank* (p. 78) in 4 hrs. The path is indicated by red marks (guide, 4 m., unnecessary for experts). On the top is the *Söldenkopfl* (pp. 76, 77), by a marked path; another equally easy to the right is the *Zipfelhäusl*, on the salt-water conduit, and past the *Grosse Linde* and *Maria-Kunstersweg* to Ramsau (comp. p. 77). — Ascent of the *Jenner* (6145′) by Vorderbrand (see above) and the *Krautkaser-Alpe* in 5 hrs., attractive and not difficult (guide 5 m.). Descent to the *Königsberg-Alpe* (Torrener Joch) and the village of *Königs-See*, see p. 75. — Ascent of the *Hochbrett* (7665′), by Vorderbrand and through the *Brettgabel* in 4-5 hrs., fatiguing (guide 6 m.). — **Kehlstein** or *Göhlstein* (6015'), a N. spur of the Hohe Göll, from *Vordereck* (p. 72) in 2½ hrs. with guide (4 m.), an attractive and not difficult expedition (path indicated by red marks). — The **Hohe Göll** (8265') may be ascended from Vordereck (p. 72) by the (3 hrs.) *Eckeralpe* (4660'; night-quarters) and over the *Eckerfirst* (5840'), the *Brettklammel*, and the *Göllleiten* in 4 hrs., but should be undertaken only by adepts with good guides (10 m.). Magnificent view. More difficult is the ascent from Vorderbrand, through the *Alpelthal*, or by the *Hochbrett*, the *Brettriedel*, and the *Archenköpfe* (guide 12 m.). — The **Schneibstein** (7465'), an excellent point of view, is easily ascended in 2 hrs. from the *Königsberg Alpe* (p. 75: guide 7 m.). — The **Kahlersberg** (7705') is ascended from the *Gotzenalp* (p. 74) by the *Laafeld* and the *Landthalwand* in 8 hrs. (fatiguing; guide 8 m.). The descent may be made viâ the *Seelein-Alpe* and the *Priesberg-Alpe* to the *Königsbach-Alpe* (p. 75), and to (5 hrs.) *Königssee*, or viâ *Vorderbrand* to (7 hrs.) *Berchtesgaden*. — The *Watzmann*, *Hundstod*, and *Steinerne Meer*, see pp. 77, 75; *Untersberg* (*Berchtesgadener Hochthron*), see p. 67.

The gem of this district is the clear, dark-green ****Königs-See** (1980'), or *Lake of St. Bartholomew*, 6 M. long and 1¼ M. broad, the most beautiful lake in Germany, vying in grandeur with those of Switzerland and Italy. Some of the surrounding mountains, which rise almost perpendicularly from the water, are 6500' in height. Three routes lead to the lake (4½ M.) from Berchtesgaden: (1) the carriage-road on the right bank of the Ache, crossing the Johannisbrücke, and leading through the *Wemholz* viâ *Schwöb*; (2) the road on the left bank, diverging at the *Schwöbbichl*, ¾ M. from the Johannisbrücke, and leading past *Unterstein* (Inn), with a château and park of Count Arco (not accessible); (3) a footpath, for the most part shaded, which descends the steps to the left by the royal villa, passes the salt-works, crosses the Ramsauer Ache (to the right on the slope lies *Schloss Lustheim*), and then runs first on the left, and afterwards on the right bank of the Königsseer Ache. On the bank of the lake lies the hamlet of *Königssee* (Zum Königssee; Inn at the 'Schiffmeister's'), with a small bathing-establishment. A small pavilion here contains an excellent relief-map of the district (scale 1 : 25,000) by Prof. Winkler of Munich. A picturesque path on the N.E. bank of the lake leads to the (½ hr.) *Malerwinkel* (*View) and to the (1 hr.) *Kessel* (p. 74).

The 'Schiffmeister' presides over the rowing-boats and their crews, and regulates their trips. The fares are paid to him on returning; the rowers usually receive a small gratuity. The latter are sometimes stalwart peasant-girls, the sinews of whose arms might well be coveted by heroes of the Isis or the Cam. From the middle of June to 1st Oct. there are three regular trips daily round the lake, starting at 8 a.m., 9.30 a.m., and 12.30 p.m.. and occupying about 4 hrs., including ½ hr. at the Sallet-Alp (fare for each pers. 1½ m.). Small boat (2 pers.), with one rower, to St. Bartholomä 3 m.; with two rowers (1-4 pers.) to St. Bartholomä 4½, to the Sallet-Alp 6½ m.; with three rowers (7 pers.) 6½ and 11 m.; for parties of 10 or upwards 1 m. and 1½ m. each. The best plan is to row direct to the Sallet-Alp (1½ hr.), and call at St. Bartholomä in returning. The most favourable light is in the early morning or late in the afternoon.

LAKE VOYAGE. To the left, on a promontory, is the *Villa Beust*; in the lake lies the islet of *Christlieger*, or *St. Johann*, with a small shrine. The boat passes the *Falkenstein*, a rock with a cross commemorating the wreck of a boat with a party of pilgrims. The lake now becomes visible in its entire extent; in the background rise the *Sagereckwand*, the *Grünsee-Tauern*, and the *Funtensee-Tauern*, and adjoining them on the right the *Schönfeldspitze* (8700'). On the E. bank the *Königsbach* falls over a red cliff into the lake. A little farther on, at the deepest part of the lake (616'), a long, reverberating echo is awakened by a pistol fired in the direction of the W. cliffs *(Brentenwand)*. In the vicinity, on the E. bank, not far from the Kessel Fall, is a cavern on a level with the water, called the *Kuchler Loch*, popularly fabled to be the source of the Kuchl or Golling waterfall (p. 84).

The boat touches at the *Wallner Insel*, a wooded promontory on the E. bank. Passengers disembark and ascend by a good path leading through prettily laid-out grounds and passing an artificial hermitage, to two small waterfalls of the *Kesselbach* (5 min.) in a rocky ravine. In descending, we obtain a beautiful glimpse, through the wooded foreground, of the green lake, the opposite mountains, and the Watzmann.

The boat now proceeds to the W. to **St. Bartholomä**, a green promontory, with a royal hunting château (restaurant). The vestibule contains drawings of unusually large salmon-trout *(Salmo salvelinus*, Ger. *Saibling)* caught in the lake during the last hundred years. In the cellar is a large tank for keeping the fish. The *Chapel of SS. John and Paul*, 1/2 M. from the landing-place, attracts numerous pilgrims on the festival of St. Bartholomew (24th Aug.), when the surrounding heights are lighted up with bonfires.

The **Eiskapelle**, a kind of glacier situated in a wild gully between the Hachelwand and the Watzmann, 2755' only above the sea-level, merits a visit (there and back 1¼ hr.; new path, rather rough; guide desirable).

At the S.W. end of the lake the *Schrainbach* is precipitated into the lake from a rocky gorge. The *Sallet-Alp*, a poor pasture 1/2 M. in breadth and strewn with moss-grown rocks, on which the Duke of Meiningen has recently built a country-house, separates the Königs-See from the wild and bleak *****Obersee** (a visit to which should not be omitted), a lake 1 M. long, enclosed by lofty precipices of limestone. The murmur of the brook issuing from the lake alone disturbs the repose of this wilderness. Beyond it tower the *Teufelshörner* (7855'), from which a brook descends over the *Röthwand* in several arms from a height of 1900'. On the E. bank is the *Fischunkel-Alp*, to which a narrow path (not recommended) leads on the S. bank in 1/2 hr. A good survey of the imposing Watzmann is obtained in returning.

From the Kesselbach (see above) a good path in long windings ascends to the (3 hrs.) "Gotzenalp (5525'), opposite St. Bartholomä. It passes the chalets of (1½ hr.) *Gotzenthal* and (1 hr.) *Seeau*. Farther on, we take the path to the right (that to the left leads to the *Regenalp*). Magnificent view of the Uebergossene Alm, Steinerne Meer, Watzmann, Hohe Göll, Untersberg, etc. Rustic quarters in the three chalets at the top (the

Springelhütte and others). The view towards the N. is imperfect until we reach the *Feuerpalfen* on the N.W. margin of the Alp, 10 min. from the chalets, and 200' higher. Somewhat beyond that point, from the brink of the rock lower down, the lake and St. Bartholomä are visible 3300' below us. Descent to the (2 hrs.) Kessel Fall, where a boat (previously ordered) should be in waiting; or we may proceed from the Gotzenthal-Alp to the right by the '*Hohe Bahn*' (Alpine path) to the *Königsbach-Alpe*, then cross the Königsbach, and descend to the left to the village of (4 hrs.) Königssee; or continue along the hills past the *Wasserfall-Alp* to (4 hrs.) *Vorderbrand*. Thence to (1¼ hr.) Berchtesgaden or (2 hrs.) Vordereck, see p. 72.

FROM THE GOTZEN-ALP TO THE SALLET-ALP, 4-5 hrs., for adepts only (guide from Berchtesgaden 7 m.). The path leads past the Wasserkaser chalet to the (1 hr.) *Laafeld* (used for battues), and in 10 min. more to the crest of the *Landthalwand*; descent to (25 min.) the *Landthal-Alp* and through the *Landthal* by a narrow, and at places rather steep and giddy path to (2½-3 hrs.) the *Fischunkel-Alp* (p. 74) and (½ hr.) the *Sallet-Alp*. The interest of the route is enhanced by the numerous deer and chamois frequently seen in this unused royal *chasse*. — A still more interesting excursion may be made from Berchtesgaden direct to the (5 hrs.) *Königsbach-Alp*; 1 hr. *Priesberg-Alp*; then through the *Hirschelau* and over the *Gotzentauern* to the *Regenalp* (numerous fossils) and the (2 hrs.) *Landthalwand* (see above).

FROM THE KÖNIGS-SEE TO GOLLING (7 hrs.; guide 10 m.). Footpath (indicated by red marks) by the *Königsberg-Alp* (5210'; clean chalet, whence the *Jenner*, 6155', a fine point of view, may be ascended in 1 hr., comp. p. 72) and (3½-4 hrs.) the Torrener Joch (5670'), between the *Schneibstein* and the *Hochbrett*; descent to the Upper and Lower *Joch-Alp* and through the *Blüntau-Thal* (passing the pretty *Torrener Waterfall*, generally insignificant in summer), with the *Kleine Göll* (5745') rising on the left, to *Golling* (p. 84).

Excursions in the Steinerne Meer, the wild mountain region to the S. of the Königs-See, are fatiguing (paths partly indicated by red marks, but guide necessary, see p. 72: to the Funtensee through the Saugasse 8 m., viâ Grünsee 9 m., over the Steinerne Meer to Saalfelden 16 m.). A path leads from St. Bartholomew on the margin of the lake to the *Schrainbach Fall* (p. 74). Above the fall we ascend to the right through wood to (1½ hr.) the *Schrainbach-Alp* (2930') and (½ hr.) the *Unterlahner-Alp* (3235'). We then mount the steep *Saugasse* in numerous zigzags to the (1¼ hr.) *Oberlahner-Alp* (4590'). Here a path to *Trischübel* ascends to the right (p. 76). The new path (passing the *Gjaidköpfe* on the right) now ascends the *Himmelstiege*, and then descends a little to the (1½ hr.) Funtensee-Hütte (5340'; club-inn), which lies 10 min. to the N.W. of the small *Funtensee* (5250'). — Another path (more interesting for persons with steady heads), from the *Sallet-Alp* (p. 74), ascends the steep *Sagereckwand* to (2 hrs.) the *Sagereck-Alp* (4895'), and mounts across the *Grünsee-Au* to the (¾ hr.) finely-situated *Grünsee* (5280'), whence a new path ascends to the right through the *Zirbenau* to (1½ hr.) the *Funtensee-Hütte*. [The *Feld* (6046'), an excellent point of view, is easily ascended hence in 1¼ hr.; or the *Viehkogl* (7078') in 1½ hr.; also the *Funtensee-Tauern* (8392'; 3½ hrs., fatiguing), commanding a magnificent view.] — Several passes (*Buchauer*, *Ramseider*, *Weissbachl*, and *Diesbach Scharte*) lead from the Funton-See to Saalfelden; the shortest (6 hrs.) and most interesting is the Ramseider Scharte (6895'), between the Breithorn and the Sommerstein. At the Scharte is the new *Riemann-Haus* (comp. p. 118).

From the *Fischunkel-Alp* (p. 74) rough and fatiguing routes (11-12 hrs.; guide 15 m.) cross the *Blühnbachthörl* (6670') and the *Mauerscharte* (7140') to the *Blühnbach-Thal* and *Werfen* (p. 113).

TO THE RAMSAU a road, passing the *Pension Oberhofreit* (p. 70), leads direct from the Königs-See viâ *Schönau* (p. 71) to (4½ M.) the *Ilsank-Mühle* (p. 76). A more attractive but somewhat longer route leads through the woods to the left from Schönau, at the base of the *Grünsteinkopf*, to the forester's house of *Schappach* (refreshments). Thence we may proceed either to the right to Ilsank, or to the left direct to the *Wimbach-Klamm* (p. 76).

From Berchtesgaden to Reichenhall (11 M.; diligence twice daily in 2³/₄ hrs., fare 2, coupé 3 m.; one-horse carriage 11 m. 20 pf.). The road leads past the royal villa, and through *Bischofswies*, where at (3 M.) the Neuwirth Inn the steep old road across the Doctorberg joins the better new route (³/₄ M. farther is the Brennerbascht tavern). We then cross the **Pass Hallthurm** (2275'; Inn), between the *Lattengebirge* and *Untersberg*. Fine retrospect towards Berchtesgaden, and afterwards a view of the Reichenhall mountains.

A far preferable route, however, is by the *Ramsau and the *Schwarzbachwacht* (18 M.). The road (see above) passes the royal villa at the S. end of the village, and after ¹/₂ M. (direction-post) descends to the left to the Ramsau road. We cross the *Bischofswieser Ache* by the *Gmundbrücke*. At the (3 M.) *Ilsank-Mühle* (1910'; Hôtel-Pension Haller; Gschossmann's Inn, at the Schönau bridge), a waterfall 400' in height works a pump by which the salt-water from the mines is forced up to the *Söldenköpfl*, 1200 ft higher, and over the Schwarzbachwacht to Reichenhall, a distance of 20 M.

Immediately beyond the Gmund bridge a cattle-track ascends on the right to the *Strub*; at the *Semlerlehen* we reach the brine conduit, along which a path leads to the Ilsank-Mühle. A flight of steps ascends thence to the *Söldenköpfl* (3110'; simple refreshments in the pump-house), whence a good path with fine views leads along the brine conduit to the (1¹/₄ hr.) *Zipfelhäusl* (p. 77) and the (1³/₄ hr.) Schwarzbachwacht (p. 77). — Route from Ilsank to the *Königs-See* viâ *Schönau*, 1¹/₂ hr. (p. 75).

To the left a grand view of the Watzmann; before us rises the broad Steinberg; by our side flows the impetuous Ache. The Ramsau is remarkably picturesque owing to the contrast of the luxuriant vegetation of the valley with the imposing and picturesquely-shaped grey mountains. The road ascends gradually, and then descends. On the left (1¹/₂ M.) a finger-post indicates the road to the 'Jagdschloss Wimbach'.

A path crossing the bridge to the left, and ascending to the right by the 'Trinkhalle', leads to the (20 min.) *Wimbach-Klamm. The clear blue water of the brook here forms beautiful falls in its rocky ravine, into which the sun shines about noon. We traverse the Klamm ('defile') in 6 min., and at a point 5 min. from its upper end we have a view of the wild Wimbach-Thal, enclosed by huge mountains (the imposing Watzmann, see below, on the left; the Steinberg, Hochkalter, Hocheisspitze, and Apelhorn on the right).

A visit to the upper *Wimbach-Thal, at least for ¹/₂ hr. beyond the Jagdschloss, or still better to the Gries-Alp, is recommended. A good bridle-path leads at first on the left, and then on the right bank of the brook through pine-wood, and afterwards traverses the broad mass of debris from which the stream issues, to (1¹/₄ hr.) the royal *Jagdhaus*. In 1¹/₄ hr. more we reach the *Gries-Alp* (4840'), and enjoy a magnificent view of the imposing mountains at the head of the valley (from left to right, the Watzmann, Hundstod, Palfelhorn, Alpelhorn, Hocheisspitze, Hochkalter, Steinberg). — A track, hewn in part in the rocks, leads to the S. from this point to the (1¹/₂ hr.) shooting-box of *Trischübel* (5785'), whence we may ascend the (³/₄ hr.) *Hirschwiese* (6930'), which affords an admirable view of this wild region, including part of the Königs-See. From Trischübel we proceed viâ the deserted *Sigret-Alp* to (3¹/₂ hrs.) the *Oberlahner Alp* (Steinerne Meer, see p. 75). — The Grosse Hundstod (8510'), ascended from Trischübel through the *Hundstod-Grube*, commands a magnificent view (3 hrs., fatiguing; guide from Ramsau 10 m.). The descent may be made to the *Diesbach-Scharte* (p. 119).

The ascent of the **Watzmann** (7-8 hrs.; guide 9 m., to the middle peak 11 m.) is fatiguing, but interesting. We ascend from Ilsank by the *Mitterkaser Alpe*, or from *Unterstein* by the *Kühroint Alpe* (4680'), to (3¹/₂ hrs.) the *Falz-Alpe* (5810') and (1 hr.) the *Watzmann-Haus* (club-hut) on the *Falzköpfl* (6830'). Thence we ascend the arête to the E. of the *Dürre Grube* and over the *Watzmannanger* to the (2¹/₂ hrs.) *Vordere Gipfel* or *Hocheck* (8700'). Another route leads from Ramsau to (2 hrs.) the *Grubenalp* (4310') and (¹/₂ hr.) the *Guglalp* (4995'; better night-quarters at the former). Next morning we traverse the *Guglschneid* (to the W. of the Dürre Grube) and Watzmannanger and ascend in 3¹/₂ hrs. to the summit, on which are a trigonometrical landmark and two crosses, one of the latter containing a visitors' book. The "View embraces the Gross-Glockner, Gross-Venediger, Krimmler Tauern, the vast Bavarian plain, the entire Salzkammergut and district of Berchtesgaden, with the Wimbachthal below, and the Königs-See and Obersee to the S. — From the Hocheck a new path, protected by a rail (steady head indispensable), leads along the arête in ³/₄ hr. to the top of the *Central Peak* (8905'; the highest). The "Panorama from this point is still more extensive, and besides a magnificent view of the Königs-See, embraces the entire Tauern chain from the Mallnitzer Tauern to the Oetzthaler Ferner, Zugspitze, etc. The ascent of the *Southern Peak*, or *Schönfeldspitze* (8950'), from the central peak in 1¹/₂ hr. (guide 17 m.), and the descent to the Wimbachthal are very difficult.

On the road, ¹/₂ M. above the finger-post (see above), is the "*Inn zur Wimbachklamm*, and a little beyond it the *Inn zum Hochkalter*. Then (³/₄ M.) **Ramsau** (2190'; *Oberwirth*).

A pleasant walk (diverging to the right from the road at a guide-post near the Oberwirth) leads hence through wood to (¹/₂ hr.) the pilgrimage church of *Maria-Kunterweg* (2495'), thence on to (¹/₄ hr.) the *Grosse Lärche*, whence we ascend to the right to (20 min.) the *Zipfelhäusl* (3210') on the salt-water conduit, 1¹/₂ hr. from the Söldenköpfl (p. 76; the path leading straight on up the hill goes to the *Todte Mann*, p. 72). — Another route leaves the Reichenhall road at a guide-post beyond the point where the Hintersee road diverges, and ascends to the left to (³/₄ hr.) the *Magdalenen-Kapelle* (2820'), a rocky grotto containing an altar. The "*Wartstein* (2900'), 3 min. farther on, affords a splendid view of the Hintersee, the Blauels Glacier, etc. Hence down to the *Hintersee*, 20 minutes.

Beyond Ramsau (³/₄ M.) the road divides, the branch to the Hintersee and the Hirschbühl (p. 78) leading to the left. The ROAD TO REICHENHALL ascends straight on (right), past the small *Taubensee* (2845') and through beautiful pine wood, to the (2¹/₄ M.) **Schwarzbachwacht** (2910'), a pump-house on the summit of the pass, beyond which the conduit descending from the Söldenköpfl runs parallel with the road (¹/₄ M. farther on is the *Inn zur Schwarzbachwacht*, 2840'). The road then descends into the deep wooded valley between the *Reiteralpe* on the left and the *Lattengebirge* on the right, and (3 M.) crosses the *Schwarzbach* by the *Bucherbrücke*. Facing us are the Müllnerhorn and Ristfeichthorn. At the (1 M.) *Jettenberg* pump-house (1795'; Rfmts.; view), at the end of the valley, another bridge crosses the Schwarzbach, which forms a fine cascade *(Staubfall)* here and falls into the Saalach immediately below. [A footpath, diverging to the left before the bridge, leads under the latter to the fall.] The road then skirts the right bank of the Saalach, passing opposite *Fronau*, to (4¹/₂ M.) *Reichenhall* (p. 79).

The OBER-WEISSBACH ROAD (see above) crosses the Ache (picturesque ravine) twice (beyond the first bridge, footpath to the left to the Hintersee, see below) and ascends to the (1½ M.) sequestered green **Hintersee** (2550'), overshadowed by the *Hochkalter*. At the beginning of the lake, near the small *St. Antoni Chapel*, is *Sollacher's Pension & Restaurant* ('pens.' 4½ m.; pretty view). The royal shooting-lodge (*Anzinger's Inn*, adjacent) and the Bavarian custom-house are ¾ M. farther on.

EXCURSIONS from the Hintersee (guide, Jac. Gruber). A visit to the **Blaueis Glacier**, between the Hochkalter and Steinberg, the northernmost glacier in the German Alps, is fatiguing but very interesting; to the foot of the glacier (6280') 3½ hrs. (guide 5½ m.); chamois are sometimes seen on this route. — **Edelweisslahnerkopf** (6405'), 4 hrs. (guide 5 m.); beautiful 'Edelweiss' at the top. — The **Mühlsturzhorn** (7830'; admirable view of the Tauern) may be climbed by adepts in 5 hrs. (guide 8 m.). — **Hochkalter** (8625'), through the *Ofenthal* in 5-6 hrs. (guide 9 m.), not difficult for experts.

Those who desire to proceed to Reichenhall from the Hintersee take the road to the left at the N. end of the lake, turn to the left again 10 min. farther on, and in ½ hr. reach the Reichenhall road below the Taubensee (see p. 77). — A pleasant return-route to Ramsau (indicated by red marks) skirts the E. bank of the Hintersee, and after crossing the brook at a lock (ferry to Sollacher's Restaurant) continues through a finely-wooded dale to the Ramsau road (p. 77), which it strikes about 2 M. from Ramsau.

The beautiful valley between the *Hochkalter* (left) and the *Mühlsturzhorn* (right) is now ascended to the (5 M.) **Hirschbühl** (3780'; *Inn*), the Austrian custom-house, formerly a fortified pass, which was fiercely contested by the Austrians and Bavarians in 1809.

The *Kammerlinghorn* (8176'), ascended from the Hirschbühl in 3-4 hrs. (somewhat fatiguing; guide 4 m.), is an admirable point of view (Steinerne Meer, Tauern, etc.). — Experts may ascend the **Hocheisspitze** (8260') in 1/2-3/4 hr. from the Kammerlinghorn, partly over smooth and giddy rocks. The descent viâ the *Aipel-Scharte* (7280') to the Wimbachthal (4 hrs. to the Jagdschloss) is steep and difficult. — To the W. of the Hirschbühl a path (with red marks) crosses the **Kleine Hirschbühl**, which affords a very fine view of the mountains bounding the Saalachthal, to *Wildenthal* and (1¾ hr.) *St. Martin* on the Lofer road (p. 176).

The road ascends a few hundred paces farther to its highest point (3870'), and then descends into the Saalachthal. Before us rise the imposing *Leoganger Steinberge*. Near the saw-mill, 2¼ M. farther on, a finger-post indicates the way to the *Seisenberg-Klamm*, a profound and very narrow gorge, hollowed out by the action of the *Weissbach*, which dashes over huge blocks of rock below. The narrow cleft above, through which the light falls, is overgrown with bushes entirely concealing the sky and imparting a peculiar colouring to the gorge. At a (25 min.) mill at the lower end of the ravine we reach the Saalachthal; and a road leads hence to (½ M.) **Ober-Weissbach** (2180'; *Auvogl*, near the church), where we rejoin the road from the Hirschbühl (to the left). The *Inn zur Frohnwies* lies ½ M. to the S.

About ½ M. to the W. of Ober-Weissbach, on the Lofer road, is the **Lamprechts-Ofenloch**, a large cavern with an imposing entrance which is accessible in winter only, when the brook is frozen. It is proposed to render it accessible at all times by diverting the course of the brook. — About 6 M. to the N. (carr. in 1½ hr.), reached by a pleasant and well-shaded road, is the interesting *Vorderkaserklamm* (p. 177). The Vorderkaserklamm, the Seisenbergklamm, and the Lamprechts-Ofenloch may all be easily visited in one day from Frohnwies or Oberweissbach; and most conveniently in the order given.

The road to Saalfelden (one-horse carr. from Frohnwies 4, two-horse 6-7 fl.; omnibus daily in summer, 1 fl.) traverses a defile *(Diesbacher Hohlwege)*, 6 M. long, on the right bank of the Saalach. Near the village of *Diesbach*, a pretty waterfall on the left. The valley then expands, and the Tauern become visible towards the S.

9½ M. *Saalfelden*, on the Salzburg and Tyrol Railway, see p. 118.

15. From Salzburg to Reichenhall.
Comp. Map, p. 68.

14 M. Railway in 55 min. (express from Munich to Reichenhall in 3 hrs. 55 min.).

To (4½ M.) *Freilassing*, see p. 56. The line here diverges to the left and ascends on the right bank of the *Saalach*. On the right the wooded *Högelberg*; on the left the Gaisberg and Untersberg. From (8 M.) *Hammerau* a shady forest-path ascends (¾ hr.) the *St. Johanns-Högel* (Inn), from which a fine view is obtained. On the right, near (11 M.) *Piding*, at the base of the abrupt Hochstauffen (p. 82), stands the ruin of *Stauffeneck*. The train then crosses the Saalach to —

14 M. **Reichenhall**. — **Hotels**: °Cur-Hôtel Burkert, near the Curpark, R. & A. from 3 m., B. 1, D. 3 m.; Curhaus Achselmannstein, with garden, R. & L. 4½, D. 3 m.; °Louisenbad, R. from 2½ m., D. 3 m.; °Maximiliansbad; °Marienbad *(Dr. Hess)*; °Bad Kirchberg (p. 80), all for a prolonged stay. Apartments with pension: °Villa Hessing, in an elevated and picturesque situation; °Villa Schader, near the station; Villa Salve; Villa Mann, etc. — °Löwe, with garden, R., L., & A. 3, D. 3 m.; °Russischer Hof, R. 2, D. 2½ m.; °Post (or Krone), R. 2 m.; Hôtel Bahnhof, Goldner Hirsch, unpretending.

Cafés, etc.: *Café Mayr*, also a restaurant and lodging-house (R. & A. 1½ m.), with garden; *Staimer*, by the Curgarten; *°Niedermaier's Café-Meierei*, prettily situated ¾ M. to the N. of the Gradirpark, in the direction of the Saalach; *Fischerbräukeller*, with garden. — *Schiffmann*, confectioner.

Visitors' Tax (for a stay of more than eight days) 15 m. (less in proportion for members of a family). *Reading Room* at the Achselmannstein Hotel.

Post and Telegraph Office in the market; post-office (poste restante) also at the station. — Money may be changed at *M. Grundner's*, Bahnhof-Str., near the Gradirhaus.

Carriage to Gross-Gmain, Karlstein, Molkenbauer, with one horse 3, with two horses 6 m.; to Jettenberg 4½ or 8; Thumsee 5 or 9; Mauthhäusl 6 or 10½; Schnaizlreut 7 or 12; Schnaizlreut and Mauthhäusl 8 or 14; Melleck 10 or 17; Melleck and Mauthhäusl 11 or 18; Unken 12 or 24; Lofer 15 or 27; Berchtesgaden viâ Hallthurm 10 or 15; the same, and the Königs-See 13 or 22; Ramsau 12 or 20; Ramsau and Berchtesgaden viâ Jettenberg 13 or 22; the same, with the addition of the Hintersee 15 or 27; the Königs-See viâ Jettenberg, Ramsau, and Berchtesgaden 18 or 30; Salzburg 10 or 16 m.; fee 1 or 1½ m. per ½ day, 1½ or 2½ m. per day. The return-fare is included in each case, and will not be deducted unless by special agreement.

English Church Service in summer.

Reichenhall (1580'), a favourite watering-place on the *Saale*, or *Saalach*, rebuilt after a fire in 1834, is very picturesquely bounded on three sides by an amphitheatre of mountains, the *Untersberg* (6480'), *Lattengebirge* (5700'), *Reitalpgebirge* (6460'), *Müllnerhorn* (4500'), *Ristfeichtkogl* (5315'), *Sonntagshorn* (6430'), and *Hoch-Stauffen* (5948'). This is the central point of union of the four principal Bavarian salt-works, which are connected by conduits of an aggregate length of 50 M. The surplus brine from the Berchtesgaden mines is conducted to Reichenhall, which in its turn supplies Traunstein (p. 55) and Rosenheim (p. 53). The large *Salinengebäude*, or salt-work buildings, in the market-place, contain the offices on the right, and four *Sudhäuser* ('boiling-houses', from 'sieden', Engl. seethe, suds) on the left, opposite which is the handsome *Hauptbrunnhaus*, or pump-house. In the latter (second door) tickets of admission (1 m.) to the springs and the salt-pans are obtained.

The sources of the saline springs of Reichenhall, fifteen in number, are about 50' below the surface of the soil, and are reached by a flight of 72 steps. Five of them are so strongly impregnated (Edelquelle, 25^1/$_2$ per cent) that they are at once conducted to the salt-pans. The water of the other ten springs is conducted to the Gradirhaus (see below), and also supplies the fountain in the Gradirpark. The fresh-water springs are conveyed to the Saalach by means of a shaft 1^1/$_2$ M. in length and 8 ft. in height. The pump-house contains the two huge wheels by which the pumps are worked. On the second floor is a chapel in the Byzantine style, with stained-glass windows. In the court are two fresh-water fountains adorned with statues of SS. Virgilius and Rupert.

The *Principal Church*, restored in the Romanesque style, is adorned with frescoes by *Schwind*. A new *Protestant Church* adjoins the Kurgarten. Rising above the town appears the old castle of *Gruttenstein* (1680').

Reichenhall is resorted to by patients suffering from general debility, chronic rheumatism, pulmonary affections, asthma, etc., who find relief in the mild and highly ozonized air, as well as from the salt-baths, saline and pine-needle inhalation, whey-cure, etc. The patients reside for the most part in the *Curvorstadt*, a suburb or district of the town consisting of hotels, bath-houses, and villas. The chief rallying-point of visitors is the new *Curgarten*, beside the *Gradirhaus* (behind the Hôtel Burkert), with a covered promenade, a café, etc., where a band plays from 6.30 to 8 a.m. and from 5 to 7 p.m. (on Tues. and Frid. afternoons at Bad Kirchberg, see below). The Curanlagen contain the *Soolsprudel*, a salt-water fountain 20' in height. The *Gradirwerk* (evaporating-house), 180 yds. long, is exclusively devoted to the purposes of the inhalation cure.

About ^{1}/$_2$ M. to the S.W., on the left bank of the Saalach, is the **Kirchberg Bath-House* (Dr. Pachmayr; salt and mineral baths and whey-cure; music, see above), near which are a number of villas.

ENVIRONS. One of the chief attractions of Reichenhall for invalids consists in the numerous shady woodland walks in the immediate neighbourhood of the town, some level and some gently ascending, e. g. in the *Nonner Wald*, *Forstplantage*, *Kirchholz*, etc. These are all marked with letters and numbers at intervals of 500 or 600 paces, and the visitor who is provided with *Bühler's Map of Reichenhall*, has little difficulty in finding his way from point to point. — On the Salzburg road, ¹/₂ M. to the N.E. of the Curhaus, lies St. Zeno (*Hofwirth; Schwabenbräu*), once an Augustine monastery, of very ancient origin, but suppressed in 1803, and fitted up in 1858 as a nunnery and school. (Pleasantest way to St. Zeno by the promenade at the foot of the Kirchholz, passing the handsome *Villa Korg*.) The church, originally Romanesque and recently restored, possesses a handsome portal of the 12th cent., an ancient font, and finely-carved choir-stalls. One of the pillars in the cloisters (12th cent.) bears an old marble relief of Charlemagne. — The **Königsweg**, a winding path among the fine pines of the *Kirchholz*, begins behind the monastery and ascends gradually to (¹/₂ hr.) the *Klosterhof* (1770'; café, see below). Descent hence direct to St. Zeno, 10 min.; by the *Eichen-Allee* and past the *Moltke Oak* to Reichenhall, 25 min.; or across the hill to Gross-Gmain, 20 minutes. Another path to (25 min.) Gross-Gmain turns off to the left about 5 min. farther up the hill, beyond the Klosterhof, and runs along the edge of the wood, commanding charming views.

Pleasant walk of 40 min. to **Gross-Gmain.** The route (footpath by Staimer's café. or carriage-road past the Villas Hessing and Langenfeld) crosses the hill, turns to the left by an old lime-tree. and descends gradually. Fine view of the Untersberg and Lattengebirge all the way. The pleasant little village (1710'; *Untersberg; Kaiser Karl*) lies on the right bank of the *Weissbach*, just beyond the Austrian frontier. The rococo church, with a Gothic tower, contains four paintings by Zeitblom (?) and a Madonna, in artificial stone, said to have been executed by Archbishop Thiemo in the 11th century. — The picturesque ruined castle of *Plain* (popularly called *Salzbüchsel*) lies 1¹/₂ M. to the E., at the base of the Untersberg. — We may return by the Weissbach road to (5 min.) the *Bachbauer* (reached also by a footpath from the church. or through the garden of the Kaiser Karl), whence we ascend to the left to the *Städlbauer*. Hence we may either continue to the left over the hill (view of the Hohe Göll, etc.), past the *Schöne Aussicht* (a farm) and *Langenfeld* (see above), to (³/₄ hr.) Reichenhall; or keep straight on to the Klosterhof (see above). — Another return-route follows the road running to the E. from Gross-Gmain to the (20 min.) *Batzenhäusl*, where it joins the Berchtesgaden road (opposite the Alpgarten, see below). Then to the right to (¹/₂ hr.) Reichenhall.

On the Berchtesgaden road, 1¹/₄ M. to the E. of Reichenhall (but shorter from the Curhaus to the old lime-tree, mentioned above, and then to the right), is the *Whey Dairy* in connection with the Curhaus, and ¹/₄ M. farther on the *Restaurant zum Alpenthal*, situated at the entrance to the **Alpgarten**, a rocky gorge. which we may ascend as far as (10 min.) the 'Klause'. — The road then leads between the Untersberg on the left and the Lattengebirge on the right, and across the *Weissbach*, to (3¹/₄ M.) the *Pass Hallthurm* (p. 76), to which also a shady and picturesque path leads from the entrance of the Alpgarten, at first skirting the Reichenhall water-conduit and crossing the foot-bridge at the pump-house (1¹/₂ hr.). — From the dairy we may return to Reichenhall in 25 min., passing the *Streitbühl* (private property, not open to the public) and the old *Schloss Gruttenstein* (p. 80).

To the W. of the Gradirpark, beyond the (¹/₂ M.) *Nonner Steg* (bridge across the Saalach), extends the *Nonner Wald*, which is intersected by numerous paths. The most frequented leads straight on (where it forks, we pass through the fence to the right) to (³/₄ M.) **Non** (1590'; *Fuchsbauer's Restaurant*), a village at the foot of the Hochstauffen, with an old church containing a Gothic *Altar of the 15th century. — The raised path to the left, just beyond the Nonner Steg. leads to (1¹/₂ M.) *Bad Kirchberg* (p. 80). Other paths lead past the 'Eichenrundel' and through the *Weitwiesen* to (2¹/₂ M.) the *Kutil*, on the Lofer road (p. 82); to the *Buchenhof* and (1¹/₂ M.) the *Poschen-Mühle* (Rfmts.; *View); etc. — The *Padinger Alpe* (2170'; 650' above Reichenhall) may be reached in 1¹/₄ hr., either viâ Non (see above) or by a zigzag path from Buchenhof; on the top is a café (splendid view of the Reichenhall valley). — The **Listsee** (2040'; 1 hr.), a small lake embosomed among woods at the foot of the Zwiesel, is reached by ascending beyond the Buchenhof (see above), chiefly through wood. Return-route by *Langacker* to (2¹/₂ M.) *Bad Kirchberg* (p. 80).

The **Molkenbauer** (1625'; *Inn*), on the left bank of the Saalach (1 M.), affords a good view of the valley of that stream. The path (generally in shade) farther on follows the left bank (the road running on the opposite bank, p. 77) to (1½ hr.) *Fronau*, and crosses the Jettenberg bridge to (20 min.) *Jettenberg* (p. 77). — The Bürgermeister-Alp (2420'; 1 hr.) is ascended by a zigzag path from the Molkenbauer (or we may diverge to the right immediately beyond the Saalach bridge) through wood, and through the *Teufelshöhle*, to the *Vordere Aussicht* (view of Reichenhall). We then retrace our steps through the grotto, and take the path to the left to the *Hintere Aussicht* (Lattengebirge, Saalach valley, etc.). On the N. side is a path leading direct to Kirchberg (not recommended). — The **Kugelbachbauer** (2085'; ¾ hr.), reached by a path ascending to the left beyond Bad Kirchberg, commands a pretty view (refreshments at the farm). About halfway up, a few minutes to the right, is the *Reischlklamm*, a rocky cleft, spanned by a bridge. — Route to (4½ M.) Jettenberg and the *Staubfall* (by the Ramsau road through the valley of the Saalach), see p. 77.

The Lofer road (p. 178) leads to the W. from Reichenhall, passing Bad Kirchberg, to (1½ M.) the *Kaitl Inn* (well spoken of) and ascends a wooded ravine. About ½ M. farther on, by a mill on the left bank of the *Seebach*, is a flight of 277 steps ascending to the right to (20 min.) the **Chapel of St. Pancras** (1800'), commanding an extensive view. On the higher eminence facing it on the W. stands the ruin of **Karlstein** (reached by the first footpath to the right beyond the steps to St. Pancras), another good point of view. — About ¾ M. farther on (1 hr. from Reichenhall) we reach the pretty **Thumsee** (1730'), ½ M. long and ¼ M. broad. The road ascends from the W. end of the lake through the picturesque *Nesselgraben* to the (½ hr.) pump-house of *Obernesselgraben*, at the summit of the pass (2120'), and ¼ M. farther on divides. The left branch descends abruptly to *Schnaizlreut* and *Unken* (p. 177); while the right branch, known as the *Neuweg*, maintains its high level above the valley of the *Weissbach* (opposite rises the huge *Ristfeichthorn*, 5315'; to the S.E. the *Watzmann*), and reaches the (1½ hr.) **Mauthhäusel** (2070', *Inn*), in a most picturesque situation above the profound gorge of the Weissbach. This is a favourite excursion from Reichenhall (carriages, see p. 79; omn. daily in summer, starting from the Achselmannstein Hotel at 2.30, returning at 6 p.m.; return-fare 1½ m.). A narrow path (not adapted for inexperienced climbers) leads down to the *Gorges of the Weissbach* and the *Schrainbach Fall* in the ravine beneath. — Beyond the Mauthhäusel the road goes on, past *Weissbach* and *Inzell*, to *Traunstein* (comp. p. 55). — An attractive return-route to Reichenhall from the Mauthhäusel leads through the *Höllenbachthal* in 3 hrs.

ASCENTS (guide, J. Kuglstatter). An admirable point of view near Reichenhall is the *Zwiesel* (6030'; 3½-4 hrs., bridle-path; guide unnecessary), the W. and highest peak of the *Stauffengebirge*. We may drive from Bad Kirchberg, turning to the right at the *Kaitl* (see above), to (¾ hr.) the farm of *Langacker* (Rfmts.), and thence follow the cart-track leading up through wood to (½ hr.) a guide-post, which indicates the footpath diverging to the right through wood to (1½-2 hrs.) the *Zwiesel* or *Schwaig Alp* (4790'; Inn, bed 2 m.), 1 hr. below the summit. A shorter and more picturesque route leads from Reichenhall via the Nonner Steg and through the Oberlandl to (1 hr.) the *Listsee* (p. 80), whence we reach the Zwiesel route through a cleft to the left, turning to the right at the (10 min.) guide-post (see above). The summit (the highest peak is about 10 min. to the N. of the cross) commands a magnificent mountain-panorama, extending from the Gaisberg on the E. to the Kaisergebirge on the W. (Schafberg, Untersberg, Dachstein, Tennengebirge, Hohe Göll, Hochkönig, Watzmann, Schönfeldspitze, Wiesbachhorn, Mühlsturzhorn, the Lofer and Leogang Steinberge, Glockner, Venediger, and Sonntagshorn), and a view of the plain to the N.E., with its numerous lakes. — A steep path ascends from the Zwiesel-Alp across the *Weitscharte* in 2½ hrs. to the **Hochstauffen** (5950'), the E. peak of the Stauffengebirge, marked by a large cross. The ascent on the N. side by a good new path from *Piding* is preferable (p. 79).

The *Stoisser Alpe* on the *Teisenberg* (4375'), easily ascended from stat. *Piding* (p. 79) in 3½ hrs., is another very interesting point. Carriage-road by *Mauthhausen*, *Anger*, and *Kohlhäusl* to the chalet, ¼ hr. from the top. Descent to *Siegsdorf* (p. 57) or *Teisendorf* (p. 56).

Delightful drive of one day by *Jettenberg*, the *Schwarzbachwacht*, *Ramsau* (*Wimbachklamm*) and *Königssee* to *Berchtesgaden*, returning by *Hallthurm*. Two days: by *Melleck*, *Unken*, and *Lofer* to *Ober-Weissbach*, returning by *Hirschbühl*, *Ramsau*, the *Schwarzbachwacht*, and *Jettenberg*.

16. From Salzburg to Hallein and Golling.
Comp. Map, p. 68.

18 M. RAILWAY (*Gisela-Bahn*, comp. R. 22) to (11 M.) Hallein in 40 min.; to (18 M.) Golling in 1¼ hr.

Soon after starting, the train diverges to the right from the Linz line, and describes a wide curve round the Capuzinerberg p. 65). To the left lies the château of *Neuhaus* (p. 108). 2½ M. *Parsch* (*Gaisberg Railway*, see p. 66); 4½ M. *Aigen* (p. 65). The Salzach is now approached, and the precipitous Untersberg becomes more prominent, with the Watzmann and Hohe Göll adjoining it on the left. To the right, on the opposite bank of the river, is the château of *Anif* (p. 66). 6 M. *Elsbethen*, with a château, a monastery, and the school of *Goldenstein*. [St. Jakob am Thurn (p. 65) lies 1½ M. to the N. The *Elsbether* or *Todte Klammen* (½ hr.; guide 30 kr.) deserve a visit.] Beyond (9½ M.) *Puch* the train passes the village of *Oberalm* (left), and the large brewery of *Kaltenhausen*, on the left bank of the Salzach, and crosses the *Alm*.

11 M. **Hallein** (1450'; *Vogl's Inn* and *Salt Baths*, near the station, R. 80 kr.; *Post* or *Schwarzer Adler*; *Sonne*; *Auböck*; *Stampflbräu*; *Ortner's Restaurant*, with rooms, at the station), an old town on the left bank of the Salzach, noted for its salt-works, which produce 16,500 tons of salt annually. The **Dürnberg**, whence the salt-water is obtained, rises above the town. The mode of extracting the salt from the earthy matter with which it is mingled is described at p. 94. About 350 miners are employed here. Those who have not yet explored a salt-mine may avail themselves of this opportunity (but the Berchtesgaden mine is preferable, p. 69). Permission is obtained at the office of the salt-works at Hallein (one pers. 3 fl., a party 1½ fl. each). The route to the (¾ hr.) Dürnberg ascends on the W. side of the town through a narrow lane, to the right before the church is reached, commanding several fine views. After ¼ hr. the road turns into the valley to the right, and beyond the *Inn Zur Gemse* enters a gateway to the left. At the (12 min.) *Inn Zum Jägergut*, the road divides, the right branch leading to Berchtesgaden (p. 84), the left to the Dürnberg.

DÜRNBERG SALT MINE. At the foot of the hill (2525'), which is crowned by the picturesque miners' church, constructed of marble in 1598, is the mining-office, where visitors present themselves. The donning of mining attire and the mode of 'travelling in the interior' are much the same as already described (p. 69). The total length of this mine is about 3000 yds., breadth 1320, depth 400. The visit occupies 1-1½ hr. — From the Dürnberg the *Raspenhöhe* (2930'; view) may be ascended in ½ hr.

The **Kleine Barmstein** (2740') commands a magnificent view of the surrounding mountains and of the valley of the Salzach. A marked path leads from Hallein by *Theresenruhe* and the ruins of *Dierndl* to (1½ hr.) the summit, which consists of a narrow plateau, with abrupt precipices on three sides. The *Grosse Barmstein* (2750'), ½ hr. from the Kleine Barmstein, is less interesting. This expedition may also be advantageously made from Berchtesgaden (3 hrs.), following the Zill road (see below) and on the plateau turning to the left to (2½ hrs.) the hamlet of *Mehlweg* (view), which lies about ½ hr. from the top of the Kleine Barmstein.

The *Rossfeld* (*Hennenköpfl*; 5040'), the N. spur of the Hohe Göll, may be ascended in 3 hrs (guide unnecessary). We follow a marked path leading viâ the Dürnberg and through wood to the (2 hrs.) *Pechhäusl* (3680'; Inn) and thence proceed viâ the *Rossfeld-Alp* (Rfmts.) to the summit (1 hr.). — The ascent of the Hohe Göll (8264') from Hallein is fine but fatiguing (7½ hrs.; guide 7 fl.). From the (2 hrs.) Pechhäusl (see above) we proceed viâ the *Rossfeld-Alp* and the *Ahorn-Alp* to the (2 hrs.) *Ecker-Sattel* or the *Ecker-Alp* (p. 85), and ascend thence to (3½–4 hrs.) the top (comp. pp. 73, 85).

The view from the *Schlenken* (5400'), which is easily ascended by a marked path viâ *Adnet* in 5 hrs., resembles that from the Gaisberg. A new path leads from the Schlenken viâ the 'Jägernase' to the (¾ hr.) *Schmittenstein* (5555'), a height resembling a ruined castle and commanding a fine panorama.

To BERCHTESGADEN (7 M.). The following road, recommended to walkers (steep at the beginning and end, and not very suitable for driving), is the shortest way from Hallein (and Salzburg) to Berchtesgaden. To the *Jägergut* (p. 83) the route is the same as that to the Dürnberg. The road here turns to the right, passes the (½ M.) Austrian custom-house (2140'), and reaches the (¼ M.) Bavarian custom-house of Zill (2165'; *Inn*). The road then traverses a hilly plateau, sprinkled with farms and picturesque groups of trees (view of the Untersberg to the right), and finally descends rapidly through the wooded *Essielthal-Graben* to the (3 M.) Salzburg-Berchtesgaden road (p. 70). — Besides this road a carriage-road runs viâ *Au* (p. 71) direct to (9 M.) Berchtesgaden or to (9 M.) Vordereck (p. 71); and a footpath (¼ hr. longer; guide advisable) leads from Au by the *Laros Conduit* and through two tunnels (p. 71) to the salt-mine (p. 69).

To the Almbachstrub, an attractive excursion from Hallein. Road by *Wiesthal* (or *Almthal*) to the (10 M.) *Neuhäusl* (Inn). Then by the *Franz-Reyl-Steig*, high on the right bank, to the ravine of the *Strubbach* (discharge of the Hintersee), flanked with huge precipices (to the *Leopoldinenklause* 1 hr.). Road thence to (1¼ M.) *Faistenau* (2580'; Inn). 2 M. to the S. of which is the *Faistenauer Hintersee* (2250'). To the E. of Faistenau an easy path leads over the (3 hrs.) *Faistenauer Schafberg* (5110'; fine view) and through the *Tiefbrunau* to (2 hrs.) *Fuschl* (p. 108).

The train follows the right bank of the Salzach and crosses the *Taugelbach*, which issues from a deep gorge, 1 M. to the E. From (16 M.) *Kuchl* (1525'; Hepflinger; Neuwirth; Seethaler), an old village with a Gothic church, a path leads to the right across the bridge direct to the (2¼ M.) Schwarzbach Fall (see below).

18 M. Golling (1440'; *Hôtel Bahnhof*, in an open situation at the station; *Alte Post, Neue Post, Metzger Holzherr*, in the village), lying on a hill, ¼ M. from the station, with an old *Castle*, the seat of a district-court, derives some importance from the attractions of the environs. On the E. side is the *Bachstatt*, a spur of the *Rabenstein*, with pleasant grounds and fine points of view. The route to the (2¼ M.) *Schwarzbach Fall cannot be mistaken (one-horse carr. for 1-2 pers. 1½, 3 pers. 2 fl.). Starting from the station, we cross the railway to the right, and then the Salzach, and walk in the direction of the white church of (1½ M.) *St. Nicolaus*, on a

to Golling.   GOLLING.   *II. Route 16.* 85

hill, where a finger-post on the left indicates the way. In about 5 min.
we reach *Meidler's Inn*, and at the mill ¹/₄ M. beyond it is the
inn *Zum Wasserfall*. From the wooded slope of the Hohe Göll
the *Schwarzbach* is precipitated from a cavern (1900' above the
sea-level) and through an aperture in the rock, over a cliff 200'
high, in two vast leaps. Masses of rock projecting over the abyss
form a natural bridge. The Schwarzbach is said to be one of the
outlets of the Königs-See, which lies about 7 M. to the S.W. and
78' higher. This is not improbable, as in 1823, 1866, and 1882,
when the surface of the lake was lower than the Kuchler Loch
(p. 74), the Schwarzbach ceased to flow. Between 10 and 11 a.m.
the sunshine forms a rainbow in the spray. Easy paths, protected
by railings, lead past the lower to the upper fall and to (¹/₄ hr.) the
point where the Schwarzbach issues in a clear and copious stream
from the rocks.

Pedestrians on their way to Hallein save an hour, if, instead of returning to Golling, they proceed direct from the falls to (³/₄ hr.) *Kuchl* (p. 84), crossing the Schwarzbach at the mill (see above; several finger-posts).

FROM GOLLING TO BERCHTESGADEN (5-6 hrs.; guide, 4 fl., unnecessary for experts). By *St. Nicolaus* (p. 84), or crossing the brook beneath the fall, we proceed to (1 hr.) the '*Kohlstatt*' in the *Weissenbachthal*. Then a path (indicated by red marks) ascends the N. side of the valley (opposite are the precipices of the Hohe Göll, forming the *Wilde Freithof*) to the (2 hrs.) *Dürrfeichten-Alpe* (4425') and the (¹/₂ hr.) Eckersattel (4700'), between the *Eckergrat* and *Mitterberg* (view of the Hohe Göll, Tennengebirge, Dachstein, and Salzachthal). Lastly we descend to (1 hr.) *Vordereck* (p. 71) and (2¹/₂ hrs.) *Berchtesgaden*. A longer (by 1¹/₂ hr.) but finer route from the Dürrfeichten-Alp leads to the right across the (1 hr.) Rossfeld (*Hennenköpfl*, 5040'), which commands a view of the Salzachthal as far as Salzburg; then down by *Au* to the *Laroswacht* (p. 71). A third route crosses the Ahornbüchsen (5260'), the summit of the Mitterberg between the Eckersattel and the Rossberg, which affords a good view of Berchtesgaden (2 hrs. from the Dürrfeichtenalp to Vordereck, by the *Ahornalp*). — The Hohe Göll (8205') may be scaled from the Eckersattel by the *Eckerfirst* in 3¹/₂-4 hrs. (see p. 73; guide from Golling 8 fl.). The night may be spent at the *Ecker-Alpe* (4060'), below the saddle, to the W.

From Golling to the *Königs-See* by the *Torrener-Joch*, 6-7 hrs., see p. 75.

The *Oefen*, 2 M. to the S. of Golling, on the W. side of the
high-road to Werfen, are curious and picturesque ravines, filled
with huge blocks of rock heaped together in wild confusion, between which the Salzach has forced its passage for upwards of a
mile. These rocks, partly overgrown with wood, and undermined
by the action of the water, are rendered accessible by paths and
bridges in every direction. At the N. and S. entrances to the Oefen
are finger-posts indicating the approach, and not ¹/₄ M. apart, whilst
the walk through the rocky wilderness occupies ¹/₂ hr. (one-horse
carr. from Golling for 1-2 pers. 1¹/₂, 3 pers. 2 fl.; halfway is the
Duschen Inn). A path leads along the left bank of the Salzach to a
point of view ('der Oefen Ende') commanding the best survey of
the Oefen as well as a glimpse of the Salzachthal, and to the
Croatenhöhle, a fortified cave on the slope of the Hagengebirge, at
the entrance of the Pass Lueg (p. 86). — At the S. entrance to

the Oefen is the *Maria Brunneck Chapel* (1815'), whence the best view is obtained of the *Pass Lueg* (see below) and the grey precipices of the *Hagengebirge*.

The *Pass Lueg, a grand ravine of the Salzach, 6 M. in length, between the *Tennengebirge* on the E. and the *Hagengebirge* on the W., forms a fitting portal from the lower to the higher Alps. (It should be traversed on foot or in an open carriage as far as Sulzau, see below; one-horse carr. 4 fl.) The pass is frequently mentioned in the records of the struggles of 1809. At the entrance, $1/4$ M. from the chapel of Maria Brunneck (see above), are fortifications constructed in 1836; opposite is the *Croatenhöhle*, mentioned at p. 85. About $3/4$ M. farther on, on the left bank, are a tunnel and bridge of the *Gisela Railway* (see p. 112). The road follows the right bank, passing (2 M.) an *Inn*, to ($1^1/_2$ M.) *Sulzau* (station, p. 112; no inn).

Route from Golling to *Abtenau* and *Gosau*, see p. 102; the *Lammeröfen* are about $6^1/_2$ M. from Golling, and the *Aubach Fall* about 9 M. (one-horse carr. for a visit to both and back, in 4-5 hrs., 4 fl., two-horse carr. 6 fl.). — From (3 M.) *Scheffau* (p. 103), the Schwarzberg (5190') may be easily ascended, by the *Lehngriesalp*, in 3 hrs. (guide useful); fine view from the summit.

17. From Linz to Salzburg.

$77^1/_2$ M. RAILWAY. Express in $2^3/_4$-3 hrs; ordinary trains in $4^3/_4$-$5^3/_4$ hrs. Linz (*Erzherzog Carl; *Goldner Adler; *Rother Krebs; *Kanone, the nearest to the station; etc.), see Baedeker's *S. Germany and Austria*. Soon after starting, a number of the forts of Linz are seen on the low hills to the right; above them in the distance rises the *Pöstlingberg* with its church. Stations *Hörsching, Marchtrenk*.

15 M. Wels (1025'; *Bauer zum Adler; *Post; *Kaiserin von Oesterreich*, at the station; *Rail. Restaurant*), the *Ovilava* of the Romans, a small town on the *Traun*, with an old castle of Prince Auersperg and a modern Gothic church, is the junction for Passau.

The line now traverses a wooded district. 20 M. *Gunskirchen*.
— 24 M. **Lambach** (1100'; *Rail. Restaurant*, with rooms; *Rössl*), a small town with several large buildings. Among these is a *Benedictine Abbey* (founded in 1032), containing a collection of engravings, specimens of early printing, MSS., and nine large altar-pieces by *Sandrart*. From a wooded height on the right bank of the Traun, below the mouth of the *Ager*, peeps the pilgrimage-church of *Baura*, triangular in form, with three towers. and paved with marble of three different colours, founded in 1722 by an abbot of the monastery in honour of the Trinity.

FROM LAMBACH TO GMUNDEN ($17^1/_2$ M.), branch-line in $1^1/_2$-2 hrs. The line (an ill-constructed narrow-gauge line, used as a tramway from 1821 to 1855) crosses the *Traun* and runs towards the S., in view of the *Traunstein* (p. 90), the outline of which is said to resemble the profile of Louis XVI.; to the left beyond it the glaciers of the Dachstein. to the right the Höllengebirge. 3 M. *Railham*; $8^1/_2$ M. *Traunfall*, from which a path descends to the right, through wood, to the (20 min.) *Traun Fall*

(*Inn*). A long, indented ridge of conglomerate extends halfway across the river towards the left bank, over and through which the clear green Traun is precipitated from a height of 45'. The fall is best seen from the bridge below it, and from the projecting rock with the railing below the bridge. On the right bank of the river is a *Canal* ('Der gute Fall'), 400 yds. in length, constructed in 1552, with a fall of 50', which carries the saltbarges past the waterfall (twice a week, usually between 11 and 12 o'clock). For a fee of 20-30 kr. one of the miller's men closes this canal and so causes the whole of the water to be precipitated over the rocks. The descent from Gmunden to the falls by one of the barges (a favourite excursion; fee 1½ fl.) is a novel and pleasant trip, quite unattended with danger; the start is made on Tues. or Frid. between 9 and 11 and the fall reached in 1½ hr.; passengers (who must give notice the day before to the bargemaster Moser) disembark about ¾ M. lower down, and return by train.

Next stations *Eichberg-Steyermühle* with a large paper-mill, *Laakirchen*, *Oberweis*. Then *Gmunden* (Seebahnhof, 1½ M. from the station of the Salzkammergut line; see p. 88).

Beyond Lambach the line quits the Traunthal and enters the valley of the *Ager* (discharge of the Attersee, p. 109). On the left are the Traunstein and the Höllengebirge. From (28 M.) *Breitenschützing* a branch-railway runs to the right to *Wolfsegg*. 30½ M. *Schwanenstadt* (3 M. to the N.W. of the Traun Fall, p. 86). — 34½ M. **Attnang** (1320'; *Rail. Restaurant; Inn* at the station), the junction of the Salzkammergut Railway (R. 18).

FROM ATTNANG TO SCHÄRDING, 41 M., railway in 2½ hrs., see Baedeker's *S. Germany*. From the second station (7 M.) *Manning-Wolfsegg* a pleasant road leads to the E. to (2 M.) **Wolfsegg** (°*Hättl*, with view; *Post*), a small town charmingly situated on the slope of the *Hausruck*. The park of Count St. Julien (particularly the 'Schanze') commands a beautiful view of the hilly environs, with numerous villages, beyond which rise the Styrian and Salzburg Alps, from the Todte Gebirge to the Untersberg and Watzmann. Excursion to the (1¼ M.) prettily-situated *Kohlgrube* (coal-mine; miners' band plays on Sundays). Another to (4 M.) the *Thomasroith* coal-mine (train, by *Holzleithen*, in ¾ hr.).

To the left, farther on, is the ancient château of *Puchheim*; in the background the Höllengebirge (p. 94). 37½ M. **Vöcklabruck** (1430'; *°Mohr; Post*) is a little town on the Ager, with old gate-towers and remains of walls. On a height to the E. is the old Gothic church of *Schöndorf*. To the *Attersee*, see p. 109.

The train crosses the Ager twice. 40 M. *Timelkam*. Beyond (43 M.) *Neukirch-Gampern* the line enters the valley of the *Vöckla*, which falls into the Ager here. 45 M. *Redl-Zipf* (Traumüller), with a large brewery (right); 47½ M. *Vöcklamarkt;* 50 M. *Frankenmarkt* (1760'), a market-town. The railway now quits the Vöckla, and winds through the wooded hills which form the watershed between the Traun and the Inn. The highest point is near *Ederbauer* (1960'). To the left, above (58½ M.) *Rabenschwand-Oberhofen*, we observe the overhanging summit of the Schafberg and the Schober (p. 110). — 60½ M. *Strasswalchen* (1775'). Route to the Mondsee, see p. 110. — 62 M. *Steindorf*, the junction for *Braunau;* 63 M. *Neumarkt-Köstendorf*.

The **Tannberg** (2572'; °*Inn*), ascended from the station in 1¼ hr., is a splendid point of view (°Inn). Descent to *Mattsee* (2 hrs.; see p. 88).

Beyond (65½ M.) *Weng* the train skirts the pretty little *Waller-*

88   *II. Route 18.*   GMUNDEN.   *From Salzburg*

see, or *Lake of Seekirchen*, on which a small steamboat plies. — 69 M. *Seekirchen* (1675'; Inn), ³/₄ M. from the S.W. end of the lake. A diligence plies daily in 1½ hr. from Seekirchen to (8 M.) **Mattsee** (1650'; *Iglbräu*), charmingly situated on a headland between the *Ober-Trumersee* and *Nieder-Trumersee* (the '*Mattseen*'); 1¼ M. to the N.W. is the smaller *Grabensee*. The *Schlossberg* (1855'; ¼ hr.) affords a good survey. Hence to the top of the *Tannberg*, 3 hrs., see p. 87.

The train then enters a wooded tract and crosses the deep ravine of the *Fischach* (outflow of the Wallersee) several times. 71 M. *Eugendorf*; 73 M. *Hallwang-Elixhausen*. The train now turns sharply to the S. and runs through a wooded ravine into the valley of the *Salzach* (to the left the rounded Gaisberg, to the right the Hohe Göll, Untersberg, and the Stauffen). 75 M. *Berg-Mariaplain* (p. 67). — 77½ M. *Salzburg*, see p. 60.

18. From Salzburg to Ischl and Aussee. Salzkammergut.

92 M. RAILWAY to (43½ M.) *Attnang* in 1½-2½ hrs.; from Attnang to (48½ M.) *Aussee* in 2½-3 hrs. — From *Vienna* to Ischl viâ *Attnang* (178 M.), express in 6¾ hrs.; viâ *Amstetten* and *Selzthal* (202 M.), express in 8¾ hrs. (view from last carriage in the train, comp. p. 112).

The "Salzkammergut (an imperial domain, literally 'salt-exchequer-property', the sale of salt being a monopoly of the Austrian government), a mountain-region between Styria and Salzburg, about 250 sq. M. in area, with 18,000 inhab. (5000 Prot.), is characterised by picturesque green valleys and beautiful sequestered lakes. It is intersected by the *Traun*, which connects the lakes of Hallstadt and Gmunden, and forms near Lambach the waterfall mentioned at p. 87. There is probably no district in Germany or Austria which presents such a variety of charming scenery within so small a compass, and the traveller may pleasantly spend weeks or even months in exploring it.

To (43 M.) *Attnang*, see p. 87. The Salzkammergut Railway crosses the *Ager* (on the right *Schloss Puchheim*, p 87) and the *Aurach*, and then follows the smiling *Aurachthal* to (47½ M.) *Aurachkirchen* (1525') and (51 M.) *Gmunden*; the station (Rail. Restaurant, dear) lies above the town to the W., 1½ M. from the lake, and halfway between Gmunden and *Pinsdorf*.

Gmunden. — Hotels. *HÔTEL AUSTRIA*, *BELLEVUE* (Pl. a), both first-class, on the lake, with view; *GOLDENES SCHIFF* (Pl. b), R. & L. from 1 fl., A. 30 kr.; *HÔTEL MUCHA* (formerly *Lauffhuber*), on the lake, near the Seebahnhof, with garden (see below); R. 1½ fl., L. & A. 50 kr.; *KRONE* (Pl. c), Casino-Platz; *POST*; *GOLDENER BRUNNEN* (Pl. e) above the lock of the Traun, good wine; *GOLDENE SONNE* (Pl. f); *HÔTEL KOGL* (Pl. d), ¼ M. from the lake, fine view; *GOLDENER HIRSCH* (Pl. g), plain. — Cafés. *Nüstlinger, Pürstinger*, both in the See-Platz; *Detwinger* (*Goldnes Schiff*); *Paradeisgarten*, at the end of the esplanade. — Confectioner's in the Kiosk on the esplanade. — *"Kursaal* (Pl. i), on the lake, with restaurant, large terrace, reading-room, etc. (adm. free). Garden-restaurant at the *Hôtel Mucha* (see above), on the lake; also at the *Hôtel Bellevue*, *Mühlwang*. *Goldner Brunnen*, *Kogl*, etc.

Baths of all kinds at the *Bellevue* and *Austria*; *Fischill's Baths*, at the bridge over the Traun; *Theresienbad*, Elisabeth-Str. 77; *Swimming Baths*, by the Esplanade, for ladies and gentlemen (bath with towel, etc., 30 kr.). *Hydropathic Establishment*, with inhaling-room for saline and pine-needle vapour, pneumatic room, etc., adjoining the Bellevue.

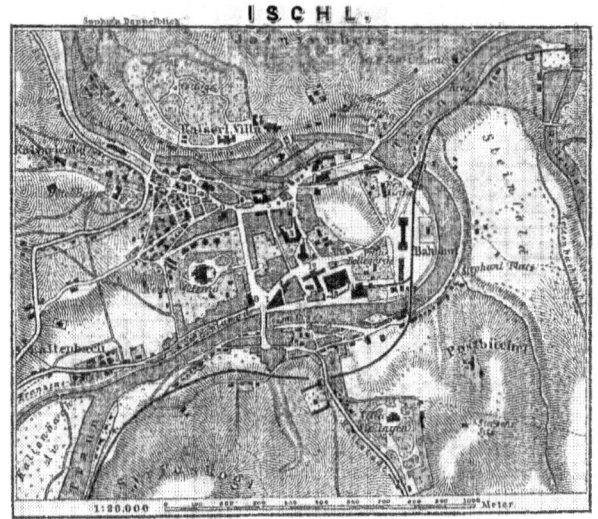

Trinkhalle for mineral waters, whey, etc., on the Esplanade. — *Theatre* (Pl. 3), from June to September, in the Graben, adjoining the Kursaal. — *Visitors' Tax*. Visitors staying more than 6 days pay a tax of 4 fl. each; additional members of the same family less in proportion; the tax is demanded a second time from visitors staying more than 12 days.

Carriages. Drive within the town, one-horse carr. 70 kr., two-horse 1 fl.; to the West Station 1 or 1½ fl., at night 1 fl. 30 kr. or 2 fl.; to the Traun Fall (2½ hrs.) 3½ or 6 fl.; *Kammer* on the Attersee (4 hrs.) 6 or 10 fl.; Almsee (6 hrs.) 9 or 15 fl.; Langbath-Seen (whole day) 7 or 12 fl.; no extra charge for returning, and a stay of 1 hr. allowed, beyond which 50 or 70 kr. per hour is charged for waiting; gratuity 1 fl. to 1 fl. 20 kr. per day. — **Boats.** To Ort or Weyer with one rower 80 kr., Grünbergergut 50 kr., Prillinger 70 kr., Altmünster or Kleine Ramsau 1 fl., Ebenzweier or Hoisengut 1 fl. 10. Staininger 1 fl. 60 kr., Lainaustiege 2 fl. (return-fare included); with two rowers, about one-half more; for waiting, 10 kr. per ¼ hour; boat per hr. with one rower 60, with two rowers 90 kr. — *Donkey* per hour 1 fl., each additional hour 60 kr., ½ day 2 fl. *Mänhardt's* lending library, etc., in the See-Platz.

Gmunden (1395'), the capital of the Salzkammergut, is a busy town (6600 inhab.) and favourite watering-place, charmingly situated at the efflux of the Traun from the Traunsee. The *Parish Church* contains an altar in carved wood by Schwanthaler, of 1656. Handsome modern *Protestant Church* in the English Gothic style. The *Museum of Forestry*, in the Forestry Office, and the *Industrial Museum*, in the public school, are worth a visit. The shady *Esplanade* (band 11.30 to 12.30 and 6.30 to 8; Sundays 12-1), on the W. bank, commands a good survey of the lake: to the left is the wooded *Grünberg* (3295'), then the *Traunstein* (5548'), rising almost perpendicularly from the lake, and the *Erlakogl* (5150'); farther to the right, in the background, the *Wilde Kogel* (6865'); the *Kleine Sonnstein* (3030'), apparently terminating the lake, with Traunkirchen at its base; to the right of it the *Sonnstein-Höhe* (3430'), and in front the broad *Fahrnau* (3940'); then the long *Kranabetsattel* (p. 91). *Höllengebirge* (p. 91), and *Hochlekengebirge* (p. 109). Pleasant gardens and villas in the environs.

Short Walks (routes all indicated by marks). To the N.W. the (10 min.) *Wunderburg* and (5 min. farther) the *Calvarienberg*; to the W. the *Hochkogel* (1770'), with the *Marienwarte* (¼ hr.; at its foot the Hôtel am Kogel, p. 88); the (25 min.) *Villa Satori*, with a charming park, beautiful points of view, a chalet (refreshments), and a dairy; to the S.W. *Schloss Ort* (1½ M.), on the lake, connected with the mainland by a bridge, 70 yds. long. To the N.W. *Rosenkranz* (25 min.), to the N.E. *Baumgarten* (¾ hr.), and to the E. *Sieberroth* (¾ hr.), on the slope of the Grünberg, all with restaurants. On the right bank of the Traun (footpath over the Marienbrücke) lie the shady *Kronprinz-Rudolfs-Anlagen* (pleasuregrounds), with a café and a restaurant (½ hr.). Adjacent is the large new château of the Duke of Cumberland.

Longer Walks. By the high-road, past the villas of the Grand-Duchess of Tuscany and the Duke of Würtemberg, to (2 M.) *Altmünster*, (3 M.) *Ebenzweier*, and (7 M.) *Traunkirchen* (p. 90). — Past the Villa Satori (see above), and then by a path indicated by finger-posts and streaks of paint, to the (1½ hr.) *Gmundner Berg* (2700'; fine view; Inn at the top); descend to (1 hr.) the *Reindlmühle* (Inn) in the Aurachthal, and return by (1 hr.) Ebenzweier (4½ hrs. in all). — Descend on the left bank of the Traun to the *Theresienthal* cotton-mill, (2 M.) *Altmühle*, and (4½ M.) *Ohlstorf* (Inn). — Past the Salzkammergut station to *Pinsdorf*, the (4½ M.) *Dichtlmühle*, and (6 M.) the *Rabenmühle*. From the Dichtlmühle we may ascend the *Hongar* (3095'; Inn), with view of the Attersee. — The **Traun Fall** may be visited on foot (3½ hrs.), or better by the Lambach railway (p. 86) or by one of the salt-barges mentioned at p. 87. — On the E. bank: the *Grünberger-Gut* (½ hr.), *Prillinger* (40 min.), *Kleine Ramsau* (50 min.), the *Hoisengut* (Zum Traunstein; 1 hr.), *Staininger* (König v. Hannover; 1½ hr.), all with restaurants; if the traveller prefer to go one way (or both) by water, a boat should be ordered at Gmunden (p. 89). In the afternoon the steamer touches at the Kleine Ramsau, Hoisengut, and Staininger.

LONGER EXCURSIONS. Across the (1¼ hr.) *Himmelreich-Wiese*, the (½ hr.) *Schnee-Wiese*, and the (½ hr.) *Hochgeschirr* (3140'), with a view of the glaciers of the Dachstein, to the (1 hr.) Laudach-See (2890'), picturesquely situated on the E. side of the Traunstein; return either by *Franzl im Holz* (2 hrs.), or by (1¾ hr.) the Kleine Ramsau, and take a small boat or the steamer thence to Gmunden. Finger-posts on this route, so that a guide may be dispensed with. (Shortest route from the Kleine Ramsau to the Laudachsee: from the landing-place ascend in ¼ hr. to the *Waldrast*; then follow the path indicated by marks on the trees, which leads to the lake in 2 hours. Return by the same route for ½ hr., cross a meadow to the right and ascend into the wood, and regain Gmunden by the Hochgeschirr, the Schneewiese, and the Himmelreichswiese.) — **Traunstein** (5518') ascended in 5 hrs. from Gmunden, interesting (guide, advisable, 4 fl.; A. Reitter of Gmunden recommended; permission necessary from the 'Forstverwaltung'). The lake is crossed by the *Lainaustiege* (to which also the 'Miesweg', a path constructed by the Austrian Tourist Club, leads on the bank of the lake in 2½ hrs.), whence we ascend to the (1 hr.) *Kaisersitz* (20 min. above which is the prettily-situated *Mayralm*). At this point the path, indicated by red marks, turns to the left, passes the *Touristenbründl*, and ascends to the (3 hrs.) plateau of the Traunstein, overgrown with underwood, from which rise the *Traunkirchnerkogel*, the *Mitterkogel* (with a stone monument and a vane), and the *Alpenspitze* (the highest peak, with a trigonometrical signal). Magnificent view, particularly of the Priel group and the Dachstein. In the foreground, far below, lie the Traunsee on the W. and the Laudachsee on the E. — From the Mayralpe over the *Hohe Scharte* to the *Laudachsee* 2½ hrs.; path indicated by marks (better in the reverse direction).

Ascent of the **Sonnstein** (3080'), a pleasant afternoon's excursion; charming view of the mountains encircling the lake, and of the valley of Ebensee (guide advisable for the inexperienced). From Traunkirchen the Ebensee road is followed for 1 M., after which the path to the right, indicated by marks, leads to the top in 1½ hr. (last 20 min. over rocks).

The **Almsee**, reached by carriage in 6 hrs. The road leads by (9 M.) *Mühldorf* (*Inn) in the pretty *Almthal*, and (3 M.) *Grünau*, whence the *Kassberg* (5720') may be ascended in 3½ hrs. (marked path), to (2 M.) the *Almsee* (1930'), grandly situated on the N. margin of the Todte Gebirge (*Inn kept by the forester). — From the Almsee the *Hohe Pfad* leads to the *Offensee* (p. 92) in 4 hrs. (guide from Grünau to Ebensee 5½ fl.). From the Almsee by the *Weisshorn*, the *Wilde See* (5100') and the *Wildensee-Alpe* to *Alt-Aussee* (p. 97), 8 hrs., fatiguing (guide to Aussee 10½ fl.). — Through the *Bernerau* to *Stoder*, see p. 390.

FROM GMUNDEN TO ISCHL (steamboat to Ebensee in 1 hr., fare 1 fl., preferable to the railway; tickets are issued available both for the steamboat and the train; views to the left). The train passes the back of the Duke of Wurtemberg's Villa, and at *Altmünster*, with the oldest church in the district, approaches the beautiful *Traunsee or **Gmundner See** (1385'; 7½ M. long). — 54½ M. (from Salzburg) *Ebenzweier*, with a château formerly belonging to Count Chambord (now a girl's school); pretty retrospect of Gmunden, with the Traunstein to the left. The scenery becomes more severe as the S. end of the lake is approached, the green slopes gradually giving place to lofty mountains. Behind the Traunstein are the *Hochkogl* (4865') and the fine cone of the *Erlakogl* (see below). 57 M. *Traunkirchen;* then round a bay of the lake and through two tunnels to (57 1/2 M.) *Traunkirchensee*, the station for the village of **Traunkirchen** (*Hôtel am Stein, 1 M. to the N., on the lake, near the station of Traunkirchen, with shady garden: *Post, on the S. side of the village; *Burgstaller*, with a terrace overlooking the lake; *Swimming Bath*), charmingly situated on a peninsula, and the most beautiful point on the lake. The church contains a quaintly carved wooden pulpit in the form of a ship, with nets and fish. The finely situated convent, now the parsonage, also deserves a visit.

Fine view from the *Calvarienberg*. On a rock jutting into the lake is the *Johanniskapelle*. On the opposite bank of the lake, in a cave on the N. slopes of the *Erlakogl* (p. 92), is the interesting **Röthelsee**: boat across the Traunsee 1/2 hr.; then a steep ascent of 1 hr. by a new path (guide with torch necessary; boat for 4 pers. on the lake). — *Sonnstein*, see p. 90.

The train passes through a short tunnel, and then the *Sonnstein Tunnel*, 1570 yds. in length. (On the road, which runs between the Sonnstein and the lake, is a lion hewn in stone, commemorating the construction of the road.) The railway skirts the lake for a short distance, stops at (60 1/4 M.) *Traunsee*, a steamboat-station, crosses the *Traun*, and reaches (61 M.) **Ebensee-Langbath** (1395'; *Hôtel Lehr*, near the station; *Post, at the quay; *Preimesberger; Rail. Restaurant*), at the S. end of the Traunsee, with extensive salt-works (about 30,000 tons annually) and a large ammonia-factory. Vast stores of wood lie in the Traun and on its banks, and numerous rafts are constructed here and floated down the Traun to the Danube. The salt-water evaporated at Ebensee is brought from Ischl and Hallstatt (p. 98) in wooden pipes.

EXCURSIONS (guides, *Joh. Stummer, Karl* and *Josef Wallner*). Pleasant walk on the left bank of the Traun, along the brine-conduit, to (3/4 hr.) the *Steinkogl* (°Inn), a fine point of view, opposite the station of that name (p. 92), and (1 hr.) the °*Fall of the Rinnbach* (Rfmts. at the mill). The °**Lakes of Langbath** (2 1/2 hrs.) deserve a visit (omnibus from stat. Traunsee-Ebensee to the Vordere See at 8 and 11.30 a.m., returning from the Kreh at 3 and 6 p.m.; there and back 1 1/2 fl.). The road ascends the *Langbath-Thal* to (1 1/2 M.) the *Kreh* (2130'; Inn) and (1 M.) the *Vordere Langbath-See* (2215'), whence a footpath leads to the smaller but finer (3/4 hr.) *Hintere See* (2385'). Between the two lakes is the *Valerien-Aussicht* (3/4 hr., with guide), affording a good view of both lakes. We may also reach the Valerien-Aussicht by crossing the Vordere See by boat (gratuity) and following the green path to the left (*not* the gravel-path immediately opposite), turning to the right farther on. A visit to the two lakes takes about 2 hrs. — To the *Attersee*, see p. 109.

The **Kranabetsattel**, the E. spur of the *Höllengebirge*, a range which extends for a distance of 20 M. between the Traunsee and Attersee, is easily ascended from Langbath in 3 1/2-4 hrs. (guide 2 fl.). The *Feuerkogel* (5220'), the nearer peak, commands an admirable survey of the Salzkammergut, and of the plains of Austria as far as the Bohemian Forest and the Styrian Alps; the view from the *Alberfeldkogel* (5600') is still more extensive. The usual route leads from Ebensee across the Calvarienberg and through the *Gsoll* (4020'), but the ascent may also be made from the Kreh-Alp (steep and stony). Accommodation at the chalets near the top.

92   *II. Route 18.*   ISCHL.   *Salzkammergut.*

The **Erlakogl** (5150'; 3½ hrs guide), a fine point of view, is ascended from Ebensee by the *Spitzlstein-Alpe* and *Müller-Alpe* (rough at places). The line follows the pretty Traunthal to (62½ M.) *Steinkogl* (¼ M. to the E. the *Mariengasthof*, with shady walks).

The *Kronprinz Rudolf Bridge* crosses from the station to the °*Steinkogl Inn*, on the left bank of the Traun. From the bridge a good and shady path, joining that from Ebensee in the Gsoll, leads to the (3 hrs.) *Kranabetsattel* (p. 91).

To the *Offensee* (2135'; 6 M.) a road leads through the *Traunweissenbachthal*. The lake, with an imperial hunting-seat (good accommodation at the forester's), lies picturesquely in a green basin, commanded on the S. by the *Todte Gebirge* (p. 97). From the Offensee a pass leads by the *Hohe Pfad* to the (4 hrs.) *Alnsee* (p. 90; guide from Ebensee 5½ fl.); another (fatiguing) by the *Wilde See* and the *Wildensee-Alpe* to (7-8 hrs.) *Alt-Aussee* (p. 97; guide from Ebensee to Aussee 10½ fl.).

The **Hohe Schrott** (5350') is ascended from Steinkogl by the *Gimbach-Alpe* (road thus far) and the *Dielau-Alpe* in 4½ hrs. (fatiguing, but interesting; guide 4 fl.; better from Ischl, comp. p. 94).

The train now crosses the *Traunweissenbach*. 65 M. **Langwies**. 67½ M. *Mitter-Weissenbach* (Drei Mohren; road to *Weissenbach*, on the Attersee, see p. 109). A rock in the Traun near Ischl is surmounted by a lofty cross. The train crosses the Traun.

70 M. **Ischl**. — **Hotels**. °KAISERIN ELISABETH (Pl. 1); °HÔTEL VORMALS BAUER (Pl. 2), charmingly situated on a height above Ischl, high charges; °POST (Pl. 3). R. from 1 fl., L. & A. 60 kr.; °GOLDENES KREUZ (Pl. 5). R. from 1 fl. 20 kr., L. & A. 70 kr.; °HÔTEL AUSTRIA, on the Esplanade, with garden; °VICTORIA (Pl. 4), with garden-restaurant; ERZHERZOG FRANZ CARL (Pl. 6). — Second-class: °STERN (Pl. 7), with good restaurant; °KRONE (Pl. 8), with a garden on the Ischl; °BAYRISCHER HOF (Pl. 9); GOLDNER OCHSE, at Gries, moderate. — °HÔTEL-PENSION RUDOLFSHÖHE, with café-restaurant (see p. 94), prettily situated at the W. end of the Esplanade; °PENSION FLORA, with sanatorium; HÔTEL GARNI RAMSAUER; ATHEN; REDLICH. — °*Dr. Hertzka's Hydropathic Establishment*, ½ M. from the end of the Esplanade, well fitted up, pension 25-32 fl. per week.

°KURSALON, with café, reading-room, etc. (see p. 93). — *Café Ramsauer*, opposite the post-office; *Café Walter*, *Café Zauner*, Esplanade; *Café Rudolfshöhe* (see above). — °*Railway Restaurant*, with rooms. — *Swimming Bath* and '*Gymnastische Heilanstalt*', on the left bank of the Ischl. — *Manhardt*, bookseller, in the Pfarrgasse. — *Theatre* (Pl. 16) during the season.

Visitors' Tax (*Kurtaxe*). Patients whose stay exceeds 12 days pay a tax of 8 or 6 fl. each, according to their means; ladies 3, children 1 fl. (For 6-12 days half these charges.) Music-tax 3 fl., each addit. member of a family 1 fl. — The band plays in the Rudolfsgarten (or, in bad weather, in the Trinkhalle) from 6.30 to 7.30 a.m.; from 12 to 1 p.m. on the Esplanade; and from 6.30 to 8.30 p.m. in front of the Kursalon or on the Esplanade.

Carriages. To *Strobl* in 1½ br., one-horse 3 fl. 30 kr., two-horse 6 fl. (including return, 5 fl. or 8 fl. 40 kr.); *St. Wolfgang* in 2 hrs., 4 or 7 fl. (including return, 5 fl. 60 kr. or 9 fl. 50 kr.); *Steg* in 1½ hr., 3 fl. 30 kr. or 6 fl.; *Hallstatt* in 2½ hrs., 6 or 10 fl.; *Gosau-Schmied* in 4 hrs., 8 or 15 fl., *Weissenbach* on the *Attersee* in 2½ hrs., 5 or 9 fl.; *Chorinsky Klause* in 1¾ hr., 4 fl. 50 kr. or 8 fl. 20 kr. These fares include the driver's fee. — To or from the station 60 kr. or 1 fl.; at night 80 kr. or 1 fl. 40 kr. — Within the town, for one hour, 90 kr. or 1 fl. 70 kr.; each additional hour 70 kr. or 1 fl. 30 kr.

English Church Service in the season at 10.30 a.m. and 4 p.m.

Ischl (1535'), the central point of the Salzkammergut, beautifully situated on a peninsula formed by the *Traun* and the *Ischl*, first came into notice as a watering-place in 1822, and is now a fashionable and expensive resort. Pop. (including Gries) 5300, of the commune 7800. Besides the salt-baths (which contain 25 per cent of salt), there are mud, sulphur, pine-cone, vapour, and other baths, in addition to the whey-cure and the saline and sulphureous drinking-springs. Well-kept walks, with shady resting-places, intersect the beautiful valley in all directions.

The shady Bahnhof-Strasse leads from the station, on the E. side of the town, past the *Rudolfsgarten*, with a bust of Archduke Rudolf, and the *Rudolfsbad*, to the *Parish Church* (Pl. 11), built under Maria Theresa, restored in 1852, and adorned with altarpieces by Kupelwieser and with modern ceiling-paintings (from the life of St. Nicholas) by Mader. In the Kaiser-Ferdinands-Platz, to the S. of the church, are the *Trinkhalle* (Pl. 12), with a covered promenade, where whey and mineral water are dispensed in the morning, and beyond it, to the right, the *Wirerbad* and the *Giselabad*. To the left are the extensive *Salt Works* (Pl. 13) and the *Salt-Water Vapour Bath* (Pl. 14).

From the Kaiser-Ferdinands-Platz the Pfarrgasse leads to the W. to the Franz-Carl-Platz, which contains a handsome bronze fountain in memory of the parents of the Emperor Franz Joseph (Archduke Franz Carl, d. 1878, and Archduchess Sophie, d. 1872), and to the Traun Bridge. On the left bank of the Traun at this point begins the *Sofien-Esplanade*, with its pleasant avenues, the favourite evening promenade of visitors (music, see p. 92). The centre is embellished with a small bronze statue of Hygieia, with an inscription to the effect that 'it is a great blessing to *be* healthy but a still greater to *become* so'.

On the W. side of the Wirer-Strasse, which leads out of the Franz-Carl-Platz on the N., is the *Wirer-Park*, with the *Kur-Salon* or *Casino*, containing a café-restaurant, etc. To the E., in the Wirer-Strasse, is a colossal bust of *Dr. Wirer von Rettenbach* (d. 1844), who first brought Ischl into notice. In the grounds to the N.W. of the Casino are a small *Bazaar* and a *Museum* (adm. daily, 10-12 and 3-7, 30 kr.), containing natural history specimens and other objects from the Salzkammergut.

WALKS. The *Imperial Villa*, with its beautiful garden and grounds (no admission during the residence of the family, usually from July to September). — The (3/4 M.) *Karolinen-Panorama* and (2 M.) the *Neue Schmalnau*, two cafés to the left of the road to Ebensee, afford good views of Ischl; we return by the (1 M.) *Gstätten Inn* and follow the brine-conduit to (1 1/2 M.) Ischl. — The *Sofiens-Doppelblick* (café; view of Ischl, the Dachstein, and the Wolfgang-Thal) may be reached in 1/2 hr. This walk may be prolonged to (the 1/4 hr.) *Dachstein-Aussicht* and the *Hohenzollern Waterfall*; we return either to the right by *Trenkelbach* (1/2 hr.), or to the left through the *Jainzenthal* (1 1/2 hr.). A path, indicated by marks (guide 1 fl. 30 kr.) ascends from the waterfall to the (1 1/2 hr.) *Saigerbach-Alpe* (3445'); charming view from the 'Schneeröselkogl'. — Right bank of the Traun: Ascent of the *Siriuskogel* or **Hundskogel** (1960': 1/2 hr.); finest view of Ischl and its environs from the *Kaiser-Franz-Josefs-Warte* on the top (small restaurant). Across the lower bridge to the (1/2 hr.) *Rettenbach Mill* and the (1/4 hr.) **Rettenbach-Wildniss** (a pretty ravine); return by *Sterzen's Abendsitz* (fine view) to (3/4 hr.) Ischl. — To the W. by the (1/4 hr.) *Cal-*

varienberg to the (1/2 hr.) *Ahornbühl*, and thence past the café *Zur Schwarzen Katz* to (3/4 hr.) the dairy of *Lindau*, or (turning off to the right 1/4 hr. before the dairy) to (1 1/2 hr.) the pretty little *Nussen-See* (1970'), with a restaurant and swimming-bath (also accessible from Ischl by carriage). — From the Esplanade through the *Franzens-Allee* to the *Fürst-Metternich-Platz* (above, to the right, is the *Café Rudolfshöhe*, p. 92), and by the *Fürstenweg* to the *Villa Waldeck*, where we diverge to the right to the (1/2 hr.) *Kaiser-Franz-Josefs-Platz*; or proceed beyond the Villa Waldeck, viâ the *Franz-Karl Promenade* and past the *Hydropathic Establishment* (p. 92) and the fish-breeding ponds, to the ruin of (1 hr.) **Wildenstein**, on the slope of the Katergebirge. Through the valley of the Traun by the shady promenade (*Kaiser-Ferdinands-Morgenweg*) to the Hydropathic Establishment and the *Erzherzog Rudolfs-Brunnen*, with new pleasure-grounds; and thence by the pleasant path following the salt-water conduit to (1 hr.) *Laufen* ("Restaurant zum Rössl). — By the Ischl road and across the Pfandl Bridge into the *Zimitz-Thal*, with the *Zimitz-Wildniss* (Inn) and the *Zimitz-Graben* (2 hrs.); returning on the left bank of the Ischl viâ the *Trenkelbach Mill*.

To the **Ischl Salt Mine** (*Ischler Salzberg*). We follow the Laufen road (see below) to (1 M.) *Reiterndorf* (°**Bachwirth**), and then ascend the road to the left in the Sulzthal to (2 M.) *Pernegg*, where the permission to visit the mine, previously procured at the 'Salinenamt' in Ischl, is shown at the mining-office. Thence to the mine 1/2 hr. more. The mine consists of 12 horizontal shafts or galleries, one above the other. The entrance is by the central shaft, named 'Empress Maria Ludovica' (3170'). A visit to this mine, or to those of Berchtesgaden (p. 70), or Hallein (p. 83), is interesting, but the veins of salt are too much mixed with clay to present a brilliant appearance (as at Wieliczka). During the bath-season the mine is illuminated once weekly, but for the reason stated visitors are apt to be disappointed. (The illumination at other times costs about 5 fl.) The brine, which is conducted to Ebensee and there evaporated, is obtained by filling the different chambers with fresh water. After 4-6 weeks it becomes highly saturated with salt, and is then drawn off. — A finger-post near the mine indicates the way to the (1 1/2 hr.) *Hütteneckalp*. We ascend by a steep path and by about 800 steps through the wood, and then cross the *Reinfals-Alp* (3345') to the (1 1/2 hr.) "**Hütteneck-Alp** (4185'; Rfmts.), which affords a magnificent view of the Dachstein and other peaks, with the Lake of Hallstatt below. Hence by the *Rossmoos-Alp* to the top of the *Predigtstuhl* (see below) in 3/4 hr. Descent by the *Gschwand-Alp* to (1 1/2 hr.) *Goisern* (p. 95).

MOUNTAIN EXCURSIONS (guides, *Furtner*, *Grieshofer*, *Bromberger*, *Putz*, *Riecher*, *Reisenauer*, and *Seitner*). Ascent of the Zimitz (*Leonsberg-Zinken*, 5990'), through the *Zimitzthal* and by the *Schütt-Alp* in 5 hrs., rather fatiguing (guide 3 fl.); "View of the Dachstein, St. Wolfgangs-See, Mondsee, and Attersee. — The **Hohe Schrott** (5850'), by the *Kothalpe*, interesting but fatiguing (see p. 92; 4 1/2-5 hrs.; guide 4 fl.). — The **Hainzen** (N.E. peak of the Katergebirge; 5370'), from the Franz-Karl Promenade in 3 1/2 hrs. (3 fl.); back by the *Ahornfeld* and through the *Schiffauthal* to the Inn zur Wacht, on the Salzburg road (p. 108). — The **Predigtstuhl** (or *Thörlwand*; 4186') is ascended viâ *Reiterndorf* and *Obereck* in 3 hrs. (1 fl. 30 kr.), or from the salt-mine viâ the *Rossmoos-Alp* in 1 1/2 hr., view similar to that from the Hütteneck-Alp (see above). — The **Hohe Kalmberg** (6010'), the highest peak of the *Ramsauer Gebirge*, is ascended from Goisern, viâ *Ramsau* and the *Trockerthon-Alpe* or the *Schartenalpe* in 4 1/2 hrs. (3 fl.); admirable view. Descent by the *Iglmoos-Alpe* to Gosau, 2 hrs.

FROM ISCHL TO ALT-AUSSEE direct (6 1/2 hrs.; with guide; fatiguing). We ascend the *Rettenbachthal* (p. 93) to the (2 1/2 hrs.) *Rettenbach-Alpe* (2090'), at the S. base of the *Hohe Schrott*, and through the *Fludergraben* to the Alp of that name, whence we descend to the *Brandwies-Hütten* and through the *Augstbachthal*, between the Sandling and Loser, to *Fischerndorf* (p. 97).

EXCURSIONS BY CARRIAGE OR RAILWAY. 1st. *Hallstatt*, half-a-day (p. 98). — 2nd. *Gosau* (p. 100), a day. — 3rd. *Hallstatt* and *Gosau*, 1 1/2 day: in the afternoon by rail to Hallstatt; on foot to the Waldbach-Strub and back;

Salzkammergut.   LAUFEN.   *II. Route 18.* 95

next morning drive (by omnibus or one-horse carriage, ordered on arriving in Hallstatt) to the Gosau Schmied in 2½ hrs.; walk to the Gosausee and back; return to Hallstatt; and take the train to Ischl. This excursion may also be accomplished in one day by taking the first train from Ischl to Gosaumühl (p. 100), ferrying over to the Gosau Mill, and thence driving to Gosau-Schmied and back to Hallstatt, where we arrive in time to visit the Waldbach-Strub in the afternoon, before returning to Ischl. But a carriage is not always to be had at the Gosau Mill. — 4th. *St. Wolfgang* and the *Schafberg* (p. 103), 1½ day: drive in the afternoon to St. Wolfgang, ascend the Schafberg, spend night at the top, descend to St. Wolfgang or St. Gilgen (Scharfling, Unterach), and return thence to Ischl. — 5th. *Traunsee* and *Traun Fall* by railway and steamboat in one day, dining at Gmunden (p. 88). — 6th. '*Three Lakes Tour*', recommended: circular-tickets viâ Strobl, St. Gilgen, Scharfling, Mondsee, See, Unterach, Weissenbach, and Ischl (or in the reverse order, from Ischl to Strobl) may be obtained for 6 fl. in the Hôtel Post at Ischl. Those going viâ Strobl start at 6, those going viâ Weissenbach at 7 a.m.; returning from Weissenbach at 8, from Strobl at 8.40 p.m.

FROM ISCHL TO AUSSEE (22 M.). The train (views to the right) returns to the right bank of the Traun and passes the suburb of *Gries* (short tunnel). It then skirts the river and the base of the *Siriuskogel* (p. 93), crosses the Traun, and reaches (74 M. from Salzburg) **Laufen**. The picturesque village lies on the opposite bank, ¾ M. to the S. (1570'; *Rössl*, with garden; *Krone*). The rapids of the Traun here are called the 'Wilde Laufen'. Pleasant footpath to Ischl, see p. 94. The *Laufener Höhe*, ascended by a marked path in ½ hr., is a good point of view. — The train again crosses the Traun. 75½ M. *Anzenau*. On the opposite bank lies *Ober-Weissenbach*, with extensive stores of timber.

The **Chorinsky Klause** (2055'), a large dam with three sluice-gates, in the Weissenbachthal, about 3 M. above its mouth, is used to accumulate the water of the *Weissenbach* sufficiently to float timber down to the Traun when the gates are opened. This is usually done once a month, and visitors at Ischl are apprised of the day by advertisement. One-horse carriage from Ischl 4 fl. 50, two horse 8 fl. 20 kr (1¾ hr.). — A good forest-path, to the left at the mouth of the Weissenbachthal, ascends (¾ hr.) the Hochmuth (*Jochwand*), which affords a charming view of the valley, the mountains of Aussee, and the Lake of Hallstatt.

The valley expands. On the right are the Ramsauer Gebirge, on the left the Sarstein (p. 99).

76½ M. **Goisern** (1640'; *Zur Wartburg*; *Steinmaier's Bräuhaus*; *Bär*; rooms at *Rundhammer's*), a considerable village (4400 inhab.), containing the largest Protestant community in the Salzkammergut and frequented as a summer-resort. About ½ M. to the N. are the small sulphurous and iodine baths of *Goisern*, with the *Marie-Valerie-Quelle*.

EXCURSIONS (guides, *Franz Neubacher, Johann Scheutz, M. Unterberger*). The *Hütteneck-Alp* (4195'; p. 94) is ascended hence in 2 hrs.; the descent may be made to (2 hrs.) Ischl or (3 hrs.) Aussee (guide not indispensable). — *Kalmberg* (6010'; p. 94), 3-4 hrs. (guide desirable; G. M. Putz of Ramsau recommended). Descent to Gosau 2-2½ hrs. Or we may proceed over the *Knall-Thörl* (4796'), along the *Jäger-Kogl* (6040'), and past the imposing *Wilde Kammer* (p. 101) to the (3 hrs.) '*Gamsfeld* (6640'), whence we descend viâ the *Andenkar-Alp* to (1½ hr.) *Russbachsag* (p. 101). — *Predigtstuhl* (4185'; p. 94), 1½-2 hrs. — The excursion through the *Leisling-Graben* to (2 hrs.) *Alt-Aussee* is not advisable except in dry weather (guide desirable).

96   *II. Route 18.*   AUSSEE.   *Salzkammergut.*

From *Stambach*, ³/₄ M. to the S. of Goisern, the old *Pötschen-Strasse* ascends to the left by *St. Agatha* to (10 M.) *Aussee*. 78 M. *Steg* (Petter's Inn), at the N. end of the **Lake of Hallstatt** (p. 98). The train skirts the E. bank of the lake (on the W. runs the road to Hallstatt, p. 98), the line, 50' above the water, having been hewn at places in the precipitous rocks of the *Sarstein* (p. 99). On the right are the Gosauhals and Gosau Mill, and, farther on, the Plassen and the mountains at the head of the lake (the Krippenstein, Zwölferkogl, and Hirlatz). Beyond (81 M.) *Gosaumühl* (p. 100) the train passes through a tunnel and crosses the deep *Wehrgraben* by an iron bridge. 83 M. **Hallstatt**; the station is opposite the town of that name (p. 98). We then pass to the rear of the small château of *Grub*, with its four towers.

84 M. **Obertraun** (*Zum Sarstein*, at the station), at the S.E. angle of the lake.

FROM OBERTRAUN TO AUSSEE, over the *Koppen* (1955'; 3 hrs.). a pleasant route, chiefly through wood. A visit to the **Koppenbrüller-Höhle** (in the *Brüllergraben*, to the left below the road. 4 M. from Obertraun) is interesting in spring only, when the brook, which rushes in a subterranean course through the cavern, is swollen by melting snow (guide and torches requisite).

The train now runs through the wild and narrow *Koppenthal*, close to the foaming Traun, a picturesque defile resembling the Gesäuse in the Enns valley (p. 379). The train passes through a tunnel and crosses the river three times. The gorge expands, and we soon reach (92 M.) the station of *Aussee* (2130'; Railway Restaurant), at *Unter-Kainisch* (salt-work), about 1 M. to the S. of the town.

Aussee. — Hotels. *ERZHERZOG FRANZ CARL; *HACKL, R. 1½ fl., L. & A. 50 kr.; *ERZHERZOG JOHANN; SONNE; WILDER MANN, R. 1½ fl., L. 15 kr. — *Café Vesco* in the Cur-Platz. — CURHAUS, with reading-room, etc., Mecsery Promenade.

Visitors' Tax for a stay of more than a week 3 fl.; band 2½ fl.

Baths of all kinds in the *Curanstalt Alpenheim* (see below), at the *Badehôtel Elisabeth*, at *Rastl's*, etc. Swimming Baths on the Traun and on the Grundlsee.

Carriage from the station to the town 1 fl., with two horses 1½ fl.; to the Grundlsee (Schramml), or to Alt-Aussee, 1 fl. 80 kr. or 3 fl.; there and back, with stay of 1 hr., 3 fl. 40 or 4 fl. 60 kr. (from the station, 4 or 6 fl.); to Gössl via Grundlsee and back (tour of the three lakes), with stay of 1 hr., 4 fl. 30 or 6 fl. 60 kr. (from the station 5 fl. 30 kr. or 8 fl.), each additional hour's stay 60 kr. or 1 fl.). These fares include the driver's fee. — *Omnibus* from the station to the town 30 kr.

Aussee (2145 ft.), a Styrian market-town, with extensive saltworks, charmingly situated on the *Traun*, the three arms of which (Alt-Aussee, Grundlsee, and Oedensee Traun) unite here, is much visited as a watering-place (salt-baths, etc.) and summer-resort. Close to the town are fine pine-woods, traversed by pleasant walks. The small *Spitalkirche* contains a good early-German winged altarpiece of 1449. A short distance to the N., on the road to Alt-Aussee (p. 97), is *Dr. Schreiber's Curanstalt Alpenheim* (hydropathic establishment, with various baths), open all the year round, and about ½ M. farther on is the *Badehôtel Elisabeth*.

EXCURSIONS (guides, *Stefan Hopfer* and *Alois Grieshofer*; key-plan to the system of marked paths kept in the Kurhaus). A good survey of the environs is obtained from *Sixtleithen*, 10 min. from the Kurhaus. Other pleasant walks: to the *Tauscheria* (10 min.), with fine view of the Sarstein, Loser, Driesselwand, and Todte Gebirge; to the *Cramer Promenade* and the *Café Loitzl* in Obertressen (1/2 hr.); to *St. Leonhard* (1/2 hr.); to the *Schmiedgut* (1/2 hr.); and to the *Wasner* (3/4 hr.). All these points have cafés and command views of the Dachstein.

To (3 M.) *Alt-Aussee, a drive of 3/4 hr. (carriage, see p. 96); omnibus thrice daily from the railway-station, in 1 hr. (70 kr.). The road (adjoining the Elisabeth Promenade) follows the wooded valley of the *Alt-Ausseer Traun*, which it crosses thrice, to *Alt-Aussee* (Kitzerwirth) and *Fischerndorf* (°Seewirth). Both lie on the beautiful *Alt-Aussee Lake* (2320'; 2 M. long and 1/2 M. broad), overshadowed by the precipitous Trisselwand on the E., the Tressenstein on the S., and the Loser and Sandling on the N. Boats at the Seewirth. The (1 hr.) *Seewiese*, at the N.E. end, commands a good view of the Dachstein. About 1/2 hr. farther on is the chaos of rocks called the *Gaisknechtstein*. — From Alt-Aussee to the ruin of *Pflintsberg*, with waterfall and fine view, 1 1/4 hr.; thence to the *Bachwirth*, 3/4 hr. — To the *Aussee Salt Mine* at the *Sandting*, 1 hr.; the mine resembles that at Ischl (p. 94). The *Hohe Sandling* (5630') may be ascended from the mine in 2 1/2-3 hrs. with guide (3 fl.), by a good path, indicated by marks, and provided with wire-ropes at the steepest points. The *Loser* (6020'; 3-3 1/2 hrs.; guide 3 fl.), an admirable point of view, presents no difficulty. It may be ascended from the end of the lake by a steep path in 2 hrs.; or more easily by a route passing through the *Augstbach-Thal*, and mounting on the W. side of the mountain in 2 1/2 hrs. to the *Loserhütte* on the *Augst-Alp* (4500'; Inn in summer). The summit (3/4 hr. more) commands an extensive and beautiful view. The *Bräuningzinken* (6200'), reached in 1 1/2 hr. from the Loserhütte by a path (improved and marked) leading past the little *Augstsee*, enjoys a still more comprehensive panorama. — From Alt-Aussee to *Ischl*, see p. 94; to the *Almsee* or the *Offensee*, see pp. 90, 92.

To the (4 M.) *Grundl-See, a beautiful drive of 3/4 hr. (as far as Schramml's Inn; carriage, p. 96; omnibus from the Sonne thrice daily, in 1 hr., fare 70 kr.). The road leads for the most part through wood, skirting the Grundlsee Traun, which it crosses at the (3 M.) *Seeklause*, and then along the lake to the (1 M.) *Schramml Inn* (generally crowded in summer), a charming point of view. [Walkers may follow the right bank of the Traun or the Cramer Promenade, 1 1/2 hr.] The road next leads past the (2 M.) *Inn zum Ladner* to (1 1/2 M.) *Gössl* (see below). The *Grundlsee* (2325'), 3 3/4 M. long and 1/2 M. wide, is enclosed by wooded mountains and abounds in fish. The E. background is formed by the bare precipices of the *Todte Gebirge*. From the Seeklause a small screw-steamer, owned by Hr. Schramml, plies five times daily in summer to Schramml's Inn and to Gössl, at the upper end of the lake. From *Gössl* (°Veit) a path skirts the base of the perpendicular *Gösslwand* to (1 M.) the beautiful "Toplitz-See (2350'), 1 1/4 M. long, with two waterfalls (boat across in 25 min., boatman to be brought from Gössl). About 1/4 M. beyond the Toplitz-See lies the sequestered *Kammersee*, in a grand situation at the base of the Todte Gebirge. This 'Drei-Seen-Tour', or tour of the three lakes, makes a very charming excursion (from the Grundlsee to the Kammersee and back, 2 hrs.; fare from Schramml's Inn to Gössl and back, including the ferry across the Toplitz-See, 1 fl.). — At the *Ranftmühle*, 20 min. from Gössl, is a picturesque waterfall.

FROM ALT-AUSSEE TO THE GRUNDLSEE, direct, across the *Sattelsteig*, 2 1/2 hrs. (guide 1 1/2 fl., unnecessary). The path (finger-posts) leads to the right from the S.W. end of the Alt-Aussee lake and ascends (for the most part blasted through the rock, but quite safe) the almost vertical *Steigwand* to the (1 1/2 hr.) *Tressensattel* (3140'), whence we survey Aussee and the mountains of the Aussee basin. The path then descends through meadow and wood, passing *Lammersberg* and *Mosern*, and rejoins the road at the W. end of the Grundlsee. An easy ascent of 1 hr. leads from the saddle

98   *II. Route 19.*   HALLSTATT.

to the top of the *Tressenstein* (3985'); equally attractive but longer (2½ hrs.; path marked) is the ascent of the *Trisselwand* (5815').
   Ascent of the *Pfeifer-Alm* or *Pfeiferin* (1½ hr. from Aussee), and of the *Sarstein* (5 hrs.; p. 99), interesting. — The **Zinken** (6090') is an attractive ascent of 3½ hrs. (with guide) from the railway-station (path marked with red). — The exploration of the **Todte Gebirge** is interesting but attended with fatigue. From the Ladner Inn (p. 97), we may ascend to the *Grosse Lahngang-See* (5100'; club-hut) in 3 hrs. with guide; thence past the *Kleine Lahngang-See* to (1 hr.) the shooting-box in the *Elmgrube* and the (¾ hr.) *Etm-See* (5420'); then across the plateau to (4½ hrs.) the summit of the *Grosse Priel* (8250'; a fatiguing ascent), and down to *Stoder* (comp. p. 390; guide 10 fl.). — From Gössl to Hinterstoder over the *Salzsteig* (8-9 hrs.; guide 8 fl.), an interesting route: we cross the *Schneckenhöhe* and enter the *Salzathal*, ascend the *Salzsteig* to the *Oedernalm*, cross the *Oedernthörl* (5210') to the *Gross-See* and the *Tauplitz-Alm*, on the picturesque *Steyrer See*, and reach the *Schwarzsee* (see p. 391), where the route joins that from Klachau viâ Tauplitz.
   Railway from Aussee to *Steinach* and *Selzthal*, see pp. 392, 393.

19. From Ischl to Hallstatt, and to Abtenau and Golling viâ Gosau.

Comp. Map, p. 112.

   RAILWAY to (12½ M.) *Hallstatt* station in 40-50 minutes. — STEAMBOAT between the station and town of Hallstatt in 10 min., in connection with each train (fare 30, return 50 kr.). Railway-tickets may be obtained including the ferry to the town of Hallstatt (railway and steamboat tickets are issued at the post-office in the Hôtel Seeauer). — OMNIBUS between Hallstatt and Gosau-Schmied in summer daily in 2½ hrs.; fare 1½ fl., there and back 2 fl. (leaving Hallstatt at 7.30 a.m. and Gosau-Schmied at 3.30 p.m.). Diligence (3 seats) from *Steg* to *Gosau* (Kirchenwirth) daily in 2½ hrs.; fare 1 fl. 20 kr. (leaving Steg at 8 a.m. and Gosau at 5 p.m.). Carriages may be hired in Steg at a house on the right bank of the Traun, opposite the railway-station. — One-horse carr. from *Ischl* to *Hallstatt* in 2½ hrs., 6 fl. 10 kr.; two-horse carr. 10½ fl.; to *Gosau* (Brandwirth) in 3½ hrs., 7 fl. 15 or 12 fl. 30 kr.; to *Gosau-Schmied* in 4 hrs., 8 fl. 15. or 14 fl. 30 kr. (driver's fee included). One-horse carr. to Gosau-Schmied and back, from Hallstatt 8 fl. (incl. fee), from Gosaumühl 6 fl. — DILIGENCE from Gosau to *Abtenau* daily at 10 a.m. (returning at 3.30 p.m.) in 3½ hrs. (1 fl. 70 kr.); from Abtenau to *Golling* daily at 6 a.m. (returning at 11 a.m.) in 3 hrs. (1 fl. 30 kr.); one-horse carr. from Abtenau to Golling 4, two-horse 8 fl., and 1 fl. to the driver.
   Railway from Ischl to (12½ M.) *Hallstatt* station, see pp. 95, 96. The *Hallstätter See* or **Lake of Hallstatt** (1620'), which is 5 M. long and ½-2 M., broad, is bounded on three sides by lofty mountains (E. the Sarstein; S. the Krippenstein, Zwölferkogl, and Hirlatz; W. the Plassen, Gosauhals, and Ramsauer Gebirge). The finest combination of lake and mountain scenery is between Hallstatt and Obertraun. A steamboat conveys travellers to view this part of the lake, without landing, at 8.30 a.m. and 2 p.m. (fare 50 kr.), but only if there are at least 10 passengers, or if ten fares are paid.
   Hallstatt (**Hôtel Seeauer*, R. 1 fl. 20, L. & A. 50 kr.; **Bellevue*, both on the lake; *Restaurant zur Lahn*, with rooms), a long village (1100 inhab., ½ Prot.), confined within very narrow limits between the mountains and the lake, lies at the N.W. end of the latter. In the middle of the village the *Mühlbach* forms a waterfall. The old *Parish*

Church contains an altar in carved wood of the 15th cent.; numerous skulls are preserved in the ossuary. The *Protestant Church* is modern. About ³/₄ M. to the S., on the *Lahn*, a small plain formed by the alluvial deposits of the *Waldbach*, are the *Salt Works*. Hallstatt is so situated that it does not see the sun from 17th Nov. to 2nd Feb.

The *Rudolfsthurm* (2920' above the sea, 1300' above the lake; tickets of admission to the mine obtained here), occupied by the manager of the mine, is reached by a good zigzag path in 1 hr. (horse 3 fl. 50, to the mine 4 fl. 70 kr.).

An inscription by a bench, halfway up, dated 1504, records that the mines were visited in that year by Emp. Maximilian. The little garden in front of the house affords a fine view of the lake. Excavations made since 1810 have brought to light an ancient burial-ground in the vicinity. The graves (of which about 2000 have been opened) are probably those of Celtic salt-miners of the 3rd or 4th cent. B. C. Numerous relics, especially bronze ornaments, have been discovered. The most important of these are now in the cabinet of antiquities at Vienna, and in the Museum Francisco-Carolinum at Linz.

The mining-offices and the entrance to the *Hallstatt Salt Mine*, 754' above the Rudolfsthurm, are reached in ³/₄ hr. more. A visit to the interior is more fatiguing than to that of the Ischl mine (p. 94; tickets of adm. at the Rudolfsthurm).

Robust walkers may proceed hence (with guide, 1 fl.) across the hill and down the *Gangsteig* (steep but perfectly safe) to the (1 hr.) Waldbach-Strub. — Path by the brine-conduit from the Rudolfsthurm to the (1¹/₄ hr.) Gosau-Zwang, see p. 100.

The *Waldbach-Strub*, in the beautiful *Echernthal*, 1 hr. to the S.W. of Hallstatt, is precipitated in three leaps from a height of 330' through a cleft in the rocks. The path leads to the right from the Lahn (see above), passes (¹/₂ hr.) *Lackner's Inn* and the (10 min.) *Binderwirth*, and ascends steeply, latterly by a flight of steps, to (18 min.) a point of view opposite the fall. The *Schleier Fall*, of about equal height, descends into the same abyss. Both are insignificant in dry seasons. — About 1 hr. farther up is the *Waldbachursprung* (2955), a point of no great interest, reached by a rough path. — A picturesque path ('Malersteig') leads along the right bank of the Waldbach from Lackner's Inn (see above) to the Lahn and back to Hallstatt.

MOUNTAIN ASCENTS (guides, *M. Fischer*, *V. Riezinger*, *Franz Rott*, *Alois Scheutz*, *M. Schupfer*, *Al. Wimmer*, *P. Zavner*). **Steingrabenschneid** (or *Schneidkogel*, 5055') bridle-path in 3 hrs.; guide (2 fl.) not indispensable; fine view of the Dachstein, the Hallstätter See, Traunthal, etc. — **Plassen** (6405'); steep ascent of 2¹/₂ hrs. from the salt-mine viâ the *Schiechling-Alpe* (guide 3 fl.); magnificent view, particularly of the Dachstein range towering immediately to the S., the Alps of Salzburg and Styria, and the valleys of the Traun and the Gosau. The descent may be made by the *Schreier-alp* and the *Rossalp* to (3 hrs.) *Gosau*. — The **Hierlatz** (*Feuerkogl*; 6430'), ascended by the *Wiesalp* (p. 100) and the deserted *Hierlatz-Alpe* in 5¹/₂ hrs., and the **Zwölferkogl** (6490'), ascended in 5¹/₄ hrs., command striking views of the Hallstätter See (guide 3 fl.). — The **Sarstein** (6375'; 4¹/₂–5 hrs.; guide 3 fl.) is best ascended from Obertraun by the *Hüttelalp* and the (3¹/₂ hrs.) *Vordere Sarstein-Alp* (5510'); we then mount the broad rounded back of the mountain (*Steinhüttelgrat*) to the (¹/₂ hr.) *Hohe Sarstein-Alp*, and thence to the (³/₄ hr.) summit. View one of the most extensive in the Salzkammergut. The ascent may also be made from the *Pötschenstrasse* (p. 95) viâ the *Niedere Sarstein-Alp* or *Scharten-Alp* (easiest route), or from Aussee (p. 96) viâ the *Pfeiferin* and the *Brand-Alpe*. — **Krippenstein** (6905'; 6 hrs.; guide 3 fl.), another fine point. From Obertraun we cross the Traun by the *Köhlerbrücke* to the S., and ascend to the right to the (2½ hrs.) *Untere Schafeck-Alpe* (3940'), and the (20 min.) *Obere Schafeck-Alpe* (4430'). We then proceed through the *Krippengasse* to the (³/₄ hr.) *Krippenbrunnen* (5085') and the (½ hr.) *Krippeneck* (5700'), turn sharply to the left, round the *Niedere Krippenstein*, and reach (1½ hr.) the summit of the *Hohe Krippenstein*, which affords an excellent survey of the Dachstein range. About 20 min. to the W. of the Krippeneck lies the *Gjaidalpe* (about 5900'). To the S. of it a path marked with stakes crosses the Stein and the *Feisterscharte* to the *Ramsau* (see p. 396; guide to Schladming 7 fl.). — **Hohe Gjaidstein** (9140'; 7½ hrs.; guide 7 fl.), another fine point: ascent from the (4 hrs.) *Gjaidalpe* (see above) viâ the *Taubenkogl* and *Niedere Gjaidstein* in 3½ hrs. (or from the *Simony Hut*, mentioned below, in 2½-3 hrs.).

The **Hohe Dachstein** (9830'), the second highest peak of the N. Limestone Alps (Parseier Spitze 9910', Zugspitze 9710'), is usually ascended from Hallstatt (9-10 hrs.; trying; guide 10, with descent to Schladming 15, to Gosau 13 fl.; to the Simony Hut 5 fl.). The route (bridle-path) leads through the *Echernthal*, and ascends rapidly to the (4 hrs.) *Wiesalpe* (5480') and the (³/₄ hr.) *Ochsenwiesalpe* (6000'), which is occupied in summer only; then across the *Ochsenwieshöhe* and through the *Wildkar* to the (1½ hr.) *Simony Hut* (7250'), erected by the Austrian Alpine Club. The hut lies on the margin of the *Karls-Eisfeld* or *Hallstatt Glacier*, which descends from the Dachstein to the N.E. between the Hohe Kreuz and the Gjaidstein, and affords an admirable view of the Dachstein group. From the hut we cross the glacier, which seldom presents any difficulty, to the (2 hrs.) foot of the Dachsteinwand (fine view from the 'Dachsteinwarte'), follow the new path, which avoids the 'Randkluft' (formerly the most difficult point) by a circuit to the left, and lastly mount by means of iron pegs driven into the rock and with the aid of a wire-rope, to the (1-1¼ hr.) summit. Superb view, embracing the Schneeberg, Terglou, Kanin, Tauern, Stubaier Ferner, and the Bohemian Forest. Ascent from *Gosau*, see p. 101; from *Schladming*, see p. 396.

The road from HALLSTATT TO GOSAU skirts the lake to (2 M.) *Gosaumühl* (*Inn), about (2 M. to the N.W. of *Steg* (p. 96), at the mouth of the *Gosaubach*. [Pedestrians should take the more interesting *Soolenleitungsweg*, or path by the brine-conduit, which leads from the Rudolfsthurm along the mountain-slope, with a constantly varying view of the lake; at the Gosau-Zwang, 1½ hr. from Gosaumühl, it joins the road.] At the Gosau Mill the road turns to the W., passes under the *Gosau-Zwang* (an aqueduct, 146 yds. long and 140' high at the highest part, by which the salt-water conduit crosses the valley), and ascends the narrow wooded ravine of the *Gosau-Bach*. Near the long village of (6 M.) **Vorder-Gosau** (2510'; *Brandwirth; *Kirchenwirth*) the valley expands. An imposing background is formed towards the S. by the barren and precipitous pinnacles of the *Donnerkogeln* (6730 ft.).

The carriage-road ends at the (3 M.) *Gosau-Schmied* (2490'; *Inn) in *Hinter-Gosau*. We now ascend on foot through the wood to the (³/₄ hr.) beautiful green ***Vordere-Gosau-See** (2980'), 1 M. long, ¼ M. broad, surrounded by woods (small tavern at the sluice). To the S.E., in the background, towers the lofty Dachstein with the two Gosau Glaciers; to the left the Hohe Kreuz, to the right the Thorstein and Donnerkogeln. Rowing to the S. end of the lake (30 kr.), or walking round by the S. bank, we next ascend by a steep and stony path, passing the *Gosaulacke*, to the (1½ hr.) light-green *Hintere Gosau-See* (3790'), a lakelet about half the size of the Vordere See, grandly and wildly situated. To the left rise the slopes of the Gschlösskogel, to the right the Kopfwand, and in the background the huge Thorstein.

At the upper end of the latter lake lies the *Hintere Seehütte Alp*. The path on the S. bank, crossing rocky debris (1½ hr.), is fatiguing (better to take a boat). About 1½ hr. above the lake (path steep at places), 5 hrs. from the Gosau-Schmied, we reach the *Grobgestein Hütte* (5410'), built by the Austrian Alpine Club, the starting-point for the Dachstein and the Thorstein (both difficult). Ascent of the **Hohe Dachstein** (two guides, 10 fl. each): from the hut a laborious ascent of 2 hrs. to the *Great Gosau Glacier*; we then mount the snowy terraces of the glacier, in which there are several large crevasses, to the (1½ hr.) *Obere Windlucke* (8860'), between the Mitterspitze and the Dachstein, and follow the W. arête to the (1 hr.) summit (see above). — Ascent of the **Thorstein** (9605'), 4½ hrs. (guide 12 fl.): to the (2 hrs.) *Gosau Glacier* as above; here we turn to the right and ascend between the Mitterspitze and Thorstein to the (1½ hr.) *Untere Windlucke* (8990'), where we turn to the right and ascend round the S. side of the Thorstein, by a steep and difficult route, to the (1 hr.) summit. °View remarkably imposing and picturesque. Descent by the *Windleger Scharte* (about 7550') to Filzmoos or to Ramsau, rather steep (comp. p. 396). — Guides at Gosau: *Mich. Gamsjäger, Jos. Sam. Höhenegger* and *Chr. Urstöger*, all at the Gosau-Schmied; *G. Gapp*, at the Brandwirth's.

From the Vordere See a somewhat toilsome but interesting path (constructed and marked by the Austrian Alpine Club) leads over the *Scharwandalpen*, the *Armkaar*, and the (3½ hrs.) **Steigl** (6900'), between the *Bischofsmütze* and the *Gosauer Stein*, down to the (1 hr.) *Hofer Alp*, 3½ M. by road from *Filzmoos* (p. 397).

From Gosau to Abtenau, 13 M. From Vorder-Gosau the carriage road ascends for nearly 3 M. to the *Pass Gschütt* (3185'; Inn), the boundary between the Salzkammergut and the district of Salzburg. View of the Tennengebirge to the W., and of Gosau with the Donnerkogeln to the S. E. The road now descends to (2¼ M.) *Russbachsag* (2660'; Inns), at the foot of the *Gamsfeld* (6640'), which may be ascended hence, viâ the *Andenkar Alp*, in 3 hrs. (path marked in red; extensive view); the rocky gorge on the N. side is named the *Wilde Kammer*. From Russbachsag the road continues through the *Russbachthal*, a valley abounding in fossils, to the (5 M.) *Lammerbrücke*, passing on the left the road to the Handlhof (p. 102), and then ascends to (3 M.) **Abtenau** (2335'; *°Post; Rother Ochs*), a large village, near which are the pretty *Schwarzbach Falls*.

The route over the *°Zwiesel Alp* (5195') is, however, far preferable to the above-mentioned road (from Vorder-Gosau to Abtenau 6 hrs.; ascent of the Zwiesel Alp from Vorder-Gosau 3, from the Gosau-Schmied 2¼ hrs.; guide 30 kr. per hr.; to Abtenau 3 fl.; chair-porters to the Zwiesel Alp 11 fl.). The bridle-path from Vorder-Gosau, indicated by finger-posts and red marks, diverges to the right from the road to the Gosau-Schmied at (20 min.) the last houses, and ascends gradually, chiefly through wood, latterly affording fine views of the Gosau-Thal, the lakes, and the Dachstein. At the foot of the peak, beyond an enclosure, the path to the right leads to the *Ed-Alp* (see below) and approaches the summit from the N.W.; the path to the left, ascending on the E. side, is shorter and steeper. — From the Gosau-Schmied our path (indicated by red marks) ascends to the right through wood by a finger-post, 20 min. on the way to the Gosau Lake, and can hardly be mistaken (2 hrs.). Or we may ascend direct from the Vorder-See, passing close below the Donnerkogeln (2 hrs.; this path also indicated by red marks). At the top are a table and bench. To the N. W., $1/4$ hr. from the top, is the *Ed-Alp* (*Inn). The Zwiesel Alp is one of the favourite points of view in the Salzkammergut. The panorama is grand and picturesque, but as little water is visible it is inferior to that from the Schafberg (p. 103).

"VIEW. To the S., in the distance, immediately behind the Donnerkogeln, rises the Hochalpenspitze, then the Tauern chain, and the conspicuous Gross-Glockner, with its snow-fields; adjoining it is the Wiesbachhorn; to the right, through an opening, the Gross-Venediger is partly visible. To the S. W., in the foreground, the Tennengebirge; more to the left, the Uebergossene Alp and the Hochkönig. To the W. the Hohe Göll; to the right, rather more distant, the long Untersberg. To the E., above the Gosau-Thal, rises the Dachstein, with the Gosau glaciers; far below lie the Gosaulacke and the small green Hintere Gosau-See. From the slope, a few hundred paces to the E., an admirable survey is obtained of the Vordere Gosau-See.

To the PINZGAU. Travellers bound for the *Pinzgau* proceed to the W. in $1/2$ hr.(to the three chalets below the summit of the Zwiesel Alp. Marked path thence in 2 hrs. to *Annaberg* (2550'; Larbacher; Post), whence a road leads by (6 M.) *St. Martin* (Inns) to (7$1/2$ M.) *Hüttau* (p. 397).

To FILZMOOS (5$1/2$-6 hrs.). From the Zwiesel Alp an attractive but laborious path (guide advisable) leads round the W. side of the *Donnerkogeln* to the (1$1/2$ hr.) *Stuhlalp* (4500'), which affords a fine view of the Tauern. It then crosses the *Stuhllochhöhe* (5250') to the (2 hrs.) *Sulzkaralpe*, whence we proceed viâ the *Hackelplatten* (4830') to the (1 hr.) *Anaipe* and (1 hr.) *Filzmoos* (p. 397). — The *Grosse Donnerkogel* (6730') may be ascended from the Zwiesel Alp in 2 hrs., with guide.

FROM THE ZWIESEL ALP TO ABTENAU (3 hrs.). The path descends from the Ed-Alp (see above) to the depression on the N.W., leaving the fence to the right. Beyond the meadows straight in front, it turns to the left and follows the guide-posts, passing at first through wood, beyond which ($3/4$ hr.) we obtain a fine view of the Lammer-Thal, with the Tennengebirge and Uebergossene Alp to the W. Then past three farms to a ($3/4$ hr.) bridge over the *Lammer*. We may now either cross the bridge and follow the Annaberg road to (4$1/2$ M.) *Abtenau*; or, without crossing, follow the cart-track to the right to the (1$1/2$ M.) *Hôtel-Pension Zwieselbad-Handlhof*, with a mineral spring and baths, in a quiet and sheltered situation (good quarters for travellers; carriages; two-horse carriage to Golling 10 fl.). The road hence to (3$1/2$ M.) Abtenau descends the course of the Lammer and reaches the Gosau road (p. 101) at the influx of the Russbach. (From Abtenau to the Zwiesel Alp, guide advisable, 2$1/2$ fl.)

FROM ABTENAU TO GOLLING (11 M.; diligence and carriages, see p. 98). The new road ascends gradually to the N.W. to *Döller-*

hof and (1½ M.) *Mühlrain* and then descends into the deep and prettily wooded valley of the *Schwarzbach*, which it crosses close to its junction with the *Lammer* (1½ M.). We then follow the left bank of the latter, passing (¼ M.) the Voglau Inn, opposite the farm-houses of *Pichl* (right bank). The valley contracts and is shut in by lofty wood-clad cliffs. ¾ M. Finger-post indicating the way (to the right) to the (5 min.) **Aubach Fall*, which descends over a rocky wall in three stages from a height of 330' (20 kr.). About 1 M. farther on, to the right, below the road, is the *St. Veit's Bridge*, which affords a fine view of the wild Lammeröfen. [A path, protected by a rail, descends into the gorge, but is not recommended to those inclined to giddiness.] The road now descends to (1 M.) the *Lammerbrücke*, where we meet the steep old road, descending on the left from the *Strubberg* (Brückenwirth, on the right bank). Crossing the river here, the road follows the right bank to (3 M.) *Scheffau* and (3 M.) *Golling* (p. 84).

At the point (½ M. before Golling) where the road leaves the *Lammer*, a path to the left crosses the fields to a bridge over which the Salzburg and Gastein road passes. This bridge is about ½ M. from the entrance to the *Oefen* (p. 85), which the traveller not proceeding farther S. should now visit, instead of going first to Golling, and thus save 1 hr. — From Scheffau to the top of the *Schwarzberg*, see p. 86.

20. From Ischl to Salzburg viâ St. Gilgen. Schafberg.
Comp. Maps, pp. 88, 68.

34 M. POST-OMNIBUS to Strobl in summer daily at 9.30 a.m. in 1½ hr., fare 90 kr.; from Strobl by STEAMBOAT to St. Gilgen in 50-60 min. (1 fl.); POST-OMNIBUS from St. Gilgen to Salzburg in 4½ hrs. (at 12.45 p.m., arriving at 5.15 p.m.), fare 3 fl. (From Salzburg at 7 a.m., arr. at St. Gilgen at 11.30 a.m., Strobl 2.40, Ischl 4.10 p.m.) — CARRIAGES, see p. 92. — STEAMBOAT from Strobl to St. Gilgen four times a day in 1 hr. (to St. Wolfgang in 14 min.).

No traveller should quit the Salzkammergut without having visited the **Schafberg*, one of the finest points of view in the Austrian Alps. It is usually ascended from Ischl viâ St. Wolfgang; but the ascents from St. Gilgen and Scharfling are easier, and that from Unterach (see p. 106) more interesting. *Guide* from St. Wolfgang to the summit 2½ fl. (incl. 17 lbs. of luggage); across the Schafberg to St. Gilgen or Scharfling 3 fl. 20 kr.; bed in the Schafberghaus 70 kr. Chair (4 bearers) 14 fl.; horse or mule 9 fl., across the Schafberg to St. Gilgen 10 fl. 40 kr., to Scharfling 11 fl. 45 kr. Similar charges from St. Gilgen, Scharfling, and Unterach.

The Ischl and Salzburg road follows the right bank of the *Ischl*, a brook descending from the Lake of St. Wolfgang, to (1½ M.) *Pfandl* (Inn). Beyond the bridge the direct road to (8 M.) St. Wolfgang, viâ *Russbach* and *Schwarzenbach*, diverges to the right. Near (3 M.) *Aigen* (Wacht Inn), the road returns to the right bank. Farther on we pass *Weinbach*, with a large paper-mill, on the right. — 4½ M. **Strobl** (**Hôtel am See*, R. & L. 1 fl. 20 kr.; *Post* or *Platzl*), at the E. end of the *St. Wolfgang-See* (see p. 107). A road leads hence to the N., round the *Pürglstein*, and then along the N. bank of the lake to (4½ M.) St. Wolfgang, but it is preferable to proceed thither by steamer.

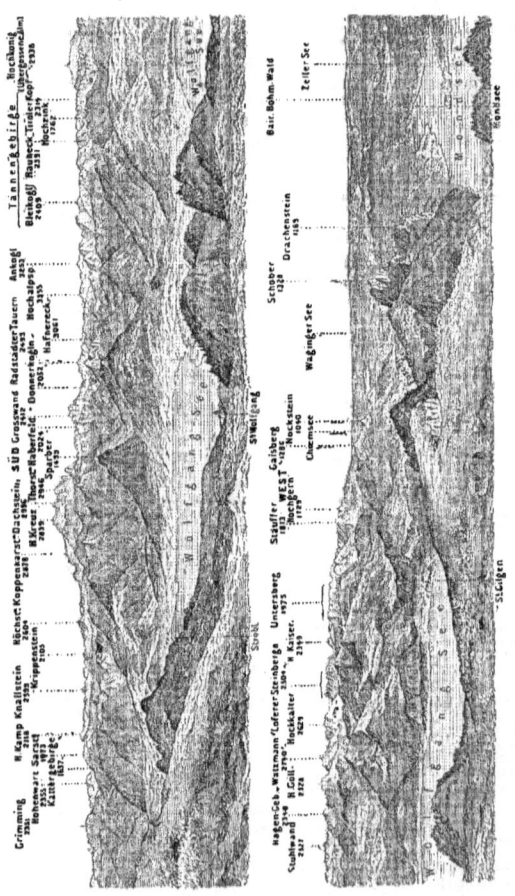

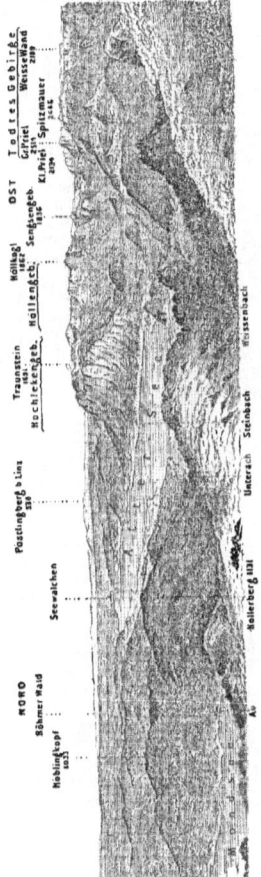

St. Wolfgang (*Hotel-Pension Peterbräu*, in an elevated situation facing the lake; *Drassl zum Weissen Ross*, at the steamboat-quay; *Schader's Gasthof zum Touristen*, well spoken of; *Kortisenbräu*, at the W. end of the village; *Hirsch*, *Weisser Bär*, plain; *Restaurant Peterbräu*, on the lake, moderate), a considerable village, prettily situated on the lake of that name, is frequented as an Alpine healthresort and summer-retreat (pleasant lake-baths). The Gothic church contains a winged *Altarpiece, carved in wood by *M. Pacher* in 1481, with old German paintings (by Wohlgemuth?) on the wings. In the entrance-court is a fountain with good reliefs, cast at Passau in 1515.

Fine view of the lake from the garden of *Dr. Zach* (adm. on Tues. and Frid.). — Pleasant walks to the (10 min.) *Lighthouse*, the *Cyclamenwiese* (*Steins-Ruhe*; 1/4 hr.), the *Dietlbach-Wildniss* (20 min.; p. 106), etc. — A pleasant excursion (3 1/2-4 hrs., with guide) may be taken by the *Holzbauer* to the (1 1/2 hr.) *Schwarze See*, at the S. base of the Schafberg, then across the moor to the (1 hr.) *Holzstuben*, and thence either to (1 1/4 hr.) *Unter-Burgau*, or through the *Burggraben* to (1 1/4 hr.) *Unterach* on the Attersee (p. 109).

The *Schafberg (5840' above the sea-level, 65' lower than the Rigikulm), an isolated mass of Alpine limestone, rising between the St. Wolfgang-See, the Mond-See, and the Attersee, commands one of the finest and most picturesque views among the German Alps. There are four routes to the summit, starting respectively from St. Wolfgang, St. Gilgen, Scharfling, and Unterach (see p. 103). Guides are not indispensable on the first three of these routes, but they will be found useful in carrying baggage (tariff, see p. 103).

Ascent of the Schafberg from St. Wolfgang (3-3½ hrs.; route mostly in shade in the morning; marked with blue and not to be missed). Starting from the (5 min.) Kortisen-Garten, at the W. end of the village, we proceed in a straight direction for 3 min. and then ascend to the right. Avoiding (10 min.; finger-post) the path diverging to the left to the *Dietlbach-Wildniss* (a mill in a gorge), we follow the path to the right, and after 4 min. descend a little to the left, passing a house, to (5 min.) a bridge. Hence a steep ascent leads up in 8 min. to the highest farm (Grabnerbauer). At the division of the paths (6 min.), we follow the bridle-path to the left. ¼ hr. Bridge in a stony ravine; 8 min. Bench on the saddle, a little beyond which is a clearing affording a fine view of the St. Wolfgang-See; ¼ hr. Bench, where we turn to the right; 5 min. Bridge, where we ascend to the right, along the enclosure, to the (5 min.) *Dorner Alp* (3130'). Farther on we mount a fatiguing flight of wooden steps through the wood and finally ascend the bare slopes in zigzags to the chalets of the (1 hr.) *Obere Schafbergalp* (4795'), where on the right is *Aschinger's Inn*, at the base of the highest peak. (Magnificent view to the W.; the Thorstein, Hochkönig, Hohe Göll, Watzmann, and Untersberg.) Thence to the summit 1 hr. more. *Grömmer's Inn* at the top (R. 1-2 fl.).

Ascent from St. Gilgen (3½ hrs.; new path, available for vehicles as far as the Upper Alp; guide unnecessary). We follow the Mondsee road on the W. side of the lake to (1½ M.) *Winkel* (p. 108), leave it at a lime-tree with benches (finger-post), and ascend to the right to (5 min.) the *Reithberger Inn*. A few paces farther on we avoid a cart-track descending to the right (to Fürberg, see p. 108), and ascend the steep path (with red marks) to the left. After ¼ hr. a glimpse of the St. Wolfgang-See is obtained. Farther on the path ascends in windings through the wood to the (½ hr.) *Untere Schafbergalp* (3180'; water bad). We then ascend in a straight direction, and afterwards again in windings through woods to the (1 hr.) *Obere Schafbergalp* (see above).

Ascent from Scharfling (p. 109; 3¼ hrs.; guide, 4 fl., unnecessary; horse, kept overnight, 9 fl.). We follow the St. Gilgen road (p. 108) to the S., ascending through wood past the small *Eylsee*. After 1 M. (finger-post) we take the good bridle-path to the left, which leads mostly through wood, past the *Elisabethhöhe* (pretty view of the Mondsee), to the (¾ hr.) *Kesselalpe* (Rfmts.), where we have a view of the Krotensee and St. Gilgen. In about 40 min. more the path emerges from the wood, and skirts the mountain-slope to the right to the (½ hr.) *Obere Schafbergalp*, where it joins the routes described above.

Ascent from Unterach (p. 109; 3½-4 hrs.; the finest route, recommended to experts; guide advisable). We follow the Mondsee road to ($^1/_2$ M.) a guide-post indicating a path leading over a bridge to the left, and ascending the right bank of the Ache through fine wood. Where the path forks ($^3/_4$ M.), we take the branch to the left (the footpath to the right leads to the Mondsee, p. 109), and follow the red marks on the trees to (1$^1/_2$-2 hrs.) the *Eisenauer Alpe* (3350'), six chalets at the base of the steep cone of the Scharfberg (refreshments in the third chalet; good spring beside the last). Hence in $^3/_4$ hr. to the *Suissenalm*, above the picturesque little *Grünsee* (almost dry in midsummer); we then ascend again for about 5 min. and skirt the rocks of the Schafberg to the right by an almost level path for 25 min. (fine view of the Attersee and Mondsee). Finally, beyond the *Kaiserquelle*, the path ascends in zigzags and by steps cut in the rock to the *Himmelspforte*, a passage hewn through the rocks of the *Schafloch*, on emerging from which we have a magnificent view of the Dachstein and Hochkönig, previously concealed. A few paces farther on we reach the ($^1/_2$ hr.) *Schafberg Hotel* (p. 106).

The **VIEW from the summit of the Schafberg is little inferior to that from the Rigi. The mountains and lakes of the Salzkammergut, Upper Austria as far as the Bohemian Forest, the Alps of Styria and Salzburg, and the Bavarian plain as far as the Chiemsee and Waginger See are all distinctly visible in clear weather. The fantastic surging of the mists in the valleys sometimes presents a curious sight. The largest sheet of water visible is the Attersee, 12$^1/_2$ M. long, at the N.E. base of the Schafberg; to the right (E.) rises the Höllengebirge, with the Hochgrenseck, Rottenkogl, and Höllkogl; beyond them the Traunstein; then the Kleine and Grosse Priel, Spitzmauer, Hohe Schrott, Grimming, Hoheuwart, Sarstein, and Hochwildstelle; then, on the lake below, the Rettenkogl, Rinnkogl, and Sparber, beyond which towers the huge Dachstein group; next come the Gamsfeld, the peaks of the Donnerkogeln near Gosau, the Radstädter Tauern, Hafnereck, Hochalpspitze, and Ankogl; to the S. the long, indented Tennengebirge, the Hochkönig rising above the Pass Lueg, the Steinerne Meer, the Hohe Göll, Watzmann, Hochkalter, Loferer Steinberge, Hochkaiser, Untersberg, Stauffen, Gaisberg near Salzburg (with the Nockstein, a protuberance on the right), the Fuschlsee, and at the N.W. base of the Schafberg the Mondsee with the perpendicular Drachenstein. Compare the annexed Panorama. — Pleasant walk to the '*Adlerhöhle*', a cavern 120' long, 30' broad, and 30' high, $^1/_4$ hr. from the inn (finger-posts); picturesque view from it of the Attersee, Traunstein, etc.

The **St. Wolfgang - See**, or **Aber - See**, a greenish-blue lake (1800'), 7$^1/_2$ M. long, 1$^1/_4$ M. broad, and 374' deep, is bounded on the N. by the Schafberg, while on the S., beyond the wooded banks, rise the Sparber, Hohe Zinken, Königsberghorn, and other picturesquely-shaped mountains. The banks approaching each other above St. Wolfgang divide the lake into an *Upper* and a *Lower* part. At the narrowest point, $^1/_2$ M. to the W. of St. Wolfgang, at the mouth of the Dietlbach, rises a *Lighthouse*, erected in 1844. About 1 M. beyond it, on the wooded promontory of *Frauenstein*, is the *Villa Cotins*, with its pretty grounds (no admission). At the *Falkenstein*, farther on, there is a fine echo. Farther to the E., on the rocks on the same side, are two crosses. The *Hochzeitskreuz* ('wedding-cross') is to the memory of a wedding party who were amusing themselves on the frozen surface of the lake and were drowned through the breaking of the ice. The *Ochsenkreuz* ('oxcross') commemorates the exploit of a butcher, whose ox became unmanageable and plunged into the lake. The bold butcher followed, and grasping the ox by the tail reached the opposite bank in safety. From the station of *Fürberg* (*Ebner), prettily situated in a wooded bay on the N. bank, a road runs direct to *Winkel* and (3³/₄ M.) *Scharfling*, which is preferable to the road from St.Gilgen (see below). At the W. end of the lake lies **St. Gilgen** (*Post*, with restaurant on the lake; *Kendler*), on the Salzburg road, 15 M. from Ischl.

The ROAD FROM ST. GILGEN TO THE MONDSEE (one-horse carr. to Scharfling. 4¹/₄ M., 2¹/₂-3 fl.), ascends past the handsome *Villa Billroth* to (1¹/₂ M.) *Winkel* (Inn; ascent of the Schafberg, see p. 106). Farther on, on a hill to the right, rises *Schloss Hüttenstein*. Beyond (³/₄ M.) the dark *Krotensee* (Inn), the road rises through wood to (¹/₂ M.) its highest point, at the *Schanzbichl* (1990'), whence it descends in curves to (1¹/₂ M.) *Scharfling* (p. 109).

Beyond St. Gilgen the Salzburg road ascends, commanding a fine retrospect of the lake, and enters a picturesque hilly district. Beyond **Fuschl** (*Mohr, Brunnenwirth*, both unpretending), we reach the small *Fuschlsee* (2170'), and ascend near its S. bank. Pleasing retrospect. On a height by the lake below stands a square castellated château.

From Fuschl through the *Tiefbrunau* to the top of the **Faistenauer Schafberg** (5110'), 4 hrs., interesting and not difficult. Descent to *Faistenau*, and thence viâ *Wiesthal (Almbachstrub)* to (7 hrs.) *Hallein*, see p. 83.

24¹/₂ M. **Hof** (2420'; *Post*). The road descends, and passes the *Nockstein*, a rocky excrescence of the *Gaisberg* (p. 66). On the last height (*Guggenthal*, 2000') before Salzburg are a church and a brewery. To the left, farther on, rises *Schloss Neuhaus*, erected in 1424 by Abp. Eberhard III. von Neuhaus, now the property of Count Thun, by whom it has been restored. The road then skirts the N. base of the Capuzinerberg.

34 M. **Salzburg**, see p. 60.

21. The Attersee and Mondsee.
Comp. Map, p. 88.

RAILWAY from Vöcklabruck to Kammer, 7¹/₂ M., in 33 minutes. STEAMBOAT on the Attersee from *Kammer* to *Unterach* twice daily in summer (8 a.m., and 3 p.m.) in 2 hrs. (fare 1 fl. 60 or 1 fl. 3 kr.); on the Mondsee thrice daily from *See* to *Mondsee* in 1 hr. 10 min. (fare 1 fl. 10 kr.; to *Scharfling* four times daily in 22 min., 62 kr.).

Vöcklabruck, see p. 87. The Attersee line diverges from the Salzburg and Linz railway a little to the W. of Vöcklabruck and skirts the winding Ager. 1³/₄ M. *Pichlwang*. On the left, beyond the finely wooded hills, rise the Traunstein and the Höllengebirge. 5¹/₂ M. *Siebenmühlen*, so called from the seven mills in the *Au*, to the left. The train now crosses the Ager.

7¹/₂ M. **Kammer**, a pleasant village, with lake-baths and promenades, and a château of Count Khevenhüller, lies on a promontory at the N. end of the Attersee, and commands a charming view (*Hôtel Kammer*, with baths, R., L., & A. 1¹/₂ fl.; *Traube*, plain, well spoken of; *Miltendorfer-Keller*, pretty view; lodgings at the château and at several villas).

The ***Attersee**, or **Kammersee** (1525'), $12^1/_2$ M. in length, 1-2 M. in breadth, and 660 ft. in depth, the largest lake in Austria, is bounded by picturesque mountains at the S. end. To the right the finely-shaped Schafberg rises immediately from the water; to the left is the broad range of the Hochlecken and Höllen-Gebirge, stretching towards the Traunsee.

The steamer, leaving *Seewalchen* (good Inn) to the right, crosses the lake diagonally to *Attersee* (*Hôtel Attersee), charmingly situated at the foot of the *Buchberg*, with a pretty and conspicuous church. On the opposite bank lies *Weyeregg* (Post), a village on the site of an ancient Roman settlement. On the W. bank we next touch at *Nussdorf* and *Dexelbach*, and on the E. at *Steinbach* (Inn), prettily situated at the foot of the Hochlecken-Gebirge.

FROM STEINBACH TO THE LANGBATH LAKES (3 hrs.), a pleasant excursion. The route leads round the N. side of the Hochlecken-Gebirge to ($^3/_4$ hr.) *Unterfeicht* and ($^1/_2$ hr.) the *Untere Klause*. Then past a hut and over the *Aurachkar* to the *Taferl* (or *Obere*) *Klause*; thence to the right over the *Spielberg* or over the *Grosse Alpe* (*Inn) to the ($1^1/_4$ hr.) *Hinter-See* (p. 91). This is the shortest way from the Attersee to the Traunsee, but should not be attempted in wet weather.

The steamer now steers close to the precipitous rocks at the upper end of the lake, and touches at **Weissenbach** (*Post), whence a road leads through the sequestered *Weissenbach-Thal*, between the Höllengebirge and the Leonsberg, to (9 M.) *Milter-Weissenbach* (p. 92; omnibus to Ischl daily; see p. 95). The steamer now coasts the pine-clad *Breitenberg* to *Burgau* (*Loidl's Inn, with interesting fish-ponds) and —

Unterach (**Goldnes Schiff*; **Zur Post*, with restaurant on the lake), a summer-resort, beautifully situated at the mouth of the *Ache*.

A pleasant walk may be taken along the lake by the *Kaiserin-Elisabeth-Allée* to the ($^3/_4$ hr.) *Kaiserbrunnen* and ($^1/_4$ hr.) the *Burggraben-Rechen*, and thence to (25 min.) *Burgau* and (40 min.) *Weissenbach* (see above). [A finger-post near the Burggraben-Rechen points out the narrow path, hewn in the rock and protected by a railing, which leads to the (20 min.) romantic *Burgau-Klamm*, with a waterfall.] — Ascent of the *Schafbery* from Unterach ($3^1/_2$-4 hrs.), see p. 108.

The road from Unterach to the Mondsee (omnibus in $1/_2$ hr.; also beautiful path through the woods) follows the left bank of the Ache, through the *Au*, and reaches ($2^1/_2$ M.) the steamboat-station *See* (*Inn), at the E. end of the **Mondsee** (1570'). The Schafberg here rises abruptly from the lake; opposite us is the Drachenstein, and beyond it the Schober. The lake is 7 M. long and $1^1/_4$ M. broad, and is bounded on the N. by wooded hills of moderate height. The steamboat first calls at *Pichl* (*Hôtel Anhof, R. from 80 kr.), situated in a small bay on the N. side of the picturesque lake, and then crosses to **Scharfling** (**Wesenauer*), the landing-place for the Schafberg and St. Gilgen (p. 108). The next station is *Blomberg*, on the S. bank. Retrospect of the imposing Schafberg, in the background the Höllengebirge; to the left the Drachenstein, through which an aperture is seen near the top, then the double-peaked Schober.

Mondsee (*Post; *Krone; Traube; Adler; *Hôtel Königsbad*, on the lake, ½ M. below the village), a thriving place (1500 inhab.), with a large church and a number of country-seats, prettily situated at the W. end of the lake, attracts numerous visitors in summer. Beautiful walks on the banks of the lake. The *Mariahilf Chapel* (8 min.) affords the best survey of the lake.

Excursions (guides, *Rauchenschwandtner* and *Darnhofer*). Ascent of the **Kulmspitze** (3590'), viâ the *Stabau*, in 2-2½ hrs., easy and interesting (admirable view; new belvedere). — **Kollmanns** (or *Colomans*) **Berg** (3058'), 3 hrs., ascended by a pilgrims' path passing the (2½ hrs.) *Schernthaner* (3135'); fine view of the Salzburg Alps, but obstructed by trees. — The **Schober** (4350'; 3½ hrs., with guide) requires a steady head: steep ascent by the so-called *Drahtzug* to the (2½-3 hrs.) ruin of *Wartenfels*, a good point of view; then by a rocky path to the top. The descent may be made to Fuschl (p. 108). — **Drachenstein** (3885'), from Blomberg (p. 109), in 3 hrs., with guide, rather fatiguing. — The **Höllkar** (3895'), easy and well worth the effort, may be ascended in 2½ hrs. (path indicated by green marks) from *Wichlafen*, on the road between Blomberg and Scharfling; or direct through the *Zepezau*, in 2½-3 hrs., by another easy path.

To **Strasswalchen** (p. 87), a station on the Linz and Salzburg railway; post-omnibus in 2½ hrs., starting at 5 and 11.30 a.m. (fare 1 fl.). The road passes the picturesque *Zeller-See* or *Irr-See* (1750'). 3 M. *Zell am Moos* (Bahn). Pleasing retrospect from the height at the end of the lake. At *Oberhofen* the road crosses the railway and proceeds to the left to *Irrsdorf* and Strasswalchen.

To **Salzburg** post-omnibus daily at 1 p.m., in 4¼ hrs., viâ *Thalgau* (fare 1 fl. 35 kr., including gratuity).

III. THE GISELA RAILWAY. THE HOHE TAUERN.

22. From Salzburg to Wörgl 112
    The Blühnbachthal, 113. — Hochkönig. Hochkail. Dientner Schneeberg. Hochgründeck, 113. — The Liechtensteinklamm. The Grossarlthal and Kleinarlthal, 114. — From Schwarzach to Dienten viâ Goldegg. Heukaareck, 115. — Kitzlochklamm, 116. — The Zeller See, 117. — Schmittenhöhe. The Pinzgauer Spazierweg, 117. — The Glemmthal. Excursions from Saalfelden. Kühbühel. Lichtenberg, etc., 118. — The Steinerne Meer, 118. — Breithorn. Schönfeldspitze, etc., 119. — The Urslauthal. Hochkönig. Birnhorn. Spielberg, 119. — From Fieberbrunn to Waidring viâ St. Jacob im Haus, 119.

23. The Gastein Valley 120
    Gamskarkogl. Türchlwand,121. — Excursions from Wildbad Gastein. Windischgrätzhöhe. Kötschachthal. Graukogl. Tisch. Kreuzkogl. Böckstein and the Nassfeld, 123, 124. — The Anlaufthal. Over the Hochtauern to Mallnitz. Ankogl, 124. — From Gastein to Rauris across the Bockhart-Scharte or the Riffel-Scharte, 125. — To Ober-Vellach over the Mallnitzer Tauern, 126.

24. The Rauris 126
    The Bernkogl, 126. — From Rauris to Heiligenblut over the Heiligenbluter Tauern, 127. — Excursions from Kolm Saigurn, Herzog Ernst, Schareck, 127. — Sonnblick, Hochnarr, 128. — From the Rauris Gold Mine to Frägant by the Goldberg-Tauern; to Döllach by the Klein-Zirknitz-Scharte, the Windisch-Scharte, or the Tramer-Scharte, 128.

25. The Fuscher Thal. From Ferleiten to Heiligenblut . 128
    The Hirzbachthal. Imbachhorn, 128. — From Fusch to Kaprun by the Hirzbachthörl, 129. — Excursions from Bad Fusch. Kasereck. Kühkarköpfl. Schwarzkopf, 129. — Excursions from Ferleiten. Durcheckalp. Käferthal, 129. — Trauneralp. Walcheralp. Hochtenn. Wiesbachhorn, etc., 130. — From Ferleiten to Heiligenblut over the Fuscherthörl and the Heiligenbluter Tauern, 130. — Brennkogl. Ferleiten to Heiligenblut over the Pfandelscharte, 131. — From Ferleiten to Heiligenblut over Fuscherkarscharte and Bockkarscharte, 132.

26. The Kaprun Valley 132
    The Mooserboden, 133. — Imbachhorn. Kitzsteinhorn. Schmiedinger. Wiesbachhorn. Riffelthor. Kapruner Thörl, 134.

27. From Zell am See to Krimml. Upper Pinzgau . . . 134
    Gaisstein. Pihapper Spitze, 135. — The Hollersbachthal, 135. — Over the Plenitz-Scharte or the Weisseneckerscharte to Oschlüss. The Habachthal. Wildkogel, 136. — Sulzbach Fall. By the Obersulzbachthal to the Kürsinger Hütte and the Gross-Venediger, 136. — From Krimml to the Ahrnthal by the Krimmler Tauern, 137. — From Krimml to Gerlos over the Pinzgauer Platte, 138.

28. From Lienz to Windisch-Matrei and Prägraten.
    The Iselthal 138
    The Weisse Wand. Hochschober. The Defereggerthal, 138. — Passes from the Defereggerthal to the Isel, Gsies, Rein, and Ahrn Valleys, 139. — Excursions from Windisch-Matrei.

Rottenkogl, 139. — Zunigkopf. Nussingkogl. Gschlöss, 140.
Ascent of the Gross-Venediger from the Prager Hütte, 140. —
From Windisch-Matrei to Mittersill over the Velber Tauern,
141.—Lasörling, 141.—Excursions from Prägraten. Berger-
kogl. Gross-Venediger. Obersulzbach-Thörl. Krimmler
Thörl. Maurerthal. Maurerthörl and Reggenthörl, 141-143.
— From Prägraten to St. Jakob in the Defereggerthal by the
Mullitzthörl or the Bachlenke, 143.—Excursions from the
Umbalthal. Röthspitze. Dreiherrnspitze. Simonyspitze.
Malhamspitze. Daberspitze. Schwarzes Thörl, 144. To
Kasern over the Umbalthörl, 144.

29. From Windisch-Matrei to Kals and Heiligenblut . . 145
From Huben to Kals through the Kalser Thal. From
Uttendorf to Kals through the Stubachthal, 145. — Granat-
spitze. Kalser Tauern, 146. — Excursions from Kals.
Gross-Glockner. Romariswandkopf. Hochschober.
Gornetschamp. Rothenkogel. Muntaniz, etc. 146, 147.

30. From Lienz to Heiligenblut 148
Geiersbühl. Ederplan 149. — The Möllthal. Ragnaschlucht.
Lanza. Polinik, 149. — Schoberthörl, Stellkopf. Pet-
zeck. Stanziwurten, 150. — Excursions from Heiligen-
blut. Franz-Josefs-Höhe. Hofmannshütte. Fuscherkar-
kopf. Sonnenwelleck. Bärenkopf. Hohe Burgstall.
Wiesbachhorn. Johannisberg. Hohe Riffel. Schnee-
winkelkopf. Gross-Glockner. Sandkopf, 151-153. —
From the Glocknerhaus to Kals by the Berger Thörl;
over the Riffelthor to the Kapruner Thal; over the
Obere Oedenwinkelscharte to the Stubachthal, 154. —
From Heiligenblut to the Rauris Gold Mine by the
Fleiss and the Goldzechscharte. Hochnarr, 154.

22. From Salzburg to Wörgl.

119 M. RAILWAY in 5¼-8 hrs. — The *Salzburg-Tyrol Railway*, or *Gisela-
Bahn*, an interesting line through a beautiful mountainous country, constructed in 1873-75, affords communication between Salzburg (and Vienna)
and Innsbruck (but longer by 28 M. than the line viâ Rosenheim, see
RR. 11, 31), and greatly facilitates a visit to the Tauern (RR. 23-30). —
Good railway-restaurants at Bischofshofen and Saalfelden; dinner, at a
charge of 1 fl., will be handed into the carriages at either of these places, if
previously ordered through the guard, — The end-carriage in each train on
the Austrian mountain-railways is generally an open first-class carriage,
with an unimpeded view on every side; second-class passengers may use
this carriage between any two stations by taking a supplementary third-
class ticket ('Ergänzungsbillet') for that distance. For circular tours,
however, travellers are advised to take first-class tickets. (Views generally to the right.)

From Salzburg to (18 M.) *Golling*, see pp. 83, 84. The railway
traverses the broad valley towards the S., passing on the right the
entrance to the *Blüntau-Thal* (p. 75) and on the left that of the
Lammer-Thal (p. 103). It then crosses the *Lammer* and *Salzach*,
passes through a tunnel (1000 yds. long) piercing the *Ofenauer
Berg*, a spur of the Hagengebirge, and again crosses the Salzach by
a slanting iron bridge of 70 yds. span, beyond which it enters the
Pass Lueg (p. 86), a grand defile flanked with huge masses of
rock, piled one above another. 24½ M. *Sulzau* (1660′); 27 M. *Con-*

to Wörgl. WERFEN. *III. Route 22.* 113

cordiahütte, the station for the iron-works of that name on the left bank, at the entrance to the *Blühnbach-Thal*.

A cart-track leads through the Blühnbach-Thal, a favourite haunt of the chamois, on the left bank of the Blühnbach, between the *Imlauer Gebirge* on the left and the *Hagengebirge* on the right, to the (2 hrs.) *Shooting Lodge* (2685'), where, except during the shooting-season, beds and guides may be procured. From the head of the valley (*Tennboden*) fatiguing passes lead to the W. across the *Blühnbach-Thörl* (6670') and the *Mauerscharte* (7140') to the (9 hrs.) *Obersee* (p. 74), and another to the S., over the *Thorscharte*, or *Hintere Urslauer Scharte* (7490'), to (7 hrs.) *Hinterthal*, in the upper *Urslauer-Thal*, and thence either to the right to (3 hrs.) *Saalfelden* (p. 118), or to the left by the *Filzensattel* (p. 119) to *Dienten* and (5½ hrs.) *Lend* (p. 115).

The line follows the right bank, and crosses several torrents. On the left rises the abrupt *Tennengebirge*, with the *Raucheck*. To the right, farther on, romantically perched on a rock 345' above the Salzach, is the well-preserved *Schloss Hohenwerfen*, built in 1076, restored in the 16th cent., and now the property of Count Thun.

29 M. **Werfen**. The important-looking village (**Post*; *Tirolerwirth*) lies on the opposite bank, overlooked by the jagged rocks of the *Uebergossene Alp* (see below). 29½ M. *Pfarr-Werfen*. The valley expands. The train crosses the *Fritzbach* (p. 397), issuing from a narrow gorge, and then the Salzach.

33 M. **Bischofshofen** (1795'; **Rail. Restaurant & Hotel*, R. & L. 1 fl. 20 kr.; **Maier's Inn*, R. 70 kr.; *Böcklinger*), an old village with three churches, is the junction for the upper Ennsthal Railway (R. 71). The (¼ hr.) *Fall of the Geinfeldbach* is easily reached and worth seeing. To the W. rises the *Ewige Schnee* ('perpetual snow') group of mountains, with the *Wetterwand* and *Manndlwand*.

On the plateau of this huge limestone group lies a glacier (*Ewige Schnee* or *Uebergossene Alp*), about 3½ M. long and 2 M. broad, on the S. side of which towers the **Hochkönig* (9640'). The ascent presents no difficulty to experts (guide 7 fl.; Jos. or Joh. Aigner and Ludw. Lercher at Mühlbach, or one of the Mühlbach miners; apply to the Manager). A road leads from the *Mitterberg* station (see below) through the narrow *Mühlbachthal* to (6 M.) **Mühlbach** (2800'; **Neuwirth*), and then ascends to the right, passing some copper-mines, to (6 M.) *Mitterberg* (4965'; Inn; a shorter way from Bischofshofen leads by *Geinfeld*, 3½ hrs. with guide). The mines have been worked from time immemorial; and various prehistoric discoveries (stone and bronze tools, etc.) are exhibited in the house of the Manager. Thence in ¾ hr. to the *Mitterfeld-Alp* (5840'), then by the *Gaitsnase* into the *Ochsenkar*, past the *Manndlwand* (good echo), and between the striking *Thorsäule* (8300') on the right and the *Kleine Bratschenkopf* (8810') on the left, by a path, indicated by red marks, over rocks to (3 hrs.) the glacier. Lastly an ascent of 1 hr. over snow to the summit (refuge-hut). The **Panorama* is extensive and magnificent. Descent to (3½ hrs.) *Hinterthal*, see p. 119. — The **Hochkail* (3736'), ascended from Mitterberg in ¾ hr. (guide not indispensable), commands an admirable view of the Tauern and (E.) the Dachstein. — Another interesting ascent is that of the **Dientner Schneeberg** (6290'), from Mühlbach in 3 hrs. (guide 4 fl.).

The **Hoch-Gründeck* (5964') may be scaled without difficulty in 3 hrs. from Bischofshofen by a new marked path, leading to the E. viâ *Arzberg*. The summit (Inn in summer) affords a splendid view of the entire chain of the Tauern, the Uebergossene Alp, the Hagengebirge, the Tennengebirge, the Dachstein, etc (panorama by A. Baumgartner). We may descend either on the N. W. to (2 hrs.) *Hüttau* (p. 397), or to (2 hrs.) *St. Johann* (p. 114).

BAEDEKER's Eastern Alps. 6th Edit. 8

The line traverses the broad valley, on the left bank of the Salzach; fine retrospect of the bare and jagged peaks and precipices of the Tennengebirge, which form the entire background to the N. 35½ M. *Mitterberg*, at the entrance of the *Mühlbachthal* (see p. 113). 38 M. St. **Johann im Pongau** (1845'; **Pongauer Hof*, at the railway-station; **Post*, R. ³/₄-1 fl.; **Franz Prem*; **Zum Andrä'l*; **Goldnes Kreuz*, the last three with gardens; **Lackner*; *Brückenwirth*; *Schwaiger*, near the church, R. from 60 kr.), a large village, ³/₄ M. from the station, with a fine modern Gothic church and a mineral bath. The situation renders it a suitable place for a stay of some time. — A pretty walk may be taken to the *Rabenkanzel* (¹/₄ hr.).

A very interesting excursion from St. Johann is to the *Liechtenstein Klamm* (on foot there and back 3 hrs.; one-horse carr. from the station in 1 hr., there and back, including a stay of 1½ hr., 2 fl. 20 kr.; two-horse carr. 3 fl. 60 kr.; also omnibus, 80 kr.). The road from the station crosses the Salzach and after ¼ M. the *Wagreiner Bach* (to the right), and passes a chapel. We now follow the Grossarl road (see below), skirting the base of the mountain, to the village of (2 M.) *Plankenau* (*Winkler's Inn*, beyond the village; *Zur Schönen Aussicht*, ¼ M. farther on, on the footpath to the Klamm). The new road (private property; toll 10 kr.) diverges here to the right, passes the deserted foundry of *Oberarl*, and ascends the prettily wooded valley of the *Grossarler Ache*. The road ceases at a (1½ M.) *Restaurant*, 3 min. from the entrance to the Klamm. Crossing the Grossarler Ache, we now enter the wild rocky gorge by a path constructed by the local Alpine Club (adm. 20 kr.). The Ache descends through the gorge in a series of cascades. The path, hewn in the rock in many places, is 970 yds. in length from the entrance of the defile to the tunnel, and is perfectly safe, being a yard wide and provided with a railing. At the end of the first gorge is a huge caldron with rocky sides, 380' high. The path winds round a projecting cliff and enters the second *Gorge*, one of the finest in the Alps, only three or four yards broad, and apparently closed overhead. The path crosses the Ache and leads through a tunnel, beyond which the best view of the gully is obtained, to a *Waterfall*, 175' in height (¼ hr. from the beginning of the gorge). From the end of the gorge the path, which soon loses its attractions, leads in ½ hr. to the very primitive 'Bad', whence it ascends in 25 min. by flights of steps (fine view of another gorge) to the Grossarl road, about ¼ M. from the inn *Zur Wacht* (see below). — A path to the left of the entrance to the Klamm crosses the hill to (1 hr.) stat. Schwarzach.

The *Hochgründeck (5064') may be easily ascended in 3½ hrs. by a marked bridle-path, most of which is in shade (guide not indispensable; mule 5, up and down 7 fl.). Comp. p. 113.

The Grossarl-Thal (20 M. long), the easternmost of the valleys stretching down from the Hohe Tauern mountain-chain to the Salzach, is traversed by a road leading to the left from (³/₄ hr.) *Plankenau* (see above), and passing at a considerable elevation above the Liechtenstein Klamm (footpath through the Klamm, see above), to the (1¼ hr.) picturesque defile of *Stegenwacht* (Inn *Zur Wacht*). Thence it descends steeply to the Ache and continues at first on the left and then on the right bank to (1½ hr.) Grossarl (3020'; *Linsinger*; carriages, and guides). From Grossarl we may easily reach Dorf Gastein by the *Arthörl* (6910') in 4 hrs.; Hof-Gastein in 5½ hrs., with guide, by the *Aigen-Alpe* and the *Schmalzscharte* (7110'); and Bad Gastein in 7-8 hrs. with guide, by the *Bacher-Alpe* and the *Gamskarkogl* (p. 124), or in 6-7 hrs. with guide, by the *Toferer-Alpe* and the *Throneck-Sattel* (6850'). The ascent of the Gamskarkogl (1 hr. from the saddle) may also be conveniently combined with the latter route. — The road proceeds, crossing the Ache several times, to the deserted copper-mines of (2 hrs.) *Hüttschlag* (Inn), and to (³/₄ hr.) *Karteis*

(3655'), at the entrance of a valley of the same name, where it degenerates into a mountain-track. [An interesting expedition (4½ hrs. with guide) may be taken hence viâ the *Kardeis-Alps*, the *Kardeisthörl*, and the *Tappenkar-See*, to *Kleinarl* (see below).] The cart-track continues to ascend to (1 hr.) *Stockham* (4410'), the last farm, and (¼ hr.) the shooting-box of *Lehen am See*. From this point a fatiguing route leads to the W., over the *Kräh-Alp* and the *Murthörl* (7425'), into the *Lungau* (6-7 hrs. to *Rothgülden*, p. 398). Another leads to the S. through the *Schöder-Thal*, past the small *Schöder Lake* and over the *Artscharte* (7385'), to (5½-6 hrs., with guide; Felix Laimböck of St. Johann recommended) the *Etendhütte* in the *Maltathal* (p. 399). An ascent of the *Keeskogel* (9435'), commanding a splendid view, may be easily combined with the latter route.

A road runs eastward from St. Johann viâ (6 M.) *Wagrein* (2740'; °Arlwaldwirth) to (12 M.) *Radstadt* (p. 397). Immediately to the S. of Wagrein opens the **Kleinarl-Thal**, the most westerly valley of the *Niedere Tauern*. This valley is traversed by a road leading past (1½ hr.) *Mitter-Kleinarl* (3325'; °Inn) to the little *Jäger-See*, on which is a shooting-lodge belonging to Prince Liechtenstein. At (1 hr. farther) the innermost recess of the valley the road makes a steep ascent to (1 hr.) the °**Tappenkarsee** (5780'), situated amid magnificent scenery (to *Kardeis*, see above). An easy pass (guide necessary) leads hence to the S.E. across the *Hastloch*, to the N. of the *Klingspitze* (7975'), to the *Zederhauswinkel* in the Lungau (to *Zederhaus* 6¼ hrs., *St. Michael* 3 hrs.; see p. 398).

42 M. *Schwarzach-St. Veit*. The prettily-situated village of **Schwarzach** *(Wallner; Sattlegger)* lies ½ M. to the W. In 1729 the Protestant peasantry and miners held their last meeting here, after which Leopold, Archbishop of Salzburg, issued a decree banishing no fewer than 22,151 'heretics' from his dominions.

The inn, where the peasantry solemnly ratified their league by the ancient custom of dipping their fingers in salt, still contains the table at which the ceremony took place, with a rude painting representing the event. A book on the table bears the inscription: '*Dilexerunt tenebras magis quam lucem. Joan. c. 3, v. 19*'.

The churchyard of *St. Veit* (½ hr.) affords a good survey of the Grosse Wiesbachhorn. — From Schwarzach a road leads to (2 M.) **Goldegg** (2700'; two rustic inns), prettily situated in a fertile plateau, with a small lake and an old château of the extinct knights of Goldegg (partly destroyed by fire in 1747), containing an interesting room with coats-of-arms. The road then leads past the *Lang-See* and the *Scheibling-See*, and through the ravine of the *Dientenbach*, to (10 M.) *Dienten* (p. 119).

Ascent of the °**Heukareck** (6865'; 4 hrs.; guide unnecessary for mountaineers) from Schwarzach recommended. Superb view of the Tauern and the Salzburg Alps.

The train crosses the Salzach, and continues to follow the narrow valley, passing through a tunnel and several cuttings in the rock. It soon crosses the Salzach again and reaches —

47 M. **Lend** (2070'). The village *(*Straubinger*, R., L., & A. 1½ fl.; *Post; Baldauf; Pens. Rieser),* with the old smelting-works of the Rauris and Böckstein mines, lies on the opposite bank. — Road to *Gastein*, see p. 120. Below the village (½ M.) a fine *Waterfall is formed by the *Gasteiner Ache* just before it joins the Salzach. The bridge below the fall forms the boundary between the Pongau and Pinzgau.

Above Lend the line crosses the Salzach twice, in order to avoid the *Eschenauer Plaike* and the *Embacher Plaike* (slopes of loose stones), and then penetrates the *Unterstein*, a spur of slate-rock on the left bank, by a tunnel, 352 yds. long. We then skirt the Salzach and reach (51½ M.) *Rauris-Kitzloch*, at the entrance of the Rauristhal (p. 126), ¾ M. to the E. of Taxenbach (see below).

°**Kitzloch Klamm.** A visit to this magnificent ravine (1½ hr. there and back) is strongly recommended. We cross the Salzach to the '*Restaurant & Pension Embacher*', and then the *Rauriser Ache* (leaving the *Restaurant Taxwirth* to the left), and ascend the right bank of the latter (adm. 20 kr.). At the (15 min.) beginning of the ravine the path crosses to the left bank and leads past a small stalactite grotto to the (8 min.) *Kessel*, into which the *Ache* is precipitated in four leaps from a height of 330 ft. (°*Kitzloch Fall*). We cross the bridge and ascend in zigzags and by wooden steps, passing a projecting platform from which we obtain a good survey of the seething abyss. At the top we turn to the right and pass through three tunnels, one of which is 58 yds. long. Between two of the tunnels is 'Embacher's Schreckbrücke', named after the constructor of the path. The bridge beyond the long tunnel (85 min. from the station) commands a striking view of the chasm, and of the Oedwandspitze in front. From the beginning of the long tunnel we return to the upper end of the wooden steps, where we ascend to the right through two short tunnels, and then descend by a good path to the (¾ hr.) station of Rauris-Kitzloch. (At the entrances to the tunnels are some interesting traces of shaft-cutting, attributed to the Romans.) Or we may pass through the long tunnel and follow a good path, gradually ascending on the right bank of the Ache, to the (½ hr.) *Landsteg* (Inn, primitive) and (1 hr.) the village of *Rauris*. Thence we follow the road leading by *Embach* (3325'; from the pilgrimage-church *Maria im Elend* splendid view of the Pinzgau) to (1¼ hr.) the station of Rauris-Kitzloch.

Immediately beyond Rauris-Kitzloch the train traverses a tunnel (297 yds.) under the Taxenbach Schlossberg. 53 M. **Taxenbach** (2330'; *Taxwirth*; **Post*). The village, on an eminence ¾ M. to the E. (½ M. from the station of Kitzloch), has two castles, the newer of which, below the village, on a rock above the Salzach, is the seat of the district-court.

The valley now expands. To the right, on a hill near (56 M.) *Gries*, is the church of *St. Georgen* (2705'), a fine point of view. On the left the ice-clad *Hochtenn* (11,050') rises from the *Fuscherthal*. The train crosses the Salzach and the *Fuscher Ache*.

59 M. **Bruck** (2470'; **Zum Kronprinzen v. Oesterreich*, at the station; **Gmachl zum Bräu*; **Mayr zum Lukashansl*) lies opposite the entrance to the *Fuscherthal* (see p. 128). To the N.W. (¼ hr.) rises **Schloss Fischhorn*, the property of Prince Liechtenstein, tastefully restored by Schmidt of Vienna, and commanding a fine view of the Zeller See and the Tauern. — The train crosses the Salzach for the last time, traverses the *Zeller Moos*, which has of late been brought under cultivation, and reaches the *Zeller See*, running on an embankment partly built out into the lake.

62 M. **Zell am See** (2475'; **Hôtel Kaiserin Elisabeth*, at the station and on the lake, R. from 1½ fl.; **Krone*, **Hôtel am See*, both on the lake; **Post*; *Bodingbauer*; *Neuwirth*; **Lebzelter*, **Metzger Rupert Schwaiger*, both moderate; *Café Geister*, on the lake; *Pichler*, confectioner), beautifully situated on a peninsula on the W. bank of the lake, is a favourite summer-resort. The choir of

the old church contains interesting sculpture. The Schloss is now occupied by the forestry authorities. During an insurrection in 1626 the Zellers remained faithful to their archbishop, who as a reward for their loyalty permitted them to undertake an annual pilgrimage to Salzburg, at the conclusion of which they were regaled at his expense.

The *Zeller See is $2^1/_2$ M. long, 1 M. broad, and 240' deep. The water is pleasant for bathing (bath-houses; bath 40 kr.). A small steamer plies on the lake, making the round seven times a day (65 kr.). Stations: *Thumersbach* and *Seehäusl* (Restaurant Haring), at the N.W. end of the lake. From Zell to Thumersbach 4 times daily (fare 20 kr.). Small boats may be hired (ferry to Thumersbach 1 pers. 20, 2 pers. 30, 3 pers. 35, 4 pers. 40 kr.; per hour 40, 60, 70, 80 kr.). The finest *View of the environs is obtained from the middle of the lake: to the S. we obtain a striking survey of the Tauern (due S., between Fusch and Kaprun, are the Imbachhorn and the Hochtenn, to the left of which are the Brennkogl and Schwarzkopf, to the right the Bärenkopf, Johannisberg, Hohe Riffel, Grieskogel, Hohe Eiser, and, in the foreground, the beautiful Kitzsteinhorn with the Schmiedinger Kees); to the W., above Zell, extends the broad Schmittener Höhe; N. the Birnhorn group, the Steinerne Meer, with the Kammerlinghorn, Hundstod, Breithorn, and, in the background, the three Mühlsturzhörner; E., at the end of the Thumersbach-Thal, the bald Hundstein. Evening light most favourable; the phenomenon known as the 'Alpglühen' is often witnessed. On the E. bank of the lake lies *Thumersbach* ('Bachler's Restaurant and Inn, with terrace), a favourite resort of boating-parties. At a point about $^1/_4$ M. from the landing-place, between the old maple trees on the left bank of the brook, we obtain a good survey of the environs. — A good view of the lake is afforded by the *Parapluie*, a small pavilion, the way to which ($^3/_4$ hr.) is indicated by a finger-post at the S. end of the village. — The *Rudolfs-Promenade* (ascent from the Fischhorn road by a finger-post on the right) and the ($^3/_4$ hr.) *Ebenberg-Alpe* (Rfmts.) are also fine points of view. A *Promenade* leads from the park of the Hôtel Elisabeth (open to the public) along the banks of the lake to another good view-point. — An ancient custom of illuminating the lake and mountains on the 23rd of June is still kept up (worth seeing).

The *Schmittenhöhe (6348') is one of the best and most accessible points of view in the Austrian Alps (3 hrs.; guide $2^1/_2$ fl., unnecessary; horse $5^1/_2$, there and back 9, or, if a night be spent on the top, $10^1/_2$ fl.; carr. for one pers. 9, there and back 12, incl. night on top 15 fl.). The route leads to the W. from Zell through the Schmittener Thal to ($^1/_4$ hr.) *Schmitten*; here we turn to the left, and follow an easy bridle-path, practicable for light vehicles, which ascends in windings, mostly through wood, passing ($^1/_2$ hr.) a bench commanding a good view (to the left is the route to the *Ebenberg Alpe*, see above), to the (1 hr.) *Mittelstation* (*Schweizerhütte*, with five beds; mule thence to the top 2 fl. 75 kr.) and ($^1/_2$ hr.) *Brunner's Inn zum Gross Glockner* (fine view), and finally mounts the crest of the hill to the broad summit (*Hubinger's Inn*, 70 beds, R. with one bed $^3/_4$-1 fl., with two beds $1^1/_2$-3 fl., L. 20 kr.; rooms may be ordered at Jos. Fill's in Zell). The superb panorama embraces to the S. the entire Tauern range from the Ankogl to the Gross-Venediger (particularly fine the view of the Kapruner Thal, the whole of which is seen, surrounded by the Hochtenn, Wiesbachhorn, Glockerin, Bärenkopf, Gross-Glockner, Glocknerwand, Johannisberg, and Kitzsteinhorn); to the W. the depression of the Hoch-Gerlos; to the N. the limestone Alps from the Kaisergebirge to the Dachstein (including the Watzmann, to the right of the Hundstod); on the E. the Kleine Tauern, Hafnereck, Hochalpspitze, etc.; immediately below us the Zeller See. (Comp. the Panorama.) The 'Ranggelfest' (wrestling matches) celebrated on the Schmittenhöhe on the third Sunday of August is accompanied by interesting old customs. In descending avoid apparent short-cuts. — The **'Pinzgauer Spazierweg'**, which at places is a little indistinct, leads from the Schmittenhöhe along the crest of the hill to the (8 hrs.) *Gaisstein* (p. 174), and commands a series of splendid views of the Tauern from the Ankogl to the Dreiherrnspitze. It is, however, somewhat monotonous and fatiguing. Provisions necessary; guide advisable (from Zell to the Gaisstein 8 fl.; Jos. Eder and Joh. Buchner at Zell are recommended). From the Schmittenhöhe the path at first descends to the W. into a basin, then ascends, and follows the crest of the hill (about 5900') on the S. side to the (5 hrs.) *Sommerscharte* (*Wehnachtscharte* in the special map; pass from Uttendorf into the Glemmthal). To the N. rises the huge Birnhorn. Farther on the path leads above the *Mühlthal* to the (1½ hr.) *Murnauer Scharte* (6675') and the (1¼ hr.) *Bürglalpe* (p. 135), and ascends the (¾ hr.) *Gaisstein* (p. 174) from the W. side. We may then descend by the *Obere* and *Untere Sintersbach-Alpe* to (3½ hrs.) *Jochberg* (p. 174). — Visitors to the *Kapruner Thal* may descend by a rough path direct from the Schmittenhöhe to Fürth (p. 135).

The *Hundstein* (6940'; 4 hrs.; guide 4½ fl.) and the *Hönigkogl* (6080'; 3 hrs.; guide 3½ fl.), both to the E. of the Zeller See, afford views similar to that from the Schmittenhöhe.

From Zell am See to the *Kapruner Thal*, see p. 132; to *Mittersill* and *Krimml* (*Ober-Pinzgau*), see p. 135.

The train quits the lake at *Schloss Prielau*. 64½ M. *Maishofen* (2495'), on the flat watershed between the Salzach and the *Saalach*; to the left the château of *Saalhof*, at the mouth of the *Glemmthal*, from which the Saalach issues.

A road (diligence from Zell thrice a week) runs through the Glemmthal (18 M. long), passing *Vishhofen* (Oberwirth), to *Saalbach* (3595'; Oberwirth; Unterwirth), 9 M. from Maishofen and 11 M. from Zell. The *Gaisstein* (7746') may be easily ascended in 4 hrs. from Saalbach (comp. p. 174). A road, practicable for carriages, runs to the N. from Saalbach, viâ the *Alte Schanze* (4270'), to the W. of the *Spielberg* (6636'; ascent of 2 hrs. from the Schanze; *View from the top), to (12 M.) *Fieberbrunn* (p. 119).

The train crosses the Saalach. The broad grassy valley of the *Mitter-Pinzgau*, with a fine view of the *Steinerne Meer* (see below) on the right, is next traversed. — 70 M. **Saalfelden** (2380'; *Ringler*; *Rail. Restaurant*). The village (*Oberschneider*; *Neuwirth*; *Post*; omnibus 20 kr.), ¾ M. to the E. of the railway, is prettily situated on the *Urslauer Ache*, in the middle of the broad and sunny valley. Fine view from the cemetery above the village (or from the station): N.W. the Leoganger Steinberge, N. the Steinerne Meer, E. the Hochkönig (Uebergossene Alp), S. the Hochtenn, Kitzsteinhorn, etc.

The tower on the **Kühbühel** (2815'), ½ hr. to the S. (gradual ascent, passing a bath-house, with peat and other baths) commands a still more extensive view. — To the N., on a spur of the Steinerne Meer, at the base of the towering *Persalhorn*, stands the (¾ hr.) castle of **Lichtenberg** (2090'); adjacent are a hermitage, with four cells hewn in the rock, and the Chapel of St. George, with a rock-hewn pulpit (*View of the Zeller See and the Tauern). In the valley below lie *Schloss Dorfheim*, to the S.E. of Saalfelden, and *Schloss Farmach* to the E. — About 2 M. to the E. are the prettily-situated baths of *Fieberbrunn* (2780'; Restaurant).

The **Steinerne Meer** (comp. p. 75) is most easily visited from Saalfelden (guides, Alois and Joh. Moshammer). A good path, at first partly through wood, afterwards hewn in the rock, and provided with railings and staples (guide to Königs-See, 8 fl., unnecessary for mountaineers), crosses the Ramseider Scharte (6895') to the (6 hrs.) *Funtensee* (interesting fossils in the 'Salzstatt'). A little above the Scharte, and under the slope of the Sommerstein (3½ hrs. from Saalfelden), is the *Riemann-Haus* (6990';

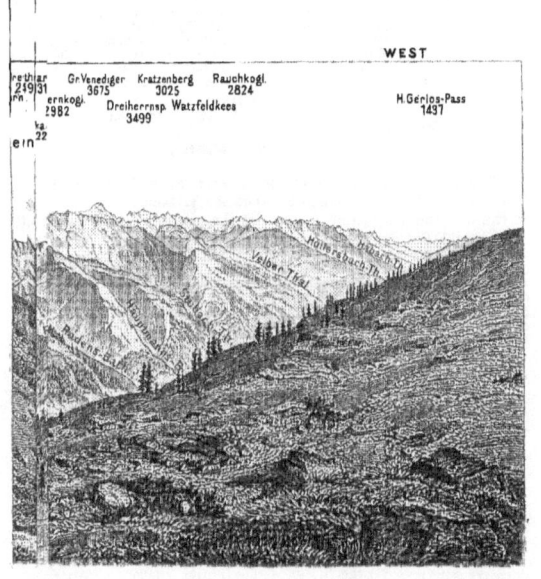

118 *III. Route 22.*   SAALFELDEN.   *From Salzburg*

a little indistinct, leads from the Schmittenhöhe along the crest of the hill to the (8 hrs.) *Gaisstein* (p. 174), and commands a series of splendid views of the Tauern from the Ankogl to the Dreiherrnspitze. It is, however, somewhat monotonous and fatiguing. Provisions necessary; guide advisable (from Zell to the Gaisstein 8 fl.; Jos. Eder and Joh. Buchner at Zell are recommended). From the Schmittenhöhe the path at first descends to the W. into a basin, then ascends, and follows the crest of the hill (about 5900') on the S. side to the (5 hrs.) *Sommerscharte (Wethnachtscharte* in the special map; pass from Uttendorf into the Glemmthal). To the N. rises the huge Birnhorn. Farther on the path leads above the *Mühlthal* to the (1½ hr.) *Murnauer Scharte* (6675') and the (1¼ hr.) *Bürgtalpe* (p. 135), and ascends the (¾ hr.) *Gaisstein* (p. 174) from the W. side. We may then descend by the *Obere* and *Untere Sintersbach-Alpe* to (3½ hrs.) *Jochberg* (p. 174). — Visitors to the *Kapruner Thal* may descend by a rough path direct from the Schmittenhöhe to Fürth (p. 135).

The *Hundstein* (6940'; 4 hrs.; guide 4½ fl.) and the *Hönigkogl* (6080'; 3 hrs.; guide 3½ fl.), both to the E. of the Zeller See, afford views similar to that from the Schmittenhöhe.

From Zell am See to the *Kapruner Thal*, see p. 132; to *Mittersill* and *Krimml (Ober-Pinzgau)*, see p. 135.

The train quits the lake at *Schloss Prielau*. 64½ M. *Maishofen* (2495'), on the flat watershed between the Salzach and the *Saalach*; to the left the château of *Saalhof*, at the mouth of the *Glemmthal*, from which the Saalach issues.

A road (diligence from Zell thrice a week) runs through the **Glemmthal** (18 M. long), passing *Viehhofen* (Oberwirth), to *Saalbach* (3595'; Oberwirth; Unterwirth), 9 M. from Maishofen and 11 M. from Zell. The *Gaisstein* (7746') may be easily ascended in 4 hrs. from Saalbach (comp. p. 174). A road, practicable for carriages, runs to the N. from Saalbach, viâ the *Alte Schanze* (4270'), to the W. of the *Spielberg* (6696'; ascent of 2 hrs. from the Schanze; *View from the top), to (12 M.) *Fieberbrunn* (p. 119).

The train crosses the Saalach. The broad grassy valley of the *Mitter-Pinzgau*, with a fine view of the *Steinerne Meer* (see below) on the right, is next traversed. — 70 M. **Saalfelden** (2380'; *Ringler; *Rail. Restaurant*). The village (**Oberschneider*; **Neuwirth*; **Post*; omnibus 20 kr.), ¾ M. to the E. of the railway, is prettily situated on the *Urslauer Ache*, in the middle of the broad and sunny valley. Fine view from the cemetery above the village (or from the station): N.W. the Leoganger Steinberge, N. the Steinerne Meer, E. the Hochkönig (Uebergossene Alp), S. the Hochtenn, Kitzsteinhorn, etc.

The tower on the **Kühbühel** (2815'), ½ hr. to the S. (gradual ascent, passing a bath-house, with peat and other baths) commands a still more extensive view. — To the N., on a spur of the Steinerne Meer, at the base of the towering *Persailhorn*, stands the (¾ hr.) castle of **Lichtenberg** (2090'); adjacent are a hermitage, with four cells hewn in the rock, and the Chapel of St. George, with a rock-hewn pulpit ("View of the Zeller See and the Tauern). In the valley below lie *Schloss Dorfheim*, to the S.E. of Saalfelden, and *Schloss Farmach* to the E. — About 2 M. to the E. are the prettily-situated baths of *Fieberbrunn* (2780'; Restaurant).

The **Steinerne Meer** (comp. p. 75) is most easily visited from Saalfelden (guides, Alois and Joh. Moshammer). A good path, at first partly through wood, afterwards hewn in the rock, and provided with railings and staples (guide to Königs-See, 8 fl., unnecessary for mountaineers), crosses the Ramseider Scharte (6895') to the (6 hrs.) *Funtensee* (interesting fossils in the 'Salzstatt'). A little above the Scharte, and under the slope of the Sommerstein (3½ hrs. from Saalfelden), is the *Riemann-Haus* (6990';

Inn in summer), built in a picturesque situation by the Pinzgau section of the German Alpine Club. From this point the *Breithorn* (8170') is easily ascended in 1½ hr. by those who have steady heads (pavilion at the top; splendid view). The ascent of the *Schöneck* (8085'), 1¼ hr., is laborious; that of the *Schönfeldspitze* (*Hochzink*, 8700'), 2½ hrs., is difficult and should be attempted by experienced mountaineers only. — From the Funtensee to the *Königs-See*, see p. 75. — Other passes to the Königs-See are the *Diesbachscharte* (6990'), to the S. of the Grosse Hundstod (p. 76); the *Weissbachl-Scharte* (7365'), between the Hollermaishorn and the Achselhorn, and the *Buchauer Scharte* (7485'), to the E. of the *Schönfeldspitze* (see above).

A road ascends the **Urslau-Thal** to the E. to (3½ M.) *Alm* (2610'; guide, Joh. Herzog) and (4½ M.) *Hinterthal*; 1½ M. farther is *Bad Hinterthal* (3430'), picturesquely situated at the base of the **Hochkönig** (9640'), which may be ascended hence by a new path, viâ the *Hinterthaler Wetterwand* and the *Teufelslöcher*, in 5-6 hrs. (guide; comp. p. 113). At Hinterthal our path turns to the right and leads across the *Filzensattel* (4240') to *Dienten* and (15 M.) *Lend* (p. 115). From Hinterthal across the *Thor-Scharte* or *Hintere Urschlauer-Scharte* (7160') to the *Blühnbachthal* (to the shooting-lodge 7 hrs., fatiguing), see p. 113.

From Saalfelden viâ *Ober-Weissbach* to *Reichenhall*, see pp. 79, 177; to *Berchtesgaden*, see p. 78. Diligence to Lofer daily (at 3 p.m.) in 3½ hrs. (1½ fl., to Frohnwies 1 fl.). One-horse carriage to Frohnwies 4, two-horse 6 fl.; to Lofer 6 or 10 fl.; across the Hirschbühl to Berchtesgaden (including trace-horse) 24 or 40 fl. (driver extra). — The °*Seisenbergklamm* (p. 78) is within a walk of 3½ hrs., or a drive of 1½ hr., from Saalfelden. The *Lamprechts-Ofenloch*, see p. 78; the °*Vorderkaserklamm*, see p. 177.

The train now turns to the W., crosses the Saalach and the *Leogang*, enters the *Leogang-Thal*, and ascends rapidly at the base of the *Birnhorn* (8628') to (75 M.) *Leogang* (2750'; Inn), with baths. The **Birnhorn** (8630'; 6½ hrs., with guide) may be ascended through the *Birnbachgraben* and the *Melcherloch* (fatiguing, but repaying). The descent by the *Gruber-Alp* to *Frohnwies* (p. 79) is difficult.

The train crosses the *Weissbach* and *Griessenbach*, and beyond *Pass Griessen* (2835'), which was once fortified, crosses the Tyrolese frontier. — 81 M. **Hochfilzen** (3170'; *Inn*), the highest point on the line, lies on the watershed between the Saalach and the Inn.

From Hochfilzen a carriage-road leads to the W., past the little *Wiesensee*, to (9 M.) *St. Ulrich am Pillersee* see below). — A footpath runs past *Taubach*, *Grimmbach*, *Willeck*, *Schittdach*, and *Dalsen* to the *Vorderkaserklamm* in 2½-3 hrs. (comp. p. 177). — The ascent of the °**Spielberg** (6696') may be made from Hochfilzen or Fieberbrunn viâ the *Spielberg-Alp* in 3½ hrs., with guide. The view from the top is little inferior to that from the Gaisstein. We may descend by the *Alte Schanze* into the *Glemmthal* (see p. 118), or to the N.E. into the *Leogang-Thal*.

The train now descends a sharp gradient (1 : 44) on the right side of the *Pramau-* or *Pillersee-Achenthal*, crossing several lateral ravines. — 87 M. **Fieberbrunn** (2610'; *Inn*, at the station); the village (**Obermaier; Post*) lies below, to the left.

From Fieberbrunn a carriage-road leads to the N. to (3 M.) *St. Jacob im Haus* (2800'; Inn), a little village on the low saddle between the Pramauthal and the Strubachenthal. Thence it runs past *Flecken* ('Strassweit') to (3 M.) *St. Ulrich am Pillersee* (p. 176), and through the *Oefen* to (4½ M.) *Waidring* (p. 175). — From Fieberbrunn the *Kitzbühlerhorn* (6512') may be ascended viâ the *Oberrheinthal-Alp*, in 4½ hrs. (fatiguing; comp. p. 174).

We next pass *Schloss Rosenberg* and the *Pillersee* iron-works

120   *III. Route 23.*   KLAMM PASS.

(with the Loferer Steinberge, Flachhorn, Ochsenhorn, etc., on the right), and continue to descend rapidly through the somewhat monotonous valley. The *Pillersee Ache* is crossed.

92 M. **St. Johann in Tirol** (2165'; *Post; *Bär; *Zum Hohen Kaiser*, at the station), pleasantly situated in the broad *Leukenthal*, or valley of the *Grosse Ache*, which is here formed by the confluence of the *Pramau*, the *Kitzbühler*, and the *Reitner Ache*, is commanded by the rugged *Kaisergebirge* (p. 175) on the W., and the *Kitzbühler Horn* (6542') on the S. (better ascended from Kitzbühel, see p. 174). — To *Waidring* and *Lofer*, see pp. 175, 176.

The right bank of the *Kitzbühler Ache* (on the left the Kitzbühler Horn) is now followed. — 95 M. *Wiesenschwang-Oberndorf*.

98 M. Kitzbühel (2420'; *Tiefenbrunner; *Hinterbräu; Haas*, near the station), and railway thence to (119 M.) *Wörgl*, see pp. 174-171.

23. The Gastein Valley.

DILIGENCE from *Lend* (p. 115) to (15¹/₂ M.) *Wildbad Gastein* thrice daily (6 a.m., 1 and 3.45 p.m.) in 4 hrs. (3 fl. 40 kr.). Two-horse carriage from Lend to Hof-Gastein 10 fl., to Wildbad Gastein 13 fl. (there and back 26 fl.; less before and after the height of the season). — The Gasteiner Thal below Wildbad is scarcely picturesque enough to repay the pedestrian. During the season accommodation is not easily procured at the Wildbad. A stay of 6-8 hrs. is enough for a flying visit to Wildbad.

Lend (2070'; *Straubinger; *Post*), see p. 115. The Gastein road ascends rapidly from the 'Post', and carriages require 'Vorspann', or the aid of an additional horse. In the valley on the left are the waterfalls of the Ache. At the top of the hill (2476'), near the beginning of the pass proper, stands a (2 M.) *Chapel*.

The *Klamm Pass* is a profound and sombre gorge in the limestone rock, through which the Ache has forced a passage. Down to 1821 the defile was closed by a gate and railing, and guarded by a small fort; but these were destroyed by a landslip, and afterwards swept away by an inundation. A fragment of the old wall still stands near the (1 M.) *Klammstein-Brücke* (2550'), at the end of the pass. To the right, from the chain which separates the valley of Gastein from the Rauris, rises the double-peaked *Bernkogl* (p. 126); to the left is the *Arlspitz* (7240'); and in the background to the S. the *Tisch* (8080').

We now enter the broad green valley of Gastein and pass the villages of *Mairhofen*, (4 M.) *Dorf Gastein* (2740'; Edler), and (5¹/₂ M.) —

12¹/₂ M. **Hof-Gastein** (2850'; *Moser*, R. 1 fl. 20 kr.; *Müller*, with a large dining-hall, R., L., & A. 85 kr.; *Bieber zum Boten; Blaue Traube; Neuwirth ; Café Viehauser*), the capital of the valley, which in the 16th cent., when its mines still produced considerable quantities of gold and silver, was the wealthiest place in

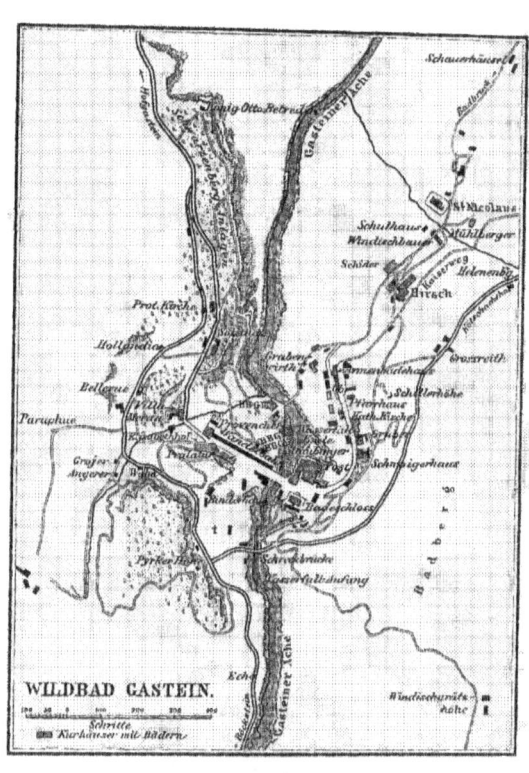

HOF GASTEIN.   *III. Route 23.* 121

this district next to Salzburg. Most of the miners (chiefly Saxons) and many of the natives of the valley were formerly Protestants. Of the 22,151 persons exiled in 1731 by the intolerant Archbishop of Salzburg (p. 115) no fewer than 1000 belonged to this region. Several of the houses, with decorations of the 16th cent., still testify to the ancient prosperity of the place, especially that of *Moser*, with arcades on each floor. Near it, in the court of the baker Embacher, are two richly-ornamented columns of serpentine of the same period. The *Cemetery* contains handsome monuments of the Strasser, Weitmoser, and other families (16th cent.).

The *Military Hospital*, with the two corner-turrets, once a guildhouse, was fitted up for its present use in 1832, by Lad. Pyrker, Archbishop of Erlau. — The open space in front of it is adorned with a gilded bust of Emp. Francis I., commemorating the construction in 1826 of a conduit, upwards of 3 M. long, which brings the thermal water hither from the springs at Wildbad. The temperature of the water falls during its transit from 102° to 93° Fahr. Baths at the 'Actienbadhaus', the Gutenbrunn Badhaus, etc. Living is less expensive here than at the Wildbad, but there is a lack of shady walks.

CARRIAGES. With one horse to the Wildbad 3, with two 5 fl.; to the Kötschachthal and Böckstein 5 or 8; Dorf Gastein 3 or 5 fl.; driver's fee 60 kr. or 1 fl. extra. If the carriage is not used for returning, 1 or 1½ fl. deducted; if kept the whole day, 80 kr. or 1½ fl. is added.

EXCURSIONS (guide, *Josef Deissl*). The *Gamskarkogl (8085'; 4 hrs.; horse and attendant 9 fl.; guide, 4 fl., unnecessary for the experienced) is ascended from Hof-Gastein by a good path. After an ascent of ½ hr. we leave the chapel to the right, and a few paces beyond it take the less trodden path to the right, ascending through the woods in the *Rastetzen-Thal*, to the (2 hrs.) *Rastetzen-Alp* (5665'; refreshments). To the summit (refuge-hut) 2 hrs. more. The view embraces the surrounding mountains only, and little or no vegetation is visible except in a small part of the valley of Gastein. The ice and snow-mountains of the Ankogl and Tischlerkar are most conspicuous to the S.; to the W. the lofty double-peaked pyramid of the Gross-Glockner and the prominent Wiesbachhorn; N. the Ewige Schneegebirge; N.E. the Dachstein and the Hochgolling. Descent to Wildbad Gastein, see p. 124. — The *Türchlwand (8440'; 5½ hrs.; guide 4½ fl.), ascended from Hof-Gastein by the *Angerthal* (see below) and the *Bockfeld-Alpe*, commands a splendid view (ascent somewhat fatiguing). — An easier ascent is that of the *Haseck (6950'), the top of which is reached from Dorf Gastein in 4½-5 hrs. by a marked path viâ *Grub* and the *Mairhofer Alp*. It commands a splendid view of the Salzachthal, the N. Limestone Alps, and the Tauern.

The road to the Wildbad (3 M., by carriage in 1 hr.) traverses a marshy part of the valley and then ascends on its W. side. On the right is the entrance of the *Angerthal*. (By the *Stanz* to *Bucheben*, see p. 127.) On the left we obtain a view of the *Kötschachthal*, commanded by the *Bocksteinkogl* and *Tischlerkar-Kees*, to the left of which rises the *Gamskarkogl*; on the right the *Graukogl*, *Feuerseng*, and lastly the pyramidal *Kreuzkogl*. We next pass the *Englische Kaffehaus* (café).

15½ M. Wildbad Gastein (3430'). — Hotels. °STRAUBINGER (POST), generally crowded in summer; °BADESCHLOSS, opposite Straubinger's;

122 III. Route 23. WILDBAD GASTEIN. *The Gastein*

*HÔTEL WEISMAYR, adjoining the Wandelbahn; *SCHERNTHANER (GRABENWIRTH), opposite the lower fall of the Ache, R. 1 fl. 20, D. 1 fl. 30 kr.; *HIRSCH, 1/4 M. from Straubinger's, finely situated; HAMBURGER HOF; all these with baths. — Lodging Houses (with baths): *ELISABETHHOF, opposite the Wandelbahn, R. 2 1/2 fl.; *GRUBER; OBERKRÄMER; *MOSER; *DR. SCHIDER; *MÜHLBERGER; *GERMANIA; TAXENHAUS; *BELLEVUE; SOLITUDE; *VILLA HOLLANDIA; LAINER; SCHÖPF; WINDISCHBAUER; the CUR- UND -MIETHHÄUSER, Nos. 1, 2, & 3, below the Wandelbahn; VILLA GROJER; VILLA ANGERER; WARA. — In July and Aug. it is often difficult to obtain good rooms at the Wildbad; the visitor should never enter into a contract without assuring himself by personal inspection that the rooms are neither damp nor otherwise undesirable. Notices posted up at the entrance to the Hôtel Straubinger and in the railway-stations of Salzburg, Bischofshofen, and Lend give information as to the accommodation at the Wildbad. — *Post Office* at Straubinger's Hotel. — *Visitor's Tax* during the season (May-Sept.), for a stay of five days or upwards, 8 1/2-10 fl. according to the class in which the visitor is ranked; additional members of a family and servants proportionally less.

Guides (*Johann Niederretter, Frz. Wurzer, A. Waggerl*, and *R. Hacksteiner* at Bad Gastein; *Joh. Schneeberger* and *Alois Stöckl* at Böckstein). To the summit of the Gamskarkogl 4 fl.; to the Nassfeld 2 fl. 40 kr.; to the Bockhartsee 3 fl.; to the Nassfelder Tauernhaus 5; to Mallnitz 7; to Kolm-Saigurn over the Bockhartscharte 5; to Prossau in the Kötschachthal 3; the Graukogl 4; the Anlaufthal as far as the Radeck-Alp 3 1/2; the Ankogl 10; the Schareck 8; by the Stanz to Bucheben 5 1/2; by the Riffelscharte and Zirknitzscharte to Döllach 18; by the Elendscharte to Gmünd 16 1/2 fl. — Carriages. Two-horse carriage to Lend, see p. 120; one-horse carr. to Hof-Gastein 4, two-horse 7; Böckstein 4 or 6; to the 'Aufzug' 5 or 10 fl.; driver's fee included on a half-day's drive, for a whole day 1-2 fl. extra. — Horses. To the Kötschachthal as far as the Himmelwand 2 fl. 80 kr.; Prossau 6 fl.; Rudolfshöhe, Windischgrätzhöhe 1 fl. 80 kr.; Nassfeld 5 fl. 40; Radeck-Alp 6 fl. 00; from Böckstein to the Nassfeld 3 fl. 60, the Tauernhaus 7 fl. 80, Mallnitz 10 fl. 80 kr.; fee included in each case.

Most of the older houses of the Wildbad, built of wood, lie on the E. slope of the valley, which is so steep that the door of one is frequently on a level with the chimneys of its neighbour. Of recent years, however, chiefly owing to the annual visits of the late Emperor William (d. 1888), the Wildbad has become a fashionable and thriving place, with numerous handsome villas. The chief rallying-points of visitors are the small *Schloss-Platz*, between the Straubinger and Badeschloss hotels (music daily at noon and 6.30 p.m.), and the *Wandelbahn* (at the W. end of the bridge), a long covered glass-gallery, used as a promenade in wet weather. On the right side of the valley is the new *Roman Catholic Church*, a handsome Gothic building, and on the left side is the *Protestant Church* (p. 123).

The Ache, which flows through the valley, is precipitated here through narrow gorges, forming two magnificent *Waterfalls*, the upper 207', the lower 280' high, vying in grandeur with those of Krimml (p. 137). The upper fall is best viewed from the bridge by Straubinger's, the lower from a platform near the Grabenwirth. Nervous persons will find it difficult to habituate themselves to the perpetual thunder of the falls.

The springs (77° to 120° Fahr.), known as early as the 7th cent., rise on the E. slope of the valley, at the foot of the *Graukogl*, and yield about 770,000 gallons of water daily. The water, which has neither taste nor smell, contains a very small proportion of mineral ingredients, but possesses exhilarating properties, and is beneficial in cases of debility, nervous affections, gout, &c. The visitors to the baths (about 6000 annually) belong chiefly to the higher ranks. The usual routine consists of 17-21 baths, but for some patients 11-14 suffice. The season lasts from 15th May to 30th September.

*WALKS. The road to Hof-Gastein on the W. side of the valley passes the Wandelbahn and the *Villa Meran*. Higher up, on the left, is the *Bellevue* (café; fine view), to which a path ascends from the Elisabethhof, and beyond it is the *Villa Hollandia*. The road next reaches the *Solitude* (right), the property of Countess Lehndorff-Steinort, and the small *Protestant Church* (service during the season on Sun. at 11 a.m., and on Thurs. at 5 p.m.). At this point, to the right, below the road, begin the *Schwarzenberg Grounds*, with various views of the waterfalls, while the *König-Otto Belvedere* here overlooks the Gastein valley. A road to the left leads to the Straubinger Quarry, passing in the wood a large glacier-basin known as the 'Gasteiner Taufbecken' ('font'). More to the left is the new *Erzherzog-Johann Promenade*, with splendid view. At the end of the grounds is * *Stöckl's Restaurant*. Farther down the road is the *Englische Kaffehaus* (p. 121). — The road to Böckstein ascends to the left, 3 min. beyond the Protestant church, passing the villas *Hollandia* and *Bellevue*, and skirting the *Pyrkerhöhe* (see below), to a (3/4 M.) *Saw Mill*, where it divides: the branch to the left leads to the *Schreckbrücke* (see below), that to the right to (1/2 M.) the *Patschger* (see below). From the latter, 1/4 M. farther on, a path diverges to the right to the (10 min.) *Pyrkerhöhe*, which commands a view of the Gastein and Böckstein valleys, and the Uebergossene Alp with the Hochkönig towards the N.

On the right (E.) side of the valley a charming walk is afforded by the new *Kaiserweg*, which passes above the Hirsch Inn and the *Church of St. Nicholas*, and follows the slope of the hill to the (20 min.) *Habsburger Hof* (fine view of Hof-Gastein and the Nassfeld Tauern) and to (25 min.) the Café zum Grünen Baum in the Kötschachthal (p. 124). — The **Schwarze Lisl*, a café with an admirable view, is reached in 10 min. by a path diverging to the right shortly before reaching Stöckl's Restaurant. — Shady paths with steps ascend to the right and left from the Badeschloss Hotel to the (6 min.) *Schreckbrücke*, with a view of the upper fall. — The best ascent to the (5 min.) *Schillerhöhe* is from Gruber's. — The view from the *Rudolfshöhe* is more open than that from the Schwarze Lisl, to the right of which the path to it ascends (5 min.). — The * *Windischgrätz-Höhe* (3/4 hr.), on the slope of the Badberg, affords a survey of the valleys of Gastein and Böckstein, of the Schareck with the Schlapperebenkees, and of (N.) the Wetterwand with the Hochkönig. The path to it ascends from the Schreckbrücke (right bank), and an easier route leads from the Patschger (to the left, by the small chapel). — The *Patschger* (*Inn), on the Böckstein road, is 1¼ M. from the Wildbad. — Past the church of St. Nicholas to *Badbruck* and (³/₄ hr.) *Kötschach* (café); cross the Ache below Kötschach and ascend to the *Englische Kaffehaus* (p. 121); thence back by the road (2 hrs. in all).

The picturesque **Kötschachthal** may be reached either by the Kaiserweg (on foot; see p. 123) or by the road leading from the Schreckbrücke past the Villa Helenenburg and the Schwarze Lisl, and round the angle of the hill. The latter then descends between trees to the (2 M.) *Café zum Grünen Baum* (fine view), whence a bridle-path ascends the valley past the precipitous *Himmelwand*, affording a good view of the Bocksteinkogl and Tischlerkarkees, with the considerable *Kees Fall* on the left, to (1½ hr.) *Prossau*, the last Alp (4220'; refreshments). — A fatiguing pass, rarely used, leads hence to the left across the *Kessel-Alp* and the *Klein-Elend-Scharte* (8220') to the *Malta-Thal* in Carinthia (to the Elendhütte 6 hrs., see p. 399; guide as far as Gmünd 16 fl.). — Pleasant excursion from the Grüner Baum to the *Reedsee* (5915'; 2½ hrs.; with guide). Thence on to the *Gamskartsee* and over the *Lainkarscharte* to the *Anlaufthal*, see below.

The *Gamskarkogl* (8085') is frequently ascended from Bad-Gastein by the Kaiserweg and the Kötschachthal (better from Hof-Gastein), in 4½ hrs. (guide 4 fl.; horse and attendant 9 fl.). — The Graukogl (8172'; from Wildbad by the *Reihilben-Alp* in 4½–5 hrs.; guide 4 fl.) affords a view similar to that from the Gamskarkogl; the glaciers, however, are much nearer, and at its E. base lie the pretty *Reedsee* and *Palfner-See*. — The view from the Tisch (8075') also repays the ascent. The route leads to the W. from the Wildbad past the *Zitterauer Alpe* (6180') and through the *Hirschkaar* (4½ hrs.; guide 4 fl.). — The Kreuzkogl (8800'), the highest peak of the *Radhausberg* (p. 126), commands an extensive panorama. The path leads from the Böckstein bridle-path to the (2 hrs.) gold-mine (*Hieronymus-Bergbau*, 6235'), and thence in 2½ hrs. to the summit, the last part fatiguing (guide 5 fl.). — The *Schareck (10,270') may be ascended in 4–5 hrs. from the Nassfeld by a new path (guide 8 fl.; comp. p. 127).

Böckstein and the *Nassfeld* are two favourite points for excursions from the Wildbad. The former, a village at the head of the valley in which the baths lie, is reached on foot in 1 hr., or by carriage in ½ hr. The road leads from the Schreckbrücke (p. 123), following first the left, then the right bank of the Ache, and passes the (½ hr.) *Patschger* (Inn). Opposite to us rises the *Kreuzkogl*; to the right, the snow-clad *Schareck*. After ¼ hr. a footpath diverges to the right, leading to Böckstein in 7 min., while by the road it takes twice as long. Böckstein (3700'; *Kettl's Hotel & Kurhaus*, with garden, pens. 5 fl.; *Gruber*, unpretending) is situated opposite the mouth of the *Anlaufthal* (fine view of the Ankogl). Good drinking-water. The round building on the hill is a church, erected in 1766; near it Count Czernin has built a new château.

Anlaufthal. A good path, rather fatiguing at the end, leads from Böckstein past (1 hr.) the *Anlauf-Alpe*, the *Herkar Fall*, and (1½ hr.) the *Tavern Fall* to (1 hr.) the *Radeck Alp* (4970'; refreshments and hay-beds), the loftiest pasture in the valley, with a fine view of the magnificent scenery at its head (Ankogl, Höllthorspitze, etc.) The Ankogl (10,670') is occasionally ascended from Radeck (in 5 hrs.), but is difficult and should not be attempted except by experts with trustworthy guides (10 fl.; comp. pp. 126, 400). — An easy and attractive path leads over the Hochtauern, or *Korntauern* (8080'), to *Mallnitz* (p. 126) in 8 hrs. (guide 7 fl.). Near the Tavern Fall (see above) we ascend to the right to the summit of the pass (5 hrs. from Böckstein), whence a fine view is enjoyed; descent by the *Seebachthal*, 3 hrs. — An interesting but somewhat difficult path leads from the Anlaufthal to the *Kötschachthal* (p. 124), ascending to the left opposite the Tauern Fall (p. 124) to the **Lainkarscharte** (7875'), to the S. of the *Kreuskopf* (see above), and then descending past the small *Gamskart-See* (7365') and the *Reedsee* (5915'; from Böckstein to Gastein 7-8 hrs.).

The route to the *Nassfeld* (from Böckstein $1^1/_4$-$1^1/_2$ hr.) is by a road as far as the ($1^1/_4$ M.) point where the '*Aufzug*' formerly began. This was a kind of wooden tramway, 700 yds. long, for the transport of the miners and the ore from the gold mine on the *Radhausberg* above. We then ascend by a path through the *Asten*, a rocky gorge about 1 M. in length, in which the Ache forms a series of cascades. At the entrance is the *Kessel Fall*, at the end the *Bären Fall*, near both of which new points of view have been opened. Below the latter the stream which drains the *Bockhart-See* (see below) falls into the ravine over a precipice 330' high, forming the graceful *Schleier Fall* ('veil-fall'). By the bridge, 5 min. farther on, the path enters the *Nassfeld (5890'), a sequestered green valley, 3 M. in length and $1^1/_2$ M. in breadth, through which winds the Ache, fed by the snow and ice of the surrounding mountains (from left to right, the *Geiselkopf*, *Murauer Kopf*, *Sparanger Kopf*, *Schlapperebenspitz* with the *Schlapperebenkees*, *Strabelebenkopf*, and the lofty, pyramidal *Schareck*; to the right the *Bockhartgebirge* rising over the *Siglitzthal*). Near the last bridge, just below the mouth of the Siglitzthal, stands the new *Nassfeldhaus* of the German Alpine Club (Inn, with 16 beds). About $^3/_4$ hr. farther on is the *Schweizer Hütte* or *Straubinger Hütte*, at the S.E. end of the Nassfeld. As, however, nothing more is to be seen at the upper than at the lower end of the valley, the traveller need not go beyond the Nassfeldhaus.

FROM GASTEIN TO THE RAURIS GOLD MINE there are two passes, one over the *Bockhartscharte*, and the other over the *Riffelscharte*. The former route (6 hrs., guide 5 fl.) is easier and preferable. From the Nassfeldhaus we ascend the *Siglitzthal* to the right to the (10 min.) *Moserhütte*, where we take the path to the right (indicated by red marks) and ascend the *Bockhart-Thal* to (1 hr.) the beautiful *Untere Bockhart-See* (6070'); on its N. side is the *Straubinger-Alp*. Thence past deserted mines to the ($^3/_4$ hr.) *Obere Bockhart-See* (6760'), between the Kolbenkaar on the left and the Silberpfennig on the right, and to the ($^1/_2$ hr.) **Bockhartscharte** (7340'), marked by a cross, between the Seekopf and the Silberpfennig, whence a fine view is obtained of the Rauris glaciers and the Ankogl. [A more extensive view is obtained from the *Silberpfennig* (8520'), easily ascended from the pass in 1 hr.] We descend to the right for 100 paces and then to the left by the *Filzen-Alpe* and the *Durchgang-Alpe* to the ($1^1/_2$ hr.) *Kolm-Saigurn* (p. 127).

The RIFFELSCHARTE route to the gold mine is somewhat toilsome (6 hrs., guide 6 fl.). To the ($2^1/_2$ hrs.) *Moser-Hütte*, in the *Siglitz-Thal*, see above. The path ascends rapidly to the (2 hrs.) *Riffelscharte (7890'), a magnificent point of view. We then descend to the left by the steep '*Verwaltersteig*' ('manager's path') to the *Neubau* (p. 127) and again ascend to the ($1^1/_2$ hr.) *Knappenhaus am hohen Goldberg* (p. 127).

FROM WILDBAD GASTEIN TO OBER-VELLACH over the *Nassfelder* or *Mallnitzer Tauern*, 10 hrs., a tolerable bridle-path; guide unnecessary in fine weather (to the Tauernhaus 5, to Mallnitz 7 fl.; horse, incl. fee, 12 fl. 80 kr., or, to the Tauernhaus only, 7 fl.; the steep descent beyond the latter is disagreeable on horseback). To the *Schweizer-Hütte* (5400') in the Nassfeld (3¼ hrs.), see p. 125. The bridle-path, indicated by stakes and not to be missed, winds up a steep slope (good spring at the top), and then ascends less steeply through the valley (behind us the Hochnarr and Bockhartsee) to the (2½ hrs.) **Mallnitzer**, **Nassfelder**, or **Niedere Tauern** (7920'), a depression forming the boundary between Salzburg and Carinthia, on which are two finger-posts. The bell on the second is sometimes rung as a guide to travellers in bad weather. The view is limited. A few hundred paces below the saddle stands the *Tauernhaus* (rustic Inn; bed 40 kr.); farther down, a limited view is obtained to the S. as far as the Terglou, and to the W. as far as the Glockner, while the Mallnitzer-Thal lies far below. The path passes a chapel, reaches the highest chalets (*Mannhart-Alp*), and crosses to the right bank of the brook. It then descends, at first steeply, but afterwards more gradually through wood and meadows, passing the mouth of the *Seebach-Thal* (fine view of the Ankogl to the left), to the prettily-situated village of (2½ hrs.) **Mallnitz** (3885'; °*Drei Gemsen*). [An ascent of the °**Ankogl** (10,670') may be made from this point in 7 hrs. (fatiguing; guide 7 fl.; Josef Gfrerer and P. Rosskopf of Mallnitz recommended). The route leads through the Seebachthal to the (4 hrs.) *Hannoverhaus* on the *Elschesattel* (8020'), where the night is spent; thence to the summit 3 hrs. (magnificent view).] The narrow and often rough road next leads to (¾ hr.) *Lassach*. (To the left, forming the background of the *Dössener Thal*, is the *Säuleck*, p. 399.) It then descends, crossing the brook and passing through wood at places, to (1 hr.) *Ober-Vellach* (p. 149) in the Möllthal. (One-horse carr. to Sachsenburg station in 2 hrs., 3½, two-horse carr. 6½ fl.).

Travellers on their way to HEILIGENBLUT (p. 150) need not go to Ober-Vellach, but proceed to the right from Lassach (see above) to (2½ hrs.) *Flattach* (p. 150), skirting the flank of the hill, and passing above the restored castle of *Groppenstein* (view of the Möllthal), thus saving an hour.

24. The Rauris.
Comp. Map, p. 120.

The **Rauris Valley**, which opens to the S. of the Rauris-Kitzloch station, is traversed by a monotonous road leading across the *Heiligenbluter Tauern* to *Heiligenblut*. (A more interesting route is that from the Fuscher Thal over the *Fuscher Thörl*, p. 130.) The head of the *Hüttwinkel-Thal* (p. 127), or S.E. arm of the Rauris, noted for its gold-mines, is enclosed by magnificent glacier-scenery, which mountaineers will find it well worth their while to explore (good accommodation at Kolm Saigurn).

Rauris-Kitzloch station (½ M. to the E. of the village of Taxenbach), see p. 116. The shortest and pleasantest route for pedestrians into the Rauris leads through the *Kitzlochklamm* (p. 116). The path crosses the Ache by the (1 hr.) *Landsteg* (Inn), whence the road leads on the left bank (soon affording a view of the head of the valley, the Schareck, Hochnarr, etc.) to (3 M.) **Rauris** (3110'; *Bräu, R. & A. 90 kr.), the chief place in the valley, and a summer-resort, prettily situated.

EXCURSIONS (guides, *Jos. Grabmaier*, *Vitus Oberfeichtner*, and *Jos. Trigler*). The °**Bernkogl** (7615'; 3½-4 hrs.; guide, 3 fl., unnecessary) commands a fine view of the Tauern, the Uebergossene Alp, etc. From Rauris the route proceeds to the E. into the *Gaisbachthal*, and turning to the left in ¼ hr. by a finger-post, ascends the slopes of the *Grubereck* (6900') to the (3 hrs.) refuge-hut on the saddle between that mountain and the *Sladinkopf* (7560'). Thence over debris to the base of the Bernkogl-wand, and by a good zigzag path to the (1 hr.) summit. Marked paths also lead from *Dorf-Gastein* (p. 120) and from the *Kitzlochklamm* (see above) to the summit in 4½ hrs.

At *Wörth* (3060'; Pfeiffenberger, with a collection of minerals), 3 M. farther on, the valley divides into the *Seidlwinkel* (right) and the *Hüttwinkel* (left). (Over the *Weichselbach-Höhe* to *Bad Fusch*, see p. 129.)

The TAUERN ROUTE (guide to Heiligenblut, 7 fl.) leads through the **Seidlwinkel** or **Seitenwinkelthal**, with the scattered village of *Seidlwinkel*, and past the *Schockhütten*, the *Maschel-Alp*, and the *Fall of the Spritzbach*, to the (3 hrs.) *Rauriser Tauernhaus* (4965'; rustic inn). It then ascends more steeply, passing the *Litzlhofhütten* and the *Einöder Wirthsalpe* (6240'), and (guide desirable; not always to be found at the Tauernhaus) crossing tracts of slaty debris and snow, to the (2 hrs.) *Fuscher Wegscheide* (way-post), where the path from the Fuscher Thörl joins ours on the right (p. 130). Passing a deserted miners' house, we next reach the (³/₄ hr.) *Hochthor des Heiligenbluter Tauerns* (8440'; limited view). Descent to (2 hrs.) *Heiligenblut*, see p. 131.

The first place in the **Hüttwinkel** above Wörth is (3 M.) *Bucheben*(3750'; Frohn Inn; guides, Chr. Langreiter and Victor Pelzler). A tolerably easy path (guide desirable, 5¹/₂ fl.) leads hence over the **Stanz** (6900') and through the *Angerthal* to (6 hrs.) *Hof-Gastein* (p. 120).

The road crosses the Ache twice, and afterwards the *Krumelbach*. In front of us rises the Ritterkopf, to the left the Herzog Ernst and Schareck. At the (1¹/₂ hr.) *Bodenhaus* (4020') the path crosses to the right bank of the Ache, and ascends in windings through wood opposite the *Grieswies-Alp* (5170'), where the head of the valley with its glaciers comes into view (on the right the Hochnarr and Goldbergspitze, on the left the Herzog Ernst), to the (1¹/₂ hr.) **Kolm Saigurn** or *Kolben* (5240'), the headquarters of Herr Rojacher's works, where about 20-25 lbs. of fine gold is annually extracted from the ore by amalgamation (good quarters; electric lighting; horses for hire). Visitors are allowed to inspect the various interesting processes to which the ore is subjected. We may now ascend in 12 min. by means of the 'Aufzug' (p. 125; 50 kr.; steady head necessary) to the *Maschinenhaus* (7142') and thence in 8 min. by the 'Rollbahn' to the Knappenhaus (see below). The bridle-path from Kolm-Saigurn (guide unnecessary; horse 6 fl.) ascends on the E. side of the 'Aufzug', over the *Melcherböden*, to the (2 hrs.) deserted *Neubau*, on the *Kälberriedel*, a little to the E. of the Maschinenhaus. About ¹/₂ hr. farther up is the **Knappenhaus am hohen Goldberg** (7680'; Inn), magnificently situated on a moraine on the margin of the *Goldberg Glacier (Vogelmaier-Ochsenkarkees)*, which has covered part of the old workings.

MOUNTAIN ASCENTS (guides, *Simon Neumaier*, *G. Poberschnigg*, *Blasius Zraunigg*, *Jos. Eder*, *Jos. Winkler*). The **Herzog Ernst** (9620') may be ascended from the miners' house in 2 hrs. (interesting and not difficult; guide 3 fl.). — The **Schareck** (10,270'), which commands a still more extensive view, may be reached from the Herzog Ernst by a path following the arête (impassable after snow) in 1 hr., or may be ascended from the mining-house viâ the *Goldberg-Tauern* and the *Wurtenkees* in 2½-3 hrs. (guide 4½ fl.). — The *Sonnblick* (10,180'), ascended by the *Goldberg Glacier* in 3 hrs., is another fine point (guide 4 fl.). At the top is the *Sonnblickhaus* (*Inn), a meteorological station inhabited throughout the year. The descent may be made viâ the *Kleine Fleisskees* to the (2½ hrs.) *Seebichlhaus* (p. 154), or by the *Brettscharte* to the *Grosse Zirknitzthal* and (4-5 hrs.) *Döllach* (p. 150). — The ascent of the *Hochnarr* or *Hohenaar* (10,690'), the highest of the Goldberg group, takes 5-6 hrs. (fatiguing but well worth the trouble; guide 5 fl., or descending to Heiligenblut 8½ fl.; comp. p. 154). We follow the 'Erfurter Weg' to the *Hochnarrkees*, and then ascend to the summit either by the *Goldzechscharte* (p. 154) or by the snow-ridge extending to the E. from the Hochnarr to the *Griesswies-Schwarzkogel* (*View). The pass from the Hochnarr to the *Sonnblick* is difficult (4 hrs.)

PASSES. To *Fragant* by the **Fraganter** or **Goldberg Tauern** (9065') in 8-9 hrs. (guide 6 fl.). We ascend to the left from the Knappenhaus past some deserted shafts, then cross the Goldberg glacier to the (2 hrs.) summit of the pass (8855'), between the Herzog Ernst and the *Goldbergtauernkopf* (9090'). Descent over the *Wurten Glacier* into the *Wurtenthal* and so to *Inner* and *Ausser-Fragant* (p. 150). — To *Döllach* by the Zirknitzscharte (8850') in 6-7 hrs. (guide 6 fl.). The summit of the pass lies to the E. of the *Alteck* (9640'). Descent to the right over the *Wurten* and *Klein-Zirknitz Glaciers* into the *Kleine Zirknitzthal*, and to the right again, above two small lakes (*Gross-See* and *Keffele-See*), to the (2 hrs.) highest chalet. The *Kleine* and *Grosse Zirknitz* unite about ½ hr. lower down. Thence a better path (bridle-path) past the *Neun Brunnen* (waterfall) and across the *Hohe Brücke* to (2 hrs.) *Döllach* (p. 150). — By the Windisch-Scharte (8945'), between the Alteck and the *Tramerkopf* (9200'), or by the Tramer-Scharte, between the Tramerkopf and the *Goldbergspitze*, descending across the *Gross-Zirknitz Glacier* into the *Gross-Zirknitzthal*, and to Döllach 6-7 hrs. (guide 6 fl., both laborious).

Over the *Bockhart-Scharte* or the *Riffel-Scharte* to *Gastein*, see p. 125 (guide to the Moserhütte 3 fl.); over the *Goldzech-Scharte* and the *Fleiss* to *Heiligenblut*, see p. 154 (guide 6 fl.).

25. The Fuscher Thal. From Ferleiten to Heiligenblut.
Comp. Maps, pp. 144, 120.

A visit to the beautiful *Fusch Valley* is strongly recommended, as there is probably no other valley among the E. Alps which introduces the traveller so quickly and so easily to the grandest Alpine scenery. CARRIAGE ROAD as far as the *Bär Inn* (one-horse carr. from Bruck 5, two-horse 9 fl., from Zell 8 or 12 fl.); thence a steep and rough road, hardly suitable for driving, leads to *Ferleiten*. (Tolerable road from the Bär Inn to the baths of *Fusch*, see below; one-horse carr. 5, two-horse 9 fl.). Routes to HEILIGENBLUT, see pp. 130, 149.

Bruck (2470'), see p. 116. The road follows the left bank of the *Fuscher Ache* past *Judendorf* to (4½ M.) **Fusch** (2665'; *Schernthaner*; *Zum Imbachhorn*, with baths), the chief place in the valley. Beyond the church (¼ hr.) the *Hirzbach* forms a fine *Waterfall*; and 20 min. to the N.E. opens the *Sulzbach-Klamm*, in which there is another waterfall.

EXCURSIONS (guides, *Georg Schranz, Jakob Oberhollenzer, Josef Oblasser*; tariff as from Ferleiten, to which the guides carry wraps, etc., without extra charge). A steep path ascends the Hirzbachthal, which opens here on the W., to the (3 hrs.) *Hirzbach-Alpe* (5635'), whence the Imbachhorn (8100'; 2½ hrs; guide 4 fl.), a fine point of view, is ascended (descent to Kaprun, see p. 134). At the end of the valley, which bends to the S. at the Alp, is the

FERLEITEN. *III. Route 25.* 129

Hirzbach Glacier, above which rises the Hochtenn (11,050'). The ascent of the Hochtenn from this point (4-5 hrs., with guide) is difficult. A better route leads from the village of Fusch viâ the *Schmalzgrubenalpe* to the *Zottingköpfel* (N. E. summit, 10,270') and then crosses snow-slopes to the *Hochtenn-Gletschergipfel* (10,928') and the (7 hrs.) *Hochtenn-Bergspitze* (11,050'). The view is very fine.

FROM FUSCH TO KAPRUN by the Hirzbachthörl (9915'), 8 hrs. to the Rainerhütte (guide 6 fl.), somewhat fatiguing. From the (3 hrs.) Hirzbachalp we ascend by a steep route through the *Zwing*, and over snow to (3 hrs.) the summit of the pass, between the *Bauernbrachkopf* and the *Hochtenn* (fine view). Descent across debris and steep grassy slopes to (2 hrs.) the *Rainerhütte* (p. 133).

The road follows the left bank of the Ache, crosses it twice, passes *Embach* on the left, and reaches the (1½ M.) *Bär Inn* (2690'; charges high).

[On the E. opens the *Weichselbachthal*, in which a winding road ascends to (3 M.) **Bad Fusch**, or **St. Wolfgangs-Bad** (3750'; **Weitguni; Flatscher*), a sheltered spot, with excellent drinkingwater and well-kept promenades.

A good footpath leads direct from Fusch to the Bad in 1½ hr., crossing the Ache to the left just above the village, and gradually ascending (fine view of the Hochtenn and the Wiesbachhorn). Another path leads direct from the Bad on the right bank of the Ache, chiefly through wood, to (1½ hr.) *Ferleiten* (guide unnecessary; several finger-posts).

EXCURSIONS from Bad Fusch (guide, *Joh. Untersatnberger*). A pleasant walk may be taken to the (2 hrs.) *Dixenhütte*, viâ the *Thallmayerhütte* and the *Marienhütte*, returning by the *Embachalp* (Rfmts.). — Another point for a walk is the *Loninger-Alpe*. — The Kasereck (5200'; 1 hr.; guide unnecessary, 80 kr.) affords a fine view; steep ascent on the right bank of the brook to the *Reiter-Alpe* (Rfmts.), then to the left (W.). At the top is a refuge-hut. — A more extensive panorama, including the N. Limestone Alps, is obtained from the **Kühkarköpfl** (7430'; 3-3½ hrs.; guide 2½ fl.), ascended viâ the Reiteralpe and *Fletschenalp* (Rfmts.). Refuge-hut (*Adelenhütte*; key kept at Bad Fusch) 20 min. from the top. — The *Schwarzkopf* (9065'; 4½ hrs.; guide 4), with descent to Ferleiten 4½ fl.) is a superb point of view. The route, which is somewhat fatiguing, leads to the S.E. to the *Rieger-Alpe*, then traverses a ravine, rounding the *Schwarzschädel* to the left, passes the small 'Blaue Lake', and ascends over debris and the broad arête to the summit. Descent to the W. by the *Durcheck-Alp* (see below) to *Ferleiten* in 2½ hrs. — From Bad Fusch across the **Weichselbachhöhe** (7270') to *Wörth* in the Rauris (p. 127), 6½ hrs., with guide (5 fl.), an easy and attractive route.]

The valley contracts. The road, now narrow and rough, ascends, at first rather abruptly, to (3½ M.) **Ferleiten** (3760'; *Lukashanslwirth*, in an open situation on the right bank of the Ache, dear; *Tauernhaus*, on the left bank, plain), a hamlet and chapel situated on the level floor of the valley, and commanding a fine view of the Sonnenwelleck, Fuscherkarkopf, and other imposing mountains at its head.

EXCURSIONS (guides; *Joh. Burgsteiner, Matth. Holleis, Anton* and *Franz Hutter, Peter* and *Rupert Mittereurzer, Georg Riess, Aug.* and *Jos. Rupitsch, Peter Schernthaner,* and *Egid. Höltzl*). The finest view is obtained from the *Durcheck-Alpe (5445'; refreshments; 2 hrs.; guide unnecessary, 1½ fl.). A good winding path ascends from Ferleiten to it on the E. side of the valley, passing through a gate to the left 5 min. beyond the first chalet. (Ascent of the *Schwarzkopf*, and descent to Bad Fusch, see above.) — The *Käferthal (guide desirable, 1½ fl.). We follow the road on the left bank of the Ache to the (2 M.) finger-post opposite the *Hundsdorfer Alpe* (see below), passing the *Vögalalp*, where the imposing *Wiesbachhorn* suddenly comes into view on the right in its full extent; 10 min. beyond the Hundsdorfer Alpe we diverge to the right and follow a broad cart-track across meadows (marshy at places; the narrow path ascending to the right, through wood and over grass, is drier) to the (1 hr.) *Juden-Alpe* (4870'). Passing round the foot of the *Hohe Dock*, we may now ascend the valley for a greater or lesser distance, enjoying fine views of the imposing Fuscher Eiskar (see below). At the head of the valley is a lofty waterfall formed by the melting of the Bockkarkees and the Fuscherkarkees, two glaciers seen high above. — To the (1¾ hr.) *Trauneralpe*, on the way to the Pfandelscharte, see below.

MOUNTAIN ASCENTS. The **Hochtenn** (11,050'), by the *Walcher Alpe* and the *Ferleiten Glacier* in 6-7 hrs., guide 8 fl.; fatiguing (better from Fusch; see p. 129). — The **Grosse Wiesbachhorn** (11,755'), 8-9 hrs., guide 8, or with descent to the Rainer Hütte 13 fl.; difficult. By the *Vögalalpe* to (4 hrs.) the *Schwarzenberghütte* (7550'), built by the Austrian Alpine Club, and thence over the *Hochgruber Glacier* and the *Wielinger Scharte* to (4-5 hrs.) the summit. Comp. pp. 134. 158. — The Brennkogl (9892'), 7 hrs., guide 6, or with descent to Heiligenblut 7¼ fl.; see p. 131.

FROM FERLEITEN TO HEILIGENBLUT there are two passes, one over the *Fuscher Thörl* and the *Heiligenbluter Tauern* (8½-9 hrs.), the other over the *Pfandelscharte* (9, or including the Franz-Josefs-Höhe 11 hrs.). The Tauern route affords magnificent views as far as the Fuscher Thörl, after which it becomes monotonous. Those who have not seen the Pasterze should select the Pfandelscharte route, coupled with a visit to the Franz-Josefs-Höhe, especially as they thus save the day which a visit to the Pasterze from Heiligenblut would occupy. (Travellers bound for Kals should pass the night in the Glocknerhaus, and proceed thence direct to the Berger Thörl.) Guide and provisions necessary on both routes; but on the Pfandelscharte route the Glocknerhaus on the Elisabethrast affords good quarters.

a. TO HEILIGENBLUT OVER THE TAUERN (guide 6 fl.). A broad track on the left bank of the Ache is followed to (40 min.) a finger-post, which indicates the way to Heiligenblut to the left. Here we cross the brook to the left, pass the three chalets of the *Hundsdorfer Alpe*, and ascend to the right by a well-defined path (marked by stakes), somewhat steep at places, commanding a magnificent view of the head of the valley. The path afterwards turns sharply to the left and leads through the *Untere Nassfeld* to the *Petersbrunnen* (7010'), a clear spring, 3 hrs. from Ferleiten. From this point we enjoy a superb *View of an imposing amphitheatre of snow-clad peaks and glaciers: from E. to W., the Brennkogl, Klobon, Spielmann, Sonnenwelleck, Fuscherkarkopf, Fuscherkarscharte, Breitkopf, Bockkarscharte, Eiswandbühel, Hohe Docke, Hochgruber Glacier, Grosse Bärenkopf, Bratschenkopf, Glockerin, Grosse and Kleine Wiesbachhorn, and Hochtenn. We next ascend through the *Obere Nassfeld*, at first in zigzags over debris, to the (¾ hr.) ***Fuscher Thörl** (7900'), between the *Brennkogl* (9892') on the right and the *Bergerkogl* (8445') on the left, before reaching which the Gross-Glockner suddenly comes into view to the S.W., next to the Sonnenwelleck. We now descend into a basin (with a spring) to the right, skirt the base of the Brennkogl, and then remount to the (1¼ hr.) *Mitter-Thörl* (7830'), a depression in the ridge descending from the Brennkogl, and over stony slopes to (³/₄ hr.) a finger-post, where the path comes up from Rauris on the left (p. 127). The path here turns to the right, past a deserted miners' house, and ascends, in some seasons over patches of snow, to the (³/₄ hr.) **Hochthor of the Heiligenbluter Tauern** (8440'), the boundary between Salzburg and Carinthia. View limited (to the E. the Weissenbachköpfe; to the N., in the distance, the Uebergossene Alp). A fair bridle-path descends from the Hochthor to the (¼ hr.) *Säumerbrunnen* (7925'), a good spring, crosses the brook, and skirts the slope to the left, soon affording a fine view of the Gross-Glockner. At the (³/₄ hr.) *Kasereck* (6285'), where the Mölltthal comes into view, the path descends abruptly to the right by an old chapel to (³/₄ hr.) *Heiligenblut* (p. 151). [A longer but easier path descends to the right, about ¼ hr. before the Kasereck is reached, to the *Gutthal-Alp*, and passes the *Mariahilf* chapel.]

Mountaineers may without much difficulty combine the ascent of the **Brennkogl** (9892') with the passage over the Fuscher-Thörl (see above); the route ascends a stony slope to the S.W. of the *Mitter-Thörl* (see above), and mounts the W. arête to the (2 hrs.) summit (splendid view); the descent may be made into the *Gutthal* (see above).

b. To Heiligenblut over the Pfandelscharte (guide to the Glocknerhaus 5½, including the Franz-Josefs-Höhe 6½ fl.; riding practicable as far as the 'Frühstückstein' near the glacier). Travellers should start from Ferleiten not later than 5 a.m., in order to reach the snow before it is softened by the sun. To the (40 min.) finger-post, see above; straight on for 20 min. more; then to the left across the brook, and up to the (40 min.) *Trauner Alpe* or *Lukashansl Alpe* (5010'), which overlooks the Käferthal and the majestic mountains surrounding it (see p. 130). We now descend slightly to the right through a basin, cross the brook coming from the Brennkogl, and then ascend abruptly by a good path, enjoying fine retrospects of the Fuscher Thal. To the right, far below, is the *Pfandelbach*. An ascent of 1½-2 hrs. brings us to the *Pfandelscharte Glacier*, the lower part of which is steep, and in 1½ hr. more we reach the summit of the **Pfandelscharte** (8760'), between the *Spielmann* (9928') on the left and the *Bärenkogl* (9325') on the right. Fine view in both directions: left the Gross-Glockner, right the Wiesbachhorn, N. the Steinerne Meer. We now descend across the *Racherin* or *S. Pfandelscharten Glacier* towards the S., and then over gravelly and grassy slopes to the (1½ hr.) *Glocknerhaus* (p. 152; hence to the *Franz-Josefs-Höhe* and back 2½ hrs.).

In dry weather we may also descend through the *Nassfeld* to the *Franz-Josefs-Höhe*, but the better plan is to visit the latter from the Glocknerhaus. Those, however, who wish to try the Nassfeld route turn sharply to the right at the top of the pass, quit the glacier after 20 min., and descend by the lateral moraine on the right, and afterwards by a narrow and steep path over stony and grassy slopes, to the (1 hr.) *Nassfeld*, a level basin intersected by numerous streams, which form the *Pfandelscharlenbach*, descending to the Pasterze. Crossing this obliquely, we descend on the right side to the (20 min.) *Schäferloch*, a shepherd's hut, where the path divides: the branch to the left leads to the (20 min.) *Wallnerhütte* and (¹/₄ hr.) the *Glocknerhaus;* that to the right ascends to the (³/₄ hr.) *Franz-Josefs-Höhe* (p. 152).

Two other passes lead from Ferleiten to Heiligenblut: one over the FUSCHERKARSCHARTE, and the other over the BOCKKARSCHARTE to the Pasterze (suitable for adepts only; able guides, ropes, and ice-axes necessary). The first of these routes ascends steeply to the left from (1³/₄ hr.) the *Juden-Alpe* (4870'; see p. 130) to the *Fuscherkarkees*, and crosses the fatiguing and crevassed glacier to the (4-5 hrs.) **Fuscherkarscharte** (9435'), the opening between the *Breitkopf* and the *Fuscherkarkopf*. It then descends to the highest part of the *Pasterze* and to the (1¹/₂ hr.) *Hofmannshütte*. The ascent of the *Fuscherkarkopf* (10,806'), an excellent point of view, adds 2¹/₂ hrs. to this expedition (guide 8¹/₂ fl., ; comp. p. 152). — The **Bockkarscharte** (9790') lies to the N.W. of the Fuscherkarscharte, between the Breitkopf and the *Eiswandbühel*. The route ascends abruptly from the *Schwarzenberghütte* (p. 130), to the *Remskopfl* (7595'; the E. spur of the *Hohe Docke*, 10,710'), and then crosses the *Hohe Gang*, a ledge covered with detritus, to the *Bockkar Glacier* and the Scharte. Descent to the head of the Pasterze and the *Hofmannshütte* (p. 152; or by the *Riffithor* to Kaprun, comp. p. 134); guide to the Glocknerhaus 8, to the Rainerhütte 10 fl.

26. The Kaprun Valley.
Comp. Map, p. 144.

The **Kapruner Thal**, one of the grandest valleys of the Tauern, 15 M. in length, is wooded in its lower part, and contains numerous waterfalls, while the *Mooserboden at the head of the valley presents a magnificent view of glacier-scenery, which is paralleled in the E. Alps by the Pasterze (p. 152) alone. It may easily be visited from Zell am See or Bruck. The former is connected by a carriage-road with (6 M.) Kaprun, beyond which a bridle-path extends to the (4 hrs.) Rainerhütte. CARRIAGE from Zell to Kaprun and back, with one horse 4¹/₂, with two horses 7¹/₂ fl., ; if the horses are ridden thence to the Rainerhütte, a charge of 12 fl per horse is made (including the drive to Kaprun; from Bruck 10 fl.), if kept overnight 16 fl. Guide to the Rainerhütte (unnecessary) 3 fl. Lanterns should be taken if the ascent is made in the evening.

The ROAD from Zell to Kaprun diverges to the left from the Mittersill road at (4¹/₂ M.) *Fürth* (p. 135), and crosses the Salzach and the Kaprun moor to (1¹/₂ M.) that village. PEDESTRIANS follow the Mittersill road to (2¹/₄ M.) the second road coming from Bruck, and proceed by the latter to the left as far as the footpath (to the right) constructed by the German Alpine Club. After ¹/₂ hr. the path crosses the Salzach, and then leads along the foot of the hills and below the ruin of *Schloss Kaprun* to the (¹/₂ hr.) village of **Kaprun** (2465'; *Orgler, plain; *Mitteregger*), prettily situated at the entrance to the valley, on both banks of the *Kapruner Ache*.

A cart-track on the right bank of the Ache ascends the valley from Kaprun, crossing the *Kesselbühl*, which forms a barrier across the valley. (The footpath on the left bank, passing a fine gorge of the Ache, is preferable. It diverges to the right, 20 min. from the

Neuwirth, and before the Wüstelau recrosses to the right bank.) The road then passes several farm-houses in the broad and smiling valley, and reaches the (1 hr.) *Hinterwaldhof* in the *Wüstelau* (2945'; Inn, not adapted for night-quarters). On the right are the falls of the *Grubalmbach* (p. 134). After 1/4 hr. more we enter the *Ebenwald*, and ascend gradually, passing (20 min.) a small grotto called the *Küsketler* ('cheese-cellar'). Near this point, 5 min. below the path (finger-post), is a wild gorge *(Kesselklamm)* with an imposing waterfall, which, however, should be approached with caution. Beyond the wood the path becomes steeper and mounts a grassy slope strewn with rocks, skirting the brawling cascades of the Ache. Above the (3/4 hr.) *Stegfeld Bridge* (3840') the Ache issues from a narrow cleft and forms a fine waterfall, and lower down it dashes below the *Devil's Bridge*, a huge rock lying across the stream. The path now rapidly ascends on the left bank and winds up the *Hochstegfeld*. From (1 hr.) the top of the hill, where the path enters the highest reach of the valley, we obtain a fine retrospect, extending to the Steinerne Meer, Hundstod, Hochkalter, and Birnhorn. The route then follows the left bank of the Ache, running high above its bed for some distance, to the (20 min.) *Limberg-Alpe* (5140'), at the beginning of the **Wasserfallboden** (with the majestic *Wiesbachhorn* on the left), and then leads past the *Bauern-Alp* (on the right bank) to the (25 min.) **Orgler Hütte* (bed 1 fl.) and (6 min.) the *Rainerhütte* (5240'; Mayr's Inn, with accommodation for 30 persons). On the opposite bank is the *Wasserfall-Alpe*. Fine view of the Hochtenn, Wielinger Glacier, Fochezkopf (with the Kaindlhütte, high up on the arête, see below), Glockerin, and Bärenköpfe. To the right, in the background of the valley, the falls of the Ache and the Ehmatbach.

The ***Mooserboden** (6330'), 1 hr. from the Rainerhütte, is the chief attraction in the Kapruner Thal, which the traveller should on no account fail to visit (guide from the Rainerhütte 1 fl., unnecessary). We cross the brook to the Wasserfall-Alpe. We may then either follow a path to the right through the valley, which crosses the brook after 10 min., and ascends in zigzags on the left bank (after 8 min. we take the narrower path to the left); or we may ascend by a preferable path to the left from the Wasserfall-Alpe, which crosses the hill to the N. of the *Höhenburg* (p. 134) and leads round the back of it, at first coinciding with the way to the Kaindlhütte (p. 134), and then ascending gently to the right through the valley. The majestic amphitheatre of mountains and glaciers surrounding the *Mooserboden*, the highest part of the Kapruner Thal, presents a most impressive spectacle. From left to right are the Hochtenn, Fochezkopf, Glockerin, Bärenköpfe, Riffelthor, Hohe Riffel, Todtenkopf, Thorkopf, Kapruner Thörl, Grieskogl, and Kitzsteinhorn. In the centre is the imposing *Karlinger Glacier*, descending from the Riffelthor. A path on the left bank of the stream leads over detritus to the (½ hr.) end of the glacier, where the Grosse Wiesbachhorn becomes visible next to the Fochezkopf.

A fine survey of the Mooserboden is obtained from the **Höhenburg** (6990'), a barrier which separates it from the Wasserfallboden (ascend to the left from the Wasserfall-Alp, 1 hr.; guide, 1½ fl., unnecessary). The *Johannisberg* (11,578'), beyond the Riffelthor, is also visible from this point.

ASCENTS FROM THE KAPRUNER THAL (guides, *Ant.* and *Jos. Hetz*, *Thom. Altenberger*, *Thom. Lechner*, *Joh. Mairhofer*, *Franz Nussbaumer*, *Andr. Rupitsch*, and *Joh. Höllwerth*). The **Imbachhorn** (8100'), a splendid point of view, is easily ascended from Kapren, viâ the *Riedlalpe*, in 5 hrs. (guide 4, with descent to Fusch 5 fl.) — The **Kitzsteinhorn** (10,480'; 7½ hrs.; guide 7 fl., with descent to the Rainerhütte 9 fl.) is ascended without difficulty from the *Wüstelau* (p. 133; path practicable for horses as far as the Salzburger Hütte). We ascend past the fall of the *Grubbach*, and through the *Grubalm Valley*, to the (4 hrs.) *Salzburger Hütte* on the *Obere Häuslalm* (c. 6660'; Inn) and then across the extensive *Schmiedinger Glacier* (steep part at the end facilitated by a wire-rope) to the (3½ hrs.) summit. View very striking. Descent to the Rainerhütte by a new path in 2½ hrs. (ascent 4½ hrs.). — The *Schmiedinger* (9615') may be scaled in 3 hrs. from the Salzburger Hütte (guide 6 fl.); also interesting.

The **Grosse Wiesbachhorn** (11,735') is a difficult ascent of 7-8 hrs. (guide 10 fl.; with descent to Ferleiten 11, or the Glocknerhaus 14 fl.). From the Rainerhütte to the *Kaindlhütte* (9075') on the *Fochezkopf*, a laborious ascent of 4 hrs.; we then ascend the *Kaindlgrat*, a sharp arête of névé with precipitous sides, high above the *Lower Wielinger Glacier* (a steady head necessary), to the (2½-3 hrs.) *Wielinger Scharte* (9865'), a ridge of névé between the Fochezkopf and the Wiesbachhorn, and lastly to the left to the (¾ hr.) summit, which commands an imposing view. Descent by the *Keilscharte* to the (4 hrs.) *Hofmannshütte* (p. 152), or by the *Hochgruber Glacier* to the (3 hrs.) *Schwarzenberghütte* and to (3½ hrs.) *Ferleiten*, comp. p. 130.

PASSES. Over the **Riffelthor** (10,140') to the Glocknerhaus (10 hrs. from the Rainerhütte; guide 12 fl.), see p. 154. Over the Riffelthor and the *Bockkarscharte* (9790') to Ferleiten (11-12 hrs.; guide 10 fl.), see p. 131. Both these are imposing glacier-routes, but difficult, particularly the ascent of the crevassed *Kartinger Glacier*. The ascent of the *Johannisberg* (11,578') adds 3 hrs. to either route (guide 13 fl.; comp. p. 163).

Over the **Kapruner Thörl** (8640') to the *Stubachthal* (from the Rainerhütte to the Rudolfshütte 5½, to Kals 10½ hrs.; guide from Kaprun 7, to Uttendorf 10, to Kals 13 fl.), rather fatiguing. From (1½ hr.) the end of the Mooserbodeu across the *Kartinger Glacier* and the steep *Thörl Glacier*, covered with débris, to the (2 hrs.) Thörl, a depression between the *Thorkopf* on the left and the *Kleine Eiser* on the right (fine retrospect of the Mooserboden, Wiesbachhorn, etc.). Descent over the *Riffl Glacier*; then to the left under the precipices of the *Todtenkopf* and the *Hohe Riffl*, and across the moraine of the *Oedenwinkel Glacier*, to the (2 hrs.) *Rudolfshütte* (p. 146). — Over the **Geralscharte** (9120 ft.) to the Stubachthal (to the Rudolfshütte 7 hrs.), fatiguing. — Ascent of the *Hocheiser* (10,510') from the Scharte difficult (3 hrs.; guide 8 fl.). The ascent from the Rainerhütte by the *Birkscdlgrat* is better.

By the *Hirzbachthörl* (9920') to *Fusch*, 8-9 hrs. from the Rainerhütte, with guide, see p. 128. — A fatiguing pass leads to Ferleiten across the **Wiesbach-Thörl** (9765'), between the Kleine Wiesbachhorn and the Hochtenn, descending past the *Walcher Alpe* (7-8 hrs.; guide 9 fl.)

27. From Zell am See to Krimml. Upper Pinzgau.

Comp. Maps, pp. 144, 140, 172.

35½ M. POST-OMNIBUS from Zell am See to Krimml daily in 9½ hrs. (leaving Zell at 6.30 a.m., Mittersill at 11 a.m., and Neukirchen at 1.30 p.m., and arriving at Krimml at 4 p.m.; returning from Krimml at 7 p.m. and

8.30 a.m., leaving Neukirchen at 5 a.m., and arriving in Zell at 11 a.m.). — CARRIAGE from Zell to Mittersill with one horse 6, with two 12 fl.; from Mittersill to Krimml 6-7 or 12 fl. — The scenery of the Upper Pinzgau is somewhat monotonous, but the Krimml waterfalls are highly interesting. The 'Pinzgauer Spazierweg' (p. 117) from Zell to Mittersill viâ the Gaisstein is recommended to pedestrians.

Zell am See, see p. 116. The road skirts the lake for $3/4$ M. and then turns to the right. It is soon joined on the left by the Bruck and Zell road, and farther on by that between Bruck and Mittersill. The valley of the Salzach is here upwards of $1^1/_2$ M. broad, and is swampy at places. The road leads on the N. side, skirting the mountain, to *Aufhausen* and ($3^3/4$ M.) *Fürth*, where the road to the *Kapruner Thal* (p. 132) diverges to the left. At the entrance to the valley of Kaprun lies the village of that name, commanded by the *Kitzsteinhorn*.

Farther on, at (1 M.) *Piesendorf* (Inn), the range between the Kaprun and Fusch valleys comes into view on the S.E., with the *Hochtenn* and the *Wiesbachhorn* (p. 134). Passing *Walchen*, on the boundary between the upper and lower Pinzgau, and *Lengdorf*, we next reach ($4^3/_4$ M.) *Steindorf* (Post, well spoken of). Opposite, on the right bank of the Salzach, lies the hamlet of *Niedernsill*, at the entrance to the *Mühlbachthal*, from which in 1798 three torrents of mud descended into the valley of the Salzach, causing fearful devastation. Near (3 M.) *Uttendorf* (2535'; Post; Liesenwirth; Bäckerwirth) opens the *Stubachthal*, with the *Schneewinkelkopf* (11,590'; route over the *Kalser Tauern* to *Kals*, see p. 145). Above Uttendorf the whole valley was formerly occupied by the river and its numerous stony islands, but much of this area has lately been reclaimed. The road leads by *Stuhlfelden* and the small sulphur-baths of *Burgwies* to ($4^1/_2$ M.) —

Mittersill (2560'; *Schwaiger; Grundmer; Post*), on the left bank), the principal village in the valley. The well-preserved old *Schloss*, on a height on the left bank, 500' above the river, belongs to Count Larisch. (Fine view thence; to the S. the *Velber-Thal*, with the *Tauernkogl*, 9780'.)

EXCURSIONS (guides, *Silvester Nussbaumer, Joh. Brugger*, and *Alois Brunner*). The *Gaisstein* (7745'), a very fine point of view, is ascended without difficulty from Mittersill through the *Mühlthal* in 5-6 hrs. (guide necessary; the night may be spent in the *Bürgthütte*, $3/4$ hr. below the summit, bed 80 kr.). — The *Pihapper Spitze* (8230'), ascended by the *Lach-Alpe* in 6 hrs. (guide), is another fine point. — Road over *Pass Thurn* to *Kitzbühel*, see p. 174. Bridle-path over the *Velber Tauern* to *Windisch-Matrei*, see p. 141 (a route which may be shortened by spending a night at the Schösswender Tauernhaus, 2 hrs., or Spital, 3 hrs. from Mittersill).

The road crosses the Salzach and next reaches (3 M.) *Hollersbach* (2710'), at the mouth of the valley of that name; in the background rises the snowy *Kratzenbergkopf* (9925").

Through the **Hollersbachthal**, a valley about 10 M. long, a path ascends on the right bank of the stream, which forms numerous fine waterfalls, to the *Leitner-Alpe* and the (3 hrs.) *Rossgrub-Alp* (4290'), at the N.E. base of the *Lienzinger Spitze* (9012'). After another hour, above the *Ofner Alpe* (5020'), the valley forks: through the right (W.) branch a

136   *III. Route 27.*   NEUKIRCHEN.   *From Zell am See*

fatiguing route leads past the *Kratzenberg-See* or *Rasberg-See* (7065'); on the right is the *Kratzenberg-Kopf*, 9925', with its glacier, and on the left the *Abreder-Kopf*, 9745') to the **Plenitz-Scharte** (8800'; fine view of the Venediger, Krystallwand, etc.). We may then descend to the left (steep) to (1½ hr.) *Inner-Gschlöss* (p. 140), or (better) to the right, across the *Viltragen Glacier* and round the E. side of the Kesselkopf, to the (2 hrs.) *Prager-Hütte* (p. 140). — In the left (E.) arm of the valley the path first ascends past the *Ochsen-Alpe* over the pastures of the *Weissenecker Alpe*, and then toils over a stony tract to the (3½ hrs.) **Weissenecker Scharte** (8600'), between the *Dichtenkopf* (9250') on the right and the *Fechtebenkopf* (9415') on the left. The steep descent leads past a small ice-tarn to the Velber-Tauern route, where we proceed to the left to the (2½ hrs.) *Matreier Tauernhaus* (p. 140).

Beyond Hollersbach we return to the left bank of the Salzach and reach (2¼ M.) *Mühlbach*, with sulphur-mines (path thence to *Pass Thurn*, see p. 174); then (¼ M.) *Picheln*, (1½ M.) *Bramberg*, and (1½ M.) *Weierhof*, with a ruined castle (Inn, with good old wood-carvings). Opposite is the mouth of the *Habachthal*, with the *Habach Glacier*, the *Hohe Fürleg* (10,750'), and the *Grün-Habachkopf* (9725') in the background.

A difficult pass leads through the wild Habachthal and over the *Habach-Scharte* to *Gschlöss* (10-11 hrs.; guide 7 fl.; Alois Wurnisch of Bramberg recommended). The path leads from Weierhof across the Salzach to the hamlet of *Habach*, and ascends first on the W., and then on the E. bank of the brook to the (3 hrs.) *Mayer-Alp* (4090'); thence through the narrow *Kothgasse* to the (1 hr.) *Keesau*, whence we ascend to the left to the (1¼ hr.) *Gross-Weitalpe* (7300'), which affords a fine view of the head of the valley. Hence across the *Habach Glacier* to (3 hrs.) the *Habach-Scharte* (c. 9500'), between the Schwarzkopf and the Grün-Habachkopf; then descend over the *Viltragen Glacier* to (3-3½ hrs.) *Inner-Gschlöss* (p. 140). — Over the *Kesselscharte* (8740') to the Lower Sulzbachthal, not difficult.

On the left, beyond (3 M.) **Neukirchen** (2800'; *Schett; Kammertander*), a considerable village, is the *Sulzau*, a district at the junction of the *Unter-* and *Ober-Sulzbachthal*, which are separated by the *Mitterkopf*.

Excursions (guides, *Dom. Kronbichler, Jos. Lechner, Lor. Lentgeb, Caj. Nussbaumer,* and *Joh. Unterwurzacher*). The *Rechteckbauer*, on the slope of the *Russberg*, 1 hr. to the N.W., affords a splendid view of the Venediger and the two branches of the Sulzbachthal. A far grander view is obtained from the *Wildkogel (7200'; 4 hrs.; guide, unnecessary, 2 fl.; new bridle-path), particularly of the imposing pyramid of the Venediger at the end of the Habachthal and the Grosse Rettenstein, towering immediately to the N. (Refuge-hut at the top; inn in summer.) The traveller may descend to Pass Thurn, to Jochberg, or to Kirchberg (guide in this case 5-6 fl.).

Pleasant walk to the *Untersulzbach Fall (¾ hr.). This good new path leads along the left bank of the stream, mostly through wood, affording fine views of the waterfall (160' high). — A steep path ascends through the Untersulzbachthal, on the right bank of the stream, past an abandoned copper-mine, the *Wagner-Alp*, and the *Abichel-Alp*, to the (3½ hrs.) *Innere Hochalp* or *Aschham Alp* (5520'; poor quarters). ¾ hr. below the end of the crevassed *Unter-Sulzbach Glacier*. The *Venediger* (see below) may be ascended from this point in 8-9 hrs. (arduous, and not recommended). Over the *Unter-Sulzbach-Thörl* (9265') to *Gschlöss* (p. 140), 8 hrs., difficult.

A tolerable path (guide to the Körsinger Hütte 4½ fl.; to the Gross-Venediger 9, with descent to the Matreier Tauernhaus 14, to Windisch-Matrei 16, by the Velber Tauern to Mittersill 15 fl.) ascends the **Ober-Sulzbachthal** on the right bank of the stream, past several Alps and waterfalls (one at the *Wegeralp* upwards of 300' high), to the (4 hrs. from

Neukirchen) *Ascham-Alp* (3390'; riding practicable thus far). Then a steep ascent by the *Stierlahner Wand* and *Keeslahner Wand* to the (3 hrs.) *Kürsinger Hütte* (8990'; Inn in summer) in the *Keeskar*. Magnificent *View of the huge *Ober-Sulzbach Glacier* (the ice-fall of which is called the 'Türkische Zeltstadt'), surrounded by the peaks of the Venediger group: the *Gross-Venediger*, *Grosse Geiger*, *Maurerkeesköpfe*, *Sonntagskopf*, and *Schlieferspitze*. The ascent of the Venediger (12,050'; 4-5 hrs.) from the hut is somewhat laborious (see pp. 140, 142); in the Obersulzbach glacier is a wide crevasse, crossed by a ladder. Over the *Ober-Sulzbach-Thörl* or the *Maurer-Thörl* to *Prägraten*, see pp. 142, 143; over the *Zwischen-* and the *Unter-Sulzbach-Thörl* to *Gschlöss*, see p. 141; over the *Krimmler Thörl* to the *Karalpe* in the Krimmler-Thal, see p. 142 (these all difficult).

The road crosses a mound of debris at the mouth of the *Dürnbachgraben* (view of the Venediger from the chapel to the left), passes the ruin of the *Hiebury* (right), and reaches (3 M.) *Wald* (2865'; *Strasser's Inn), where the direct route to (13 M.) *Gerlos*, viâ *Ronach*, diverges to the right (p. 181). Our road turns to the left and crosses the (1½ M.) *Salza*, which here unites with the Krimmler Ache to form the *Salzach*. It then leads round a projecting rock called the *Falkenstein*, and ascends in the broad valley to (3 M.) —

Krimml (3410'; *Waldl*, R. 70 kr.; guide, *Joh. Scharr*), a pleasant village, chiefly visited on account of its magnificent **Waterfalls**, the finest among the German Alps.

The *Krimmler Ache*, the discharge of the great Krimml Glacier, is precipitated in three falls into the valley below, a depth of about 1400'. The three falls are not seen simultaneously except from a distance; the highest only is visible from the inn. The finest points of view are rendered easily accessible by the new *Walks on the left bank, constructed by the German and Austrian Alpine Club. Guide unnecessary. A road leads from the back of the inn in the direction of the falls as far as a (¼ hr.) finger-post, where we go straight on (while the old Tauern path crosses the bridge to the left), soon reaching the new path, which ascends in rocky steps. In ¼ hr. we reach the first point of view ('Kürsinger-Platz'), where we view the *Lowest Fall* as it thunders into its basin at our feet and bedews us with its spray, in which the sun forms beautiful rainbow hues. Returning a few paces from this point, we then ascend to the *Regenhäuschen*, a pavilion which commands another admirable survey of the lowest fall, and to (5 min.) a third point of view overlooking the same fall. We next pass a platform at the foot of the *Central Fall* and reach the (¼ hr.) *Riemann's Kanzel* (named after the late president of the Pinzgau branch of the German Alpine Club), a projecting rock with a parapet and seats above the beginning of the lowest fall, in a wild and grand situation. Passing another view of the second fall, we visit (¼ hr.) a projecting rock which affords a fine view towards Krimml, and then ascend over the *Schönangerl* (refreshments at the chalet on the right bank) to the (¼ hr.) 'Jung-Kanzel', the first point of view for the *Highest Fall*, which descends in two leaps from a height of about 650'. (Those who do not care to mount to the top of this fall should at least ascend for a few hundred paces more in order to obtain a complete view of it.) About 10 min. higher is the 'Sendtner-Kanzel', and near the top of the fall (20 min.) is another coign of vantage. At the top of the falls, close to the brink of the rocks over which the Ache is precipitated, a bridge ('Schett-Brücke') crosses the stream to the Tauern path on the right bank. We return to Krimml by the same route. (From Krimml to the foot of the highest fall and back 3 hrs.)

OVER THE KRIMMLER TAUERN TO KASERN, 10 hrs. (guide as far as the Tauernthörl advisable; to Kasern 7 fl.; comp. Map, p. 140). From the head of the upper fall (4400'; see above) the path gradually ascends the sequartered *Krimmler Achenthal* to the (3½ hrs. from Krimml) *Krimmler Tauernhaus* (5320'; poor inn). At the *Unters-Alp* (5145'), ½ hr. farther on, the path quits the Achenthal (in which, 1¼ hr. higher up, is the *Karalpe*, whence the route described at p. 142 leads over the *Krimmler Thörl* and *Obersulzbach-Thörl* to Prägraten), and ascends somewhat steeply to the S.W. in the bleak *Windbachthal*. Fine view of the extensive *Krimmler Glacier*, enclosed by the *Schliefer-Spitze*, the *Sonntagskopf*, the *Maurerkees-köpfe*, the *Simony-Spitze*, and the *Dreiherrn-Spitze*; to the W. is the triple-peaked *Windbachthalkopf* (9295'). From the (3 hrs.) **Krimmler Tauern** (8645') a splendid *View is obtained, to the S., of the Dreiherrn-Spitze, the Rödt-spitze, and the Rieserferner. Then follows a rapid descent to (2 hrs.) *Kasern* (5135'; Hofer's Inn, rustic), the highest village in the *Prettau*, or upper *Ahrnthal*.

From Krimml to Gerlos over the Platte (3½ hrs.), see p. 181; guide (2 fl. 60 kr.) unnecessary, if the traveller is shown the way as far as the ascent through the wood. Over the *Plattenkogl to Gerlos (5 hrs.), guide advisable (3½ fl.). Horse to the Plattenkogl 4 fl., over the Platte to Gerlos 7, to Zell 13 fl.

28. From Lienz to Windisch-Matrei and Prägraten. The Iselthal.

Comp. Map, p. 140.

Post-Stellwagen from Lienz (Traube) to *Windisch-Matrei* (18½ M.) daily at 9.30 a.m. in 5½ hrs. (fare 1 fl. 50 kr.; to Huben 1 fl.); from Windisch-Matrei to Lienz at 12.30 a.m. (to Huben 50 kr., from Huben to Lienz 1 fl.). — One-horse carr. to Windisch-Matrei (4 hrs.) 7, two-horse 10 fl.; to Huben 4 or 6 fl.; to St. Johann im Wald 3 or 4½ fl.; from Windisch-Matrei to Lienz 6½ or 11½ fl.; to Huben 2½ or 4½ fl.

Lienz (2190'), see p. 334. The lower *Iselthal* is monotonous and unattractive for walkers. The road passes the shooting-ranges (to the S. the Lienz Dolomites, to the E. the Schleinitz) and *Schloss Bruck* (p. 334), crosses to the left bank of the Isel, and then leads through scanty wood, leaving *Ober-Lienz* on the right (in the background the *Maurer Glacier* in the Virgenthal is visible). Beyond (4½ M.) *Ainet* (Egger), the road leads straight on along the Isel, passing the *Schloss* and *Bud Weierburg*, to (4½ M.) **St. Johann im Wald** (2400'; *Inn), where we recross the stream.

The **Weisse Wand** (7960'), a good point of view, is ascended from St. Johann in 5-6 hrs. (fatiguing; with guide, 5 fl.), viâ the *Michelbach-Alpe*. — The **Hochschober** (10,640'; 7-8 hrs.; difficult; guide 8 fl.) commands a superb view. From St. Johann we ascend rapidly to the E. to (1½ hr.) *Ober-Leibnig* (4025'), and thence through the wooded *Leibniger-Thal* to the (2 hrs.) *Leibniger-Alpe* (scanty accommodation) and to the (1½ hr.) small *Gattensees*, on the saddle between the Lemnitz and the Hochschober. Thence we proceed towards the N.W., over loose stones, rock, and snow to the (2 hrs.) top. The descent may be made through the *Lesach-Thal* to *Kals* (see p. 148).

The road passes the ruined *Kienburg*, just beyond which, to the left, at the mouth of the *Defereyger-Thal*, 10 min. above the road, s the **Glockner-Aussicht*, affording a striking view of the Glockner. — 9 M. **In der Huben** (2570'; *Scheitz). Thence to *Kals*, see p. 145. Ascent of the *Rottenkogel*, see p. 139.

The **Deferegger-Thal** (24 M. long) presents little attraction, with the exception of the upper part, terminated by the Rieserferner group and the Röthspitze. The natives are in the habit of emigrating as carpet-dealers, and return home after having amassed a competency. Hence the superior dress and language of many of the inhabitants. The cart-road ascends abruptly from Huben and reaches the valley at (3½ M.) *Hopfgarten* (3575'; Inn, primitive), on the left bank of the *Schwarzach* (*Deferegger Bach*). [From this point, with a guide, through the *Zwenewald-Thal* and over the *Villgratner-Joch* (8465') to the *Winkelthal*, and viâ *Ausser-Villgraten* to *Sillian* (p. 383). 6-7 hrs.; the pass affords an admirable view of the Glockner, the Venediger, and the Dolomites.] The valley contracts; to the right lies *St. Veit*, high above us; in the background the peaks of the Rieserferner. Then (9 M.) *St. Leonhard*, situated on a mound of debris at the broadest part of the valley, and (1½ M.) **St. Jakob** (4525'; °*Ladstätter; Zum Untereiner*, well spoken of), at the mouth of the *Trojer Thal*. [Passes: From St. Jakob to the N. to Prägraten or Virgen over the *Mullitzthörl* (8-9 hrs.; guide 5 fl.), see p. 143; this route is easily combined with the ascent of the Lasörling (p. 142). — To Prägraten over the *Bachlenke* (8 hrs.; guide), see p. 143. — From St. Jakob to the S.W. through the *Lapplhal* and over the *Gsieser Thörl* (7200'), with fine view, to (4 hrs.) *St. Magdalena*, in the Gsieser Thal, and (4 hrs.) *Welsberg* (p. 330).]

The village of (3½ M.) **Erlsbach** (5055'; *Stampfer*) is the last in the valley, which here turns towards the N.W. The cart-track passes the mouth (left) of the *Staller-Thal* (traversed by the route to *Antholz* over the *Staller-Sattel*, p. 330), and then that of the *Patscher-Thal*, at the head of which the *Hochgall* (p. 389) is for a short time visible, and reaches the (2 hrs.) *Seebach-Alpe* (6155'). To the W. rises the Fleischbachspitze, to the E. the Todtenkorspitze and the Panargenspitze. About ½ hr. farther up the valley divides: the main branch, now called the *Schwarzachthal*, stretches towards the N. (the *Affenthal*, to the W., see below). [Over the *Schwarze-Thörl* (9650') to the Daberthal and Umbalthal, see p. 144; another pass crosses the *Rothenmannjoch* (about 9510'), between the *Röthspitze* (p. 144) and the *Kemetspitze* (10,164'), and descends across the *Röthkees* to the *Röthlhal* and to (7 hrs.) *Kasern* in the Prettau, p. 190; trying, and fit for proficients only.]

In the *Affenthal*, the N.W. arm of the valley, 20 min. farther up, lies the **Jagdhaus-Alpe** (6600'), with numerous chalets and a chapel. Thence over the *Klammi-Joch* to the (3 hrs.) *Reinthal*, see p. 340; over the *Merbjöchl* to the *Prettau*, see p. 191.

The new road from Huben to (6 M.) Matrei, completed in 1885, gradually ascends through wood on the right bank of the Isel, and crosses that river about 1 M. before reaching —

18½ M. **Windisch-Matrei** (3190'; *Hamerl*, with baths; *Wohlgemuth*, well spoken of; *Schneeberger's Brewery*), prettily situated, the chief village (2600 inhab.) in the Iselthal, the upper part of which beyond this point is called the *Virgenthal*. In the vicinity the Tauernthal ascends towards the N. The village is protected by huge stone dams against the ravages of the *Bürgerbach*, which descends from the Bretterwand on the E. — To the N.W. is the (¼ hr.) château of *Weissenstein* (3380'), now a *Hotel and Pension, adapted for a stay of some time.

EXCURSIONS (guides: *Franz Raneburger*, *Andr. Eder*, *Andr. Köll*, *Virgil Oberfelner*, *Joh.* and *Andr. Untersteiner*, *Franz Asslaber*, *Vinc. Ganzer*, *Simon Penzl*, and *Joh. Wibmer*; the guides' office is at Hamerl's). Pleasant walk past the old church of *St. Nikolaus* and the *Guggenberger Höfe* to the (1½ hr.) Lukaskreuz, commanding an admirable view of the Lasörling and the glaciers at the head of the Virgenthal. A more extensive view is obtained from the **Reiterboden** (7500'), reached viâ Guggenberg and the *Arnitz-Alpe* in 4 hrs. (guide).

The **Kals-Matreier Thörl** (7235'; p. 145), a splendid point of view, is ascended in 3½-4 hrs.; guide unnecessary (1 fl. 80; to Kals 2 fl. 80 kr.).

The **Rettenkogel** (9045'; 5 hrs.; guide 4 fl.) is very attractive. We follow the route to the Kalser Thörl for ½ hr., diverge to the right, and

140 *III. Route 28.*   GSCHLÖSS.   *From Lienz*

cross the (1½ hr.) *Rainer Alp*; then for 2 hrs. over detritus, fatiguing; lastly we ascend the rocky *Gamsleiten* to the (¾ hr.) summit. The ascent may also be made from Huben (p. 138; viâ *Matterberg*, 6 hrs., with guide).

The **Zunigkopf** (9075'; 5 hrs.; guide 3 fl.), the E. peak of the range separating the valleys of Defereggen and Virgen, is another fine point of view.

An excellent view of the Glockner, Venediger, etc., is obtained from the **Nussingkogel** (9796'; 5½ hrs.; guide 4 fl.). The route ascends, partly through wood, past Schloss Weissenstein and the hamlet of (1¼ hr.) *Stein* (4545'; see below) to the (1¼ hr.) *Untere Steiner Alpe* (5675; beds). Thence by the *Obere Steiner Alpe* to the (3 hrs.) summit, not difficult.

To **Gschlöss** (there and back, 11 hrs.; guide 3½ fl., needless; horse 9 fl.), a very fine excursion. A broad bridle-path (Pinzgauer Tauernweg, see below) ascends through the *Tauernthal* towards the N., passing *Schloss Weissenstein* (see above) on the right, and after 25 min. crosses to the right bank of the *Tauernbach*, which here issues from a grand but inaccessible gorge. About ½ hr. beyond *Proseck* (fine retrospect of Windisch-Matrei; opposite us on the left bank, the lofty *Steinbach Fall* and the houses of *Stein*) the path returns to the left bank of the deep ravine. At (1½ hr.) *Gruben* the narrow *Frosnitzthal* opens on the left. Thence the path gradually ascends, crossing the brook twice, to the (1½ hr.) *Landecksäge* (4240'; 'Inn, plain), at the mouth of the (E.) *Landeckthal* (p. 146), through which an interesting pass leads across the *Granatscharte* (c. 9800') to the (6-7 hrs.) *Rudolfshütte* (see p. 146). Then a rather steeper ascent to the (1½ hr.) *Matreier Tauernhaus* (4080'; Inn, dear). The good new path to the Gschlöss diverges to the left at the *Ganzer Alp*, ¼ hr. higher, crosses a bridge (fine fall of the Tauernbach, with the Venediger in the background), and reaches the chalets of (½ hr.) *Ausser-Gschlöss* and (¾ hr.) **Inner-Gschlöss** (5590'; Rfmts. at the last chalet on the right bank). The *Schlaten Glacier*, which in the last 15 years has lost very much of its former magnificence, here falls into a green basin, overshadowed by the Klein-Venediger, the Gross-Venediger, the Schwarze Wand, and the Krystallwand. To the right, separated from this glacier by the Kesselkopf, is the *Viltragen Glacier*. The chapel hewn in a huge block of gneiss is interesting.

EXCURSIONS FROM GSCHLÖSS. (Guides must be brought from Windisch-Matrei, p. 139.)

The **Rothe Säule** (8420'; 3½ hrs.; guide 2 fl.), not difficult; ascent across pastures, and then loose stones; good view of the Venediger. The descent may be made to the *Hollersbachthal* (see p. 136).

The *°**Gross-Venediger**° (12,050'; one guide suffices for 1-3 pers., two for 4-5 pers.; from Windisch-Matrei 11, with descent to Prägraten 11½, to the Kecsalpe in the Krimmler Thal 15 fl.; to the Prager Hütte alone in one day 5, two days 7 fl.), a most interesting excursion, presenting little difficulty to proficients (comp. p. 142). From Inner-Gschlöss the route leads by the left bank of the Gschlössbach and across the discharge of the *Viltragen Glacier* at the foot of the Kesselkopf, and ascends, at first over turf, and then for some distance over the lateral moraines of the Schlaten Glacier, to the (3-3½ hrs.) **Prager Hütte** (about 8700'; *Inn* in summer), grandly situated on the S. slope of the Kesselkopf. A new path ascends from the hut over rocky debris to the *Schlaten Glacier*, which we ascend gradually towards the *Niedere Zaun* (10,050'), a crest of rock separating it from the Viltragen Glacier. The *Klein-Venediger* (11,415') remains on the right. The *Rainerhorn* (p. 142) soon becomes visible on the S.; then, facing us, the rounded summit of the Venediger, which is reached on the S.E. side in 4-4½ hrs. from the Prager Hütte. It is not advisable to go to the extreme and highest point of the long snow-clad crest, as the overhanging masses of snow render it difficult and sometimes impossible of access. The °View, hardly inferior to that from the Gross-Glockner, comprises to the E. the Glockner (the Gross-Glockner appearing like a slender pinnacle) and Schober groups; to the S., the wild and serrated Dolomites; W., the Dreiherrnspitze, Röthspitze, Daberspitze, and Rieserferner Ms., and, in the distance, the Adamello, Ortler, Bernina, the Oetzthal, Stubai, and Zillerthal Alps; N., the Kitzbühel

Mts., the Chiemsee, and the N. Dolomites as far as the Dachstein; immediately at our feet lie the huge ice-cataracts by which the mountain is encircled. — Descent to Prägraten: we traverse the snow of the Schlaten Glacier to the saddle between the *Hohe Aderl* and the *Rainerhorn*, cross the *Rainer Glacier* to the *Defreggerhütte* on the *Mullwitz-Aderl* and to the *Johannshütte* (comp. p. 142; to Prägraten, 4½-5 hrs.). — TO THE OBER-SULZBACHTHAL the descent is difficult: first between the Gross and Klein-Venediger to the *Unter-Sulzbach Glacier* (descent to the *Unter-Sulzbachthal* somewhat hazardous); then to the W. over the *Zwischen-Sulzbach-Thörl* (9440') to the *Ober-Sulzbach Glacier* and (3 hrs.) the *Kürsinger Hütte* (p. 137). — The descent to the *Karalpe* in the Krimmler Thal, see p. 142.

Other passes from Gschlöss: Over the *Plenitz-Scharte* or the *Weissenecker Scharte* into the *Hollersbach-Thal* (p. 136); over the *Unter-Sulzbach-Thörl* to the *Unter-Sulzbachthal*, difficult (comp. p. 137).

FROM WINDISCH-MATREI TO MITTERSILL in the Pinzgau, 12-13 hrs. (guide, unnecessary for adepts, 8 fl.; horse to the Matreier Tauernhaus 7, Velber Tauern 15 fl.). This trip is better made in two days, in combination with a visit to the Gschlöss (p. 140). To the (4½ hrs.) *Matreier Tauernhaus*, see p. 140. At the *Ganzer Alp* our path ascends steeply to the right, affording a fine view of the Schlatenkees and the Venediger, and then follows the left bank of the *Tauernbach*, through a bleak valley and past two refuge-huts, to the (3 hrs.) **Velber Tauern** (8330'). The view here is limited, but the *Tauernkogl* (9780'), to the W., ascended from the Tauern in 1½ hr., commands a splendid prospect. The path crosses loose stones and descends steeply to the *Nassfeld*, with its two small lakes (*Platlsee* and *Lackelsee*); to the left rise the *Tauernkogl* (9780') and the sombre *Freiwand*. The path then follows the *Velber Thal* (the *Hintersee*, 4275', remaining there, to the left) to the (2½ hrs.) *Tauernhaus Spital* and the (¼ hr.) *Tauernhaus* on *Schösswend* (3530'; good quarters and guides), ½ hr. below which the *Ammerthaler Oed* opens on the right. Then, crossing the *Velber Bach* several times, to (1½ hr.) *Mittersill* (p. 135).

FROM WINDISCH-MATREI TO THE VIRGENTHAL. A rough road leads to (11 M.) Prägraten (horse to Virgen 3½, to Prägraten 5, porter 2½ fl.). Driving is possible as far as Virgen, but is not recommended. The icy regions of the Venediger group are not visible from the bottom of the valley, but are disclosed to view when the Johannshütte is reached (p. 142). The road crosses the Tauernbach and ascends through wood on the left bank of the Isel, viâ *Mitteldorf*, to (5 M.) **Virgen** (3900'; *Bräu*). On the hill to the right is the ruin of *Rabenstein*; to the left the *Lasörling*.

The **Lasörling** (10,150'; 6-7 hrs., fatiguing; guides, *Joh.* and *Jos. Mariacher* or *Jak. Resinger*, 5 fl.) is a very fine point of view. From Virgen or Welzelach (see below) we proceed to the S. through the *Mullitzthal* to the (1½ hr.) *Stadler-Schutzhaus* (5250'; Rfmts. and beds); then over a slope of detritus, and round the arête, which stretches to the S.E., to the (2½ hrs.) S. base of the peak, which is attained after a laborious ascent of 1½ hr. more over debris. View imposing: N., the Venediger group; W., the Rieserferner; E. the Glockner and Schober; S., the distant Ampezzo Dolomites. — The *Mullitz-Thörl*, see p. 143.

The cart-track to (6 M.) Prägraten leads on the right bank of the Isel viâ (3 M.) *Welzelach*. The footpath by (20 min.) *Obernauer*, running high up on the N. slope, and descending through wood to (50 min.) *Bowojach* and (½ hr.) Prägraten, is preferable.

Prägraten (4275'; *Stainer's Inn, below the church), a prettily-situated village, is a good starting-point for excursions among the Venediger group.

EXCURSIONS. Guides: *Thom. Ploner*, *Thom. Mariacher*, *Jos. Berger*,

Alois Weisskopf, *Simon Mair*, and *Jakob Stainer*. Application should be made to the inn-keeper *Isaias Stainer*, the chief of the guides' association. The tariff is given in connection with the different excursions. The guides provide themselves with food. The return-journey is paid for if the guide is dismissed at a distance from home. Each guide is bound to carry 15lbs. of luggage; overweight 2 kr. per lb. per hour.

The **Bergerkogl** (8700'; 3½-4 hrs.; guide 3 fl.) commands a very fine view, particularly of the Venediger group. We ascend to the S., through the *Zopetnitzthal*, to the (2 hrs.) *Berger See* (7115'), and in 1½ hr. more to the top. Similar view from the **Toinig** (8720'; 2½ hrs.; guide 5 fl.), between the *Lasnitzthal* and the *Kleinbachthal*.

The **Lasörling** (10,150'; 6-7 hrs.; guide 5 fl.) may be ascended from Prägraten through the *Losnitzthal* (difficult); better from *Welzelach* and through the *Mullitzthal* (p. 141).

The *Gross-Venediger* (12,050'; guide 6 fl., with descent to Gschlöss 10, to the Kürsinger Hütte 10, to the Karalpe 11 fl.), a most interesting ascent, and not difficult for adepts. Travellers who ascend from Prägraten spend the night at the Johannshütte or the Defreggerhaus. We follow the cart-track through the valley to the W., pass the (½ hr.) *Bühel*, and ascend the bridle-path to the right, and in ½ hr. turn into the *Kleine Iselthal*, which near its mouth forms a deep gully. Below are the houses of *Hinterbühl*. On the left, the precipices of the *Schlüsselspitze* and the *Niklaskopf*. The *Islitzbach* with its numerous falls remains on the left, and farther on rushes through a wild subterranean channel. Near the *Gumpach-Krenz* (6425') a view is suddenly disclosed of the Venediger, Hohe Aderl, Rainerhorn, and the Dorfer, Rainer, and Mullwitz glaciers. Then past a herdsmen's hut to (3 hrs. from Prägraten) the **Johannshütte** (6850'), in a small hollow, the property of the Austrian Alpine Club. Immediately beyond the hut we cross the discharge of the Mullwitz Glacier, ascend over slopes of turf, detritus, and rock, and then skirt the *Capunizachköpfl* (9060') towards the right (the *Mullwitz Glacier* lies to the right; the extensive *Dorfer Glacier* below, to the left) to the (3-3½ hrs.) **Defregger-Schutzhaus** (10,330'; Inn in summer), opened by the Austrian Tourist Club in 1887, on the *Mullwitz-Aderl* (10,614'), a rocky crest between the *Mullwitz* and *Rainer Glaciers*. We now descend by a ladder to the surface of the Rainer Glacier, and ascend across it to the snow-saddle between the *Hohe Aderl* (11,486') and the *Rainerhorn* (11,660'), whence we obtain a view, to the right, of the *Schlaten Glacier*, descending to the Gschlöss. We then ascend the upper névé of the glacier to the (2 hrs.) summit. — Descent by the *Schlatenkees* to the *Prager-Hütte*, see p. 140; to the *Obersulzbachthal* or *Krimmlerthal*, see p. 141.

Passes. To the Obersulzbachthal over the Obersulzbach-Thörl (to the Kürsinger Hütte 8, to Neukirchen 12 hrs.; guide 7 or 10 fl.). From the Johannshütte (see above) we cross the gradually-sloping *Dorfer Glacier* to the (3 hrs.) *Obersulzbach-Thörl* (9400'; 6 hrs. from Prägraten, guide 4 fl.): admirable view of the N. side of the Venediger group, to the left the Sonntagskopf and Schlieferspitze, to the right the Keeskogel. Descent, steep and fatiguing, over the *Obersulzbach Glacier*, and then to the right, above its fall ('Türkische Zeltstadt'), to the (2 hrs.) *Kürsinger Hütte* (p. 137); to *Neukirchen* (p. 136) 4 hrs. more.

To Krimml by the Obersulzbach-Thörl and Krimmler Thörl, very interesting, and free from danger (from the Johannshütte to the Karalpe 7 hrs., to Krimml 4-5 hrs. more; guide 7½ fl.). By this pass the long circuit by the Umbalthörl and the Krimmler Tauern is avoided. From the Johannshütte to the (3 hrs.) *Obersulzbachthörl*, see above. We then descend to the highest névé of the *Obersulzbach Glacier*, describe a circuit to the left of the Grosse Geiger and the Maurerkeesköpfe, in the direction of the slopes of the Sonntagskopf, and thus reach the ice-clad depression of the (2 hrs.) Krimmler **Thörl** (9280'). Steep descent between the *Sonntagskees* on the right and the fissured *Krimmler Glacier* on the left, and across the level tongue and the moraine of the latter, to the (2 hrs.) *Innerkees-Alpe* or *Karalpe* (p. 138). — Through the *Maurerthal* to the Krimmler Thörl (shorter, and not difficult), see p. 143.

Maurerthal. Maurer-Thörl. Reggen-Thörl. The **Maurerthal**, to the W. of the Kleine Iselthal (p. 142), and parallel with it, has hitherto been little visited, but is well worthy of notice. We follow the Iselthal as far as (1 hr.) *Streden* (4510'), the last farm (see below), cross the Maurerbach, and enter the valley to the right; 5 min., the *Maurer-Alp;* cross the brook to the (10 min.) *Görlach Alp*; then ascend gradually on the left bank. As soon as the forest zone is quitted, a beautiful amphitheatre of snow-mountains and glaciers is disclosed: to the W., the Malham-Spitze and Gubach-Spitze, between them the Reggenthörl; N.W., the Simony-Spitze; N., the Maurerkeesköpfe and Grosse Geiger; E., the Grosse Happ and Kleine Happ. We next pass a cow-shed and ascend the pastures to the (1¼ hr.) tongue of the *Maurer Glacier.* The route to the Maurer-Thörl (with guide and rope, safe) traverses the gradually-ascending Maurer Glacier, and finally mounts a rocky slope 100' in height, in 3 hrs. (from Streden 4½ hrs.) to the **Maurer Thörl** (9500'), to the E. of the *Hintere Maurerkeeskopf.* View similar to that from the Obersulzbach-Thörl. Then a walk of 1 hr., free from danger, across the gently-sloping snow of the *Ober-Sulzbachfirn,* to the *Krimmler Thörl* (p. 142), or of 2 hrs. to the *Kürsinger Hütte* (p. 137). — Ascent of the **Grosse Geiger** (11,000') difficult, both from the Maurer and the Dorfer Glacier.

REGGEN-THÖRL. We ascend the slopes of the *Dellacher Keesflecken,* between the Maurer and Simony glaciers, take to the latter, and follow the left margin of the S. arm of the glacier, crossing furrowed snow-slopes, steep at places, to the flat snow-saddle of the **Reggen-Thörl** (9980'), a pass between the *Malham-Spitze* and the *S. Gubach-Spitze* (5½ hrs. from Streden). Fine survey of the Dreiherrenspitze and the Umbal Glacier. Gradual descent of 3 hrs. (little crevassed) to the *Clara-Hütte* in the Umbalthal (see below). Those bound for the Prettau may go direct from the Reggenthörl to the (2 hrs.) *Hintere Umbal-Thörl* (see p. 144).

The DEFEREGGERTHAL may be reached from Prägraten by the *Mullitz-thörl* or by the *Bachlenke.* The path to the former (to St. Jakob 8-9 hrs.; guide 5 fl.) ascends from (1 hr.) *Welzelach* (p. 141) to the S. through the *Mullitzthal* to the (1½ hr.) *Stadlerhütte* (5250') and along the S.E. base of the *Lasörling* (p. 141). It then turns to the left, crosses the brook, and ascends abruptly to the (3 hrs.) **Mullitz-Thörl**, or **Prägratner Thörl** (8910'), whence we obtain a fine view of the Venediger behind us, and of the Lasörling to the right. Descent into the *Tegischthal*, and to the right to (2½-3 hrs.) *St. Jakob* (p. 139). — The route over the *Bachlenke* is finer (8-9 hrs.; guide 5½ fl.). From Prägraten we ascend the valley to the (1½ hr.) *Pebell-Alpe* (see below), above which we turn to the left, cross the Isel, and mount through the picturesque *Grossbachthal*, with its numerous waterfalls, to the *Untere Alp.* Thence a steep ascent (on the left a fine *Waterfall) to the *Obere Alp*, and over slopes of turf and debris to the (3½ hrs.) **Bachlenke** (or *Trojer Thörl;* 8850'). Shortly before reaching the top of the pass we enjoy a beautiful retrospect of the Venediger and Dreiherrnspitze. We descend, at first turning to the right, and passing a small lake on the left, into the upper *Trojer Thal* (opposite the *Panargenspitze*), follow the steep grassy slopes on the left side of the valley (path soon improving) to the *Upper* and *Lower Trojer-Alp* (5960'), and traverse the picturesque and narrow valley to (3 hrs.) *St. Jakob.*

A visit to the *Umbalthal, or highest region of the Iselthal, is recommended (from Prägraten to the Clarahütte 4 hrs.; guide for the inexperienced 3 fl.). The road in the valley leads past the *Bühel*, crossing the *Islitzbach* (p. 142) at the houses of *Hinterbühl*, to (1 hr.) *Streden* (4510'), the last farm, at the mouth of the *Maurerthal* (see above; in the background rise the *Maurerkeesköpfe*). At the *Pebell-Alpe* (4925'), ½ hr. farther on, the path crosses the Isel (to the left the beautiful fall of the *Grossbach*, see above), and then ascends on the right bank, passing a (10 min.) second waterfall. A steeper ascent, through wood, passing a fine fall of the Isel on the right, brings us to a higher region of the valley. After 1 hr. we cross the brook and follow a narrow path on the steep grassy slopes of the left bank, passing a (1/2 hr.) shepherd's hut. To the left opens the *Daberthal* (see below), at the head of which rise the Todtenkorspitze and the Panargenspitze, with their glacier; facing us is the Röthspitze with the Welitzkees (see below). The path now crosses a rocky barrier, and then descends to the (3/4 hr.) *Clarahütte* (6900'), a club-hut belonging to the Austrian Alpine Club. — About 1/2 hr. higher the magnificent *Umbal Glacier* (not visible from the hut) descends into the valley.

MOUNTAIN ASCENTS. The **Dreiherrnspitze** (11,480'; 5-6 hrs.; guide 7 1/2 fl.) is fatiguing, and fit only for experienced mountaineers. We first cross the lower, nearly level part of the *Umbal Glacier* (1 1/2 hr.), then ascend the grassy and rocky slopes of the *Schlattner Keesflecken* to the upper region of the glacier, and cross the latter towards the N.E., below the *Althausscheid*. Lastly a steep ascent to a rock projecting towards the S.E., which we mount (with caution owing to its friable nature) to a snowy plateau immediately below the summit, whence we reach the top by traversing a snowy arête. *View extensive, but obstructed towards the N.E. by the Venediger. The descent may be made by the *Hintere Umbalthörl* to Kasern. (Descent over the *Prettaukees* or *Lahnerkees* not advisable.)

The *Röthspitze (*Welz*, 11,400'; 4-5 hrs.; guide 6 1/2, with descent to Kasern 10 fl.), a very fine point of view, is also toilsome. The brook is crossed to the W. of the Clarahütte, and the steep grassy slopes are ascended in zigzags, the end of the *Welz Glacier* being avoided by keeping to the left. The névé of the glacier is then ascended (rather steep) to the arête between the Daberspitze (Hohe Säule, see below) on the left and the Röthspitze on the right. We then ascend the latter, avoiding the 'Scharte', and mount over rock and snow to its broad rocky summit. °View little inferior to that from the Venediger. — Descent to the N.W. across the *Röthkees* to the (2 1/2 hrs.) *Lenkjöchlhütte* and the *Röththal* (p. 191), or to the S.W. across the *Rothenmannjoch* to the *Schwarzachthal* (trying; see p. 139).

The **Simonyspitze** (11,415'; 5-6 hrs.; guide 8 fl.) and the **Malhamspitze** (10,090'; 4-5 hrs.; guide 6 1/2 fl.) may also be ascended from the Clarahütte. The **Daberspitze** (*Hohe Säule*, 11,145'; 5-6 hrs.; 8 fl.) is more difficult.

PASSES. OVER THE VORDERE UMBALTHÖRL TO KASERN in the Prettau, 5 1/2-6 1/2 hrs., a remarkably fine route, somewhat trying, but unattended with danger (guide 7 1/2 fl.). From the Clarahütte to the *Umbal Glacier* 1/2 hr., then over the moraine and across the glacier (1/2-3/4 hr.), the first part only being somewhat steep. On the W. side of the glacier we ascend abruptly over debris and rock, and finally over snow to the (1 1/2-2 hrs.) *Vordere Umbalthörl (9720'), to the S. of the *Agner-* or *Eiss-Kopf*. During the whole ascent we enjoy magnificent views of the extensive snow-fields at the head of the Umbal Glacier, and of the Dreiherrn-, Simony-, Gubach-, and Malham-Spitze; from the top of the pass the long chain of the Zillerthal Alps becomes visible to the W. Descent by the *Windthal* to *Kasern* (2 1/2 hrs.), see p. 191; or better, by the *Lenkjöchl* and the *Röth Glacier* to the *Röththal* (p. 191; 3 1/2 hrs. to Kasern). — The passage of the **Hintere Umbalthörl** (9270') is also free from danger, and presents no difficulty when the ice is in good condition. We cross the Umbal Glacier and ascend a snowy slope, between the *Schlattner Keesflecken* and the *Agnerkopf*, to the Thörl. The descent to the *Windthal*, at first steep, crosses the brook in the valley, and follows its left bank to *Heiligengeist* and (5 1/2-6 hrs.) *Kasern* (see above). — Immediately to the S. of the Vordere Thörl is the *Virgl-Joch* (10,200'), seldom traversed.

A laborious route (for experts only, with guide) leads through the wild *Daberthal*, or *Sulzbachthal* (see above), and over the **Schwarze Thörl** (9050'), between the *Thörlspitze* (10,010') and the *Rothe Mann* (10,070'), to the *Schwarzachthal* and the (6 hrs.) *Jaydhaus Alp* (p. 139).

29. From Windisch-Matrei to Kals and Heiligenblut.

To Kals from Windisch-Matrei the most attractive route is by the *Matrei-Kalser Thörl* (see below; bridle-path, to the Thörl 3¹/₂-4, to Kals 5¹/₂ hrs.; guide not indispensable). — From Lienz to Kals, 7 hrs.; road as far as *Huben* (p. 138); then a footpath through the *Kalser-Thal* (see below). — From Uttendorf in the Pinzgau to Kals over the *Stubacher* or *Kalser Tauern*, 12-13 hrs., an interesting route (better in two days, with a night at the Rudolfshütte, see p. 146). — From Heiligenblut to Kals by the *Berger Thörl*, 7¹/₂ hrs. (see p. 148).

Windisch-Matrei, see p. 139. Above the church we ascend the pilgrimage-path in zigzags through larch-wood, go straight past the (20 min.) chapel, pass a cross, and begin to ascend to the right at (¹/₄ hr.) two houses. Then successively past two more houses, a solitary house on the right, and a large farm-house on the left, to a (40 min.) guide-post. The path now continues to ascend less steeply through woods and past a chapel, keeping above the gorge of the *Bürgerbach*. In 40 min. we cross a brook, and in 25 min. more emerge from the wood at a guide-post where the inn at the Thörl comes in sight. The incline now becomes steeper, and the path, crossing two brooks, mounts in zigzags, partly through wood, to (1¹/₄ hr.; 3³/₄ hrs. from Windisch-Matrei) the summit of the *Kals-Matreier Thörl* (7230'; *Hamerl's Inn*, poor). Splendid view of the Venediger, Glockner, and Schober group. (Comp. the annexed Panorama, after J. Stüdl.) The view is much finer from the second height, to the S., with a trigonometrical column, easily reached by following the crest of the hill for 1 hr. (guide unnecessary).

The path to (1¹/₂ hr.) Kals descends towards the left, and then leads through wood. At the bottom of the valley we avoid the broad path to the left which leads first to the *Grossdorf*, a circuit of ¹/₄ hr., and cross the fields straight towards the church at the lower (S.) end of Kals. Then, descending to the *Kalser Bach*, we follow the rough track along the right bank of the brook, cross the bridge, and descend either to the right to the Unterwirth, or ascend to the left to the Oberwirth, beside the church.

From Huben (p. 138) to Kals through the **Kalser Thal**, 3¹/₄ hrs., a fair path. We turn to the right beyond the inn, and traverse meadows to a (2 min.) bridge over the Isel. Then through wood, ascending to the left at a (20 min.) hut, to (¹/₂ hr.) *Ober-Peischlach* (the village remains to the left), where the route turns into the *Kalser-Thal*. Beyond this point the track is generally good, ascending slightly, and at places skirting the profound ravine of the foaming Kalser Bach. Near (40 min.) *Staniska*, a magnificent view of the *Gross-Glockner*, with the Glocknerwand and the Ködnitz and Teischnitz glaciers, is disclosed. The valley expands at (40 min.) *Haslach* (3730'; Inn); to the right a fine waterfall. Farther on we observe numerous traces of the ravages of mud-torrents, which sometimes destroy the path in rainy weather. To the right, at the entrance to the *Lesachthal* (p. 147), lies the hamlet of *Lesach* (in the background the *Gödis* and *Ganot*). Farther on, where the valley is broader, the path crosses the deposits of a torrent, and soon reaches (1 hr.) *Kals* (p. 146).

From Uttendorf (p. 135) to Kals through the *Stubachthal* and over the *Kalser Tauern*, by an attractive route of 13-14 hrs. (to the Rudolfshütte 8 hrs.; guide necessary to the Tauern Pass, 6 fl.; to Kals 10 fl.;

Alois Täubl or *P. Dürnberger* of Uttendorf). Road as far as the (7 M.) *Vellerer Bauer* (3200') and the (³/₄ M.) *Schneideralm* (Inn; horses for hire), at the base of the *Teufelsmühle* (8190'); to the right opens the *Dorfer Oed*, at the head of which rises the *Landeckkopf* (9530'). From this point a bridle-path (steep and stony at places) ascends, turning to the right at a (35 min.) guide-post, to (20 min.) a waterfall, beyond which it crosses the *Bürchl* and a bridge leading to the left bank of the *Wurfbach*. It then ascends across pastures to the right to the *Enzinger Boden*, as this region of the valley is called, and (2¹/₄ hrs.) the picturesque *Grünsee* (5600'). Farther on it skirts the slopes of the *Schafbühel* (see below) to the *Weiss-See* (7300') and the (1¹/₂ hr.) magnificently situated Rudolfshütte (7380'; Inn in summer), erected by the Austrian Alpine Club. The *Hintere Schafbühel* (7675'; ¹/₄ hr.) commands a superb view of the *Oedenwinkel Glacier* and its imposing environs, the Hohe Kasten, Eiskögele, Johannisberg, and Hohe Riffel; to the W. rises the Granatkogel group with the Sonnblick Raberkopf, and Granatspitze. — From the Rudolfshütte over the *Kaprimer Thörl* to the *Mooserboden*, see p. 132; over the *Obere Oedenwinkelscharte* to the *Pasterze*, see p. 153. — The Granatspitze (10,110') and the Sonnblick (10,120') may be ascended from the Rudolfshütte, viâ the *Sonnblick Glacier* and the *Granatscharte* (c. 9800'), between the Granatspitze and the Sonnblick, without difficulty (each 3-3¹/₂ hrs.; guide 2¹/₂-3 fl.). Descent over the *Granatspitze Glacier* and through the *Landeckthal* to Windisch-Matrei (p. 130).

From the Rudolfshütte the path ascends over rock and a patch of snow to the (1 hr.) Stubacher or Kalser Tauern (8500'); view limited. Then a steep and stony descent to the (1¹/₄ hr.) *Dorfer-See* (6300'), along the left bank of the Kalser Bach, and across the streams draining the *Laperwitz* and *Frusnitz* glaciers. The picturesque valley (*Dorfer-Thal* or upper Kalser-Thal) contains upwards of 50 chalets. Lower down (1³/₄ hr.) the brook runs through a narrow gorge, and the path ascends the *Stiegenwand* by stone steps. Fine view from the top. Descent to *Kals*, 1 hr. more.

Kals (4335'; *Unterwirth* or *Glocknerwirth*, kept by Thomas Groder, with a small Alpine library and the interesting 'Glocknerbuch', containing accounts of ascents from Kals; *Oberwirth Bergerweiss* '*Zum Alpenverein*', near the church, good cuisine; *Michael Groder*), a village pleasantly situated in a broad basin, is a good starting-point for expeditions among the Glockner group.

Guides: *Michael, Thomas, Peter,* and *Joseph Groder, Joh. Gräfler, Kasp. Gorgasser, Joseph, Andrä*, and *Johann Kelerer, Peter* and *Sebastian Huter, Lorenz Koller, Alois Schnell, Peter Unterberger, Joh. Ausserhofer, Rup. Entstrasser, Chr. Holaus,* and *Karl Rogl*. The office of the guides' society (president, P. Groder) is near Groder's Inn.

Tariff, see the separate excursions. For each excursion on which a night is spent in the Erzherzog-Johannshütte on the Adlersruhe the charge is 1¹/₂ fl. more. The guide provides himself with food, and carries 17 lbs. of luggage (overweight 2 kr. per lb. per hr.). Fee for a tour of 5 days or upwards, 4 fl. 20 per day (10 hrs. walking), for a longer day 5 fl. 20, half-day 3 fl. 20, day of rest 2 fl. 20 kr.; same rates for the return-journey if the guide is dismissed at a distance from home.

The ascent of the *Gross-Glockner* (12,460'; to the Stüdlhütte 4¹/₂. to the top 3-4 hrs. more; guide 7¹/₂ fl., with descent by the Hofmannsweg to the Glocknerhaus 10 fl.) from Kals is shorter and cheaper than from Heiligenblut (p. 153), but is recommended to experts only. Route to (1¹/₄ hr.) *Groder*, see p. 148. Then crossing the Ködnitzbach, we turn to the left at (¹/₂ hr.) a guide-post and ascend the *Ködnitzthal*, passing the (25 min.) *Jörgenhütte* (6425') and the (1 hr.) *Lucknerhütte* (7460'; to the right are the *Lange Wand* and the *Ködnitzkees*). We then ascend the slope of the *Freiwand* to the left to the (1¹/₂ hr.) Stüdlhütte, on the *Vanitscharte* (9480'), erected by Hr. Stüdl of Prague, and well fitted up (Inn in summer). The Vanitscharte, a depression between the Freiwand and the arête descending from the Glockner between the Teischnitz and Ködnitz Glaciers (on which arête the 'Stüdlweg' leads to the top, see below), commands a fine °View of the Ampezzo Dolomites to the S.W., beyond the Kalser Thörl. If we ascend the Freiwand to the S. for a short distance, we obtain a view of the peak of the Glockner to the N., apparently quite near; to the N.E. are the Ködnitz Glacier and the Adlersruhe; to the W. is the Teischnitz-Thal, with the Teischnitz and Graue Glaciers, overshadowed by the Kramul, Gamsspitze, and Zollspitze. Our route ascends to the N. from the Stüdlhütte, over detritus, to the arête, between the *Teischnitz* and *Ködnitz Glaciers*, and mounts the arête, which becomes steep towards the end, to the (2½ hrs.) Erzherzog-Johannshütte, erected in 1879-80 by the Austrian Alpine Club on the *Adlersruhe* (11,300'; Inn), where this route joins the Heiligenblut route (p. 153). Ascent from the Adlersruhe at first gradual, then more rapid, over snow and rock, to the (¾ hr.) *Klein-Glockner* (12,350'). On the N.W. side of this peak we descend steeply about 25' (facilitated by iron pegs and a wire-rope) to the *Obere Glocknerscharte*, a gap between the Little and the Great Glockner, consisting of a ridge 30' long and 1-2' wide (descending on the right to the Pasterze, and on the left to the Ködnitz Glacier) the passage of which requires a steady head, but is facilitated by a wire rope attached to the rocks. Lastly a steep ascent over rock (wire and pegs) to the summit of the Gross-Glockner (20-30 min. from the Klein-Glockner).

[Another route, the '*Stüdlweg*', ascends the rocky arête between the Teischnitz and Ködnitz glaciers (see above) with the aid of wire-ropes and iron stanchions attached to the rocks. This route avoids the Klein-Glockner and the Scharte, but is difficult in certain states of the snow and is now seldom attempted.]

The **View is almost unrivalled in extent and magnificence (panorama in the Stüdlhütte). Towards the W. it extends to the Rhaetikon chain and the Silvretta; on the S.W., to the Bernina and Adamello; S., to the Adriatic Sea, which is sometimes visible as a bright streak on the horizon; S.E., the Terglou; E., the Carpathians; N.E., the Moravian and Bohemian Mts.; N., the Bavarian plain, as far as Ratisbon. On the summit are a wooden pyramid, used in Sept., 1879, in connection with the measurement of latitude, and an iron cross about 9' high, erected by the Austrian Alpine Club in 1880. — Descent by the *Hofmannsweg* to the *Pasterze*, difficult, see p. 153; to *Heiligenblut* by the *Leiter Glacier*, see p. 153. — In 1879 the Gross-Glockner was ascended by Hr. Gröger of Vienna, attended by Chr. Rangetiner, for the first time by the N.W. arête (*Untere Glocknerscharte* or *Teischnitzscharte*, about 11,500'; very difficult). The only time the direct ascent from the Pasterze to the *Obere Glocknerscharte* (see above) has been accomplished was by the Marquis Pallavicini in 1876 (see p. 151).

The °**Romariswandkopf** (11,035'; 6-7 hrs.; guide 6½ fl.) commands a splendid view, hardly inferior to that from the Gross-Glockner. From the (4½ hrs.) Stüdlhütte we ascend to the *Teischnitz Glacier*, which we cross in the direction of the Glocknerwand. We then cross the flat *Kramul-Sattel*, to the N.E. of the *Kramul* (10,670'), to the *Frusnitz Glacier*, and ascend to the top without much difficulty by the snowy Glockner arête.

The **Hochschober** (10,640'; 7-8 hrs.; guide 6½ fl.), is reached by the *Lesachthal*, the *Lesacher-Alp* (5865'; night-quarters), and the *Ralf Glacier*; fatiguing but interesting (comp. p. 138). — The **Gornetschamp** (9020'; 4 hrs.). the W. spur of the Schober group, between the Ködnitzthal and the Lesachthal, which presents no difficulty, affords a splendid view of the Glockner, Schober, and Venediger groups. — °**Rottenkogel** (9045'; 4 hrs.; guide 4 fl., to Windisch-Matrei 5½ fl.), see p. 139. — The **Grosse Muntaniz** (*Laimetspitze*, 10,590'; 6-7 hrs.), the highest peak between the Kalserthal and the Tauernthal, is a fine point of view, but fatiguing. — The *Granatspitze* (10,110'), see p. 146.

Over the °**Kals-Matreier Thörl** (7236') to Windisch-Matrei (4½ hrs.; guide, 2½ fl., not necessary), see p. 145. The noble °View from the Thörl amply repays a visit to it, even by those who do not proceed to Matrei.

10*

From Kals to Heiligenblut over the Berger Thörl, 7½ hrs. (guide 4 fl.), attractive. A tolerable bridle-track leads past the church, and ascends the *Ködnitzthal* to the (1¼ hr.) hamlet of *Groder*; 25 min. farther up the path crosses the Ködnitzbach, and ascends abruptly to the right (guide-post; path to the left to the Städlhütte, p. 147) over Alpine pastures to the (2 hrs.) broad saddle of the **Berger Thörl** (8600'). Admirable view: S. the Schober, S.W. the Defereggen Mts. and the Dolomites, N.W. the Hochgall, E. the Gastein Mts. with the Hochnarr, Sonnblick, etc. In descending we obtain a view of the Leiter Glacier, Adlersruhe, and Glockner to the left. The path descends steeply into the *Leiterthal* (N. the Schwerteck and Leiterköpfe), crosses the brook to the (1½ hr.) *Upper Leiterhütte* and (8 min.) the *Lower Leiterhütte* (6650'), on the right bank, and then descends on the left bank by the *Lower Katzen-Steig*, 130-160' above the *Leiterbach* (no difficulty). In ½ hr. we cross the brook again and ascend to (20 min.) the *Troyalp* (6100'), beyond which the path descends through wood, soon coming in sight of Heiligenblut. In 1 hr. more we cross the *Gössnitzbach* (the *Gössnitz Fall*, in the ravine to the right, is not visible from the path), then (25 min.) the *Möll*, and ascend again to (¼ hr.) *Heiligenblut*. — The *Peischlag Thörl* (8135'), to the S. of the Berger Thörl, is not recommended, as the path is bad.

Travellers bound for the *Franz-Josefs-Höhe* or *Ferleiten* save a day by proceeding from the Leiterhütten to the left, round the *Vordere Leiterkopf* and along the *Obere Katzensteig* (requiring a steady head at places), and across the *Marxwiesen* and the *Lower Pasterzenkeesboden*, direct to the (2 hrs.) *Glocknerhaus* (see p. 154; from Kals to this point 6-7 hrs.; guide 4 fl., to Heiligenblut 5 fl. 80 kr., to Ferleiten viâ the Glocknerhaus, Franz-Josefs-Höhe, and Pfandelscharte 9 fl.).

30. From Lienz to Heiligenblut.

Comp. Maps, pp. 334, 120, 144.

From the South, Heiligenblut is most conveniently reached from *Dölsach* in the Pusterthal by the new road viâ *Winklern* (24 M.). Diligence from Dölsach daily, starting at noon and reaching Heiligenblut at 8.25 p.m. (leaving Heiligenblut at 8 a.m. and reaching Dölsach at 4.40 p.m.). One-horse carriage from Dölsach to Heiligenblut and back 12 fl., two-horse carr. 20 fl.; one-horse carr. from Winklern to Heiligenblut 5, to Döllach 3 fl.; porter from Dölsach to Winklern 1½ fl. — From *Möttbrücken* (1¼ M. to the E. of *Sachsenburg*, p. 336) to (29 M.) *Winklern* a small post-vehicle runs daily in 11 hrs., the night being spent at Stall or Ober-Vellach (not recommended). A post-gig also plies twice daily from Möllbrücken to Ober-Vellach in 2½ hrs. (fare 1 fl.). One-horse carr. from Sachsenburg to Ober-Vellach in 2¼ hrs., (3½ fl.), from Ober-Vellach to Winklern in 4½ hrs. (6 fl.). — From *Kals* to Heiligenblut over the *Berger Thörl*, see above.

From the North, the most attractive route to Heiligenblut leads through the *Fuscherthal* and over the *Pfandelscharte* (p. 131). — From *Rauris* over the *Hochthor* of the *Heiligenblut-Rauriser Tauern*, see pp. 127, 131; across the *Goldzechscharte* and the *Fleiss* (glacier-excursion, for experienced mountaineers), see p. 154. — From Gastein over the *Mallnitzer Tauern* to the *Möllthal* and to Heiligenblut, see p. 126. — From the *Kapruner Thal* a

WINKLERN. *III. Route 30.* 149

difficult glacier-pass leads over the *Riffelthor* to the Pasterze (p. 134); a similar pass from the *Stubachthal* crosses the *Obere Oedenwinkelscharte* (p. 153).
From *Lienz* to *Dölsach* (3 M. by railway; 10 min.), see p. 335. The village of Dölsach (2350'; *Putzenbacher*) lies 1 M. to the N. of the station. The church contains an altarpiece (Holy Family) by *Defregger* (born near Dölsach in 1835). The new road (9 M. to Winklern) ascends in wide curves (a shorter, but steep and stony footpath diverges beyond the inn) to (3³/₄ M.) the hamlet of *Iselsberg* (3645'), commanding fine views of the valley of the Drave, Lienz, and the jagged crests of the Lienz Dolomites. A footpath from Lienz also ascends viâ *Nussdorf* and *Debant* to (2 hrs.) Iselsberg. About 1¹/₂ M. farther on, beyond the *Inn zur Wacht*, we cross the boundary of Carinthia, and in ³/₄ M. more we reach the summit of the **Iselsberg** (3950'). Thence the road descends to (¹/₄ M.) the *Badhaus zum Gross-Glockner (Inn), and through wood to (2¹/₄ M.) **Winklern** (3140'; *Aichenegg, *Post, both belonging to the same landlord; *Geiler*, plain; *Fercher*, well spoken of), a summer-resort, finely situated on a slope high above the *Mölltal*.

EXCURSIONS (guides, *Jos. Schober*, *Joh.* and *Jos. Suntinger*). The *Geiersbühl (6228'), ascended viâ *St. Benedikt* in 3 hrs., commands a view of the Schober group, the Lienz Dolomites, etc. — A still finer view is obtained from the *Ederplan (6500') which is easily ascended in 3¹/₂ hrs. The bridle-path diverges to the left, after ¹/₂ M., from the Iselsberg road and ascends along the N. slope of the *Stronachkopf* to the small chapel of *Zwischenbergen* and the summit (refuge-hut; comp. p. 335).

[The **Mölltal** opens off the Pusterthal near station *Sachsenburg* (p. 336). A carriage-road (diligence to Winklern daily in 11 hrs., see above) ascends the valley. It crosses the Möll at *Möllbrücken*, and leads viâ *Mühldorf*, *Kolbnitz*, and *Stallhofen*, below the castle of *Falkenstein*, to (13 M.) **Ober-Vellach** (2250'; *Post; *Pacher*), the chief village in the lower Mölltal, pleasantly situated near the mouth of the *Mallnitzthal*. The Gothic church contains a winged altarpiece by Joh. Schoreel (1520).

EXCURSIONS (guides, *Joh. Weichslederer* and *Jos. Zaderer*). Pleasant wood walks to the *Potinik Fall* and the *Klausen Fall* (¹/₂ hr.), and to (¹/₂ hr.) the fine *Groppensteiner Waterfall of the Mallnitzbach. On a crag above the last rises the picturesque *Schloss Groppenstein (2805'), built in the 10-13th cent., and recently restored in the ancient style. Fine view from the tower. — To the *Raggaschlucht (near Flattach), ¹/₂ hr.'s drive, or 1¹/₄ hr. on foot through the woods. This striking gorge, over the four terraces of which the *Raggabach* descends in a series of cascades, has been rendered accessible by means of bridges and paths. The uppermost fall, 80' high, may be reached in about ¹/₂ hr. from the entrance. — The **Lanza** (7105'), ascended without difficulty in 5 hrs. (guide), viâ Groppenstein and the *Steiner Alpe*, is a fine point of view.

The ascent of the **Polinik** (9120'), the highest summit of the *Kreuzeck* group (p. 336), makes an attractive expedition of 5¹/₂-6 hrs. (guide 5 fl.). The route leaves Ober-Vellach on the S., and traverses the *Böden* and the *Spitalwiese* to (3 hrs.) the *Stampfer Alpe* (6900'; refuge-hut, with refreshments). We reach the base of the peak in 1 hr. more and in another 1¹/₂ hr. scale the rocky slope to the summit, affording a magnificent panorama of the Carinthian and Tyrolese Alps as far as the Ortler and the Adriatic Sea.

To (2 hrs.) *Mallnitz* and over the *Mallnitzer Tauern* to (8 hrs.) *Gastein* guide from Mallnitz 4 fl.), see p. 126.

From Ober-Vellach the road leads past *Semslach* (to the right the castle of *Groppenstein*, p. 149) to (3 M.) *Flattach* (Scheiflinger), opposite the mouth of the Raggathal (p. 149), and to (1½ M.) *Ausser-Fragant* (Inn), at the entrance to the *Fragant-Thal*. An easy pass (see below) leads from Flattach or Ausser-Fragant, past *Inner-Fragant* and over the **Schober-Thörl** (7730'), to *Döllach* (8 hrs., with guide). Still more interesting is the ascent of the *Stellkopf* (9335'), to the N.W. of the Thörl (1½ hr.), with descent to Döllach (see below). — Route through the Fragant-Thal (the upper part of which is called the *Wurtenthal*) and over the *Goldbergtauern* (9070') to Rauris (8-9 hrs. to the Goldberg-Knappenhaus), see p. 128.

The Möllthal now contracts. The road passes (4½ M.) *Wöllatratten*, at the mouth of the *Wöllathal* (p. 336), *Stall* (1½ M.; Inn), with the ruin of *Wildegg*, and (4¾ M.) *Rangersdorf* (Hassler). It then leads across the Möll to (2¼ M.) *Lainach*, a prettily situated village and bath, on a tongue of land formed by the deposits of the *Zlainitzbach*. 3 M. *Winklern* (p. 149).]

The road from Winklern to (15 M.) **Heiligenblut** descends into the valley and crosses the Möll. At (4½ M.) *Mörtschach* (3160'; Inn, rustic) the *Astenthal* opens to the right; at (1½ M.) *Stampfen* the picturesque *Wangenitzthal* diverges to the left. To the right is *Sagritz*. At (3 M.) **Döllach** (3370'; **Ortner; Post*), at the mouth of the *Zirknitzthal*, which has been impoverished by the exhaustion of its mines, rises the old castle of *Gross-Kirchheim*. (Over the *Klein-Zirknitz* or the *Tramer-Scharte* to the *Rauris Gold Mine*, see p. 128.) Near the inn the Zirknitz bursts forth from a wild rocky gorge; farther on is the (½ M.) *Alexisklamm*, with the fine *Zirknitz Fall, 200' in height.

EXCURSIONS (guides, *Karl Brugger & Joh. Zlöbl*). The *Stellkopf (9335'), which affords a splendid survey of the Goldberg, Glockner, and Schober groups, may be easily ascended from this point, viâ the *Astnerhütten*, in 5-6 hrs. (with guide). — The *Petzeck* (10,745') the E. summit of the Schober group, ascended hence in 7-8 hrs. (laborious), through the *Gradenthal* and past the *Gradenalpe* (hay-beds), also commands a magnificent view. — An interesting and less fatiguing ascent is that of the **Stanziwurten** (8830'; 4½-5 hrs.), viâ the *Zirknitzbauer*, the *Kulmer-Alp*, and the *Riegel-Alp*. — Over the *Schober-Thörl* (7730') to *Ausser-Fragant* (see above), 8-9 hrs., with guide.

Beyond Döllach the road next reaches (1½ M.) *Putschall* (3470'), at the entrance to the wild *Gradenthal*, and crosses to the right bank of the Möll, returning to the left 1¼ M. farther on. On the left (½ M.) is the *Jungfernsprung*, a waterfall 420' high. At (1¼ M.) the hamlet of *Pokhorn* (3560'), with the Gothic church of St. Martin, the Möllthal appears to be terminated by a hill, which the road ascends in zigzags. From the top the Gross-Glockner is visible; to the left the Möll forms a fine waterfall *(Zlappfall)*, 260' high. The road ascends to the right and soon reaches (2 M.) —

Heiligenblut (4600'; *Schober's Inn*, near the church), finely situated in a green Alpine valley, overlooked by the bold snow-pyramid of the Gross-Glockner. It derives its name from a phial of the 'Holy Blood' said to have been brought from Constantinople by St. Briccius. This relic is now preserved in an elegant ciborium, 42' in height, in the church here, an edifice of the 15th century, which also contains a handsome carved altar and the monument of St. Briccius (in the crypt). In the churchyard are the graves of the Marquis Pallavicini (p. 147) and Herr Crommelin, with the guides Rangetiner and Rubesoier, who all lost their lives on the Glocknerwand on June 26th, 1886. The *Calvarienberg* ($^1/_4$ hr.) affords a good view of the Gross-Glockner; to the left the three Leiterköpfe, to the right the Romariswandkopf (p. 147), in the background the Johannisberg (p. 153).

The Obere Fleiss, $^3/_4$ hr. to the E. of Heiligenblut, is a finer and more open point of view. The path descends to the left by Schober's Inn, crosses the brook, and ascends to the left (route to the Calvarienberg). By the (10 min.) large house we go straight on, following the upper path (good and well-defined) at a nearly uniform level; 25 min., the chalet *Zur Untern Fleiss*. In 5 min. more the path descends and crosses the *Fleissbach* (p. 154), and then ascends to the right through wood to the (10 min.) *Inn zur Obern Fleiss* (ca. 4900'; rustic). The *Fleisskapelle*, a little farther on, is the best point of view. — A direct path (fine views) leads from the Fleiss along the hills to ($2^1/_2$ hrs.) Döllach (p. 150), passing the scattered huts of *Apriach* and *Mitlen*. The descent is steep.

EXCURSIONS (guides, *Johann Kramser, Joseph Trübuser, Anton, Veit,* and *Lorenz Grauögger, Georg Bäuerle, Georg Bernhard, Anton Wallner, Matt. Aslaber, Anton, Franz,* and *Georg Lackner, Jos. Bernstein, P. Neuhauser, Jos. Kellner, Joh. Moser, Jak. Pichter,* and *Joh. Rupitsch*). The president of the guides is to be found every evening at the inn for the purpose of making arrangements as to guides and porters. — HORSE from Heiligenblut to the Glocknerhaus 5, Franz-Josefs-Höhe 6 fl. (with side-saddle 1 fl. extra); to the Pfandelscharten Glacier 6 fl. 30 kr.; to the Hochthor only, $3^1/_2$ fl. — *One-horse Carriage* to Döllach 3, Winklern 5, Dölsach 10 fl.

The chief attraction near Heiligenblut is the view from the *FRANZ-JOSEFS-HÖHE, vying with the most sublime in Switzerland. A good bridle-path (guide unnecessary; to the Glocknerhaus 2 fl., there and back 2 fl. 60 kr.; to the Franz-Josefs-Höhe and back 3 fl.) ascends to the Glocknerhaus in 3 hrs.; thence to the Franz-Josefs-Höhe 1 hr. more (descent to Heiligenblut 3 hrs.). Immediately beyond Heiligenblut we descend to the left, and after 10 min. cross to the right bank of the Möll. By a ($^1/_4$ hr.) chapel, where the path to the Leiterthal (p. 154) diverges to the left, we recross the stream. By the (5 min.) houses of *Winkel* (4720') we cross the *Gutthalbach*, and then ascend. To the left, on the opposite slope, is the *Kessel Fall*, partly concealed by pines, while the Möll, the discharge of the Pasterze, is precipitated over the rocks far below. On the height, where the path turns to the right, a fine retrospect is obtained of the Möllthal. To the E. is the Floiss Glacier, beyond which lies the gold-mine (p. 154). A few paces farther on the Pasterze Glacier comes in sight. For a time the path is now level, leading partly through wood to the ($1^1/_2$ hr. from Heiligenblut) *Briceiuscapelle* (5290'), opposite the *Leiter Fall*. Close by is a good spring.

Then another ascent. After 40 min. the path ascends by means of steps hewn in the rock, called the *Ochsenplatten*, or *Böse Platte*, beyond which the Glockner is disclosed to view. We next mount a rocky saddle by zigzags. At the ($^1/_2$ hr.) top (the *Brettboden*, 6815') the path divides (the footpath in a straight direction, leading round an angle of rock, being shorter than the bridle-path to the right, but soon rejoining it). We then ascend the pastures to the (20 min.) **Glocknerhaus** on the *Elisabethruhe* or *Elisenrast* (6980'), built by the Austrian Alpine Club, and affording an excellent view of the Pasterze and the Glockner (*Inn*, bed 1 fl. 60 kr., in separate room dearer; hay-bed 50 kr.; admission by day 20 kr.; telephone to Heiligenblut).

The Franz-Josefs-Höhe is reached in another hour (guide 1 fl., unnecessary). The path crosses the *Pfandelschartenbach* (p. 131) to the ($^1/_4$ hr.) *Wallnerhütte* (6940'). Above the hut we ascend to the right, by the brook; at a (5 min.) spring we turn to the left, rounding an angle of the *Freiwand*, high above the magnificent fall of the bluish-green glacier. In $^3/_4$ hr. more we reach the ****Franz-Josefs-Höhe** (7870'), a point of view on the rock-strewn flank of the Freiwand, which commands a complete survey of the huge *Pasterze Glacier*, the second-largest among the German Alps (6 M. in length; at the Hofmannshütte $^3/_4$ M., and in the upper basin about 3 M. in width; the Gepatsch Glacier is $^3/_4$ M. longer). The view is finest in the direction of the white pyramid of the Johannisberg, which becomes visible here. Immediately before us towers the Gross-Glockner, with its two peaks; to the left of it are the Adlersruhe, Burgwartscharte, Hohenwartkopf, Kellersberg, Schwerteck, and the three Leiterköpfe; to the right of the Glockner rise the serrated Glocknerwand (Hofmannspitze), Romariswandkopf, Schneewinkelkopf, Untere Oedenwinkelscharte, Johannisberg, Obere Oedenwinkelscharte, and Hohe Riffel; the three rocky peaks in the upper basin of the Pasterze are the Kleine, Grosse, and Hohe Burgstall. A slab of marble on a rock on the Franz-Josefs-Höhe, protected by an iron door, is to the memory of Carl Hofmann of Munich, a distinguished Alpine traveller, who fell at Sedan in 1870.

Few travellers extend their walk beyond the Franz-Josefs-Höhe; but, if time permit, it is well worth while to prolong it to the *Hofmannshütte* (guide advisable; from the Glocknerhaus, there and back, 1 fl. 80 kr.). The path descends a little, skirting and traversing the moraine, and then crosses a nearly level part of the glacier to the (1$^1/_2$ hr.) Hofmannshütte (7965'), in the *Gamsgrube*, a hollow at the base of the *Fuscherkarkopf*. The hut, erected by Archduke John (and formerly called *Johannshütte*), and repaired in 1870 by Hr. Hofmann and Hr. Südl, is the starting-point for a number of fine excursions, although most travellers prefer to spend the night at the Glocknerhaus.

ASCENTS FROM THE HOFMANNSHÜTTE OR FROM THE GLOCKNERHAUS (for experts only, with competent guides; the charges given are from the Glocknerhaus, where guides are always to be found). — The Fuscherkarkopf (10,896'; guide 4 fl.), affording an excellent survey of the Glockner group, is ascended from the Hofmannshütte in 3 hrs. by the Gamsgrube and the S.W. arête (steep at first). — The **Sonnenwelleck** (10,660'), the E. neighbour of the Fuscherkarkopf, is ascended from the Glocknerhaus by the Freiwand and the *Freiwand-Kees* in 4 hrs.; fine survey of the Fuscherthal. (From the Fuscherkarkopf to the Sonnenwelleck, by following the sharp arête, which sinks towards the centre, 1 hr.)

The **Mittlere Bärenkopf** (11,045') is ascended from the Hofmannshütte in 3 hrs. (guide 5 fl.). The route, at first the same as that to the Bockkarscharte (p. 132), crosses the arm of the upper Pasterze which descends from the *Breitkopf* (10,312'); then, leaving the Bockkarscharte to the right, it leads to the (2 hrs.) *Eiswandbühel* (10,465') and ascends a snow-arête to the (1 hr.) *Mittlere Bärenkopf* (11,045'). We may descend to the N.E. to the *Keilscharte* (see below), and return by the *Bockkarscharte* to the Hofmannshütte. (Descent to the *Schwarzenberghütte* by the *Hochgruber Glacier*, difficult.) — The **Hohe Burgstall** (9730'), reached from the Hofmannshütte in 2 hrs. by crossing the upper plateau of the Pasterze, commands a good survey of the glacier. This expedition may be combined with the preceding, by going direct from the Burgstall to the (1 hr.) *Eiswandbühel* (see above).

The **Grosse Wiesbachhorn** (11,735'; from the Hofmannshütte 6-7 hrs.; guide 9, to Ferleiten 12, to the Rainerhütte 14 fl.). We cross the Bockkar-Scharte (p. 132) to the *Bockkar Glacier*; then ascend to the left to the *Keilscharte* (10,250'), the pass between the *Mittlere* and the *Hohe Bärenkopf* (see above), skirt the latter by keeping to the left and traversing the névé, pass the *Glockerin* (11,230'), between the *Vordere* and the *Hintere Bratschenkopf* (11,235'), and thus reach the *Wielinger Scharte* (p. 134), from which we have a steep ascent to the snowy summit. Descent to the *Kaindlhütte*, see p. 134; to *Ferleiten*, see p. 134.

The **Johannisberg** (11,400'; from the Hofmannshütte 4-5 hrs.; guide 6 fl.). The route lies across the upper Pasterze Glacier; then avoids the fall of the highest Pasterze basin by passing between the *Glocknerwand* (12,235') and the *Kleine Burgstall* (8890'), traverses wide expanses of snow, and lastly ascends somewhat steeply to the summit by the snow-arête on the E. side. On the W. side the mountain descends in huge precipices to the Oedenwinkel Glacier in the Stubachthal. Splendid survey of the Glockner group, and extensive view towards the N. (Zeller See, etc.). This ascent may easily be combined with the route over the Obere Oedenwinkelscharte or the Riffelthor (see pp. 154, 134).

The **Hohe Riffel** (10,960'; 5 hrs.), from the Hofmannshütte past the Riffelthor (p. 154), and lastly up a steep snow-arête, is another fine point.

The **Schneewinkelkopf** (11,200'; from the Hofmannshütte 4-5 hrs.; guide 6 fl.). As far as the upper basin of the Pasterze Glacier we follow the Johannisberg route (see above). Then a wide circuit, leaving the Untere Oedenwinkelscharte (see p. 154) on the right, to the depression between the *Eiskögele* (11,280') and the Schneewinkelkopf, whence a snow-arête leads to the summit. Descent to Kals by the *Laperwitz Glacier*, 6 hrs., without difficulty (guide 11 fl.).

The ascent of the ***Gross-Glockner** (12,460'), 9-10 hrs. from Heiligenblut, is fatiguing but not very difficult for practised mountaineers (guide from the Glocknerhaus 9, with descent to Kals 12 fl., in each case 1½ fl. more if a night be spent at the Erzherzog Johannshütte). It was ascended for the first time in 1799 by Count Salm, Bishop of Gurk, attended by 29 guides. The first ascent from Kals (p. 146) was made in 1855.

From Heiligenblut or the *Glocknerhaus* (where the previous night may be spent) the usual ascent follows the Kals route (see below) to (2 hrs.) the *Leiterhütte* (6650'). We then ascend to the right to the (2½ hrs.) *Salmshütte* (9200'), on the *Schwerteck*, and thence mount the fatiguing *Leiterkees* to the (1½ hr.) *Hohenwart-Scharte* (10,400') and the (¾ hr.) *Erzherzog-Johannshütte* on the *Adlersruhe* (11,360'), where the route unites with the old Glockner route from Kals (see p. 147). Thence to the summit (1½-1½ hr.). This route is rendered easier by spending the night in the Salmshütte (primitive) or the Erzherzogs-Johannshütte (see p. 147), and ascending thence early in the morning.

Another route, the ***Hofmannsweg**, is much more arduous than this Leiterweg, and should be attempted only by thoroughly seasoned mountaineers, and only when there is abundance of snow in a favourable condition. This route, starting from the Glocknerhaus, crosses the Pasterze Glacier, and traverses the *Aeussere Glocknerkar Glacier* to (3½-4 hrs.) the *Adlersruhe*. Thence to the summit 1-1½ hr.

ASCENTS FROM HEILIGENBLUT. The *Sandkopf* (10,118'), easily ascended in 5 hrs. (with guide), is a fine point of view. From the Fleiss Inn (p. 151) we ascend across the pastures of the *Münichberg*, passing two crosses (7920' and 9035'). The last part of the ascent is over debris and rock. — The Brennkogl (9890') is ascended through the *Gutthal* in 5 hrs. (guide; comp. p. 131). — The *Hochnarr* (10,690') and the *Hintere Sonnblick* (10,180') may each be ascended from the Seebichelhaus in about 3 hrs. (see below; better from the Rauris, p. 128).

PASSES. FROM THE GLOCKNERHAUS TO KALS BY THE BERGER THÖRL (6-7 hrs.; guide 5 fl.; provisions necessary), see p. 148. From the Wallner-Hütte (p. 152) we cross the lower Pasterze basin to the *Marxwiesen*, with a fine view of the Pasterze, Glockner and Johannisberg; and thence follow the 'Upper Katzensteig', a narrow but safe path, round the *Vordere Leiterkopf* to the (2 hrs.) *Leiterhütte* (p. 148), in the *Leiterthal*. Thence a steep ascent leads to (2 hrs.) the *Berger-Thörl*, from which we descend in 2 hrs. to Kals (p. 146).

OVER THE RIFFELTHOR TO THE KAPRUNER THAL (to the Rainerhütte 9 hrs.; guide 9 fl.), laborious. The Riffelthor (10,140'), between the *Hohe Riffel* (10,960') and the *Vordere Bärenkopf* (10,676') is reached viâ the upper Pasterze basin and past the *Johannisberg*. Descent across the *Karlinger Glacier*, keeping to the right above the ice-fall (caution necessary owing to the wide, though not numerous crevasses, which often intersect the whole glacier), to the *Mooserboden* and the *Rainerhütte* (p. 133).

OVER THE OBERE OEDENWINKELSCHARTE TO THE STUBACHTHAL (to the Rudolfshütte 8 hrs.; guide 10 fl.), also trying. The route to the Riffelthor (see above) is followed as far as the middle of the Pasterze basin. Here we turn to the left and ascend to the Obere Oedenwinkelscharte (10,785'), which lies between the *Hohe Riffel* and the *Johannisberg*. The descent to the *Oedenwinkel Glacier* and the *Rudolfshütte* (p. 146) is precipitous and difficult. — The Untere Oedenwinkelscharte (10,415'), between the Johannisberg and the Eiskögele, crossed by Messrs. Hofmann and Südfl for the first time in 1869, is very difficult and dangerous.

Over the *Pfandelscharte*, *Fuscherkarscharte*, or *Bockkarscharte* to *Ferleiten*, see pp. 131, 132 (the first accomplished most conveniently from the Glocknerhaus); over the *Hochthor* of the *Heiligenbluter Tauern* to *Rauris* or *Ferleiten*, see p. 131.

FROM HEILIGENBLUT TO THE RAURIS GOLD-MINE (and Gastein) BY THE FLEISS. ASCENT OF THE HOCHNARR. This interesting glacier-tour requires a trustworthy guide (to Gastein 10, incl. the Hochnarr 12 fl.). The *Fleissthal* (p. 151), divides 1 hr. to the E. of Heiligenblut into the *Grosse Fleissthal* to the N. and the *Kleine Fleissthal* to the E. We ascend the latter to the (2½ hrs.) *Seebichthaus* (8085'; Inn in summer) and the (½ hr.) *Zirm-See* (8220'), a small lake in a rocky basin at the foot of the *Goldzechkopf* (10,010'). The *Gjaidtroghöhe* (9790), between the Kleine and the Grosse Fleiss, is easily ascended from this point in 2 hrs. and affords a fine view of the Glockner and Goldberg groups. Another good point of view is the *Hintere Sonnblick* (10,180'), ascended from the Seebichlhaus in 3 hrs. by the gap to the S.W. of the Goldzechkopf and the *Kleine Fleisskees* (better from the Knappenhaus on the Hohe Goldberg, p. 127). — We next ascend over ice and rock, past a deserted miners' house, to the (1½ hr.) Goldzechscharte Pass (9220'), lying between the Hochnarr on the N. and the Sonnblick on the S. [From the pass to the summit of the Hochnarr or *Hohenaar* (10,690'), an easy ascent of 1½ hr. (from Heiligenblut 6 hrs.); view magnificent.] We descend from the pass over the *Goldzechkees* (sometimes much crevassed) by the 'Erfurter Weg' to (3-4 hrs.) *Kolm Saigurn* (p. 127). Thence to *Rauris*, see p. 127; over the *Bockhartscharte* to *Gastein*, see p. 125.

IV. NORTH-EASTERN TYROL. THE ZILLERTHAL ALPS.

31. From Munich to Innsbruck viâ Rosenheim and Kufstein 156
    Excursions from Brannenburg. Ramboldplatte. Wendelstein, 156. — Brünnstein. Traithen, 156. — Thierberg. Duxerköpfl. Kaiserthal. Stripsenjoch. Haltspitze. Sonneneck. Pyramideuspitze. Nauuspitze, 157, 158. — From Kufstein to Söll, 158. — Excursions from Brixlegg. Kramsach. Strass. Reith. The Alpbachthal. Gratlspitze, 159. — Tratzberg. St. Georgenberg, 159. — Keller-Joch. Lamsen-Joch. Stanser Joch. The Vomper Thal. Absam, 160. — The Gnadenwald. The Haller Salzberg. The Volderthal. Over the Navisjoch to Steinach, 161.

32. Innsbruck and Environs 161
    Schloss Amras. The Lanserköpfe. Ampass. Weiherburg. Mühlau. The Kranewitter Klamm. Schloss Mentelberg. Patscher Kofel. Saile. Hafelekar, etc., 168-171.

33. From Wörgl to Mittersill. Hohe Salve 171
    The Kelchsauthal. Over the Salzachjoch or the Filzensattel to the Pinzgau. The Spertenthal. Grosse Rettenstein, 172. — Kitzbühler Horn. Gaisstein, 174.

34. From Wörgl to Reichenhall viâ Lofer 175
    The Kaisergebirge. The Hintersteiner See, 175. From St. Johann to Waidring viâ St. Jakob im Haus, 175. — Excursions from Waidring. Pillersee, etc., 176. — Excursions from Lofer. Loferer Hochthal. Loferer Alpe. Hinterhorn. Ochsenhorn. From Lofer to Oberweissbach, 176. — The Vorderkaser-Klamm. Schwarzbergklamm. Staubfall. Sonntagshorn, 177.

35. The Zillerthal 178
    Kellerjoch. Wiedersberger Horn. Wilde Krimml, 179. — Excursions from Zell. Klöpfelstaudach. Marchkopf. Gerloswand, 179. — From Zell to Gerlos (Schönachthal, Wilde Gerlos, Thorhelm, Brandberger Kolm, Wildgerlosspitze, Reichenspitze) and Krimml, 179-181. — Peukenberg, Ahornspitze. The Zillergrund. Hörndl-Joch, Hundskehl-Joch, Heiligengeist-Jöchl. The Stilluppthal. Over the Keilbach-Joch or Frankbach-Joch to the Ahrnthal, 182. — The Tuxer Thal. Wery-Hütte. Riffelscharte, 183. — Floitenthal. Löffler. Trippach Saddle. Mörchenscharte. Tristner, 184. — The Gunkel. Gross-Ingent, etc., 185. — Schwarzensteingrund. Berliner Hütte. Rothkopf. Ochsner. Feldkopf. Kleine and Grosse Mörchner. Schwarzenstein. Hornspitzen. Greiner, 185, 186. — From Breitlahner to Sterzing over the Pfitscher Joch. Olperer Hütte. Schlegeisthal, 186. — Wiener Hütte. Hochfeiler, Weisszint, Wilde Kreuzspitze, etc., 187. — Schlüsseljoch. Pfünderjoch, 188.

36. The Ahrnthal 188
    The Mühlwald-Lappacher Thal, 188. — Hochfeiler. Weisszint. Ringelstein. Tristenspitze. From Lappach to Pfunders over the Passenjoch, the Rieglerjoch, or the Eisbruckjoch; to Pfitsch over the Untere or Obere Weisszintscharte; to Schlegeis over the Schlegeisscharte or over the Neves-Sattel; to Weissenbach over the Nevesenjoch or over the Lappacher Jöchl, 189. — The Weissenbachthal. Nevesenjoch Hütte. Mösele. Thurnerkamp. Passes to the Zillerthal, 189. — Schwarzenbachthal. Schwarzenstein. Daimerhütte, 190. — Grosse Löffler. Frankbachjoch. Röththal. Leukjöchl-Hütte. Röthspitze. Dreiherruspitze. Excursions from Prettau, 191, 192.

31. From Munich to Innsbruck viâ Rosenheim and Kufstein.

Comp. Maps, pp. 40, 52, 172, 40.

109 M. RAILWAY. Express in 4¼ hrs.; ordinary trains in 6-8½ hrs. From Munich to (40 M.) *Rosenheim*, see R. 11. The line turns to the S. and follows the left bank of the *Inn*. On the opposite slope, beyond (45 M.) *Raubling*, lies *Neubeuern* (*Auer), with walls and gates, commanded by a château on a rock above.

49 M. **Brannenburg** (1660'; *Inn at the station; *Schlosswirth*, in the village). The village, a summer-resort, with a château, lies at the base of the mountains, ¾ M. to the W. (Beautiful view from the Bierkeller, to the S. of the village.)

EXCURSIONS (guides, *Mart. Holzner* and *Jos. Huber*). *Schwarzlack-Kapelle*, ½ hr. to the N.W., with a fine view of the plain; *Biber* (1710'), a hill with pretty forest-paths and views, ½ hr. to the S.E.; *St. Margarethen*, at the mouth of the *Reindler-Thal* (¾ hr. to the S.); *In den Grund* (valley of the *Förchenbach*), with a fine waterfall (1¼ hr.; thence through a tunnel 100 yds. long to the *Tatzelwurm* in 1¼ hr.; comp. p. 52); ascent of the *Petersberg* (see below), an admirable point of view, 2 hrs. (from Fischbach 1¼ hr.). — The *Ramboldplatte (4605')*, ascended viâ the *Schiefgraben-Alpe* and the *Rambold-Alpe* in 2½ hrs., commands a fine view of the Chiemsee, the Kaisergebirge, etc. — *Wendelstein (6030'), 4½-5 hrs. (guide advisable; provisions should be taken). The new route (bridle-path) passes *St. Margarethen* and enters the *Reindler-Thal*, through which it ascends to (2 hrs.) the *Mitter-Alpe* (3810') and (1 hr.) the *Reindler-Alpe* (4090'). It then skirts the N.W. side of the Wendelstein, crosses the *Schweinberg* saddle, and follows the Birkenstein route (p. 50) to (1½ hr.) the *Wendelsteinhaus*. [The old path ascends to the left above the Mitter-Alpe, leaving the Reindler-Alpe to the right (above), to the (½ hr.) *Reindlerscharte* (5350'), whence it ascends on the E. of the cone of the Wendelstein to (½ hr.) the *Zellerscharte* (5445'), and then keeps along the left side of the 'Kessel' (Wendelstein Grotto, see p. 51) to the saddle on the side next the (½ hr.) *Wendelsteinhaus* (p. 51). The final ascent begins on this side of the saddle.

At (51 M.) *Fischbach* (Bräuhaus) the line approaches the Inn. On a rock to the right is the ruin of *Falkenstein*, and high above it is the pilgrimage-chapel on the *Petersberg*. On the opposite bank rise the *Heuberg* (4490') and *Kranzhorn* (4475'). The train crosses the *Aubach* to (56 M.) **Oberaudorf** (1580'; *Hofwirth*; *Zum Brünnstein*, at the station; *Niederauer*, rustic), near which is the ruined *Auerburg*.

EXCURSIONS (guides, *Isidor März Junior* and *Senior, Joh. Bapt. März*). To the *Weber an der Wand* (¼ hr.); *Gfaller Mühle*, with a small cascade (¾ hr.; Wolfschlucht Inn); to the *Tatzelwurm* (fine waterfall) in the *Aubachthal*, 2½ hrs. (thence to *Bairisch-Zell*, see p. 52). — Brünnstein (5355'), an interesting ascent of 4 hrs., with guide. The path leads up the valley from the Gfaller Mühle to *Wildgrub* and (3 hrs.) the *Himmelmoos-Alp*, prettily situated, whence it ascends to the right to the (¾ hr.) chapel on the S.E. peak. Magnificent view of the Kaisergebirge, Tauern, Inn Valley, etc.; to the right, the Wendelstein. Descent to the Tatzelwurm (2½ hrs.), fatiguing. — The easy and interesting ascent of the Traithen (6160'; comp. p. 52) may be made from Oberaudorf in 4½ hrs. viâ the *Unterberg-Alpe* and the *Unterberger Joch*; the *View extends from the Dachstein to the Oetzthaler Ferner. — Route to *Kössen* and *Reit im Winkel*, see p. 58.

59½ M. *Kiefersfelden* (Schrecker's Inn; Restaurant zum Kiefer) has a rustic theatre, in which the peasants perform popular dramas (every Sun. in summer). Near the *Otto-Capelle*, erected to commemorate the departure of King Otho of Greece (1833), the train crosses the frontier of the Tyrol, enters the *Klause* (see below), a narrow defile, and approaches —

62 M. **Kufstein** (1600'; *Auracher Bräu*, with garden on the Inn; *Post*, on the Inn, pens. from 2½ fl.; *Drei Könige*, moderate; *Zur Gräfin*; *Hirsch*; *Eggerbräu*; *Rail. Restaurant*, dear; wine at *Schickedanz's*), an ancient fortress on the opposite (right) bank of the Inn, with new fortifications on both banks. It was besieged in 1504 by Maximilian I. The Bavarian commandant, believing it impregnable, caused the walls to be swept with brooms, in derisive allusion to the impotence of the emperor's cannon. The latter, however, sent for some heavy ordnance from Innsbruck, destroyed the walls, and executed the commandant for his temerity. Kufstein was the only frontier-fortress retained by the Bavarians at the end of the campaign of 1809. The sole approach to the fortress (now a barrack) is very steep; provisions are drawn up by means of a windlass. Fine view from the *Calvarienberg*, immediately beyond the cemetery (½ M. from the Inn bridge); to the W. rises the Pendling. To the left, near the chapel in the cemetery, is the grave of *List*, the political economist, who shot himself here in 1846. On the Kienbichl, in the vicinity, are the baths of *Kienbergklamm* (also a Pension), well fitted up (bath 30-40 kr., very agreeable water).

EXCURSIONS (guides: *Kasper Pirkner* at Kufstein, *Jos. Bichler* at Veitenhof, *Jos. Auer* at Schwendt, *Mich. Wurzenrainer* at Bärnstatt, *Thom. Widauer* and *Jos. Zintinger* at Hintersteln). On the left bank of the Inn, 10 min. from the station, is the *Zeller Burg*, or *Nackelburg* (*Inn), at the foot of the wooded *Zeller Rain*. Walk viâ *Zell*, and past the swimming-baths (well fitted up), to the (¾ hr.) *Ed* (°Inn); by the high-road along the Inn to (40 min.) the *Klause* (see above; *Inn, good cuisine; view). — Ascent of the °*Thierberg* (2370'; 1 hr.). The path ascends through wood to the left below the railway-station, and passes the two *Thierberg Farms*. Beautiful view from the tower, which dates from the 11th cent. (key kept by the 'hermit', 10 kr.). We may return by an attractive route from the *Lower Thierberg Farm*, passing the (¾ hr.) °*Hechtsee*, embosomed in wood, and affording an admirable view of the Kaisergebirge, to the (½ hr.) *König-Otto-Capelle*, and (40 min.) *Kufstein*; or to the W., through beautiful woods, to the *Ed* (see above). Hence to the railway-station 20 minutes. — *Thiersee-Thal*, *Landl*, and *Bairisch-Zell*, see pp. 52, 51 (one-horse carr. from Kufstein to Ursprung 12 fl.). An easy and well-marked route leads from Vorder-Thiersee to the top of the *Pendling* (5124'; 2½ hrs., with guide); steep descent to Langkampfen (p. 158).

Duxerköpfl (2418'; 1 hr.), with fine view of the Innthal, Kaisergebirge, etc.: ascent by the Calvarienberg to the left through wood; easy descent by the *Hochwand* to (¾ hr.) *Bad Kienbergklamm* (see above). — The **Brandkogel** or **Gamskogel** (4750'), the highest point of the *Brentenjoch* range, ascended in 3 hrs. by the *Duxer Alpe* and the *Brentenjoch Alpe*, affords an excellent survey of the Kaisergebirge (guide 2 fl., including descent into the Kaiserthal 2½/2, to Hinterstein 3 fl.). Descent viâ the *Bettlersteig* to (2 hrs.) the *Triftklause* in the Kaiserthal (see below), or by the *Steinberger Alp* and *Walter Alp* to (3 hrs.) the *Hintersteiner See* (p. 175).

°**Kaiserthal** (half-a-day, guide unnecessary). A road leads to the N. to (1¼ M.) *Sparchen*, a mill and iron-work at the narrow mouth of the valley, where the *Sparchenbach* forms a fine fall (best viewed from the

158   *IV. Route 31.*   WÖRGL.   *From Munich*

bridge). We ascend the path beyond the bridge, just behind the mill, and (3 min.) the steps to the right by the crucifix; 10 min., a bench (*'Neapelbank'*), affording a fine view of Kufstein, overshadowed by the Pendling, and of the Inn Valley up to the Stubaier Ferner. Thence by a good path, high above the valley, passing the six 'Kaiserhöfe' (*Veitenhof*, the third, is a rustic tavern; a chapel near the *Pfandlhof*, the fourth farm, affords the best survey of the valley). [From the *Veitenhof* a marked path leads to the top of the *Teufelskanzel*.] The (1½ hr.) last farm (*Hinterkaiserhof*, 2790'; a few beds), which commands a fine view of the huge precipices of the *Wilde Kaiser* (comp. p. 175), is the usual turning-point. The prolongation of the path descends through wood to the (1 hr.) *Triftklause* on the Sparchenbach, and then crosses the *Bärenbach*, and, leaving the *Vordere Bärenbach-Alpe* on the right, ascends along the *Stripsenbach* to (3/4 hr.) the **Bärenbad Club Hut**, on the *Hintere Bärenbadalp* (2725'; Inn in summer). An interesting pass (guide, 4½ fl., unnecessary; path marked) leads from this point across the (2½ hrs.) Stripsenjoch (5265'), between the *Todtenkirchl* on the right and the *Stripsenkopf* (5900'; an easy ascent of 3/4 hr. from the col) on the left to (2½ hrs.) *Griesenau* in the *Kaiserbachthal*, where we may either turn to the left to *Schwendt* and (2½ hrs.) *Kössen* (p. 58), or to the right to *Gasteig* (Inns, primitive) and (2 hrs.) *St. Johann* (p. 175). — An interesting, but difficult ascent is that of the **Elmauer Haltspitze** (7792'), the highest summit of the Kaisergebirge, which may be accomplished from the Bärenbad Hut in 5 hrs. (guide 4 fl., including descent to Elmau 5 fl.), viâ the *Untere* and *Obere Scharlinger Boden* and the *Rothe Rinnscharte* (comp. p. 175). — Ascent of the **Sonneneck** (7380'), a splendid point of view, from the Bärenbad Hut, through the *Gamskarl*, and across the *Gamskarlköpfl*, in 4½ hrs. (guide 5 fl.), interesting, but rather fatiguing. Descent by the *Wiesberg*, the *Kaiserhochalpe*, and the *Kaiserniederalpe* to (3 hrs.) *Bärnstatt* (p. 175), steep at first. — Route from the Vordere Bärenbad Alp (see above) over the **Feldalpe** (4265') and through the *Habersauer-Thal* to (6 hrs.) *Walchsee*, also attractive (with guide, p. 58). — From the *Veitenhof* (see above) a path over the *Hintere Kaiserfellenalpe* (4920') and the saddle of *Egersgriun* ascends the **Pyramidenspitze** (6550'), the highest peak of the *Hintere* or *Zahme Kaiser* (p. 175), an interesting ascent of 5 hrs. (from Kufstein 6-7 hrs.; guide 2½ fl.). The summit, which is surmounted by a cross, commands a magnificent view. — Another interesting point is the **Naunspitze** (5380'), the westernmost peak of the Hintere Kaiser, ascended from the Pfandlhof viâ the *Pfandler-Alpe* and the *Vordere Kaiserfellen-Alpe* in 2½-3 hrs. (guide 2 fl.). A path, indicated by red marks (guide advisable), leads from the Naunspitze across the plateau, and past the *Zwölferkogel*, the saddle of *Egersgriun* (see above), and the *Elferkogel* to (2 hrs.) the Pyramidenspitze.

FROM KUFSTEIN TO SÖLL (3½ hrs.; shortest way to the Hohe Salve). The path diverges to the left from the road at the foot of the fortress, and runs across meadows to (½ hr.) the *Bairische Hof* (Inn), and thence through the pretty *Weissachthal* or *Glemmachenthal* (cement-works) to (½ hr.) a bridge over the *Gaisbach*, from which a steep path ascends to the inn of (½ hr.) *Eiberg* or *Neuberg*. Then, high above the right bank of the Weissach and across to (1½ hr.) *Söll* on the left bank (p. 175). — To the **HINTERSTEIN LAKE** (p. 175.), 2½ hrs. (guide not indispensable). About 3/4 M. beyond Neuberg we leave the high-road to the left (guide-post) and ascend the *Steinerne Stiege*, a path hewn in the face of the cliff (without danger). From the top (25 min.) we continue straight on to (½ hr.) the Hinterstein **Lake** (3630'), the N. side of which we skirt to (¼ hr.) the *Bärnstatt Inn* (p. 175).

From Kufstein to *Kössen* and *Reit im Winkel*, see R. 12.

Between (67 M.) *Langkampfen* and (70 M.) *Kirchbichl* (Oberreitner) the train crosses the Inn. On the left rises the green *Hohe Salve*, with its chapel (p. 174). We cross the *Brixenthaler Ache*.

72 M. **Wörgl** (1660'; **Rail. Restaurant and Inn*), the junction of the Salzburg line (RR. 33, 22). The village *(Post; Lamm; Zur*

Hohen Salve) lies ¹/₂ M. to the S. Near it is the small *Bad Eisenstein* (Restaurant, with rooms; bath 30 kr.; fine view). — Ascent of the *Hohe Salve, see p. 171; to *St. Johann* viâ *Elmau*, see p. 175.

To the left beyond (76 M.) *Kundl*, on the high-road, is the church of *St. Leonhard*, said to have been founded by Emp. Henry II. in 1019. On the N. side of the broad Innthal extends the long *Brandenberger Joch* (4945'). On the S.W. side of the old town of *Rattenberg* (*Stern; Krämerbräu; Adler) the train threads a short tunnel.

81¹/₂ M. **Brixlegg** (1680'; *Vogl; *Gold. Hirsch or Judenwirth; *Herrenhaus*; *Restaurant*, with beds, near the station), situated at the confluence of the *Alpbach* with the Inn, with lead and copper smelting-works, is a favourite summer-resort. Passion-plays are performed here every few years. On the Alpbach, ¹/₂ M. to the S., are the baths of *Mehrn*.

EXCURSIONS (guides, *Jos. Kirchner* of Brixlegg, *J. G. Hörhager*, *R. Laimgruber*, and *Joh. Lettenbichler* of Kramsach). To (³/₄ hr.) **Kramsach** (*Zum Glashaus*, brewery and pension), prettily situated on the left bank of the Inn, at the mouth of the *Brandenberger Ache*. On the left bank of the Ache is *Achenrain*, with a château and brass-foundry; ¹/₄ hr. farther on is the convent of *Mariathal*; ¹/₂ hr. farther up, at the base of the *Brandenberger Joch*, is the small *Rainthaler See*; and still farther up (³/₄ hr.) is the picturesque *Perlsteiner See*. — To **Strass**, at the end of the Zillerthal, 1¹/₂ hr.: the road leads past the castles of *Matzen* and *Lichtwehr* (*In der Au Inn*, in the vicinity) to *St. Gertraud* (on the right the ruin of *Kropfsberg*, on the left the *Reitherkogl*, see below), and then crosses the Ziller (fine view of the valley) to *Strass* (p. 178). — A pleasant excursion may be made to (1 hr.) Reith (Inn), and (1 hr.) the top of the *Reitherkogl* (4376'). — Through the Alpbachthal to (2¹/₂ hrs.) the prettily-situated village of *Alpbach* (3200'; Knollenwirth); from the head of the valley we may proceed to the W., past the *Wiederberger Horn* (p. 179), to *Fügen* in the Zillerthal. — Gratlspitze (6200'), 4 hrs., with guide, not difficult. Splendid view. (Small inn on the *Holzalpl*, ³/₄ hr. below the top.) — To *Steinberg* (6 hrs., viâ *Aschau*; guide advisable), see p. 47. — Through the *Brandenberger Thal* to *Fatepp*, 9-10 hrs.; see p. 50.

The train crosses the Inn. On the right bank, on the rocky hills between the river and road, rise the old castles of *Matzen* and *Lichtwehr*, and, farther on, the extensive ruin of *Kropfsberg*, at the mouth of the *Zillerthal* (p. 178).

85¹/₂ M. **Jenbach** (2825 ft.; *Toleranz, near the station; *Hôtel Jenbach*; *Post, R. 70 kr.; *Zum Bräu, above the village, ¹/₂ M. from the station, view from the veranda, pension 2¹/₂ fl.), a large village with smelting-works and forges, is the station for the Achensee (R. 9) and the Zillerthal (R. 35).

EXCURSIONS. The imposing château of **Tratzberg**, on the hill-side (2000'), ³/₄ hr. to the W., is said to have 365 windows. It was tastefully restored by its late owner, Count Enzenberg, and contains a collection of arms (castellan 40 kr.). Excellent view of the Innthal from the grounds above it. — An attractive excursion (from Tratzberg 1¹/₄ hr.; from Schwaz viâ *Vicoht* 1¹/₂ hr.) may be made to the pilgrimage-church of ***St. Georgenberg** (3025'), in the *Stallenthal*, to the W., romantically perched on a rock overhanging a wild ravine. (Inn.)

90¹/₂ M. **Schwaz** (1775'; *Rail. Restaurant*). The town (*Stern; *Zum Freundsberg*; *Post*) lies on the opposite bank of the Inn, commanded by the château of *Freundsberg*. The silver-mines worked here in the middle ages are exhausted, but the iron and copper mines are still productive. The *Church*, roofed with copper, has a fine façade, completed in 1502, and an altarpiece by *Schöpf*. The cloisters of the *Franciscan Monastery* are adorned with old frescoes. To the right, $^1/_2$ M. from the station, rises the Benedictine abbey of *Viecht* (now a school), restored after a fire in 1868.

EXCURSIONS (guide, *Lindner*). *Keller-Joch (7675'; 4$^1/_2$-5 hrs.), by a marked path (guide desirable) viâ *Freundsberg* and *Anzingerhof* to the (3$^1/_2$ hrs.) *Kellerjoch Hut* of the local Alpine Club and to the (1$^1/_4$ hr.) summit (descent to Fügen, see p. 179). — FROM SCHWAZ TO HINTER-RISS ACROSS THE LAMSEN-JOCH, an interesting excursion of 8-9 hrs. (with guide). The path diverges to the left from the St. Georgenberg route beyond Viecht, and ascends to (1$^1/_2$ hr.) the *Bauhof* and along the right side of the wooded *Stallenthal* to (1$^1/_2$ hr.) the *Lower Stallenalpe* (4310'). Thence we ascend to the left to (1$^1/_2$ hr.) the **Lamsen-Joch** (6370'), between the Rothmandlspitz and Schafjöchl, and proceed to ($^1/_2$ hr.) a second pass at the foot of the *Lamsenspitze* (8540'), whence we descend to the ($^3/_4$ hr.) *Binsalp* and to the *Eng* (4 hrs. to Hinter-Riss, p. 43). — OVER THE STANSER-JOCH TO THE ACHENSEE, in 7$^1/_2$ hrs., a somewhat fatiguing path (guide necessary). From St. Georgenberg we mount rapidly over the *Stanser Alp* to (3$^1/_2$ hrs.) the **Stanser-Joch** (6880'; view). Descent through the *Weissenbachthal* to (2 hrs.) *Maurach* or *Seespitz* (p. 49).

About $^3/_4$ hr. above Schwaz is the mouth (N.) of the **Vomper-Thal**, one of the wildest valleys of the N. Limestone Alps, about 12 M. long, which has lately been rendered accessible. A path leads through the village of *Vomp*, crosses the brook and enters the gorge, known as the *Vomper Loch*. On the N. side (3 hrs. from Vomp viâ *Vomperberg*) is the shooting-box of *Im Zwerchbach*. From this point a trying route (guide) crosses the *Ueberschall* (6260') to the *Haller Anger* in the *Lavatsch-Thal* (p. 36).

To the right appears the village of *Vomp*, with the château of *Sigmundslust*. The train crosses the *Vomperbach* and approaches the Inn. Stations *Terfens* and *Fritzens*. On the opposite bank are the villages of *Wattens* (*Angerer), a summer-resort, with a pretty waterfall, and *Volders* (Post). The latter lies at the mouth of the *Volderer Thal* (p. 161), near the castle of *Friedberg*. We now enter the broad basin of Innsbruck. On the left rise the Patscherkofl and Saileſpitze; on the right, the serrated range on the N. side of the Inn valley (p. 162).

102$^1/_2$ M. **Hall** (1835'; *Bär; *Post; *Stern; *Rössle*, moderate; *Hirsch; Kaiser Brewery*), a quaint old town of 5000 inhab., with salt-works, to which the brine is conveyed from a distance of 6 M. (see p. 161). The evaporating houses near the station contain a cabinet of models. On the S.W. side of the town, near the *Residenz* (palace) built by Archduke Sigismund in 1480, is a curious old tower called the *Münze*, a relic of the ancient 'mint' once situated here. The *Casino* (formerly 'Trinkstube') dates from the beginning of the 16th century. The *Parish Church* contains valuable old church utensils. On the outer wall is a small monument to *Speckbacher* (d. 1820; the companion-in-arms of the patriotic Andrew Hofer), who in 1809 succeeded three times in storming the bridge over the Inn, the key to the position of the French and Bavarians.

EXCURSIONS (guide, *Rathgeber* at Absam). The village of **Absam** (*Bogner*, with garden and view; *Ebner*), situated on a height, $^1/_2$ hr. to the

N., with a pilgrimage-church, was the birthplace of Jacob Stainer (d. 1683), the famous violin-maker, whose house is denoted by a marble tablet with an inscription.

To reach the **Gnadenwald**, the hills on the N. bank of the Inn, we follow the road to the Salzberg (see below) for 2½ M., and then ascend to the right to (¾ hr.) *St. Martin* (Speckbacher), *St. Michael* (½ hr.; 2870'), and (½ hr.) the *Gungl Inn*. From this point we descend to (¾ hr.) the church of *Maria-Larch* and (½ hr.) *Terfens*. A very interesting expedition may be made from St. Michael to the top of the **Walder Alpe** (5340'); fine views from the *Walder-Joch* (5340'), 20 min. to the E. (to the N. the deep gorge of the *Vomperthal*), and from the *Hinterhornalm* (4990'), ½ hr. to the W. The descent on the N. side leads to the *Gan Alp* in the Vomperthal, and then to the right, round the ridge, to *Ummelberg* and (2½ hrs.) *Terfens*.

The **Haller Salzberg** (2½ hrs.). The road leads to the N., past (left) *Absam* (the path viâ Absam, which joins the road in 1 hr., is preferable), and ascends the *Hallthal*, between the *Zunderkopf* (6414') on the left and the *Bettelwurfspitze* (8976') on the right, to the shafts of the Salt Mines, 2780' above Hall (tavern at the '*Herrenhaus*'). A visit to the mines is interesting (1½ hr.; fee 40 kr.). The *Zunderkopf* (ascended by a new club-path) commands a fine view. — About ½ hr. above the Herrenhaus is the *Issenanger*, in a wild situation. An attractive pass leads hence over the *Lavatscher Joch* (6815') and through the *Hinterauthal* (carriage-road beyond the shooting-lodge) to (7 hrs.) *Scharnitz* (comp. p. 36); another (fatiguing) pass crosses the *Stempeljoch* (7190') to the *Gleirschthal* (to Scharnitz 7-8 hrs.; comp. p. 36).

The **Volderthal.** The road leads to the E. across the bridge over the Inn to (3 M.) *Volders* (1835'; Inn), whence a steep cart-track ascends on the E. side of the valley to the (1½ hr.) *Volderer Wildbad* (3650'; good and cheap quarters), prettily situated in the woods. The °*Glungetzer* (8780') is ascended hence without difficulty in 5 hrs. (with guide). — ACROSS THE NAVISJOCH TO MATREI (on the Brenner railway), 8½ hrs., easy and interesting (guide unnecessary in good weather; Ant. Angerer of Volders recommended). From the Voldererbad we follow the left bank of the brook to (2 hrs.) the *Vorberg-Alpe* (5580'), cross to the right bank, recross near the (1 hr.) *Steinkaseralpe* (6560), and reach (1½ hr.) the **Navisjoch** (8200), immediately to the W. of the Sonnenspitze, with a fine view of the Tux and Stubai Alps. Descent through the Navisthal to the *Zehenter-Alp* and the *Stipler-Alp* and over steep meadows to (2 hrs.) *Naris* (4400'; quarters at the curé's), whence a cart-track leads to (2 hrs.) *Matrei* or *Steinach* (p. 220).

The train quits the Inn and traverses the broad valley towards the W. On the right rise the *Zunderköpfe*, with the white *Franzenspyramide*; at their base lie the villages of *Thaur, Rum,* and *Arzl*. To the left, on the lower hills, at the foot of the *Glungetzer* (8780'), is the village of *Rinn*, the birthplace of Speckbacher (b. 1768). Farther down is the château of *Amras* (p. 168). The train crosses the Inn, above the influx of the *Sill*, opposite *Mühlau* (p. 170), and traverses the valley on a long, unsightly viaduct.

109 M. *Innsbruck.*

32. Innsbruck and Environs.

162   IV. Route 32.   INNSBRUCK.   *Situation.*

Maria-Theresien-Str., adjoining the post-office; *Hirsch (Pl. f; B, C, 3);
Krone, by the triumphal arch, well spoken of; *Goldner Löwe; Rother
Adler (Pl. g; D, 3), Seilergasse; *Grauer Bär (see below), moderate;
Weisses Rössl; Goldne Rose, near the Goldne Dachl. — On the left bank
of the Inn: *Pension Kayser (p. 170), charmingly situated 1/2 M. from the
bridge, adapted for a stay of some time, pens. with R. from 2 1/2 fl. per
day (also a café-restaurant). Second-class: Goldner Stern (Pl. h; B, 2)
frequented by the clergy; *Mondschein (Pl. i; B, 3), by the bridge;
Mohren, Mariahilf-Str. — In summer it is advisable to order rooms in
advance. — *Pension Schloss Mentelberg, see p. 170.
  Cafés and Restaurants. *Kraft* (military music frequently), *Hierhammer*, both in the Museums-Strasse; *Grubhofer*, Erler-Str.; *Katzung*,
under the Lauben; *Kreid*, Margarethen-Platz; *Kayser (see above), with
view-terrace. — Beer. *Breinössl*, *Passerl*, Maria-Theresien-Str. 12 & 21,
both with shady gardens; *Bierwastl*, Ursulinergraben; *Summerer*, Viaduktgasse, near the station (often military music); *Adambräu*, Adamsgasse. Good
wine at the *Grauer Bär*, with garden, Universitäts-Str. — *Rail. Restaurant.*
  Carriages (driver included). To or from the station, with bag, one-horse 80 kr., two-horse 1 fl.; drive in the town, first hour 1 or 2 fl., each
additional hour 80 kr. or 1 fl.; 1/2 day 4 or 6, whole day 7 or 10 fl. To
the Berg Isel and back (with stay of 1 br.), one-horse 1 1/2 fl., two-horse
2 fl.; Mentelberg 1 or 2 fl.; Mühlau 1 fl. 20 kr. or 2 fl.; Weiherburg 2 or 3;
Weiherburg, and back by Mühlau, 2 1/2 or 4; Amras 2 or 3; Kranewitten
2 1/2 or 4; Lans 4 or 7; Lans and Igls 5 or 8; Igls via Vill 4 or 6; Stefansbrücke 2 1/2 or 4; Schönberg 5 or 8; Neustift 9 or 16 fl. — Omnibus from
the Anna-Säule (p. 163) to the Berg Isel (10 kr.) and Amras (20 kr.),
in 1 hr., starting at 9, 11, 3, and 5 o'clock, returning from Amras at 10.15,
12, 4, and 6 o'clock.
  Railway to Munich, see R. 31; by Wörgl and Saalfelden to Salzburg,
see RR. 33, 22; to Botzen, see R. 41; to Landeck, see R. 43. *Porter* from the
station to the hotel for luggage under 33 lbs. 10 kr.for each package, under
1 cwt. 15 kr., above 1 cwt. 20 kr.
  Baths. *Swimming and other Baths* in the Adamsgasse, adjoining the
Margarethen-Platz, near the station, well fitted up (for ladies 8-11 a.m.).
Kaiserkrone, Herzog-Otto-Str. (restaurant); *Swimming and other baths* at
the *Giessen*, on the left bank of the Inn, above the rifle-range; *Erzherzog-Maximilians-Bad*, at St. Niklaus.
  Summer Theatre (rustic comedies) at *Pradl* (p. 168) on Sun. afternoons.
  Post and Telegraph Office (Pl. C, 4), Maria-Theresien-Str. — Carved
wood, photographs, etc., at *F. Unterberger's*, Museums-Str., and *Crichna's*,
Herzog-Friedrich-Str. 1 and Rudolf-Str., near the Hôtel de l'Europe.
  English Church Service in the Redoute building at 11 a.m. and 6 p.m.

Innsbruck (1910'), the capital of Tyrol, with about 30,000 inhab. and a garrison of 2000 men, is charmingly situated on the
Inn, not far from the influx of the *Sill*, and next to Salzburg is
the most picturesque town among the German Alps. In every direction, particularly towards the N., the eye is met by striking groups
of bold and fissured limestone mountains (*Brandjoch*, *Frauhütt*, *Seegrubenspitzen*, *Hafelekar*, *Rumerjoch*), towering above the cultivated
slopes of the valley; while towards the S., above the wooded *Berg Isel*,
rise the noble outlines of the *Saile-Spitze* and *Waldraster-Spitze*.
To the S.E., nearer the foreground, above the *Lanser Köpfe*,
peeps the rounded summit of the *Patscher Kofel*.

Leaving the station (Pl. D, 4), we pass between the handsome
new hotels and first reach the Margarethen-Platz (Pl. C, D, 4),
where the *Rudolfsbrunnen* (Pl. 2), in red Tyrolese marble, erected in
1863-77, commemorates the 500th anniversary of the union of Tyrol

with Austria (1363). At the top is a bronze statue of Duke Rudolf IV., 10' in height, by Grissemann, and around the basin below are four water-spouting dragons and four griffins as shield-bearers.

We next reach the Maria-Theresien-Strasse (Pl. C, 3, 4), the busiest street in the town, which contains the *Landhaus*, the *Post Office* (formerly the palace of Prince Thurn and Taxis, Pl. C, 4), and other handsome buildings of the 17-18th cent., and is embellished with the *Anna-Säule* (Pl. C, 4), erected in 1706 'ob hostes tam Bavarum quam Gallum A. 1703 Tyrolim invadentes depulsos'.

On the W. side of the street is the former *Oesterreichische Hof*, now private property; the façade of the 'Saalbau', in the court, is adorned with excellent *Frescoes (female figures, over life-size, typifying Industry, Good Fortune, Ability, and Thrift; above, groups of cupids), executed in 1886 from designs by Ferd. Wagner. — Near the column is the house in which the Tyrolese poet *Herm. v. Gilm* (d. 1864) was born, with a bust of him in marble.

The Maria-Theresien-Str. is continued towards the N. by the Herzog-Friedrich-Strasse, a street flanked with arcades ('Lauben'), which leads direct to the Goldne Dachl.

The '**Goldne Dachl**' (Pl. C, 3), a gilded copper roof, covering a rich late-Gothic balcony constructed in 1425, belongs to a palace which Count Frederick of the Tyrol, nicknamed 'with the empty pockets', is said to have built at a cost of 30,000 ducats (about 14,000*l*.) in order to refute the imputation. The paintings on the outer wall, representing the Emp. Maximilian and his two wives, and the well-executed armorial bearings in marble commemorate the restoration of the balcony by that emperor about the year 1500. — The adjoining *Stadtthurm* or *Feuerthurm*, a handsome old tower, commands a fine view.

Further on, to the right, we reach the **Franciscan Church**, or **Hofkirche** (Pl. C, 3), in the Renaissance style, erected in 1553-63, in compliance with the will of Emp. Maximilian I. (d. 1519; interred at Wiener-Neustadt, p. 363), whose sumptuous *Monument occupies the centre of the nave. Maximilian is represented in a kneeling posture, in bronze, on a massive marble sarcophagus, surrounded by 28 bronze statues of his heroic ancestors, in the guise of mourners and torch-bearers. The completion of this imposing work occupied several generations, and the emperor himself ordered its execution as early as 1509; but the original plan having been lost, the monument was not erected till the time of Ferdinand I. and the Archduke Ferdinand, and was not finished till about 1583. The superintendence of the work was entrusted to *Gilg Sesselschreiber* of Augsburg, the court-painter, who designed more than half of the statues. The figures were cast by *Stephan Godl* (who succeeded Sesselschreiber in 1518), *Bernhard Godl*, *Gregor Löffler*, *Hans Lendenstreich*, and others; and the famous *Peter Vischer* of Nuremberg, to whom the figure of King Arthur, the finest of all, is attributed, also took part in the work.

On the right: 1. Clovis of France; 2. Philip I. of Spain, son of Maximilian; 3. Emp. Rudolph of Hapsburg; 4. Duke Albert the Wise; *5. Theodorich, King of the Ostrogoths; 6. Ernest, Duke of Austria and Styria; 7. Theodobert, Duke of Burgundy; *8. Arthur, King of England (1513); 9. Archduke Sigismund; 10. Bianca Maria Sforza, second wife of Maximilian; 11. Margaret, their daughter; 12. Zimburga, wife of Duke Ernest; 13. Charles the Bold of Burgundy; 14. Philip le Bon, father of the last.

On the left: 15. Johanna, Queen of Philip I. of Spain; 16. Ferdinand the Catholic, her father; 17. Cunigunde, sister of Maximilian; 18. Eleonora of Portugal, mother of Maximilian; 19. Maria of Burgundy, his first wife; 20. Elisabeth, wife of Albert II.; 21. Godfrey de Bouillon, with a crown of thorns; 22. Emp. Albert I.; 23. Frederick IV., Count of Tyrol, 'with the empty pockets' (p. 163); 24. Leopold III., the Pious, who fell at Sempach; 25. Count Rudolph of Hapsburg, grandfather of the Emperor; 26. Leopold the Saint; 27. Emp. Frederick III., Maximilian's father; 28. Emp. Albert II.

Most of these statues were cast under Ferdinand I. at the bronze foundry of Mühlau near Innsbruck, which was established by Maximilian I.

On the sides of the sarcophagus are 24 reliefs in marble, representing the principal events in the emperor's life. The first four are by *Bernhard* and *Albert Abel* of Cologne; the other twenty, by *Alex. Colin* of Malines (1558-66), who received 240 fl. for each, have been pronounced by Thorvaldsen the most perfect works of their kind. Many of the heads are portraits; the features of Maximilian at different periods of his life are unmistakable; and the characteristics of the different nationalities are faithfully rendered. The reliefs are covered with glass and enclosed by a railing. The sacristan shows the monument and the Silberkapelle (50 kr.).

1st Relief. Nuptials of the Emperor with Maria of Burgundy, 1477; 2. Victory over the French at Guinegate, 1479; 3. Taking of Arras, 1482; 4. Coronation as Roman king at Aix-la-Chapelle, 1486; 5. Victory of the Tyrolese over the Venetians at Calliano on the Adige, 1487; 6. Entry into Vienna, after its abandonment by the Hungarians, 1490; 7. Taking of Stuhlweissenburg; 8. Return of his daughter Margaret from France; 9. Expulsion of the Turks from Croatia; 10. Alliance between Maximilian, Pope Alex. VI., the Republic of Venice, and the Duke of Milan, against Charles VIII. of France; 11. Investment of Ludovico Sforza with the duchy of Milan; 12. Marriage of Philip le Bel, son of Maximilian, with Johanna of Arragon; 13. Victory over the Bohemians at Ratisbon, 1503; 14. Siege of Kufstein (p. 52); 15. Submission of Duke Charles of Guelders, 1505; 16. League of Cambrai; 17. Surrender of Padua to Maximilian, 1509; 18. Maximilian Sforza reinstated as Duke of Milan; 19. Second battle of Guinegate, 1515; 20. Meeting of Maximilian and Henry VIII. of England at the siege of Tournai, 1513; 21. Battle of Vicenza against the Venetians; 22. Attack of the Venetian camp at Marano; 23. Marriage of Maximilian's grandson Ferdinand and his granddaughter Maria, with Maria and Lewis, children of Vladislaw, King of Hungary, 1515; 24 Defence of Verona against the French and Venetians, 1516.

The steps to the right, at the beginning of the right aisle, lead to the *Silberne Kapelle*, so called from a silver statue of the Virgin, and embossed representations in that metal of the 'Lauretanian Litany' on the altar. On the left wall are 23 bronze statuettes of saints, cast at Innsbruck, and probably once destined for the monument of Maximilian. The tomb of Archduke Ferdinand II. (d. 1595), executed by Colin during the duke's lifetime, is adorned with the arms of the Austrian provinces admirably inlaid in stone, and with four scenes in relief from the life of the deceased. The tomb of Philippina Welser of Augsburg (d. 1580), first wife of the archduke (see p. 168), is embellished with two reliefs by Colin. The old organ is said to have been a gift of Pope Julius II.

At the entrance to the left aisle is the *Monument of Andreas Hofer*, in Tyrolese marble, executed by *Schaller*, with a relief by *Klieber*. Hofer was shot by the French at Mantua, 20th Feb., 1810; and in 1823 his remains were brought to Innsbruck, and solemnly interred here. In relief are six Tyrolese, who represent the six districts of the Tyrol, binding themselves by an oath over the lowered banner. At the sides are the tombs of *Speckbacher* and *Haspinger*, with memorial tablets. Opposite these is a monument to all the Tyrolese who have fallen in the defence of their country since 1796, with the inscription: 'Absorpta est mors in victoria'. — In this church, on 3rd Nov., 1654, Christina of Sweden, daughter of Gustavus Adolphus, embraced the Roman Catholic faith.

ANDREW HOFER, born in 1767 at the *Sandhof Inn* (p. 254), near St. Leonhard in the Passeyr, was originally an innkeeper and dealer in wine and horses. In 1796 he began his public career as the leader of a corps of riflemen against the French on the banks of the Lago di Garda. In 1803 he promoted the reorganisation of the militia, in 1808 he took an active part, under Hormayr, in a rising against the Bavarians, and in 1809 took the command of the Tyrolese, whose struggle for liberty was crowned with marked success on three occasions at Innsbruck (see above), as well as elsewhere. Hofer now assumed the position of civil and military governor of the Tyrol, and resided at Schloss Tyrol for about six weeks, during which period he conducted the administration with his characteristic simplicity and shrewdness. After the Peace of Vienna, on 14th Oct., the Emperor of Austria himself exhorted the Tyrolese to submit to the foreign yoke; but Hofer, misled by false reports, was induced once more to lead his countrymen against the French and their Bavarian allies. His patriotic efforts, however, being speedily crushed, he dismissed his followers and retired to his native mountains, where he sought refuge in the Kellerlahn chalet (p. 254). His hiding-place was betrayed to the French by one Raffl, whose secret was extorted by threats of death, and on 20th Jan., 1810, Hofer and his family were taken prisoners. He was conveyed to Mantua and tried by court-martial, the majority of the judges in which were opposed to his execution. Notwithstanding this he was shot on 20th Feb., by order of Napoleon himself.

Hofer's most undaunted coadjutors were the Capuchin monk HASPINGER (b. 1776, d. 1858), who distinguished himself as a soldier, as well as in his sacred office, and SPECKBACHER (b. 1758, d. 1820), another Tyrolese, who was originally a farmer and chamois-hunter, but afterwards took up arms in defence of his native country, and terminated his career as a major in the Austrian service.

To the left, on leaving the Franciscan Church, we observe the imperial palace, or **Hofburg** (Pl. C, 3), erected in the rococo style in 1770, on the site of a castle built by Maximilian I. and enlarged by Ferdinand I. — Tickets of admission to the Burg (9-12 and 2-4; the *Riesensaal* with portraits and the *Chapel* are worth seeing) and also to Schloss Amras (p. 168) are obtained at the intendant's office ('Schloss-Kanzlei', first door on the E. side, then to the left).

Opposite the Burg are the *Redoutensäle* (Pl. 19) and the *Theatre* (Pl. C, 3). In front of it lies the Rennweg, embellished with a small equestrian *Statue* (Pl. 1) in bronze, on a disproportionately large pedestal, erected by Claudia de' Medici to her husband Archduke Leopold V. The figure was originally designed for a fountain. — To the N. of this point is the well-kept **Hofgarten** (Restaurant).

Next the Hofkirche in the Universitäts-Strasse is the *Theresianum*, formerly a school for the sons of the nobility, and now a *Gymnasium* (Pl. 5). In the same street, beyond the entrance to the Botanic Garden (see below), is the **University** (Pl. C, D, 3), founded by Emp. Leopold in 1672 and restored in 1826. A medical faculty was added in 1869. It is attended by about 800 students and possesses the usual collections. The **Jesuitenkirche** or *University Church* (Pl. 9), erected in 1627-40 in the baroque style, is crowned with a dome 200' high. The former Jesuits' College, adjoining, contains the **University Library** (Pl. 25), a collection of 80,000 vols. (open 9-12 and 3-6).

The **Botanic Garden** (Pl. D, 2, 3; entrance opposite the back of the Gymnasium) contains upwards of 600 species of Alpine plants with the different kinds of rock on which they grow, arranged orographically.

The **Capuchin Monastery** (Pl. D, 2, 3), begun in 1598, was the first of this order in Germany. A cell built by Archduke Maximilian, Master of the Teutonic Order (d. 1618), where he annually spent some time according to the rules of the Order, still contains reminiscences of the founder.

Near this point, in the Museums-St., rises the handsome Renaissance building of the **Landes-Museum** (*Ferdinandeum*; Pl. C, D, 3), a private institution, founded and maintained by 600 members (open daily, except Sun. afternoon, in summer 9-5, in winter 10-3; admission 50, catalogue 20 kr.). The façade, which was erected by Tommasi in 1883, is adorned with busts of twenty-two eminent natives of Tyrol (Angelica Kauffmann, J. A. Koch, etc.).

GROUND FLOOR. In the vestibule are Roman and mediæval monuments in stone and bronze. The central hall, containing portraits of the founders and supporters of the museum, is intended for temporary exhibitions; and the side-rooms contain the natural history collections and the library.

FIRST FLOOR. The Corridor contains plaster-casts. — Room I.: Collection of arms. — R. II.: Pre-Roman and Roman antiquities. — R. III.: Ethnographical collection. — R. IV.: Geographical objects and instruments; standard weights and measures. — R. V.: Collections illustrating the history of civilization. — R. VI., a circular apartment containing patriotic and historical relics and curiosities: statue of Hofer; his tombstone from Mantua; his sabre, amulet, coins struck during his brief rule, his rifle, &c.; Speckbacher's sabre and belt; Haspinger's hat and breviary; a Neapolitan six-pounder; the flag of a Venetian volunteer corps, captured from the Italians by a corps of Innsbruck students in 1848; a mountain-gun of the same period. — The *Radetzky Album*, a memorial of the marshal of that name, contains over 1000 autographs; the most interesting leaves are exhibited in frames on the wall. — R. VII.: Sculptures, and plaster-casts of works by Tyrolese artists. — R. VIII.: Small objects of art in porcelain, glass, etc. — R. IX.: Objects of art in metal. — R. X.: Coins.

SECOND FLOOR. The *Picture Gallery* here occupies seventeen rooms and cabinets. To the right of the staircase, Cab. I.-III. Tyrolese artists of the 15-16th centuries. — Cab. IV.: *Cranach*, St. Jerome. Works by *Paul Dax* and *M. de Vos*. — Cab. V. *Seb. Scheel* of Innsbruck. — Rooms I.

and II.: Tyrolese masters of the 17-18th centuries. — R. III.: Works by *J. A. Koch* and other Tyrolese masters of the first part of the 19th century. — R. IV. ('Defregger Room'): *Defregger* (p. 149), Speckbacher and his son Anderl; six copies of Defregger's chief pictures, touched up by himself. — R. V.: Modern Tyrolese and German masters. — R. VI.: Copies of Italian and other paintings. — R. VII.: Dutch, German, and Italian pictures of the 17-18th cent., chiefly belonging to the Tschager Collection (bequeathed to the museum in 1856), including works by *Van der Helst*, *Terburg*, *Rembrandt*, and *G. Dou*. — Five other cabinets contain watercolours, engravings, and drawings.

The **Church of St. James** (*St. Jakob*; Pl. C, 3), not far from the Goldne Dachl, re-erected in 1717, contains a picture of the Virgin over the high-altar by *L. Cranach*, surrounded with a painting by *Schöpff*; and the tomb of Archduke Maximilian, Master of the Teutonic Order, designed by K. Gras and cast by H. Reinhart.

The handsome *Bridge (Pl. B, 3), which leads to the suburbs of *St. Nicolaus* and *Mariahilf* on the left bank of the Inn, affords the best survey of the environs. Below the bridge, on both banks, extend pleasure-grounds, at the lower end of which the river is crossed by an iron foot-bridge (1 kr. toll). In the *Inn-Allée* on the left bank are a pillar with a barometer, and a zinc *Statue of Walther von der Vogelweide* (p. 263).

At the S. end of the Maria-Theresien-Strasse is a **Triumphal Gate**, erected by the citizens in 1765, on the occasion of the entry of Emp. Francis I. and the Empress Maria Theresa, to commemorate the marriage of Prince Leopold (afterwards Emp. Leopold II.) with the Infanta Maria Ludovica. The emperor died before the conclusion of the festivities.

Beyond this gate, to the right, is the *Tyrolese Glass-Painting and Mosaic Establishment* (Pl. 24; B, 5); in the adjacent Fallmerayer-Str. stand the *Imperial Law Courts* (Pl. B, 4, 5), the *Commercial School* (Pl. 6), and the *Pädagogium* (teachers' seminary; Pl. B, C, 4). The garden of the last contains a department for Alpine plants, and a large and interesting *Relief Model of Tyrol* (scale 1 : 7500; vertical scale 7 : 15,000), by *Prof. Schuler*, covering an area of about 100 sq. yds., and reproducing accurately the geological peculiarities of the different districts. In the Anich-Str. rises the *Technical School* (Pl. 21), built by Tommasi; more to the S.W. are the *University Clinical Institutions* (Pl. A, B, 4, 5), and the new *Public Hospital*. Towards the S.W., in the direction of the Inn, is the *Pathological and Anatomical Institute* (Pl. A, 5), and in the same quarter lies the well-kept **Cemetery**, containing handsome modern monuments by Knabl, Grissemann, and other Tyrolese sculptors, and that of A. Colin, the sculptor (p. 164), in the Renaissance style. In the vestibule of the chapel are frescoes by A. Plattner, a pupil of Cornelius (1863-1873), and sculptures by M. Stolz.

About ³/₄ M. from the gate, on the Brenner road (p. 227), is the Premonstratensian Abbey of **Wilten**, or *Willau*, the Roman *Veldidena*. By the church-portal are statues of the giants *Haimon*, the traditional founder of the abbey, and *Thyrsus*. The church is sumptuously decorated with stucco, frescoes, and gilding.

In 3 min. more the road brings us to the foot of the ***Berg Isel** (2455'), where a notice indicates the way to the rifle-practice ground of the Tyrolese Riflemen ('Kaiser-Jäger'). Ascending the hill, we reach in 10 min. the park-like plateau with its monuments and buildings. The rifle-range is on the side next the Sillthal (officers' practice on Saturday afternoons, with military music). The *Belvedere* affords a charming survey of the Innthal and the town.

At the sides are two obelisks, commemorative of the various wars in which the Tyrolese have been engaged. One of them bears the inscription: '*Donec erunt montes et saxa et pectora nostra Austriacae domui moenia semper erunt.*' The dates 13th April, 29th May, and 13th August, 1809, refer to the repeated capture of the town from the Bavarians by the brave Tyrolese peasants under *Andreas Hofer*, whose attacks were chiefly directed against it from the Berg Isel and the hills adjoining it on the E. as far as Schloss Amras. — The smaller *Pyramid* of white marble records the names of Tyrolese officers and soldiers who fell in the campaigns of 1848, 1849, 1859, 1863, and 1878 in Tyrol, Italy, Hungary, and the Herzegovina. — The belvedere contains portraits of Hofer, Speckbacher, and Haspinger, trophies, uniforms, etc. (adm. 20 kr.).

On a spur of the Mittelgebirge, or lower hills, 3 M. to the S.E. of Innsbruck, stands Schloss Amras, the direct road to which leads by *Pradl*. (A shorter footpath leads to the right below the railway-station and crosses the Sill to the gas-works; here we go towards the right for a few hundred paces, and then follow a field-track to the left, which leads to the road in 10 min.) Another road to the Schloss viâ *Wilten* is longer, but pleasanter. It leads to the left under the Brenner Railway at the foot of the Berg Isel, and crosses the Sill Canal and the *Sill* (farther up is a weir, and on the left bank is seen the mouth of the first tunnel of the Brenner line), and then leads straight to the château along the base of the mountains. (*Schlosskeller Restaurant*, to the right, near the entrance.)

*Schloss Amras or *Ambras* (2045'), originally erected in the 13th cent., owes its fame chiefly to Archduke Ferdinand, son of Emp. Ferdinand I., and husband of Philippina Welser, daughter of a wealthy patrician of Augsburg, whom he had met at the diet of Augsburg in 1547 and secretly married in 1557. The archduke, an enthusiastic lover of art, who became governor of the Tyrol in 1563, extended the château considerably and filled it with treasures of art. His historical collection of armour established here, but transferred to Vienna in 1806, is to this day one of the finest in existence, and many of the greatest treasures of the collections and library at Vienna were originally purchased by the archduke for this château. The Schloss gradually fell into decay, but when Archduke Karl Ludwig (governor of Tyrol in 1856-58) selected it as his residence, it underwent a thorough restoration. In 1880 the collection of objects of art were considerably increased by contributions from the imperial collections in Vienna, and in 1882 the château was opened as a museum (open from June to Oct. daily, except Mon., 9-12 and 2-5, in winter 10-12 and 1-3; tickets of admission are obtained gratis at the Hofburg in Innsbruck, daily, except Mon., 9-12 and 2-5; see p. 165).

The outer court contains 8 Roman milestones, from the time of Septimius Severus (193-211 A. D.), found on the road from Wilten to Schönberg. The visitor is shewn successively the 'Unterschloss', the 'Spanish Saloon', and the 'Hochschloss' (fee for each). In the Unterschloss ('lower castle'), two large halls to the right contain the valuable *Collection of Weapons*, from the 15th cent. to the present time, arranged in chronological order. At the entrance to the Hochschloss is the large *Spanish Saloon*, 140' long, 32' broad, and 18' high, with marble pavement, fine wooden ceiling, and artistically inlaid doors; on the walls are portraits of counts and dukes of Tyrol from 1229 to 1600. Built in 1570-71, this hall was thoroughly restored in 1856-77. — The *Ground Floor* of the **Hochschloss** ('upper castle') contains a restored Gothic chapel of the 15th cent., with frescoes by Wörndle; and a bath-chamber said to have been used by Philippina Welser. — *First Floor*: Rooms I-VI, Collection of furniture (in R. V. fine antique panels from Meran). R. VII: Models of stone buildings. R. VIII.: Models of wooden buildings, wax-reliefs, etc. R. IX.: Objects in metal, and textile fabrics. R. X.: Oriental and Asiatic articles. R. XI.: Marble sculptures. R. XII.: Works in wood, ivory, horn, amber, etc.; small sculptures in stone; mosaics and paintings upon stone. R. XIII.: Coral. — The *Second Floor* (N. side) contains a historical portrait-gallery in nine rooms. Among the portraits in RR. III. and IV. are those of the Archduke Ferdinand (d. 1595), at various ages, Philippina Welser (d. 1580), and their sons Andrew (d. 1600 as cardinal), and Charles, Margrave of Burgau (d. 1618). Room V. contains a fine old panelled ceiling. The religious and historical pictures in the last four rooms are of little value.

The pretty *Park, with its miniature waterfalls, is also accessible (entrance near the Spanish Saloon), and as the gate at the lower end is generally open, it is not necessary to return to the château.

About ³/₄ M. nearer the town than Schloss Amras a path with pilgrimage-stations ascends towards the S. into the wood to the *Tümmelplatz* ('tournament-ground'), a small open space, with chapels, crosses, and votive offerings This was the burial-place of about 8000 soldiers who perished during the wars of 1797-1805, when the Schloss was used as a military hospital.

The finest of the excursions from Innsbruck is the ascent of the *Lanser Köpfe (3100'; 1¹/₄-1¹/₂ hr.; carriage and pair from Innsbruck and back, in 4 hrs. including stay of 1 hr., 6 fl.). Beyond the bridge over the Sill at Wilten, by a finger-post to the right, we ascend the *Paschberg*, soon obtaining a fine view of the Inn valley; by the (12 min.) red cross, where the carriage-road viâ *Igls* diverges to the right (see below), our path ascends to the left round the Lanser Köpfe to the point where carriages stop; thence from the S. side to the top. A shorter way diverges to the right from the above route, 18 min. from the red cross; by a (3 min.) farm-house we ascend to the left by a pleasant forest-path, the route being distinctly indicated by red marks on the trees; at the (8 min.) top of the hill we follow the broad path to the left, and at (8 min.) another finger-post we turn to the right and (6 min.) reach the N.E. summit (390' above the Mittelgebirge; marked by a column 42' high, with a vane), whence we enjoy a charming *View of the valley of the Inn from the Martinswand to the Kellerjoch and Kaisergebirge, and of the Stubaier Ferner, Habicht,

Waldrasterspitz, Saile, etc., towards the S. (see the mountain-indicator). — We may return past the small round *Lanser See* (rustic baths, 20 kr.) to (20 min.) *Igls* (2900'; Iglerhof, high charges), and past (3/4 M.) *Vill* (*Inn) to (3 M.) Innsbruck; or we may proceed to the left from the Lanser See to (1 M.) *Lans* (Traube; Wilder Mann), and follow the road (carriages, see p. 162) viâ *Aldrans* to (2 M.) *Amras* (p. 168; a path leading to the left immediately to the N. of Lans saves 3/4 M.).

The hill near the church of **Ampass** commands a view similar to that from the Lanser Köpfe and is much more accessible. From Amras we proceed viâ (1/4 hr.) *Bad Egerdach* to (10 min.) the old 'Salzstrasse' ('salt road' from Hall to Matrei (see below). We then ascend this road till the church of Ampass comes in sight and mount by a good path on the E. side of the hill to (5 min.) the tower on the top.

A pleasant walk may be taken on the left bank of the Inn, by *St. Nikolaus* (p. 167), the château of *Büchsenhausen* (with a brewery), and the *Pension Kayser* (p. 162), to (1/2 hr.) **Schloss Weiherburg** (2210'; Restaurant) with a view-terrace (mountain-indicator) commanding a fine view of the valley of the Inn, the Glungetzer, Patscher Kofel, etc. We may then return by (20 min.) **Mühlau** (*Stern; *Pension Edelweiss*). About 800' above the Weiherburg (ascent of 40 min.) is the farm-house of *Maria-Brunn* (the '*Hungerburg*'; *Restaurant), which commands a *View extending to the Stubaier Ferner. — About 3/4 M. from Mühlau is the wild *Mühlauer Klamm*, or gorge. From Mühlau we return to (1 1/4 M.) Innsbruck by the handsome suspension-bridge.

The **Kranewitter Klamm** is well worth a visit. Taking the first turning to the left in the Höttinger Gasse, which ascends from the bridge over the Inn, we cross the *Höttinger Brook*, and continue straight on to (3/4 M.) a chapel. Keeping to the right of the hill, we proceed for about 2 1/4 M. between meadows and wood, and then ascend to the right to (1/2 hr.) the *Kerschbuchhof*, where we have a view of the Saile, the Kalkkögel, and the Tuxerferner (Olperer). The Klamm lies about 1/4 hr. below in the wood (in wet weather visitors should beware of the stones which occasionally fall on the path). The most convenient return-route is by railway from *Vöts* (p. 231), which we reach by descending from the Klamm to the (1/4 hr.) Hotel at *Kranewitten* and crossing the *Inn* by ferry (apply at the hotel). — A rough path (guide to Zirl 2 1/2 fl.) leads through the Klamm to (2 hrs.) the *Zirler Mähder*, whence it descends to the *Zirler Klamm* and (2 1/2 hrs.) *Zirl* (p. 232). — A finer route to the Kranewitter Klamm is by the '*Stangensteig*', which begins at the (3/4 hr.) *Planitzenhof* and ascends thence direct, through wood (fine views), to (1 hr.) the *Kerschbuchhof* (guide 1 1/2 fl.). — A walk may also be taken from the Planitzenhof, through wood, to the (1/2 hr.) solitary and most romantically situated *Höttinger Bild* (guide 1 fl.).

Schloss Mentelberg (*Hotel-Pension and *Restaurant*), finely situated 3 M. to the W. of Innsbruck (road viâ Wilten), is a favourite excursion, for the sake of the fine view it commands. — Another pleasant excursion may be made by the *Brenner Road* (p. 227), either on foot or by carriage, past the *Ferrarihof* (Restaurant, with pretty view), to the (1 1/2 M.) *Stefansbrücke (thence to *Ober-Schönberg*, etc., see p. 227). — By the Arlberg Railway to *Kematen* (*Kaiser Ferdinand Waterfalls*) and to *Zirl*, see pp. 231, 232.

MOUNTAIN ASCENTS (guides, *B. Gheri, Al. Hochraincr*, and *Fr. Rumggaldier*). The **Patscher Kofel** (7205'; 5-5 1/2 hrs.; guide from Heiligwasser 2 fl.) commands a very extensive view. We take the road to *Vill* and (1 1/2 M.) *Igls* (see above), cross the 'Salzstrasse' from Matrei to Hall, and ascend

HOHE SALVE.   *IV. Route 33.* 171

to the small pilgrimage-church of (1 hr.) *Heiligwasser* (4040'; Inn). Thence with guide (path, indicated by red marks, steep at places) past the *Ochsenalpe* (good water) to the broad summit (refuge-hut) in 2½ hrs. more. There is no single point from which the whole panorama can be surveyed. A steep path leads from the Ochsenalp through wood to (1½ hr.) *Patsch* (p. 219). — The **Saile** or **Nockspitz** (7880'), a toilsome ascent of 5 hrs. with guide (4 fl.), vià *Mutters* and *Kreit* (p. 227), offers fewer attractions than the Patscher Kofel.

Among the limestone-mountains on the N. side of the Inn, the **Hafelekar** (7485') is the most interesting (5 hrs., not difficult; guide, unnecessary for adepts, 3 fl.; path marked with yellow). Passing the church of Hötting, we reach the quarries on the W. side of the Hungerburg, and then beyond the *Titschenbrunnen* (3445'), the (3 hrs.) *Arzler Rossalpe* (5080'), about 2 hrs. below the summit. Fine view. Good spring ¼ hr. to the W. (36° F.).

33. From Wörgl to Mittersill. Hohe Salve.

40 M. RAILWAY (*Giselabahn*, comp. R. 22) from Wörgl to (22 M.) *Kitzbühel* in 1½-2 hrs. One-horse carriage from Kitzbühel to Pass Thurn 5 (two-horse 10), Mittersill 7, Krimml 14 fl.

Wörgl (1665'), see p. 158. The railway follows the left bank of the *Brixenthaler Ache* (on the other bank is the *Kaiserstrasse*, p. 175), to (2½ M.) *Leukenthal*. Below *Schloss Itter*, which stands on a spur of the Hohe Salve to the left, the train enters the *Brixenthaler Klause*, a rocky gorge, in which, beyond a short tunnel, it crosses the Ache.

5½ M. **Hopfgarten** (2030'; *Post* or *Paulwirth*; *Diewald*; *Staffner's Restaurant*, at the station), a large village, the seat of the district-court, ¾ M. from the station (omn. 10 kr.).

The **Hohe Salve** (5985'), the Rigi of the Lower Innthal, is one of the most popular and most accessible points of view in the German Alps. The conspicuous summit of the mountain is covered with turf, and forests and farm-houses extend more than halfway up its slopes. The ascent may be made from Hopfgarten, Brixenthal, Söll, or Itter (new path), but is easiest from Hopfgarten (3 hrs.). Travellers approaching from Kitzbühel ascend from Westendorf or Brixen (the shortest route, 2½ hrs.). The ascent from Söll (3 hrs.), on the N. side, has this advantage that the view towards the S. is concealed until the summit is reached, when it is suddenly disclosed in all its grandeur. — Guide (unnecessary) from Hopfgarten to the top and back, including a stay of 3 hrs., 1½ fl.; to the top and back by Brixen 2 fl. 20, back by Söll 2 fl. 50 kr. (9 kilogr. of luggage free). Horse or mule with attendant to the Tenn Inn 3, to the top 5 fl.; 'chaise-à-porteurs' 12 fl. (Same tariff from Westendorf.)

From *Hopfgarten* station the route proceeds to (¼ hr.) the village, then follows the high-road and ascends to the left by the (5 min.) fingerpost (path rough at places); ¾ hr. a spring; ¼ hr. a mill; ¼ hr. fingerpost pointing to the left; 5 min., the *Tenn Inn* (good quarters), 1½ hr. from the summit. The path now ascends a little to the left, and then to the right (numerous short-cuts); 40 min. the *Vorder-Hütten*; 25 min., the path from Söll joins ours; ¼ hr. the summit.

From *Brixen* (Mairwirth) we ascend to the right at the W. end of the village; at the (1 hr.) chalets turn to the left; by the (¾ hr.) chapel again turn to the left to the Alp; lastly a steep zigzag ascent to the (¾ hr.) summit.

From stat. *Westendorf* a bridle-path, with way-posts, and not to be mistaken, ascends at first through wood and then over pastures. The last part of the route is in bad preservation (porters [and horses to be had at Soitner's Inn, see p. 172).

From *Söll* (p. 175) there is a bridle-path to the top, which cannot be mistaken. Good walkers may prefer the following route: first towards the S. to the *Stampfanger Graben*, passing (20 min.) a chapel on an isolated rock on the right, and ascending straight on; $1/4$ hr., pass through the gate to the brook (path to the left to be avoided), and ascend steeply on the other side through wood; beyond (20 min.) the solitary house of *Romsen*, ascend in zigzags over pastures; $3/2$ hr., a large and conspicuous farm-house with a bell, where the bridle-path is joined. Then ($1^1/2$ hr.) a spring, 5 min. beyond which the route joins that from Hopfgarten, at a point 20 min. from the summit.

At the top are a chapel and an *Inn* with outbuildings (40 beds at 80 kr.; early arrival advisable in fine weather). The *View*, although less varied than that from the Rigi or the Schafberg owing to the absence of lakes, is magnificent, particularly to the S., where the complete Tauern chain is visible from the Hochtenn and Wiesbachhorn to the Zillerthaler Ferner. Due S. rises the Gross-Venediger, to the left of which is the fantastic-looking Grosse Rettenstein in the Spertenthal; farther W. are the distant Ortler, the N. Limestone Alps with the Zugspitze, and the Steinbergerspitze, not unlike a church; to the N., the Miesing, Wendelstein, and, on the S. side of the deep valley of the Inn, the imposing, serrated ridge of the Kaisergebirge; E. the Salzburg Alps, the Loferer Steinberge, the Steinerne Meer, and, in the foreground, the Kitzbühler Horn (comp. Panorama).

To the S. of Hopfgarten opens the Kelchsauthal, traversed by two rarely-used passes: one to the right leading through the *Lange Grund* to (10 hrs.) *Gerlos*, the other to the left through the *Kurze Grund* and over the *Salzachjoch* (6485') to (9 hrs.) *Ronach* in the Upper Pinzgau (both unattractive; guide necessary). — A third route leads through the *Windauthal* (see below) and over the *Filzensattel* (5590') to (9-10 hrs.) *Wald* in the Pinzgau (with guide).

At *Haslau* above Hopfgarten (where we observe the ruin of *Engelsberg* on the right, at the entrance of the *Kelchsauthal*) the train crosses the Brixenthaler Ache, which here forms a waterfall, and turns to the right into the *Windauthal*, on the left side of which it ascends a steep gradient. Beyond a tunnel, 360 yds. long, the line bends back, and crosses the valley and brook to the opposite slope by means of an embankment 60' high and a bridge 75' high. A second tunnel (220 yds. long) then leads to the upper part of the Brixenthal. The train crosses the Lauterbach and reaches (12 M.) **Westendorf** (2490'; *Soitner's Restaurant*), the station for the large village of *Brixen* (Mairwirth), $1^1/2$ M. to the W. (Ascent of the Hohe Salve, see p. 171.) About $1/2$ M. to the S. of the village is the *Maria-Luisen-Brunnen* (Inn), a chalybeate spring.

The train continues to traverse the broad valley, passing (14 M.) *Lauterbach*, and crosses the watershed between the Brixenthaler and Kitzbühler Ache. — 16 M. **Kirchberg** (2690'; *Bächlwirth*; *Katswirth*; *Rail. Restaurant*), prettily situated at the entrance to the *Spertenthal*.

Through the Spertenthal a cart-track leads from (5 M.) *Aschau* (3280'; rustic inn), where the valley forks. The W. branch is the *Untere Grund*; through which an easy pass leads over the *Geige* (6560') to (5$1/2$ hrs.) *Neukirchen* (p. 136) in the Pinzgau; while from the E. branch, or *Obere Grund*, another easy pass leads over the *Stange* (5780') to (7 hrs.) *Mühlbach* (p. 136). — A fine excursion from Aschau is the ascent of the Grosse Rettenstein (7745'; $4^1/2$ hrs., with guide). The route leads through the Untere Grund and over the *Sonnwendalpe* to the (3 hrs.) *Schönthalalpe*, and thence in $1^1/2$ hr. to the top (imposing view).

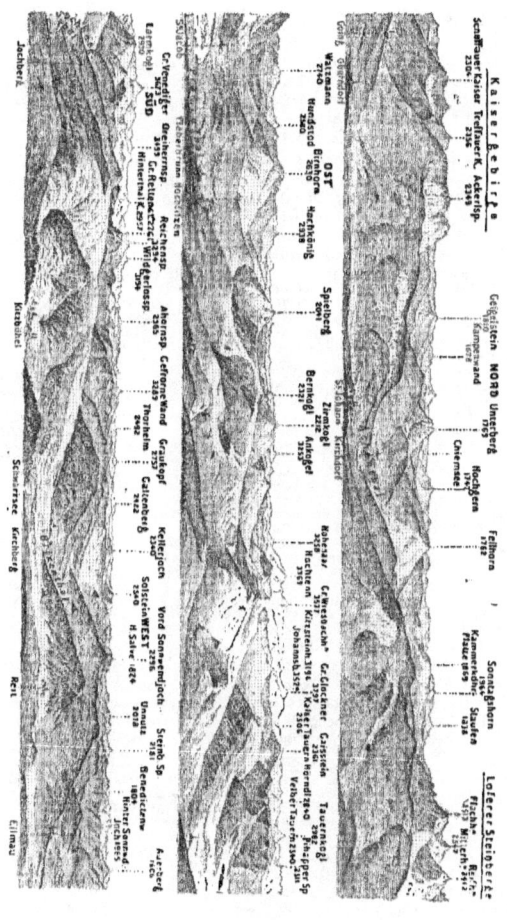

At *Klausenbach* the train crosses the *Aschauer* or *Reitner Ache* (N., the *Kaisergebirge*, p. 175), and soon passes the *Schwarzsee* on the left (station). It next crosses the *Kitzbühler Ache* and the Pass Thurn road, and reaches —

22 M. **Kitzbühel** (2420'; *Tiefenbrunner* or *Post*; *Hinterbräu*; *Stern*; *Rössl*; *Hechenberger*; *Haas*, at the station; *Schwarzer Adler*, moderate; *Oberaigner*; *Beer Garden*, opposite the station; furnished rooms at *Frau Stainer's*, *Pirchl's*, etc.), a small town (3000 inhab.), charmingly situated on the Kitzbühler Ache, and much frequented for summer-quarters. About 3/4 M. to the S. is the *Kitzbühler Bad* (inexpensive), with a chalybeate spring.

EXCURSIONS. Pleasant walk to the N.E. to (1/2 hr.) the *Griessenau*, with a good view of the Kaisergebirge; S.E. to (3/4 hr.) the *Ebnerkapelle*, with a fine view of the Venediger, thence by a new path through the woods to (1/4 hr.) the *Schleier Fall* ('veil-fall'), in the *Kögelsgraben*, and back through the *Zephirau* to (1 hr.) Kitzbühel; S.W. to (1/2 hr.) the *Ehrenbachwasserfall*, in a romantic ravine; W. to (1/2 hr.) the château of *Lebenberg* and the (3/4 hr.) *Schwarzsee* (Inn).

The *Kitzbühler* **Horn** (6542'; 3 1/2 hrs., guide, 3 1/2 fl., unnecessary; horse to the inn 4, to the top 5, there and back 8 fl.) is an admirable point of view. The route leads to the S. from the station, past the Hôtel Haas, and along the Ache; the (4 min.) second turning to the left is then taken, the railway crossed, and a good bridle-path, provided at doubtful points with way-posts, is ascended through wood and over pastures (several good springs) to the new (2 1/2-3 hrs.) *Inn* (bed 80 kr.), above the *Trattalpe*. The summit, on which stands a chapel, is reached in 3/4 hr. more. The view, particularly of the Tauern, surpasses that from the Hohe Salve, and is remarkable for the picturesque grouping of the valleys; to the E. are the imposing Loferer Steinberge, to the N.E. the Chiemsee. Compare the Panorama. About 10 min. from the inn is a small stalactite cavern.

— Descent on the N. side by the *Hofsralpe* to *St. Johann* (p. 175); on the E. side by the *Oberrheinthal-Alpe* to *Fieberbrunn* (p. 119; guide desirable).

— FROM THE KITZBÜHLER HORN TO THE GAISSTEIN (see below), a highly interesting route, marked by the local Alpine Club, in 8-9 hrs. The route runs along or near the ridge which stretches to the S., crossing the *Lämmerbühl*, and passing the *Dischof*, *Staffkogel*, *Tristkogl*, and *Gamshag*. Refreshments are to be had at various chalets on the way.

RAILWAY from Kitzbühel to **Zell am See** and *Salzburg*, see R. 22.

The Mittersill road crosses the Ache, and leads by the *Kitzbühler Bad* (see above) and (left) *Aurach* to *Wiessneck* (to the S. the Gross-Venediger). Then a steeper ascent past a deserted copper-stamping mill to (5 1/2 M.) **Jochberg** (3000'; *Wagstätten*; *Adler*, moderate).

The ascent of the *Gaisstein* (7745'; 4 1/2 hrs.; with the shoemaker as guide) from Jochberg is recommended (no difficulty). The route ascends through the steep *Sintersbachgraben* to the *Lower* and (3 1/2 hrs.) Upper *Sintersbach-Alpe*, and in 1 hr. more to the summit, which affords a magnificent view of the Tauern. Descent to the *Bürglhütte* (*Stuhlfelden* or *Mittersill*), see p. 135; to Saalbach, see p. 118; to the Kitzbühler Horn, see above. The *Pinzgauer Spazierweg* to the (8 hrs.) *Schmittenhöhe*, see p. 118 (provisions necessary; guide advisable).

The road ascends gradually, past the *Zur Wacht Inn*, to (4 M.) *Jochberg-Wald* (Waldwirth), and then in long windings (which a path to the left cuts off), to the (4 M.) **Pass Thurn** (4180'; *Inn*), the boundary between Tyrol and Salzburg. A hill 1/4 hr. to the W. affords a fine survey of the Tauern; still finer view from the *Resterhöhe*

(6100'), farther up, to which a path leads from the inn in 1½ hr. — The road now descends, passing a second (10 min.) *Inn*, and affording a magnificent view of the Pinzgau with its reedy swamps, and of the Tauern, and then winds down to (4½ M.) *Mittersill* (p. 135).

Walkers on their way to *Krimml* save 1 hr. by taking the footpath to the right at the bend of the road, about 200 paces below the second inn (see above), which descends through pastures and wood direct to (1 hr.) *Mühlbach* (see p. 136).

34. From Wörgl to Reichenhall viâ Lofer.

Comp. Maps, pp. 172, 68.

56 M. HIGH-ROAD. From St. Johann to (9 M.) Waidring,'diligence daily in 1¾ hr. (fare 1 fl.). From Lofer to Reichenhall a Stellwagen daily in 4 hrs. (fare 1 fl. 55 kr.); one-horse carr. 6½, two-horse 12½ fl.

Wörgl (1665'), see p. 158. The road (called the '*Kaiserstrasse*', from the *Kaisergebirge*, which rises to the N.) crosses the railway (p. 171) and the *Brixenthaler Ache* at the station of (2½ M.) *Leukenthal*, and ascends (in view of *Schloss Itter*) to the low saddle separating the *Sölland*, or valley of Söll, from the Achenthal.

7 M. Söll (2320'; *Post;* ascent of the Hohe Salve, see p. 172). The wooden houses in this district are interesting. The road next passes (3 M.) *Scheffau*, on the hill to the left, and the *Plaiken Inn*.

The Kaisergebirge consists of two ranges separated by the *Kaiserthal* (p. 157): the N. chain is the *Hintere Kaiser*, while the S. chain, at the base of which our road runs, is called the *Vordere* or *Wilde Kaiser*. The latter and higher chain culminates in the *Elmauer Haltspitze* (7792'), *Treffauer Kaiser* (7730'), *Scheffauer Kaiser* (7560'), and *Ackerlspitze* (7706'). These peaks are difficult of ascent owing to the steepness of the upper parts, and should not be attempted except by adepts (guide indispensable; comp. p. 137). The highest peak, the *Elmauer Haltspitze*, takes 7-8 hrs. from Elmau (guide 4-5 fl.; comp. p. 158). The ascent of the *Scheffauer Kaiser* is easier (from Bärnstatt by the *Kaiserhochalpe* in 4 hrs.; guide 2½ fl.). The *Sonneneck* (7380'; guide 3 fl.) is ascended in 4½ hrs. from Bärnstatt viâ the *Kaiserhochalpe;* see p. 158.

Pleasant excursion from the Plaiken Inn viâ Scheffau to the (1 hr.) **Hintersteiner See** (3040'), a lake 1¼ M. long and ½ M. broad, picturesquely situated at the base of the *Zettenkaiser*. About ¾ hr. from the E. end, near the St. Leonhardskapelle, is the rustic inn of *Bärnstatt*. We may now descend the *Steinerne Stiege* to (2½ hrs.) *Kufstein*, see p. 157.

3 M. **Elmau** (2655'; *Post; Hochfilzer*) is prettily situated at the highest point of the road, which now descends by *Going* and *Rettenbach*, and follows the *Reitner Ache* to the *Leukenthal*.

6½ M. **St. Johann in Tirol** (2130'; *Post; *Bär; *Zum Hohen Kaiser*, at the station), a station on the Salzburg-Tyrol Railway (p. 120), lies at the N. base of the *Kitzbühler Horn* (p. 174).

The following route is more attractive than the monotonous high-road to Erpfendorf and Waidring: by railway to *Fieberbrunn* (p. 119); then walk by *St. Jacob im Haus* to *Pillersee* and (3½ hrs.) *Waidring* (p. 176). — From St. Johann to *Kössen* by *Gasteig* and *Schwendt*, see p. 58; over the *Stripsenjoch* to *Kufstein*, see p. 157.

The road leads from St. Johann to the N. through the wide valley of the *Grosse Ache (Leukenthal)*, quits it at (4½ M.) *Erpfendorf* (1900'; route to *Kössen*, see p. 58), and turns to the E. into the *Ausserwaldthal*. On the left rises the *Fellhorn* (5780'), and farther off, above Waidring, the *Kammerköhr-Platte* (6132').

4½ M. **Waidring** (2560'; *Post*), a thriving village, finely situated on the watershed between the Achenthal and the Saalachthal, is a summer-resort. To the S. rise the *Loferer Steinberge*.

By the *Grünwaldhütte* to the **Kammerköhr-Alp** and through the *Schwarzbergklamm* to (6 hrs.) *Unken*, see p. 177 (guide necessary). The *Kammerköhr-Platte* (6132') may be ascended from the (2 hrs.) Alp without difficulty in 1 hr.; view very fine. — Ascent of the **Fellhorn** (5780') by *Reiterndorf* and the *Eckalpe*, 4 hrs., toilsome; better from Reit im Winkel (p. 56).

Pleasant walk (road) from Waidring to the S. through the *Oefen*, a gorge of the *Strubache*, and past the chapel of *St. Adolari* to the (1¼ hr.) sequestered blue **Pillersee** (2740'), at the S. end of which lies the (1½ M.) village of *St. Ulrich* (Seewirth). To the E. rise the *Loferer Steinberge* (p. 175). — From St. Ulrich by *St. Jacob im Haus* to (2 hrs.) *Fieberbrunn*, see above.

The road from Waidring almost all the way to Reichenhall leads through grand mountain-scenery. The profound and picturesque valley of the *Strubache*, between the Hochplatte and the Steinberg, gradually contracts. In the narrowest part is the *Pass Strub* (2255'), the frontier between the Tyrol and Salzburg, which was once fortified, and was heroically defended by the Tyrolese peasants in 1805 and 1809 (obelisk erected in 1887). The *Saalachthal* is entered at —

6 M. **Lofer** (2095'; *Post*; *Bräu*; *Zum Schweizer*), where the Pinzgau road joins ours. A good view of the beautiful environs of Lofer is afforded by the (10 min.) *Calvarienberg*. On the E. are the *Reiteralpe* and *Mühlsturzhörner*; S.W. the huge peaks of the *Loferer Steinberge* (*Breithorn, Ochsenhorn*, etc.).

EXCURSIONS (guides, *M. Scholz, Andr.* and *Joh. Walder*). Beautiful walk to the (25 min.) *Gesundheitsquelle* or *Exenbachquelle* (*Loferer Bründl*), a spring to the S. of the Waidring road, at the entrance to the *Loferer Hochthal*, a grand rocky valley (4½ M. long) enclosed by the precipitous sides of the Steinberge. From this point the 'Salzburgerweg' leads across the *Wechsel Sattel* (4165') to (2½ hr.) *Maria-Kirchenthal* (see below), whence we may return by a marked path (blue and white), viâ the *Rauchenberg* and *Carolinenhöhe*, to Lofer. — Other pleasant walks may be taken to the S. along the Saalfelden road to the (½ hr.) *Hochmoos*, with its mud-baths, near St. Martin; viâ St. Martin to the (1 hr.) pilgrimage-church of *Maria-Kirchenthal* (2880'); to (1½ hr.) *Wildenthal*, on the right bank of the Saalach, on the road to the Kleine Hirschbichl (p. 78); to the N. down the Saalachthal viâ the *Teufelssteg* to the (½ hr.) *Eberl* (Inn), and from Maurach (p. 177) to the right, crossing the Saalach, to the (1¼ hr.) *Mairbergklamm*, etc. — The Loferer **Alpe** (4795'; rustic inn; 3 hrs.; guide 2½ fl.) is another fine point (view from the *Ganiskopf*, 5110'); thence to the Schwarzbergklamm, p. 177. — Ascent of the **Hinterhorn** or **Mitterhorn** (8212'), the second-highest peak of the *Loferer Steinberge*, laborious (6-7 hrs.; guide 4½ fl.). We ascend through the Loferer Thal to the (2½ hrs.) *Steinbergalm-Hütte* (4190'; club-hut); then through the *Grosse Wehrgrube* or *Wirlgrube*, and up the arête to the (3½-4 hrs.) summit (imposing prospect; path recently improved and marked). We may descend by the *Anderl-Alm* and round the *Blaue Wand* (guide 5 fl.). — The **Ochsenhorn** (8215'; 4 hrs.; guide 5½ fl.), another fine point, is ascended from the Steinbergalm Hut through the *Kleine Wehrgrube*.

To OBER-WEISSBACH (Saalfelden or Berchtesgaden). The road follows the Saalach as far as (1½ M.) *St. Martin* ("Weissbacher; carriages to be had), where the road viâ *Wildenthal* to the Kleine Hirschbichl, mentioned at p. 78, diverges to the left, and then crosses the *Pass Luftenstein* 2070'; Inn), which was formerly fortified.

to *Reichenhall.*   UNKEN.   *IV. Route 34.* 177

About half-way between Lofer and Ober-Weissbach, and 3 M. to the S. of St. Martin, in the *Schüttachgraben* or *Schiedergraben*, is the *Vorderkaser-Klamm* (Rfmts. at the chalet), a magnificent ravine, rendered accessible in 1881. This curious defile, 2¼′ to 20′ in width, and flanked with rocks about 230′ high, contains interesting water-worn cavities and several fine waterfalls. From the upper end of the Klamm we may return by the (20 min.) *Almberg-Alpe* to the (1 hr.) high-road, but the return through the gorge is more interesting. The visit takes about 1 hr. (the whole excursion from St. Martin and back 3½-4 hrs.). If, as is often the case, the water is low, the traveller should have the sluice opened (fee 40 kr.). From Ober-Weissbach (p. 78) the Klamm is reached on foot in 1¾ hr., or by carriage in 1½ hr. (carr. with one horse 3, two horses 6 fl.). We may reach the railway station at *Hochfilzen* (p. 119), from the Vorderkaser-Alpe, in 2½-3 hrs., by a route passing *Dalsen*, *Schildach*, and *Willock*.

The road now passes (right) the *Lamprechts-Ofenloch* (p. 78), crosses the *Saalach*, and reaches (3 M.) *Ober-Weissbach* (°Inn). Thence to (18 M.) *Berchtesgaden* over the *Hirschbühl*, see p. 78; to (12 M.) *Saalfelden*, see p. 79. (About ¼ hr. to the N. of Ober-Weissbach is the interesting *Seisenberg-Klamm*, p. 78.) — One-horse carriage from Lofer to Frohnwies 2, two-horse 4 fl.; to Saalfelden 6½ or 12½ fl. (diligence daily at 8 a.m. in 3½ hrs., fare 1½ fl.); to Waidring 2 fl. 30 kr. or 4 fl. 30 kr; to St. Johann in Tirol 6½ or 12½ fl; to Berchtesgaden 18 or 32 fl.

The Reichenhall road leads to the N. on the left bank of the Saale, passing the *Antonikapelle* and *Maurach*, where the route to the Mairbergklamm diverges to the right (see above). We then pass through the *Kniepass* and reach —

6 M. **Unken** (1880′; *Post; Lamm*), a summer-resort, about ½ M. to the S. of which lie the small baths of *Oberrain* (*Hotel). To the right is the *Reiteralp-Gebirge.*

EXCURSIONS (guides, *Joh. Auer* and *Ferd. Buchmayer*). Very attractive excursion to the (2½ hrs.) °**Schwarzbergklamm** or **Unkner Klamm** (guide, needless, 1½, horse 4½ fl.). A bridle-path ascends the *Unkenthal* to the W. from Unken or Oberrain, and after ¾ hr., at the *Friedl* (Rfmts.), mounts rapidly to the left. We pass a small waterfall in a gorge to the left, and reach the (½ hr.) *Eibelklamm*. We next pass a workmen's hut ('Engstübl', generally closed), and reach the (1 hr.) entrance to the Klamm, or gorge of the *Schwarzbach*, which was rendered accessible in 1880 by means of paths and bridges. This is one of the grandest ravines of the kind among the German Alps, and is especially remarkable for the screw-shaped contortions of the huge rocky sides, which nearly meet at places. At the entrance is the inscription: 'Gutta cavat lapidem non vi sed saepe cadendo', placed there by order of Lewis I. of Bavaria. The gorge, ½ M. long, is quitted at the upper end by flights of wooden steps leading to the *Schwarzberg*, a hunter's hut, where there is an excellent spring. — Thence over the *Kammerköhr-Alp* (5055′) to *Waidring* (p. 176) in 4 hrs. (guide necessary, 3½ fl.). By the **Loferer Alpe** (see p. 176) to *Lofer* 4-5 hrs. (guide necessary, 3 fl.). By the *Winkelmoos-Alpe* to *Reit im Winkel* 4½ hrs. (guide to the Alp desirable; see p. 57). — The *Staub Fall* (3 hrs.) is a fine cascade, especially after rain. Same road as to the Schwarzberg-Klamm for about 2 M.; we then diverge to the right by the road into the *Heuthal*, with the *Sonntagshorn* rising on the N.; where the road divides, we ascend the valley to the left to the fall (620′ in height). The path leads behind the fall. (Through the *Fischbachthal* to *Seehaus* and *Ruhpolding*, see p. 57.) These two excursions may be combined, but not without a guide (3 fl.). — The ascent of the °**Sonntagshorn** (6444′) by the *Heuthal* and the *Unkner Hochalpe* is interesting (bridle-path, 4½ hrs.; guide 3, horse to the Hochalpe 6 fl.); superb view. (A shorter route, marked with red, and unmistakable, leads from Mellock through the *Steinbachthal* and the *Rosskar*, 4 hrs.)

The Austrian and Bavarian frontier below Unken is guarded by

BAEDEKER's Eastern Alps. 6th Edit.   12

the *Stein Pass*, a fortified gateway. The road then ascends rapidly to (2¼ M.) **Melleck** (2015'; *Inn*, with fine view), the seat of the custom-houses of both countries. Here, on 17th Oct., 1809, the Tyrolese under Speckbacher sustained a disastrous defeat from the Bavarians, and Speckbacher's son was taken prisoner. The road now passes *Ristfeicht*, and descends the *Bodenbühl*, where several engagements took place during the wars of 1800, 1805, and 1809, to (3 M.) *Schnaitzreut* (1670'; *Inn), a group of houses in the broad floor of the valley. A few hundred yards farther on, a footpath diverges to the right to *Jettenberg*, on the Ramsau and Reichenhall road (p. 77). We now rapidly ascend the *Weissbach-Thal*, between the *Müllnerhorn* on the right and the *Ristfeichthorn* on the left; before we reach the top of the pass, the road to Inzell and Traunstein (p. 55) diverges to the left. At the summit we observe the (2¼ M.) brine-conduit from Reichenhall to Traunstein and two pump-houses *(Untere* and *Obere Nesselgruben)*. The road now descends gradually through the picturesque *Nesselgruben* (the old road is on the other side of the valley) to the (1½ M.) green *Thumsee* (1730'), a small lake well stocked with fish, and then through a wooded ravine, past the ruin of *Karlstein*, the *Chapel of St. Pancras* (p. 82), and *Bad Kirchberg*.

3½ M. *Reichenhall* (1570'), see p. 79.

35. The Zillerthal.

Comp. Map, p. 46.

From *Jenbach* (p. 159) or *Brixlegg* (p. 159) to Zell, 16½ M. — STELLWAGEN from the railway-station and the 'Toleranz' at Jenbach to Mairhofen daily in summer, starting at 9 a.m. and reaching Zell at 1 and Mairhofen at 3 p.m. (leaving Mairhofen again at 11 a.m. and Zell at 1 p.m., arriving at 5 p.m.). Another diligence runs from Jenbach to Zell, starting at 2.45 p.m. and arriving at 6.40 p.m. (return from Zell at 3.45 a.m., arriving at 8 a.m.). Carriage from Jenbach to Fügen with one horse 3, to Zell 6½, to Mairhofen 9 fl.; carr. and pair to Zell 10, to Mairhofen 14, and fee of 1 fl. (one-horse carr. from Brixlegg to Zell 6-7 fl.). The incivility and obstinacy of the postmasters and drivers in the Zillerthal is complained of.

The **Zillerthal** is at first broad, fertile, and somewhat monotonous, enclosed by pine-clad heights and smiling pastures. Towards Zell it contracts, and the background is formed by snow-mountains and glaciers. The clear green *Ziller*, seldom visible from the road, flows on the E. side of the valley. Some of the inner ramifications of the valley (*Gründe*; p. 181), which have been rendered more accessible by numerous paths and huts constructed by the German and Austrian Alpine clubs, are well deserving of a visit.

Jenbach, see p. 159. The road to the Zillerthal crosses the Inn by the *Rothholz* bridge, leads to the left through the Schloss of that name, and joins the Innsbruck high-road. 3 M. *Strass* (1700'; Neuwirth), at the entrance to the Zillerthal. (To the left, at the foot of the *Reitherkogel*, is the ruin of *Kropfsberg*, p. 159.) To the right, on the *Schlittersberg*, is the *Brettfall* chapel, a good point of view (½ hr.). Near (2 M.) *Schlitters* (Jäger; Stern) the *Brandberger Kolm*, the *Gerloswand*, and the *Ahornspitze* become visible; behind us rises the *Vordere Sonnwendjoch* (7300'). Then *Gagering*, and (2 M.) **Fügen** (**Post; *Stern; Aigner; *Sonne*, moderate), capital of the lower Zillerthal.

The **Kellerjoch* (7675'; 5 hrs., not difficult; guide 8½, horse 6 fl.), ascended from Fügen, commands a magnificent and extensive view, embracing the Inn Valley, the N. Limestone Alps, the Zillerthal, Stubai, and Oetzthal Glaciers, the Tauern, etc. (descent to Schwaz, p. 160; 3 hrs.). — The **Wiedersberger Horn** (6965'), on the opposite (E.) side of the Zillerthal, is less interesting (4½ hrs.; guide 2½ fl.).

Beyond *Kapfing* the road crosses the *Finsingbach*, and next reaches (2¼ M.) *Uderns* (Pachmair), *Ried*, and (2¼ M.) *Kaltenbach* (*Post), where the broad *Ziller* is approached. On the opposite bank lies the village of *Stumm*.

Ascent of the **Kreuzjoch** (8205'; 5 hrs.; guide 2½ fl.) from Kaltenbach, easy and repaying. — Viâ the **Wilde Krimml** to *Gerlos*, 8 hrs. (guide 4 fl.), not difficult. We ascend past the *Hendacher-Alpen* and *Kapauns-Alpe* (6230') to the (4 hrs.) saddle (7940') between the *Rifflerkopf* (8190') and the *Kreuzjoch* (8205'). We then descend into the *Wilde Krimml*, pass the *Langensee* (7300'), and proceed through the *Krummbachthal* to (3 hrs.) *Gerlos* (see below).

Beyond (2¼ M.) *Aschau*, from a point where the road ascends slightly, a pleasing retrospect is obtained. 2¾ M. *Zell*, which is not visible until it is nearly reached.

Zell am Ziller (1880'; **Post, *Bräu, Daviter*, on the left bank; **Welschwirth, *Greiderer, *Neuwirth*, on the right bank; *Holzeisen's Café*, near the Post), the chief place (1200 inhab.) in the valley, which is here broad and fertile, lies at the confluence of the *Gerlosbach* with the *Ziller*. To the E. rise the *Hainzenberg* (with the *Maria Rast Capelle* on a projecting spur) and the lofty *Gerloswand* (7095'), resembling a wall; S. the *Ahornspitze* (9730'), the blunted pyramid of the *Tristner* (9080'), and the snow-fields of the *Ingent* (9565'). At the foot of the Hainzenberg, 1½ M. to the E. of Zell, the *Gerlosbach* forms a fine cascade. The adjacent gold-mine is no longer worked.

Excursions (guides, *Franz* and *Heinr. Schönherr* and *Georg Waibl* of Zell). Pleasant walk to (½ hr. from the 'Post') **Klöpfistaudach**, a farm-house, with a terrace commanding an excellent view, on a spur of the Zellberg, to the W. of Zell. — The **Marchkopf** (8190'; 5½ hrs., with guide), ascended by the Zellerberg, and the **Gerloswand** (7094'; 4½ hrs., with guide), reached by the village of *Hainzenberg* (see below) and the *Gerlosstein-Alp*, are both fine points of view, which present no difficulty.

[To the E. of Zell opens the **Gerlos**, through which a well-trodden bridle-path leads to the upper Pinzgau. To Gerlos 4 hrs., from Gerlos over the Platte to Krimml 4, over the Plattenkogl 5 hrs. (horse from Zell to Gerlos 4, to the Platte 7, to Krimml 9 fl.; guide from Zell to Krimml over the Platte 4 fl. 20 kr., from Gerlos 3 fl.). The route leads from Zell to the S.E. to the (¼ hr.) foot of the *Hainzenberg*, and rapidly ascends this hill (roughly paved cart-track), past the (20 min.) *Maria Rast Chapel* (2290'; Inn), to the village of (½ hr.) *Hainzenberg*. The view, at first limited, afterwards embraces the whole of the lower Zillerthal, with the mountains on the N. bank of the Inn in the background. At the (1/2 hr.) *Oetschen Inn* (3350') a small wooden platform affords a capital view of Zell. The hilly path, leading chiefly through wood, now skirts the *Gerlosbach*, which flows through a gorge on the left, passes (1/4 hr.) *Marteck* (two houses), and crosses the (10 min.) *Schönbach* and the (1/2 hr.) *Zaberbach*. We next cross the (20 min.) *Weissbach*, the (10 min.) *Schwarzach*, and the (20 min.) *Wimmerbach*, and immediately afterwards the Gerlosbach, and reach (5 min.) the hamlet of *Gmünd*, where the valley expands. The path crosses (20 min.) to the left bank of the Gerlosbach, recrosses (5 min.) to the right, and then leads across the stony *Riederbach* to the (20 min.) long village of **Gerlos** (4110'; **Alpenrose*, at the lower end, near the church, R. 60 kr.; *Stöckl*; **Kammerlander*, 8 min. farther on).

EXCURSIONS (guide, *Jakob Hochstaffl*). Up the Schönachthal to the (11/4 hr.) *Obere Iss-Alpe* (ca. 4900'); fine view of the head of the valley (Schönach Glacier, Zillerkopf, etc.). — From the *Durlassboden* (see below), to the right, up the Wilde Gerlos, to the (11/2 hr.) *Doissen-Alp;* at the head of the valley is the extensive *Gerlos Glacier*, over which tower the Reichenspitze and Wildgerlosspitze. — The Ebenfeldalpe (ca. 5575'), to the N.W., easily reached in 11/2 hr., affords a fine view of the Schönachthal, with the Wildgerlosspitze and the Zillerkopf. — Ascent of the **Thorhelm** (8176'; 4 hrs., with guide), interesting and not difficult: the route ascends the *Krumbach-Thal* to the N. to the end of the valley (*Wilde Krimml*), then turns to the right to the saddle between the Thorhelm and the Katzenkopf, and mounts the W. side to the summit (excellent survey of the Zillerthal group). The *Kreuzjoch* (8205'), to the S. of the Wilde Krimml, commands a similar view. — The ***Brandberger Kolm** (8845'; 51/2 hrs.; guide 41/2 fl.), the top of which affords a fine view of the Zillerthal Glacier, offers no difficulty to experts. We proceed through the *Schwarzachthal*, passing the Alp of that name, to (41/2 hrs.) the *Brandberger Joch* (7550'), between the Thorhelm and the Brandberger Kolm, and thence to the S. to the (1 hr.) top. Descent from the Brandberger Joch to *Brandberg* (p. 182), 2-21/2 hrs. — Another splendid point of view is the **Wildgerlosspitze** (10,760'), ascended through the *Schönachthal*, viâ the *Schönach* and *Ziller Glaciers*, in 7 hrs. (fatiguing; night spent at the *Bausteinhütte;* guide 7 fl.). — The ascent of the **Reichenspitze** (10,803'; 8-9 hrs., guide 71/2 fl.) is difficult and suitable for adepts only. We proceed through the Schönachthal to the (3 hrs.) *Baustein-Alpe*, where the night is spent; thence over the *Schönach*, *Ziller*, and *Kuchelmoos Glaciers* to (4-5 hrs.) the summit. Descent to the *Kuchelmoos-Alp* (p. 182) in the Zillergrund very steep (guide 9 fl.). — From Gerlos to *Kaltenbach* through the *Krummbachthal* and the *Wilde Krimml* (8 hrs), with guide), see p. 179.

The path follows the right bank of the Gerlos, passing the entrance to the *Schönachthal* (at the head of which is the glacier of that name, with the Wildgerlosspitze and the Zillerkopf), crosses the (1/4 hr.) *Krumbach*, and ascends through wood to the (3/4 hr.) highest region of the valley, called the *Durlassboden* (4000'), where we pass a timber-dam. The valley bends to the S. (*Wilde Gerlos*), and the background is formed by the *Reichenspitze* and its glaciers. The path (marked) continues to follow the N. side of the valley and crosses the (25 min.) *Hollenzenbach*, the frontier of Salzburg and Tyrol. About 5 min. farther on is a fingerpost pointing to left to Gerlos, and to the right to Krimml. The direct route to the Pinzgau turns to the left and ascends along the

Hollenzenbach, crossing the stream twice. It then turns sharply to the N. and reaches (3/4 hr.) the flat saddle of the **Hohe Gerlos**, or *Pinzgauer Höhe* (4780'), beyond which it descends to (1/2 hr.) *Ronach* (4755'; Inn, plain), *Waldberg* (3/4 hr.; 3840'), and (3/4 hr.) *Wald* (p. 137).

A far more attractive route crosses the PINZGAUER PLATTE to KRIMML. The path turns to the right (S.E.) by the finger-post (p. 180), and ascends the N.W. slope of the Plattenkogl; it then ascends to the left to the (3/4 hr.) *Millerplatten-Alpe* (ca. 5575'; Rfmts.). Proceeding towards the E., past the (1/2 hr.) *Leitner-Alpe*, we reach (10 min.) a hut with a finger-post ('Weg nach Gerlos'), beyond which the Pinzgau and the Krimmler-Thal and its cascades come in sight. The bridle-path now descends through wood to (1 hr.) *Krimml* (p. 137). — A still finer route, but 1 hr. longer, crosses the *Plattenkogl*, or *Hintere Platte* (guide advisable on account of the marshy places; from Gerlos to Krimml 3 fl. 60 kr.). The path diverges to the right from the Platte route at the (3/4 hr.) *Millerplatten-Alpe* (see above), and ascends to the S.E. to (40 min.) three chalets, where a post points the way (E.) to the (20 min.) summit of the ***Plattenkogl** (6656'). The admirable view embraces the Pinzgau, the Dreiherrnspitze to the S.E., the Reichenspitze and the Wilde Gerlos to the S.W., and, far below, Krimml with the waterfalls. No defined path descends hence to Krimml. The route leads towards the N.E., at first skirting a precipice on the right, and passing the *Handthütten*. At the (40 min.) last hut, by the finger-post, we rejoin the Platte route (see above).]

The road from Zell to (4 1/2 M.) Mairhofen (diligence daily at 2 p.m., returning from Mairhofen at 11 a.m., 40 kr.; one-horse carr. 2 1/2 fl.) follows the right bank of the Ziller, viâ *Bühel*, *Eckartau*, and *Hollenzen*; but the path on the left bank (1 3/4 hr.), by *Laimach* and *Hippach*, passing the chapel of *Burgstall*, an excellent point of view, is more attractive.

Mairhofen (2095'; **Stern*, with the post-office, R. 50 kr.; **Neuhaus; *Alte Post*), the highest village in the lower Zillerthal, is beautifully situated on a green plateau amidst lofty mountains (see above). To the W. we have a pleasant glimpse of the Tuxer Thal with the village of *Finkenberg*, commanded by the *Grünberg*. The valley divides here into four branches ('Gründe'): E. the Zillergrund, S.E. the Stillupthal, S.W. the Zemmthal, W. the Tuxerthal.

GUIDES: *Simon* and *Josef Fankhauser* at Lindthal (both good). *Max Egger*, *Jos. Hausberger*, *Michael Mayrl*, and *G. Moser* of Mairhofen, *Jos. Kröll* of Dornauberg, and *Franz Wechselberger* of Rosshag (guides should be brought from Zell or Mairhofen, as they are not always procurable at Rosshag). Tariff: to the Karlssteg in the Dornaubergklamm and back (3 1/2 hrs.) 1 fl.; to the Karlssteg and back by the Teufelssteg (4 hrs.) 1 fl. 20 kr.; to Ginzling (3 hrs.) 1 1/2, Rosshag (4 hrs.) 2, Breitlahner (5 hrs.) 2 1/2, the Berliner Hütte on the Schwarzenstein-Alp (8 hrs.) 5, to the Dominicushütte (7 hrs.) 4, Olperer Hütte (10 hrs.) 6, Hinter-Tux (5 hrs.) 2 1/2, Zell on the Ziller (2 hrs.) 1 fl. — Mule to Ginzling 5, to Breitlahner 7, to the Berliner Hütte 10 fl.

The *Penkenberg* (*Gschösswand*; 6860'), commanding an excellent survey of the 'Gründe' of the Zillerthal, is easily ascended in 4-5 hrs. from Mairhofen viâ *Finkenberg* (see below) and the chalets of *Im Altenstall* (guide 2½ fl.). — The °*Ahornspitze* (9730'; 6-7 hrs.; guide 5 fl.; laborious), between the Zillergrund and the Stilluppthal, commands a magnificent view. We proceed viâ the *Fellenberg-Alpe* to the (4 hrs.) *Edel-Hütte* in the *Fellenbergkar* (7710') and thence to 2 hrs. the top. [From the Stilluppthal (see below) we ascend from the Vincenzhütte by the *Popberg-Alpe* and the *Popbergschneide* in 4½ hrs.].

The **Zillergrund**, which opens to the E. and is drained by the *Zillerbach*, is traversed by several passes leading to the Ahrnthal. The most frequented of these crosses the *Hundskehljoch* (12-13 hrs. from Mairhofen to St. Peter; guide from Brandberg, not indispensable, 7 fl.). From Mairhofen, a steep ascent on the right bank of the Ziller to (1½ hr.) *Brandberg* (3515'; Tanner); thence to (1½ hr.) *Häusling* and (1¼ hr.) *In der Au* (4030'), opposite a shooting-box of that name (Inn; guides to be had). Through the *Sondergrund*, which opens here to the S., a fatiguing route crosses the **Hörndljoch** (8360'; fine view) to (7-8 hrs.) *St. Jakob* in the Ahrnthal (p. 191; guide from Mairhofen 7 fl.). By the *Bärenbad-Alpe* (4700'; opposite, on the left bank, the *Sutzenalpe*), 1 hr. farther up the Zillergrund, our path (recently improved and indicated by posts) ascends to the right through the desolate *Hundskehlgrund*, and past the *Neuhütten-Alp*, the *Mitterhütten*, the *Oberhütte*, and three small lakes, to the (4 hrs.) **Hundskehljoch** (or *Karscharte*, 8960'), with view of the Rieserferner, Dreiherrnspitze, etc., and descends thence to (2½-3 hrs.) *St. Peter* in the Ahrnthal (p. 191). — Above the Bärenbad, in the upper part of the Zillergrund ('Zillergründl'), are the (1 hr.) *Zillerhütten-Alpe* (5650'), the (½ hr.) *Kuchelmoos-Alpe* (5920'), and a sterile pasture called the *Höhenau-Alpe*, from which a toilsome pass crosses the (3½ hrs.) **Heiligengeist-Jöchl** (8700'; *View*), to (2½ hrs.) *Kasern* (p. 191).

The **Stilluppthal**, stretching to the S.E., between the *Ahornspitze* on the left and the *Tristner* on the right, up to the main range at the head of the Zillerthal, will repay a visit (provisions should be taken). The Zillerbach is crossed at *Strass*. At the (20 min.) hamlet of *Haus* we cross by the (¾ hr.) *Klammsteg* (3000') to the left bank of the *Stilluppbach*, ascend a stony slope of the *Fitzenberg*, and traverse a wild ravine to the upper part of the valley, passing near (½ hr.) the chalets of the *Lackneraste* (3410'; on the right bank). We continue to follow the left bank, enjoying a fine view of the glaciers at the head of the valley, and at the fourth bridge cross to the (1½ hr.) *Vincenz-Jagdhaus* (3590'). Those who merely wish a view of the valley go on for ¼ hr. more to the *Niestalpe* and turn there. The ascent of the Grundschartner (10,050'; laborious) may be made hence viâ the *Madereckl-Alpe* and the *Madereckikar* in 6 hrs. (guide). — Continuing to follow the right bank of the Stilluppbach we pass the *Steimeralpe* and reach the (2 hrs.) *Texachhütte* (4870') nd the (1 hr.) upper *Stopfenalp* (5455'; poor accommodation), in a desolate basin at the end of the valley. From this point over the *Stillupp Glacier* and the **Keilbach-Joch** (9310') to *Steinhaus* or *St. Johann* in the Ahrnthal (p. 190), a fatiguing but interesting route of 8-9 hrs. (guide from Mairhofen 7 fl.). — The **Frankbachjoch** (9370'), between the Grosse Löffler and the Keilbachspitze, is difficult and fit for experts only.

Through the **Tuxerthal**, or *Duxerthal*, the most populous of the above valleys, a well-trodden route leads from Mairhofen to (1½ hrs.) *St. Jodok* on the Brenner Railway (p. 220). The road crosses the *Zemmbach* by the (35 min.) *Untere Steg* (see p. 184), and ascends to (1 hr.) *Finkenberg* (2900'; *Neuwirth*; Eberle, rustic). [To the Karlssteg by the 'Schumannweg', see p. 184. In place of the old Teufelssteg, the deep ravine of the Tuxerbach is now crossed by the substantial wooden 'Persallbrücke'.] At *Freithof*, 1 hr. above Finkenberg, the path crosses to the right bank of the Tuxer Bach (fine retrospect of the Ahornspitze, etc.), and at (1 hr.) *Vorder-Lanersbach* (*Kapellenwirth) it recrosses to ($1/2$ hr.) *Lanersbach*, or *Vorder-Tux* (4130'; *Stock; Brückenwirth, plain). Farther up we obtain a view of the Kasererspitze, Olperer, Gefrorne Wand, etc. We next reach ($1^3/4$ hr.) **Hinter-Tux** (4840'), the highest village in the valley, consisting of a few wooden huts, a Bath-house (rustic; water 71° Fahr.), and an *Inn. Grand environs, enhanced by the *Gefrorne Wand*, a considerable glacier, below which there is a magnificent waterfall (well seen from the *Kaseralpe*, $1^1/2$ hr. from Hinter-Tux, and from the *Frauenwand*, see below).

EXCURSIONS (guides, *M. Stock* of Vorder-Tux, *Dav.* and *Mich. Kirchler* of Hinter-Tux). In a picturesque situation on the E. side of the Gefrorne Wand, $3^1/2$ hrs. from Hinter-Tux (path steep and toilsome), is the **Wery-Hütte** (about 8200'), built by the Austrian Tourist Club, serving as a starting-point for the ascent of the *Riffler* (10,625'; 3 hrs.), the *Gefrorne Wandspitze* (10,790'; $3^1/2$ hrs.), the *Olperer* (11,415'; 4-5 hrs.), and the *Grosse Kasererspitze* (10.700'; 4 hrs.). — From Hinter-Tux a very fine route crosses the **Riffelscharte** (9440') and the *Federbett Glacier* to (8 hrs.) *Rosshag* (p. 185; guide 6 fl.). With this route may easily be combined ascents of the *Riffler* (see above and p. 185; from the Riffelscharte viâ the Federbett Glacier, 1 hr.) and the *Realspitze* (10,000'; $3/4$ hr. from the Federbett). — Over the *Riepensattel* to the *Dominicus-Hütte* (8 hrs.; guide 6 fl.), see p. 186.

The *Dornauberg* (p. 184) may be combined with the Tuxer-Thal by an addition of $2^1/4$ hrs. to our walk, if we follow the route described below to the Karlssteg (from Mairhofen $1^3/4$ hr.) and then return along the W. side of the mountain, ascending the *Schumannweg* (see p. 184), to the ($1^1/4$ hr.) *Persallbrücke* (see above); beyond the bridge, at the chalets of Persall, we proceed either to the right to ($1/4$ hr.) *Finkenberg*, or to the left to *Lanersbach* and (4 hrs.) *Hinter-Tux*.

From Hinter-Tux the steep and stony path (guide, not indispensable, to Kasern $2^1/2$, to St. Jodok 3 fl.) ascends opposite the Gefrorne Wand, passing several waterfalls, to the ($2^1/2$ hrs.) **Tuxer** or **Schmirner Joch** (7665'). From the cross we overlook the bleak *Weidenthal* to the right, which descends to the E. to Hinter-Tux. Here we turn sharply to the left (finger-post) and reach on the saddle a second cross, from which we descend to the chalet in the basin lying before us, and thence by numerous zigzags into the *Schmirner Thal*. — The ascent of the *Frauenwand* (8300'), $3/4$ hr. to the S. of the Joch, will reward the traveller with a splendid view of the Gefrorne Wand, etc.

We now descend the somewhat monotonous Schmirner Thal to ($1^1/2$ hr.) *Kasern* (poor and dear quarters at the chalets) and (1 hr.) *Inner-Schmirn* (4020'; Inn), at the mouth of the *Wildlahner Thal*, to ($1^3/4$ hr.) *St. Jodok* (p. 220).

The Zemmthal divides at Breitlahner (see p. 185) into the Zemmgrund or Schwarzensteingrund to the left (E.; in the direction of the Ahrnthal) and the Zamser Grund to the right (W.; route over the Pfitscherjoch to Sterzing). These strikingly picturesque valleys are now traversed by good bridle-paths and may be visited without a guide. Beyond Mairhofen, at the (10 min.) hamlet of *Strass*, the road crosses the *Zillerbach*, and then, beyond the hamlet of *Haus* (finger-posts), the (¼ hr.) *Stilluppbach* (see p. 182), which forms a fine waterfall here. We now turn to the left and reach (10 min.) the covered bridge, known as the *Hochsteg* (*Untere Steg* to the right, leading to the Tuxerthal, see p. 182), crossing the *Zemmbach*, which here emerges from a wild ravine. The road then ascends on the left bank across the pastures of *Lindthal*, passing the Linde Inn and the Lindthal Café, to the *Dornauberg-Klamm*, a profound ravine, enclosed by lofty, pine-clad rocks, between which the Zemmbach is precipitated in numerous cascades. The scenery as far as the (1 hr.) *Karlssteg* is very striking, vying with, and at places surpassing the Via Mala in the Grisons.

The *Karlssteg* (2795′), 1¾ hr. from Mairhofen, 1¼ hr. from Ginzling, crosses the brook which here dashes wildly over huge rocks. (The 'Schumannweg', ascending by rocky steps to the right, leads to Finkenberg, see p. 183.) In the background rises the snow-clad *Ingent* (9565′). The Zemmbach forms the boundary between two bishoprics; the farms on the right bank and the inn of Ginzling belong to the parish of Mairhofen (bishopric of Salzburg, green towers), while those on the left bank, with the chapel, belong to the parish of Finkenberg in the see of Brixen (red towers). Beyond this point the track ascends gradually from the Karlssteg on the right bank of the Zemmbach, passing (10 min.; on the right) a group of rocks which form a pointed vault, and (20 min.) a hut with memorial-tablets. We next reach (¾ hr.) —

Ginzling (3200′; *Kröll*, 18 beds), prettily situated on the right bank of the Zemmbach, at the mouth of the *Floitenthal*.

EXCURSIONS from Ginzling (guides, see p. 184; to the Berliner Hütte 3½, to the Olperer Hütte 3½ fl.).

To the S. E. opens the wild Floitenthal, which is worthy of a visit (9 M. long; guide unnecessary). Steep ascent to the (1 hr.) *Höhenberg-Alp* (3800′), a little before reaching which a view of the glaciers is obtained. Then a gradual ascent to the (¼ hr.) *Sulzen-Alp* (4265′; bed at the *Franzens-Jagdhaus*, belonging to Prince Auersperg and occupied by the gamekeeper, Gregor Eder), the (½ hr.) *Bockach-Alp* (4795′), and the (¾ hr.) *Baumgarten-Alp* (5100′). At the head of the valley lies the extensive *Floiten Glacier*, encircled by the *Löffler*, *Schwarzenstein*, and *Mörchner*. — The ascent of the **Grosse Löffler** (11,096′) is very fatiguing (from the Vincenz-Jagdhaus, p. 182, across the crevassed *Floitenkees* and the *Floitenjoch* (10,500′) in 8 hrs.; two guides, 7 fl. each); superb panorama (descent by the *Trippachferner* to *St. Johann*, see p. 190). — Over the Floiten Glacier to the **Trippach Saddle** (10,040′), between the *Floitenspitze* and *Schwarzenstein*, and down over the *Rothbach Glacier* to the *Daimerhütte* (9 hrs. from the Vincenz-Jagdhaus), an imposing glacier-route (comp. p. 191). — A difficult route leads across the **Mörchenscharte** (9700′), between the *Kleine Mörchner* and the *Feldkopf*, to the *Berliner Hütte*, in 7-7½ hrs. from the Vincenz-Jagdhaus. Fine view of the Floitenthal, with the Löffler, and of the Schwarzensteingrund.

Ascent of the **Tristner** (9080′; 5 hrs.; guide 4½ fl.), easy and repaying. We ascend to the (2 hrs.) beautifully-situated shooting-box of *Wandeck* (small inn), from which a steep climb of 3 hrs. (the huntsman acts as guide, 2 fl.) brings us to the summit (splendid view).

To the **Gunkel**, 1½ hr. (guide unnecessary; provisions should be taken). We follow the right bank of the Zemmbach to the (½ hr.) saw-mill; then ascend to the left through wood, passing (½ hr.) a fine fall of the *Gunkelbach*, to the (1¼ hr.) *Jagdhaus in der Gunkel* (4790'), which affords a fine view of the environs of the valley (Feldkopf, Rothkopf, etc.). From the head of the valley an interesting, but somewhat difficult pass leads over the *Gunkelplatte* and the **Melkerscharte** (8790'), between the Feldkopf and Rothkopf, to the Schwarzsee and the (5-5½ hrs.) Berliner Hütte (see below). — The **Feldkopf** (*Zsigmondyspitze*; 9940') may be ascended from the Gunkel viâ the Melkerscharte and the S.E. arête (more easily reached from the Berliner Hütte) in 4½-5 hrs. (very difficult).

The path crosses the Zemmbach near the chapel of *Dornauberg*, and leads past the falls of the *Gunkelbach* on the left and the *Pitzerbach* on the right to the (1 hr.) **Rosshag-Alp** (3630'; *Faukhauser's Inn, bed 40 kr.; provision-depôt of the German Alpine Club).

MOUNTAIN ASCENTS (guides, see p. 184). The **Gross-Ingent** (9565) is ascended through the *Ingentkar* in 5-6 hrs. (toilsome; guide 5¼ fl.; better from the Gunkel through the *Gunkelkar*, in 5 hrs.). — Ascent of the ***Riffler** (10,625'; 6-7 hrs.), trying but very fine (guide 6 fl.). The path leads past the *Birglberg-Alpe* to the (3 hrs.) *Riffler-Hütte* (7380'), picturesquely situated below the small *Rifflersee*, and then across the *Federbett Glacier* to (3½ hrs.) the summit (magnificent view). Descent to the N. to the *Riffelscharte* (p. 183), to the W. (difficult) to the *Wery-Hütte* by the *Gefrorne Wand*, or to the S. to the *Friesenberg-Kar* and the *Olperer-Hütte* (p. 186). — The **Realspitze** (10,000'; 6 hrs., with guide), easy but not so remunerative as the Riffler. — From Rosshag over the *Riffelscharte* to *Hinter-Tux* (8½ hrs., with guide), an easy and attractive route, see p. 183.

The path continues to follow the left bank of the Zemmbach, passing through wood, and then crosses by a covered bridge to (1 hr.) **Breitlahner** (4070'; *Inn*, clean, bed 30 kr.), finely situated at the junction of the Zemmgrund with the Zamserthal.

[To the S.W. here opens the ***Zemmgrund** or **Schwarzensteingrund**, a highly-picturesque valley, rich in minerals. (Guides, see above; unnecessary for those who visit the Berliner Hütte only.) From Breitlahner the path follows the right bank of the stream, which here forms a small ravine, and ascends slightly to the (40 min.) *Schwemm-Alp* (4395'), situated in a broad basin covered with rocky debris. To the right rises the *Grosse Greiner* (see below.) The steeper ascent begins 20 min. farther on. The good path rapidly ascends the slopes of the *Grawander Schinder* (passing a fine fall of the Zemmbach on the right) to the finely-situated (1 hr.) *Grawand-Alp* (5690'), beyond which the path is narrow at places; 40 min. *Alpenrose Inn*, opposite the *Waxeck-Alp* (6120'); 25 min. *Schwarzenstein-Alpe*. A few yards beyond the last is the splendidly situated **Berliner Hütte** (6745'; *Inn and provision-depôt, with a ladies' room), erected by the German Alpine Club. To the S.E. the *Schwarzenstein Glacier*; S. the *Horn* and *Waxeck* glaciers, over-topped by the *Rothkopf*, *Kleine* and *Grosse Mörchner*, *Hornspitzen*, *Thurnerkamp*, *Rossruck*, *Mösele*, *Schönbichler Horn*, and *Grosse Greiner*. The best point of view is the small *Schwarzensee* (8340'), 1½ hr. to the N. of the hut (path indicated by marks).

MOUNTAIN ASCENTS from the Berliner Hütte. (Tariff for guides from Dornauberg, see p. 184; to the Berlinerhütte 3½ fl.). **Rothkopf** (9730'),

3½ hrs., interesting but somewhat difficult (guide 5 fl.). — The ascent of the *Ochsner (10,190'; 4 hrs.; guide 6 fl.) is a little more arduous, but the view is much finer. — The **Feldkopf** (*Zsigmondyspitze*; 9910'), ascended by the S.W arête in 4 hrs., should not be attempted except by adepts (see p. 185). — The **Kleine Mörchner** (10,480'; 5 hrs.; guide 7 fl.), somewhat difficult, commands a splendid view. — The **Grosse Mörchner** (10,740'; 5 hrs.; guide 7 fl.) presents no difficulty when the condition of the snow is favourable (fine view). — The *Schwarzenstein (11,045'; 5 hrs.; guide 7 fl.) commands a splendid panorama. The route ascends the Zemmbach and then crosses it to (1¾ hr.) a 'stone man', beyond which it ascends over debris and snow to (¾ hr.) the *Schwarzensteinkees* and over the *Trippach-Sattel* to the (2½-3 hrs.) summit. The descent may be made viâ the *Trippachsattel* and the *Rothbachkees* to the (3½ hrs.) **Daimerhütte** and to **Luttach** (comp. p. 189; guide 10 fl.). The ascent of the **Hornspitzen** (first peak, or Berlinerspitze, 10,860'; second peak 10,610'; third peak 10,601'; 4-5 hrs.; guide 6 fl.) presents no great difficulty and is repaying. — The **Grosse Greiner** (10,455'), ascended from the Alpenrose Inn in 6-7 hrs. (guide 7½ fl.), is difficult. — The *Grosse Mösele* (11,415') and the *Thurnerkamp* (11,200') are scarcely ever attempted from the Zemmgrund, as their N. sides present great difficulty (better from the Neveserjoch, p. 190). — Passes to Taufers over the *Schwarzenbachscharte*, the *Schwarzenbachjoch*, *Mitterbachjoch*, *Rossruckjoch*, and *Tratterjoch*, see p. 190 (each about 8 hrs., guide 8 fl.). Over the *Metkerscharte* to the Gunkel, see p. 185; over the *Mörchenscharte* to the Floitenthal, see p. 184. — Over the *Schönbichlerscharte* (10,000') to the *Furtschagelhütte*, 6 hrs. (guide), fine and not difficult; an ascent of the *Schönbichlerhorn* (10,275') is easily combined with this route.]

Over the PFITSCHER JOCH TO STERZING, 10 hrs. from Breitlahner, a fine route on the whole, but rather long. (Bridlepath; guide from Mairhofen to St. Jacob 7, to Sterzing 9 fl., unnecessary for experts.) The path crosses the Zemmbach to the W. and ascends the *Zamserthal* rapidly on the left bank of the *Zamser Bach* over the *Breitlahner* or *Zamser Schinder*. Farther on it ascends more gradually, crosses several tributary torrents, and reaches the (2 hrs.) **Dominicus-Hütte** (5510'; *Inn*), situated opposite the entrance to the magnificent *Schlegeis-Thal*, with its glacier-clad background. On the right bank of the stream is the humble *Zamser-Alpe* (5535').

A good, but at first rather steep path ascends from the Dominicus-Hütte to the (2 hrs.) **Olperer Hütte** (8355'; bed 60 kr.), a club-hut erected in 1881, overlooking the beautiful Schlegeisthal with the Furtschagel and Schlegeis glaciers, above which, from left to right, rise the Kleine and Grosse Greiner, the Schönbichler Horn, Mösele, Mutnock, Breitnock, Weisszint, Hochfeiler, Hochfernerspitz, and Hochstaller. This hut is the best starting-point for the ascent of the *Olperer (11,445'; 3-4 hrs.; guide 7½, or with descent to Hinter-Tux 9 fl.). The last part is steep, but presents no special difficulty to those who have steady heads, if the rocks are clear of snow or ice (stout worsted gloves should be taken). The Olperer Hütte is also the best starting-point for the ascent of the *Gefrorne Wandspitzen* (N. or highest peak 10,790) via the *Riepensattel* (4-5 hrs.; not difficult) and the *Schrammacher* (11,190'; 6 hrs.; fatiguing). — PASSES. From the Olperer Hütte over the Alpeiner Scharte (9710') between the Fussstein and the Schrammacher, to the *Alpeiner* and *Valser Thal* and (9 hrs.) *St. Jodok* (p. 220), an interesting but laborious route. — Over the Riepensattel (10,000'), between the Olperer and the Gefrorne Wandspitzen, to the *Wery-Hütte* (p. 184), 5 hrs. (to Hinter-Tux 8 hrs.), an attractive glacier expedition, free from difficulty (guide 6½ fl.).

The *Schlegeisthal well repays a visit. A good path, indicated by marks, leads from the Dominicus-Hütte via the *Herbig-Alpe* to (2½ hrs.)

the *Furtschagel-Hütte* (7575'), at the foot of the *Furtschagel-Kees*. From this point, which commands a magnificent survey of the surrounding glaciers (from W. to E.: Hochsteller, Hochfernerspitze, Hochfeiler, Weisszint, Breitnock, Mutnock, Grosse Mösele, Schönbichlerhorn, Talgenköpfe, Greiner), the *Schönbichter Horn* (10,275') and the *Grosse Talgenkopf* (10,580') may be ascended in 2½-3 hrs. (with guide). The ascent of the *Grosse Mösele* (11,415'), by the *Furtschagel-Kees*, is difficult (4-5 hrs.; see p. 190). The *Mutnock* (10,200') and the *Breitnock* (10,510'; difficult at places) are ascended viâ the *Schlegeis Glacier* in 4-4½ hrs. The ascent of the *Weisszint* (10,965'; 3 hrs.), viâ the same glacier and the N.W. arête, is grand but very difficult. — Over the *Neves-Sattel* or the *Schlegeis-Scharte* to *Lappach*, see p. 189; over the *Schönbichlerscharte* to the *Berliner Hütte*, see p. 186.

The path crosses to the right bank above the Dominicus-Hütte, and, gradually ascending, passes the *Lovitz-Alpe*, and intersects the highest reach of the valley (on the right is the *Stampfl Glacier*, from which issues the Zamserbach). Following the way-posts, we now ascend to the (2½ hrs.) **Pfitscher Joch** (7320'; Inn), which affords a fine view, to the left, of the *Rothwand* (9415'; ascended without difficulty from the Joch in 2 hrs.; interesting), the Oberbergspitzen, and (from a point 100 yds. to the W. of the Joch) of the Hochfeiler. In the foreground, far below, are the green Pfitschthal and the serrated ridge which separates it from the Pfundersthal, with the Pletzenhorn, Rothe Beil, and Grabspitz; at the end of the Pfitschthal rises the Amthorspitze; and to the W., in the distance, are seen the Ortler and the Stubai Alps. In a basin to the left below the pass lie three small lakes. The path on the other side of the Joch, steep at places, now descends to (¾ hr.) the *Bärenbach*, which it crosses, and follows the right bank to (¾ hr.) Stein and (½ hr.) **St. Jacob** in the *Inner-Pfitschthal* (4660'; **Rainer's Inn*; provision-depôt).

A path (steep at places; guide, advisable for novices, 3 fl.) leads to the E. from St. Jacob through the *Unterberg-Thal* to the (4½ hrs.) **Wiener Hütte** (8755'; built by the Austrian Alpine Club in 1881, and well fitted up), finely situated on a rocky knoll above the *Glieder-Ferner* and a little to one side of the small but beautiful *Weisskar Glacier*. From the hut experienced mountaineers may ascend the ***Hochfeiler** (11,500'; 2½-3 hrs.), the highest of the Zillerthal Alps, a superb point of view. — The ascent of the **Weisszint** (N. or highest peak 10,965'; 3 hr.) another fine point of view, viâ the *Glieder-Ferner*, is laborious. — From the Wiener Hütte to Lappach over the *Untere* or the *Obere Weisszint-Scharte* (5 and 6 hrs. respectively), see p. 189. — Guides in the Pfitschthal: *Martin Tötsch, Jac. Hofer ('Holzer') Chr. Pircher, Jac. Hofer ('Walderer')* of St. Jacob, and *Joh. Obermüller* of Kem tien. Tariff: To the Wiener Hütte 3; Hochfeiler 6 (if the night is spent. 7); Weisszint-Scharte to Lappach 7; head of the Pfitscher-Joch 2½; Breitlahner 6; Schlüsseljoch to the Brenner 4 fl.

Beyond St. Jacob we proceed through the level floor of the valley, either by the footpath along the stream, or by the road, which describes a wide circuit to the right. 1 hr. *Kematten* (*Hofer); ¼ hr. *Wieden* (4525'), opposite the entrance to the *Grossbergthal* (p. 188).

ASCENTS (guides, see above). The ascent of the ***Wilde Kreuzspitze** (10,270'; 5½-6 hrs, with guide) is fatiguing but highly remunerative. From (½ hr.) *Burgum* (see p. 188) we proceed through the Burguiner-Thal to the (3 hrs.) *Burgumer Alp*, and ascend thence over debris, ice, and rock to the (2½-3 hrs.) N. or higher peak, which commands a magnificent view. The descent may be made past the finely situated *Wilde See* to *Freienfeld* (comp. p. 224). — The *Kramerspitze* (9660'), easily ascended viâ the Burgumer Alp in 2 hrs., is also a fine point of view. — From Kematten over the **Schlüsseljoch** (7310') to the *Brennerbad* (p. 221; 4 hrs.; with guide), an easy and attractive route, preferable to that to Sterzing through the valley. — The route from *Wieden* through the *Grossberg-thal* and over the **Pfunderajoch** (8700') to (7 hrs.) *Pfunders* (p. 328) is somewhat toilsome.

The houses of *Burgum* are seen on the left bank. Near (³/₄ hr.) the *Wehr Inn* (4265') the cart-track crosses to the left bank and descends very abruptly through wood (driving unadvisable), skirting the margin of the ravine, through which the brook forces its way to a lower part of the valley. Below the ravine it recrosses to the right bank. On the left bank remain the houses of *Tuffer*. Farther on we cross the stream twice. 1½ hr. *Wiesen* (3100'; Elephant), a considerable village with a handsome church. The track now turns to the left round a projecting hill, passes under the railway, and leads to the right to the station of (½ hr.) *Sterzing* (p. 222).

36. The Ahrnthal.
Comp. Maps, pp. 178, 140.

The **Tauferer Thal** or **Ahrnthal**, 35 M. in length, which opens into the Pusterthal at Bruneck, extends at first towards the N. to Luttach, and then N.E., between the Zillerthal-Ferner and the Rieser-Ferner, towards the Tauern chain. The central part of the valley from Luttach to St. Peter is called the *Ahrnthal*, while the upper end is known as the *Prettau*. Numerous passes lead from this valley to the Zillerthal and the Pinzgau on the N., and the Virgenthal and Deferreggerthal on the E. — DILIGENCE from Bruneck to (9 M.) Taufers twice daily in 2 hrs., fare 70 kr.; OMNIBUS, daily at 7 p.m., fare 70 kr. (from Taufers at 5 p.m.); One-horse carr. 4-5, two-horse 7-8 fl. — From Taufers to Luttach in ³/₄ hr. (with one horse 1 fl. 80 kr.), to Steinhaus in 1½ hr. (3 fl.), to St. Valentin in 4 hrs. (6 fl.). If necessary the traveller may drive as far as Kasern. — Guides at Taufers. *Joh.* and *Georg Niederwieser* ('*Stabete-Hansl*' and '*Stabete-Jörgl*'), *Stef. Kirchter* ('*Gröber-Steffl*'), *Jos. Auer* ('*Feuerschwenter*'), *Jos. Auer* ('*Stockmair-Seppl*'), *Joh. Reden* ('*Huter-Hansl*'), *Mart. Reden* ('*Huter-Martl*'), *Mich. Oberteiler* ('*Matznicht*'), comp. also Kasern, p. 191, and Rein, p. 339.

From Bruneck to (9 M.) **Taufers** (2835'; *Post*; *Elephant), see p. 337. At *Mühlen*, 2½ M. below Taufers, the *Mühlwalder Thal* opens to the W.

[The entrance to the **Mühlwald-Lappacher Thal** (12 M. long) consists of a deep ravine, called the *Aussermühlwalder Klamm*; (10 min. from Mühlen is the pretty *Mühlener Wasserfall*, to which a path, protected with railings and without danger, leads along the water-conduit). There is a path on each side of the valley. The usual route (at first a carriage-road) leads to the S. from Taufers parallel with the post-road, for 1 M., and then ascends to the right on the N. side of the valley, passing above Mühlen, which lies to the left. On the S. side ('Schatten-Seite') another path ascends the valley from Mühlen, somewhat steeply at first, to the (³/₄ hr.) *Grüner-Brücke*, below which the brook forms sev-oral falls before it disappears in the gorge. Beyond the bridge the path joins the route on the N. side (see p. 188), and follows the left bank of the stream. Near (1½ hr.) **Mühlwald** (4035'; *Inn*, rustic), with its loftily-situated church, we obtain a view of the Speikboden (p. 338) to the right, and of the Reisnock and Stechwand in front. The track now leads up and down hill (better descend by the church and follow the path on the left bank). By a (³/₄ hr.) chapel the valley turns towards the N.W. (opposite is a waterfall), and a fine view is enjoyed of its head with the snow-clad *Weisszint* (10,720'). At (1 hr.) **Lappach** (4665'; *Inn*, primitive) the *Zesenthal* opens to the W.; above this point the main valley, stretching to the N., is called the *Nevesthal*.

ASCENTS. For most of the following excursions the best starting-point is the *Neves-Ochsenhütte* (6110'), 1½ hr., or the club-hut known as the *Neveserjoch-Hütte* (see below), 3½ hrs. above Lappach. The **Hochfeiler** (11,500'), is ascended from the Ochsenhütte by the *Untere Weisszintscharte* (see below) and the (5 hrs.) *Wiener Hütte* (p. 187); thence to the top in 3 hrs. more; (guide 6, with descent to Pfitsch 8 fl.). — The **Weisszint** (highest peak, 10,965'), free from serious difficulty, is ascended from the Ochsenhütte in 5-6 hrs. (guide 5 fl., with descent to Pfunders 7, to Pfitsch 8 fl.). — The **Ringelstein** (8300') ascended from Lappach viâ the *Lappacher-Jöchl* (p. 190) in 3½ hrs. (3 fl.), and the **Tristenspitze** (8905'), ascended (more laborious) by the *Lappacher Jöchl* in 4½ hrs. (guide 4 fl.), are also fine points of view. — The *Grosse Mösele* and the *Thurnerkamp*, see p. 190.

PASSES. FROM LAPPACH TO PFUNDERS: over the **Passenjoch** or **Posenjoch** (7930'), 5 hrs. (guide 3 fl.); through the *Zesenthal* and over the **Rieglerjoch** (7885'), 5 hrs. (3 fl.); through the *Nevesthal* and over the **Eisbruckjoch** (8355'), 7 hrs. (4 fl.), all unattended with difficulty. — To **PFITSCH**: over the *Eisbruck-Joch* and the **Untere Weisszintscharte** (about 9600'), 8 hrs. (to the Vienna Hut 5 hrs.), or (somewhat longer) over the **Obere Weisszintscharte** (about 10,500'), 9 hrs. (to the Vienna Hut 6 hrs.; guide 6 fl.). — To **SCHLEGEIS** (p. 187): over the **Schlegeisscharte** (10,095'), 7 hrs. from the Ochsenhütte to the Furtschagel-Hütte, difficult; over the **Neves-Sattel** (10,000'), 6-7 hrs., very trying — To **WEISSENBACH** (see below): over the **Neveser Joch** (5900'), with its hut and fine view of the Rieserferner, etc., 7 hrs. (3½ fl.); or through the *Rinsbachgraben* and over the **Lappacher Jöchl** (7730') 5 hrs. (3 fl.).

Above Taufers the valley contracts. The road, gradually ascends on the left bank of the Ahrnbach, below Schloss Taufers, and then (1¼ M.) crosses to the right bank. It next passes the fall of the *Bojerbach* on the right, and traverses the gradually widening valley (continuous view of the Hornspitzen and the Schwarzenstein) to (1½ M.) **Luttach** (3175'; *Unterstock Inn*, on the road; another by the church). On the W. opens the *Weissenbachthal*.

The *Weissenbachthal* is well worthy of a visit. From the Unterstock Inn we ascend a hill of debris to the left, in the direction of the church, cross the stream, and mount somewhat abruptly on the left bank, finally over meadows, to (1 hr.) *Weissenbach* (4300'; Inn, very primitive). The church contains a fine old carved altar. To the N. opens the *Mitterbachthal*, and farther up the valley bifurcates into the *Tristenbachthal* on the left and the *Trattenbachthal* on the right (N.W.).

ASCENTS (guides, see p. 188). The *Speikboden* (8264') is ascended in 4 hrs. (guide 3 fl.); descent to Taufers viâ Michelreiss, see p. 338. — Interesting excursion to the **Neveserjoch-Hütte** (7910'; 3 hrs.), through the *Trattenbach-Thal*, viâ the *Göge-Alpe* and *Stieralpe*. The hut, built by the German Alpine Club in 1880, and affording an excellent survey of the Rieserferner, the Tauern, and the neighbouring Zillerthaler Ferner, lies on a rocky knoll to the S. of and about 30' above the *Neveser-Joch* (see p. 189), and at the N. base of the *Schaftlanernock* (8520'), which is ascended hence by a new path in ³/₄ hr. (very striking view; also ascended from Weissenbach through the *Tristenthal* in 4-5 hrs., by a good path passing the *Tristensee*). To the N of the Nevesjoch Hut rises the *Gamslanernock* (9785'), another fine point, ascended in 2 hrs., the last part, up the arête, fatiguing. From the Gamslanernock to the summit of the *Pfaffnock* (9888'), 1 hr., difficult (guide 3¹/₂ fl.). — The *Ringeltelein* (8360'; 3¹/₂ hrs.; guide 3 fl.), see p. 189. — The **Grosse Mösele** (11,415') is reached from the Neveserjoch-Hütte in 4-5 hrs., a trying ascent; the route leads from the hut across the *E. Neves Glacier* to the *E. Mösele-Scharte* (10,725'), between the Mösele and the Rossruckspitze, and then climbs the rocks (grand view; guide 6, with descent to Weissenbach 7, to Waxeck 8 fl.). Descent over the *Waxeck-Kees* to *Waxeck*, or over the *Furtschagetkees* to the *Schlegeisthal* difficult (guide 6, with descent to Lappach 7, to Schlegeis or Waxeck 8 fl.). — The °**Thurnerkamp** (11,168'; 6-7 hrs. from the Neveserjoch-Hütte over the *E. Neveser Glacier*; guide 6 fl.) is difficult.

PASSES. To MÜHLWALD over the **Mühlwalder Joch** (7700'; 6 hrs.; 3 fl.), an interesting route. — To LAPPACH over the *Lappacher Jöchl* (7780'; 5 hrs.; 3 fl.), or over the *Neveser-Joch* (9240'; 6¹/₂ hrs.; 3¹/₂ fl.), see p. 189. — To THE BERLINER HÜTTE (p. 185) over the **Rossruckjoch** (10,565') between the Thurnerkamp and the Rossruckspitze, with descent over the *Horn Glacier*, 7-8 hrs., a trying route. Over the **Tratterjoch** (9750') between the Thurnerkamp and fifth Hornspitze, in 8 hrs. (6 fl.), a fatiguing excursion; the fifth Hornspitze may be easily ascended from the Joch in ¹/₂ hr. The route over the **Mitterbachjoch** (10,430'), immediately to the S.W. of the third Hornspitze (10,605'), is fine but trying (8 hrs.; guide 6¹/₂ fl.).

We cross the *Weissenbach* to (³/₄ M.) *Ober-Luttach*. In the ravine of the *Schwarzenbach* (1 M. to the W.) is the fine *Luttach Waterfall*; at the head of the valley rise the *Hornspitzen*.

A difficult route leads through the steep gorge of the **Schwarzenbach** and over the *W. Schwarzenbach-Joch* (about 10,200'), or over the *Schwarzenbach-Scharte* (9430') to (7-8 hrs.) the *Berliner Hütte* (p. 185). The *Zweite Hornspitze* (10,620') is ascended without difficulty from the Schwarzenbach-Joch in ³/₄ hr.

The ascent of the °**Schwarzenstein** (11,045'; 7 hrs.; guide 5 fl.) is very fine and not difficult; view magnificent. The route ascends from Oberluttach through wood to *Brunnberg*, where it enters the *Rothbachlthal*, ascending by an Alpine track to (2¹/₂-3 hrs.) the **Daimerhütte** on the *Obere Rothbach-Alpe* (6070'; Inn). Thence a new path leads to the moraine of the *Rothbach Glacier*, and across it to the (3 hrs.) *Trippachsattel* (10,040'), and then to the left to (1 hr.) the summit. Descent to the N.W. by the *Schwarzenstein Glacier* to the *Berliner Hütte* (p. 185), 8 hrs., not difficult; to the N.E. over the *Floiten Glacier* to the *Floitenthal* (difficult descent), 5-6 hrs. to Ginzling (guide 7 fl.); comp. p. 184.

The valley now bends to the N.E.; and the E. part of the Zillerthal ridge comes into full view (from W. to E., the Hornspitzen, Schwarzenstein, Löffler, Keilbachspitze, Rothwandspitze, Napfspitze, and Wagnerschneid). The road traverses the immense deposits of the *Rothbach*, from which rise the chimneys of a copperfoundry, destroyed in 1878; and about 1 M. farther on reaches the lower end of the *Lake*, formed by the floods of 1878. About ¹/₂ M. along the W. bank is *St. Martin*, with an ancient church. The road next crosses the deposits of the *Trippach* (the Trippachferner and Löffler rising on the left) to (³/₄ M.) **St. Johann** (3325'; *Inn*, rustic). Fine view, from the churchyard-wall, of the Dreiherrnspitze to the E.

The **Grosse Löffler** (11,090'; 8 hrs.; guide 5½ fl, to Ginzling 7½ fl.) is trying (comp. p. 184). To the *Hofer-Alpe* in the Trippach valley (6140'; night-quarters), 2½ hrs.; then over slopes of turf, moraines, and the extensive *Trippachferner* to the (4½ hrs.) *Floitenjoch* (ca. 10,500'), between the *Floitenspitze* (10,528') and the *Trippachspitze* (10,785'), and round the W. side of the latter, and across the *Floitenfirn*, to (¾ hr.) the summit. Descent over the *Floiten Glacier* to the *Floitenthal* steep and difficult (guide 7½ fl.).

The road now leads past the *Frankbachthal* (terminated by the Frankbach Glacier and Löffler) to (3 M.) **Steinhaus** (3440'; **Gewerkschaft; Neuwirth*), a pleasant village with several substantial houses.

From Steinhaus over the *Keilbach-Joch* to the *Stillupthal* (11 hrs. to Mairhofen; guide 7 fl.; Martin Nothdurfter of Steinhaus), see p. 182. — Another grand but difficult pass (for adepts) is the **Frankbachjoch** (about 9680'): from St. Johann or Steinhaus to Mairhofen 11 hrs.; descent over the *Löfflerkees* to the Stillupthal very steep. With this route we may combine the ascent of the *Keilbachspitze* (10,056'), a good point of view.

Ascending more steeply and crossing the Ahrenbach twice, we next pass (2¼ M.) **St. Jakob** (3930'), which lies on the hill to the left. (Route over the *Hörndljoch* and through the Zillergrund to Mairhofen 12 hrs., see p. 182.) Beyond (3 M.) *St. Peter* (3940'; rustic inn) the valley contracts to a narrow gorge, in which there is barely room for the road and the stream. At the end of the defile we enter the *Prettau*, the highest region of the valley, and next reach (4½ hr.) **St. Valentin** or *Prettau* (4580'; *Wieser*, rustic). The road ends, 1½ M. farther on, at *Neuhaus*, with the copper mines of the Ahrner Co., beyond which are (¼ hr.) **Kasern** (5300'; *Hofer*, rustic), the last hamlet, and (¼ hr.) the church of *Heiligengeist*.

Ascents (guides, *Jos. Voppichler* of Prettau, *Peter* and *Matt. Griesmair* of Kasern.) The **Röththal** deserves a visit (3½-6 hrs. there and back). By the copper-works we ascend through wood, past the copper-mines of *St. Jakob* (6330'; the highest ruined shafts are interesting), to the (2 hrs.) *Inner Röth-Alpe* (about 7200'; accommodation), which affords a fine view of the grand head of the valley (Röthspitze, with the glacier of that name, Kemetspitze, and Löffelspitze). Thence we may proceed over the easy *Röth Glacier* to the (1¼ hr.) **Lenkjöchl-Hütte**, finely situated on the *Judenlacke*, just below the *Lenkjöchl* (8440'). The ***Röthspitze** (11,455'), a splendid point of view, is easily ascended hence in 3 hrs. (guide) via the Röth Glacier (descent to the *Clara-Hütte*, see p. 144). The ascent of the **Dreiherrnspitze** (11,480'; 5-6 hrs.; guide 7 fl.), via the *Hintere Umbalthört* (p. 144), also offers no serious difficulty (comp. p. 144). Over the *Umbalthörnl* to Prägraten, see p. 192.

The **Rauchkofel** (10,656'), steep at places, may be ascended from St. Valentin by the *Wieser-Alpe* in 5 hrs. (4 fl.); admirable view of the Reichenspitze and the Venediger group.

Passes. From St. Peter over the **Hundskehljoch** (8380') to the Zillergrund (to Mairhofen 12 hrs.; guide 7 fl.), see p. 182. — From St. Peter through the *Hasenthal* and over the **Ochsenlenke** (about 8530') to *Knutten* (p. 340), 6 hrs., with guide, without difficulty (from Knutten to Jagdhaus or Rein, see p. 340). — From St. Valentin over the **Merbjöch** (9300') to the *Jagdhaus-Alpe* (p. 139) in the Defereggen-Thal, 7 hrs. (4 fl.), a fatiguing route. (From the S. side of the pass we may proceed to the *Klammt* and Rein, see p. 340.) Over the **Rothenmann-Joch** (9055'), 7 hrs. from Kasern to Jagdhaus (for experts only; 5 fl.), see pp. 139, 340. — From Kasern over the **Heiligengeist-Jöchl** (8760') to the Zillergrund (to Mairhofen 12 hrs.; 7 fl.), see p. 182. — Over the **Krimmler Tauern** (8645') to Krimml,

192 *IV. Route 30.*   BIRNLÜCKE.   *Ahrnthal.*

10 hrs. (6 fl.), see p. 138. The route ascends the valley on the right bank to a finger-post pointing the way to the Tauern, and then more abruptly to the left to the *Tauern-Alpe* (6230'), and past the *Herzogsbrunnen* (a good spring) to the (3 hrs.) summit of the pass, which affords a splendid view of the Röthspitze and Dreiherrnspitze. Descent through the *Windbachthal* to the *Krimmler Tauernhaus* and to *Krimml* (p 137). — Over the **Birnlücke** (8730') to Krimml, 10 hrs. (6 fl.), laborious; in descending, we overlook the extensive Krimml Glacier (p. 138). — Over the Vordere (9720'), or the **Hintere Umbalthörl** (9270'), to *Prägraten*, 9-10 hrs. (7 fl.), toilsome but interesting (p. 143). The ascent to the Vordere Thörl from the *Lenkjöchl-Hütte* (p. 191) takes 1½ hr., to the Hintere Thörl 2 hrs. (comp. p. 144).

V. NORTH-WESTERN TYROL. BRENNER RAILWAY. THE OETZTHAL ALPS.

37. From Bregenz to Landeck. The Arlberg Railway . . **195**
Excursions from Bregenz. Gebhardsberg. Pfänder, etc., 196. — Excursions from Dornbirn. Zanzenberg. Gütle, etc., 197. — Hohe Kugel, 197. — From Götzis viâ Klaus and Rötis to Rankweil, 198. — The Laternser Thal. The Hohe Freschen, 198. — Excursions from Feldkirch. Margarethenkapf, 198. — Maria-Grün. Aelpele, etc., 199. — From Feldkirch to Buchs, and to Mayeufeld. Liechtenstein, 199. — The Saminathal. Naafkopf. Schönberg. Gallinakopf, 199. — The Gamperton-Thal, 200. — The Grosse Walserthal. Over the Schadona-Sattel to the Schrecken, 200. — The Hohe Frassen. Brandner Thal. Lüner See. Seesaplana, 201. — From Dalaas to the Montavon over the Kristberg, 202. — From Langen to St. Anton by the Arlberg, 203. — Excursions from St. Anton. The Moosthal. Schneidjöchl. Rendelspitze. Fervallthal, 203. — Konstanzer Hütte. Almejurjoch. Kaiserjoch, 204. — Blankajoch. Rüfler, 205.

38. From Bregenz to the Schrecken. The Bregenzer Wald **206**
From Egg viâ Hittisau to Oberstaufen or Oberstdorf, 206. — From Schwarzenberg to Dornbirn over the Lose. The Hochälple, 207. — Excursions from Mellau. Mörzelspitze. Canisfluh, etc., 208. — From Au to Bludenz or to Rankweil viâ Damüls, 208. — Excursions from the Schrecken. Widderstein, Kinzelspitze, etc., 209. — From the Schrecken to Oberstdorf by the Genischeljoch. To the Arlberg, 209.

39. From Reutte to the Arlberg through the Upper Lechthal **210**
From Weissenbach across the Dirschentrittjoch to Nassereit. Thaneller, 210. — Namlosthal. Steinjöchl, 210. — From Elmen to Imst by the Hochtenn Sattel, 210. — Memminger Hütte. Grossbergjoch. Flirschjoch. Alperschonjoch. Kaiserthal, 211. — From Lech to Stuben by the Flexensattel, 211. — From Lech viâ the Formarin-Alp to Dalaas and to the Grosse Walserthal. The Rothewandspitze, 212. — To Klösterle viâ the Spullersee. Schafberg, 212.

40. The Montavon and Patznaun Valleys **212**
Excursions from Schruns. Tschagguns. Vandans. Bartholomäberg. Silberthal, 213. — Monteneu. Tanzkopf. Gapelljoch. Sulzfluh. To the Lünersee through the Rellsthal or the Gauerthal, 214. — Passes to the Prätigau (Schweizerthor, Drusenthor, Partnun-Pass, Plasseggenjoch), 214. — To St. Anton on the Arlberg through the Silberthal, 214. — The Gargellenthal. St. Antönicajoch. Schlapinajoch. Heimspitze. Madriser Spitze, 215. — Excursions from Gaschurn. Valschavielthal. Ganerathal, 215. — Schaffodenberg. Maderer, etc., 216. — By the Gaschurner Winterjöchl to St. Anton. Vallülaspitze, 216. — From Patznen to the Patznaun by the Zeinisjoch or the Bielerlöbe, 216. — From the Madlenerhaus to Klosters over the Kloster Pass or the Rothe Furka, 217. — Jamthal Hütte. Piz Buin. Vermunt Pass, Futschöl Pass. Jamjoch. Fluchthorn, etc., 217. — From Ischgl through the Fimberthal

to Samnaun and Finstermünz or Stuben, 218. — Finber Pass. Schneidjöchl. Blankajoch. Peziner Spitze, 218.

41. **From Innsbruck to Botzen over the Brenner** 219
From Patsch to the Stubaithal, 219. — Maria-Waldrast. Mieselkopf, 220. — Blaser. Pendelstein. The Gschnitzthal. Pflerscher Pinkl. Tribulaun, 220. — The Obernbergthal. Padauner Kogl 221. — Kraxentrager, Dornspitze. Schlüsseljoch, 221. — Amthorspitze. Pflerschthal. Magdeburger Hütte. Ellesjoch. Aglsjoch, 222. — Rosskopf. Zinseler, 222. — Ridnaunthal. Teplitzer-Hütte, 223. — Over the Schneeberg to the Passeir and Oetzthal, 223. — Wilde Kreuzspitze, 224. — Vahrn. Schalderer Thal. Vellthurns. The Plose, 225. — The Villnössthal. Over the Raschötz-Alp to Gröden and over the Wurzen to Enneberg, 225. Latzfons. — Bad Dreikirchen, 226.

42. **The Stubaithal** 227
Waldrasierspitze, 227. — Hohe Burgstall, 228. — From Neustift to Gschnitz over the Pinniser-Joch. Habicht. Oberberg. Alpeiner Ferner. Schwarzenbergjoch. Brunnenkogeljoch, 228. — Pfandler Alpe. Valbesonthal, 229. — The Langethal. Nürnberger Hütte. Passes to Gschnitz, Pflersch, Ridnaun, and Passeir. Wilde Freiger, 229. — Sulzenau. Pfaffennieder. Sonklarspitze. Over the Mutterberger Joch to Längenfeld, 230. — Eggessengrat. Bildstöckljoch. Schaufelspitze, 230. — Zuckerhütl, 231.

43. **From Innsbruck to Landeck** 231
The Selrainthal, 231. — Martinswand. Solstein, 232. — Anich Refuge Hut. Stamser Alpe, 233. — Excursions from Imst. Tschürgant. Mutterkopf, 234. — Excursions from Landeck. Lötzer Klamm. Thialspitze. Rothbleisskopf. Venetberg. Parseierspitze, 235.

44. **The Oetzthal** 235
The Stuiben Fall, 236. — The Sulzthal. Gamskogel. Schrankogl, 237. — From Längenfeld to the Pitzthal by the Breitlehner Jöchl, 237. — Brunnenkogl, 237. — Nöderkogl, 238. — Excursions from Vent. Breslauerhütte. Kreuzspitze, Ramolkogl. Wildspitze, Weisskugel, etc., 238, 239. — Taufkarjoch. Sextenjoch. Taschachjoch. Seiterjöchl. Tiefenbachjoch. Gepatschjoch. Guslarjoch. Kesselwandjoch. Langtauferer Joch. Oberettenjöchl. Hintereisjoch Steinschlagjoch, 239, 240. — Schalfkogel, Similaun. Hochvernagt Glacier, 241. — Excursions from Kurzras. Langgrubjoch. Taschljoch. Weisskugel, 242. — Excursions from Gurgl. Gurgler Glacier. Langthaler Eissee. Gaisbergferner. Mutberg. Hangerer. Schalfkogl, etc., 243. — From Gurgl to Vent over the Ramoljoch; to the Passeir over the Timbler Joch, the Königsthal-Joch, the Rothmoosjoch, or the Langthaler-Joch; to the Schnalser Thal over the Gurgler Joch, 244.

45. **The Pitzthal** 245
From Wenns to Prutz over the Pillerjoch, 245. — Rofelewand. Lolbiser Joch. Excursions from Mittelberg. Mittelberg Glacier. Taschach Glacier, 245. — Riffelsee. Mittagskogel, etc., 246. — Pitzthaler Jöchl. Oelgrubenjoch. Madatschjoch. Verpailjoch. Tiefenthal Joch. Niederjöchl,246

46. **From Landeck to Meran. Finstermünz** , . . 246
The Kaunser Thal. Gepatschhaus. Oelgrubenspitze, 247. —

Passes to the Pitzthal, the Oetzthal, and the Langtauferer Thal, 248. — The Radurschel-Thal, 248. — Excursions from Nauders. Pitzlat. Schmalzkopf, 249. — The Langtauferer Thal. Excursions and passes, 250. — Excursions from Glurns. Glurnser Köpfl, Piz Ciavalatsch, etc., 251. — From Mals to St. Maria in the Münsterthal, 251. — The Matscher Thal, 251. — The Laaser Thal, 252.

47. The Passeierthal 253
From St. Leonhard to Sterzing over the Jaufen, 254. — From St. Leonhard to Sölden over the Timbler Joch, 254.

37. From Bregenz to Landeck. The Arlberg Railway.

Comp. Maps, pp. 8, 212, 216.

76½ M. Railway in 4-5¾ hrs. (to Innsbruck, 104 M., in 5¼-8¼ hrs.). The **Arlberg Railway** (*Arlbergbahn*), built in 1880-84 at an expense of 42 million florins (3,350,000 *l.*), with its numerous tunnels, viaducts, retaining walls, and protective works, is one of the most interesting examples of mountain-railway engineering, while at the same time it commands a series of magnificent views (from Bludenz to Langen the best views are to the right, from St. Anton to Landeck to the left). The steepest gradient on the W. side (from Bludenz to Langen) is 31:100 (St. Gotthard railway 26:100), and on the E. side (from Landeck to St. Anton), 26:100. — View-carriages, see p. 112: holders of second-class tickets from Bregenz to Landeck pay 8 fl. extra, and in circular tours it is better to take first-class tickets at once. The express-train makes no halt for dinner; but dinners are handed into the carriages at Landeck (1 fl. 20 kr.).

Bregenz. — Hotels. *Hôtel Europa*, at the station and quay, finely situated; *Oesterreichischer Hof*, on the lake, R. & A. 1½-2 fl., B. 50 kr.; *Hôtel Montfort*, near the station; *Weisses Kreuz*, Römer-Strasse, R. & A. 1½ fl., B. 55 kr.; Krone; *Schweizerhof*; Löwe; Lamm; Heidelberger Fass, with garden, moderate; Tiroler Hof.
Restaurants and Cafés. *Railway Restaurant*, with view of the lake from the veranda; *Café Austria*, at the harbour; *Café Sonntag*, near the station. Wine at *F. Kinz's* ('Bürgermeister'), Kirchgasse; '*Old German' Wine-Room*, opposite the station; *Gmeinder*, with rooms; *Franz Ritter*, at the foot of the Gebhardsberg (see p. 196). Beer at the *Hirsch*; *Forster*, with garden; *Hörburger*; *Neue Welt*; *Löwe*; *Zur Schanz*, on the Lindau road; *Schützengarten*, on the Berg Isel; *Zum Engel*, see p. 196.
Baths (swimming, etc.) at the harbour and on the Lindau road.

Bregenz, the capital of the Vorarlberg (district 'before the Arlberg'), the *Brigantium* of Strabo and Ptolemy, with 4800 inhab., lies at the base of the *Pfänder*, at the E. end of the *Lake of Constance* (Ger. *Bodensee*, Latin *Lacus Brigantinus*). The *Old*, or *Upper Town*, of irregular quadrangular shape, situated on a height, occupies the site of the *Roman Camp*, and formerly had two gates, of which that to the S. has been removed. (Adjoining the old tower on this side of the town is a mediæval castle.) Over the gateway of the old inner tower in the Autrachgasse, is an ancient relief of Epona, goddess of horses. The handsome *Church*, with an ancient tower, is situated on another hill to the S. The *Pier* commands a good survey of the town and neighbourhood. The *Vorarlberg Museum* (near the station; adm. 25 kr.) contains natural history specimens, coins,

13*

196   *V. Route 37.*   BREGENZ.   *From Breyenz*

pictures, and Roman antiquities found on the *Œlrain*, a plateau $1/2$ M. to the S.W., and at other spots near the town.

Pleasant *WALK along the Lindau road, past the *Schanz* inn, to the (1 M.) *Klause*, the tower of which commands a charming view (evening light best). Thence to the ($1^1/_2$ M.) *Bäumle* (*Anker; Thierheimer's Pension) near *Lochau* (p. 7) and to ($3/_4$ M.) the '*Zech*' *Taverna*, just beyond the Bavarian frontier. — To the S. the Gallus-Strasse or old road leads over the *Œlrain* and past the *Villa Taxis* to ($3/_4$ M.) *Franz Ritter's Restaurant*, prettily situated at the foot of the Gebhardsberg; $1/2$ M. farther on is the restaurant *Zum Engel*, at the bridge over the *Ach*, near which is the *Riedenburg*, now a girls' school. We may return either by the new road ($1^1/_2$ M.), which commands a pretty view of the lake; or by the village of *Rieden*, to *Vorkloster* (see below), passing the '*Gletscherfeld*', a tract shewing interesting traces of glacier action. — To the W. a walk may be taken to ($1^1/_2$ M.) *Vorkloster* (warm sulphur-baths; omn. from the 'Kreuz' four times daily); and to *Mererau*, a Cistercian abbey, with a handsome new church in the basilica style. — To the E. is the ($3/_4$ M.) *Berg Isel*, a tavern and rifle-range, with a pleasing view (finer from *Weissenreute*, the farm-house above it). To ($5^1/_2$ M.) the little village of *Fluh*, see below.

The *Gebhardsberg (1945'; ascent $3/_4$ hr.) is reached by a good road passing the church and the handsome *Villa Raczynski*, and traversing wood. The summit, on which are the scanty ruins of the castle of *Hohenbregenz*, now surmounted by a small church, and a rustic inn, commands an extensive prospect, embracing the Lake of Constance, the valley of the Bregenzer Ach and the Rhine, the Alps, and the snow-mountains of Appenzell and Glarus; the foreground is formed by very picturesque pine-clad mountains. — A carriage-road leads round the face of the Gebhardsberg to ($2^1/_4$ M.) *Kennelbach* (Krone), prettily situated on the right bank of the Ach, crosses the Ach to *Schloss Wolfurt* ($1^1/_2$ M.), and ascends to the left via *Rickenbach* to (6 M.) *Bildstein* (2145'), frequented by pilgrims and affording a fine view. Return by ($2^1/_4$ M.) *Schwarzach* (see below).

The *Pfänder (3476'), which commands a very striking and extensive view, is ascended by several routes. The best ($1^1/_2$-2 hrs.) leads past *Berg Isel* (see above) to *Weissenreute*, and then ascends to the right through wood (indicated by white marks) to *Hintermoos* (refreshments). Another path diverges to the right from the Lindau road beyond the barracks, ascends to the left by a finger-post, and passes a bench affording a pleasing view; it then becomes steeper, and leads through wood to the (1 hr.) *Halbstation Pfänder* (refreshments); 12 min., last houses of *Hintermoos*; lastly a gradual ascent of 20 min. to the large *Hôtel-Pension Pfänder* (R. from 1 fl. upwards, L. & A. 40, B. 50 kr., pens. $3^1/_2$-4 fl.; telephone to Kinz's wine-room, p. 195), and of 10 min. more to the summit. The view from the top embraces the Bregenzer Wald, the Algäu and Vorarlberg Alps, the Rhætikon, the mountains of Glarus and Appenzell, and the whole of the Lake of Constance. — The carriage-road, which is rather longer (2-$2^1/_2$ hrs.) leads past *Berg Isel* (see above), chiefly through wood, to ($1^1/_4$ hr.) *Fluh* (Krone) and ($1^1/_4$ hr.) the hotel. — From *Lochau* (p. 7) also the summit may be reached by a good path ($2^1/_2$ hrs.) which follows the telegraph-posts as far as the *Hagenmühle*, and then ascends to the left to the hamlet of *Riese* and the hotel. — From the Pfänder by *Möggers* and *Scheidegg* to *Röthenbach* (6 hrs.), see p. 6.

The *Hirschberg (3570'), $1^1/_4$ hr. to the E. of the Pfänder, affords a better survey of the Bregenzer Wald, but the view is otherwise inferior (ascent from Bregenz 3 hrs., viâ *Fluh*, *Oeserberg*, and *Ahornach*).

From Bregenz viâ *Weiler* to *Oberstaufen*, see p. 6.

THE VORARLBERG RAILWAY skirts the *Gebhardsberg* (see above), crosses the *Bregenzer Ach* at *Rieden*, and at ($2^1/_2$ M.) *Lauterach* (junction for *St. Margarethen*, a station on the Coire and Rorschach Railway, see *Baedeker's Switzerland*) enters the broad valley of the Rhine. — $5^1/_2$ M. **Schwarzach** (1340'; *Bregenzwälderhof*, at the station; *Post or Löwe, on the Alberschwende road) is the station for the Bregenzer Wald (p. 206). The large village lies 1/4 M. from the railway. About 1 hr. to the N.E. is *Bildstein* (p. 196), a resort of pilgrims, with a fine view.

7 1/2 M. **Dornbirn** (1415'; *Hirsch; *Dornbirner Hof; Mohr; Scharfeck; Restaurant Weiss, opposite the station), the principal market-town in the Vorarlberg, with 9800 inhab., is a busy, well-built place upwards of 2 M. long, situated on the *Dornbirner Ach*. It consists of the four quarters of *Markt*, *Oberdorf* (E.), *Haselstauden* (N.) and *Hatterdorf* (S.; the last two are railway-stations), and contains four churches. The horizon on the S.W. is bounded by the mountains of Appenzell, the Kamor and Hohe Kasten, the snow-clad Sentis, and the indented Churfirsten. A new road, commanding a series of picturesque views, runs N.E. from Dornbirn through the populous Mittelgebirge to (6 M.) *Alberschwende* (p. 206).

EXCURSIONS (guide, *Herm. Wehinger*; paths all indicated by marks on the trees, etc.). Fine views from the °**Zanzenberg**, 1/2 hr. to the E., with pavilion and tavern, and from the hamlet of (3 M.) *Kehlegg* (Inn), reached through the *Steinebachthal*. — In the valley of the Dornbirn Ach, 3 M. to the S.E., lies the **Gütle** (*Restaurant*), with several factories, aqueducts, and a fountain, which plays to a height of 180'. About 1/2 M. farther up is the newly-opened °*Rappenloch Gorge*, through which dashes the foaming Ach, spanned at a dizzy height by a covered bridge (route to the Hohe Freschen, see below). The return may be advantageously made via the Zanzenberg (see above; 4 1/2 M. to Dornbirn). — About 2 M. to the S. of Dornbirn, at the base of the *Breitenberg*, lies the small *Bad Haslach*, 3/4 M. from which is the fine *Fall of the Fallbach*.

From Dornbirn over the *Lose* to *Schwarzenberg*, see p. 207; ascent of the °*Hochälple* (by Kehlegg in 3 hrs., over the Lose in 3 1/2 hrs.), see p. 207. — The *Mörzelspitze* (5093'; 5 hrs.; with guide) is another fine point; descent to Mellau 3 hrs., comp. p. 208. — The upper part of the *Hohe Freschen* (6565'; 6 1/2 hrs.; guide 6 fl.) requires a steady head (better from Rankweil, see p. 198).

12 1/2 M. **Hohenems** (1405'; *Post*), a well-to-do village (4500 inhab.), with large factories and a brisk timber-trade, lies very picturesquely at the foot of precipitous rocks, commanded by the ruins of *Alt*- and *Neu-Ems*. The half-ruined château belonged to the once powerful Counts of Hohenems.

A new and shady path leads to (40 min.) the insignificant ruins of *Alt-Ems*. Splendid °View from the plateau (small inn) and from the 'Sätzle' (Rheinthal, Vorarlberg Alps, etc.). The castle of *Neu-Ems*, also called the *Tannenburg*, boldly perched on the precipitous *Glopper*, is partly preserved and occupied. Farther to the N., on a plateau affording several fine views, lie the houses of *Emser-Reute*. — At the base of the *Götznerberg*, 3/4 M. to the S. of Hohenems, is the small *Bad Schwefel*.

The flat alluvial plain of the Rhine is relieved at places by rocky and wooded heights, the chief of which is the *Kummenberg* (2175'; easily ascended from the S.W. side via *Koblach*; fine view), on the right. Near (15 1/2 M.) **Götzis** (*Goldner Adler; Engel*; *Zum Bahnhof*), with a modern Romanesque church, is the ruined castle of *Neu-Montfort*. To the right, near the railway, is the ruined *Neuburg*.

The **Hohe Kugel** (5390'), a fine point of view, is easily ascended from Götzis via *Frasern* in 3 1/2 hrs. (guide), or from Rankweil via *Ebnit* in

4½ hrs., (guide). — The following walk or drive from Götzis is recommended: past the ruin of *Neu-Montfort* and the pilgrimage-chapel of *St. Arbogast*, and through a wooded ravine, to (2¼ M.) *Klaus* (Adler; fine view by the church) and (¾ M.) *Weiler* (*Summer*) with the small château of *Hahnenberg*, and thence past (¾ M.) *Rötis* (*Bad*) and (¾ M.) *Sulz* to (1½ M.) *Rankweil*. The *Victorsberg* (2890'; Inn), a splendid point of view, may be ascended from Sulz in 1½ hr.

Beyond the small stations of *Klaus-Koblach* and *Sulz-Rötis*, the train crosses the *Frutzbach* to (20½ M.) **Rankweil** (1510'; *Hohenfreschen*, at the station; **Hecht*; *Schwert*; *Goldner Adler*; *Schwarzer Adler*), a village with a picturesquely situated church, at the entrance to the *Laternser Thal*, which is watered by the Frutz. Charming view from the outer gallery of the church on the *Frauenberg* (1670').

Pleasant excursion to the S.E. viâ *Rheinberg* to (1½ hr.) *Uebersaxen* (2950'; Inn), an elevated village commanding a fine view; or to the N.E. viâ *Muntlix* and *Batschuns* to the (1½ hr.) *Stöck Inn* (fine view), and to (¾ hr.) the village of *Laterns* (2090'; Inn), in the *Laternser Thal*, above the deep gorge of the Frutzbach. At the head of the Laternser Thal is the (2 hrs.) *Hinterbad*. Thence over the *Furkel* to *Damüls* and *Au*, see p. 208.

The ascent of the ***Hohe Freschen** (6565'; 5-6 hrs.; guide 4½ fl., F. Barbisch and Leonhard Weber of Rankweil recommended) is a very fine excursion. The usual path by *Stöck* (see above) and the Alps *Furx*, *Alpwen*, and *Tschuggen* is bad at places and very muddy after rain, but nowhere steep or difficult. About ¾ hr. from the top is the *Touristenhaus* (well fitted up). Magnificent panorama from the summit, embracing the mountains of the Algäu, Lechthal, and Patznaun, the Silvretta, Rhätikon, Glarus, and Appenzell Alps, the Bregenzer Wald, and the Lake of Constance.

The train now threads a defile on the E. side of the wooded and vine-clad *Ardetzenberg*, where a junction-line to Buchs diverges to the right (see p 199), and soon reaches —

22½ M. **Feldkirch** (1490'; **Englischer Hof*, R. 1 fl., B. 45 kr.; *Löwe*; *Schäfle*, well spoken of; *Ochs*; beer at the *Rössl*; *Railway Restaurant*), a well-built, thriving town (3600 inhab.), enclosed by mountains which form a natural fortress, once the key of Tyrol, and commanded by the ancient castle of *Schattenburg*. Many of the houses have covered arcades in front of them. The *'Stella Matutina'* is a large school conducted by Jesuits. The Gothic *Church*, erected in 1487, possesses a Descent from the Cross attributed to Holbein and a fine pulpit; the *Capuchin Church* also contains a good Descent from the Cross. Opposite the hospital is the *Kurhaus*, presented to the town by Burgomaster von Tschavoll, with pleasant promenades. The grounds of the *Gymnasium* contain interesting Alpine plants.

The terrace in front of the (10 min.) *Schattenburg* (now a poor-house) is a good point of view. A pleasant walk may be taken hence along the *Gäfiserweg* to the *Waldfestplatz* and the (25 min.) *Känzel*, in the *Steinwald*; returning viâ *Stein* and the *Upper Illklamm* to (½ hr.) Feldkirch.

A fine view of the valley of the Rhine, from the Falknis to the Lake of Constance, and of the gorge of the Ill, is obtained from the '**Margarethenkapf** (1828'), a hill ½ hr. to the W. of Feldkirch, on the left bank of the Ill, with the villa and grounds of Herr v. Tschavoll. (Ascend to the right beyond the lower bridge over the Ill; admission by cards obtained at the hotels in the town or on presentation of a visiting-card. The villa contains excellent pictures by Matt. Schmid, illustrating local legends.) — Similar views from the **Veitskapf** on the Ardetzenberg, on the opposite (N.) side of the gorge of **the Ill** (road ascending to the right on this side of the bridge; 20 min.), and from Maria-Grün (Restaur. with garden), ¹/₂ hr. to the S., reached by ascending from the lower bridge over the Ill to the left by the *Leize* (return by the upper bridge). The *Stadtschrofen*, 10 min. from Maria-Grün, affords a pretty glimpse of the town.

Pleasant excursion by the **prettily-situated village** of *Amerlügen* (Inn) to the (2¹/₂ hrs.) **Aelpele** (4545'), a splendid point of view. Thence ascend the (1¹/₂ hr.) *Rojaberg* (*Frastanzer Sand*, 5850'), another fine point. Ascent of the **Drei Schwestern** (6880'; 3¹/₂ hrs.; guide from Feldkirch 4¹/₂ fl.), viâ the *Sareuen-Alp* and the *Garsella-Alp*, fatiguing, and to be attempted only by adepts. Guide, Ign. Steurer ('Rothgärtner') of Feldkirch.

From **Feldkirch** to **Buchs**, 11 M., railway in ³/₄ hr. The line skirts the Ardetzenberg (p. 198), crosses the *Ill* at *Nofels*, traverses the plain of the Rhine to *Nendeln* and *Schaan* (2 M. to the S. of which is *Vaduz*, see below), and near *Buchs* crosses the Rhine (comp. *Baedeker's Switzerland*).

From **Feldkirch** to **Matenfeld**. About 9 M. to the S. of Feldkirch (2 M. from Schaan, see above), lies **Vaduz** (1525'; °*Linde; Engel; Löwe*), the capital of the small principality of Liechtenstein (42 sq. M. in area), at the base of the *Drei Schwestern* (see above). The castle of *Liechtenstein*, or *Vaduz*, stands on a (20 min.) hill which overlooks the picturesque little town and affords a charming view (Inn). The road continues to traverse the plain of the Rhine, skirting the mountains, and at (8 M.) *Triesen* (Adler) approaches the river. Beyond (3¹/₂ M.) *Balzers* (°Post, good wine), by the St. Katharinen-Brunnen (1605'), the boundary of the Canton of the Grisons is reached. The road now ascends between the *Falknis* (8420') on the left and the *Fläscherberg* (3045') on the right, to the (3¹/₂ M.) **St. Luziensteig** (2885'), a fortified pass. The highest blockhouse commands a magnificent prospect. Then a descent by the Swiss custom-house (Inn, wine) and the ancient *Church of St. Lucius* to (1¹/₂ M.) *Mayenfeld* (1706'; Rössl; Sonne), a railway-station opposite Ragatz (see *Baedeker's Switzerland*).

Above and below Feldkirch the Ill has forced a passage through the limestone rocks by means of the *Obere* and *Untere Illklamm*. The train passes through a tunnel below the Schattenburg, enters the Obere Klamm, and crosses the Ill. — 25¹/₂ M. **Frastanz** (1500'; *Kreuz; Löwe*), at the entrance to the *Saminathal*, from which tower the jagged crests of the *Drei Schwestern* (6880').

The *Gurtisspitze* (5880'), ascended by *Gurtis* in 4 hrs., commands an admirable view (guide necessary).

A rough path leads through the wild and narrow **Saminathal** viâ *Amerlügen* (see above) and the *Gaudenz Alp*, at the entrance to the *Vallorsch Thal*, to the (5 hrs.) *Steg Alp* (4240'). An easier road leads from Vaduz (see above) viâ *Triesnerberg* and the *Kulm* (4785') to the same point in 3¹/₂ hrs. Beyond the tunnel of the Kulm is the *Sücka Alp* (Rfmts.) from which we survey the Saminathal from the Naafkopf to the Lake of Constance. Thence to the *Steg Alp*, ¹/₂ hr. To the E. of Steg opens the *Malbun-Thal* (1¹/₂ hr. to the *Malbun-Alp*, 5655'), out of which a pass leads to the E. over the *Sareiser Joch* or *Seves-Joch* to the *Gamperton-Thal*. The easy and attractive ascent of the **Schönberg** (6900') may be made in 2 hrs. from the Malbun-Alp, viâ the shooting-box of *Sass* and the *Schaaner Fürkele* (pass to the Vallorschthal). The **Gallinakopf** (7205'), ascended in 3 hrs. viâ the Schaaner Fürkele and the *Matter-Alp*, is another interesting point; the descent may be made from the Matler-Alp to the *Vallorsch-Thal* (see above), or by the *Guschgfieljoch* to the *Gump-Alp*, and through the *Gallinathal* to *Latz* and (4 hrs.) *Frastanz*. — A cart-track leads from Steg through the upper Saminathal to (³/₄ hr.) *Valüna* (4580'), the last Alp, whence the Naafkopf (*Grauspitze* or *Rothewand*, 8425') may be ascended in 3¹/₂ hrs., by the *Gritsch Alp* and the saddle of *Vermales* (pass to the Gamperton valley). — From Valüna over the *Jes-Fürkele* (*Samina-Joch*, 7795') to (6 hrs.) *Seewis* in the Prätigau, an attractive route.

The valley, from this point to Bludenz called the *Inner-Walgau*, now expands. The train crosses the *Gallinabach* and follows the left bank of the Ill to (30 M.) **Nenzing** (1655'; *Sonne; Zur Gamperdona*), a large village at the mouth of the *Gamperton-Thal*. On a hill 1/2 hr. to the W. is the ruin of *Ramschway* (2100'; fine view).

The picturesque *Gamperton-Thal* will repay a visit. A good path leads first on the right and then on the left bank of the *Mankbach*, which flows through the valley between the precipices of the *Exkopf* and *Ochsenkopf* on the right and those of the *Fundelkopf* on the left, to (4 hrs.) the *Gamperton-Alpe*, with the church of *St. Rochus* (4470'), in a beautiful basin called the *Nenzinger Himmel* (club-hut; **Inn** zur Himmelssonne). The ascent of the *Naafkopf* (8425') from St. Rochus, viâ the *Vermales-Alpe*, 4 hrs. (guide) is interesting; so also that of the *Fundelkopf* (*Matschonspitze*, 7868'; 4 hrs.; with guide). Passes: W. over the *Sareiser-Joch* to the *Malbun-Thal* and *Samluathal* (p. 193); E. over the *Matschon-Joch* and the *Patäd-Alpe* to (4 hrs.) *Braud* (p. 201); S. over the *Grosse Furka* (*Barthümmel-Joch*, 7195'), between the *Naafkopf* and *Ochsenberg*, or over the *Kleine Furka* (*Salaruel-Joch*, 7420'), between the *Horaspitze* and *Panülerschroffen*, to **Seewis**.

The train crosses the *Münkbach* and the Ill, and reaches (32 M.) *Strassenhaus*, the station for the *Grosse Walserthal*, at the foot of the **Hohe Frassen** (p. 201).

THROUGH THE GROSSE WALSERTHAL TO THE SCHRECKEN, 11 hrs., a fine route on the whole (guide necessary from Buchboden to the Schrecken). A carriage-road (omn. from Bludenz to Thüringen twice daily; fare 40 kr.) leads from **Strassenhaus** viâ *Ludesch* to (1½ M.) **Thüringen** (1800'; *"Hirsch"*), a village with large factories, at the entrance to the valley. We now ascend a cart-track to the right, which runs high up on the right side of the valley of the *Lutzbach*, making numerous descents into the transverse ravines from the N., and leading to (1½ hr.) *St. Gerold* (below which, on the right, is a monastery belonging to the Abbey of Einsiedeln) and (1½ hr.) *Blons* (2975'; opposite lies *Raggal*). It then descends past the mouth of the *Garsella-Tobel* to the Lutzbach, and remounts to (1½ hr.) **Sonntag** (2915'; *"Löwe; Krone"*), the capital of the valley, where the cart-road ends. (Thence by *Fontanella* and over the *Faschina-Joch* to *Damüls* and *Au*, see p. 208.) [An excellent route for pedestrians from Bludenz to the Walserthal leads viâ *Latz* and *Ludescherberg*, and round the flank of the *Hohe Frassen*, to (2½ hrs.) **Raggal** (Röss), at the entrance to the *Marulthal* (route to *Alp Laguiz, Formarin*, etc., see p. 212); it then descends into the deep *Lasanka-Tobel*, whence it remounts to *Plazera, Garsella* (where it crosses the *Lutzbach*), and (2 hrs.) *Sonntag*.] — From **Sonntag** we follow the right side of the valley to (1½ hr.) *Buchboden* (3010'; Inn, plain), opposite the entrance to the *Hattler-Thal*. (Viâ the Alp *Klesenza* to *Laguiz*, see p. 212.) In the *Rothenbrunnen-Tobel* (on the left bank of the Lutzbach), ¾ hr. above Buchboden, are the chalybeate baths **and inn** of *Rothenbrunn* (3100'; rustic). Beyond Buchboden we follow the right bank for ½ hr. more, and then ascend sharply to the left (path bad at places), past the *Alp Itschgerney* (on the left, above us), to the (3 hrs.) **Sehadona-Sattel** (5975'), between the *Rothhorn* on the right and the *Kunzelspitze* (ascent from the pass in 2 hrs.) on the left. Fine retrospect of the Walserthal, the Seesaplana to the S.W., the Kleinspitze to the S., and the pyramidal Widderstein to the E.; far below us lies the little church of the *Schrecken* (p. 209), which is reached from the saddle in about 2 hrs. (part of the route in the valley is uphill).

Beyond Strassenhaus the train next passes *Nüziders*, a small watering-place, and the ruins of *Sonnnenberg*.

36 M. **Bludenz** (1905'; *"Bludenzer Hof"*, R. 1 fl., D. 1 fl. 20 kr.; *Seesaplana*, *"Arlberger Hof"*, all three near the station; *"Eisernes Kreuz, Post, Krone"*, in the town; good **beer** at the *Fohrenburg*

Brewery, 1/4 M. to the W.), a place of 2100 inhab., is prettily situated. Above it rise the church and the château of *Gayenhofen* (now government offices). To the S. is the picturesque ravine of the *Brandnerthal*, with the ice-peak of the *Scesaplana* and the broad snowy saddle of the *Brandner Glacier* in the background.

EXCURSIONS (guides, *Ferd. Heine*, *Fidel Khüny*, and *Chr. Neyer* of Bludenz; *Adam*, *Jacob*, and *Leonh. Beck*, *Phil. Bitschi*, *Bern.*, *Joh.*, and *Paul Meyer*, *Joh.*, *Simon*, and *Wolfg. Kegele*, and *Jos. Sugg* of Brand; tariff high, 'night-money' 1 1/2 fl. — A good survey of the environs is obtained from the (10 min.) refuge-hut of *Montiggel*, above the château (Restaurant); the view is more extensive from the *Ferdinandsruhe*, 20 min. higher up, towards the E. From this point we may follow the ridge to the *Hintere Ebene*, descend to the village of *Rungelin*, and return to the town (1 1/2 hr.) viâ the convent of *St. Peter* or the *Haide*.

The °**Hohe Frassen** (*Pfannenknecht*, 6480'; 3 1/2-4 hrs.; guide, not absolutely necessary, 4 fl.), ascended from Bludenz (several finger-posts), affords an admirable view of the Vorarlberg Alps (panorama by Waltenberger). The path ascends to the N.W. to the hamlet of *Obdorf*, descends across the *Galgentobel*, ascends in zigzags through meadows and wood, turns to the left at a small chapel and to the right by a bench (waypost) and reaches a second chapel. Beyond this it leads to the left, for a short distance through wood, passes the houses of *Muttersberg*, afterwards traverses underwood again, and ascends to the (3 hrs.) *Pfannenknecht-Alp* (Inn) and to the (3/4 hr.) top.

To THE LÜNER SEE AND THE SCESAPLANA, a very interesting excursion. To (2 1/2 hrs.) Brand there is a narrow carriage-road, thence to the (3 1/2 hrs.) Douglashütte a footpath. Leaving the station, we cross the Ill to (1/4 hr.) *Bürs*, cross the *Alvierbach*, and ascend to the right, through wood, to (1 hr.) *Bürserberg* (2850'), prettily situated on the deep *Gschisertobel*, or *Schesatobel*. The charming *Brandner Thal* is now traversed; on our left rise the *Wasenspitze* (6588') and *Zimbaspitze* (8600'); opposite us is the *Scesaplana* with the *Brandner Glacier*; to the left, below us, is the deep gorge of the Alvierbach. In 1 1/4 hr. we reach Brand (3275'; °*Beck*, moderate, 'pens' 1 fl. 80 kr.; *Kegele*, well spoken of), prettily situated at the base of the *Mottenkopf*. (Over the *Matschon-Joch* to the *Gamperton-Thal*, see p. 200.) We now cross the stream and follow its right bank to the *Schattenlagant Alp*. On the right are the precipices of the Scesaplana, with several cascades, and farther on those of the Zirmenkopf or Seekopf, with large masses of debris at their base; on the left is the Saulenkopf. At the head of the valley a waterfall, the discharge of the Lüner-See, issues from the rock on the left. Here we turn to the right and ascend in zigzags over slopes of loose stones at the base of the Seekopf to the rocky saddle on the N.W. side of the picturesque dark-green °**Lüner See** (6310'), 4 M. in circumference, the largest lake among the Rhætian Alps. On the W. side is the (3 1/2 hrs.) *Douglashütte* (Inn in summer, bed 1 fl.). A boat may be obtained here for a row on the lake.

The ascent of the **Scesaplana** (9720'; 3-4 hrs.), the highest peak of the Rhätikon chain, is rather fatiguing, but without danger. (Guide, including night-fee, from Bludenz 9 1/2, from Brand 7 1/2, with descent to Seewis 15 1/2 or 13 1/2 fl.) The route from the club-hut skirts the lake for a short way, and then ascends to the right, at first over grassy slopes, and afterwards over debris and rocks (*Todten-Alp*). Lastly we climb through a rather steep gully to the arête, which we then follow without difficulty to the summit. The magnificent view embraces the whole of Swabia as far as Ulm on the N., the Vorarlberg and Algäu Alps to the N.E., the Oetzthal, Stubai, and Zillerthal Alps to the E., and to the S. and W. the Swiss Alps from the Silvretta and Bernina to the Gotthard and the Bernese Alps, the Prätigau, the valley of the Rhine, the Appenzell Mts., and the Lake of Constance; immediately below us on the N. are the extensive Brandner Glacier and the Brandner-Thal. — Descent to the *Schamella Club Hut* and to (3 hrs.) *Seewis* in the Prätigau.

see *Baedeker's Switzerland*. — From the Läner-See through the *Rellsthal* or the *Gauerthal* to *Schruns*, see p. 211.
From Bludenz to the *Montavon*, see p. 213.

At the nunnery of *St. Peter* the *ARLBERG RAILWAY quits the Ill, which here issues from the *Montavon* (p. 213), and enters the *Klosterthal*, watered by the *Alfenzbach*. A beautiful view up the valley is soon disclosed; on the left rises the *Rogelskopf* (7448'), At (40½ M.) **Bratz** (2310'; *Löwe; Rössl) the line leaves the bottom of the valley and begins to ascend along the N. slope. Viaducts and tunnels follow each other in rapid succession. Traversing three tunnels and crossing the *Schanatobel Bridge* (85 yds. long), the train stops at (43½ M.) **Hintergasse** (2700'), beyond which it crosses the *Griffettobel*. Then follow a vaulted cutting (snow-shed), a tunnel (132 yds. long), in the *Engelwäldchen*, a bridge over the *Brunnentobel*, and the *Engetwand Tunnel* (303 yds. long). To the right, as we emerge from the last, is the *Fallbachwand*, with a pretty waterfall. A huge viaduct, 130 yds. long and 160' high, next carries the line over the *Schmiedtobel*, and beyond two tunnels, another viaduct, 138 yds. long, spans the *Hötlentobel* (to the left the precipitous crags of the *Saladinaspitze*, 7306').

46 M. **Dalaas** (3055'; *Paradies*, well spoken of), the station lying 300' above the village (*Post*) which is charmingly situated far below to the right. From the station we obtain a beautiful view down the valley to the Sentis; to the N.W. the Rogelskopf; to the N. the Saladinaspitze and Pfaffenspitze; and to the E. the Burtschakopf. — To the (4 hrs.) *Formarin-See*, see p. 212.

FROM DALAAS TO THE MONTAVON over the Kristberg (4875'), an interesting route (guide unnecessary; 4 hrs. to Schruns). From the Post we ascend by a steep route through the woods, past a chapel, to (2 hrs.) the top of the pass, with a crucifix; fine view of the Silberthal, Lobspitze, Sulzfluh, Seesaplana, etc. Descent to the interesting Gothic *Chapel of St. Agatha*, and thence by a good path to the right across pastures to the conspicuous church of (1¼ hr.) *Inner-Bartholomäberg*, or *Innerberg* (3770'), from which we descend to the left to (¾ hr.) *Schruns* (p. 213).

Beyond Dalaas the line skirts the mountain-slope at a considerable elevation, commanding a splendid view up the valley (on the left the Rhonspitze, and on the right the Albonkopf). Then across the picturesque *Radona Gorge* (viaduct, 87 yds. long) and two smaller torrents (in the valley to the right is *Wald*) to (49½ M.) *Danöfen* (3520'; to the *Spullersee* and *Schafberg*, 6 hrs., see p. 212). The train crosses the *Spreubach* (p. 212); looking back we obtain a brief glimpse of the *Seesaplana*, adjoining the dark *Timskopf*. Traversing a long snow-shed, the train next reaches the fine *Bridge* which spans the *Wäldlitobel* with a single arch (206' high, 140' wide). In the valley to the right is *Klösterle* (3470'; Löwe), at the mouth of the narrow *Nenzigast-Thal*. At the head of the latter rises the *Kalteberg* (9500') with the *Wildebene Glacier* (ascent fatiguing, 6 hrs., with guide; comp. p. 204). — 52½ M. Langen (3990'; Railway Restaurant; *Post; Zum Arlberg).

FROM LANGEN TO ST. ANTON BY THE ARLBERG (4 hrs.), a very interesting route for pedestrians. The Arlberg road, passing the end of the great tunnel (see below), ascends through a wild and sequestered valley, and crosses the Alfenz four times in rapid succession. On the left rise the *Rhonspitze* and *Erzberg*. ³/₄ hr. **Stuben** (4650'; *Sonne*), the last village in the valley. (Over the *Flexensattel* to *Lech*, see p. 211.) The road ascends in windings, which afford fine retrospects of the Klosterthal as far as the Seesaplana, with the Erzberg and Roggelspitze on the left, and the Peischelkopf on the right. It then traverses a bleak valley to the (1³/₄ hr.) **Arlberg Pass** (5895'), the watershed between the Rhine and Danube, and the boundary between the Vorarlberg and the Tyrol. Snow frequently lies here in the early summer. View limited. On the E. side, ¹/₄ M. from the summit, is the old hospice of *St. Christoph*, with a small chapel. The road descends to (20 min.) the *Kalte Eck*, then turns sharply to the left. Fine view, on the right, of the Patteriolspitze, the Kartell Glacier, the Riffler, etc.; before us rise the mountains of the Stanzer-Thal as far as the Eisenkopf and Parseier Spitze. Then a winding descent past the *Waldhäusl Inn*, and through the *Rosanna-Thal*, to (1¹/₄ hr.) *St. Anton* (see below).

The train now crosses the Alfenzbach, and after affording us a glimpse to the left of the Erzberg and Trittkopf, plunges into the great *Arlberg Tunnel. This tunnel, 6³/₈ M. (or 10¹/₄ kilomètres) long, 26' wide, and 23' high (3 M. shorter than the St. Gotthard Tunnel) was begun in June, 1880, and was finished in November, 1883; the total cost of construction was 16 million florins (about 1,300,000*l*.). It ascends at a gradient of 15:100 to its highest point (4300'; 1595' below the Arlberg Pass), and descends thence at a gradient of 1:50 to St. Anton. The kilomètres are marked by numbers (I-IX) on coloured lamps. The transit (very smoky) lasts 20-25 min., and the temperature is 59°-64° Fahr. An obelisk, to the left of the E. end of the tunnel, bears a portrait in relief of *Jul. Lott* (d. 1883), the first chief engineer of the line. Beyond the tunnel the line curves to the left, and enters the station of —

59 M. **St. Anton** (4270'; *Post; Adler; Rail. Restaurant*), the highest village in the Rosanna-Thal, which above St. Anton is called the *Fervall-Thal*, and below it the *Stanzer-Thal*. This village is an excellent centre for excursions.

EXCURSIONS AND MOUNTAIN-ASCENTS (comp. Map, p. 216; guides, *Jos. Ladner*, *Alois Schwarzhans*, *Ferd. Matdies*). The **Moosthal** repays a visit (guide not indispensable). The route crosses the Rosanna opposite the E. end of the tunnel, and ascends to the right, mostly through wood, to (2 hrs.) the *Vordere Taya* (chalet) of the *Rossfall-Alpe* and past the poor huts of the *Hintere Taya* (*Geisslerhütten*; 6400') to the (2 hrs.) grandly situated *Darmstädter Hütte* (6900'), built by the German Alpine Club in 1888. Fine view of the imposing head of the valley (Kartell Glacier, Rautekopf, Küchelspitzen, Kuchenspitzen; right the Faselfadspitze, Ochsenberglerkopf, and Sulzköpfe). A rough pass leads hence over the **Schneidjöchl** (about 9180'), between the *Seekopf* (9970') and the *Samspitze* (9910'), to (5-6 hrs.) *Ischgl* in the Patznaun (comp. p. 218; descent from the pass through the *Vergrössker* bad; better round the Seekopf and through the *Madleinerthal*). Over the *Kuchenjoch* to the *Konstanzer Hütte*, see below. — The **Ochsenberglerkopf** (9510'; 5 hrs., with guide), ascended through the Moosthal, and the **Rendelspitze** (9245; 4¹/₂ hrs., with guide), ascended by the *Fervall-Alpe*, are interesting points, easily accessible. — Still more interesting is the **Samspitze** (9910'), scaled in 5¹/₂ hrs. from the Hintere Taya viâ the *Hintere Kartell Glacier*; fine view of the Küchelspitze, Kuchenspitze, Silvretta, etc.

The **Fervallthal**, or upper Rosannathal (to the Konstanzer Hütte 3 hrs.

guide not indispensable), is also worth visiting. A tolerable path, branching
off to the left from the Arlberg road after about 1½ M., ascends along the
Rosanna, mostly through wood, and passing the entrance of the *Maroithal* (see below), reaches (2½ hrs.) the **Konstanzer Hütte** (6100'). This
hut, at the junction of the *Fasulthal* with the Fervallthal, is the starting-
point for the ascents of the *Patteriolspitze* (10,020'; dangerous from falling
stones; guide 9 fl.), **Küchelspitze** (10,205'; guide 10 fl.), and *Kuchenspitze*
(10,300'; guide 10 fl.), all three difficult and fit only for experts with perfectly steady heads; and also for the ascents of the *Scheiblerkopf* (9400'),
Kalteberg (see below), *Fasulspitze*, *Schönbleiskopf*, *Pflunspitzen*, etc. A
laborious pass leads from the Konstanzer-Hütte across the Kuchenjoch
(7875'), between the Kuchenspitze and the Scheiblerkopf, and over the
Küchel Glacier, into the *Moosthal* (p. 203; to St. Anton 7½ hrs.). — Another
fatiguing pass leads through the wild *Fasulthal* and over the **Schafbuchjoch** (about 8200') to (5 hrs.; from St. Anton 8 hrs.) *Mathon* in the Patznaun (p. 218); in ascending we enjoy fine views to the right of the Patteriol,
Fasul Glacier, etc., and to the left of the Kuchenspitze and Küchelspitze.

The route from the *Gaflnuer Winterjöchl* descends from the W., opposite the Konstanzer Hütte (comp. p. 215). — In the **Schönfervall**, or upper
Fervallthal, a path leads on the right bank of the Rosanna to the
(1½ hr.) *Hintere Brannwesinhütte*, where the route to the *Silberthaler
Winterjöchl* diverges to the right (7 hrs. to Schruns; see p. 213). About
1 hr. farther up, beyond the *Ochsenhütte*, the path quits the Rosanna and
ascends to the (1 hr.) flat saddle on the **Scheidsee** (or *Verbelluer Winterjöchl;*
7420'), grandly situated: to the N.E. is the Patteriol, N. the Valschavielkopf
or Albonakopf, W. the Strittkopf. Descent along the *Verbellabach*, with
a fine view of the Hochmaderer and Litzner group, to the (1½ hr.) *Inner-
Ganifer Alp*, where the path joins the route from the Zeinisjoch, and
to (1 hr.) *Patenen* (p. 214).

Route from St. Anton to *Stuben* by the *Arlberg Pass*, see p. 203. —
From the (1½ hr.) hospice of *St. Christoph*, the **Peischelkopf** (7900'), which
affords an admirable survey of the Fervall mountains, is easily ascended
in 2 hrs. — The **Galzig** (7180'), the summit of the Arlberg to the E. of
the pass, is ascended without difficulty from St. Anton, through the *Steissbachthal*, in 2½ hrs. (guide hardly necessary for experts); descent to
St. Christoph 1¼ hr. — Another easy ascent is that of the **Schindlerspitz**
(8600'), accomplished from St. Christoph in 3 hrs., or from St. Anton, via
the *Steissbachthal*, in 4½ hrs. Fine view; E. the Pärseierspitze, W. the
Zimbaspitze and Scesaplana. — The **Kalteberg** (9500'; 6 hrs., with guide),
a toilsome ascent, from St. Anton through the *Maroithal* (see above) or
from the Konstanzer Hütte through the *Pflunthal*. The summit affords a
magnificent view.

ACROSS THE ALMEJURJOCH INTO THE LECHTHAL, an easy and attractive
expedition (6½ hrs. to Steg; guide not indispensable for experts). Leaving
St. Anton, the route passes the hamlets of *Nasserein* and *Bach*, ascending
at the latter to the left on the bank of the *Schönbach*. Then to the right
through woods and across meadows to (3½ hrs.) the Almejurjoch (7300'),
on the W. side of the **Stanskogel** (*Gesteinsspitze*, 9040'), which may be
easily ascended from the pass in 1½ hr. (fine view). We descend through
the *Almejurthal* to (2 hrs.) *Kaisers* and (1 hr.) **Steg** (p. 241).

Beyond St. Anton the railway gradually descends through the
Stanzer Thal and crosses the Rosanna twice. Above, to the left, is
the hamlet of *St. Jacob*. In front of us fine view of the *Eisenkopf*
(9250'), and the limestone cliffs adjoining it on the N.; to the right
are the *Riffler* and the *Blankahorn* (p. 205), with its precipitous
glacier. — 62½ M. **Pettneu** (3925'); the village (3975'; *Adler;
Hirsch*), lies to the left, at the foot of the *Stanskogel* (see above).

EXCURSIONS (guides, *Joh. Dicht*, *Jos. Muir*, *Jakob Müller*, *Al. Tschiderer*,
L. Zangerl). A pleasant and not difficult route leads across the **Kaiserjoch**
(7590') to *Steg* in the Lechthal (6 hrs.; route marked, guide not indispensable;

comp. p. 211). From the (2½ hrs.) *Kaiserjoch-Haus*, at the head of the pass, the *Grieskopf* (8530') may be ascended in ¾ hr. (splendid view).

The route to *Kappl* in the *Patznaun*, through the *Malfonthal* and over the Blankajoch (8810'), is somewhat arduous (6-7 hrs.; guide, Jos. Mair of Pettneu). The summit of the pass lies between the *Blankahorn* (10.350') and the *Weisskogel* (9765'); a little below it, on the S. side, are the small *Blanka-Seen*. — On the W. side of the Blankajoch, 3½ hrs. from Pettneu, in the *Upper Kapplerboden*, is the *Edmund Graf Hut* of the Austrian Tourist Club (about 8200'), from which the *Riffler* (N.E. and highest peak, 10,590') may be ascended in 3½ hrs. viâ the saddle between the Blankahorn and the Kleine Riffler (guide; not difficult for adepts). Magnificent and extensive panorama from the top.

The railway now crosses to the right bank of the Rosanna. To the left is **Schnann** *(Stanzer Wirth)*, at the mouth of the *Schnanner Klamm*, a gully of the Schnannerbach (worth visiting; there and back from Flirsch 2 hrs.). We cross the Rosanna twice more. — 67 M. Flirsch (3680'); the village (*Post), ½ M. to the N. on the left bank, is pleasantly situated at the base of the *Eisenkopf* (9252'). — Over the *Flirschjoch* or *Alperschonjoch* to the Lechthal, see p. 211.

The valley contracts; the rapid and brawling Rosanna forms several waterfalls. As far as Landeck the railway remains on the right bank, crossing successively the courses of the *Ganderbach*, the *Obere Klausbach*, and the *Untere Klausbach* (the second is carried across the line by an aqueduct, 70' broad). — 69½ M. **Strengen** (3940'), 125' above the village *(Post; Trientl)*, which lies to the left. The construction of the next portion of the railway (as far as Pians) was attended with great engineering difficulty, and its inspection well repays a walk from Flirsch or Strengen to Landeck. Supported by massive retaining-walls, the line is carried across the *Upper Moltertobel* (tunnel 60 yds. long, adjoined by an aqueduct 22 yds. long), the *Lower Moltertobel*, and the *Raurismuhre* (aqueduct 23 yds. long). Here opens a magnificent view down the valley as far as the Innthal; in the distance rises the pyramidal Tschürgant; and to the right is seen the large Trisanna viaduct. Then follows a tunnel, 220 yds. long, immediately beyond which an imposing *Bridge*, 280 yds. long and 180' high (central span 390'), crosses the *Trisanna*, which issues from the *Patznaunthal* (p. 219) and unites with the Rosanna to form the *Sanna*. Far below to the left is the covered bridge across which runs the road to the Patznaunthal. On the right bank, at the foot of the picturesque castle of *Wiesberg*, is the station of the same name (7½ M.; to the Patznaunthal, see p. 219). The line is now conducted along the *Majenwand*, high above the Sanna, by a series of viaducts and cuttings; it then crosses the *Ganderbach*, and reaches the station of —

72½ M. **Pians-Patznaunthal** (2900'). Below, to the left, on the other side of the river and at the mouth of the *Luttenbach*, lies the picturesque village of *Pians* (2730'; *Alte Post; *Neue Post, moderate); above it, on the verdant Mittelgebirge, is *Grins* (2320') and farther off is *Stanz*, at the base of the huge *Parscierspitze* (9955'); ascended from Grins in 6 hrs.; see p. 235.

The line now descends the right bank of the Sanna at a steep gradient to (74½ M.) *Perfuchs* (below, to the left, is *Bruggen*), and then, leaving the Stanzer-Thal in a wide curve, crosses the rapid *Inn* below Landeck, by a bridge with nine arches (170 yds. long and 60' high; central span, 196'). To the right we obtain a picturesque view of Landeck, dominated by the *Venetberg*; high up on the left rises the red church-tower of *Stanz*, at the base of the *Brandjöchl*; still farther to the left are the *Ochsenberg* and the *Parseierspitze*; and behind us the beautiful pyramid of the *Riffler* (p. 205). A lofty embankment now carries the railway over the high-road, and the train enters the station of —

76½ M. **Landeck** (2550'), situated 1¼ M. from the town (p. 234).

38. From Bregenz to the Schrecken. The Bregenzer Wald.
Comp. the Maps, pp. 8, 194.

The **Bregenzer Wald**, as the N. part of the Vorarlberg is called, is a diversified mountain-region watered by the *Bregenzer Ach*, and bounded by the Rhine, the Ill, the Lech, and the Iller. It is rich in beautiful scenery, which will amply repay the pedestrian. A distinction is made between the *Vordere*, or *Aeussere* (outer) *Wald*, a thickly-peopled hill-country, with moderate heights covered with grass and wood, and the *Hintere*, or *Innere Wald*, which in part exhibits the characteristics of an Alpine district. *Schwarzach* (diligence to *Bezau* twice daily in 5 hrs.) and *Dornbirn* (new road to Alberschwende, 6 M.) are the best starting-points for a visit to this district. The most interesting routes are to the *Schrecken* (about 40 M. from Schwarzach or Dornbirn) viâ *Schwarzenberg* or *Bezau*; and thence either to the *Arlberg*, or across the *Gentscheljoch* to *Obersdorf*.

Railway from Bregenz to (5 M.) *Schwarzach* in 22 min., see p. 196. The road ascends through the picturesque *Schwarzachtobel*, passing a slate-quarry and two inns, to (4½ M.) **Alberschwende** (2350'; *Taube*, plain), a prettily-situated village, with a handsome church containing good altarpieces by Deschwanden, whence a road diverges to *Dornbirn* (p. 197), and a pleasant path, marked with green and white, crosses the *Lorena* (3575') to (2 hrs.) *Schwarzenberg* (p. 207). The road then skirts the hill-side in a wide circuit, affording a splendid view of the valleys of the Rothach, Bregenzer Ach, and Weissach, which unite far below. At the (3 M.) *Krönle Inn* the road to Lingenau (see below) diverges to the left. After ¾ M. the road divides again, the rugged road to the right leading viâ *Wieden* and *Stangenach* to (3 M.) *Schwarzenberg* (p. 207), while the high-road descends into the valley and leads across the Ach and the *Schmidlebach* to (1½ M.) **Egg** (1835'; *Löwe; Adler*).

Travellers bound for Oberstaufen, or Oberstdorf viâ Hittisau, follow the road from the *Krönle* Inn (see above), which descends past *Müselbach* to the Ach, and then ascends to (6 M. from Alberschwende) *Lingenau* (Ochs), and (3 M.) Hittisau (2715'; *Krone*), a large village, beautifully situated on the hill between the *Bolgen-Ach* and *Subers-Ach*. [Excursions: to the *Hüttsberg* (4350'; 2 hrs.) and the *Hochhäddrich* (5128'; 2½ hrs.) with fine views; through the *Lecknerthal* to (1½ hr.) the small *Leckner-See* (refreshments at the *Höfle-Alpe*), and across the *Lehen-Alpe* to

to the Schrecken. SCHWARZENBERG. *V. Route 38.* 207

the top of the (3 hrs.) *Hochgrat (Fahnengrat; 6170').* To *Oberstdorf* viâ *Sibratsgfäll* and *Rohrmoos*, see p. 13.] — A road (diligence thrice daily) leads from Hittisau towards the N. viâ *Riefensberg*, to (6 M.) *Springen* (custom-house) and then follows the *Weissachthal*, past *Ach* and *Weissach*, to (6 M.) *Oberstaufen* (p. 5). — FROM LINGENAU TO EGG (4½ M.): the road descends in windings into the ravine of the Subers-Ach, and then re-ascends viâ *Grossdorf*. A shorter path (through the *Alte Tobel*) diverges to the right, 10 min. to the S. of Lingenau (to Egg, 1 hr.).

[**Schwarzenberg** (2275'; **Hirsch*, D. 90 kr.; *Lamm; Krone*), charmingly situated at the foot of the *Hochälple* (see below), affords pleasant quarters for a prolonged stay (chalybeate spring). The church contains an altarpiece (Glorification of the Virgin) by Angelica Kaufmann (b. at Coire 1741, d. at Rome 1807), whose parents lived here, as a memorial tablet below a marble bust of the artist in the left aisle of the church records. The *Angelikahöhe* (10 min.) commands a charming view.

Footpath across the *Lorena* to *Alberschwende*, see p. 206. An enjoyable, but more fatiguing path crosses the *Lose* (3645') to (3 hrs.) *Dornbirn* (p. 197), or, descending to the right beyond the pass, and skirting the wood, to (3 hrs.) *Schwarzach*. The °*Hochälple* (4706') rises immediately to the S. of the saddle, from which it is easily ascended in 1 hr. It affords a fine view of the Bregenzer Wald, the valley of the Rhine, the Lake of Constance, and the mountains of Appenzell (refuge-hut near the top). — The direct route from Schwarzenberg to the top of the Hochälple ascends to the right by the 'Hirsch'; where the road divides, we may either take the bridle-path to the right, or the shorter footpath to the left; beyond the last four chalets we take (½ hr.) the path to the left, which leads in 20 min. to two huts just below the wood; at the first of these our path turns to the right, towards the corner of the wood, and then traverses the wood; ¼ hr., chalets; ¼ hr., other chalets (refreshments). Our route, however, enters the wood to the right before reaching these last chalets, and ascends the slope to (¾ hr.) the grass-grown summit.

FROM SCHWARZENBERG TO MELLAU (6 M.). A narrow road descends to the S. from Schwarzenberg, passing the hamlet of *Loch* and crossing a torrent, to the Ach, which here flows through a rocky gully. The bold new *Bersbuch Bridge* (beyond which a path leads up to the road from Egg to Bezau, see below) remains on 'the left. We then proceed through wood on the left bank, passing (1 M.) a second bridge. [The road to Bezau runs on the right bank; those who wish to proceed thither cross this bridge and turn to the right.] The road to Mellau, which now becomes broader, keeps to the left bank, passing (1 M.) *Hof*, (¾ M.) *Bayen*, and (¼ M.) a third bridge (to the right the conical *Mittagspitze*, 6860'). On the right bank lies the hamlet of *Ellenbogen*, whence roads lead to (left; ¾ M.) *Bezau* and (right; 1 M.) *Reute* (p. 208). Our road follows the left bank, winds round the wooded *Bayenberg*, and leads past *Klaus*, where the footpath from Reute joins the road on the left, beside the covered bridge (see p. 208), to (3 M.) *Mellau*.]

FROM EGG TO BEZAU. The road follows the right bank of the Ach to (1½ M.) *Andelsbuch*, ½ M. to the E. of which are the chalybeate baths of that name (moderate; adjacent is **Dr. König's Hôtel-Pension*). Then past *Büchl* and *Bersbuch*, and round the projecting *Bezegg* (see p. 208) to (6 M.) **Bezau** (2090'; **Gemse*;

Post; Restaurant Bär, prettily situated on the Bezegg road, 1/2 M. from the village), the chief place of the Innere Wald, and seat of the district court. A private house contains eight pictures by Angelica Kaufmann, which are shown to visitors (fee).

A path (shorter than the road) leads from Büchl across the **Bezegg** (3165') to Bezau in 1 1/4 hr. On the top (halfway) a Gothic column has been erected as a memorial of the wooden Rathhaus, in which the 'popularly elected Landammann and Council of the Innere Bregenzer Wald' managed the affairs of the community for several centuries, and which stood here till 1807. — A few min. to the S. of this point is a fine mountain-view.

FROM BEZAU TO MELLAU (3 1/2 M.; diligence to Au daily in 2 hrs.; two-horse carr. 8 fl.). The road crosses the Ach at *Ellenbogen* (p. 207). About 3/4 M. to the S., in the pleasant *Bizauer Thal*, are the small chalybeate baths of *Reute* (plain, but good), whence a path, affording pretty views, crosses the *Hebung* (2425') to *Hinterreute*, and to the *Klausbrücke* over the Ach (to Mellau in 1 hr., see p. 207).

Mellau (2365'; *Bär*, with chalybeate baths, pens. 2 fl. 40, bath 30 kr.; *Sonne; Adler*), charmingly situated in a finely-wooded valley, is recommended for a prolonged stay. To the S.E. rise the precipitous walls of the *Canisfluh* (6696'); on the W. opens the narrow *Mellenbach-Thal*, between the *Hohe Koien* and *Guntenhang*, with the *Hohe Freschen* in the background.

EXCURSIONS (guide, Matt. Wüstner). Ascent of the *Mörzelspitze* (5991'), through the Mellenbachthal, 3 1/4 hrs. (view limited towards the S.). — The Hohe Freschen (5566'), 7 hrs., with guide (4 1/2 fl.); better from Rankweil (p. 198). — The **Canisfluh** (6695), 4 1/2 hrs., with guide (4 fl.), rather fatiguing (better from Au, see below); the route crosses the *Hofstätten-Alp* and the *Canis-Alp*, and ascends steep grassy slopes to the summit (admirable view).

The road crosses the Ach, skirts the wooded slope of the *Gopfberg*, with the long ridge of the Canisfluh on the right, and leads viâ *Hirschau* to (3 1/2 M.) Schnepfau (2415'; *Krone; Adler*).

FROM REUTE (see above) TO SCHNEPFAU, more direct path in 1 1/2 hr by *Bizau* and the Schnepfegg (2915). At the top, near *St. Wendelins-Kapelle*, we enjoy a striking view of the Canisfluh, Mittagsfluh, etc.

The road follows the right bank of the Ach, between the Canisfluh on the right and the Mittagsfluh on the left, while the Kinzelspitze faces us. **3 M. Au** (2580'; *Krone*, good beer; *Rössle*, beyond the bridge), pleasantly situated in a broader part of the valley.

The interesting and not difficult ascent of the **Canisfluh** (6695'; see above) may be made from Au viâ *Argenstein* and the *Vorsässhütten* in 3 1/2 hrs. (guide). — A pleasant route leads to the GROSSE WALSERTHAL, through the *Damülser Thal*, which ascends towards the S.W. Skirting the right bank of the *Argenbach* as far as the *Hinterbödmen Alp*, we there turn to the left to the Faschinajoch (4920'), and descend to *Fontanella* and (6 hrs.) *Sonntag* (p. 200). — The road to (9 1/2 hrs.) RANKWEIL is also interesting. It first ascends the valley towards the Faschinajoch, then ascends to the right to (2 1/2 hrs. from Au) *Damüls* (4688': Inn, rustic), a loftily-situated village, from which the *Mittagspitze* (6860') may be ascended in 2 1/2 hrs., with a guide (not difficult for practised climbers). The route then leads on past *Oberdamüls* (4820') and the (1 1/2 hr.) Furkel (5905') into the *Laterner Thal*, and to (4 1/2 hrs.) *Rankweil* (p. 198).

Walkers need not return from the 'Rössle' to the high-road, but may follow the left bank until opposite (20 min.) *Lugen*, where a bridge crosses the Ach. The road (short-cut by a path through the meadows to the right) ends at (1/2 hr.) **Schoppernau** (2730'; *Krone; Adler*), the birthplace of F. M. Felder, the peasant-poet (d. 1869), to whom a monument has been erected in the churchyard. To the S. rises the imposing *Kinzelspitze* (7570'), and to the left, in the foreground, the pyramidal *Uenschellerspitze* (6676'). To *Mittelberg* via the *Starzeljoch*, see p. 10.

A good bridle-path ascends gradually from this point, past the small sulphur-baths of *Hopfreben* (3350'), to (2 1/2 hrs.) the **Schrecken** (4135'; *Ochs*, R. 60-80 kr.), a little village in a green basin, around which mountains rise to a height of 7000-8000 ft., covered with forest and pasture at their bases, and snow on their summits *(Juppenspitze, Mohnenfluh, Rothhorn, Kinzelspitze)*.

MOUNTAIN ASCENTS. *Widderstein (8305'), 4-4 1/2 hrs. from the Schrecken, not difficult for experts. Starting from (1 1/2 hr.) *Hochkrumbach* (see below) with a guide (P. Schwarzmann, the host of the inn, or one of his sons), we follow the path to the Gentscheljoch (see below), turn to the left from the pass, and ascend through a rocky basin on the S. side of the mountain (path recently improved) to the arête and (2 1/2 hrs.) the summit. Magnificent view of the Algäu and Lechthal Alps, the Tauern, the Œtzthal and Rhætian Alps, the Ortler, the Bernina, the Glarus and Appenzell Alps, and the Lake of Constance. — *Hochkinzelspitze* (7570'), 5 hrs. with guide, over the Schadona Pass (p. 200), fatiguing; *Mohnenfluh* (8335'), also fatiguing. — *Kleinspitze*, or *Braunarlenspitze* (8680'), 6 hrs., with guide, difficult.

PASSES. TO OBERSTDORF OVER THE GENTSCHELJOCH (8 1/2 hrs.), an interesting route. A tolerable bridle-path ascends past the small *Kalbl-See* to (1 1/2 hr.) *Hochkrumbach*, or *Krumbach ob Holz* (5620'; Inn, rustic), a scattered group of houses in a barren valley, inhabited in summer only. Hence we ascend to the left by a zigzag path across steep pastures to (1 hr.) the wooden cross on the summit of the **Gentscheljoch** (6480'), at the S.E. foot of the *Widderstein* (see above); fine retrospect of the Aarhorn, Mohnenfluh, etc. The descent (to the right) is steep and stony as far as the *Upper Gentschelalp*, or *Genstelalp* (5580'), after which it improves. The route then runs high up on the left side of the picturesque *Gentschelthal* (to the right the precipices of the *Liechtkopf* and *Zwölferkopf*), passing at one point along a sheer wall of rock, where it is protected by a low parapet, and leads to the *Lower Gentschelalp* (4270'). The path remains on the left bank of the brook, passes the hamlet of *Bödmen*, crosses the *Breitach*, and reaches (2 hrs.) *Mittelberg* (3980'; Krone), the principal place in the Kleine Walser or Mittelberger Thal. From this point to (4 hrs.) *Oberstdorf* there is a carriage-road (comp. p. 10). — To Oberstdorf via the *Haldenwangereck* or the *Schrofen Pass*, see p. 13.

FROM THE SCHRECKEN TO THE ARLBERG (to Stuben 5 hrs.; guide unnecessary). A good but steep bridle-path ascends the right side of the deep defile of the *Auenfeldtobel*, at first through wood. On quitting the wood (20 min.) we obtain a striking view of the Juppenspitze and Mohnenfluh, and, farther on, of the lofty Kleinspitze (Braunarlonspitze, 8680') with its glacier. After 1/4 hr. we reach the *Aelpele* (refreshments), traverse a broad basin between the Juppenspitze on the right and the Aarhorn on the left, where the Bregenzer Ach takes its rise, and ascend gradually to the *Auenfeld-Alp* (5730'). [Travellers from Lech keep to the right as far as the first chalet, then to the left to the Ach, cross in 5 min. to the right bank, and descend along it.] We now descend to the right, cross (1/2 hr.) a bridge, and ascend a wooded hill, on the other side of which we descend into the Lechthal (our path being joined on the left by that from *Warth*, p. 211), and cross the *Lech* to (40 min.) *Lech* (p. 211). Hence to (2 1/2 hrs.) *Stuben*, see p. 211. — From the Schrecken to the *Upper Lechthal* (to Reutte 16 hrs.), see R. 39; to *Bludenz* across the *Schadona Sattel* and through the *Grosse Walserthal*, see p. 200.

BAEDEKER, Eastern Alps. 6th Edit. 14

39. From Reutte to the Arlberg through the Upper Lechthal.

Comp. Maps, pp. 14, 8, 216.

Carriage-road (poor at places) to (33 M.) *Steg* (diligence daily in 8 hrs.), beyond which the route proceeds by cart-tracks and bridle-paths. The lower part of the valley is monotonous and offers few temptations to linger (driving preferable to walking), but the uppermost part (Tannberg) is highly picturesque and well worthy of a visit (more conveniently reached from the Arlberg or Schrecken, see pp. 209, 211).

Reutte (2770'), see p. 18. The road crosses the *Lech* to *Aschau*, and follows the left bank of the river viâ (2¹/₄ M.) *Höfen* (*Krone) to (3¹/₂ M.) **Weissenbach** (2890'; *Löwe*), with an interesting church. The road from the *Pass Gacht* (p. 22) here joins ours on the right; to the left (E.) is the *Thaneller* (7675').

A carriage-road leads to the E. to (1¹/₂ hr.) the *Ehrenberger Klause* (p. 18), viâ *Rieden* and across the saddle (3340') between the Schlossberg and Thaneller. — OVER THE TIRSENTRITTJOCH TO NASSEREIT (8 hrs.), a fatiguing and not very interesting route. A cart-track runs through the wooded gorge of the *Rothlechthal* to (2 hrs.) *Rinnen* (3935'; Inn, poor), whence the *Thaneller* (7675') may be ascended viâ the high-lying village of *Berwang* (4395'; *Rose) in 4 hrs. (fine view and refuge-hut on the summit; guide, Martin Riml at Berwang, 2 fl.). Beyond *Anrauth* and (1 hr.) the last village *Mitteregg* (4880'), the route traverses the ravine of the Rothlechbach to (2 hrs.) the *Hintere Alm* (6060'), where the valley turns to the E. Crossing the Tirsentrittjoch (5185'), at the N. base of the imposing *Heiterwand* (8055'), we then enter the bleak *Tegesthal*, and finally reach (3 hrs.) *Nassereit* (p. 20).

The road now returns to the right bank of the Lech. 3 M. *Forchach* (2970'); 3 M. farther on, beyond the narrow opening of the *Schwarzenwasserthal*, is *Stanzach* (3115'; Inn).

To the left opens the monotonous Namlosthal, with the hamlet of (2¹/₂ hrs.) *Namlos* (3870'), whence the *Wetterspitze* (8356'; fine view) may be ascended in 4 hrs. Easy passes lead hence eastwards viâ *Kelmen* (4490') to *Anrauth* (see above), and southwards viâ the *Grubegg* and the *Steinjöchl* (7215'), with a fine view, to the *Hochtenn-Sattel* (see below; to Imst 6 hrs.).

On the left bank of the Lech, at the mouth of the *Hornbachthal* (p. 13), appears *Vorder-Hornbach*, and farther on is *Mortenau*, at the foot of the *Glimmspitze* (8075'). — 3 M. **Elmen** (3130'; *Post*, rustic), rebuilt for the most part after a fire in 1881.

ACROSS THE HOCHTENN TO IMST, an interesting expedition of 6-8 hrs. (guide not needed by proficients; Erh. Wolf of Haselgehr recommended). Bridle-path through the *Bschlabs-Thal*, passing *Bschlabs* (accommodation at the curate's), *Boden* (Inn, rustic; guide, Lechleitner), and *Pfafflar*, to the (4 hrs.) Hochtenn-Sattel (6250'), to the N. of the *Muttekopf* (p. 234), whence we descend viâ *Alp Maldon* and through the *Salvesen Thal*, at the S. base of the massive grey *Heiterwand*, to (3¹/₂ hrs.) *Imst* (p. 234).

We next pass the *Rautherhof*, said to be the oldest house in the valley, and recrossing the Lech at *Unterhöfen*, reach (3¹/₄ M.) *Häselgehr* (3310'; Bräuhaus). To the S. opens the *Gramaisthal*, through which a fatiguing route leads viâ the *Kofelyras-Joch* (7720') to (9-10 hrs.) *Schönwies* (p. 234); farther on, at (1¹/₂ M.) *Unter-Schönau*, is the short *Griesthal*. — 2¹/₄ M. **Elbigenalp** (3400'; *Post), a large village pleasantly situated at the mouth of the *Bernhardsthal* (interesting gorge). *View from the *Calvarienberg*.

Farther on are the hamlets of *Untergiebeln* (*Hirsch) and *Obergiebeln*, at the latter of which Joseph Koch, the painter, was born in 1768. We cross the Lech once more to reach (3 M.) **Bach**, or **Lend** (3460'; *Traube), at the mouth of the *Alperschonbach*.

EXCURSIONS (guides. *Al. Knittel* and *Joh. Schiffer* of Elbigenalp, *Ans. Klotz* of Stockach). A bridle-path leads hence along the left bank of the brook to (4½ M.) the hamlet of *Madau* (4035'), where the valley divides into the *Rothtal* to the E., the *Parseierthal* to the S., and the *Alperschonthal* to the S.W. We follow the Parseierthal to (¾ hr.) the *Ochsenalpe* (4800'), whence we ascend to the left (steep, marked path) to the (2½ hrs.) **Memminger Hütte**, near the *Lower Seebi-See* (7380'). About 1 hr. farther on, in the upper part of the *Patrolthal* (p. 235), is the *Oberloch-Alp*, whence we may either descend to the E. to (2½ hrs.) *Lötz*, or ascend the (3½-4 hrs.) *Galschkopf* (9650'; new path; *View) and then descend to (1 hr.) the *Augsburger Hütte* (p. 235). The ascent of the *Parseierspitze* (9955') from the N. side is very difficult (better from the Augsburger Hütte, p. 235). — From the *Rothtal* a path leads across the *Lahmsjoch* (7900') and through the *Madriolthal* to *Lötz* and (9 hrs.) *Landeck* (p. 234). — From the *Alperschonthal* we may either cross the *Flirschjoch* (about 7870') to (7 hrs.) *Flirsch* (p. 205), or the *Alperschonjoch* (7610') to (6½ hrs.) *Schnann* (p.205).

Above *Stockach* we continue on the left bank of the Lech to (4½ M.) **Holzgau** (3635'; *Hirsch; *Post; *Bräu; *Bär*), a thriving village, picturesquely situated at the opening of the *Heckbachthal* or *Höhenbachthal* (over the *Obermädele-Joch* to *Oberstdorf*, see p. 13). The carriage-road passes *Hägerau* and ends at (4½ M.) *Steg* (3670').

To the S. opens the **Kaiserthal**, watered by the *Almejurbach*. At the village of (4½ M.) *Kaisers* (4970'; *Adler) the valley divides into the *Kaiserthal*, to the left, and the *Almejurthal*, to the right (viâ the *Kaiserjoch* or the *Almejurjoch* to the Arlberg Railway, see p. 204).

The valley now contracts. The bridle-path, at first on the right bank, crosses the Lech beyond *Ellenbogen*, and then rising high above the profound gorge of the stream, passes the opening of the *Hochulpenthal* (p. 13), and reaches (9 M.) **Lechleiten** (5050'; *Stern*), situated among green meadows at the foot of the *Biberkopf* (8515'; over the *Schrofen Pass* to *Oberstdorf*, see p. 13). A fine view opens here of the upper Lechthal with the Omishorn and Schafberg to the S.W., and the Warthorn and Widderstein to the W. The path now descends rapidly, and after crossing the *Krumbach*, a tributary of the Lech, again ascends to (¾ hr.) *Warth* (4900'; Rössle, poor), the first village of the *Tannberg*, or uppermost district of the Lech, prettily situated at the base of the *Warthorn*. From this point we may either turn to the right, and skirt the right bank of the Krumbach to (3 M.) *Hochkrumbach* (p. 209); or follow the good path to the left, leading round the slope of the Warthorn, through the deep gorge of the Lech, and passing below the highlying village of *Bürstegg* (5625'), to —

4½ M. **Lech** (4720'; *Krone*; *Adler*), the chief place in the Tannberg, picturesquely situated at the foot of the *Omishorn* (8438'; path hence viâ the *Auenfeldalp* to the *Schrecken*, see p. 209).

ACROSS THE FLEXENSATTEL TO STUBEN, 2½ hrs. A cart-road leads from Lech along the right bank of the *Zürsbach*, between

212   V. Route 39.   FORMARIN-SEE.

the *Omishorn* and *Rauchespitz*, past (1¼ hr.) *Zürs* (Inn, rustic), to (¼ hr.) the **Flexensattel** (5775'), which commands a view to the S. of the *Kalte Berg* (9500') and the *Wildebene-Ferner*. The road next descends on the right side of a deep and narrow valley, in which the *Stubenbach* forms a series of cascades, winding along a precipitous rocky slope. It then crosses the brook and joins the Arlberg road above (1 hr.) *Stuben* (p. 203).

FROM LECH BY THE FORMARIN - ALP TO DALAAS, 6 hrs., interesting (guide advisable; provisions should be taken). The track follows the left bank of the Lech to (¾ hr.) *Zug*, where the path to the Spuller-See across the Bratzer Staffel diverges to the left (see below), and to the (1 hr.) *Aelple*, with a large cheese-dairy, situated on a broad expanse of meadow-land; on the left rises the *Schafberg*, and facing us are the *Johanneskopf* and *Hirschenspitze*. After ½ hr. the path crosses the Lech, and ascends to (10 min.) the *Tannleger-Alp* (fine retrospect); on the left opens the *Kälberthal*, through which runs another path to the (3 hrs.) *Spuller-See*, viâ the *Spullers-Alpe* and *Dalaaser Staffel*. In ¼ hr. more we recross the brook and ascend its left bank. In its bed are several stoplike terraces, the water trickling from which forms a subterranean discharge of the Formarin-See, one of the sources of the Lech. In 1¼ hr. we reach the *Formarin-Alp* (6070'); 10 min., the small, green *Formarin-See (5980'), at the foot of the towering *Rothewandspitze* (see below). We may either walk round the lake by the N. and W. sides, or turn to the left and choose the shorter but inferior path on the E. slope to (½ hr.) the summit of the pass (6235'), which affords a view of the Rhaetikon, Sulzfluh, etc. The descent leads by (½ hr.) the *Ruckstaffel-Alp*, 5 min. below which is an excellent spring; thence in numerous windings to (¾ hr.) the *Mustarin-Alp*, on the right bank, and to the left to (1 hr.) *Dalaas* (p. 202). — TO THE WALSERTHAL AND BLUDENZ. A rugged path leads to the N.W. from the Formarin-See across the saddle between the *Pitschköpfe* and *Rothewandspitze* to (2 hrs.) the *Lagutz-Alp* (5050'; chalet), and then to the W., along the slope of the *Alpilla*, to *Garfälla* and (2 hrs.) *Marul* (Inn) in the *Marulthal*; opposite rise the wooded slopes of the *Hohe Frassen* (p. 201). The Marulthal unites about 1 hr. lower down with the *Grosse Walserthal* (p. 200; viâ *Garsella* to *Sonntag*, 2 hrs.). The route to Bludenz leads to the left across the deep *Lasankatobel* to (1 hr.) *Raggal* (Inn), and winds round the W. side of the *Hohe Frassen* to (2½ hrs.) *Bludenz* (comp. p. 201). — Ascent of the **Rothewandspitze** (8860') from the Lagutz-Alp in 4-5 hrs., with guide, difficult; shorter and easier from the *Klesenza-Alp*, 1 hr. to the N. of Lagutz, in the upper *Buttler Thal* (2 hrs. from Buchboden), which may be also reached from *Tannleger* (see above) direct, in 2½ hrs., by crossing the *Johannesjoch* (6920'), between the Rothewandspitze on the left and the Hirschenspitze on the right.

FROM LECH TO KLÖSTERLE BY THE SPULLER-SEE, 5 hrs., also interesting. At (¾ hr.) the village of *Zug* we cross the Lech to the left, and ascend the bank of the *Stierlochbach* to the *Stierloch-Alpe*, whence we cross the *Bratzer Staffel* to (2½ hrs.) the grandly-situated *Spuller-See (5710'; boat). To the N. rises the imposing °*Schafberg* (8780), the summit of which is easily reached from the lake in 3 hrs. (path recently improved; guide required); splendid view. The descent from the lake to (1½ hr.) *Klösterle* (p. 202), or to the right through the *Spreubach-Tobel* to (2 hrs.) *Danöfen* on the Arlberg railway, is steep.

40. The Montavon and Patznaun Valleys.
See also Maps, pp. 194, 216.

DILIGENCE from Bludenz to (3½ M.) *Schruns* twice daily (at noon and 6 p.m.) in 2 hrs. (fare 80 kr.); from Schruns to *Gaschurn* post-gig (three seats) daily, at 2.30 p.m., in 3½ hrs. (fare 1 fl. 20 kr.). If desired, the post-gig goes on to Patenen, but the last part of the road is very rough.

One-horse carriage from Bludenz to Schruns 3½, two-horse 6 fl.; from Schruns to Gaschurn 4 or 7 fl. Beyond Patenen driving is not practicable. A new road through the Patznaun valley was opened in 1887.

The **Montavon** (*davo*, 'behind'), or Upper Illthal, a well-wooded green valley, is inhabited by a race of Rhætian origin, as the names of many of the places still indicate, through German only is now spoken. This valley, which is separated on the S. from the Prätigau in the Grisons by the *Rhätikon Chain*, affords a number of attractive excursions, for which *Schruns* and *Gaschurn* form the best headquarters. A visit to the **Patznaun**, a wild and narrow valley, with beautiful Alpine pastures and famous for its cattle, has been facilitated by the construction of the new road (see above); the S. lateral valleys (Jamthal, Fimberthal) are especially interesting.

Bludenz (1905'), see p. 200. The road into the Montavon (new road in progress) intersects the Arlberg railway at the hamlet of *Brunnenfeld*, beyond *St. Peter* (p. 202), and crosses the *Alfenzbach* above its junction with the Ill. It then traverses the defile of *Stebösi*, crosses the Ill, and reaches (2¼ M.) *Lorüns*. (Road on the left bank to Vandans, see below.) The Ill is again crossed to (2¼ M.) *St. Anton* (Adler; Schäfle), a hamlet on a hill of debris at the base of the *Davennakopf*. The road then follows the right bank (opposite are *Vens* and *Vandans*, at the mouth of the *Rellsthal*, commanded by the bold *Zimbaspitze*, see p. 214), past the Inn *Zum Kalten Brunnen* and the Capuchin monastery of *Gauenstein*, to —

3¼ M. **Schruns** (2250'; *Löwe*, at the upper end of the village, D. 1 fl., S. 70 kr., 'pens.' 2½-2¾ fl.; *Taube*, R. 1½, D. 1 fl.; *Stern*, 'pens.' 2½ fl.; *Schäfle*; *Rössle*; *Pension Gauenstein*, ¾ M. to the W., with a fine view), the chief place in the Montavon, charmingly situated in a broad part of the valley, on the *Litzbach*, which descends from the *Silberthal*, and a favourite summer-resort.

WALKS. To the W. to the (20 min.) monastery of *Gauenstein*, with a charming view from the terrace (adm. on week-days, 9-10 and 4-5). — To the S.W. to (³/₁ M.) **Tschagguns** (*Löwe*), on the left bank of the Ill, at the mouth of the *Rosafeibach*, which descends from the Gauerthal. Hence we may ascend to the right viâ *Landschau* to (¾ hr.) *Ober-Landschau*, with a fine view of the Sulzfluh, Drusenfluh, etc.; or on the right bank of the Rosafeibach to the top of the (1 hr.) *Ziegerberg*, which also offers a good view. On the W. slope of the Ziegerberg, in the *Gampadellthal* (p. 214), is the simple *Bädle* (Inn), 1¼ hr. from Tschagguns. — **Vandans** (3 M.) may be reached either viâ Tschagguns and along the left bank of the Ill, or by following the road to Bludenz to (½ hr.) the *Inn zum Kalten Brunnen* (see above), crossing the Ill there, and taking the pretty woodland path to the village (Sonne), which is prettily situated at the entrance of the *Rellsthal*. A pleasant path leads on, chiefly through wood, viâ *Vens*, to (¾ hr.) *St. Anton*, or on the left bank of the Ill to (1 hr.) *Lorüns* (see above). — To (1¼ hr.) **Ausser-Bartholomäberg** (3625'): we cross the Litzbach (see above), ascend to the right by the guide-post, and then take the first path to the left, which leads past the *Inn zum Grünen Wald* to the high-lying church (Adler, plain). Good view of the Rhätikon chain, the Illthal, and Silberthal. Thence to the *Rellsereck* in 1¼ hr., a pleasant walk. To (1½ hr.) *Inner-Bartholomäbery* and over the *Kristbery* to (3 hrs.) *Dalaas*, see p. 202. — To the **Silberthal** (p. 214) we follow the pretty new road on the left bank of the *Litzbach*, and after about 1 hr. cross the stream. (To the village of *Silberthal*, 1 hr. more, by a monotonous road; see p. 214.) From this point we enjoy a fine retrospect of the Mittagspitze, Drusenfluh, Seesaplana, etc. — Another pleasant promenade is afforded by the shady road running to the E. Into the valley, along the base of the Gapelljoch, to (1 hr.) the hamlet of *Gampretz*, just on this side of the *Landbrücke* over the Ill (see p. 215).

MOUNTAIN ASCENTS (guides, *Christ. Zudrell, Jos. Bitschnau, H. Durig*, and *Franz Vergut*; high charges). *Monteneu* (6560'), an easy and attractive ascent, viâ Ausser-Bartholomäberg in 3½-4 hrs., with guide. — **Tanzkopf** (*Itonskopf*, 6810'; 3½-4 hrs., with guide), viâ Inner-Bartholomäberg, only slightly more difficult. — The *Vorder-Gapelljoch* (7800'; 5 hrs., with guide) is a very interesting point, commanding a highly picturesque view. The route leads by *Gamplasche* to (3½ hrs.) the *Vordere Gapell-Alpe*, and thence through the depression between the Gapelljoch and the Hochjoch (8255'), first to the N. peak and then to the slightly higher S. peak. The *Hochjoch*, which affords a still more extensive view, may be reached by the arête in 1½ hr. from the S. peak. The descent may be made on the N. side viâ the *Gampell Alpe* to Silberthal (see below), or on the S. (steep and toilsome) through the *Zamanglobel* to Gaflenkirch (p. 215). — **Mittagspitze** (7100'; 4 hrs.), viâ the Ziegerberg and *Alp Alpilla*, somewhat fatiguing; Schwarzhorn (8000'; 6 hrs.), toilsome. — Zimbaspitze (8680'; 8-9 hrs.), from Bludenz viâ the Brandner-Thal and Sarotla-Thal, very difficult, and fit for adepts only.

The ascent of the **Sulzfluh** (9200'; 7 hrs.; guide 7½, if kept overnight 9 fl.) is very interesting and not difficult. The route leads from *Tschagguns* to the left viâ *Ziegerberg* to (2¼ hrs.) the *Gampadal-Alpe* in the *Gampadel-Thal*. Beyond the Alp we turn to the right, ascend the meadow straight on for 10 min. (following the red marks), and again strike a path, leading along the slope of the *Schwarzhorn* (below to the left lies the *Walser Alpe*) to a rocky barrier, beyond which is (2 hrs.) the *Tilisuna-Hütte* (6010'; inn, bed 1 fl.), lying above the small blue *Tilisuna-See* (adepts may dispense with a guide to the Hütte; the landlord acts as guide hence to the summit, 2-3 fl.) Thence to the left to the *Verspalagrat*, then over a broad rocky plateau, and lastly across the uncrevassed *Sporer Glacier*, to the (2½ hrs.) summit, which commands a magnificent panorama. Descent viâ the *Bilkengrat* into the *Gauerthal* (see below) by a steep new path.

The *Lünersee* is reached by a route through the Rellsthal (from *Vandans* a steep ascent on the left bank of the Rellsbach) to the *Lüner Alpe*, and over the *Schafgafalljoch* (*Lüner Krinz*) to the lake (6 hrs. to the Douglashütte, see p. 201). A far preferable route (7 hrs.; guide 5½ fl.) ascends from *Tschagguns* viâ *Landschau* to the saw-mill on the *Geyensporn*, and thence across the Rosafeibach and along its right bank through the **Gauerthal**, passing the Mittagspitze and Schwarzhorn on the left, with a fine view of the imposing head of the valley (*Sulzfluh, Drei Thürme, Drusenfluh*). We next reach the *Untere* and the (3 hrs.) *Obere Sporer-Alp*, a group of forty huts in a basin on the S. side of the *Ocisspitze* (7658'). Then a steeper ascent through the *Ocfentobel*, and past a few patches of snow, to the (1½ hr.) **Oefen** or **Sporer Pass** (about 7875'; view of the Scesaplana on the W. and the Patznaun Mts. on the E.). The path now descends, past the imposing "*Schweizerthor* (7055'; peep of the Grisons), ascends again to the (1½ hr.) **Alp-Vera Jöchl** (7550'), and lastly descends to the left to the (1 hr.) *See-Alpe* and on the S. bank of the Lüner-See to the (½ hr.) *Douglashütte*. Ascent of the *Scesaplana*, and descent through the *Braudner-Thal* to *Bludens*, see p. 201.

To THE PRÄTIGAU, several passes. Through the *Rellsthal* and over the **Schweizerthor** (7055') to (10 hrs.) *Schiers* (steep descent). — From the Douglashütte across the **Gafalljoch** or **Cavelljoch** (7330') to Schiers or Seewis, 6 hrs., fatiguing. — From Tschagguns through the *Gauerthal* and over the **Drusenthor** (7220') to Schiers, 9 hrs., toilsome. The pass lies between the Sulzfluh and the Drei Thurnien. — Through the *Gampadel-Thal* to the *Tilisuna-Alpe* and over the **Partnun** or **Gruben Pass** (7280'), or over the **Plassegen-Joch** (7900'), to *Küblis* in 8 hrs., two attractive routes. (On the *Partnuner Staffel*, below the small lake of that name, is the "*Hôtel Sulzfluh*, finely situated; 5865'.) — The *St. Antönien-Joch* and the *Schlapina Joch*, see p. 215.

To ST. ANTON ON THE ARLBERG THROUGH THE SILBERTHAL, 11-12 hrs.;

guide and provisions necessary. We ascend the left and then the right bank of the *Litzbach* by a new path to the scattered village of (2 hrs.) **Silberthal** (2920'; *Hirsch*, well spoken of), with a bathing establishment. On the E. rises the *Lobspitze* (8545'; ascent through the *Wasserstubentobel*, in 5-6 hrs., fatiguing). The valley now contracts; the path ascends, generally through wood, first on the right and then on the left bank of the rapid Litzbach to the (2 hrs.) *Alp Gieseln* (4280'), where the valley bends to the E., and (1/2 hr.) the *Alp Unter-Gaſtuna*, at the mouth of the *Gaſtunathal* (see below). On the left tower the rugged *Geisslerspitzen*, farther on the *Madererspitze* (see below). The path through the Silberthal crosses to the right bank of the Litzbach and ascends through wood, past the *Fräsch-Alp* and the little *Pfannensee*, to the (2½ hrs.) **Silberthaler Winterjöchl** (*Fräschenlücke*, 6378'), between the *Trostberg* on the left, and the *Wannenköpfe* on the right; fine view of the bold *Patteriolspitze* (p. 204) to the E. Descent to the *Schönferrall* and (3 hrs.) *St. Anton* (p. 203).— The route through the *Gaſtuna-Thal* (see above), and over the *Gaſtuner-Winterjöchl* (7740') to (13 hrs.) St. Anton is fatiguing and devoid of interest.

Above Schruns the valley contracts; on the left is the *Zamungspitze* (7820'), on the right the *Geweilkopf* (8045'). The road crosses the Ill by means of the 'Landbrücke', and ascends rapidly through the *Fratte*, a defile which divides the Montavon into the *Ausser-* and *Inner-Fratte*. At *Kreuzgasse* a road diverges to the right to the *Gargellenthal* (see below), whence the *Suggadinbach* issues (with the *Madriser-Spitze*, 9075', in the background). Crossing this stream at *Gulgemuel*, farther on, we recross to the right bank of the Ill, pass a small cascade formed by the *Vermühlbach* on the right, and reach (6 M.) **St. Gallenkirch** (2730'; *Adler*; *Rössle*, moderate; *Kreuz*), situated on a hill at the mouth of the *Zamangtobel*. To the E. rises the *Vallülaspitze* (p. 216).

EXCURSIONS (guide, *J. A. Kessler*). **Zamangspitze** (7820'; 4-5 hrs., with guide), by the *Lifinar Alp*, toilsome but repaying. — A cart-track leads through the smiling Gargellenthal to *Reute* and (3 hrs.) *Gargellen* (5160'; Madriser Gasthof), a prettily-situated hamlet, to the S. of which are the *Schmalsberg*, the *Rietzenspitzen*, and the *Madriser-Spitze* (9075'), with a small glacier. About ½ hr. farther up the valley divides into the *Vergaldner-Thal* on the left and the *Vatzerſenz-Thal* on the right. A much-frequented route (guide not necessary, but advisable in the beginning of summer after snow; the sons of the inn-keeper Tschofen may be recommended) leads from Gargellen to the W. across the **St. Antönien-Joch** (7665') to (6 hrs.) *Küblis*; another to the S. over the **Schlapina-Joch** (7100') to (5 hrs.) *Klosters* in the Prätigau. The **Heimspitze** (9095'; 4½ hrs.; guide), ascended by the *Vergalda-Alpe*, and the **Madriser Spitze** (9075'; 5 hrs., guide), are two fine points (the latter is fit only for experts). — Over the *Vergaldner Jöchl* (8385') to the Ganera-Thal and Gaschurn, 7 hrs., rather fatiguing.

The hilly road follows the right bank, passing several solitary farm-houses and *Gurtepohl*, to (3½ M.) **Gaschurn** (3120'; *Rössle* or *Post*, R. 70, B. 40 kr., D. 1 fl., 'pens.' 2 fl. 30 kr.; crowded in summer), with a modern Romanesque church, prettily situated at the mouth of the *Ganerathal*.

EXCURSIONS (guides, *Rud. Kleboth*, *Vinc. Salner*). To the N. into the **Valschavielthal** as far as the *Valschavieler-Alpe* (2 hrs.), at the foot of the *Madererspitze* (see p. 216). — To the S., via (1¼ hr.) the *Ganeu-Alp*, to (½ hr.) the solitary *Ganera Lake* in the **Ganerathal**. About ¾ hr. beyond the lake is the poor *Ganera-Alp*, whence an arduous route leads across the *Ganera-Joch* (8160') to (6 hrs.) *Klosters* in the Prätigau. From the Ganerathal across the *Vergaldner Jöchl* to *Gargellen*, 4 hrs., see above.

— The **Schafbodenberg** (7700'), ascended viâ the *Alp Ganeu* in 4 hrs., the *Hochmaderer* (9255'), viâ the *Ganera-Alp* in 6 hrs., and the **Versailspitze** (7005'), viâ the *Ibau Alp* in 5 hrs., are all fine points and not difficult of access. More serious ascents are those of the Plattenspitze (9450'), reached through the Ganerathal in 8 hrs., and the **Madererspitze** (*Valschavieler Maderer*, 9075'; 7 hrs.), reached from the W. by the arête above the *Netzenthal*, to which we ascend through the Valschavielthal.

FROM GASCHURN TO ST. ANTON OVER THE GASCHURNER WINTERJÖCHL, 11-12 hrs., with guide, an interesting expedition. The route ascends by the *Valschavieler-Alp* and *Mardusa-Alp* to the (5 hrs.) Gaschurner Winterjöchl (about 7320'), between the *Strittkopf* and the *Atbonakopf*, with six lakelets and fine views of the Patteriolspitze and Maderer, and descends viâ the *Schönferwatt* to (6-7 hrs.) *St. Anton*. An easy and attractive route diverges at the Gaschurner Winterjöchl, and skirts the Strittkopf to (1 hr.) the *Verbetlner Winterjöchl* on the *Scheidsee* (p. 204); thence back to Patenen.

3 M. **Paténen** or *Parthenen* (3435'; *Sonne*, well spoken of), the last village in the Montavon, lies in a sequestered basin.

EXCURSIONS (guides, *Chr. Lerch* and *Pfefferkorn*, vulgo 'Essigwirth', the landlord of the Sonne). The **Vallüla**, or *Flammspitze* (9220'; 5-6 hrs.; guide 9 fl.), fit for experts only, is ascended by the *Vallüla-Alp* (or from the Madlenerhaus in 4-5 hrs.). View strikingly grand.

From Patenen to *St. Anton*, on the Arlberg Railway, over the *Verbetlner Winterjöchl* (10-11 hrs.; guide 12 fl.), see p. 202.

FROM PATENEN TO THE PATENAUN, two passes. The shorter crosses the **Zeinisjoch** (4 hrs. to Galtür; path marked with red and unmistakable). We begin to ascend beyond the last houses, cross (½ hr.) the *Verbeltabach*, recross (½ hr.) to the right bank, and reach the *Inner-Ganifer Alp* (on the left a fine waterfall). Thence the path ascends in steep zigzags, past a (¼ hr.) finger-post ('Weg nach Tirol'; to the left the path to the Verbellenthal, p. 204), through the *Flächeln*, a number of curiously weather-worn crags, to the shrine on the *Allhöh*, and thence across wet pastures to (3/4 hr.) the *Zeinis-Alp* (5970'; refreshments). The path then traverses a moor and reaches (20 min.) the summit of the pass (6075'), between the *Muhspitze* and *Fädnerspitze* or *Vettspitze* on the N., and the *Baltimspetze* on the S. side. (The Fädner-Spitze, 9140', with a fine view, may be easily ascended from the pass in 2½-3 hrs.) The path then descends past a large mass of rock to *Wirl* in the Patznaunthal. Then across the *Vermunibach* to (1½ hr.) *Galtür* (p. 217). — The longer, but much more interesting route leads through the **Vermunt-Thal** (to Galtür 6½-7 hrs.; path marked with red, but guide desirable). Above Patenen (¼ hr.) it crosses the Ill; in 10 min. more it returns to the right bank, and then ascends the *Gross-Vermunt-Thal* to a steep rocky barrier (*Cardatscha*), over which the Ill is precipitated in an imposing double fall (*Stüber Fall* or *Hölle*). To visit the fall (path indicated by marks), we cross to the left bank, 40 min. from the second bridge mentioned above, and ascend rapidly to the (35 min.) top of the rocky barrier, from which we may look down into the abyss (guarded by a railing). The path returns to the right bank ¼ hr. farther up, near the huts of *Schweizer-Vermunt*, and regains the direct route to the pass. View here of the picturesque *Litznergruppe* (*Plattenspitze*, *Seehorn*, *Klein-Litzner*, *Gross-Litzner*, and *Lobspitzen*) to the S., the *Hochmaderer* to the W., and the *Cresperspitze* to the E. The path, marshy at places, ascends gradually through the upper Vermunt-Thal, which soon turns to the E. (view, to the right, of the *Cromer That* with the Litzner glacier), passes the *Alp Gross-Vermunt*, and reaches the (1½ hr.) **Madlener**haus (about 6300'; inn in summer), 20 min. below the **Bielerhöhe**, or **Pillerhöhe** (6710'), which affords a survey of the grand environs. On the right rises the Lobspitze, on the left the pyramidal Hohe Rad; between the two lies the Ochsenthal with the Gross-Vermunt Glacier, the source of the Ill; to the left of the Hohe Rad is the serrated chain between the Vermunt-Thal and the Jamthal. [The *Hohe Rad* (9530'), affording an admirable survey of the Silvretta group, may be ascended from the Madlenerhaus in 3½ hrs., with guide (marked path, fit for experts only).]

Descent on the left bank of the Pillerbach through the wild *Klein-Vermunt-Thal* (to the left the *Vallüla*, to the right the *Hochnörderer-Spitze*), and past two small lakes to (2¼ hrs.) *Wirl* and (¾ hr.) *Galtür* (see below).

Over the "*Vermunt Pass* to *Guarda* in the Lower Engadine, 7 hrs. from the *Madlenerhaus*, a fatiguing route (better from the *Jamthalhütte*, see below).

OVER THE KLOSTER PASS TO KLOSTERS in the Prätigau, 7-8 hrs. from the Madlenerhaus, with guide, not very difficult. We ascend the *Klosterthal*, which branches off to the left, on the left bank of the Ill, and crossing a small glacier descending from the *Gross-Litzner* (the large *Klosterthal Glacier* lies to the left) reach (4 hrs.) the **Kloster Pass** (about 9180'). A steep descent takes us in 3-4 hrs. past the *Silvretta Alp* and *Sardasca* to *Klosters*. — OVER THE ROTHE FURKA TO KLOSTERS, 9-10 hrs., laborious. We cross the *Klosterthaler Glacier*, and in 5-6 hrs. reach the **Rothe Furka** (8910'), on the E. side of the *Thälihorn* (9015'); descent in 4 hrs. to *Klosters*, across the *Silvretta Glacier* and past the *Silvretta Hut*.

TO THE JAMTHALHÜTTE the shortest way from the Madlenerhaus (3½-4 hrs., with guide; easy and attractive) leads through the *Piltthal* and across the *Piltthaler Glacier* to the saddle overtopping the *Todtenfeld Glacier*. In descending we traverse the latter and (farther down) the lower *Jamthaler Glacier*, and cross the *Jambach* to the club-hut (see below).

At **Wirl**, the highest village in the **Patznaun-Thal**, the routes from the Zeinisjoch and the Pillerhöhe unite. A cart-track leads through the sequestered valley, surrounded with lofty mountains, and across the *Vermuntbach* to (¾ hr.) **Galtür** (5040'; *Rössle* or Post), at the entrance to the *Jamthal*. Retrospect of the Gorfen, Ballunspitze, and Vallüla.

EXCURSIONS (guides, *Gottlieb* and *Ignatz Lorenz*, *Johann* and *Benedikt Walter*). A good path (guide not indispensable) leads through the narrow and deep *Jamthal* to (3 hrs.) the **Jamthalhütte** (7240'; well fitted up by the German Alpine Club), in a picturesque situation above the junction of the *Futschölbach* and the *Jambach*, commanding a magnificent view of the majestic Fluchthorn to the E., and the Augstenberg and the great Jamthal Glacier to the S. The hut is the starting-point for the *Fluchthorn* (11,120'; 5 hrs.; difficult, requiring a steady head; guide 8 fl., with descent to the Fimberthal 10 fl.); *Augstenberg* (10,590'; 4½-5 hrs.; 6 fl.); *Piz Falschauv* (10,430'; 5 hrs.; 7 fl.); *Jamspitze* (10,010'; 4½ hrs.; 6 fl.); *Grenzeckkopf* (9990'; 3 hrs.; 4½ fl.), etc.

*Piz Buin (10,870'; 6-7 hrs.; guide, with descent to the Madlenerhaus, 9½ fl.), the highest peak in the Voralberg, a fatiguing ascent, but not dangerous for adepts. We cross the *Jamthal Glacier* in the direction of the *Gemsspitze* (10,400') and the *Dreiländerspitze* (10,495') and ascend (steep) to the (5 hrs.) *Vermunt Glacier*. Beyond this we cross (1½ hr.) a rocky ridge and reach (1 hr.) the 'Kamin', or chimney, a trying point, beyond which we meet no other difficulty. The *View is magnificent. We now descend to the N.E. across the Vermunt Glacier, in the direction of the rubble-strewn slopes of the *Ochsenthal*. Farther on our route leads high above the (2½ hrs.) *Source of the Ill*, following the right bank and passing the deserted 'Vellliner Hüsli' and the mouth of the *Klosterthal* (see above). Lastly we cross the marshy *Gross-Vermunt-Alpe* and reach the (2 hrs.) *Madlenerhaus* (p. 216).

PASSES. OVER THE VERMUNT PASS TO GUARDA, in the Engadine, 6-7 hrs. (with guide), a grand but fatiguing route. To the (3 hrs.) *Vermunt Glacier*, see above. In ½ hr. more we reach the *Vermunt Pass (9205'), to the W. of the *Piz Buin* (see above). Descent through the *Val Tuoi* or *Gtozza* to (2½ hrs.) *Guarda*; see *Baedeker's Switzerland*.

From the Jamthalhütte over the **Futschöl-Pass** (9165'), between the *Augstenberg* and the *Grenzeckkopf*, to Ardetz or Fettan in the Lower Engadine, 8-9 hrs., with guide (8 fl.), trying. A more interesting pass leads over the great *Jamthaler Glacier* (to which a path has recently been made) and the **Jamjoch** (about 9360') between the *Jamspitze* (see above; easily climbed from the pass) and the *Gemsspitze* (10,400'); descending thence

218 V. Route 40.   KAPPL.

across the *Urezas-Glacier* to the *Val Tasna* and to (8-9 hrs.) *Ardetz* (guide 8½ fl.). — To the *Madlenerhaus*, see p. 217.

The new road through the Patznaun descends gradually along the *Trisanna*, past *Tschafein*, to (3½ M.) *Mathon* (4760'; Inn), at the mouth of the *Larcinthal*, with its glaciers. (Across the *Schafbuchjoch* to the *Fasulthal*, see p. 204.) Beyond Mathon the road is level. At the hamlet of *Patznaun* it crosses the stream to (3½ M.) **Ischgl** (4730'; *Wälschwirth or Sonne; *Post; Adler), a well-to-do village, finely situated on a green hill at the entrance to the *Fimberthal*. To the N. is the *Madleinerthal*, with the *Seekopf* (9970').

Through the Fimberthal to Samnaun and Finstermünz or Stuben, 10-11 hrs., an attractive route (guides, *Franz Pöll* of Mathon, *H. Ganahl* and *Fz. Oesterer* in Ischgl; 9 fl.). The path ascends the steep Calvarienberg, and then through a wooded valley, after 40 min. crossing the *Fimberbach* and passing a chapel. By the (20 min.) *Pürschtig-Alp*, the huge *Fluchthorn* (11,120'; see p. 217) comes in sight at the head of the valley; on the right is the *Bergterkopf* (9445'). In ¾ hr. more we reach *Im Boden* (5950'; rustic Inn), a meadow on the left bank of the stream, where we cross the Fimberbach and ascend to the E. through the *Vesilthal*, and past the *Campenalp*, first on the left and then on the right bank of the Vesilbach. At the head of the valley, the *Vesilhütte* remains on the right. The path turns sharply to the left and leads over grass to the (2¼ hrs.) Zeblesjoch (8840'), between the *Vesilspitze* (*Piz Vadret*, 10,145') on the right and the *Paulinerkopf* or *Pellinkopf* (9340') on the left. Fine *View of the Oetzthal Glaciers, the towering Fluchthorn (to the S.W.), the Stammerspitz (S.E.), and (as we descend) the Muttler and the Piz Mondin. We descend rapidly (keeping to the left) over a patch of snow, loose stones, and turf, cross the brook after ½ hr., and follow the left side of the valley. At the bottom of the valley we return to the right bank and cross pastures to (1½ hr.) *Samnaun* (6010'; Inn, rustic), the first village in the Samnaunthal, a Swiss valley. To the S. rise the Muttler and Stammerspitze. Then on the left bank of the *Schergenbach* by *Ravelsch* and *Plan*, and past the villages of *Loreth* and *Compatsch* ("Piz Ureza Inn, plain; the landlord is also a guide), which remain above us to the left, to the (1½ hr.) *Spisser Mühle* (5330'), the boundary of Tyrol, with the Austrian custom-house. The valley now becomes a wild, wooded ravine, in which the *Schalkbach* forms a series of cascades. The path crosses the stream repeatedly, and then ascends on the left bank through wood to the (1½ hr.) hamlet of *Noggls*, opposite the imposing *Piz Mondin* (10,380'). Where the route divides, 20 min. farther on, we descend to the left to (1½ hr.) *Stuben* (p. 248), or to the right (rough path; guide advisable) to (¾ hr.) *Alt-Finstermünz* (p. 249).

From Ischgl over the **Fimber Pass** (*Engadiner Joch*, 8545') to *Remüs* in the Lower Engadine, 10-11 hrs., with guide (9 fl.), interesting and not difficult.

A fatiguing pass leads from Ischgl through the *Madleiner Thal* and over the **Schneidjöchl** (about 9150') to (8 hrs.) *St. Anton* (p. 203).

Below Ischgl the road recrosses to the left bank, and passes the hamlets of *Platt, Ubnich, Sinsen, Wiesen,* and *Höfen*. To the left, above the road, is (7 M.) **Kappl** (4085'; *Löwe*), the chief place in the valley.

From Kappl over the **Blankajoch** (8810') to *Pettnen* (p. 204), 7 hrs., with guide, a toilsome but attractive route. The *Riffler* (10,895') may be easily scaled from the *Edmund Graf Hut*, on the W. side of the pass, in 2½-3 hrs.; comp. p. 205. — The Fetziner-Spitze (8350', 5 hrs.; with guide), ascended viâ *Langesteí* (p. 219), is easy and interesting.

Fatiguing passes lead to the S. from Kappl through the *Visnitz-Thal* and the *Gribele-Thal* to the (6 hrs.) *Spisser Mill* in the Samnaun (see above).

The road follows the left bank of the Trisanna. On the slope of the *Petziner-Spitze* (see p. 218), to the left, lies the village of *Langestei* (4860'; Inn). On the right are passed the mouths of the *Flath-Thal* and the *Istalanz-Thal*, through the latter of which a path, affording fine views, leads over the *Furgler Joch* (9120') to *Serfaus* and (7 hrs.) *Ried* (p. 248). The road now descends abruptly through the wild *Gfäll-Schlucht*, to the (7½ M.) *Gfäll Inn*, and opposite the castle of *Wiesberg* crosses the *Trisanna* (3000'). On the right bank we either follow the footpath ascending to the right to the (1 M.) *Wiesberg* station (p. 205), before reaching the huge viaduct of the Arlberg railway (p. 205), or pass below the viaduct and cross the Sanna (to the left) to (2¼ M.) the village of *Pians* (p. 205). Thence by the Arlberg road to Landeck, 3½ M. The station *Pians-Patznaunthal* on the Arlberg railway lies on the other side of the Sanna, 1 M. from the village and 262' above it.

41. From Innsbruck to Botzen by the Brenner.
Comp. Maps, pp. 178, 226, 246, 320.

80 M. RAILWAY. Express in 5 hrs., ordinary trains in 6½ hrs. Good refreshment-room at Franzensfeste. Best views to the right as far as the Eisak bridge below Sterzing; beyond it, generally to the left. The *Panoramas* published by the Railway Co. ('Südbahn') are useful (60 kr. each).

The **Brenner** (4470'), the lowest pass over the main chain of the Alps, is traversed by the oldest of the Alpine routes, once used by the Romans, and rendered practicable for carriages in 1772. The railway, opened in 1867, one of the grandest works of the kind (30 tunnels; 60 large, and many smaller bridges), is the shortest route between Central Germany and Italy. The steepest gradient, 1:40, occurs five times between Innsbruck and the summit; and thence to Sterzing the gradient is 1:44. The total cost was 32,000,000 fl. (2,500,000 l.). The most interesting parts of the line are between Innsbruck and stat. *Gossensass*. — A *Walk* from Innsbruck to Sterzing by the Brenner road is also repaying.

Innsbruck (1910'), see p. 161. The train passes the abbey of *Wilten* (right), traverses a tunnel 750 yds. long under *Berg Isel*, and then the *Sonnenburg Tunnel* (270 yds.), and crosses the *Sill* by a stone bridge, 78' in height. Further on it runs through the narrow *Wippthal*, high above the brawling river. On the left bank is the high-road; to the S. rises the beautifully-formed *Waldraster-* or *Serles-Spitze* (8905'). Two more tunnels follow before (3¾ M.) *Unterberg*; opposite is the bold *Stefansbrücke*, across which runs the road to the Stubaithal (p. 227). Beyond three other tunnels we reach (5 M.) **Patsch** (2550'); the village lies on the hill to the left, and is not visible from the train. To the W., beyond the Sill, is the wooded *Burgstall*, concealing the mouth of the *Stubaithal*.

FROM PATSCH TO THE STUBAITHAL (comp. R. 42). We descend from the station to the Sill, which is crossed by a bridge, ascend the steep left bank (good path) to the Brenner road, follow this road to the left to the *Ober-Schönberg* post-station, and turn to the right to the (¾ hr.) village (*View, comp. p. 227). Or we may cross the Brenner road and ascend the forest-path in a straight direction (½ hr.; keep to the right at the top).

Three more tunnels, including the *Mühlthal Tunnel* (1035 yds.), the longest on the line. Near Matrei the line penetrates the Matreier Schlossberg. On the right, close to the railway, flows the Sill in its artificial rocky channel. The train crosses the Sill to (12 M.) **Matrei** (3240'; *Stern; *Krone*, good beer; *Kreus; Lamm*, moderate), the *Matreia* of the Romans, a beautifully situated village, with the château of *Trautson*, the property of Prince Auersperg.

EXCURSIONS (guide, *Jos. Steiner*). A tolerably easy route leads from Matrei to the W., viâ the pilgrimage-church of (2 hrs.) **Maria-Waldrast** (5355'; *Inn & Pension*), on the N.E. flank of the *Waldraster* or *Serles-Spitze*, to (1½ hr.) *Mieders* (p. 227), or (pretty forest-path) to (2 hrs.) *Neustift* (p. 228). Fine view from Waldrast; more extensive from the *Gleinser Jöchl* (6080'), to the N., ascended by a bridle-path in ½ hr. — Ascent of the *Waldraster Spitze* (3 hrs. from Maria-Waldrast), see p. 227.

The *Mieselkopf* (*Pfonserjoch*, 8570') easily ascended from Matrei by *Pfons* in 4 hrs., with guide, is an interesting point. — Through the *Navisthal* to the (8 hrs.) *Volderbad*, see p. 161.

The railway and the road follow the valley of the Sill. To the left is the church of *St. Katharina*, at the mouth of the *Navisthal*. The Sill is again crossed. — 14½ M. **Steinach** (3430'). The village (*Post; *Steinbock*, moderate; *Wilder Mann*) lies on the left bank of the Sill, at the mouth of the *Gschnitzthal*.

EXCURSIONS (guides, *Alois, Georg*, and *Joh. Pillracher* of Gschnitz). The *Blaser* (7345') and *Pendelstein* (7840') are easily ascended from Steinach (each 3½-4 hrs.; guide 2½ fl.; paths recently improved and marked).

The **Gschnitzthal** is worthy of a visit (comp. Map, p. 226). Road as far as (3 M.) *Trins* (3885'; *Heidegger*), a pleasant village at the S. base of the *Blaser* (see above; ascended from this point in 3 hrs.). The (5 min.) *Calvarienberg* commands a fine view of the glaciers at the head of the valley. We then pass the picturesque château of *Schneeberg* in the narrowing valley, and reach (1¾ hr.) *Gschnitz* (4070'; quarter's at the Curé's), at the base of the *Kirchdachspitze* (9370'). To the S. rises the *Tribulaun* (10,168'), to the N. the *Habicht* (10,740'), and at the head of the valley the *Feuerstein* and *Schneespitze* with the *Simming Glacier*. About 1½ hr. farther up the valley (in which we pass a fine cascade on the left) is the highest Alp, *Lapones* (4635'), 2½ hrs. from the foot of the *Simming Glacier*. From the Alp over the *Simmingjöchl, Schönjöchl*, or the *Trauljoch* to Ranalt in the Stubaithal, see p. 229. — From Gschnitz over the *Pinniser-Joch* to Neustift (7-8 hrs.; guide 4 fl.), and ascent of the *Habicht* (from the Innsbrucker-Hütte 3½ hrs., with guide), see p. 228. — A toilsome but repaying route leads from Gschnitz to the S. through the *Sandesthal* and over the Pfierscher Pinkl (about 8880'), to the W. of the *Kleine Tribulaun* (*Goldkappe*, 9100'), to (7 hrs.; guide 4 fl.) *Inner-Pflersch* (p. 222). — The **Grosse Tribulaun** or *Scharer* (10,160') may be ascended from Gschnitz viâ the *Sandesjoch* in 7-8 hrs. (guide 8 fl.; very difficult; grand view).

The train now begins to ascend rapidly on the E. side of the valley (in view of the *Habicht*, to the right, for a short distance), and then, near the village of *Stafflach* (*Lamm*), which lies on the Brenner road below, to the right, it enters the *Schmirner Thal*. (Above us, on the other side of the valley, is seen the mouth of a tunnel through which the train afterwards passes.) Below us, to the right, at the mouth of the picturesque *Valser-Thal*, with the glaciers of the Tux Mts. in the background, lies the charmingly-situated village of (16½ M.) **St. Jodok** (route across the Tuxer Joch to the Zillerthal, see p. 183; 7½ hrs. from St. Jodok is the *Wery-Hütte*, p. 183).

The line describes a long curve, crosses the *Schmirner Bach*, penetrates the hill between Schmirn and Vals by means of a curved tunnel, and crosses the *Valser Bach* (view of the Valser Thal now to the left). The train next ascends the S. slope of the valley (to the right, 225' below, lies the route already traversed), regains the Sillthal through another curved tunnel, and runs towards the S., high on the slope of the *Padaunerkogl*.

19½ M. **Gries** (4100'). The village (*Aigner*), a summer-resort, lies below on the road, at the mouth of the *Oberbergthal*.

EXCURSIONS (guides, *Joseph* and *Thomas Spörr*). A road leads through the picturesque **Obernbergthal**, skirting the *Seebach* and passing *Venaders*, to (2 hrs.) the prettily situated village of *Obernberg* (4555'; Ochs); and a cart-track runs thence by the little *Untere See* and past the *Rainsalpen* to the (¾ hr.) *Hintere See* (5220'), beautifully situated at the foot of the *Obernberger Tribulaum* (*Portmader*, 9080'). Milk, etc., may be obtained at the *See-Alpe*, at the S. end of the lake. A route, indicated by marks (but guide advisable; 3½ fl.), leads hence over the *Port-Jöchl* (*Grubjoch*, 7020') to the (4 hrs.) station of *Pfersch* (see below).

The *Padaunerkogl (6765'), a splendid point of view, is ascended from Gries (or from Stafflach) without difficulty in 3 hrs. (with guide). From Gries a good forest-path ascends to the (1½ hr.) *Padauner Sattel* (5245'; view of the Olperer, etc.); thence to the (1½ hr.) top a steep climb over moss-grown rocks.

The line describes a long curve, high above the Sillthal, passing the small green *Brenner-See* (4300') and crossing the *Vennabach*. To the left rises the *Kraxentrayer*, with a small glacier. The *Sill*, which rises to the E., at the foot of the *Wildseespitze*, is now crossed for the last time, and we reach the station of (23½ M.) **Brenner** (4485'; *Buffet*), in a valley devoid of view forming the watershed between the Black Sea and the Adriatic. The *Eisak* forms several falls to the right of the station. On the road opposite is the old *Post Inn*.

Fine view from the *Postalpe* (1½ hr.), on the E. side of the valley. — The ascent of the **Kraxentrager** (9825'; 4 hrs.; with guide), through the *Vennathal*, and that of the **Wolfendorn** (9095'; 3½ hrs., with guide; marked path), viâ the *Lueger-Alpe* and the *Wolfenberg-Alpe*, are very interesting and free from difficulty. — The *Amthorspitze* (9010') is better ascended from Gossensass (see p. 222).

From the Brennerbad over the **Schlüsseljoch** (7315'; guide) to *Kematten* in the Pfitsch valley (p. 187), 4 hrs., an interesting and easy route.

The train follows the course of the Eisak, at first traversing a level, grassy valley to the (27 M.) **Brennerbad** (4350'; *Sterzinger Hof* or *Wildbad Brenner*, R. 1½ fl., D. 1 fl. 20 kr.; *Badhaus*, with rooms), the mineral water of which resembles that of Gastein, and then descending rapidly by means of a long embankment and two tunnels to (29 M.) *Schelleberg* (4065'). One of the most curious parts of the line is between this point and Gossensass (p. 222), which lies 588' almost perpendicularly below Schelleberg. The line turns suddenly to the right into the *Pferschthal*, which opens here, gradually descends on its N. slope, enters the side of the valley by the curved *Aster Tunnel*, 840 yds. long, and emerges lower down, but in an opposite direction. A fine view of the Pferschthal glaciers, and of the Feuerstein, Schneespitze, etc., is obtained to the left on entering, and to the right on emerging from the tunnel 31 M.

Pflersch. — 33 M. **Gossensass** (3480'; **Gröbner*, fine view from the veranda, pens. 2½-3 fl.), often crowded with summer-visitors.

Excursions (guides, *Joh.* and *Jos. Krahl*). The ***Amthorspitze** (*Hühnerspiel*, 9010'; 4-4½ hrs.; guide not indispensable; path indicated by marks), a fine point of view, is ascended from Gossensass by a good bridle-path leading through wood to (1½ hr.) the *Amthor-Alpe* (Inn, good wine), whence the ascent continues over turf to the (2½-3 hrs.) summit. Splendid view (panorama by Lergetporer).

In the **Pflerschthal** (comp. Map, p. 226), a rough road leads from Pflersch viâ *Anichen* to (1¼ hr.) *Boden* or *Inner-Pflersch* (4100'; Inn; quarters also at the Curé's), at the foot of the massive *Pflerscher Tribulaun* (10,150'), which may be ascended hence viâ the *Sandesjoch* in 7-8 hrs. (difficult; good guides necessary, see p. 221). By the chalets of *Erl* we cross the brook to (½ hr.) *Stein*, and then ascend steeply past the *Hölle* (grand waterfall) to the (2 hrs.) shepherd's hut on the *Furt-Alpe* (5440') and to the (1½ hr.) **Magdeburger Hütte** (about 7870'), opened in 1887, on the verge of the plateau next the *Stuben Glacier*, commanding a magnificent view. The ascent of the *Schneespitze* (10,405'; 2½-3 hrs., with guide; Joh. Teissel, Joh. Windisch, and Joh. Mühlsteiger of Pflersch) from this point by the Stuben Glacier is remunerative and easy. That of the *Oestliche Feuerstein* (10,740'; 5-6 hrs., with **guide**) is laborious. — Over the *Pflerscher Hochjoch* to *Stubai* (7-8 hrs. to the Nürnberger-Hütte), see p. 229; over the *Pflerscher Pinkl* to *Gschnitz*, see p. 220. — From **Inner-Pflersch** to *Ridnaun* over the **Allrissjoch** (about 8200'), between the *Wetterspitze* (8880') and the *Mauerspitze* (8594'), uninteresting (6 hrs. to St. Lorenz). More interesting, but also more difficult is the **Aglsjoch** (about 8880'), between the *Agls-Spitze* and the *Lorenz-Spitze* (9440') affording a fine survey of the great *Üeblenthal Glacier*. Descent past the *Pfurnsee* to the *Untere Agls-Alpe* or to the **Teplitzer-Hütte** (see p. 223).

The train crosses the Eisak at the influx of the *Pflerschbach*, follows the old bed of the river for some distance, while a tunnel now conducts the river through the projecting rocks, and then leads high up on the left side of the narrow wooded valley. To the left, above, is the ruin of *Strassberg*; on the high-road, to the right, the village of *Ried*. We now enter the broad basin of —

38 M. **Sterzing** (3105'; **Rose;* *Alte Post or *Sterzinger Hof*; **Schwarzer Adler;* **Krone;* **Neue Post;* *Stoetter's Hotel*, with restaurant, at the station). The clean little town (1400 inhab.), with its picturesque old buildings, arcades, balconies, and turrets, lies ½ M. from the station, on the right bank of the Eisak, which is confined between strong embankments. The town owes its prosperous appearance to the mines formerly worked here; marble-polishing is still actively carried on. The interesting *Church* (16th cent.) has a Gothic *Choir and nave and aisles restored in the rococo style, adorned with ceiling-paintings by Adam Mölckh (1753).

Excursions (guides, *Peter Platzer, Alois* and *Joh. Steiner*). A good view of the valley is obtained from the hill to the W., behind the *Capuchin Monastery*; also from the (¼ hr.) *Custozza Restaurant*, near the church, and from the castles of *Sprechenstein* (¾ hr.) and *Reifenstein* (¾ hr.), the latter of which is well-preserved and worth visiting (see p. 224). — More extensive views, embracing the Stubai and Zillerthal snow-mountains, the Eisakthal, etc., are afforded by the **Rosskopf** (7175'), reached without difficulty by *Raminges* in 3½ hrs. (guide 2½-3½ fl.), and by the **Zinseler** (*Stilfser Joch;* 7930'), ascended viâ *Rust* in 4½ hrs. (marked path; guide 4 fl.). — The **Amthorspitze** (9010') may be ascended from Sterzing by a new bridle-path in 5 hrs. (guide 4 fl.), but is better approached from Gossensass (see above). — *Wilde Kreuzspitze*, see p. 224. — Over the *Penser*

Joch to Botzen, see p. 261 (guide to Sarntheim 5 fl.); over the *Pfitscher Joch* to the Zillerthal, see p. 187; over the *Jaufen* to Meran, see p. 254 (guide 8 fl.).

OVER THE SCHNEEBERG TO THE OETZTHAL, a well-trodden route leading through the **Ridnaun-Thal**, which opens here to the W. (to Gurgl or Sölden two days). The road (constructed for the mining-traffic) extends to the Kasten (see below), but is interrupted by three 'Bremsberge' ('brake-hills'), up which the trucks are drawn by a wire-rope. Driving is therefore practicable to the foot of the first 'Bremsberg' only, near Mareit. The road ascends gradually on the right bank of the *Gailbach*, by which the valley is watered, to *Gasteig*, at the entrance to the *Jaufenthal* (p. 254), passes the mouth of the *Ratschinges-Thal*, and reaches (6 M.) *Mareit* (3625'; *Stern), with the picturesque château of *Wolfsthurn*. It then ascends more steeply, passing the *St. Magdalenenkirche* (4660'; fine view of the head of the valley, with the Botzer, Sonklarspitze, and Freiger), to (2 hrs.) *Ridnaun-Mayrn* (4430'; Inn).

[TO THE TEPLITZER HÜTTE, an interesting excursion (from Ridnaun 3½ hrs.; guides, P. Braunhofer of Mareit, Jos. Eder and P. Kotter of Ridnaun). By the stamping-mill at the entrance to the Lazzachthal (see below) we diverge to the right from the road by a recently improved path, ascending through the *Burgstall-Wald*, and then descend to the Mareiter Bach, and follow its left bank to the desolate *Agls-Boden* (above which, to the right, is the *Untere Agls-Alp*). We next ascend steeply on the left bank of the stream descending from the glacier to the (3 hrs.) **Teplitzer-Hütte** (7275'), on the upper *Blosse Bügel*, 100' above the great Ueblenthal-Ferner. Best survey of the grand environs from the *'Ippeleskogel*, 1 hr. from the club-hut. Passes cross the glacier from this point to the Stubai and Passeir (Teplitzer Scharte, Freigerscharte, Pfaffennieder, Botzerscharte, etc.; comp. p. 229). The *Wilde Freiger* (11,245), the *Wilde Pfaff* (11,370') the *Zuckerhütl* (11,480'), the *Sonklarspitze* (11,415') the *Botzer* (10,680'), and other peaks may also be ascended hence viâ the Ueblenthal Glacier. A fine route leads over the flat tongue of the glacier (*Ebener Ferner*) and through the *Sennesregerten-Thal*, to the (3 hrs.) top of the **Schwarzseespitze** (9815'), whence we descend to (2 hrs.) *St. Martin* (see below; guide from Sterzing viâ the Teplitzer-Hütte to the Schwarzseespitze and back to Sterzing viâ Schneeberg, 2-2½ days, 9 fl.).]

By the stamping-mill ¼ hr. above Ridnaun-Mayrn the road reaches the second 'Bremsberg' (steep ascent), enters the *Lazzacher Thal*, and ascends through a rather monotonous region (with the Krapfenkar and the Moarer Spitze on the right) to the (2 hrs.) *Kasten-Alpe* (wine, etc.), where the road ends (third 'Bremsberg'). We now (with a guide) ascend the slope to the (¾ hr.) *Kaindl* (7610'), a shaft 800 yds. long pierced through the crest of the Schneeberg. A light is necessary for the passage of this tunnel (10 min.). The traveller had better get a miner from the Kasten to propel him through the shaft on one of the trucks called 'Hunde'. When the mine is being worked the shaft is not passable, in which case the traveller must cross the hill (¾ hr. longer), but the view repays the trouble. From the shaft we follow the cable-tramway to (¼ hr.) **St. Martin am Schneeberg** (7650'; poor inn), grandly situated. The mines (zinc and lead), which were known in the 15th cent., are again actively worked. The *Schwarzseespitze* (9815'; 2 hrs.; with guide) and the *Botzer* (10,680'; 4 hrs.; with guide), two fine points of view, may be ascended from St. Martin. — We may now descend to (1½ hr.) *Rabenstein* (p. 254), and again ascend to *Schönau* and the *Timbler Joch* (p. 254; 5½ hrs. to Zwieselstein; instead of descending to Rabenstein we may follow the slope on the right bank of the brook direct to Schönau.) Or (2 hrs. longer, but a far finer route) we may ascend from St. Martin to the N.W. to the (1 hr.) *Gürtelscharte* (8520'), which affords a capital survey of the *Timbler Mulde* and its grand surroundings. We then descend to the *Timbler Alpe* (7700') and cross the *Schönauer Alpe* to the Timbler Joch.

The train crosses the *Pfitscher Bach* (p. 188), and runs between river and rock, close under the castle of *Sprechenstein*. On the opposite bank rise the castles of *Thumburg* and *Reifenstein* (a good specimen of a mediæval stronghold), at the mouth of the *Ridnaunthal* (p. 223), at the head of which rise the lofty snow-clad Botzer, Sonklarspitze, and Freiger. The line traverses the marshy *Sterzinger Moos* by a long embankment and reaches (40$^1/_2$ M.) **Freienfeld** (*Neuhaus*, 'pens.' 2$^1/_2$ fl.). On the hill to the left lies the village of *Trens*, and on the other side *Stilfes* and the little watering-place of *Möders*.

The ascent of the *Wilde Kreuzspitze* (10,270'; 7$^1/_2$ hrs.; guide 6 fl.) from this point is difficult but repaying. We proceed through the *Senges-Thal* to the *Senges-Alp* and the crest facing the *Valser-Thal*, behind which nestles the picturesque *Wilde See*. Then over steep grassy slopes, debris, and snow to the N. peak (comp. p. 187). Descent to the *Burgumer Alp* and to (3 hrs.) *Burgum*, see p. 187.

The train crosses the Eisak and the *Eggerbach*, which descends from the *Penser Joch* (p. 261), and stops at the (42$^1/_2$ M.) station of **Mauls**. The village, with the ruin of *Wolfsberg*, lies on the opposite bank, at the mouth of the *Sengesthal* (see above). The train now enters a narrow defile, in which lie (45 M.) *Grasstein* (2745') and (47 M.) *Mittewald* (Post). Marshal Lefebvre was defeated here by the Tyrolese under Haspinger and Speckbacher in 1809. At *Oberau* 550 of his Saxon troops were taken prisoners, and the pass is still called the *Sachsenklemme*.

The mouth of the defile, called the *Brixener Klause*, near *Unterau* (2460'), was strongly fortified in 1833-38. These works (**Franzensfeste**), which are very conspicuous when seen from the S., command the Brenner route and the entrance to the Pusterthal. 49 M. *Franzensfeste Station* (**Rail. Restaurant*, D. with wine 1 fl. 20 kr., bed 1 fl.; *Zum Reifer; *Hofer*, below the bridge, both unpretending) lies upwards of 1 M. from the fortress. The *Pusterthal Railway*, see R. 60; immediately below the railway-bridge the highroad into the Pusterthal crosses the Eisak by the *Ladritsch Brücke*, an old wooden bridge 160' above the stream.

The group of houses to the left in the valley below, beyond the hill, is the Augustinian monastery of *Neustift*, founded in 1142 (imitation of the Castello S. Angelo at Rome; church richly decorated with stucco, and worth seeing. To the right, near (54 M.) *Vahrn* (stat.), opens the *Schalderer Thal* (see p. 225). The vegetation assumes a more southern character, and vineyards and chestnuts begin to appear.

56$^1/_2$ M. **Brixen**, Ital. *Bressanone* (1830'; *Elephant, next door to the post-office, $^3/_4$ M. from the station; *Stern; *Sonne*; *Goldnes Kreuz*; *Goldner Adler, all in the town), for nine centuries the capital of a spiritual principality, which was suppressed in 1803, and now an episcopal see, still exhibits traces of its ecclesiastical period. It contains several churches of the last century, with altarpieces by Tyrolese masters. The *Cathedral*, with its two copper-roofed towers, was completed in 1754. To the right of the

to Botzen. KLAUSEN. *V. Route 41.* 225

portal is the entrance to the *Cloisters*, containing old mural paintings and numerous tombstones, one of the first of which, to the left of the portal, is that of the minstrel Oswald von Wolkenstein (d. 1445). Opposite to it is a finely-executed little relief of the Resurrection in copper, in memory of Hans Kessler, a coppersmith (d. 1654). At the S.W. end of the town, to the right of the entrance to the station, is the *Episcopal Palace*, with an extensive garden.

A good view is obtained from *Krakofel*, on the spur between the Eisak and the Rienz, 20 min. to the N.; also from *Köstland* (Bräuhaus), an ascent of 1/2 hr. to the E.; more extensive from *St. Andrä* (1 hr.; reached viâ *Mitland*). — Pleasant walk to the N. to (3/4 hr.; railway in 1¼ min.) the charmingly-situated village of **Vahrn** (*°Pension Mayr*, pension 2 fl. 70 kr., often full; *Waldsaeker*), with its fine old chestnuts, commanded by the ruin of *Salern*, and through the richly-wooded **Schalderer Thal** to the (1 hr.) *Schalderer Bad*. (Thence over the *Schalderer Joch* to *Durnholz* 5 hrs., see p. 261.) — Interesting excursion to the S.W., viâ *Tschötsch* (see below), to (2½ hrs.) **Feldthurns** (*Oberwirth*), with a château of Prince Liechtenstein (rooms with fine panelling); thence down to the (1/2 hr.) highroad, or (with guide) viâ *Leitach* and the nunnery of *Säben* to (1½ hr.) *Klausen* (see below). — The *°Plose* (8205'; 5 hrs.; guide not necessary) commands an admirable survey of the Oetzthal and Zillerthal Alps, the Dolomites, etc. The easy and interesting ascent (marked path, shaded in the morning) leads by (1½ hr.) the small baths of *Burgstall* and (1 hr.) the farm of *Platzbon* to (2½ hrs.) the *Plosehütte* (Inn in summer), on the crest of the mountain, 20 min. (level path) from the W. peak (*Fröttspitze* or *Telegraph*; 8205'). A still more extensive view is enjoyed from the highest peak (*Gabler*, about 8530'), which may be reached from the Fröllspitze in 1½ hr. (skirting the *Pfannspitz*, 8515'). Easy descent viâ *Afers* to (4 hrs.) Brixen.

The Eisak is again crossed. To the right, on the hill, lies the village of *Tschötsch*, the birthplace of Fallmerayer (d. 1861), the Orientalist. To the left rises the handsome château of *Pallaus*, and farther on, at the entrance to the *Aferser Thal*, stands the church of (59 M.) *Albeins*, beyond which a glimpse is obtained of the wild *Geislerspitzen* (10,438') at the head of the valley. The Eisakthal contracts. At (60 M.) *Villnöss* opens the *Villnöss-Thal*.

The **Villnöss-Thal**, 15 M. in length, offers special attractions to the geologist. A road, diverging to the right from the Brixen road at the *Schmelz*, ascends the ravine (passing *Gufidaun* on the right, above us, and *Theiss* on the left) to the (3 M.) custom-house of *Mileins* (Inn). In the woods above, on the right, is the small *Bad Froi*. The road now leads past *St. Josef* (the *Flitzthal*, with a mineral spring, lying to the right) and the churches (on the hill to the left) of *St. Jakob* and *St. Valentin*, to (4½ M.) **St. Peter**, or *Villnöss* (3565'; *°Zeltenwirth*; *°Kabesuirth*; guide, Lor. Grossrubatscher), the chief place in the valley, frequented as a summer-resort. An easy and attractive pass (marke dpath) leads hence to the S. viâ the *°Raschötzer-Alp* (7540'; fine view) to (6 hrs.; guide 3½ fl.) *St. Ulrich* in the Grödener Thal (p. 264). — The road in the Villnösthal ends at (3½ M.) *St. Magdalena* (4330'), grandly situated. To the S.E. tower the wild and lofty *Geister-Spitzen* (p. 264); to the S. is the *Raschötzberg*, to the E. the *Sobutsch* and *Ruefenberg*. From this point to the Enneberg viâ the *Wurzen* or *Poma Pass* (7845') and the *Petzes-Alp* (to *Campill*, p. 342, 5 hrs.; with guide), an interesting route.

60½ M. **Klausen** (1695; *°Lamm*; *Post*), consisting of a single narrow street, and lying in a defile, as its name imports, has always been regarded as an important military point. The Benedictine nunnery of *Säben* (2460'), crowning the cliffs on the right and command-

BAEDEKER'S Eastern Alps. 6th Edit. 15

ing a fine view, was successively a Rhætian fortress, a Roman castle (*Sabiona*), an episcopal residence down to the 10th cent., and a baronial castle. A painted crucifix on the tower projecting to the N. was placed there in memory of a nun who was pursued by the French in 1809 and threw herself from the battlements. The *Loretto Chapel*, adjoining the **Capuchin Monastery** (where visitors apply for admission), contains the most curious collection of ecclesiastical treasures in Tyrol, presented by the founder of the monastery (1699), who was confessor to the wife of Charles II. of Spain. The Capuchin Haspinger (p. 165), one of the bravest leaders of the insurrection of 1809, belonged to this monastery. A monument was erected here in 1875 to the Minnesänger Leutold von Säben.

EXCURSIONS (guide, *Ant. Marageiter*). Pleasant walk to (1 hr.) *Fonteklaus*, a fine point of view, and (3/4 hr.) *Gufidaun* (2383'; Stern), two summer-resorts; then back direct, or through the Villnösthal (p. 225) to (1 hr.) Klausen. Others along the right bank to (1½ hr.) *Villanders*, and viâ *Säben* to (2 hrs.) *Feldthurns* (see p. 225). — A path (marked with red) leads through the ravine of the *Dinabach* to the (1½ hr.) *Garnsteiner Pochwerk* (stamping-mill), and mounts rapidly thence to (1 hr.) Latzfons (3750'; Inn), from which we may ascend in 3 hrs. to the *Latzfonser Kreuz* (7550'; Inn rustic), an admirable point of view. [A still finer point is the *Kassianspitze* (8470'), easily ascended from the Inn in 1 hr. Thence over the *Lückl* (*Latzfonser Joch*, 7765') to *Reinswald* and (3 hrs.) *Astfeld*, in the *Sarnthal* (p. 261).

65½ M. **Waidbruck** (1520'; *Krone*, at the station; *Sonne*, by the church) lies at the mouth of the *Grödener Thal*. To the left, high above it, rises the *Trostburg* (2040') with its numerous towers and pinnacles, the property of Count Wolkenstein.

To the *Grödener Thal*, see p. 263; viâ *Kastelruth* to the *Seisser Alp*, see p. 265. — A tolerable road (preferable to those from Atzwang and Botzen) leads past *Lengstein* and the '*Erdpyramiden*' to (4 hrs.) *Klobenstein* (p. 259).

From *Kollmann*, on the right bank of the Eisak, 3/4 M. to the S. of Waidbruck, a tolerable cart-road, steep at the beginning only, leads viâ *Barbian* to (2 hrs.) the charmingly-situated **Bad Dreikirchen** (3630')

The train crosses the Grödener Bach, and then the Eisak, in a defile of porphyry rock, called the *Kuntersweg* (after the supposed constructor of the road in the 14th cent.). 69 M. *Kastelruth*, the station for the village of that name (3395'), situated high up on the left bank (p. 265; 2 hrs.). From (71 M.) **Atzwang** (1240'; *Post*, in Unter-Atzwang), at the mouth of the *Finsterbach* (p. 260), a steep road ascends to the right to (2½ hrs.) *Klobenstein* on the Ritten (p. 259). — To *Seis*, *Ratzes*, and *Völs* (with ascent of the *Schlern*), see pp. 265, 266.

Again crossing the Eisak, passing through several tunnels, and crossing the *Mühlbach* at stat. *Steg* (Inn; to the left, high up, the château of *Prössels*; in the background the *Schlern*), we next reach (74 M.) *Blumau* (1020'; Bräu), at the mouth of the *Tierser Thal* (p. 262). On the right bank, beyond the next tunnel, begin the vine-clad slopes of the *Botzener Leitach*. 77½ M. *Kardaun*, at the mouth of the *Eggenthal* (p. 261; above, to the left, the castle of *Karnsid*). The train now crosses the Eisak, and enters the broad and lux-

uriant basin of Botzen *(Botzener Boden)*, which resembles a vast vineyard. Botzen, with its fine Gothic tower, is visible in the distance.
80 M. *Botzen*, see p. 256.

42. The Stubaithal.

Comp. Map, p. 238.

The *Stubaithal*, the main valley of the Stubai Alps, which may in a wider sense be included in the Oetzthal Group, presents within a small compass a series of superb Alpine scenes. ROAD to a point 6 M. beyond Neustift. STELLWAGEN from Innsbruck to Vulpmes daily in 4½ hrs., starting at 2 p. m.; fare 90 kr. (from Vulpmes at 5 a.m.; fare 80 kr.). One-horse carr. from Innsbruck to the Stefansbrücke 3 fl., two-horse 4 fl. 80 kr.; to Schönberg 5 fl. 60 kr. or 9 fl., Vulpmes 8 or 13, Neustift 10 or (7)½ fl. PEDESTRIANS should follow the Brenner road to the (4½ M.) Stefansbrücke, and then ascend along the left bank of the *Rutzbach* (path marked) to (2 hrs.) *Vulpmes* (see below); or they may go by train to *Unterberg* (only two trains daily) and proceed thence across the Sill to the Stefansbrücke. A finer but longer route (4½ hrs. to Vulpmes) leads viâ *Ober-Schönberg* (see below), which may be reached either by the Brenner road or from stat. *Patsch* by the way described at p. 219. Another interesting route ascends to the right from the *Gärberbach Inn* (see below) to (½ hr.) *Mutters*, and leads along the slope of the *Saile* (p. 171), viâ *Kreit* (Inn), and through fine larch-wood, with beautiful views of the Waldrasterspitze, Habicht, Sulzenau Glacier, etc., to (2 hrs.) *Telfes* and (½ hr.) *Vulpmes* (p. 228).

Innsbruck, see p. 161. The Brenner road ascends the *Berg Isel* in long windings (p. 168; the old road, to the left at the first bend, is shorter), and then leads high up on the left side of the deep *Sillthal* (in which, to the left, below us, runs the Brenner Railway with its tunnels). past the (2¼ M.) *Gärberbach Inn* and the *Schupfen Inn* (the headquarters of Andreas Hofer in 1809), to the (2¼ M.) *Stefansbrücke*, which in a bold span of 140' crosses the *Rutzbach*, descending from the Stubaithal. At *Unter-Schönberg* (2310'; Inn), beyond the bridge, the road divides: the old Brenner road ascends somewhat steeply to the right; the new road winds to the left round the slope and leads through the Sillthal to (3½ M.) **Ober-Schönberg** (3290'). The old road is shorter, and for walkers far more interesting. By the (2¼ M.) *Custom House*, the first house in Ober-Schönberg, we obtain a fine *Survey of the Stubaithal*, with the Sailespitze on the right, the Waldrasterspitze and the Habicht on the left, and the ice-crowned background (Wilde Freiger, Pfaffenkamm, Sulzenauferner); below us lie the ravine of the Rutzbach and the villages of Mieders, Vulpmes, etc. On the hill, about 200 paces farther on, is *Domanig's Inn*, which commands a splendid view, particularly from the 'Aussicht', 2 min. distant.

We now descend gradually to (2¼ M.) **Mieders** (3100'; *Blaue Traube; Seewald; Kreither*), the capital of the valley and seat of the district-court, prettily situated at the foot of the rugged *Waldraster-Spitze* or *Serles-Spitze*.

EXCURSIONS (guide, *Jos. Danler*). Route viâ *Maria-Waldrast* to (3½ hrs.) *Matrei* (guide, not indispensable, 2½ fl.), see p. 220. — Ascent of the *Waldrasterspitze* (8905'; 3 hrs.; guide 4 fl.), from Maria-Waldrast, laborious (path recently improved). Fine view.

Crossing the Rutzbach, and passing the village of *Telfes* on the right, we next reach (3 M.) **Vulpmes** (3040'; *Pfurtscheller, *Lutz*), on the *Schlickerbach*, with busy iron manufactories.

EXCURSIONS (guides, *Franz* **Kapferer** and *Ant. Siller*). The **Hohe Burgstall** (8560'; 5 hrs.; guide 3 fl.), an admirable point of view, is ascended without difficulty, either from the N. side by the (2 hrs.) *Schlicker Alpe* (5140') and by the saddle between the Kleine and the Hohe Burgstall; or from the S. by the *Froneben Alpe* and the *Kaserstatt-Alpe*. Descent to the *Bärenbad*, or by *Haslergruben* direct to *Neustift* (see below).

Instead of going to Vulpmes we may follow the road on the right bank to *Medraz* (small baths), *Neder* (Inn), at the entrance to the *Pinnis-Thal* (see below), and (4¼ M.) **Neustift** (3240'; *Zum Salzburger*, kept by *Jennewein*; *Hofer*, unpretending; *Volderauer*), the last village in the valley. At *Milders*, ¾ M. farther up, the valley forks into the *Oberberg* on the right and the *Unterberg* on the left.

GUIDES: *Franz, David, Georg,* **and** *Jos. Pfurtscheller, Peter Tanzer* ('*Urbas-Peter*'), *Thom. Siller, Matth. Schönherr, Fried. Jennewein, And. Gunpold, Seb. Ranalter, Mich. Egger, Jos. Kindl, Joh. Danler, Seb. Huter, Jos. Karmalter, Mart. Metz, Jos.* and *Peter Percht, Jos. Volderauer,* and others.

OVER THE PINNISER-JOCH TO GSCHNITZ, an interesting pass (8-9 hrs.; guide 4 fl.). We return to (2 M.) *Neder* (see above), and ascend the *Pinnis-Thal* to the *Alp Issenanger* (4600'), and the (2 hrs.) *Pinnis-Alp* (5010'). Night-quarters at the *Karalp*, ½ hr. farther up. Then a steep ascent to the (2½ hrs.) **Pinniser-Joch** or **Alfachjoch** (7755'), with fine view of the **Tribulaun**, etc. On the S. side, a little below the Joch, is the *Innsbrucker Hütte* (7740') of the Austrian Tourist Club. Descent to (2½ hrs.) *Gschnitz* (p. 220). — The ascent of the **Habicht** (10,740'), a famous point of view, may be accomplished from the Innsbrucker Hütte without serious difficulty, in 3½ hrs. (path recently improved; guide 5, with descent to Gschnitz 10 fl.).

The **Oberberg (Alpeiner Thal)** is worthy of a visit (to the Alpeiner Glacier 5 hrs.; guide, unnecessary, 3 fl.). The path follows the right bank of the Oberbergbach to the (1 hr.) *Bärenbad* (4125'), a very primitive little bath (Ascent of the *Hohe Burgstall* 4 hrs.) Then past the *Zigidack* or *Seeduck Alp* to the (2 hrs.) *Sibeklen Inn* (5470'; four beds) and the (½ hr.) *Ober-Iss Alp* (6000'), finely situated. (Over the *Hornthaler Joch* (*Villerscharte*) to the *Lisenser Thal,* sec p. 232.) Lastly a steep and stony ascent, with the wild gorge of the Oberbergbach on the left, to the (1 hr.) *Alpeiner Alp* (6700'), and the (½ hr.) **Franz-Senn-Hütte** (about 6890'), finely situated on a spur near the extensive *Alpeiner Glacier*. The latter hut is the starting-point for the ascents of the *Seespitze* (11,195'), *Ruderhofspitze* (11,420'), *Schrankogel* (11,475'), *Wilde Thurm* (10,968'), *Brunnenkogel* (10,900'), *Fernerkogel* (10,805'), etc. The glacier (7300') may be safely visited, except when fresh snow has fallen; on the way are some fine 'Gletscherschliffe', or marks of glacial friction, and on the tongue of the glacier are a number of 'glacier-tables'. A fine, but toilsome route (guide necessary; to Längenfeld 9 fl.) leads hence over the Schwarzenbergjoch (10,000') to the (4½ hrs.) *Amberger Hütte* (p. 237) in the Sulzthal. Another, shorter but more difficult, crosses the Brunnenkogeljoch (about 10,170'), between the **Wilde Hinterbergl** and the *Brunnenkogel*, and descends steeply into the *Schrankar* and to the *Vordere Sulzhalalp* (p. 237).

Through the *Unterberg*, or main valley, which stretches to the S.W., a road gradually ascends on the right bank of the brook, passing *Schaller, Kressbach,* and *Gasteig,* to (3½ M.) *Volderau*. It then crosses the brook, leads through wood, recrosses the stream near *Valbeson,* and rounds a projecting rock to (3½ M.) **Ranalt** (4480'; *Vikoler's Inn*), the last hamlet in the valley, finely situated.

EXCURSIONS (guides, see p. 228). Interesting excursion to the *Pfandler Alp* (7055'; 3 hrs.; guide 2 fl.). The path ascends steep grassy slopes on the left side of the valley (better path viâ *Schöngelair* and *Schellegrübl*, see below) to the (2¼ hrs.) Alp, and then leads to the W. to the (3¼hr.) *Tumbichlgrat* (8030'), a spur of the *Scheckbühelgrat*, affording a fine view of the Stubai Mts., the **Wilde Freiger**, Sonklarspitze, Zuckerhütl, etc.; directly opposite is the Sulzenau waterfall (see below). The descent may be made by a path (lately repaired) to *Schellegrübl* (Rfmts.), *Schöngelair* (see below), and Ranalt; or by the **Scheckbühel Alp** and *Grabanock Alp* to *Mutterberg* (p. 230). The latter steep route (no path) is the shortest way to the Dresdner Hütte.

The **Valbesonthal** also deserves a visit. On the right bank of the Valbesonbach the path ascends rapidly, passing the (1¾ hr.) *Ochsenalpe*, to the (1¼ hr.) *Hohe Moos-Alp* (7460'), with a fine view of the head of the valley (Hohe Moos-Ferner, Ruderhofspitze, Kreilspitze, Knotenspitze, etc.). Keeping to the right and skirting the Moosalp, we next reach the foot of the Hohe Moos Glacier, and ascend rapidly on the right side to the (2½ hrs.) *Grabagrubennieder* (about 9200'), where we obtain a fine view of the Pfaffen group, etc. Descent either to the left to *Schellegrübl* and over the Pfandler Alp (see above) to (2 hrs.) Ranalt, or to the right to the *Alp Grabanock* and *Mutterberg* (p. 230). — The **Ruderhofspitze** (11,420'), ascended from Schellergrube or Grabanock in 5 hrs. (difficult; guide from Ranalt 7 fl.), commands a magnificent view.

[About 20 min. above Ranalt diverges the **Langethal**, which is well worthy of a visit. A good and partly new path ascends on the W. side of the valley, high above the *Langenbach*, here flowing in a deep ravine, to (2½-3 hrs.) the **Nürnberger Hütte** (7870'), built in 1887 at the foot of the *Gamsspitze* (9120'), ½ hr. from the end of the extensive *Grübl Glacier*. Fine view of the head of the valley. Numerous interesting expeditions may be made from this point (guides, see p. 228).

TO THE GSCHNITZTHAL over the **Simming-Jöchl** (about 8880'), between the *Innere Wetterspitze* and the *Simming Glacier*, an attractive but toilsome route (6 hrs. to *Lapones*, the highest Alp, p. 220). Other fatiguing passes (guide necessary) lead over the **Schönjöchl** (9035'), between the *Innere* and the *Aeussere Wetterspitze*, and over the **Trauljoch** (9140'), between the *Innere Röthenspitze* and the *Aeussere Wetterspitze*, in 5½-6 hrs., to Lapones. — TO THE PFLERSCHTHAL over the **Pflerscher Hochjoch** (10,340'), difficult (to the *Magdeburger Hütte*, 7-8 hrs.; p. 222). — TO RIDNAUN (p. 223). An easy route crosses the W. branch of the *Grübl Glacier* to the **Teplitzer Scharte** (ca. 9550'), to the W. of the *Hoch-Grindt* (9910'), and descends across the *Hangende Ferner* to the (4 hrs.) *Teplitzer Hütte* (p. 223). More difficult passes cross the *Rothegrat-Scharte* (about 9600'), to the W. of the Teplitzer Scharte, and the *Enge Thürl* (9350'), farther to the E., between the Hochgrindl and the *Westliche Feuerstein* (10,700'), the ascent of which may be combined with the pass. Another toilsome pass leads over the **Freigerscharte** (9680'), lying to the E. of the *Wilde Freiger*, then traverses the *Uebleuthal Glacier*, and descends through the *Ueble Thäler* to the (5 hrs.) *Teplitzer Hütte*. The *Wilde Freiger (11,245'), an admirable point of view, may be ascended from the Freigerscharte in 1½ hr. — *Sonklarspitze*, see below. — TO THE PASSEIR. This route leads over the *Freigerscharte* and traverses the *Uebleuthal Glacier* to the **Botzer-Scharte** (9415'), between the *Botzer* (10,680') and *Königshof* (10,150'), whence it descends steeply to the *Timbler Alps* (see below); or over the *Hohe Ferner*, the *Röthenferner*, and the *Timbler Ferner* to the *Schwarzsee-Scharte*, and past the *Schwarzsee* to (9-10 hrs.) *Schneeberg*, a long but very grand glacier-tour, unattended with danger (able guides required).]

The main valley (*Mutterberger Thal*) bends to the W. The path crosses to the left bank of the stream, and leads past the Alps of

Schöngelair and (1½ hr.) *Graba* (4900'; opposite the imposing *Sulzenau Fall*, 460' high) to the (¾ hr.) **Mutterberger Alpe** (5640').

The **Sulzenau.** From the Alp *Graba* (see above) a steep path ascends the wooded slope on the left of the waterfall to the (1 hr.) *Sulzenau-Alpe* (6060'), in a rock-girt basin (on the left the *Apere Freiger*, on the right the *Apere Pfaff*). In the background two glacier-streams form cascades. — A difficult route leads hence over the *Sulzenau-Ferner* and the Pfaffennieder (10,400'), the saddle between the *Oestliche Pfaff* and the *Wilde Freiger*, to the *Uebtenthal-Ferner* (see p. 229), and then either over the *Schwarzwandscharte* (10,070') or over the *Hohe Stellen-Scharte* (10,105') to the (8-9 hrs.) *Timbler Alpe* (p. 223). From the Uebtenthal-Ferner we may also cross the *Botzerscharte* (see above) to Schneeberg, or descend on the left side of the glacier through the *Ueble Thäler* to the *Teplitzer Hütte* (p. 223). Experienced guides essential. — The **Sonklarspitze** (12,300'; splendid view) may be ascended from the Sulzenau viâ the Pfaffennieder and the *Sonklarscharte* in 5-6 hrs., or from the *Teplitzer Hütte* viâ the *Uebtenthal-Ferner* in 5 hrs. (difficult).

OVER THE MUTTERBERGER JOCH TO LÄNGENFELD, 8 hrs., toilsome (guide 6 fl.). From Mutterberg we ascend abruptly to the W. to the highest chalet and through the *Glammergrube* (the small *Mutterberger-See*, 8250', lying above us on the right); then mount a fatiguing slope of snow to the (4 hrs.) **Mutterberger Joch** (9890'), between the *Bockkogl* on the right and the *Daunkopf* on the left. View limited. The path now descends the dry bed of a torrent to a large expanse of detritus, crosses the *Sulzthaler Ferner* (in view of the magnificent *Schrankogel*; p. 237), and leads down the left lateral moraine into the *Sulzthal*, to (2 hrs.) the *Amberger Hütte*, (1½ hr.) *Gries* (4960'; quarters at the Caplan's), and (1 hr.) *Längenfeld* (p. 237).

Beyond Mutterberg the path, at first rather steep, ascends to the S.W. to the (1½ hr.) *Dresdner Hütte, in the *Obere Fernau* (about 7870'; rebuilt in 1887, Inn in summer).

The *Eggessen Grat (8650'), to the N. of the hut, ascended without difficulty in ¾ hr., commands the best survey of the magnificent environs. To the S. is the Pfaffenkamm with the Apere Pfaff and Zuckerhütl, more to the right the Schaufelspitze, W. the Bildstöckljoch and Daunkopf, N. the Hölltalspitzen, Ruderhofspitze, etc.

OVER THE BILDSTÖCKLJOCH TO SÖLDEN, 7 hrs., a very interesting pass, and not difficult (guide from Ranalt 8; viâ the Schaufelspitze 9 fl.; a single traveller should take two guides; provisions obtainable at Ranalt). The route ascends from the Dresdner-Hütte to the right over grassy slopes, then over moraine-deposits and rocky debris to the *Schaufel Glacier*, which is crossed (at the end rather steep) to the (2½-3 hrs.) *Bildstöckljoch (10,270'), a rock-strewn ridge to the W. of the *Schaufelspitze* (see below). Fine retrospect of the N. Stubai group, the Ruderhofspitze, Schwarzenberg, etc.; below, the Mutterberger-See. We now descend slightly to the left, passing a small ice-tarn, to the W. side of the Joch (the best resting-place), affording a striking view of the upper Oetzthal chain (Wildspitze, Weisskugel, Hintere Schwärze, etc.). The route next descends to and crosses the *Wipdach Glacier* (in ½ hr.; caution necessary on account of the crevasses; the rope should be used), and then leads down a steep water-course, over several patches of snow, and lastly over grassy slopes (a long and steep descent) to the (2 hrs.) *Windach-Alp* (6500'; Inn, 2 beds), in the *Windach-Thal*; then through wood, with the stream in a deep gully on the left, to (1½ hr.) *Sölden* (p. 237). The route in the reverse direction, from Sölden to the Dresdner Hütte, takes 9 hrs. (guide to the Mutterberger-Alp 7 fl.). — The *Schaufelspitze (10,920') may be ascended without much difficulty from the Windacher Ferner in 1½ hr. (or the ascent may be combined with the Bildstöckljoch route, to which it adds 1½ hr.; guide from Ranalt to the Schaufelspitze and Sölden 9 fl.). Superb view (Zillerthal, Oetzthal, and Stubai Alps, and Dolomites).

The **Zuckerhütl** (11,480'), the highest peak of the Stubai Alps, may be scaled from the Dresdner Hütte in 5-6 hrs., a laborious ascent, but free from danger for experts (guide 7, from Neustift 9 fl.). The route leads over the *Fernau Glacier* towards the *Fernau Joch*, then to the left over the *Pfaffengrat* to the *Sulzenau Ferner* and up to the *Pfaffensattel* (10,950'), between the Zuckerhütl and the Oestliche Pfaff; then a steep climb to the top. View very imposing. [The *Oestliche* or *Wilde Pfaff* (10,470') is easily ascended from the Pfaffengrat in 1/2 hr.] The descent over the *Pfaffen-Ferner* to the *Windach-Thal* is steep and toilsome (to Sölden 5-6 hrs.); better over the *Ueblenthal-Ferner* to the *Teplitzer Hütte* (p. 223).

A fine 'high-level' walk, which may be accomplished by adepts in favourable conditions of the snow in about 12 hrs., may be taken from the Dresdner Hütte viâ the *Zuckerhütl*, *Wilde Pfaff*, and *Wilde Freiger* to the *Nürnberger Hütte* (or to the *Teplitzer Hütte*).

Over the *Daunkogel-Ferner* to the *Sulzthal* (to the *Amberger Hütte* 5 hrs.), see p. 237.

43. From Innsbruck to Landeck.

Comp. Maps, pp. 14, 226, and 216.

45 1/2 M. RAILWAY (*Arlbergbahn*, see R. 37) in 1 1/2-2 1/2 hrs. Best views to the right.

Innsbruck, see p. 161. The line diverges to the right from the Brenner railway (on the left the abbey of Wilten and Berg Isel), and approaches the Inn in a wide curve. On the slope to the left rises *Schloss Mentelberg* (p. 170). 4 1/4 M. *Völs*, among orchards, with the *St. Blasienkirche* on a projecting hill (to the *Kranewitter Klamm*, see p. 170). Then across meadows, with a view of the massive Martinswand (see below) to the right. Before we reach (7 M.) **Kematen** (2000'; *Tiefenthaler; Weiss*) the Selrain-Thal, with the Lisenser Glacier in the background, opens on the left.

About 1 1/2 M. to the S.E. of the station are the *Kaiser Ferdinand Waterfalls*, three pretty cascades of the *Sendesbach*, in a picturesque gorge made accessible in 1885 by the Austrian Tourist Club.

The shortest way for pedestrians into the lower Oetzthal leads through the **Selrain-Thal**. A cart-track (carriage-road under construction) leads from Kematen to (2 M.) the picturesquely situated village of *Ober-Perfuss* (2030'; Inn), the church of which contains the tomb of Peter Anich (d. 1766), the famous Tyrolese mathematician. Thence we descend abruptly past *Kammerland* to (3 1/2 M.) *Selrain*, or *Rothenbrunn* (2955'; Inn), with a chalybeate spring, in the *Melachthal*. At a considerable elevation to the N. is the *St. Quirinus-Kapelle*, which enjoys a wide prospect. Ascent of the *Rosskogl* (8658'; 4 hrs.; guide; path marked with red and white), interesting. Guides. *Joh. Hepperger* and *Alois Jordan* of Rothenbrunn, and *Jos. Pairst* of Ober-Perfuss. — At (4 1/2 M.) *Gries* (3960'; Inn) the Selrainthal divides into the *Lisenserthal* (see below) to the left and the **Selrainer Oberthal** to the right. We ascend the latter to (1 1/4 hr.) *St. Sigmund* (4925'; Inn, rustic); thence through the *Gleirscher-Thal* and over the *Gleirscher Jöchl* (8980') to *Umhausen* in the Oetzthal 6-7 hrs., fatiguing (guide 4 fl.). Beyond St. Sigmund the path in the Oberthal leads viâ *Haggen* (Inn) and the *Zirnalp* (at the junction of the path from the Kreuzjoch, p. 233) to the flat saddle of the *Stockach-Alpe* (6590'), a little beyond which is (2 1/2 hrs.) **Kühtai** (6460'; *Brugger's Inn*), finely situated. (Ascent of the *Birchkogl*, 9275'; 3 hrs., with guide; repaying.) Picturesque excursions hence to the *Finsterthal Lakes* (7410'), 1 hr.; the *Plenderle Lakes* (6890'), 1 hr.; to the top of the *Birchkogl* (9275'), 3 hrs., with guide; etc. Route over the *Feldringerboden* or the *Kreuzjoch* to the *Stamser Alpe*, see p. 233. — We may now either descend viâ (1 3/4 hr.) **Ochsengarten** (5010; good accommodation at the Curé's) and by a pleasant forest-path along the

232   *V. Route 43.*   ZIRL.   *From Innsbruck*

Stuibenbach, viâ *Au* and *Ebene*, to (2½ hrs.) *Oetz* (p. 236); or (better) guide to Umhausen 6 fl.) pass the *Finsterthal Lakes* and cross the glacier of the same name to (2 hrs.) the **Finsterthal-Scharte** (about 9050'), on the W. side of the *Kraspesspitze* (9560'), with a view of the Sulzthal glaciers. Then descend by a steep path through the *Weisse Kaar* to (1½ hr.) the *Zwiesel-bacher Alp* (6405') and along the *Horlachbach* to (1½ hr.) *Niedertai* (5485'; accommodation at the Curé's). Thence we either proceed past the *Stuiben Fall* to (1 hr.) *Umhausen*, or viâ *Lehen* and *Wiesle* (5270') to (2 hrs.) *Längenfeld* (p. 237).

Ascending the **Lisenser Thal** (see above) from Gries, we reach (1½ hr.) *Praxmar* (5340', *Schöpf), a summer-resort, and (¾ hr.) the finely situated Alpine farm of *Lisens* (*St. Maria Magdalena*, 5325'), the property of the convent of Wilten. At the head of the valley is the imposing *Lisenser Glacier*, commanded by the *Fernerkogl* (10,805'); a good view of it is obtained from the *Längenthaler Alp* (6500'; rustic quarters), 2 hrs. above Praxmar. The route hence across the *Winnebach Ferner* and the **Griesjoch** (8650'), and down past the *Winnebach-See* to (5-6 hrs.) *Gries*, is attractive on the whole. Another pass (fatiguing) leads to the S.E. from Lisens to the **Hornthaler Joch** (*Villerscharte*, 9160'; fine view), and then descends abruptly to the (6 hrs.) *Stöcklen Inn* in the Alpeinerthal (p. 228). — Ascent of the *Fernerkogl* (10,805') laborious (5-6 hrs. from the Längenthaler Alp; superb view).

The train crosses the *Melach* (in front fine view of the broad valley of the Inn, with the Hohe Munde in the background) passes *Unter-Perfuss*, and skirts the crumbling cliffs of the *Reissende Rangen*, on an embankment (550yds. long) in the Inn.

91½ M. **Zirl** (1955'; *Zur Marntinswand*, at the station). The village (2035'; *Post or Stern, *Löwe) is picturesquely situated on the left bank of the Inn, 1 M. to the N. High above is the castle of *Fragenstein* (p. 37).

EXCURSIONS (guides, *Martin Satler*, *Frz. Schnaiter*, and *Joh. Gulleben*). Beautiful view from the (½ hr.) *Calvarienberg*; to the S. are the jagged peaks of the Selrain, Tuxer Ferner (Olperer, Fusstein), etc.; to the N. is the huge gorge of the *Ehbach*, descending from the Solstein. The gorge is best reached by going to the foot of the Calvarienberg, and taking a workman from the cement-works there as guide.

On the left, about 1 M. beyond Zirl, is the **Martinswand** (3650'), rising 1000 ft. perpendicularly above the valley. In 1493 the Emp. Maximilian, having lost his way while pursuing a chamois above the Martinswand, missed his footing, and rolled down to the brink of the precipice, where he clung to a projecting rock, but was unable to move from the spot. His peril being observed from below, the pastor of Zirl, with numerous members of his flock, repaired to the foot of the rock with the host, by the raising of which he granted the emperor absolution. At this juncture, according to tradition, an angel suddenly came to the rescue of the exhausted monarch, and conducted him by unknown paths to a place of safety. The 'angel' was a chamois-hunter, who was afterwards ennobled under the name of Hollaner. The scene of the emperor's perilous adventure is marked by a cross in a small cavern 900' above the Inn, accessible since 1883 by a safe and easy path (1½ hr. from the station). A bust of the emperor, by Klotz, was placed in the cavern in 1884.

The **Grosse Solstein** (8330'; 6 hrs.; with guide) is ascended from Zirl by the *Erlalp* (club-hut to be built) and the *Erlsattel* (p. 36) without serious fatigue. Extensive and striking view. — The ascent of the higher *Kleine Solstein* (8710'), to the N. of the Grosse, is difficult.

From Zirl to *Scharnitz* and *Mittenwald*, see R. 6.

At (10½ M.) **Inzing** (Klotz) the *Hundsthal* opens on the left, with the *Peiderspitze*, *Kofterspitze*, and *Rosskogl* in the background; to the right the *Hohe Munde* and the *Mieminger Hochplatte*. 12½ M.

to Landeck. TELFS. *V. Route 43.* 233

Hatting; 13½ M. *Flaurling* (2000'), at the entrance of the valley of the same name, above which rises the *Grieskogel* (9458').

16½ M. **Telfs** (2045'; *Seiser's Inn,* at the station); the village (**Post;* **Löwe; Traube;* **Schöpfer's Inn,* prettily situated near the bridge), with an extensive cotton-factory, lies on the left bank. The corner-house opposite the 'Löwe' is embellished with a marble bust of *Joseph Schöpf,* the painter (d. 1822), who was a native of Telfs.

EXCURSIONS (guides, *Ant. Gredler, Mich. Spiegl,* and *Joh. Staudacher*). The chapel of *St. Moritz* on the Calvarienberg, ½ hr. to the W., affords a beautiful view. Other fine points are the pilgrimage-church on the *Birkenberg,* ¾ hr. to the N., and the ruin of *Hörtenberg,* 40 min. from the station (beyond *Pfaffenhofen*). — The **Hohe Munde** (8495'; 5 hrs., guide 5 fl.) is ascended on the E. side from Telfs viâ *Buchen* (laborious; fine view from the top; comp. p. 35).

From Telfs to *Nassereit,* see p. 20. — Marked paths lead to the N. from Telfs viâ *Buchen* to (3 hrs.) *Leutasch,* and viâ *Mösern* to (3 hrs.) *Seefeld* (p. 37). — Over the *Niedermunde-Sattel* (6770') to the (5 hrs.) *Tillfuss-Alpe* in the *Gaisthal,* and thence to (3½ hrs.) *Lermoos* (guide 5 fl.), see p. 19. — To the top of the *Zugspitze* (11-12 hrs. from Telfs, with night at the Knorrhütte; guide 7½ fl.), see p. 33.

20 M. *Rietz* (Haas); above the village, on the slope to the left, rises the *Chapel of St. Anthony.*

An easy route leads through the *Klauswald* to (3 hrs.) the **Peter Anich Refuge Hut** of the Austrian Tourist Club, on the *Untere Seben-Alpe* (6560'), whence the *Hocheder* (9106') may be ascended in 2½ hrs., and the *Grieskogel* (9458') in 3 hrs. (guide 5 fl.).

28 M. *Stams* (Stamserwirth); the village (*Speckbacher), 1 M. to the S., contains an extensive Cistercian monastery, founded in 1271 by Elizabeth, mother of Conradin, the last of the Hohenstaufen. The library contains manuscripts, incunabula, coins, etc.

The **Stamser Alpe** (6090'; 3½ hrs., with guide; *Inn), ascended from Stams, affords a good view of the Inn Valley and of the N. Limestone Alps. Thence to the *Birchkogel* (9275'; 3 hrs., with guide), easy and attractive (descent to Kühtai, see p. 231); to the *Grieskogel* (9458'; 3½ hrs.), viâ the *Kreuzjoch* (8410'; pass hence to Selrain, p. 231), another easy expedition (see p. 231). A good path leads to the S. from the Stamser Alp to (1½ hr.) *Ochsengarten* (p. 231), viâ the *Feldringerboden* (6685').

A bridge across the Inn leads from (23 M.) *Mötz* to the village of *Mötz* (Kaiser) and to *Ober-Mieming* (p. 20). — 24½ M. **Silz** (2130'; *Railway Restaurant;* *Post or *Steinbock, Löwe,* in the village, ¼ M. distant), with a handsome modern church. To the left rises the *Peterberg*, with a château of Count Wolkenstein-Rodenegg; to the right the sheer cliffs of the *Tschirgant* (p. 234). Beyond (27 M.) *Haiming* we traverse sparse fir-woods to —

28½ M. **Oetzthal** (2165'; **Sterzinger's Hotel,* at the station, with carriages for hire), the station for the Oetzthal (R. 44). The line is carried by a long embankment over the huge masses of debris with which the *Oetzthaler Ache* has here strewn the valley of the Inn, and crosses the former river by a bridge, 65' high (central span 260'). To the left, fine view of the Oetzthal with the Acherkogl; to the right the Weisse Wand, with its masses of debris.

Beyond (31 M.) *Roppen* (Klocker; carr. to the Oetzthal, see

p. 235), begins the most striking part of the line, which is here sometimes carried along the sheer precipices of the S. bank by means of galleries, and sometimes supported by works projecting into the stream. The train crosses the *Pitzenbach* by a boldly-constructed bridge (to the right the high-lying village of *Karres*, with its slender Gothic church-tower) and reaches —

34¹/₂ M. Imst (2345'). The station occupies a site on ground reclaimed from the Inn; the large village (*Post; *Lamm; *Sonne*, moderate), situated 2 M. to the N., on a terrace on the N. side of the *Gurgler Thal*, is divided by the *Malchbach* into the *Obermarkt* and *Untermarkt*. The (¹/₄ hr.) *Calvarienberg* affords the best view of the neighbourhood: to the N. the Muttekopf, Platteinkogl, Heiterwand, Rauchberg, and Wanneck; to the E. the Tschirgant; to the S. the Oetzthal mountains, and the Pitzthal, lying between the Wildgrat and the Venetberg.

The road from the station to the village passes (³/₄ M.) Brennbichl, where, at *Mayr's Inn*, Frederick Augustus, King of Saxony, died on 9th Aug., 1854. The spot where the king was thrown from his carriage and received a fatal kick from one of the horses is marked by a small chapel with a green roof just beyond the bridge over the Inn.

EXCURSIONS AND MOUNTAIN ASCENTS (guides, *Alois Dialer*, *G. Kammerlander*, *J. A. Schrott*). To the *Aussichts-Pavillon*, ¹/₄ hr. to the S.W.; *Gungl-grün*, above the Landeck road, ³/₄ hr. — To the Rosengartl-Schlucht, beyond the Calvarienberg, to the E. Passing the *Johannskirche* we follow the path, partly hewn in the rock, over 4 bridges to (10 min.) a waterfall (30' high); thence to (20 min.) the *Katzenbödele*, a fine point of view. — A new path leads from (³/₄ hr.) *Tarrenz* (p. 20) across the deep *Salvesen-Klamm* to (1 hr.) the ruins of Alt-Starkenberg. A new track descends into the Klamm, crosses the bridge (320' above the narrow rocky channel of the stream), and ascends the opposite bank to (1 hr.) the brewery of *Neu-Starkenberg* (p. 20). Thence back to Imst, 1¹/₄ hr.

The Tschirgant (7766'; 5-6 hrs.; guide 3 fl.; marked path) is frequently ascended from Imst. A footpath leads to the *Karöster Alp*, viâ *Karösten*, in 2¹/₂ hrs.; thence to the summit 2¹/₂-3 hrs. more (no water on the route except a scanty spring, ¹/₂ hr. above the Karöster Alp). The striking view comprises the Oetzthal and Pitzthal glaciers, the N. Limestone Alps, and the Innthal from Landeck to Innsbruck. — The Muttekopf (9,090'; 5-6 hrs.; guide 5 fl.) is another very fine point of view. The last part of the ascent is fatiguing. We ascend the *Malchbach* to (2¹/₂ hrs.) the *Obermarkt-Alpe* (refreshments) and to the *Muttekopfhütte*, near the *Beisselstein*; thence over turf and rocks to the (1¹/₂-2 hrs.) top.

From Imst to *Nassereit* and over the *Fern Pass* to *Reutte*, see R. 3; over the *Hochtenn* to the *Lechthal*, see p. 210. Walkers from Imst to the *Oetzthal* (p. 236) follow the Innsbruck road to Brennbichl and (2¹/₄ M.) *Karres*, whence a footpath leads to the right to (2 M.) *Roppen* (p. 233).

The train now traverses meadows to (37¹/₂ M.) *Imsterberg*, passing *Mils* (on the right) with a waterfall of the *Larsenbach* 39¹/₂ M. *Schönwies* (Kölle), in a fertile expansion of the valley. Then once more through a defile, and beneath the ruins of *Kronburg* (3450'), situated on a high cliff, to (43¹/₂ M.) *Zams*, with a large nunnery of Sisters of Charity.

45¹/₂ M. Landeck (2670'; *Rail. Restaurant*). The large village (*Post*, R. 1 fl., B. 50 kr.; *Schwarzer Adler*, well spoken of; *Goldner Adler*; *Zum Schrofenstein*, both mediocre), 1¹/₂ M. to the S.W., is situated on both banks of the Inn and is commanded by the ancient *Feste Landeck*. A few spare hours here may be devoted to visiting the Lötzerklamm (see below) or to a walk on the road ascending the Inn, which forms several rapids above the village. Fine view from the loftily-situated *Parish Church*, which dates from 1471: to the N. the *Stanzerwand* and *Silberspitze*; to the N.W. the *Parseierspitze*; to the W. the *Riffler* with its glacier; to the S.W. the *Thialspitze*; to the E. the slopes of the *Venetberg*.

A pleasant excursion may also be made to the **Lötzer Klamm**. We follow the road to the station for about 1 M., but turn to the left just before reaching the station, and cross the bridge to *Perjen*. Thence a path leads along the left bank of the Inn to (1½ M.) the hamlet of *Lötz*, at the back of which, in a wild ravine, is the fall of the *Lötzerbach* (key at the mill, 10 kr.). An alternative way back (¼ hr. longer) leads viâ the considerable village of *Zams* (Gemse). — The **Lötzer Thal** (*'Zamser Loch'*) divides farther up, at the *Unterloch-Alp*, into the *Madriol-Thal* to the right and the *Patrol-Thal* to the left (route across the *Lahmajoch* to Lend in the *Lechthal*, see p. 211).

The village of *Stanz*, beautifully situated at the foot of the *Brandjöchl*, above Perjen, commands a splendid view. The path thither ascends to the left from the Lötz road beyond Perjen (1½ hr. from Landeck); from Stanz to the ruin of *Schroffenstein*, ½ hr. — A picturesque walk leads to (2 hrs.) the *Kronburg* (see above; rustic Inn about ¼ hr. to the S., below the ruin); descent thence to (40 min.) *Schönwies* (see above).

Ascents. The *Thialspitze* (7810'; 4½ hrs.; guide 3½ fl.) is worth ascending. — The *Rothbleisskopf* (9620'), ascended through the *Urgthal* in 6 hrs. (with guide), commands a magnificent view; at the top is the new *Ascherhütte*. — The *Venetberg* (8230'; 5 hrs.; guide 4 fl.), another fine point, is best ascended from the *Attenzoll* (p. 247), viâ *Fliess* and the *Goylesalpe* (new refuge-hut on the top). — The *Parseierspitze* (9965'; 7-8 hrs.; guide 7 fl., Jos. Neuner, Nik. Waldner, and Al. Staggl of Grins, Karl Reich of Pians), the highest peak of the N. Limestone Alps, is not difficult for adepts. From *Grins* (3320'), which lies ½ hr. from *Pians* (p. 205) and 1½ hr. from Landeck, we reach in 4 hrs. the magnificently situated **Augsburger Hütte** (about 7710'; Inn in summer); thence by the *Tawin-Ferner* and the E. arête to the (2½-3 hrs.) summit. Very striking view. — The ascent of the **Gatschkopf** (9652'), from the Augsburger Hütte in 2 hrs., is attractive. A marked path leads over the Gatschkopf to the (5 hrs.) *Memmingerhütte* (p. 211).

From Landeck over the *Arlberg* to *Bludenz*, see R. 37; viâ *Finstermünz* to *Meran* or to the *Stilfser Joch*, see RR. 46 and 50.

44. The Oetzthal.

Comp. Maps, pp. 226, 238, and 246.

Stellwagen from the Oetzthal station daily at 7.30 and 11.30 a.m. to Oetz (1 hr.; 40 kr.), to Umhausen (3 hrs.; 80 kr.), and Längenfeld (5½ hrs.; 1 fl. 20 kr.); on the return-journey it leaves Längenfeld at 5.30 a.m. and 2.30 p.m., reaching Oetzthal at 10 a.m. and 7.15 p.m. An Omnibus also plies several times daily from the same station to Oetz (¾ hr.; 40 kr.). A *Carriol-Post* (3 seats) starts daily from Längenfeld at 8.30 a.m. for Sölden (3 hrs.; returning from Sölden at 1.15 p.m.). — Carriages. With one horse from the Oetzthal station to Oetz 3, to Umhausen 6, with two horses 12 fl. (similar charges from Roppen). New road from Oetzthal to Oetz; tolerable road from Oetz to Umhausen, but bad from Umhausen to Sölden. — Distances. From Oetzthal station to Oetz 3½ M. (from Roppen 4 M.), Umhausen 9½, Längenfeld 16, Sölden 25½, Zwieselstein 28½ M.; from Zwieselstein to Vent 4, to Gurgl 3 hrs. (from Gurgl over the Ramoljoch to Vent 7 hrs.); from Vent over the Hochjoch to Unser Frau

236 V. *Route 44.*   UMHAUSEN.   *Oetzthal.*

S. over the Niederjoch 7 hrs., from Unser Frau to Naturns 4 hrs.; — Guides, see the different excursions. From Umhausen to Gurgl or Vent 5½ fl. (unnecessary). The guide is bound to carry 9 kilogrammes (about 19 lbs.) of luggage; for each additional kilogramme 4 kr. is added to each florin of the tariff-charge. — Mule from Sölden to Vent or Gurgl 5 fl.; from Vent to Unser Frau, with sledge over the Hochjoch (if the state of the snow permits) 7-8 fl.

The *Oetzthal*, the longest lateral valley of the Inn, well watered, and remarkable for the varied charms of its scenery, is broad and fertile in the lower part, contracts higher up to a number of wild ravines and in its highest region branches off in several arms towards the S., terminating in a vast expanse of snow and glacier. The valley is much exposed to the ravages of mud-torrents and avalanches, the former being most frequent in the lower part of the valley, especially near Umhausen and in the Maurach, the latter occurring in the higher regions in winter and spring only. The roads have lately been much improved, but even in summer they are liable to be damaged, so that enquiries should be made beforehand as to their condition. Where there are no inns, accommodation may be procured at the houses of the curés.

Oetzthal Station (2260'; *Sterzinger's Inn), see p. 233. The new road ascends through fir-wood, approaches the *Oetzthaler Ache*, and leads along the right bank, past *Brunnau* and across the *Stuibenbach*, which here forms a pretty waterfall (see below), to the hamlet of *Ebene* (on the opposite bank of the Ache is the large village of *Sautens*), and to (3½ M.) **Oetz** (2690'; *Kasselwirth, R. 60 kr.; *Zum Alpenverein; guides, Alois and Jos. Plattner), a thriving village, visited as a summer-resort, amidst fields of maize, at the base of the *Acherkogl* (9860').

Before reaching Oetz this road is joined by the carriage-road from *Roppen* (p. 233) viâ *Sautens* (5 M.; the best route for walkers entering the Oetzthal from Imst). — A pleasant walk leads from Oetz to the (¾ hr.) *Piburger See* (3130'), on a plateau on the left bank of the Ache. — Another pleasant excursion may be made to the *Auer Klammen*, at the end of the *Ochsengarten-Thal* (p. 231), in which the *Stuibenbach* forms a series of cascades (new path on the right bank). — Route by *Kühtai* to *Selrain* (guide 4 fl. 40 kr.), see p. 234.

At *Habichen* we cross the Ache and ascend the new road winding along the *Gsteig*. Fine retrospect of the rich valley and the wild slopes of the Tschürgant (p. 234). Near *Tumpen* the road recrosses the stream, skirts the lofty and almost perpendicular *Engels wand*, and leads to (6 M.) **Umhausen** (3400'; *Krone*).

Excursions (guides, *J. A. Doblander*, *Joh. Holzknecht*, *Matth. Schmid*). Pleasant walk to the (¾ hr.) °**Stuiben Fall** (guide unnecessary). The path crosses the *Horlachbach* at the church, and ascends its right bank in the direction of the gorge, from which the spray of the fall rises to a great height. After ½ hr. we cross the stream (fine larch-wood), ascend for ¼ hr. more, and arrive opposite the imposing cascade, which is precipitated from beneath a natural bridge of rock in two vast leaps, together 490' in height. A new path, constructed by the German Alpine Club, leads up past the waterfall, crosses the brook above it by the *Frischmannbrücke*, and returns to (1 hr.) Umhausen. — Travellers proceeding to Längenfeld need not return to Umhausen, but may descend, at the bridge below the fall, to the left by the conduit and through meadows and fields of flax to the carriage-road on the bank of the Ache (guide advisable). — Route across the *Gleirscher Jöchl* to *Selrain* or over the *Finsterthal-Scharte* to *Kühtai*, see p. 231.

We now enter the wild defile of *Maurach*, an old moraine with dreary slopes of clay and loose stones, and cross the Ache twice. After a short ascent between blocks of rock, scantily clothed with pines, the road enters a broad green plateau of the valley, in which lie the hamlets of *Au* and *Dorf*, and, farther on, *Längenfeld* and *Huben*. In the foreground the *Hauerkogl* (8160'); farther back the *Hallkogl*, *Berglerkogl*, and (left) *Gamskogl* (see below). By a chapel at the end of the Maurach a short-cut diverges to the left, which passes *Au* and *Dorf* on the right.

6¹/₂ M. **Längenfeld** (3820'; **Oberwirth* or *Goldner Stern*, by the church; **Unterwirth Gstrein* or *Hirsch*) lies at the mouth of the *Sulzthal*, from which the rapid *Fischbach* descends.

EXCURSIONS (guides, *Franz Gstrein*, *Sigm. Guster*, *Georg* and *Oswald Schöpf*, and *Chr. Steinmüller* of Längenfeld, *Joh. Brugger* and *Quir. Gritsch* of Gries). The **Sulzthal** is worthy of a visit. A good path (the beginning of which should be asked for) ascends rapidly from Unter-Längenfeld through wood on the right bank of the deep ravine of the Fischbach (crossing the brook and soon recrossing it), afterwards becoming level, to the village of (1½ hr.) Gries (4960'; Inn at the curé's), opposite the grand *Schrankogel*. The **Gamskogel** (9220'), a splendid point of view, is easily ascended from Gries in 4 hrs. by a new path. — Farther on our route leads through wood and across the extensive *Vordere Sulzthal-Alpe*, passing some waterfalls and the rocky gorge of the Fischbach, to the (2 hrs.) *Hintere Sulzthal-* or *Gries-Alpe* (6535') and to the (½ hr.) *Amberger Hütte* (7710'; built in 1888), which commands a fine view of the *Grosse Sulzthal-Ferner* at the head of the valley. (A pond near the chalets contains lukewarm sulphur-water.) The **Schrankogel** (11,475'; 4¹/₄-5 hrs.; two guides, 9 fl. each, with descent to the Franz-Senn-Hütte in the Alpeiner Thal 11 fl.), is ascended from this point (toilsome, but free from danger; magnificent view). — From the Sulzthal over the *Mutterberger Joch* to the *Stubaithal* (guide 4 fl.), see p. 230; over the *Schwarzenberg Joch*, see p. 228. — A route free from difficulty crosses the *Sulzthal-Ferner* and *Daunkogl-Ferner* to the Dresden Hut (p. 230; 6 hrs. from the Griesalp). — Via *Winnebach* to *Setrain* (guide 4 fl.), see p. 231.

FROM LÄNGENFELD TO THE PITZTHAL a somewhat laborious route crosses the *Hundsbacher* or *Breitlehner Jöchl* (8660'); to Trenkwald (p. 245) 7 hrs.; guide 4 fl. 40 kr. — From Huben over the *Loibiser Joch* to Plösmös, see p. 245.

At (2 M.) **Huben** (good quarters at the curé's) the *Hohe Geige* (11,125') appears on the right, beyond the Hallkogl. (Pedestrians may follow the field-path which diverges to the left 1-1¹/₄ M. beyond Längenfeld, and which, leaving Huben to the right, follows the right bank of the Ache to the second bridge beyond Huben, where it rejoins the road.) Above Huben the valley contracts, and the road becomes bad. Beyond the *Aschbach Inn*, at the *Brand*, we cross the Ache and ascend through wood; then descend to the stream again, cross it twice, and reach (7¹/₂ M.) —

Sölden (4595'; **Grüner zum Alpenverein*, near the church; **Unterwirth Gstrein*; **Oberwirth Riml*), a village charmingly situated on the slope to the right. To the S. rises the *Nöderkogl* (10,364'), separating the Gurgler-Thal from the Venter-Thal.

EXCURSIONS (guides, *Ant. Fender*, *Alois Fiegl*, *Kasp. Grüner*, *Franz Kneist*, *Vinc. Schöpf*). To the *Edelweisswand* (2 hrs.; guide 1½ fl.), on which there is abundance of Edelweiss. — The ascent of the *Brunnenkogl* (9058'; 4 hrs.; guide, 2 fl., not required by adepts) is interesting (stony at places). A well-made path crosses the Oetzthaler Ache and the *Windach*

238   V. Route 44.   VENT.   Oetzthal.

(p. 230) and ascends steeply through wood to (1½ hr.) the *Falkner Inn* (6185'; well spoken of); thence over pastures, detritus, and rocks (path marked with red) to (2½ hrs.) the *Brunnenkogelhaus* (Inn) on the summit, which affords a fine panorama. — The *Grieskopf* (9570'; 3½ hrs.; with guide, 1 fl. 3 kr.) and the *Gaislachkogel* (10,015'; 4½-5 hrs.; guide 3 fl., or with descent to Heiligkreuz 4 fl.) are also interesting points (ascent of the latter not difficult). — To the *Stubaithal* over the *Bildstöckljoch*, see p. 230 (to *Neustift* 12-13 hrs.; guide to the Dresdener Hütte 6 fl.). A pleasant excursion may also be made to the (2 hrs.) *Windacher Alpe* (Fiegl's Inn; see p. 230). — To the *Pitzthal* by the *Pitzthaler Joch*l, see p. 246 (guide 4 fl. 40 kr.). — Carr. and pair from Sölden to Längenfeld 4 fl.

Beyond **Sölden the road** becomes rougher. It soon crosses the brook and ascends through a grand and wild rocky ravine of the Ache, called the *Kühtreien*. At the (3 M.) hamlet of **Zwieselstein** (4775'; *Prantl*; *Traube*, moderate), at the foot of the Nöderkogl, the valley divides into the *Gurgler Thal* (p. 243), which ascends to the left, and the *Venter Thal* to the right.

Besides the road through the valley, another route (club-path), about 1 hr. longer but commanding a series of fine views, leads from Sölden to Heiligkreuz viâ **Gaislach** (about 6560'). Over the *Gaislachkogel* (7-8 hrs. to Heiligkreuz), see above. — Ascent of the **Nöderkogl** (10,365'; 5 hrs.; guide 3 fl.; Sigisb. Prantl or Alois Santer) from Zwieselstein rather fatiguing, but the view remarkably fine. Descent to (3-4 hrs.) *Gurgl* steep.

The path into the **Venter Thal** turns to the right, by a fingerpost, before the first houses of Zwieselstein are reached, crosses the Ache, and follows a stony slope on the left bank of the brook to (1¾ hr.) *Heilig-Kreuz* (5375'; good quarters at the Curé's), the white church of which, rising conspicuously on a precipitous height, is seen an hour before we reach it. Opposite is the range separating the Venter Thal from the Gurgler-Thal, on which several glaciers are visible high above us. Above Heilig-Kreuz we cross the brook by the second bridge to the hamlet of *Winterstall* on the right bank, and soon return to the left bank, which we follow to (2¼ hrs.) **Vent** or *Fend* (6205'; good quarters at the Curé's; *Tappeiner*, clean and moderate, R. 80 kr.), an Alpine hamlet on a green pasture at the foot of the *Thalleitspitze* (11,165'), and (like Gurgl, p. 243) an admirable starting-point for glacier-excursions.

EXCURSIONS AND ASCENTS. (Guides: *Joh. Falkner*, *Quirin Fiegl*, *G. Praxmarer*, *Jos. Scheiber*, *Osw. Schöpf*, and *Jos. Spechtenhauser*; the other Oetzthal guides are also usually to be found at Vent. Here and at Gurgl the guides will not start on Sundays till after mass.) Fine views from the *Feldkögele*, ½ hr. to the N. A very interesting excursion (guide, 2 fl.. recommended to the less experienced) may be made to the W. by a well-made new path over the steep mountain-pastures of *Stablein* to the (2½ hrs.) **Breslauer Hütte** (about 9550'), built and well fitted up by the German Alpine Club, in a magnificent situation at the foot of the *Oetzthaler Urkund* (ascent of the *Wildspitze*, see below). A similar but wider view is enjoyed from the *Wilde Mannle* (9910'; viâ Stablein; 3 hrs.; guide 2 fl. 20 kr.), the S. spur of the Wildspitze. Fine views may also be obtained from the *Motboden* (8650'; 2½ hrs.; guide 2 fl. 20 kr.) on the W. side of the valley, and from the *Mutock* (about 8530'; 2 hrs.; guide 1 fl. 40 kr.) on the E. side of the valley, at the foot of the Ramolkogel (route diverging to the left from that to the Ramoljoch at the shepherd's hut on the *Seeboden*). — To the *Samnoar Hut* (2¾ hrs.), see p. 241.

The ascent of the "Kreuzspitze (11,332'; 5 hrs.; guide 4 fl.), one of the finest and easiest of the longer excursions from Vent, is made either from the Hochjoch or from the Niederjoch. From the Niederjoch route we diverge to the right by the (2¾ hrs.) *Sanmoar-Hütte*, and ascend steep grassy slopes to the (1 hr.) *Kreuzhütte* or *Brizzhütte* (9575'), and over detritus and rocks to the (1¼ hr.) summit. Magnificent °Panorama of the Oetzthal Mts., with a distant view of the Zillerthaler Ferner, Tauern, Dolomites, Adamello, Ortler, Bernina, Silvretta, etc. — Descent to the *Hochjoch Hospice* (2 hrs.), first by the S. arête, then across the *Kreuz-Ferner* (much crevassed, caution advisable; two guides necessary when the snow is unfavourable); lastly over stony slopes to the inn.

The °**Vordere Ramolkogl** (11,630'; 5 hrs., somewhat laborious; guide 4 fl.) is another magnificent point of view. We follow the route to the Ramoljoch (see p. 244) for 2 hrs., then diverge to the left and ascend by a tolerably good path into the *Rothe Kar*, traverse slabs of rock and loose stones, and lastly mount the arête (sometimes difficult) to the (3 hrs.) summit. View similar to that from the Kreuzspitze, but more open towards the E. — Direct descent over the *Kleine Ramolkogl* to the *Ramoljoch* very difficult, and not advisable.

The **Wildspitze** (12,388'; 6½ hrs.; guide 7 fl.), the highest peak of the Oetzthal Alps, presents no unusual difficulty. From the (2½ hrs.) *Breslauer Hütte* (see above) a new path crosses the *Mitterkar-Ferner* to the *Mitterkar-Joch* (about 11.480') and ascends the uppermost ice-slopes of the *Taschach Glacier* from the W. side to the (3 hrs.) S. peak (12,370'), which is connected with the N. peak (18' higher) by a narrow arête (where the overhanging masses of snow necessitate caution). The distant view is magnificent. Descent over the *Taschach Glacier* to the *Pitzthal*, difficult (see p. 246).

The °**Weisskugel** (12,272'; fatiguing) is ascended from the Hochjoch Hospice in 7 hrs. (two guides, 10 fl. each, or with descent to Kurzras 11 fl., or to Matsch 13 fl.). [Easier and shorter ascent from the Karlshader Hütte, see p. 251.] The route descends at first across the steep tongue of the *Hochjoch Glacier* (largely melted away), rounds the *Obere Berg*, and crosses the *Hintereis Glacier* (the *Langtauferer-Spitze*, 11,640', remaining on the right) to the *Hintereis-Joch* (p. 250), between the *Innere Quellspitze* (11,470') and the Weisskugel. Thence to the right by a snowy arête (1 hr. long) to the summit. The °View is of surpassing grandeur. Descent to (4-5 hrs.) *Kurzras* (p. 242), to the *Matscher-Thal* (p. 251), or to the *Langtauferer-Thal* (p. 250).

The *Similaun* (11,808'; two guides, 4 fl. each), ascended in 6 hrs. from Vent, see p. 241. The °*Schalfkogl* (11,600'; 5½-6 hrs.; two guides, 5 fl. each; comp. pp. 241, 213), the *Fluchtkogl* (11,772'; 6-7 hrs.; guide 5 fl.; comp. p. 175), the *Hochvernagtspitze* (11,575'; 7 hrs. viâ the Vernagt Glacier; guide 5 fl.), and the *Finailspitze* (11,515'; 4 hrs. from the Hochjoch Hospice; two guides, 6 fl. each) are also fine points. More difficult is the *Hintere Schwärze* (11,900'; 5 hrs. from the Sanmoar Hut, by the Marzell-Ferner; two guides, 6½ fl. each).

From Vent over the °*Ramoljoch* to (7-8 hrs.) *Gurgl*, a very interesting route, and not difficult, see p. 244 (guide 4 fl. 40 kr.).

OVER THE TAUFKAR-JOCH TO MITTELBERG IN THE PITZTHAL, 8-9 hrs. (two guides at 7 fl.), a rather fatiguing route, but free from danger and very grand. We follow the path towards the Breslauer Hütte (p. 238) for 1 hr. Then to the right, past the *Wilde Mannle* and over fragments of rock and glacier-deposits, to the (2½ hrs.) *Taufkar Glacier*, which we cross; lastly a steeper ascent to the left to the (1 hr.) summit of the °**Taufkar-Joch** (about 10,500'), between the *Taufkarkogl* on the left and the *Weisse Kogl* (11,210') on the right (both of which may be ascended from the Joch without difficulty). Admirable view of the E. Oetzthal Mts. (Ramolkogl, Firmisanspitze, Schalfkogl, Hintere Schwärze, Thalleitspitze; immediately to the left the imposing Wildspitze). We descend across the extensive snow-fields at the head of the large °*Mittelberg Glacier* (on the left the *Hohe Wand* and *Rechte Fernerkogl*), then skirt the *Linke Fernerkogl* and traverse the crevassed lower part of the glacier. Above the ice-fall we cross it to the right to the *Karles Glacier* (observing on the right the *Hangende Ferner*, with its fantastic ice-formations), and reach the (2½ hrs.) *Rothe Karle* (9400'), a buttress of rock affording the finest °View of the huge

Mittelberg Glacier and its imposing ice-fall. To the W. are the snow-clad mountains separating the Pitzthal from the Kaunserthal, and the green Riffelsee at the base of the Verpailspitze; far below lies the Pitzthal. We descend to the right by a new path skirting the ice-fall, over rock, debris, and steep stony slopes; in the valley it crosses the lofty moraine, traverses the flat tongue of the glacier, and leads through underwood on the left bank to (2½ hrs.) *Mittelberg* (p. 245). — This tour may be very pleasantly prolonged by crossing the *Oelgrubenjoch* to the *Gepatschhaus* (p. 247), and thence either returning over the *Gepatsch Glacier* to Vent or crossing the *Weisseejoch* to the *Langtauferer-Thal* and *Mals* (comp. p. 248).

To the PITZTHAL over the Sexten-Joch (10,620'; 9 hrs. to the Taschach Hut; two guides at 7 fl.), a fatiguing route. The pass lies between the *Hochwernagt-Ferner* and the *Sechsegerten-Ferner*, to the N.E. of the *Hochvernagtspitze* (11,575'). — The Taschach Joch (10,670'; 10 hrs. to the Taschach Hut; two guides at 7 fl.), between the *Hochvernagt-Ferner* and the *Taschach-Ferner*, is difficult. — The Seiter-Jöchl (10,140'; to Mittelberg 8 hrs.; guide 7 fl.) between the *Innere* and the *Aeussere Schwarze Schneide*, and the **Tiefenbach-Joch** (10,640'; 7-8 hrs.; guide 7 fl.), between the *Innere Schwarze Schneide*, and the *Linke Fernerkogl*, are also trying routes.

To the KAUNSERTHAL over the **Gepatsch-Joch** (10,580'; 10 hrs. to the Gepatschhaus; two guides at 8½ fl.) a difficult route; better over the **Kesselwand-Joch** (9-10 hrs.; two guides at 8½ fl.). From the Hochjoch Hospice we cross the *Hintereis-Ferner* to the *Hintereiskamm;* then, skirting the grand ice-fall of the *Kesselwand-Ferner*, ascend steep grassy and stony slopes to the flat upper part of the glacier, and thus reach the **Kesselwand-Joch** (10,710'), where we obtain a survey of the huge *Gepatsch-Ferner*. The direct descent over the 'Sumpf', or fissured surface of the glacier, is hazardous; we therefore make a circuit to the left, in the direction of the *Weissseespitze*, and then turn to the right to the *Rauhe Kopf* (9790'), on the flanks of which are the imposing ice-falls of the glacier. Descent, toilsome and steep, between the Grosse and Kleine Rauhe Kopf to the refuge-hut of the German Alpine Club (p. 247); lastly over the flat tongue of the glacier to the Gepatschhaus (p. 247). — Another route to the Kesselwand-Joch leads from Vent over the *Plattei* (8880'), the *Vernagt-Ferner*, and the *Gustar-Ferner* to the Gustar-Joch (10,010'), between the *Kesselwandspitze* (11,160') and the *Fluchtkogl* (11,770'; ascended from the Joch in 1 hr.; *View), and then across the *Kesselwand-Ferner* to the *Kesselwand-Joch* (see above). — A route (partly new) leads also from the *Breslauer Hütte* (p. 238) to the Vernagt-Ferner, commanding magnificent views of glacier-scenery.

To LANGTAUFERS over the **Langtauferer Joch** (10,400'), an interesting route (to Hinterkirch 10-11 hrs.; two guides, 9 fl. each). From the Hochjoch Hospice we cross the *Hintereis Ferner* to the Joch, which lies between the *Vernagelwand* and the *Langtauferer Spitze*. Descent over the *Langtauferer Ferner* to the *Malager-Alpe* and to *Hinterkirch* (p. 250).

To the MATSCHER-THAL over the **Oberetten-Jöchl** (10,710'; the shortest passage from the Oetzthal to the upper Vintschgau, an interesting route (from the Hochjoch Hospice to the Karlsbader Hütte 6 hrs.; guide 7 fl.). The route diverges to the right from that to Kurzras at the *Teufelseck* beyond the Hochjoch (p. 242), follows a new club-path to the *Steinschlag-Ferner*, which it crosses to the Joch (p. 252); and descends across the *Oberetten-Ferner* to the *Karlsbader Hütte* (p. 252). — Over the **Hintereis-Joch** (11,340'; the highest pass of the Oetzthal), a fatiguing but grand expedition (from the Hochjoch Hospice to the Karlsbader Hütte 7 hrs.; two guides at 8½ fl.); comp. *Weisskugel* (p. 239). — To KURZRAS over the **Steinschlag-Joch** (about 9850'), 6 hrs. from the Hochjoch Hospice (2 guides, 6½ fl. each), an attractive glacier-route. We cross the *Hintereis-Ferner* to the snowy crest to the left of the Hintereis-Jöchl; then a very steep descent over the *Steinschlag-Ferner* and to Kurzras (p. 242).

The ROUTE OVER THE **Niederjoch** (to Unser-Frau 7 hrs.; guide 5 fl. 40 kr.) crosses the *Niederthaler Ache* and ascends its left bank, passing the Ochsenhütte, to the (1½ hr.) *Klotzhütte*. It then mounts more steeply, above the tongue of the *Marzell-Ferner*, to the (1¼ hr.) **Sanmoar-Hütte** (8275'; Inn, 20 beds at 80 kr.), splendidly situated opposite the great *Schalf-Ferner* and the *Mutmal-Ferner*, which unite with the Marzell-Ferner below, and encircled by the *Marzellspitzen, Mutmalspitze, Schalfkogl*, and *Diemkogl*.

Fine survey from the mountain-terrace of *Kilfeben*, at the foot of the Diemkogl (1 hr.). — The Sanmoar Hut is the starting-point for the *Kreuzspitze*, the *Similaun*, the *Hintere Schwärze*, and the **Schalfkogl** (11,600'). The route to the last (comp. p. 243) ascends the Schalf-Ferner to the (3 hrs.) *Schalfkogljoch*, between the Schalfkogl and the *Kleinleitenspitze*, and then mounts by the arête, which becomes very narrow, to the (1 hr.) summit. (A shorter but steeper ascent is over the *Diemjoch*, between the *Hintere Diemkogl* and the Schalfkogl; the direct ascent from Vent, over the Diem-Ferner, also crosses this Joch.) — From the Sanmoar Hut to the *Ramoljoch*, see p. 244.

Beyond the hut we soon reach the *Niederjoch Ferner*, which presents no difficulty, and in 1½ hr. more the **Niederjoch** (9840'), to the W. of the *Similaun*, where we obtain a view of the Ortler chain. We now descend by a narrow path, over steep rocky slopes, into the *Tisenthal*, passing the chalets of *Raffein* and *Tisen* (wine), and reach *Ober-Vernagt* and (2½ hrs.) *Unser-Frau* (p. 242).

The *Similaun* (11,808'; two guides required by the less experienced, 4 fl. each, or with descent to Unser Frau 6 fl.) may be ascended from the Niederjoch in 2½ hrs. (steep at places). The best route ascends the snowy slopes to the left before the Niederjoch is reached. The grand view extends E. to the Gross-Glockner, S. to the vicinity of Verona, W. to the Bernese Alps. — Other passes from the Sanmoar Hut to the Schnalserthal (all toilsome and fit for proficients only) are the *Similaunjoch*, between the Similaun and the Marzellspitzen; the *Rossbergjoch*, to the E. of the Hintere Schwärze; and the *Fanatjoch* (about 10,500'), between the Fanatspitze and the Karlesspitze.

Most travellers prefer the easier route from Vent across the Hochjoch (to Unser Frau 8 hrs.; guide 5 fl. 40 kr., to Kurzras 4 fl. 50 kr.; mules, see p. 236). From Vent we traverse pastures to (½ hr.) *Rofen* (6570'), where Frederick with the Empty Pockets (p. 163) found an asylum with the families of Klotz and Gstrein. When this prince re-established his authority, he exempted the hamlet from taxation, a privilege which it enjoyed down to 1849. Above Rofen (5 min.) the path crosses the Ache and ascends slowly on the right bank, passing (¼ hr.) a memorial-stone to Cyprian Granbichler, a guide who lost his life here in 1868. In ½ hr. more we reach the moraine of the *Hochvernagl-Ferner*, piled high up on the right side of the valley, which we cross in ¼ hr. (On the other side of the valley is the broad and stony bed of the glacier. A small part only of the glacier is seen higher up.)

The **Hochvernagt Glacier**, which has receded greatly of late, has frequently advanced rapidly (as in 1677, 1680, and 1770) so as to fill the whole valley and dam up the discharge of the Hintereis and Hochjoch glaciers. A lake called the *Rofensee* was thus formed, the overflow of which has caused great devastation on several occasions. The last disaster of the kind occurred in 1845, when the ice in the valley was no less than 650' in thickness. At the upper Rofenhof a borer is still shown which was sent from Vienna in 1772 to tap the glacier!

An ascent of 1 hr. more (with view of the Wildspitze and the

Weisskugel) brings us to the **Hochjoch-Hospiz** (7970'; bed 1 fl.), situated on the brink of the *Hochjoch Glacier*, which descends precipitously into the valley. To the right are the *Hintereis* and *Kesselwand Glaciers*, with their large moraines.

Ascent of the *Kreuzspitze* (3 hrs.), see p. 239; *Finailspitze*, see p. 239; *Weisskugel*, see p. 239; *Kesselwandjoch*, see p. 240; *Langtauferer Joch, Hintereisjoch, Steinschlagjoch*, see p. 240. Over the *Finailjoch* (about 10,200') to Unser-Frau (a route which may be combined with the ascent of the Finailspitze), 5 hrs.; laborious, but interesting.

Beyond the hospice we cross the moraine for $1/4$ hr. and reach the glacier, which is traversed without difficulty in $1^1/_2$ hr. from E. to W. The **Hochjoch** (9430') lies near its S. end. Retrospect of the Rofenthal and Wildspitze; to the S.E. the Schnalserthal with the Salurnspitze, and beyond it the Martell mountains; N.E., the Stubai glaciers.

We reach the end of the glacier in 20 min. more and descend on the right side of the *Oberbergthal* by a good bridle-path, which winds down to ($1^1/_4$ hr.) **Kurzras** (6600'; rustic *Inn* at the *Kurzenhof*, with a horse for hire), the highest cluster of houses in the **Schnalser Thal**, splendidly situated.

Excursions (guides, *Joh. Garber, Ant.* and *Wend. Nischler, Gabriel Spechtenhauser, Rochus Raffeiner*). Over the *Langgrub-Joch* (9975) or the *Oberetten-Jöchl* (10,710') to the *Matscher Thal* (to the *Karlsbader Hütte* 6 hrs.), fatiguing, see p. 252 (guide 5 fl. 40 kr.). — A route which is trying at places leads to the S. over the **Taschl-Joch** (9135'), affording an admirable view, into the *Schlandernaun-Thal* and to (7-8 hrs.; guide 5 fl.) *Schlanders* (p. 252; shortest way from the Oetzthal to the Martellthal; a bridle-path is being constructed). — The **Weisskugel** (12,272') may be ascended from Kurzras in 7-8 hrs. (guide 10 fl. 80 kr.), viâ the *Steinschlag* and *Hintereis Glaciers* and the *Hintereisjoch*; very fatiguing (better from the Matscher-Thal, pp. 239, 251).

A well-trodden path leads from Kurzras on the left bank of the *Schnalser Bach*, through meadows and larch, to ($1^1/_2$ hr.) *Ober-Vernagt*, where it unites with the Niederjoch route (on the left the Finailspitze and Similaun, on the right the Salurn-Spitze), and to ($1/_2$ hr.) **Unser Frau** (4760'; *Mitterwirth zum Adler; Kreuz*, well spoken of). The valley contracts. After 1 hr. the path crosses to the right bank of the brook, and ascends to ($1/_4$ hr.) *Carthaus* (4355'; *Weisses Kreuz; Rose*, beer), an old monastery. To the N., far below, is seen the mouth of the *Pfossenthal*. The church of *St. Catharina* is seen on a steep height on the opposite bank.

A bridle-path leads through the deep **Pfossen-Thal**, passing the chalets of *Vorderkaser* and *Mitterkaser*, to the (3 hrs.) *Eishof* (6785'; accommodation), the highest farm in Tyrol, situated at the foot of the *Falschungspitze* (across the *Gurglerjoch* or *Eisjoch* to *Gurgl*, see p. 214). An arduous pass (guide necessary, 5 fl.) leads hence over the **Eisjöchl am Bild** (9475'), between the *Hochwilde* (11,405') and the *Hochweisse* (10,754'), and descends steeply over ice and rocks to *Lasnu* and (5 hr.) *Plan* (p. 204), in the *Pfelders-Thal*. A hut is to be built on the S. slope of the Hochwilde.

We now descend rapidly to (1 hr.) **Neurattels** (Inn), where the new road begins (Stellwagen to Naturns at 10 a.m. and 7 p.m. in $1^1/_2$ hr., fare 1 fl.; one-horse carr. $3^1/_2$ fl.). It crosses the stream below (1 M.) **Ratteis** (2810'; Inn) and leads through the wild and

Oelzthal. GURGL. *V. Route 44.* 243

picturesque defile, where it is frequently hewn in the rock or supported by embankments of masonry, to the (3½ M.) Vintschgau postroad (p. 253), reaching it 1½ M. from *Naturns* (*Post*). Thence to (9½ M.) *Meran* diligence thrice daily in 1½ hr., starting at 9 a.m., 2.30 p.m., and 6.15 p.m.; one-horse carriage 3 fl., two-horse 5 fl. 30 kr.

The **Gurgler Thal**, beginning at *Zwieselstein* (p. 238), is the S. ramification of the Oetzthal. Crossing the *Gurgler Ache* at Zwieselstein, the path ascends abruptly on the left bank, and (1 hr.) above the mouth of the *Timbler Bach* (p. 254) returns to the right bank. We again cross the stream twice, pass the chalets of *Pillberg* and *Königsrain* or *Unter-Gurgl*, and reach (2 hrs.) **Ober-Gurgl** (6265'; quarters at the Curé's), the loftiest village in Tyrol, situated in the midst of imposing scenery (to the S. the Gurgler Ferner, Falschungspitze, Firmisanschneide, etc.).

Excursions (guides, *Alois* and *Peter Paul Gstrein*, *Joh. Grüner*, *Joh.* and *Jos. Ant. Klotz*, *Mich. Raffl*, *Vinc. Santer*, *Alois*, *Josef*, *Martin*, *Method.*, *Rupert*, and *Valentin Scheiber*).

To the Gurgler Ferner and the Langthaler Eissee, 2½ hrs., interesting (guide advisable, 1 fl. 80 kr.; to the Steinerne Tisch 3 fl.). The **Gurgler** or **Grosse Oetzthaler Ferner**, the third largest of the Oetzthal group of glaciers, forms a barrier across the mouth of the *Langthal* and dams up the discharge of the Langthal glacier. A lake 1650 yds. long and 660 yds. broad is thus formed when the snow melts in spring. This is the **Langthaler Eissee** (7820'), which, like the Rofensee (p. 241), formerly caused disastrous inundations, but now finds a regular outlet in summer under the Gurgler Ferner. The path (guide advisable) ascends from Gurgl to the left, crossing the torrents issuing from the *Gaisberg-Ferner* and *Rothmoos-Ferner*, to the *Grosse Gurgler Alpe* (occupied by cattle from Schnals), and then, rounding the *Langthaler Eck*, high above the tongue of the Gurgler Ferner, enters the Langthal (p. 244). A small part only of the Gurgler Ferner is seen from this point; a better view is obtained by descending to the glacier below the Eissee and traversing its right side (guide necessary) to the (1½ hr.) *Steinerne Tisch* (about 9500'). A good survey of the Gurgler Glacier and the Eissee is obtained from the Ramol route (see below).

A walk to the **Gaisberg-Ferner** is recommended (3 hrs. there and back; guide 1 fl. 80 kr.). From the bridge over the Gaisberg-Ache (see above) we ascend to the left to the glacier (about 7870'), which may be safely explored from the N. lateral moraine. Grand surroundings (Granatenwand, Seeberspitze, Kirchenkogl, etc.; in the opposite direction the ridge separating Gurgl from Vent).

The **Mutberg** (8725'; 2 hrs., with guide), which rises between the Gaisbergthal and the Rothmoosthal, affords an excellent survey of these two valleys with their glaciers. Beyond the bridge over the Gaisberg-Ache the path ascends the grassy slopes to the right. — The **Hangerer** (9900'; 4 hrs., viâ the Gurgler Alpe; guide 3 fl.), rising more to the S., between the Rothmoosthal and the Langthal, commands a very much more extensive prospect.

Ascents. The ascent of the **Schalfkogl** (11,600'; 10 hrs.; two guides, 7½ fl. each), with the descent to Vent, is recommended to good walkers. From the (3½ hrs.) Ramolhaus (see below) we diverge to the left and ascend the slope, over grass and rocks, and then over snow, passing the *Firmisan-Schneide* (11,380'), and thus reach (2½-3 hrs.) the summit on the N. side. Admirable survey of the Oetzthal glaciers. Descent over the *Schalfkogeljoch* and across the *Schalf-Ferner* to (4 hrs.) Vent.

The *Hohe Wilde* (11,405'; 8-9 hrs.; two guides, 8 fl. each), *Hohe Fürst*

16*

(11,190'; 7-8 hrs.; two guides, 5½ fl. each), and *Liebener Spitze* (11,100'; 5-6 hrs.; guide 5½ fl.) are all difficult and fit for adepts only.

Passes. Over the Ramoljoch to Vent, a magnificent route, free from difficulty (7 hrs.; guide 4 fl. 40 kr., or including the Ramolkogel 7 fl.; mule to the Ramolhaus 4-5 fl.). Crossing the Ache near the 'Widum', or parsonage, we ascend by a tolerable path (best for riding in the early morning) on the left side of the valley, enjoying an admirable view of the Gurgler and Langthaler Glaciers and of the bed of the Eissee (empty in summer). We then mount more rapidly over rock and debris to the (3½ hrs.) *Ramolhaus* on the *Köpfle* (10,105'; Inn, rustic), and again for a short way over loose stones to the *Ramol Glacier*, which we ascend without difficulty to the (¾ hr.) *Ramoljoch (10,440'), a sharp ridge strewn with rocky debris, between the *Kleine Ramolkogl* on the right and the *Hintere Spiegelkogl* on the left. Beautiful view towards the E., embracing the vast expanse of névé at the head of the Gurgler and Langthaler glaciers, over which tower the Hochwildspitze, Falschungspitze, and other peaks, while the Gross-Glockner is said to be visible in the distance; to the W. is the majestic Wildspitze. We descend over the large and easily-passable *Spiegel Glacier* and the moraine on its right side, and then by a better path over grassy slopes high up on the right side of the *Niederthal*. Fine view, to the left, of the Niederjoch glacier, as far as the pass to the right of the dazzling Similaun; more to the right is the Kreuzspitze, and facing us is the Thalleitspitze. The path then descends in zigzags, finally through pine-wood, into the Venter-Thal, and crosses the Ache to (3 hrs.) *Vent* (p. 238). — The ascent of the **Vordere Ramolkogl* (11,630') adds 8½ hrs. to this route (best from the Spiegel Glacier through the *Rothe Kar*; see p. 239; from the Joch very difficult).

[From Gurgl to the Niederjoch. Instead of descending to Vent, the traveller may follow a new path direct from the Ramoljoch to the Sanmoar Hut and thus save about 2 hours. The path crosses the Spiegelferner to a heap of stones on the left side-moraine, then traverses debris and grass, skirting the base of the Vordere Spiegelkogl, and enters the grand and wild *Diemthal*, enclosed by the Firmisanschneide, Schalfkogl, and Dicmkogl. Below the Diem-Ferner we cross the brook, descend rapidly into the Niederthal, cross the bridge over the Ache, and ascend to the Klotzhütte and the (3½-4 hrs. from the Joch) *Sanmoar Hut* (p. 241). A good walker, starting from Gurgl early, and crossing the Ramoljoch and the Niederjoch, may therefore reach Unser-Frau in one day (12 hrs.; guide 10 fl.).]

To the **Passeir** over the Timbler-Joch (8135'), 5½-6 hrs. from Gurgl or Zwieselstein to *Schönau*, see p. 254 (guide 4 fl.; from Schönau over the *Schneeberg* to *Sterzing*, see p. 228). — Over the **Königsthal-Joch** (about 9190') to the *Seeberthal* and *Schönau* (6-7 hrs.; guide 4 fl.), fatiguing. — Over the **Rothmoos-Joch** (about 9850') to (7½ hrs.) *Plan* in the *Pfeldersthal* (p. 254), laborious (guide 5 fl.). — A grand but toilsome route leads over the **Langthaler-Joch** (about 9880') to *Lazins* in the *Pfeldersthal* (8 hrs.; two guides at 5½ fl. each). From the (2½ hrs.) *Gurgler Eissee* (p. 243) we cross the *Langthaler Glacier* to the (3½ hrs.) pass, between the *Langthalerjoch-Spitze* (10,340') and the *Hochweilde* (11,405'), whence the descent to (2 hrs.) *Lazins* (5090'), at the head of the *Pfeldersthal*, is very steep. From Lazins we may either descend the valley to (½ hr.) *Plan* (Inn) and (2½ hrs.) *Moos* in the *Passeierthal* (p. 254); or ascend to the right through the *Lazinserthal* to (3 hrs.) the *Spronser-Joch* (8790') and past the *Spronser Lakes* (p. 275) to *Dorf Tirol* and (6 hrs.) *Meran* (p. 270).

To the **Schnalser-Thal** over the Gurglerjoch or Eisjoch (9950'), a difficult route, to Carthaus 10-11 hrs. (two guides at 6½ fl.). The route crosses the whole of the *Gurgler* or *Grosse Oetzthaler Glacier* (p. 243) to the (6 hrs.) pass between the *Falschungspitze* (10,384') on the W. and the *Hochwilde* (11,405') on the E. View limited. Descent very steep and disagreeable, to (2½ hrs.) *Eishof* (5785') in the *Pfossenthal*, and thence down the valley to (2 hrs.) *Carthaus* (p. 242).

45. The Pitzthal.

Comp. Maps, pp. 226, 238.

A visit to the **Pitzthal**, a valley running parallel to the Oetzthal on the W., is recommended not only to mountaineers, who will find many attractions here, but also to less ambitious travellers who desire to obtain a glimpse at the Oetzthal glacier-region. A cart-track leads as far as *Mittelberg*, about 30 M. from Imst (horses or mules may be hired at Imst, Wenns, and St. Leonhard); but travellers will avoid the necessity of accomplishing this long distance in one day, if they arrange so as to spend the previous night at Wenns.

Stat. *Imst* (2345'), on the right bank of the Inn, 2¼ M. to the S. of the village, see p. 234. A cart-track ascends to the left from the station to (1½ M.) *Arzl* (Inn), picturesquely situated on a terrace at the foot of the *Burgstall* (3440'). To the left runs the *Pitzbach* in its deep ravine. We now ascend the smiling valley, enlivened by numerous farms, past (3¾ M.) the little *Bad Steinhof* (Inn; fine views from the garden), which lies ¼ M. to the right of the road, to (1½ M.) **Wenns** (3195'; **Post; Zum Ochsen*, well spoken of; *Kuprian*, unpretending), a prettily-situated village.

OVER THE PILLERJOCH TO LANDECK OR PRUTZ, 6 hrs., an easy and pleasing route. Good path viâ the village of *Piller* (4415') to the *Gache Blick* (5160'), the top of the pass, on the brink of the deep Innthal. Descent by *Fliess* to the *Altenzoll* (p. 246).

The road now descends to the left, crosses the Pillerbach and ascends the narrow valley of the Pitzbach (passing *Jerzens*, on the left, above) to the (2 M.) Inn *Auf der Schön* (to the right the *Stuibenbach* forms a picturesque fall). It again crosses the brook several times and leads past the hamlets of *Ritzenried, Wiesen* (Inn), *Zaunhof*, and *Hairlach* to (11 M.) **St. Leonhard** (4580'; *Sonne or *Lisele*; *Alte Post, at *Plösmös*, on the right bank). On the right is the fall of the *Fitscherbach*, descending from the *Rofelewand*; to the left (S.E.) rise the *Hohe Geige* (11,125") and the *Puikogl* (10,960').

EXCURSIONS (guides, *Alois Rauch, Alois Neururer*, and *Hieron. Elter*). The *Rofelewand* (10,995'; 6 hrs., with guide; fatiguing), ascended viâ the *Arzler Alp* and the *Todlenkar-Ferner*, commands a striking view. — OVER THE LOIBISER JOCH TO HUBEN 6-7 hrs. (guide 4 fl. 40 kr.), repaying, and shorter than the *Breitlehner Jöchl* (p. 246), but for proficients only. From Plösmös the path ascends the steep terraces of the E. slope of the valley, and then traverses snow and the *Reiser Glacier* to the **Loibiser Joch** (about 8860'), between the *Loibiskogl* and the *Reiserkogl*. Steep descent to the *Breitlehn-Alp* and to *Huben* (p. 237). — Over the *Niederjöchl* or the *Wallfahrtsjöchl* to the *Kaunserthal*, see p. 248.

Passing the fall of the *Leklebach* (on the right) and *Trenkwald*, we next reach (7½ M.) *Plangeross* (5280'; Inn), the last village, and (3½ M.) **Mittelberg** (5880'; **Kirschner's Inn*), the last farm, beautifully situated within view of the **Mittelberg Glacier* (p. 240), the imposing fall of which is 1 hr. farther up the valley. A visit to the glacier is interesting. We reach the end of it in ¼ hr., and then cross its flat and easily-passable tongue to the (1 hr.) right lateral moraine. (To the *Rothe Karle*, see below.)

EXCURSIONS FROM MITTELBERG (guides, *Tob. & Joh. Jos. Ennemoser, Alois Schöpf, Alois, Franz, & Jos. Dobler, Engelbert, Franz, Jos., & Alois Kirschner, Jos. Santeler, Alois Ostrein*, and *Caspar Elter*). To the °**Taschach Glacier**

246   V. Route 45.   PITZTHAL.

(3 hrs.; guide 8 fl.; a most interesting excursion when combined with a visit to the Riffelsee, see below). The route leads to the S.W. from Mittelberg, on the right side of the *Taschachthal*, to the (1³/₄ hr.) end of the glacier, **and** traverses the arched tongue to the left lateral moraine (caution necessary, as deep crevasses are sometimes encountered). The path then ascends grassy slopes to the (1¹/₄ hr.) *Taschachhütte* (7990'), built and well fitted up by the German Alpine Club on a spur of the *Pitzthaler Urkund*, and affording a fine view of the **Taschach Glacier**, with its imposing ice-falls and its environment of glistening snow-peaks (on the left the *Hintere Brochkogl*, 11,026'); on the W. is the *Sechsegerten Glacier* (see below). — To the Riffelsee (7330'; 2 hrs.; guide 1¹/₂ fl.), attractive. The path ascends abruptly from the *Taschach-Alp*. The height to the E. of the lake (*Am Mutten*, 7675') affords a fine survey of the Mittelberg and Taschach glaciers, **and of the Hohe Geige**, Puikogl, and other peaks. We may descend into the upper Taschach-Thal (fine views of the Taschach and Sechsegerten glaciers), reach the path to the Taschachhütte (see above) near the end of the glacier, and return by it to Mittelberg. — The **Mittagskogl** (10,360'; 4¹/₂ hrs.; guide 4 fl.) affords a fine survey of the three glaciers.

The ascent of the *Wildspitze* (12,388') from Mittelberg takes 7-8 hrs. (two guides at 8 fl., to Vent 10 fl.); last part of the way very steep (comp. p. 239). — The *Hohe Geige* (11,125'; guide 5 fl.), *Vordere Brunnenkogl* (11,145'; 5¹/₂ fl.), *Hintere Brunnenkogl* (11,270'; 5¹/₂ fl.), *Blickspitze* (11,055'; 6 fl.), and *Puikogl* (10,960'; 5¹/₂ fl.) may also be ascended from Mittelberg.

PASSES. To SÖLDEN over the *Pitzthaler* (*Söldener*) **Jöchl** (9945'), 6¹/₂-7 hrs. (guide 5 fl.). The route traverses the lower end of the Mittelberg Glacier, and then ascends to the left over steep slopes of grass, debris, and rock to the Joch on the S. side of the *Polles-Ferner*. Descent over the *Rettenbach Glacier* and through the *Rettenbachthal* to Sölden (p. 237). — To VENT over the *Taufkarjoch* (comp. p. 239; 8-9 hrs.; two guides at 7 fl.), a much finer route. Ascent to the *Rothe Karle* by a new path constructed by the German Alpine Club. — The *Seiterjöchl*, *Tiefenbachjoch*, *Sexten joch*, and *Taschachjoch*, see p. 240 (the last two grand but trying). — The *Breitlehner Jöchl* (6 hrs. from Trenkwald to Huben). see p. 237.

To THE KAUNSERTHAL over the *Oelgruben-Joch* (9870'), 7¹/₂ hrs., a fine route, and not difficult (guide 6 fl.). To the (3 hrs.) *Taschachhütte*, see above. We descend on the W. side of the hill to the left to the *Sechsegerten Glacier*, which we ascend without difficulty (enjoying, farther up, a fine retrospect of the Wildspitze and the lofty crest of névé stretching from it towards the W.) to the (2¹/₂ hrs.) *Joch*, a flat snow-saddle between the *Innere* and *Aeussere Oelgrubenspitze* (the former easily ascended from the Joch in ³/₄ hr.; superb view). View limited. (To the left, below, is the small *Oelgruben Glacier*, with its huge moraines.) Descent by an improved path, over debris and grassy slopes, to the (2 hrs.) *Gepatschhaus* (p. 247). — Other passes into the Kaunserthal: the **Madatsch-Joch** (about 8000'), between the *Watzekopf* and the *Schwabenkopf* (from Plangeross to Feuchten 6-7 hrs., not difficult; guide 5 fl.); the **Verpail-Joch** (9100'), between the *Schwabenkopf* and the *Sonnenkogel* (from Trenkwald to Feuchten 8 hrs., laborious; guide 4 fl. 40 kr.); the **Tiefenthal-Joch** or **Wallfahrts-Jöchl** (9050'), between the *Peuschelkopf* and the *Tristkopf* (from St. Leonhard to Kaltenbrunn or Feuchten 7 hrs., trying; guide 4 fl. 40 kr.); the **Niederjöchl** (7835'), from Rietzenried to Kaltenbrunn, past the *Krumpensee*, in 5 hrs. (not difficult; guide 4 fl. 40 kr.).

46. From Landeck to Meran. Finstermünz.

Comp. Maps, pp. 216, 226, 238.

80 M. DILIGENCE (landau with four seats) daily at 3.30 a.m in 15¹/₂ hrs. (10 fl. 32 kr.). STELLWAGEN daily at 8 a.m. from Landeck to Mals (arr. 8.30 p.m.). and from Mals to Meran (7.30 a.m., arr. 4.15 p.m.) DILIGENCE daily at 12.20 p.m. from Landeck to Nauders, in connection with the Swiss diligence to Schuls-Tarasp. Another Stellwagen plies daily from Schlanders (Kreuz) to Meran in 4 hrs (starting at 6 a.m.). EXTRA-POST with two horses,

PRUTZ. *V. Route 46.* 247

without changing carriages, from Landeck to Nauders 23 fl. 90, to Mals 35 fl. 79, to Eyrs 42 fl. 77, to Meran 64 fl. 38 kr.; from Meran to Naturns 10 fl. 14, to Eyrs 25 fl. 81, to Mals 32 fl. 79, and to Landeck 67 fl. 54 kr. (these charges include all fees, etc.).

Landeck (2670'), see p. 234. — The road passes the Schloss and skirts the right bank of the *Inn;* on the left are the slopes of the *Venetberg* (8228'). The river forces its way through a narrow gully and forms several rapids; in the background rise the peaks of the Alps of Kauns. On the left bank is a waterfall of the *Urgbach*, high above which lies the village of *Hochgallmig*. To the left are *Fliess* and *Schloss Bidencck*. (Over the *Pillerjoch* to the Pitzthal, see p. 245.) The road ascends to *Altenzoll* (Inn), and descends to the (6 M.) *Pontlatzer Brücke* (2770'), where the Tyrolese 'Landsturm' nearly annihilated the Bavarian invaders in 1703 and 1809.

On a precipitous rock, to the right, above Prutz, stand the ruins of *Schloss Laudeck*, near which is the village of *Ladis* (3880'), 1 hr. from Prutz, with sulphur-baths (moderate). About 1/2 hr. higher lies *Obladis* (4530'), a well-organised bath-house, with a famous mineral spring, beautifully situated at the foot of the *Schönjöchl* (8160'; easy and repaying ascent of 3 hrs.).

9 M. **Prutz** (2825'; *Post* or *Rose*), where the road returns to the right bank, lies in a marshy plain, at the entrance to the *Kaunser Thal*, the mountains of which have been visible for some time.

The **Kaunser Thal** runs to the E. as far as Kaltenbrunn, then towards the S., parallel with the Pitzthal, to the central mass of the Oetzthal Mts. A good bridle-path leads over the hill formed by the deposits of the *Faggenbach* at its exit from the valley, crosses the stream near the church of *Faggen*, and ascends on the right bank to (3/4 hr.) *Kauns* (3530') and (1 1/4 hr.) *Kaltenbrunn* (4140'; *Eckhardt*), a prettily-situated resort of pilgrims. (Over the *Niederjöchl* to the *Pitzthal*, see p. 246.) The path then leads past *Nufels* and *Vergelschen* (on the left the fine waterfalls of the *Gsallbach*) to (1 1/2 hr.) *Feuchten* (4160'; *Hirsch*), the last village in the valley. (Over the *Verpailjoch* or the *Madatschjoch* to Plangeross, see p. 246.) Farther up, the route crosses the brook twice, and then follows the right bank, passing the chalets of *Wolfkehr*, *Platt*, and *Riefenhof* (occupied in summer only). Above the (2 1/2 hrs.) *Rostitz-Alp* we cross to the left bank, then return to the right by the second bridge, and ascend the steep *Gepatschloch* to the (2 hrs.) **Gepatschhaus** (about 6230'; *Inn*), picturesquely situated on a hill clothed with Alpine cedars, opposite the imposing *Gepatsch Glacier*, the largest in Tyrol (upwards of 7 M. long). About 20 min. farther up, on the left bank of the *Faggenbach*, which forms three falls before reaching the glacier, is the extensive *Gepatsch-Alp*.

Excursions from the Gepatschhaus (guides, *Praxmarer*, *Mich. Auer*, *Thomas Mark*, *Franz & Joel Gfall*, *Ser. Lentsch*, and *J. J. Penz*). A good view of the Gepatsch Glacier is afforded by the *Nöderkogl* (8060'; 3 hrs.; guide 2 1/2 fl.); more extensive from the *Wonnetbery* (9282'; 3 hrs., with guide), a spur of the Innere Oelgrubenspitze; descent over the Gepatsch Glacier. — The ***Aeussere Oelgrubenspitze** (10,980'; 4 1/2-5 hrs.), a splendid peak, is ascended by following the route to the Oelgrubenjoch (p. 246) for 1 1/2 hr., then turning to the left by a narrow path, over detritus, snow (steep at places), and finally rocks to (2 1/2-3 hrs.) the summit. Magnificent view of the Oetzthal mountains. — The *Weissseespitze* (11,580'; 5 1/2-6 hrs.), see below. — The **Glockthurm** (10,994'; 4 1/2-5 hrs.), fatiguing. Ascent through the *Krummgampenthal* to the Scharte between the *Krummgampenkopf* and the *Glockthurm*; then by the arête, over rock and debris, to the top (striking view). Descent, if preferred, by the *Krummgampen-Ferner* and the *Glockthurmjoch* to Radurschel (p. 249), or by the *Krummgampenschartl* to Langtaufers.

PASSES (comp. Map. p. 238). To MITTELBERG in the Pitzthal over the *Oelgrubenjoch* (9870'), 8 hrs. (guide 6 fl.), see p. 246. — To VENT (p. 238) over the *Gepatschjoch* (10,080'), 9-10 hrs., difficult; better over the *Kesselwandjoch* and *Guslarjoch* (p. 240). This route has lately been made easier by the erection of a refuge-hut on the *Kleine Rauhe Kopf*, in the middle of the Gepatsch Glacier, 3 hrs. from the Gepatschhaus. — To LANGTAUFERS over the *Weissseejoch* (9660'; 6 hrs.; guide 5½ fl.; mule to the Joch 4 fl.), a fine route, free from difficulty. From the Gepatsch-Alp we ascend to the right over grassy slopes to the first terrace of the *Nöderberg*, affording an admirable view of the glacier (see above), over which rise the Fluchtkogel and Kesselwände. To the W. is the *Glockthurm* (10,994'). We next cross the Faggenbach, turn to the right round the flank of the Nöderberg, and traverse the moraine of the *Weisssee Glacier* to the (2 hrs.) *Weisssee* (8515'), at the foot of the imposing *Weissseespitze* (11,580'; ascent from the lake in 4 hrs., fatiguing but very interesting; direct descent on the S.W. side very steep, and not recommended; better descent to the *Falginjoch*, between the Weissseespitze and the Karlspitze, and over the Falgin-Ferner to Malag). Our route now ascends abruptly to the right over turf and debris, and then traverses the *Seejoch Glacier* to the (1½ hr.) Joch, between the *Vordere Karlesspitze* and the *Nasse Wand*. (Another pass, marked by a small shrine, to the right of the Nasse Wand, may be traversed if the snow beyond the Weissseejoch is troublesome.) The descent from the pass leads at first over a very steep, and generally hard-frozen slope of snow (caution necessary; better to follow the stony slope to the right of the snow); then over debris and turf (3/4 hr., a good spring), and by a better path into the *Malag-Thal*, commanding a good survey of the mountains enclosing the Langtauferer-Thal (*Freibrunnerspitze*, *Weisskugel*, *Langtauferer Spitze*). Above the hamlet of *Malag* we turn to the right and descend to (2½ hrs. from the Joch) *Hinterkirch*, in the *Langtauferer-Thal* (p. 250), and to (2 hrs.) *Graun* (p. 250). — To the RADURSCHEL-THAL through the *Kaiserthal* and over the *Kaiserjoch* (9625'), laborious (to the *Radurschel-Haus*, see below, 5 hrs.; guide 3½ fl.). The *Riffeljoch* (about 9500'), to the N. of the Glockthurm, and the *Glockthurmjoch* (about 9500'), to the S. of it, are both fatiguing.

9½ M. **Ried** (2850'; *Post; Maass*), a thriving village, with the castle of *Siegmundsried*, the seat of a district-court. The road to Ladis (p. 247) diverges here to the right. On a hill on the left bank lies *Serfaus*(4700'), whence an interesting route leads over the *Furgler-Joch* (9120') to (6-7 hrs.) *See* in the Patznaun (comp. p. 219).

The road now ascends gradually over the extensive alluvial deposits at the mouth of the *Stallanzer Bach*. To the right, the ruined church of *St. Christina*. It then descends, close by the river, to (4¼ M.) *Tösens* (3045'; Wilder Mann), crosses (½ M.) the Inn again, and next reaches (4¼ M.) —

18½ M. **Pfunds** (3185'), consisting of two villages, *Stuben* (*Traube, R. 50-80 kr.; Post) on the high-road on the left bank of the Inn, and *Pfunds* (*Inn) on the right bank, picturesquely situated at the entrance to the *Radurschel* or *Pfundser Thal*. To the S.W. towers the *Piz Mondin* (10,374'), belonging to the N. Engadine chain; to the S.E. rise the *Glockthurm* (10,994') and other peaks of the Oetzthal snow-mountains.

The **Radurschel Thal**, at first a narrow ravine, expands higher up into a beautiful Alpine valley with luxuriant pasturage and wooded slopes. In the background to the S.E. rises the lofty *Glockthurm* (10,994'). A good path, steep at the beginning only, leads through wood on the left side of the valley, past the mouths of the *Pfunder Tscheythal* (left) and the (1½ hr.) *Sadererthal* (right); then on the right bank (passing after ¾ hr. a shooting-lodge on the left bank, at the entrance to the *Nauderer Tscheythal*) to the beautifully-situated *Radurschelhaus* (5880'; Inn). About ½ hr. farther up is the fine *Alpel Fall*, formed by the Radurschelbach. — From the Radurschelhaus to the top of the *Glockthurm* (10,994'; 6 hrs.; with guide), very laborious (comp. p. 247). — From the Radurschelhaus over the *Kaiserjoch* (9625'), the *Glockthurmjoch* (9500'), or the *Riffeljoch* (10,170') to the (5 hrs.) *Gepatschhaus*, see p. 247. Other passes lead from the head of the valley to the S. over the *Radurscheljoch* (9800'), to *Hinterkirch* in Langtaufers (see p. 250); from the *Nauderer Tscheythal* to the S. over the *Tscheyer Schartl* (9200') to Langtaufers, and to the W. over the *Tscheyjoch* (8750') to Nauders; and from the *Sadererthal* over the *Saderer* or *Labauner Joch* (7870') to Nauders (6 hrs. from Pfunds, easy and interesting; the ascent of the *Labauner Kopf*, mentioned below, may easily be combined with this pass).

From Stuben or Finstermünz to *Samnaun* and across the *Zeblesjoch* to the *Patznaun* valley, see p. 218.

Above Pfunds (1½ M.) the road crosses the Inn, and gradually ascends on the right bank, being hewn in the perpendicular rock at places, passing through three tunnels and two avalanche-galleries, and occasionally supported by buttresses of masonry. Picturesque views of the narrow valley of the Inn. The finest point is at (23 M.) **Hoch-Finstermünz** (3730'; *Inn*), a group of houses on the road-side, 420' below which is *Alt-Finstermünz*, with a tower and a wooden bridge over the Inn. Opposite are the slopes of the Piz Mondin, to the left the Piz Lat and other mountains of the Engadine. — The road now quits the Inn and enters (to the left) a small lateral valley leading to Nauders. Farther on, a fine waterfall is passed. The end of the defile is guarded by small fortifications *(Fort Nauders)*. The road then ascends in a long bend (old road shorter for walkers) to (1¼ hr.) —

27 M. **Nauders** (4470'; *Post; Löwe*, moderate; *Mondschein*), a large village, almost rebuilt since a fire in 1880, with the old *Schloss Naudersberg*, the seat of the local authorities. The *Cemetery*, on a hill about ¼ M. to the E., commands a fine view of the Ortler.

High-road to the W. to the *Engadine* viâ *Martinsbruck*, see Baedeker's *Switzerland*. The *Piztat* (9200'; 4 hrs.; with guide), the highest point of the range separating our route from the Innthal, the base of which is skirted by the road, affords a fine view of the Engadine Mts.; another good point is the *Labauner Kopf* or *Schmatzkopf* (8928'; 4 hrs.; Jos. Patscheider of Nauders recommended as guide), to the N.E., in the direction of the Radurschel (see above).

The road gradually ascends on the right bank of the *Stille Bach* to (4 M.) the **Reschen Scheideck** (4900'), its culminating point, the watershed between the Inn and the Adige. A little beyond the village of (½ M.) *Reschen* (4890'; *Stern*, rustic), which lies near the small green *Reschen-See*, a very striking *** View is disclosed. The background is formed by the snow and ice-fields of the Ortler chain; on the left the *Laaser Spitze* and the *Tschengiser Hochwand*, farther distant the *Cevedale*, then the lofty pyramid of the *Königsspitze*, and lastly, to the right, the *Ortler* (p. 291), forming the central point of the picture the whole way to Mals.

The **Etsch**, Ital. *Adige*, rises near Reschen, flows through the lake of Reschen, and afterwards through the *Mittersee* and *Heidersee*. We next reach (1½ M.) *Graun* (Traube), a poor village at the entrance to the *Langtauferer Thal* (in the background the Weissseespitze and Vernagelwand).

The smiling **Langtauferer Thal** is traversed by a good track on the right bank of the *Carlinbach*, passing *Bedross* and *Kapron* (Inn), to (2½ hrs.) *Hinterkirch*, or *Grub* (6150'; rustic Inn, 5 min. below the church). At the chalets of *Malag* (6260'), ½ hr. farther up, the magnificent glacier-girt head of the valley (Langtauferer Spitze, Weisskugel, Freibrunnerspitze, etc.) is disclosed to view.

EXCURSIONS FROM LANGTAUFERS (guide, *Christian Hoheneger*.) The *Weisskugel* (12,272') may be scaled in 7 hrs. by the *Bärenbart-Ferner* and the *Bärenbart-Joch* (between the *Bärenbartkopf* and the Weisskugel), or in 7-8 hrs. by the *Langtaufer Glacier*, the *Weisskugeljoch*, and the *Hintereisjoch*, a laborious ascent (comp. p. 239). — The *Freibrunnerspitze* (11,056'), through the *Langgrub* and over the *Rotheben-Ferner* in 5-6 hrs., also fatiguing; magnificent view. — *Schafkopf* (9830'), to the N. of Hinterkirch, in the direction of Radurschel, 3 hrs., repaying, and not difficult. — *Danzebell* (10,300'), from Kapron through the *Kühthal* in 5-6 hrs., fatiguing; magnificent view. The descent may be made through the *Planait-Thal* (see below) to (4 hrs.) *Mals*.

PASSES. Over the *Weisssecjoch* to *Gepatsch* (6 hrs.), see p. 248. — Over the *Langtauferer-Joch* to *Vent* (10-11 hrs.), see p. 240. — To the *Matscher-Thal* over the *Matscher Joch* (10,500'), between the Freibrunnerspitze, and the Bärenbartkogel, or over the *Bärenbartjoch* (about 11,150'), between the Bärenbartkogel and the Weisskugel (to the Karlsbader Hütte, 7 hrs.), trying glacier-tours (p. 251). — To *Radurschel*, see p. 249.

The road crosses the *Carlinbach*, here confined by embankments, and leads past the *Mittersee* to (3½ M.) —

37 M. **St. Valentin auf der Heide** (4695'; *Post, ½ M. to the S.), formerly a hospice, situated between the Mittersee and the *Heidersee*. Below the latter lake begins the monotonous *Malser Heide*, which the road traverses, still commanding a view of the majestic Ortler. On the left opens the *Planailthal*. To the right, at the foot of the hills, lies the village of *Burgeis* (3975'; Kreuz), with its red spire and the castle of *Fürstenburg*, once a summer-seat of the bishops of Coire, now occupied by poor families. Farther on, the Benedictine Abbey of *Marienberg* lies on the hill to the right. We next pass *Schleis*, with the entrance to the *Schlinigthal* on the right.

42 M. **Mals** (3430'; *Post*, or *Adler; Bär; Hirsch*), a village of Roman origin, in the *Upper Vintschgau* (Ital. *Val Venosta*, so named from the Venosti who once inhabited the valley). The church contains a good picture by *Knoller*, representing the Death of Joseph.

The mountain-slope to the E. (opposite the Post, 5-10 min. ascent) has been laid out as *Pleasure Grounds*, with benches, etc., and commands a fine view of the Vintschgau; immediately in front rises the wooded pyramid of the *Glurnser Köpfl*, to the right the entrance of the Münsterthal, and to the left the snowy dome of the Ortler, the Tschengiser Hochwand, the Laaser Spitze, etc. — There are various other good points of view in the neighbourhood, *e.g.* near the mill, 5 min. from the Post (through the old ruin and past the tower).

PEDESTRIANS on their way to Prad and **Trafoi** may avoid the sunny and fatiguing route through the Valley of the Adige from Mals to Prad viâ Spondinig by proceeding southwards from Mals to (1¼ M.) *Glurns* (see below), crossing the artificial bed of the *Adige*, and skirting the base of the mountains to (4¼ M.) *Lichtenberg* (°Inn), charmingly situated amidst fruit-trees, and commanded by a castle of the same name (see below), to (1¼ M.) *Agums*, a village with a ruined castle, and lastly to (³/₄ M.) *Prad*. — Glurns (3000'; *Sonne; *Steinbock*), a small town enclosed by walls, with an ancient church, is the chief place in the *Upper Vintschgau* and the starting-point for several interesting excursions. (Guides, *Alois Blaas* and *Jos. Plangger*.) Ascent of the *Glurnser Köpfl (7838'; 3¹/₂ hrs.; guide 3, with descent to Gomagoi 4 fl.), very attractive, and not difficult; splendid view of the Vintschgau, the Ortler, and the Oetzthal snow-mountains. The *Piz Ciavalatsch* (9040'; 6-7 hrs.; guide 5, with descent to St. Maria in the Münsterthal 5¹/₂, to Trafoi 6 fl.) affords a striking view of the Ortler. Other ascents: *Norkenspitze* (*Hohes Joch*, 8185'; 4¹/₂ hrs.; guide 3¹/₂ fl.); *Piz Maipitsch* (10,400'; 7¹/₂ hrs.; 5 fl.); *Piz Seesvenna* (10,568'; 8-9 hrs.; 6 fl.), etc.

To the MÜNSTERTHAL. A good new road leads from Glurns first on the right, then on the left bank of the *Rambach*, to (4 M.) *Taufers* (4010'; 'Post), a loftily-situated village with three churches and overlooked by three ruined castles (Stellwagen every afternoon to Schlanders viâ Glurns). About ³/₄ M. farther on is the Swiss frontier and (³/₄ M.) *Münster*, Rom. *Mustair* (4100'; Piz Ciavalatsch; Hirsch), the first Swiss village, with a large Benedictine abbey-church. The road now descends and crosses the Rambach, passes the *Aua da Pisch*, a fine waterfall in a wooded ravine on the left, and leads viâ *Stelva* to (2 M.) St. Maria (1550'; *Piz Umbrail; Weisses Kreuz*, both expensive), a large village at the entrance to the *Val Muranza*, which is traversed by the path to the Wormser Joch (p. 280). From this point over the *Ofener Pass* to *Zernetz* and through the *Val da Scari* to *Schuls*, see *Baedeker's Switzerland*.

On quitting Mals we pass the venerable tower of the *Frölichsburg*. The road leads through *Tartsch* (Hilpold, well spoken of) to (3³/₄ M.) *Schludérns* (3010'; Schweizerhof), at the mouth of the *Matscher Thal*. To the left rises the *Churburg*, a château of Count Trapp, containing a valuable collection of armour (not always accessible).

The Matscher Thal. A tolerable cart-track leads from Tartsch (see above; a better road leads from Mals direct in 2 hrs.) to (4 M.) *Matsch* (5100'; *Stadt Karlsbad; Telser) in the Matscher-Thal, prettily situated on a mountain-terrace, with a fine view of the Vintschgau, Ortler, etc. About ¹/₂ M. below, on a rocky knoll in the ravine of the Saturnbach, are the ruins of *Ober-Matsch* and *Unter-Matsch*. The track leads hence through pleasant pastures to the (2 hrs.) *Glieshöfe* (5940'; good accommodation) and the (³/₄ hr.) *Innere Matscher-Alpe* (6560'), where a good view of the grand head of the valley is obtained: to the N. the *Matscher Ferner* with its imposing ice-fall, the *Freibrunnerspitze, Bärenbartkogel, Weisskugel*, etc. A bridle-path leads hence over mountain-pastures in (2 hrs.) the Karlsbader Hütte (8080'; well fitted up), at the foot of the *Oberettenferner*.

ASCENTS from the Karlsbader Hütte (guides, Jos. Tschiggfrei, Jos. Heinisch, Franz & Ser. Thanei, and Franz Guntsch of Matsch.) The *Weisskugel (12,272'), over the *Matscher Glacier* and the *Hintereisjoch*, 4-5 hrs. (guide 5, with descent to the Hochjoch Hospice 7, to Kurzras 7, to Langtaufers 11 fl.; two guides advisable); shortest route for this ascent (comp. p. 239). — *Freibrunnerspitze* (11,056'), over the *Matscher Glacier*, 3¹/₂ hrs. (guide 4, or with descent to Langtaufers 7 fl.); *Schwemser Spitze* (11,335'), over the *Oberetten-Ferner* in 3¹/₂ hrs. (guide 4¹/₂, with descent to Kurzras 6¹/₂ fl.); *Innere Quell-Spitze* (11,466'; 3¹/₂ hrs.; guide 4¹/₂ fl.); *Aeussere Quellspitze* (11,180'; 3 hrs.; guide 4 fl.); *Saturnspitze* (11,256'), from the Innere Matscher Alpe over the *Saturn-Ferner*, 4¹/₂-5 hrs. (guide 5 fl., with descent to Kurzras 6¹/₂ fl.); five difficult ascents, fit for adepts only. — *Remsspitze* (10,500'; 5 hrs. from Matsch; guide 4 fl.), a fine point, free of difficulty.

PASSES. Over the *Matscher Joch* or the *Bärenbartjoch* to Langtaufers, see p. 250; over the *Hintereisjoch* to Vent, see p. 240 (to the Hochjoch

Hospice 6 hrs.; guide 5½ fl.). — Over the Langgrub-Joch (9975') to the *Schnalser Thal* (from the Innere Matscher Alpe over the *Saturn-Ferner* to Kurzras, 5½ hrs.; guide 5½ fl.), a fatiguing route. A preferable route leads from the Karlsbader Hütte over the Bildstöckeljoch (10,780'), to the S. of the *Schwemser* (from the Karlsbader Hütte to Kurzras 5 hrs., guide 5 fl.). The shortest route from the Karlsbader Hütte to the Hochjoch leads over the Oberettenjöchl (10,710'), between the *Aeussere Quellspitze* and the *Schwemser;* descent across the *Steinschlag-Ferner*, whence a new path to the left leads to the *Hochjoch* (comp. p. 240; to the Hochjoch Hospice 6 hrs., guide 6 fl.).

In the distance to the right, beyond the Adige, rises the ruined castle of *Lichtenberg* (see above). At (3¾ M.) *Neu-Spondinig* (2915'; *Hirsch), the Stelvio road (p. 277) diverges, intersecting the plain to the right. In the distance are the glaciers of the W. Ortler range. — Then (2 M.) —

52 M. **Eyrs** (2950'; *Post; Krone*). Opposite is *Tschengls*, a village almost entirely burnt down in 1885, with an old castle, commanded by the *Tschenglser Hochwand* (11,060'). In the vicinity are the small baths of *Schgums*. 4 M. *Laas* (2850'; Sonne), with extensive marble-works, in which the fine marbles of Laas and Göflan are prepared for sculptors and architects. The *Laaser Thal* here opens to the right. To the S. rises the ice-peak of the *Laaserspitze* (10,824').

MOUNTAIN EXCURSIONS in the Laaser Thal (guides: Joh. Tscholl and Franz Tappeiner). The *Laaserspitze* (10,824'; 6-7 hrs.; guide 6 fl., to Gand 7 fl.) is not difficult. We proceed past the chapel of *St. Martin* and the marble-quarries to the (2 hrs.) *Lower Laaser Alp* (about 6170'); thence over the *Schluderscharte* (about 9840'), between the Laaserspitze and the Schluderspitze, in 4½ hrs. to the top (descent to Gand, see p. 286). *Schluderspitze* (10,585'; 6-7 hrs.; guide 6 fl.); *Kleine Angelus* (10,860'; 4 hrs.; guide 5½ fl.), from the *Upper Laaser Alp*, which lies to the W., about 720' above the Lower Laaser Alp; *Pederspitzen (Aeussere*, 11,158', *Mittlere*, 11,345'; 4½-5 hrs.; guide 6½ fl.): all these are toilsome ascents. — The *Hohe Angelus* (11,585'; 5½ hrs.; guide 6½ fl.), over the *Angelus-Scharte*, difficult (descent to Sulden, 3-4 hrs., see p. 289). — A somewhat arduous route leads over the *Laaser Glacier* and the *Rosimjoch* (10,435') to Sulden (10 hrs.; guide 7 fl.; comp. p. 293), with which the ascent of the *Vertainspitze* (11,614'; 1½ hr. from the pass; guide 1¼ fl. extra) may be conveniently combined. — Over the *Laaser Scharte* (10,170') to the Martell-Alm (9½ hrs.; guide 7 fl.), toilsome; the ascent of the *Lyfi-Spitze* (10,975'; 1 hr. from the pass; guide 1½ fl. extra) may be incorporated with this route.

The road crosses a large mound of debris (the top of which commands an extensive view over the Vintschgau, and of the Laas Mts. with the Hochofenwand and Hohe Angelus on the S.) and then descends to *Kortsch* (2600') and (3¼ M.) —

59 M. **Schlanders** (2365'; *Post; Weisses Kreuz*, moderate), at the entrance to the *Schlundernaun-Thal* (p. 242; guides, Joh. Gruber and Engelb. Nollet). At *Göflan*, in the vicinity, are quarries of white marble. The road crosses (2 M.) the Adige above *Goldrain* (with the Schloss of that name on the right), and then the rapid *Plima*, which descends from the *Martellthal* (p. 285) on the S. On a hill at the mouth of that valley stand the castles of *Unter-* and *Ober-Montan*. Opposite, on the N. slope, is *Schloss Annenberg*, high above which stands the pilgrimage-church of *St.*

Martin auf dem Kofel. Beyond (2 M.) **Latsch** (2110'; **Hirsch*) the road recrosses the Adige, and runs high above the narrow and rocky bed of the river, to (2¹/₂ M.) *Castelbell* (Mondschein), where we reach a vine-growing region. To the left, on a rock near the road, rises the picturesque ruined château of Castelbell, which was burned down in 1842. The road now traverses a broad, and at places marshy valley, to *Tschars* (opposite *Tabland*), **Leimer's Bad Kochenmoos*, with a sulphur spring (passing travellers also received), and (3¹/₂ M.) *Staben* (1800'), at the foot of a barren slope. High above Staben is the half-ruined castle of *Juval*, past which the route into the Schnalser Thal formerly led (p. 242).

Below Staben the road passes the narrow mouth of the *Schnalser Thal* (on the left bank of which runs the new road to *Neuratteis*, p. 242), and leads to (2 M.) —

71 M. **Naturns** (1675'; **Post*), with a ruined castle. On a hill on the opposite bank is *Schloss Dornsberg*. Beyond (3³/₄ M.) *Rabland* the valley contracts. A saddle, called the *Töll* (1665'), separates the Vintschgau from the Adige district. The road passes an *Inn* (to the N.W. of which lies *Partschins* at the base of the *Tschigatspitze*; in the valley, the *Partschins Waterfall*, p. 274), and soon crosses the (1¹/₂ M.) rocky bed of the river, which forms several rapids lower down. On the right bank of the Adige are the small baths of *Egart*. The road now descends the slope of the *Marlinger Berg* (p. 273) in a wide curve, affording a striking view of the beautiful Valley of Meran, which resembles a vast orchard of vines, chestnuts, and walnuts, enlivened with villages, churches, and castles, and enclosed by beautifully-formed porphyry mountains. At the foot of the hill (1 M.) we pass on the right the *Forst Brewery*, ¹/₄ M. beyond which is *Schloss Forst* on the left (p. 274). The road here crosses the Adige, and soon reaches (2¹/₄ M.) —

80 M. *Meran* (1050'), see p. 270.

47. The Passeierthal.
Comp. Map, p. 246.

From Meran to St. Leonhard 5, thence over the Jaufen to Sterzing (p. 222) 7 hrs. — From Meran viâ St. Leonhard to Moos 7, thence (with guide) over the Timblerjoch to Sölden in the Oetzthal (p. 237) 9 hrs.

The Passeierthal is intimately associated with the memory of ANDREAS HOFER, the Tyrolese patriot (b. 1767, shot at Mantua 1810; see p. 165). The lower part of the valley presents few natural attractions, but those who cross the Jaufen to Sterzing, or the Timbler Joch to the Oetzthal, will be rewarded with some grand scenery, especially on the latter route.

Meran, see p. 270. The wild *Passer* flows through the valley. A rough paved track on the right bank passes the *Zenoburg* (p. 272) and the narrow entrance of the *Spronser Thal* (or *Fineleloch*, p. 273), crosses the *Finelebach*, and leads to *Kuens* and (1¹/₂ hr.) *Rifflan* (1770'; high up on the opposite bank stands the castle of *Schönna*, p. 273). It then descends to (¹/₂ hr.) *Saltaus* (1560'; **Inn* in the old Schildhof), where the vineyards terminate. In rainy weather the torrents descending from the E. slopes sometimes dissolve the crumbling soil of the *Kellerlahn*, a fissured slope near St. Martin, and thus give rise to dangerous mud-avalanches ('Lahn'). 2 hrs. St. *Martin* (*Unterwirth), above which are the *Pfandlerhof*, Hofer's asylum in 1809, and, ³/₄ hr. higher, the *Pfandlerhütte* or *Hoferhütte*, where he was captured in 1810, with a memorial tablet. We next reach the (¹/₂ hr.) *Sandhof* (Inn), in which Hofer was born, and mementoes of him are shown. Adjacent is the new *Hoferkapelle*.

Above (¹/₂ hr.) **St. Leonhard** (2130'; *Einhorn* or *Strobtwirth*; *Brühwirth*), the chief village in the valley, rises the *Jaufenburg*, a ruin on an isolated green hill (view). The Tyrolese peasantry stormed the churchyard in 1809, and drove out the French.

OVER THE JAUFEN TO STERZING, 7 hrs., bridle-path (guide useful, 4¹/₂ fl.; riding not recommended). The path leads through the *Waltenthal*, to the E. (pretty retrospect of the glaciers of the Pfelderthal), to (2 hrs.) the little village of *Walten* (Inn, rustic), and ascends rapidly to the Jaufenjoch (6870') in 2 hrs. more (two primitive inns, one on each side of the pass). Several splendid views of the Oetzthal snow-mountains. Descent through the *Jaufenthal*, or by the regular Jaufen path on the S. slope of the *Ratschingesthal* via *Kalk* to **Gasteig** (p. 223) and (3 hrs.) *Sterzing* (p. 222).

FROM ST. LEONHARD TO SÖLDEN IN THE OETZTHAL (10¹/₂ hrs.; guide to Zwieselstein 6 fl.; Jos. *Gögele* and *Joh. Oettl* at **St. Leonhard**, *Seb. Pfitscher* and *Seb. Pixner* at Pfelders, *Joh. Gadner* in Rabenstein). The Passeierthal turns to the W. above St. Leonhard. The *Grafellweg*, a good bridle-path, leads on the left bank of the turbulent Passer, past the toll-house of *Grafell*, where a small toll is exacted, to (2 hrs.) *Moos* (3340'; Hofer). Opposite the village is a fine waterfall of the *Pfelderer Bach*, above which is the hamlet of *Platt*. [About 3 hrs. up the *Pfelders Thal* (tolerable path) lies the hamlet of *Pfelders* or *Plan* (5340'; °Inn), and ¹/₂ hr. farther up is *Lazins* (5090'), the last hamlet; to the right rise the precipitous walls of the *Gurgl-Passeirer Kamm*. Passes over the *Eisjöchl* to the *Pfossenthal*, over the *Langthaler Joch* or the *Rothmoosjoch* to Gurgl, and over the *Sprouser Joch* to Meran, see p. 244.]

At Moos the Passeierthal turns to the N. The path first traverses a stony chaos on the left bank, then crosses to the right bank, skirting the rock by means of a gallery, ascends a steep slope, and descends to the (1¹/₂ hr.) *Seehaus* (Inn, tolerable). The *Kummersee*, formed by landslips in 1401, frequently devastated the valley by its overflow, but was drained in 1774 (now a pasture).

The next villages are (³/₄ hr.) *Rabenstein* (4405'; Inn; to *St. Martin* and over the *Schneeberg* to the *Ridnaunthal*, see p. 223) and (1 hr.) *Schönau* (5040'; °Inn), at the mouth of the *Seeberthal* (over the *Königsthaljoch* to *Gurgl*, see p. 244). The path ascends to the right to the (³/₄ hr.) *Schönauer Alpe* (6020'), to which the route from the Timbler Alpe descends (p. 223); it then crosses the Passeierbach to the left and ascends steeply through the *Moosthal* over debris to the (2 hrs.) **Timbler-** or **Tümmel-Joch** (8135'; view limited). Descent at first steep, over rock. After 1¹/₂ hr. we cross to the left bank of the *Timblerbach*, recross to the right bank in ³/₄ hr., and then follow the hill-side, on the right bank of the *Gurgler Ache*, to (³/₄ hr.) *Zwieselstein* and (1 hr.) *Sölden*. Travellers bound for Gurgl descend the slope by the path diverging to the left before the second bridge over the Timbler Bach, and at *Pillbery* (p. 243) join the route to (3¹/₂ hrs. from the pass) *Ober-Gurgl* (p. 243).

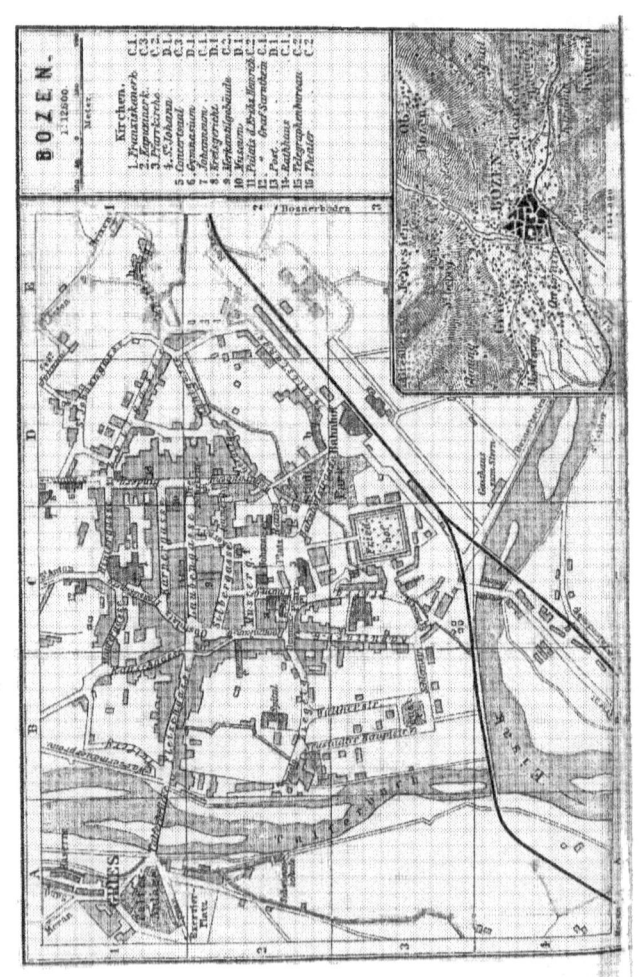

VI. SOUTH-WESTERN TYROL.

48. Botzen and Environs 256
 The Calvarienberg. Virgl. Haselburg. Badl. Kollern. Gries, 257, 258. — Jenesien. Glaning. Altenberg. The Ritten. Oberbotzen. Klobenstein. Lengmoos. Ritterhorn, 258, 259. — The Sarnthal. Runkelstein. Sarnthein. Over the Auen Joch or Kreuzjöchl to Meran; over the Penser Joch to Sterzing. The Eggenthal, 260. — Birchabruck. Over the Satteljoch to Predazzo. Deutschnofen. Weissenstein. Weisshorn. Schwarzhorn. Welschnofen, 261. — Over the Caressa Pass to Vigo, 262. — The Tierser Thal. To Fassa over the Tierser Alpel. Rosengarten. Grasleiten Pass. Kesselkogel. Vajolett Pass. Santner Pass. Rosengartenspitze, 262. — Gröduer Thal. Seiser Alp. Schlern, 263-266. — Ueberetsch. Kaltern. Mendel Pass. Monte Roën. Penegal, 266-268.

49. From Botzen to Meran 268
 From Botzen to Meran viâ Nals, Tisens, and Lana. The Gaul, 268. — Excursions from Meran. Schloss Tirol. Lebenberg. Schönna. Fragsburg, etc., 272-274. — Vigiljoch. Rothsteinkogel. Mutspitze. Spronser Thal. Gfallwand. Jünger. Hirzer. Laugenspitze, 274, 275. — From Meran to the Baths of Rabbi through the Ultenthal, 276.

50. From Eyrs (Landeck, Meran) to Colico on the Lake of Como. Stelvio Pass 276
 The Three Holy Springs, 277. — Ascent of the Ortler from Trafoi, 278. — Tartscher Alm. Korspitze. Kleinboden. Hochleitenspitze and over the Hochleitenjoch to Sulden, 278. — Excursions and Passes from Franzenshöhe and from the Stelvio Pass, 279, 280. — Wormser Joch. Piz Umbrail, 280. — Excursions from Bormio. Monte delle Scale, 281. — Excursions from S. Caterina. Forno Glacier. Monte Confinale. Val Zebrù, etc., 282. From S. Caterina to Ponte di Legno by the Gavia Pass; to Pejo over the Sforzellina Pass, 283. — Val Malenco. Excursions from Chiesa. Monte della Disgrazia, 284. — Val Masino. Badile, 285.

51. The Martellthal 285
 Cevedale. Innere Pederspitze. Zufrittspitze. Veneziaspitze, etc., 286. — From Martell to Rabbi over the Süllent-Joch; to Pejo over the Hohenferner-Joch or the Fürkele-Scharte; to St. Gertrud in the Ultenthal over the Soy-Joch or Flim-Joch, 286. — To S. Caterina over the Cevedale Pass. From Martell to Sulden over the Madritsch-Joch or the Eissee Pass, 287.

52. The Suldenthal 287
 Rosimboden. Schaubachhütte, 288. — The Hintere Grat and End der Welt. Schöneck. Payerhütte. Hochleitenspitze. Tabarettaspitze. Vertainspitze. Hintere Schöntaufspitze. Pederspitzen. Plattenspitze. Cevedale, 289. — Königsspitze. Monte Zebrù. Suldenspitze. Ortler, 291. — From Sulden to S. Caterina over the Eissee and Cevedale Passes; to Martell over the Madritsch-Joch; to Trafoi over the Hochjoch and Ortler Pass, 292. — To Laas over the Rosim-Joch, 293.

53. From Botzen to Verona 293
 Monte Bondone, 294. — Monte Stivo, 295.

54. **From Trent to Riva. Lago di Garda** 296
 From Terlago over the Monte Gazza to Molveno, 296.
 — From Alle Sarche viâ Comano to Riva, 296. — Excursions from Arco, 297. — Excursions from Riva. Full of the Ponale. Monte Brione. Gorge of Varone. Monte Baldo, 299. — Valle di Ledro. Val Ampola, 300. — Excursions from Gardone, 302.

55. **The Val Sarca. Giudicaria** 303
 From Mezzolombardo to Stenico viâ Molveno, 303. — Val d'Algone, 304. — From Riva to Tione direct by the Durone Pass, 304. — Dosso del Sabione. From Pinzolo to the Val di Sole viâ Campiglio, 305. — From Pinzolo to Molveno over the Bocca di Brenta, 305. — Cima Tosa. Cima di Brenta, 306. — Val di Genova, 306. — Bedole. Leipsic Hut. Adamello. Lares Hut, 307. — From the Leipsic Hut to Val Camonica by the Passo del Lago Scuro, the Passo del Lago Ghiacciato, or Passo Presena. Presanella. Val di Daone and Val di Fumo, 308.

56. **From S. Michele to Tirano. Val di Non. Val di Sole. Tonale Pass. Passo d'Aprica. Val Camonica** ... 309
 From Cles to Meran over the Gampen Pass, 310. — S. Romedio, 311. — From the Baths of Rabbi to Pejo over the Cercena Pass, 311. — From Pejo to S. Caterina and to the Martellthal, 311. — Passo di Montozzo. Val d'Avio, 312. — Passo del Mortirolo. From Edolo to Brescia through the Val Camonica. Lago d'Iseo, 313.

48. Botzen and Environs.

Comp. Maps, pp. 246, 304, 320.

Hotels. °KAISERKRONE (Pl. a; C, 2), Muster-Platz, R. from 1 fl., L. 30, A. 30 kr., D. 2 fl., B. 60 kr.; °HOTEL VICTORIA (Pl. b; D, 2), at the station, R. 1-1½ fl., L. & A. 75, B. 60 kr.; °SCHWARZER GREIF (Pl. c; C, 2), Johannes-Platz, with baths, 'Old German' wine-room, and good cuisine, R. & L. from 1 fl.; °MONDSCHEIN (Pl. d; D, 1), Bindergasse, R. 80, D. (incl. wine) 80 kr.; °ERZHERZOG HEINRICH (Pl. e; B, C, 2), Dominikanergasse, R. & L. 70 kr.; °HÔTEL DE L'EUROPE (Pl. f; C, 2), Johannes-Platz, with Kräutner's Restaurant (see below); R. & L. 1 fl. 20 kr.; °STIEGL (Pl. h; C, 1), in the Zollstange, ¼ M. to the N. of the station, with shady garden, moderate. — °BADL (Pl. d) and others at Gries, see p. 258.

Restaurants. °*Kräutner* (beer), Johannes-Platz; °*Schgraffer*, opposite, with shady garden; °*Zum Bürgersaal*, with garden; °*Rozner Hof (Schluff)*, at the foot of the Calvarienberg; °*Forsterbräu (Natje)*, Laubengasse 10 *Vilpianer Bierquelle*, to the S. of the station; *Tschugguel*, Dominikanergasse; *Larcher*, Bindergasse; *Schlernwirth*, Schlern-Str. 14, Neustadt; *Bräuhaus*, at Gries, opposite the Badl. Wine at the *Pfau*, next to the post-office, at the *Zallinger Buschn*, Rauschgasse 4, and at the *Patzenhäusl*, Zollgasse 14.

Cafés. *Kusseth*, next to the Kaiserkrone; *Walther*, next door to the Schwarzer Greif; *National*, Pfarr-Platz 10.

Money-Changers. *Schicart Söhne*, Johannes-Platz; *Tschurtschenthaler*, Obst-Platz, corner of the Lauben; *A. Decorona*, in the Lauben; *Wilh. Schwarz*, near the Badl at Gries.

Theatre in the rear-building of the Kaiserkrone (see above); performances four times weekly in winter.

Preserved Fruits. *Actiengesellschaft für Conservirte Früchte*, Lauben 7; *Al. Tschurtschenthaler*, Zollgasse. Fresh fruit (a staple commodity): Süd-

tiroler Früchte-Export-Gesellschaft, Rauschgasse; *J. Holzknecht*, **Karnergasse**; *P. Rieger*, **Mustergasse**. Dried Alpine plants (Edelweiss, etc.): *Santner*, Bindergasse.

Photographs: *Moser*, Johannes-Platz; *Augschiller*, Korn-Platz.

Baths (swimming and others) at Gries, below the Talferbrücke (reserved for ladies 8-10 a.m.).

Stellwagen to **Kaltern** (p. 267), thrice daily in summer, in 3 hrs. (fare 80 kr.; starting from the railway-station and the Mondschein). — To the *Mendel*, see p. 267.

Botzen, Ital. *Bolzano* (880′), a town with 10,640 inhab., was the chief depôt of the traffic between Venice and the North in the middle ages, and is now the busiest commercial town in Tyrol. It is charmingly situated at the confluence of the *Talfer*, which descends from the *Sarnthal* on the N., and the *Eisak*, which falls into the Adige 3 M. below the town. The E. background, beyond the Eisakthal, is formed by the picturesque and fantastic dolomite peaks of the Schlern and the Rosengarten, while to the W. the view is bounded by the long ridge of the Mendel, stretching from Mte. Roën to the Gantkofel and rising above the castled hills of Ueberetsch. Fine view of the environs from the Talfer bridge.

The traffic of the town centres in the *Laubengasse*, with its arcades and shops, and the adjoining *Obst-Platz*. In the former the chief buildings are the *Rathhaus* and the *Mercantilgebäude*, with a hall for exhibitions. Shady *Promenades* have been laid out between the station and the town. In summer, when the heat in the basin of Botzen is very oppressive, the *Wassermauer* on the Talfer affords a cool walk after sunset (approached from the Talferbrücke, to the right, or from *Zwölfmalgreien*, the N. suburb). In July and August the wealthier citizens retire to their country-seats on the Ritten, at Kollern, Jenesien, etc., returning to Botzen in September.

The Gothic *****Parish Church** (Pl. 3; C, 2), of the 14-15th cent., has a W. portal with two lions of red marble, in the Lombard style, and a fine open tower, completed in 1519. Behind the high-altar is the vault of Archduke Rainer (d. 1853), with a marble relief. Altarpiece by Lazzarini, a pupil of Titian. — The gateway on the E. side, with the inscription '*Resurrecturis*', leads to the **Cemetery** (Pl. C, 3), surrounded by arcades. In the S.W. corner is the vault of the Giovanelli family, with a Madonna under a Gothic canopy, designed by Schnorr.

The **Franciscan Monastery** (Pl. 1; C, 1) possesses a finely-carved old German altar (in a chapel adjoining the sacristy). Fine cloisters; in the fore-court (to the right) is a reproduction of the grotto of Lourdes, generally surrounded by worshippers. — Horticulturists should visit the gardens of the Archduke Henry and Dr. Streiter, on the Oberbotzener Berg, of the late artist Moser in the Raingasse, and of Count Sarnthein, Franziscanergasse 2. In the last is an ancient Roman memorial marble.

ENVIRONS. The *****Calvarienberg** (950′) commands a fine view of the town and its W. environs (25 min.: turn to the left from the highroad by the Botzener Hof beyond the Eisak bridge, cross the railway, and ascend to the right). The oratories on the path to the summit contain curious life-size groups in wood. A more extensive view is obtained from the square powder-tower at the hamlet of *Virgl*, 25 min. farther up, or from the *Wendlandthof* (1695'; Inn), 10 min. higher. — Another walk follows the lime-tree avenue to the right of the Eisak bridge, turns off by the ($^1/_4$ hr.) footpath to the left after crossing the railway, and ascends through wood to the ($^3/_4$ hr.) partly preserved *Haselburg, or castle of *Kühbach*, picturesquely situated on the brink of a precipice, and commanding an excellent view of the valley of the Adige (Restaurant).

The footpath continues to the S. beyond the Haselburg and in $^1/_4$ hr. divides at a moss-grown rock (1570'). The right branch leads to the ($^1/_2$ hr.) *Statterhof* (refreshments) and descends viâ *St. Jakob* to ($^1/_2$ hr.) the highroad, beside which it runs through meadows to (1$^1/_4$ hr.) Botzen; the left branch rapidly ascends the *Langenwand* to (1 hr.) *Seit* (2715'), crosses the ridge of the *Kollerer Berg*, and leads through fine wood to (1$^1/_4$ hr.) *Bauernkollern* (3755'; *Baumgartner), and thence viâ *Badl* back to (2 hrs.) Botzen. The direct road to Badl (*Bad St. Isidor*; 2990') ascends to the left on the bank of the Eisak immediately beyond the Eisak bridge (see above), turning to the right before reaching the church of *Kampil*, and mounting to (1$^1/_2$ hr.) *Kampenn*, with a small château. Thence it again ascends to the right to ($^1/_4$ hr.) a finger-post indicating the way to the 'Badl', which it reaches in $^3/_4$ hr. more (*Inn, rustic, open in summer only). St. Isidor and Kollern (*Bauernkollern* 3755', *Herrenkollern* 3860'), situated $^3/_4$ hr. farther up, are favourite summer-quarters (horse from Botzen to Badl 4; to Kollern 6 fl.). Beautiful wood-walks and charming views. Marked paths ascend from Bauernkollern or Herrenkollern (1$^1/_4$ hr. in each case) to the *Titschen* (5290') and the *Rothwand* (4945'; splendid view).

Gries (900'; *Hotel-Pension Austria, *Hotel-Pension Bellevue, *Grieser Hof, Sonnenhof, these four first-class, with gardens; *Badl, beyond the Talfer bridge, with baths; *Kreuz; *Pension Trafoier; apartments at numerous villas), a village on the right bank of the Talfer, lies in a sheltered situation at the base of the *Guntschna-Berg*, and is frequented in winter by persons with delicate chests, the mean temperature being 4$^1/_2$° Fahr. higher than that of Meran. The *Curhaus* contains a café-restaurant, reading-rooms, etc. (music three afternoons a week). The *Stiftskirche* contains frescoes by Knoller. Fine view of the Dolomites from the Cemetery.

The *Guntschna-Berg*, the S. buttress of an extensive plateau similar to the Ritten, lies between the valleys of the Talfer and Adige and extends nearly as far as Meran. Its surface is sprinkled with villages (*Jenesien*, *Flaas*, *Mölten*, etc.) and farms. Jenesien (4180'), occupying a lofty and pleasant situation 6 M. from Botzen, a summer-resort of the townspeople, is worthy of a visit. From Gries we proceed to the N.E., crossing the *Fagenbach*, to *Trojenstein*, pass the *Gescheibte* (round) *Thurm* (said to be of Roman origin), and ascend in windings to the (1 hr.) village of *St. Georg* (1980'). (Charming view near the church.) *Jenesien* (3545'; *Oberwirth; Unterwirth), 1$^1/_2$ hr. farther on, is not visible until we are close to it. A little before reaching it we pass a barren hill on the left (the 'Krumme Bühel') which commands a splendid view of the Dolomites. — An excursion to *Glaning* and *Greifenstein* is also interesting. By the old parish-church of Gries we ascend by a steep track to the village of (1$^1/_2$ hr.) Glaning (2360'; *Messner Inn*), lying on a spur of the *Atten* (see below) and affording a picturesque view. We then descend to the ($^1/_2$ hr.) ruin of *Greifenstein* or *Sauschloss* (2445'), perched on a rock high above the Adige, and then either return as we came, or descend (very steep and

and its Environs. KLOBENSTEIN. *VI. Route 48.* 259

rough) to (3/4 hr.) *Siebeneich* and follow the Meran-road (p. 269) to *Moritzing* and (1½ M.) Botzen. — The *Altenberg (4010'), which commands a splendid view, is easily ascended from Glaning in 1½-2 hrs., or from Gries by a marked path viâ the *Trattnerhof* in 3 hrs. Return to (1½ hr.) Botzen by *Siebeneich* (p. 269) and the Meran road, or by train.

The **Ritten**, a lofty and extensive plateau to the N.E. of Botzen, between the Talfer and the Eisak, is a favourite summer-resort. The chief villages are *Oberbotzen* and *Klobenstein*. The new bridle-path (shady in the morning; horse to Oberbotzen 5, to Oberbotzen and Klobenstein 10 fl.) leads by (3/4 M.) *St. Anton* (p. 260) and ascends to the right to *St. Peter*. Here we turn to the right and ascend by a somewhat steep paved path, and then by a broader road, to a (3/4 hr.) cross, and thence to the left (the track to the right leads to *Ploner*), chiefly through wood, to (2 hrs.) **Oberbotzen** (3825'), which commands a fine *View of the Dolomites from the Latemar to the Geislerspitzen. *Menz's Aussichtswarte*, or belvedere, affords an admirable view towards the W. (Ortler, Oetzthal Alps). From (¼) *Maria-Schnee* (Unterhofer, tolerable) a picturesque road (with varying views of the Schlern, etc.) leads to (3/4 hr.) *Wolfs-gruben* (3925'), with its small lake, and (1 hr.) **Klobenstein** (3765'; *Staffler Inn, pens. 2½-3 fl.), the busiest and most beautifully-situated village on the Ritten, with a magnificent view of the long chain of the Dolomites. The best point of view is the *Belvedere*, ¼ hr. to the E., to the left of the road to *Lengmoos*, which is now almost a part of Klobenstein: to the extreme left are the Geislerspitzen between the Villnöss and the Gröden, then the Langkofel, Puflatsch, Schlern, Rothwaud, Latemar, Zangen, Weisshorn, etc., the Mendol terminating the range on the W. About ½ hr. farther to the N., in the valley of the *Finsterbach*, are the curious *Earth Pyramids, columns of the debris of an old moraine, worn into their present shapes by the action of rain-water, and preserved from farther destruction by stones or trees on their summits. A road from Lengmoos crosses the ravine by a wooden bridge to (3/4 hr.) *Mittelberg*, whence we may proceed to *Lengstein* and *Waidbruck* (p. 226; 3 hrs. from Klobenstein). — The direct route from Botzen to Klobenstein (3½-4 hrs.) is by a rough road (not suitable for driving), viâ *Rentsch*, *Kleinstein*, and *Unterinn*. From Klobenstein to Atzwang (p. 226), or to Steg, a steep bridlepath (2 hrs.).

The ***Rittnerhorn** (7405'; guide 2 fl., A. Lobis or 'Spänglertoni' of Klobenstein; horse 3½ fl.), ascended from Oberbotzen or Klobenstein by a marked path in 3½ hrs., is an admirable point of view. The route from Klobenstein ascends gradually to (2 hrs.) *Pemmern* (Inn, poor; Badl, ¼ hr. to the E., better), and thence by the *Rittner-Alpe* to the summit (new refuge-hut). Extensive survey (panorama by Seelos): to the E. the Dolomites from the Peitlerkofel to the Mts. of the Fleimserthal; to the S. the Alps of Trent, Monte Baldo, Bocca di Brenta, Adamello, Presanella; to the W. the Ortler and the Oetzthal Alps; to the N. the Stubai and Zillerthal snow-mountains, and the Tauern as far as the Gross-Glockner. Descent, if preferred, viâ the *Villanderer Alp* and *Villanders* to (4½ hrs.) *Klausen* (p. 225); or viâ *Barbian* to (3 hrs.) *Waidbruck* (p. 226); to *Sarnthein* through the *Tanzbachthal* or over the *Sarner Scharte*, fatiguing.

17*

Sarnthal (one-horse carr. to Runkelstein 3 fl.). Immediately to the N.W. of Botzen opens the *Sarnthal*, a deep valley intersecting the porphyry mountains, watered by the *Talfer*, and sometimes contracting to a wild ravine. The narrow road to (13½ M.) Sarnthein leads to the N. from the Obst-Platz through the Franziskanergasse to the (1½ M.) spinning-mill of *St. Anton* and *Schloss Klebenstein*. (Walkers follow the Wassermauer, passing *Schloss Maretsch*.) On the right, above, is the church of *St. Peter*, and on the left the *Gescheibte Thurm* (p. 259). The road to the left over the bridge leads to Gries (wine at the *Stegwirth* and the *Sandwirth*, on the right bank). Our road, however, keeps to the right, following the left bank of the Talfer, and passes below (1 M.) *Runkelstein, a castle belonging to the Emperor of Austria, built in 1237 and thoroughly restored in 1884-88 (adm. daily, 10-12 and 4-7). It is adorned with curious mediæval frescoes (Inn). To the left, farther on, rises *Schloss Ried* (*Staffler's Inn), on a rock on the right bank of the Talfer. Beyond this, also to the left, are the *Sarnerhof Hotel*, and then, high above the road, the ruined *Rafenstein* or *Sarner Schloss* (2130'). On the hill to the right is the ruin of *Wangen* or *Langegg*. Passing the (1½ M.) inn *Zum Sarner Zoll* (toll 2 kr.), we enter (1¼ M.) the *Mackner Kessel*, a wild rocky chaos, beyond which the *Johanniskofel*, a nearly perpendicular porphyry rock, 330' high, on which is perched a chapel *(Johanniskirchlein)*, arrests the attention. We cross the Talfer, pass Meier's Inn, recross to the left bank at the (1 hr.) *Bader Inn*, and reach the (20 min.) *Tourist Inn*, 7½ M. from Botzen. The valley now expands, and we next reach (6 M.) **Sarnthein** (3200'; *Gänsbacher* or *Post*; *Schweizer*; *Braunwirth*), the principal village in the valley, pleasantly and healthily situated, and much visited in summer. To the E. rise the ruins of *Reineck* and *Kranzelstein*, to the N. the *Kellerburg*.

Attractive passes lead from Sarnthein to the W. over the Auen-Joch (6370') and *Hafling* (p. 275; 6 hrs.), and over the Kreuzjöchl (6500') and by *St. Katharina in der Schart* (p. 275) to *Meran* (7 hrs.; guide in each case 5 fl.). — At *Astfeld* (3200'; Inn), 3 M. above Sarnthein, the valley divides: the right (E.) branch is named the Durnholzer Thal, the left (W.) branch the *Penser Thal*. In the former lies (3 hrs.) the hamlet of *Durnholz* (5150'; quarters at the curé's), with a small lake; the route to it passes *Reinswald*, on the slope to the right, by which the path from the *Latzfonser Joch* descends (p. 226; from Durnholz over the *Schalderer Joch* to Schalders, see p. 225). — A tolerable road ascends the **Penser Thal**, passing *Aberstücki* (4205'), situated in a side-valley to the left, at the base of the *Hirzer* (p. 275), and (7 M.) *Rabenstein* (4090'; *Inn), with the lead and silver mines of Mr. Wilberforce, to (2 M.) *Ausser-Pens* (4330'; Inn) and (3 M.) *Pens* (4690'; poor Inn). From Pens a marked path leads by *Asten* to the **Penser Joch** (7250') and through the *Jaufen-Thal* to (6 hrs.) *Sterzing*, or through the *Eggenthal* to (5 hrs.) *Mauls* (p. 224), uninteresting (guide from Sarnthein 6 fl.; Jos. Aichner or Jos. Wassermann of Sarnthein).

Eggenthal. The lower part of the *Eggenthal*, which unites with the Eisakthal about 2¼ M. above Botzen, is remarkably picturesque and deserves a visit. (Carr. with one horse from Botzen to the waterfall and back 5 fl.) We drive to (2 M.) *Kardaun*

(950'), following the Brixen road to *Rentsch* (Lamm), and there crossing the Eisak and the railway. Here we turn to the right through a gateway (toll 2 kr.) into the narrow ravine, watered by the *Karneidbach*. On a precipitous rock to the left rises the picturesque castle of *Karneid* (1570'). After 2 M. the road passes through two short tunnels; under the bridge before the first of these the Karneidbach forms a picturesque fall. This is the finest point in the valley, which expands higher up. On the slopes to the left are several 'earth-pyramids' (p. 259). 6 M. (10 M. from Botzen) **Birchabruck** (2850'; *Lamm*), charmingly situated, with a superb view of the Latemar to the right, and the Rothe Wand and Rosengarten to the left. The valley ramifies here, the *Welschnofener Thal* diverging to the left, and the *Unter-Eggenthal* to the right.

In the Unter-Eggenthal a road ascends among the scattered houses of the village of that name to (1½ hr.) the upper *Church* (4500'). Thence we proceed to the (2 hrs.) *Reiterjoch-Alpe* (6555'), with remains of old fortifications, between the *Reiterjoch* or *Cima della Valsorda* (9080') on the left, and the *Zangenberg* or *Pala di Santa* (8160') on the right, the latter (splendid view) ascended from the Alp in 1¼ hr. We then either descend to the right, through the *Val di Stava*, to (2½ hrs.) *Tesero*, or ascend to the left to the (½ hr.) **Satteljoch** (7010'), between the Reiterjoch and *Mte. Agnello*, and descend thence by the *Val Gardeno* to (1½ hr.) *Predazzo* (p. 321); an attractive excursion. — A pretty path through the woods leads along the foot of the Latemar from Unter-Eggenthal to the (1¼ hr.) *Untere Karrersee* (see below).

On the plateau between the Eggenthal and the Etschthal, 6 M. to the S.W. of Birchabruck, lies **Deutschnofen** (4430'; *Adler*; *Rössl*), a considerable village, prettily situated. It may also be reached from stat. *Branzoll* (p. 293) in 3½ hrs., viâ *Leifers* and the *Brandenthal*. Charming excursion from Deutschnofen to the beautifully-situated monastery and pilgrimage-church of (1¾ hr.) *Weissenstein* (4950'; *Inn*), and thence across the plateau, affording admirable views of the valley of the Adige and the mountains beyond it, to (1½ hr.) *Aldein* (Inn) and (1½ hr.) stat. *Auer* (p. 293). — The *Weisshorn* (7585'), an excellent point of view, may be ascended without difficulty from Weissenstein in 2½, from Deutschnofen in 3, or from Aldein in 3½ hrs. (guide advisable). The descent may be made to the S. to the (½ hr.) *Joch Grimm* (6725'; Inn), and thence either to the W. by the *Grimm-Alp* and *Radein* to *Fontana Fredda* (p. 321), or to the E. by the *Lavazze-Alp* to (2½ hrs.) *Cavalese* (p. 321). — The **Schwarzhorn** (7995'), to the S. of the Weisshorn, commands a more extensive view (from the Joch Grimm 1¼ hr; from Cavalese by the Lavazze-Alp, 4 hrs., comp. p. 321).

To the E., a road ascends from Birchabruck along the *Welschnofener Bach* to (3½ M.) **Welschnofen** (3885'; *Rössl*; *Kreuz*; *Krone*), known in the Fassa as *Nova Italiana*, and occupying a fine open situation. To the right rises the serrated ridge of the Latemar, to the left the imposing Rosengarten. From Welschnofen over the *Caressa Pass* to Vigo 4½ hrs. (guide 3 fl., not indispensable; Joh. Kaufmann, Leop. Huck, and G. Munter of Welschnofen recommended). The route ascends gradually past several farms, and enters the wood. At a (¾ hr.) saw-mill we cross the brook and pass the (¾ hr.) *Untere Karrer-See* (5280'), picturesquely situated in the wood at the base of the Latemar. The path then ascends the *Moar-Thal* to the (¾ hr.) *Alpenrose Inn*, on the *Costalunga Alp*, and to the (¼ hr.) **Caressa**, **Costalunga**, or **Karer Pass** (5740'), between the *Latemar* (8980') on the right and the *Rothwand* (9125') on the left. Opposite are seen the Dolomites of Fleims and the Fassa (with the Cimon della Pala in the background); to the W., in the distance, is the Ortler range. We may now either descend to the right, through the *Costalunga Valley*, to (1¼ hr.) *Moëna* (p. 322), or by a good path to the left to *Vallonga* and (1½ hr.) *Vigo* (p. 322).

The Tierser Thal, which runs parallel with the Eggenthal on the N., descends towards the W. from the Rosengarten to the Eisakthal at Blumau (p. 226). A road ascends along the *Breinbach* to the (3½ M.) *Zoll Inn*, and then to the left to the (3½ M.) village of *Tiers* (3210'; *Rose; Krone). From this point an attractive and not difficult route leads over the TIERSER ALPEL to *Campitello*, in 6½–7 hrs. A tolerable path ascends the *Tschaminthal*, passing the chapel of *St. Cyprian* and the (1 hr.) unpretending *Weisslahnbad* (3703'), to (1½ hr.) the *Rechte Leger* or the *Ochsenalpe* (chalets), at the mouth of the wild *Bletschenthal* (p. 265), where we obtain a fine view of the Rosengarten chain, and to the (¾ hr.) imposing culdron of the (¾ hr.) *Bärenloch* (way-post). Thence we ascend the *Stieye*, a rocky cliff rising in successive ledges like a staircase, to (1 hr.) the depression of the Tierser Alpel (8000'; *View), between the Rosszähne on the left and the Molignon on the right. We descend through the *Duronthal* to (2½ hrs.) *Campitello* (p. 328). Those who are not seasoned mountaineers are recommended to take a guide (5 fl.; *Alois Villprattner* or '*Löwenloisl*', Jos. Damian or '*Messnerseppel*', and *Alois Ratschgier* of Tiers).

There are several other passes between Tiers and the Fassathal, crossing the **Rosengarten Chain**. The Grasleiten Pass (8–9 hrs. to Vigo, guide 5 fl.) is the least arduous. From the (3¼ hrs.) *Bärenloch* we ascend to the right through the wild *Grasleittenthal* to the (¾ hr.) splendidly situated *Grasleiten-Hütte* (7100') and to the (1 hr.) pass (about 8220'), between the *Kesselkogel* (9785') on the left and the *Grosse Valbonkogel* (9200') on the right. We may descend either to the right to the (1½ hr.) *Sojat Chalets* in the magnificent *Vajolett-Thal*, which is enclosed by the precipitous sides of the *Dirupi di Larsec* and the *Rosengarten*, and thence reach (1¼ hr.) *Perra* (p. 322); or to the left by the cliffs of the *Antermojakogel* (9285') to the *Antermoja Lake* (p. 322) and then through the *Duronthal* to Campitello. — The *Kesselkogel* (9785'), the highest peak of the Rosengarten group, may be ascended from the Grasleiten-Hütte or from the Antermoja-See (p. 322) in 2½–3 hrs. (not difficult; guide from Vigo or Campitello 6 fl.). The ascent was first made in 1874 by Mr. Tucker. — The *Antermojakogel* (9285'), the *Molignon* (9120'), and the *Grosse Valbonkogel* (9200') may also be ascended from the Grasleiten-Hütte. Ascent of the *Schlern* (3½ hrs.), see p. 266.

Another and more difficult route leads over the **Vajolett Pass** (7½ hrs. to Vigo; guide 5 fl.). We turn to the right at the chapel of *St. Cyprian* (see above), ½ hr. from Tiers, and ascend on the right bank of the *Purgametschbach* through wood to the *Traunwiesen*, and thence to (1½ hr.) the *Fetsegger Schwaige* (chalet). Steep stretches of debris and snow lie between this point and the (2½ hrs.) Vajolett Pass (8150'), to the N. of the *Three Towers of Vajolett* (9160'). Magnificent view. Thence a steep descent to (1 hr.) the *Sojat Chalets* and (1¼ hr.) *Perra*.

The **Santner Pass** (10 hrs. to Vigo) should be attempted by expert climbers only. From the (2 hrs.) *Felsegger Schwaige* (see above) we turn to the S., and proceed at first through wood and then over stony meadows to the *Rosengartenwand*, which we ascend by an exceedingly steep and difficult climb to the *Gartl* (Rosengartenfeld), and then to the **Santner Pass** (about 8850'), immediately to the N. of the *Rosengartenspitze* (see below). A very steep descent leads down to (2 hrs.) the *Sojal Chalets* and (1¼ hr.) *Perra*. — The **Rosengartenspitze** (*Catinaccio*, 9765'), a difficult ascent which should be attempted only by those who are free from dizziness (guide from Vigo or Campitello 8 fl.), may be accomplished from the Gartl in 2 hrs.

Farther to the S. are the comparatively easy *Tschagerjoch* (*Forca di Davoi*, 8866'), to the S. of the Rosengartenspitze, and the *Vajolon-Joch* (about 8200'), to the N. of the *Rothwand* (9175'), which may be crossed in 7 hrs. from Welschnofen or Tiers to Vigo.

Grödner Thal. Seiser Alp. Schlern (comp. Map, p. 320). The narrow **Gröden Valley** (Romanic *Goerdeina*, Ital. *Gardena*), 18 M. in length, traversed by the brook of that name, consists of bright green meadows flanked with dark pine-forest. The N. slopes are thickly sprinkled with neat dwellings, and the background towards the E. is formed by huge Dolomites. The dialect of the valley is 'Ladin', but German is generally understood by the men. The road (diligence to St. Ulrich daily at 4.45 p.m. in 3 hrs., fare 1 fl. 10 kr.; omnibus in summer daily at 12.30 p.m., fare 1 fl 20 kr.; one-horse carr. to Plan 8 fl.) ascends the narrow valley to the left from *Waidbruck* (p. 226). On the height to the N. is *Lajen*, with the *Vogelweidhof* (3470'), said to have been the home of the poet Walther von der Vogelweide (a pleasant walk of 50 min. from Waidbruck). On the S. are the slopes of the *Puflatsch* (see below). 5 M. *Bräuhaus St. Peter* (3130'), near which, above, to the left, lies the village of the same name. Farther on we pass *Pontives*, leaving the village of *Pufels*, in the valley of the *Pufler Bach*, to the right. The Langkofel, Sella, and Mesules now become visible.

3½ M. **St. Ulrich** (3845'; **Rössl*; **Adler*; **Mondschein*; beer at the *Engel*), Ladin *Ortisei*, the chief village in the valley, is frequented as a summer-resort. Near the church is *Purger's* depôt of carved wood.

EXCURSIONS (guides, *Franz Fistil, Engelhard Nagler, Alois Harder*, and *J. B. Vinatzer*). A new road leads to the E. to (3 M.) St. Jakob (4960'), with an ancient church and a splendid view of the Langkofel. (By St. Jakob to St. Christina, 1¼ hr., a far finer route than the road in the valley.) To the N. the **Raschötz** (7470'; the W. summit of the *Raschötzer-Alp*, see p. 225), may be ascended in 2½ hrs. (guide, not indispensable, 1½ fl.; porter 1½ fl.). — To the S. the ***Puflatsch** (7112'; guide 2½ fl.) may be ascended in 3 hrs. by a new bridle-path (*Schnürlsteig*) passing *Pufels* (guide, not indispensable, 2½ fl.); descent by the *Schgaguler Schwaige*, at the foot of the *Pitzberg* (6900'), and through the ravine of the *Pitzbach*. (Descent by the Seiser Alp, and by a rough paved path to Kastelruth or Ratzes, not pleasant.; see p. 265). To the E. to the **Rodella* (see below) 3½ hrs. — To the *Villnössthal*, see p. 225.

We next reach (2½ M.) **St. Christina** (4615'; **Dosses Inn*, at the end of the village). On the right towers the huge *Langkofel* (10,430'), with the château of *Fischburg* at its base.

The mountain-pastures above St. Christina to the N. afford a good survey of the grand environs: to the N. the Raschötz, Pitschberg, Geiselspitzen, Col delle Pieres; E. the Spitzkofel and the Sella group; S. the Langkofel, Plattkofel, Puflatsch, and the more distant Rosengarten and Schlern.

MOUNTAIN ASCENTS (guide, *W. Kostatter* of Wolkenstein). The **Langkofel** (10,430') may be ascended from St. Christina in 7 hrs. (difficult; good guides, rope, etc., necessary). The first ascent was made by Hr. Grohmann in 1869, and the second highest peak (*Grohmannspitze*, 10,412') was reached for the first time in 1880. Comp. p. 323. — The **Plattkofel** (9700'; 5½ hrs.; guide 3½, with descent to Campitello 5 fl.), is not difficult. We proceed through the Christiner Wald to the *Zallinger Alp* (Rfms.) and the (3 hrs.) *Fassa-Joch* (p. 323), and then ascend to the left, across the sloping rocky plateau, to (2½ hrs.) the summit, — The Geislerspitzen (highest peak, *Sass Rigais*, 10,440'), a difficult ascent, made from St. Christina in 7-8 hrs. We proceed through the *Tschister Thal* to (2 hrs.) he finely situated *Regensburger-Hütte* (6890'), and ascend thence over debris and crumbling slopes to the summit.

The road crosses the *Tschisterbach* and leads over a hill (fine glimpse of the head of the valley) to (2¼ M.) *St. Maria* or *Wolkenstein* (*Hirsch, near the church; guide, W. Kaslatter). To the left, at the mouth of the *Langenthal*, is the ruin of *Wolkenstein*.

FROM ST. MARIA TO CORVARA OVER THE GRÖDNER JOCH, an easy and pleasant route (4 hrs.; guide hardly necessary). Road to (1½ M.) *Plan* (5180; inn, rustic) at the head of the valley. Here we ascend to the left, at first steeply through wood, and then more gradually across pastures (*Ferara Alp*, with the huge slope of the Sella on the right), to the (1½ hr.) Grödner Joch (6990'), between the *Spitzkofel* and the *Sella (Mesules);* behind us towers the Langkofel. Descent to (1½ hr.) *Colfosco* (p. 343); below we cross the brook to the right and then ascend to (½ hr.) *Corvara* (p. 343). Thence to *St. Cassian* (p. 342) 2 hrs. (before reaching the Stern we descend to the right and follow the Grossbach, cross it above its influx into the Murz, and ascend on the left bank of the latter).

TO CAMPITELLO OVER THE SELLA-JOCH (4 hrs.; path marked with red; guide unnecessary). From *Plan* (see above) the bridle-path ascends to the right to the (2 hrs.) Sella-Joch (7315'), between the Pordoi and the Langkofel (splendid view of the Marmolada, the Sella group on the left, and the Plattkofel and Langkofel on the right; still finer from the *Col di Rodella*, 8146', to the W. of the Joch, easily ascended in ¾ hr.). From the pass we descend to the left by a well-trodden path through the grassy valley. (To the right is the path to the Rodella, which ascends gradually.) After a few minutes we diverge to the right by an indistinct path across the pastures and descend on the right slope of the valley, to (1¼ hr.) *Campitello* (p. 323). — Those who ascend the Rodella (see above) do not require to return to the Sella Pass, but may descend direct to Campitello by a path (steep and rough at places; guide advisable) on the S.W. side.

The Seiser Alp is a lofty and undulating grassy plateau, 12 M. long and 8-9 M. broad, bounded by the Eisakthal on the W., the Grödner Thal on the N., the Schlern and Rosszähne on the S., and the Langkofel and Plattkofel on the E. side. It is the largest pasture in Tyrol, and is sprinkled with about 70 chalets and 365 hay-sheds. The greater part of it belongs to the parish of Kastelruth (see below). The margin of the plateau (N.W. the Puflatsch, 7130', Pitzberg, 6900'; S. Mahlknecht-Joch, 7255') is considerably higher than the centre (5900'). Guide desirable, particularly before the hay-harvest. (From Kastelruth over the Mahlknechtjoch to Campitello 4 fl.; ascent of the Schlern 3, or with descent to Campitello 5½ fl.)

The Seiser Alp is approached from the stations of *Atzwang*, *Kastelruth*, or *Waidbruck* (p. 226). FROM ATZWANG a bridle-path, steep at first, and turning to the left after ¾ hr. (the path to the right goes to Völs, see p. 265), leads to the (1½ hr.) church of *St. Konstantin*, and thence by *Strasser* (inn, rustic) to (1¼ hr.) *Seis* (3260'; *Unterer Wirth; guide, Anton Marsoner, nicknamed 'Bergler'). Opposite, on the slope of the majestic Schlern, is the *Hauensteiner Wald*, with the ruins of *Salegg* and *Hauenstein*, once the home

of the Minnesänger Oswald von Wolkenstein. In the wild and wooded ravine of the *Frötschbach* or *Tschapitbach*, $^3/_4$ hr. above Seis, are the **baths** of **Ratzes** (3930'; *Inn, 'pens.' incl. R. $2^1/_2$ fl.), with a spring containing iron and sulphur. (Travellers bound for Ratzes need not go as far as Seis, but ascend to the right through wood by a finger-post, 55 min. from St. Konstantin and 50 min. from the baths. In the wood lies a small, sequestered lake.) —
FROM THE KASTELRUTH STATION (p. 226) we cross the Eisak by the *Tergöler Brücke* and ascend by a steep bridle-path to (2 hrs.) **Kastelruth** (3395'; *Lamm ; Rössl*), the seat of the district-court, in a fine open situation, with pleasant views, attracting many summer-visitors. Thence viâ *St. Valentin* to Seis 1 hr., to Ratzes $1^1/_4$ hr., to the Seiser Alp direct $2^1/_2$hrs. — FROM WAIDBRUCK (p. 226) a new road leads along the E. slope of the valley of the Eisak, passing through a tunnel (110 yds. long) below *Tiesens* and finally ascending in windings through wood, to ($7^1/_2$ M.) Kastelruth.

A rough cart-road, paved at places, which is soon joined by the road from Ratzes on the right, leads from Seis to the Seiser Alp. On reaching the plateau ($1^1/_2$ hr.) we enjoy a fine view: to the S. the Schlern and Rosszähne, and to the S.E. the Langkofel and Plattkofel. A still finer point is the (1 hr.) **Puflatsch** (7130'): to the N. a picturesque peep into the Gardena, to the W. the Ritten and Rittnerhorn , in the distance the Ortler, to the N. the Zillerthaler Ferner, to the E. the Dolomites of the Enneberg and the Fassa. (Descent to St. Ulrich, see p. 263.) — The path now ascends gradually towards the S.E., rounding the N.E. spur of the Rosszähne, to the ($2^1/_4$ hrs.) *Mahlknecht-Alp* (6720'; Alpine fare), and in $^1/_2$ hr. more to the **Mahlknecht-Joch** (7255'), which commands a view of the Fassa Dolomites, the Marmolada, etc. Descent through the *Duron Valley* to (2 hrs.) *Campitello* (p. 323), not to be mistaken.

On the S.W. the Seiser Alp is bounded by the huge dolomite mass of the °**Schlern** (8400'), which may be ascended from Kastelruth, Seis, Ratzes, Völs, Campitello, or Tiers. The best starting-point is Ratzes (see above; guide, $2^1/_2$-3 fl., not indispensable; Jac. Fill, or 'Larmjockl' of Ratzes, and R. Leitner of Kastelruth), whence we ascend by the *Touristensteig* (bridlepath) and then in windings through the ravine of the *Frötschbach*, passing the mineral spring, to (3 hrs.) the Schlern plateau and ($^1/_2$ hr.) the °*Schlernhaus* (8070'; club-hut; Inn in summer), $^1/_2$ hr. below the rocky summit. [The highest summit is called the *All-Schlern* or *Petz* (8400'); the N.W. peak the *Junge Schlern* (7823'); to the N. is the *Burgstall* (7580'), with the rocky pinnacles of the *Euringer-Spitze* and the *Santnerspitze* (7620').] — The shortest way from Atzwang (Blumau or Steg) leads viâ ($1^1/_2$ hr.) the finely situated village of **Völs** (3060'; °*Weisses Kreuz*; °*Wenzerwirth*; guide, Chr. Rassler) to the *Untere* and ($2^1/_2$ hrs.) *Obere Schlern-Alp*, where a boy may be obtained to show the way; it then climbs the steep S. slope of the Schlern (see below) to the (1 hr.) chapel of *St. Cassian* (7670') and (20 min.) the Schlernhaus. — From Tiers several routes ascend through the *Tschaminthal* (p. 262) to the Schlern, one by the *Bärenfalle*, another by the °*Jungbrunnenthal* (with ladders, etc.), and a third by the *Bletschenthal*. These routes (each $5^1/_2$ hrs. to the Schlernhaus) should not be attempted except by experts, with guides ($3-3^1/_2$ fl.). An easier route ascends from the ($3^1/_4$ hrs.) *Bärenloch* (p. 262) viâ the 'Stiege' to the (1 hr.) *Tierser Alpel* (p. 262), to which also the approach from Campitello through the Duronthal leads; thence to the left to the *Rothe Erde*, and along the whole of the Schlern ridge to the (3 hrs.) Schlernhaus (5 hrs.). [This is a pleasanter descent to Campitello than the route viâ the Mahlknechtjoch.] — The summit commands a magnificent Panorama: on the W., far below us, is the valley of the Adige with the long ridge of the Mendel, beyond which rises the Ortler group; to the right of the Ortler are the Oetzthal, Stubai, Zillerthal, and Rieser Ferner, and the Tauern (Venediger): N.E. the extensive Seiser Alp, and the wild Geisterspitzen and other Enneberg Dolomites towering over the pine-forests of the Grödner Thal; E. the Plattkofel, Langkofel, and Bôë, and farther back the Antelao and Pelmo; in the foreground the serrated Rosazähne, above which are seen the snow-fields of the Marmolada; S.E. the Rosengarten chain with the Kesselkogel, Monte Alto, and Rothwand; S. the Latemar, Zangen, Weisshorn, and Trentine Alps, the Brenta, Adamello, and Presanella (see panorama by Siegl). — A few paces to the W. of the summit we get a view of the wild *Schlern-Klamm*, with the rocky walls of the *Schlernalm* on the left, the broad back of which is also visible from Botzen.

Ueberetsch. Kaltern. (Stellwagen, see p. 257.) Beyond the Talfer Bridge the road diverges from the Meran road to the left, traverses vineyards and fields of maize and reeds, crosses the Meran Railway near (3 M.) stat. *Sigmundskron* (p. 268), and is carried across the Adige by a new iron bridge. On a rock to the left rises the conspicuous and still partly-preserved castle of *Sigmundskron* or *Formigar* (1100′), founded in the 9th cent., rebuilt by Duke Sigismund in the 15th, and now used as a powder-magazine. (A path, marked with red, ascends to it in 20 min.; good view.) The road forks at the Ueberetscher Hof (Inn). The new road (to the left) ascends gradually viâ the *Katzenleiter* to (3 M.) *Girlan* (1415′; Rössl) and (2¼ M.) *St. Michael* (see below). The branch to the right leads to the S. to the (½ M.) hamlet of *Frangart* (see below); it then turns to the right, skirts the foot of the hill, ascends to the left at the *Pillhof*, and again forks, one arm leading to the left through the *Warlthal* (new Mendel road, p. 267) to (4½ M.) *St. Michael*, and the other running to the right through the *Pautsner Höhle*, passing the ruins of *Wart* and *Altenburg*, to (3½ M.) **St. Pauls** (1270′; *Adler*), a large village, with a handsome Gothic church. The tower, which contains a fine peal of bells, commands a beautiful survey of the vine-clad environs, of the rich basin of Botzen, and of the Etschthal up to Meran.

Pleasant walk (path marked with blue and white) viâ the castle of *Korb* (left), the ruin of *Boimont* (left), and the village of *Missian* (right) to the beautifully-situated ruin of (1 hr.) **Hoch-Eppan** (2300′), the ancestral seat of the counts of that name. Return by the ruin of *Boimont*. — Ascent of the Gantkofel (6415′) from **St. Pauls**, viâ the *Buchhöfe* and *Monte Dentro* (5285′), interesting (4 hrs.; with guide; view similar to that from Monte Roën).

The road now leads to the S. across a lofty and fertile plain to (1¼ M.) **St. Michael**, or *Eppan* (1345′; *Rössl*; *Sonne*, with post and telegraph office; *Traube*), a well-built and thriving village. Road over the *Mendel*, see p. 267.

The *Gleifcapelle (1780′), above the village, to the W. (½ hr.), commands an admirable survey of the valleys of the Adige and the Eisak. — An interesting excursion (¾ hr.; path marked with white and red) may be made viâ *Schloss Gandegg* to the 'Eislöcher', on the *Gandberg*. These 'ice-caverns', formed by overthrown masses of rock, are remarkable for the lowness of their temperature (Alpine roses in the neighbourhood). The walk may be prolonged along the Mendel road (see below), or to *Ober-Planitzing* and (1¼ hr.) *Kaltern*.

The road next leads by **Unter-Planitzing** and past the *Calvarienberg* (on the left) to (3 M.) **Kaltern** (1380'; *Rössl), the capital of the Ueberetsch, with a considerable wine-trade ('Seewein' the best). The churchyard-wall at the back of the church, and the terrace of Baron Dipauli's villa of *Windegg* (admittance on application), command a charming view of the Kalterer See and the environs.

Pleasant excursion to (1½ hr.) the **Montiggl Lakes**. By the Calvarienberg we descend to the right (path marked with blue and red), bear slightly to the left by the wall, and at the (¼ hr.) cross go straight on (avoiding the ascent to the left). After 20 min. more we ascend to the left through wood to (25 min.) the village of *Montiggl* (1610'; Inn). About 10 min. beyond the village, in the midst of wood at the foot of the *Mittelberg*, which separates the lofty plain of Eppan from the Etschthal, is the *Great Montiggler Lake* (1660'), and ¼ hr. higher up is the *Small Montiggler Lake*. [From *Sigmundskron* a path, marked with red, leads direct across the *Schreckbühel* to the larger Montiggler Lake in 2½ hrs.] A steep path (marked with blue and yellow) leads across the Mittelberg from Montiggl to *Pfatten* and (1 hr.) *Branzoll* (p. 293).

To the RAILWAY from Kaltern there are two carriage-roads. One on the E. bank of the *Kalterer See* (775'), passing the ruin of *Leuchtenburg* on the Mittelberg (to the left), goes to (5 M.) *Gmund*, crosses the Adige by a ferry, and leads along the railway to (1 M.) stat. *Auer* (p. 293). The other road leads on the W. side of the lake to (6½ M.) *Tramin* (890'; *Adler), famous for its wine, and then crosses the plain of the Adige to (2 M.) stat. *Newmarkt*, which is about ¾ M. from the village of that name on the left bank of the Adige. A pleasanter route, but 7½ M. longer, traverses the hills on the right bank of the Adige, by *Kurtatsch* (*Rose) and *Margreid* (*Greif; Hirsch), and descends to the railway at *Salurn* (p. 293).

*MENDEL ROUTE. An omnibus (open vehicle) plies daily in summer from Botzen over the Mendel Pass to Malè and back. It starts from Botzen (Schwarzer Greif) at 6 a.m., reaching the Mendel Pass at noon, Fondo at 1 p.m., and Malè at 6 p.m.; it starts on the return-trip from Malè at 10 a.m., reaching Fondo at 2, Mendel at 5, and Botzen at 8.15 p.m. (fares, from Botzen to Mendel 2½, to Fondo 3, to Malè 0½ fl.; return-tickets from Botzen to Mendel 3½-4, to Malè 6½-7½ fl.). A second omnibus leaves Botzen at 2 p.m. for the Mendel Pass (arrival at 7.30), whence it returns on the following morning at 6.30. A third vehicle runs daily at 6 a.m. from Botzen (Hotel Mondschein) across the Mendel to Cavareno and Cles. One-horse carr. from Botzen to the Mendel Pass and back 14, carr. and pair 24 fl.; to Fondo 18 and 30 fl. — These *Mendel Excursions* form a most enjoyable and convenient expedition for a day from Botzen. The splendid new road, which was constructed in 1880-84, for strategic purposes, ascends from Sigmundskron through the *Warlthal* to (4½ M.) *St. Michael* (p. 266), passes *Ober-Planitzing* (near which, to the right, are the *Eislöcher*, p. 266), on the *Gandberg* (2965'; left), and ascends in a wide curve to the (8½ M.) *Matschatscher Hof* (2730'; Rfmts.), with a villa of Baron Dipauli. Thence it ascends the steep slope of the Mendelwand in numerous windings, commanding a magnificent view of the Eschthal, the Dolomites, the Schlern, Rosengarten, Latemar, Schwarzhorn, Weisshorn, and, far below, of Ueberetsch and Kaltern, with its lake. In 1¾ hr. more it reaches the **Mendel Pass** (4470'). The *Mendelhof Inn*, charmingly situated ¼ M. beyond the pass, is suited for a stay of some time (R. 60 kr., pens. 3 fl.). Adjacent are a few villas. The 'Schöne Aussicht' (¼ hr.) affords a charming view of the valleys of the Adige and Noce. — The **Monte Roèn** (6735'), the highest peak of the Mendel, or Mendola Mts., ascended from the inn viâ the *Roèn-Alp* in 3 hrs. (path indicated by red marks; guide not indispensable; mule 2½-3 fl.), commands a superb view: to the E. the Dolomites as far as the Tauern; to the S. the Brenta,

Adamello, and Presanella; to the W. the Ortler; to the N. the Oetzthaler and Stubaier Ferner, etc.; at our feet stretches the beautiful Etschthal. Descent on the W. side to (3 hrs.) *S. Romedio* (p. 310), easy. — The *Penegal* (5685'), easily reached in 1¼ hr. by a path (white and red marks) leading to the N. from the Mendelhof Inn, commands a view little inferior to that from the Monte Roen.

The Mendola forms the boundary between the languages, the villages on the W. side being Italian. The track leads down for most of the way through wood to (½ hr.) *Ruffrè* or *Fondoi*, where it divides; the branch to the left leads viâ *Ronazano* and *Sarnonico* to (1¼ hr.) *Cavareno* (3190'; Coruna; Chiave), on the road to Cles and Mezzolombardo (p. 309); that to the right viâ *Malosco* to (1½ hr.) Fondo (3200'; *Post; Hôtel Fondo; see p. 310). The route from the Mendola to Fondo is comparatively uninteresting; so that those who wish to return to Botzen will find their account in alighting at the pass, and in spending the interval before the return of the omnibus from Fondo in ascending the Penegal. — From Ruffrè by *Amblar* to *S. Romedio* (an easy day's excursion from the Mendel Hotel), see p. 310.

49. From Botzen to Meran.
Comp. Map, p. 246.

20 M. RAILWAY in 1½-2 hrs. (no second class).

PEDESTRIANS who prefer the picturesque route to Meran over the hills on the right bank of the Adige (8-9 hrs., rough at places) should take the train (see below) to (10 M.) *Vilpian*, there cross the Adige to (1½ M.) *Nals* (785'; *Sonne; *Löwe), and ascend to the left through the ravine of the *Prissianer Bach* (waterfalls), passing the castle of *Fahlburg*, to (1 hr.) *Prissian* (2185'), charmingly situated, and (½ hr.) *Tisens* (2050'; *Adler), lying amidst fruit-trees at the foot of the wooded *Gall*. Fine view from the little church of *St. Christoph*, on the brow of the hill, ¼ hr. to the E.; still more extensive from the chapel of *St. Hippolyt* (2475'), ¾ hr. to the N., on a conspicuous rocky hill. From Tisens a bridle-path gradually descends past *Naraun* and St. Hippolyt (on the left), the ruin of *Leonburg*, and the châteaux of *Alt*- and *Neu-Brandis*, and through a beautiful chestnut-grove, to (3½ M.) *Unterlana* (920'), with its interesting Gothic church. We may now regain the railway at (1½ M.) stat. *Lana* (p. 269); or we may follow the Brandis conduit on the hill-side, passing the *Schwarze Wand* and the ruin of *Braunsberg*, to (1½ M.) Oberlana (see below). The pleasant road viâ Völlan is ½ M. longer: from Tisens it crosses the plateau to the N.W., leaving the chapel of St. Hippolyt (see above) on the right, and leads through the ravine of the Völlaner Bach to (3 M.) *Völlan* (with the ruined *Mayenburg* on the right), from which we descend by a roughly-paved road to (2½ M.) *Oberlana* (*Rössl; Adler), at the entrance to the *Ultenthal* (p. 276). — Pleasant walk from Oberlana into the *Gaul*, the wild gorge of the *Falschauer-Bach*, which descends from the Ultenthal (there and back ½ hr.; key at the Rössl, 10 kr. for each person). From Oberlana a road leads to the E. to (2½ M.) stat. Lana (see below); another to the N., viâ *Tscherms* (*Schloss Lebenberg*, above, to the left, p. 273), to (5 M.) Meran.

The train crosses the *Talfer* (to the left the Calvarienberg and the Haselburg, to the right the Sarnthal with its castles) and ascends towards the W. on the bank of the Eisak through vineyards and then through a wooded tract to (3½ M.) *Sigmundskron* (Sigmundskron; Mendlhof; Ueberetscher Hof, on the other side of the Adige), at the foot of the castle of that name (p. 266). We next traverse embankments on the left side of the Adige or Etsch, enjoying a view to the right of Botzen, the Schlern, Rosengarten, etc. On the hill to the left are the ruins of *Boimont* and *Hoch-Eppan* (p. 264), overshadowed by the *Gantkofel* (6115'). To the right, on a precipitous rock, rises the ruined *Greifenstein* (p. 259). Beyond *Siebeneich* (right) is the ruin of *Neuhaus* or *Maullasch*, on a low rocky hill to the right, a castle which once completely commanded the valley. To the left, beyond the Etsch, lies the village of *Andrian* with the ruin of *Felsenstein*.

8 M. **Terlan** (800'; Rail. *Restaurant*, good white 'Terlaner'; *Oberhauser*), famous for its wine, has a Gothic church of the 14th cent. with remains of old frescoes, which have been recently restored. The old leaning tower was taken down in 1884 as dangerous. — 10 M. **Vilpian** *(Post)*, with a brewery, on the *Möltener Bach* (fine waterfall). Beyond the Etsch we observe the large village of *Nals* (p. 268) and the hills of *Tisens*, overtopped by the wooded summit of the *Gall* (5335'); more in the background, the *Laugenspitze* (p. 267). The train next traverses maize-fields and woods on the bank of the Etsch. Beyond (12½ M.) *Gargazon* we cross the *Aschler Bach*, which by the Treaty of Verdun (843) was constituted the boundary between Germany and Italy, and in 1810-13 separated Bavaria from Italy. From (15 M.) *Lana-Burgstall* a road crosses the Etsch to the left to *Ober-Lana* (see above), at the mouth of the *Ultenthal* (p. 276). The line traverses the old bed of the river. To the right the castle of *Katzenstein* and the lofty *Fragsburg* (p. 274); to the left, on the slope of the *Marlinger Berg*, rises *Schloss Lebenberg* (p. 273); in the background are *Meran* and *Schloss Tirol*. 18¾ M. *Unternais* (p. 270), immediately below the Marling bridge (p. 273). The train quits the Etsch, traverses a high embankment, crosses the Passer, and enters the station of (20 M.) *Meran*, on the right bank of the Passer. Omnibuses and cabs at the station, see p. 270.

Meran. — **Hotels.** *Post or Erzherzog Johann*, conveniently situated in the Sand-Platz, with a beautiful garden; *Habsburger Hof*, *Tiroler Hof*, both at the station; *Hassfurther*, comfortable, good cuisine; *Graf von Meran* (in these, R. from 1 fl., B. 40 kr., D. 1½-2, pension 3½-5 fl.); *Hôtel Walder*, Schiessstand-Platz, near the Gisela Promenade, R. from 80 kr.; Hôtel Forsterbräu, with garden-restaurant, R., L., & A. 1 fl.; *Erzherzog Rainer*, *Hôtel Austria*, at Obermais; *Maiserhof*, in Untermais; Hôt. Bæcker in the *Meraner Hof*; *Sonne* (R. 70 kr.), Kreuz, etc., in the town. — **Pensions.** Germania, Fortuna, Passerhof, Pircher, Moser, *Neuhaus*, all in the Gisela Promenade (the best situation); Euchta, Stefanicpromenade; beyond the Passer, Adelheid; Deutsches Haus, Dr. Putz, Villa Fanny, Sandhof, Bellevue, Holstein, Edelweiss, Tschoner, all in the Anlagen (promenades); Vindobona, in the Habsburger-Str.; Villa Hoch, Meinhard-Str.; Felsenrck, on the Küchelberg, outside the Passeirer Thor. At Obermais (see p. 272): *Weinhart*, *Mazegger*, Dr. Mazegger, Villa Regina, *Warmegg, Aders, Rolandin, Tannheim, Freihof, Körberhof, Lichtenegg, Matscher, Nirdl, Behrmayr, Schillerhof, Bavaria, Villa Stefanie, Elsenhain, Friedheim, etc. Pension in all these, 3-4 fl. per day; R. with a S. aspect, without board, from 20 fl. a month (R. to the E. or W. 12-18 fl.). Less expensive (from 2 fl. per day): in the town. Starkenhof, Holzeisen, Holzknecht, Andreas Hofer, etc.; at Untermais, Villa Maja, Berthasheim, Flora, Fröhauf, Hermann; at Obermais, Petersburg, Stainer; to the W. of the town, on the road to Forst and Gratsch, Villa Claudia, Ladurner, Dohlhof, and Martinsbrunn. The châteaux of Trautmannsdorff Ra-

METZ, MADER, LEBENBERG, WINKEL, PLARS, JOSEFSBERG, etc., are also fitted up as pensions. A number of the villas are let to families. When a stay of some time is contemplated it is of importance to have all the arrangements with the landlord reduced to writing (with the advice and assistance of the directors of the baths).

Cafés. *Kurhaus* (see below); *Café Wieser*, *Café Paris*, both under the arcades, with gardens; *Café Meran*, Pfarr-Platz; *Schönbrunn*, Habsburger-Str.

Restaurants, at the above-mentioned hotels. Wine at *Putz's*, Habsburger-Str. 44, and at *Jos. Marquetti's*, Laubengasse. Beer: *Kurhaus* (see below; on the ground-floor); *Raffl*, Pfarr-Platz; *Forsterbräu*, with a garden.

Kurhaus, in the Gisela Promenade, with handsome Kursaal, café and reading-room, restaurant (table d'hôte at 12.30 p.m., 1 fl. 10 kr.), baths, pneumatic apparatus, etc.; subscription 1½ fl. per week, 3 fl. per month, 7 fl. per quarter, 12 fl. per half-year; members of a family at reduced rates; season-tickets (1st Sept. to 1st July) 15, for a family of two persons 20, of more than two 25 fl. (tickets sold by the attendant at the casino). — *Visitors' Tax* 1 fl. per week (for a stay of more than three days); for the autumn season (to 1st Nov.) 4 fl., winter season (to 1st April) 6 fl., spring season (to end of May) 4 fl.; tickets for all three seasons, adults and children over 12 years, 10 fl., younger children 5 fl., servants 2 fl. Subs. to the band 1 fl., for all three seasons 2 fl.

Photographs. *Pötzelberger* (also lending library), Pfarr-Platz; *Plant*, Gisela Promenade. — Money-Changers. *Biedermann*, by the Post Office; *Blümel*, Landstrasse; *Fickenscher*, under the arcades.

English Church Service in the Erzherzog Johann.

Carriage from the station to the town, with one horse 60 kr., two horses 1 fl.; to Obermais 1 or 2 fl. From Meran to Schönna and back 4 fl. 70 or 7 fl. 70 kr.; to Forst and back 2 fl. 70 or 4 fl. 50 kr., or returning by Marling 3 fl. 90 or 6 fl. 60 kr.; to Töll and back 3 fl. 20 or 5 fl. 50 kr.; to Laua and back 3 fl. 60 or 6 fl. 60 kr. (these charges include half of 2 hrs., and fees and tolls). By time: in the town, ¼ hr. 30 or 60 kr., ½ hr. 60 kr. or 1 fl. 20 kr., 1 hr. 1 fl. 5 or 2 fl. 10 kr.; each addit. ¼ hr. 20 or 80 kr.; double fares at night. Outside the town: ½ hr. 70 kr. or 1 fl. 40 kr., 1 hr. 1 fl. 40 or 2 fl. 80 kr., etc. — Horse to Schloss Tirol, Schönna, Goyen, Lebenberg, Josefsberg, Töll, Partaching, or Hallbauer, 2 fl.; fee to attendant 40 kr.

Meran (1050'), with 5334 inhab., the ancient capital of Tyrol, occupies a delightful and sheltered situation at the base of the vine-clad *Küchelberg*, on the right bank of the *Passer*, ½ M. above its confluence with the Etsch, and is much frequented in winter by persons with pulmonary complaints on account of the mildness and equableness of its climate. There is also a whey-cure in spring and a grape-cure in autumn. On the opposite bank of the Passer lie the villages of *Untermais* and *Obermais* (the latter higher and cooler), with numerous villas, old castles, and vineyards. The business quarter of Meran is a long street intersecting the town from E. to W., flanked with arcades ('Unter den Lauben'). In this street, in the court of the 'Magistratsgebäude', is situated the *Burg*, once the residence of the Counts of Tyrol, dating from the 15th cent., and containing old frescoes, armorial bearings, etc.; it has been restored and deserves a visit (adm. 30 kr.). — The Gothic *Church* (14th cent.) contains a good altarpiece by *Knoller* (d. 1804), representing the Assumption. — A tablet, placed in 1884, marks the house in the Rennweg, in which Andreas Hofer spent the last night before he was taken to Mantua (1810).

The *Gisela Promenade*, with its fine old poplars, the chief rallying-point of visitors, lies on the right bank of the Passer below the Botzen bridge, having been laid out on the broad and substantial bulwark which protects the town against the inundations of the river. Adjoining it is the handsome *Kurhaus* (see p. 270), in front of which a band plays in winter, and farther on is the new *Stefanie Promenade*, with the Protestant Church, finished in

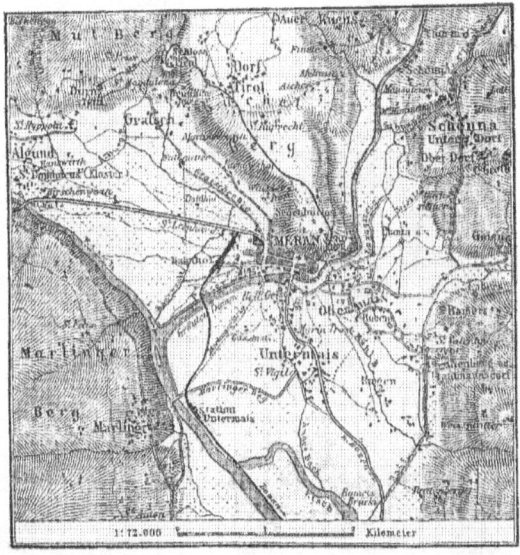

1885. Above the *Spitalbrücke* there are tasteful pleasure-grounds on both banks of the river. On the right bank is the *Untere Winter-Anlage (Kurgarten)*, very sheltered and sunny, and the favourite walk of delicate persons (smoking prohibited). Farther up is the *Obere Winter-Anlage* at the end of which is the upper bridge. On the left bank are the *Untere* and *Obere Sommer-Anlage*, or 'Maria-Valeria-Garten', where the band plays in the evening in spring and autumn. These grounds extend along both banks, beyond the *Steinerne Steg*, to the *Elisabethgarten* at Obermais, on the left bank, which contains a large covered promenade and a café-pavilion (band twice weekly), and to the new *Gilf-Anlage* on the right bank, at the foot of the Zenoburg (see below). — The mountains visible from Meran, or better from the road to Dorf Tirol, are, to the N.W., the Muthspitze, Röthelspitze, and Tschigatspitze; then above Partschins, the Zielspitze, Texelspitze, and Gfallwand; to the E., above the lower spurs, the Ifinger, to the right of which is the loftily-situated little church of St. Katharina in der Scharte; from the Etschthal rises the precipitous Gantkofel and in the distance is the Cima d'Asta, one of the Alps of Trent; to the S.W. the Marlinger Berg.

Pleasant walk from **Obermais** towards the E., past *Schloss Rubein* with its cypress-avenue, and across the *Naif* (two cafés by the bridge), to the (20 min.) church of *St. Valentin*, which commands a charming view; then back by *Schloss Rametz* (p. 274), or to the S. by *Schloss Trautmannsdorff*, with a park and a terrace at the back, which is another fine point of view. (A direct and attractive route leads hence to the *Weissplatter* on the way to the Fragsburg, p. 274.) — *Lazagsteig*, see p. 273. — The most interesting of the numerous old châteaux of Obermais are the ivy-clad *Planta* and *Schloss Rottenstein*, the latter belonging to the Archduke Karl Ludwig (garden generally open to the public). The garden of the *Schillerhof*, the property of Hr. v. Redwitz, contains a bust of the poet.

EXCURSION TO SCHLOSS TIROL (there and back $3-3^1/_2$ hrs.). Three paths, paved at places, and affording little shade, ascend to the castle. The best route leads past the Pfarrkirche and through the N.E. town-gate (**Passeirer** Thor; where we observe the picturesque *Zenoburg*, with its curious Romanesque portal, to the right, rising above the Passer), and then ascends to the left (finger-post) to (55 min.) *Dorf Tirol* (2050'; Zum Rimmele, with a terrace affording a beautiful view; Zum Schloss Tirol). We next ($1/_4$ hr.) pass through the 'Knappenloch', a tunnel 100 paces long (passing the picturesque ruin of the *Brunnenburg* in the ravine to the left), and in a few minutes more reach the entrance to the castle. — Another and longer route ($1^3/_4$ hr.), rough at places, but level for the first $1/_2$ hr., passes through the N.W. town-gate (Vintschgauer Thor), diverges from the high-road to the right opposite the convent (the middle path), and ascends by the village of *Gratsch* (wine at Villa Wessobrunn), the old château of *Durnstein*, and the church of *St. Peter*, to the castle. This route is recommended for the descent ($1^1/_4$ hr.; beautiful views). — The shortest route to Dorf Tirol ascends from the back of the Pfarrkirche on the S.W. side of the Küchelberg. This path is steep and destitute of shade.

*Schloss Tirol (2140'), situated on the N.W. side of the Küchelberg, was the earliest residence of the Counts of Tyrol, who possessed considerable power as early as the 12th cent. and gave their name to the whole country. It is now in a dilapidated condition, having been partly destroyed by a landslip. The only ancient parts of the building are a porch and the two interesting marble portals of the Rittersaal and the chapel, the latter, with a representation of the Fall of Man, being particularly rich. Magnificent *View from the windows of the Kaisersaal, best by evening-light, embracing the valley of the Adige to a distance of 20 M., bounded on the left by a chain of porphyry mountains extending to Botzen, and on the right by the cliffs of the Hohe Mendel and the Ultenthal Mts.; to the W. stretches the luxuriant valley of Meran, with the falls of the Adige (which descends 600' from the Töll to Meran); in the background the Laaser Ferner (fee 20-30 kr.).

About 1½ M. to the N.E. of Dorf Tirol is the well-preserved old château of *Auer*, below which the *Finelebach* issues from the deep *Spronser Thal* (p. 275).

The château of *Lebenberg (1865'; now a pension, 3 fl. per day; Rfmts.), charmingly situated in the midst of rich vegetation 5 M. to the S. of Meran, formerly the property of Count Fuchs, is still in excellent preservation, and some of the rooms are adorned with paintings illustrative of its history. The shortest route to it is as follows. Follow the 'Marlinger Steig', which crosses the fields to the (1½ M.) *Marlinger Brücke*, above the station of *Untermais* (p. 269). Beyond the latter follow the road to the left to the (1½ M.) bridge over the *Lebenberger Graben*; on the other side ascend by the field-path past several mills, and then by the carriage-road to the (40 min.) castle. The short-cuts through the vineyards are barred in autumn, but a payment of 5 kr. to the mediævally-attired watchers ('Saltner'), with their grotesque feathered caps, will secure permission to pass. — In returning we may choose the charming route along the slope by *St. Anton* and *Marling*.

Among the numerous old castles visible from Meran, that of *Schönna (1900') at the entrance to the Passeir, built in the 12th cent., the property of Count Meran, son of Archduke John (d. 1859), and containing a collection of old weapons and other curiosities, is one of the most interesting and picturesque. Of the different routes to it the easiest is the carriage-road by Obermais (3½ M.; fingerpost by the well near the 'Erzherzog Rainer'). A shorter but steeper route is the '*Stickle Gasse*'. Or the *Lazag-Steig*, ascending by the Passer to the left from Pension Mazegger, may be followed to (1 hr.) *Dorf Schönna* (*Inn), the last part steep. The Gothic *Chapel, on the projecting platform of masonry near the church, contains the tomb of Archduke John and commands as fine a *View as the castle itself (fee to the steward for castle and chapel 60 kr. - 1 fl.).

The walk may be very pleasantly prolonged as follows (best by morning-light). From Dorf Schönna we return by the road to the (10 min.) *Unterdorf*, then ascend to the left to the (5 min.) *Oberdorf*, and follow the hill-side, shaded by fine chestnuts and affording charming views of Meran, to the beautifully-situated château of (½ hr.) *Goyen* (no admittance). We next descend by a long curve into the *Naifthal*, beyond which we remount through wood to (1/2 hr.) *Schloss Rametz*, now a pension. We may now either return to Meran viâ Obermais in 1/2 hr.; or again ascend by the 'Freiberger Weg', which passes the *Stegerhof* and the *Weissplatter*, and skirts the hill. After 1 hr. the track divides, the branch to the right leading to the (10 min.) *Hallbauer*, that to the left to the (40 min.) Fragsburg (2395'; no admittance), loftily situated, and commanding an extensive view of the Etschthal. In a gorge, 20 min. farther on, is a fine waterfall of the *Sinachbach* (visitors to which must have written permission from Hr. Erwin, the proprietor of the castle).

From the saw-mill by the approach to the castle a steep path descends to the (1/4 hr.) Hallbauer. Meran may be regained by the same path; or we may make a circuit by the (20 min.) castle of *Katzenstein*, and descend to the *Rametzbrücke* over the Naif. We may now return to (2 M.) Meran by the Botzen road, or we may ascend to the right on the left bank of the Naif, past *Schloss Trautmannsdorff* (p. 272), to the upper Naif bridge and reach the town viâ Obermais (1 hr.).

The Vintschgau road leads from Meran to the W. (passing on the right, just outside the gate, the pleasant walk, 'Unterm Berge' to *Pension Martinsbrunn*; 1/2 hr.), to the (1 3/4 M.) bridge over the Etsch, immediately beyond which, on the right, is the ruin of *Forst*, and 1/2 M. farther on the *Forster Brewery*, with a view of Meran. A still finer view of the town is obtained from the small château of *Josefsberg*, 1/4 hr. higher up (pension 2 1/2-3 fl.).

The road ascends in a wide curve on the S. side of the valley to the (1 M.) saddle of the **Töll** (1665'; *Inn*), from which the Etsch descends in a series of rapids (p. 253). Beautiful walk from this point to the (1 1/2 hr.) *Partschins Waterfall*, passing *Partschins* (2070'; *Zur Stiege*), and ascending the *Zielthal* by a somewhat steep path. From the Töll we may return to Meran by the picturesque *Old Road* (*View of the falls of the Etsch), or by the *Plarser Wasserleitung* (fine views of the Etschthal) on the hill-side, to (1 hr.) *Algund* and (3/4 hr.) Meran.

Excursion to *Ober-Lana* and the 'Mittelgebirge' of *Völlan* and *Tisens*, see p. 268; the *Ultenthal*, p. 276; the *Passeir*, p. 253.

ASCENTS FROM MERAN (guides, *Jos. Buchensteiner*, *Alois Schussegger*). The finest expedition for a whole day is the ascent of the *Vigiljoch* or 'Jocher' (5870'). The route leads by *Marling* (p. 273) to *St. Felix*, ascends to the right by a somewhat steep, but good and unmistakable path to the N.E. angle of the *Marlinger Berg*, and then winds up to the (3 hrs.) *Eggerbauer* (4210'; tavern), with its chapel. Or we may follow the Vintschgau road as far as the Töll, and then ascend to the left viâ the *Quadrathöfe* (2740'), by a good path through wood, to the (3 1/2 hrs.) Eggerbauer. Beyond this point a guide is advisable, and it is better to bring one from Meran or Marling (3 1/2, or returning by St. Pankraz 4 1/2 fl.). The path ascends gradually to the S.W., through wood, to the (2 hrs.) old *Vigilkapelle* on the *Vigiljoch*, adjoining which is the *Jocherbauer* (Rfmts.; better night-quarters at the *Gamperhof*, 5 min. below it, to the S.). The view is very grand: to the N. the Oetzthaler Ferner form the background of the Schnalser Thal; to the W. is the Vintschgau, bounded on the S. by the Laaser Ferner and the Ortler, and close to us rise the peaks enclosing the Ultenthal (Hasenohr, etc.); to the S. are the Laugenspitze, the Mendel as far as Monte Roën, and the Etschthal as far as Sigmundskron; to the E. the Dolomites, from the Peitlerkofel and the Geislerspitzen on the N. (Langkofel, Plattkofel, Marmolada, Rosengarten, Latemar, Schwarzhorn, Weisshorn) to the vicinity of the mouth of the Avisio, beyond which the peaks of the Trentine Alps may be descried; to the N.E. are the Ifinger, Hirzer, and, beyond the Jaufen, the Tuxer Ferner. A more extensive view is obtained from the

Ifinger. MERAN. *VI. Route 49.* 275

Lärchbühel (5968'), 20 min. to the E., and a still finer point is the *°Rauhe Bühel* (6630'), 1¼ hr. to the S.W. — We may return by the *Lebenberger Alp* and *Schloss Lebenberg* (3½ hrs. to Meran), or by the longer and more interesting route past the scattered village of *Pawigl*, with its picturesque church, to (1¾ hr.) *Ausserhof* in the Ultenthal (p. 276), and thence by *Tscherms* (p. 268) to (2½ hrs.) *Meran*. — The ascent of the Hochwart (8450') from the Jocher is not difficult, and will amply repay the fatigue (3 hrs.; guide from Meran 6 fl.).

The **Rothsteinkogel** (5150') is also interesting (8 hrs.; guide 3-3½ fl.). We ascend by *Katzenstein* (p. 274) and through the *Haftingerschlucht*, past the *Fragsburg Waterfall*, to the *Hochplatter*, the highest farm-house belonging to Meran (Kfmts.). On the margin of the Vöran plateau we diverge to the left from the path to Vöran, and soon reach the summit, distinguished by its girdle of sandstone. The view embraces the Etschthal, the Dolomites, Ortler, etc. We return either by *Vöran* (3970'; Lercher's Inn) and *Vilpian* (p. 269), or by *Hafling* and *Katharina in der Schart* (p. 272).

The **Muthspitze** (7300'; 5½ hrs.; guide 4 fl.) is less interesting: from Dorf Tirol to the *Mulhhöfe*, then a fatiguing ascent, partly through wood.

To the **Spronser Thal**, with its ten lakes, a fatiguing but attractive expedition (there and back 14-15 hrs.; guide 3½, or with descent to Plan 5 fl.). The path ascends by Dorf Tirol and *Schloss Auer* to the (3½ hrs.) farm of *Langfall* or *Longvall* (3390') in the Spronser Thal; thence over the *Langfall-Alpe* (5120') to the (3½ hrs.) *Kasersee* (to the left of which is the *Pfitschsee*), and past the *Grünsee* to the (¾ hr.) *Meran Club-Hut*, magnificently situated near the *Langsee* (4700'), the largest of the lakes (4½ M. in circumference). The ascents of the *Röthelspitze* (8615'; 2 hrs.; with guide) and the *Tschigatspitze* (9820'; 2½ hrs.; with guide) are interesting expeditions from this point. — Instead of returning by the same route (5-6 hrs.), we may cross the (¾ hr.) *Spronser Joch* (8790'; °View of the Gurgler glaciers) to *Plan* and (3 hrs.) *Pfall* in the Pfelderthal (comp. p. 254), and return to (9 hrs.) Meran via *Moos* and the *Passeir*.

The **°Gfallwand** (10,420'; 1½ day; guide 6½ fl.), between the Zielthal and the Schnalser Thal, is the finest of the loftier peaks near Meran. Drive in the afternoon to *Naturns* (p. 263); walk or ride thence in 4 hrs. to the *Mayrulpe* (good quarters); next morning ascend to the plateau on the summit in 3½ hrs. (refuge-hut). View magnificent. A shorter but rough path leads from the Töll through the Zielthal to the (4½ hrs.) *Zieler* or *Muth-Alpe* (poor quarters), and thence to the (2 hrs.) top.

The **Ifinger** (8370'; 6 hrs.; guide 3½-4 fl.), fatiguing. The path leads by *Goyen* and *Alfreid* to the (3½ hrs.) *Gsteirhof* (4435'; Alpine fare); then a toilsome ascent over the *Ochsenboden* and the *Rothwand* to the (3 hrs.) nearer peak, a fine point of view. (The farther and higher peak, 8450', is very difficult of access.) Descent to (1 hr.) the *Naifer Pass* (6650'), at the head of the Naifthal; thence to the S.W. to (1½ hr.) *St. Katharina in der Schart* (3565'; Sulfner Inn), and by the *Eggerbauer* and *Rametz* to (2 hrs.) Meran, or to the N.E. by the *Leiseralm* and the *Missenstein Pass* (6880') to (3 hrs.) *Aberstückl* in the Pensarthal (p. 260); pleasant detour by the *Kratzberg See*; or to the S.E. through the *Oettenbach-Thal* to (3½ hrs.) *Sarnthein* (p. 260).

The ascent of the °**Hirzer** (*Prennspitze*, 9124'; 9½ hrs.; guide 6 fl.) is a very fine excursion. A good bridle-track leads by *Schönna* to (2 hrs.) *Verdins* (2990'; Inn), a small 'Bad'. Crossing the romantic *Masulschlucht*, it next leads to (2 hrs.) *Tall* or *Prenn* (Inn, rustic), and ascends to the (2½ hrs.) *Hirzerhütte* on the *Taller-Alp* (6725'; night-quarters), from which a somewhat toilsome path, recently improved, leads to the (2-3 hrs.) summit. The superb °Panorama embraces, to the N., the Oetzthal, Stubai, and Zillerthal Alps, the Hohe Tauern as far as the Glockner, E. the Dolomites, S. the Brenta and Presanella, W. the Ortler and the distant Piz Linard. Steep descent to *Aberstückl* in the Sarnthal; better by *Videgg* to Schönna.

The °**Laugenspitze** (7970'; guide 6 fl.), one of the most famous points of view in this district, is best scaled from the *Ultner Mitterbad* (see p. 276; bridle-path, 4 hrs.), from *Platzers* (1½ hr. above Völlan, p. 268;

18*

in 3 hrs.), or from *Unser Frau im Walde* (p. 311; 3 hrs.). Near the top is a club-hut (six beds). Splendid and extensive view (panorama by F. Plant).

From Meran to the Baths of Rabbi, through the Ultenthal (12 hrs.), not a very attractive route. At (4½ M.) *Tscherms* (p. 268) the ascent begins with the *Eichberg*; *Oberlana* (p. 268) lies below, to the left. The road passes beautiful groups of old chestnuts, and commands fine views of the Etschthal and the opposite heights, the Fragsburg, the Ifinger, etc. The first house in the Ultenthal is (1¼ hr.) *Ausserhof*; 50 min., ruins of *Eschenloh* on the left, with gigantic pines in the vicinity; ½ hr., *St. Pankraz* (2415'; *Ausser-Wirth*; guide, Matth. Gamper). The road now descends to the bottom of the valley. After 35 min. it divides at the 'Wälsche Sägen'. The road bearing to the left and crossing the bridge leads through the *Maraunethal* to the (½ hr.) **Mitterbad** (3100'), a little watering-place with a chalybeate spring and a good bath-house, whence the *Laugenspitze* (7970') may be ascended without difficulty in 4 hrs. (guide 3½, with descent to Unser-Frau 4, to Proveis 4½ fl.). Over the *Hofmahd* to *Proveis*, 4 hrs., see p. 311. The road in the main valley, to the W., leads past the *Innerbad* or *Lotterbad* to the (1½ hr.) *Eck Inn* (on the hill to the right of which is the church of *St. Walburg*); then to (1 hr.) *Kuppelwiese* (3720'; Inn), to (½ hr.) *St. Nicolaus* (4125'), and to (1¼ hr.) *St. Gertrud* (4820'; very poor inn), with a handsome parsonage. (Passes to the Martell see p. 286; guide, Joh. Trafoier at St. Nicolaus.) Thence by a bridle-path through the *Kirchberger Thal* to the (2 hrs.) *Lach-Alm* (7090') and the (1 hr.) Kirchberger Joch or **Rabbi Joch** (8130'), near the *Lake Corvo*, where a new mountain-view is disclosed. Descent by a stony path to the (¾ hr.) *Cespede Alp*, the path to the right before which must be avoided. Lastly viâ *Piazzola di Rabbi* to the (1¼ hr.) *Baths of Rabbi* (see p. 311).

From Meran over the *Gampen Pass* to *Cles*, see p. 310; over the *Auener Joch* or the *Kreuzjöchl* to the *Sarnthal*, see p. 260.

50. From Eyrs *(Landeck, Meran)* to Colico on the Lake of Como. Stelvio Pass.

Comp. Maps, pp. 246, 288, 304.

99 M. Diligence from Landeck to Mals (42½ M.) daily in 9½ hrs.; to Eyrs (52 M.) daily in 10¾ hrs.; from Meran to Eyrs (28 M.) daily in 5 hrs. (also Stellwagen in both directions). An omnibus, in connection with the diligence over the Stelvio, plies daily in summer from *Mals* to Prad in 1½ hr., leaving Mals at 5.30 a.m. and Prad at 4.25 p.m. — Diligence from Eyrs to Bormio over the Stelvio (32 M.) in summer (10th July to 30th Sept.) daily in 11½ hrs. (8 fl. 40 kr.; open vehicles), leaving Eyrs at 6.30 a.m., and reaching Prad at 7.15, Trafoi 10, Franzenshöhe (where dinner is taken) 1 p.m., S. Maria 3.45, and the Baths of Bormio at 6 p.m.; from Bormio 6.30, S. Maria 10.45 a.m., Franzenshöhe 1.45, Trafoi 3, Prad 4.50, arrival at Eyrs 5 p.m. — Italian Diligence from Bormio to Sondrio (41 M.) twice daily in 8 hrs.; Railway from Sondrio to Colico (26 M.) in 1 hr. 35 minutes. — Carriage from *Eyrs* to Gomagoi, one-horse 7, two-horse 8 fl.; to Trafoi 10 and 11½ fl. (extra horse for the hills, when more than 66 lbs of luggage, 4 fl. 60 kr.); to Franzenshöhe 15 and 17 fl.; to Bormio 32 and 34 fl. (extra horse 10 and 14 fl.); from *Mals* to Gomagoi 8 and 9½ fl.; to Trafoi 11 and 12½ fl.; to Franzenshöhe 16 and 18 fl.; to Bormio 32 and 34 fl. Extra-Post with two horses from Mals to Trafoi 12 fl. 50 kr.; from the Baths of Bormio to Trafoi 55, to Sondrio 70 fr.

The route over the *Stelvio (Giogo di Stelvio*, Ger. *Stilfser Joch)*, the highest carriage-road in Europe, 9045' above the sea-level, constructed by the Austrian government in 1820-25, is exceedingly interesting, and gradually carries the traveller from the huge glaciers and snow-fields of the Ortler and Monte Cristallo to the vine-clad slopes of the Val Tellina, and the luxuriant vegetation of the banks of the Lake of Como. The finest scenery is on the Tyrolese side of the pass; and the construction of the road itself is an object of interest on the Italian side.

PEDESTRIANS crossing the pass are strongly recommended not to take any short-cuts, as the road affords the finest view. At Mals, Eyrs, and Laas, however, the dusty high-road may be avoided by following footpaths straight across the valley.

From Landeck or Meran to *Eyrs*, see R. 46. The Stelvio road crosses the Etsch to the left at *Spondinig* (2915'; *Hirsch), 2 M. to the W. of Eyrs, and then runs straight across the valley, which is here 1 1/2 M. broad and is covered with debris and rendered marshy by the inundations of the *Trafoier Bach*. At —

3 1/2 M. **Prad** or *Brad* (2940'; *Alte Post; *Neue Post; good ice-axes at Dialer's), a small village at the entrance to the Trafoier Thal, the road is joined on the right by the direct route from Mals viâ Glurns and Lichtenberg (p. 251). At the *Schmelz* (Inn) the road begins to ascend, the valley contracts, and the brawling Trafoier Bach forms several waterfalls. On the hill to the right lies the poor village of *Stilfs*, Ital. *Stelvio*, whence the route derives its name. A little farther on we cross the stream, and soon obtain a fine view of the Trafoi snow-mountains (see below). In the opposite direction (N.) towers the broad snowy pyramid of the *Weisskugel* (p. 239). Near (4 1/2 M.) —

8 M. **Gomagoi**, Germ. *Beidewasser* ('gemelle acque', 4265'; *Reinstadler's Inn*), with a small fort, to the S.E., opens the wild *Suldenthal*.

To *Sulden* (bridle-path to St. Gertrud, 2 1/4 hrs.), see p. 287. A direct path, constructed by the German Alpine Club, leads from Gomagoi to the (5 1/2 hrs.) *Payerhütte* (p. 291). This route diverges to the right from the Sulden road immediately beyond the bridge over the Trafoier Bach, and leads mostly through wood.

The road ascends more rapidly and crosses the Trafoier Bach four times. As we approach (3 1/4 M.) Trafoi the *Monte Livrio* (10,470') first becomes visible, and adjoining it on the right the *Naglerspitze* (10,685'). A magnificent panorama is soon disclosed: to the left the huge *Ortler* (the summit itself is not visible); to the right of it the *Pleisshorn* (10,312'); then the *Untere Ortler Ferner* and the *Trafoier Ferner*, separated by the *Nashorn Spitze* (9442'), and crowned by the *Trafoier Eiswand* (11,240'); next, the black *Vordere Madatschspitze* (10,174'), the *Madatsch-Ferner*, the *Kristall-Spitzen* (11,300'), and the *Geisterspitze* (11,355').

11 M. **Trafoi** (5080'; *Post, R. & L. 1 fl., B. 30 kr.; *Zur Schönen Aussicht*), a small village, is grandly situated.

EXCURSIONS AND ASCENTS (guides, Joh. *Mazag*, *Math. & Joh. Thöni*, and *Jos. Platzer* of Trafoi, *Alois Pichler* of Stilfs, and *Georg & Jos. Pichler* of Gomagoi; comp. p. 284). Interesting walk (guide unnecessary) from Trafoi to the (3/4 hr.) HEILIGE DREI BRUNNEN. The path, which is nearly level the whole way, descends from the road to the left, about 250 paces above the 'Post', runs at first below the pine-wood and then through it, crosses the three arms of the brook, which afterwards unite, and reaches the 'Three Holy Springs' (5260'). Under a wooden roof are three rude figures representing Christ, the Virgin, and St. John, from whose breasts flows the ice-cold 'holy water'. Adjacent are a chapel and a house used as a tavern when a pilgrimage takes place. Opposite rises the huge and nearly perpendicular Madatsch, from the dark limestone cliffs of which two brooks are precipitated from a great height. To the left, above us, are the ice-masses of the Trafoi and Untere Ortler Glaciers, overshadowed by the Trafoier Eiswand. The whole scene is very picturesque and impressive. The interior of the chapel is interesting (keys kept by the Curé at Trafoi). — A steep and toilsome footpath (not recommended), diverging to the right shortly before the Three Springs, ascends to the Franzenshöhe (p. 279).

The ascent of the *Ortler (12,812') from Trafoi (from which 1000' more have to be ascended than from Sulden) has been much facilitated by the erection of the *Payerhütte* (p. 291), which enables the traveller to divide the excursion into two days. (Ascent, 8-9 hrs. in all; guide 10 fl.. with descent to Sulden 11½ fl.; to the Payerhütte and back 4 fl., by the Payerhütte to Sulden 5½ fl.). Comp. p. 291. The route crosses the Trafoibach halfway to the Holy Springs, and ascends by a new path through wood, and then through the *Tabarettathal* over grass and debris and across the little *Tabaretta Glacier* to the (4½ hrs.) *Payerhütte* (10,060'), where it unites with the club-paths from Gomagoi (about 5½ hrs.; see above), and from Franzenshöhe (5-6 hrs.; p. 279). Hence to the summit, see p. 292. [The old route passed the Holy Springs, and ascended to (1 hr.) the *Bergl-Hütte* (6230'), a small refuge-hut erected by Dr. Arning of Hamburg (d. 1886). It then either crossed the *Stickle Pleiss*, a small and precipitous glacier and ascended the saddle to the N. of the *Pleisshorn* ('Bulliner's Route'), or made a circuit to the left through the *Hohe Eisrinne* (p. 292) to the *Obere Ortler Glacier* and to the summit ('Tuckett's Route'). The latter affords the shortest descent to Trafoi (comp. p. 292).]

An admirable survey of the Ortler group is obtained from the Tartscher Alm (6170'), 1 hr. to the S.W. of Trafoi (guide, unnecessary, 1 fl.); still more extensive views are afforded by the *Schwarze Wand* (7020'), 1½ hr. farther up, and by the *Korspitze* (9600'), 4½ hrs. from Trafoi (same way to both; good path almost to the top; guide 3 fl.). — From the Korspitze across the *Seejoch* (9500'; a toilsome pass leading to the Münsterthal, less attractive than the Wormser Joch) to the *Röthelspitze* 3/4 hr.. and descent to the Stelvio Pass, very interesting, see p. 280. — The Kleinboden (7435'; 2 hrs.; guide 1½ fl.) affords a fine view of the Ortler. Stelvio, Oetzthaler Ferner, etc. — Other ascents are described under Franzenshöhe and the Stelvio Pass, pp. 279, 280.

OVER THE HOCHLEITENJOCH TO SULDEN, with the ascent of the *Hochleitenspitze (9160'), 6½-7 hrs. (guide 5½ fl.). The path crosses the brook at the Trafoi Mill and ascends by a wide circuit to the left, through wood. It then becomes steeper, and leads through the *Hochleitenthal*, over abrupt slopes of grass and detritus, to the (3½ hrs.) *Hochleitenjoch* (8056'), from which we ascend the rocky arête to the (¾ hr.) summit without difficulty. Magnificent view of the Sulden Alps: from left to right, Tschengelser Hochspitze, Kleine and Hohe Angelus-Spitze, Vertainspitze, Plattenspitze, Pederspitze, Schöntaufspitze, Madritsch-Spitze, Cevedale, Suldenspitze, Schrötterhorn, Kreilspitze, and finally the huge Ortler, which seems quite near. Far below, to the E., is the Suldenthal; to the W. the Trafoithal, with the Stelvio road and the sombre Madatsch; N. the Ober-Vintschgau, with Mals and the lakes of the Etsch. — Descent partly over steep and crumbling rocks, slopes of turf and debris. and lastly through wood and meadows to (2½-3 hrs.) *St. Gertrud* (p. 288).

By the *Payerhütte* to Sulden (6 hrs.; guide 5½ fl.), see p. 291.

The road ascends in bold windings on the left side of the valley. As the best views are obtained from some of the bends, the short-cuts should be avoided. The finest point is (2½ M.) the *Weisse Knott*, a platform with a marble obelisk (erected in 1884) to the memory of *Josef Pichler* ('P'sseyrer Josele'), who, in 1804, made the first ascent of the Ortler. Facing us is the sombre Madatsch, to the right the Madatsch Glacier, and to the left the Trafoi and Untere Ortler glaciers, separated by the Nashornspitze and overlooked by the snowy summits of the Eiskogl, Fernerkogl, Thurwieserspitze, Trafoier Eiswand, and Hintere Madatschspitze. More to the left, in the foreground, rises the Pleisshorn with the Hohe Eisrinne (p. 292). Far below, amid dark pine-trees, lies the sequestered chapel of the Three Holy Fountains. About 1/2 M. farther on, just before the kilomètre-stone marked 18, is the spot (indicated by a marble tablet) where Madeleine de Tourville, an English lady, was thrown down the slope and murdered by her husband, a Walloon, on 16th July, 1876. Just beyond this point a rough and steep path (not recommended) descends to the left to the Heilige Drei Brunnen, p. 277. Immediately opposite the superb Madatsch glacier, which, however, has greatly receded, is the (3/4 M.) Cantoniera al Bosco, which was destroyed by irregular Italian troops in 1848. The zone of trees is now quitted, and stunted dwarf-pines only are occasionally seen. At (1 1/4 M.) —

16 M. **Franzenshöhe** (7160'; *Inn*), the highest peak of the Ortler becomes visible for the first time.

A splendid view, particularly striking by evening-light, is obtained by ascending the grassy slopes of the *Vordere Grat* behind the inn for 1/2-1 hr.; to the *Untere Signalkuppe* 3/4-1 hr., to the °*Obere Signalkuppe* (9048'), 2 hrs. In the foreground is the Madatsch glacier with its magnificent ice-fall, and above it rises the Madatsch, behind which is seen the Ortler in all its grandeur; in the background to the N.E. are the Oetzthaler Ferner. — Franzenshöhe is one of the best headquarters for MOUNTAIN ASCENTS in the W. Ortler district (guides, *Joh., Alois, & Anton Theiner, Matth. Fahrner*). The *Geisterspitze* (11,400'; 4 hrs.), see p. 280. Other easy peaks are the *Grosse Naglerspitze* (*Cima Vitelli*, 10,682'; 3 1/2 hrs.; guide 3 1/2 fl.), the *Payerspitze* (11,300'; 4 hrs.; guide 4 1/2 fl.), and the *Tuckettspitze* (11,384'; 5 hrs.; guide 4 1/2 fl.). Adepts only should attempt the *Madatschspitzen* (*Vordere*, 10,174'; *Mittlere*, 10,964'; *Hintere*, 11,280'), the *Hohe Schneide* (11,856'; 5 hrs.; guide 5 fl.), or the *Krystallspitze* (11,312'; 5 1/2 hrs.; guide 5 fl.). Still more difficult are the *Grosse Schneeglocke* (11.240'; 5 1/2 hrs.; guide 5 fl.), and the *Grosse Eiskogel* (11,720'; 7 hrs.; guide 6 fl.). Very difficult are the *Trafoier Eiswand* (11,750'; 8-9 hrs.; guide 12 fl.) and the *Thurwieserspitze* (11,975'; 8-10 hrs.; guide 14 fl.). — The *Ortler* (pp. 278, 201) may also be ascended from Franzenshöhe. The 'Alpine Club Route' crosses the tongue of the *Madatsch Glacier*, skirts the *Vordere Madatschspitze*, and then traverses the *Trafoier* and *Untere Ortler Glaciers* to the *Bergl* (p. 278) and the (5 1/2 hrs.) *Payerhütte* (guide 4, to Sulden 5 1/2, to the top of the Ortler 10, and with descent to Sulden 11 1/2 fl.).

PASSES. To STA. CATERINA over the *Ortler Pass* (10,975'), between the Ortler and the Grosse Eiskogel, 8 hrs. to the *Milan Club Hut* in Val Zebrù, difficult. The *Thurwieserjoch* (11,384'), between the Grosse Eiskogel and the Thurwieserspitze (8-9 hrs. to the Milan Hut; guide 9 fl.), is also difficult. Other fatiguing or difficult passes are the *Glockenjoch* (10,840'), between the Trafoier Eiswand and the Grosse Schneeglocke, 7 hrs. to the Milan hut or to the *Malga Prato Beghino* in the Val Zebrù (guide 5 1/2 fl.); the *Trafoierjoch* (10,785'), between the Kleine Schneeglocke and the Hintere Madatschspitze (7 hrs.; guide 5 1/2 fl.); the *Tuckettjoch* (11,020'), between the Hintere Madatschspitze and the Tuckettspitze (6 hrs.; guide 5 1/2 fl.); the *Madatschjoch* (10,985'), between the Tuckettspitze and the Krystallspitze (6 hrs.; guide 5 1/4 fl.); and the *Geisterjoch* (*Passo di Sasso Rotondo*, 10,685'), between the Geisterspitze and the Hohe Schneide. — To SULDEN over the *Ortler Pass* (see above) and the *Hochjoch* (11,635'), between the Ortler and the Zebrù (14 hrs.; guide 12 fl.), very difficult, see p. 292.

The road ascends in long windings on slopes of talc-slate.

About halfway up is the dilapidated Casetta, a road-menders' hut. On the summit of the **Stelvio Pass** (*Stilfser Joch*, or *Ferdinandshöhe*, 9045'), 5½ M. from Franzenshöhe, is a workman's house. A column to the left marks the boundary between Austria and Italy. The Bernina, the next highest Alpine pass crossed by a carriage-road, is 7660' in height.

A path by the house, traversing mica-slate, ascends in steep zigzags to the (20 min.) *Dreisprachenspitze* (about 9180'; a spur of the Röthelspitze, see below) which commands an imposing view, particularly of the Ortler, the snowy dome of which appears quite near. Below, in the foreground, are the gorges of the Stelvio road. The barren red **Monte Pressura** (*Röthelspitze*, 9940'), which intercepts the view of the Münsterthal to the N., may be ascended in 1 hr. more (from Franzenshöhe direct in 2½ hrs.; view similar to that from the Umbrail).

The *Geisterspitze (11,400'), a very fine point, may be ascended from the pass in 3, or from Franzenshöhe in 4 hrs. (guide 4 fl.). The route ascends gradually across the *Eben Glacier*, between *Monte Livrio* on the left and the *Naglerspitze* and *Hohe Schneide* on the right, to the W. base of the Geisterspitze, a sharp, snow-clad ridge. Then a steep ascent to the narrow arête at the top (no serious difficulty; but a steady head necessary), which commands an admirable view of the Ortler, etc. Far below lies the green Val Furva.

To the left, close to the road, is the glittering ice of the *Eben* (*Cristallo*) and *Stelvio Glaciers*. The road is seldom entirely free from snow except in warm seasons; snow 6-8' deep is sometimes seen by the road-side in July, and long icicles frequently hang from the roofs of the galleries. The road then descends in windings, which may be avoided by short-cuts, to (1½ M.) —

23 M. **S. Maria** (8315'; *Inn*), the fourth Cantoniera and the Italian custom-house.

A bridle-path, formerly the only route between the Vintschgau and Val Tellina (valleys of the Adige and Adda), diverges from the Stelvio route to the right near the Cantoniera S. Maria, crosses the **Wormser Joch** (8240'), or *Umbrail Pass*, and descends (in 3 hrs., ascent 4 hrs.) through the *Muranza Valley* to the Swiss village of *S. Maria* in the Münsterthal (p. 250); thence by *Taufers* to (9 M.) *Mals* (p. 250) in the valley of the Adige (or Etsch). This forms a very pleasant excursion.

The ascent of the *Piz Umbrail (9950'; 1½ hr.; guide, advisable, 5-6 fr.), the E. and highest peak of the serrated mountain-range which bounds the valley of the Braulio on the N., is recommended. We diverge by the Dogana to the right, and ascend first a grassy slope and then a stony zigzag path to the jagged summit (the Umbrail glacier is no longer crossed). Magnificent view. To the E., towering above the red Monte Pressura, is seen the Ortler, with its series of snowy peaks, Zebrù, Königsspitze, Thurwieserspitze, Trafoier Eiswand, Tuckett-Spitze, Cevedale, Monte Cristallo, Geisterspitze; to the S. the distant Adamello, then the Alps of the Val Tellina (Cima di Piazza, Cima di Lago Spalmo, Corno di Dosdè, etc.); W. the Bernina; N. the Alps of the Lower Engadine (Piz Linard, Piz Buin, Fluchthorn), then the Oetzthal Alps with the Weisskugel, Similaun, and, in the background, the Venediger and Glockner. A good panorama by Faller may be seen at the cantoniera. — Those approaching from Bormio ascend the Umbrail from the third cantoniera (see below); the route (no path) diverges to the left from the road, near a post on the right, about ½ M. above the cantoniera, and ascends the hill-side to (1 hr.) a small lake, whence it climbs over rocks to the (1 hr.) top. Descent to S. Maria.

We next reach the (1 M.; third) *Cantoniera al Piano del Braulio*

(7590'; Inn well spoken of), near the *Abitazione del R. Cappellano* and a chapel, and then the *Casino dei Rotteri di Spondalonga* (7100'), a house occupied by road-menders.

The road descends in numerous windings, which the pedestrian can generally cut off. (In the gorge to the right are the *Falls of the Braulio*, precipitated over rocky terraces.) We cross the brook descending on the left from the *Val Vitelli* by the *Ponte Alto*, and reach the (second) *Cantoniera al Piede di Spondalonga* (6500'), which was destroyed by the Garibaldians in 1859. To the right rises the abrupt *Mte. Braulio* (9780'). The road skirts the mountain slope and is carried through the *Diroccamento Defile (Wormser Loch)* by covered galleries. Farther on is the (first) *Cantoniera di Piatta Martina* (5585'), beyond which the *Adda* dashes forth from the wild *Val Fraele* on the right and unites with the Braulio. (A brook springing from a rock at the mouth of the Val Fraele is sometimes erroneously called the source of the Adda.)

Beyond the last gallery but one the valley and the road turn towards the S., and a beautiful view is disclosed of the valley of Bormio as far as Ceppina. To the S.W. rise the *Corno di S. Colombano* (9915'), the *Cima di Piazzi* (11,280'), and the *Piz Redasco* (10,300'); to the S.E. are the *Mte. Valaccetta* (10,325') and the ice-pyramid of *Piz Tresero* (11,820'). On the right, beyond the deep gorge of the Adda, tower the abrupt slopes of the *Mte. delle Scale*. The *Bagni Vecchi* (plain but good quarters) or Old Baths of Bormio (7¼ M. from S. Maria), now come into view, perched on the rocks below the road. Before the last tunnel is reached, a road descends to them direct. At the egress of the last tunnel (the *Galleria dei Bagni*), a slab on the rock to the left records that this 'Via a Burmio ad Athesim per Braulii juga', begun in 1820, was completed by the architect Donegani in 1825. Fine view from the bridge.

The *New Baths of Bormio, or *Bagni Nuovi* (4395'; also a hotel, R. 2-4, L. & A. 1½, B. 1½, D. 4, 'pens.' from 8 fr.; closed on 15th Oct.), ½ M. lower down, a handsome building on a terrace, rebuilt in 1859, command a fine view of the valley of Bormio and the surrounding mountains. The baths are much frequented in July and August. The thermal water (92-100° Fahr., almost without mineral ingredients) is conducted hither by pipes from the springs at the old baths, to which, besides the road, a pleasant footpath ascends (¼ hr.). The springs, which are mentioned by Pliny, issue from the dolomite cliffs above the deep gorge of the Adda. The old Roman baths hewn in the rocks are interesting. — The diligences over the Stelvio and through the Val Tellina arrive at and start from the New Baths, where luggage from the N. addressed to Bormio is usually left.

Across the *Val Viola Pass* to the *Bernina*, and across the *Foscagno Pass to Livigno*, see *Baedeker's Switzerland*. — The ascent of the **Monte delle Scale** (8210; 3½ hrs.; guide convenient) is recommended. The route descends to the W. from the Baths, crosses the Adda at *Premadio*, and ascends by a good bridle-path on the N. slope of the *Val Viola* (edelweiss abundant) to the two towers of the (2 hrs.) *Scale di Fraele* (6515'), a well-known pass in the middle ages, commanding fine views of the Piz Tresero, Cima di Piazza, etc. About 1/4 hr. farther on is the beautiful little *Lago di Scale* (Chalet; Rfmts.), where the bridle-track ends. From this point a climb of 1 1/4 hr., the last 1/2 hr. steep, brings us to the plateau of the *Mte. delle Scale*, with its two peaks. Magnificent view to the E. of the Ortler group, the Val Viola, Val Furva, and Valle di Sotto, while immediately below are the gorge of the Adda and the Baths of Bormio. — The *Corno di S. Colombano* (9915'; 4-5 hrs.) and the *Monte Valaccetta* (10,325'; 4-5 hrs.), are both interesting ascents presenting no difficulty. The difficult ascent of the *Cima di Piazza* (11,280'; 8 hrs.) should be attempted only by adepts.

The windings of the road end, 1 1/4 M. lower down, at —

32 M. **Bormio**, Ger. *Worms* (4010'; *Posta*, moderate; *Alb. della Torre*, Piazza Cavour), an antiquated little Italian town at the entrance to the **Val Furva**, with many dilapidated towers.

FROM BORMIO TO STA. CATERINA, 9 M. (diligence twice daily in 1 1/2 hr.; one-horse carr. there and back 12 fr.), a very attractive expedition. The tolerable road leads through the *Val Furva*, which is picturesque at first, but afterwards monotonous, viâ *S. Niccolò* and (3 M.) *S. Antonio*, at the mouth of the *Val Zebrù* (see below), which is terminated by the precipices of the Cristallo, to (6 M.) Sta. **Caterina** (5700'; *Stabilimento di Bagni*, much frequented by Italians in summer, closed after 15th Sept.; *Hôtel Tresero*, well spoken of), a bath of some repute, with a spring impregnated with carbonic acid. Sta. Caterina is very finely situated between the Monte Confinale on the N., the Mte. Tresero on the E., and the Mte. Sobretta on the S., and is a good starting-point for exploring the S. side of the Ortler.

EXCURSIONS (guides, *P. Compagnoni*, *L. Bonelli*, *Batt. Confortola*, *Fil. Cola*, and *Pietrogiovanna*). To the *Forno Glacier*, a beautiful walk (3 1/2 hrs. there and back; guide not indispensable). We follow the right bank of the Frodolfo, the path being level at first, and then ascend the wild *Val Forno*, which contains remarkably fine Alpine cedars (skirting the deep gorge of the Frodolfo on the right). The path, steep and stony at places, leads to the (2 hrs.) *Baita del Forno* (ca. 7550'; rustic accommodation), grandly situated opposite to the huge *Forno Glacier*, which descends to the valley in an imposing ice-fall, and surrounded by the finely-shaped Piz Tresero, Punta di S. Matteo, Mte. Saline, etc. To the *Val di Cedeh* and the *Cedeh Hut* (8530'), see below and p. 291.

Very interesting and moderately easy is the ascent of *Monte Confinale* (11,055'; 4-5 hrs., with guide), to the N. of Sta. Caterina, between the Val Zebrù and the Val Furva. Admirable survey of the Ortler chain from the summit; W. the Bornina and Piz Linard, S.W. the Monte della Disgrazia, S. the Presanella.

FROM STA. CATERINA TO THE VAL ZEBRÙ (10-11 hrs. there and back; guide necessary), attractive. From the (2 hrs.) *Baite del Forno* (see above) we ascend on the W. side of the *Val di Cedeh*, over grass, debris, and snow, to the (2-3 hrs.) *Passo del Zebrù* (9910'). Fine view of the Königsspitze, Zebrù, Thurwieserspitze, and Mte. Cristallo. Descent over snow to the (1 1/2 hr.) *Baita del Pastore* (7255'), in the Val del Zebrù, and thence to the (1/2 hr.) *Malga Prato Beghino* (6345'), and viâ (2 hrs.) *S. Antonio* back to (2 hrs.) *Sta. Caterina*. On the edge of the *Zebrù Glacier*, 2 hrs. above the Pastore Alp, is the **Milan Hut** (*Capanna Milano*, 9440'), of the Italian Alpine Club, the starting-point for the ascents of the *Mte. Zebrù* (12,270'; over the *Hochjoch* in 4 hrs.), the *Thurwieserspitze* (11,980'; 5-6 hrs.; either from the S. or viâ the *Thurwieserjoch*), the *Königsspitze* (12,664'; over the *Colle Pale Rosse* in 6-7 hrs.; see p. 291), and the *Ortler* (12,812'; by the Hochjoch in 8-9 hrs.; see p. 292). All these ascents should be attempted only by experienced mountaineers, with steady heads and good guides.

From Sta. Caterina over the *Cevedale Pass* and the *Eisses Pass* to

Sulden, and ascent of the *Königsspitze* and *Cevedale*, see R. 52. Over the *Cevedale Pass* to the *Martelltal*, see p. 287; over the *Glockenjoch*, *Madatschjoch*, *Ortler Pass*, etc., to *Trafoi*, see p. 279. — The following S. peaks of the Ortler group (all fatiguing) may be ascended from Sta. Caterina by experts with an able guide: *Piz Tresero* (11,820') in 5½ hrs. (the last part only steep); *Punta S. Matteo* (12,090') in 6 hrs.; *Mte. Vioz* (11,940') in 7-8 hrs.; *Palon della Mare* (12,160') in 7-8 hrs.

FROM STA. CATERINA TO PONTE DI LEGNO, over the **Gavia Pass** (8700'), 7 hrs., easy and interesting (guide unnecessary in clear weather, but advisable in the reverse direction). A tolerable but steep bridle-track ascends on the W. side of the valley, crosses the stream by the (1¼ hr.) *Ponte delle Vacche* (6590'), and again ascends to (1 hr.) the top of the E. side of the valley. On the left are the precipices of the *Piz Tresero* (11,820'). Farther on, the path crosses, by the *Ponte di Pietra* (7890'), the discharge of the *Dosegù Glacier*, which descends on the left from the *Punta S. Matteo* (good view of the glacier from the hill to the left beyond the bridge). We then traverse a more level valley, following the right bank of the stream (way marked by crosses and heaps of stones), pass the *Lago Bianco*, and reach the (2 hrs.) summit of the pass, between the *Corno dei Tre Signori* (11,020') and the *Monte Gavia* (10,575'; fine retrospect of the Ortler group). On the other side of the pass the *Lago Nero* (9510') lies on the right. The path descends to the left, past a spring ('Acqua Benedetta'; marble tablet with inscription of 1619), to the (2 hrs.) small baths of *S. Apollonia* (5180'; beds), in the *Val delle Messi*, from which a carriage-road follows the bank of the *Oglio*, passing *Pezzo* on the hill to the left, to (3 M.) *Ponte di Legno* (p. 313).

FROM STA. CATERINA TO PEJO, over the **Sforzellina Pass** (9860'; 9½ hrs.; with guide), laborious and devoid of interest. The route is at first identical with that to the Gavia Pass; above the Ponte di Pietra, where the more level valley begins, we diverge to the left, and cross loose stones and snow in the direction of the opening to the N. of the *Corno dei Tre Signori* (11,020'). The summit of the pass, 4½ hrs. from Sta. Caterina, affords little view. Then a rapid descent into the small *Val Bormina*, a rough walk of 2 hrs. through the valley to the *Val del Monte*, and thence to *Pejo* (p. 312) in 2 hrs. more.

The road, which will repay pedestrians as far as Bolladore, crosses at (1 M.) *S. Lucia* the muddy *Frodolfo*, which falls into the Adda below the bridge, and then turns towards the S. The broad green valley *(piano)* of Bormio ends at (2¼ M.) *Ceppina*, beyond which we pass the hamlet of *S. Antonio*, and then *Morignone*, in the green *Valle di Sotto*, with its church on the hill above. The *Serra di Morignone*, a defile 3½ M. in length, here separates the district of Bormio, 'Paese Freddo', or 'cold region', from the *Val Tellina*, which belonged to the Grisons down to 1797, then to Austria, and since 1859 has been united to Italy. The broad valley is watered by the *Adda*, the inundations of which often cause great damage, and its slopes yield excellent red wine. The *Ponte del Diavolo* was destroyed by the Austrians in 1859. Near the end of the defile, on the right, are the ruins of a fort. The valley now expands, and the vegetation becomes richer. To the left lies *Le Prese*, prettily situated at the mouth of the *Val di Rezzo*; then *Mondadizza*. On the slope to the W. rises the church of *Sondalo*.

45 M. **Bolladore** (2840'; *Posta* or *Angelo*, high charges; *Hôtel des Alpes*). At (1½ M.) *Tiolo* a bridle-path diverges to the left and leads over the *Passo del Mortirolo* to *Edolo* (p. 313). Near (2 M.) *Grosio* (2170') we cross the Adda, and at the large village of

(1½ M.) *Grossotto* (Leone d'Oro) the *Roasco*, which issues from the *Val Grosina*. (At the entrance to the valley, on the left, are the well-preserved ruins of the handsome castle of *Venosta*.) At (1½ M.) *Mazzo* the road recrosses the Adda. To the W. rises the precipitous *Piz Masuccio* (9140'), a landslip from which in 1807 blocked up the narrow channel of the Adda, and converted the populous and fertile valley into a large lake. The road then descends by *Tovo*, *Lovero*, and *Sernio*, passing vine-clad hills, to —

57 M. **Tirano** (1475 ft.; *Alb. d'Italia*, with the post-office, bargaining advisable; *Posta; Hôtel Stelvio*, by the lower bridge), a small town which has also often suffered from the inundations of the Adda, with old mansions of the Visconti, Pallavicini, and Salis families.

About ¾ M. farther on, on the right bank of the Adda, lies **Madonna di Tirano** (*S. Michele*, R. 3, B. 1 fr.), a small village built in a wide circle round the imposing pilgrimage-church, an edifice of the 17th century. (The road which diverges here to the right leads to *Poschiavo*, and across the Bernina to the Upper *Engadine*; see *Baedeker's Switzerland*.) — The road next crosses the *Poschiavino*, which descends from the Bernina glaciers. At *Tresenda* (1220') the road over the Monte Aprica diverges to the left (comp. p. 314, and *Baedeker's Northern Italy*). On the N. slope of the valley rises the old watch-tower of *Teglio* (2945'), which gives its name to the valley *(Val Teglino)*. On the hill to the right, near Sondrio, stand the churches of *Pendolasco* and *Montagna*.

73 M. **Sondrio** (1140'; *Posta; Maddalena; Ristoratore del Marino*, with rooms, well spoken of), the capital (7000 inhab.) of the Val Tellina, with a considerable wine-trade, is prettily situated on the *Malero*, a torrent which has frequently endangered the town, but is now conducted through an artificial channel.

The beautiful *Val Malenco*, which opens here to the N., deserves a visit. A tolerable road leads on the right bank of the *Malero* viâ *Torre* to (10 M.) *Chiesa* (4280'; Inn, dear), the chief place in the valley, very finely situated (N. the Bernina, W. Monte della Disgrazia). Thence over the *Muretto Pass* (8390') to the *Maloja* (8 hrs.), or through the *Val Lanterna* (ascending to the N.E.) and through the *Val Campo Moro* to the *Canciano Pass* (8360') and *Poschiavo* (9-10 hrs.); see *Baedeker's Switzerland*. Picturesque walks in the vicinity: to the *Lago di Palù* (6300'), beautifully situated; viâ *Lanzada* to the waterfall at the head of the *Val Lanterna*; to the *Pirlo Lakes* (6890'), etc. — The **Monte della Disgrazia** (12,070') may be ascended from Chiesa in 14 hrs. (very fatiguing and difficult). The previous night may be spent in the *Capanna della Disgrazia* of the Italian Alpine Club, on the *Corna Rossa Pass* (8850'), between the Val Malenco and the Val di Sasso Bissolo, 7 hrs. from Chiesa. Hence the summit, on which there is a small refuge-hut, may be attained in 7 hrs. Magnificent view. The ascent from the Val Masino (see below) is shorter. The route leads from *Cataeggio* through the *Val di Sasso Bissolo* and the *Val di Pietra Rossa* to the (5 hrs.) *Capanna Cecilia* (8280'), another hut of the Italian Alpine Club, whence the top is reached in 5 hrs.

The RAILWAY skirts the hill of *Sassella*, producing a well-known wine, on the right bank of the Adda. 76½ M. *Castione;* 79½ M. *S. Pietro-Berbenno*. At (84 M.) *Ardenno-Masino* the interesting *Val Masino* opens to the right.

The road in the Val Masino ascends to the right from the station, viâ *Masino*, *Pioda*, and *Cataeggio*, at the mouth of the *Val di Sasso Bissolo* (see p. 284), to (7½ M.) *S. Martino* (3755'), where the valley divides: to the right is the *Valle di Mello*, to the left the *Valle dei Bagni*. In the latter lie (1¼ M.) the *Bagni del Masino*, with a good *Bath-house (4350'). The valley, called the *Val Porcellizza* above this point, now turns to the N. At its head (3½-4 hrs. from the Bagni), and at the base of the precipitous *Badile* group, is the *Badile Hut* (8530'). The E. peak (*Piz Trubinasca*, 9575') and the W. peak (*Piz Cengalo*, 11,050') present no difficulty to experts with good guides. The central peak (*Pis Badile*, 10,850') is very difficult. — Passes to the Val Bregaglia (*Bondo Pass, Forcella di S. Martino*, etc.), see *Baedeker's Switzerland*.

The train crosses the Adda above its junction with the *Masino*. 87 M. *Talamona*. 89½ M. **Morbegno** (850'; *Regina d'Inghilterra*), noted for its silk-culture, has a 17th cent. church. 91½ M. *Cosio-Traona*. The village of *Traona* lies on the other side of the Adda, at the foot of the mountains. 94 M. *Delebio*. The lower part of the Val Tellina is rendered marshy and unhealthy by the inundations of the Adda.

99 M. **Colico** (700'; *Albergo Piazza Garibaldi*, on the lake; *Isola Bella*) is situated at the N.E. end of the *Lake of Como*; see *Baedeker's N. Italy*, or *Baedeker's Switzerland*.

51. The Martellthal.

Comp. Maps, pp. 288, 246, 304.

The **Martellthal**, or **Martellthal**, the longest valley in the Ortler Alps (15 M.), affords the shortest route from the lower Vintschgau to Sulden. The lower part of the valley (as far as the Marteller Alp) is rather mountainous, but the glacier-scenery at its head is magnificent. The best starting-point for excursions is the club-hut on the Zufall-Alp (see p. 286). — Guides: *Paul* and *Math. Kobald, Joh., Jos., Math.*, and *Mart. Eberhöfer* of Gand; *Joseph* and *Math. Holzknecht* of Salt (see also Sulden guides, p. 288).

At the mouth of the valley lies the village of *Morter* (2380'), reached in 20 min. from *Goldrain* (p. 252), or in 40 min. from *Latsch* (p. 253). The path from the latter quits the village on the S.W. side, to the right, crosses the *Plima* after 35 min., and in 5 min. more reaches the road up the valley, at the upper end of the village of Morter. On a hill to the left are the ruined castles of *Unter-* and *Ober-Montan* and the ancient *Chapel of St. Stephen*. The road (10 min.) crosses the brook and begins to ascend rapidly. The floor of the valley is strewn with rocks and debris, over which dashes the Plima. Near Salt are large marble quarries.

1 hr. *Salt*, a small chalybeate bath, lies a few hundred paces above the road, to the left (plain but good quarters). To the right, on the hill on the left bank, lies *Martell*, or *Thal* (4270'; Inn, near the church, rustic), a scattered village. We next cross the *Flimbach* to (¾ hr.) the long village of **Gand**, or *Gand* (*Eberhöfer*, rustic), traverse wood (on the right the precipitous *Schluderhorn*, 9005'), and pass the solitary chapel of (1¼ hr.) *Maria-Schmelz* (5060'). We then (½ hr.) recross the stream and traverse a large

Alp, with numerous chalets and hay-sheds. High up, on the left, is the *Untere Zufritt Ferner*. At the end of the Alp (¼ hr.) the path again enters the wood and ascends, skirting a projecting spur, beyond which the two snowy peaks of the Cevedale are suddenly disclosed; this magnificent picture, however, soon disappears. We next reach the (½ hr.) **Untere Marteller Alp** (5975'), on the right bank, and the (10 min.) *Obere Marteller Alp*, finely situated on the left bank (opposite which, to the S., are the *Vordere Rothspitze* and the *Gramsen-Ferner*).

The path now ascends through wood on the left bank, crosses the (1 hr.) *Pederbach* (shortly before reaching which we pass an excellent spring), and ascends to the right. On the first buttress of the mountain (where the route to the *Madritsch-Joch* diverges; see p. 287), we turn to the left, cross the *Madritschbach*, and ascend the steep rock to the (1 hr.) **Zufall-Hütte* (6885'; **Inn* in summer), prettily situated on a grassy hill near the *Zufall-Alpe*, and the best starting-point for the Cevedale, the Eissee Pass, etc. To the W. the imposing *Zufall Glacier* descends in two arms into the valley (left, the *Fürkele-Ferner*; right, the *Langen-Ferner*). On the left is the *Hohen-Ferner* with the *Veneziaspitze* and *Schranspitze*.

ASCENTS (guides, see above; the charges given are from the Zufall-Hütte; guide from Gand to the hut 2½ fl.). The ascent of the °**Cevedale** (*Zufall-Spitze*, 12,380'; 5½-6 hrs. from the Zufall-Hütte; guide 6, with descent to Sulden 8½, to Sta. Caterina 9½ fl.) is troublesome, but most interesting (comp. p. 289). From the hut we ascend to the W., through the *Hutweidenthal*, on the slope of the *Mutspitze* (9585'), to the foot of the *Hintere Wandln*; then across the *Langen-Ferner* to the *Cevedale Pass* (see p. 287), and thence to the left to the top (p. 289). — The **Innere Pederspitze** (10,764'), which commands a splendid view of the Ortler, is ascended from the Zufall-Hütte in 4 hrs. (rather toilsome; guide 3, with descent to Sulden 6 fl.). The *Plattenspitze* (11,286'; 4½ hrs.; guide 3 fl.), the *Aeussere Pederspitze* (11,158; 5 hrs.), the *Mittlere Pederspitze* (11,315'; 5 hrs.), and the *Schildspitze* (about 10,820'; 4½ hrs.; 2½ fl.) may also be ascended from the Zufall-Hütte. — *°Hintere Schöntaufspitze*, see p. 289. — The ascent of the *Zufritt-Spitze* (11,256') from the Untere Marteller-Alp is laborious but interesting (7-8 hrs.; guide 6 fl.). The same remark applies to the *Venezia-Spitze* (11,090'), ascended from the Zufall-Hütte by the *Hohenfernerjoch* in 5 hrs., and to the *Hintere Rothspitze* (10,960'), reached from the Zufall-Hütte by the *Schran-Ferner* and *Gramsen-Ferner* in 4 hrs. (guide 4½, with descent to Pejo over the *Caresen-Ferner* 9½ fl.). — The *Laaser Spitze* (10,822') and the *Schluderspitze* (10,585') are both comparatively easy (from Gand 5-6 hrs.; guide 4 fl., with descent to Laas 6½ fl.); comp. p. 262.

PASSES. To THE BATHS OF RABBI (p. 311) from the Zufall-Hütte or the lower Marteller Alp over the **Sällent-Joch** (9900') between the *Gramsenspitze* and the *Sällentspitze*, 10 hrs., laborious (guide 8 fl.). — To PEJO (p. 312), from the Zufall-Alp, either over the Hohenferner-Joch (10,510'), on the W. side of the *Venezia-Spitze* (see above; ascended from the pass in 1 hr.), in 10½ hrs. (guide 8 fl.), or over the Fürkele-Scharte (9900') to the E. of the Cevedale, in 10 hrs. (guide 7½ fl.), both fine but fatiguing routes. — To ST. GERTRUD in the *Ultenthal* (p. 276), several passes. From the lower Alp over the Zufritt-Joch (10,680'), to the W. of the *Zufrittspitze* (see above), down the rocky slope called '*In der Neuen Welt*', and past the *Gränsee* to the *Weissbrunner Alp*, laborious but interesting (10 hrs.; guide 7½ fl.). From Gand to St. Gertrud over the Soy-Joch (9900'), to the N E of the Zufrittspitze, 7½ hrs., or over the **Flim-Joch**, to the W. of th Hasenohr, 7 hrs., two attractive routes, free from difficulty (guide 6 fl.). — To STA. CATERINA over the **Cevedale Pass** (10,730'), a grand glacier-tour of 8 hrs. from the Zufall-Hütte (guide 7 fl.), with which the ascent of the *Cevedale* may be combined (3-4 hrs. more; comp. p. 289).

To SULDEN, 10 hrs. from Sult, over the **Madritsch-Joch** (10,340'), which forms the usual exit from the Martellthal, a somewhat fatiguing route, but highly interesting when combined with the ascent of the *Hintere Schöntaufspitze* (guide 7½/2, including the Schöntaufspitze 8 fl.; from the Zufall-Hütte 6 and 6½ fl.). From the upper Marteller Alp to the (1 hr.) bridge over the *Pederbach*, see p. 286. We then ascend to the right through wood and across pastures in the *Madritschthal*, and lastly over a steep slope of debris to the (2½-3 hrs.) summit of the pass. On the way up, a fine retrospect is obtained of the Zufrittspitze, the Vordere Rothspitze, and the Venezia-Spitze with their glaciers, and from the summit a stupendous view is disclosed of the mountain-giants mentioned at p. 285, all apparently within gun-shot. The *Hintere Schöntaufspitze* (10,892'), immediately to the N. of the pass, and easily ascended in ½ hr., commands a still grander and more extensive panorama (see p. 290). Descent from the Joch over the *Ebenwand Ferner*, which presents no difficulty, to the (1½ hr.) *Schaubachhütte* and to (1½ hr.) Sulden (p. 288). — If the night has been spent at Sult, the long ascent through the valley to the Joch is fatiguing, the more so as the steeper portions must be faced during the midday heat. The traveller may therefore prefer to spread the walk over two days, spending a night in the *Zufall-Hütte*. In the reverse direction (from Sulden, and still more easily from the Schaubachhütte) a good walker may cross the Madritsch-Joch, climb the Schöntaufspitze, and reach *Latsch* (p. 253) in one day.

Another grand route to Sulden is by the **Eissee Pass** (10,500'; from the Zufall-Alp 7 hrs.; guide 6½ fl.). We follow the Cevedale route as far as the névé of the *Langen-Ferner* (p. 286), and then proceed to the right to the (3½ hrs.) top of the pass, lying to the right of the *Suldenspitze* (11,105'), and commanding a magnificent view of the Suldenthal, with the Königsspitze and the Ortler on the left. Descent over the *Sulden Glacier* to the (1½ hr.) *Schaubachhütte* and (1½ hr.) *Sulden*.

52. The Suldenthal.

Comp. Maps, pp. 246, 304.

The imposing *Ortler Group*, situated between the sources of the Adige and the Adda, and notable for their boldness of form, great height, and magnificent glacier-scenery, present a most interesting field to the tourist, and have accordingly attracted numerous visitors in recent years. The best starting-point for excursions is *Sulden* or *St. Gertrud*, beautifully situated (good quarters and good guides), 2¼ M. from Gomagoi on the Stelvio route (porter 1 fl. 90 kr.; horse with guide 5 fl. and fee). — For good walkers the finest route (4-5 days) to the Suldenthal and the Ortler region is from *Innsbruck* through the Stubaithal and over the Bildstöckljoch (p. 230), to Sölden; thence over the Hochjoch, or better the Niederjoch, to Naturns; from Naturns by carriage to Latsch (or over the Hochjoch and Taschljoch to Schlanders); and then through the Martellthal and over the Madritsch-Joch to Sulden.

At *Gomagoi* (p. 277), on the Stelvio road, the **Suldenthal**, a valley 9 M. in length, opens to the E. The new road, which has been commenced, but not carried on very far, descends to the right by the inn, crosses the *Trafoibach* in its narrow gorge, and then, skirting the wooded slope to the left, enters the valley and (¾ M.) crosses the wild *Suldenbach*. A cart-track (not suited for driving, but easy for walking) ascends in zigzags through the woods on the right bank (to the left beyond the bridge), and then gradually as-

cends the N. side of the valley to the (40 min.) *Unter-Thurnhof*
(Inn), beyond which it degenerates into a stony bridle-path. We
pass the *Gandhof* and then (¹/₄ hr.), beyond a small chapel, cross
the *Razoibach*, which separates Ausser- and Inner-Sulden, the
former of which belongs to the parish of Stilfs. The white
mantle of the Ortler now becomes visible on the right; to the
left, farther on, are the Schöntaufspitze, Pederspitze, and Plattenspitze. After 25 min. the path crosses the Suldenbach, ascends
steeply on the left bank to the highest plateau of the valley,
and (now nearly level) traverses wood and the broad moraine of
the *Marlt Glacier* (p. 291). Before the (25 min.) first house is
reached, the path leads to the right through a gate, and crosses
the meadows to the (10 min.) church and parsonage of **St. Gertrud**
or **Sulden** (6055'; *Hôtel Eller*, kept by the sisters of the curé, often
crowded in summer; *Zum Ortlerhof*, to the left, beyond the gate and
the brook). The view from this point is limited : E. the *Vertainspitze*
(11,614'), *Plattenspitze* (11,286'), *Innere Pederspitze* (10,768'),
and the *Hintere* and *Vordere Schöntaufspitze* (10,892' and 10,100');
W. the *Ortler* (12,812') with its lofty snowy crest, and to the
right of it, the *Tabarettaspitze* (10,255', with the *Tabarettascharte*,
the route to the Ortler, on the right); lastly the *Hochleitenspitze* (9160'). We now descend to the left by the inn, cross
the brook, ascend to the right across meadows, and cross the
Zaibach to the Gampenhöfe (6160'), ¹/₂ hr. beyond the church,
where the magnificence of the scene is fully disclosed. Opposite to
us (S.) rises the *Schrötterhorn* (11,148'), with the *Suldenspitze*
(11,105') on the left and the *Kreilspitze* (11,096') on the right;
then the *Königs-Spitze* (12,648') and the huge rocky precipices of
the *Ortler* (12,812'). Between the Königs-Spitze and the Kreil-
Spitze lies the *Königsjoch* (11,060'), and between the Kreil-Spitze
and the Schrötterhorn the *Oedeh-Pass* (10,940'). — From these
mountains descends the vast *Sulden Glacier*, which in 1818 and
1856 advanced rapidly into the valley, but afterwards receded, leaving its walls of rubbish behind.

Excursions. Guides: *Peter Dangl, Johann, Alois*, and *Joseph Ping-
gera*, all first-rate; *Jos. Reinstadler* of Putzenhof; *Jos., Peter, Paul*. and
Vinc. Reinstadler of Gomagoi; *Josef* and *Alois Angerer, Alois Schöpf, Jos.
Tembl, Simon Reinstadler* of Gampenhof; *Jos. Reinstadler* of Völlensteinhof;
Joh. Reinstadler of Pichlhof; *Jos. Kössler, Franz Zischg*, and *Alois Knüner*.
Comp. p. 277. On Sundays the Sulden (like the Oetzthal) guides will not
start before mass (8.30 a.m.). — To the Rosimboden 1¹/₂ hr. (guide 1 fl.
75 kr.; horse 4¹/₂ fl.). We may either cross the Zaibach, and below the
saw-mill (20 min. from St. Gertrud; fine survey of the Ortler) ascend to
the left through wood; or, beyond the Gampenhöfe, ascend to the left by
the wood by a somewhat steeper path. Where the wood terminates we
reach a height called the *Kanzel* (about 7800'), which affords a magnificent
View of the Ortler, with the small End-der-Welt Glacier (p. 289).

To the *Schaubachhütte* (9430'; 2 hrs.; guide 2¹/₂ fl.), a very fine excursion. The path leads from the Gampenhöfe to the S., crosses the *Rosin-
bach*, and ascends the *Legerwand*; to the right are the huge moraines of
the *Sulden Glacier*. After about 1 hr. the path mounts the old E. lateral

Ortler District. CEVEDALE. *VI. Route 52.* 289

moraine, and finally, bending to the left, ascends in zigzags over grassy slopes, to the *Schaubachhütte*, on the *Ebenwand*, splendidly situated in view of the Sulden Glacier. Opposite to us rises the imposing Königsspitze; to the right are the Zebrù and Ortler, to the left the Königsjoch, Kreilspitze, Cedeh Pass, Schröttorhorn, and Suldenspitze. The hut (Inn in summer, bed 1 fl.) is the best starting-point for the Königsspitze, the Cevedale, Zebrù, Eissee Pass, etc.

The **Hintere Grat** and **End der Welt** (there and back 4½ hrs.; guide 2½ fl.). The route diverges to the right at the (½ hr.) Gampenhöfe (see p. 288), crosses the brook, and ascends to the (¾ hr.) *Schönleitenhütte*, and thence to the (1¼ hr.) small *Grat-See*, in a wild situation at the base of the precipitous *Hintere Grat*. Thence over grassy slopes to the (1 hr.) summit of the *Hintere Gratspitze* (0815'), with fine view. We descend over grass, then over the huge moraines of the *End-der-Welt Glacier* (to the left of which tower the gigantic precipices of the Ortler), and return across the *Kuhberg* and through wood to (2 hrs.) St. Gertrud.

The **Schöneck** (10,240'), opposite St. Gertrud, on the right side of the Zaithal, ascended without difficulty in 3 hrs. (guide 3 fl.; horse 7 fl.), commands a splendid view of the Ortler group.

To the **Payerhütte** (10,058'; 3-4 hrs.; path marked with red; guide 4 fl.), see p. 291; recommended even to those who do not intend to ascend the Ortler. — **Hochleitenspitze** (9160'; 3 hrs.; guide 4 fl.), an interesting ascent and not difficult (best combined with the passage of the *Hochleitenjoch*; see p. 278). — **Tabarettaspitze** (10,255'), from the Payerhütte across the *Tabaretta Glacier*, ½ hr. (guide from Sulden 4½ fl.), laborious; strikingly grand view of the Ortler.

The ascent of the *Vertainspitze (11,614'; 5 hrs., not very difficult; guide 5 fl.) is specially recommended. The route is by the Rosimboden (see above) to the *Rosim Glacier*, part of which is crossed; it then ascends over rocks and loose stones, and lastly a snow-field. 'The Vertainspitze is an admirable point of view for the three huge pyramids of the Ortler, Zebrù, and Königsspitze. Magnificent mountain-scenery is disclosed on every side: the Monte Cevedale, the beautiful Laas group with its numerous lofty peaks (Pederspitze, Orgelspitze, Ofenwand), the Tschengelser Hochwand, and the E. slopes of the Martellthal (Zufrittspitze), many of them remarkable for picturesqueness of form. Then the Stubai and Oetzthal snow-mountains (the Venediger and Glockner being also visible), those of the Grisons, the Bernina, the Finsteraarhorn group, and the Adamello-Presanella Alps. Lastly, at a prodigious depth below the spectator, lie the houses of Sulden and the Malser Heide, which is visible almost as far as Nauders.' (Payer.) — A better and shorter route for adepts leads through the *Zaithal* and by the couloir between the Vertainspitze and the rounded rocks to the right ('Schnorrweg'), over snow and ice (steps sometimes required), to the saddle, and across rocks and debris to (4-5 hrs.) the summit. — Descent by the *Rosimjoch* into the *Laaser Thal*, see p. 252.

The *Hintere **Schöntaufspitze** (10,892'; 4½ hrs.; guide 4½ fl.) is another admirable point, free from difficulty. The route leads from the *Schaubachhütte* (p. 288) over grass and moraine debris and across the *Ebenwand Glacier*, to the (2 hrs.) *Madritsch-Joch* (10,340'), and thence to the left by the arête to the (1½ hr.) summit. Magnificent *View (comp. the Panorama, p. 290). The ascent is generally combined with the passage of the Madritsch-Joch to the *Martellthal* (comp. p. 287). — The *Innere Pederspitze* (10,768'; 5 hrs.; guide 5 fl.), the *Plattenspitze* (11,286'; 5 hrs.; 4½ fl.), and the *Madritschspitze* (10,602'; 4½ hrs.; 4½ fl.), peaks similar to the Schöntaufspitze, are also occasionally ascended. More fatiguing are the *Mittlere Pederspitze* (11,315'; 5-6 hrs.; 5½ fl.), the *Hohe Angelus* (11,588'; 6 hrs.; 5½ fl.), and the *Tschengelser Hochwand* (11,060'; 5 hrs.; 5 fl.).

The *Cevedale (12,380'; 7 hrs., or from the Schaubachhütte 4½-5 hrs.; guide 8 fl.), a magnificent point, is easy for adepts. The preceding night should be spent in the *Schaubachhütte* (p. 288), whence we traverse the *Sulden Glacier* to the (2½ hrs.) *Eissee Pass*; see p. 292. We leave the *Cevedale Pass* (p. 292) to the right, ascend gradually to the left over terraces of snow, and lastly mount the steep Cevedale ridge, where steps must some-

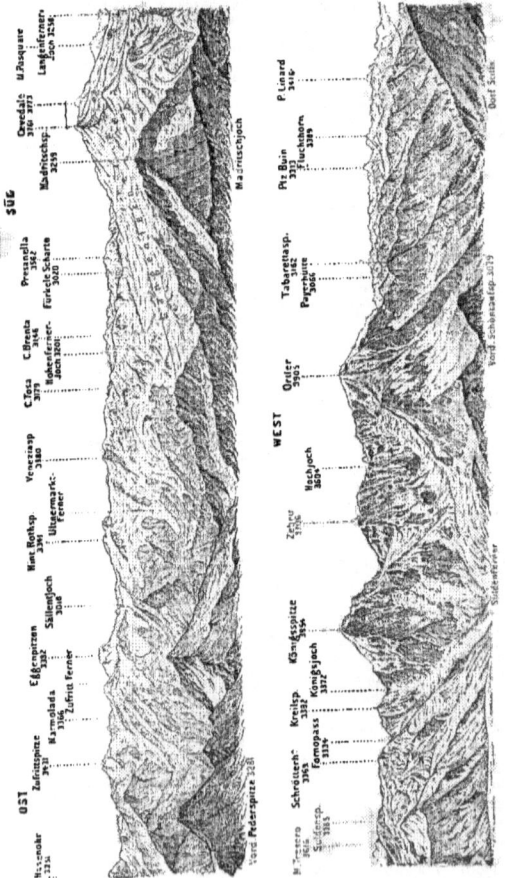

Panorama from the Hintere Schöntaufspitze (10,892').

Ortler District.   ORTLER.   *VI. Route 52.* 291

times be cut, to the saddle between the central and the S. peak and follow the arête to the (2-3 hrs.) S. and highest peak. (The Cevedale, called in the Martelltlhal the *Zufallspitze* or *Fürkele*, forming the central mass of the Ortler Alps, and long regarded as their highest mountain, consists of three peaks: the N. 12,135', the central 12,035', and the S. 12,380'.) The °°View vies with that from the Ortler, and is by many preferred, the Ortler group itself being seen to much greater advantage. To the S.W. the Adamello, Presanella, and Brenta Alps are conspicuous. At our feet lie the Val di Cedeh (Val Furva), Val della Mare, the Martellthal, and the Upper Vintschgau. — Descent by the *Cevedale Pass* to *Sta. Caterina*, see below (5 hrs.; guide 12 fl.); by the *Langen-Ferner* to *Martell* (4½-5 hrs. to the Zufallhütte; guide 10 fl.), see p. 286. By the *Vedretta Venezia* to the *Cevedale Hut* (p. 312) in the *Val della Mare* and to *Pejo* (7 hrs.; two guides at 15 fl.).

The ascent of the **Königsspitze** (12,648') is difficult, and fit for experts only (from the Schaubachhütte 5-6 hrs.; guide 12 fl.). From the hut we cross the *Sulden Glacier* to (1½-2 hrs.) the foot of the *Königsjoch*, which we ascend in ¾-1 hr. (very steep and difficult; worst part of the route; caution necessary on account of the falling stones). At the top we turn to the right to the (¾ hr.) *Schulter*, a projection on the E. side of the Königsspitze, whence a stiff climb of 1½ hr. over snow and ice, and finally over rocks and detritus, brings us to the summit. The °View is magnificent, particularly of the Ortler, and towards the S. — The ascent on the S. side is rather easier. From the *Capanna Milano* in the Val Zebrù (p. 282) we cross the *Zebrù* and *Miniera Glaciers* to the *Colle Pale Rosse* (11,200'), then ascend direct to the left to the *Schulter* (see above; 6-7 hrs. to the top). The descent from the Königsjoch to the *Cedeh Glacier* is better than that to the Sulden Glacier. — The ascent from the N. side, by the *Payerjoch* (11,280'; guide 18 fl.), far more difficult, was made for the first time in 1878, and in 1879 the summit was reached direct from the Sulden Glacier by the N.E. slope.

The ascent of the **Monte Zebrù** (12,270'; from the Schaubachhütte by the *Hochjoch*, 6-7 hrs.; guide 12 fl.) is also difficult, but interesting; the descent may be made to the *Capanna Milano* in the Val Zebrù (p. 282). — The **Suldenspitze** (11,110'; from the Schaubachhütte over the Eissee Pass, 3½ hrs.; guide 5 fl.) is attractive and not difficult.

The °**Ortler** (12,812'), the highest of the Eastern Alps, may be ascended in 7-8 hrs. (guide 10, with descent to Trafoi 11½ fl.). The ascent is fatiguing and in an unfavourable condition of the glaciers difficult, and should be attempted only by experienced mountaineers. The preceding night is generally spent in the *Payerhütte*. — The Ortler was ascended for the first time by the Passeir hunter Joseph Pichler (see p. 273) from Trafoi in 1804, and the following year by Dr. Gebhard; then in 1826 by M. Schebelka, an officer of engineers. No successful ascent was again made till the summit was attained in 1861 by Messrs. Jacob and Walpole, and in 1864 by Mr. Tuckett, also from Trafoi. In 1865 Dr. v. Mojsisovics discovered the easier route from Sulden, and since that year ascents have been frequent.

About 5 min. below the last houses of St. Gertrud the route to the *Payerhütte* (p. 280; 3-4 hrs.; riding practicable to the foot of the Tabaretta rocks) ascends gradually to the left through wood; after ½ hr. it crosses the broad moraine of the *Marlt Glacier*, turns sharply to the left, and ascends in steep zigzags through wood, afterwards over debris and (to the right) over slopes of turf to the (1½ hr.) *Marltschneid*, a grassy height on the left side of the Marltlhal. Here we turn to the right, cross a steep slope of debris, and ascend the apparently vertical rocks of the *Tabarettawand* by a narrow but safe path, which finally leads up a flight of steps in the rock to the (1 hr.) *Tabarettascharte* or *Durchfahrt* (9330'), a depression in the Tabaretta crest, about halfway between the Bärenkopf and Tabarettaspitze (splendid °View to the W. and N.). We then follow the crest to the left to the (20 min.) **Payerhütte** (10,000'), lying in a sheltered saddle, with a view to the E. as well as to the W. From the hut we cross the *Tabaretta Glacier* to the right to the (¼ hr.) 'Scharte' below the Tabarettaspitze, whence a magnificent view is obtained of the Ortler, on this (N.

19*

VI. Route 52.   CEVEDALE PASS.   *Ortler District.*

side entirely covered with snow. We now round the shoulder of the Tabarettaspitze, and follow a good path (*'Hamburger Weg'*) made by the German Alpine Club, with steps at places, to the (^{1}/$_4$ hr.) *Upper Ortler Glacier*, which descends to the right into the valley of the *Hohe Eisrinne*. Here we ascend to the left over the glacier, at first steep (beware of the stones which occasionally fall), to the *Tschiefeck* (a rock); then over the crest of névé, steep at places, to the highest plateau. Here we pass to the right of the peak, and afterwards ascend it to the left, from the S. side. The summit (3-4 hrs. from the Payerhütte) lies at the N. and highest point of a sharp arête of snow, 200 yds. long (not difficult, but requiring a tolerably steady head). The "View, as might be expected from such a height, is most imposing. The majestic Königs-Spitze, the Cevedale, the Thurwieserspitze, and the Cristallo peaks are the most conspicuous of the Ortler group. Towards the N. is the Tauern chain, with the Glockner, the Venediger, and the Dreiherrnspitze, then the Alps of the Zillerthal, Stubai, and Oetzthal; E. the Dolomites with the Marmolada and Pala di San Martino; W. the Silvretta, Bernina, and Finsteraarhorn groups, and the Tödi; S. the Adamello and Presanella.

[Another route to the top of the Ortler ('Gebhardsweg', comp. p. 291), again brought into notice in 1872, leads from Sulden over the *Hintere Grat* (p. 289) direct to the summit in 9 hrs., but is very difficult (guide 13 fl.). A third route, discovered in 1875, leads from the Sulden Glacier over the *Hochjoch* (11,825') and the *Ortler-Vorgipfel* (guide 17 fl.). In 1879 the Ortler was ascended for the first time direct from the *End-der-Welt Glacier*, and in 1881 direct from the Sulden Glacier by the so-called '*Lawinenrinne*' — The direct descent to Trafoi leads through the *Hohe Eisrinne* (p. 278), but is very steep and at one point exposed to danger from ice-avalanches.]

Passes. FROM SULDEN OVER THE EISSEE AND CEVEDALE PASSES TO STA. CATERINA IN THE VAL FURVA, 9 hrs., a most interesting expedition, with which the ascent of the *Cevedale* (p. 289) may easily be combined (guide 9, including the Cevedale 12 fl.). The night is passed in the *Schaubachhütte* (p. 288). We descend thence to the left over grassy slopes and moraine debris to the *Sulden Glacier*, with its deep crevasses, on which we then ascend, the last ^{1}/$_2$ hr. being steep, to the (2^1/$_2$ hrs.) **Eissee Pass** (10,500'). Immediately to the right rises the huge Königsspitze (12,648'), beside which the Ortler and Zebrù look insignificant. Beyond the pass we cross the névé of the *Langen-Ferner*, which descends to the Martelthal (p. 286), and ascending slightly (with the *Suldenspitze*, 11,105', on the right) reach the (3/4 hr.) **Cevedale Pass**, or *Langenferner-Joch* (10,730'), from which a view of the S. part of the Ortler group and of the Bernina and Val Tellina Alps to the W. is enjoyed. The S. side of the Königsspitze, and of the whole Ortler group, consists of precipices of black rock. (The summit of the Cevedale is attained from the pass in 1^1/$_2$-2 hrs., see p. 289.) Descent over a long and steep slope of debris and across the *Cedeh Glacier* to the (1^1/$_2$ hr.) *Capanna Cedeh* (chalet; 8530'); then on the right side of the sequestered *Val Cedeh*, enclosed by grand mountains and glaciers, the path soon becoming well defined, to the (2 hrs.) *Baite del Forno* (p. 282; with the splendid Forno Glacier on the left, p. 282) and (1^1/$_4$ hr.) *Sta. Caterina* (p. 282). — OVER THE CEDEH PASS (10,600'), between the *Kreilspitze* and the *Schrötterhorn*, 9^1/$_2$ hrs. from Sulden to Sta. Caterina, an attractive route of no great difficulty.

To THE MARTELLTHAL OVER THE MADRITSCH-JOCH (7 hrs. to the Zufallhütte), see p. 287. The route from this side is less fatiguing, but in the reverse direction it is more striking, the view of the Ortler group being then new to the traveller. Guide to the Zufallhütte 6 fl., to Gand 7 fl. 50 kr., to Latsch 9 fl.; with ascent of the Schöntaufspitze or Madritschspitze 50 kr. more. — OVER THE EISSEE PASS (8 hrs. to the Zufallhütte; guide 6^1/$_2$ fl.), see p. 287.

To TRAFOI OVER THE HOCHLEITENSPITZE (6^1/$_2$ hrs.; guide 5 fl.), see p. 278; BY THE PAYERHÜTTE (7 hrs.; guide 5^1/$_2$ fl.), see p. 289. — Over the *Hochjoch* (11,825') and the *Ortler Pass* (10,980'; 14 hrs.; guide 14 fl.), a very difficult route, advisable only when the glacier is in a favourable condition.

To the Laaser Thal (p. 252) over the Rosim-Joch (10,430'; 9 hrs. to Laas; guide 8 fl.), rather difficult, particularly the descent over the Laaser-Ferner. An ascent of the Vertainspitze may be combined with this route.

53. From Botzen to Verona.

Comp. Maps, pp. 304, 300.

94 M. Railway. Express in $3^1/_4$-$4^2/_3$, ordinary trains in $5^1/_4$-$6^1/_4$ hrs.

Botzen (880'), see p. 256. The train crosses the *Eisak*, which falls into the *Etsch*, or *Adige*, 3 M. lower down. The latter becomes navigable at ($7^1/_2$ M.) *Branzoll* (Kreuz). On the right stretches the long porphyry ridge of the *Mittelberg* (p. 267), which separates the Eppan plateau from the Etschthal. At *Gmund*, beyond ($9^1/_2$ M.) *Auer* (Rose; Elephant), the train crosses the river; to the right is the Kalterer See, with Kaltern (p. 267) on the height above it. $14^1/_2$ M. **Neumarkt**; the village, Ital. *Egna* (*Post; Krone; Engel*), lies on the left bank of the Adige, 1 M. from the railway. Roads diverge to the Fleimserthal, to the E., both at Auer and Neumarkt (comp. p. 321). On the slopes to the right lie the villages of *Tramin*, *Kurtatsch*, and *Margreid* (p. 268). — $19^1/_2$ M. *Saturn* (Adler), the last German village, lies on the left bank, with a dilapidated castle on an apparently inaccessible pinnacle. The *Rocchetta Pass* to the right leads to the *Val di Non* (p. 309).

24 M. **S. Michele**, or *Wälsch-Michael* (705'; *Inn*, plain, at the station), with a handsome old Augustinian monastery, now suppressed, is the station for the Val di Non. The line recrosses the Adige. Near station *Atta Nave* is the *Nave S. Rocco*, a very ancient ferry over the Adige, crossing to the road from the Val di Non.

$28^1/_2$ M. *Lavis* (745') lies on the *Avisio*, a torrent descending from the *Val Cembra* (p. 320), which with its ramifications is crossed above its influx into the Adige by a curved bridge 1000 yds. long.

35 M. **Trent**. — Hotels. At the station: *Hôtel Trento, R., L., &
A. 2 fl., B. 60 kr. — In the town: *Europa, R. & A. 1 fl. 40 kr. — Second-class: Aquila Bianca, near the castle; Agnello d'Oro; Alb. ai Conti, Via S. Marco. — Restaurants. *All' Isola Nuova*, by the station, with garden; *Frassoni*, by the theatre; *Rebecchino*. — Cafés. *Europa; Specchi; Nones*, Piazza Macello Vecchio. — *Post Office*, near the cathedral. — *Swimming and other Baths* on the Fersina. — *English Church Service*, in the Hôtel Trento.

Trent (685'), or *Trento*, Lat. *Tridentum*, with 19,576 inhab., once the wealthiest town in Tyrol, founded according to tradition by the Etruscans, and mentioned by Strabo, Pliny, and Ptolemy, possesses numerous towers, marble palaces, and broad streets, and, despite many traces of dilapidation, still presents all the characteristics of an important Italian town.

The *Cathedral*, founded in 1048, begun in its present form in 1212, and completed in the 15th cent., is a Romanesque basilica, surmounted by two domes. At the N. portal, as at Botzen, is a pair of lions (p. 257). The flights of steps in the aisles are peculiar. In the S. transept are several old monuments, half-faded frescoes, and (by the wall) the porphyry tombstone of the Venetian general Sanseverino, whom the Tyrolese defeated at Calliano in 1487. The interior is at present undergoing restoration. The mouldings on the doors and windows at the back of the choir, on the outside, deserve notice. In the Piazza del Duomo, which is embellished with a fountain, are the old *Courts of Justice* and the *Torre di Piazza*.

S. Maria Maggiore (admirable organ), where the celebrated Council of Trent sat in 1545-63, contains a picture on the N. wall of the choir (covered by a curtain) with portraits of the members: 7 cardinals, 3 patriarchs, 33 archbishops, and 235 bishops. Adjoining the S. side of the choir a column was erected in 1845 to commemorate the 300th anniversary of the meeting of the Council.

The finest of the old palaces, whose façades, sometimes adorned with painting, conceal but imperfectly their dilapidated interiors, are the *Palazzo Zambelli*, opposite the Europa Hotel, erected in the 16th cent. by one of the wealthy Fuggers (fine view from the garden), and the *Palazzo Tabarelli* (now *Salvatori*), Via S. Benedetto, said to have been designed by Bramante. — The *Museum*, in the Via Larga, to the N. of the cathedral, contains Roman, Celtic, and other antiquities from S. Tyrol and a valuable collection of coins and medals.

On the E. side of the town rises the *Castello of Buon Consiglio*, with remains of ancient frescoes, once the residence of the Prince-Bishops, now a fortified barrack. The huge circular *Torre di Augusto* is said to be of Roman origin (fine view; permission to enter at the commandant's office, behind the cathedral). To the S. of the Porta Nuova are the handsome new *Law Courts (Tribunale)*.

The rocky hill of *Dos Trento* (950'), on the right bank of the Adige, at the mouth of the Buco di Vela (p. 296), affords a fine view (permission from the commandant, see above). Another good point is the terrace of the *Capuchin Monastery*, above the castle. On the S.W. side of the town is the tasteful new *Campo Santo*. — A pleasant promenade, affording picturesque views, leads along the Val Sugana road (p. 316) to (³/₄ hr.) a fine *Fall of the Fersina* (140' high), in a rocky gorge to the right (good view of the fall from the garden of the Osteria 'alla Grande Cascata'; 20 kr.).

From Trent to Venice through the *Val Sugana*, see R. 57; through the *Val Sarca* to *Riva*, see R. 54; to *Giudicaria*, see R. 55. — By *Pergine* to *Lavarone* and *Luserna*, see p. 317. — To the *Val Piné* (drive of 3 hrs. to Lavarda, back in 1½ hr.), see p. 317.

The ascent of the *Monte Bondone* (6890') is repaying. We follow the road by *Cadine* (see p. 296) to (1³/₄ hr.) *Sopramonte* (2024'); then proceed, with guide (3 fl.), via *Sta. Anna*, passing several chalets, to the (4½ hrs.) summit. Grand view. — *Monte Gazza*, see p. 296.

The train follows the broad valley of the Adige, which has been very fertile since the drainage of the marshes. To the S.W. of Trent, on the right bank, is the village of *Sardagna*, with a considerable waterfall. Then *Ravina*, at the mouth of a gorge descending from Mte. Bondone, *Romagnano*, and *Aldeno*. 39½ M. *Mattarello* (route to the *Val Sugana*, see p. 317). On a hill to the left near (45 M.) *Calliano* rises the large château of *Beseno*, the property of Count Trapp. Rocky debris here indicates the scene of an old landslip. The lower valley of the Adige, rich in fruit, and yielding excellent red wine, is called *Val Lagarina* as far as the Italian frontier. 48 M. *Villa Lagarina* (*Compatscher).

50 M. **Rovereto** (680 ft.; **Cervo; Olivo; Corona*), a busy town with 11,000 inhab., on both sides of the *Leno*, is noted for its silk-culture. The old *Castello* is interesting.

From Rovereto by *Mori* to *Riva*, omnibus twice daily, see p. 298. — **Monte Stivo** (7606'), the S. spur of the mountain-group of the *Orto d'Abramo*, between the Sarca and Adige, may be ascended from Villa Lagarina in 5 hrs. (with guide), viâ *Castellano*, the *Bordola Alp*, and the *Spiazine*. The summit commands a magnificent view of the Lago di Garda, the valleys of the Sarca and the Adige, the Tredici Comuni, Adamello, Presanella, Dolomites, etc. Descent to *Arco* (2½-3 hrs.), see p. 298. — A good road leads to the S.E. from Rovereto, viâ *Vall' Arsa* (2025'; Inn) and the *Passo delle Fugazze* (4220'; Italian frontier), to (28 M.) **Schio** (630'; *Croce d' Oro; Stella*), an industrial town with 9500 inhab. on the *Leogra*. Railway from Schio (in ¾ hr.) to (20 M.) *Vicenza*, see *Baedeker's Italy*.

On the right bank is *Isera*, with vineyards, villas, and a waterfall. On the left bank, to the E. of the railway, near *Lizzana*, is a castle in which Dante resided about the year 1302, when banished from Florence. The line follows the left bank of the Adige. 52½ M. **Mori** (*Railway Hotel*, R. from 80 kr.); the village, on the opposite slope, on the road to Riva (p. 298), is noted for its asparagus.

Near *S. Marco* are traces of a vast landslip, which is said to have overwhelmed a town in 833, and is described by Dante (*Inferno* xii., 4-9). At (56½ M.) *Serravalle*, the ancient fort guarding the defile, the valley contracts.

61½ M. **Ala** (415'; *Posta; Rail. Restaurant*), a considerable place (3800 inhab.), with velvet-manufactories which were once in high repute, lies on the slope of a steep green hill. — 62½ M. *Avio* is the last Austrian station. The village, with a well-preserved castle of Count Castelbarco, lies on the right bank.

69 M. *Peri* is the first Italian station. About 4½ M. to the S.W., in a wild and rocky gorge, is the famous pilgrimage-church of the *Madonna della Corona*, p. 299. The *Monte Baldo* (7280'; p. 299), on the W., separates the valley of the Adige from the Lago di Garda. The train now enters the celebrated *Chiusa di Verona*, a rocky passage which the Adige has forced through the limestone mountains. This important military point was defended against the Veronese in 1155 by the German army under Otho of Wittelsbach, in the reign of Frederick Barbarossa. To the left is a new fort, and farther on the new fortification of *Incanale*, commanding the defile. On a height on the right bank lies *Rivoli*, which was stormed several times by the French in 1796 and 1797 under Masséna, who derived his ducal title from this village. 75½ M. *Ceraino*.

Stations *Domegliara, Pescantina, Parona*. The train crosses the

Adige, reaches at *S. Lucia* the Verona and Milan line, and soon stops at the small station outside the Porta Nuova, and then at the main station outside the Porta Vescovo.

94 M. **Verona**, see *Baedeker's N. Italy*.

54. From Trent to Riva. Lago di Garda.

Comp. Maps, pp. 300, 304.

26 M. One-horse carriage from Trent to Riva 9, two-horse 15 fl.; STELLWAGEN daily in 6 hrs. (2 fl.). A shorter route is from stat. *Mori* (p. 295) to (10½ M.) Riva; OMNIBUS (at 6.40 and 8.30 a.m. and 7.40 p.m.; returning from Riva at 3.40 and 5.20 a.m. and 3.30 p.m.) in 2¾ hrs. (90 kr.); open supplementary carriages provided when the omnibus is full. One-horse carr. 4, two-horse 7½ fl. (from Mori to Arco 5 or 9 fl.). An omnibus also plies twice daily from *Rovereto* (Corona) to Mori and Riva in 3¾ hrs. (1 fl.). — Travellers who intend to return from Riva without going farther S., should choose the route by Mori for the sake of the magnificent view of the Lago di Garda obtained at Nago.

FROM TRENT TO RIVA. The road crosses the Adige, skirts the S.W. side of the *Dos Trento* (p. 294), and ascends through a series of wild, partly-wooded ravines, called the *Buco di Vela*, the (3 M.) upper end of which is guarded by a fort. The road now ascends in a wide curve past the hamlet of *Cadine* (1555') to the summit of the pass (1640'), and then, turning sharp to the S.W., gradually descends. To the right in the valley lies the village of *Terlago*, with its little lake (1315'), at the base of the *Monte Gazza* (6515').

OVER THE MONTE GAZZA TO MOLVENO, 5½-6 hrs., an attractive route, presenting no difficulty. A carriage-road, diverging to the right about 5 min. beyond the summit of the pass, leads round the S. end of the lake to *Terlago* (1485') and (1 hr.) *Covelo* (1910'). Thence a bridle-track, at first through wood, ascends to the saddle (about 5575') between the two summits of **Mte. Gazza** (N. peak, 6480'; S. peak, 6015'), where a magnificent °View of the Lago di Molveno and the striking Brenta group is unfolded. Descent to the N.W. (keep to the right) through meadows and wood to (1½ hr.) *Molveno* (p. 304). — The N. summit of Mte. Gazza (6480') may be ascended from the pass in ¾ hr. (easy); thence to the top of the *Dos Negro* (6580') ¼ hr., and on to the *Mte. Paganella* (6955'), 1 hr.; all excellent points of view.

The road descends past (1½ M.) *Vigolo* to (3 M.) **Vezzano** (*Stella d'Oro, *Croce*, both with gardens, good wine), a large village, and to (1½ M.) *Padergnone*, at the entrance to the *Val Cavedine*, where olives begin to appear. The road crosses by means of an embankment and bridge the narrow strait between the little *Lago di S. Massenza* (to the right), and the *Lago di Toblino*. The picturesque château of that name, the property of Count Wolkenstein, stands on a tongue of land in the latter. At (2¼ M.) **Alle Sarche** (700'; *Sommadossi's Inn*, good 'Vino Santo') the *Sarca* emerges from a deep gorge, and the road to Giudicaria diverges to the right (p. 303).

PEDESTRIANS are recommended to avoid the somewhat monotonous road through the lower part of the Val Sarca by taking the road from Alle Sarche to Giudicaria (p. 303) as far as (5 M.) *Comano*, and proceeding thence to the left through the charming mountain-scenery of Giudicaria, via *Campo, Fiave, Ballino,* and *Pranzo,* to (6-7 hrs.) Riva.

Below Alle Sarche the road crosses the Sarca and runs between the mountains and the river, traversing the debris of old landslips. 2¹/₄ M. *Pietra Murata*. Near (4¹/₂ M.) *Drò* (Inn, good wine) the Sarca is again crossed; on a rocky eminence to the left rises the ruined castle of *Drena*. Beyond *Ceniga* (Inn), an extremely fertile district, which extends to Riva, is entered. Near (3 M.) *Arco* the road regains the right bank. (On the left bank a road to *Nagò*, see below, diverges to the left.)

Arco. — Hotels. *CURNAUS, with garden, café-restaurant, baths, whey-cure, and a covered promenade, and containing 80 rooms, of which 40 have a S. aspect, 'pens.' with R. 3¹/₂-5 fl. per day; *CUR-CASINO & HÔTEL BAUER, opposite, new and handsomely fitted up; both of these have conversation and reading-rooms, etc.; *HÔTEL OLIVO, R. from 1 fl., L. & A. 40 kr., D. 1¹/₂ fl.; these three in the prettily laid out Cur-Platz; *HOTEL-PENSION ARCO, ¹/₂ M. to the W. of the Cur-Platz, in the most sheltered and warmest situation, 'pens.' with R. from 3 fl.; *CORONA, in the town. — Boarders taken 'en pension' at the hotels, and in the *Pensions Bellaria* (well situated), *Aurora*, *Rainalter*, *Villa Emilie*, *Kayser*, *Strasser*, and *Monrepos* (3¹/₂-5 fl., L. and heating extra). — Private Apartments in the *Villas Anna*, *Consolini*, *Steigerwald*, etc. (R. 30-60 fl. per month, according to the aspect). — Beer at *Jönsen's*; wine at *Giov. Povoli's*. — *Café Strasser*.

OMNIBUS to Riva at 5 a.m., 2.20 p.m., and 5.20 p.m. (fare 20 kr.). — CARRIAGE to Riva and back, with one horse 1¹/₂, two horses 3 fl.; to Castel Toblino 3¹/₂ or 6 fl.; to Mori 3¹/₂ or 6 fl.; to Trent 9 or 14 fl. — DONKEYS, 50 kr. the first hr., 30 kr. each addit. hr.; ¹/₂ day 1 fl. 60 kr., whole day 2 fl., and fee. — VISITORS' TAX 2 fl. per month; subscription to the reading-room 2 fl.

Arco (300'), an ancient town with 2400 inhab., situated in a beautiful valley, almost perfectly shut in on the N., E., and W. by lofty mountain ranges, and protected from the S. winds blowing in March by Monte Brione (p. 299), has for several years been a favorite winter-resort for consumptive and nervous patients. Near the Cur-Casino is a well-appointed *Curanstalt*, with baths of every description, saline and pine-needle vapour inhalation, etc. The vegetation resembles that of Lago Maggiore; vines, olives, cedars, magnolias, cypresses, and oleanders flourish. The Archduke Albert has a new château here, with a fine winter-garden (custodian 50 kr.). Near the handsome Renaissance church is the old town-palace of the counts of Arco, with allegorical frescoes. To the N., on a precipitous rock (390'), rises the *Castle of Arco*, destroyed by the French in the Spanish War of Succession, with a beautiful garden (key kept by the gardener, Via degli Olivi al Castello; 40-50 kr.).

EXCURSIONS. To the N. to the *Castle of Arco* (25 min., see above); to the *Casa Bianca*, *Veduta Maria*, and the '*Holm Oak*' (in all ³/₄-1 hr.; paths indicated by marks). Past the small *Laghel Lake* (dry in summer), over the hill by a stony path to *Ceniga*, and back by the right bank of the Sarca, a pleasant round of 3 hrs. — Drive to *Castel Toblino* (p. 296).

A pretty walk of 3¹/₂ hrs. leads by the road ascending on the right of the château through groves of fine old olive-trees to the village of (¹/₄ hr.) *Chiarano*, with a fine orangery and a charming view, and past *Vigne* to (¹/₄ hr.) *Varignano*. Thence we may either proceed to the left to (³/₄ hr.) *Varone*, or ascend to the right by a road, the picturesqueness of which makes up for its roughness, to the (3¹/₂ M.) village and château of *Tenno* (p. 299). We descend by *Cologna* to (2 M.) *Varone* (p. 299) and thence through the plain back to (3 M.) Arco. — Another excursion may be made over the Sarca bridge to (¼ M.) *Oltresarca*, (¾ M.) *Bolognana*, and (1½ M.) *Vignole*, where another fine view is enjoyed, including the castle-hill of Arco. — A good and level but sunny road leads to the S. to (4¼ M.) *Riva* (see below). — To the *Monte Brione* (p. 299; 1½ hr.). We ascend from the Villa Lutti beyond *La Grotta* (p. 299) and descend to Fort S. Niccolò, returning thence viâ *Torbole* and the Nago road (evening-light best), or by *Riva*. — To the *Fall of the Ponale*, the *Val di Ledro*, etc., see p. 299.

MOUNTAIN ASCENTS. *Monte Stivo* (6700'; 4-5 hrs.; guide not required by adepts), viâ *S. Giacomo* and the *Stivo-Alp*, attractive and not difficult; comp. p. 295. — *Mte. Tenera* (7060'), see p. 300. — *Mte. Baldo* (6790'), see p. 299.

The road now leads to the S.W. through the broad and beautiful valley, Mte. Brione being visible to the S., and Tenno (p. 299) on the hills to the right, to (4½ M.) *Riva*.

FROM MORI TO RIVA (conveyances, see p. 297; the omnibus starts from the station, p. 295; carriages to be had at the Station Hotel). The road, which in suitable weather will reward even the pedestrian, crosses the Adige to *Ravazzone* and (2 M.) *Mori* (600'; Adler), a long and thriving village. It then traverses the broad green valley to (3 M.) *Loppio*, the property of Count Castelbarco of Milan, passes the little *Lago di Loppio* (665') with its rocky island, and ascends in windings amid rocky debris to the (1½ M.) culminating point of the route (1050'). We now descend to (¾ M.) *Nago*, a village situated on the brink of a ravine, with the ruins of the castle of *Peneda* on a barren rock to the left. [The new road to (3 M.) Arco viâ *Vignole* diverges here to the right, see above.] Below the village the road leads through a fortified gateway, immediately beyond which we enjoy an exquisite *View of the Lago di Garda, in its entire expanse, while Torbole lies at our feet, and Arco with its castle rises to the right. The road descends rapidly to (½ M.) the village of *Torbôte* (Bertolini; small boat for 1-6 pers. to Riva 1½ fl., per hour 1¼ fl.; one-horse carr. to Riva 1 fl. 20 kr., to Arco 2, to Mori 3½ fl.), charmingly situated. It then traverses the broad valley of the Sarca, crosses that river, and leads past the precipitous *Mte. Brione* (p. 299), with the Fort S. Niccolò, to (3 M.) *Riva*.

Riva. — **Hotels.** *HÔTEL DU LAC, ¾ M. to the E., on the Torbole road, with a large garden and bath-house, R. from 80, B. 40, L. & A. 50, D. 1 fl. 30 kr., pension from 3 fl., suited for a stay of some time; *SOLE D'ORO, with a garden on the lake, similar charges; HÔTEL-PENSION SCHMID, R. ¾-1½ fl.; BAVIERA; *GIARDINO, outside the Porta S. Michele, pension 2½ fl.; MUSCH, *GALLO, ALB. DEL POPOLO, all three moderate. — Beer: *Musch; *Giardino S. Marco*, outside the Porta S. Marco; garden outside the Porta S. Michele. — *Baths* in the lake, to the E., beyond the barracks. — Money-changers: *Pernici & Co.* — *Omnibus* to Mori, see p. 296; to Arco thrice daily (fare 20 kr.). One-horse carriage from Riva to Varone 2½, two-horse 4 fl.; to Arco 3 or 5 fl.; to Mori 3½ or 7 fl.; to Trent 9 or 14 fl. — Small boat, 40 kr. per hr.

Riva, a busy town and harbour with 6000 inhab., is charmingly situated at the N. end of the *Lago di Garda*, close to the foot of the steep *Monte Giumella*. On the hill-side, high above the town, are the ruins of the round tower of a castle, which is said to have been built by the Scaligers. On the lake is the old castle of *La Rocca*, now a fortified barrack. At the entrance to the town from Arco is the *Church of the Minorites*, erected about the middle of the 16th cent. in the florid rococco style. The *Parish Church* contains modern pictures and frescoes. Riva is recommended for a prolonged stay. The climate is healthy, and the heat in summer is tempered by the lake. (Lodgings not expensive.)

EXCURSIONS. To the **Fall of the Ponale** (3-4 hrs. there and back); the best plan is to go by boat (2-3 fl.) and return on foot (steep ascent). The waterfall itself, which the Ponale forms shortly before it falls into the lake from the ravine of the Ledro, is insignificant, but its surroundings are picturesque. We disembark at the point where the disused bridle-path from the Ledro valley reaches the lake, ascend a few paces past some ruined houses, cross the old bridge, and reach the best point of view just below the fall. — The walk to the fall by the new *ROAD is also very interesting. It leads at a considerable height along the rocky precipices of the W. bank, through a succession of tunnels and galleries, to the Ledro valley, and commands beautiful views (shade in the afternoon). At the point where it turns to the right into the valley, a path descending to the left, then ascending, and again descending, leads to the waterfall. From the highest point of the road we reach in 1 hr. a hill, marked with a cross, near *Pregasina* (2130'), where we obtain a fine view of the lake, the valley of the Sarca, etc.

Torbole may also be visited by boat (1½ fl.; see p. 298). We pass Fort S. Niccolò, at the foot of the Mte. Brione, and approach the mouth of the Sarca (good trout-fishing, and interesting fish-breeding establishment). Here we have a splendid view of the lake, and the surrounding mountains and valleys, and of the valley of the Sarca as far as Arco.

The **Monte Brione** (1184'), 1 hr. to the E. of Riva, affords a fine view of the valley and almost the whole lake (best from the rifle-range). It is most easily ascended from the hamlet of *La Grotta* (Inn), on the N.W. side, 1½ M. from Riva, but the upper road requires a military permesso.

Interesting excursion to the N.W. to (2 M.) **Varone**, where there is a wild and picturesque *Gorge with a fine waterfall, lately made easily accessible (fee 20 kr. for each person; ring at the mill). Thence by *Cologna* to (2 M.) *Tenno* (1310'), with an old castle (charming view), and along the richly-cultivated slopes to *Varignano* and (4½ M.) *Arco*. — The road by *Pranzo* (p. 304) to (9 M.) Tenno is not recommended.

The ascent of the **Monte Baldo**, a range 40 M. long, between the Lake of Garda and the valley of the Adige, is interesting but rather fatiguing (later than June the heat is generally too great for the attempt; rich spring flora). It consists of two distinct ranges, the *Altissimo* on the N. and the *Monte Maggiore* on the S., separated by the indentation of the *Bocca di Navena* (4970'). The easiest route to the **Altissimo** (6790'), ascends on the E. side from Mori (p. 298) to (2 hrs.) *Brentonico* (2215'; Aquila Nera); thence with guide (landlord's son) over the Alpine pastures of (1½ hr.) *S. Giacomo* (3825'; refreshments) to the (2 hrs.) summit. [This point may also be reached by a steep path from *Nago* viâ the *Casina Alp* in 5 hrs. (with guide).] Magnificent view of the mountains, the Val Sarca, Riva, and the N. end of the Lago di Garda. We may continue our tour viâ the *Artilone Alp* (5160'; inhabited in summer only) to the Monte Maggiore, or descend direct from the Bocca di Navena to *Malcesine* (p. 301).

The ascent of the ***Monte Maggiore** (7210') is, however, much preferable. From the railway-station *Peri* (p. 295) we proceed to the (1½ hr.) celebrated pilgrimage-church of *Madonna della Corona* and thence viâ *Spiazzi* (2660'; two Inns), a village commanding a splendid view of the S. end of the Lago di Garda, the plain of the Po, and the Apennines, to (1 hr.) *Ferrara di Monte Baldo* (*Inn, plain and moderate). This point may also be reached from *Garda* (p. 301) by a good road, passing *Caprino* and *Pazzone;* from the latter (to which the traveller should drive) the road ascends in steep windings to Spiazzi and then descends slightly to Ferrara. Leaving Ferrara at an early hour, with a guide provided by the landlord of the inn, we reach the top in 3-4 hrs. The "View, one of the grandest in the S. Alps, embraces almost the whole of S. Tyrol, the Italian and Swiss Alps as far as Mte. Rosa, the plain of the Po, and the Apennines; in clear weather the Adriatic is visible to the W.; at our feet almost the whole expanse of the Lago di Garda is seen. From the summit we may return to Ferrara, or proceed viâ the *Artilone Alp* (p. 299) to the (3 hrs.) *Italian Frontier Station* (Rfmts., good wine) and to the *Bocca di Navena* (p. 299), which affords a fine view of lake, rock, and mountain. The descent may be made to *Malcesine* (p. 301) or viâ *Brentonico* to *Mori* (p. 299).

To the Valle di Ledro, another beautiful excursion (one-horse carriage to Pieve and back 4, two-horse 8 fl.; diligence daily at 3 p.m.). Beginning of the road as far as the fall of the Ponale, see p. 299. It then turns a corner high above the waterfall, enters the valley to the W., and leads to *Biacesa*, *Molina*, the pretty *Lago di Ledro* (2135'), on the N. side of which is *Mezzolago*, and *Pieve di Ledro* (9 M. from Riva; *Tourist Hotel; Albergo alla Torre, well spoken of). At *Bezzeca*, ³/₄ M. farther on, is the entrance to the *Val Concei*, in which lie the villages of (1 M.) *Enguiso* and (¹/₂ M.) *Lenzumo* (2570'), whence the *Mte. Tenera* (7060'; 4¹/₂ hrs., with guide) may be ascended for the sake of the splendid view. (From Lenzumo to *Bondo* over the *Gavardina Pass*, see p. 308.) From Bezzeca the road leads to *Tiarno*, and through the sequestered *Val Ampola* to (9 M.) *Storo* (Cavallo Bianco, mediocre and dear), in the Val Buona (p. 308). Near the *FortAmpola*, which formerly defended the road, but was destroyed in 1866 (3 M. before Storo is reached), the wild *Val Lorina* opens on the left; through this valley a rough path leads to *Magasa* in the *Val Vestino*, surrounded by lofty mountains (more easily reached from *Toscolano*, on the Lago di Garda, or from *Bondone*, on the *Lago d'Idro*, p. 309).

From Riva to *Tione*, in Upper Giudicaria, see p. 304.

The *Lago di Garda (155'), the *Lacus Benacus* of the Romans, 34¹/₂ M. long, and 2-11 M. broad, is almost entirely in Italy, a small part near Riva alone belonging to Tyrol. The lake is rarely perfectly calm, and Virgil's description *(Geor. II., 160)*, 'Fluctibus et fremitu adsurgens Benace marino', is sometimes vividly recalled. In fine weather the S. wind usually makes the water rough in the afternoon, so that the morning is the best time for boating. The mountains at the N. end are lofty and abrupt, but slope gradually towards the S. until lost in the great plain of Upper Italy. The water of the lake is of a striking azure blue. Excellent fish are *carpione*, or salmon-trout, sometimes 25lbs. in weight, *trutte* of 1-2lbs., *agone*, and *sardene*.

Steamboat along the E. BANK from *Riva* to *Peschiera* daily (except Tuesdays) at 5 a.m., in 4 hrs.; on Tuesdays at 5.5 a.m. to *Desenzano* in 4³/₄ hrs.; fares 4¹/₂ fr., 2¹/₂ fr. (stations: *Malcesine, Assenza, Castelletto, Torri, Garda, Bardolino,* and *Lazise*). The steamer returns from Peschiera at 3.20 p.m. — Along the W. BANK (between *Riva* and *Desenzano*) daily (at 6 a.m. from Riva, and at 4.15 p.m. from Desenzano), except Mon., in 4¹/₂ hrs. (fares 4 fr. 35, 2 fr. 40 c.). The stations are *Limone, Tremosine, Tignale, Gargnano, Maderno, Gardone-Riviera, Salò,* and *S. Felice di Scovolo*. — Trip round the lake in one day: by steamer along the W. bank to Desenzano, by railway to Peschiera, and by steamer thence along the E. bank to Riva. The steamboats are apt to be irregular and unpunctual. Refreshments poor.

STEAMBOAT TRIP. E. BANK. A fine retrospect of Riva is obtained as the steamer leaves the harbour. The Fall of the Ponale is passed on the right, and *Torbole* to the left, in the N.E. angle of the lake. We now approach the E. bank, from which rise the steep slopes of the long *Mte. Baldo* (see p. 299). First station *Malcesine* (Italia, tolerable), a good harbour on the E. bank, with an ancient château of Charlemagne (recently restored), for sketching which Goethe once narrowly escaped being imprisoned as a spy. Beyond it rises the rock of *Isoletto dell' Olivo*, then *Cassone*, and farther on the small island of *Trimelone*. Then stations *Assenza*, *Castelletto*, *Torri*. The promontory of *San Vigilio*, with the *Villa Brenzoni*, extends far into the lake, and is the finest point on the E. bank. The surrounding hills are planted with vines, olives, fig, and other fruit-trees. The village of **Garda** (*Tre Corone*, indifferent), in a bay at the influx of the *Tessino*, gives its name to the lake. The château and beautiful park of Count Albertini are sometimes open to the public. About 3 M. to the S. is the *Rocca* (fine view) with the ruins of an ancient German imperial castle; on a wooded hill opposite are the hermits' cells of *S. Eremo*. A pleasant walk may be taken to 2 M. (³/₄ hr.) the promontory of *S. Vigilio* (see above; Osteria, plain and moderate), with a park and extensive view of the lake.

The next places on the E. bank are *Bardolino* and *Lazise*. The steamer finally stops at the small fortress of **Peschiera**, at the efflux of the Mincio, at the S.E. angle of the Lago di Garda, ¹/₂ M. from the railway-station (*Rail. Restaurant*, poor; omnibus 35 c.).

To the W. of Peschiera, extending into the lake from the S. bank is the narrow promontory of *Sermione* (*'Sirmio, peninsularum insularumque ocellus'*), 2¹/₂ M. in length, on which the poet Catullus once possessed a villa where he composed his poems. The ruins, consisting of two vaults (*grotte*), remains of a bath, etc., still exist. A château was also erected here by the Scaligers, who for upwards of a century (1262-1389) presided over the republic of Verona.

At the S.W. angle of the Lake of Garda, to the W. of the peninsula of Sermione, lies the busy little town (4000 inhab.) of **Desenzano** (*Mayer's Hôtel Royal*, high charges; *Due Colombe, unpretending, with a small garden on the lake), another station on the Milan and Verona railway (see *Baedeker's N. Italy*; omnibus from the quay to the station 50 c., luggage 25 c.).

W. BANK. Near the W. bank, to the N. of Desenzano, and opposite the above-mentioned promontory of S. Vigilio, lie the small *Isola di S. Biagio* (St. Blasius) and the beautiful crescent-shaped *Isola di Garda*, the property of the Duca Ferrari. In a bay to the W. lies **Salò** (*Hotel Salò, with view-terrace), a town with 5000 inhab., in a luxuriantly fertile district. Charming prospect by evening-light from the *Mte. S. Bartolommeo*, the shortest way (1¹/₂ hr.) to which leads to the left through a walled farmyard, beyond the N. gate of Salò (descent to Gardone, 1 hr.). Steam-tramway to *Tormini* and *Brescia* five times daily in 2¹/₄ hrs.; see p. 309.

At this point begins the *Riviera*, a part of the banks distinguished for its warm climate and the luxuriance of its vegetation, and dotted with numerous villages and country-houses. Gardone-Riviera (*Hôtel-Pension Gardone-Riviera, 'pens.' from 7½ fr.; *Gigola's Hotel, unpretending; *Frau Königer's Pension; lodgings moderate), in a sunny and sheltered situation, at the foot of the hills and close to the lake, has of late years become a favourite autumn and winter resort of patients suffering from pulmonary and nervous affections (visitors' tax 10 fr.). The climate, the warmest in Upper Italy, is midway between that of S. Tyrol and the Ligurian Riviera. The luxuriant vegetation is wholly southern in character. Groves of olives, cypresses, and laurels flourish, and camelias, magnolias, and palms grow unprotected in the gardens. The hills afford opportunity for numerous charming excursions and command most varied and attractive views.

EXCURSIONS. To the *Barbarana Ravine*, ½ hr. — To *S. Michele*, a high-lying church, affording a fine view of the lake, 1 hr.; we may return viâ *Sopiane*. — The charming excursion (2 hrs.) to the romantic and profound *Toscolano Ravine*, with its paper-mills, may be made by carriage. — The church of *Gaino* (2 hrs.) is reached by a beautiful route, shaded with laurels. It commands a good view of the lake, which is seen to still greater advantage from the ridge above *Cecina*, ½ hr. farther to the N. — By carriage (1¼ hr.) or steamer to *Gargnano*, see below. — By boat (1½ hr.) to the promontory of *Manerba* (view of the whole lake). — By boat (¾ hr.) to the *Isola di Garda* (see p. 301), with its pretty terraces and pleasure-grounds.

ASCENTS. *Monte Bartolommeo* (1475'), ascended in 1¾ hrs., see p. 301. — Another good point of view is *Mte. Roccolo* (1310'; 1½ hr.). — The *Monte Pizzocolo* (6835'; 5-6 hrs., with guide) commands a magnificent view; the top may be reached by several different routes.

On a promontory formed by the alluvial deposits of the *Toscolano* lies *Maderno*, with an ancient church (Roman inscriptions on the wall), at the base of the *Monte Pizzocolo* (see above). Then *Toscolano*, *Cecina*, and *Bogliaco*, with the large country-seat of Count Bettoni of Brescia. Next, **Gargnano** (*Cervo*), surrounded by lemon and orange-plantations, one of the most beautiful points on the lake.

Lemons flourish here in the open air, but are covered in winter, to facilitate which pillars of brick are erected at intervals and connected by cross-beams. The lemons of Gargnano are less delicate than those of Sicily, but keep better. The yield, however, has greatly fallen off of late owing to a disease that has attacked the trees; the annual product, which amounted to 16-18 millions in 1862, is now estimated at about 3 millions.

The Riviera ends here. The mountains become loftier. *Mustone*, *Piovere*, *Tignale*, and *Oldese*, four small places on the W. bank, follow each other in quick succession. *Tremosine*, hardly visible, lies high above the lake; the path to it, ascending a precipitous rock, is not easily distinguished. Farther on, in a bay, appear the white houses of *Limōne*, amid lemon and olive plantations. We next pass the mouth of the *Ledro Valley*, with the *Fall of the Ponale* (see p. 299), and the new road (p. 299) on the face of the cliff high above the lake, and at length reach *Riva*.

55. The Val Sarca. Giudicaria.

STELLWAGEN from Trent (Café Europa) to (38 M.) Pinzolo, twice daily in summer (4.30 and 10.30 a.m.) in 8-9 hrs., fare 2 fl. 70 (banquette 3 fl. 40) kr.; and a quicker and more expensive service from the Hotel Trento to Campiglio direct (leaving Trent at 4 a.m. and reaching Campiglio at 9 p.m., or leaving Trent at 9 a.m. and reaching Pinzolo at 7 p.m.). Post-Stellwagen from Tione to Condino and from Condino to Brescia daily (passing the Lago d'Idro by night). Carriage and pair from Trent to Pinzolo 18, to Campiglio 24 fl.; from Riva to Campiglio 20 fl. — STEAM TRAMWAY from Vobarno along the post-road viâ Volciano and Gavardo to Brescia, and from Volciano to Salò.

The **Val Sarca**, to the S. of and parallel with the Val di Non (R. 56), consists of four different regions. The lowest, from Alle Sarche to the mouth of the Sarca near Torbole, is broad, and in its lower half luxuriantly fertile. At Alle Sarche the valley turns to the W.; the Sarca emerges from a profound ravine, which expands above Comano and contracts again at Stenico. This is the second region. The third begins at Tione, where the valley turns to the N.; it is fertile and well-peopled, and called *Val Rendena*. Lastly, near Pinzolo, the valley turns again to the W., being here named *Val di Genova*, and assumes a very imposing Alpine character, terminating among the rocky wilds of the Adamello-Presanella Alps. — The short valley of the Arno, the upper Val Chiese, and the Valle di Ledro, with their ramifications, also belong to Giudicaria (principal villages Stenico, Tione, and Condino).

From Trent to $(12^1/_2 M.)$ *Alle Sarche*, see p. 296. The road to Giudicaria crosses the Sarca and ascends in long windings, commanding a beautiful retrospect of the lake and castle of Toblino (p. 296), surrounded by finely-formed mountains. The Sarca has forced its way through several deep and narrow ravines, while the road follows the windings of the stream, high above it, on the S. slope. At the end of the gorge a view is disclosed of Lower Giudicaria with Stenico and its castle. The road then descends to (5 M.) the small sulphur-baths of *Comano* (1160'), efficacious in skin diseases and pulmonary complaints (to the left, above, is the village of the same name). The road continues on the right bank (on the opposite bank *Villa di Banale*, see p. 304), and crosses the *Duina* to (1 M.) the *Alle Tre Arche* inn (1300').

To the right, a road ascends in windings to (2 M.) Stenico (2180'; *Albergo Simmonini*, well spoken of), the chief village of Lower Giudicaria, finely situated, and commanded by a château of the same name (*View). Near it is a picturesque waterfall. On the W. side a steep bridle-path ascends to the high-road, $1^1/_2$ M. from the Tre Arche.

FROM MEZZOLOMBARDO TO STENICO, 27 M., a fine route on the whole. About 1 M. to the N. of Mezzolombardo (p. 309) the road diverges to the left from the Val di Non road, and ascends in windings (steep short-cut through a wooded gorge, to the left by the cemetery), affording fine retrospects of the Val di Non and the mountains of the Adige region as far as the Schlern. Beyond (6 M.) *Fai* (3115'; Inn), prettily situated in a fertile plain, the road goes on for a short distance towards the S. and then bends to the right, skirting a deep ravine and affording a beautiful view of the valley of the Adige as far as Trent. Traversing a wooded defile, and passing $(1^1/_2 M.)$ a chapel on the left, the road again skirts the slope of the *Mte. Paganella* (p. 296), now affording a beautiful *View of the Val di Non, lying far below, with its numerous villages, and of the huge rocky peaks of the Brenta to the W. We next reach $(3^1/_2 M.)$ *Andalo* (3405'; Inn), with the small lake of that name below us on the right. The road descends a little, crosses a brook, and leads through wood. As we approach (3 M.) **Molveno** (2820'; *Alb. Cima Tosa*, *Alb. delle Dolomiti*, both unpretending), a charming view is suddenly disclosed of the considerable lake of that name (2710'), beautifully situated between the Brenta and Mte. Gazza, and enclosed by picturesquely-shaped mountains. (The churchyard wall is an excellent point of view.) Thence over the *Monte Gazza* to (4½-5 hrs.) *Terlago*, see p. 296; over the *Bocca di Brenta* to *Pinzolo*, 10 hrs. (guide 8 fl.), a grand but fatiguing route, see p. 306. *Bonif.* and *Mateo Nicolussi* of Molveno are good guides. — Beyond Molveno the narrow road skirts the W. side of the lake (boat across 2 fl.), passes the small *Lago di Nembia*, crosses the brook by the mills, and then leads in long windings via *Dorsino*, *Tarodo*, and *Villa di Banale*, to (10 M.) *Comano* or (12 M.) *Stenico* (see p. 308).

From Stenico to Pinzolo through the **Val d'Algone**, 6½-7 hrs., an easy and attractive bridle-path. We ascend rapidly through the wooded *Val d'Algone*, passing a glass-work, to (4 hrs.) the saddle (6070') to the S.E. of the *Sabbione* (6875'). We then either cross the latter, or proceed through the *Vall' Agola*, past the small lake of that name (5175'), and descend into the *Val Nambino* and to (2½-3 hrs.) *Pinzolo* (see p. 305).

The Trent and Tione road follows the right bank of the Sarca, passes below Stenico, and enters a deep gorge, where it crosses the river twice (a tunnel and two galleries). The valley expands. On the opposite bank opens the steep *Val d'Algone* (see above), and farther on are the villages of *Ragoli* and *Preore*. We next pass through *Saone*, to the left of which, on the hill-side, is *Zuclò* (see below), and cross the *Arno* to (9 M.) **Tione** (1840'; *Cavallo Bianco*; *Corona*; café and beer-house in the vicinity), prettily situated at the confluence of the Arno (p. 308) and the Sarca, the principal village in Upper Giudicaria (2000 inhab.). From Tione to the valleys of the *Arno* and *Chiese*, see p. 308.

From Riva to Tione direct (6 hrs.), a beautiful route (carriage-road to Ballino. The road leaves the town by the Porta S. Marco on the N., and gradually ascends a luxuriantly fertile slope. To the right we enjoy a fine survey of the extensive and fruitful valley of Arco, and at intervals a charming retrospect of the Lago di Garda. Farther on, the road bends into the *Val Varone* (p. 299; high on the opposite slope of which lies *Tenno*, with its castle), ascends rapidly to (3½ M.) *Pranzo*, and skirts the deep ravine of the Varone. Near the (1¼ M.) pretty, green *Lago di Tenno* a road to Tenno diverges on the right. The small village of (3 M.) *Ballino* is situated on the watershed. About ½ M. farther on, the direct route to Tione diverges to the left from the road to *Fiave* (and *Tre Arche*, see p. 308), and skirts the slope, at the same level, affording a fine view of the Brenta group. After ¾ hr. we descend, cross the *Duina*, and ascend again to (20 min.) *Cavrasto* (2335'), below the saddle of the (¾ hr.) *Durone Pass*, which commands an admirable view of the S.E. peaks of the Adamello: to the right is the lofty *Carè Alto* (11,355') with the extensive Vedretta di Lares; at our feet lies the Val Sarca. The path now descends gently to (¾ hr.) *Zuclò* and (¼ hr.) *Bolbeno*, and crosses the Arno to (¼ hr.) *Tione*.

The Val Sarca here turns suddenly towards the N., and this part of it is called the **Val Rendēna**. At (2¼ M.) *Villa di Rendena* the *Val di S. Valentino* opens on the left, through which a fatiguing route leads over the *Col di Mezzo* or the *Passo di Valentino* into the *Val di Fumo* (comp. p. 308). *Javrè*, *Darè*, and *Vigo*, the next villages, are close together; then (2¼ M.) *Pelugo* (2140') at the mouth of the *Val Borzago*, at the head of which the *Vedretta di Lares* (p. 308) is visible for a short time. The road passes a mortuary chapel with old frescoes. The next villages, *Borzago*, *Spiazza*, and *Mortaso*, belong to the parish of *Pieve di Val Rendena*. Beyond *Strembo* and *Caderzone* the road crosses the Sarca and leads by *Giustino* to (6 M.) **Pinzōlo** (2475'; *Corona; Hôtel Succursale di Campiglio; Aquila Nera*), a good starting-point for excursions among the Adamello, Presanella, and Brenta Alps. The valley of the Sarca (now called *Val di Genova*) turns here to the W., and the *Val Nambino* ascends to the N.E.

EXCURSIONS (guides: *Ant. Dalta Giacoma*, nicknamed *Lusion*, *Felice*, *Giac.* and *Lib. Collini, Pio Bolleri, Vittore Clementi, A. Ferrari, L. Pedri, A. Sanda,* and *Ognibene Bonapace;* the brothers *Nicolussi* of Molveno, good guides for long tours, are often to be found here). — On the road to Campiglio (see below), 3/4 M. to the N. of Pinzolo, is the interesting mortuary chapel of *S. Vigilio*. On the exterior of the S. wall is a Dance of Death of 1539, with Italian verses; traces of still older frescoes are visible where the whitewash has fallen off. In the choir are scenes from the life of St. Vigil, bordered with arabesques in the best Renaissance style. — The *Dosso del Sabbione* (0876'; 3½ hrs.; guide 3 fl.), easily ascended, viâ the *Ciocca Alp* or *Giustino* (see above), affords a splendid survey of the Brenta, Adamello, and Presanella. The descent may be made into the *Val d'Algone* or through the *Vall' Agola* to Campiglio (comp. p. 304).

TO CAMPIGLIO AND THE VAL DI SOLE, an attractive route (to Dimaro 6½ hrs.; one-horse carriage to Campiglio 1 pers. 3, 2 pers. 4½ fl.; carriage and pair 6 fl.). The road passes the chapel of *S. Vigilio* (see above; *Carisolo* lies to the left), and follows the left bank of the *Sarca di Nambino* to the (2 M.) bridge above the mouth of the *Val Nambron*. It then ascends (footpath shorter) to (2 M.) *S. Antonio di Mavignolo* (fine retrospect of the *Vedretta di Laris, Carè Alto*, etc.). Still gradually ascending, we follow the N. side of the *Val Nambino* (opposite the Brenta chain, with the *Vall' Agola*, *Val Brenta*, and *Vall' Asinella* far below us), which afterwards turns to the N. (To the E. rises the Mte. Spinale, see below.) We next reach (6 M.) **Madonna di Campiglio** (5250'), an old monastery, now the *Grand Hôtel des Alpes* (R., L., & A. 2 fl., B. 60 kr., D. 1¾, board 3 fl.), a pleasant and sheltered summer-resort situated on a grassy plateau among fine fir-woods. Pretty walks lead to the *Victoria-Platz*, near the waterfall in the *Val Vallesinella* (1 hr.), to the *Lago di Nambino* (5970'; 2 hrs.), to the *Lago di Ritorto* (6670'; 2½ hrs.), etc. The *Mte. Spinale* (6616'; 1¼ hr.; good path, guide not indispensable), the *Mte. Ritorto* (7890'; 3½ hrs.; with guide), and the *Mt. Nambino* (8770'; 4 hrs.; with guide), with a trigonometrical pyramid and a fine view, are worthy of a visit. — Beyond Campiglio the bridle-path (guide unnecessary) ascends to the (1½ hr.) *Ginevrie-Alp* at the summit of the *Campo Pass* ('Campo Carlo Magno', 5385'), and then descends, past a spirit distillery and through the wooded *Val Selva*, first on the left, afterwards on the right, and then again on the left side of the *Meledrio*, to (2½-3 hrs.) *Dimaro* (p. 311). Or we may turn to the right about ½ hr. before reaching Dimaro and descend direct to *Malè* (p. 311; 4 hrs. from Campiglio).

FROM PINZOLO TO MOLVENO OVER THE BOCCA DI BRENTA, 10-11 hrs., a fatiguing but grand route (guide 7 fl.). To (4 M.) *S. Antonio di Mavignolo*, see above. A good path here leads through the meadows to the right, crosses the *Sarca di Nambino* by the saw-mill, and ascends through wood to the (1½ hr.) *Lower Brenta Alp* (4095'). This point may also be reached from Campiglio by a direct path viâ the Victoria-Platz (see above; good beer at the *Palud del Spinale*, near the Alp). The superb and beautifully-wooded *Val di Brenta* consists of three vast terraces, which the path to the Bocca ascends. The lower region of the valley (*Brenta Bassa*) ends in a basin enclosed by precipices which seem to defy further progress. A steep and narrow path ascends hence on the left side of the valley, behind a rocky slope, to the (1½ hr.) *Alp Brenta Alta* (5630'), a well-watered and partly wooded plateau enclosed by huge rocky peaks: to the left the *Campanile*

306   *VI. Route 55.*   CIMA TOSA.   *Val Sarca.*

Alta (9935'), and *Torre di Brenta* (10,056'), to the right the immense rocky mass of the *Crozzon di Brenta* (10,188'), and behind it the *Cima Tosa* (see below). From the end of the terrace we make our way with difficulty through the remains of a landslip of 1882, and then ascend to a rock-girt basin, filled with debris, beyond which we mount a long, steep and fatiguing snow-slope to the (2½ hrs.) Bocca di Brenta (8355'), a gap between the *Cima Brenta Alta* (9960') on the left and the *Cima Brenta Bassa* (9120') on the right. View to the E. limited; to the N. rises the Ortler chain. — We descend over snow (behind the rocky saddle to the right is the Tosa Hut; see below), and then by a rough and toilsome path over steep slopes of debris and grass, through the *Val delle Seghe*, passing imposing rocks, especially the *Croz dell' Altissimo* (7615') at the entrance to the *Val Persa*, on the left. Farther down we enter the wood. The path improves, crosses the *Massodi* brook, and ascends high above a deep ravine on the left. It then descends (in view of the Lago di Molveno), crosses the brook, and again ascends to the left to (3½-4 hrs.) *Molveno* (p. 304).

The *Cima Tosa* (10,430'), the highest peak of the Brenta group, may be ascended by mountaineers from the Bocca (3-4 hrs.; guide from Pinzolo 8 fl.). From the snow-field at the E. base of the Bocca we ascend to the right to the (10 min.; from the Bocca 20 min.) *Tosa Hut* (wine and beer), lying on a broad rocky saddle (8700'), above the hollow known as the *Pozza Tramontana*. The path leads to the right from the hut, skirts the inner side of the Pozza Tramontana, and then crosses the *Tosa Glacier*, mounting from the lower to the upper glacier by means of an almost perpendicular 'cheminée' (about 100' high; not difficult for experts). The summit commands a magnificent view, particularly of the huge rocky pinnacles of the Brenta group: to the W. the beautiful Adamello and Presanella groups; to the N. the Ortler and the Alps of the Oetzthal and Stubai; to the N.E. the Zillerthal Alps and the Tauern; to the E. the Dolomites; and to the S. a part of the Lago di Garda and the plains of Italy.

The Cima di Brenta (10,320'), the central summit of the N. Brenta group, may be ascended from the Tosa Hut in 5-6 hrs. (difficult, suited for adepts only), viâ the *Bocchetta dei Armi* (9010'), between the Torre di Brenta and Cima dei Armi, and the *Vedretta dei Fulmini*. A steep descent crosses the *S. Vallesinella Glacier* to the *Val Vallesinella* and *Campiglio*.

The *Val di Genŏva, a beautiful, wild Alpine valley, 12 M. in length, ascends from Pinzolo to the W. into the heart of the Adamello-Presanella Alps (cart-track at first, then a footpath; provisions should be taken; guide, unnecessary, to Bedole 3, to the Leipsic hut 5 fl.). The road leads from Pinzolo to the N.W. through the broad valley to the (1 M.) chapel of *S. Maria de' Poveri*. Here we may either take the lower road to the left, passing the glass-works, and after 10 min. ascend to the right to the upper road, or we may ascend to the right, by a pilgrimage-path flanked with fine old chestnut-trees, to the (10 min.) solitary church of *S. Stefano*, on an eminence commanding a fine *View. The exterior is embellished with interesting frescoes of 1519 and 1534. We next reach (10 min.) a saw-mill at the beginning of the lowest part of the valley, called the *Pian di Genova*. On the right are masses of rocky debris, above which tower the smooth sides of the Presanella. To the right, farther on (½ hr.), is a fine waterfall, 320' high, of the *Piss di Nardis*, the discharge of the Vedretta di Nardis (to the Presanella hut, see p. 308). On the left, ½ hr. farther on, opposite the Fontana Bona (good water), opens the narrow *Val di S. Giuliano*, with a small cascade framed in dark woods, descending from a little lake of the same name, 3 hrs. higher up, where St. Julian is said to have once done penance. The track now ascends to a higher region of the valley. To the left are the picturesque *Falls of the Sarca*, and near the ($^1/_2$ hr.) *Alp Caret* (3595') are those of the *Lares*, the discharge of the Vedretta di Lares (see below), descending in three leaps. The path ascends a steep hill, from the top of which ($^1/_2$ hr.) a fine retrospect of the valley and the Brenta is obtained, and reaches the (10 min.) Alpine hamlet of *Tedesca*. To the left is the *Fargorida Fall*. The valley now bends to the N.W. The path ascends to ($^1/_2$ hr.) the *Malga Caret* (4625'), and follows the left bank of the Sarca, round the wooded *Mte. Meniciyolo* (8685'), which projects conspicuously towards the S.; on the right tower the formidable precipices of the Presanella. Beyond the corner a view is disclosed of the fine *Mandron Glacier*, which has receded greatly of late years, and of the broad valley of **Bedöle**. To the left is the *Cascata del Pedrüc*, another fine waterfall formed by the Sarca. At the (1 hr.) head of the valley is the *Casina Botognini* (5015'; *Inn, kept by the guides Felice and Liberio Collini).

A fine view of the Madron and Lobbia glaciers is obtained from the path to the *Venezia Alp* (an ascent of $^1/_4$ hr. enough). The path to the *Matterott Alp*, commanding a still finer view, was destroyed in 1887. Another good view of the Lobbia glacier is obtained at a point on the way to the Leipsic Hut, 20-30 min. above the Casina Bologuini.

On the plateau at the base of the Mandron chain, $2^1/_2$ hrs. above Bedole, is the grandly-situated **Leipsic Hut** (*Refugio del Mandron*, 8100'; Inn in summer), which forms the best starting-point for excursions in the N. Adamello region. The path to it (guide from Pinzolo, desirable for novices, 5 fl.) ascends by the Bolognini Hut, at first through wood, and then steeply through the *Ronchina Ravine*, and on the plateau leads to the left to the hut, situated near the small *Mandron Lakes*, and affording a fine survey of the Mandron and Lobbia glaciers.

EXCURSIONS (guides, see p. 305). The *Monte Adamello (11,035') may be ascended with no great difficulty from the Leipsic Hut, viâ the *Mandron* and *Adamello Glaciers*, in $5^1/_2$-6 hrs. (guide from Pinzolo 10 fl.). Superb view from the top. The descent may be made on the S. to the (3 hrs.) *Rifugio di Satarno* (7400'), and through the valley of the same name (farther down called the *Val di Brate*) to (5 hrs.) *Cedegoto* (p. 313); or on the N.W. to the *Val d'Avio*. For the latter, we retrace our steps to the foot of the *Corno Bianco* (11,265'), then ascend to the left to the (2 hrs.) *Bocchetta di Val d'Avio*, and thence descend over rock, snow, and debris, and finally by a poor bridle-path, passing several waterfalls, to the (3 hrs.) *Malga di Mezz* (milk), finely situated on the *Lago d'Avio* (6170'); thence to *Ponte di Legno* $3^1/_2$ hrs. (comp. p. 312). - The *Lobbia Bassa* (9505'; 3 hrs.), *Monte Venerocolo* (10,770'; $3^1/_2$ hrs.), and *Corno Bianco* (11,205'; 5 hrs.) may also be ascended from the Leipsic Hut. (The route to the Adamello viâ the *Corno Bianco* and *Monte Falcone* is scarcely longer than the direct ascent.) — For the E. peaks of the Adamello, the *Carè Alto* (11,355'; 5 hrs.; guide 9 fl.), *Cima di Lares* (11,000'; $3^1/_2$-4 hrs.; guide 8 fl.), etc., the best starting-point is the **Lares Hut** (9200') of the Trent Alpine Club, at the foot of the *Vedretta di Lares*, 5 hrs. from Pinzolo. Over the *Passo di Lares* to the *Rifugio di Satarno* (9 hrs., with guide), see p. 313.

20*

308 VI. Route 55. CONDINO.

PASSES (paths marked). Over the **Passo Lagoscuro** (9350') to Ponte di Legno, 6-7 hrs., with guide, fatiguing. The route ascends from the Leipsic Hut, past the small and sombre *Lago Scuro* (8730'), to the (1½-2 hrs.) top of the pass, between the *Punta Lagoscuro* on the left and the *Punta di Pisgana* on the right, where we enjoy a striking *View of the Adamello, Presanella, and Ortler. We then descend through steep and difficult snow-couloirs and over extensive slopes of detritus into the *Val Narcane*, which we follow to (4 hrs.) *Ponte di Legno* (p. 312). — The **Passo del Lago Ghiacciato** (9630'), so named from a small lake on the E. side, is equally laborious (from the Leipsic Hut to Ponte di Legno 6-7 hrs.). — A less troublesome and somewhat shorter route is the *Passo Presena (9766', from the hut to Ponte di Legno 5-6 hrs.). It ascends from the Leipsic Hut to the N.E., up the slope of the *Cima del Zigolon*, latterly over steep banks of detritus and snow, to the head of the pass, which lies to the W. of the *Cima Presena* (a second pass to the W. is less advisable). It then descends across the easily-passable *Presena Glacier* to the *Laghi Presena*, and either to the right (marked path) to the Tonale Inn or into the Val Vermiglio (to Fucine, p. 312), or to the left over a steep rocky slope (where a steady head is required) to the W. slope of the Tonale and Ponte di Legno. Guide for each of these three passes 12 fl.

Towards the N. a high ridge of rock connects the Adamello with the lofty **Presanella** range. The ascent of the highest peak, the *Cima Presanella* (11,636'), presents no difficulty to experts, and amply repays the trouble (guide 9 fl.): from Pinzolo through the *Val Nardis* (p. 306) to the *Malga di Nardis* 2½ hrs., to the *Malga dei Fiori* 1 hr., to the *Presanella Hut* (7200'), 1 hr., thence to the summit 4 hrs. (best direct over the *Nardis Glacier*, but the Italian guides usually ascend the rocks to the right). View most imposing. The ascent on the N. side, through the *Val Stavel*, is very difficult, see p. 312.

The high-road through South Giudicaria ascends from Tione (p. 304) to the S.W. on the left bank of the *Arno*, and crosses the river near (3 M.) *Bondo* (2675'), where it issues from the *Val Breguzzo*, opening on the right. An easy path leads hence to the E. through the *Val Gaverdina*, and over the pass of that name, into the *Val di Concei*, and to *Lenzumo* and *Pieve di Ledro* (p. 300). Between Bondo and (1½ M.) *Roncone* (2750') we cross the watershed between the Sarca and Chiese, and descend viâ *Lardaro* and *Strada* to (4½ M.) *Creto*, on the *Chiese*, which issues from the *Val di Daone* (W.).

The only village in the **Val di Daone** is *Daone*, ½ hr. from *Strada*. The highest part of the valley, enclosed by huge mountains and glaciers, is called the *Val di Fumo*. Over the *Col di Mezzo* to Rendena, see p. 304. A route leads by the *Lago di Campo* over the *Passo del Campo* (7500'), between *Mte. Campellio* (9215') on the right and *Mte. Castello* (9480') on the left, and descends by the *Lago d'Arno* (6880') to the *Val di Sariore* and to *Cedegolo* (p. 313).

The road next leads through the pleasant valley to *Cimego* and (4½ M.) **Condino** (1445'; *Torre di Londra*), the chief village in the *Val Buona*, or upper valley of the Chiese. At (3 M.) *Dazio* the road to the *Valle di Ledro* (p. 300) crosses the river to the left. The valley expands; (1 M.) *Darzo*; (1 M.) *Lodrone* (1245'), with the ruins of two castles of the family of that name, situated on the *Caffaro*, which forms the Italian frontier (on the left bank the Austrian, on the right the Italian custom-house). — The *Cima Spessa* (5950') on the E. side of the valley, easily ascended in 4½ hrs., affords a fine survey of the environs.

About 1½ M. lower down, the road reaches the **Lago d'Idro** (1200'), 6 M. in length, ¾-1 M. in width, and skirts its W. bank. Above, to the left, lies the hamlet of *Bondone*. (To the *Val Vestino*, see p. 300.) Then (3½ M.) *Anfo*, with the mountain-castle of *Rocca d'Anfo*. On the opposite bank, to the S.E., lies the village of *Idro*. At (3 M.) *Lavenone*, at the S. end of the lake, begins the picturesque *Val Sabbia*, of which the chief village is (3 M.) *Vestone* (Tre Spade). At (3 M.) *Barghe* the road divides: the branch to the W. leads by *Preseglie* and through the *Val Garza* to (15 M.) *Brescia*; that to the E. by *Sabbio*, *Vobarno* (tramway hence, see p. 301), and *Tormini* (junction of the Brescia line), to (12 M.) *Salò*, on the Lago di Garda (p. 301).

56. From S. Michele to Tirano. Val di Non. Val di Sole. Tonale Pass. Passo d'Aprica. Val Camonica.

Comp. Map, p. 304.

From S. Michele, a station on the Botzen and Verona Railway (p. 293), a STELLWAGEN (uncomfortable) runs twice daily to (25½ M.) *Malè* in 8 hrs. (2 fl. 10 kr.), and from Malè to (10 M.) *Fucine* twice daily in 2½ hrs. (80 kr.). From Fucine over the Tonale to (13½ M.) *Ponte di Legno* diligence (if passengers enough present themselves) daily at 6 a.m. in 6 hrs. (5 fr.). From Ponte di Legno to (13 M.) *Edolo* diligence daily at 2 p.m. in 3½ hrs. (3 fr.). From Edolo to (25 M.) *Tirano* post-conveyance daily in 6 hrs. (6 fr.). — One-horse carriage from Mezzolombardo to Cles 6-8 fl.; carriage and pair, to Rabbi 24, to Pejo 30 fl. — From Botzen over the *Mendel Pass to *Malè* omnibus in summer daily in 12 hrs., see p. 268.

The VAL DI NON and VAL DI SOLE, the *Anaunia* of the Romans, are among the most interesting valleys in S. Tyrol. Although bearing different names, they are in reality a single valley, watered by the *Noce*, about 30 M. in length, several miles in width, well-cultivated, and occasionally broken by narrow ravines. The slopes enclosing the valley are gradual, and cultivated nearly to the summit. The rapid *Noce* is generally concealed from view in its deep channel. It is visible from the road only at the *Rocchetta*, and from the lofty *Mostizoll Bridge*, which crosses it at the point where the Val di Non terminates and the Val di Sole begins. The language and character of the natives are Italian, except in a few communities in the extreme N. ramifications of the valley (Unsere Frau im Walde, Proveis, Laurein, and St. Felix).

S. Michele, or *Wälsch-Michael*, see p. 293. Fine view from the station of *Mte. Paganella*, *Mte. Bondone*, etc., towards the S. The road crosses the broad valley of the Adige to the W. (omnibus 15 kr.) to (1½ M.) **Mezzolombardo**, or *Wälsch-Metz* (865'; *Rosa*; *Corona*), a large village on the right bank of the Noce. (Route to *Fai* and *Molveno*, see p. 304.) On the opposite bank, 1½ M. to the N., is *Mezzo Tedesco*, or *Deutsch-Metz* (*Martinelli), at the foot of huge precipices, in which there is a large cavity above the village containing the ruined castle of *Kron-Metz*. Above Wälsch-Metz the rocks soon approach each other so as to form a defile, called the *Rocchetta, for the defence of which a fort was built in 1860. On the right, high above it, is the *Torre della Visione* (2065'), an ancient watch-tower, said to be of Roman origin. In this gorge the road twice crosses the Noce, the broad stony bed of which it quits on entering the **Val di Non** or **Nonsberg**. It now begins to ascend rapidly (several short-cuts), and (6½ M. from *Mezzolombardo*) reaches the prettily-situated village of *Denno* (1380'). To the right, beyond the valley of the Noce, rises the château of *Thun*. Crossing a fertile plateau, which yields wine and silk, we next reach *Flavon* (Ger. *Pflaum*) and *Terres*; then descend in a wide circuit into the deep *Tresenya Ravine*, and again ascend laboriously in windings to (5 M.) *Tuenno*, a thriving village, and (2½ M.) —

15½ M. **Cles** (2140'; *Corona*; *Aquila Nera*), the capital of the Val di Non (3000 inhab.), situated high above the confluence of the *Novella* and the Noce. The *Dos-Pez*, 5 min. to the N. of the church, is the best point of view. On the slope below the village, at the point where the road to Fondo (p. 268) descends into the valley, stands the well-preserved château of *Cles*, built in the 16th century. Cles possesses a school for wood-carving, the products of which are not expensive.

From Cles over the *Mendel Pass* to *Botzen*, see p. 268.

FROM CLES OVER THE GAMPEN PASS TO MERAN (12 hrs.), an interesting expedition. From Cles we either descend to the N.E., passing the château, to the Noce bridge above the mouth of the *Novella*, and ascend thence to (1½ hr.) *Revò* (p. 311); or we descend to the S.E., by a new road passing *Majano*, to the new iron *Ponte Justina*, 330' above the river, and ascend thence by the Mezzolombardo road (comp. p. 311), viâ *Sanzeno*, *Romeno*, and *Cavareno*, to (5 hrs.) Fondo (3200'; *Posta*; *Hôtel Fondo*), a considerable village, with the château of *Malosco* and a handsome new church, 5 M. to the W. of the Mendel Pass (see p. 268).

[From Fondo an interesting excursion may be made to *Lauregn* and *Proveis*, two German villages. The road (see below) runs to the N.W. to (1½ M.) *Castelfondo* (3100'), whence a bridle-track (guide advisable) leads over the *Jöchl* (about 4660') to (2 hrs.) *Laurein*, Ital. *Lauregno* (3300'), and thence to the high-lying (1½ hr.) Proveis (4640'; quarters at the curé's, or in the school-house, during the summer-holidays), finely situated on the E. slope of the *Gampen* (5950'), high above the *Pescara*. There is a school for lace-making at Proveis, where cheap specimens of the work may be bought. The inhabitants, who are civil and obliging, are said to be of Saxon origin. About 4 M. to the S. of Proveis are the small baths of *Mocenigo* (3445'), whence a road runs viâ *Rumo*, *Livo*, and *Scana* (p. 311) to the *Mostizoll Bridge* and (10 M.) *Cles*. Attractive footpaths lead from Proveis over the *Laureiner Alp* (*Malga di Lauregno*) to (2½ hrs., with guide) *Unsere Frau im Walde*; and to the N. over the *Hofmahd* (*Spitzenjöchl*, 5930') to (3 hrs.) the *Ultener Mitterbad* (p. 276).]

From Fondo we ascend for 3 hrs. more, viâ *Tret* and *St. Felix* (Inn), to the pilgrimage-church of *Unsere Liebe Frau im Walde*, Ital. *Senale* (4410'; rustic inn by the church), whence the *Laugenspitze* (p. 276) may be easily ascended in 2½-3 hrs. Another ¾ hr. brings us to the top of the **Gampen Pass** (5140'). We descend by *Gfrill* (small *Inn; ascent of the Laugenspitze 3½ hrs., with guide), *Tisens* (p. 269), and *Lana* (p. 269) to (6 hrs.) *Meran*.

Travellers from MEZZOLOMBARDO TO FONDO need not go to Cles, but follow the road diverging to the right in the *Rocchetta* (see above) on the left bank of the Noce. (Diligence from Mezzolombardo to Fondo daily in 6¾ hrs., starting at 11.15 a.m.; in the reverse direction in 4 hrs., starting at noon.) As the Rocchetta is quitted, the handsome château of *Thun* (1975') is seen on the right, high above *Vigo*. The road ascends gradually viâ *Tajo* and *Dermulo* to (16 M. from Mezzolombardo) *Sanzeno*, situated on a mountain-spur, with a large Romanesque-Gothic church.

Then viâ *Romeno* and *Cavareno* (p. 268) to (9 M.) *Fondo* (p. 310). — Pleasant excursion from S. Zeno to (1 hr.) S. Romedio (*Inn*), a resort of pilgrims. The route leads through the wild *Romedio Ravine* to the precipitous rock on which is perched the hermitage with its five old chapels, one above another (Inn). A visit to the hermitage may also be combined with the route viâ *Don* and *Amblar* to *Ruffrè* and the *Mendel*; comp. p. 268.

The **Val di Sole**, or *Sulzberg*, is wilder and has a colder climate than the Val di Non. The road ascends to the (1 M.) village of *Dres* (*View from the chapel of *S. Chiatar*), and then descends to the (3 M.) *Mostizoll Bridge* over the *Noce*, which dashes through a profound rocky gorge. This bridge forms the boundary between the Nonsberg and the Sulzberg.

To FONDO, 5 hrs. The road ascends on the left bank of the Noce, crossing the *Bresimo*, to (1½ M.) *Scana* (2210'), where a road diverges to the left to *Mocenigo* and *Proveis* (see p. 310). Here we turn to the right, cross the *Pescara*, and proceed to *Cagno* and (3 M.) *Revò* (2360'; Inn), whence the *Osol* or *Oken* (5090'; fine view) may be easily ascended in 2½ hrs. Thence along the right side of the profound valley of the *Novella* to *Cloz* and (7 M.) *Brez*, and over arched bridges of stone, spanning the ravines of the *Rabiala* and *Novella*, to *Castelfondo* and (3 M.) *Fondo* (p. 310). — From Revò we reach the Mendel route directly by crossing the Novella and passing (1¼ hr.) *Dambel* and (1½ hr.) *Cavareno* (see above). Thence we follow the Mendel road viâ *Sarnonico* and *Ronzano*, or take a direct forest-path to (1¼ hr.) *Ruffrè* and (³/₄ hr.) the *Mendel Pass* (p. 268).

We next reach (4½ M.) *Caldes*, with two old castles of the Counts of Thun, and then cross the *Rabbi Brook* to (1½ M.) —

25½ M. **Malè** (2530'; *Corona*), chief village in the Val di Sole. In the *Val di Rabbi*, to the N.W., 7 M. from Malè (diligence daily in 2½ hrs., viâ *Magras*, *Pracorno*, and *S. Bernardo*), are the **Baths of Rabbi** (4100'; *Hôtel Rabbi*; *Hôtel Pangrazzi*, with Cur-Salon), the most important in Tyrol, the water of which, strongly impregnated with iron, resembles that of Selters. The season extends from 15th June to 15th September. — From the Baths (guides, *C. A. Dallaserra*, *Sim. Pangrazzi*, and *A. Mengon*) through the *Ultenthal* to *Meran*, see p. 276; over the *Sältent-Joch* (9900') to the *Martellthal*, see p. 286. — An attractive route leads over the **Cercena Pass** (8515') to *Pejo* (p. 312) in 6-7 hrs. (guide 4 fl.). The pass commands a splendid view of the S. Ortler peaks: Pallon della Mare, Mte. Vioz, Saline, Taviela, Punta Cadini, Punta di S. Matteo, etc., and (to the S.) of the Presanella. Descent through the Val della Mare to Pejo (p. 312).

From Malè the road runs at nearly the same level in the broad valley to (3 M.) *Dimaro* (*Corona*), which lies to the left, at the mouth of the *Meledrio*, crosses the Noce, and then recrosses it. (Route by *Campiglio* to *Pinzolo*, see p. 305.) Above Dimaro the valley is wilder. On the S.W. rise the lofty granite buttresses of the Presanella. We next pass (3½ M.) *Mezzana*, on a height to the right, and *Castello* on the right, high above the road, and reach (2¾ M.) *Cusiano*. Opposite to us, towards the W., is the Tonale; to the left are portions of the Presanella; to the right a beautiful glimpse of the *Val di Pejo*, with lofty ridges of ice in the background (Mte. Taviela, Vioz, Cevedale, etc.). The road now crosses the Noce to (³/₄ M.) **Fucine** (3900'; *Zanella*, to the right; *Leone*). To the left lies *Ossana*, with its large ruined castle.

The *Val di Pejo*, which is traversed by a good road, divides at (4 M.) *Cogolo* (Morescini). To the W. runs the *Val del Monte*, at the mouth of which (1¹/₄ M.) lie the small baths of **Pejo** (4450'; *Hôtel Oliva*, and four other inns). The baths are in the valley; the village on the N. slope, ³/₄ hr. higher. The lofty peaks of the S. Ortler region (*Pallon della Mare*, 13,160'; *Punta San Matteo*, 12,090'; *Mte Vioz*, 11,940', etc.) may be ascended from Pejo by mountaineers. (Guides, *A. Casserotti, G. Groaz, Antonio* and *Ign. Veneri* of Cogolo.) The *Cima di Vioz* (8190'), ascended without difficulty from the village of Pejo in 3 hrs., affords a good survey of the grand environs. — Through the *Val del Monte* (the upper part of which is called *Val Bormina*) and over the *Sforzellina Pass* to *S. Caterina* and *Bormio*, see p. 283. — To the N. is the *Val della Mare*, through which a tolerable route leads from the baths of Pejo past (2¹/₂ hrs.) the *Malga Ponte Vecchio* (5770') to the (1 hr.) *Malga la Mare* (5985'), thence ascending the steep *Scala di Venezia* in the bleak *Val Venezia* to the (2 hrs.) well-equipped **Cevedale Club Hut**, opposite the *Vedretta la Mare*, a good starting-point for the *Cevedale* (5-6 hrs.), *Pallon della Mare, Cima Venezia*, etc. Across the *Fürkelescharte* or the *Hohenfernerjoch* to the *Zufall Hut*, see p. 236. Instead of returning to Martell, we may cross the *Eissee Pass* to *Sulden* from the Fürkelescharte, or descend across the *Cevedale Pass* to *Sta. Caterina*; comp. p. 292. — A trying glacier-route leads over the *Col della Mare* (11,160') to Sta. Caterina in 6-7 hrs.

Near Fucino the Monte Tonale road (13¹/₂ M. to Ponte di Legno) quits the Noce, which descends from the Val di Pejo, and ascends to the S.W. through the *Val Vermiglio* in long windings to the pass. Towards the S. we enjoy a series of splendid views of the jagged and ice-girt crests of the *Presanella*, the highest peak of which (*Cima Presanella*, 11,686'; ascent from the N., through the *Val Stavel* and over the *Presanella Glacier*, difficult, see p. 308) is repeatedly visible. The road leads by (2¹/₂ M.) *Pizzano* (Alb. Matteo; Austrian custom-house) and (3 M.) *Strino* (5110'), an Austrian fort built to guard the valley in 1866, and past the (2¹/₂ M.) *Cantoniera* (rustic inn), to the (1 M.) **Tonale Pass** (6150'), a broad grassy valley, the boundary between the Tyrol and Italy. (To the left, on the old road, is the Italian guard-house.) In 1799 and 1808 several sharp conflicts took place here between the Tyrolese and the French, and again in 1848 and 1866 between the Italians and the Tyrolese. The road descends gradually, passing several chalets and the mouth of the *Val Narcane* (left; p. 308), and then forming several long bends to the right (which the old road and footpaths cut off), to (4¹/₂ M.) **Ponte di Legno** (4140') in the *Val Camonica*, which is watered by the *Oglio*.

Over the *Gavia Pass* to *Sta. Caterina* (guide advisable for the less experienced), see p. 283; to the Val di Genova, see p. 308. — To the N. of Ponte di Legno an easy route crosses the *Passo di Montozzo* (8585') to (7 hrs.) *Pejo* (see above). — For travellers from Sulden, Ponte di Legno is the best starting-point for the ascent of the *Adamello* (p. 307); the route leads through the *Val d'Avio* (diverging at *Pontagna*, see below) to the *Malga di Mezzo* (5 hrs.; bed of hay) and to the top in 6-7 hrs. more; descent to the *Leipsic Hut* (p. 307), 3¹/₂-4 hrs. A refuge-hut is being built on the Lago d'Avio. — Guide, *Bastanzini*, at Ponte di Legno.

From Ponte di Legno (one-horse carriage to Edolo 10 fr.) the road follows the *Oglio* to Pontagna, Stadolina, Vezza (at the mouth of the *Val Grande*), Incudine, and (13 M.) —

Edolo (2285'; **Leone; Due Mori*, fair; *Gallo*), finely situated on the Oglio, and commanded on the E. by *Mte. Ariolo* (9450').

VAL CAMONICA. *VI. Route 56.* 313

TO THE UPPER VAL TELLINA over the **Passo del Mortirolo** (6235'; 7½ hrs. to Bolladore; guide not required by adepts), an easy and attractive expedition. A bridle-track, diverging to the left 40 min. above Edolo and before Incudine, ascends the *Val Mortirolo* past *Monno* to the (3½ hrs.) modest *Osteria della Fontana*, just on this side of the summit of the pass. Descent, with fine view of the Val Tellina, to (2½ hrs.) *Tiolo*, 1½ M. below *Bolladore* (p. 283).

FROM EDOLO TO BRESCIA (54 M.). Post-omnibus daily in 7 hrs. to Lovere and Pisogne (one-horse carr. 20 fr.); thence by steamboat and railway (see below). The road leads through the °**Val Camonica**, one of the most beautiful of the S. valleys of the Alps. The upper part is narrow and enclosed by chestnut-clad slopes; the lower part is fertile and well-cultivated, and its chief products are silk and iron wares. The valley is watered by the *Oglio* (p. 312). The road crosses the stream several times, and passes the villages of *Sonico*, *Malonno*, and (7½ M.) *Cedegolo* (splendid view from a chapel near the road, 1 M. above the village). To the E. opens the *Val di Saviore*, watered by the *Poglia*; about 3 M. farther up the valley divides into the *Valle Adame* to the right and the *Val di Brate* to the left. In the last-named, beyond *Ponte* and the picturesque *Lago di Salarno* (6685'; marked path), is the *Rifugio di Salarno* (7395'), a hut of the Italian Alpine Club, near the glacier of that name, and a starting-point for the ascent of the *Adamello* (11,660'; 4½ hrs.; guide, Brisio of Saviore; comp. p. 307). From the Rifugio di Salarno across the *Passo di Fumo* and the *Passo di Lares* (10,285') to the *Lares Hut* (p. 307), 9 hrs., a fine glacier-route, but to be undertaken only by adepts. The ascent of the *Cima di Lares* may easily be included. Over the *Passo del Campo* to the *Val di Daone*, see p. 308.

The road next passes the villages of *Sellero* and (11 M) **Capo di Ponte** (1315'; *°Alberge S. Antonio*). — Beautiful excursion from Capo di Ponte to the W into the *Val Clegna*, at first by a bridle-track, then by a path across pastures to the (4 hrs.) *Passo di Campelli* (6200'), on the N. slope of the furrowed *Mte. Baghetta*, with °View of the Adamello and Presanella groups. Descent to (2 hrs.) *Schilpario*, (1¾ hr.) *Vilminore* (°Bonicelli), and (1 hr.) *Dezzo* in the *Val di Scalve*; then through the grand *Dezzo Ravine* to (4½ hrs.) *Darfo* and (2½ hrs.) *Lovere* (see below).

16 M. **Breno** (*Pellegrino*; °*Italia*, well spoken of) is the chief place in the lower Val Camonica. The Oglio here flows through a rocky defile. The road crosses to the right bank. To the E. towers the bold *Mte. Frerone* (8675'). Beyond the defile, on the left bank, lies the village of *Cividate*, over which rise the ruins of a monastery. The valley expands. Near *Darfo*, which lies on the left bank, the road to *Pisogne*, *Iseo*, and *Brescia* crosses the stream.

30½ M. **Lovere** (°*Leone d'Oro*; *S. Antonio*; *Roma*), a busy harbour, is prettily situated at the N.W. end of the *Lago d'Iseo*, near the influx of the Oglio. Boat to Iseo in 4 hrs., 6 fr. — A good road leads hence to the W. through the *Val Cavallina* to (18 M.) *Bergamo*.

The **Lago d'Iseo** (*Lacus Sebinus*, 620'), 15 M. long, 1-3 M. broad, and 1000' deep in the middle, vies with the Lago di Garda in the loveliness of its banks, which are luxuriantly clothed with vegetation, while to the N. rises the snow-clad Adamello. In the middle of the lake lies a picturesque rocky island, *Montisola*, with the fishing-villages of *Peschiera d'Iseo* and *Siviano*. STEAMBOAT twice daily from *Lovere* to *Sarnico* (°Leone d'Oro), at the S.W. end, in 2¾ hrs.; stations, *Pisogne* (Croce Verde), *Riva di Sotto* (W.), *Marone* (E.), *Sale Marasino* (E.), *Tavernola* (W.), *Peschiera e Sulzano* (E.), *Iseo* (°Leone d'Oro), *Predore*, and *Sarnico* (near which is the *Villa Montecchio*, an admirable point of view). — RAILWAY from *Iseo*, in 1¼ hr., to (15 M.) *Brescia*, and from *Paratico* (on the left bank of the Oglio, opposite Sarnico), in 26 min., to *Palazzolo*, a station on the railway from Lecco to Brescia (to Bergamo about 1 hr.); comp. *Baedeker's N. Italy*.

The new ROAD TO TIRANO (25 M.; one-horse carriage in 6 hrs., 25 fr.) ascends gradually on the N. side of the *Val di Corteno*, commanding fine retrospects of the Val Camonica, with the snowy peaks of the Adamello in the background. Opposite ($4^1/_2$ M.) *Cortenedolo* (2975′) lies the large village of *Santicolo*, on the right bank of the Corteno. From (2 M.) *Galleno* (3290′) a rough footpath leads to the N. over the *Mte. Padrio* (6230′) to Tirano. The road follows the left bank of the Corteno, and beyond the hamlet of *S. Pietro* reaches the (6 M.) summit of the **Passo d'Aprica** (3875′). About $^3/_4$ M. beyond the pass, near the poor village of *Aprica*, stands the inn *Dell' Aprica*.

A view of the Val Tellina, with Sondrio in the background, is soon disclosed. The broad gravelly bed of the *Adda* (p. 283), with traces of the devastation caused by the river, is also well surveyed. Several of the snowy spurs of the Bernina come into view towards the N.; on the lower mountains above Tresenda rises the square watch-tower of *Teglio* (p. 284). On the road is the *Belvedere* (3010′; Inn), $1^1/_4$ M. from Aprica. Fine view of the valley. The road now descends through chestnut groves, describes a wide circuit by *La Motta*, penetrates the rock by two cuttings, and reaches the bottom of the valley. Before ($4^1/_2$ M.) *Tresenda* (p. 284) the Adda is crossed.

In dry weather, when no inundation of the Adda is to be apprehended, pedestrians may quit the high-road a few hundred paces beyond the point where it bends to the W. by a path, somewhat steep at first, which crosses a brook near the hamlet of *Stazzona*, passes through an opening in the wall, and leads (to the right) to *Madonna di Tirano* (p. 284) in $1^1/_2$ hr.; or the embankment of the Adda may be followed direct to ($1^3/_4$ M.) *Tirano* (p. 284). This route effects a saving of about 5 M.

From Tresenda to (6 M.) *Tirano*, see p. 284. Travellers bound for *Sondrio* (p. 284) need not go to Tirano, unless to hire a carriage, as conveyances are seldom to be had at Tresenda.

VII. SOUTH-EASTERN TYROL. PUSTERTHAL AND THE DOLOMITES.

57. From Trent to Bassano (and Venice) through the Val Sugana 316
   Val Pinè. Val Fiorozzo, 317. — Lake of Caldonazzo. Lavarone and Luserna, 317. — To Asiago viâ Vésena, 318. — Val di Sella. Cima Dodici. From Borgo to Primiero by Castel Tesino and the Brocon Pass, 318. — Sette Comuni. Grottoes of Oliero, 319. — Possagno, 320.

58. The Valley of the Avisio (Fiemme and Fassa Valleys) 320
   From Cavalese to the Schwarzhorn, 321. — From Moëna to Cencenighe by the Passo di S. Pellegrino; to Paneveggio over the Lusin Pass, 322. — Monte di Campedie. Sasso di Dam. Rothe Wand. From Vigo to Campitello through the Vajolett and Duron Valleys. Antermoja Lake, 322. — From Campitello to the Seiser Alp and to Gröden. From Canazei to Buchenstein over the Pordoi Pass. From Penia to Caprile by the Fedaja Pass or the Contrin-Joch, 323. — Serrai di Sottoguda. Marmolada, 324.

59. From Predazzo to Primiero 324
   Cima di Bocche. From Paneveggio to Cencenighe over the Vallès Pass, 325. — From Paneveggio to S. Martino di Castrozza over the Colbricon Pass, 325. — Excursions from S. Martino. Tognazza. Tognola. Rosetta. Cima di Fradusta. Cimon della Pala. Cima Vezzana. Cima di Ball. Pala di S. Martino. Rosetta Pass. Comelle Pass. Forcella Gesuretta. Passo di Ball, 325, 326. — From S. Martino to Caurta. Cima d'Asta. Canale S. Bovo, 326. — Excursions from Primiero. Castel la Pietra. Calaita Lake. Val della Noana. Monte Pavione. Val di Pradidali, 327. — From Primiero to Feltre, 327.

60. From Franzensfeste to Villach. Pusterthal 327
   Valser Thal. Gitsch. Pfunderthal. Eidechsspitze, 328. — Excursions from Bruneck. Kronplatz. Rammelstein, 329. — Antholzer Thal. Over the Staller-Sattel to the Deferegger-Thal, 329, 330. — Pragser-Thal. Over the Plätzwiesen to Schluderbach and over the Kreuzjöchl to St. Vigil, 330, 331. — Excursions from Niederdorf, 331. — Excursions from Toblach. Pfannhorn. Sarnkofel, 331, 332. — Sexten-Thal. Helm. Innerfeld-Thal, etc. 332. — Fischeleinboden. Zsigmondy-Hütte. Passes to the Ampezzo and Auronzo. From Sillian to Kötschach in the Gailthal, 333. — Paralba, 334. — Excursions from Lienz. Schönbüchele. Kerschbaumer Alp. Böse Weibl. Schleinitz. Ederplan. Hohe Zieten, 334, 335. — Hochstadl. From Oberdrauburg to Tolmezzo viâ Kötschach and the Plöken, 335. — From Greifenburg to Paternion through the Weissensee-Thal. From Greifenburg to the Gailthal over the Kreuzberg. Kreuzeckspitze. The Millstätter See, 336.

61. From Bruneck to Taufers. Reinthal 337
   The Mühlbach-Thal. Grosse Windschar. Passes to Rein and Antholz, 337. — Excursions from Taufers. Speikboden. Wasserfallspitze. Grosse Mostnock, 338, 339. — Excursions from Rein. Rieserferner-Hütte. Hochgall,

Wildgall, etc., 339. — From Rein to Defereggen over the Klammul-Joch. From Rein to Taufers, 340.

62. **The Enneberg Valley or Gaderthal** 340
Excursions from St. Vigil. To the Val Ampezzo by the Fodara Vedla Alp. Seekofel. Joch Limo, 341. — Peitlerkofel. Heiligkreuzkofel, 342. — From St. Cassian to Andraz over the Castello Pass; to Cortina viâ Tra i Sassi or the Col di Lodschia, 342. — From St. Cassian to Buchenstein viâ Prelongei, 343. — Puez Alp. From Corvara to Buchenstein over the Campolungo and Incisa saddles. From Corvara to the Val Fassa by the Grödener Joch and Sella Pass, 343.

63. **From Toblach to Belluno. Val Ampezzo** 344
Excursions from Landro and Schluderbach. Rienzibal. Monte Pian, Dürrenstein. Flodige. Toblinger Riedel. Paternsattel. Cristallino. Monte Cristallo. Hohe Gaisl. Drei Zinnen. Hochebenkofel, 345-347. — Excursions from Ospitale. Through the Val Grande to Cortina, 347. — Excursions from Cortina. Belvedere on the Crepa. Grotte di Valpera. Lago Ghedina. Lago da Lago. Zumeles. Faloria. Seletta. Nuvolau. Val Travernanzes. Seekofel. Tofana. Cristallo. Sorapiss, 349, 350. — From Cortina to Schluderbach by the Passo Tre Croci, 350. — Misurina Lake, 351. — Excursions from S. Vito. Sorapiss. Antela. Pelmo, 351. — Cadore, Comelico, and Auronzo Valleys, 352. — Val di Zoldo, 353. — From Polpet to Vittorio, 354. — From Belluno to Feltre and Primolano, 354, 355.

64. **From Cortina to Belluno viâ Agordo. Cordevole Valley** 355
Pieve di Livinalongo, or Buchenstein. Col di Lana, 356. — Excursions from Caprile. Monte Migion. Monte Fernazza, 856. — From Cortina to Caprile over the Monte Giau, 356. — From Caprile to S. Vito over the Forcella Forada or Col di Ponia, 357. — Mte. Coldai, 357. — Val Biois. Cima di Pape. Monte Alto di Pelsa, 357. — From Agordo to Primiero over the Cereda Pass, 358. — From Agordo to the Val di Zoldo over the Duran or Moschesin Pass, 358.

57. From Trent to Bassano *(and Venice)* through the Val Sugana.

Comp. Map, p. 320.

57 M. OMNIBUS from Trent to (21 M.) Borgo thrice daily in 4½ hrs. (starting alternately from the railway-station and the Café Europa; fare 1 fl. 20 kr.); from Borgo viâ Primolano to (36 M.) Bassano daily in 7 hrs. (fare 2½ fl.). [To Primolano in 3 hrs., fare 1 fl.; thence to Feltre daily, see p. 355.] RAILWAY from Bassano to (30 M.) *Padua* in 1¾ hr., from Padua to *Venice* in 1-1½ hr., see *Baedeker's N. Italy*. — One-horse carriage from Trent to Levico (Lago di Caldonazzo) and back 4 fl.

Immediately beyond Trent the road ascends, and soon enters the ravine of the *Fersina*, being at places hewn through the overhanging rocks, or supported by masonry. The fall of the Fersina (p. 294) lies to the right, below the road, about 2¼ M. from Trent. At the narrowest part of the valley the road is defended by new fortifications, and farther on is the larger fort of *Chreszano*, above which, to the left, is the village of that name. At *Maso Barisetti* (1245′), 4 M. from Trent, the road to the Val Piné diverges to the left.

The pretty **Val Piné**, formerly inhabited by Germans, is worth a visit (a day's trip from Trent, carr. and pair there and back 10 fl.). The road crosses the *Silla* and ascends the left bank viâ *Nogarè* (2255'), passing *Fornace* and *Baselga* (on the left), to the (4 M.) pretty *Lago Serraja* (3050'; Alb. al Pavone, at the lower end, fair, carriages for hire), and then, passing the smaller *Lago delle Piazze*, to the (3½ M.) *Lavarda Inn* (3345'), at the mouth of the *Val Regnana*. To the left, high up, lies *Bedole* (3715'). From this point an easy pass leads to the S.E. to (2 hrs.) *Palù*, in the Val Fierozzo (see below). — A cart-track leads along the N. side of the *Val Regnana* to (2 hrs.) *Segonzano*, with its celebrated clay-pyramids (comp. p. 260; *Sledro Inn*), whence we go on across the *Avisio* to (1½ hr.) *Faver*. Road hence viâ *Cembra* (2170'; Lanzinger) to (9 M.) the railway-station of Lavis (p. 293).

The road crosses the *Silla* and then, near (3 M.) Pergine, the Fersina. On the right are *Roncogno* and *Cimirlo*, with a new fort.

7 M. **Pergine** (1580'; *Hôtel Voltolini* or *Post*; *Cavalletto*, unpretending), a well-to-do village, is charmingly situated at the mouth of the *Val Fierozzo* and commanded by an old château of the bishops of Trent. Signor Chimelli has a large silk-spinning factory here, to which visitors are admitted.

The **Val Fierozzo**, or *Val dei Mòcheni* (Ger. *Fersenthal*), which here stretches to the N.E., contains several German communities in the midst of an Italian population: *Gereut*, *Eichleit*, *St. Franziskus*, *St. Felix*, and *Palau*. A visit to this pretty valley is recommended. The road ascends to (3 M.) *Canezza* (1955'), crosses the stream, and reaches (1½ M.) *Gereut*, Ital. *Frassilongo* (Holzer). Thence mostly through wood past *St. Franziskus*, with a charmingly situated little church, and *St. Felix*, two hamlets of the parish of *Florus* (*Fierozzo*, *Vierhof*; the curés receive travellers) to (6 M.) *Palau* or *Palù* (4600') at the head of the valley. Thence to (1½ hr.) *Lavarda* in the *Val Pinè*, see above.

The road now crosses a hill extending to the S.E. between the lakes of Levico and Caldonazzo (see below), and descends to the small *Lago di Levico* (1435'), the N. side of which it skirts.

To the W. of this lake, and separated from it by a small chain of hills, lies the larger and more beautiful *Lago di Caldonazzo* (1465'), the source of the *Brenta*. The walk from Pergine between the two lakes, viâ *Ischia*, *Tenna*, and the ruined castle of *Brenta*, to (2 hrs.) Levico, is far preferable to the road and commands charming views of the *Terrarossa*, which rises on the W.. and of the loftier *Mte. Scanupia*. Or we may follow the road on the W. side of the Lago di Caldonazzo, passing *Calceranica*, with the oldest church in the valley, to (7 M.) Levico. From Calceranica a steep path descends by *Vigolo-Vattaro* (Inn) and *Valsorda* to (2 hrs.) the station of *Mattarello* (p. 295); a good cart-track, with fine views of the valley of the Adige, also descends to the right from Valsorda, to (3½ hrs.) Trent. This tour may be agreeably extended as follows: from Calceranica we proceed to (1½ M., 2¾ M. from Levico) *Caldonazzo* (1595'; *Hôtel Caldonazzo*), a thriving village, then ascend the *Val Centa* by a good road, often hewn through the rock, to (2½ hrs.) **Lavarone**, Ger. *Lafraun* (3840'; *Inn*), with a small lake, grandly situated on the watershed between the Brenta and Astico. We then follow the new road, passing *Gionghi*, to the (4½ M.) *Laghetto Alp* (3935'), whence a bridle-path (to the right) skirts the E. side of the *Retorto Gorge*, through wood, to (1½ hr.) **Luserna**, Ger. *Lusern* (4370'; *Lusarner Hof*, plain), grandly situated on a bleak plateau (730 inhab.). [From this point a mule-track descends along the wooded slope of the *Oberleiten* and through the *Val Torra* to (2 hrs.) *Casotto*, the Austrian frontier-village, in the *Val d'Astico*, whence a road runs viâ *S. Pietro Val d'Astico* to (4 M.) *Pedescala* (to Asiago, see p. 319).] From Luserna we return viâ the Laghetto Alp to (1¾ hr.) the *Monterover Inn* (4130'), and descend the steep slope of the *Cimone* (5000') to (2 hrs.) *Cal-*

318 *VII. Route 57.*   LEVICO.   *From Trent*

donazzo. Or from Lavarone we may descend by *St. Sebastian* (Inn) and (2 hrs.) *Folgaria* (3770'; Inn) to (2 hrs.) the station of *Calliano* (p. 295). The *Monte Scanupia* (7045'; fine view) may be easily ascended from Folgaria or St. Sebastian in 3 hrs. — To ASIAGO (p. 319). From Lavarone a fine new road leads viâ (4½ M.) the *Laghetto Alp* (see p. 217) to (3 M.) **Vésena** (4620'; Inn), beautifully situated amid luxuriant Alpine meadows. [Excursions may be made hence to the *Cima Vesena* or *Pizzo* (6250'; 1½ hr.), the *Cima Mandriola* (6715'; 2 hrs.), *Mte. Verèna* (6625'; 3 hrs.), and *Luserna* (1½ hr.).] Beyond **Vésena** we proceed through the *Val d'Assa*, viâ *Termine* (Inn; Italian frontier), *Ghertele, Rastello,* and *Camporovere,* to (18 M.) *Asiago* (p. 319).

Before reaching (5½ M.) **Levico** (1655') we pass the *Baths* of the same name *(Curhaus; Bellevue; Deutscher Hof; Hôtel Comfortable; Concordia; Corona)*, with sulphur-springs, much patronized by Italians, especially in August. The chief spring rises at the little *Vitriolo Bath* (4590'), situated on the slope of the *Fronte*, a hill to the N. (bridle-path, 3 hrs.).

At this point begins the **Val Sugana** proper. Numerous villages testify to the fertility of the valley, in which mulberries and vines are chiefly cultivated, and many of the surrounding heights are crowned with ruined castles.

The road skirts a hill crowned with the large château of *Selva*, passes *Novaledo* (beyond which, on the slope to the left, lies *Roncegno*, with a well-appointed bath-house), and leads over the *Brenta* to (8½ M.) —

21 M. **Borgo di Val Sugana** (1230'; *Hôt. Val Sugana; Croce*), with 4380 inhab., the capital of the valley, and seat of the local authorities. On a height to the N. rises the château of *Telvana* (still partly occupied), once the seat of the powerful counts of Caldonazzo, high above which are the remains of the castle of *S. Pietro.* To the S. are the precipices of the *Cima Dieci* and the *Cima Dodici* (7645').

A road leads from Borgo to the S. to (1½ M.) *Olle*, at the entrance to the **Val di Sella**, in which (2 hrs.) lies a Stabilimento di Bagni, with a large stalactite cavern near it. The *Cima Dodici* (7615'), fatiguing but repaying, is ascended from Olle in 4-5 hrs. (guide).

FROM BORGO TO PRIMIERO (9-10 hrs.). The road (diligence to Castel Tesino twice daily in 3½ hrs.) leads viâ *Strigno*, on the N. side of the *Val Chiepina*, to (8 M.) **Pieve Tesino** (2700'; *Hôtel Tesino*), descends into the *Val Tesino*, crosses the *Grigno*, and remounts to (2 M.) *Castel Tesino* (2920'; Inn), where the women wear a picturesque costume. A bridletrack leads hence, round the E. slopes of the *Mte. Agaro* (6770'), to the (2½ hrs.) *Osteria del Brocon* (5260'), a little below the *Brocon Pass*, descends by *Ronco* to (2 hrs.) *Canale S. Bovo* (p. 326), and then crosses the *Gobbera* saddle (p. 326) to (3 hrs.) *Primiero* (p. 326).

The road now follows the left bank of the *Brenta*. It crosses the broad gravelly channel of the *Ceggio*, and then, beyond (1½ M.) *Castelnuovo*, the *Maso*, which descends from the *Val Calumento*. At the (1½ M.) *Alle Barricate Inn* the road into the *Val Tesino* diverges to the left (see above). On the wooded rock to the N. is the handsome château of *Ivano*, the property of Count Wolkenstein-Trostburg. *Ospedaletto* is passed on the left. Skirting the base of the *Cima Lasta* (5495'), we next reach (7½ M.) *Grigno* (855'; Alb.

Morandelli), where the *Grigno* issues from the Val Tesino. The Austrian custom-house is at (3 M.) *Le Tezze*, the Italian about 1 M. beyond it.

38 M. **Primolano** (730'; *Posta*, poor), a poor village, 2¹/₄ M. farther on, is remarkable for its confined situation. Severe engagements took place here in 1866 between Italian and Austrian troops. A road to the N., on which a large fort is being built, ascends in windings to Feltre and Belluno (p. 354), while the Bassano road enters the *Canale di Brenta, a wild and imposing ravine, bounded by lofty precipices. In a rocky grotto beyond the village, 100' above the road, is perched the old fortress of *Covolo*, a mediæval stronghold, which is now inaccessible. On the opposite height (4¹/₂ M. from Primolano) lies the large village of *Eneyo* (2430'; Tre Pini; Aquila), with a ruined castle of the Scaligers, whence a bridle-track leads to (5 hrs.) Asiago (see below). About 3 M. farther on the road crosses a handsome bridge over the *Cismon*, descending from the well-wooded *Val Primiero* on the left (p. 327). The village of *Cismon* is ³/₄ M. lower down. We next pass (6 M.) *Carpanè* (Cavallino), opposite which on the right bank of the Brenta, at the mouth of *Val Frénzela*, lies *Valstagna* (510'), where broad-brimmed hats are largely manufactured.

A bridle-path to the W. ascends the wild and romantic *Val Frénzela* or *Frénzena*, viâ *Buso* (with a church and inn), *Ronchi* (road beyond this point), and *Gallio*, to (4 hrs.) **Asiago** (2975'; *Croce Bianca; Fortuna; Rosa*), the chief place of the *Sette Comuni*, with 6200 inhab., two churches, a number of handsome buildings, and a museum of prehistoric and other antiquities. The **Sette Comuni** are seven isolated German parishes, in the midst of an Italian population. In the 16th cent. the inhabitants were considered by Italian savants to be descendants of the Cimbri, who were defeated by Marius at Verona in the year 100 B.C., as no affinity could be traced between their language and the written German of the period. They are probably, however, descended from the Alemanni who flocked to Theodoric, the Ostro-Goth, after the battle of Tolbiac in 496, as their dialect bears most resemblance to the Swabian. Most of the 30,000 inhabitants of this bleak upland plain now speak Italian only. Their chief occupations are cattle-breeding and straw-hat-making. Down to 1797 the Sette Comuni formed a small republic under the protection of Venice. The nearest railway-station to Asiago is (15 M.) *Arsiero* (Alb. Bortolau), the terminus of the line to *Schio* (p. 295) and (32 M.; 2¹/₂ hrs.) *Vicenza* (see *Baedeker's N. Italy*). To reach it we proceed to the S.W. to *Canove*, cross the deep *Val d'Assa*, and, beyond (1¹/₂ hr.) *Roana*, descend viâ *Rotzo* and *Castelletto* to (2 hrs.) *Pedescala*, in the *Val d'Astico*. Here we turn to the left for (1¹/₄ hrs.) *Arsiero*. — An interesting route leads to the S.E. of Asiago over the *Campo di Mezzavia* (3380'), at the N. base of the *Mte. Bertiaga* (4440'; ascent recommended; 1 hr., through the *Val de' Bonati*), to (6 hrs.) *Bassano* (see p. 320).

From this point there is another road to (8 M.) Bassano, following the right bank of the Brenta and passing *Oliero*, *Campolongo*, and *Campese*.

A visit should be paid to the **Grotte di Oliero**, from which the *Oliero* issues in a copious stream which soon pours itself into the Brenta. The grottoes are the property of the Parolini-Agostinelli family, and tickets of admission are obtained at the Cartoleria Righetti, Piazza Vittorio Emanuele, Bassano (guide, Giov. Bonato).

At (5¼ M.) *Solagna* the ravine at length expands. At a bend in the road we obtain a view of the extensive olive-clad plain of (3¾ M.) —

57 M. **Bassano** (440'; *S. Antonio*, near the principal piazza; *Mondo*), a finely-situated town (13,700 inhab.) and seat of an archbishop, with old ivy-clad walls. The houses in the market-place still bear traces of the old façade-paintings, with which the Venetian towns used to be adorned in the 15th and 16th centuries.

Near the market is the TOWN MUSEUM (open daily, 10-3; admission at other times on payment of a fee), containing several interesting pictures by the *Da Ponte* family of artists, who are usually surnamed *Bassano*, after their native place.

The CATHEDRAL contains pictures by *Jacopo Bassano*. A little before reaching it we pass the *Piazza del Terraglio*, which affords an admirable view of the town, the river, and the Alps. Immediately beyond the bridge is a small café on the right with a balcony. — Near the N.W. gate is the old castle of the Ghibelline tyrant Ezzelino, part of which is now occupied by the 'arciprete' or dean of the cathedral (fine view).

The *Villa Rezzonica*, 1½ M. from the town, contains the Death of Socrates, a painting by Canova, and other works of art. The *Villa Parolini*, in the suburb of Borgo Leon, stands in a beautiful park.

On 8th Oct., 1796, Napoleon, having marched from Trent to Bassano in two days, defeated the Austrians here under Wurmser, four days after the battle of Rovereto. The covered wooden bridge over the Brenta occupies the site of a bridge blown up by the French on that occasion. In 1809 Napoleon erected the district of Bassano into a duchy, with which he invested Maret, his secretary of state.

Possagno (950'; *Alb. Socal*), the birthplace of *Antonio Canova* (1757-1822), is beautifully situated at the base of the *Monfenera*, 10 M. to the N.E. of Bassano. A good road leads to it by *Romano*, the birthplace of the tyrant Ezzelino, and *Crespano*. The church (*Tempio*), in the form of a circular temple, like the Pantheon at Rome, was designed by Canova, and contains his tomb and a fine bronze relief of the Entombment. The altarpiece was painted by him. Canova's house contains models and casts of his works.

RAILWAY from Bassano viâ (9 M.) *Cittadella* to (30 M.) *Padua* and (58 M.) *Venice*, see *Baedeker's N. Italy*.

58. The Valley of the Avisio (Fiemme and Fassa Valleys).

The **Valley of the Avisio**, 60 M. long, consists of three sections: the lowest, from Lavis to Val Floriana (21 M.), called the *Cembra* (or *Zimmers*); the central part, as far as Moëna (24 M.), the *Fiemme* (or *Fleims*); and the highest region, extending to Penia (15 M.), the *Fassa* (*Evas*), which is famed for its DOLOMITES (comp. p. 344).

From *Lavis* (p. 293), where the *Avisio* emerges on the plain of the Adige from a narrow rocky gorge, the valley is seldom visited (from Lavis to *Cavalese* 27 M.). The usual route is from stat. *Auer*, or stat. *Neumarkt* (p. 293), direct to the central part of the valley.

OMNIBUS from *Neumarkt* to (16¼ M.) *Cavalese* thrice daily in 5 hrs.,

PREDAZZO.   *VII. Route 58.*   321

fare 1 fl. 30 kr. (from Cavalese to Neumarkt in 3½ hrs., 1 fl.). Omnibus from Cavalese to *Vigo* every afternoon in 5 hrs. (from Vigo every forenoon in 4 hrs.). — Carriage and pair from Neumarkt to Cavalese 12, to Predazzo 20 fl.; one-horse carriage from Cavalese to Moëna 5 fl., from Predazzo to Vigo 5, to Campitello 7 (carr. and pair 8 and 12 fl.); one-horse carr. from Vigo to Campitello 3, to Penia 4, to Predazzo 4, to Cavalese 6 fl. — The shortest routes for pedestrians from the valley of the Adige into the *Upper Fassa Valley* lead from Botzen through the *Eggenthal* and over the *Caressa Pass* (p. 262), or through the *Grödner-Thal* and over the *Sella Pass* (p. 264), or lastly over the *Seiser Alp* (p. 205).

Neumarkt (920'), see p. 293. The road at first ascends rather rapidly, and on the (2 M.) first plateau of the mountain, above the ruined *Castell Feder*, unites with the road coming from *Auer* (p. 293). On the slope to the right lies the village of *Montan* (Löwe; Rose), with the well-preserved old château of *Enn*, which the new road does not touch (walkers should follow the old road through the village). The new road ascends in long windings, affording fine views of the valley of the Adige with the Kalterer See, the hills of Ueberetsch, and the Mendel, and then bends round the N. slope of the wooded *Cislon* into a green valley, through which the *Hohlenbach* (on the left) has cut itself a deep rocky channel. We first reach (4 M.) *Kalditsch* (*Inn), prettily situated; then (3½ M.) the brewery of *Fontana Fredda*, or *Kaltenbrunn* (3115'; Inn; ascent of the *Weisshorn* viâ *Radein*, see p. 262). A road to the right diverges to the German village of (2 M.) *Truden* (3770'), a summer resort of the Neumarkters. — From the (2½ M.) culminating point of the road, near *S. Lugano* (3600'), a view is obtained of the Fiemme mountains. The road now descends to the left, passing the sulphur-baths of *Carano*, above the road to the left, and *Castello* to the right, to (4½ M.) **Cavalese** (3230'; *Ancora; Uva, fair, R. 70 kr.; *Stella*; guide, Fr. Ventura), the principal place (2500 inhab.) in the *Fiemme* valley. The ancient palace of the Bishops of Trent, with a painted façade, is now a prison. The Gothic parish-church, with its marble portal of the 11th or 12th cent. and pictures by native artists, stands on a hill to the E.

The **Schwarzhorn** (*Cima di Rocca*, 7895') may be ascended from Cavalese in 4 hrs. (with guide), viâ the *Lavazze Alp* and the *Grimm Pass* (attractive and not difficult; comp. p. 262).

The *Fiemme*, or *Fleimserthal*, is an Alpine valley of moderate width, watered by the *Avisio*, which is always visible from the road. The slopes are clothed with pines, interspersed with green pastures, villages, and solitary houses. Viewed from the church-hill, the villages of (3½ M.) *Tesero*, (1¼ M.) *Panchia*, and (¾ M.) *Ziano* seem quite near, but the intervening gorges necessitate frequent circuits. Beyond Ziano we enter another reach of the valley, the broad dale of (2½ M.) **Predazzo** (3335'; *Nave d'Oro; Rosa; B. Guadagnini, guide), an excellent field for the mineralogist. The visitors' book at the 'Nave' contains autographs of many eminent men of science. To the E. opens the *Val Travignolo* (to *Primiero*, see R. 59); in the background rise the Cimon della Pala and the Cima Vezzana.

The last part of the Fiemme is a narrow, sequestered dale. The road, still level, leads by (3 M.) *Forno* to (3 M.) **Moëna** (3870'; *Capello di Ferro*; *Corona*, well spoken of), the first village in the Fassa.

FROM MOENA TO CENCENIGHE (7 hrs.). A cart-road (shadeless and uninteresting) leads through the *Val S. Pellegrino*, which opens to the E., to the (9 M.) church of *S. Pellegrino* on the **Passo di S. Pellegrino** (6270'); descent to *Falcade* (p. 357) and (4 hrs.) *Cencenighe* (p. 357). — OVER THE LUSIA PASS TO PANEVEGGIO, 4½ hrs., interesting. We follow the S. Pellegrino road for 1 M., diverge to the right, and ascend to the (2 hrs.) *Lusia Pass* (6670'), which affords a fine view (Cimon della Pala, Cima Vezzana, Colbricon, and to the W. as far as the Rosengarten and Marmolada ; in the background the Ortler and Oetzthal Alps). Descent to the S.E. (to the right, *not* the road to the left) over the *Malga di Bocche* ((p. 325), to (2 hrs.) *Paneveggio* (p. 325).

From Moëna or Vigo to *Botzen* over the *Caressa Pass*, see p. 262.

Immediately to the left rise the dolomite rocks (p. 344) of the *Rosengarten*, *Rothwand*, etc., the W. side of which presents so striking an appearance from Botzen. To the N. the *Langkofel* (10,430'), adjoined by the *Plattkofel* (9700'), rears its white summit above the valley. To the right is the *Punta di Valuccia* (8648'). The road crosses the Avisio, and at (1½ M.) *Soraga* (3945') recrosses the stream; it becomes more stony and rugged, but is practicable for carriages as far as Penia. We next reach (2 M.) *S. Giovanni*, the church of **Vigo di Fassa** (4500'; *Corona*, good cuisine; *Rosa*), the chief village in the Val Fassa, ½ M. higher up, to the left.

EXCURSIONS (guides, *Ant.* and *Gius. Dacchiesa* and *Fr. Zacchia*). The *Monte di Campedie* (6550'), the E. spur of the *Mugoni*, between the valleys of *Vajolon* and *Vajolett*, is an admirable point of view (2 hrs.; guide desirable). Beyond the village we diverge to the right from the road to *S. Giuliano*, enter a gorge, and ascend by a tolerable path. From the summit we obtain a magnificent view of the wild Vajolett valley and of the lofty pinnacles of the Rosengarten (Ital. *Vajolone*), which rise immediately opposite; to the N. are the rugged Dirupi di Larsec, and the Langkofel and Sella; E. the Punta di Valuccia and the Sasso di Mezzogiorno, to the left of which is the Marmolada, and to the right the Cima di Lasté. — The *Sasso di Dam* (8053'), on the E. side of the valley (ascended by Pozza in 3 hrs.; guide 2½ fl.), commands a more extensive prospect: to the S. is the Val Monzoni, terminated by the syenite mass of the Riccobetta; to the E. rise the Marmolada, Sasso di Valfredda, etc. — The *Rothe Wand* (9175'), ascended without difficulty from Vigo through the Vajolon Valley (3½- 4 hrs.; guide 5 fl.), commands a fine view.

FROM VIGO TO CAMPITELLO THROUGH THE VAJOLETT AND DURON VALLEYS, 8-9 hrs. (guide 5 fl.), a fatiguing but highly interesting route. The path ascends to the left from (¾ hr.) *Perra* (see below) to the (1¾ hr.) *Sojal* or *Gardeccia Chalets* (about 6865'), and thence through the wild Vajolett Valley, flanked by the huge precipices of the *Rosengarten* and the *Dirupi di Larsec*. From the rock-strewn head of the valley, the *Antermoja Pass* (about 8850'), between the *Cima di Scalieretti* (*Cima di Larsec*, 9406') and the *Kesselkogel*, leads to the N.E. to the Antermoja Valley, in which lies the (4 hrs.) little *Antermoja Lake* (8120'), grandly situated at the foot of the *Fattwand* (ascent of the *Kesselkogel* 9785', from this point in 3 hrs., with guide; comp. p. 263). About ¼ hr. farther down the Antermoja Valley narrows to an inaccessible ravine, and the path turns to the left, crosses the *Donnajoch*, the upper end of the little *Val Donna*, enters the *Duron Valley*, and reaches (2 hrs.) *Campitello* (see p. 323).

From Vigo to *Tiers* by the *Vajoletl Pass*, *Grasleiten Pass*, etc., see p. 263.

The road descends viâ *Pozza*, at the mouth of the *Val Monzoni*, which abounds in minerals, to (2½ M.) *Perra* (*G. Batt. Rizzi*). At

(1/2 M.) *Monzon* it crosses the *Sojul*, which descends from the Rosengarten through the wild *Vajolett Valley* (p. 322). We then cross the Avisio, and recross it near (1 1/2 M.) *Mazzin*, a hamlet picturesquely situated at the mouth of the *Val Antermoja* (p. 322). — 2 1/4 M. **Campitello** (4665'; *Batt. Bernard 'al Mulino'*, fair; *Valentini*), at the influx of the *Duron* into the Avisio, well situated for excursions in the upper Val Fassa.

EXCURSIONS (guides, *Giory.*, *Ant.*, *Luigi*, and *Leon. Bernard*, and *Antonio Mazzel.*) The **Langkofel** (10,430') may be ascended from Campitello viâ the *Sella Joch*, in 6 hrs. (difficult, comp. p. 264; two guides necessary, 12 fl. each). — The *Plattkofel* (9700'; 5-6 hrs.; guide 4 fl.) is laborious but not difficult (comp. p. 264).

FROM CAMPITELLO TO THE SEISER ALP (guide to the Mahlknecht 2, to Ratzes or Kastelruth 4 1/2 fl.) A bridle-track ascends the *Duron Valley* to the W., in the direction of the stream, to the (1 1/4 hr.) *Duroner Alp* (5980') and the (1 hr.) *Soricia Alp* (6425'). Here the path ascends to the right, in the direction of the pinnacles of the *Rosszähne* (8180'), to the (1 hr.) **Mahlknecht-Joch** (7255'). Thence across the Seiser Alp to (3 hrs.) *Ratzes* or (4 hrs.) *Kastelruth* (p. 265). — FROM CAMPITELLO TO GRÖDEN (the Gardena) over the **Palatsch** or **Fassa Pass** (7550'; to St. Christina, 4 hrs.). From the valley of the *Duron*, above the second bridge, we ascend to the right and proceed across the *Laris Alp* to the (2 1/2 hrs.) pass, immediately to the W. of the *Plattkofel* (ascent, see p. 264). We then descend to the *Zallinger Alp* (Rfmts.) and thence through wood, high up on the right side of the *Saltrie Gorge*, to (1 1/2 hr.) *St. Christina* (p. 264). — To TIERS across the **Tierser Alpel** (8000'), ascending to the left by the *Soricia Alp* (from Campitello 7 hrs., guide 5 fl.), see p. 262. — From Campitello to *Gröden* or *Enneberg* over the *Sella Pass*, see p. 264.

The Val Fassa now turns to the E.; the scenery is attractive and imposing. 1 1/2 M. *Gries*; 3/4 M. *Canazei* (4790'; small inn), where the path mentioned at p. 264 descends from the Sella Pass. (Guides, *Ant. Soraperra*, *Sim. Micheluzzi*, and *L. Pitscheider*.)

FROM CANAZEI TO BUCHENSTEIN (5 1/2 hrs.; guide 4 fl.). The ascent for the first 1/2 hr. is by the Sella path; we then turn to the right and ascend to the (2 hrs.) **Pordoi Pass** (7390'), between the *Cima Pordoi* (9068') on the N. and the *Cima di Rossi* (7800') on the S. [The ascent of the latter, 3/4 hr. from the pass, is recommended; splendid "View of the Marmolada, Langkofel, and Rosengarten.] Then an uninteresting descent, skirting the *Cordevole* part of the way, to (1 1/2 hr.) *Araba* (5240'; Inn) and (1 1/2 hr.) *Pieve di Livinalongo* (see p. 356).

At *Canazei* the Val Fassa turns to the S.E. About 3/4 M. farther on we pass *Alba* (*Larzonej's Inn), on the hill to the right, and then reach (3/4 M.) *Penia*, at the mouth of the *Contrin Valley* (p. 324), the last village in the Fassa, which here again turns to the E.

FROM PENIA TO CAPRILE BY THE FEDAJA PASS (5-6 hrs.), a most attractive route, chiefly owing to the immediate proximity of the huge Marmolada (guide from Campitello to Caprile 5, to the summit of the pass 2 1/2 fl., unnecessary for experts). The bridle-track ascends on the right bank of the Avisio (passing a fine waterfall after 1/4 hr.), at first gradually through the broad valley, and afterwards more abruptly on the margin of a wooded ravine, from which rise the colossal cliffs and pinnacles of the *Vernel* (10,820'), a part of the Marmolada mass. The (1 3/4 hr.) *Fedaja Alp* (6500') is a sequestered Alpine valley 1 M. long, with a few chalets (*Terra's Inn*, to the right of the track, well spoken of; farther on, a second inn, with plain fare and high charges), overshadowed on the right by the snowclad Marmolada. At the E. end of the valley we reach the small *Fedaja Lake* (6555'), with grey glacier-water, immediately beyond which is the

21*

324   *VII. Route 58.*   MARMOLADA.

Fedaja Pass (6700'; the frontier between Italy and Tyrol). On the N. is the *Mte. Padon* (8665'); fine view of the Langkofel to the W. and the huge Civetta to the S.E. from its slopes. By the *Forcella di Padon* to *Buchenstein*, see p. 356. — We now descend, at first rapidly over pastures, into the *Val Pettorina*, and skirt the huge white precipices on the E. side of the Marmolada. On the S.E. rises the pyramidal *Sasso Bianco*. On the right, in the valley far below, is the mouth of the *Val Ombretta* (see below). The path then enters the imposing "**Serrai di Sottoguda**, a ravine with huge perpendicular walls, $^3/_4$ M. long and so narrow at places that the path has to be carried on wooden galleries above the brawling stream. At the end of the ravine lies the poor village of (2 hrs.) *Sottoguda* (4280'), which was almost entirely burned down in 1881. The valley expands. We cross the *Pettorina*, pass ($^3/_4$ hr.) *Rocca* (3885'), descend steeply, and cross the Cordevole to ($^1/_2$ hr.) *Caprile* (p. 356). Travellers from Caprile to the Fedaja Pass must ascend the valley to the right (N.) beyond the Sottoguda Ravine; the footpath passes a saw-mill and traverses pastures. — Another very interesting but fatiguing path leads to Caprile by the S. side of the Marmolada, through the *Contrin Valley* (see p. 323) and over the **Forcella di Ombretta**, or **Contrin-Joch** (9050'), between the Marmolada and the *Sasso Vernale* (10,310'). Descent through the *Val Ombretta* (see above; to Caprile 10 hrs.; guide 7 fl.).

The *Marmolada is a huge group with several peaks: the W. and highest, the *Marmolada di Penia* (11,020'); the central, the *Marmolada di Rocca* (10,584'); the E. peak, the *Serauta* (9750'). The N. slope is gradual, and is covered with a vast mantle of snow, while the S. side descends in huge and almost vertical precipices. The ascent, 4 hrs. from the Fedaja Pass, presents no material difficulty to adepts. Good guides (from the pass 5 fl.), rope, etc., are necessary (guides at Canazei and Campitello, see p. 323). From the pass to the foot of the glacier 1 hr.; then along the W. margin of the glacier, which is sometimes much crevassed and troublesome, to the (3 hrs.) W. peak. (About 1 hr. below the summit, in the rocks to the left of the glacier, is a *Refuge Cavern*, fitted up by the Italian Alpine Club, but practically unavailable.) The *View from the summit is superb.

59. From Predazzo to Primiero.

Comp. Map, p. 320.

26 M. DILIGENCE in summer daily, except Sundays, at 6 a.m., in 11 hrs. (4 fl.); returning from Primiero at 5.30 p.m. and stopping for the night at S. Martino di Castrozza. One-horse carriage from Predazzo to Primiero 12 fl. two-horse-carr. 20 fl. (8 hrs.). Omnibus daily in summer from Primiero to Feltre and to Primolano. — The picturesque **Val di Cismone** is well worthy of a visit. The best places for a prolonged stay are *Primiero* and *S. Martino di Castrozza* (often crowded in summer; rooms should be ordered beforehand). Since the completion of the road from Monte Croce to Fonzaso the Primiero and Sugana valleys may be included in a very attractive round, taking four days by carriage (1st day, from Neumarkt to Paneveggio; 2nd day, to Primiero; 3rd day, to Borgo di Val Sugana; 4th day, to Trent). Carriage and pair for 4 pers., 15-20 fl. per day (at the Posta at Neumarkt or at Gennari's in Trent.).

Predazzo (3335'), see p. 321. The road follows the right bank of the *Travignolo*, at first level and afterwards ascending to the left (short-cut for walkers), to ($4^1/_2$ M.) *Bellamonte* or *Madonna di Neve*, an Alpine hamlet with three poor taverns. To the S., beyond the thickly-wooded foreground, rises a chain of bare porphyry peaks, culminating in the *Cima di Vallon*, *Cima di Lastè*, and *Colbricon*. We cross (1 M.) a gorge descending from the left, and then ascend through wood, round the rock-strewn flanks of the

Dossaccio (6024'), to (4½ M.) **Paneveggio** (5170'; *Inn*, R. 80 kr.), formerly a hospice, in a pine-clad valley. To the E. the *Cimon della Pala* (10,970') and *Cima Vezzana* (10,270') tower majestically over the intervening green hills.

The ascent of the **Cima di Bocche** (9000'; 4 hrs.; with guide) forms an interesting excursion viâ the *Malga di Bocche*; magnificent panorama of the Dolomites of the Fassa and Primiero from the top.

FROM PANEVEGGIO TO CENCENIGHE OVER THE VALLÈS PASS, 5½ hrs., (guide not indispensable). A cart-track (road in progress) follows the right bank of the *Juribrutt*, (½ hr.) passes on the right (without crossing) the (1½ hr.) bridge leading to the *Val Veneggie* and by the *Juribell Alp* to the Rolle Pass (comp. p. 357), and (¼ hr.) crosses and recrosses the stream. Then a steeper ascent to the (1 hr.) **Vallès Pass** (6680'; Italian frontier). We descend through the *Val di Vallès* to (1½ hr.) *Falcade* (4290'), in the *Val Biois*, and thence by *Forno di Canale* to (2 hrs.) *Cenenighe* (p. 357). — From Paneveggio to *Moëna* over the *Lusia Alp*, see p. 322.

The road crosses the Travignolo, and ascends in long windings (short-cuts following the telegraph-poles), through beautiful wood (supplying the masts of the Austrian navy) and afterwards over poor pastures, to the (4½ M.) **Rolle or Costonzella Pass** (6415'; rustic inn beyond the summit). The pass commands an imposing view of the *Cimon della Pala* (10,970'), a huge rocky pinnacle, the 'Matterhorn of the Dolomites', and of the jagged chain which culminates in the *Pala di S. Martino* and extends to the *Sasso Maggiore*. The crest of the *Mte. Castelluzzo* (7460'), to the E., ascended from the inn without difficulty in 1 hr., affords the best survey of the Cimon della Pala and the Cima Vezzana, with their two small glaciers and the wild ravine in which the huge slopes of detritus descend.

The road now descends gradually on the left side of a barren valley to the Alp *Fosse di Sopra*, above which we enjoy a good survey of the valley, winds down a barrier of rock, crosses the *Cismone*, and leads through wood in windings, which may be avoided by the old bridle-path, to (4½ M.) **S. Martino di Castrozza** (4800'), originally a monastery, beautifully situated in a richly wooded basin at the foot of the Dolomites (**Hotel des Dolomites* or *Albergo Alpino*, R. 1, D. 1 fl. 40 kr., 'pens.' 3½ fl.; *Alb. alla Rosetta*, moderate). Towards the S. a striking view is obtained of the Primiero valley with the chain of the Vette di Feltre; to the W. are the Cavalazza, Cima di Colbricon, and Cima di Lastè. Beautiful walks in the neighbouring woods.

Another pass, less interesting than the high-road, leads from Paneveggio to S. Martino over the **Colbricon Pass** (6270'), between the *Cima Colbricon* (8530') and the *Cavalazza* (8275'). Two small lakes are passed near the head of the pass. Descent by the Alp *Ces*.

MOUNTAIN ASCENTS from S. Martino (guides, *Mich. Bettega, M. Cordella*, and *G. Feldkircher*; comp. p. 327). To the W. are the **Tognazza** (7728') and **Tognola** (7885'), two easy peaks, ascended by the *Tognola-Alp* in 2½-3 hrs. (guide 3 fl.) and affording magnificent views. — To the E. are the *Rosetta* (9235'; 3½-4 hrs.; guide 3 fl.) and the **Cima di Fradusta** (9745'; 5½ hrs.; guide 6 fl.), both ascended by the *Rosetta Pass* (see p. 326) and presenting no serious difficulty. — More important ascents, for experts only, are the following: the **Cimon della Pala** (10,970'; guide 12 fl.; from the Rolle Pass 6-7 hrs., difficult and dangerous owing to falling stones).

first ascended by Mr. Whitwell in 1870. — The **Cima Vezzana** (10,270';
5^1/$_2$ hrs.; guide 7 fl.) is not quite so difficult. We ascend from S. Martino
viâ the *Comelle Pass* (see below) to the (4^1/$_2$ hrs.) *Passo di Travignolo*
(9920'), between the **Cimon della Pala** and the Vezzana, and thence to the
summit in ^{3}/$_4$ hr. more. The direct ascent from the Rolle Pass is dangerous on account of the frequent falls of stone. — The **Cima di Ball**
(9290'; 6^1/$_2$ hrs.; guide 9 fl.; fatiguing) is ascended by the *Val Roda* and
the *Passo di Ball* (see below). — The **Pala di S. Martino** (10,645'; 7 hrs.;
guide 14 fl.; very difficult), ascended for the first time by Herr Maurer
and the Marchese Pallavicini in 1878, is a magnificent point of view. —
The *Cima di Canali* (9600'; 8 hrs.; guide 12 fl.) and the *Sasso Maggiore* or
Sass Maor (9225'; 8 hrs.; guide 12 fl.) are also very difficult ascents.

PASSES. A toilsome but grand route (guide indispensable) leads from
S. Martino to the N.E. over the *Pala Alp* and the (3 hrs.) **Rosetta Pass**
(8375'), between the Cimon della Pala and the Rosetta, to the (20 min.)
Comelle Pass (8545'); we then descend rapidly into the *Val delle Comelle*,
and through the fine gorge of the *Liera*, passing (3 hrs.) the beautifully
situated village of *Gares* (4000'; Rfmts. in the lowest cottage), to (1^1/$_2$ hr.)
Forno di Canale (p. 357; to Cencenighe 2 hrs. more; guide 8 fl.). Instead
of descending the Val delle Comelle to Gares, we may cross to the E. by
the **Forcella Gesuretta** (about 6230'), to the *Val di S. Lucano*, *Taibon*, and
Agordo (12 hrs. from S. Martino; guide 9 fl.). — Another route leads from
S. Martino over the arduous **Passo di Ball** (about 7870'), between the Pala
di S. Martino and Cima di Ball, to the *Val Pradidali* (p. 327; to Primiero,
6^1/$_2$ hrs.; guide 5^1/$_2$ fl.). The route **over the Passo di Pradidali** (8800'; to
Primiero 8 hrs.; guide 6 fl.) is also grand though fatiguing; comp. p. 327.

A bridle-path (guide desirable) leads from S. Martino to the W. viâ
the *Tognola Alp* to the *Tognola Pass* (6520'), and descends through the *Val
Sorda* to (6 hrs.) **Cauria** (2755'; Inn), in the *Val di Canale*, at the N.E.
base of the *Cima d'Asta* (9330'; which may be ascended through the *Val
Regana* in 6 hrs.; guide 7 fl.; Giuseppe Loss of Cauria, nicknamed
'Tabarro'). A rough road descends the Val Canale, which is watered by
the *Vanoi*, past a lake formed by a landslip in 1819-23, to (2 hrs.) **Canale
S. Bovo** (2475'; *Albergo Borso*, tolerable). Thence over the *Brocon Pass* to
Castel Tesino, see p. 318; to *Imer* in the Primiero Valley (p. 327) over the
saddle of *Gobbera* (3260'), 2 hrs. The valley farther down contracts
into an almost impassable ravine, and joins the Val di Cismone below
Monte Croce Pontet (p. 327).

The road follows the right side of the Cismone valley, at first
through wood, passing a tavern, and afterwards runs on the shadeless
hillside, high above the river. Opposite tower the rocky pinnacles
of the *Rosetta* (9235'), the *Cima di Ball* (9290'), and the *Sass
Maor* (*Sasso Maggiore*, 9225'); to the S. lies the beautiful Val
Primiero with the *Vette di Feltre*, and to the right the *Monte Pavione*. Finally the road descends in windings (footpath shorter)
and crosses the Cismone to (6 M.) *Siror* and (1 M.) **Fiera di
Primiero** (2345'; *Albergo Gilli*, moderate; *Aquila Nera*, kept
by the brothers Bonetti), the capital of the valley, which once
possessed valuable silver-mines, with an early-Gothic church and
several interesting old houses (such as the castellated court-house
near the church). The environs are rendered extremely picturesque
by the contrast between the rich southern vegetation (maize, chestnuts, mulberries, etc.) and the huge barren peaks of the Dolomites
on the N.

The best °SURVEY of the charming valley is obtained from a cross,
10 min. above the village, to the W. (Ascend to the right by the church,
and keep to the left where the path forks.) Below, in the richly-culti-

to Primiero. MTE. PAVIONE. *VII. Route* 59. 327

vated valley, lie the villages of La Fiera, Tonadico, and Transacqua; on the left towers the Sass Maor or Sasso Maggiore, and farther back the Pala di S. Martino; in the middle distance, beyond the picturesque Castel la Pietra, rise the Rocchetta, Tacabianca, and Cima d'Oltro; farther to the right, above Transacqua, is the Sasso della Padella; and to the S., in the background, are the Vette di Feltre, with the fine pyramid of the Mte. Pavione.

EXCURSIONS (guides: *Enrico Taufer, Girol. Trotter, Mich. Cordella*, and *Giac. Feldkircher*; comp. also p. 325). To the (1 hr.) **Castel la Pietra** (3330'), see p. 358; 1/4 hr. farther to the N., in the *Val di Canali* (see below), is a shooting-lodge of Count Welsperg, commanding an excellent survey of the lofty Dolomites at the head of the valley. — By Siror (see p. 326) to the (2½ hrs.) picturesque **Calaita Lake** (5220'), and thence in 2½ hrs. to the top of the *Cima d'Arzon* (7080'), a splendid point of view. — The **Val della Noana**, a wild and imposing ravine, which joins the valley of the Cismone at Imer (see below), is sufficiently seen by ascending the cart-track through it for 1 hr. Farther on it forks into the *Val Fonda* on the right, through which an unattractive route leads over the *Passo della Finestra* to Feltre (p. 354), and the *Vall' Asinozza* on the left, at the head of which rise the *Piz di Sagron* (8110') and the *Sasso di Mur* (8380'; see p. 358). — The *Monte Pavione* (7650') may be ascended by *Imer Mezzano* (see below) and the *Agnerola Alp* (5165'; good quarters) in 5½-6 hrs. (guide 5 fl.). It affords a superb view of the Dolomites on the N., and of the plain as far as the Adriatic on the S. Rich flora. — The **Val di Pradidali** (sometimes erroneously called 'Pravitale'), a wild glen containing a small lake (7050') surrounded by lofty limestone peaks, is reached by ascending to the left from the Val di Canali (4½ hrs. from Primiero). On the N. side of it tower the *Cima di Canali* (9600'), and the *Cima di Fradusta* (9745'; on the N.W., the *Pala di S. Martino* (10,645'); on the W. the *Cima di Ball* (9220') and the *Sasso Maggiore* (9225'). — Toilsome passes lead hence over the *Passo di Ball* (p. 326) to S. Martino; over the *Passo di Pradidali* (8860') to the plateau, and thence either to the W. by the *Rosetta Pass* to S. Martino, or to the N. by the *Passo di Comelle* to Gares (p. 326); and over the *Passo di Canali* (*Forcella d'Angoraz*, about 8200') to the *Val d'Angoraz*, the *Val di S. Lucano*, and *Agordo* (p. 358). — Across the Gobbera saddle to *Canale S. Bovo* and *Cauria* (3½ hrs.; guide 2½ fl.), see p. 326.

FROM PRIMIERO TO AGORDO over the *Cereda Pass* (7 hrs.; guide 6 fl.), see p. 358. — To FELTRE (8 hrs.) omnibus twice daily in summer (to PRIMOLANO once daily). The road leads through the valley of the Cismone, viâ *Mezzano* and (1 hr.) *Imer*, to the (1½ hr.) custom-house of Primolano or *Pontet* (1230'; Inn), on the Italian frontier. Thence a fine new road, in many places hewn in the rock, leads along the wild and romantic gorge of the Cismone on the left bank of the stream. At (1½ hr.) *Moline* we cross, and 1½ hr. farther on recross the stream, and finally descend, viâ (½ hr.) *Fonzoso* (1080'; *Angelo; Due Mori*), to (½ hr.) *Arten*, on the road from Feltre to *Primolano* (p. 355). — To BORGO DI VAL SUGANA over the *Brocon Pass* (10 hrs.), see p. 318.

60. From Franzensfeste to Villach. Pusterthal.

Comp. Maps, pp. 320, 334.

132 M. RAILWAY in 7½-8½ hrs. Passengers should take refreshments with them, as there are few restaurants on this line. Dinners (1 fl.) are handed into the carriages at Lienz, if previously ordered through the guard (comp. p. 112).

The **Pusterthal**, one of the longest valleys in Tyrol, consists of the valleys of the *Rienz* and the upper *Drave* or *Drau*, separated by the low saddle of Toblach. The W. part is German, while to the E. of Lienz the inhabitants and the names of the places betray indications of Slavonic origin. The scenery is pleasing, but has no claim to grandeur except at Franzensfeste, near Lienz, and at a few other points. Between Niederdorf and Liena the bold forms of the Dolomites are visible from time to time beyond the green hills enclosing the valley. The Ahrenthal, Iselthal, Mollthal, and other lateral valleys afford many beautiful excursions; and, since the completion of the railway, the Ampezzo valley, in particular, has attracted numerous visitors.

Franzensfeste (2460'), see p. 224. The train passes through part of the fortifications and crosses the *Eisak* by an iron bridge supported by six piers of granite, 200 yds. in length, and 260' above the impetuous torrent in the gorge beneath. About 100' lower is the *Ladritsch Bridge* (p. 224). Beyond *Aicha* is a tunnel 275 yds. long, beyond which we obtain a view of the *Schlern* to the S. (p. 266). At (3 M.) *Schabs* the line passes through the watershed between the Eisak and *Rienz* by means of long cuttings, turns to the left into the Pusterthal, and is carried along the hill-side by a lofty embankment. On the right is *Rodeneck*, the ancestral castle of the counts of Wolkenstein-Rodeneck. To the left on the hill lies the village of *Spinges*. — 5 M. **Mühlbach** (2540'; *Sonne*, with garden; *Linde*, well spoken of), a considerable village in a sheltered situation at the mouth of the *Valser Thal*, is a summer-resort. Opposite, on the left bank of the Rienz, are the (1 1/4 M.) small baths of *Bachgart*.

Pleasant walk through the **Valser Thal**, past the *Valser Bad*, to (6 M.) *Vals* (Maierwirth). Back by the high-lying village of *Meransen* (4640'; rustic inn), with a fine view of the Dolomites to the S. — Ascent of the **Gitsch** (8216'), by Meransen in 4 hrs. (with guide), interesting and not difficult.

Beyond Mühlbach the valley contracts to a narrow ravine called the *Mühlbacher Klause*, once defended by fortifications, which were destroyed by the French in 1809. Beyond it the valley expands. — 9 M. **Vintl** (2495'), near the village of *Unter-Vintl* (*Post), at the mouth of the *Pfundersthal*.

A road leads through the **Pfundersthal** to *Weitenthal* and (2 1/2 hrs.) *Pfunders* (3790'; Inn), a prettily-situated village. Thence across the *Weitenberg-Alpe* and over the *Pfunders-Joch* to (6 hrs.) *Kematten* in the *Pfitscher-Thal*, see p. 188; to *Lappach* (and *Taufers*) by the *Passen-Joch*, *Riegler-Joch*, or *Eisbruck-Joch*, see p. 189. — The Eidechsspitze (8960'), ascended from *Ober-Vintl*, viâ *Terenten* (3940'; Inn) and the *Terenten Valley*, in 5-6 hrs. (guide), is somewhat fatiguing; beautiful view, embracing the Zillerthal and Riesorferner snow-mountains, the S. Limestone Alps, etc.

The train crosses the Rienz, which at this point as well as farther up, at Bruneck and Welsberg, caused great devastation by inundations in the autumn of 1882. To the left are the villages of *Ober-Vintl*, *St. Sigmund* (where some trains stop), and *Kiens*. In a valley to the right lie the small sulphur-baths of *Illstern*. 14 M. *Ehrenburg*, with a château of Count Künigl. Several deep cuttings. Near *St. Lorenzen* (*Rose; Mondschein; Löwe) the train crosses the *Gader*, which descends from the Enneberg (p. 340). To the left is the dilapidated monastery of *Sonnenburg*; on a rock to the right the *Michaelsburg*.

19 1/2 M. **Bruneck** (2670'; *Post*; *Stern*; *Sonne*; *Krone*; *Hirsch*; *Bräu*; *Lamm*; *Hôtel Niederbacher*, at the station, well spoken of; wine at *Jos. Maier's*), the chief place in the W. Pusterthal, charmingly situated at the mouth of the *Tauferer Thal* (p. 337), with two bathing-establishments, is much frequented in summer. The *Château*

(2880'), formerly a seat of the Prince-Bishops of Brixen, is now a prison; the tower (visitors admitted) affords a fine survey of the environs. The *Church*, destroyed by a fire in 1850, and rebuilt in the Romanesque style, contains frescoes by Mader and altarpieces by Hellweger.

WALKS. To the S.W., through the new grounds on the *Kuhbergl*, to the (1/2 hr.) *Kresswasserl* (an excellent spring) and (1/2 hr.) *St. Lorenzen* (good inns); we may then visit the adjacent *Sonnenburg* and *Michaelsburg* (see p. 328), and return by the high-road (2 M.) or along the river viâ *Stegen*. The *Kaiserwarte*, a wooden view-tower on the top of the *Kuhbergl* (3295'; 1/2 hr.), commands a fine panorama. — To the S.E. by (2 M.) *Reischach* (°Kappler), at the base of the Kronplatz (see below), to the (25 min.) *Lamprechtsburg*, picturesquely situated above the gorge of the Rienz, and now occupied by peasants; back by the new promenade on the left bank of the Rienz (1/2 hr.). — On the right bank of the Rienz to (1/4 hr.) *Dietenheim* (Bock, near the church), affording a fine view of Bruneck (from the crucifix); to (1/2 hr.) *Aufhofen*; to the (11/2 hr.) hill of *Amelen*, with fine views; to the (13/4 hr.) castle of *Kehlburg* (p. 337).

MOUNTAIN ASCENTS (guides. *Georg Engl*, *Joh. Lindner*, and *Fr. Schuster* of Bruneck, *Franz Taferner* of Olang, and *Silv. Zingerle* of Gaiselsberg). The ascent of the °**Kronplatz** (Romanic, *Plang de Corones*; 7444'), which rises to the S., is very attractive, whether made viâ *Reischach* and the *Ochsen-Alpe* (accommodation; shortest route, but rather steep) in 4 hrs., or viâ the beautifully-situated little baths of *Schartl* and the *Kappler Alpe* in 41/2 hrs. (guide desirable, 31/2 fl.). The expedition is shorter and easier from *Olang* (see below); from the station we ascend by *Mitter-Olang* to (1/2 hr.) *Gaiselsberg* (°Inn), from which the top is reached in 21/2-3 hrs. (guide 11/4-2 fl.). [About 1/2 hr. below the top, on the Enneberg side, is a refuge-hut, with beds.] The °View embraces the *Tauern*, the Rieserferner, Zillerthaler Ferner, and Oetzthaler Ferner on the N., and the Limestone Alps from Ampezzo to the Schlern on the S. The lower, N.E. peak is named the *Spitzhörndl* (7014'). — The descent may also be made over the *Furkel* to (2 hrs.) *St. Vigil* in the Enneberg; comp. p. 341.

The **Rammelstein** (8136') may be easily ascended from *Oberwielenbach* (°Mayr), 6 M. to the N.E. of Bruneck, in 3 hrs.; with guide (Joh. and Georg Niederwolfsgruber). — The *Grosse Windschar* (10,010'; 71/2 hrs.), viâ *Bad Mühlbach*, see p. 337.

The train crosses the Rienz, describes a wide curve round the town (fine glimpse of the Tauferer Thal with the Löfflerspitze, Frankbachsattel, and Keilbachspitze), and passes through a tunnel 350 yds. long, opposite the *Lamprechtsburg* (see above). At *Percha* it recrosses the stream, the left bank of which it follows by means of cuttings and viaducts. Beyond two more tunnels we reach (281/2 M.) **Olang** (3320'), the station for the villages of *Nieder-*, *Mitter-*, and *Ober-Olang*, situated at the mouth of the *Gaiselsberger Thal*. (Ascent of the *Kronplatz*, see above; over the *Furkel* to *St. Vigil* in the Enneberg, see p. 341.) Opposite, by the village of *Rasen*, opens the *Antholzer Thal*, from which rise several peaks of the Rieserferner. To the S. are the slopes of the *Hochalpe* (8408').

Antholzer Thal. From the station at Olang we cross the Rienz by the imposing new *Windschnur Bridge* to the (3/4 M.) *Windschnur Inn* (carriages). Thence a good road leads by (11/2 M.) *Nieder-Rasen* and (1 M.) *Ober-Rasen* to the (3 M.) unpretending *Antholzer Bad*, or *Salomonsbrunnen* (3585'), the water of which is a cure for female ailments. The road continues thence to (11/2 M.) *Niederthal*, or *Antholz*, and (3 M.) *Mitterthal*, or *Gassen* (4070'; °Brugger, unpretending; guides, Ant. Messner and Jos. Rohracher), where it terminates. (Passes hence into the Mühlbacher Thal and

Reinthal, see pp. 337, 339.) Beyond Mitterthal a path leads over meadows and through wood (guide advisable; to St. Jakob 2½ fl.) to the (1½ hr.) beautiful *Antholzer See* (5390'), at the base of the *Riesenferner (Wildgall, Hochgall, Ohrenspitzen;* see p. 339). The path (better on the S. side) skirts the lake for ½ hr., ascends past the small *Obersee* (6600') to the (1¼ hr.) *Stalter Sattel* (6740'), and then descends past (5 min.) the small *Stalter See* (6600') into the *Stallerthal*, the S.W. ramification of the *Defereggerthal*, and to (1½ hr.) *Erlsbach* (5055'; Stumpfer) and (1¼ hr.) *St. Jakob* (see p. 139).

Beyond Olang the train runs in numerous windings high up on the left side of the deep ravine of the Rienz, which wrought great havoc here in 1882, and passes through a short tunnel, which had to be constructed in a tubular form owing to the loose nature of the soil. 33 M. **Welsberg** (3585'; *Löwe; *Lamm; Rose*), is pleasantly situated at the mouth of the *Gsieser Thal*. (To the Deferegger-Thal viâ the *Gsieser Thörl*, see p. 139.) To the N. rise the ruins of *Welsberg* and *Thurn;* to the S., opposite the station, are the unpretending baths of *Waldbrunn*.

[About 2 M. to the E., halfway to Niederdorf, the attractive **Pragser Thal** opens to the right (road to it passing under the railway). A road leads from Niederdorf round the foot of the *Golser Berg* (or we may take the shorter path diverging to the left at the railway-station, crossing the hill, and passing the *Lercher Höfe*) to the *Gräberhof* (fine view) and the (3 M.) *Hofstatt* in *Ausser-Prags*, where the valley divides into *Ausser-* or *Alt-Prags* on the left (E.), and *Inner-* or *Neu-Prags*, on the right (W.). About 1½ M. up the E. branch of the valley (road) lie the baths of **Alt-Prags** (4520'; *Inn*), amidst superb scenery (E., the Sarnkofel and Dürrenstein; S., the lofty Hohe Gaisl; W., the Rosskofel group). Pleasant walk to the (20 min.) *Heinrichshöhe*.

Ascent of the *Sarnkofel* (7738'; guide, not indispensable, 2½ fl.) from this point, easy and attractive, see p. 332. The *Rosskofel* (8190'; 4 hrs.; guide 3½ fl.), ascended viâ the *Gufidaun Alp*, is interesting; the descent may be made to the Pragser Wildsee. Robust mountaineers may proceed (a fine route) viâ the Gufidaun Alp and Rossalp to the *Forcella di Cocadain*, to the E. of the Seekofel, and descend viâ Fosses to the Ampezzo road (guide 5 fl.; comp. p. 347). — A footpath leads from Alt-Prags along the left bank of the brook and skirting the foot of the hill to Neu-Prags. — To **Schluderbach** an easy and very fine route crosses the *Plätzwiesen* (1½ hrs.; guide 3 fl., not indispensable). A road (marked with red) leads past the base of the *Heimwaldkofel* and up the valley for 1 hr., and a cart-track then ascends a wooded slope to the left (with the Daumkofel and the Schwalbenkofel on the right) to the extensive pastures of the (2 hrs.) **Plätzwiesen** (6490'; Hôtel *Dürrenstein*, destroyed in winter 1887-88, and now being rebuilt), at the N. base of the *Dürrenstein* (8300'), which may be easily ascended by a new path in 2 hrs. (see p. 346). On the right rises the imposing *Hohe Gaisl* (Rothwand, 10,280'). Our route crosses the plateau. Before us rise the *Cadini* (p. 345), and the huge *Cristallo* afterwards appears in the foreground. At the (1½ hr.) end of the pastures the path crosses a low rocky saddle. It then descends to the left, past the *Knollkopf* (7218'), into the *Seelandthal*, and through wood (keep to the left) to (1 hr.) **Schluderbach** (p. 345).

Through the *Inner-Prags*, or W. arm of the valley, a tolerable road leads from the Hofstatt (see above), viâ the hamlet of *Schmieden* (3400'; Inn), to the unpretending baths of (2 M.) **Neu-Prags**, or

Mösel-Bad (4335'; *Inn); opposite, on the left bank of the Pragser Bach, lies the village of *St. Veit*. Thence by a good path, crossing the brook 8 min. above the baths, in 3/4 hr. to the beautiful, dark-green *Pragser Wildsee (4850'), in which the huge *Seekofel* (9215') is reflected (boats for hire). On the left rise the precipitous sides of the *Herrstein* (8366'), to the right is the *Schwarzberg* (10,250').

The ascent of the *Seekofel (9215'; 4 hrs.) from the Pragser Wildsee, through the *Nabige Loch* and the *Ofen*, is toilsome (comp. p. 341; guides, Andr. Müller and Joh. Steiner of Inner-Prags).

A path leads on the wooded W. bank to the (1/4 hr.) S. end of the lake. To the W. of this point opens the *Grünwald-Thal*, through which an uninteresting route leads over the *Kreuzjöchl* to (4 hrs.) *St. Vigil* in the Enneberg. Leaving the lake, this route leads past the *Grünwaldhütte* and *Altkaserhütte* to the (2 hrs.) *Hochalpe* (retrospect of the Rosskofel, Seekofel), Ricegon; to the S., Mte. Sella di Senes), and the (1/2 hr.) *Kreuzjoch* (7395'), with a small lake, between the *Paratsch* on the left and the *Dreifingerspitze* on the right. We then descend through the narrow *Vogedura-Thal* to (1 1/2 hr.) *St. Vigil* (p. 340).]

The train crosses the *Pragser Bach* (to the right the Hohe Gaisl, p. 347), and ascends slightly to (35 1/2 M.) **Niederdorf** (3800'; *Schwarzer Adler*, D. 1 fl. 30 kr.; *Post; Bräu*, moderate), a large village in a broad green valley, much resorted to in summer. About 1/2 M. to the E. is the *Weiherbad* (*Pension Moser).

WALKS. To *Bad Maistatt* (4080'), on the hill-side, 1/2 hr. to the S.E., with pleasant wood-walks. By Weiherbad to (3/4 hr.) *Gratsch* (Fink's Inn) and to (1/4 hr.) *Toblach* (see below.) To (40 min.) the village of *Aufkirchen* (4340'), to the N., on a terrace of the *Eggerberg*, and to the (1/2 hr.) *Wetterkreuz*, with an admirable view of the Prags and Höhlenstein Dolomites. The (3/4 hr.) *Thaler Bauer* (refreshments) and the *Schöne Aussicht* (1/2 hr. farther on) are also good points of view. — To the *Pragser Thal*, see p. 330 (one-horse carr. to Alt-Prags or Neu-Prags and back 3 1/2, to both places and back 4 1/2 fl.; hirers should take care that the charge for their luggage is included in the fare).

At *Gratsch* the train crosses the Rienz, which descends from the Höhlensteiner Thal, for the last time, and soon reaches the *Toblacher Feld* (3950'), the watershed between the Rienz and the Drave, the highest point on the line, and the boundary between the upper and lower Pusterthal. 38 M. **Toblach** (*Südbahn-Hotel Toblach*, a large house, opposite the station, finely situated close to the wood, R. from 1 fl. 20, D. 1 fl. 80 kr., board 2 1/2 fl.; *Hôtel Ampezzo*, at the station, R. 3/4-1 fl.). The village (*Mutschlechner's Inn*, R. 60 kr., 'pens.' 2 1/2-3 fl.; *Schwarzer Adler; *Goldenes Kreuz*), with its handsome new church, lies 3/4 M. to the N. of the station. Traces of gilding may still be seen in one room of the old château of Emp. Maximilian I., now occupied by a cobbler. The road into the Ampezzo valley (p. 344) here diverges to the S. Fine view from Toblach of the narrow mouth of the valley guarded by pinnacles of dolomite (to the left the Nennerkofel, to the right the Sarnkofel and Dürrenstein), with the Cristallino in the background.

EXCURSIONS from Toblach (guides, Alois Kühbacher, Jos. Obexer, Jos. Schacher, etc.). A picturesque walk follows the new path by the *Toblacher Wildbach* to the (3/4 hr.) *Silvester Thal*, where large embankments have been constructed to prevent floods; as we return we have a pretty view of the Dolomites. On the *Ehrenberg*, the wooded spur of the *Haselberg*, to the E. of Toblach, are laid out the pleasant shady grounds of the '*Kaiser-Park*', affording charming views of the Toblacher Feld and the Dolomites of Prags and Ampezzo. — The *Wetterkreuz* (¹/₂hr.), *Gratsch*, *Maistadt*, *Aufkirchen*, *Niederdorf*, see p. 331. To *In die Rienz*, a brewery ³/₄ M. to the W. of the station. To the (²/₄ hr.) *Toblacher See* (p. 344). To the (1 hr.) *Hackhoferkaser*, at the foot of the Neunerkofel, etc. — The ascent of the *Pfannhorn* (8730') is easy and interesting (4-5 hrs.; guide for the inexperienced 3¹/₂ fl.; provisions necessary). A bridle-path (imperfectly marked; in doubtful cases, keep to the left) ascends gradually over the gently-sloping Alpine pastures of *Wahlen* and *Kandellen*, with pretty view of the wooded valleys. From the summit excellent view of the Dolomites (Dreischusterspitze), the Tauern, the Zillerthal Alps, etc. (see the indicator). — The ascent of the *Sarnkofel* (7730'; 3¹/₂ hrs.; guide 2¹/₂ fl.), which rises about ³/₄ M. beyond the Toblacher Wildsee, is made with some difficulty through wood and over steep slopes of debris. It commands a splendid view of the Pusterthal, the Tauern, the Rieserferner and Zillerthal snow-mountains, and the S. Limestone Alps. Descent to *Alt-Prags* (p. 330).

The train now descends, passing the insignificant source of the Drave on the right, to (43 M.) **Innichen** (3825'; *Bär*, R. 60 kr.; *Schwarzer Adler*; *Goldner Stern*, 'pens.' with R. 2 fl. 50-2 fl. 70 kr.; Pension *Saxonia*; *Rössle*; *Sonne*), another summer-resort, prettily situated at the mouth of the *Sextenthal*. The Romanesque *Stiftskirche*, dating from the 13th cent., possesses an interesting and very ancient portal. To the S.E. rises the *Helm* (see below), a fine point of view; to the S. are the lofty *Dreischusterspitze* (10,365') and other Sexten Dolomites.

[The road into the **Sexten-Thal** (one-horse carr. to Bad Moos 3¹/₂ fl., two-horse 6 fl.; diligence from Sexten to Sillian daily in 1 hr.) turns to the S. at the Bär Inn, crosses the *Sextner Bach*, and ascends on the left bank. After 1¹/₄ M. a road diverges to the right to the (¹/₂ M.) *Innicher Wildbad* (4370'; *Bath House*), in the woods above the main road (fine view from the Herminenhöhe, 5 min.). The road then passes the mouth of the *Innerfeld-Thal* (fine view of the Hannold on the right, and the Gsellknoten and Dreischuster on the left), crosses the *Ixenbach* at the *Sommerermühle*, and reaches (4¹/₂ M.) **Sexten** or *St. Veit* (4300'; *Post; Rose*, well spoken of), the capital of the valley. Above the village is a new fort.

The ascent of the *Helm* (7970'; 3 hrs. from Sexten; guide, not indispensable, 2¹/₂ fl., or with descent to Sillian 3¹/₂ fl.), a splendid point of view, viâ the *Tschurtschenthaler Hof* (accommodation), is recommended. (Guides, Ant. Bergmann and Alois Micheler, at Innichen; Franz, Jos., Sebast., and Veit Innerkofler at Sexten.)

[An interesting route leads through the wooded **Innerfeld-Thal**, and over the *Wildgraben-Joch*, to (6 hrs.) Höhlenstein (guide indispensable, 4¹/₂ fl.). From the Sommerermühle viâ the *Hochgriesel* to the *Unterhütte* (5400') at the end of the valley, 2 hrs.; the route then ascends to the right to the (³/₄ hr.) *Oberhütte* (6375'), which affords a fine view of the Dreischusterspitze, Schusterkofel, Schwalbenkofel, Bullköpfe, etc. Thence through the *Innicher Wildgraben*, past the *Wasserklamm*, to the (1¹/₂ hr.) **Wildgraben-Joch** (ca. 7220'), lying between the *Schwabenalpelkopf* and the *Schwalbenkofel*, and affording a capital view of the Cristallo, Sorapiss, Marmarole, Antelao, and other peaks. Descent to the Rienzthal and (1¹/₂ hr.) *Höhlenstein* (p. 344). — The ascent of the *Hochebenkofel* (9648'), from the Oberhütte, viâ the *Lückel* (8300') in 3¹/₂ hrs., presents no difficulty to the expert (guide 4½ fl.; comp. p. 347). — The *Haunold* (9645'; from the Unterhütte in 5 hrs.) is very laborious. — The *Dreischusterspitze* (10,365'), 6 hrs. from the Sextner Bad (see below), is difficult.]

About ½ hr. above St. Veit (passing the direct path to the baths, which diverges to the right, 2 min. from St. Veit) we reach *Moos*, or *St. Joseph* (4365'), where the valley forks (two new forts on the right and left). In the right arm lies (¼ hr.) the unpretending **Sextner Moosbad**, whence a beautiful walk may be taken (pleasant path on the left bank of the brook) to the ***Fischeleinboden** (4755'), which affords an admirable view of the imposing head of the valley (Gsellknoten, Dreischusterspitze, Schusterplatte, Oberbacherspitze, Einserkofel, Eilferkofel, Zwölferkofel, and Rothwandspitze); the traveller should go as far as (1 hr.) the point where the ascent begins and the valley branches into the *Altenstein-* or *Bödenthal* to the right (S.W.) and the *Bacher-Thal* to the left (S.E.).

A tolerably easy route leads through the former (route marked; guide for the inexperienced 4½ fl.), viâ the *Sextner Böden* and the small *Böden Lakes*, to the *Dreizinnenhütte* on the Toblinger Riedel (7845'); descent through the *Rienzthal* to (2½ hrs.) *Höhlenstein* (p. 344), or over the *Paternsattel* to the *Rimbianco Alp* (p. 346), or direct to *Misurina* (p. 351; from Sexten 8 hrs.). — In the *Oberbacherthal*, 3½ hrs. from Sexten, is the **Zsigmondy Hütte** (7415') of the Austrian Alpine Club, the starting-point for the ascent of the *Oberbacherspitze* (8785'; not difficult), the *Hochbrunnerschneide* (10,130'; toilsome), the *Zwölferkofel* (10,120'), and the *Eilferkofel* (10,088'; the last two very difficult). Attractive but toilsome passes lead hence to the W. across the **Oberbacherjoch** (8325'), between the Santebühel and the Oberbacherspitze, to the *Forcella di Marzon* (8890') and to the (4 hrs.) *Rimbianco Alp* (p. 346; or over the *Joch Büttele*, 8430', immediately to the E. of the Paternkofel, to the Altensteinthal and back to Sexten); to the S. over the **Giralba-Joch** (8190'), lying between the Zwölferkofel and the Hochbrunner-Schneide, in 5-6 hrs., or over the Santebühel-Joch (8230'; between the Zwölferkofel and the Santebühel) and the *Forcella Cengla* (8340'), in 7 hrs., to *Auronzo* (p. 352).

From Bad Moos the Sextenthal road ascends steeply to the (2 hrs.) Kreuzberg, or *Monte Croce* (5350'; three poor inns), where it crosses the Italian frontier. Thence to the *Val Comelico* and viâ *S. Stefano* to *Auronzo* or *Sappada*, see p. 352. From the Monte Croce to the *Schuss* or *Coltesei* (6280'), the extreme E. spur of the Rothwandspitze, a pleasant walk of ¾ hr.; fine view, to the S., of the Val Comelico, etc.]

Beyond Innichen the line follows the right bank of the Drave to (48 M.) **Sillian** (3600'; **Post; Adler*). To the N., at the mouth of the *Villgrattenthal*, stands the well-preserved castle of *Heunfels*.

EXCURSIONS (guide, *Martin Pranter*). About 1¼ M. to the W., in a sheltered position on the S. side of the Pusterthal, are the baths of *Weitlahnbrunn* (good quarters). — The *Helm (7970'), ascended from Sillian viâ the *Forscher Alp* in 4 hrs. (with guide), is an admirable point (see p. 332). To *Defereggen* over the *Villgrattenjoch*, see p. 139.

FROM SILLIAN TO KÖTSCHACH (p. 423), 13-14 hrs., unattractive. The route (at first a narrow carriage-road) ascends on the left side of the *Kartitsch-Thal*, viâ *St. Leonhard* or *Kartitsch*, to (3 hrs.) '*In der Innerst*' (4950'), the head of the pass, and the watershed between the Drave and the Gail, and descends through the *Lesachthal*, as the upper Gailthal is called, to (1½ hr.) *Ober-Tilliach* (4745'; inn) and (2½ hrs.) **Maria-Luggau** (3720'; **Post; Paternwirth*), a pilgrimage-resort. (Over the *Kofel* to *Lienz*, 6-7 hrs., see p. 336.) The road from this point to (6-7 hrs.) Kötschach is very bad, and scarcely practicable even for the lightest vehicles. It leads over very hilly ground, and is intersected by innumerable water-courses descending from the Kreuzkofel chain. From (1 hr.) *St. Lorenzen* ('Mitterberger; Werzer) the *Paralba*, or *Hochweisssstein* (8825'; 7 hrs., with guide), a splendid point of view, which is visible towards the S.E., may be ascended without much difficulty; to the Brennhütte in the *Frohnthal* 3 hrs.; thence over the *Forcella dell' Oregione* or *Hochalpeljoch* (7550') to the top 3 hrs. (descent through the *Val Sesis* to *Sappada* 3½ hrs.; see p. 352; through the Val Degano to *Forni Avoltri*, see p. 436). Guides, Lexer and Hauser of St. Lorenzen, and Salcher of Luggau. The next places are (¾ hr.) *Liesing* (Salcher), (1½ hr.) *Bierbaum* (Inn), (1¾ hr.) *St. Jakob* (*Inn), and (1½ hr.) *Kötschach* (p. 423).

The train crosses the Drave and descends to (53 M.) *Abfaltersbach* (3100'). Charming view down the valley. To the right the Lienz Dolomites with the *Spitzkofel* (8990') are seen. The scene becomes wild and lonely. The line, rebuilt since the floods of 1882, is carried along the hill-side by lofty embankments and descends rapidly (gradient 1:40). 57 M. *Mittewald*; 61 M. *Thal* (2625'). Opposite is the entrance to the wild *Gamsthal* (interesting walk of 40 min. as far as the waterfall, 230' in height, at the end of the first gorge). After traversing a defile 8 M. long the train reaches the *Lienzer Klause*, which has often been successfully defended by the Tyrolese.

66 M. **Lienz** (2190'; *Post, R., L., & A. 1 fl., B. 30 kr.; *Weisses Lamm; *Rose, with garden, R. 60-80 kr.; *Traube; *Adler; Sonne; Fischwirth, on the left bank of the Isel; *Rait. Restaurant, with beds, R. 1 fl. 30 kr.), the *Aguontum* of the Romans, the easternmost town in Tyrol, is delightfully situated near the confluence of the Drave and the *Isel*, a river three times as large. The **Lieburg**, a large edifice of the 16th cent. with two towers, in the Platz opposite the Post, is now the seat of the district-authorities. To the N.W., on the slope of the Schlossberg (20 min.), rises *Schloss Bruck*, once a seat of the counts of Lurn and Pusterthal, now a brewery (rooms let in summer); the tower affords a good survey of the town and its environs; the chapel contains some interesting old frescoes. Travellers from the N. here obtain their first view of the Dolomites, to which the chain of the *Kreuzkofel*, or *Lienz Dolomites*, separating the valleys of the Drave and Gail belongs. To the S. of Lienz, on the opposite side of the Drave, rise the wild and jagged *Rauchkofel* and *Spitzkofel*.

From Lienz to the *Iselthal* (Windisch-Matrei, Prägraten), see R. 28; to Kals, see R. 29; to the *Mölthal* (Heiligenblut), see R. 30. The interesting excursion to the *Kaiser Thörl* (p. 145) may be made in one day from Lienz by driving to Windisch-Matrei (starting at 4 a.m.), and ordering the carriage to be in waiting at Huben at 6 p.m.

WALKS. To the new *Schiessstand* on the Schlossberg, with verandah commanding a fine view (indicator); thence (or from *Schloss Bruck*) to (20 min.) the *First* and (20 min. more) the *Second Venediger View*, overlooking the valley of Lienz, with the surrounding mountains, and the Iselthal, with the Gross-Venediger in the background. To (30 min.) *Schloss Bruck* (see above; beer-garden at the foot of the hill). To (½ hr.) *Bad Leopoldsruh*, with a fine view of Lienz. To *Amlach* (*Inn, pretty garden), 1¼ M. to the S., on the right bank of the Drave. Via *Tristach* to the (1¼ hr.) pretty *Tristacher See* (2600') and to (¼ hr.) the baths of *Jungbrunn*.

MOUNTAIN EXPEDITIONS (guides, *Ant. Eyger, Joh. Pichler, Franz Gassler,* and *Jon. Gufler*).. The **Schönbüchele** (6630'), the highest peak of the Schlossberg, is easily ascended in 3½ hrs. (guide 2 fl. 70 kr.) by a new path via the Venediger Views (see p. 334) and the *Taxer-Hasl* (splendid view; route hence to the *Böse Weibl*, 1½ hr., see below). — To the (4½ hrs.). **Kerschbaumer Alp**, a fine route. We proceed by *Amlach* or *Leisach* to (1½ hr.) the mouth of the imposing "*Galizenbach-Klamm* (made accessible by paths and bridges) and follow this ravine (passing through a tunnel 230' long) to the (1 hr.) *Klammbrücke* (6050'); thence in 2 hrs. to the grandly situated Alp (5800'). Rich flora. From the Alp to the *Spitzkofel* (8790'; 3½ hrs.; guide 6 fl.) fatiguing but repaying (about ½ hr. from the summit is the *Linderhütte*, 8810', of the Austrian Tourist Club); the ascent of the *Kreuzkofel* (8825'; 3 hrs.; guide 6 fl.) is also repaying. A trying route leads from the Alp over the *Kofel* or *Zochen Pass* (7390') to (4 hrs.) *Maria-Luggau* (p. 333). — A visit to the **Laserz Lake** (7875'), in a grand mountain valley of the Kreuzkofel group, is very interesting; the route leads through the *Galizenklamm* (see above) and past the *Instein Alp* (5½ hrs.; guide 3½ fl.; new refuge-hut). — The **Böse Weibl** (8260'), an excellent point of view, is reached via the *Schönbüchele* (see above) in 5 hrs. (guide 4 fl.). — Another very attractive point is the **Schleinitz** (9520'), the S. peak of the Schober group (6½ hrs.; guide 5 fl.). The path ascends steeply to the N., via *Oberdrum* in the *Schleinitzlobel*, to the (3½ hrs.) *Feldwaibl-Alp* (6520'); thence to the top fatiguing (grand prospect). — The ascent of the Ederplan (6500'; 3 hrs.; guide 3 fl.) from Dölsach or Nikolsdorf (bridle-path) is interesting; the refuge-hut on the top was erected by Defregger the painter. — The **Hohe Zieten** (8140'; 4 hrs. from Nikolsdorf; guide 4½ fl.; 2 hrs. from the Ederplan) also commands a fine view. — The *Weisse Wand* and *Hochschober*, see p. 138.

The train crosses the Isel and traverses the broad valley of the Drave to (69 M.) *Dölsach* (Putzenbacher's Inn; road over the *Iselsberg* to the Mölltal and to Heiligenblut, see p. 149). To the right we have a picturesque glimpse of the Dolomites of the Gailthal. — 72½ M. **Nikolsdorf** (2070'), the last Tyrolese village.

The **Hochstadl** (8785'; refuge-hut), the E. peak of the Lienz Dolomites, rises here to the right (ascent by *Birkabergl* and the *Birkner Kammern* in 6 hrs., with guide, 6 fl.). — *Ederplan* and *Hohe Zieten*, see above.

The Drave and the frontier of Carinthia are now crossed. — 77½ M. **Oberdrauburg** (2000'; *Post), an unimportant place with an old château of Prince Porzia and pleasant grounds. About 1½ M. to the S. is the picturesque *Silber Fall*.

TO TOLMEZZO via *Kötschach* and the *Plöken* (12 hrs.), an interesting route. As far as Mauthen a good road (diligence daily; carriage with one horse 4 fl.); thence to Paluzza a cart-track or bridle-path, beyond it a post-road. The road, the ancient Roman route from Aguontum (Lienz) to Aquileia, crosses the Drave, and mounts a steep wooded slope to the (1 hr.) *Gailberg Sattel* (3325'). It then descends towards the S. to (1½ hr.) *Kötschach* (p. 423), and crosses the Gail to the solitary village of (25 min.) **Mauthen** (2330'; *Ortner; Huber*), the Roman *Loukium*, at the mouth of the *Valentin Valley*. The road (practicable for small vehicles for 2 hrs.) now ascends the Valentin-Thal, leading straight through the wood at the bifurcation, to (3 hrs.) the **Plöken-Alpe** (4125'; *Inn), prettily situated in a green Alpine valley. To the E. rises the *Polinigg* (7825'; 3½ hrs.; guide 4 fl.; A. Riebler of Mauthen), a fine point of view, easily ascended; to the W. the *Kollinkofel* (9220'; 4½-5 hrs. from the Plöken Inn), laborious but remunerative. Pleasant excursion (guide 3 fl.), via the *Untere* and *Obere Valentin-Alp*, the *Valentinthörl* (7000'), the *Kollinkofel*, and the *Kellerwand* (9180') to the (3½ hrs.) *Wolayer See* (6550'), grandly situated. (Route over the Wolayer Joch to *Forni Avoltri*, see p. 436.) — Then an ascent of 20 min. more, passing several Roman milestones and inscriptions, to the **Plöken Pass** (*Monte Croce*, 4500'), commanding a fine view to the S. and E. The path now descends in zigzags to the *Val Grande*, (1³/₄ hr.) *Timau* (2730'; Becc), and (1¹/₂ hr.) *Paluzza* (1985'; *Locanda Grighero*, primitive), the principal village in the *Val di San Pietro*, which is watered by the *But*. Good road hence through the picturesque valley to the small baths of *Arta* (several inns), *Zuglio* (*Julium Carnicum*, with Roman remains), and (7¹/₂ M.) *Tolmezzo* (Leone Bianco), in the Val Tagliamento, and (6 M.) *Stazione per la Carnia*, on the Pontebba Railway (p. 436).

The train crosses the Drave (passing the old fortress of *Stein* on the right), and follows the left bank. To the right of (85 M.) *Dellach* rises the *Reisskofel* (7960'). Below (89¹/₂ M.) **Greifenburg** (1900'; *Post; Assam) the Drave is navigable.

To PATERNION a direct and on the whole interesting route leads through the *Weissensee Thal* in 9 hrs. The road leads by *Waisach* to the (3¹/₂ M.) *Kreuzwirth*, where it forks, the right branch continuing to Weissbriach (see below), the left to *Gatschach* and (3 M.) *Techendorf* (Post, with baths); on the N. bank of the narrow **Weissensee** (2040'), here spanned by a bridge. At (8 M.) *Weissenbach*, at the E. end of the lake, numerous relics of lake-dwellings have been discovered. The lake should be traversed by boat, as the path on the N. bank is indifferent. Carriage-road again from Weissenbach to (3¹/₂ M.) *Stockenboi* (Fischer), with iron-mines, and through the pretty Weissensee-Thal, which opens into the valley of the Drave at *Feistritz* (p. 337). — To the GAILTHAL. Pleasant road over the *Kreuzberg* (3595') to *Weissbriach*, and through the wooded *Gitschthal* to Hermagor (p. 428), 15 M.

A path (impossible to mistake) leads to the N. from Greifenburg through the wooded *Gnoppnitz-Thal*, passing several chalets, to (5 hrs.) the *Feldnerhütte* on the *Glanzsee* (7200'), whence the **Kreuzeckspitze** (8825') may be ascended by a new path in 1¹/₄ hr. Splendid view. Descent to the S. to the *Kreuzeck-Thörl* (8070'), and then to the W. to the *Staller Alm* and through the *Wölla-Thal* to (4 hrs.) *Wöltatraten* in the Mölthal, ¹/₂ hr. from *Stall* and 1¹/₂ hr. from *Fragant* (p. 150).

92 M. **Steinfeld im Drauthal**; 97 M. *Kleblach-Lind*. — 104 M. **Sachsenburg** (1840'; *Kapeller*; *Post; Taschler*, at the station), a village at the mouth of the *Möllthal* (p. 149), partly enclosed by the Drave, and more than ¹/₂ M. from the railway. The train crosses the *Möll* and traverses the fertile plain of the *Lurnfeld*. 107 M. *Lendorf*. At *St. Peter in Holz*, in the vicinity, several traces of a Roman settlement have been discovered. On the slope to the right is the ruin of *Ortenburg*.

109 M. **Spital** (1770'; *Post; Ertl, at the station), a considerable village on the *Lieser*, with a handsome château of Prince Porzia.

To the *Millstätter See (1900'), a very attractive excursion (post-omnibus twice daily 00 kr.; one-horse carr. 2¹/₂, two-horse 5 fl.). Good new road on the right bank of the Lieser to (1¹/₄ M.) the dye-works near *Seebach*. Here we cross the Lieser and continue viâ *Seeboden* (Peterwirth) to (6 M.) Millstatt. Or (far preferable for walkers) we follow the *'Liesersteig', a beautiful walk on the left bank of the Lieser, to the dye-works, then descend to the road, cross the outlet of the lake, and follow it to the right to the (1 hr. from Spital) bath-house (Inn) at the W. end of the lake, and row thence to (³/₄ hr.) **Millstatt** (*Hôtel Seevilla*, on the lake, dear; in the village, ¹/₄ M. from the lake, *Burgstaller*; *Deffner*; *Post; Rainer*, all with gardens; *Café Marchetti*, on the lake, with bathing-establishment and rooms to let), charmingly situated on the N. bank of the lake, with lake-baths, and ancient abbey-buildings (Romanesque cloister; very aged lime-tree in the court). The lake, which is very deep and well stocked with fish, is 7¹/₂ M. long and ¹/₂-³/₄ M. broad. Fine excursions from Millstatt are the ascents of the *Millstätter Alpe* (6840'; 3¹/₂ hrs.; with guide), and the *Mirnock* (6000'; 5 hrs.; with guide; comp. p. 422), both excellent points of view.

MÜHLBACH-THAL. *VII. Route 61.* 337

From Spital to *Radstadt*, over the *Radstädter Tauern*, see R. 72. — To the N. of Spital lies (9½ M.) *Gmünd*, at the mouth of the *Mallathal* (p. 399), which is best visited from Spital (diligence twice daily in 2½ hrs.). The train crosses the *Lieser*. On the *Schüttbach*, beyond the Drave, rises *Schloss Oberaich*. 113 M. *Rothenthurm*, with a red-roofed château (to the Millstätter See, path indicated by marks, 1½ hr.); 119 M. *Paternion-Feistritz*, two villages on the right bank of the Drave, at a distance from the railway (to the Weissensee, see p. 336). 127 M. *Gunmern* (on the right the *Dobratsch*, p. 422). Then (132 M.) **Villach** (p. 422).

61. From Bruneck to Taufers. Reinthal.

Comp. Map, p. 178.

From Bruneck to Taufers (9½ M.) DILIGENCE twice daily in 2 hrs. (70 kr., coupé 1 fl.); OMNIBUS daily at 7 a.m., returning from Taufers at 5 p.m. (70 kr., coupé 80 kr.). One-horse carriage 4-5, two-horse 7-8 fl. (comp. p. 188).

Bruneck, see p. 328. The Taufers road diverges to the left, just beyond the Rienz bridge, ascends a little, and crosses the railway. Fine retrospect: to the S.E. rise the Prags Dolomites, and to the N. the Frankbachsattel and Keilbachspitze. We then descend to (1½ M.) *St. Georgen*, traverse a fertile tract, and next reach (1½ M.) *Gais* (2795'; Inn); on the hill to the right stands the *Kehlburg* (3800'). Before reaching Gais we obtain a view of the *Löffler* to the left. To the S., above the lower hills, towers the Peitlerkofel (p. 342).

About 4 M. up the **Mühlbach-Thal**, which opens here to the E., lies the village of *Mühlbach* (4795'), 2½ M. above which is the rustic *Mühlbacher Bad* (6050'). A new path (not very difficult) ascends the *Grosse Windschar* (9945') from the Bad in 4 hrs. (guide Jac. Mairhofer, nicknamed 'Auerjackl', of Gais). Fine view from the top. The *Grosse Rauchkofel* (10,230'), and the *Grosse Fensterlekofel* (10,430'), may also be ascended from this point (experience and a good guide necessary). To REIN a fatiguing route crosses the *Grubscharte* (9250') and the *Elferscharte* (9320') and descends over the *Rauchkofel Glacier* into the *Gelltthal* (7 hrs. to Rein); another rough route crosses the *Mühlbacher Joch* (9715'), between the *Morgenkofel* (10,060') and the *Schwarze Wand* (10,175'; both ascended from the col without difficulty), and descends over the *Gelltthal Glacier* to the *Gelltthal* and (8 hrs.) *Rein* (p. 339). The Gelltthal Glacier may also be crossed to the (¾ hr.) *Gänsebichljoch* (9405') and (3 hrs.) *Mitterthal*, in the Antholzer Thal (comp. p. 330).

The road crosses the Ahre and leads past the ruin of *Neuhaus* on the left to (2½ M.) *Uttenheim* (2750'), with the ruin of that name perched on the rock above (4035'). It then traverses meadows, dotted with alders, to (2½ M.) *Mühlen* (2810'), at the mouth of the *Mühlwalder Thal*, which opens on the W. (p. 188).

Beyond Mühlen the *Tauferer Boden* is entered. To the N.E., beyond the mouth of the *Reinthal*, rises the *Grosse Mosinock* (10,030'), on the slope of which lies the village of *Ahornach* (p. 338); on the left rises the precipitous *Pursteinwand* (p. 338). We next reach (¾ M.) the Gothic parish-church of *Taufers*, of the 16th cent., with the much more ancient chapel of St. Michael adjoining it. Then (³/₄ M.) **Taufers** (2830; *Post, R. 70 kr. to 1 fl., D. 80 kr.; *Elephant; Plankensteiner; Mohren), consisting of the villages of *Sand* on the right, and *St. Moritzen* on the left bank of the stream, most picturesquely situated, and commanded by the old castle of *Taufers*. This is the capital of the valley and the seat of a district-court. To the N. is the Schwarzenstein (p. 190), with the Trippach Glacier on the right and the Schwarzenbach Glacier on the left, while more to the left rise the Hornspitzen.

WALKS. [The paths are all indicated by marks; maps in the inns; guides, see p. 188.] The *Schiessstand* (rifle-range), 5 min. to the E. of the 'Post', reached by a path across the meadows, commands an unimpeded view of the valley and of the glaciers to the N. By the targets the path divides; that to the left leads to (¹/₂ hr.) *Bad Winkel*, plainly fitted up (Inn), that to the right to (¹/₂ hr.) *Kematen* (Stockmaier). By the last house of Kematen a path ascends somewhat steeply to the left over pastures, crosses a torrent, and leads in zigzags to the (¹/₂ hr.) *St. Walburgkapelle* (3370'), an excellent point of view. The lower *Reinbach Falls* (there and back 1¹/₂-2 hrs.) may be reached either by taking the path to the left of the rifle-range through the fields to *Winkel*, or from *Sand*, on the left bank of the Ahrenbach, viâ *St. Moritz* and *Winkel*. The path crosses the *Reinbach* and gradually ascends on the left bank to the (³/₄ hr.) broad *Lower Fall*, which issues from a cleft in the rocks. A path to the right ascends from the lower fall to the (20 min.) larger *Second Fall*, in a wild gorge which we view from above. We next ascend the path to the right and cross the hill to the *Schupfenboden*, a shady spot in the forest, strewn with fragments of rock, and return thence by a direct path through the wood.

Schloss Taufers (3130'; 25 min.). By the last houses of Sand we cross the bridge to the right and ascend by a rough paved track. From the (10 min.) chapel we may either ascend to the right by a zigzag path direct to the castle, or follow the broader path to the left, round the castle-rock, and approach the castle from the back. (This second path is also reached by following the Luttach road for ¹/₂ M. beyond the castle, and then ascending to the right.) The Schloss, the ancient seat of the knights of Taufers, is still in part occupied. The old chapel and an inscription on the panelling in one of the rooms are objects of interest. The windows on the S. side overlook the Tauferer Boden, and those on the N. survey the glaciers. — From the Schloss we may ascend to (1¹/₄ hr.) *Aschbach*, and follow a tolerable forest-path to the right to the high-lying church of (1 hr.) *Ahornach* (4365'), which affords an admirable survey of the Rieserferner and the Enneberg Dolomites; or from Aschbach we may go to the left to (1 hr.) *Bojen*, another striking point of view.

A picturesque walk by the Ahrnthal road leads to (1 hr.) *Luttach* (one-horse carriage 1 fl. 80 kr., comp. p. 190). The finest point is reached about ¹/₂ M. before the village. Visitors, however, should make a point of continuing to the (¹/₂ hr. farther) *Lake of St. Martin*, where extensive traces of the great inundation of 1878 are still visible.

To *Ober-Purstein*, 1¹/₂ hr. We follow the road to Bruneck for ¹/₄ M., and then ascend to the right. The clearing above the chalets affords a magnificent view of the glaciers to the N.

LONGER EXCURSIONS. Ascent of the *Speikboden* (*Speikberg*, 8235'; 4¹/₂-5 hrs.; guide 3 fl.; returning by Mühlwald or Weissenbach, 3 fl. 80 kr.), easy and attractive. The path diverges to the left from the Luttach road, after about 1 M. (guide-post), crosses the Ahrnbach, and ascends through pastures and woods, to (1 hr.) *Michelreiss*, a cluster of houses visible from below, commanding a fine survey of the Rieserferner, Hornspitzen, Schwarzenstein, etc. Thence through wood, steep at places, to the (1³/₄ hr.) *Michelreisser Alp* (good spring by the last hut; 6125'). We now ascend to the right through rhododendrons, and mount a stony slope to a basin filled with debris. Turning to the left here, we regain the path a little farther up, and ascend to the summit without difficulty in 1³/₄ hr. more. Splendid *Panorama: N., the chief range of the Zillerthal Alps, from the Weisszint to the Birnlucke; E. the Tauern, with the Simonyspitze and Dreiherrnspitze, the Rieserferner; S., the Dolomites; S.W., the Adamello and Ortler; W., part of the Oetzthaler Ferner. Below the summit, 5 min. to the W., lies the *Sonklarhütte* (7875'), commanding a good view. — Descent through the *Mühlwalder Thal*. The path descends abruptly from the chalet over pastures and loose stones, through woods, and over meadows to the (1¹/₂ hr.) upper farm of *Mitterberg* (milk). The path, generally good, here turns to the left and leads chiefly through wood, finally joining the cart-track to (2 hrs.) *Taufers* (Mühlen lies below on the right, comp. p. 188).

The arduous but interesting ascent of the **Wasserfallspitze** (8694'; 5-6 hrs.; guide 3¹/₂ fl.) may be made viâ *Kematen* (p. 338) and the *Kofel-Alp*.

The **Grosse Mostnock** (10,080'; 6¹/₂ hrs.; guide 4 fl.) is ascended by *Ahornach* (direct route, but trying), or by *Bojen* (see p. 338) and the (3 hrs.) *Bojer Alpe* (6575'), where the night is spent; next morning we ascend on the W. side, chiefly over fragments of rock, to the (3 hrs.) summit. View very striking, particularly of the Rieserferner, towering immediately opposite. Descent to (3 hrs.) *Rein* (see below), laborious.

A visit to the *****Reinthal** is recommended (to Rein 3-3¹/₂ hrs.; guide, 2 fl. 60 kr., unnecessary; provisions should be taken). Beyond St. Moritz we ascend gradually to the left through wood (by the upper path) to the (³/₄ hr.) *Plattenschmied* (3510'; Inn, plain). We then follow a paved track to the (¹/₂ hr.) *Tobel Waterfall*, cross the bridge (passing on the left the scanty remains of an old convent on the Burgkofel), and ascend through the *Reinwald*, on the left side of the brook, with its numerous falls. The path is bad at places. After 1 hr. we cross to the right bank by the second, broader bridge, and in ¹/₄ hr. reach the unpretending *Sager Inn* (4950'); to the right opens the *Geltthal* (to the *Innere Geltthal Alpe*, 1¹/₂ hr., interesting), between the *Putzernock* (8210') on the right and the precipitous *Galternock* (9570') on the left. The path then leads past the chapel, through the level valley of the *Reiner Au*, and crosses two bridges. At the bifurcation of the path we may ascend to the left to the (³/₄ hr.) church of **Rein** or **St. Wolfgang** (5240'; *Oberer Wirth*, *Unterer Wirth*, both rustic). The village lies most picturesquely at the junction of the (N.) *Knuttenthal* with the (E.) *Bacherthal*, which is encircled by the snow-clad *Rieserferner*. A good point of view is at the cross, 5 min. to the N. of the church (from E. to W., the *Stuttennock*, *Lengstein*, *Riesernock*, *Hochgall*, *Wildgall*, and *Schnebige Nock*).

ASCENTS (guides, *Jos.*, *Joh.*, and *Bartlmä Ausserhofer*). The startingpoint for most of the ascents is the **Rieserferner-Hütte** (7400'), at the foot of the *W. Rieserferner*, 3 hrs. from Rein (rough and steep path). — The **Schnebige Nock** (11,122'; 3¹/₂ hrs. from the Rieserferner Hut; guide 5 fl.), a grand point of view, is not difficult for proficients. — The *****Hochgall**, the highest peak of the Rieserferner (11,292'; 4¹/₂-5 hrs. from the hut; 7 fl.), a splendid point of view, and the **Wildgall** (10,725'; 4¹/₂ hrs.; 7 fl.) are both troublesome. — The **Stuttennock** (8986'; 3¹/₂-4 hrs. from Rein; 3 fl.) is easy and interesting. — The **Grosse Lengstein** (10,615'; from Rein in 6 hrs.; 5 fl.) is a fine point of view, and not very difficult. — The **Grosse Mostnock** (10,030'; from Rein in 4¹/₂ hrs.; 4 fl., with descent to Taufers 5 fl.) is fatiguing (see above).

PASSES. To MÜHLBACH from the *Geltthal* by the *Elferscharte* and the

Grubscharte, or by the *Mühlbacher Joch* (each about 8 hrs.; toilsome), see p. 337. — To the ANTHOLZER THAL from the *Gsellthal* (see p. 339), over the Gänsebichljoch (9400'), 8 hrs. to Mitterthal (p. 329), fatiguing; or from the Bacherthal over the Antholzer Scharte (9000'), 6 hrs. from the Rieserferner Hut to Mitterthal, steep descent (guide 6 fl.). — OVER THE KLAMML TO THE DEFREGGERTHAL (to Jagdhaus 3½, to St. Jakob 8 hrs.), not very attractive; guide unnecessary (to Jagdhaus 2 fl. 80 kr., to St. Jakob 5 fl.). From the church the path ascends the *Knutienthal* (with retrospect of the Schnebige Nock) to the (1¼ hr.) Alpine hamlet of *Knutten* (6190'), crosses the bridge, and mounts to the right, passing the small *Klamml-See*, to (1½ hr.) the Klamml-Joch (7600'). Steep descent (on the left a good spring) over pastures to the *Affenthal*, or upper Defereggerthal, and the (¾ hr.) Alpine hamlet of *Jagdhaus* (6600'; quarters). — Ascent of the *Fleischbachspitze* (10,330'; 3½ hrs. from Jagdhaus, with guide), interesting and not difficult. The *Röthspitze* (11,400'; 5-6 hrs., with guide), ascended through the *Schwarzachthal* and over the *Schwarzach Glacier*, is difficult (descent over the *Röth Glacier* to the *Röththal*, p. 191; to the Clara Hut in the Umbalthal, p. 144). — From Jagdhaus to *Erlsbach* and *St. Jakob*, see p. 139; over the *Schwarze Thörl* to *Prägraten*, see p. 144; over the *Merbjöchl*, or the *Rothenmann-Scharte*, to *Prettau*, see p. 191.

FROM REIN TO TAUFERS, interesting return-route viâ *Ahornach* (guide desirable). The route turns to the left (N.W.) at the church of Rein and ascends mountain-pastures for 1 hr., affording a fine survey of the Rieserferner. We then skirt the slope by a tolerable path, and, as soon as we obtain a view of the bottom of the valley, follow the margin of the wood to the left. The Zillerthaler Ferner are gradually disclosed to view. We now descend by a rough path to the (1¼ hr.) church of *Ahornach* (see p. 338), and viâ *Aschbach* to (1½ hr.) *Sand*.

From Taufers to *Kasern* (*Ahrnthal*), see pp. 188-191.

62. The Enneberg Valley or Gaderthal.

Comp. Map, p. 320.

From Bruneck to St. Vigil 10½ M., to Corvara 25½ M. ROADS as far as St. Vigil (one-horse carriage 8, two-horse 12 fl.) and St. Leonhard (one-horse carr. 12-15, two-horse 20 fl.); driving possible, but not pleasant, as far as Corvara. The only other means of communication in the valley are cart-tracks or bridle-paths. — The LANGUAGE spoken in the Enneberg, Gardena (p. 263), and Livinalongo (p. 356) valleys is '*Ladin*', which resembles the Romanic of the Grisons. Each of these valleys has a slightly different dialect. Philologists may consult *Joh. Alton's* 'Ladinische Idiome in Ladinien, Gröden', etc. (Innsbruck, 1879) and 'Beiträge zur Ethnologie von Ostladinien' (Innsbr., 1880); also *Vian's* 'Der Grödner u. seine Sprache' (Botzen, 1874), and *Gartner's* 'Grödner Mundart' (Linz, 1879). In the Gardena, however, Italian is gradually superseding Ladin, and the prayer-books in common use are almost all Italian. Of the twelve pastors in that valley eight preach in Italian, three in Ladin, and one in German; but every one understands and speaks German. In the Enneberg, on the other hand, German is becoming the predominant language.

By the first houses of *St. Lorenzen* (p. 328) the new road into the **Enneberg Valley**, or **Gaderthal**, diverges to the left, leads viâ *St. Martin* (the Michaelsburg to the left; p. 328) to the Gader. and ascends gradually through the deep valley of that stream to *Pulfrad* (Inn) and (7½ M.) *Lunghiega*, Ger. *Zwischenwasser* (3290'; Inn), near the junction of the *Vigilbach* and the Gader.

[The name *Enneberg* strictly belongs to the *Vigilthal*, which opens here to the S.E., and above St. Vigil is called the *Rauthal*. St. Vigil, in Ladin *Plung da Marò* (3000'; *Stern*), the chief place in this valley, and a summer-resort, lies 3 M. above Lunghiega, amid grand scenery. (A path to the right after 1¹/₄ M. is a shortcut.) To the right rise the Crostafels or Paresberg, Eisengabel, Neunerspitze, and Lavinores; to the left are the Col di Lasta, Mte. Sella di Senes, Paratsch, Peresspitze, and Kronplatz. About ³/₄ M. to the S., on the stream, are the small baths of *Cortina*, efficacious in rheumatic affections (bath 15 kr.).

EXCURSIONS (guides, *Fc. Flöss*, *A. Peskoller*.) To the Jöchl (5200'; leading to Piccolein), with °View as far as the Marmolada, 1 hr. (steep descent to Piccolein, ¹/₂ hr.). — To the top of the *Kronplatz* (7444') viâ the *Furkel* (see below), 3¹/₂ hrs., very attractive (descent to *Gaiselsberg* and *Olang*, or by *Bad Scharll* to *Bruneck*, see p. 329). — The *Peresspitze* (8215'; 4¹/₂ hrs.) and the *Hochalpe* (8415', 5¹/₂ hrs.), both ascended viâ the *Kreuzjoch* (p. 331), are easy and attractive (guide advisable). — To OLANG (p. 329) over the *Furkel*, an easy excursion of 3 hrs.; descent by *Gaiselsberg* or past the small baths of (2 hrs.) *Perfall* and along the *Furkelbach*. — To PRAGS over the *Kreuzjoch*, see p. 331. — To ST. CASSIAN (p. 342), a charming expedition (guide): over the saddle *Bus dal Lega* (6150') to (3 hrs.) the upper *Wengenthal* (p. 342); then over the lofty Alpine terraces of *Armentara*, which command a splendid prospect, skirting the slopes of the *Rosshauptkofel* and the *Heiligkreuzkofel* on the left, to the (1¹/₂ hr.) church of *Heiligkreuz* (p. 342) and to (¹/₂ hr.) *St. Cassian*.

The VAL AMPEZZO is reached from St. Vigil by two attractive routes (provisions should be taken). — a. OVER THE FODARA VEDLA (to Cortina 7¹/₂-8 hrs.). The road leads through the *Rauthal* to the (2¹/₄ M.) small *Kreidensee* (to the right, below the road, is the source of the *Vigilbach*, at the foot of the *Crostafels*), and then past the entrance of the *Kripes Valley* to (1¹/₂ M.) the *Tamers Alp* (4770'). A bridle-path leads hence to the (³/₄ hr.) grand head of the valley, known as *Pederü* (4975'). We then mount rapidly, keeping to the right at the top, to (1¹/₄ hr.) the extensive Alp Fodara Vedla (*Rudo di Sotto*, 6500'), which affords an admirable survey (from the cross) of the *Hohe Gaisl*, Lavinores, Crepa di Rudo, Eisengabel, and other peaks. Then a steep descent to the (1 hr.) *La Stuva Alp* (5655') in the *Val Campo-Croce*, and thence to the (³/₄ hr.) Ampezzo road, which is reached at the apex of the long curve below Peutelstein (comp. p. 348). — The ascent of the **Seekofel** (9215') is easily combined with this route (interesting, and not difficult for experts). In this case we turn to the left 40 min. beyond Pederü (see above), and ascend to the (1 hr.) splendidly-situated *Senes Alp* (*Rudo di Sora*, 7010'); thence to the W. peak of the Seekofel, which commands a strikingly grand view, in 2¹/₂ hrs. more. Descent by the *Forcella di Cocadain* and through the *Nabige Loch* to the *Pragser Wildsee* (p. 331), by the Forcella di Cocadain and the *Rossalp* to Alt-Prags (p. 330), or by the *Fosses Alp* and *La Stuva* to the Ampezzo road (p. 347).

b. VIÂ FANES (to Cortina 8¹/₂-9 hrs.). From (3 hrs.) *Pederü* (see above) this route leads through the *Vallon di Rudo*, to the W. of the *Col de Rü*, and past the little *Pischodel Lake* (5900') to the (1³/₄ hr.) *Klein-Fanes Alp* (6650'), magnificently situated near the little *Grünsee*. We then turn to the S.E., and proceed viâ the **Joch Limo** (7070') and the *Limo-See*, or *Fanes-See*, to the (³/₄ hr.) *Gross-Fanes Alp* (6860'), where the route from the *Col de Lodschia* (p. 343) descends on the right. We next traverse the *Ampezzo Fanes Valley*, between the *Vallon Bianco* (8820') on the right, and the *Croda del Becco* (9150') and *Col Becchei di Sotto* (8205') on the left, to the *Ponte Alto di Progoito* (p. 350), in the *Plan dell' Ova*, and to the (1³/₄ hr.) Ampezzo road (p. 348).]

The new road crosses the Vigilbach and ascends the right bank of the Gader (to the right, high up, the village of *Welschellen*), passing the mouth of the *Untermoi Valley*, to (3 M.) *Piccolein* (3640';

*Zingerle, plain), with an old foundry (over the *Jöchl* to *St. Vigil*, see p. 341). *St. Martin* (3665'; Tasserwirth), with the old castle of *Thurn*, is seen on the left bank of the Gader. — We next reach (1½ M.) *Preroman*, at the mouth of the *Campill Valley*.

About 6 M. up the Campill Valley lies *Campill* (4590'; Inn), whence the *Peitlerkofel* (9430'; magnificent view) may be ascended by the *Peitlerscharte* in 4½-5 hrs. (with guide; new path; not difficult for experts). — Over the *Wurzen Pass* to *Villnöss*, see p. 225.

The road exhibits several interesting geological phenomena. At (2¼ M.) *Pederoa* (Inn) opens the *Wengenthal*, with the hamlet of *Wengen* and the small baths of *Rumaschlung*. Farther on we pass through a ravine, crossing the tracks of several large mud-torrents, which destroyed parts of the road almost as soon as they were completed. After 3 M. the road crosses to the left bank of the Gader and next reaches (2¼ M.) *Pedratsches* (Nagler's sulphur-baths; Zingerle), opposite to which, on the right bank (new iron bridge), lies —

St. Leonhard (4450'; *Craffonara's*), or *Abtei*, Ladin *Badia*, the capital of the valley (here called the *Abtei-Thal* or *Val Badia*), overshadowed by the precipitous *Heiligkreuz-Kofel* (9530'). On the W. rises the *Gardenazza* (8750').

Pleasant walk to the (2 hrs.) pilgrimage-church of *Heiligkreuz* (6686'; Inn, rustic); admirable view and echo. — Ascent thence of the *Heiligkreuzkofel* (9530'; 2½-3 hrs.; with guide, Franz Fistil or Joh. Ninz of St. Leonhard), not difficult. We ascend to the right to the pass, and moreover detritus to the summit, which affords a noble prospect. Descent to the *Klein-Fanes Alp*, and thence to the N. to *St. Vigil*, or to the E. by *Gross-Fanes* to *Cortina*, see p. 341.

From St. Leonhard a cart-road leads along the right side of the Abtei-Thal (from which the Corvara Valley diverges 1 hr. farther up; see p. 343) to *Valle* and (4½ M.) **St. Cassian** (5000'; *Inn*), near which fossils abound. Travellers from Corvara to (2 hrs.) St. Cassian descend to the right at Stern (p. 343), cross the Corvara or Grossbach at its confluence with the *Sorè*, ascend the left bank of the latter through wood, finally cross the fourth bridge, and ascend steeply to St. Cassian.

FROM ST. CASSIAN TO CORTINA VIÂ TRA I SASSI (6-7 hrs.; with guide, Joh. Canins and Jos. Rudiferia), an interesting route. We ascend through pastures and past the mouth of the *Lagazuoi Valley* (see below) to the (1¼ hr.) *Valparola-Alp* (5665'). Below the chalets we cross the brook and ascend steeply through wood, and afterwards over grass and loose stones, to the (1½ hr.) **Castello Pass** (about 6800'), which commands a retrospective view of the Enneberg Valley, the Kreuzkofel, the Peitlerkofel, and the Zillerthal Mts. (to the N., in the distance). Beyond the pass, above a small lake, the path divides. The lower and better route descends to the right, soon affording a fine retrospect of the huge Marmolada, and afterwards leading through wood, to *Buchenstein* (to the *Castell Andraz*, p. 355, 1¼ hr.). The upper path follows the slope to the left, traversing dreary tracts of debris, crosses the pass Tra i Sassi (ca. 7220'), between the *Lagazuoi* on the left and the *Sasso di Stria* on the right, and reaches the *Falzarego Road* on the summit of the pass; to the hospice 1½ hr., and to Cortina 2 hrs. more (see p. 355; horse from St. Cassian to Cortina 9 fl.). — TO THE AMPEZZO VALLEY OVER THE COL DU LODSCHIA, a laborious route (to Cortina 7 hrs., to Schluderbach 7½ hrs.).

After 1/2 hr. we diverge to the left from the Valparola route (see p. 342) and ascend along the *Sorè* (to the right the wild *Lagazuoi Valley*) to the (2 hrs.) **Col de Lodschia** (6870'), between the *Conturinspitze* (10,080') on the left and the *Mte. Casale* (9765') on the right. We then descend to the (1 hr.) *Gross-Fanes Alp* (9860') and proceed through the Fanes Valley to the Ampezzo road (comp. p. 344). — To BUCHENSTEIN over the *Castello Pass* (to Andraz 4 1/2 hrs.), see p. 342. Another pleasant route (guide advisable) leads viâ **Prelongei** (7010'), with fine view of the Marmolada, etc., to (4 1/2-5 hrs.) *Pieve di Livinalongo*. Extensive panorama from the "*Sett Sass* (8395'), reached from Prelongei by following the crest of the hill for 1 1/2 hr. to the E.

The road from Pedratsches (p. 342) to Corvara follows the bank of the Gader to the (1 M.) *Sonnpunt Bridge* (4450') and then ascends to the right to (1 1/2 M.) *Stern* (4815'; Inn), where the Corvara Valley opens off the Abtei-Thal. It then runs to the right to *Verda*, descends to the *Corvara*, and ascends a little on the right bank to (3 3/4 M.) **Corvara** (5160'; *Inn*), a finely-situated village. About 1 1/4 M. farther up the W. arm of the valley, which ascends to the Gardena Pass, lies *Colfosco* or *Kolfuschg* (5390'; *Cappella, at the end of the village), the most picturesque point in this interesting dolomitic region (S. the Sella group, with the Boè, Pizzadoi, and Mesules; N. the Sass Songer, Puez, and Tschampatsch).

EXCURSIONS (guides, *Joseph Rottonara* of Corvara and *Vigil Alton* of Colfosco). A most attractive excursion may be made to the °**Puez Alp** (3 hrs.). From Colfosco we follow a marked path to the N.W. to the (1 1/2 hr.) *Puez Hut*, magnificently situated on the small *Tschampatsch Lake* (6940'); thence we ascend to the left to (3/4 hr.) the *Tschampatsch Joch* (7835'), between the Puezberg on the right and the Piz Tschampatsch on the left. From the pass we proceed across the Puez Alp, surrounded by huge Dolomite peaks, either to the left, viâ *Crespena* and the *Forca Rossa* (adjoining the *Spitzkofel*, 8525'), to the (1 1/2 hr.) *Grödner Jöchl* (see below), or to the right, through the *Langethal*, to (2 hrs.) *St. Maria* in the Gardena Valley (p. 264). The *Puezberg* (8780'), the *Piz Tschampatsch* (8725'), and the *Spitzkofel* (8525') may each be ascended from the Puez Hut in 2 hrs. (all three attractive).

FROM CORVARA TO BUCHENSTEIN. One route, a bridle-track (marked with red), leads over the saddle of **Campolungo** (6200') and then divides: to the right to *Araba* (see below), to the left to *Varda* and (3 1/2 hrs.) *Pieve* (p. 356); another and more attractive path crosses the **Incisa Saddle** (about 6560'), which affords a fine survey of the Marmolada, Civetta, etc., and descends viâ *Cherz* and *Corte* to (3 hrs.) *Pieve*.

FROM CORVARA TO THE VAL FASSA there are two routes: one leading as above to (2 hrs.) *Araba*, and then crossing the *Pordoi-Joch* (p. 323) to Canazei in 3 1/2 hrs.; the other, far more attractive, crosses the **Gardena Pass** and the **Sella Pass** to (6 hrs.) Campitello. This route ascends from Corvara to the (2 hrs.) *Gardena Pass*, or *Grödener Joch* (see p. 264). Descending through the upper region of the valley (*Ferara Alp*, see p. 264), we follow an ill-defined path to the left, close to the precipices of the Sella (descent to S. Maria to be avoided), and ascend to a low pass. The path then leads down to a ravine, descending from the Sella, and crosses the stony bed of a brook, where the bridle-path from S. Maria is reached. We now ascend to the (2 1/4 hrs.) *Setta Pass* (p. 264), and descend thence to (1 1/2 hr.) *Campitello* (p. 323).

TO THE GARDENA VALLEY, over the *Gardena Pass* (5 hrs.) from Corvara to St. Ulrich, see p. 264.

63. From Toblach to Belluno. Val Ampezzo.

Comp. Maps, pp. 320, 348.

67 M. POST-OMNIBUS from the *Toblach* station to (18½ M.) *Cortina* daily at 7.30 a.m. in 4 hrs., returning at 5 p.m. (fare 1 fl. 70 kr., coupé 2 fl.). The SÜDBAHN OMNIBUS (a comfortable open vehicle, starting from the Südbahn Hôtel) plies daily between Toblach and Cortina, 4½ hrs. each way (from Toblach at 1 p.m., from Cortina at 6.30 a.m.); fare 1 fl. 80 kr. (to Landro 1 fl., Schluderbach 1 fl. 20 kr., from Schluderbach to Cortina 1 fl.), return-ticket 3 fl. 30 kr. — CARRIAGE with one horse from Toblach to Landro 2½, with two horses 4 fl.; to Schluderbach 3 and 5 fl.; to Cortina 6 and 11 fl. To Cortina and back, with one horse 8, two horses 14 fl., if kept overnight 10 and 16 fl.; to Cortina viâ Misurina, and back by the high-road, with two horse 20, if kept overnight 22 fl. From Cortina to Schluderbach, one-horse carr. 4, two-horse 8 fl., to Landro 4½ and 9 fl.; to Toblach 6 and 11 fl. — POST-OMNIBUS from Cortina daily at 11.40 a.m. to *Borca* (fare 60 kr.) and Italian diligence thence to *Belluno* (fare 6 fr. 80 c.), arriving at 11 p.m.; halt of ¾ hr. at Tai di Cadore, during which the diligence runs to Pieve di Cadore and back. Carriage with one horse from Toblach to Vittorio (2½ days) 35, with two horses 64 fl.; from Cortina to Belluno 15½ and 29 fl., to Vittorio 24 and 45 fl.

A visit to the Limestone Alps of S. Tyrol, enclosed by the Drave, Rienz, Eisak, Adige, Brenta, and Piave, and generally known as the **Dolomites** (from Dolomieu, the geologist, who first examined this magnesian limestone formation), is greatly facilitated by the Pusterthal railway. Strictly speaking, the term *Dolomite* belongs to the Fassa Mts., the Langkofel, Rosengarten, and Schlern, but does not apply to the Cristallo, Hohe Gaisl, Tofana, Sorapiss, Antelao, Pelmo, and other peaks of the Ampezzo Limestone Alps; but as these mountains are widely known as the 'Ampezzo Dolomites', the popular nomenclature is adhered to in the Handbook. Alike to the man of science and the mountaineer the curiously fissured Dolomites offer a rich and varied field of interest, in their innumerable large and small peaks, pinnacles, caverns, cañons, and subterranean water-courses. The most striking formations are generally found about halfway up the mountains, as from the summits as well as from the valleys many of their most characteristic features are lost to view. Comp. *The Dolomite Mountains*, by *Gilbert and Churchill* (London).

The *AMPEZZO ROAD (called by the Italians 'Strada d'Allemagna') quits the Pusterthal at the *Toblach* station (3950'; *Hôtel Toblach; Hôtel Ampezzo; comp. p. 331), leads due S., between the *Sarnkofel* on the right and the *Neunerkofel* on the left, into the *Höhlensteiner Thal*, watered by the *Rienz*, and passes the small, dark *Toblacher See* (4045'). The valley soon contracts to a wild gorge. To the left the *Nasse Wand* is conspicuous; to the right rises the jagged spurs of the *Dürrenstein*. The view up the valley to the S. is bounded by the *Mte. Pian* (p. 345). Above the *Klausbrücke* (4310') the *Rienz* (p. 345) issues from its subterranean channel. On the left slope of the valley rises a curiously-shaped isolated rock, called by the natives the *Muttergotteskofel*. The road passes a toll-house and a road-keeper's house, and before Landro, a new fort.

6 M. **Höhlenstein**, Ital. *Landro* (4615'; *Post, kept by *Baur*, D. 1½, pension 4-6 fl.), is a pleasant summer-resort. At the head of the valley of the *Schwarze Rienz*, which opens here to the left, rise the lofty and glistening *Drei Zinnen* (9720'). A few paces farther on, at the N.W. base of the Mte. Pian, is the light-green *Dürrensee*. In the background rise the huge *Monte Cristallo*

(10,600'), with its glacier, and its neighbours, the *Piz Popena* (10,335') and the *Cristallino* (9318'), presenting a most striking picture. The lake, into which the *Schwarze Rienz* flows, is sometimes dry in autumn, but fills again in spring. The road skirts the W. side of the lake (passing the Mte. Pian on the left), and 1½ M. from Landro reaches —

7½ M. **Schluderbach** (4730'; *Zum Monte Cristallo*, kept by *Ploner*, generally full in midsummer, R. 1 fl., D. 1 fl. 36 kr.; one-horse carr. to Cortina and back 6, to Lago Misurina and back 3 fl.), beautifully situated at the mouth of the *Val Popena* (see below). The Monte Cristallo is here concealed by the sombre *Rauhkofel* (7665'), and the lower *Cristallino* only is visible. To the right rises the vast red limestone pyramid of the *Croda Rossa* (*Rothwand*, or *Hohe Gaisl*, 10,280'), which forms the boundary between the German and Italian tongues. To the left, at the head of the Val Popena, are the *Cadini*.

WALKS AND EXCURSIONS from Höhlenstein and Schluderbach. Round the *Dürrensee*, part of the way lying in wood. — From Schluderbach to the (½ hr.) *Eduardsfelsen*, at the entrance of the *Val Fonda* and the base of the Cristallo; to the (½ hr.) *Sigmundsbrunnen* in the *Schönleitenthal*; through the fine woods of the *Seelandthal* to the (1½ hr.) *Plätzwiesen* (pp. 330, 345).

A stony track from Höhlenstein traverses the **Rienzthal** as far as the foot of the (¾ hr.) rocky barrier which seems to close the valley, and above which tower the Drei Zinnen; to the right, the Mte. Pian. A steep path ('Katzenleiter'), beginning opposite the shepherd's hut, ascends the *Val Rimbianco*, backed by the Cadini, to the (1 hr.) *Rimbianco Alp* (p. 346). — The path to the left in the Rienzthal divides in ½ hr.; one branch leading steeply to the N. through the *Grosse Wildgraben* to the (1½ hr.) *Wildgraben-Joch* (p. 332); the other running to the E. over the *Rienzböden* to the (2 hrs.) *Toblinger Riedel* (p. 346).

From Schluderbach, by the 'Ernstrasse' through the *Val Popena* to the (2 hrs.) °*Lago Misurina*, see p. 351. The route by Misurina and °*Tre Croci* to (5 hrs.) Cortina is better from Schluderbach than in the reverse direction, for in the former case the ascent is more gentle and the finest views are always in front, see p. 350 (guide, 4 fl., unnecessary).

MOUNTAIN ASCENTS (guides, *Michael Innerkofler*, a guide of the first rank; *Joh.* and *Jos. Innerkofler*). The °**Monte Pian** (7530') may be ascended from Schluderbach without difficulty in 2½-3 hrs.; guide not indispensable (one of the men at the hotel, 2 fl.). We ascend the *Val Popena* by the Auronzo road (see p. 351), from which we diverge to the left by a (2¾ M.) finger-post, and follow a steep path (marked with red) over the *Forcella Alta* to the (1½ hr.) summit, an extensive plateau, with curiously fissured rock-formations. The highest point is on the W. margin, facing the Rienzthal. Stones painted red indicate the way to the (20 min.) best point of view (refuge-hut). The panorama is very fine: to the S. are the Cristallo, Sorapiss, Antelao, Marmarole, Cadini, and the Lago Misurina; S.W., the Tofana and the distant Marmolada; to the W., far below, lie Schluderbach and Höhlenstein (Landro), with the Dürrensee, beyond which rise the Hohe Gaisl and Seekofel; N., the Schwalbenkofel, Birkenkofel, and Dreischusterspitze, with the Zillerthaler Ferner, Rieser Ferner, and Tauern in the background; E., the Drei Zinnen and the Mts. of Auronzo. The part of the mountain towards Höhlenstein, from which it appears to be the highest summit, should also be visited, for in some particulars the view from it is finer; grand fissures on the Rienzthal side. — The Monte Pian may also be ascended from *Höhlenstein* (p. 344) through the *Rienzthal* and viâ the *Katzenleiter*, *Rimbianco Valley* (p. 346), and *Forcella*

Alta, without much difficulty. The route through the woods from Rimbianco to the Forcella is, however, not easily found; it may be recommended for the descent. — Descent to the *Lago Misurina*, see p. 351.

Ascent of the *Dürrenstein (9305'; 4 hrs.; guide 3 fl., unnecessary), very attractive. The route (red marks) leads through the *Seelandthal* to (2 hrs.) the *Hôtel Dürrenstein*, on the Plätzwiesen (p. 345), whence a new path ascends to the right to the (2 hrs.) summit. View similar to that from Monte Pian, but more extensive. The ascent may conveniently be combined with the route to Prags (p. 345). Another path, indicated by red marks, leads from Höhlenstein (p. 344) to the summit. It follows the bleak *Hellthal*, crosses the saddle above the Plätzwiesen, where the Hohe Gaisl suddenly comes in sight, and then ascends the slope diagonally. The descent in any case should be made to Schluderbach for the sake of the fine view of the Mte. Cristallo, which is especially effective by evening-light.

The **Flodige** (6 hrs. there and back from Höhlenstein). The route diverges to the W. from the Ampezzo road a little beyond the (1½ hr.) Toblacher See, and ascends (red marks) into the *Sarl* (5600'), a beautiful sequestered valley between the Sarnkofel (right) and the Flodige Schneide (left). From the (2½ hrs.) *Sarl Sattel* (6890'), to the N. of the *Sarlköfele* (7570'), we obtain a picturesque glimpse of the Prags valley. From this point we ascend by an easy route to the *Flodige Schneide* (6890'), immediately in front of the rugged precipices of the Dürrenstein; then descend over grass and follow the path (indicated by marks) through the *Flodige Valley*, striking the Ampezzo road at the (2 hrs.) Klausbrücke (p. 344).

A tolerable path (indicated by marks) ascends through the *Rienzthal* (see p. 345) to the **Toblinger Riedel** (7845'; 3½ hrs.), a saddle strewn with needle-like rocks, between the *Paternkofel* (8925') on the right and the *Toblinger Knoten* (8560') on the left. On the Riedel stands the *Dreizinnenhütte* of the German Alpine Club, in a grand situation opposite the perpendicular cliffs of the *Drei Zinnen* (p. 347). The *View embraces the Rienzthal, Mte. Cristallo, Hohe Gaisl, etc., to the W., and the Altensteinthal to the E., with the *Böden Lakes*, lying but a few yards below the Riedel. (Through the Altensteinthal to Sexten, or over the Oberbacherjoch to the Zsigmondy Hut, see p. 333.) — A stony but tolerable path diverges to the left a short distance down the path to Landro, skirts the rubble-strewn flanks of the *Paternkofel*, and finally ascends again to the (1 hr.) **Paternsattel** (*Forcella di Lavaredo*; 8135'), between the Paternkofel and the Œstliche Zinnen. View hence of the Cadini, Marmarole, and Antelao to the S. We now skirt the S. side of the castellated *Drei Zinnen* (ascent on this side, see below), to the *Forcella di Marzon* (6890'), and descend over loose stones and grass and then through wood to the (1½ hr.) *Rimbianco Alp* (6120'; Rfmts.). Thence we may regain (1½ hr.) *Höhlenstein* viâ the Katzenleiter and the Rienzthal; or follow the cart-track, which is at first good, but rapidly deteriorates, viâ the *Forcella Bassa*, to (1 hr.) *Misurina*. — Another path leads from the **Toblinger Riedel** to the terrace of the *Lange Alm*, immediately beneath the N. precipices of the Drei Zinnen, and thence over steep slopes covered with debris and round the W. spur of the Drei Zinnen to Rimbianco.

The ascent of the **Cristallino** (highest peak, 9318', the fourth from the left as seen from Landro; 3½-4 hrs.; guide 3½ fl.) is attractive and not difficult for adepts. The view from the summit embraces the valley of Höhlenstein as far as Toblach, the Tauern in the distance, and in the immediate foreground the wild precipices of the Popena and Cristallo.

The **Monte Cristallo** (10.699'; 6-7 hrs.; guide 8 fl.) is highly interesting, but fitted only for expert climbers with steady heads. The route leads through the *Val Fonda* (*Val del Monte Cristallo*) to the (2½ hrs.) *Cristallo Glacier*, which it crosses to (1½ hr.) the *Cristallo Pass* (9270'), between the Mte. Cristallo and the Popena. We then ascend the 'Lange Band' on the S. side of the Cristallo and finally clamber over rocks (the worst point being the 'Böse Platte') to the arête and the (2-3 hrs.) summit. The view is magnificent. The descent may be made from the pass over snow and debris to *Tre Croci* and *Cortina* (p. 348).

The **Hohe Gaisl** or *Rothwand* (*Croda Rossa*, 10,280'; 7-8 hrs.; guide 9 fl.) is ascended by a very toilsome and difficult route viâ the *La Rosa Alp* and the *Val Buones*. — Of the **Drei Zinnen** (9205', 9720', 8185') the central peak (4-5 hrs. from Rimbianco viâ the Forcella di Marzon; guide 9 fl.) is both the highest and the easiest, but is fit only for experts with steady heads. The *Kleine Zinne* is a dangerous ascent.

The **Hochebenkofel** (9515'; 5 hrs.) is accomplished without difficulty from Höhlenstein over the *Toblacher Schafalm*. It is connected with the slightly higher *Birkenkofel* (9580'), to the N., by a narrow arête, requiring a steady head. Descent to the *Innerfeldthal* and *Sexten*, see p. 333.

FROM SCHLUDERBACH TO AURONZO viâ *Misurina*, see p. 351. Shorter but more toilsome passes lead from the (2 hrs.) *Rimbianco Alp* (see p. 346) over the *Forcella di Marzon* (6890') or the *Forcella di Rimbianco* (7220') to the *Val Marzon* and (5-6 hrs.) *Auronzo*.

The road ascends, crosses the *Seelandbach*, and then the bed of the *Knappenbach*, which is generally dry, and reaches the *Gemärk*, or *Cima Banche*, the low watershed (5000') between the Rienz and the Boite, which forms the boundary of the Ampezzo district. To the right rises the majestic *Hohe Gaisl* (10,280'), with the precipices of the *Col Freddo* (8954'), and next it the *Croda di Rancona* (see below), appearing above the wooded hills of the *Crepi di Zuoghi*; before us the peaks of the *Tofana* overtop the *Col Rosà*; to the left is the *Cristallo*; behind us, the *Monte Pian* and the *Cadini*. The road descends gradually, passing the shallow *Lago Bianco* (4865') on the left, and crosses the *Rufreddo*, which descends from the right and has formed a deep and rocky channel for itself lower down. We next cross the *Gottresbach* and soon reach (4 M.) **Ospitale** (4960'; *Inn*), once a hospice, picturesquely situated at the base of the *Crepi di Zuoghi*. Opposite is the *Punta del Forame* (9395'), with the valley of that name, watered by the *Felizon*, which here unites with the Rufreddo. Farther down is the *Val Grande*, flanked on the W. by the *Pomagagnon*, beyond which rise the *Tofana*, *Col Rosà*, and *Vallon Bianco*.

Beautiful WALK in the *Gottres Valley*, between the *Col Freddo* on the right and *Monte Cadini* on the left, to the (1¾ hr.) **La Rosa Alp** (6700'), which commands a fine view of the mountains of Fanes and Travernanzes (p. 318), and, to the right, of the Seekofel (p. 341). We may then either descend to the (½ hr.) *La Stuva Alp* (5655') and through the narrow valley of the Boite to (¾ hr.) Peutelstein (p. 348) on the Ampezzo road; or (somewhat toilsome) follow the slope to the right, by the *Forcella di Giraibes* (7220'), to the large sheep-pasture of (1½ hr.) *Fosses* (7015'), with its two small lakes. [From Fosses we may ascend the (1½ hr.) *Seekofel (comp. p. 341), a splendid point of view; descent over the *Forcella di Cocodain* (p. 339) to *Alt-Prags* or *Neu-Prags*.]

THROUGH THE VAL GRANDE TO CORTINA (4½ hrs.), attractive. A good track descends, crosses the *Felizon*, and ascends to the S. in the *Val Grande*, between the *Pomagagnon* (7515') on the right and the Cristallo on the left, to the (2 hrs.) *Padeon Alp* (6080'). Thence we ascend to the right to the (1 hr.) **Zumeles Joch** (6790'; fine view), and descend steep slopes of debris to (1½ hr.) *Cortina*: or we may proceed to the left from the Alp to the (1 hr.) **Forca** (6880'), and descend to the (40 min.) *Tre Croci Pass* (p. 350).

For some distance the road, now level, skirts the slope of *Monte Cadini* (*Croda di Rancona*, 7740'), the side of which is pierced by an aperture high above us. On the left are the ravine of the *Felizon* and the *Val Grande*. (A finger-post by the telegraph-post numbered 463 indicates a short-cut which crosses the deep gorge of the Felizon by the *Ponte Felizon, rejoining the road below the Ponte Alto. The road, however, is more attractive in point of scenery.) The road ascends for a short distance, and then descends. About 1¼ M. beyond Ospitale the conspicuous *Peutelstein* (4944') rises on the left. The rock was formerly crowned with the ruins of the castle of that name (Ital. *Poddestugno*), which were removed in 1866. The road bends sharply to the right, and winds down into the valley of the *Boite*. In the foreground is the *Col Rosà*, overtopped on the right by the *Vallon Bianco*, to the right of which are the *Col Becchei di Sotto*, *Taè*, *Croda d'Antruilles*, and *Lavinores*. The apex of the long curve, where a finger-post indicates the way to the Ranthal to the right (comp. p. 341), commands a fine survey of the valleys of *Fanes* and *Travernanzes*, and (right) that of the Boite; in the distance to the S. are the Cima di Formin, Becco di Mezzodì, and Pelmo.

The road now descends to the S., skirting precipitous slopes, and on the S. side of the Peutelstein crosses the deep gully of the *Felizon* by the (1¾ M.) *Ponte Alto* (to which the above-mentioned path descends from the Ponte Felizon). The following stretch of the valley is monotonous; the Boite flows through a broad stony bed, between pine-clad banks, over which tower the rocky masses of the Tofana on the right and the Pomagagnon on the left. About ¾ M. farther on a finger-post indicates the route to the right to St. Cassian (p. 342) viâ Travernanzes and Fanes; and after ¾ M. more we pass the two houses of *Flammes* (small inn to the right). Facing us is the jagged Sorapiss (p. 350). The road then (1½ M.) quits the wood, and affords a view of the beautiful valley of (1 M.) —

18½ M. **Cortina.** — *AQUILA NERA, the dining-room and the exterior of the dépendance of which are decorated with good paintings by the sons of the late landlord *Ghedina*; *HÔTEL CORTINA, R. 1-1½ fl., L. & A. 60 kr., D. 1½ fl., 'pens.' 3-4 fl.; °STELLA D'ORO; °CROCE BIANCA, R. 90 kr., D. 1 fl. 20 kr., S. 70 kr., 'pens.' 3 fl., civil landlord; °ANCORA, — Guides (bargaining advisable): *Alessandro Lacedelli*, *Fulgenzio* and *Pietro Dimai*, *Ang.*, *Gius.*, *Luigi*, and *Tobia Menardi*, *Ant. Soravia*, *Sim. Ghedina*, *Arcangelo Dibona*, *Mans.* and *Giov. Barbaria*, and *Gius. Colli*. Most of the guides speak a little German. — *English Church Service* in the Aquila Nera.

Cortina di Ampezzo (3970'), superbly situated and admirably adapted for a prolonged stay, is the capital of the valley and the seat of the district-authorities, and carries on a considerable trade in timber and cattle. The parish is said to be the wealthiest in Tyrol, and its inhabitants and their dwellings present a well-to-do appearance. The industrial school founded here in 1869 deserves a visit (filigree-work and wood-mosaic tasteful and not expensive).

The *Church*, adjoining which is a new promenade, contains a rich altar, wood-carvings by Brustolone, etc. The gallery of the handsome detached *Campanile* (about 200' in height; 235 steps) commands an admirable survey of the surrounding landscape. On the N.E. rises the Cristallo group, with the Pomagagnon and the highest Cristallo peak; E., the Tre Croci saddle; S.E. the Sorapiss and Antelao; S., the Pelmo, and (nearer) the Rocchetta and Becco di Mezzodì; S.W., Croda di Formin, Nuvolau, the Cinque Torri, and, in the foreground, the Crepa; W., Lagazuoi and Tofana; N., Col Rosà, Lavinores, Seekofel, and the Cadini.

A fine survey of the valley, for which the evening-light is most favourable, is obtained from the (1¹/₄ hr.) *Belvedere on the *Crepa (5085'), a prominent rocky hill on the W. side of the valley. We ascend the Falzarego road to (3 M.) a finger-post indicating a steep path to the left (to the inn, 10 min.), or (easier) we may follow the road for ¹/₂ M. more, to a finger-post on the hill beyond the Crepa, and proceed thence to the left to (5 min.) the *Inn* on the nearer side of the rock (guide unnecessary; horse 2, light carriage 2¹/₂ fl.). In the wood, beyond the Belvedere, are several deep fissures in the rock, of which the traveller should beware. — A path, diverging to the left from the way to the Crepa after about ³/₄ M., leads through the hamlet of *Mortisa* to the *Grottoes of Maria di Zanin* or *di Valpera*, at the S.E. foot of the Crepa, 40 min. from Cortina. These ravines, with their grotesque rock-formations, were made accessible in 1883. Below, at the foot of the mountain at the end of the Costeana ravine (1 hr. from Cortina), lie the baths of *Campo di Sotto*, destroyed by an inundation in 1882.

Another attractive walk leads to the (³/₄ M.) beautiful *Lago Ghedina*, embosomed in woods at the foot of the Tofana (guide necessary; horse 2 fl.). — A good path through the woods leads by *Campo di Sotto* (see above) and the *Federa Alp* to the (3¹/₂ hrs.) little **Lago da Lago** (6700'), picturesquely situated at the foot of the *Croda da Lago* (8815'; first ascended in 1881) and the *Becco di Mezzodì* (8430'). Thence to the *Forcella d'Ambriz*, see p. 353.

To the *Zumeles (6795'; 2 hrs.), a very pleasant expedition. The best route ascends to the left before the Tre Croci (p. 350) are reached, and crosses the *Forca* (p. 347); we may return through the *Val Grande*, across the *Felison Bridge* to the *Ponte Alto*, and by the high-road to (4 hrs.) Cortina. — To the *Tondi di Faloria, on the *Monte Casadio* (3¹/₂ hrs.). The path diverges to the right from the Tre Croci route (p. 350) by a finger-post about ¹/₄ hr. below the pass, and ascends to the clearing of *Pian della Bigontina*. We cross (10 min.) a bridge, and (¹/₄ hr.) where the path divides we proceed to the right across the grassy hill of the *Tondi*, to the (1 hr.) *Crepedel* (7815'), which commands a splendid survey of the Ampezzo Valley, the Tofana, Cristallo, Drei Zinnen, Cadini, etc.; to the S. is the lofty *Punta Nera* (9030'), with the rocky range stretching from it to the N.E. to *Cesta* (9070') and the *Cadin del Laudo*, and separating the Mte. Casadio from the Val Sorapiss. — Experts are recommended to mount the **Seletta** (8700'), the col to the N.E., between the Punta Nera and the Cesta. It commands a superb view of the Val Sorapiss and of the huge perpendicular sides of the Sorapiss. From the bifurcation of the path at the beginning of the Pian della Bigontina to the summit of the pass, 2 hrs., the last hour very steep (guide requisite). Descent from the Selcita to the *Val Sorapiss* and the *Sorapiss Lake* (6325'), steep but unattended with danger; thence either down to the *Val Buona* (p. 353), or (laborious) across the col *Sora la Cengia del Banco* (8495'), between the Punta Nera and the *Foppa di Mattia* (a peak of the Sorapiss; 10,800'), to *Chiapuzza* (p. 351), in the valley of the Boite.

The ascent of the *Nuvolau (S. peak, 8445'; 4 hrs., guide, 3¹/₂ fl., not necessary for adepts; horse to the Cinque Torri 5¹/₂ to the top 7 fl.) is very attractive and not difficult. Driving is practicable by the Falzarego road (p. 355) as far as the *Cinque Torri di Averau* (3 hrs.; good water); thence we ascend in the direction of the *Nuvolau Saddle* (7875'), between the N. and S. peak, and then to the left, over the broad ridge to the (1 hr.) *Sachsendank Club Hut* (8440'), on the S. peak, which commands a noble *Panorama: to the W., the Marmolada, adjacent to which appears the distant Ortler, and then the Rosengarten Mts.; N.W., the Mts. of the Gaderthal (Boè, Gardenazza, Geislerspitzen), with the Zillerthal and Oetzthal snow-mountains in the background; N. the triple-peaked Tofana; farther back, part of the Tauern; then the Cristallo and Cadini, E., the Sorapiss and Antelao, with the Croda di Formin (or del Lago) and the Becco di Mezzodì; S.E., the Pelmo; S., the Civetta; S.W., the Pala di S. Martino. — The ascent of the higher (N.) peak (8600') is difficult. — From the Nuvolau saddle an easy descent may be made to *Colle S. Lucia* (p. 357) and (2¹/₂ hrs.) *Coprile* (p. 356), or by the *Potorre Joch*, between the Nuvolau and Cinque Torri, to the (1¹/₂ hr.) hospice of *Falzarego* (see p. 355).

The interesting **Val Travernanzes** (8-9 hrs. to the Tofana and back; guide not indispensable for experts; horse to the Alp 6 fl.) is well worth a visit. At the (1¹/₄ hr.) guide-post on the Ampezzo road beyond *Fiammes* (p. 348) we turn to the left and enter the (¹/₂ hr.) *Pian dell' Ova*, an imposing rocky basin, where the Boite is reinforced by the brooks of Antruilles, Fanes, and Travernanzes. Crossing the Boite and then the Travernanzes brook we skirt the foot of the *Col Rosà* to the left to the (¹/₂ hr.) *Ponte Alto di Progoito*, spanning at a height of 260' the gorge of the Travernanzes brook, at the point where the road from the *Gross-Fanes Alp* in the Fanesthal (p. 341) debouches. Beyond the bridge we turn to the left, pass the entrance of the *Val Fiorenza* (see below), recross the stream in ¹/₄ hr., and ascend the narrow and profound *Val Travernanzes*. To the left rise the huge cliffs of the *Tofana*, and to the right the *Vallon Bianco*, *Mte. Casale*, *Mte. Cavallo*, and *Fannesspitze*. About 2 hrs. farther on is the poor *Travernanzes Alp* (6435'), whence we ascend in 1¹/₄ hr. (butterly no path) to the *Col dai Bos* (7775'), between the *Tofana di Razes* (10,550') on the left and the *Cima Falzarego* (8395') on the right. Beyond the pass we obtain a splendid view of the Marmolada (still finer from the Cima Falzarego, easily ascended in ³/₄ hr.). The descent leads across steep Alpine pastures to the (1 hr.) Falzarego road (p. 355), where we proceed to the left to (1 hr.) the *Pocol Alp* and (³/₄ hr.) Cortina.

The *Seekofel (9215') is reached from Cortina in 6 hrs. (guide 6 fl.). We follow the Ampezzo road to the (1¹/₂ hr.) guide-post indicating the route to the *Raulhal* (p. 341), then turn to the left and ascend to (1 hr.) the *Stuva Alp*, and proceed by the (2 hrs.) *Fosses Alp*, to the (1¹/₂ hr.) summit (comp. p. 341).

Among the more important ascents from Cortina, all fit for adepts only, that of the **Tofana** (*Tofana di Mezzo* 10,725'; *Tofana di Fuori* 10,705'; *Tofana di Razes* 10,550') is comparatively the easiest. The night is spent in the *Tofana Hut*, on the *Forcella di Tofana* (7610'), 4¹/₂ hrs. from Cortina; thence to the Tofana di Mezzo 2¹/₂ hrs., to the Tofana di Razes 2 hrs. (guide 7 fl.). — More difficult are the **Cristallo** (10,095'), ascended from the *Tre Croci* viâ the *Passo Cristallo* in 5-6 hrs. (guide 7 fl.; comp. p. 346). and the **Sorapiss** (10,860 ft.), ascended by *Chiapuzza* and the *Forcella Grande* (7535') in 8-9 hrs. (guide 12 fl.). In ascending the latter it is customary to pass the night in a cavern (Landro) near the Forcella Grande. The ascent, though without serious difficulty, is very long and fatiguing, owing to the numerous digressions which must be made in order to reach the best places for scaling the rocks.

From Cortina to Schluderbach by the Passo Tre Croci (4¹/₂-5 hrs.), a very attractive route (preferable in the reverse direction, comp. p. 345; guide, 4 fl., including Monte Piano 5¹/₂ fl., unnecessary; light vehicle, including return by the Ampezzo road, with one horse 7, two horses 12 fl.). The narrow and stony carriage-road skirts the ravine of the Bigontina, and ascends at first between houses and fields, then over pastures and through wood, passing a (1¹/₂ hr.) finger-post pointing to [the right to Faloria (p. 349), to the (¹/₂ hr.) **Passo Tre Croci** (5955'; rustic tavern), a depression between the Sorapiss and Cristallo, so called from the wooden crosses which stand here. A magnificent *View* is obtained hence of the green Ampezzo Valley and the lofty Tofana to the W., to the left of which, between the Torre di Averau and Nuvolau, is the snow-clad Marmolada; to the N. rise the Cristallo and Popena; to the E. is the upper Aurenzo Valley (Val Buona), with the wall-like chain of the Marmarole; N.E., the Cadini; S., the Sorapiss. After descending for ¹/₂ hr.

we diverge to the *left* from the road leading into the Val Buona (p. 252), and follow the wooded slope at the same level, enjoying beautiful views of the Sorapiss and Marmarole to the right, and the huge slopes of the Cristallo on the left. In ³/₄ hr. we reach the road ('Erzstrasse') from the Val Auronzo to Schluderbach, constructed for the mineral traffic (see p. 252). The road ascends slightly across the *Misurina Alp* (passing a large cheese-dairy on the left), affording a fine survey of the Cristallo, Sorapiss, Antelao, Marmarole, Cadini, and the imposing Drei Zinnen, and passes the (40 min.) ***Lago Misurina** (5890'), a pale-green lake abounding in trout, its E. bank fringed with sombre pines (*Alb. Misurina*, at the upper end, unpretending). After a slight ascent to the (5 min.) *Col S. Angelo* (5900'), the road descends through the wooded *Val Popena* (right, Mte. Pian) to (1¹/₂ hr.) Schluderbach (p. 345). — The ascent of **Mte. Pian* (p. 345) may be combined with this excursion by a digression of 3 hrs. (guide from the Lago Misurina to Schluderbach 2 fl.; unnecessary for adepts). The route leads over the *Forcetta Bassa* to the (1¹/₂ hr.) plateau; descent by the *Forcetta Alta* (p. 345). — From the Lago Misurina over the *Patern-Sattel* to *Sexten* (8 hrs.; with guide), see pp. 333, 346.

Pleasant day's drive to *Pieve di Cadore (see below; one-horse carr. there and back 7, two-horse 13¹/₂ fl.; returning by Auronzo and Tre Croci, 14 and 26 fl.). — From Cortina to *Buchenstein* and *Caprile*, see p. 355; to *St. Cassian*, see p. 342; to *St. Vigil*, see p. 341.

The road next reaches *Zuel* (splendid view down the valley) and then (3 M.) *Acquabuona*, the last Tyrolese village, crosses the (1¹/₂ M.) Italian frontier, and descends rapidly to (1¹/₂ M.) *Chiapuzza* (3475'), the first Italian hamlet, and (¹/₂ M.) **S. Vito** (3415'; **Alb. all' Antelao*, plain), with the Italian custom-house, finely situated at the base of the Antelao. The old church, *La Difesa* (1512), has some curious old frescoes. The new church contains a fine altarpiece by Francesco Vecelli, Titian's elder brother. To the right (S.W.), above the wooded hills, towers the *Pelmo* (10,394'), a colossal rock, forming the most conspicuous feature in the landscape.

ASCENTS from S. Vito (guides, *G. Giacin, G. Zanucco, Luigi Cesaletti, Gius. de Vido,* and *L. Giustina*; tariff lower than that at Cortina). The ascent of the **Sorapiss** (10,860'; 6-7 hrs.), viâ the *Forcetta Grande*, is laborious; comp. p. 350. — The ***Antelao** (10,660'; 6-7 hrs.), a superb point of view, scaled by the *Forcetta Piccola*, though fatiguing, offers no special difficulty to experts (guide from Cortina 9¹/₂ fl., from S. Vito 15 fr.). — The *Pelmo* (10,394'; 7-8 hrs.; guide 10¹/₂ fl.), now generally ascended from S. Vito (guide 18 fr.; from Cortina 10¹/₂ fl.) is difficult, and should be attempted only by expert climbers with perfectly steady heads (comp. pp. 355, 357).

From S. Vito (or *Borca*) over the *Col di Ponta* or the *Forcetta Forada* to *Caprile*, see p. 357. To the E. over the *Forcetta Piccola* (6960'), between the Sorapiss and the Antelao, and through the *Val Oten*, to *Pieve di Cadore* (see below), 5-6 hrs. (with guide).

Between S. Vito and *Borca* (3200'; Alb. al Pelmo) the road runs high above the Boite on the slopes of the Antelao, a landslip from which in 1814 overwhelmed the villages of Marceana and Taulen. The road then leads past *Cancia, Vodo* (Alb. d'Italia), and *Peajo* to (9 M.) —

34¹/₄ M. **Venas** (2895'; * *Alb. Borghetto*), below which the *Vallesina* unites with the Boite. Then (2 M.) *Valle* (Leon Bianco; route to *Zoldo*, p. 353), finely situated opposite the mouth of the *Val Cibiana*, (1¹/₄ M.) *Tai di Cadore* (2795'; Inn), and (1 M.) —

38¹/₂ M. **Pieve di Cadore** (2905'; *Progresso; Angelo; Sole*, civil

352   *VII. Route 63.*   AURONZO.

landlady; *Tiziano*), the capital of the *Val Cadore*, beautifully situated on a mountain-spur high above the *Piave*. In a corner of the chief Piazza stands the humble dwelling in which Titian was born in 1477 (d. 1575), denoted by a tablet. In 1880 a bronze statue of the great painter, by Del Zotto, was erected in the Piazza. The Palazzo Comunale is adorned with a marble relief of the master and with a monument to P. F. Calvi ('morto per la patria' 1855). The school contains a small *Museum* of natural history objects, coins, and antiquities, and Titian's patent of nobility with his armorial bearings. The church possesses an altarpiece (the Child adored by a bishop) and other pictures by Titian (?), Palma, etc.

The (1/4 hr.) old *Castello* (3140') affords a splendid view up and down the Val Piave. Attractive excursions to the *Cappella S. Dionigi* (3-4 hrs.), to the top of the *Mte. Vedorchia* (3 hrs.), etc. — The *Mte. Zucco* (3986'), easily ascended from Tai in 1 1/4 hr., commands a superb survey of the Pelmo, Antelao, Marmarole, etc., and of the Val Piave.

From Pieve a good road leads through the beautiful Val Cadore, which is enclosed by picturesque Dolomites (right, the *Mte. Cridola;* left, the *Marmarole*), to *Domegge* and (7 M.) *Lozzo* (2480'; Osteria alla Fortuna). At (1 1/2 M.) *Pelos* it crosses the Piave by the *Ponte Nuovo* (2870'; route to *Tolmezzo* over the *Mauria Pass*, see p. 436), and again at (3/4 M.) *Tre Ponti*, (2400'; Inn, rustic), at the influx of the *Ansiei*, which descends from the Val Auronzo (see below; handsome bridge).

[**Val Comelico.** Above Tre Ponti the Piave dashes through a series of wild ravines. A good road runs from *Gogna* (see below) through the narrow valley, crossing from the right to the left bank by the *Ponte della Lasta*, to (7 M.) **S. Stefano** (3030'; *Aquila Nera; Umiltà*), the capital of the *Comelico Inferiore*, pleasantly situated at the junction of the *Padola* and the Piave. (By the *Kreuzberg* to *Sexten*, see below.) From S. Stefano we ascend the valley of the Piave past *Campolongo* and *Presenajo* to the (4 1/2 M.) *Ponte del Cordevole* (4130'), above the confluence of the Piave with the *Cordevole*, which emerges here from the deep *Val Visdende*, to the N. We then follow the right bank of the Piave to (3 1/2 M.) *Granvilla* (4025'; "Kratter, by the church; *Stern), the chief hamlet of the parish of *Sappada*, Ger. *Bladen*, picturesquely situated at the foot of the *Mte. Ferro*. The villagers are Germans, probably mediæval immigrants from the Pusterthal. A cart-road leads from Granvilla by *Cima* to (2 hrs.) *Forni Avoltri* (p. 436). Route over the *Hochalpel* to (8-9 hrs.) *Lorenzen* in the Gailthal, see p. 384 (with which may be combined the ascent of the *Paralba*; guide 15 fr.). — From S. Stefano a good road leads to the N.W., making a wide bend past *S. Nicolò* in the *Upper Comelico Valley*, to (5 M.) *Candide* (4095'; *Alb. alle Alpi*), whence it continues on the left bank of the Padola viâ *Dosoledo* (4180'), passing (1 1/4 M.) *Padola* (4430'; Due Nazioni) on the right bank, and crosses the (2 hrs.) *Kreuzberg* (or *Mte. Croce*; 5355') to *Sexten* and (4 hrs.) *Innichen* (p. 333).]

In the **Val Auronzo** (road to Schluderbach; diligence from Pieve to Auronzo daily), 3/4 M. above *Tre Ponti* (see above), lies *Gogna* (route into the Comelico, see above), and 3 M. farther up is **Auronzo** (2910'), consisting of the villages of *Villapiccola*, with a large new church, and *Villagrande* (*Alb. alle Alpi; Alle Grazie; Vittora;* from Pieve to this point a drive of 2 1/2 hrs.). The *Mte. Calvario* affords a good survey of the environs. A highly-attractive route, with splendid views, leads to the N. over the *Forcella di Mte. Zovo* to (3 hrs.) *Padola* (see above). — The road through the upper Val Auronzo, or *Val Buona*, follows the left bank of the *Ansiei* (opposite the imposing chain of the *Marmarole*), and leads viâ (3 1/2 M.) *Giralba* (route to *Sexten*, see p. 332), at the mouth of the *Val Marzon* (on the right; at its head rise the *Drei Zinnen* or *Tre Cime di Lavaredo*), and the (3 M.) *Miniera Argentiera* (lead and zinc mines) to (3 M.) *Stabiziane* and (1 1/2 M.) the solitary frontier-house of *S. Marco* (3710'; quarters)

About 2¼ M. farther on is the Tyrolese frontier, a few hundred yards beyond which is the *Bastianshütte*, a shooting-lodge (4555'; Rfmts.), with a good view of the *Sorapiss*. (To the *Sorapiss Lake*, 2 hrs., with guide, a pleasant trip; comp. p. 349.) The road now forks; a road (not very good) to the left leads over the (4½ M.) *Passo Tre Croci* (p. 350) to (4½ M.) Cortina, while the new 'mineral road' to the right follows the Italian or left bank of the *Misurina* brook, the boundary stream, to the (4½ M.) *Lago Misurina* and (4½ M.) *Schluderbach* (comp. p. 351).

From Tai the road describes a long circuit round the *Mte. Zucco* (see p. 352), and descends in windings, being hewn in the rock and supported by masonry at places, to the (4½ M.) valley of the *Piave*, into which the Boite here falls.

43 M. **Perarolo** (1735'; **Corona d'Oro*, carr. and pair to Vittorio 25 fr.; *Alb. Sant' Anna*). The Piave runs for many miles through a narrow ravine, in which there is barely space for the road. 1½ M. *Macchietto*, with the small pilgrimage-church of *S. Maria della Salute*, opposite the entrance to the *Val Montina*. Farther on are the villages of *Rucorvo* and *Rivalgo*. To the right, near (3½ M.) *Ospitale*, is a fine waterfall; opposite the hamlet of (2 M.) *Termine*, on the left bank of the Piave, is a second fall (*La Pissa*). The road now passes through a cutting, 50' deep, and reaches (1¼ M.) *Castel Lavazzo*, the ancient *Castellum Laebatium*, as appears from an inscription found here. Then (2½ M.) —

54 M. **Longarone** (1470'; *Posta*, R. & A. 2½ fr.; *Albergo di Roma, unpretending; *Lepre*), charmingly situated at the junction of the *Maè*, which issues from the *Val Zoldo*, with the Piave.

The attractive, but little-known Val di Zoldo is entered by a narrow ravine, through which a road (diligence from Longarone daily, in 2 hrs., 1½ fr.) leads to (10 M.) **Forno di Zoldo** (2855'; *Cercena), the capital of the valley, with iron-works. To the N. rise the three huge rocky peaks of the **Mte. Pelmo** (10,395'), with its small glacier, which may be ascended either from Forno viâ *Zoppè* and the *Rutorto Alp* in 7-8 hrs., or from Fusine (see below) in 5-6 hrs. (difficult; able guides requisite, comp. p. 351). Easy and attractive routes lead from Forno to the N.E. over the **Forcella Cibiana** (5100') to (4 hrs.) *Venas*; to the N. over the **Col Potei** (5300') to (4 hrs.) *Vodo* (p. 351); to the N.W. over the **Passo di Rutorto** (6800') to (6 hrs.) *Borca* (p. 351); to the S. through the *Val Pramper* and over the *Moschesin Pass* (p. 358) to (6 hrs.) *Agordo* (p. 358). — Above Forno lies (¾ hr.) **Dont di Zoldo** (3115'; *Alb. al Pelmo*), where the route from *S. Tiziano di Goima* and the *Duran Pass* descends from the left (p. 358). The church contains a handsome monument (by Besarel) to the sculptor *Andrea Brustolon* (d. 1782), a native of the village. — The bridle-path then leads to the right through the narrow valley of the Maè, viâ *Fusine* (rustic inn) and *S. Nicolò*, to (1½ hr.) **Mareson** (4486'; *Locanda Filippi*, two beds), where the valley forks for the last time. Through the W. branch an easy and interesting path leads by *Pecol*, at the E. base of the huge *Civetta* (p. 354), and over the *Passo Coldai* (6100'), to (3 hrs.) *Alleghe* (p. 357). — Through the N. branch (*Val Pattafavera*) a path ascends, with admirable views of the Pelmo and Civetta, to the (2 hrs.) **Forcella di Staulanza** (5935'), between the Pelmo on the right and the Mte. Crot on the left, and then descends to the (½ hr.) *Fiorentina Alp*, in the *Val Fiorentina*. We may now descend the valley to the left, viâ *Pescul* and *Selva*, to (3 hrs.) *Caprile* (p. 356); or proceed to the right over the *Forcella Forada* or the *Col di Ponta* (p. 357) to (3½ hrs.) *Borca* (p. 351); or, lastly (very attractive), follow the heights to the N. and cross the *Durona Alp* to the (2 hrs.) **Forcella d'Ambrix** or *da Lago* (7546'), between the *Becco di Mezzodi* and the *Croda da Lago*, whence we descend by the *Federa Alp* to (2 hrs.) *Cortina* (p. 349). — The Civetta (10,420'), reached from *Mareson* (p. 353) viâ the *Forcella di Grava*, in 7-8 hrs. (guide), first ascended in 1867 by Mr. Tuckett, is difficult and dangerous on account of the frequent falls of stone.

Beyond Longarone the valley expands, without at first losing its wild character. The road crosses several torrents, reaches (3 M.) *Fortogna*, and divides at **Polpet**, 3½ M. farther on, the left branch leading to Vittorio, the right to Belluno.

The road to VITTORIO (20½ M.; diligence from Belluno daily in 5 hrs.; one-horse carr. from Longarone 20 fr.; two-horse carr. from Cortina 45, one-horse 24 fl.) crosses the *Piave* at (½ M.) **Ponte nelle Alpi** or *Capodiponte* (1205'; *Campana*, plain and moderate; *Stella*), turns to the E., and follows the left bank of the *Rai*, which issues from the (6 M.) *Lago di S. Croce* (1225'; 2½ M. long). At the S. end of the lake is the hamlet of *S. Croce*. The road then crosses the debris of an extensive old landslip (*Cima Fadalto*; 1650') and descends steeply to *Fadalto*. It next skirts the E. bank of the *Lago Morto* (925'), passes two other small lakes, and traverses a picturesque defile, at the end of which lies (12 M.) *Serravalle* (510'), connected by a fine avenue, ¾ M. long, with the larger village of *Ceneda*. These two places together form the town of Vittorio (*Hôtel Vittorio*, not far from the station, with garden; *Giraffa*, in the town). In the Piazza is a **statue of Victor Emanuel II.**, by Del Favaro, erected in 1882. RAILWAY from Vittorio to *Venice* viâ *Conegliano* in 2⅓ hrs., see *Baedeker's N. Italy*.

The BELLUNO ROAD (omnibus from Longarone to Belluno, at 4 and 7 p.m., in 2 hrs.; fare 1½ fr.) turns to the right at *Polpet* (see above), ½ M. from the Ponte nelle Alpi (see above), and follows the broad valley of the Piave to (4½ M.) —

64½ M. **Belluno** (1330'; *Cappello*; *Leon d'Oro*), the capital of the province, with 10,000 inhab., situated on a hill between the *Ardo* and the *Piave*, which here unite. The exterior of the town is Venetian in character. The *Cathedral*, built by *Palladio*, was partly destroyed by an earthquake in 1873, but has been restored. The massive campanile, 230' high, commands a beautiful view. An old sarcophagus, locally prized as a work of art, adorns the piazza in front of the church of S. Stefano. The triumphal arch outside the W. gate, completed in 1815, and dedicated to the Emp. Francis, was, like that at Milan, begun in honour of Napoleon.

FROM BELLUNO TO PRIMOLANO IN THE VAL SUGANA (38 M.). Railway to (19½ M.) *Feltre* in 1-1¼ hr.; from Feltre to Primolano diligence daily in 3½ hrs., starting at 9 a.m. — The railway traverses the broad valley of the Piave, generally at a distance from the river. Mulberries, maize, and vines indicate the character of the climate. On the slopes, and on the line itself lie numerous villages. Beyond (8 M.) *Sedico-Bribano* (route to *Agordo*, see p. 358) the train crosses the *Cordevole*. Near (10½ M.) *S. Giustina*, to the right, rises the *Mte. Pizzocco* (7175'). 15 M. *Cesio-Busche*. Near Feltre the valley contracts; the line skirts the Piave, and then quits it entirely.

19½ M. **Feltre** (*Hôtel Vapore*), an ancient town of 12,000 inhab., the *Feltria* of the Rhætians, presents rather a dilapidated appearance. The principal street, with the poor Albergo, leads through the modern town, skirting the hill on which lies the dirty and intricate old town. The *Piazza* in the latter is surrounded by the new, Venetian-Gothic *Palazzo Guarnieri*, adorned with mural paintings, the church of *S. Rocco*, in a debased style, the ruinous old *Castle*, and a building embellished with the gilded lion of St. Mark, the lower story of which is used as a school and the upper as a theatre. In the centre of the piazza rise statives of two distinguished natives of Feltre: *Vittore Rambaldoni*, educationalist (1378-1446), erected in 1868, and *Panfilo Castaldi* (b. 1308), for whom the inscription claims the honour of having invented movable types, erected by the printers of Milan in 1866. — From Feltre to *Cornuda* and *Treviso*, see *Baedeker's N. Italy*; to *Primiero* (omn. twice daily in summer, see p. 327).

FROM FELTRE TO PRIMOLANO (12½ M.). The beautiful road to Primolano passes *Arten (Fonzaso*, on the Primiero road, remaining on the right; p. 327), leads across the *Cismone* (p. 319) to (9 M.) *Arsie*, and descends through the Val Brenta in windings to (12½ M.) *Primolano* (p. 319).

64. From Cortina to Belluno viâ Agordo. Cordevole Valley.

Comp. Maps, pp. 348, 320.

The picturesque *Val Cordevole is well worth visiting. The lake of Alleghe and the environs of Agordo are among the finest points in the dolomite region, and many of the lateral valleys (Val Fiorentina, Val Forno, Val di S. Lucano, etc.) present magnificent scenery. Only the N. ramifications of the valley (Livinalongo or Buchenstein) belong to Tyrol; the Italian frontier lies to the N. of Caprile.

FROM CORTINA TO CAPRILE, there are two routes: the easier (18 M.) leads by *Falzarego* (road to the summit of the pass; one-horse springless carr. to the hospice 5½ fl., two-horse 10 fl ; driving thence to Caprile not recommended); the more attractive (also easy) is by the *Mte. Giau* (p. 356), or by the *Nuvolau* (p. 349; 6½-7 hrs.; guide hardly necessary for experts). FROM CAPRILE TO AGORDO (12 M.) a carriage-road; one-horse carr. in 4 hrs., 10-12 fr. (quite enough, though more may be demanded); from Agordo to SEDICO-BRIBANO (p. 358) diligence twice daily in 3½ hrs. (3 fr. 20 c.). — FROM CORTINA TO THE FASSA, either direct over the Fedaja Pass, or by the longer, but interesting route viâ Agordo and the Cereda Pass to Primiero, and thence by the road viâ S. Martino di Castrozza to Predazzo (comp. p. 321).

Cortina (3970'), see p. 348. Our road descends to the right immediately to the W. of the church, crosses the *Boite*, and ascends on the right bank through meadows and fields, skirting the *Crepa* (p. 349), and at places rather steep, to the (3½ M.) *Pocol Alp* ('behind the hill'), where the route to the Giau Pass (p. 356) diverges to the left. The road then ascends the N. slope of the wooded *Costeana Valley* (passing on the right the huge slopes of the *Tofana*, high up in which is a cavern, 'Il Buso della Tofana', and on the left the fissured *Croda da Lago*, the *Croda di Formin*, the *Cinque Torri* with the curious *Mte. Averau*, and the *Nuvolau* with the Sachsendank Hut) to the (4½ M.) unpretending *Hospice of Falzarēgo* (6535') and the (1¼ M.) **Falzarēgo Pass** (6950'), a wide, rock-strewn depression between the *Nuvolau* on the S. and the *Lagazuoi* on the N. To the S.W. appears the snow-crowned *Marmolada*, in the foreground are the *Sasso di Stria* and *Col di Lana*. The path in a straight direction leads between the *Sasso di Stria* and the *Lagazuoi* to the pass *Tra i Sassi* and to St. Cassian (p. 342). The road to Buchenstein turns abruptly to the S. before the Sasso di Stria, and terminates beyond the pass, on the frontier of the Ampezzo district, whence we descend by a steep and rough cart-track past the picturesque ruin of *Andraz* (5625'; to the right the route over the Castello Pass to St. Cassian, p. 342) to (3 M.) **Andraz**

23*

(4695'; *Col. Finazzer, good beer), a village at the base of the *Col di Lana*, in the E. branch of the Buchenstein Valley.

A good path, with fine views of the valley, leads from Andraz round the slope of the Col di Lana, and past *Salesei*, to (1 hr.) **Pieve di Livinalongo**, or **Buchenstein** (4815'; *Posta; Fel. Finazzer*), the chief place in the *Val Livinalongo*, or upper *Cordevole Valley*, picturesquely situated high above the ravine of the Cordevole. Thence by *Prelongei* to *St. Cassian*, see p. 343; by *Campolungo* or *Incisa* to *Corvara*, see p. 343; over the *Pordoi Pass* to the *Fassa*, see p. 323. — A highly interesting route leads to the S.W. from Pieve over the **Forcella di Padon** (7800'), which affords a splendid view of the Marmolada, etc., to the (3½-4 hrs.) *Fedaja Pass* (p. 324; the shortest way from Cortina to the Marmolada). — The **Col di Lana** (8070'), ascended from Pieve in 2½ hrs. (with guide) commands a superb view; the route leads mostly over grass, and is steep at places. — A rough and unattractive path leads from Pieve direct to Caprile in 1½ hr., viâ *Salesei* and *Digonera*.

The cart-track from Andraz to Caprile crosses the stream at a saw-mill, and then runs, at first through wood, high up on the left side of the *Val Cordevole*, passing several hamlets, and commanding a fine view of Pieve, the Col di Lana, Val Livinalongo, and the long Croda di Boè. Farther down, on a spur of *Mte. Migion*, rises the tower-like *Sasso di Ronch;* to the S. appears the vast Civetta. The road descends steeply, crossing the extensive stony deposits with which the meadows of the valley were covered by the inundations of the Cordevole in 1882, to (6 M.). —

18 M. **Caprile** (3375'; *Albergo delle Alpi*), picturesquely situated in a beautiful valley.

EXCURSIONS (guides, *Ball.* and *Bortolo dalla Santa, Clem. Callegari, Nepom. del Buos, Pellegrino & Ant. Pellegrini, Giac. Fabiani*.) The **Monte Migion** (7835'; 3½ hrs., with guide), rising to the N. between the Val Pettorina and the Val Livinalongo, commands an admirable view of the Marmolada, Civetta, etc. — An easier and also very attractive point is the **Mte. Fernazza** (ca. 6890'), to the E. of Caprile (2 hrs.); ascent through wood and then over pastures. Splendid view of the Pelmo, Civetta, Marmolada, Tofana, etc., and of the valleys of the Cordevole (with the Lago d'Alleghe far below) and the Fiorentina. The descent may be made over the *Forcella d'Alleghe* (5935') to Alleghe or to Pescul in the Val Fiorentina (see below).

FROM CORTINA TO CAPRILE OVER THE MONTE GIAU, 6½-7 hrs., easy and interesting (guide 5½ fl.; horse to the pass 5½ fl.). The route descends to the left from the Falzarego road at (3½ M.) Pocol (p. 355), and at the (20 min.) *Pezzié di Parú Alp* it crosses the *Falzarego* or *Costeana*, beyond which it crosses the *Giau* and ascends through wood, leading to the right at the bifurcation, and after ½ hr. recrossing the stream. Quitting the wood (25 min.) we next ascend the pastures of the *Giau Alp* (with the jagged crest of the *Croda di Formin* on the left, the *Nuvolau* on the right, and the *Tofana* behind us), cross the stream below a chalet, which we leave on the right, and soon reach the (1 hr.) °**Giau Pass** (7380'), on the right side of the *Col Giatei* (7260'), a low grassy eminence, on the left side of which another pass leads to *Selva* in the *Val Fiorentina* (see p. 357). Superb °View, towards the N., of the rocky walls of the Nuvolau, Tofana, Hohe Gaisl, and Cristallo; E., the Sorapiss, Croda di Formin, and Monte Carnera; W., the majestic Marmolada, the Boè, and other peaks. We now descend by a steep and narrow path, pass several huts, and soon obtain a fine view of the huge Civetta and (farther down) of the Pelmo. In the valley (¾ hr.) we turn to the right, cross the *Codalongu*, at the junction of the path descending from the Nuvolau (p. 319), and then descend (to the right) the wooded slope of the *Mte. Frisolet* (1875'), the path being at first alternately level and hilly, and afterwards descending over meadows to (1¼ hr.) **Colle** di S. Lucia, or *Villagrande* (4830'; Finazzer), beautifully situated on a mountain-terrace, with a striking view of the Val Fiorentina, the colossal Pelmo, and the (S.) Civetta. From Colle to *Caprile*, ½ hr.

FROM CAPRILE TO S. VITO on the Ampezzo road (p. 351), an easy route (new carriage-road on the left bank of the Fiorentina as far as Selva), thence bridle-path) leads in 6 hrs. through the *Val Fiorentina*, past the villages of *Selva* (4480'), *Andria*, and *Pescul*, and over the **Forcella Forada** (6895'), on the N. side of the Pelmo, or over the Col di Ponia (6890'), a little to the N. The *Pelmo* (10,395') may be ascended from the *Val Fiorentina* (difficult, comp. pp. 351, 533; from Selva, where guides may be procured, 9-10 hrs.). — Over the *Forcella d'Ambriz* to Cortina, and over the *Forcella di Staulanza* to Zoldo, see p. 353.

From Caprile by *Rocca* to the *Val Pettorina* (" *Sottoguda Gorge*), the *Fedaja Pass*, and the ascent of the *Marmolada*, see p. 324 (experts require no guide for the Fedaja Pass; from Caprile to Campitello 10 fr.).

The ROAD FROM CAPRILE TO AGORDO (12 M.) follows the left bank of the rapid Cordevole (leaving *Callónèghe* on the right bank) to the beautiful "**Lake of Allèghe** (3220'), 1½ M. long, the E. bank of which it skirts. The lake owes its origin to a landslip from the *Mte. Forca*, which in 1772 buried three villages. The surface of the green water reflects the towering rocks of *Mte. Civetta* (10,420'). On the E. bank lies (1½ M.) the hamlet of *Allèghe* (3235'; Inn, poor), charmingly situated at the mouth of the *Val Lander*. (Pleasant walk from Caprile to Alleghe; then across by boat to a hill on the W. bank which commands the finest view of the lake, and back to Caprile via Calloneghe; 2 hrs. in all.)

The '**Mte. Coldai**, to the E. of Alleghe, ascended through the *Val Lander* in 3 hrs. (guide, *Ag. Soppela* of Alleghe), commands an admirable view of the Civetta, Pelmo, etc. To the N. of the Coldai an easy route crosses the **Passo Coldai** (3720') to the *Val di Zoldo* (p. 353).

At the S. end of the lake the road crosses the Cordevole (the canal here for floating timber, constructed by Sign. Manzoni of Agordo, is interesting) and traverses the scene of the abovementioned landslip. It then leads through a picturesque and richly wooded valley, in view of the *Cima di Pape* and *Pale di S. Lucano*, with the *Mte. Alto di Pelsa* on the left, to (4½ M.) **Cencenighe** (2540'; *Osteria Vecchia*, plain), a hamlet at the confluence of the *Biois* with the Cordevole.

In the **Val Biois (Val Canale)** a carriage-road leads to (3 M.) *Forno di Canale* (3200'; °Gallo, moderate), picturesquely situated at the mouth of the *Val Comelle* (p. 326); from Forno there is a bridle-track on the left bank of the Biois to (1¼ hr.) *Falcade* (4290'), at the head of the valley. Thence over the *Vallès Pass* (6880') to (4 hrs.) *Paneveggio*, see p. 326; those who are bound for S. Martino di Castrozza need not go as far as Paneveggio, but ascend to the left below the *Veneggia Alp* and cross the *Juribell Alp* direct to the *Rolle Pass* (see p. 325). — Over the *Pellegrino Pass* to *Moëna*, see p. 322; over the *Comelle Pass* and *Rosetta Pass* to *S. Martino di Castrozza*, see p. 326. Guides, *Val. Bonelli* of Forno di Canale and *P. Lorenzi* of Garès.

The **Cima di Pape** (8238'), a very fine point of view, is ascended from Cencenighe or Listolade (p. 358) without serious difficulty (5 hrs.; guide, *Cesare Lazzarini* of Cencenighe). — Another attractive and not difficult ascent is that of the **Monte Alto di Pelsa** (7910'; 5½ hrs., with guide), accomplished from Listolade viâ the *Val di Comparsa* and the *Manzoni Alp*.

The road crosses the Biois, and at (¾ M.) *Puè*, the *Cordevole*, and enters an imposing, rock-strewn gorge, at the end of which lies the (3 M.) hamlet of *Listolade*, at the mouth of the wild *Val di Comparsa*. To the left rises the *Cima di Framont*. To the right, at (1 M.) *Taibon*, opens the *Val di S. Lucano* (p. 326), with the precipices of the *Pale di S. Lucano* (8530') on its N. side. Then (1½ M.)—

12 M. **Agördo** (2000'; *Albergo alle Miniere*, reading-room of the Italian Alpine Club on the ground-floor, open to strangers; *Alb. alle Alpi Dolomitiche*, new), the capital of the valley (3000 inhab.), beautifully situated in a rich valley amid imposing mountains (N., Mte. Alto di Pelsa and Cima di Framont; E., the Pramper Mts.; W., Pale di S. Lucano, etc.). In the extensive piazza stands the mansion of Cavaliere Manzoni.

FROM AGORDO TO PRIMIERO OVER THE CEREDA PASS, 7-8 hrs., easy and attractive (guide 7 fr.). At (10 min.) *Brugnach* we cross the Cordevole and ascend to the left, obtaining fine retrospects of the Val Agordo (to the W. the *Croda Grande*, 9120'), pass *Voltago* and *Miana*, and reach (1½ hr.) the picturesquely situated village of *Frassenè* (3600'; Inn). About ¾ hr. farther on (short-cut to the right, by the last house) is the *Forcella Aorine* (4325'), between *Mte. Luna* and *Mte. Gardellon*. Thence we descend again to (½ hr.) *Gosaldo* (Inn), in a lateral valley of the *Mis*, at the foot of lofty dolomites (*Sasso di Campo, Cima d'Oltro*, etc.). We now follow the upper path, high above the **Mis valley** (opposite *Sagron*, see below, above which is a long rocky ridge with the picturesque *Piz di Sagron*, 8105'), to (1 hr.) *Mis*, cross the stream (Austrian frontier), and ascend to the (¾ hr.) *Osteria*, ½ hr. below the low, grassy summit of the Cereda Pass (4500'). On the other side the broad, stony track descends gradually through meadows and woods to the (1 hr.) *Castel della Pietra*, a ruin most picturesquely perched on an inaccessible rock at the mouth of the *Val di Canali*. (Before the castle is reached the route to the *Val di Pradidali* diverges to the right, see p. 326.) A rough track now descends the hill and crosses a (¼ hr.) bridge, whence a good road leads viâ *Tonadico* to (2 M.) *Fiera di Primiero* (p. 326). — Another route from Agordo to the Cereda Pass leads viâ *Tiser, Ren, Valalta* (quicksilver mines, interesting to geologists), and *Sagron*, but is longer and less attractive than the path by Gosaldo. — The *Piz di Sagron* ('1 Piz', 8105') and the *Sasso di Mur* (8380') to the S. of it, may be ascended from Sagron by the *Comedon Pass* (7220'; both very difficult). Guides, *Arcangelo Gariet, Nic. Valconezza, Gius. Pretoran* of Agordo, *Tom. dal Col* of Voltago.

FROM AGORDO TO FORNO DI ZOLDO over the Duran Pass (5360'), easy (5 hrs; guide not indispensable for experts). The path ascends viâ *Rif, Piasent*, and *Dugon* to the pass, between *Mte. Mojazza* and *Mte. S. Sebastiano*. Descent either direct, or by *S. Tiziano di Goima* (4175'), to *Dont* and *Forno* (p. 353). — From Agordo to Zoldo over the **Moschesin Pass** (6315') and through the *Val Pramper* to (6 hrs.) Forno, another easy route (bridle-path; guide not indispensable).

Below Agordo the valley contracts. The road is flanked with huge masses of rock. It leads over the *Ponte Alto, and farther on crosses the Cordevole three times more in this magnificent defile (*Canal **d'Agordo**), the narrowest part of which is guarded by a new fort. The valley expands at (10 M.) *Peron* (Inn), and at the hamlet of (1 M.) *Mas* the road forks, the left branch traversing a hilly district to (6 M.) *Belluno* (p. 354), the right skirting the Cordevole to (4½ M.) *Sedico-Bribano*, on the railway from Belluno to Feltre (p. 354).

VIII. ALPS OF UPPER AND LOWER AUSTRIA. STYRIA. CARINTHIA. CARNIOLA. KÜSTENLAND.

65. From Vienna to Gratz 361
   Kaltenleutgeben. Anninger, 361. — Helenenthal. Eiserne Thor. Merkenstein. Gutenstein, 362. — Forchtenstein. Rosaliencapelle. From Neustadt to Aspang. Wechsel, 363. — Gfiederberg. Schloss Wartenstein. Kirchberg on the Wechsel. Reichenau, 364. — The Höllenthal. From the Singerin over the Nasskamm to Kapellen. Schneeberg, 365. — Raxalpe, 366. — Sonnwendstein, 367. — Stuhleck. Drahtekogel. Hohe Veitschalp, 368. — Rennfeld, Bärenschütz. Hochlantsch. Hochalpe, 369. — Oleinalpe, 370.

66. From Mürzzuschlag to Mariazell and Bruck on the Mur 370
   Schneealpe. Hohe Veitsch, 371. — From Mürzsteg to Mariazell viâ Freiu and the Freinsattel, 372. — Excursions from Mariazell. Bürger-Alpe. Erlaufsee. Lassing Fall. Oetschergraben, 373. — From Mariazell to Gaming; to Schrambach, 373, 374. — From Wegscheid to Weichselboden over the Kastenriegel, 374. — Hochschwab. Mitteralpe. Filzstein. St. Ilgen. Messnerin. Karlhochkogel. Sonnschien-Alpe, 375.

67. From Mariazell to Gross-Reifling viâ Weichselboden and Wildalpen 376
   The Ring. Hochschwab, 376. — Hochstadl. Excursions from Gschöder. Riegerin, Ebenstein, etc. Excursions from Wildalpen, 377. — From Wildalpen to Eisenerz over the Eisenerzer Höhe. Schafhals-Sattel, 378. — Krausgrotte, 379.

68. From Vienna to Linz 379
   From St. Pölten to Leobersdorf. Reisalpe. Hocheck. Schöpfl. Steinwandklamm, 379, 380. — From Pöchlarn to Kienberg-Gaming. Oetscher, 380. — Göstling. Lunz. Dürnstein. Hochkaar. From Göstling to Weyer. Voralpe, 381. — From Amstetten to Klein-Reifling. Waidhofen and its environs, 381, 382. — Environs of Linz, Freinberg. Jägermayr. Pöstlingberg. Giselawarte, 382, 383.

69. From Linz to St. Michael viâ Steyr 383
   Excursions from Steyr. Damberg. Schoberstein. Through the Steyrthal to Windisch-Garsten, Hohenock, 383, 384. — St. Gallen. Spitzenbachgraben. Voralpe. Carl-August-Steig, 384. — Hartelsgraben. Tamischbachthurm. Luganer. From Hieflau to Leoben viâ Eisenerz and Vorderneberg, 385. — Frauenmauerhöhle. Tragösstthal. Brockgraben, 386. — Johnsbachthal. Excursions from Admont. Schloss Röthelstein, 387. — Kaiserau. Grosse Buchstein. Natterriegel. Grosse Pyhrgass, 388. — From Trieben to Judenburg viâ Hoheutauern. Bösenstein, 389. — Zeiritzkampel. Hoch-Reichart. Seckauer Zinken. Gösseck, 389.

70. From Linz to Liezen viâ Kirchdorf and Windisch-Garsten. Stoder 389
   Bad Hall. Excursions from Kirchdorf and Michidorf. Steyrlingthal. To the Almsee viâ the Berneran, 390. — Excursions from Stoder. Kleine Priel. Grosse Priel. Spitzmauer. To Klachau over the Salzsteig, 391. — Excursions from Windisch-Garsten. Source of the Piesling.

Gleinker See. Warscheneck, etc. Through the Laussa to Weissenbach, 394. — From Spital am Pyhrn to the Grosse Pyhrgass and over the Pyhrgass-Gatterl to Admont, 392.

71. **From Selzthal to Aussee and Bischofshofen** . . . 392
Hochmölbing, 392. — Irdning. Möllhegg. Grimming. Lopernstein. Gumpeneck, 393. — Pass Stein. The Sölkthal. Grosse Knallstein. Predigtstuhl. Stoder-Zinken. Kammspitze. Seewigthal, 394. — Excursions from Schladming. Ramsau. Austriahütte. Dachstein. Scheichenspitze, etc., 395, 396. — Riesach-See. Klafferkessel Hochwildstelle. Hochgolling. Preuneggthal. Filzmoos, 396. — Röthelstein. Bischofsmütze. Rossbrand. Grieskareck. From Radstadt viâ Wagrein to St. Johann in the Pongau, 397.

72. **From Radstadt to Spital over the Radstädter Tauern** 397
The Murwinkel. Rothgülden-See. Hafnereck, etc., 398. — The Lungau. Excursions from Tamsweg. Lasaberg-Alpl. Preberspitze. From Tamsweg to Scheifling, 398. — Excursions from Gmünd. Tschirneck. Königsstuhl. Reiseck. Maltathal. Gössgraben. Passes to Mallnitz, Gastein, and St. Johann, 399, 400.

73. **Gratz and Environs** 400
Buchkogl. Schöckel. Tobelbad, 404. — From Gratz to Köflach and over the Stuhalp Pass to Judenburg, 404. — From Gratz viâ Schwanberg to Klagenfurt. The Schwanberg Alps. Koralpe, 404, 405.

74. **From Gratz to Trieste** 405
Radkersburg. St. Urban, 406. — The Baths of Robitsch. Donatiberg. Krapina-Töplitz. Baths of Neuhaus, 407. — The Sannthal Alps, 407-9. — The Franz-Josephs-Bad, 409. — Excursions from Laibach. Gallenberg. Krimberg. Gottschee, 410. — Quicksilver Mines of Idria. Javornik. Zirknitzer See. Schneeberg, 411. — Stalactite Caverns of Adelsberg. Lueg. Präwald. The Nanos, 412. — Abbazia. Monte Maggiore. Crown Prince Rudolf Grotto. Cascades and Grottoes of St. Canzian, 413.

75. **From Marburg to Villach** 414
Welka Kappa. Windischgratz. Ursulaberg. The Lavantthal, 415. — From Wolfsberg to Judenburg viâ St. Leonhard. The Petzen, 416. — From Kühnsdorf to Krainburg viâ Eisenkappel and the Vellacher Bad. Hochobir. Grintouz. Skuta, 417, 418. — From Klagenfurt to Krainburg over the Loibl, 419. — The Stou. Bärenthal. From Klagenfurt to Waidisch and Zell, 420. — Rosegg. Sternberg, 421. — Excursions from Villach. Bad Villach. Faaker See. Mittagskogel. Gerlitzen-Alp. Treffen. Dobratsch, 422, 423. — The Gailthal, 423.

76. **From Bruck to Villach** 424
From St. Lorenzen to Seekau. Zinken. From Knittelfeld to the Gleinalpe. Ingering-Thal. Hoch-Reichart, 424. — Excursions from Judenburg. Zirbitzkogel. Schafkogel. Roseukogel, etc., 425. — Oberwölz. Hohenwart. Grebenzen. From Friesach to Feldkirchen viâ Flattnitz and St. Leonhard. Eisenhut, 426. — Gurk. Hoch-Osterwitz. Magdalenaberg. St. Georgen am Längsee. From Launsdorf to Hüttenberg. The Grosse Saualpe, 427. — From Glandorf to Klagenfurt through the Zollfeld, 428.

77. From Laibach to Villach 429
    From Bischoflaak to Tolmein. Veldes, 429. — The
    Wochein. Schwarzenberg. Baža Pass. Skerbinja-Joch.
    Ascent of the Terglou, 430. — The Terglou Lakes. To
    Moistrana over the Kerma Sattel. The Stou. Urata
    Valley. Over the Luknia Pass to Flitach, 431. — Pi-
    schenza Valley. Over the Verschitz Sattel to Flitsch.
    Weissenfels Lakes, 432.
78. From Villach to Udine. Pontebba Railway 433
    Excursions from Tarvis. Graf-Carl-Steig. Bartolograben.
    Göriacher Alp. Römerthal, 433. — Luschariberg. Seisera
    Valley. Bärenlahnscharte. Dogna Pass. Uggowitzer
    Alp. Osternigg. Mittagskofel, 434. — Over the Lusnitzer
    Alp to Dogna. Poludnig. Rosskofel. Gartnerkofel, 434, 435.
    — From Tolmezzo viâ Forni Avoltri and Ampezzo di
    Carnia to Cadore, 436.
79. Trieste and Environs 437
    Miramar. Občina. Capo d'Istria, etc., 440, 441.
80. From Trieste to Villach viâ the Predil 441
    Excursions from Tolmein. Dante Grotto. Kern, 442. —
    Excursions from Flitsch. Prestreljenik. Kanin. Rombon.
    Baumbachhütte, 442. — Excursions from Raibl. Lake
    of Raibl. Kaltwasserthal. Mangart. Wischberg. Braun-
    kofel, 443. — From Raibl to Chiusaforte through the
    Raccolana Valley, 444.
81. From Trieste to Pola and Fiume 444

65. From Vienna to Gratz.

141½ M. RAILWAY. Express-trains in 5½-6¼ hrs.; ordinary in 8-9 hrs. 'View-carriage' as far as Semmering; views generally to the left.

Vienna, see *Baedeker's S. Germany and Austria*. The line runs at a considerable height, affording an extensive view to the E. as far as the Leitha Mts., and to the W. overlooking the city, numerous villas, and populous villages at the base of a picturesque range of hills. To the left lie the cemetery of Matzleinsdorf and the Protestant cemetery. The suburbs of the city extend as far as (2 M.) *Meidling*. 2½ M. *Hetzendorf* (with an imperial château); 5 M. *Atzgersdorf*; 6 M. *Liesing*; 7 M. *Perchtoldsdorf*.

A branch-line runs hence (22 min.) to (4½ M.) **Kaltenleutgeben**, a village charmingly situated in the valley of the *Dürre Liesing*, with many villas and two hydropathic establishments. A very pleasant excursion may be made to the (3½ M.) *Höllenstein* (2120'), where the '*Julienthurm*' commands a splendid view.

8 M. *Brunn*, with iron-works. From (10 M.) *Mödling*, an old town at the entrance to the picturesque *Brühl*, a branch-line diverges on the left to *Laxenburg*, an imperial château in a fine park.

The *Anninger (2215') may be ascended from Mödling in 2½ hrs. We ascend by the 'Goldne Steige' to the *Wilhelmswarte*, which commands a magnificent view (more open to the N. and W. from the *Sophienwarte*, on the *Eschenkogel*, 2130', reached in 25 min.). A little below, near the *Buchbrunnen*, is the *Anningerhaus* (Inn in summer). The Anninger may also be ascended (paths marked) from Gumpoldskirchen, Baden, etc.

13 M. *Guntramsdorf*; 14 M. *Gumpoldskirchen*, famous for its wine.

17 M. **Baden** (695'; *Stadt Wien; *Grüner Baum; Rechtberger; Hirsch; *Schwarzer Adler; Goldener Löwe) is a famous watering-place, the warm springs of which (72-97° Fahr.) were known to the Romans (*Thermae Pannonicae*). The chief spring (*Römerquelle*, or *Ursprung*) rises copiously in a cavern in the shady *Park*, at the base of the *Calvarienberg* (1070'). The best view of the town is obtained from the Calvarienberg (20 min.).

A pretty walk leads through the *Helenenthal, on the bank of the Schwechat, to the (1 M.) *Weilburg*, a château of Archduke Albert, and thence to the (1 hr.) *Urtelstein* and the (1/2 hr.) *Krainerhütten*; on the heights to the right and left. are the ruins of *Rauhenstein, Rauheneck*, and *Scharfeneck*. — To the *Eiserne Thor (Hohe Lindkogel*, 2726'; 3 hrs. from Baden) is another attractive excursion. We reach the shooting-lodge in the *Weichselthal* in 1¼ hr., and follow thence the route indicated by red and blue marks to the (1¾ hrs.) summit, on which there is a view-tower and hut (restaurant). Well-defined routes also ascend the Hohe Lindkogel from the *Krainerhütten* (see above) and from *Merkenstein* (see below) in 1½-2 hrs.

A little beyond Baden the ruins of Rauhenstein and Rauheneck (see above) are visible from the train on the hills to the right. The broad plain to the left, sprinkled with villages, is bounded by the *Leitha Mts*. Near (19½ M.) **Vöslau** (800'; *Hôtel Back; Hallmayer*), another watering-place, the finest Austrian wine is produced, the best vineyards being above the church of *Gainfarn*, which yield 'Oberkirchner'.

Immediately adjoining Vöslau is the prettily situated village of Gainfarn (*Weintraube*) with a favourite hydropathic establishment. — Excursion to (1½ hr.) *Merkenstein*, with a ruined castle, a château, and a belvedere in the park. Pavilion with refreshments, outside the park Thence to the *Eiserne Thor*, 1½ hr., see above.

Near (22 M.) *Leobersdorf* (870'; Adler) the *Schneeberg* (p. 365) appears on the right. To the E. is (1¼ M.) *Schönau*, with a beautiful park.

FROM LEOBERSDORF TO GUTENSTEIN, 24 M., railway in 1½ hr. The line diverges to the left from the Pölten railway beyond (1¾ M.) *Wittmannsdorf*, passes *Matzendorf*, and enters the smiling valley of the *Piesting*. Stations *Steinabrückl, Wöllersdorf* (with large sandstone-quarries), and *Unter-Piesting* (Löwe; Hirsch), 3 M. to the N. of which is *Hornstein*, the finely-situated château of Archduke Leopold. About 1½ M. to the S. of (13½ M.) *Ober-Piesting* (Grüner Baum) is the extensive ruin of *Starhemberg*, once a seat of Frederick 'der Streitbare'. Beyond *Wopfing* we reach (15½ M.) *Waldegg*, the station for the villages of *Waldegg* and *Peisching* (*Singer's Hotel). Interesting excursion to the **Hohe Wand**. The marked path (steep at places, and provided with wire-rope and ladders) leads through the *Dürnbachthal* (waterfall), passing Schönthaler's Inn, to the (2 hrs.) *Waldegger Hütte* (3290'; view-tower), a little to the S. of which is the game-park of Archduke Leopold, containing mountain-goats and mouflons. — The *Mandling* (3040'; 1½ hr.) may also be ascended from Waldegg.

The valley contracts. The train runs through deep cuttings and crosses a viaduct. 17½ M. *Oed* (Gscholder), with a large wire-factory; thence to the S., across the *Miesenbach*, to (9 M.) *Buchberg* (p. 365), interesting. Then past *Ortmann* (with a wool-factory) to (21 M.) *Pernitz* (1410'; Adler; Singer), in a broad and pleasant valley. About 2 M. to the N.W. lies *Muckendorf* (Herzog), from which the *Unterberg* (4400'; splendid view) is ascended in 3 hrs. (but shorter from Gutenstein through the *Steinapiesting-Thal*); about ½ hr. below the top is a new club-hut (3820'; 10 beds). Above Muckendorf is the (20 min.) fine *Mira Fall* (Karner's Inn). Viâ *Greith to Gratz.* NEUSTADT. *VIII. Route 65.* 363

and the *Steinwandklamm* to the *Further-Thal*, see p. 380. — 24½ M. Gutenstein (1580'; *Bär*; *Löwe*), a prettily-situated village. Fine views from the ruined castle (access across the *Lange Brücke* through the gorge of the Steinapiesting, from several points in the park of Count Hoyos, and from the (¾ hr.) *Mariahilfberg* (2315'; Inn), with a pilgrimage-church. A road leads from Gutenstein through the *Klosterthal*, and over the *Klosterthaler Gscheid* (2575'), to the (10 M.) *Hähbauer* (from this point to the *Schneeberg*, see p. 366), and to the (3 M.) *Singerin*, at the head of the Höllenthal (p. 365).
From Leobersdorf to *St. Pölten*, see p. 379.

26 M. *Felixdorf*; 28½ M. *Theresienfeld*.

31 M. **Wiener-Neustadt** (930'; *Hirsch*; *Kreuz*; *Rössl*), a manufacturing town with 23,500 inhab., has been almost entirely rebuilt since a fire in 1834, which destroyed all but fourteen houses. On the S.E. side of the town is the ancient ducal *Castle* of the Babenberg family, built in 1192, and altered by Emp. Frederick III. in 1457. In the court, over the entrance, is a statue (of 1453) of the Emp. Frederick, whose favourite and bombastic motto A. E. I. O. U. ('Austria erit in orbe ultima', or 'Austriæ est imperare orbi universo') is inscribed on different parts of the walls. The building was converted into a military academy (400 pupils) by Maria Theresa in 1752. The garden contains a statue of the empress by Gasser. In the interior are portraits of the foundress and of several pupils. Beneath the high-altar of the chapel Emp. Maximilian I. is interred (comp. p. 163).

Interesting excursion by the *Oedenburg Railway* (see *Baedeker's S. Germany and Austria*), viâ *Neudörfl*, *Sauerbrunn* (the *Neustädter Warte*, on the *Gespitzte Riegel*, 1925', 3 M. to the S.W., commands a fine view), and *Wiesen*, to (11 M., in ½ hr.) *Mattersdorf*, whence we ascend to the left by *Forchtenau* to the (5 M.) château of *Forchtenstein*, the property of Prince Esterhazy, conspicuously situated on a limestone rock (1080'), and containing a collection of family-portraits, captured weapons, etc. (castellan 50 kr.; Inn adjoining the château). — On the top of the *Heuberg*, ¾ hr. farther on, rises the *Rosaliencapelle* (2440'), a pilgrimage-church erected in 1695, with an extensive prospect. A picturesque path (indicated by blue and white marks) descends from this point through the *Kaiserwald* to the *Ofenbach Graben* and to (2½ hrs.) *Klein-Wolkersdorf* (see below).

FROM NEUSTADT TO ASPANG, 22 M., railway (from a station on the E. side of the town) in 1¼ hr. (from Vienna to Aspang 3 hrs.). Stations: *Klein-Wolkersdorf*, *Erlach*, and (8 M.) [*Pitten* (Inn), an old village with an extensive ruin, beyond which the line follows the pleasant *Pittenthal*. — 10½ M. *Seebenstein* (*Fuchs*; Apold) is commanded by the handsome castle of that name, erected in 1092, the property of Prince Liechtenstein, and still partly preserved, containing an interesting armoury. (A pleasant forest-path leads hence to the *Türkensturz*, in ¾ hr.) — 14 M. *Scheiblingkirchen*. 16½ M. *Edlitz* (1170'; *Schnöcker*); pleasant excursion thence to the (1 hr.) *Grimmenstein-Warte* on the *Kulmriegel* (2484'). — 22 M. Aspang (1555'), consisting of *Unter-* and *Ober-Aspang* (Aspanger Hof; Goldner Adler; Schwarzer Adler), with the château of Count Pergen, the terminus of the railway. This is the best starting-point for the ascent of the **Wechsel** (5 hrs.). We may either follow the road to the W. through the *Klosterthal* ('Grosse Klause') to (2½ hrs.) *Mariensee* (Dorfstetter), and ascend by the (2 hrs.) *Mariensee Schwaig* (3810'; Inn); or ascend by a steep road to (2½ hrs.) *Mönichkirchen* (3215'; Windbichler; Treitner), a high lying village with a fine view, and thence by the *Vorauer Schwaig* (4840' tavern) in 3½ hrs.; or mount in 4 hrs. by the *Steinerne Stiege* (4305') and the *Niedere Wechsel* (5475') to the summit (*Hochwechsel* or *Hohe Umschuss*, 5700'), marked by a trigonometrical pyramid (splendid view). Descent by

the *Kranichberger Schwaig* (4920'; *Inn*) to (3½ hrs.) *Kirchberg* (see below).
— From Aspang to (8 M.) *Kirchberg* diligence daily viâ *Feistritz* in 1¾ hr.; see below.

To the right beyond Neustadt the *Schneeberg* is visible from the summit nearly to the base; to the left the Leitha Mts. Large fields of maize, and then pine-woods are passed. On the hills to the left in the distance stands *Schloss Seebenstein* (p. 363). 35½ M. *St. Egyden*; 40½ M. **Neunkirchen** (1210'; *Hirsch*), a manufacturing place. Scenery picturesque and varied. At (43 M.) *Ternitz*, a place with a large steel-foundry, the train crosses the *Sierningbach*.

Through the *Sierningthal* to *Buchberg*, see p. 365. To the W. of Ternitz rises the conical **Gösederberg** (1990'), which may be easily ascended from (1½ hr.) *St. Johann-im-Steinfelde* (Inn) in ½ hr.; charming view from the tower.

45½ M. *Pottschach*, with manufactories. — 47½ M. **Gloggnitz** (1430'; *Rail. Restaurant; *Alpenhorn; *Adler; Rössl; Touristenruhe*), at the base of the Semmering. On a hill is *Schloss Gloggnitz*, with its numerous windows, a Benedictine abbey down to 1803, and now the seat of the district-authorities.

On a spur of the *Otterberg*, 4½ M. to the S.W., rises the picturesque **Schloss Wartenstein** (2490'), with an extensive view from the tower. The château, now in the possession of Princess Liechtenstein, dates from the 12th cent., and has recently been restored in the style of that period. — A road leads from Gloggnitz to the S.E., viâ *Schloss Kranichberg* (the property of the Archbishop of Vienna) and the *Rams* (2080'; Inn), to (7½ M.) Kirchberg *on the Wechsel* (1890'; *Hirsch; Grüner Baum; Dannhäuser*), from which the *Wechsel* (5700') may be ascended viâ the *Kranichberger Schwaig* in 5 hrs. (see above). — To the W. of Kirchberg is the (¼ hr.) *Hermannshöhle*, a fine stalactite cavern, recently rendered accessible (adm. 50 kr.; the visit takes 2-3 hrs.). — To the E. of Kirchberg (3¾ M.) lies *Feistritz*, with a château of Prince Sulkowski, sumptuously fitted up (but the collections are only shown to those who have obtained permission at Vienna). Thence to (4¼ M.) *Aspang*, see above.

The *Semmering Railway, which begins at Gloggnitz, the oldest of the great continental mountain-railways, constructed by Hr. v. Ghega in 1848-53, is remarkable for the boldness of its engineering and the grandeur of the scenery it traverses. Between Payerbach and Mürzzuschlag, a distance of 20 M., there are 15 tunnels and 16 viaducts. The maximum gradient is 1:4. The line reaches its highest point (2940') in the long tunnel (p. 367). The construction of the line cost about 2,000,000*l*.

The train now ascends. Schloss Gloggnitz presents a handsome appearance; in the valley flows the green *Schwarzau*, on which is the large paper-manufactory of *Schlöglmühl*. On the left rises the *Sonnenwendstein*, with its three peaks; to the W., in the background, the *Raxalp* (p 366). The line describes a wide circuit round the N. slope of the mountain to (55 M.)' **Payerbach** (1510'; *Mader; *Rail. Restaurant*, with beds).

To REICHENAU AND THE HÖLLENTHAL, a very attractive excursion from Payerbach (omnibus from the station to Reichenau). The road passes under the railway-viaduct and reaches (1½ M.) Reichenau (1600'; *Fischer*, R. 1½ fl., L. 15 kr. good wine; *Goldner Anker; *Waisnix*, prettily situated in the *Thalhof*, ½ M. to the N.), in a sheltered situation in the beautiful green valley of the *Schwarzau*, a fashionable resort of the Viennese, with many new villas and lodging-houses. (On the left bank of the Schwarzau is the *Rudolfsbad*, a hydropathic, well fitted up.) The road then passes the *Villa Warthols*, the seat of Archduke Karl Ludwig, and the new château of Baron Nathaniel Rothschild, at the mouth of the *Preinthal* (p. 366), and reaches (2 M.) *Hirschwang* (1620'; Inn), with its large ironworks. The valley now contracts (on the left rises the *Grünschacher*, on the right the *Feuchter*, *Ochsenwand*, and *Stadelwand*), and we enter the *Höllenthal*. The road crosses the Schwarzau several times, and next reaches (2 M.) *Kaiserbrunn* (1760'; °Schnepf's Inn). Adjoining the inn-garden is the walled enclosure of the *'Kaiserbrunnen'*, which, together with the Stixensteinquelle in the Sierningthal, supplies Vienna with excellent drinking-water. A steep path ascends from this point through the *Klausgraben* to the summit of the Schneeberg (see below; to the Baumgartner 3 hrs.). We now pass through a very picturesque part of the valley. After 2 M. a finger-post indicates the way to the (3/4 M.) °*Grosse Höllenthal* (2130'), a grand basin, enclosed by the rocky slopes of the *Loswand* on the left and the *Kloben* on the right, with the *Losbühel* to the left in the background. (Chamois, which are preserved here, are often seen.) Good view from the (20 min.) large clearing. Ascent of the *Raxalp*, see p. 366.

The main road next passes (2 M.) the rustic *Weinzettel Inn*. The valley becomes more open, and we reach the (2 M.) inn *"Zur Singerin* (1890'), at the mouth of the *Nassthal*. The Schwarzauthal now turns to the N., and after 1½ M. again ramifies. The road through the *Vois-Thal* to the right ascends to the (1½ M.) *Höhbauer* (ascent of the Schneeberg, see below), and crosses the *Klosterthaler Gscheid* (2565'), to (12 M.) *Gutenstein* (p. 363).

Few tourists proceed beyond the Grosse Höllenthal, or at farthest the Singerin; but the following prolongation of the excursion is very attractive. From the Singerin we ascend the *Nassthal*, with the scattered village of *Nasswald* (a Protestant community, founded at the end of the 18th cent. by woodcutters from Gosau), to the (1½ M.) *Reithof* (°Inn) and (½ M.) *Oberhof* ('Dangl; diligence to Payerbach daily in 3 hrs.; 1 fl. 30 kr.), a few hundred paces beyond which is *'Engleitner's Inn*. The valley again contracts, and we cross the *Saurüsselbrücke* to the Nasswald properly so called, and (3 M.) the *Schütter Inn* (2380'), situated in a charming dale. The *Reisthal*, at first a narrow gorge, diverges here to the S.; at the upper end of it is the rustic *Binder Inn* (2655'), with the *Scheibwald-Mauer* on the left and the huge *Kohlmauer* beyond it. Thence to the Raxalp, see p. 366. — From the Binder Inn we ascend through beautiful wood to the (3 M.) *Nasskamm* (3055'), a saddle between the *Raxalp* and *Schneealp*. (Ascent of the latter, see p. 371; from the Nasskamm over the *Gamsecksteig* to the Raxalp, see p. 366.) We then descend to the *Nassbauer*, and proceed via *Altenberg* to (6 M.) *Kapellen* (p. 370).

The **Schneeberg** (6810') is usually ascended from *Payerbach* or from *Buchberg* (guide there and back 4 fl. if a night be spent out 5 fl.; Ant. Hirand and Lor. Mauser recommended). From the Payerbach station (the shortest and most frequented route) the path ascends steeply to the right to the (1½ hr.) *Schneedörfel* and through wood, passing the *Thalhof* (see above; path indicated by notices and red streaks) to the (½ hr.) *Eng*, a defile between the Schnalzwand and the Sanrüssel. We then mount the new *Marienateig* and through the *Gansriese* (a timber-slide in a steep gorge) to the (1½ hr.) *Lackerboden* (4040'; Inn). We next ascend in a straight direction by the Pürschhofweg, turn to the left to the *Alpeleck*, at the foot of the *Hochalpal*, and mount the *Krummbachsattel* (4300') in windings to the (1½ hr.) *Baumgartner-Haus* (1500'; Inn, bed 1, pension 3 fl.), situated on the steep S. slope of the Hoch-Schneeberg. From this point we ascend either by the *Emmysteig* (shorter but more fatiguing), or to the right past the *Fischer-Ruhe* (view-point with benches) to the *Luchboden*, and round the S. slope of the *Warriegel* (6180'), to the (1½ hr.) *Damböckhaus*, a hut on the *Ochsenboden* (5910'), and to the right, by a path marked by posts, to the (1 hr.) *Kaiserstein* (6760'; refuge-hut), and thence to the (½ hr.) summit of the *Klosterwappen* or *Alpengipfel* (6810'). The view is very extensive, stretching to the W. as far as the Dachstein. The ascent is easier from *Buchberg* (Doppler), 9 M. to the N.W. of station *Ternit*: (p. 362; road through the charming *Sierning-Thal*, passing *Schloss Stixenstein*, diligence daily; one-horse carr. 4-5 fl.). From Buchberg a good bridle-path (practicable for driving) ascends the *Hengsthal*, passing the (2 hrs.) excellent *Kalte Wasser* spring (3875'), to the (1 hr.) *Baumgartner-Haus* (p. 365). — The 'ascent from the *Höhbauer* (p. 363) is by a somewhat steep path, at first through wood, to the (2 hrs.) *Innere Hütten* (Alpine fare), on the N. margin of the *Kuh-Schneeberg* (5090'); then across a furrowed plateau, past the *Aeussere Hütten*, to the (4 hrs.) Kaiserstein.

The ascent of the Raxalpe, an extensive plateau bounded on every side by precipitous slopes, with numerous chalets, offers special attractions to the botanist (guide to the Heukuppe 3 fl.; if a night be spent out 4 fl.). The highest point is the *Heukuppe* (6590'), on the S.W. side. In the middle of the plateau rises the *Scheibwaldhöhe* (6380'). The buttress projecting into the Höllenthal and culminating in the *Jacobskogel* (5700') is called the *Grünschacher*. The ascent is best made from Prein (2260'; *Eggl's Inn; °Draxler; Joh. Darrer, a good guide), 6 M. to the S.W. of Reichenau, in the *Preinthal*, which diverges from the main valley near *Hirschwang* (p. 365; omnibus from Payerbach to Prein on Sat., Sun., and Mon., fare 60 kr.). From Prein we follow the road to the E. as far as the (3 M.) *Preiner Gscheid* (3510'), the watershed between the Schwarzau and the Mürz, and the frontier of Styria. (The continuation of the road descends to *Kapellen*, p. 370; 6 M.) We now ascend to the right through the *Siebenbrunnenthal* (a fine rocky basin) to the (⅔ hr.) *Halterhütte* (4320'), and thence by the *Schlangenweg* (practicable for carriages) to the (1¼ hr.) Karl-Ludwigshaus (5915', built by the Austrian Tourist Club, and used as an °Inn), situated on the plateau. From this point, passing the *Lackenhofer-Hütte* (6450'), we reach the summit of the *Heukuppe* in ¾ hr. more (extensive and beautiful view). A shorter route is afforded by the *Reisthaler Steig*, which ascends direct from Gscheid through the *Raxenmäuer* (wire-rope) to the (1½ hr.) Lackenhofer Hütte. — The *Grünschacher* is ascended as follows at the point where the Prein road divides, 1½ M. from Reichenau, we keep to the right, and ascend to the (1 hr.) *Knappendorf* (2700'). Hence we either ascend direct viâ the *Thörlsteig*, or (less steep) go across the *Gsollwiese* to the plateau and over the *Thörl* to the (2½-3 hrs.) *Jakobskogel* (5700'), distinguished by its rich flora, and ascend by the *Seehütte* and the *Trinkstein-Sattel* to the (2½ hrs.) *Karl-Ludwigshaus*. — From *Kapellen* (p. 370), on the S. side of the Rax, there are several different routes to the summit. One route leads through the *Rexenthal* to the (6 M.) *Gscheid*, and as above to the Karl-Ludwigshaus. Another leads to the N. to (3½ M.) *Altenberg* (°Perl), and ascends through the *Kern-Graben* to the right to the (1½ hr.) *Karrer Alm* (4855'); it then proceeds to the left to the *Hohe Stein* ('View) and mounts by a good path in windings to the (1 hr.) plateau (6060'), near the *Gamseck* (6090'), whence it ascends to the right to the (½ hr.) Heukuppe. A third route leads viâ Altenberg to the (2½ hrs.) *Nasskamm* (3955'; see above), proceeds to the right to the (¾ hr.) deserted *Grüberalm* and thence to the (20 min.) *Gupfhüttel*, and lastly ascends by the steep and stony, but perfectly safe *Gamsecksteig* (with steps, chains, and a ladder) to the (1½ hr.) cairn on the plateau and to the (½ hr.) Heukuppe. — From the *Grosse Höllenthal* the '*Liststeig*' ascends (at one point by an iron ladder, 13' high) past the *Gaislochs* to the *Rax* (to the *Eishütten* on the *Grünschacher* 3 hrs.); thence over the *Trinkstein-Sattel* to the Karl-Ludwigshaus 1½ hr.). More interesting, but difficult, is the *Losbühelsteig*, leading through the *Teufelsbadstube* to the (2½ hrs.) top of the Loswand. Thence to the *Hofhait* (herdmen's hut) 1 hr., and to the Eishütten ¾ hr. (see above). — A number of other routes, varying in difficulty and danger (*Jagdsteig, Rudolfsteig*, etc.) lead from the Höllenthal to the plateau. — Several paths also ascend from the *Reisthal* to the Rax (fit for experts only; guides, Daniel Innthaler and Ant. Winter). One route leads from the Binder Inn, viâ the *Kaisersteig*, to the (1½ hr.) *Zikafahnler Alp* (small inn); thence to the (1 hr.) *Pehofer Inn*, on the *Wassriegel* (6260'; °View), the (1 hr.) *Liechtensterm-Hütten*, and the (1½ hr.) Karl-Ludwigshaus. Other paths (suitable only for travellers with steady heads) lead from the Binder over the *Grosse Gries* to the (2½ hrs.) Pehofer Haus, and by the *Grosse Gries*, the

Bärenloch, the *Wildfährte*, or the *Zerbenriegel* to the (3 hrs.) Karl-Ludwigshaus.

Beyond Payerbach the train crosses the Schwarzau by an imposing viaduct of 13 arches (pretty view to the right of the valley of Reichenau, and to the left of the Payerbach valley), and then ascends (gradient 1 : 40) the S. slope of the valley. The paper-manufactory of Schlöglmühl again becomes visible far below, while to the W. the Raxalp still forms the background. Two short tunnels; to the left an extensive view of the plain. Gloggnitz lies 560' below this part of the line.

The train next skirts the *Gotschakogel* (two tunnels). On a rocky pinnacle, at (61½ M.) **Klamm** (2255'), rises an old castle of Prince Liechtenstein, once the key of Styria, but now half destroyed. Far below runs the old Semmering road, with several manufactories and the white houses of *Schottwien* in a ravine. Beyond the next tunnel a picturesque retrospect of the castle of Klamm. Farther on, a fine view is obtained of the deep valley with its rocky walls and pinnacles. The train traverses a long gallery, with apertures for light, and a bridge, skirting the *Weinzettelwand*, and reaches (66 M.) *Breitenstein* (2540'). Two more tunnels. It then crosses the *Kalte Rinne* by a viaduct 310 yds. long and 150' high, the loftiest on the line, and ascends in a wide sweep (fine retrospect, in the background the Raxalp) to the last large viaduct (175 yds. long, 90' high), which spans the *Untere Adlitzgraben*.

After three more tunnels (station *Wolfsbergkogel*, beyond the second, see below) the train stops at (70½ M.) **Semmering** (2840'; *Inn*), 1¼-1¾ hr. from Gloggnitz. A monument to *Karl von Ghega* (p. 364), the constructor of the railway, has been erected on the rocks to the right.

On the slope of the *Kartnerkogel*, about 1 M. to the N. (omnibus at the station), is the *Semmering Hotel, built by the S. Railway Company, in a fine situation (3255'), frequented as a summer-resort. A little lower are the two 'dépendances' belonging to the hotel, and the *Restaurant Wolfsbergkogl*, at the station of the same name (see above). Numerous picturesque walks in the neighbourhood. Thus we may follow the '*Hochweg*' (carriage-road) to the (½ hr.) *Erzherzog Johann Hotel*, at the highest point of the Semmering road (3220'; ¼ hr. from Semmering station), with a monument in honour of Emp. Charles VI., the constructor of the road. Or we may walk to the top of the (¾ hr.) *Pinkenkogel* (4235'; refuge-hut; fine view); to the (¾ hr.) *Adlitzgraben* (see above), etc.

The *Sonnwendstein or Göstritz (4996'; guide unnecessary), ascended by a new track in 2 hrs., commands an extensive and beautiful panorama. Far below in the foreground is the railway. About 7 min. below the summit is a club-hut (*Inn). — A zigzag path ('Fischerweg') descends on the N. side to (1 hr.) *Maria-Schutz* (2490'; *Westermaier's Inn), a resort of pilgrims, in a charming situation. Thence by the old Semmering road to *Schottwien* (1890'; *Ehrendörfer) and (6 M.) *Gloggnitz* (see above).

The line now avoids a farther ascent of 276' by means of a tunnel, 1564 yds. in length, which penetrates the **Semmering**, the boundary between Austria and Styria. The middle of the tunnel is the culminating point of the line (2940'). The train then descends rapidly. From *Steinhaus* onwards it is carried high up on the N.

side of the picturesque *Fröschnitzthal* by means of long embankments and deep cuttings. — 78 M. **Spital** (2520'; Schwan; Hirsch).

The **Stuhleck** (5850'), ascended through the *Kaltenbach-Graben* or viâ the *Hocheck* and the *Spitaler Alpe* in 3½-4 hrs. (marked path), commands a fine and extensive view. About 5 min. below the summit (N.W.) is the *Gustav-Jäger-Schutzhaus* of the Austrian Tourist Club. The descent may be made by the *Schwarzkogel-Alpe* and *Schöneben* to (2½ hrs.) Mürzzuschlag (path marked).

82½ M. **Mürzzuschlag** (2200'; *Erzherzog Johann*; *Adler*, R. 60 kr.-1 fl.; *Post*, R. 1 fl. 20 kr.; *Hôtel Lambach*, prettily situated ½ M. from the station; *Rail. Restaurant*, R. 1 fl. 20 kr.), an old town with iron-works, picturesquely situated on the Mürz, is a summer-resort, with a new Curhaus and tasteful promenades.

Short walks lead hence to the (¼ M.) *Ganster*, the (1½ M.) *Grüblbauer*, the (1½ M.) *Rauchengraben*, the *Steinbauer*, and the (1½ hr.) top of the *Ganselein* (2860'; refuge-hut). — An easy route (indicated by blue marks) leads to the N from the station to the (3 hrs.) top of the *Drahtekogel* (5140'), which offers a fine view of the Schneeberg, Raxalp, Schneealp, &c. Descent by the *Kamp-Alpe* to (2 hrs.) Spital (see above). — From Mürzzuschlag to *Neuberg* and *Mariazell*, see p. 370.

The line follows the pleasant, pine-clad valley of the *Mürz*, which is enlivened with a number of iron-forges. Near (87½ M.) *Langenwang* (2110'), on a height to the left, is the ruin of *Hohenwang* or *Hochschloss* and to the right of the line is the château of *Neu-Hohenwang*. 90 M. *Krieglach*; 92 M. *Mitterdorf* (Grünwald) with coal-mines and a large gun-factory. To the right, at the mouth of the *Veitschthal*, rises *Schloss Püchl*, with its four towers.

The **Hohe Veitschalp** (6500'; 5 hrs.; comp. p. 371), a fine point of view, deserves a visit. Road in the Veitschthal to (3½ M.) *Veitsch* (2180'; Briller; Wedl), where the valley divides into the *Grosse* (W.) and *Kleine Veitschthal* (E.). Road through the former to the (1½ M.) *Inn im Bad* (2690'); then an ascent to the left to the (1 hr.) *Schaller Alpe*, and by a new zigzag path over the *Hundschupfen* to the (1½ hr.) *Graf Meran Refuge Hut* (6230'; Inn in summer), on the plateau, and the (½ hr.) summit (*Hoch Veitsch*, 6500); extensive view. Descent by the *Rothsohlhütten* and through the *Aschbachgraben* to (3½ hrs.) *Wegscheid* (p. 374); or through the *Fischgraben* or the *Dürnthal* to (3 hrs.) *Mürzsteg* (p. 371).

Farther on, near *Wartberg*, to the right, is the ruin of *Lichteneyg*. The train makes a wide sweep round the *Wartberg-Kogel*, crossing the Mürz twice, and reaches (97 M.) *Kindberg* (1820'; Krone; Adler), with the handsome château of *Oberkindberg*, the seat of Count Attems. 102 M. *Marein*. 106 M. *Kapfenberg* (1580'; Ramsauer), with *Schloss Wiedhof*, and to the left, high above us, the picturesque ruin of *Oberkapfenberg* (2315'). At the mouth of the *Thörlthal* (p. 376), ¾ M. to the W., lies *Bad Steinerhof* (pine-cone baths).

109 M. **Bruck an der Mur** (1590'; *Post*, at the station; *Lamm*; *Adler*) is a small town (400 inhab.) at the confluence of the Mürz and the *Mur*, with a Gothic church of the 15th century. The old castle, with Romanesque arcades, once belonged to the princes of this district. The *Calvarienberg*, on the right bank of the Mur, affords the best survey of the town and environs. On a crag to the N. of the station rises the old castle of *Landskron*, which was burned down

in 1792. — To *St. Michael* and *Villach*, (see R. 70; to *Mariazell*, see R. 66.

The train now enters the narrow valley of the *Mur* (comp. Map, p. 424). At (115½ M.) **Pernegg** (1555'; *Linde*) is the large château of the Lipith family, built in 1582. Above it are the ruins of an interesting older castle, in plan resembling the Wartburg.

Ascent of the **Rennfeld** (5345') from Pernegg, interesting and easy, either through the *Gabraungraben* in 3½ hrs., or through the *Breitenau* and the *Feistergraben* in 5 hrs.; descent to the N. to (1½ hr.) *Frauenberg* (*Maria-Rehkogel*; 3085), a favourite resort of pilgrims, and thence either to (3½ M.) *Kapfenberg* (p. 368) or (5 M.) *Bruck*.

118 M. **Mixnitz** (*Schartner*), a village picturesquely situated at the foot of the *Röthelstein* (4050').

EXCURSIONS (guide, Peter Stengg, vulgo 'Weber'). On the slope of the Röthelstein, about 1550' or 1½ hr. above the village, is an extensive stalactite cavern, called the **Drachenhöhle** or *Kogellucken* (visit fatiguing, guide 1 fl.). — A pleasant excursion may be made to the *Bärenschütz. The route leads through the valley of the *Mixnitzbach* to (1¼ hr.) a charcoal-burner's, and thence (guide-post) for 20 min. along the cliff, to the *Bärenschütz* (2665'), where the Mixnitzbach breaks through the rocky wall (rendered easily accessible).

The **Hochlantsch** (5650'; 4½-6 hrs.; guide 4-5 fl.) is also well worthy of a visit. We follow the right bank of the Mixnitzbach to the (1¼ hr.) charcoal-burner's (see above), thence to the left to the (½ hr.) *Schwaigerbauer*, and to the (¾ hr.) Inn (way-post). Then either to the left to (¾ hr.) *Schüsserlbrunn* (4055'), a pleasantly situated pilgrimage-chapel (two inns), and by the arête to the (1¼ hr.) summit; or (the usual route) from the way-post (see above) over Alpine pastures and along the Mixnitzbach to the (1½ hr.) *Teichalpe* (3855'; Alpine fare) and the (2 hrs.) summit, which commands an admirable view of the Styrian Alps and possesses a rich flora. Descent by Schüsserlbrunn, and through the *Breitenau* to (4 hrs.) *Pernegg* (see above); or from the Teichalp through the *Turnauer Graben* to (3 hrs.) *Frohnleiten*.

125 M. **Frohnleiten** (1425'; *Stadt Strassburg*, with view from the terrace; *Austria*; *Fleischer*), with forges and a hydropathic establishment. To the right of the railway is *Schloss Neu-Pfannberg* or *Grafendorf*, and on a height to the left are the ruins of the castle of *Pfannberg*.

The **Brucker Hochalpe** (5370') is most conveniently ascended from stat. *Frohnleiten*. We follow the Bruck road thence for 1½ M. to the N.W., turn to the left into the *Gamsgraben*, passing *Schloss Weyer*, and reach the (2 M.) *Traminger Inn*, at the bifurcation of the valley. We then ascend to the right through the Gamsgraben ('Diebsweg'), turning to the left at (1 hr.) the cross, to the (1 hr.) *Almwirth* (3865') on the ridge, and thence to the right (route marked) over the 'Schneide' to the (1¾ hr.) summit, where a fine panorama is enjoyed. (About ½ hr. from the top, to the S.W., are the *Hochalpenhütten*.)

On a rock on the right bank is the recently-restored castle of *Rabenstein*. The valley now expands for a short distance, and then contracts to a narrow defile, through which the line is carried along the *Badlwand* by means of a gallery of 35 arches (440 yds. long). Above the railway runs the high-road. At (129½ M.) *Peggau* (Brewery) the *Schöckel* (p. 404) is seen to the left. Opposite, at the mouth of the *Uebelbach*, lies the small town of *Feistritz*, with lead and zinc smelting-works. Near it, on the left bank of the Mur, are some interesting caverns (the *Badlhöhle* the most convenient to visit, 1 hr., with guide).

The Gleinalpe is an interesting point (7½-8 hrs.). From *Peistritz* (Bräuhaus) we follow the road on the left bank of the *Uebelbach*, through its pretty valley, to (3 M.) *Waldstein*, with a château and ruined castle, and the village of (5 M.) *Uebelbach* (1895'; Jägerwirth; Bräuhaus; Köhlinger). The road terminates at *Hojer* (Inn), 7 M. farther up the valley. Thence an ascent of 2 hrs. to the *Alpen-Wirthshaus* (5210'), an inn beside a church, 1¼ hr. from the top of the **Speikkogel** (6525'), the highest peak of the Gleinalpe, commanding an extensive and interesting view. We now descend from the inn to the (2¼ hrs.) *Krautwasch Inn* (3740'), and then through wood and past the *Sattlwirth* to the (1½ hr.) *Abraham Inn* (2100'), in the *Stübinggraben*. From this point we ascend to the right to the (1 hr.) *Pleschwirth* (3335'), whence the *Pleschkogel*, 3488', a good point of view, may be ascended in ¼ hr.). Lastly we proceed by the 16th cent. church of (1½ hr.) *Rein* to (1½ M.) the rail. stat. *Gratwein* (see below), whence Gratz is reached by train in ½ hr. (Descent from the Gleinalpe to the *Murthal* and *Knittelfeld*, see p. 424.)

The train crosses the Mur, and follows the right bank to Gratz. At (132 M.) *Stübing* (Hirsch) is the handsome château of Count Palffy. The line then runs between the river and a wall of rock to (134½ M.) *Gratwein* (1290'; Fischerwirth), where there is a large paper-mill. The valley expands. Near (136½ M.) *Judendorf* (Kreuzwirth; Railway Inn), on an eminence to the right, stands the pilgrimage-church of *Maria-Strassenget*, a pleasing Gothic building with an open tower (1355). The train now skirts a height which is crowned with the ruined castle of *Güsting* (p. 404), and enters a fertile basin, where the isolated Schlossberg of Gratz rises on the left, with the ancient capital of Styria at its base.

141½ M. Gratz, see p. 400.

66. From Mürzzuschlag (*Vienna*) to Mariazell and Bruck on the Mur.

Railway from Mürzzuschlag to (7½ M.) *Neuberg* in 34 minutes. — Diligence from Neuberg to *Mariazell* (29 M.) twice daily in 6⅔ hrs. (3½ fl.); two-horse carr. in 4 hrs., 10 fl. (there and back 15 fl.); one-horse carr. from Neuberg to Mürzsteg 2, two-horse 3 fl. — Between Mariazell and *Bruck* (40 M.) Diligence twice daily in summer in 7½ hrs. (fare 5 fl. 50 kr.). — From *Gaming* to Mariazell, see p. 373; from *St. Pölten* viâ *Schrambach* to Mariazell, see pp. 379, 374.

Mürzzuschlag, see p. 368. The Neuberg line diverges here to the right from the main line, crosses the *Mürz*, and ascends the wooded valley of that stream, passing several iron-works, to (4½ M.) *Kapellen* (2310'; Hirsch; route to the *Raxalpe*, see p. 366; ascent of the *Schneealpe*, p. 371; viâ the *Nasskamm* to the *Singerin*, p. 365). Following the right bank of the Mürz, the train reaches —

7½ M. **Neuberg** (2400'; *Hôtel Adler, with garden; *Stern*; *Hirsch*; *Zur Hinterbrüht*, moderate), finely situated at the base of the *Schneealpe* (see below). The handsome Gothic *Cistercian Church*, with its fourteen slender octagonal pillars and large rose-window, was consecrated in 1471, and has recently been restored. From the well-preserved cloisters, which contain portraits of all the abbots, we enter the elegant crypt, in which are the coffins of the Margrave Otho, his two wives, and his two sons. The abbey was suppressed by the Emp. Joseph II. in 1785. The E. wing of the extensive abbey-buildings is the residence of the emperor during the spring shooting-season. A little to the N. of Neuberg are the extensive iron-works of the Alpine Montangesellschaft (shown on application to the director). At the foot of the Calvarienberg, above the town, is a pyramid with a portrait in relief, carved from the rock in 1882 as a monument to the *Archduke John*.

The **Schneealpe** (6245'; 3½-4 hrs.; guide 4-5 fl.) is ascended from Neuberg or from Kapellen (p. 370), the best route being that leading through the *Lichtenbachgraben*, the mouth of which lies between these two places: to the *Michelbauer*, 1½ hr.; then by a steep ascent viâ the *Kampel* (4795') to the plateau and the *Schneealphütten* (Inn) 2 hrs.; to the summit (*Windberg*, 6245') ½ hr. more. Extensive view of the Styrian Alps. — The shortest route from Kapellen ascends past the cemetery, to the right of the *Kapellenkogl*, to the (½ hr.) chalets *Im Greith*, and to the (1½ hr.) *Kampel* (4795') and the (1 hr.) Schneealphütten. — From *Altenberg* (p. 366) a marked path leads to the W., through the *Almgraben*, to (2½ hrs.) the Schneealphütten. From *Krampen* (see below) a carriage-road ('Kaiserweg') runs to the N.W. through the *Innere Krampengraben*, past the (½ hr.) hamlet *Im Tirol*, to the (1½ hr.) *Eisern Thörl* (4420'; see below), and then to the W., viâ the *Grossbodenalp*, to the (3 hrs.) Windberg. From the Schneealphütten viâ the *Ameisbühel* and the *Nasskamm* to the *Raxalp* (p. 366), 5 hrs.

From the *Eisern Thörl* (see above) a pleasant walk may be taken to the S.W., viâ the *Luchalphütten*, to the **Lachalpe** or *Blassstein* (5135'), a good point of view. — From the Thörl the road goes on to (2 M.) the *Jägerhaus* in the *Nasskühr* (Inn), ½ M. to the N. of the imperial Jagdschloss (4510'). Thence a marked path leads viâ the *Hinteralpe*, and past the *Rosskogel* and *Hochriegel*, to (1½ hr.) *Frein* (p. 372).

Above Neuberg the valley becomes narrower and more picturesque. The road, skirting the clear and rapid *Mürz*, side by side with a shady forest-path, ascends to (2¼ M.) *Krampen* (2480'; *Forelle) and the pretty village of (5½ M.) —

8 M. (from Neuberg) **Mürzsteg** (2570'; *Post), with an imperial shooting-box. To the S.W. stretches the *Hohe Veitschalpe*.

The **Hohe Veitschalpe** (6500'; 4½ hrs.), an interesting point, is easily ascended from Mürzsteg. We follow the Wegscheid road for 1½ M., diverge to the left, and ascend the *Fluchgraben* by a good path to the (1 hr.) shooting-lodge on the *Senkstein* (4200'; Rfmts.); thence over the plateau by a path indicated by blue and white marks to the (3 hrs.) summit (comp. p. 368). Another route, entering the *Bärengraben* about 1 M. before Mürzsteg, ascends past the *Dürnthalhütten* to the (2½ hrs.) finely-situated *Veitschalpenhütten* (1690'); thence across the plateau to the summit 2½ hrs. more. From *Neuberg* (see above) a path indicated by blue marks ascends viâ the *Veitschbachthörl* (4610'), the *Heinzelkogel* (4200'), and the (4 hrs.) *Veitschalpenhütten*. — From the *Niederalpel* (see below) to the Hohe Veitsch viâ the *Sohlenalpe* (4480') a path (indicated by red marks) ascends in 4 hrs. — The descent may be made on the S.W. side to the (1 hr.) *Rothsohlhütten* (4605'), through the Rothsohl-Graben to the *Aschbachthal*, and by road to (6 M.) *Wegscheid* (p. 374).

The valley divides here. The high-road ascends the *Dobrein-Thal* to the W., and crosses the **Niederalpel** (4000'; fine view of the Veitschalp and Hochschwab) to (27½ M.) *Wegscheid*, a village 9½ M. to the S. of Mariazell (p. 374).

24*

The new ROAD VIÂ FREIN is much preferable (from Krampen to Frein over the Eisern Thörl, see p. 371). This runs to the N. through the gradually widening valley of the Mürz to the (3½ M.) *Scheiterboden* (2700'; Inn), and then leads through wild ravines, between the cliffs of the *Rosskogl* on the right and the *Proleswand* on the left, close by the side of the foaming stream. [The path through the gorge was formerly carried above the stream by a wooden gallery resting on iron bars inserted in the rock.] In the midst of this rocky wilderness a small waterfall descends from a cavity above, called the *Todte Weib* (2730') from a peasant-woman having been found dead at this spot many years ago. A flight of wooden steps, passing a hermitage, ascends to the orifice whence the cascade issues. The valley soon expands into a green dale, surrounded by lofty, pine-clad mountains, in which lies the hamlet of (2½ M.) **Frein** (2840'; two *Inns*).

From Frein the road continues to the W. through the *Freiner Thal*, passing (3 M.) *Gschwand*, and then ascends in wide curves to the (2½ M.) *Hühnerreith-Sattel* or *Schönebensattel* (3750'), between the *Student* and the *Fatlenstein*. Descending to (1 M.) the *Schöneben Inn* (3630'), we either take the marked path to the right, through the *Wasshubenwald*, on the flanks of the Student, to (2¼ hrs.) *Mariazell*, or follow the road through the pretty *Fallensteiner Thal* (to the left is the *Tonion Alpe*, 5575') to the (5½ M.) *Gusswerk* (p. 374), on the road from Bruck to (3½ M.) *Mariazell*.

The FOOTPATH from Frein over the *Freinsattel* to Mariazell (4½ hrs.) is more attractive and saves 1 hr. but is wet and slippery at places after rain. Guide (3 fl.) not necessary. The path diverges from the road to the right (way-post; white marks) at *Gschwand*, 3 M. from Frein, and ascends into the wood to (¾ hr.) an image of a saint on the summit of the **Freinsattel** (3670'). To the left rises the *Student* (4960'), and to the S.W., in the background, the bald summit of the *Oetscher* (6210'). Then a steep descent. After 20 min., we descend by the path to the left (following the brook) to the *Hallthal*, and in ½ hr. cross the *Salza* to the St. Æygd and Mariazell road (*Inn Zum Touristen*). We now follow the road descending the stream, ascend to the saddle of the *Kreuzberg* (2995'; view of the Hochschwab, Dürnstein, Oetscher, etc.), and finally descend to (2 hrs.) Mariazell.

29½ M. **Mariazell** (2830'; **Schwarzer Adler*, the old Post; **Löwe*, moderate; **Weintraube*; **Greif*; **Krone*, the new Post; *Sandwirth*; *Cepek*, and many others), very picturesquely situated in a wide basin, surrounded by beautiful wooded mountains of varied forms, is the most frequented shrine in Austria, being visited annually by upwards of 200,000 pilgrims. The village consists almost entirely of inns and taverns, all of which are crowded at the time of the great pilgrimages (from Vienna on 1st July, from Gratz on 14th Aug.) and during the latter half of August. In the centre of the village rises the imposing church, erected at the end of the 17th cent., with its four towers, of which the handsome Gothic central tower belongs to the original structure of the 14th century. The miraculous wooden image of the Virgin and Child, 20 inches high, was presented by a priest of the Benedictine abbey of St. Lambrecht (mother-church of Mariazell) in 1157. A chapel erected here for its reception by the Margrave Henry I. of Moravia in 1200 was replaced in 1363 by a larger edifice, by Lewis I. of Hungary, after a victory over the Turks, to which the reliefs over the portal refer.

Interior, 300' long and 110' broad. The CHAPEL containing the small miraculous image is sumptuously decorated with 12 columns of silver, &c. The PULPIT consists of a large block of red porphyry. Over the HIGH ALTAR is a large cross of ebony, with two life-size figures in silver, representing God the Father and God the Son, presented by Emp. Charles VI. Beneath the cross is a silver globe, 6½ ft. in diameter, round which a serpent is coiled. In the corner to the right is a long table on which the devout place their rosaries and other objects for consecration. Round the upper galleries are suspended numerous small votive pictures. The larger and older pictures above the arches represent various miraculous events connected with Mariazell. A staircase in the S.W. tower leads to a chamber containing the 'KRIPPLEIN' (manger), a plastic representation of the Nativity: right, the Adoration of the Magi; left, a group of Styrian peasants with various offerings. — The TREASURY contains a valuable collection of ecclesiastical vessels in gold and silver, reliquaries, jewels, miniature altars made of precious stones, old mass-books, &c. The altarpiece, a Madonna in the early Italian style, was presented by King Lewis of Hungary.

At the numerous adjoining booths every variety of refreshment for soul and body may be purchased by the pious.

EXCURSIONS (guide, *Ferd. Kalisch*). To the *Calvarienberg* (¼ hr.), by the rifle-range; the adjacent *Carolinenhöhe* commands a charming view. View also of the Hochschwab, etc., from the *Luckele Kreuz* (½ hr.), on the Hallthal road (p. 372). — The *Franz-Karl-Warte* on the **Bürger-Alpel** (4155'; 1¼ hr.; forest-path indicated by red marks) commands a striking view of the Œtscher, Dürrenstein, and Hochschwab. A path, indicated by yellow marks, descends hence to the (½ hr.) interesting cavern in the *Hohlenstein*, with stalactites and a small waterfall; thence we may regain (1¼ hr.) Mariazell by a path (white marks) viâ the *Hundseck* and the Calvarienberg.

Pleasant excursion (one-horse carr. 3 fl.) through the *Grünau* (Marien Waterfall; refreshments at the Klitznerbauer's) to the (5½ M.) **Erlaufsee** (2740'; °*Seewirth*, at the upper end, trout; lake-baths; boats for hire), from which we may return by the direct road on the S. bank (3 M.).

To the °**Lassing Fall**, 3½ hrs., very interesting. We follow the road to the N. to *Mitterbach* and then the old road over the *Josefsberg* (3230') to the (9 M.) *Wienerbrückl* (°Burger), and descend thence to the left to the (½ hr.) fall, 286' high, which the Lassing forms before its union with the Erlau, amidst grand rocky environs. (The fall, in itself insignificant, may be improved by the opening of a sluice; fee 2 fl.; tickets at Burger's Inn.) By the drawbridge we descend to the left, crossing the Lassing and the *Erlauf*, and then follow a narrow path (yellow marks) to the left, which is hewn for the most part out of the rock and leads through the romantic °**Oetschergraben** and past the *Mira Fall* to the (2 hrs.) *Klause*. From this point we may follow a path through wood to the (1 hr.) *Spielbichler* (a good rustic inn), ascend rapidly to the (1 hr.) *Riffelsattel* (4210'), between the Grosse and the Kleine Oetscher (p. 381), and descend in a straight direction to (1 hr.) *Lackenhof* (p. 381), and to the right to (20 min.) the *Œtscherhaus* (red marks), and thence ascend to the top of the (1¼ hr.) °*Œtscher* (8200'; comp. p. 381). From the Œtschergraben a marked path leads direct back to Mariazell viâ *Hangen* and (1½ hr.) *Mitterbach* (see above; from the Œtscherklause to Mariazell 3½ hrs.). — A picturesque path leads from the Lassing Fall through the beautiful *Erlaufthal* to (5 hrs.) *Gaming* (p. 380).

FROM MARIAZELL TO GAMING (25 M.). The road leads past the *Erlaufsee* (see above) and over the *Zellerrain* (3510'), the boundary of Lower Austria, and the watershed between the Erlauf and the *Ybbs*, to (8½ M.)

374   *VIII. Route 66.*   BRANDHOF.   *From Mariazell.*

Neuhaus (3290'; Konrad), with a fine new church; and then through the picturesquely wooded *Neuhauser Thal*, between the *Zwieselberg* (4710') on the left and the *Buchalpe* (4840') on the right, and past the *Hotzknecht-Hütten*, with a large shooting-lodge, belonging to Baron Rothschild, to (6¹/₂ M.) *Langau* (2260'; Bretschneider; Frühwald), in the *Oisthal*, or valley of the *Ybbs*. The route to *Lackenhof* diverges to the right; 1¹/₂ M. farther on, and that to *Lunz* (p. 380), by the *Durchlass*, to the left. The road follows the Ybbs for 3¹/₄ M. more, ascends to the N., over the *Föllbaumhöhe*, to the (2¹/₄ M.) *Grubberg* (p. 381), and then descends to (3 M.) *Gaming* (p. 380).
   FROM MARIAZELL TO SCHRAMBACH (34¹/₂ M.), diligence daily in 6¹/₄ hrs. (fare 2 fl. 70 kr.). The road leads through the Lassingthal, viâ *Mitterbach* and *Wienerbrückl* (see above), to (15¹/₂ M.) *Annaberg* (3180'; Post), with its pilgrimage-church, and then descends the wooded *Steinbachthal* to (9¹/₂ M.) *Türnitz* (1510'), with an old church, prettily situated at the influx of the Türnitzbach into the *Traisen*. The road now follows the Traisen to (5¹/₂ M.) *Freiland* (where a road diverges to the right viâ *Hohenberg* to *St. Aegyd*) and (4 M.) *Schrambach* (Am Steg), the terminus of a branch-line viâ *Lilienfeld* (Zur Porte; Schrittwieser), with its famous Cistercian abbey (late-Romanesque abbey-church of the 13th cent., with splendid cloisters) and (5¹/₂ M.) *Scheibmühl-Traisen* (p. 379) to (17¹/₂ M.) *St. Pölten* (p. 379).
   From Mariazell to *Weichselboden*, *Wildalpen*, and *Eisenerz*, see R. 67.

The ROAD FROM MARIAZELL TO BRUCK (40 M.) leads through the pretty valley of the *Salza*. To the right, on a wooded rock, stands the *Sigmundscapelle*, originally fortified and surrounded with lofty walls to protect it against the Turks, who in the 16th cent. frequently invaded these remote valleys. At the (3¹/₂ M.) **Gusswerk** (2450'; *Inn), with important iron-works, the road to *Weichselboden* diverges to the right (see p. 376). Our road now quits the Salza, ascends the *Aschbachthal* to the S.E., uniting after 2¹/₂ M. with the road from *Frein* (p. 372), and reaches (3¹/₂ M.) the small village of **Wegscheid** (2670'; *Post*). — From Wegscheid to *Mürzsteg* across the *Niederalpl* (3¹/₂ hrs.), see p. 371.
   FROM WEGSCHEID TO WEICHSELBODEN OVER THE KASTENRIEGEL, a pleasant route (carriage-road, 11-12 M.). About ¹/₂ M. to the S.W. of Wegscheid the road turns to the right by a finger-post into the narrow entrance of the *Ramnerthat*, and ascends through wood and meadow to the (5 M.) **Kastenriegel** (3545'), a depression between the *Zeller* and *Aflenzer Staritzen* (6525'), at the head of the *Hütte* (p. 376). It then descends, running at first high up on the S. slope in wide curves (short-cuts for walkers), and afterwards passing the mouth of the *Untere Ring* (p. 376), to (6¹/₂ M.) *Weichselboden* (p. 376).

The road ascends by the *Gollradbach* to (3³/₄ M.) the important iron-mines of *Gollrad* (to the left lies the *Knappendorf*, inhabited by the miners), and 1¹/₂ M. farther on reaches the **Brandhof** (3660'), formerly a shooting-lodge of Archduke John (d. 1859), and now the property of his son, the Count of Meran, surrounded by fine groups of trees.
   The villa is adorned with stained glass, statues, and reminiscences of the chase. The garden contains a choice collection of Alpine plants. The small Gothic chapel, with two paintings by Schnorr, is interesting. One of the saloons contains statues of Ferdinand of Tyrol, Charles II. of Styria, Emp. Maximilian I., Francis I., and Maria Theresa. In the 'room of the chase' are portraits of Maximilian I. and Hofer; beneath the latter Hofer's rifle; also weapons, antlers, sportsmen's gear, &c.

The road now ascends steeply to the (1¹/₂ M.) **Seeberg Pass**

(4115′), where we enjoy a fine view of the *Seethal*, enclosed by the rocky walls of the Hochschwab chain, and then descends in long windings (short-cut to the left) to (2 M.) the village of —

18½ M. **Seewiesen** (3175′; *Post), picturesquely situated.

The **Hochschwab** (7475′; 5 hrs.; guide to Weichselboden 5 fl.) is frequently ascended from Seewiesen. We ascend the Seethal to the (1½ hr.) *Untere* and (1¼ hr.) *Obere Dullwitzhütten* (5430′), follow the valley for ¼ hr. more past the *Goldbrunnen*, and then ascend to the right, skirting the *Wetterkogel*, to the (1¼ hr.) *Schiestlhaus*, on the *Schwabenboden* (7380′; Inn in summer), and to the (½ hr.) summit, on which are a trigonometrical pyramid and an iron memorial tablet. Extensive "View, reaching to the Danube on the N., and embracing the whole of the E. Alps from the Schneeberg to the Dachstein. On the S. side the Hochschwab descends in a sheer precipice. — Descent by the *Edelboden* to (3 hrs.) *Weichselboden*, or through the *Antengraben* to *Gschoder*, see pp. 376, 377. To *St. Ilgen*, see below.

The road traverses the *Seegraben*, passing the small *Dürrensee* (2970′); at *Grassnitz* it turns to the W. into the *Stübmingthal* and soon reaches (9 M.) **Aflenz** (2510′; *Post*; *Karlon*), a thriving village with an old church.

Ascent of the *Bürgeralpe* (4940′; 2 hrs.; good path), a pleasant excursion. Thence over the *Schönleiten* and the *Zlacken-Sattel* (5720′) to the (2½ hrs.) **Mitter-Alpe** (6490′), a plateau bounded by huge precipices on every side. (Fine view from the *Kampl*, the highest point.) Easy descent to the E. over the *Hacken-Alp* to (2¼ hrs.) *Seewiesen*; to the W. over the (½ hr.) *Fölz-Alpe* (4830′) to (2½ hrs.) *Aflenz*. Ascent of the (1½ hr.) **Fölzstein** (6635′) from the Fölz-Alpe, attractive; thence an easy ascent of ½ hr. more to the top of the *Karl-Hochkogel* (see below) and past the *Karlhütten* to (2½ hrs.) *St. Ilgen* (see below). Guides, *Simon Heitzlhofer* and *Jos. Frühauf* of Aflenz.

At **Thörl** (2065′; *Sumrauer*), a village with wire-works, 2½ M. to the S. of Aflenz, the brooks from the S. slopes of the Hochschwab combine to form the *Thörlbach*. Above the village rises the picturesque ruin of *Schachenstein*.

A road leads from Thörl to the N.W. through the pretty *St. Ilgner Thal* to (3½ M.) **St. Ilgen** (2400′; *Pierer*). Road thence by *Ober-Zwain* to *Buchbery* and the (4½ M.) *Bodenbauer Inn* (2875′), beautifully situated at the head of the valley, and a good starting-point for excursions. (Guide, Jos. Leggerer.) Ascent of the **Messnerin** (6025′; 3½ hrs.) by the *Pfütsteiner Alpe*, interesting (from St. Ilgen also in 3 hrs.; descent to *Oberort* in the *Tragösthal*, p. 386, 2 hrs.). — The **Karl-Hochkogel** (6870′), a fine point of view, is reached by the *Trawiesen-Alpe* and the *Gehackt-Brunnen* in 3 hrs., or from St. Ilgen by the Karlhütten in 3¾ hrs. Descent by the *Trawies-Sattel* to (3 hrs.) *Seewiesen*; to the *Fölzstein* (1¼ hr. from the Karlhütten) and to *Aflenz*, see above. — The **Sonnschien-Alpe** (4970′), the finest Alp in the Hochschwab group, is ascended by the *Häusel-Alpe*, the *Sackwiesen-Alpe*, and the *Sackwiesen-See* in 3 hrs. (quarters at the wood-cutter's hut). We may thence ascend the *Ebenstein* (6970′), a superb point of view, in 2 hrs.; also the *Brandstein* (6570′), by the *Andrathhütten* in 2 hrs., another fine point. — The **Hochschwab** (7475′) is ascended by several routes. The easiest leads by the *Hänsl-Alpe* (see above) to the (2¼ hrs.) *Hochstein-Hütten* (5600′), and ascends thence through the *Hirschgrube* and viâ the *Kloben* and the *Zarkenboden* to the (2½ hrs.) summit. A more interesting route is by the *Trawiesen-Alp* to the (2½ hrs.) *Gehackt-Brunnen* (see above); then, skirting the slopes of the *Gehacktkogel* and over the '*Gehackte*', by a path indicated by red marks to the (¾ hr.) plateau and the (½ hr.) summit. Descent to Seewiesen, to Weichselboden, or to Gschoder, see above and pp. 376, 377. — A good bridle-path leads from the Bodenbauer to the N. over the *Hochalpe* (5105′) and through the *Antengraben* to (5 hrs.) *Gschoder* (p. 377). Another fine route crosses the *Sonnschien-Alpe* and the *Schafhals-Sattel* (5100') to the valley of the *Sieben Seen* and (6 hrs.) *Wildalpen* (with which route an ascent of the *Ebenstein* or the *Brandstein* may easily be combined; see p. 375).

We next traverse the narrow *Thörlthal*, passing several ironworks, and reach the (3 M.) *Jägerwirth*, at the E. base of the *Floning* (5205'; *View), which is easily ascended hence in 2 hrs. The road then leads viâ *Bad Steinerhof* (p. 368) to (4½ M.) *Kapfenberg* (p. 368) and (2 M.) —

40 M. *Bruck an der Mur* (p. 368).

67. From Mariazell to Gross-Reifling viâ Weichselboden and Wildalpen.

Comp. Map, p. 384.

44 M. ONE-HORSE CARRIAGE to Weichselboden (15½ M., in 4 hrs.) 6 fl.; thence to Wildalpen (11 M., in 2¼ hrs.) 4 fl.; from Wildalpen to Reifling (17½ M., in 4 hrs.) 6 fl. A tolerable WALKER takes 5½-6 hrs. from Mariazell to Weichselboden, thence to Wildalpen 4 hrs., and from Wildalpen to Reifling 6 hrs.

The road, practicable for light vehicles only, quits the Bruck road at the (3½ M.) *Gusswerk* (p. 374), and leads to the S.W. through the picturesque valley of the *Salza*. 5½ M. *Greith* (2275'; Inn, primitive). The Salza in its deep ravine turns towards the S., while the road ascends to the W. through wood to the *Hals* (2785'; view of the Hochschwab). We then descend in windings (short-cut to the left) to (6½ M.) —

15½ M. **Weichselboden** (2220'; *Haselwander; *Schützenauer, in the Vordere Hölle, 1 M. to the E.), a small village at the union of the *Radmerbach* with the Salza, in a sequestered basin surrounded by lofty mountains.

The road from Wegscheid over the *Kastenriegel* and through the *Hölle* is preferable (comp. p. 374; from Mariazell to Weichselboden 20 M.). — The neighbouring mountains abound in game, especially the *Hölle* and the *Ring*, formerly the chasse of the Archduke John. Pleasant walk through the *Vordere Hölle* (*Inn, see above) to the (¾ hr.) *Jägerhaus* (2530'), and thence (with guide) to the *Untere* and (2 hrs.) *Obere Ring* (5415'), a magnificent rocky basin, into which hundreds of chamois are driven on the occasion of a grand battue. The heath-cock, with the feathers of which the Styrian huntsmen decorate their hats, also abounds here.

The **Hochschwab** (see p. 375) is frequently ascended from Weichselboden. We may either ascend direct viâ the *Weichselleiten*, or ascend to the right (steep), 10 min. beyond the Schützenauer, over the *Miessattel* (4885'), to the (¾ hr.) *Edelboden* (4385'; rustic quarters at the forester's), and ascend thence by the *Saumstatt* and the (2¼ hrs.) *Weihbrunnkessel* to the *Ochsenreich-Kaar* and the (1 hr.) *Schiestlhaus*, the path being indicated by red marks (guide unnecessary for experts; P. Fahrenberger or Georg Plachl of Weichselboden). Descent to Gschöder, see below; to Seewiesen, see p. 375; to the Bodenbauer, see p. 375. — FROM THE HOCHSCHWAB TO EISENERZ THROUGH THE FRAUENMAUERHÖHLE (9-10 hrs.; guide, not indispensable for adepts, 12 fl.). The first part of the route leads by the *Grosse Speikboden*, the *Kleine Speikboden*, and the *Hundsboden* (the landlord of the Schiestl Inn acts as guide to this point) to the *Hirschgrube* and then viâ the *Hiäusl-Alpe* to the (3½ hrs.) *Sackwiesen* (p. 377). Above the houses we ascend to the right to the saddle and skirt the near side of the Sackwiesen Lake to the (1 hr.) *Sonnschien-Alpe* (p. 375). Farther on, beyond the *Hörndl-Alpe*, we at first ascend, then descend a little, and proceed to the right, by a path high up on the right side of the valley (indistinct at first), under the precipices of the *Hörndlmauer*, to the *Kulm-Alp* and the (1½ hr.) *Neuwaldegg-Alp* (4400'). The 'Sennerin' in the uppermost chalet keeps the keys of the (25 min.) *Frauenmauer-Höhle*, through which we now proceed, under her guidance, to (2¼ hrs.) *Eisenerz* (p. 385).

The **Hochstadl** (6300'; new refuge-hut), ascended without difficulty from Weichselboden viâ *Rothmoos* in 5 hrs., affords a good survey of the Styrian Alps, and particularly of the Schwaben chain. Other paths ascend from *Gschöder* (see below; viâ the *Bärenbach-Sattel*, in 4½ hrs.) and from *Wildalpen* (over the *Nasenbauer-Alp*, in 5 hrs.).

The ROAD TO WILDALPEN (11 M.) follows the rocky ravine of the *Salza*, the fine scenery of which will reward even the pedestrian. At the (1¼ M.) *Brescení-Klause* (timber-dam) the road passes through a small tunnel; it then (¾ M.) crosses to the left bank, and reaches the (3 M.) hamlet of **Gschöder** (2050'; *Gasthof zur Gemse*, rustic), at the mouth of the *Antengraben*, a good starting-point for excursions.

Excursions (guide, *Schüttbauer Michel*). To the **Hochschwab** (see above), several routes. The easiest leads through the *Antengraben*, with its grand rocks, to the (1½ hr.) lower huts in the *Antenkar* and the (1½ hr.) *Hochalpenhütten* (rustic quarters at the Sommerauer Hütte; 5400'); then by the 'Dollnensteig' (path with red marks), viâ the *Speikböden* and the *Zarkenboden*, to the (3½ hrs.) summit. Or from the lower huts in the Antenkar to the left to the (¾ hr.) *Kartalpe*; then between the *Grosse* and *Kleine Hochwart* to the *Grosse Speikboden* and the (3 hrs.) summit (path with blue marks). — The **Riegerin** (6370'; 4 hrs.; with guide), ascended through the Antengraben, is an attractive point. — The **Ebenstein** (6970'; 5½ hrs.) is reached by the *Hochalpe* and the *Polster;* the last part difficult (see below).

A fine route (good bridle-path) leads from Gschöder to the S., viâ the *Hochalpenhütten* (5100') and the *Häusl-Alpe*, to the (5½ hrs.) *Bodenbauer* (p. 375). From the Hochalpenhütten we may ascend by the *Hochalpe* (6085') and cross the saddle between the *Seemauer* and the *Wilde Kirchen* to the (1½ hr.) *Sackwiesen-See* (4660'; see p. 376), and thence proceed across the *Pletscherboden* to the *Klamm-Alpe* and (2½ hrs.) *Oberort* in Tragöss (p. 385); or from the Hochalpe nearly to the Sackwiesen-See, and then to the right to the (2 hrs.) *Sonnschien-Alpe* (p. 375), from which we may cross by the *Andralt-Hütten* and the *Fobesthört* (p. 370) to the (4½ hrs.) *Leopoldsteiner See* (p. 385), or through the *Frauenmauerhöhle* to (4 hrs.) *Eisenerz* (see above).

The road next leads between the precipices of the *Riegerin* (6370') on the left and the *Hochstadl* (6300') on the right, and past the entrance of the (3 M.) *Brunnthal*, with its small lake, above which tower the rocks of the *Riegerin*, *Ebenstein*, and *Griesstein*, to (3 M.) —

11 M. **Wildalpen** (2000'; **Zisler*, R. & A. 1 fl. 20 kr.), a thriving village and summer-resort, charmingly situated on the *Wildalpenbach*, which here falls into the Salza.

A visit to the *Arzberghöhle* is interesting. We descend the road in the Salzathal to the 'Steinbruchmauer' inn and ascend to the left to the (½ hr.) cavern. The *Thorsteinhöhle*, 1½ hr. from the inn, is also worth visiting (guide to the Arzberghöhle 1 fl. 80 kr.; Thorsteinhöhle 6 fl.). — Ascent of the *Hochstadl*, see above. The *Brandstein* (6570'; 5½ hrs.; with guide) and the *Ebenstein* (6970'; 5½-6 hrs.; with guide), ascended by the *Schafhals-Sattel* (p. 378), are also fine points. — To the *Hochschwab* (see above) the direct route from Wildalpen is through the *Brunnthal;* we follow the road to the E. to the (3½ M.) entrance of the valley, and then a level path to the right for ¾ hr., after which we ascend steeply, skirting the *Thurm* and *Stadurzkogel* to the (2 hrs.) *Hochalpenhütten* (p. 377). Guide (3-4 fl.) necessary.

From WILDALPEN TO EISENERZ, direct, over the *Eisenerzer Höhe*, an attractive route (7 hrs.). Guide not indispensable. From Wildalpen we ascend the course of the *Wildalpenbach* towards the S.; ³/₄ M., where the road divides, we follow the Wildalpenbach, with its numerous waterfalls, to the right, and reach (3 M.) *Hinter-Wildalpen* (2680'). Here we take a footpath to the left (red marks; the path in a straight direction leads over the *Goss* to *Gams*, p. 379), cross a small bridge, skirt an enclosure, and gradually ascend to the (25 min.) *Raninger Bauer*. We now ascend rapidly through the green, flower-carpeted ravine of the *Eisenerzer Bach*, cross a bridge (³/₄ hr.), and (¹/₄ hr.) ascend a steep and stony slope, avoiding the level path which goes on in a straight direction. After 10 min. more the path divides, that to the left being somewhat shorter, but the branches soon re-unite. 10 min. Eisenerzer Höhe (5060'). View of the Kaiserschild, Reichenstein, and, on the left, of part of the Schwaben chain.

The steep path now descends over loose stones and rock straight to the (20 min.) chalets of *Erzboden* (4305'), a little beyond which we reach a carriage-road, hewn in the rocks and protected by a parapet. On the right rises the perpendicular cliff of the *Zargenmauer*, 1000' above the road; on the left lies a profound, pine-clad ravine, 1000' below, while before us is the sharp rocky ridge of the *Kitzstein* (4485'). This is the finest point on the route. After a short distance at the same level (avoiding the turn to the left by a small house), we descend in long and somewhat steep windings to the base of the mountain, where (1¹/₄ hr.) a forester's house is situated in the beautiful meadows of the *Seeau* (2142'). The path now crosses the Seebach, which falls into the *Leopoldsteiner See* (p. 386), ascends slightly through dense pine-forest, crosses the *Seeriegel*, and finally descends to the (1 hr.) high-road, which (to the left) leads to (1¹/₂ M.) *Eisenerz* (p. 385).

A longer but more picturesque route crosses the *Schafhals-Sattel* (7¹/₂ hrs. from Wildalpen to Eisenerz; guide necessary). We ascend the Wildalpenthal to the (³/₄ M.) bifurcation (see above); here we ascend on the bank of the *Seisenbach* to the left to (40 min.) *Siebensee*, a pretty valley with seven small lakes, and past the Jagdhütte on the (1 hr.) *Kreuzpfäder* to the (2 hrs.) Schiffwald-Sattel or Schafhals-Sattel (5100'), between the *Brandstein* on the right and the *Ebenstein* on the left (see p. 377). Descent to the right by the *Fobesthört* to the (1¹/₄ hr.) *Halterhütte* (4270'), the (2 hrs.) forester's house in the *Seeau* (see above), and (1¹/₂ hr.) *Eisenerz*. — From the *Schafhals-Sattel* the traveller may prefer to go to the (1 hr.) *Sonnschien-Alpe* (p. 376); and then either to the right to (2¹/₂ hrs.) *Oberort* in the Tragoss valley (p. 386), or to the left over the *Räckwiesen* and *Häusl-Alpe* to the (2 hrs.) *Bodenbauer* (comp. p. 375).

The ROAD TO REIFLING (17¹/₂ M.) follows the narrow, wooded valley of the Salza. After 4¹/₂ M. the *Lassing*, and 5 M. farther on the *Mändling*, join the Salza on the right. At the junction of the latter (Gemse Inn) the road through the valley of the Mändling to *Lassing* and *Göstling* (p. 381) diverges to the right. Continuing to follow the Salza we next reach (1 M.) *Palfau*, a commune consisting of *Auf der Lend*, *Allerheiligen* (picturesque church, and inn), and other hamlets. The road now divides. The shortest route to the Ennsthal and the railway follows the right bank of the Salza to its confluence with the *Enns*, and then crosses the latter to (7 M.) —

17¹/₂ M. *Gross-Reifling* (railway-station, see p. 384).

From the bifurcation just mentioned a longer but more picturesque road leads to *Hieflau* (diligence daily in 3¹/₄ hrs.). It descends to the Salza, ascends on the left bank to the (2 M.) *Eschauer Inn*, and then leads towards the S. through the *Gamsgraben* to (3 M.) *Gams* (Schwager; Haidacher).

About 1½ M. above *Gams* is the wild and imposing gorge *In der Noth*, with the *Krausgrotte, an extensive cavern rendered accessible by Hr. Kraus in 1884, and containing beautiful stalactites and crystals (electric light; key and guide at Gams). Adjacent are some warm baths, with a large swimming-basin (bath, incl. towels, 30 kr.). By the *Carl-August-Steig* to *Gross-Reifling*, see p. 384. To *Wildalpen* over the *Goss* (4370'), 6 hrs.; guide to the saddle advisable.

The road now turns to the right and crosses a hill (1950'; fine view of the Ennsthal from the top), and then descends to (3½ M.) *Lainbach* and (3 M.) *Hieflau* (p. 385).

68. From Vienna to Linz.
Comp. Map, p. 384.

117½ M. RAILWAY. Express train in 3¾-4 hrs., ordinary in 6½ hrs. For further particulars as to the environs of Vienna, the Danube, etc., see *Baedeker's S. Germany and Austria*.

The train starts from the *Westbahnhof* (*Restaurant), outside the Mariahilf line. Soon after starting we observe the imperial palace of *Schönbrunn* on the left. 2 M. *Penzing*, and opposite to it *Hietzing*, both with numerous villas. On a height to the left stands the archiepiscopal château of *Ober St. Veit*. To the left, beyond (3¾ M.) *Hütteldorf-Hacking*, are the walls of the extensive imperial park. A little to the left lies *Mariabrunn*, with its pilgrimage-church and old monastery, now a school of forestry. 5½ M. *Weidlingau-Hadersdorf*, with a château and park of Prince Dietrichstein. 7½ M. *Purkersdorf*, with numerous villas. The line here quits the old road and runs to the left, through the *Wolfsgraben* and the *Pfalzau*, to the hills of the *Wiener Wald*. To the S.W. of (12½ M.) *Pressbaum* are the sources of the *Wien*. The train traverses a wooded region, and beyond (15½ M.) *Rekawinkel* crosses the *Aichgraben*. 23½ M. *Neulengbach*, prettily situated on a height, with a château of Prince Liechtenstein above it. To the N.E. rises the *Buchberg* (1520'). 27½ M. *Kirchstetten*; 30½ M. *Böheimkirchen*, on the *Perschlingbach*. Beyond (33½ M.) *Pottenbrunn* the train quits the hills and crosses the *Traisen*, on which lies —

38 M. **St. Pölten** (875'; *Rother Krebs; **Kaiserin v. Oesterreich*; *Löwe*; *Hirsch*), a well-built town with 10,015 inhab., and the seat of a bishop. The *Abbey Church*, founded in 1030, was restored in a degraded style at the beginning of last century. The S. aisle contains good stained glass.

FROM ST. PÖLTEN TO LEOBERSDORF, 47½ M., railway in 3 hrs. The line traverses the *Steinfeld* to the S., on the left bank of the *Traisen*. On the left, *Schloss Ochsenberg*. 7½ M. *Wilhelmsburg*, a large village; 12 M. *Scheibmühl* (branch-line to *Schrambach*, p. 374). The train now turns to the E. into the valley of the *Gölsen*. 15 M. *St. Veit an der Gölsen* (Inn), from which the *Reisalpe* (4585'; 5 hrs.), a fine point of view, is ascended. — 20 M. Hainfeld (1380'; *Witzmann; *Traube*; *Post*; *Rail. Restaurant*), a manufacturing place and summer-resort (1000 inhab.), at the influx of the *Ramsau* into the *Gölsen*, with a number of iron-works in the vicinity. Pleasant excursion to (3 M.) *Ramsau* (*Götz*), whence the *Unterberg* (4400') is easily ascended in 3½ hrs. (comp. p. 362); also to (6 M.) *Klein-Zell* (1540'; Weintraube) in the *Hallbachthal*, at the N.E. base of the *Reisalpe* (see above; ascent hence, with guide, 3 hrs.).

The train crosses the watershed (1885') between the Traisen and the Triesting and descends to (27½ M.) *Kaumberg* (2615'; Bär). In the *Triestingthal* we next reach (30½ M.) *Altenmarkt-Tenneberg*, the former (Lamm; Elephant) to the E., the latter (Drei Löwen) to the W. of the station. Ascent to the S., of the (2½ hrs.) Hocheck (3400'), with tower affording an extensive view. To the N., by *Klein-Maria-Zell* and *St. Corona* (Inn), to (3¼ hrs.) the summit of the Schöpfl (2930'), another fine point.

In the narrow valley we next reach (35½ M.) *Weissenbach an der Triesting* (Inn), at the mouth of the *Further Thal*. [About 3 M. from Weissenbach is the *Furthner Inn*, at the entrance to the narrow *Steinwandgraben*, in which, about 4 M. up, is the very interesting *Steinwandklamm*, rendered accessible by the Austrian Tourist Club by means of bridges and ladders. From the upper end a picturesque path (indicated by marks) leads through the *Türkenlucken*, a rock-grotto, to the (½ hr.) hamlet of *Greith* ("View of the Schneeberg and other peaks), whence it descends to (40 min.) *Muckendorf* (p. 362).] — The valley of the Triesting expands. 38 M. *Pottenstein*; 40 M. *Berndorf*, with a large metal-ware factory 41 M. *Triestinghof*; 42 M. *St. Veit an der Triesting* (Krone). 44½ M. *Enzesfeld*, with the château of that name on the hill to the right (Baron Rothschild's). 46½ M. *Wittmannsdorf*, junction of a line to Gutenstein (p. 362). — 47¼ M. *Leobersdorf*, see p. 362.

43 M. *Prinzersdorf*, on the *Pielach*, a good fishing-stream. On a hill to the right is the castle of *Hoheneggs*. 44½ M. *Markersdorf*; 46½ M. *Gross-Sierning*; 49½ M. *Loosdorf*, with a large cement-factory, the interesting château of *Schallaburg* (S.), and the dilapidated castles of *Sitzenthal*, *Albrechtsberg*, and *Osterburg* (N.). Beyond the *Wachberg Tunnel* we reach the finest point on the line at (53 M.) Melk or *Mölk* (*Lamm*; *Ochs*; *Hirsch*), on the *Danube*, at the foot of a rock which is crowned with a famous *Benedictine Abbey* (185' above the river), founded in 1089, and rebuilt in the Italian style in 1701-38. The church, richly embellished with marble and gilding, the library with its valuable incunabula and MSS., and various other art-treasures deserve a visit. The terrace commands a beautiful *View of the Danube.

The train crosses the *Melk* and descends to the Danube. On the opposite bank is the ruin of *Weitenegg*, and higher up the river, on the hill, is *Artstetten*, a handsome château of Archduke Karl Ludwig. 58½ M. Pöchlarn *(Pleiner)*, on the *Erlauf*, the Roman *Arelape*, the traditional seat of Rüdiger of Bechelaren, one of the Nibelungen heroes.

FROM PÖCHLARN TO KIENBERG-GAMING, 23½ M., railway in 1¾ hr. Beyond (3 M.) *Erlauf* the train crosses the Erlauf, and passes *Wieselburg* and *Purgstall* (with a château of Count Schaffgotsch). — 17 M. Scheibbs (1050'; *Rainöhl*; *Hirsch*), a summer-resort, prettily situated among wooded hills, with the Oetscher in the background. Beautiful walks in the environs; charming view from the (1½ hr.) *Blassenstein* (2700'). — 49½ M. *Neubruck*, at the mouth of the *Jessnitz*. — 23½ M. *Kienberg-Gaming*, 2 M. (omnibus 20 kr.) from the pleasant village of Gaming (1410'; *Hallriegl*; *Pascher*), with the interesting ruins of a Carthusian monastery, suppressed in 1782.

EXCURSIONS FROM GAMING. Through the romantic *Erlaufthal* to the (6 hrs.) *Lassing Fall* (comp. p. 373). — ASCENT OF THE OETSCHER, recommended. We follow the Lunz road (see below) to (3 M.) the cross-roads near the *Grubberg* (2470'; Inn), diverge there to the left by a road crossing the *Föllbaumhöhe* (2680') to the *Oisthal* or upper *Ybbsthal*, and ascend to the left to (2½ hrs.) *Lackenhof* (2740'; *Jagersberger; guide, Matt. Reiter), which may also be reached from Gaming by a good path viâ *Jägerreith* and *Oberpolzberg* (3 hrs.). Thence by a path indicated by marks (guide unnecessary) over pastures and through wood to the (1¼ hr.) *Riffelsattel* (4210'), between the Kleine and the Grosse Oetscher, and (left) to the (20 min.) *Oetscherhaus* (4660'; *Inn); lastly we ascend over the *Kreuzboden* to the (1¼ hr.) pyramid on the top of the ***Grosse Oetscher** (6210'; superb and extensive view). — The *Oetscherhöhlen*, ice-caverns on the S. slope on the side next the Erlaufthal, are reached from the summit in 1½-2 hrs. (with guide). — Descent through the *Oetschergraben* to *Mariazell*, see p. 373 (direct route from the Mira Fall to *Mitterbach*, see p. 373).

From Gaming to Göstling, 13 M., diligence daily in 3½ hrs. (one-horse carr. to the Lunzer See, 3½ fl.), viâ (6 M.) **Lunz** (1950'; **Schadensteiner; Dieminger; Leichtfried*), charmingly situated on the Ybbs, and pleasant for a lengthened stay. To the E. is the (½ M.) *Lunzer See* (2025'; 1¼ M. long). From the (1½ M.) *Seehof* (Inn), at the upper end of the lake, we may cross the *Durchlass* (2485') to the (1½ hr.) *Oisthal* (see above), the road in which leads to the left to (2 M.) *Lackenhof* (see above), and to the right to (1½ M.) *Langau* (p. 374). — The ***Dürrenstein** (6160') is ascended from the Seehof in 5 hrs. (guide, M. Ritzinger): through the *Seebachthal*, between the *Seemauer* and *Hetzkogl* and viâ (½ hr.) *Länd* to the grandly situated (¾ hr.) *Mittersee* and (½ hr.) **Obersee*. Thence we ascend by the *Herrenalpe* to the (2½ hrs.) summit, which affords an excellent view. Descent through the *Steinbachthal* to *Göstling*, see below.

The high-road leads through the Ybbsthal from Lunz to (7 M.) **Göstling** (1745'; **Reichenpfader; Berger*), prettily situated at the mouth of the *Göstlingbach*. Fine view from the *Calvarienberg*. Beautiful walk to the **Steinbachthal*, and through the grand ravine of the *Noth* (with its bold bridge) to the (1¼ hr.) hunting-lodge of Baron Rothschild (splendidly situated). — The *Dürrenstein* (see above) may be ascended in 6 hrs. from Göstling, through the Steinbachthal. — The ***Hochkaar** (5935'), a superb point of view, deserves a visit. We take the road through the Göstlingthal to (5 M.) *Lassing* (2275'; Inn), and at the Moosbauer or Oberhaus ascend to the left through the *Wassergraben* to the (2½ hrs.) *Lassinger Alpe* (4710'; quarters) and the (1½ hr.) top. — Beyond Lassing the road descends the *Mändlingthal* to the (3½ M.) Salzathal (p. 378), in which (Jagersberger's Inn 'Zur Gemse') we may eitherpr oceed to the left to (10 M.) Wildalpen, or to the right to (1 M.) Palfau (diligence from Göstling to Palfau daily in 3¼ hrs.; from Palfau to Wildalpen in 3 hrs., to Hieflau in 3¼ hrs.).

From Göstling to Weyer (18½ M.). The road leads through the Ybbsthal to (5 M.) *St. Georgen am Reith*, where the road to *Waidhofen* (see below) diverges to the N., and (6 M.) *Hollenstein* (1600'; Dietrich), charmingly situated at the mouth of the *Lassing*. Then by *Klein-Hollenstein*, where the road quits the Ybbsthal, and over the *Saurüssel* to (7½ M.) *Weyer* (p. 381). Ascent of the **Voralpe** (5665'; 4 hrs., with guide; H. Fürnholzer) from Hollenstein recommended; descent by the *Esslingalpe* to (3 hrs.) *Altenmarkt* (p. 384).

Beyond Pöchlarn the train crosses the *Erlauf*. On the right *Marbach*, and on the hill above it the pilgrimage-church of *Maria-Tafert* (1450'). 61½ M. *Krumnnussbaum;* 64 M. *Säusenstein*. Near (67 M.) *Kemmelbach-Ybbs* (the latter 1½ M. from the station) we quit the Danube and cross the *Ybbs*, the valley of which we now follow. 69½ M. *Neumarkt-Karlsbach;* 72½ M. *Blindenmarkt*. — 77½ M. **Amstetten** (900'; *Railway Hotel & Restaurant; Huber*, at the station), prettily situated.

To Klein-Reifling, 29½ M., railway in 1¼-2½ hrs. The train soon turns to the S. and crosses the *Ybbs*. Stations *Utmerfeld*, *Hilm-Kematen*, *Rosenau*, *Sonntagberg*. Then across the Ybbs to (14½ M.) **Waidhofen** *on the*

Ybbs (1170'; *Infär; Goldner Löwe; Reichsapfel; Goldner Stern*), an old town and summer-resort, once fortified, lying in a pleasant dale. Adjoining the old Schloss is the church of St. Magdalena, of 1279, containing an interesting silver monstrance of the 15th century. On the right bank of the Ybbs (view from the bridge) lies the village of *Zell*, below which there is a good bath-house on the Urlbach. On the *Buchenberg*, to the S. of the town, are extensive shady walks. Beautiful excursions in the vicinity: ascent of the *Sonntagberg* (2310'; 1½ hr.), with pilgrimage-church, inn, and fine view (or ascended direct from stat. Sonntagberg in ¾ hr.); ascent of the *Spindeleben* (3495'; 3 hrs.), through the *Redenbachthal*; through the *Ybbsthal* to (7 M.) *Ybbsitz* and (8 M.) *Opponitz*; and thence to the right to (7½ M.) *Hollenstein* (p. 381), or to the left to (9½ M.) *Göstling* (p. 381).

The train now quits the Ybbsthal, ascends the *Seeberger Thal* to the S., and at (20 M.) *Oberland* (1690') crosses the watershed between the Ybbs and the Enns, the frontier between Lower and Upper Austria, marked by an old so-called Turkish entrenchment. We now descend viâ *Gaflenz* to (25½ M.) Weyer (1300'; *Pachbauer; Schnellinger*), prettily situated in a narrow dale. (Thence to Hollenstein, etc., see p. 381.) We then cross the Enns to *Kastenreith* and (29 M.) *Klein-Reifling*, on the Rudolfbahn (p. 384).

The train quits the Ybbsthal. 82 M. *Mauer-Oehling*; 84½ M. *Aschbach*; 90 M. *St. Peter* (1½ M. to the S. of which is the large Benedictine abbey of *Seitenstetten*); 94 M. *Haag* (with *Schloss Salaberg* on the left). — 102½ M. St. Valentin (870'; *Rail. Restaurant*), the junction of lines to *Budweis* and *St. Michael* (p. 383). The train then crosses the *Enns*, the boundary between Lower and Upper Austria, to —

106½ M. **Enns** (920'; *Krone; Ochs*), an old town on the site of the Roman *Laureacum*, picturesquely situated. On a height stands Prince Auersperg's château of *Ennseck*, with pleasant grounds. — 109½ M. *Asten*. Near (114 M.) *Kleinmünchen* the train crosses the *Traun*.

117½ M. **Linz**. — *Erzherzog Karl*, R. from 1 fl., L. & A. 60 kr.; *Goldner Adler*, R. from 80 kr.; both on the Danube, near the steamboat-quay. Above the bridge: *Rother Krebs*, R., L., & A. 1 fl. 90 kr. In the town: *Löwe* and *Stadt Frankfurt*, in the Franz-Josefs-Platz; *Kanone*, Landstrasse, the nearest to the railway-station; *Goldnes Schiff*, *Herrenhaus*, Landstrasse.

Linz (870'), the capital of Upper Austria, with 41,687 inhab., lies on the right bank of the *Danube*, across which an iron bridge, 300 yds. long, leads to the suburb of *Urfahr*. The large *Franz-Josefs-Platz*, which ascends from the river, is embellished with a lofty '*Trinity Column*', erected by Emp. Charles VI. in 1723. On the busy *Promenade* are the *Landes-Theater* and the *Museum Francisco-Carolinum*, containing historical and scientific collections (daily 10-12). In the vicinity is the new *Cathedral*, in the Gothic style, designed by Statz, and containing handsome altars and good stained glass. — For a more detailed account of Linz, see *Baedeker's Southern Germany & Austria*.

Environs. The *Freinberg is reached from the Capuchin church in ½ hr., by a path passing large deposits of quartzose sand. Archduke Maximilian of Este (d. 1863) erected a fortified tower here, by way of experiment, before executing his plan for fortifying Linz, but the works have long since been abandoned. The tower on the Freinberg was afterwards converted into a church and handed over to the Jesuits. *View from the platform very fine (ladies not admitted; men not after 7 p.m.).

A good level path leads thence to the N. to the (¼ hr.) *Jägermayr (Inn) and the new promenades of the public-spirited 'Verschönerungs-Verein' of Linz, with numerous points of view. To the S., in the distance, stretches the chain of the Alps of Salzburg and Styria, as far as the eye can reach, the Traunstein being especially conspicuous. — The Jägermayr lies just above the Danube bridge, from which it may be reached in a straight direction in ¾ hr.; but the pleasantest route to it, 20 min. longer, skirts the Danube as far as the Calvarienberg, and ascends thence.

The view from the *Pöstlingberg (1762'), on the left bank, to the N.W., 1 hr. from Urfahr, is still more extensive, and is particularly fine by evening-light. (Good panorama by Edlbacher.) A pilgrimage-church and rustic inn on the top.

St. Magdalena, a small pilgrimage-church with an inn, a charming point of view, ¾ hr. to the N. of Urfahr, attracts many visitors. About 2 hrs. beyond it is the *Giselawarte (3130'), a tower commanding an extensive distant view.

From Linz to *Salzburg*, see R. 17; to *Kremsmünster* (Bad Hall) and *Windisch-Garsten*, see R. 70.

69. From Linz to St. Michael viâ Steyr.

142 M. Railway in 5¾-10 hrs. (dinner, 1 fl., handed into the carriages at Klein-Reifling, Selzthal, and St. Michael). A seat should be secured in the last carriage for the sake of the view (see p. 112), at least from Hieflau to Admont.

To (15½ M.) *St. Valentin* (880'), see p. 382. Our line (Rudolfbahn) here diverges from the Westbahn to the S.W., and at (20 M.) *Ernsthofen* enters the valley of the *Enns*. 25½ M. *Rammingdorf*.

28 M. **Steyr** (990'; *Hôtel Eiselmeyr; Löwe; Schiff*), a town with 17,200 inhab., at the confluence of the *Steyr* with the *Enns*, is noted for its iron-wares. The old town, situated between the two rivers, is connected with its suburbs *Ennsdorf* and *Steyrdorf* by two bridges. On a hill rises *Burg Steyr* (10th cent.), the property of Prince Lamberg, the tower of which commands a fine view. (Admission to the park on application to the gardener.) The Gothic *Church*, begun in 1420, contains fine stained glass and a font in bronze, with reliefs of 1560; also a modern votive-altar in carved wood. The new *Rathhaus* and the extensive *Austrian Rifle Factory* (adm. on application) are also worthy of notice. The ground-floor of the *Public School* is occupied by the *Collections of the Styrian Industrial Society*.

Walks. To the N.: to (¼ hr.) *Tabor*, with view of the town; to *Gleink* (¾ hr.), formerly a Benedictine convent, with inn and a fine view. To the W.: to *Christkindl* (¾ hr.), a pilgrimage-church. To the S.: *Garsten* (½ hr.), a village on the left bank of the Enns, with a large Benedictine convent, now used as a prison; to the *Hohe Ennsleithen* (1½ hr.); to *St. Ulrich* (¾ hr.), a charmingly situated hamlet. Pretty walk to *Sand* (1¼ hr.), on the 'Eisenstrasse' (see below). — The tower on the *Damberg* (2450') affords a splendid survey of the Alps and the valley of the Danube. Crossing the Enns bridge, we walk straight through Ennsdorf and the Damberger Gasse (finger-post), and pass under the railway-embankment. The path, indicated by reddish-yellow marks, leads to (1 hr.) the *Schoiber Inn* (verandah with view), and thence ascends to the edge of the wood, where we turn to the right to the *Laurenzikapelle*, and in ¾ hr. reach the tower (panorama by Gründler). A path indicated by red marks diverges to the left to *St. Ulrich* (see above), whence we may return to Steyr. The **Schoberstein** (4190'), the shortest really Alpine expedition from Steyr, may be scaled from *Ternberg* (see below) in 3½ hrs., viâ *Trattenbach*.

A road, following the left bank of the river, leads through the pretty **Steyrthal** (enlivened with iron-works), to *Unter-* and *Ober-Grünburg* and (16 M.) *Leonstein* (1415'; Bräu). Opposite, below the mouth of the *Krumme Steyerling*, lies the (1½ M.) beautifully-situated village of *Molln* (Wegscheider), noted for its manufacture of Jew's-harps. [Very attractive walk from this point (fit for mountaineers only, with a guide and provisions), viâ *Ramsau* and the *Gopfing*, to the (5 hrs.) *Feuchtau Lakes* (4558') and the top of the (2 hrs.) Hohencck (6430'), the highest peak of the *Sengsengebirge* (p. 391), with an extensive view. Descent to (3 hrs.) *Windisch-Garsten* (p. 391).] — At *Herndl*, 4½ M. farther on, our road joins the high-road from Michldorf. (Thence to *Windisch-Garsten* and *Lietzen*, see p. 390.)

Near (30 M.) *Garsten* the train crosses the Enns and then follows the left bank, opposite the road (called 'Eisenstrasse', from the iron-ore traffic). 36½ M. *Ternberg* (Derfler); 42 M. *Losenstein* (Grösswang), a village inhabited principally by nail-makers, with an old church and a ruined castle. 45½ M. *Reich-Ramming* (1145'), at the mouth of the *Rammingbach*, has extensive brass and iron-works. 50 M. *Gross-Ramming*. The village lies on the right bank, at the mouth of the romantic *Pechgraben*, in which, about 4½ M. from the station, is a large granite boulder bearing an inscription (1857) in honour of Leopold von Buch, the geologist (pleasant walk; *Stieglechner's Inn, in the Aschach, near the boulder). Then across the *Hammergraben* by a viaduct, and through the *Ennsberg Tunnel*, 350 yds. long, to (55½ M.) *Kastenreith*, at the confluence of the *Gaflenzbach* with the Enns (p. 382). 57½ M. **Klein-Reifling** (1200'; *Rail. Restaurant; Mitterhuber's Inn*, ¾ M. from the station), junction of the line to *Amstetten* (p. 381). We now traverse a picturesque valley, pass through two tunnels, and cross the *Laussa* (see above) to (66 M.) *Weissenbach-St. Gallen* (Gruber), 1 M. to the N.E. of which lies *Altenmarkt* (Lohner).

A road leads from (2 M.) *St. Gallen* (1680'; *Haller*), with the castle of *Gallenstein*, built by the abbots of Admont to command the valley, through the *Buchau* to (12 M.) *Admont*. Pleasant excursion from St. Gallen to the romantic **Spitzenbachgraben*; from (1¼ hr.) its farther end a marked path leads viâ the *Sauboden* to the (2½ hrs.) *Maiereck* (5785'), an excellent point of view. — From Altenmarkt through the *Lauszathal* to (20 M.) *Windisch-Garsten*, see p. 392. — The ascent of the Voralpe from Altenmarkt is recommended (path marked): by the *Esslinger-Hütten* to the S. peak (*Tanzboden*, 5665'), 4 hrs.; extensive view of the plain of the Danube as far as the Bohemian Forest, of the Styrian Alps to the S., the Dachstein to the S.W., etc.; the descent may be made to *Hollenstein* (p. 381).

At (72½ M.) **Gross-Reifling** (1400'; *Baumann*) the *Salza* falls into the Enns. (To *Wildalpen*, see R. 67.)

A very pleasant expedition may be made by the 'Carl-August-Steig', a footpath constructed by the Austrian Tourist Club, to *Gams* (to the *Krausgrotte*, p. 379). Leaving the railway-station we cross the Enns, and then the *Salza* (by the Salzahauernbrücke), and follow the path (indicated by red marks, and provided with railings and benches) along the precipitous S. bank of the latter to (1½ hr.) *Gams* (p. 379).

The train threads two tunnels, and crosses the Enns. Beyond (75½ M.) *Landl*, near *Lainbach*, the *Schrabl-Thal* opens on the left (to *Gams*, see p. 379). The Ennsthal contracts. Two short tunnels. Then (79 M.) **Hieflau** (1700'; *Steuber, or Post; *Steinberger*), with important iron-works, finely situated at the confluence of the *Erzbach* and the Enns.

EXCURSIONS. To the **Hartelsgraben** and back, 4½-5 hrs. We follow the road to the Gesäuse (p. 386), and beyond the (1 hr.) second bridge ('Hartelsbrücke') cross the railway and ascend the romantic ravine by a good path to (2 hrs.) the *Jägerhaus* above the *Höllboden* (across the *Sulzkaar* to *Johnsbach*, see p. 387). Hence we cross the saddle to the E., between the *Goldeck* and the *Polster*, to the *Waggraben*, and follow the carriage-road back to (4½ M.) Hieflau. — The **Tamischbachthurm** (6670'; with guide) may be ascended from Hieflau, viâ the *Hochscheiben*, in 4½ hrs. (better from Gstatterboden, see p. 386); the ascent may also be made from *Gross-Reifling*, and from *St. Gallen* viâ the *Bärensattel*, in 5-5½ hrs. — The Luganer (7235'; 4 hrs.; guide), ascended viâ the *Waggraben* and the *Schenkegg-Alp*, is also recommended.

FROM HIEFLAU TO LEOBEN viâ EISENERZ (27½ M.). Railway to (9½ M.) *Eisenerz* in 1 hr. The line and the 'Eisenstrasse' (see p. 384) turn to the S.E. into the picturesque ravine of the *Erzbach*. To the right, at (2½ M.) *Radmer*, diverges the *Radmer-Thal*, in which, at the foot of the *Luganer* (7235'), 4½ M. distant, lies the village of *Radmer an der Stube* (2395'; Mühlenwirth; Kirchenwirth); to the E. rises the *Kaiserschild* (6830'). Hence across the *Radmerhals* (4300') to Eisenerz, 3½ hrs., attractive; to *Johnsbach*, see p. 387. — On a height to the left, farther on, stands the château of *Leopoldstein*; beyond it (not visible from the line) lies the beautiful, dark-blue *Lake of Leopoldstein* (2030'), over which tower the bold precipices of the *Seemauern* and the *Pfaffenstein*.

9½ M. **Eisenerz** (2445'; *Schardinger, R. 60-80 kr.; *König v. Sachsen; Moser*; *Rudolfsbahn*, near the station), with 4000 inhab., an old mining-town, as its name ('iron-ore') imports, is commanded on the E. by the abrupt *Pfaffenstein* (6140'), and on the W. by the *Kaiserschild* (6830'). The *Church of St. Oswald*, a Gothic structure of 1279, is an interesting example of a mediæval fortified church.

To the S. the red *Erzberg* (5030') closes the valley. This 'ore-mountain' is so productive that the ore is quarried in summer without the aid of mining operations. In winter, however, the subterranean mode of excavation is more convenient. The lower part of the mountain belongs to the Alpine Montangesellschaft, the upper and more productive part is the property of the community of Vordernberg. The mines, some of which have been in operation for 1000 years, employ about 5000 hands and yield 300,000 tons of iron annually. Permission to visit the mines is obtained at the mining-office (ticket 1 fl. 20 kr. for 1-4 pers.). We ascend past the *Chapel of St. Barbara* to the *Kaiserlisch*, and thence to the (2½ hrs.) summit, marked by a colossal cross erected by the Archduke John. The top of the hill commands a beautiful survey of the Seemauern, Pfaffenstein, Schwarzenstein, Kaiserschild, and Reichenstein. In the neighbourhood is the Vordernberg Mining-house (Restaurant), whence a tramway (interesting), for the ore, descends to the Prebühl (see below). — From Eisenerz viâ the *Eisenerzhöhe* to (6-7 hrs.) *Wildalpen*, see p. 378.

The road from Eisenerz to Vordernberg (8 M.; Stellwagen in summer daily in 2¼ hrs.) leads to the E., skirting the foot of the Erzberg, to (1½ M.) *Trofeng* (Zur Frauenmauer), whence it ascends abruptly to the (3¼ M.) **Prebühl Pass** (4025', Inn), a saddle between the *Polster* (6270') on the left and the *Vordernberger Reichenstein* (7105') on the right. It then descends to (3¼ M.) **Vordernberg** (2685'; *Post; *Schwarzer Adler*), a prosperous place with a brisk trade in iron, from which the *Hochthurm* (6835'; 4 hrs.; with guide) and the *Reichenstein* (7105'; 5½ hrs.; guide) may be ascended. The latter may also be ascended from Eisenerz in 5½ hrs. viâ the *Erzberg*, the *Plattenalpe*, and the *Stiege*. — RAILWAY from Vordernberg (in ¾-1 hr.), viâ *Friedauwerk, Trofajach, St. Peter-Freienstein*, and *Donawitz*, to (10 M.) *Leoben*.

FOR PEDESTRIANS the route from Eisenerz through the *Frauenmauer Cavern* and the *Tragössthal* to Bruck is much more attractive (11½ hrs.; torches and guide, 3½ fl., necessary for the cavern; magnesium-wire useful). We diverge to the left from the high-road at *Trofeng* (see above), and ascend the wooded *Gsollgraben* to the (1½ hr.) *Gsoll-Alp* (3695'), at the foot of the *Frauenmauer* (6000'), a range of mountains stretching from the Schwaben chain to the *Griesmauer*. Another hour of stiff climbing, latterly over a stony slope (fine retrospect), leads to the W. entrance (4705') of the *Frauenmauerhöhle*, an imposing cavern perforating the whole mountain, 900 yds. in length, without including the numerous side-galleries. Soon after entering the cave (wraps advisable) we descend by an ice-clad and slippery ladder to the *Eiskammer*, which contains columns of ice. We then remount the ladder and traverse a series of magnificent halls, often 160-200' in height, floored with limestone debris, to the (¾ hr.) E. mouth of the cavern (5120'), where we obtain a striking view of the imposing group of the *Hochschwab*, *Ebenstein*, etc. We now descend to the *Neuwaldegg-Alpe* and through the well-wooded *Jassing-Graben*, with the *Hochthurm* (6835') rising on the S., pass the *Grüne See*, and reach (2½ hrs.) *Oberort* (2560'; *Peintinger*; *Hölzel*, moderate), the chief village in the upper **Tragössthal**. Thence a carriage-road (diligence to Bruck daily; 1 fl. 66 kr.) through the picturesque valley of the *Laimingbach*, to *Püchel*, *Oberdorf*, *St. Kathrein*, and (15 M.) *Bruck* (p. 368).

Over the *Eisenerzhöhe* to (6-7 hrs.) *Wildalpen*, see p. 378.

The Ennsthal now turns towards the W., and we enter the *Gesäuse*, a profound defile, 12 M. in length, flanked by the *Tamischbachthurm* and the *Buchstein* on the N., and the *Hochthor* and *Reichenstein* on the S., and traversed by the Enns, which forms a series of wild rapids (from Admont to Hieflau fall of 400'). The railway (best views to the right as far as Gstatterboden, then to the left) threads a short tunnel and enters the imposing ravine at the foot of the sheer rocky wall of the *Ennsbrand*. The road, which runs opposite on the left bank, well repays the pedestrian as far as the end of the Gesäuse (carriage from Hieflau to Admont with one horse 7, with two horses 10 fl.). On the left opens the *Hartetsgraben* (p. 385), from which a foaming streamlet issues. The train next pierces the *Hochsteg Tunnel* and crosses the *Kummerbrücke* to the left bank of the Enns. The rocky walls recede and the Enns flows tranquilly through the *Ennsflur*, an expansion of the valley, dominated on the right by the massive cliffs of the *Grosse Buchstein* (7296'), and on the left by the precipitous *Planspitz* (6950'). — 84½ M. **Gstatterboden** (1850'; *Hotel Gesäuse*, moderate), in a grand situation.

EXCURSIONS. Pleasant walk through wood to the (½ hr.) *Gstatterboden-Bauer*, a solitary farm in a forest-glade, encircled by imposing mountains. This is the best starting-point for an ascent of the **Tamischbachthurm** (6670'; 4-4½ hrs.; with guide). The marked path ascends to the (2½-3 hrs.) *Ennsthal Club Hut* (5250') and thence to (1½ hr.) the summit (magnificent view; panorama by L. Haas). — The *Grosse Buchstein* (A½-5 hrs.; difficult), see p. 388.

From Gstatterboden to the *Bruckgraben*, there and back 3½-4 hrs. (permission and guide, 1 fl. 20 kr., at the inn). We follow the railway for 1 hr. up the valley, then ascend the romantic gorge to the right, as far as the woodman's hut, about 10 min. below the *Triftklause* (timber dam). The guides usually make a detour adding about 1 hr. to the excursion, diverging to the left by a deserted hut before the woodman's cottage to the *Ritschergraben*, where there is a chalet (refreshments) and thence to the woodman's hut. We return over the (20 min.) *Brucksattel* (3585'), by a steep but good path (red marks) through wood, to the (1 hr.) station.

To the *Johnsbachthal*, a very interesting excursion. We follow the high-road through the Gesäuse for 2¼ M. to the W., and then ascend by a road to the left through the wild and picturesque gorge, between the *Reichenstein* to the right and the *Oedstein* on the left, to the (4½ M.) finely-situated village of **Johnsbach** (2585'; *Donnerwirth*, near the church, unpretending; *Kölbwirth*, 1 M. farther up the valley. To the W. rise the precipices of the *Reichenstein* (7372'), to the E. the *Oedstein* (7660') and the *Hochthor* (7782'), all three difficult. A magnificent view is enjoyed from the **Treffner Alp** (4855'; 2 hrs.) to the S.W., ascended from the Donner Inn through wood. (Thence over the *Flitzen-Alp* to the *Kaiserau*, 2½ hrs., see p. 388.) — A not very attractive path ascends from Johnsbach through the valley, which now trends to the E., passing the (1½ hr.) *Wolfbauer*, and a fine waterfall above it to the left, to the *Ebner Alp* and *Neuburg Alp*, and crosses the saddle to the S. of the *Haselkogel* to (4 hrs.) *Radmer an der Hasel* (2985'; accommodation at the *Schloss Greifenberg* or 'Schlössl') and (¾ hr.) *Radmer an der Stube* (p. 385) in the *Radmerthal*. — The route from Johnsbach over the *Sulzkaar* to *Hieflau* (about 5 hrs., with guide) is preferable. It ascends to the left viâ the *Wolfbauer* (see above) leads past the waterfall to the (¾ hr.) *Untere Koder Alp* (4390'), magnificently situated at the foot of the *Oedstein* (7660'), and then skirts the precipices of the *Hochthor* to the *Obere Koder* or *Stadel Alp* and to the (1½-2 hrs.) Sulzkaarhund-Sattel (5740'), to the S. of the *Hoch-Zinödl* (see below). Thence we descend to the *Sulzkaar-Alpe* (4900') and through the *Hartelsgraben* (see above) to (2½ hrs.) *Hieflau* (p. 385). With this route may be combined the ascent of the *Hoch-Zinödl* (7185'; fine view, 2 hrs. from Sulzkaarhund), which offers no difficulty to adepts.

The valley now again contracts. The railway, rounding the cliffs of the *Bruckstein* in wide curves, passes the mouth of the imposing *Johnsbachthal* (see above), and crosses the *Brucksteinbach*, which issues from the *Bruckgraben* (see above). It then runs between the *Himberstein* (3880') on the right and the *Haindlmauer* (4640') on the left, and crosses the Enns. Beyond the *Haindl-Tunnel*, 260 yds. in length, is the station *Gesäuse-Eingang*. The train then enters the broad green dale of —

93 M. **Admont** (2105'; *Post*, R. 1 fl., B. 24 kr.; *Buchbinder*; *Jerausch*; *Wölzenberger*, R. 60-80 kr.; *Bartl*, nearest the station; *Bräuhaus*; good wine at the *Stifts-Stübl*; swimming and other baths at *Haus's*), a picturesque village and summer-resort, with the handsome buildings of the celebrated Benedictine abbey of Admont ('ad montes'), founded by Archb. Gebhard of Salzburg in 1074, partly burned down in 1865, but since rebuilt. The Gothic abbey-church, *St. Blasius-Münster*, with its two slender spires, has been modernised. The valuable library, in a richly-decorated hall, comprises 80,000 vols. and 1000 MSS (open daily 10-11 and 4-5).

Above Admont, to the S., stands (½ hr.) **Schloss Röthelstein** (2680'), the property of the abbey, which affords an admirable survey of the Ennsthal; to the N.W. is the wooded *Pleschberg* (5636'), with the church on the *Frauenberg* (see below) at its base; to the N. rise the '*Haller Mauern*', consisting of the *Grosse Pyhrgass* (7360'), *Scheibelstein* (7220'), *Hexenthurm* (7156'), and *Natterriegel* (6850'); to the E. is the *Grosse Buchstein* (7296'); to the S.E. the *Sparafeld* (7366'). — Another good view of the environs is obtained from the bridge over the Enns, 1 M. from the railway-station. In the neighbourhood, on the right bank of the Enns, is the *Eichelau*,

388 *VIII. Route 69.* ROTTENMANN. *From Linz*

with shady walks. — About 2 M. to the N. is the picturesque village of *Hall* (Inn next the church); and about 2 hrs. farther *Mühlau* (Inn), charmingly situated at the foot of the Haller Mauern. Hence an attractive route (at first a cart-track, then a marked footpath) leads across the *Pyhrgassgatterl* (4420'), between the *Grosse Pyhrgass* and the *Bosruck*, to *Spital am Pyhrn* (p. 392) in 3 hrs.

A road (two-horse carr. 8½ fl.) leads from Admont towards the S. over the *Lichtmessberg*, past a scythe-work and the 'Paradies' (*Restaurant) to the (1¾ hr.) *Kaiserau Inn* (3560') and the (¼ hr.) Kaiserau (3700'), a picturesque glade surrounded by pine-woods, with an old castle belonging to the Abbey of Admont. An attractive excursion leads hence over the *Kalblinggatterl* (5050') to the (2 hrs.) *Flitzen Alpe (3935'), immediately beneath the cliffs of the Sparafeld and Reichenstein. (Thence to *Johnsbach* by the *Treffner Alp*, see p. 387; 3 hrs., with guide.) The *Kalbling* (6000') and *Sparafeld* (7300') may easily be ascended from the Kaiserau (guide in each case 5 fl.); the *Reichenstein* (7312'; 4-5 hrs.), ascended from the Flitzen Alpe, is difficult and dangerous. — Two foot-paths cross from the Kaiserau to the Paltenthal, one leading W. to *Bärndorf* and (2 hrs.) *Rottenmann*, the other S. to *Dietmannsdorf* and (1¼ hr.) *Trieben* (see below).

ASCENTS (guides, *A. Feistlinger, Marl. Metschilzer, P. Stoll,* and *Gottl. Vogel*). The **Grosse Buchstein** (7290'; 7 hrs.; guide 6 fl.) is toilsome, but repays the fatigue. The road to St. Gallen (p. 384) is followed towards the S.E. viâ *Weng* to (4½ M.) the *Buchauer Sattel* (2790'; Tonner Inn), 1½ M. beyond which we diverge to the right by a shooting-lodge; we then traverse the *Gsengschneide* and the *Gschiessgraben* and ascend a stony gully to the plateau and the (4½ hrs.) summit. Or we may go on by the road from the Tonner Inn to the (3 M.) *Eisenzieher Inn* (2750'), and ascend thence to the right (marked path) to the (1 hr.) cavern in the *Schiesswald*, then over the *Schiesswaldrücken* and through the *Klamm* to the (3½ hrs.) summit. Admirable view. Descent to the *Gstatterboden* steep and unpleasant. — The ***Natterriegel** (6650'; 4½-5 hrs.; guide 4½ fl.) is a remarkably fine point, and free from difficulty. We ascend from Admont viâ the *Pilzhütte* and the *Lärcheck* in 3½ hrs., or from *Weng* (see above) in 3 hrs., to the *Grabnerthörl*, between the *Grabnerstein* (6045') and the Natterriegel; thence a slight descent on the E. side, and finally over turf and rocks to the (1½ hr.) summit. — The **Grosse Pyhrgass** (7800'; 5-6 hrs.; guide 5 fl.) is also recommended: we proceed viâ *Mühlau* (Inn) and the *Gstattmeier Nieder-Alpe* to the (3 hrs.) *Pyhrgassgatterl* (see above); then viâ the *Brandtner-* and *Hössel-Alpe* to the arête, and thence to the right to the (3 hrs.) top.

The train follows the broad valley of the Enns. To the right, near (97½ M.) *Frauenberg*, rises the *Frauenberg* (2500'), with a handsome pilgrimage-church, and farther on lies the pretty village of *Ardning*, at the foot of the *Bosruck*. At the confluence of the *Paltenbach* with the Enns, the line turns towards the S.; to the W. rises the *Grimming* (p. 393). — 102 M. **Selzthal** (2080'; **Huber, Krone*, both at the station; **Rail. Restaurant*), the junction of the line to Aussee and Bischofshofen (for Salzburg; R. 71). The train skirts the slopes of the *Dürrenschöberl* (5700'), and enters the wooded *Paltenthal*, a valley ascending to the E. On a pine-clad height to the right rises the picturesque château of *Strechau* (2835').

106 M. **Rottenmann** (2210'; **Post; Bräu; Lebzelter*), a small town with rolling-mills and iron-works.

EXCURSIONS. Picturesque walks lead hence to various points of view in the (½ M.) *Bürgerwald*. — The ascent of the *Dürrenschöberl* (5700'; 3 hrs.) viâ the *Messner Alpe*, is easy. — That of the *Bösenstein* (8085'; 6-7 hrs., with guide) through the *Strechengraben* and across the *Bärnwitz-Alpe*, where the night is spent, is toilsome. — The *Hochhaide* (7750'; 4-5 hrs., guide), viâ *St. Lorenzen* and the *Pethaler-Alpe*, is an easy and attractive ascent.

to St. Michael. TRIEBEN. *VIII. Route 69.* 389

The train continues to follow the Paltenthal, passing (107 M.) *Rottenmann Station*; to the right rises the *Hochhaide* (7750').
112¹/₂ M. **Trieben** (2320'; *Post*), at the entrance of the *Triebenthal*.
From Trieben a road ('*Tauernstrasse*') leads to the S. to *Judenburg* (p. 425; about 31 M.). Fine scenery as far as (7¹/₂ M.) the hamlet of **Hohentauern** (4150'; *Inn*), on the top of the pass (pretty woods and waterfalls in the *Wolfsgraben*); thence through the *Pölsthal*, monotonous. A nearer way to the pass leads through the *Sunk* (2 hrs.). — From Hohentauern a path, indicated by marks (guide not indispensable for experts), leads to the top of the **Bösenstein** (8035'; 4¹/₂ hrs.) over the *Scheiblalpe* and the *Hauseck*, between the *Kleine* and the *Grosse Bösenstein-See* (5900'). The summit commands a splendid and extensive view. The Bösenstein may also be ascended from *Trieben* viâ the *Hölter-Alpe* and *Koth-Alpe* in 5¹/₂ hrs.; from *Rottenmann*, see above.

The next station, (115 M.) **Gaishorn** (2530'; *Post; Bräu*), a village of considerable size, is situated near the entrance of the *Flitzenthal* (to the left), in which tower the cliffs of the *Reichenstein* (p. 388; to the *Flitzenalpe*, 2¹/₂ hrs.). To the right lies the little *Gaishorn Lake* (2315'). The line gradually ascends to the station of (121¹/₂ M.) *Wald*, on the *Schober Pass* (2785'), the watershed between the Enns and Mur, and then descends the *Liesiny-Thal* to *Kallwang* (2470'; Fleischer; Post), the thriving village of *Mautern* (2340'; Klossner), *Kammern, Seitz*, and *Traboch-Timmersdorf*. Then (142¹/₂ M.) **St. Michael** (p. 424).

EXCURSIONS (guides, *Vincent Schueiger* of Mautern and *Thom. Rainer* of Kallwang). The Zeiritzkampel (6972'; 3 hrs.; guide 4 fl.), a fine point of view, may be ascended from *Wald* or *Kallwang* without difficulty. Rich flora (Edelweiss). The descent may be made viâ the *Kammerl-Alpe* to *Radmer* (p. 385). — Another attractive ascent is that of the **Hoch-Reichart** (7930'; 4¹/₂-5 hrs.; with guide), from Wald, Kallwang, or Mautern. Descent to *Ingering*, see p. 421. — The '**Seckauer Zinken** (7865'; 4¹/₂ hrs.) is easily ascended from Mautern, through the *Hagenbachgraben* and the *Gotsthal*. Magnificent view from the summit. Descent to *Seckau*, see p. 424. — The **Reiting** or **Gösseck** (7265') is ascended from Mautern (marked path) viâ the *Schrecker-Alp* (good accommodation) in 5 hrs. (with guide), or from *Kammern* (see above), by a route passing the picturesque ruins of *Ehrenfels* and *Kammerstein* and crossing the *Seiwaldalpe* in 4¹/₂ hrs. (guide). Grand view.

70. From Linz to Lietzen viâ Kirchdorf and Windisch-Garsten. Stoder.
Comp. Map, p. 384.

67¹/₂ M. RAILWAY (*Kremsthalbahn*) to (35¹/₂ M.) *Michelsdorf* in 3¹/₂ hrs. DILIGENCE from Michelsdorf to (32 M.) *Lietzen* twice daily in 6¹/₄ hrs.

Linz, see p. 382. The line passes the stations of *Schartinz, Weyscheide*, and *St. Martin*, crosses the Traun at (7¹/₂ M.) *Traun*, and at (10 M.) *Nettingsdorf* enters the smiling *Kremsthal*. In the distance, to the S., the *Grosse Priel* is conspicuous among the Styrian Alps. On the hills to the right, near (11¹/₂ M.) *Nöstelbach* stands *Schloss Weissenberg*. 13 M. *Linning*; 13³/₄ M. *Neuhofen*, a large village, the seat of a district court, with the ruined castle of *Gschwendt*; 15 M. *Piberbach*; 16 M. *Kematen*; 18 M. *Neu-Kematen*, at the mouth of the *Sulzbach*; 20 M. *Unter-Rohr*. On the hill to the right is the handsome château of *Achleiten*, the property of Hr. v. Boschan.

A branch-line runs (in 14 min.) through the *Sulzbachthal* to *Hohenberg* and (7½ M.) **Bad Hall** (1230'; *Kaiserin Elisabeth; °Erzherzog Karl; Budapest; Stadt Triest*), with famous springs containing iodine and salt, and tasteful promenades. The *Kurhaus* and *Baths* and the theatre are new. A road runs to the E. from Hall (post-omnibus twice daily in 2 hrs.), viâ *Sierninghofen*, to (10½ M.) *Steyr* (p. 383).

22½ M. **Kremsmünster** (1085'; *Kaiser Max; Post; Sonne*), a prettily-situated village, with the venerable Benedictine abbey of that name, founded by Duke Tassilo of Bavaria in 777, and rebuilt by Henry II. in 1004 after its destruction by the Hungarians. The palatial buildings date from the 18th century. The valuable library contains 70,000 vols, 1700 MSS., and 837 incunabula. The cabinet of antiques also contains many curiosities. The admirably-equipped observatory, eight stories in height, contains extensive natural-history collections on the lower floors. The fish-pond is worth seeing. Good wine at the tavern of the abbey.

From Kremsmünster to *Wels* (p. 86), 12 M., diligence twice daily in 2¼ hrs.

27½ M. *Wartberg;* 31 M. *Schlierbach;* 33½ M. **Kirchdorf** (1395'; *Post; Schobersberger*), a pleasant village, with the château of *Pernstein*.

A pleasant excursion may be made by the ruin of *Alt-Pernstein* to the top of the **Hirschwaldstein** (3686'; 2 hrs.), on which there is a belvedere tower commanding a wide prospect. Descent by a picturesque path through the woods, over the *Pröller*, to (1 hr.) *Micheldorf*.

35½ M. **Micheldorf** (*Strasser; Restaurant*, opposite the station) is the terminus of the railway.

Through the *Kremsthal* to the S.W. to the (¾ hr.) *Ursprung* (Baths and Inn), and thence to the right through wood to the (1½ hr.) *Graden-Alp* (quarters), a pleasant expedition. Thence to the summit of the *Pfannstein* (4672'; 1½ hr), attractive; to the summit of the *Kreins-Falkenmauer* (5246'; 2 hrs., with guide), not difficult for adepts.

The high-road leaves the Kremsbach and at (3½ M.) *Herndtschmid* enters the *Steyrthal* (p. 384). We now ascend through the *Klaus* (Inn) between the *Kremsmauer* on the right, and the *Sengsengebirge* on the left, to (3½ M.) *Neu-Preisegg*, at the confluence of the *Steyrling* and Steyr.

Through the Steyrlingthal a road leads viâ (1½ M.) *Steyrling* (Inn) and past the (3 M.) hunting-lodge of Prince Schaumburg-Lippe in the *Brunnwinkel* (view of the Todte Gebirge) to (3½ M.) *Steyrreith*. About ¼ M. higher up is the hunting-lodge in the *Barnerau* (Inn). Thence we ascend through wood to the top of the *Ring* (2936'; 1¼ hr.); and descend to the (¼ hr.) Jägerhaus in the *Hetzau* (near the small *Ödenseen*), whence an attractive path leads through the *Straneckthal* to (1¼ hr.) *Habernau* and the (½ hr.) *Almsee* (p. 90). From Steyrreith to Stoder, viâ *Hastau*, 3 hrs, with guide, attractive.

At (3 M.) *Steyrbruck* (1540'), above the influx of the *Teichtbach* the road to *Stoder* diverges to the right.

[TO THE *STODERTHAL*, a very pleasant digression. The road ascends the *Hintertambergau*, on the right bank of the Steyr, between the *Tamberg* on the left and the *Kleine Priel* on the right, passing the *Stromboding Fall*, a fine cascade of the Steyr, 84' high, to (7¹/₂ M.) Hinter-Stoder (1920'; *Jaidhaus*; *Schmalzerwirth Huemer*), situated in a beautiful green valley, enclosed by the sombre precipices of the *Todte Gebirge* (Kleine and Grosse Priel, Spitzmauer, Ostrowitz, Kraxen, and Hebenkas); to the N. rise the Sengsengebirge; to the E. the Hochmölbing and Warscheneck.

EXCURSIONS (guides, Joh. Diell. Jos. Riedler, F. Kniewasser, Eust. Priller, and Ign. Stallinger). The **Kleine Priel** (7000'; 4 hrs.; guide 3 fl.), a fine point, is ascended by the *Schnabl-Alpe* or the *Priller-Alpe* without difficulty. At the foot of the Kleine Priel is the *Kreidenlucke*, a cavern 1870' long (guide and torches necessary). — The **"Grosse Priel** (8250'; 6¹/₂-7 hrs.; guide 5 fl.) affords a splendid prospect (panorama by Mühlbacher). We ascend through the *Polsterthal* and the *Polsterlucke* (picturesque head of the valley) to the (3 hrs.) *Carl Krahl Refuge Hut* on the *Obere Polster-Alpe* (3860'; quarters), and thence over turf, loose stones, and a patch of snow by the E. cliffs of the *Brotfall* and past the *Krahlhöhle* (7770'), a cave formerly fitted up as a refuge, to the (2¹/₂ hrs.) plateau. Then to the old pyramid and across the arête to the (1¹/₄ hr.) summit, marked by an iron cross 25' high. Descent to the *Grundlsee*, 8 hrs., laborious; through the *Feuerthal* to the *Elmsee*, 4¹/₂ hrs.; to the *Grosse Lahnganysee*, 1³/₄ hr.; to *Gössl*, 2 hrs. (see p. 97). — Ascent of the **Spitzmauer** (8025'; 6 hrs.; guide 5 fl.), toilsome, either through the Polsterlucke and over the *Klinserscharte*, or through the *Dietlhöhle*, a fine Alpine valley at the base of the Ostrowitz, where a night may be spent in the *Dietlhütte* (3180').

To KLACHAU (p. 303) over the *Poppenalm* and the *Salzsteig* (5525'). The interesting route (8¹/₂ hrs.; guide 5 fl.) leads past the *Schwarze See* and *Tauplitz*. From the Schwarze See to the *Grundlsee* (guide 3 fl.), see p. 98.

From Hinter-Stoder a road leads to the E. viâ (3¹/₂ M.) *Vorder-Stoder* (2650'; *Stocker*), the highest village in Upper Austria, and (4¹/₂ M.) *Rossleithen*, with scythe-works, to (4¹/₂ M.) Windisch-Garsten (see below). A pleasant round for walkers (³/₄ hr. more) leads past the *Source of the Piesling* and the *Gleinker See* (see below).]

The road continues from Steyrbruck to (³/₄ M.) *Dirnbach* (Post) and (1 M.) *St. Pankraz* (Popp; Obermayr), and leads through the Teichlthal (with the *Sengsengebirge* on the E.) to (6 M.) **Windisch-Garsten** (1970'; *Goldne Sense*; *Erzherzog Albrecht*; *Schöne Aussicht*), a summer-resort, finely situated. The *Calvarienberg* and the *Kühberg* afford the best views of the pretty environs.

EXCURSIONS (paths well kept and indicated by marks). To the *Garstnereck* (2414'), 1¹/₂ M. to the S., a picturesque woodland walk. — Good view from the *Wurbauer Kogl* (2815'), 3 M. to the N. — By the Dirnbach road to the (1¹/₂ M.) *Teichlbruck* (Inn) and to (3¹/₂ M.) *Gradau* (Inn); by the Stoder road to the (1¹/₂ M.) *Seebachhof* (Inn), and thence to the top of the (³/₄ hr.) *Schweizersberg* (2610'). — To the **Source of the Piesling** (1³/₄ hr.), we ascend the Piesling from the Seebachhof, viâ *Rossleithen* (see above), to the *Ursprungs-Stein* and to a grotto from which the Piesling issues in a cascade. — To the **Gleinker See** (2650'; lake-baths; Rfmts. at the Seebauer's), a pleasant expedition, 5 M.; thence to the source of the Piesling viâ the *Tonnerlhof*, 2¹/₄ M.; to *Spital*, 4¹/₂ M.

ASCENTS (guide, *Joh. Stummer*). The **Hohencck** (6430'; 4¹/₂ hrs.; guide 4 fl.), the highest peak of the *Sengsengebirge*, attractive. Descent past the *Feuchtauer Lakes* to *Molln*, see p. 384. — The **Warscheneck** (7828'; 5 hrs.; guide 4-4¹/₂ fl.) is interesting and commands a fine view. It is still more easily ascended from Vorder-Stoder, viâ the *Lagelsberger Alpe*, in 4¹/₂ hrs. — A carriage-road runs to the E. from Windisch-Garsten over the *Hengst* and through the *Laussathal* to (20 M.) *Weissenbach St. Gallen* (p. 384).

The road next leads through a hilly region to (5 M.) **Spital am Pyhrn** (2120'; *Post; Huemer; Schredl*), prettily situated at the foot of the *Grosse Pyhrgass* and *Bosruck* (shorter road through the meadows on the right bank of the Teichl).

The ascent of the **Grosse Pyhrgass** (7360'; 4½ hrs.; guide 3 fl.) is attractive and not difficult. The route leads through the *Grünau* to the (2 hrs.) *Hofalpe*, and thence over the arête to the (2½ hrs.) top. Comp. p. 388. — Across the *Pyhrgass-Gatterl* to *Admont* (4½ hrs.; guide 4 fl.), see p. 388. Guides, Peter Duckkowitz and **Ferd**. Stadlhuber.

About 1 M. beyond Spital the road passes the interesting double church of *St. Leonhard*, reached also by a picturesque walk over the *Josefiberg*, in ½ hr. We then ascend past a waterfall of the *Schreiende Bach* to (4¼ M.) the **Pyhrn Pass** (3100'), between the *Brunnstein* and *Bosruck*, and thence descend along the *Pyhrnbach* to (4¼ M.) *Lietzen* (see below).

71. From Selzthal to Aussee and Bischofshofen.

Comp. Maps, pp. 384, 96.

RAILWAY from Selzthal to (30 M.) *Aussee* in 1½-2 hrs.; to (62 M.) *Bischofshofen* in 3½ hrs.

Selzthal, see p. 388. The train crosses the *Puttenbach* near the station, and runs towards the W. through the broad and in parts marshy valley of the Enns (peat-cuttings), crossing the *Enns* and the *Pyhrnbach*, to (3½ M.) **Lietzen** (2160'; *Post; Fuchs*), a small town with 1800 inhab., pleasantly situated at the entrance to the *Pyhrnthal*. Good survey of the environs from the *Calvarienberg*; to the W. the huge Grimming, S. the Hohe Trett and Blosen, and E. the Dürrenschöberl.

From Lietzen a road leads to the N. (diligence daily in summer in 2½ hrs.; also omnibus, fare 1 fl. 60 kr.) over the *Pyhrn* (see above) to (15 M.) *Windisch-Garsten* (p. 391); thence to *Stoder*, see p. 391. — The ascent of the Hochmölbing (7650'; 7 hrs., with guide; Joh. Mühlbauer of Lietzen) is recommended. We follow the road from Lietzen to the W. as far as (1½ M.) *Weissenbach*, and ascend to the right through the *Weissenbachgraben* to the (20 min.) *Bruckstaeger*; then to the left over the brook and through wood in the *Langpoltner Graben* to the (1½ hr.) *Riesshütte*, and (1 hr.) *Langpoltner-Hütte*. From this point we may either ascend by the *Niederhütte* and the *Kirchfeld*, or by the *Brunnalpe* to the (4 hrs.) summit, which commands an admirable panorama of the E. Alps from the Schneeberg to the Glockner, and a view to the N. as far as the Bohemian Forest.

The line skirts the hill-side. On the right stands *Schloss Grafeneyg*, now a brewery. At *Weissenbach* the bald rocks of the *Angerhöhe* (6742') peep from a wooded valley on the right. 9 M. *Wörschach* (2100'), with small sulphur-baths, commanded by the ruin of *Wolkenstein* on a red rock. The *Hochmölbing* (see above) may also be ascended from this point (5½ hrs.; guide).

We next pass *Maitschern* and (on the right) *Niederhofen*, with the ruin of *Friedstein*. At (12 M.) **Steinach** (2105'; *Inn*, at the station) the line divides; the right branch goes to Aussee, the left to Bischofshofen. The well-built village of *Steinach* (*Post*), lies ½ M. to the E. of the station

About 2¼ M. to the S. of Steinach station (omnibus) lies Irdning (2120'; *Rosl*; *Sigl*), at the entrance to the *Irdning-* or *Donnersbach-Thal*. Pleasant excursion thence to the (3½–4 hrs.) **Möllbegg** (6810'), affording an admirable view of the Enns Valley, the Todte Gebirge, etc.

The railway to AUSSEE soon begins rapidly to ascend the N. slope of the valley, affording fine views of the Ennsthal. The village of *Unter-Grimming*, at the base of the Grimming, lies below us, to the left. Beyond two tunnels (the second of which, the *Burgstaller Tunnel*, is 365 yds. long) the train enters the narrow and romantic *Grimmingbach-Thal*, and ascends in windings high up on the left side, while the road runs on the opposite bank. The *Wallerbach*, in its deep and narrow ravine, is crossed, and then the *Grimmingbach*. — 17 M. **Klachau** (2730'; *Meierl*, rustic), finely situated at the N. base of the Grimming. To the N.E. rise the barren peaks of the Todte Gebirge.

The **Grimming** (7710'), a huge mountain with precipitous sides, may be ascended from Klachau, viâ *Kulm* and the *Lärchkogel* (5-6 hrs.; difficult; guide Joh. Feuchter, or 'Petschpaul', of Kulm). Fine view: Ennsthal, the S. Tauern as far as the Gross-Glockner, Dachstein, Todte Gebirge. — From *Tauplitz* (rustic inn), situated on the hill-side, ½ hr. to the N. of Klachau, a fine route (guide), leading through the *Traglyebirge*, passes the *Schwarze See* and crosses the *Salzsteig* (5525') to (7 hrs.) *Hinter-Stoder* (p. 391).

From Klachau (highest point on the railway) the line runs to the W. across meadows and marsh to (20½ M.) **Mitterndorf-Zauchen** (2615'). To the right, ½ M. from the railway, lies the large village of *Mitterndorf* (*Oberascher; Post), with a sulphur-spring.

A road leads hence to the S., through the *Stein*, to (9 M.) *St. Martin* in the Ennsthal (see p. 394). — The *Lopernstein* or *Lawinenstein* (6434'), ascended from *Mitterndorf* in 3 hrs., commands an admirable view of the Todte Gebirge, Dachstein, etc.

To the left, above the green lower hills, appear several peaks of the Dachstein group. To the right, on a wooded hill, stands the pilgrimage-church of *Maria-Kunnitz*. 22 M. *Grubeck*. 26 M. *Kainisch* (2525'; Muss), on the *Oedensee-Traun* or *Kainisch-Traun*, which issues from the *Oedensee* (2570'), 1½ M. to the S.; on the right rises the *Röthenstein* (5250'). The train now follows the right bank of the wooded Traunthal, and then crosses the stream to (30 M.) **Aussee** (p. 96).

FROM STEINACH TO BISCHOFSHOFEN. The train crosses the *Grimmingbach*, passes (14 M.) *Trautenfels* (with the handsome château of that name on the right), skirts the base of the *Grimming*, and below the influx of the *Salza* crosses the Enns and reaches (17½ M.) *Nieder-Oeblarn* and (20 M.) **Oeblarn** (2225'; *Fleischer*), at the mouth of the *Walchernthal*. To the W. rises the pointed *Stoder-Zinken* (p. 394).

The *Gumpeneck (7300'), scaled from Oeblarn viâ the *Mathilden-Alpe* in 4 hrs. (guide), commands a magnificent view of the Dachstein, Todte Gebirge, Tauern, etc. — The *Salza*, which rises on the Todte Gebirge, forces its way, to the S. of Mitterndorf, through a profound gorge between the Grimming and the Kammergebirge, called the Stein, through which a road leads from *St. Martin* (on the high-road, 3 M. to the N. of Nieder-Oeblarn) to (9 M.) *Mitterndorf* (p. 393).

The train skirts the S. slope of the valley to (23 M.) *Stein an der Enns*, at the mouth of the *Sölkthal*.

The **Sölkthal**, which divides, 3 M. from Stein, into the *Gross-Sölkthal* to the left, and the *Klein-Sölkthal* to the right, deserves a visit. Following the **Gross-Sölkthal**, we reach the villages of (1¹/₄ hr.) *Gross-Sölk* (Bäckerwirth), with a château and church, (2 hrs.) *Mössna*, with a shooting-lodge belonging to the Duke of Coburg, and (³/₄ hr.) *St. Nicolai* (3090'; Inn). Fine scenery at the head of the valley. — EXCURSIONS. From Gross-Sölk to the top of the *Gumpeneck* (see p. 393), through the *Feistagraben*, in 3¹/₂ hrs., an interesting walk (path through the woods nearly the whole way: guide not indispensable). Ascent of the **Grosse Knallstein** (8525') from St. Nicolai, viâ the *Knittierberg-Alpe* in 4¹/₂ hrs. (guide); superb panorama. The descent from the *Klein-Sölker Unterthal* is fatiguing. — Over the *Sölkerscharte* (5870') to *Murau* (p. 398), 7 hrs., guide advisable.

In the **Klein-Sölkthal**, 1¹/₂ hr. above Stein, lies *Klein-Sölk* (3210'; Inn), 1¹/₄ hr. above which the valley divides into the *Unterthal* on the left (ascent of the *Grosse Knallstein*, see above) and the *Oberthal* on the right. The latter contains the (1¹/₂ hr.) splendidly situated *Schwarze See* (3780'; quarters at the gamekeeper's), whence the **Predigtuhl** (8350'; 4¹/₂ hrs., with guide) may easily be ascended. Fine view. Two toilsome passes lead hence to the *Lessach-Graben* and (8 hrs.) *Tamsweg* (p. 398), one over the *Landschitz-Scharte* (7690'), the other over the *Kaiser-Scharte* (7525'); another (repaying) crosses the *Preberthörl* (7195') to *Krakaudorf* and (10 hrs.) *Murau* (p. 398). — The *Hochwildstelle* (9010') may be ascended hence, but more conveniently from Schladming (see below).

The train crosses the *Sölkbach*, 25 M. **Gröbming** (2200'); the village (*Post; *Mandl), the district-capital, with an old Gothic church, lies 2 M. to the N., on the left bank of the Enns. To the left of the station, *Schloss Thurnfeld*.

The *Stoder-Zinken* (6715') may be ascended from Gröbming viâ the *Assacher Scharte* without difficulty in 4¹/₂ hrs. (with guide). Very striking view, especially of the nearer mountains (Dachstein, Todte Gebirge). About 300' below the summit is a refuge hut, the *Brünner Hütte*. An interesting descent (path marked) leads through the *Ahornkar*, with the *Grafenberger See* and the finely situated *Ahornsee* (4800'), to (4¹/₂-5 hrs.) *Haus* (see below). — The **Kammspitze** (7025'; 4 hrs.; with guide), the highest summit of the *Kammergebirge*, commands a magnificent view, but should be attempted only by adepts. About 1¹/₂ hr. below the summit, on the N. side, is the *Kamp* or *Karl Alpe*.

26 M. *Pruggern*; 30 M. **Haus** (*Rail. Restaurant*, with beds). On the left rise the *Höchstein* and the *Hochwildstelle*.

On the left bank of the Enns, about 4 M. to the N., is the picturesque *Grattenbach Fall*. — A visit should be paid to the **Seewigthal**, which diverges from the Ennsthal at *Aich*, ³/₄ M. to the E. of Haus, and terminates in an inaccessible gorge 2¹/₂ M. long. The road gradually ascends from *Höhenfeld*, ¹/₄ M. from the station, to the (³/₄ hr.) *Aigner*, on the W. slope of the valley, whence it continues amid pretty scenery to the (1 hr.) *Bodensee*, embosomed in woods. At this point the route begins to ascend more steeply to the (1¹/₄ hr.) beautifully situated *Hüttensee* (4930') and to the (³/₄ hr.) *Obersee*, at the imposing head of the valley, which is closed by the Hochwildstelle. A route, not difficult for experts (with guide: 4¹/₂ hrs.), leads hence across the *Höchsteinscharte* (7230'), between the Höchstein and the Hochwildstelle, to the *Riesachsee* (p. 396).

The Enns is then crossed to (32¹/₂ M.) *Oberhaus* and (36 M.) **Schladming** (2400'; *Alte Post; Bräuhaus* or *Neue Post; Fleischer; Steinerwirth*), pleasantly situated on the right bank of the Enns,

to Bischofshofen. RAMSAU. *VIII. Route 71.* 395

with two churches. To the S. opens the *Schladminger Unterthal*, which ends in the imposing *Bruckerklamm* (pleasant walk to the *Bruckerwirth*, 1/2 M.). To the N. stretch the wooded hills of the *Ramsau*, which conceal the Dachstein.

Good view of the neighbourhood from the (1/4 hr.) **Hofbauerngschloss**, a view-tower and restaurant on the edge of an abrupt cliff at the entrance of the Unterthal. More extensive view, embracing the Dachstein, etc., from the **Rohrmoosberg**, on the W. side of the Unterthal (1 hr. to the highest farm), and from the **Fastenberg**, to the E. of the Unterthal. To the *Brand* ('Postmeister Alm'; Rfmts.), 11/4 hr.; thence to the *Planai* or *Schladminger Kaibling* (6250'), the summit of the Fastenberg, 11/2 hr. (view of the Gross-Glockner, Steinerne Meer, etc.).

Pleasant excursion to the **Ramsau**, a fertile, upland plain, 5 M. long by 21/2 M. wide, 3300-3900' above the sea-level, separated from the Ennsthal on the S. by a chain of pine-clad hills, and bounded on the N. by the precipitous sides of the Edelgrieshöhe, Scheichenspitze, and Eselstein, three imposing limestone peaks of the Dachstein group, while the Dachstein and the Thorstein rise more to the W. The Ramsau is inhabited by Protestants, and is dotted with numerous farm-houses. In order to obtain a glimpse at this district, it is sufficient to go as far as the church of **St. Rupert am Kulm** (3520'; *M. Prugger's Inn*, moderate, R. 4-5 fl. per week;, carr. to Schladming 4 fl.), which may be reached either by a rough road (41/2 M.) viâ *Mauterndorf*, or, better, by a footpath (11/4 hr.), leading to the right along the Enns beyond the bridge, crossing the railway after 5 min., and ascending, at first somewhat abruptly, through wood. The traveller is recommended, however, to extend the expedition to the Brandriedel. From Kulm we follow a shadeless road, past the (11/4 M.) *Protestant Meeting House* (Perhab's Inn), to the (13/4 M.) *Karlwirth* (beer). Here we turn to the right, and ascend to the (11/4 hr.) **Austriahütte** (5350'; Restaurant in summer), above the *Brandalpe* and 20 min. below the barren summit of the *Brandriedel* (5656'), which commands a splendid view of the Dachstein, Tauern, etc. (panorama by Zoff). To the N.E. (1/2 hr.) lies the finely situated *Neustatt-Alpe*. From this point to the *Source of the Kalte Mandling*, 1 hr.; to the *Schart-Alpe*, 1 hr. (From the Schart-Alpe to *Fitzmoos*, 11/2 hr.; across the *Sulzenhals* to the top of the *Rettenstein*, 3 hrs., comp. p. 397.)

The shortest route to the top of the **Hohe Dachstein** (9830') is from the Austriahütte (51/2-6 hrs.; comp. p. 100), but is fit for proficients only (guide from the Ramsau to the summit and back 8, from Schladming 9, with descent to Hallstatt or Gosau 12 or 13 fl.; guides, *Joh. Steiner* or '*Bartlhans*', *Florian Steiner*, and *Karl Fischer* of the Ramsau, *Joh. Schrempf* or '*Auhäusler*', *Franz* and *Joh. Knauss*, of Mandling.) From the Austriahütte we cross the lower end of the *Edelgries-Schlucht* and the pastures of the *Brandstell*, then descend to the broad stretch of debris at the foot of the lower Schwadering cliffs, and cross it, ascending to the right. At the upper end the path ascends abruptly, turns to the right over rocky slopes (at first stanchions and rope) and enters the *Schwadering*, a large basin enclosed by lofty and perpendicular rocks, through which we have a long and fatiguing ascent over debris and grassy slopes (keep to the right). At the head of this basin we ascend the rocky slope to the left, traverse several steep patches of snow, cross a rocky crest, and soon reach the new path. We now ascend the *Rothe Rinne* (recognized from below by a cave to the right), a groove or channel formed by blasting the rocks, 80' high and sloping at an angle of 75°, the passage of which is facilitated by a wire-rope. The wire-rope helps us to mount other rocks, scarcely less steep, and patches of snow, and brings us to an almost perpendicular rock about 65 high, which we scale, with the aid of the rope, by means of iron stanchions driven into the rock. In a few minutes more (3 hrs. from the Austriahütte) we reach the *Hunerkogl-Scharte* (about 8200'), between the Hunerkogel and the Grosse Koppenkarstein, at the head of the *Schladming Glacier* (31/2 hrs. from the Austriahütte). We traverse the glacier, passing the two '*Dirndln*' (9185'), and reach the summit in 2 hrs. more (comp. p. 100).

Among the other peaks of the Dachstein, the **Scheichenspitze** (8734', splendid view) is the easiest (from the Kulm Inn viâ the *Feisterkar* and *Grubachscharte* in 4½-5 hrs.; guide 5 fl.). The **Grosse Koppenkarstein** (9442'; 4-5 hrs.), a difficult ascent, suitable for adepts only, is accomplished by the *Edelgries-Schlucht* (or from the *Hunerkogel-Scharte*, see above, in 2 hrs.) — The ascent of the **Thorstein** (9665'; 5-6 hrs.), from the Scharl-Alpe (see above) by the *Windlegerscharte* (7545') and the *Untere Windlucke*, is very troublesome (comp. p. 100; guide 10, with descent to Gosau 13 fl.). — The *Bischofsmütze* (8050'; guide from the Ramsau 10 fl.), see p. 397. — From St. Rupert am Kulm to the N., over the **Feisterscharte** (7250'), between the *Eselstein* (8370') and the *Sinabell* (7685'; easily ascended in ½ hr. from the Scharte; fine view), and then over the dreary rocks of the '*Stein*', viâ the *Schönbichl*, to the *Krippeneck* and to (8 hrs.) *Hallstatt* (p. 98), a toilsome route (guide 7 fl.).

Another pleasant excursion from Schladming is to the S., up the Schladminger Unterthal. About 1 M. beyond the (2½ hrs.) *Weissenwandalpe* (Rfmts.), at the point where the valley divides we turn to the left (the *Steinriesenthal* to the right, see below), and ascend the *Riesachwthal*; past the (¾ hr.) *Riesach Fall* (190' high; 3 min. to the right of the path), to the (1½ hr.) Riesach See (4370'), at the upper end of which is the (¼ hr.) *Wieserhütte*. Thence past the *Schmiedlehenhütte* and Hr. v. Vernouillet's shooting-lodge to the (½ hr.) *Kerschbaumerhütte* (quarters). A very interesting expedition may be made hence to the *Klafferkessel*, an imposing hollow containing three lakes, as far as the central or *Rauhenberg Lake* (7465'), 3-3½ hrs. with guide. The ascent of the *Greifenberg* (8745'; good view) may be made from this point in 1½ hr., with guide. We may descend through the *Steinriesenthal* to the *Untere* or *Obere Eibl-Alpe* (see below). — The *Hochwildstelle* (9010') may be ascended from the Kerschbaumerhütte by the *Brandalm*, *Neualm*, and *Wildlochscharte* in 4½ hrs., or by the *Kothalpe* and *Waldhornalpe* in 5 hrs., with guide (6 fl.; toilsome). The summit affords a magnificent view. — The **Höchstein** (8340'; 3½ hrs.; with guide), presenting no difficulty to climbers free from dizziness, is another attractive ascent, made from the Wieserhütte, viâ the *Kaltenbachhütte*. — The ascent of the **Hochgolling** (9392'; guide 7 fl., with descent to the Lungau 10 fl.), the highest mountain in Styria, is toilsome, but presents no difficulty to experts. We ascend the *Steinriesenthal* from the *Weissenwandalpe* to the (2¾ hrs.) *Franz Keil Refuge Hut*, on the *Obere Eibl Alpe* (5410'; night-quarters); thence across the (2 hrs.) *Gollingscharte* (7960') and finally on the steep N.W. side to the (1½-2 hrs.) summit. Descent from the Scharte through the *Görlachthal* to (3½ hrs.) *Tamsweg*, see p. 398.

An easy pass leads from the Schladminger Oberthal across the *Liegnitzhöhe* (6958') to (10-11 hrs.) *Tamsweg*. A slightly longer, but more picturesque route leads past the *Giglach Lakes* and across the *Giglachscharte* (*Znachsattel*, 6710') to (11-12 hrs.) *Tamsweg* (see p. 398).

The Ennsthal contracts. The line skirts the left bank of the river, passing through several deep cuttings. 39½ M. **Pichl** (*Pichlmair*), at the entrance to the *Preuneggthal*, station for the *W. Ramsau* (see p. 395; 3 hrs. to the *Austriahütte*).

An interesting excursion may be made from Pichl to (3½ hrs.) the beautifully situated *Ursprung Alpe* (5280'; quarters) in the **Preuneggthal**. From this point the *Kalkspitze* (8054'; 3 hrs., with guide), a good point of view, may be ascended. Descent to the *Giglach Lakes*, and through the *Oberthal* to (6 hrs.) Schladming.

Near (42 M.) **Mandling** (2660'; *Upper* and *Lower Inn*), the train crosses the *Mandlingbach*, the frontier between Styria and Salzburg.

Road from Mandling to the N.W., through the *Mandlingthal*, to (6 M.) **Filzmoos** (3510'; *Inn*, plain), a prettily-situated village, with a pilgrimage-church, whence the **Röthelstein** or **Rettenstein** (7365'; fine view of the Dachstein, etc.) is ascended without difficulty by the *Pilzbauer* and the *Rothe Wand* in 3½ hrs., or by the *Scharl-Alp* (p. 395) and the *Sulzenhals* in 5 hrs., with guide (see above; Franz Hofer at Filzmoos). To the N. tower the isolated pinnacles of the **Bischofsmütze** (lower peak, 7874'; higher peak, 8050'; difficult); from the *Hintere Aualp*, 4 M. from Filzmoos, in 3-4 hrs. — Over the *Steigl* to *Gosau*, see p. 101; by the 'hinter dem Stein' route to the *Zwiesel Alp*, see p. 102; *Ramsau*, p. 395.

47 M. **Radstadt** (2810'; *Post*; *Thorwirth*; *Sabin*; *Stegerbräu*), an old walled town, with 1000 inhab., stands on a rocky hill to the right of the railway. Fine view from the station of the *Tauernthal* (see below), with the *Gaisstein* and *Seekarspitze*, to the S.

EXCURSIONS (guide, *Joh. Krichmayr*). The *Rossbrand* (5800'; 2½ hrs.; guide unnecessary; path indicated by marks), ascended by the *Schwemberg Sattel* (4840'), commands a magnificent view. On the top is the *Linzerhütte*. An easy route also ascends from Filzmoos (see above), viâ the *Karalpe*, in 2½ hrs. — The **Grieskareck** (6520'; 1½ hr., with guide), ascended from *Flachau*, 6 M. to the W. of Altenmarkt (see below), is also a fine point.

A road leads from Radstadt to the W., viâ *Altenmarkt*, to (12 M.) **Wagrein** (2740'; *Neuwirth*) and (6 M.) *St. Johann im Pongau* (p. 115). — Over the *Radstädter Tauern* to *St. Michael* and *Spital*, see R. 72.

At (48½ M.) *Altenmarkt* the line quits the Enns, which rises 12 M. to the S.W. in the *Flachau*, and runs N.W. to (51 M.) *Eben* (2810'), on the watershed between the Enns and the Salzach. It then passes through a deep cutting, crosses the *Fritzbach* by a bold bridge (striking *View of the Dachstein to the right, and of the Uebergossene Alp to the left), and descends the narrow *Fritzthal* to the W., crossing the stream repeatedly. At (55½ M.) **Hüttau** (2320'; *Post*) diverges the road to the Salzkammergut viâ St. Martin and Annaberg (p. 102). Several tunnels. The train descends rapidly, crossing the Fritzbach six times, penetrates the *Kreuzberg* by a tunnel, 770 yds. long, and descends the slope to the left (view of the Salzachthal, Hochkönig, and Tennengebirge). Lastly we cross the *Salzach* to —

62 M. **Bischofshofen** (1795'; *Rail. Restaurant*; see p. 113).

72. From Radstadt to Spital over the Radstädter Tauern.

Comp. Map, p. 334.

67½ M. DILIGENCE to St. Michael in summer daily in 8¾ hrs., and thence the next morning in 6¾ hrs. to Spital. Another runs daily from Radstadt to *Scheifling* (p. 425), spending the night at Tamsweg (18 hrs.).

Radstadt, see above. The road crosses the Enns, and ascends the valley of the *Tauernache* towards the S. to (10½ M.) *Untertauern* (3295'; Post). It then ascends through the *Tauernklamm*, past the falls of the Tauernache (see finger-posts; the finest fall is the **Upper Fall* or *Johanniswasserfall*, 460', easily accessible by new paths). About 1 M. past the top of the (10 M.) **Radstädter Tauern** (5700') stands the *Tauernhaus*, a kind of hospice with a chapel and a burial-ground. The road descends steeply to (61/2 M.) —

28 M. *Tweng* (4090'; *Post*), the first village in the *Lungau*. Then through the *Tauruchthal* to (6 M.) *Mauterndorf* (*Post;

*Wallner), a small town with a well-preserved castle (tower 144' high), and across the *Staig* to (6 M.) —

40 M. **St. Michael** (3505'; *Post; Wastlwirth*), a small town on the *Mur*.

The **Speiereck** (7900'; 4 hrs., with guide) affords an excellent survey of the Lungau, Niedere Tauern, etc. Refuge-hut on the top. — The **Murwinkel** (upper Murthal; one-horse carr. to Rothgülden and back 4 fl.) is worthy of a visit. Road to the W. to (2 M.) *Niederdorf*, at the mouth of the *Zederhausthal* (to *Kleinarl*, see p. 115); then to the left through the narrow Murthal to *Schellgaden*, (6 M.) *Mur* (3630'; Gferrer), and (4½ M.) the arsenic-works of *Rothgülden* (4100'), at the mouth of the valley of the same name, in which lie the (1½ hr.) beautiful *Untere* and (¾ hr. farther up) *Obere Rothgülden-See*, at the N. base of the *Hafnereck* (10,040'; ascent difficult; better from the Maltathal, see below). — About 1 hr. above Rothgülden, on the left, opens the wild *Moritzenthal*, with its three picturesque lakes (to the *Obere Schwarzsee* 2½ hrs.). Thence 1½ hr. more to the last chalets, near the *Source of the Mur*, at the N.W. base of the *Marchkareck* (8790'). — Across the *Murthörl* to *Grossarl*, see p. 114.

The principal place in the *Lungau* (region of the sources of the Mur, belonging to Salzburg) is **Tamsweg** (3350'; *Post; Platzbräu; Lebzelter*), a pleasant little town, with the loftily-situated church of *St. Leonhard*, 9 M to the E. of *Mauterndorf* (13 M. from St. Michael; diligence to it daily from both these places). The **Lasaberg-Alpel** (6345'; 2½ hrs., with guide) affords a good survey of the environs; descent to (1½ hr.) *Ramingstein*, (2 hrs.) *Predlitz*, or (2½ hrs.) *Stadl*, on the high-road (see below). The *Preberspitze* (8990') is a splendid point of view. Cart-road to the (2 hrs.) sombre *Prebersee* (4395'), ½ hr. above which is the *Predinger-Alphütte* (spend night); lastly 3 hrs. more to the summit. — ROUTE TO SCHLADMING by the *Göttingscharte*, and ascent of the *Hochgolting*, see p. 396; through the *Liegnitzthal* and across the *Liegnitzhöhe*, see p. 396. — Another pleasant route is through the *Weisbriachthal* (11-12 hrs.). We ascend by *Maria-Pfarr* to the (2½ hrs.) *Siegthof*, and, where the valley divides (1½ hr.), ascend to the right through the *Znachthal* to the (2½ hrs.) *Znachsattel* (6710') lying to the E. of the *Lungauer Kalkspitze* (8400'); then descend into the *Gigter Thal*, passing the *Obere* and *Untere Gigtach See*, to the *Gigtach Alps* and the *Landauer See*, and traverse the *Oberthal* to (5 hrs.) *Schladming* (p. 394). — To SÖLK, through the *Lessachthal* and over the *Landschitz-Scharte* or the *Kaiser-Scharte*, see p. 394.

FROM TAMSWEG TO SCHEIFLING (37 M.). Road (diligence daily in 9½ hrs.) through the Murthal, viâ *Ramingstein, Predlitz, Stadl*, and (22½ M.) **Murau** (2610'; *Bähn; Post; Bräu*), a small town with three old churches, commanded by the castle of *Ober-Murau*, to *Scheifling* (p. 425), a station on the Bruck and Villach line (R. 76). — EXCURSIONS. Interesting ascent of the **Schilcherhöhe** (7430'), from *Ramingstein* in 3½ hrs. (guide); descent viâ *Inner-Krems* to *Kremsbruck* (see below), 3½ hrs. — A pleasant expedition may be made from *Predlitz* (Hofer) through the *Predlitzgraben* to (10 M.) **Turrach** (4135'; *Ferner; Bergmann*), with large iron-works, whence the *Eisenhut* (8000') may be ascended in 3½ hrs. (comp. p. 426), and the *Königsstuhl* (7650') in 4 hrs. (both attractive; guide necessary). From Turrach the road ascends steeply to the (4½ M.) *Turracher See* (5785'; Seewirth), and then descends on the bank of the *Seebach* to (6 M.) **Ebene Reichenau** (3560'; *Schiestl*) in the *Gurkthal*, whence a road leads to the W. viâ *Klein-Kirchheim* ("Badwirth"), *Radenthein* (Mahr), and *Döbriach* to (18 M.) *Millstatt* (p. 336). — From *Stadt* (Post; Fleischer) to *Flattnitz* (p. 426) a rough road leads through the *Paalgraben* (15 M.). — From *Murau* to *Gröbming* over the *Preberthörl* or the *Sölkerscharte*, see p. 396.

The road crosses the *Katschberg* (5385'), separating Salzburg from Carinthia, and beyond (9½ M.) *Rennweg* (3780 ft.; Post) leads through the Liesenthal by *Kremsbruck* and *Leoben* to (9 M.) —

58½ M. **Gmünd** (2400'; *Fetdner; Lax; Post; Kohlmayr*), a

small town with a new and old château of Count Lodron, at the mouth of the *Maltathal*. Good survey of the district from (³/₄ M.) the *Calvarienberg*.

EXCURSIONS. The **Tschirneck** (6830'; 4¹/₂ hrs., with guide), a good point of view, is easily ascended viâ *Oberbuch* and the *Hoferalpe*. Descent to *Mittstatt*, 3 hrs; to the *Millstatter Alpe* (p. 386), 2 hrs. — The ascent of the **Königsstuhl** or *Karlnock* (7645') is also easy and attractive. From (1¹/₂ hr.) *Leoben* (see above) we traverse the *Leobengraben* (to the right) to the (4 hrs.) *Karlbad*, an unpretending 'Bad', where we spend the night, and thence ascend to the summit in 1¹/₂ hr. Descent through the *Kremsgraben* to (5 hrs.) *Kremsbruck* and (2¹/₂ hrs.) *Gmünd*. — The **Reisseck** (9710'; 8 hrs., guide, 7 fl.) is laborious. We ascend through the *Radlgraben* to (3 hrs.) Count Latour's shooting-lodge (night-quarters), and thence to the (3 hrs.) grandly situated *Hohe See* and the (2 hrs.) summit. Magnificent panorama from the top.

The °**Maltathal** is a beautiful valley, about 30 M. in length, with numerous waterfalls. A road (one-horse carr. to the Pflügelhof and back, 3 fl.) leads from Gmünd viâ *Fischertratten* and *Hitpersdorf* to (4¹/₂ M.) *Malta* or *Mattein* (2750'; *Homann*; *Krommer*; guides, *Joh.* and *Jos. Fercher*, *Joh. Klampferer*, *Georg Karner*), with a church and château, from which the *Faschauner Thörl* (5790'), with a fine view of the E. Tauern Mts., may be ascended in 3 hrs. (guide 1¹/₂ fl.). The road is continued along the left bank of the Malta viâ *Feistritz* and *Koschach* and past the pretty fall of the *Fallbach* to (4¹/₂ M.) *Brandstatt*. A branch, crossing to the right bank at Koschach by the second bridge, leads to the (³/₄ M.) **Göss Fall**, at the mouth of the Gössgraben (see below). We cross the brook, below the fall, to the (1¹/₂ M.) *Pflügelhof* (2800'; Inn, rustic), and finally recross to the left bank of the Malta, about ¹/₄ M. before reaching Brandstatt. From the Gossgraben, a valley with numerous fine waterfalls (to the °*Zwillings-Fall*, 2 hrs., guide 1¹/₂ fl.), a fatiguing route crosses the *Dössner* or *Maltnitzer Scharte* (8780'), in 10 hrs. to *Maltnitz* (p. 126). The night may be spent at the *Tomanbauer's* or *Mentebauer's* (hay-bed), 3 hrs. from the Pflügelhof. The **Sauleck** (10,110') may be ascended from the top of the pass in 1¹/₂ hr. (guide 9, or incl. the Sauleck 10 fl.).

The path in the Maltathal (guide unnecessary; to the Blaue Tumpf 4¹/₂ fl., to Elend 5 fl.) next passes the *Schleier Fall* and reaches the *Kerschbakl-Hütten* and (40 min.) the *Fatter-Hütten*. A guide-post here indicates the path to the left to the (10 min.) *Fatter Tümpfe*, or cascades of the Malta, falling into a rocky basin. By a path leading hence to the right we regain (5 min.) the broader track which brings us after a few yards to the *Hochsteg* (3205'); far below flows the Malta through its narrow ravine; to the right is the large *Melnik Fall*. [A path, indicated by red marks, leads hence to the right to the (³/₄ hr.) °*Melnik-Alm*, which commands a fine view of the Hochalmspitze, Preimelspitze, Hochalmkees, etc.; and then descends to (¹/₂ hr.) the *Veitlbauer*.] The path now divides. The new club-path on the right bank (over the Hochsteg, then to the right) has the advantage of being shaded and of commanding finer views of the Melnik Fall and gorges of the Enns, which it crosses about ¹/₂ hr. farther on. The path on the left bank is about ¹/₂ M. shorter and leads across the *Veitlbauern-Alm*. These paths reunite immediately before the *Hochbrücke*, about ¹/₄ hr. beyond the point where the former crosses the Enns. From the Hochbrücke we gradually ascend to the (20 min.) *Traxhütte* (3770') in the *Schönau*, with a shooting-box, and the (¹/₄ hr.) °**Blaue Tumpf**, the finest point in the valley. To the left the *Hochalpenbach* forms a double waterfall, 320' ft. high, while on the right the Malta is precipitated into a basin, 65 ft. in depth, the whole scene being picturesquely framed with rock and wood. The path now becomes rougher the higher the *Lange Wand*, to the left the lofty *Preimet Fall*), and immediately before the (1 hr.) *Wolfgänghütte*, crosses to the right bank of the Malta; 1 hr., *Wastelbauerhütte* (5510'); 1 hr., the *Samerhütte*, adjoining which are a shooting-box and the **Elendhütte** (5970'), a club-hut. A steep path leads hence to the N. over the (2¹/₂ hrs.) **Arlscharte** (7385') into the *Grossarlthal* (p. 114;

400 *VIII. Route 73.* GRATZ.

guide to St. Johann 13 fl.). The Maltathal now turns to the W. and ramifies into the (left) *Gross-Elend* and (right) *Klein-Elend-Thal*. From the former a fatiguing route crosses the Plesnitz- or Gross-Elend-Scharte (8770') in 7 hrs. to *Mallnitz* (p. 126; guide 10 fl.); from the *Klein-Elend-Thal* another of similar character crosses the Klein-Elend-Scharte (8230') into the *Kölschachthal* and to (10 hrs.) *Gastein* (p. 121; guide 10 fl.). — Ascent of the **Hochalpenspitze** (11,010'; 10-11 hrs. from Mallnitz; guide 8 fl.), the highest peak of the E. Tauern, laborious. The route leads from the Hochsteg, viâ the *Straneralm* and the (3 hrs.) *Hochalpenhütte* (9360'), to the (1 hr.) *Villacher Hütte* (7710': 5 beds) on the *Lange Boden*, beneath the *Schwarze Schneide*, about 1/4 hr. from the end of the glacier. Thence to the summit about 4 hrs. Magnificent view. Interesting descent by the *Preimelscharte* (9765') and the *Grosse Elend Ferner* to the Grosse Elendthal (4-5 hrs. to the Elendhütte; see above). — The **Hafnereck** (10 040'; 6 hrs.; guide 6 fl.), ascended from the Traxhütte, viâ the *Mahr-Alm*, is fatiguing, but repaying. The **Ankogel** (10,672'; 5-6 hrs.; guide 10 fl.), from the Elendhütte past the *Schwarzhornsee* and across the *Klein-Elendkees*, presents no difficulty to proficients (easier from this side than from Mallnitz or Gastein, p. 124). — The **Grosse Sonnblick** (11,890'; 5-6 hrs.; guide 5 fl.), from the Traxhütte over the *Melnik-Alm*, is another interesting point.

FROM GMÜND TO MILLSTATT, 3½ hrs. We pass through the archwaymarked 'nach Millstatt', on the east side of the market-place, cross the Lieser, and ascend by pleasant paths (indicated by red marks) through wood to *Trefling*, where we join the carriage-road viâ *Tangern* to *Millstatt* (p. 336).

The new road from Gmünd to (9 M.) Spital leads through the profound Lieserthal, closely skirting the river, to *Lieseregg* and *Seebach* (to *Millstatt*, see p. 336).

67½ M. **Spital**, see p. 336.

73. Gratz and Environs.

Hotels. On the *right bank* of the Mur, near the suspension-bridge, ¾ M. from the station: ELEPHANT (Pl. a; C, 5), R., I., & A. from 2 fl.; *OESTERREICHISCHER HOF, Annen-Strasse; *FLORIAN (Pl. d; C, 5), Griesgasse 15 and Mur-Quai 22, R. 1 fl.; *GOLDNES ROSS and SONNE, Mariahilf-Str.; *GOLDNER LÖWE, Mur-Platz, moderate; HÔTEL DANIEL, at the station; GOLDENER ENGEL, at Gries, moderate; DREI RABEN (Pl. e; B, 5), Annen-Strasse, near the station. — On the *left bank*: *ERZHERZOG JOHANN (Pl. h; C, 5), R. 1½-2 fl., L, 50, A. 40 kr., with a good restaurant; HÔTEL RIES (*Stadt Triest*; Pl. f, D 5), Jakomini-Platz; KAISERKRONE (Pl. c; D, 4), Färbergasse; GOLDNE BIRNE, Leonhard-Str.

Cafés. *Europa* and *Pöll*, Herrengasse; *Nordstern*, Sporgasse; *Mareur*, Haupt-Platz; *Schuster*, Carl-Ludwigs-Ring, by the theatre; *Promenade*, beyond the Burgthor; *Seidl*, Glacis-Str.; *Café Wien*, Rechbauer-Str.; *Freyler*, Mehl-Platz; *Café Wirth*, in the Stadt-Park (open-air concerts frequently in the afternoon). — On the right bank of the Mur, near the suspension-bridge: *Meran*; *Englischer Hof*; *Helm*; *Oesterreichischer Hof*; *Hannick*, on the Mur-Quai. — **Confectioners** (ices): *Grünzweig*, Sporgasse; *Hasserick*, at the theatre and also in the Mur-Platz; *Schmidt's Söhne*, Herrengasse. — **Restaurants** (beer). *Daniel's Rail. Restaurant*; *Toneihoff*, Herrengasse; *Paslete*, Sporgasse; *Neu-Gratz*, Realschulgasse; *Alt-Gratz*, Bürgergasse; *Bierjackl*, Sack-Str. 10; *Bierquelle*, Badgasse; *Theatre Restaurant*; *Sandwirth*, Herrengasse and at Gries; *Pilsner Keller*, Rathhausgasse; *Zum Grünen Anger*, near the Stadt-Park, with garden. — Military music several times weekly at the *Puntigamer Bierhalle*, in the Georgigasse, and at *Sapl's*, at Gries, both on the right bank of the Mur. — On the left bank of the Mur: *Steinfelder Säle*, Münzgraben; *Maifredy Bierhalle*, Maifredygasse; *Gösser Bierhalle*, Leonhard-Str. — **Wine** (also at the cafés, etc.): *Admonterhof*, near the Paradies; *Kleinoscheg* (room in the old German style).

GRATZ. *VIII. Route 73.* 401

Herrengasse; *Römischer König*, Sporgasse; *Kriehuber*, Sack-Str. — The best wines of Styria are *Luttenberger* (strong), *Pickerer, Kerschbacher, Sandberger*, and *Nachtigaller*. The turkeys and capons of Styria are highly esteemed. Gratz biscuits ('Gratzer Zwiebaek') at *Sorger's*, Mur-Platz, *Schreiber's*, Gleisdorfergasse, etc.

Baths. *Military Swimming Bath*, above the upper suspension-bridge, at the N.W. base of the Schlossberg, 10 kr.; towels extra. The water of the Mur is very cold. — *Wastian's* swimming and other baths, Tegethoffgasse 11; *Förster*, Brandhofgasse (tramway-station); *Hirth's* swimming-bath, Lichtenfelsgasse; *Leistentritt*, vapour-baths, etc., Sack-Str. 45.

Reading Room at the *Studenten-Verein* (Stempfergasse; strangers admitted), and in the *Ressource* (introduction by a member).

Theatres. *Landes-Theater* (Pl. 11; D, 4), Franzens-Platz, daily; *Stadt-Theater* (Pl. D. 5), Carl-Ludwigs-Ring, well fitted up, operettas, etc., three times a week.

Military Music twice weekly, alternately in the *Stadt-Park* and on the *Hilmteich*; Concert almost daily in the *Stadt-Park*.

Post & Telegraph Office (Pl. 9; C, 5), Neuthorgasse. Branch-offices in the Mur suburb (near the suspension-bridge) and at the station.

Cabs. *Two-horse.* 60 kr. for the first 1/2 hr., 1 fl. for 1 hr., 50 kr. for each additional 1/2 hr.; *one-horse*, 30 kr. for the first 1/4 hr., 50 kr. for the first 1/2 hr., 80 kr. for 1 hr., 20 kr. for each additional 1/4 hr. — *To or from the Station:* middle of the town, one-horse 70 kr., two-horse 1 fl.; Mur suburb (right bank) 50 or 80 kr. — For half-a-day, for drives within a radius of 5 M., forenoon 2 1/2 fl. or 3 fl., afternoon 3 fl. or 4 fl.; whole day 5 or 7 fl.; for longer drives (10 M. radius), 3 or 4. 3 1/2 or 5. and 5 1/2 or 8 fl. respectively. — *Omnibuses* ply to every part of the environs.

Tramway (10 kr. per drive) from the principal station (Süd-Bahnhof) through the Annen-Str. and over the suspension-bridge to the Haupt-Platz; then through the Herrengasse to the Jakomini-Platz, and thence to the right to the Raab Station, and to the left along the Glacis-Strasse to the Geidorf-Platz. A branch-line runs through the Leonhard-Str. to the Elisabeth Volksschule in the vicinity of the Hilmteich.

Gratz (1170'), the capital of Styria, with about 100,000 inhab. and a garrison of 4000 men, picturesquely situated on both banks of the *Mur*, which is crossed by five bridges, is one of the pleasantest and healthiest of the Austrian provincial capitals, and is the residence of numerous retired civilians and officers, including no fewer than sixty generals. Since the middle of the century a number of handsome new streets have sprung up: on the W. the *Annen-Strasse*, leading from the station to the town, on the E. the handsome *Ring-strasse (Burg-Ring, Carl-Ludwigs-Ring)*, the *Elisabeth, Schiller, Lessing*, and *Rechbauer-Strasse*. On the site of the former glacis, between the inner town and the outlying suburbs, is the ***Stadt-Park***, charmingly laid out in the English style, and adorned with the *Auersperg-Brunnen* with its lofty jet, a *Bust of Schiller* by Gasser, the '*Waldlilie*' (a beautiful bronze figure by Brandstetter, illustrating a poem by Rosegger), and a tasteful iron *Hygrometer*. The N. part of the park, picturesquely bounded by the Schlossberg, is embellished with the **Franz-Josefs-Brunnen* (in bronze, by Durenne), exhibited in 1873 in the Vienna Exhibition. Near it are the *Café Wirth* and a *Music Pavilion* (concerts, see above).

The ***Schlossberg*** (Pl. C, D, 3, 4) towers above the town. The fortifications, constructed in the 15th cent. to protect the town against the Turks, were blown up by the French in 1809 in consequence of the armistice, after they had been successfully defended for four weeks by a garrison of 500 Austrians against 3000 French under General Macdonald. The Schlossberg is ascended on the E. side, from the Carmeliter-Platz: the road passes through an archway under the house No. 1 (with the inscription 'Am Fuss des Schlossbergs'), and passes the clock-tower. On the N. side the hill is ascended from the Wickenburggasse (Pl. C, 3). The plateau in front of the Swiss House is adorned with a *Statue of General Welden* (d. 1853), the originator of the promenades, in bronze. On the upper platform (Pl. C, 4; 1545') are a *Clock Tower*, 50' high, and two topographical indicators. The noble *View from the castle-hill is justly celebrated. The valley of the Mur and the populous basin, surrounded by mountains of beautiful form, present a most picturesque scene. To the N. rises the Schöckel, N.W. the Alps of Upper Styria, S.W. the chain of the Schwanberg Alps, S. the Bacher Mts.

The **Cathedral** (Pl. 5; D, 5), a Gothic structure of 1446-1462 (the copper roof of the tower added in 1663), has an interesting W. Portal.

Interior. The high-altarpiece in the choir, representing the Miracles of St. Ægidius, is by *Jos. Flurer*. On the walls are two votive paintings by *Peter de Pomis*: on the right the Archduke Charles II. with his whole family before the crucifix, on the left his duchess Maria of Bavaria with her 9 daughters before the Virgin. To the right and left of the approach to the choir are two ebony reliquaries on marble pedestals, the former containing the relics of St. Maxentius and St. Vincent, the latter those of St. Maxentia and the arm of St Agatha, presented to Archduke Ferdinand by Pope Paul V., and deposited here in 1617. The six small *Reliefs in ivory, choice Italian works of the 16th cent., represent the triumphs of Love, Innocence, Death, etc. (from Petrarch's 'I Trionfi').

The **Mausoleum** (Pl. 8), adjoining the Cathedral, was erected for himself by Emp. Ferdinand II. (d. 1637), who at the beginning of the Thirty Years' War sought refuge at Gratz from his Bohemian and Austrian subjects. Interior uninteresting. Archduke Charles II. (d. 1590) and his wife, parents of Ferdinand, are also interred here.

The large building opposite (Pl. 12), formerly belonging to the Jesuits, now comprises the *Grammar School*, the *Old University*, the *Ecclesiastical Seminary*, and the *University Library* (120,000 vols.). The valuable *Archaeological Museum* of the university is open on Thurs. and Sun., 11-12. The extensive new University Buildings, including *Institutes for Anatomy & Physiology, Chemistry*, and *Physics*, are situated in the Harrachgasse (Pl. E. 3), on the other side of the Stadt-Park, about ½ M. to the N.E.

The handsome new *Polytechnikum*, or *Technical High School*, stands in the Rechbauer-Strasse.

In the neighbouring Franzens-Platz (Pl. D, 4) is the **Landes-Theater** (Pl. 11), in front of which stands a bronze Statue of Francis I. (Pl. 2), in the robe of the Golden Fleece, designed by Marchesi.

CHURCHES. The *Parish Church* in the Herrengasse (Pl. D, 5), a building of the 15th cent., with an interior restored in the Gothic style in 1875, contains a high-altarpiece by Tintoretto, the Assump-

Landhaus. GRATZ. *VIII. Route 73.* 403

tion and Coronation of the Virgin. The *Leechkirche* (Pl. E, 4), a small but interesting Gothic structure (13th cent.), contains ancient stained glass. The *Herz-Jesu-Kirche* (Pl. F, 5), in the Naglergasse, a handsome modern erection, in the early-Gothic style, with a tower 350' high, was designed by Hauberrisser.

The **Landhaus** (Pl. D, 5), or *Hall of the Estates*, in the Herrengasse, the busiest street in the town, with the best shops, was erected in the Renaissance style in the 16th century. Interesting portal with two balconies.

To the right of the principal entrance is a curious old German painted notice, dating from 1588, cautioning those who enter against quarrelling or drawing their 'daggers or bread-knives'. The first court, with the arcades and a finely-executed fountain, in cast and wrought iron of the 16th cent., is particularly pleasing. Memorial tablet to *Johann Kepler*, the astronomer. The *Rittersaal* and *Landtags-Saal* ('Hall of the Diet') in the interior are destitute of ornament; but the *Landschadenbundbecher* preserved here, a masterpiece of the goldsmith's art in the 16th cent., is worth seeing (apply at the Obereinnehmer-Amt, 1st floor).

The interesting old *Landes-Zeughaus*, or *Arsenal* (erected in 1644), adjoining the Landhaus on the S., is maintained in exactly the same condition as it was 200 years ago, so that an army of 8000 men might be fully equipped from its stores with the armour of the 17th century. Among the contents are the sledge of Emp Frederick III. and the double litter of Stephen Bathory and his wife. (Admission from the Landhaus at 11 p.m. punctually, 50 kr.; Sun., 10-1, free.)

The **Haupt-Platz** (Pl. C, D, 4) is embellished with a bronze *Statue of Archduke John (d. 1859), by *Pönninger*, erected in 1878. In this square were beheaded 159 of the ringleaders of the great rebellion of the peasantry in 1516, who had been captured near Pettau. On the S. side of the Platz is the *Rathhaus* (Pl. 10), erected in 1807.

The *Joanneum (Pl. C, D, 5), founded in 1811 by Archduke John for the promotion of agriculture and scientific education in Styria, is now occupied by various collections. The *Natural History Museum* is open gratis on Thurs., 10-12, and Sun., 10-11 o'clock. The *Cabinet of Coins and Antiquities* contains a rich collection of coins and medals, interesting Celtic antiquities (particularly the 'Judenburger Wagen'), Roman tombstones, milestones, etc. The *Botanical Garden* contains a bust of the botanist *Mohs* (d. 1839). The *Provincial Library* consists of about 80,000 volumes.

The **Picture Gallery** (Pl. D, 5) of the Estates (Sun. and Thurs., 10-12, free; at other times 50 kr.) contains over 600 paintings and 1100 engravings.

In the suburb of *Karlau*, on the right (S.) bank of the Mur, about 1 M. from the suspension-bridge, is the new *Prison* (Zellengefängniss; Pl. B, 8). To the S.W., on the road to Tobelbad, about 1 M. farther on, is the new *Lunatic Asylum*.

ENVIRONS. The following short excursion is recommended: starting from the Geidorf-Platz (Pl. D, 3), we follow the Körblergasse, Rosenberggasse, and Panoramagasse, and ascend the *Rosenberg* (1570') as far as the (³/₄ hr.) *Stoffbauer* (Inn; beautiful view).

26*

Thence we ascend the (3/4 hr.) *Plutte* (2136'), an admirable point of view; then descend to (1/2 hr.) *Maria-Grün* (1460'), ascend to the (1/2 hr.) *Hilmteich* (Pl. F, 2; Restaurant), and return to Gratz in 1/2 hr. more. — Other favourite points, on the left bank of the Mur: the *Rainerkogl* (1644'; 1 hr.), affording the best survey of Gratz; *Andritz-Ursprung* (1 1/2 hr.); *Maria-Trost* (1540'; 1 1/2 hr.), a pilgrimage-church; *Riess* (Ladeuwirth, 1 hr.); *Schloss Lustbühel* (1600'; 1 1/2 hr.). On the right bank of the Mur: the château and hydropathic establishment of *Eggenberg* (3/4 hr.); by the ruin of *Gösting* (1 hr.; near which is the *Jungfernsprung*, rising abruptly from the Mur) to (2 hrs.) *Thal*; *Plabutsch* (2505'), an excellent point of view, reached viâ *Eggenberg* in 2 hrs.; *St. Oswald* (1820'), charmingly situated, reached from stat. *Judendorf* (p. 370), viâ *Schloss Plankenwart*, in 2 1/2 hrs.

The **Buchkogl** (2150'; 2 1/2 hrs. to the S.W.) may be reached by driving as far as the (4 1/2 M.) *Bründl* (*Inn) in 3/4 hr., and walking thence to the top (passing the château of *St. Martin*) in 1 hr. more. The path can hardly be mistaken. On the summit is the iron *Rudolfs-Warte*, a belvedere 36' in height, erected in 1879. The *View embraces the broad valley: N., Gratz, the double tower of the pilgrimage-church of Maria-Trost, and the Schöckel; N.W., the Upper Styrian Mts. (Hochschwab); W., the Schwanberg Alps; S., the Bacher Mts.

The ***Schöckel** (4744') is most easily ascended from *Bad Radegund* (2340'; *Hydropathic) at the S.E. base of the mountain (10 M. distant, road through the *Annenthal*; omnibus daily in 2 1/4 hrs., starting at 8 a.m.). Thence to (1 1/4 hr.) the upper *Schöckel-Kreuz* (3696') 1 hr., and towards the left to the (1/2 hr.) *Semriacher Chalet* (beside which is a club-hut) and to the (1/4 hr.) top. Extensive view (panorama by Presuhn). A direct ascent leads from the *Andritz-Ursprung* viâ *Buch* and the *Göstinger Alphütte* in 2 1/2-3 hrs.

The **Tobelbad** (1150'; *Kurhaus-Restauration*; *Zum Königsbrunn*), a watering-place prettily situated amid pine-woods, 7 1/2 M. to the S.W., may also be visited from Gratz. The road to it (carr. in 1 hr.) leads by *Strassgang*. Or we may take the train to *Premstätten* on the Köflach railway (in 28 min.), and walk thence to the Tobelbad in 25 minutes.

FROM GRATZ TO KÖFLACH, 25 1/2 M., railway in 1 3/4 hr. (comp. Map, p. 414). The line, constructed for the coal-traffic, descends the broad valley of the Mur, nearly due S., to (7 1/2 M.) *Premstätten*, where it turns to the N.W. into the valley of the *Kainach*, and ascends past (10 M.) *Lieboch* (branch-line to *Schwanberg-Wies*, see below) and a number of unimportant stations. From (25 1/2 M.) Köflach (1450'; *Brün; *Schachner*), with coal-mines and glass-works, a road leads to the N.W. over the *Stubalpe* (5000'; Inn) to *Weisskirchen* and *Judenburg* (p. 425), in the upper valley of the Mur.

FROM GRATZ TO KLAGENFURT viâ SCHWANBERG. Railway in 3 hrs. to (12 M.) *Wies*; then a carriage-road to (15 M.) *Mahrenberg*. At (10 M.) *Lieboch* (see above) our line diverges to the left from the Köflach line and leads viâ *Lannach*, *Preding-Wieselsdorf*, and *Gross-Florian* to (29 1/2 M.) **Deutsch-Landsberg** (1220'; *Frittsberg*; °*Stelzer*), a prettily-situated village with an old *of Gratz.*   SCHWANBERG ALPS.   *VIII. Route 73.*   405

château. We next pass the handsome château of *Hollenegg*, the property of Prince Franz Liechtenstein, with valuable collections and a fine view. 34½ M. **Schwanberg**; the village *(Post; Neuwirth; Fleischer)* lies 2 M. to the W.; then (40 M.) *Pölfing*; and lastly (42 M.) *Wies* (1120'; Fleischer) pleasantly situated on the *Weisse Sulm*, with iron-works and forges, commanded by the old castle of *Burgstall*. — We now follow the road towards the S.W. to (3 M.; diligence thrice daily in 50 min.) *Eibiswald* (1190'; Fleischer), with iron-works, and ascend thence by a steep but well-kept road over the *Radelberg* (2200'; Inn), which commands a fine view of the Drave Valley and the Karawanken Chain to the S., and of the Schwanberg Alps as far as Gratz on the N. The road then descends into the valley of the Drave to (12 M.) **Mahrenberg** (1220'; *Feldbach; Bräu*), a straggling village, with a château and a ruined monastery, from which we cross the Drave by means of a ferry to (2 M.) the railway-station of *Wuchern* (p. 415). To prevent disappointment, travellers coming from Klagenfurt should order carriages at Mahrenberg beforehand (to Wies 6-7 fl.).

The **Schwanberg Alps** attract many excursionists from Gratz (guides, not necessary, Alois Herk at Deutsch-Landsberg, Ant. Peierl at Schwanberg). We take the train as far as *Deutsch-Landsberg* (see above), cross the *Lassnitz*, and ascend to the right viâ (1¾ hr.) *Trahütten* (3265') and the *Parfus Inn* (3245'; fine view), to (1½ hr.) *St. Maria* or *Glashütten* (4180'; °Inn). Thence we follow the road to the right to the (1¼ hr.) boundary between Styria and Carinthia, and skirt the fence to the left across the *Weineebene* to the depression between the *Hünerstützen* and the *Moschkogel*, in which, a little below us, is (1 hr.) the *Schafhütte* or *Grillitschhütte* (5725'; refreshments obtainable if the shepherds are there). From this point we mount in 1½ hr. more through the *Kar*, to the summit of the **Koralpe** (7025'), the highest peak of the Schwanberg Alps, locally called the *Speikkogel*. The *Koralpenhaus* (6435'; °Inn), ¼ hr. from the top, is on the W. side. View to the W. of the Lavantthal, Klagenfurt with its lakes, and Villach; a considerable part of Carinthia, the Gross-Glockner, Gross-Venediger; N., the Hochschwab, Schöckel, and Gratz; S., the Mts. of Carniola; E., over Gleichenberg and Riegersburg to Hungary and Croatia. — Descent on the E. side viâ the *Brendlalp* to (4½ hrs.) *Schwanberg* (see above); on the W. viâ the *Hipfhütten* or through the *Pensgraben* to (4 hrs.) *Wolfsberg* (p. 415), or viâ the *Kollnitzer Alpe* and *Gemersdorf* to (4 hrs.) *St. Andrä* (p. 415).

74. From Gratz to Trieste.

228 M. Railway. Express trains in 9 hrs.; ordinary trains in 14 hrs.

Gratz, see p. 400. The train traverses the fertile *Gratzer Feld*, on the right bank of the Mur, at a distance from the river. 4 M. *Puntigam*. On the hill to the right stands the château of *Premstätten*, the property of Count Sauran. Beyond (8 M.) *Kalsdorf*, on the hill to the left, beyond the Mur, is *Schloss Weissenegg*, once besieged by the Turks. Near (15 M.) *Wildon* (1030') the *Kainach* is crossed; on the height is the ruined castle of *Ober - Wildon* (1480'), in which Tycho Brahe once made his astronomical observations (restaurant; fine view).

On the right are the vine-clad *Sausal-Gebirge*. At (16½ M.) *Lebring* the *Lassnitz-Thal*, and near (22½ M.) *Leibnitz* the valley of the *Sulm* (see above) open on the right. In the *Leibnitzer Feld*, a peninsula between the Sulm and Mur, numerous Roman antiquities have been found, this being the site of the Roman *Flavium Solvense*. The episcopal château of *Seckau*, 1½ M. to the W. of Leibnitz, contains a collection of Roman inscriptions.

The train crosses the Sulm and approaches the Mur. 26½ M. *Ehrenhausen*, with the château of Count Attems on a wooded height to the right, adjoining which is the dome-covered burial-chapel of the princes of Eggenberg. At *Gamlitz*, a village 1½ M. to the W., are the interesting library and museum of Prof. Ferk. — 28½ M. *Spielfeld*, with another handsome château of Count Attems. About 1½ M. to the S. is Count Lucchesi's château of *Brunnsee*, with numerous art-treasures, and a fine park.

FROM SPIELFELD TO RADKERSBURG, 10 M., branch-railway in 1¾ hr. The line traverses the fertile valley of the Mur, passing the stations of *Schwarza*, *Weitersfeld*, *Mureck*, *Gosdorf*, *Pürkla*, and *Halbenrein*. — 19 M. **Radkersburg** (675'; *Kaiser von Oesterreich*; *Kleinoscheg*), a pleasant little town with 2500 inhab., is situated on the left bank of the Mur. The handsome late-Gothic parish-church dates from the 15th century. On the opposite bank of the river is *Ober-Radkersburg*, with the loftily situated castle of Count Wurmbrand (870'; fine view). — About 6 M. to the S.E., on the right bank of the Mur and near the Hungarian frontier (omnibus from the station in ¾ hr.), lies the watering-place of **Radein** (650'; *Kurhaus*, R. ½-1 fl.), with a mineral spring. An agreeable walk may be taken hence through the woods to (½ hr.) *Kapellen* (1000'; Inn), commanding a wide prospect towards Hungary, etc. About 9 M. farther to the S.E., on the *Stainzbach*, is *Luttenberg*, a village noted for its wine.

The train quits the Mur, turns to the S. into the *Windisch-Büheln*, a range of hills separating the Mur and Drave, and penetrates the watershed by the *Egidi Tunnel* (200 yds.; station). Near (36 M.) *Pössnitz* it crosses the *Pössnitzthal* by a viaduct of 64 arches, 700 yds. in length; it then pierces the *Posruck* by means of the *Leitersberg Tunnel* (725 yds.) and descends to —

40½ M. **Marburg** (880'; *Stadt Wien*; **Erzherzog Johann*; **Stadt Meran*; **Mohr*; good restaurant at the *Casino*), a town with 18,000 inhab., the second in Styria, picturesquely situated on the left bank of the *Drave*, at the foot of the *Posruck*. The Tappeiner-Platz in front of the commercial school is embellished with a statue of *Admiral Tegetthoff* (1827-1871), who was a native of Marburg. Adjacent is the *Stadt-Park*, with *Monuments* to the *Emperor Joseph* and to the *Archduke John*, and commanding fine views of the Posruck and Bachergebirge. In the distance rises the white Petzen. Marburg, which contains the provincial pomological school, is the centre of the Styrian fruit and wine cultivation. At the suburb of *St. Magdalena*, on the right bank, are the extensive workshops of the 'Südbahn'.

The (20 min.) *Calvarienberg* and the (½ hr.) *Pyramidenberg* afford a fine survey of the town and environs. — Pleasant excursion to (2 hrs.) **St. Urban** (1950'), a pilgrimage-church on the E. spur of the Posruck, with an extensive view over Styria and Hungary (driving is practicable as far as the foot of the mountain, the ascent of which is easily accomplished in ¾ hr.). — To (7½ M.) *St. Wolfgang*, on the *Bacher* (3400'), is another interesting excursion (refreshments at the forester's).

From Marburg to *Villach* and *Franzensfeste*, see RR. 75, 60.

The train crosses the Drave by a long bridge (picturesque view of the town and the Drave Valley to the right); on the right bank the Villach line diverges here (p. 414). A broad plain is now traversed ; to the right, at the foot of the *Bacher-Gebirge*, is the château of *Haus am Bacher*. 48½ M. *Kranichsfeld* ; 52½ M. **Pragerhof**, the junction for *Budapest* (see *Baedeker's S. Germany and Austria*). The train enters a hilly district and passes through two tunnels. 56 M. *Windisch-Feistritz*. 60½ M. *Pöltschach* (Hôtel Baumann, near the station ; *Post, in the village), at the N.W. base of the *Wotsch* (3215′ ; ascended viâ *St. Nikolaus* in 2 hrs.; fine view).

Diligence several times daily to (9½ M.) the **Baths of Rohitsch**, or *Sauerbrunn-Rohitsch* (*Kurhaus ; Europa ;* apartments procurable), the water of which, impregnated with carbonic acid gas, resembles that of Selters (500,000 bottles annually exported). About 5 M. farther to the E., on the *Sottla* or *Sattlbach*, which here forms the frontier of Croatia, lies *Markt Rohitsch* (Post), at the foot of the conical **Donatiberg** (2900′), the *Mons Claudius* of the Romans (ascended by *St. Georgen* in 2½ hrs. ; splendid view). About ½ hr. below the summit is the *Fröhlich-Hütte* (2585′), of the Austrian Tourist Club. — From Rohitsch the diligence goes on to (26 M. from Pöltschach) *Krapina-Töplitz*, in the Hungarian county of Varasdin, a watering-place with powerful medicinal springs, which are specially efficacious in cases of gout and rheumatism. The water, of which there is a most copious supply (1,360,000 gals. per 24 hrs.), is almost entirely free from mineral ingredients.

German is now replaced by a Slavonic or Wend dialect. The line winds through a sparsely-peopled hill-district, intersected by narrow valleys, and richly wooded. 69 M. *Ponigl* ; 75½ M. *St. Georgen* ; 79½ M. *Storè*, with several foundries. An extensive view of the *Sannthal*, a hilly, well-cultivated, and populous plain, bounded by the *Sulzbach Alps* (see below), is now suddenly disclosed.

82½ M. **Cilli** (790′ ; *Elephant* ; *Erzherzog Johann ; *Krone* ; *Löwe*), a pleasant old town with 5393 inhab., founded by the Emperor Claudius *(Colonia Claudia Celeja)*, attracts visitors by the picturesqueness of its environs and its river-baths in the *Sann* (temperature in summer 75-85° Fahr.). The local museum contains some interesting Roman antiquities. The *Stadt-Park* is prettily laid out on the right bank of the Sann. The (¼ hr.) *Josefiberg* (984′) commands a charming view of the town, the Sannthal, and the Sannthal Alps. A still finer point is the (¾ hr.) *Laisberg* (ascend to the church of the St. Nicholas and follow the slope of the hill). On the wooded *Schlossberg* stands the ruin of *Ober-Cilli* (1350′).

The **Baths of Neuhaus** (1160′ ; *Kurhaus), frequented chiefly by ladies, lie 10½ M. to the N.W. of Cilli, on the spurs of the Sannthal Alps (diligence twice daily in 2 hrs., viâ *Hohenegg* and *Neukirchen*). The thermal water resembles that of Pfäffers in Switzerland. Charming environs, and beautiful walks in every direction, particularly to the (¾ hr.) ruined *Schlangenburg*, with a picturesque and extensive view.

A pleasant excursion may be made from Cilli by *Hohenegg* and *Schloss Sternstein* to (4 hrs.) *Gonobitz*, a pretty little town, celebrated for its wine ; another leads by Sternstein to (4 hrs.) *Weitenstein* ; a third to (2 hrs.) *Deutschenthal*, in the *Sannthal*, with a large china and earthenware manufactory (visitors admitted) ; and a fourth to the top of the *Dostberg* (2750′ ; 2 hrs.), which commands a good view.

The ***Sannthal Alps**, also known as the *Alps of Sulzbach* or *Steiner Alpen*, form the S.E. portion of the Carinthian Alps, situated on the frontier of Carinthia, Carniola, and Styria. They present many beautiful and interesting points, and are well worthy of a visit. The inhabitants are Slavonic, but most of the innkeepers and guides speak a little German.

— A road leads from Cilli (diligence as far as Laufen daily in $6^1/_2$ hrs., fare 1 fl. 55 kr.; two-horse carr. in 6 hrs., 12 fl.) to the E., on the left bank of the *Sann*, viâ *Sachsenfeld* and *Sannbrücken* (*Inn), to (19 M.) *Prassberg* (Post; Hofbauer) and ($9^1/_2$ M.) Laufen (1385'; *Krutetz*, rustic), lying in a wide basin, where the carriage-road ends. We now follow a rough cart-road to ($7^1/_2$ M.) Leutsch or *Leuischdorf* (1700'; *Messner*, *Meide*, both unpretending; guide, Ant. Dolinar), picturesquely situated at the influx of the *Leutsch* into the Sann. The Raducha (6715'), a good point of view, may be ascended hence in 4 hrs. (guide $2^1/_2$ fl.); a finer point is the **Oistritza** (7710'), the second in height of the Sulzbach Alps, which commands a superb view (6-7 hrs., with guide; laborious). The good path leads chiefly through wood to the *Planinschek* (3565'; good night-quarters), a large and prettily situated farm-house, $1^3/_4$ hr. from Leutsch. Thence in 3 hrs. to the *Koroschitza-Hütte* (5930'), where the night should be spent, and in $1^1/_2$ hr. more to the narrow arête of the summit. The descent viâ the *Skarje-Sattel* (6980') to the *Klemenschek Alp* (3920') and the *Logárthal* is steep and toilsome ($3^1/_2$ hrs. to the Plesnik, see below).

At Leutsch the Sannthal turns to the N. and becomes a wild ravine, from which the rocky sides of the *Raducha* rise on the right almost perpendicularly. The stony path, hewn in the rock at places, crosses after 25 min. to the left bank; at the (25 min.) *Nadel* (*Igla*; 1800') it leads through a rocky cleft, 3-4 ft. wide, near which is an intermittent spring, and descends to the stream. On the right bank is situated ($1^1/_2$ hr.) —

Sulzbach (2170'; *Messner*; *Maruschnik*; *Sturm*). Interesting excursion hence to the *Logarthal. In $1^1/_4$ hr. we reach the *Logarbauer* (2240'), near which the *Sann*, after pursuing a subterranean course for some distance, appears above ground; then ($1/_2$ hr.) the *Plesnikbauer* (2485'; quarters). The Logarthal is a basin, 5 M. long and $1/_2$ M. broad, the head of which is enclosed by a huge amphitheatre of Dolomites, extending from the *Oistritza* to the *Rinka*. Those who do not wish to cross the ridge should turn here. The road farther on in the valley (guide advisable, Joh. Kramer at Sulzbach, Joh. Pickarnik at the Plesnik) ascends from the Plesnik for $1^1/_2$ hr more, part of the way through pine-wood, past the *Logar-Alpe*, to the *Rinka Fall*, a fine cascade of the *Sann*, which is precipitated over a rock, about 400' high, in the S.W. angle of the valley. Thence we may continue the walk to the right, ascending a zigzag path (indicated by marks) to the ($1/_2$ hr.) *Source of the Sann* (4230'), and to the grandly-situated terrace of ($1/_4$ hr.) *Okreschel*, with a refuge-hut (4520'; N. the Merzlagora, W. the Rinka, S. the Brana, S.E. the Baba and Oistritza). The *Rinka* (8000'), the *Brana* (7370'), and the *Baba* (*Planjava*, 7818'), may be ascended from this point (each 3-$3^1/_2$ hrs.; guide 3 fl.). From the Plesnik viâ the *Skarje* to the top of the *Oistritza* (7710'; 5 hrs.; guide $3^1/_2$ fl., with descent to Leutsch 4 fl.), see above. — A repaying route (lately improved) leads from Okreschel across the Steiner Sattel (6105'), between the *Brana* and the *Baba*, to the picturesque *Feistritz-Graben* and the (3 hrs.) *Ursitz-Bauer* (1940'), and to ($3^1/_2$ hrs.) *Stein* (see below). From Okreschel across the Sannthaler Sattel (about 6880') to *Seeland* (to the Kazino, 5 hrs.), by a marked path (for experts only, with guide), see p. 418.

FROM THE NORTH-EAST the direct route to Sulzbach is from *Prevali* (p. 416): road viâ *Mies* to (9 M.) *Schwarzenbach* (2000'; Mateusch); thence along the Mieshach to ($2^1/_2$ hrs.) *St. Jacob* (rustic inn) and over the *Kopreinsattel* (4415') to ($2^1/_2$ hrs.) *Sulzbach*; or (less interesting) through the *Wistragraben* and across the *Wistra-Sattel* (4125') to (5 hrs.; guide 3 fl.) *Sulzbach*. — FROM THE NORTH-WEST, an easy route from *Eisenkappel* (p. 417): we follow the Vellach road to the S. for 1 M.; then diverge to the left through the *Remschemiggraben*, and in 20 min. enter a gorge on the right and ascend to the ($1^1/_4$ hr.) oratory of *St. Leonhard*. The shortest route from this point is by a footpath to the left, ascending to the ($1/_2$ hr.) church of *St. Leonhard* (4360'; rustic inn), crossing the (20 min.) Sulzbach-Höhe (4715'), and descending to (20 min.) *Heiligen-Geist* (4090') and ($1^1/_2$ hr.) Sulzbach. Or, instead of turning to the left by the oratory of St. Leonhard, we may proceed straight on to the ($3/_4$ hr.) Leonhards-Sattel (4675'), whence a good path leads to the *Klemenseg Farm* and past the mouths of the ($1^1/_4$ hr.) *Jeseriathal* and

(1/2 hr.) *Logarthal* to (1¼ hr.) *Sulzbach*. — From *Bad Vellach* (p. 417): a path (indicated by red marks) diverges to the right from the Eisenkappel road at the *Christoph Rock*, 1 M. to the N., and ascends past the (3/4 hr.) large farm of *Paulitsch* (fine cliff-scenery in a wooded gorge; 3/4 M. to the N.) to the (1 hr.) **Paulitsch Sattel** (4390'), from which there is a fine view. It then descends through wood, past the (1 hr.) *Zavutkbauer* (3770') and the (1/4 hr.) *Schiboutbauer* (3410') to the (20 min.) mouth of the *Jeseriathal*, whence the path mentioned above leads to (1³/4 hr.) Sulzbach (guide 2½ fl.). — FROM THE SOUTH: road from *Laibach* (p. 410; diligence twice daily in 3 hrs.; railway in progress) to (15 M.) Stein (1230'; *Fröhlich*; *Rode*; *Christof*), a small town, charmingly situated on the *Feistritz*, and adapted for a prolonged stay (water-cure and Kurhaus). Three routes lead hence to Sulzbach. The longest and least interesting is the road viâ the *Cerna-Sattel* (2960') and *Oberburg* (Joschk) to (18 M.) *Laufen* (see above). The pleasantest is the footpath viâ (6 hrs.) *Leutsch*: from Stein we ascend the Oberburg road to (2¼ hrs.) *Cerna Dolina*, then follow the *Cernabach* to the (1½ hr.) *Krainsky-Rak-Sattel* (3380'), the boundary between Carniola and Styria, and descend to *Podwoltouteg*, and through the *Leutschthal* to (2½ hrs.) Leutsch. The third route leads through the picturesque *Feistritzthal*, viâ the curious natural bridge of *Predasel* (65' high) and the *Feistritz-Ursprung*, to the (3½ hrs.) **Urschitzbauer** (quarters at the farm or at the shooting-lodge; provisions should be brought). It then crosses the *Steiner Sattel* (6165'; with guide) to (3½ hrs.) *Okreschel* (p. 408), or the *Kanker-Sattel* (5900') to the (4 hrs.) *Frischauf-Haus*; see p. 418.

Beyond Cilli the train crosses the *Sann* twice, and enters the wooded and rocky ravine of this river. This is the finest part of the line, the scenery being very picturesque as far as Sava, where the mountains are quitted. Several of the hills are crowned with churches and chapels. — 89 M. **Markt Tüffer** (760'), with the *Franz-Josefs-Bad* and a ruined château.

The **Franz-Josefs-Bad**, prettily situated at the foot of the dolomitic *Hamberg* (1920'), on the left bank of the Sann, possesses three warm springs (95-102°), resembling those at Neuhaus and Römerbad. Visitors received at the *Badhaus* (pleasant grounds) and at the hotels *Zum Flösser*, *Zur Brücke*, *Bränhaus*, *Villa Stein*, and others.

94 M. **Römerbad** (690'), Slav. *Teplitza* (*i.e.* 'warm bath'; 97°), the thermal springs of which are proved by inscriptions to have been known to the Romans, is a thriving watering-place with pleasure-grounds and a good *Kurhaus*, charmingly situated.

97 M. **Steinbrück** (*Rail. Restaurant*, with rooms), an increasing place on the *Save*, or *Sau*, which here unites with the *Sann*, is the junction for *Agram* (see Baedeker's *S. Germany & Austria*).

To the W. is the long ridge of the **Kumberg**, with the pilgrimage-church of *St. Agnes* (4000'), which may be ascended from this point in 3½ hrs. (marked path; provisions should be taken). The summit (primitive Inn) commands an extensive view.

The train now follows the narrow valley of the *Save*, enclosed by lofty and precipitous limestone cliffs. 102 M. *Hrastniyy*; 105 M. *Trifail*, with one of the most important coal-mines in Austria (yielding from 275,000 to 300,000 tons of coal annually), or rather a coalquarry, as the operations are carried on above ground. The seam is 65-80' thick, but where it has been displaced or folded over by some convulsion of nature, it measures twice or three times that thickness. — 109 M. *Sagor*, the first village in Carniola; 114 M. *Sava* (810').

The valley now expands. Beyond (118 M.) *Littai* the Save is crossed by an iron bridge; and the train passes through a short tunnel. To the right *Schloss Poganek*. 122 M. *Kressnitz*; 127½ M. *Laase*. At the confluence of the *Laibach* and the Save the line quits the latter, and then follows the right bank of the Laibach, which it crosses at (132 M.) *Salloch*. The lofty mountains towards the N.W. are the *Julian Alps*, and in clear weather the *Terglou* (p. 430) is visible.

137 M. **Laibach** (940'; *Stadt Wien; Europa; *Elephant; Süddeutscher Hof, Bayrischer Hof*, near the railway; *Zur Sternwarte*, well spoken of; *Kosler's* coffee-garden; *Rail. Restaurant*), Slavonic *Ljubljana*, the Roman *Aemona*, the capital of Carniola, with 20,284 inhab. (majority Slavonic), is situated on the Laibach, in an extensive plain surrounded by mountains of various heights. The extensive old *Schloss* towering over the town, now used as a prison, commands a beautiful view, especially towards the Terglou and the Sulzbach Alps. (Visitors admitted to the tower only when attended by the sergeant on guard.) The *Cathedral*, in the Italian style, with a dome, is adorned with stucco mouldings and frescoes of the 18th century. The neighbouring school-buildings contain the *Landes-Museum*, a collection of products of the district.

The Congress held at Laibach from 27th Jan. to 21st May, 1821, the chief object of which was the suppression of the insurrection at Naples, first brought the town into notice. The principal square, is still called the Congress-Platz *(Kongresni-Trg)*. The Stern-Allee in this Platz is adorned with a bronze *Bust of Marshal Radetzky*.

Pleasant walk through *Lattermann's Allee*, an avenue with beautiful old chestnuts, to the (¾ M.) park and château of **Tivoli**, commanding a charming view, and to (¾ M.) *Rosenbach* (café), both favourite resorts. Thence through wood to the (20 min.) *Rosenbichl*, with its conspicuous church, whence a fine view is obtained of the Grintouz and other Sannthal Alps. — Longer excursions: ascent of the **Grosse Gallenberg** (2230'), 1½ hr. from stat. *Vismarje* (p. 429); splendid view from the summit (Inn; panorama by Pernhart). — The ascent of the **Katharinaberg** (2395') from *Zwischenwässern* (p. 429), in 2½ hrs., is also interesting. — Ascent of the **Krimberg** (3680') 5½ hrs.: we follow the road to (7½ M.) *Brunndorf*, and ascend thence by a path (generally good), viâ *Iggdorf* and *Oberigg*, to the (3½ hrs.) summit (extensive panorama). — The *Sannthal Alps*, see p. 409.

To the S.E. of Laibach a road leads viâ *Gross-Laschitsch* and *Reifnitz* to (41 M.; diligence daily in 9 hrs.) **Gottschee** (1510'; *Post*), a German oasis (1150 inhab.) in the district of the Karst or Carso, with a château of Prince Auersperg. The *Friedrichsteiner Eishöhle* and other interesting caverns are in the vicinity. Diligence daily from Gottschee, viâ *Brod* on the *Kulpa*, to *Delnice*, a station on the Karlstadt and Fiume Railway, see *Baedeker's S. Germany and Austria*.

From Laibach to *Villach*, see R. 77.

The line now traverses the marshy *Laibacher Moos* by means of an embankment nearly 1½ M. long, and crosses the Laibach, which already becomes navigable here, though it issues from the mountains at *Oberlaibach*, only 2½ M. higher up. This river is probably identical with the *Poik*, which rises near stat. St. Peter (p. 412).

disappears in the cavern of Adelsberg (p. 412), re-appears at Planina (see below), and after a brief career is again lost to view to the S. of Loitsch. Such phenomena are not uncommon among the *Julian Alps*, a limestone range intersecting Carniola from N.W. to S.E.

Before reaching (151 1/2 M.) *Franzdorf* the train crosses a viaduct borne by a double series of arches, 625 yds. in length and 125' high in the centre, passes *Oberlaibach*, and stops at (160 M.) **Loitsch** (1555'; *Post* or *Stadt Triest*).

QUICKSILVER MINES OF IDRIA, 21 M. to the N.W. of Loitsch. Diligence twice daily in 4 hrs., 1 fl.; carriage there and back in 6-7 hrs., 6-8 fl.; inspection of the mines and mining appliances, 3-4 hrs. The mines are entered, nearly in the centre of **Idria** (1540'; *Schwarzer Adler*), an old town situated in a sequestered valley, by a flight of 757 steps hewn in the limestone rock (admission by ticket obtained at the mining-office, 50 kr.). Pure quicksilver occurs very rarely here, but the cinnabar, or mercury ore, contains 80 per cent or more of the pure metal. The foundries at which the ore is smelted lie on the right bank of the Idriza, to the N.E. of Idria. The quicksilver is obtained by smelting and distillation, and particularly by mixing the heated and pulverised cinnabar with unslaked lime, which combines with the sulphur and sets the metal free. The annual yield is upwards of 300 tons of cinnabar, of which 50-60 tons are converted into quicksilver on the spot. — Pleasant walk from Idria to the (3/4 hr.) romantic *Wildensee*.

The ascent of the *Javornik (Spik; 4075') is interesting. We proceed to the S.W. from Loitsch by the road through the *Birnbaumer Wald* until we reach (3 hrs.) its highest point (3000'), 2 M. from *Podkraj*; hence we ascend to the right to (1 1/2 hr.) *Pri Skvarce*, the last farm-house (where the night may be spent), and thence to the (1/2 hr.) summit, which commands a magnificent view.

The train continues to traverse the partly wooded Karst district, following the valley of the *Unz* to (167 1/2 M.) **Rakek** *(Post)*.

Of the numerous caverns in the vicinity the most interesting is the imposing *Planina* or *Kleinhäusl Grotto*, through which the Poik flows, near Planina (*Post*), 5 M. to the W. (only partly explored). — About 4 M. to the E. is the **Zirknitzer See** (1800'), the *Lacus Lugeus* of Strabo, 6 M. in length and 1 1/2-2 1/2 M. in breadth, abounding in fish. The lake is surrounded by mountains, of which the *Javornik* (4166') and the *Slivenza* (3600') are the most prominent. It is drained by means of funnel-shaped apertures and fissures in the rocks, and the water re-appears in the Laibach Valley below as the brooks *Bistriza* and *Boruniza*. The lake sometimes dries up, as was the case in 1868 and 1871; and at other times, after protracted rain, it causes inundations. Innumerable waterfowl here afford excellent sport. — Ascent of the KRAINER SCHNEEBERG, very interesting. A drive of 3 hrs. viâ *Zirknitz* and *Laas* brings us to *Iggendorf* (*Mlakar*); we then follow the new road, passing (20 min.) *Schloss Schneeberg*, to (3 hrs.) *Leska Dolina* (2628'; Inn), and ascend through wood (with guide and provisions) to a (2 1/2 hrs.) *Refuge Hut*, built by the Austrian Alpine Club in the hollow of *Nova Graschina* (5050'), and the (1 hr.) summit of the *Krainer Schneeberg (5892'), called *Schneekoppe* (Slav. *Sneznik*) by the peasants, where the beautiful Edelweiss abounds. The extensive and magnificent view includes the whole of Carniola, Istria, the Friuli, Julian, and Sulzbach Alps, the Bay of Quarnero, and the N. part of Dalmatia. The ascent is shorter and easier from stat. *St. Peter* (p. 412): we follow the old Fiume road to the S.E. to *Zagurie* and (6 M.) *Grafenbrunn* (1980'; Inn); then ascend by a road to the left, viâ *Koritenze*, to the (9 M.) head-forester's house of *Maschun* (3370'; Inn), and thence (with guide; apply to the 'Oberförster') to the summit in 3 1/2 hrs. more.

177 M. **Adelsberg** (1800'; **Adelsberger Hof*, prettily situated, R., L., & A. 2 fl., B. 60 kr., D. 1 1/2 fl.; *Krone*), Slav. *Postójna*,

is a summer-resort of the Triesters. Fine view from the *Schlossberg* or castle-hill (2215'; 25 min.), with its ruined castle of *Adelsberg*.

The celebrated *Adelsberg Cavern, known in the middle ages and accidentally re-discovered in 1818, is illuminated with electric light daily in summer (May-Sept.) at 10 a.m. (adm 2½ fl. for each person; no extras), but it may also be visited at any other time on payment of fixed charges according to tariff (ticket-office near the church). Gratuities are forbidden. Total length of the cavern, so far as accessible, upwards of 2½ M.; for more than half that distance the visitor may be conveyed by tramway (return-ticket 1 fl.; chair with four bearers 6 fl.). The visit usually takes 2½ hrs. Temperature of the interior 48° Fahr.

An avenue of lime-trees ascends to the ENTRANCE (1970'), closed by a gate, ¾ M. to the W. of Adelsberg. The cavern consists of several different chambers: 1. The *Poik Cavern*, into which the *Poik* (*Piuka*; see above) flows, 60' below the entrance, this being the beginning of its subterranean channel. Two natural bridges of rock, connected by one of masonry, lead to the — 2. *Cathedral*, 72' high, 158' broad. The dimensions of this imposing grotto appear magnified owing to the uncertain light, and the eye in vain endeavours to penetrate its sombre recesses, from the bottom of which the murmur of the Poik reaches the ear. — 3. The *Kaiser-Ferdinand Grotto*, consisting of a succession of chambers, in one of which, the *Ball-Room*, 150' long and upwards of 40' high, a ball takes place annually on Whit-Monday, with brilliant illumination. — 4. The *Franz-Joseph-Elisabeth Grotto*, one of the most spacious caverns known, 112' in height, 223 yds. in length, and 214 yds. in breadth, containing the *Belvedere*, a height composed of fragments of stalactites. — 5. The *Maria-Anna Grotto*, with the *Calvarienberg*, the farthest point from the entrance.

The most interesting feature of these caverns is the variety of stalactites (depending from above) and stalagmites (upward formations) which they contain, many of them being most fantastic in form. In some places they resemble beautiful curtains or drapery, feebly illuminated by the lights behind, at others they take the form of petrified waterfalls, fountains, palms, cypresses, columns upright or recumbent. Other formations resemble human beings and various animals, and are known by a number of fanciful names. Some of the columns have attained a diameter of 12' and upwards. The fact that the ordinary dropping of the water in these grottoes forms a scarcely perceptible deposit after a lapse of 13 years serves to convey an idea of the incalculable antiquity of these formations. — A strange and rare animal (*Proteus Anguineus*; Germ. *Olm*), of pale red colour, with gills and lungs, somewhat resembling a salamander, occurs in the grottoes of the Karst; living specimens may generally be seen at Adelsberg.

A visit should also be paid to the **Poikhöhle** (*Piuka Jama*), 4½ M. to the N. of Adelsberg, a subterranean gorge, 230' deep, through which the Poik flows; it has been made accessible by the Austrian Tourist Club. In the depths of the interior are a huge dome, with the curious *Dolenzpforte* and four small lakes.

FROM ADELSBERG TO PRÄWALD, 8 M., diligence daily in 1¾ hr. About 4 M. from Adelsberg a road diverges on the right to *Landol* and (4½ M.) Lueg (1660'; Inn), a village with a castle, situated at the foot of a wall of rock, 400' high, containing several fortified caves. At its base is a grotto, in which the *Lokva* is swallowed up. — **Präwald** (1900'; *Brauhaus*), with 350 inhab., is a summer-resort of the Triesters. The *Nanos* (4265') is sometimes ascended hence (3½ hrs., with guide). Extensive view of the Carinthian Alps, the Adriatic, and the coast of Istria.

The train now traverses the valley of the *Poik* to *Prestraneck* and (183½ M.) **St. Peter** (1785'; *Railway Restaurant*). Ascent of the *Schneeberg*, see p. 411.

From St. Peter to Fiume, 35½ M., railway in 2-3 hrs. — The line traverses the undulating district of the *Karst* (see below). After passing through three tunnels we reach (5 M.) *Källenberg* (1980'), commanding a fine view. At (10 M.) *Dornegg - Feistritz*, which possesses the ruins of a castle, the *Feistritz (Bystrica)* issues from the hill in a copious stream, which is immediately used to drive several mills. Near (19½ M.) *Sapiane* (1400') the line penetrates the watershed between the Adriatic Sea and the Gulf of Quarnero by a tunnel 2050' long, and then descends, affording a view of the island of Cherso and the sea, to (26 M.) *Jurdani*, with a large cave, and (28½ M.) *Matuglie-Abbazia* (690'), the station for (2½ M.) Abbazia (carr. with one horse 2½, with two horses 4 fl.; hotel-omn. 1 fl. 20 kr.). The high-road makes a wide bend to the E. Pedestrians will find it shorter to follow the old road, which leads to the S.W. from the station to (1¼ M.) *Volosca* (Verboscheck's Inn, at the S. end of the village, good wine), prettily situated on the *Bay of Priluca*, and thence to (¾ M.) **Abbazia** (*Hôtel Stefanie*, *Hôtel Quarnero*, both belonging to the Southern Railway; *Touristenhaus*), a village in a splendidly sheltered situation, with woods of evergreen laurel, which has quite recently become a favourite summer and winter resort. Near it is the old abbey of *S. Giacomo della Priluca*. Excursions may be made viâ Volosca (see above) to *Fiume* (carr. in 1 hr., with one horse 3, with two horses 6 fl.; steamboat daily in 1½ hr.); to the cave at *Jurdani* (see above); to the S., by the picturesque coast-road along the *Liburnian Riviera*, and past *Ichsichi* and *Ika* to the charmingly situated (4½ M.) *Lovrana*. — The **Monte Maggiore** (*Utschka*; 4580') is also a delightful object for an excursion (5 hrs.). We follow the old road to Trieste as far as the (10 M.) *Stefanie-Schutzhaus* (3115'; Inn), on the *Poklon Saddle*, then turn to the left and ascend to the (1½ hr.) summit, whence we have an extensive and beautiful view.

From Matuglie (above, to the left, is the small town of *Castua*, once capital of Liburnia) the line descends towards the sea, affording a fine view of the Bay of Quarnero, with the islands of Veglia and Cherso. 35½ M. *Fiume*, see p. 446.

Beyond St. Peter the train enters an inhospitable and dreary plain, strewn with blocks of limestone, called the **Karst** (Ital. *Carso*, Slav. *Kras*), which extends from Fiume to Gorizia (p. 441). The surface is intersected by gorges, and partly covered with underwood and loose stones; and numerous funnel-shaped cavities are observed in the rocks. The fierce N.E. wind *(Bora)* which often prevails here has been known to overthrow loaded waggons.

The train threads its way through this stony wilderness and passes through several tunnels (quick train from Adelsberg to Trieste 2 hrs.). 191 M. *Lesece*. — 198½ M. **Divača** (*Railway Restaurant*, with beds; *Mahortschitsch*), the junction for the Istrian railway (see below).

About 1 M. from the station is the *Crown Prince Rudolf Grotto, containing dazzling white stalactites of the most magnificent and varied forms, particularly in the 'Coburg-Dom'. It has been made conveniently accessible. Tickets of admission (50 kr.) at the railway-restaurant, where a guide (80 kr.) may also be obtained. Illumination extra.

A visit should also be paid to the * **Cascades and Grottoes of St. Canzian**, 1⅓ M. to the S.E. of Divača, which are among the most magnificent natural phenomena of the kind. The *Reka*, flowing straight towards a massive cliff, 320' high, on which the village and church of *St. Canzian* are situated, forces its course through it (forming the *Mahortschitsch* and *Marinitsch Grottoes*) and then winds through the *Kleine Dotine* ('funnel'), amid a labyrinth of crags and scattered rocks, to a second lofty wall of rock, through which it finds its way by another deep and narrow cañon, falling at the farther end in a beautiful cascade into a small lake in the *Grosse Dotine*. Issuing from the lake the river again enters a narrow rocky gorge, and finally disappears from the light of day, to emerge from its subterranean course 18 M. off, as the *Timavo* (p. 441). Until recently the only available path was a kind of staircase, which descended from St. Canzian to the Reka Lake (490' below the village) in about 500 steps; but now the grottoes and waterfalls are easily accessible from all sides by means of new paths and bridges constructed by the local Alpine Club. The most interesting points are the *Mahortschitsch Grotto*, the *Tomasini Bridge*, the *Guttenberg Halle*, the *Schröder Gang*, the *Oblasser Warte* (amidst foaming waterfalls, reached by a natural subterranean passage), the *Tominz Grotto*, the *Maier Grotto*, the path over the *Böse Wand*, the striking *Schmidl Grotto* (with lofty vaultings and fine stalactite formations), and the subterranean passage from the last grotto to the *Rudolf Cathedral* (into which the Reka dashes in waterfalls and rapids from the rocky gorge mentioned above) and to the sixth waterfall. Those who do not object to a rough scramble may penetrate to the twelfth waterfall. — The tower in the blacksmith's meadow at St. Canzian, on the outer verge of the Doline, commands an interesting survey; and a fine view of the open valley of the Reka may be obtained from behind the church. The *Stephanie-Warte* (1425' above the sea-level; 525' above the Reka Lake) also offers a magnificent view of both Doline's with their cataracts, St. Canzian, the Krainer Schneeberg, Gaberk, Nanos, etc. The visit requires in all about 3 hrs.; tickets of admission and guides are obtained at *Gombatsch's Hotel* at *Matavun* (¹/₂ M. to the S. of St. Canzian), the headquarters of the Alpine Club. Admission to the grottoes, 80 kr. each pers.; guide for 1 pers. 20 kr. per hr., for more than 1 pers. 10 kr. each (guide advisable for every 3-4 pers. in a party; torches, candles, magnesium wire, etc., are sold at a tariff fixed by the Alpine Club). The paths and bridges are all perfectly safe and are provided with railings wherever necessary. — From the station at Divača we may walk to Matavun viâ *Unter-Lesece* in ³/₄ hr. (carr. at Divača dear). From Trieste, Matavun is reached by carriage in about 2¹/₂ hrs., viâ *Corgnale*.

FROM DIVAČA TO POLA, 76 M., railway in 3¹/₄-5 hrs. The most important stations are: 8 M. *Herpelje-Kozina* (junction for Trieste, p. 441); 22 M. *Pinguente*; 44 M *Pisino*; 57 M. *Canfanaro* (branch to Rovigno, see p. 443); 68 M. *Dignano*. — *Pola*, see p. 444.

Beyond (204 M.) **Sessana** (1630') the train crosses the highroad and descends to (211 M.) *Prosecco*, noted for its wine (comp. p. 437), and (216 M.) **Nabresina** (*Rail. Restaurant*, with rooms), where the line to Gorizia and Venice (p. 441) diverges. As Trieste is approached by long curves, a magnificent view of the blue Adriatic is enjoyed. 224 M. **Grignano**, the last station, is in a straight direction less than 1¹/₂ M. below Prosecco. On the *Punta di Grignano*, which here projects into the sea, is the handsome château of *Miramar* (p. 440). The train passes through a tunnel at *Barcola* (p. 440) and reaches —

228 M. Trieste (see p. 437).

75. From Marburg to Villach.
Comp. Map, p. 408.

101 M. RAILWAY in 5¹/₂-6³/₄ hrs.

Marburg, see p. 406. The train diverges, on the right bank of the Drave, from the **Trieste Railway** (p. 406), and stops at the (1 M.) *Kärntner Bahnhof*, or 'Carinthian Station', near the suburb of *St Magdalena*. To the left, at the foot of the Bacher-Gebirge, rises *Schloss Rothwein*; to the right, on the opposite bank of the Drave, is the village of *Gams*, prettily situated on vine-clad hills. — 5 M. *Feistritz*, opposite which is the château of *Wildhaus*; 10 M. *Mariarast*. The line crosses the *Lobnitz*, passes through a tunnel, and reaches (14½ M.) *Faal*, with a château and park of Count Zabeo. The train follows the right bank of the Drave, high above the deep bed of the river, and describes a long curve. 16½ M. *St. Lorenzen*, at the mouth of the *Radtbach*, on which, 3 M. from its mouth, is the village of *St. Lorenzen*. 22½ M. *Reifnig-Fresen*.

A road to the S., through the *Wolka-Graben*, leads to (6 M.) *Reifnig* (2345'; Puhr), at the foot of the **Welka Kappa** (5060'), the highest peak of the Bacher-Gebirge. Ascent interesting (3 hrs.; with guide). The descent may be made on the W. side to (2 hrs.) *Windischgratz* (see below).

28½ M. **Wuchern-Mahrenberg**; the small town of Mahrenberg, (p. 405), lies on the opposite bank of the Drave. 33½ M. *Saldenhofen*, on the *Feistritz*, opposite *Hohenmauthen*, with its iron-works. — 40½ M. **Unter-Drauburg** (1195'; *Post*), at the influx of the *Miesbach* into the Drave. The village *(Domaingo; Gönitzer)*, dominated by the ruined *Drauburg*, lies on the opposite bank.

A road (diligence twice or thrice daily in 1¼ hr.) leads hence to the S.E. through the *Misslingthal* to (6½ M.) **Windischgratz** (1340'; *Günther; Goll*), a small town with iron-works and the château of *Rottenthurm*. Above (½ M.) *Altenberg* rises the *Schlossberg*, the ancestral seat of the princes of Windischgrätz, burned down in 1511; the only part now left is the church of St. Pancratius. The **Ursulaberg** (5564') is ascended hence in 4½-5 hrs.: extensive view of the E. Alps, from the Dachstein and the Tauern. as far as the Croatian Mts. (on the top a pilgrimage-church and inn). The descent may be made by *Rosank* to the *Römerquelle*, a rising little 'Bad', with a mineral spring, and viâ *Köttelach* to (2½ hrs.) *Gutenstein* (Inn), 3 M. to the E. of *Prevali* (p. 416). — Beyond Windischgratz the road leads to *Weitenstein*, *Hohenegg*, and (30 M.) *Cilli* (p. 407).

[FROM UNTERDRAUBURG TO WOLFSBERG, 24½ M., railway in 2¼ hrs. The fertile **Lavantthal** is worthy of a visit. The train crosses the *Mies* and the Drave. 6½ M. *Lavamünd* (Bendl; Goll), at the influx of the *Lavant* into the Drave; 8 M. *Ettendorf*. — 14 M. **St. Paul** (1310'; *Fischer; Klimbacher*), a prettily-situated village, is commanded by an extensive Benedictine abbey, founded by Count Sponheim in 1091, with a Romanesque church. The valuable collections of the abbey (ornaments of the 10th and 11th cent., coins, library, etc.) are shown on application.

EXCURSIONS. To the pilgrimage-chapel on the *Josefsberg* (2245') 1 hr.; to the ruin of *Rabenstein* (2265') ¾ hr., and thence to the top of the (¾ hr.) **Kasparstein* (2760'), a splendid point of view. The *Koralpe* (p. 405) is easily ascended viâ *Rojach* and *Gemersdorf* in 6 hrs.

18 M. **St. Andrä** (1420'; *Pongratz; Fischer; Waschen*), a small town prettily situated, was the residence of the prince-bishops of Lavant down to 1859, when they removed to Marburg. The old palace and the neighbouring château of *Thürn* now belong to the Jesuits. To the N. rises the handsome *Loretto Church*, in the Italian rococo style (1673-1704). — 21 M. *St. Stefan*.

24½ M. **Wolfsberg** (1510'; *Pfundner; Schellander*), the capital of the Lavantthal, with 2100 inhab., is finely situated at the base of the Koralpe. Above the town rises the handsome modern *Schloss

416 *VIII. Route 75.*   BLEIBURG.   *From Marburg*

of Count Donnersmark (1740'), in the Tudor style, with beautiful grounds and a fine view. In the wood, ½ M. to the S. of the château, rises the sumptuous *Mausoleum* of the late Countess (Princess Hardenberg, d. 1857), erected by Stüler, with a marble statue of the deceased by Kiss (shown by the gamekeeper who lives in the adjoining house).

EXCURSIONS (guides, *Joh. Fellner*, *P. Greilach*, *Alex. Regger*, and *Alb. Zanger*). To the N.W. is (½ hr.) *Schloss Kirchbichel*, the property of Baron Herbert, charmingly situated (interior also worth seeing). — To the W. lies (¼ hr.) *St. Jacob* (Fauland, with garden); to the S. (2 M.) *St. Johann*, with a fine view; *Tretschach* (3 M.) and the monastery of *Marein* (3 M.) may also be visited. — Ascent of the **Koralpe** (7025', 5-6 hrs., with guide). The route leads viâ the *Zoger-Alpe*, the *Schoberkogel*, the *Warschegg*, the *Hipflhütten*, and the *Sleinschober*, to the *Koralpen-Haus*, ½ hr. below the summit on the W. side (p. 406). — Ascent of the Grosse Saualpe (6828', 5½ hrs.). We follow the road viâ *St. Michael* to (9 M.) *Lading*, and ascend direct in 2½ hrs. to the summit; or we may ascend by *St. Margarethen* and *Forst* to the (5 hrs.) *Forst-Alpe* (6645'), and then proceed either to the N. to the (¾ hr.) *Geierkogel* (6270'), a fine point of view, or to the S. viâ the *Kienberg* and the *Gertrusk* to the (1½ hr.) top of the *Grosse Saualpe*. Descent to *Lölling* or to *St. Oswald*, see p. 427.

The road from Wolfsberg to JUDENBURG (32 M.; diligence daily in 6 hrs.) leads to the N. viâ *St. Gertrud*, through the romantic *Twimberger Graben*, a valley 6 M. long. (At the N. end of the valley is the *Schlatt-wirth*, whence a road to the left leads in ½ hr. to *Prebl*, a small Alpine watering-place, with a good bath-house.) About 12½ M. from Wolfsberg we reach St. Leonhard (2865'; *Schlaffer*; *Post*), a small town with an old Gothic church. (Route over the *Klippitzthörl* to *Mösel*, and ascent of the *Saualpe*, see p. 427; two-horse carr. to Mösel in 7 hrs., 10 fl.) The next villages are (3½ M.) *Reichenfels* (Weinberger), beyond which, at the *Taxwirth*, we cross the frontier of Carinthia, (5 M.) *Obdach*, (7 M.) *Weisskirchen*, and (1 M.) *Judenburg* (p. 425).]

The railway now quits the Drave and turns to the S. into the pretty, wooded *Miesthal*. The train passes the village of *Gutenstein*, where the valley expands (to the S. the slopes of the Ursulaberg, see above), and stops at (47½ M.) **Prevali** (1400'; *Uranschek*; *Zinnerl*; *Farcher*), a busy iron-manufacturing place. (Route to *Sulzbach*, see p. 408.) The Miesthal again contracts, and the train runs at a considerable height on its N. side; it then turns to the right into the *Langsteg-Thal*, passes through two tunnels (the latter piercing the watershed between the Mies and the Drave) and descends to (57 M.) **Bleiburg** (1555'; *Rail. Restaurant*; *Sorgendorf Brewery*, near the station). The small town (*"Elephant*; *Nemetz*), with a château of Count Thurn, lies on the *Libuska*, 1½ M. to the N. of the station.

To the S. rises the isolated Petzen (6936'; 6 hrs.; guide 2½ fl.; laborious). From stat. Bleiburg to the S. to *Feistritz* (*Krauth*) ¾ hr., to the lead-foundry 25 min., to the *Berghaus* (4870', 1m., rustic) 2 hrs., to the W. peak 2½ hrs. more. Fine view, but interrupted toward the E. by the Ursula Mts. A path, indicated by red marks, leads to the E. along the crest to the *Knieps quelle* and to (1 hr.) the top of the *Kuleps* (6968'), the summit of the Petzen. The descent may be made, if preferred, from the W. summit to the S.W. to the *Luscha* farm, and through the *Leppengraben* to (4½ hrs.) *Eisenkappel* (see below).

The *Jaunthal*, a lofty, and for the most part wooded plain between the Drave and the mountains, is now traversed to (64 M.) Kühnsdorf (1415'; *Leitgeb; Reiter*), whence a fine view is enjoyed: to the S. the long chain of the Karawanken, from the Ursulaberg and Petzen to the Mittagskogel near Villach; to the N. the green hills of the Saualpe and Koralpe. About 2¼ M. to the W. is the little *Klopeiner See*, with lake-baths (Restaurant Villa Martin, on the lake). — Kühnsdorf is the station for *Völkermarkt* (Stern; Adler; Post), a town on the left bank of the Drave, 3 M. to the N., and for *Eisenkappel*, situated to the S. (diligence twice daily in 2¾ hrs., fare 1 fl.; one-horse carr. in 2 hrs., 3 fl.).

The last-mentioned road (to Krainburg, 40 M.) leads viâ *Eberndorf*, with its old abbey, and *Gösselsdorf*, with a small lake, to (7 M.) Miklauzhof (²*Inn and Brewery*), whence the *Wildenstein Waterfall* (p. 418) may be reached in 2½ hrs. We follow the Grafenstein road past *Jerischach* to the (5 M.) *Jesernik Inn* (rustic), whence a path, indicated by red marks, leads to the left through wood to (¾ hr.) the fall. Ascent of the *Obir*, see below (guides, Jos. Gaggl and Thom. Orasch). — The Krainburg road continues through the picturesque *Rechberger Schlucht*, viâ the *Rechberg* steelworks and the smelting-works of *Viktorhütte*, to (5½ M.) Eisenkappel (1830'; ¹*Niederdorfer; Fleischhauer; Löwe*), a large village at the influx of the *Ebriachbach* into the *Vellach-Bach*, with mineral springs and baths, good headquarters for the exploration of the Karawanken and Sannthal Alps (guides, Andr. Benedeizig and Franz Wriesnig). About ¼ M. to the S. is *Schloss Hagenegg*. Among the picturesque walks that may be taken from Eisenkappel are those to the *Ebriachklamm* (1 hr.); to the *Kupitzklamm* (1¼ hr.) and *Jeravizaklamm* (2 hrs.) in the *Remschenigggraben* (p. 408); and to the *Wildenstein Waterfall* (3 hrs., viâ *Rechberg* and *Jerischach*, see above).

An interesting excursion, especially for mineralogists and botanists, is the ascent of the Hochobir (7025'; 4½ hrs., guide, not indispensable, 2½ fl., if a night is spent, 3 fl.), a very fine point of view. The shortest route ascends through the *Ebriachthal* and by the well-marked '*Jovansteig*' on the slope of the *Jovanberg* to the (2½ hrs.) *Potschula-Sattel* (4790'), then crosses the *Seealp* to the *Kalte Quelle*, and follows the telephone-line to the (1¾ hr.) *Rainer Refuge Hut* (6600'; Inn), formerly a miner's house, now a meteorological station, connected with Eisenkappel by means of a telephone 8 M. long. In 10 min. more we reach the summit. Another route (5¼ hrs.) leads to the (¾ hr.) *Baracke*, before the Ebriachklamm in the Ebriachthal, and then ascends to the right (red marks) by the miner's house of *Fladung* and the *Seealp* to the (4½ hrs.) refuge-hut. A third route follows the Kühnsdorf road for 1½ M. to the N., then following the telephone, ascends the *Zauchengraben* to the (1½ hr.) *Schäffleralp* (3630'), with its lead-mine and stalactite grottoes (permission to visit these obtained at the office of Rainer's Foundry at Eisenkappel), and traverses wood and meadows to the (1¼ hr.) *Potschula-Sattel* (see above). We may descend to the *Wildenstein Waterfall* (p. 418); or, to the S.W. of the refuge-hut, to the (2½ hrs.) *Terkl-Wirth* in the Zeller-Thal (p. 420), and thence either to the W. viâ *Zell* to (3½ hrs.) *Ferlach* (p. 420), or to the E. over the *Schaida* to (3¼ hrs.) *Eisenkappel* — The *Petzen* (6936'; 6-7 hrs.; guide 3½ fl.), the *Uschowa* (6332'; 5-6 hrs.; guide 2 fl. 70 kr.), and the *Koschuta* (6752'; 7-8 hrs.; guide 4 fl.) may also be ascended from Eisenkappel; see below and p. 416. From Eisenkappel to *Sulzbach*, see p. 408.

Beyond Kappel, 6 M. to the S., in a beautiful wood, lies the Vellacher Bad (2765'; *Badhaus*, usually crowded in summer), with its chalybeate spring. Interesting expedition hence to the top of the *Carinthian* or *Seeländer Storschitz* (6784'; 2½-3 hrs.; guide 1½ fl.), to the W. of the baths. Mountaineers may ascend the *Koschuta* (E. peak 6750'; *Koschutnik Thurm*, to the W., 7005'; 5-6 hrs., with guide). Across the *Paulitsch-Sattel* to *Sulzbach*, see p. 409. (Near the *Pautitschbauer* is an interesting '*Rock Gate*', 1¼ hr.)

From the 'Bad' the road mounts rapidly to the (3 M.) top of the Seeberg (3995'; fine view, best from the 'Kanzel', a rocky knoll by the house 8 min. to the right), descends as rapidly to the (1¼ M.) *Stullerwirth* in Ober-Seeland (2970'), near the post-office and church of *St. Andrä*, and through the valley to the (1¼ M.) *Kazino Inn* (over the *Sannthaler Saddle* to the *Logar-Thal*, see p. 405). Thence it descends the *Schanzriegel* (with traces of old entrenchments, 'Schanze') to (1 M.) *Unter-Seeland* and (¾ M.) *Podlog* (Kanonierwirth), at the mouth of the *Podstorschitz-Thal*. [From this point we may ascend, viâ the *Baschl-Sattel* (5350'), to the top of the **Krainer Storschitz** (7000'; 4½ hrs., with guide), a magnificent point of view. The descent may be made viâ *Bascht* to *Tupatitsch* (see below).] Beyond Podlog our route traverses the picturesque *Kanker-Thal* to the (1½ M.) *Factory of Herr Fuchs*. ¼ M. *Zunder Inn* (rustic); 3 M. notice-board, on the left, indicating the way to the Grintouz (see below); ¾ M. *Poschner Inn*; 1½ M. *Kanker-Pfarre* (rustic inn). — The *Grintouz* (8395'), the highest of the Sannthal Alps (p. 407), is easily ascended from the Poschner Inn in 5 hrs.; at the notice-board ¾ M. above Poschner (see above), we ascend to the E. by a path indicated by marks to the (1 hr.) farm of *Suhadotnik* (2940') and the finely-situated (1¾ hr.) *Frischauf-Haus* (4835'; tavern in summer). Thence in 3 hrs. (guide 2 fl.), by a well-defined path, to the summit, which affords a most imposing prospect. The ascent from Ober-Seeland is also interesting, but is fit for mountaineers only (7-8 hrs.; guide 3½ fl.): from the Stullerwirth through the *Obere Seeländer Kotschna* to the *Stutter-Alpe* 1½ hr., to the *Ravni* 1¾ hr., to the *Schneide* 2½ hrs., to the top 1½ hr. Descent to the (2 hrs.) Frischauf-Haus, see above. — The *Skuta* (8300'; 4 hrs.; guide 2½ fl.) may be ascended from the Frischauf-Haus viâ the *Kanker-Sattel* (5900'; laborious; pass to the Feistritzthal, see p. 401). The view resembles that from the Grintouz. — At *Tupatitsch*, 3½ M. to the W. of the church of Kanker, the valley expands (to the right lies *Höflein*, a substantial village, with good inns, frequented as a summer-resort); the road enters the broad *Sau-Thal* and reaches (5 M.) *Krainburg* (p. 429).

Beyond Kühnsdorf the train approaches the Drave, on the opposite bank of which are the château of *Neudenstein* and the provostry of *Tainach*, and crosses the river by a handsome bridge below the mouth of the *Gurk* (fine glimpse of the Obir and the Koschuta to the S.). 73 M. **Grafenstein** (1370'), with a château of Prince Rosenberg.

To the S. rises the *Skarbin* (2668'; 1¼ hr.), a fine point of view — The Hochobir (p. 417) is also ascended hence. Road through the (½ M.) village of *Grafenstein* (Seebacher) to the (4½ M.) *Annabrücke* over the Drave; then (1½ M.) *Gallizien* (1435'; Teyrowsky), and (1 M.) the village of *Wildenstein*, from which a path (red marks) ascends to the right to the (½ hr.) *Wildenstein Waterfall*, which dashes over a projecting cliff, 170' high (pretty view of the Jaunthal through the water from the hollow behind the fall). Thence a path (marks) ascends to the (¾ hr.) *Rinnerfichte* (to the left the ruined *Wildenstein*) and through the *Wildensteiner Graben* to the (1½ hr.) *Hofmannsalm* (4075'). Turning here to the left we reach the *Wildenstein Sattel* in 1¼ hr., and thence follow the telephone to the (1½ hr.) *Rainer Refuge Hut* (p. 417).

The train next crosses the Gurk and the *Glan*. On the left, *Ebenthal*, a château of Count Goëss; on the right Prince Rosenberg's turreted château of *Welzenegg*.

80 M. **Klagenfurt.** — Hotels. *KAISER VON OESTERREICH*, Heu-Platz, at the corner of the Wienergasse, R. & L. 1 fl.; *KÄRNTNER HOF*, Cardinals-Platz; *MOSER*, Burggasse; *SANDWIRTH*, Pernhartsgasse, with garden; *WEISSES LAMM*, Untere Alter Platz; *GOLDNER BÄR*, Stern-Allee. Omnibus from any of the hotels to the station 20 kr.

Restaurants. *Sandwirth*, with garden, see above; *Silberegger Bierhalle*,

Hafner, Grosse Schulhausgasse; *Sonne*, Bahnhof-Str.; *Steirische Weinhalle*, with garden, Pfarrhofgasse; *Benediktiner Kellerei*, good wine. — **Cafés**. *Madner*, Wienergasse, with garden; *Schiberth*, Bahnhof-Str.; *Dorrer*, Neuer Platz. *Joos*, confectioner, Stern-Allee.

Baths. *Römerbad*, in the town (Turkish and other baths). — *Military Swimming Baths* in the Wörther See (railway-station, see p. 421; train in 10 min.), 3 M. from Klagenfurt (a drive of 25 min.; omnibus at 4 and 6 p.m., 20 kr., there and back 25 kr.; one-horse carr. there and back, with stay of 1 hr., 1½ fl.; bath with towel 25 kr.; small restaurant with fine view). — *Maria Loretto Baths*, at the efflux of the Lend Canal from the Wörther See (p. 421), 3 M. from Klagenfurt (omnibus several times daily; bath with towel 16 kr.; *Restaurant). The various summer-resorts round the Wörther See have each their larger or smaller bathing-establishments.

Cabs. To or from the station, one-horse 50, two-horse 80 kr.; at night 1 or 2 fl. — By time: first ¼ hr., with one horse, 25 kr.; ½ hr. with one horse 50, with two horses 60 kr.; whole day 6 or 8 fl.; ½ day, forenoon, 2½ or 3½ fl., afternoon 3½ or 4½ fl.

Klagenfurt (1460'), the capital of Carinthia, with 18,749 inhab., is charmingly situated on the *Glan*, which is connected with the *Wörther See* (p. 421) by the *Lend Canal*, 3 M. in length. The fortifications, destroyed by the French in 1809, have been converted into a *Ringstrasse*. The town, which is nearly square in form, possesses broad and straight streets. The new *Museum Rudolfinum* is situated in the Ringstrasse, near the station. The first story contains the Museum of Natural History (Sun. 10-12., Wed. 2-5, free; other days 9-12, 20 kr.); in the second story are the collections of the Carinthian Historical Society (Sun. 10-12, free; other days, 9-1, 30 kr., 3-4, 50 kr.), including Roman and prehistoric antiquities, mediæval and modern works of art, a library, and the provincial archives. In one of the corridors is a large panorama from the top of the Gross-Glockner. Behind the museum lies the *Botanic Garden*, adjacent to which is the *School of Agriculture and Mining*, with a bronze bust of the emperor Joseph II. The principal hall of the *Landhaus*, or House of the Estates, built in the 16th cent. by the Estates, who were at that time Protestant, is adorned with the arms of Carinthian nobles and contains the ancient ducal throne, removed from the Zollfeld (p. 428). In the principal square is a fountain with a dragon, the heraldic emblem of the town, adjoining which is a bronze *Statue of Maria Theresa*, designed by Pönninger and erected in 1872. The Cardinals-Platz is embellished with an obelisk commemorating the Peace of Pressburg. *Herbert's* white-lead manufactory here is the largest in Austria. The gallery (164') of the tower of the parish-church commands a fine *Panorama of the environs (20 kr.). The *Franz-Josefs-Anlagen* on the *Kreuzberg* (1915), ½ hr. to the W. of the town, contain a tower (82') commanding a beautiful view of the entire chain of the Karawanken Alps, etc. (*Restaurant). A similar view is obtained from *Maria-Rain (Restaurant), situated beyond the Drave, 6 M. to the S. (carr. in 1 hr.).

FROM KLAGENFURT TO KRAINBURG (36 M.) a high-road leads over the *Loibl* (a drive of 9 hrs.; carriages to be had at Unterbergen and Neumarktl, but at the former only when previously ordered). Leaving Kla-

27*

genfurt, the road leads to the S. to the (2 M.) *Glanfurtbrücke*, and then
ascends the *Sattnitz* (from the top *View to the S., of the Karawanken
range, from the Koschuta to the Mittagskogel). It passes (3¼ M.) the
château of *Hollenburg*, situated on a precipitous rock above the Drave,
¼ M. to the left, descends in a wide curve (avoided by a footpath) to
the Drave valley (here known as the *Rosenthal*), crosses the Drave to
Kirschentheuer (Ratz), and remounts to (3½ M.) Unterbergen (*Oblasser*,
rustic; **Bräuhaus**). At (1½ M.) *Unter-Loibl* (1635'; Merlin) the valley contracts. The road ascends to the (2½ M.) top of the *Kleine Loibl* (2385'),
where the road to Bleiberg and the Bodenthal diverges to the right by
the *Chapel of St. Magdalena*; it then descends in zigzags, and is carried by
the bold *Teufelsbrücke* across the wild gorge of the brawling *Bodenbach*
(a path has recently been constructed to the picturesque waterfall). The
Loibl-Thal now begins. The road is level as far as the (1¼ M.) inn 'Zum
Deutschen Peter' and (1¼ M.) *St. Leonhard*, after which it ascends in
numerous windings (cut off by footpaths) to the (6 M.) Loibl Pass (4495'),
a cutting in the rocks marked by two pyramids with long inscriptions.
Limited but picturesque view of the St. Anna-Thal to the S., with the
Koschuta on the left and the Bogunschitza on the right. The road now
descends in zigzags to the (1½ M.) hamlet of *St. Anna* (3395'; Inn), and
thence through the picturesque *St. Anna-Thal* to (6½ M.) Neumarktl (1680';
Post), a busy little town at the influx of the *Mossenik* into the *Feistritz*.
(The *Teufelsbrücke*, in a romantic gorge 4½ M. to the N.E., is worth a
visit.) We may then either follow the left bank of the Feistritz to (8 M.)
Krainburg (p. 429); or cross the hill to the right, by a picturesque road
affording a series of fine views, to (5½ M.) *Vigaun* and (2½ M.) the station *Lees* (p. 429)

The **Stou** (*Stol* or *Stuhlberg*, 7345'), the highest peak of the Karawanken Mts, is best ascended from the *Bodenthal*, a fatiguing but
picturesque excursion from the *Kleine Loibl* (see above) we diverge to
the right towards (¾ hr.) *Windisch-Bleiberg* (3110'; rustic inn on the
right, at the entrance to the village), 10 min. before reaching which we
turn to the left into the Bodenthal to the (1½ hr.) *Bodner* (3140'), the
last chalet (spend night); thence a path, indicated by marks, ascends to
the (2½ hrs.) *Wertatscha-Sattel* and in 2½ hrs. more to the top, a striking point of view (small refuge-hut). Descent to the *Valrasor-Hütte* and
to (4½ hrs.) *Jauerburg* (p. 431). — The ascent from the **Bärenthal** is less
toilsome: beyond the Hollenburg bridge, 6 M. from Klagenfurt (see above),
a road leads to the W. to (4½ M.) *Feistritz* in the *Rosenthal* (1810'; Kraiger;
guide, Tomasch); here we ascend to the left, by the brook and through
a narrow gorge, to the (2½ hrs.) *Stouhütte* (3170'), in the highest region of
the valley, and thence over the saddle of *Weinasch* to the (4 hrs.) summit.
— An easy route, with a fine view, leads from the Bärenthal over the
Medjidoh-Sattel (5525') in 3½-4 hrs. to *Jauerburg* (p. 431). — A drawback
to travelling among the Karawanken Mts. is the fact that the natives
seldom understand any other language than their Slavonic patois.

FROM KLAGENFURT TO WAIDISCH AND ZELL, a pleasant excursion. We
diverge to the left from the Loibl road at (7½ M.) *Kirschentheuer* (see above),
and follow the road viâ *Oberferlach* to (4½ M.) *Waidisch* (1810'; Inn), a village in a narrow valley, from which the *Gerlouz* (6040'; fine view) may
easily be ascended in 5 hrs. From Waidisch a rather steep ascent of
1½ hr. brings us to Zell-Pfarr (1475'; *Inn*), beautifully situated in the
centre of the Karawanken Alps (to the N. rises the Sotitsche, to the S. the
Koschuta). A picturesque road leads hence to (1 hr.) *Zell-Freibach* (2810';
Terkl) whence the *Obir* (7024', 4½ hrs.) may be ascended (comp. p. 417).
From this point we may either cross the *Schaida* (3500') to (3½ hrs.) *Eisenkappel* (p. 417), or proceed to the N. through the picturesque gorge of the
Freibach, between the *Hoch-Obir* and *Klein-Obir* on the right, and the *Setitsche* and the *Schwarze Gupf* on the left, to (1½ hr.) *Freibach* (*Inn; 3¼ M.
to the E. is the *Wildenstein Waterfall, p. 418). From Freibach we proceed to the left, viâ *St. Margarethen* and *Unterferlach*, to (3½ hrs.) *Kirschentheuer* (see above).

From Klagenfurt to *Glandorf*, see p. 428.

On leaving Klagenfurt the train crosses the *Lend Canal*. To the left is the old abbey of *Viktring*, now a cloth-factory. In the distance, above the green lower hills, rises the indented chain of the Karawanken. At the (83 M.) *Military Swimming Baths*, the train reaches the bank of the pretty **Wörther See** (1440'), or *Lake of Klagenfurt*, 11 M. long, the N. side of which it skirts.

STEAMBOAT on the Wörther See thrice daily in summer from the Swimming Baths to Maria-Loretto, Maiernigg, Krumpendorf, Reifnitz, Maria-Wörth, Seebad Maria-Wörth, Pörtschach, and Velden. Omnibus and railway from Klagenfurt to the Swimming Baths (see p. 419).

To the left, on a promontory at the mouth of the *Lend Canal* (p. 419), is Prince Rosenberg's château of *Maria-Loretto*, with the baths already mentioned (p. 419). On the S. bank, farther on, lies *Maiernigg*, with its garden-restaurant and baths. To the S. rise the green hills of the *Sattnitz*, which separate the serpentine valley of the Drave (here called the *Rosenthal*) from the plain of Klagenfurt. 85 M. *Krumpendorf* (Inn at the station; Villa Schindler), with baths. 87½ M. *Pritschitz*; opposite, on a rocky promontory on the S. bank, the village of *Maria-Wörth* (Inn on the lake), with an ancient Gothic church. — 90 M. **Pörtschach am See** (**Wahliss's Establishment*, consisting of a hotel and villas, with restaurant, large park, etc.; **Werzer; Villa Lyro; Hôtel am See*), a favourite summer-resort, with lake-baths and a fine view of the mountains. Above Pörtschach, in the midst of wood, is the ruin of *Leonstein*, a charming point of view. The mountains on both banks of the lake become higher and are clothed with dark woods. To the S. rises the conspicuous *Mittagskogel* (7034').

94 M. **Velden** (*Ulbing, with swimming and other baths; **Wrann; Glasser*, at the steamboat-quay, ³/₄ M. from the railway-station; *Pension Buchmayer; Kornhäusl*, etc.; apartments at the *Villa Knapp, Austria*, and others, R. 1½-2 fl.; *Café Moro*), a favourite watering-place, is pleasantly situated at the W. end of the lake.

A beautiful excursion may be taken to the S. to (3 M.) **Rosegg** (1585'; *Inn* by the bridge), with a château and deer-park of Prince Liechtenstein, charmingly situated in the *Rosenthal* (see above), on a peninsula formed by the Drave, and commanding a beautiful prospect. (Park closed when the family is residing here. Enquire beforehand.) — Mountaineers will enjoy the ascent of the **Mittagskogel** (comp. p. 422): from Rosegg viâ *St. Jakob to Rosenbach* (1880'; Inn at the forester's) in 2½ hrs.; thence to the summit in 4 hrs. more. From Rosenbach over the *Rosenbacher* or **Roschiza-Sattel** (5299') to *Assling* (p. 431), 6-7 hrs., an attractive route. — The ascent of the **Sternberg** (2165') from Velden (in 1¼ hr.) or from Lend (in 1 hr.) is also recommended. It commands a delightful *View of the environs of Villach and Klagenfurt, the Karawanken, etc. The church occupies the site of an old castle (refreshments at the sacristan's).

The line quits the lake, traverses a wooded, undulating tract, passes (97 M.) *Lind-Sternberg*, and at (99½ M.) *Föderlach* (*Glasser*) approaches the Drave, which it crosses twice. On a precipitous rock to the right stands the well-preserved castle of *Wernberg*. Farther on, to the N., at the entrance to the Ossiacher Thal, are the picturesque ruins of the castle of *Landskron*. Near Villach the '*Rudolf-bahn*' diverges to the right (R. 76).

104 M. **Villach** (1665'; *Post*, R. & L. 1 fl.; *Hôtel Turmann*, near the station; *Hôtel Mosser*, opposite; *Hohenberger*; *Fischer*, with garden, well spoken of; *Rail. Restaurant*), an old town on the Drave, with 5400 inhab., the junction of the lines to Lienz and Franzensfeste (R. 60), to St. Michael (R. 76), to Laibach (R. 77), and to Udine (R. 78), is picturesquely situated in a broad, fertile basin at the base of the Dobratsch (see below). The Gothic *Parish Church* (15th cent.) contains numerous tombstones of the Khevenhüller, Dietrichstein, and other noble families; fine *View from the tower. The Hans- Gasser-Platz is adorned with a statue of *Gasser*, the sculptor (d. 1868), by Messner.

ENVIRONS (comp. Map, p. 334). At the foot of the Dobratsch, 2 M. to the S.W., lies **Warmbad Villach** (rail. stat., p. 433), with warm sulphur-springs and a good bath-house (*Restaurant). About 2 M. farther to the S., at the mouth of the Gailthal, is *Federaun*, with a ruined château, a shot-tower, and a neglected park (tickets of admission, 20 pf.; opposite the post-office at Villach; visit not recommended). — To the N., on the road to Treffen, rises the *Oswaldberg* (3190'; 1¼ hr.), with a church, commanding a charming view of the Karawanken Alps, Ossiacher Lake, etc. — The ruins of **Landskron** (2200') may also be visited hence, viâ (1 hr.) *St. Andrä* (Schüßmann, with garden), which lies about 1½ M. from the old fortress (see above). Fine view. — Pleasant walk to the S.E. viâ *Proschowitz* (observe finger-posts) or *Maria-Gail* (*Glaser's Restaurant), with its Gothic church, through the *Dobrowawald*, to the (5 M.) **Faaker See** (1840'), a lake with a small island (Rfmts. at the forester's). On a lofty rock, 3 M. farther to the S., rises the picturesque ruin of *Finkenstein* (2705'). — The ascent of the **Mittagskogel** (7035'; 6½-7 hrs.; with guide) is attractive but fatiguing the route leads viâ Maria-Gail and *Faak* to (2½ hrs.) *Latschach* and then by a marked path viâ *Obtschena* to the *Jepica Alp* and the (2½ hrs.) *Berthahütte* (5576'), on the side of the saddle next Carniola; then to the E., over the arête (new path), to the (1½ hr.) top. Panorama less extensive than from the Dobratsch; fine view of the Terglou to the S. — The **Gerlitzen Alp** (6265'), ascended from *Sattendorf* viâ *Ossiachberg* in 4 hrs., commands a view similar to that from the Dobratsch.

From Villach a road leads to the N., viâ *St. Ruprecht*, to (4½ M.) **Treffen** (1790'; *Wallner or Unterwirth), a charmingly situated summer-resort, with a château and park belonging to Count Goess. Beyond Treffen the road leads along the Afritzer Bach, passing *Winklern* and *Einöde*, at the mouth of the Arrlacher-Thal (in which, 2 M. to the right, lies *Arriach*, a summer-resort), to (6 M.) **Afritz** (2350'; *Post*). [From this point we may easily ascend the *Wöllaner Nock* (7020'; 4 hrs.) or the *Mirnock* (6800'; 4¼ hrs.), two attractive points of view. From the latter we may descend to (3 hrs.) Millstatt.] The road continues hence past the *Afritzer See* and the smaller, but more picturesque *Brennsee* to (8½ M.) *Feld* (Müllbock) and thence viâ (3 M.) *Radenthein* (p. 393) and (3 M.) *Döbriach* to (4½ M.) **Millstatt** (p. 336).

The *Dobratsch (7110'), or *Villacher Alpe*, the E. spur of the Gailthal Alps, is one of the most famous points of view among the Eastern Alps, and commands a more extensive prospect than any other peak of the same height and accessibility. Carriage-road (one-horse carr. to Bleiberg 3-4 fl.; two-horse, 6 fl.; omnibus at 5.30 p.m. in 2 hrs., returning at 8.30 a.m.; fare 70 kr.) from Villach viâ *St. Martin* (Gruber), *Vellach*, and *Mitte-wald* (*Tegritz* Inn), and through the wooded *Bleiberg-Graben* to (9 M.) **Bleiberg** (2900'; *Matelitsch*; *Wohlgemuth*), with its extensive lead-mine. A road, steep at places and stony (Rfmts. at a hut halfway), leads hence to the summit in 4 hrs. (horse 6, carr. 18 fl.; the old route through the gorge is a little shorter but more fatiguing). Good walkers should go from Villach (or take the diligence to Mittenwald, 1½ M. from Heiligengeist) to (9 M.) *Heiligengeist* (2920'; °*Winkler*; a drive of 1¾ hr. from Villach; one-horse carr. 4 fl.), whence a pleasant path (red marks), mostly through wood, leads to (1½ hr.) a broader track and (a little farther up) to the Bleiberg road; to the top 2 hrs. more. On the summit are two churches (German and Wend) erected in commemoration of the landslip of 1348 (see below), and the large *Kronprinz-Rudolf-Haus* (°Inn; bed 1-1½ fl.). The °View embraces to the N. the entire range of the Hohe and Niedere Tauern, as far as the Koralpe towards the E.; to the S. are the Karawanken, the Julian Alps with the Terglou, and the Dolomites of S. Tyrol as far as the Marmolada. In the foreground below lie the fertile valleys of the Gail and the Drave, with the lakes of Ossiach, Wörth, and Faak. Traces of an appalling landslip, which overwhelmed ten villages in 1348, and converted the Gailthal for the time into a vast lake, are still observable. — The descent to the Gailthal is made on the S.W. side viâ *Sack* to (3 hrs.) *Nötsch* (see below); the descent on the E. side viâ *Mahrhof* to the (4 hrs.) *Villacher Bad* is not recommended (better by *Heiligengeist*, in 4 hrs., see above).

The Gailthal, as far as Kötschach (55 M.), is a broad, smiling valley, with numerous villages (diligence to Hermagor, 36 M., daily in 5 hrs.; fare 2 fl.). The road diverges to the N.W. at (14 M.) *Thörl-Maglern* (rail. stat.. p. 433), and leads viâ (4¼ M.) *Feistritz* (Inn; ascent hence of the *Osternig*, 6675', viâ the Feistritzer Alpe, in 3½ hrs.; comp. p. 434), beyond which it crosses the Gail, to (1½ M.) *Nötsch* (Isepp; hence to the top of the *Dobratsch*, by a new path viâ *Sack*, in 4 hrs., see above). The road next passes (2 M.) *Emmersdorf* (Bräu) and (3½ M.) *St. Stefan* (but walkers will prefer the route across the Mittelgebirge viâ *St. Georg, Kerschdorf*, and *Tratten*), leaves the Gail beyond *Förolach*, and leads past the pretty *Presseker See* to (7½ M.) **Hermagor** (2010'; °*Post*; *Fleiss*), the principal place in the lower Gailthal, charmingly situated at the mouth of the *Gitschthal*. In the latter, through which a road (p. 336) leads to (5 hrs.) *Greifenburg*, grows the *Wulfenia Carinthiaca*, a beautiful plant with dark blue flowers, found nowhere in Europe except on the slopes of the Gartnerkofel (7210'), which rises to the S.W. of Hermagor (p. 435; ascended viâ *Möderndorf* and the *Kühweger Alp* in 5½-6 hrs., with guide).

The road then follows the left bank of the Gail to *Kirchbach* and (12 M.) *Reissach* (3265'; Inn). About 3 M. to the N. is the small *Reissacher Bad* (3265'), at the S. base of the *Reisskofl* (7772'), which may be ascended in 4 hrs. (very toilsome, but interesting. The most conspicuous of the mountains bounding the Gailthal on the S. is the *Polinigg* (7655'). The road now passes *Grafendorf* and reaches (4½ M.) *Dellach*, near which, on the *Gurina*, interesting remains of Roman and pre-Roman times have been brought to light. Beyond *St. Daniel*, another small watering-place, we next reach (4¼ M.) Kötschach (2325'; °*Rizzi*; *Post*), the principal village in the upper Gailthal, and a summer-resort, prettily situated. About 1½ M. to the S. on the right bank of the Gail, lies *Mauthen* (p. 335). The *Vorhegg* (3420'; to the W.), ascended in 1 hr., affords a fine survey of the Gailthal. — The *Jauken* (7390'), easily ascended in 4½ hrs. with a guide (J. Messer; 2½ fl.), commands an extensive panorama. The marked path ascends, at first through wood, to the (3½ hrs.) *Orsini-Rosenbery Hut* and then past a miner's house to (1¼ hr.) the summit. — From Kötschach viâ *Maria-Luggau* to *Sillian*, see p. 333; over the *Gailberg* to *Oberdrauburg* (diligence daily) and over the *Plöken* to Venetia, see p. 335.

76. From Bruck to Villach.

Comp. Maps, pp. 408, 334.

127½ M. RAILWAY (*Kronprinz-Rudolfbahn*) in 4½-7 hrs.

Bruck, see p. 368. The train diverges to the right from the main line, crosses the *Mur*, and turns to the W. into the narrow Murthal. 7½ M. *Niklasdorf*. It then crosses the Mur to —

10 M. **Leoben** (1745'; *Post; *Mohr; Stadt Wien; Adler), on a peninsula formed by the *Mur*, the centre of the mining and cognate industries of Upper Styria. A miner forms the *Fountain Figure* in the market-place. View from the height 5 min. above the modern *Church of the Redemptorists*, on the Mur. The negotiations between Napoleon and the Austrians preliminary to the Peace of Campo Formio took place at the château of *Göss* (now the property of the Vordernberg Mining Company), ½ hr. to the S. of Leoben, on 18th April, 1797. Near the town are extensive iron-works and coal-mines. — To *Vordernberg*, and over the *Prebühl* to *Eisenerz*, see p. 385.

The train describes a wide circuit round the town, and to the S. of the suburb of *Waasen* stops at the (11 M.) *Rudolfbahn Station*. It then follows the left bank of the Mur (passing *Schloss Göss* on the left, see above) to (18½ M.) **St. Michael** (1905'; *Rail. Restaurant; *Hôtel Purkhart*, opposite the station; *Ahorner*, in the village), at the mouth of the *Liesing-Thal*, the junction for *St. Valentin* (R. 69). (Seats should now be taken on the right side.) — 21½ M. *Kaisersberg*, with a ruined castle, beyond which the Mur is crossed; 28½ M. *St. Lorenzen* (1980'; Ebner; Dietrich). To the left are the spurs of the *Glein Alps*, to the right those of the *Seckau Alps*.

On the left bank of the Mur, 2 M. to the W. of St. Lorenzen, opens the *Kobenz-Thal*, in which, 4 M. from its mouth, lies the village of **Seckau** (2760'; *Kahlbacher*), formerly an episcopal residence, with a handsome abbey-church ("Monument of Duke Charles II. of Styria). Interesting ascent of the *Zinken* (7870'), an excellent point of view: through the *Steinmüller Graben* to the *Jürgbauer* (where the night may be spend if necessary) 2½ hrs., and to the top in 2 hrs. more. Descent to *Mautern*, see p. 389.

33 M. **Knittelfeld** (2115'; *Pissel; Pfinze; Stadt Meran*, at the station), a prettily-situated little town, at the mouth of the *Ingering-Thal*. About 2 M. to the W. lies *Schloss Spielberg* (2300'), commanding a fine view.

EXCURSIONS (guide, *Sim. Lechner*). The *Gleinalpe* (p. 370) may be ascended without difficulty from Knittelfeld in 4½-5 hrs. We follow the high-road to the N. to (1 M.) *Gobernitz*, turn to the right at a finger-post, then (¾ hr.) to the left, where the road divides, to (¾ hr.) *Glein* (Glandler), from which we ascend the ravine of the Glein to the (3 hrs.) *Alpen-Wirthshaus* (see p. 370).

Attractive excursion through the **Ingering-Thal**, viâ (7 M.) *Bischoffeld* (Wegscheider), and past the handsome chateau of *Wasserberg*, to (6 M.) the picturesque little *Ingering-See* (3975'), at the foot of the precipitous **Hoch-Reichart** (7930'). Refreshments at the forester's, 1½ M. on this side of the lake, from which the Reichart may be ascended in 4 hrs. viâ the *Brandstädter Alpe* and the *Brandstädter Thörl* (6615'; pass to the *Liesingthal*), comp. p. 389.

The valley of the Mur now expands to its greatest width. 37½ M. *Zeltweg* (2220'; Inn), with extensive iron-works. On the right bank of the Mur, 3 M. to the S., is the village of *Weisskirchen*; and 4½ M. to the N.W. is *Fohnsdorf*, with extensive coal-mines, some of which are upwards of 800' deep.

42½ M. **Judenburg** (2380'; *Post* or *Krone*, with carriages for hire; *Brand*; *Frank*, with garden; *Dansmeyer's Restaurant*, at the railway-station, with rooms), a very ancient town (4039 inhab.), once a Celtic settlement (*Idunum*, from *Idun*, a high hill), situated on a height on the right bank of the Mur, at the foot of the *Seethal Alps*, has been almost entirely rebuilt since a fire in 1841. In the Platz is a fountain with a large marble basin. Here, too, rises the *Römerthurm*, erected in 1509, with its Gothic portal (fine view from the top; 10 kr.). In front of the *Jesuits' Church* rises a column in memory of the plague, erected in 1717. The interesting *Church of St. Magdalena* in the suburb of that name, dating from the 9th cent., contains fine stained glass and a carved pulpit. The exterior of the 'Post' is adorned with a Jew's head in stone, upwards of 500 years old, which is regarded as the cognisance of the town. Fine view from the *Antagen* on the N. and E. sides of the town; also from the reservoir of the water-works and from the prettily-situated *Calvarienberg*. In the environs are several important iron-rolling mills and scythe-works, as well as numerous ruined castles of the old Styrian nobility. To the S. are the (½ hr.) coal-mines of *Feeberg*.

EXCURSIONS (guides, Paul Jakober and Jos. Unteregger). To the E. (¾ hr.) rise the château and the ruin of *Liechtenstein*, the latter of which was the birth-place of the minstrel Ulrich von Liechtenstein. The *Liechtenstein-Berg* (3395'), above the ruin, affords a fine view (path from the Weyer suburb, with finger-posts). — To the E. (2 M.) is the handsome Gothic pilgrimage-church of *Maria-Buch*, built in 1455. — The Zirbitzkogel (7864'; 6 hrs.), a very fine point, is best ascended via *St. Wolfgang* ('Inn), and thence either to the right via the *Lindevalpe* or to the left via the *Rothhaidenhütte*. The ascent by the *Schmelz*, with the pretty *Winterleitseen*, is more interesting, but more fatiguing. Extensive view of the Styrian and Carinthian Alps from the summit (refuge-hut; tavern in summer). — The **Schafkogel** (5730'), another fine point, is easily ascended: road to (4 M.) *St. Peter*; then to the left through the *Möschitzgraben* to the top in 1½ hr. — The **Rosenkogel** (6312'): drive by the Tauern road in 2 hrs. to *St. Oswald*; ascend thence via the *Sommerthörl* and *St. Loretto* (5965'; Inn) to the top in 2½ hrs. more. — The **Bösenstein** (8035'): drive by the Tauern road in 4½ hrs. via *St. Johann* to *Hohentauern*; thence by a marked path in 4½ hrs. (comp. p. 389).

Roads lead from Judenburg to the N.W., via *Hohentauern*, to (30 M.) *Trieben* (see p. 389); to the S., via *Weisskirchen* and *Obdach*, to (32½ M.) *Wolfsberg* (p. 415; diligence daily in 6 hrs.); to the S.W., over the *Stubalp-Pass* (5055'), to *Köflach* (p. 401).

46 M. *Thalheim*; 51 M. *St. Georgen*. The railway and the river now turn to the S. to (54 M.) **Unzmarkt** (2460'; *Post*), a village on the right bank of the Mur. On the opposite bank is the ruined *Frauenburg*, once the seat of the minstrel Ulrich von Liechtenstein (see above). The train crosses the Mur (fine view to the right, up the valley) and reaches.

58 M. **Scheifling** (2495'; *Post; Ratschiller*).

To *Murau* and *Tamsweg* (diligence daily in 8½ hrs.), see p. 398. — About 4½ M. up the *Wötzer Thal*, which opens at *Niederwölz*, 2¾ M. to the

N.W., lies Oberwölz (2715'; *Klaffensack; Fleischer*), a small town with old churches and the château of *Rothenfels*. Interesting ascent of the Hohenwart (7746'; 6 hrs., with guide): through the *Schöttlgraben* to the (3 hrs.) *Steitererhütten* (4700') and (1/2 hr.) *Lachsenhütte* (picturesquely situated); then past the (1 hr.) *Fischsee* and to the right to the arête and the (1 1/2 hr.) summit, which affords an admirable panorama. — The ascent of the **Schiesseck** (7465'; 3 1/2 hrs.; guide) is also attractive. — The road leads from Oberwölz to the W., over the *Kammersberg* (3595'), to (6 M.) **St. Peter** (2675'; *Fleischer*), on the *Katschbach* (10 M. from station *St. Lambrecht* by the road via *Teufenbach*, *Katsch*, and *Althofen*). The **Greimberg** (8105'; 4 1/2 hrs.; guide), ascended from St. Peter via the *Hartlalpe* and the *Sandkogel*, is a good point of view.

The line now skirts the village in a wide curve, passes the handsome château of *Schrattenberg* with its five towers, and quits the Murthal. 63 M. **St. Lambrecht** (2915'; *Zedlacher*, at the station), on the watershed between the Drave and the Mur. (The village of that name, with its famous Benedictine abbey, lies in the *Tayathal*, 6 M. to the S.W.) — 66 M. **Neumarkt** *(Gragger's Restaurant)*. The village *(Kofler)*, 3/4 M. to the E., pleasantly situated, attracts summer-visitors (apartments in *Schloss Pichl*, 1 M. to the N.).

EXCURSIONS. The ascent of the **Grebenzen** (6135'; 4 hrs., with guide), is easy and attractive. A marked path leads via *Graslupp* and *Zeltschach* to (2 1/2 hrs.) the *Grebenzenhütte* (4595'), whence the summit (wide view) is reached in 1 1/2 hr. more. — The *Zirbitzkogel* (7861'; 5-6 hrs.; guide) is also recommended (see p. 425).

We now pass the ruins of *Forchtenstein* (on the left) and *St. Marein*, and enter the *Klamm*, a defile in which the *Olsa* forms a series of small cascades. On the right, near (71 1/2 M.) the station of **Einöd** (2225'), are the baths of that name (warm alkaline water, a cure for gout). The castle of *Dürnstein*, the traditionary prison of Richard Cœur-de-Lion, situated on the frontier of Styria and Carinthia, guards the entrance to the Olsa-Thal.

76 1/2 M. **Friesach** (2090'; **Priemig*; *Post*; **Mohr*), an old town (1600 inhab.), still surrounded with walls and moats, and commanded by the ruined castles of *Geiersburg*, *Lavant*, and *Petersberg* (interesting; old pictures in the chapel), and the remains of the provostry of *Virgilienberg*, is picturesquely situated on the right bank of the *Metnitz*, and is much frequented in summer. Gothic *Parish Church* of the 15th cent.; *Dominican Church* of the 13th cent., in the transition style. The octagonal fountain in the market was erected in 1563.

A pretty view of the town and its environs may be obtained from the pavilion on the Fischerkogel (about 2300'), 1 3/4 M. from the station.

VIA FLATTNITZ AND ST. LEONHARD TO FELDKIRCHEN, 15-16 hrs., an attractive route. Road (one-horse carr. to Flattnitz 9 fl.) through the *Metnitzthal*, via *Grades*, *Metnitz*, *Mödring* (*Seppmüller), and *Oberhof*, to the (24 M.) **Flattnitz** or **Fladnitz Alp** (4560'), in a beautiful and sheltered situation, and frequented in summer by persons with delicate lungs (*Kottmüller often crowded in summer). — The *Eisenhut* (8010'; 5 hrs.; guide), the highest peak of the *Stangalpen Group*, on the borders of Styria, Carinthia, and Salzburg, may be ascended from Flattnitz; view very striking. Descent to (2 1/2 hrs.) *Turrach*, see p. 398. — A pleasant footpath descends from Flattnitz past the *Heidnerhöhe*, to (3 1/2 hrs.) *Grifen*, whence we may either walk or drive to (9 M.) St. Leonhard (3615'; *Wanner, R. 50-80 kr.).

an Alpine summer-resort, finely situated, commanding a noble prospect of the Karawanken, and to (9 M.) stat. *Feldkirchen* (p. 428; one-horse carr. from St. Leonhard to Feldkirchen 3, two-horse 6 fl.).

79½ M. *Hirt*. At the influx of the Metnitz into the *Gurk*, 1½ M. to the S., lies *Zwischenwässern*, with *Schloss Böckstein*, the summer-residence of the Bishop of Gurk, whose headquarters are at Klagenfurt.

A road leads hence to the W. through the Gurkthal (diligence to *Weitensfeld* daily, 1 fl.), viâ *Strassburg*, to (9 M.) **Gurk** (2070'; *Moser*; *Jernig*), which possesses a fine Romanesque minster of the 11th and 12th centuries. The porch contains several groups in carved wood of the 15th cent.; in the interior, metal-work by Raf. Donner, and in the nuns' choir well-preserved mural paintings of the 13th century. — About 5 M. farther up the valley is the village of *Weitensfeld* (2300'; Post); thence through the *Glödnitzthal* to *Flattnitz* (see above), in 4 hrs.; through the *Gurkthal* to stat. *Feldkirchen* (p. 428) in 6 hrs.

The valley of the Gurk expands. The lofty and fertile plain, with its numerous signs of industry, is called the *Krappfeld*. To the E. is the long crest of the *Saualpe* (see below); to the S. rise the Karawanken and the Terglou. At (83 M.) *Treibach* are extensive iron-works. To the left, on a hill, stands the village of *Althofen*, with an ancient watch-tower. 87 M. *Krappfeld*.

91 M. **Launsdorf** (1695'; *Rail. Restaurant*). The most interesting of the old ancestral castles of the Carinthian nobles which abound in this district is *Hoch-Osterwitz, 2 M. to the S.W. of stat. Launsdorf, the seat of the Khevenhüller family since 1571. This imposing and well-preserved stronghold, on a rock 500' in height, is reached by a winding path hewn in the rock, passing through fourteen turreted gateways, and crossing three drawbridges. The chapel, with its numerous monuments, and the armoury are in good preservation. Fine view from the balcony and the bastions.

The **Magdalenaberg** (3464'; 2 hrs.), to the S. of Launsdorf, which is easily ascended by a marked path, is a still finer point of view. (Roman antiquities found here.) The descent may be made to *Meiselberg* and (2 hrs.) *Zollfeld* (see below). — To the N.W. of Launsdorf (2½ M.), diligence twice daily in ¾ hr.) is **St. Georgen am Längsee** (1800'), with a château of Hr. von Sichel (now a "Hôtel-Pension), prettily situated near the small *Längsee*, well stocked with fish. From St. Georgen, viâ *Tagenbrunn*, with a large ruined castle, to *St. Veit* (see p. 428) 4 M.

From LAUNSDORF TO HÜTTENBERG (18½ M.) railway in 2¼ hrs. The train traverses the *Görtschitzthal*, the principal seat of the Carinthian iron-industry. 4½ M. *Brückl* (to the right of which is *St. Johann am Brückl*, with extensive iron-works); 8½ M. **Eberstein** (*Nussdorfer*), with a château of Count Kristallnigg. (Ascent hence of the *Grosse Saualpe*, 6828', viâ *St. Oswald* in 4½ hrs., attractive.) — 10½ M. *Klein St. Paul*; 13½ M. *Wieting*. From (15½ M.) *Mösel* (Moselwirth) a road leads to the N.E. to (3 M.) **Lölling** (2980'; *Stadtwirth*), with considerable iron-mines, and then through the *Stelzing* and over the *Klippitzthört* (5390') to (15 M.) *St. Leonhard* in the Lavantthal (p. 416). The **Grosse Saualpe** (6828') may be ascended from Lölling direct viâ the *Kirchberger Alpe*, in 3 hrs.; easier, however, viâ (1½ hr.) *Stelzing* (4625'; *Inn), whence we may ascend the *Geierkogl* (6270') in 1½ hr.; we then follow the crest of the Saualpe and proceed viâ the *Forstalpe* (6645'), the *Kienberg* (6710'), and the *Gertrusk* (6686') to the (2 hrs.) *Grosse Saualpe* (6828'). Descent to *Eberstein* (see above) 4 hrs., to *Wolfsberg* 3 hrs., to *St. Andrä* 3½ hrs. — 18½ M. **Hüttenberg** (2515'; *Sacherer*; *Lepuschitz*; *Kompanichütte*, with garden, near the station), the chief village in the Görtschitzthal (1200 inhab.), lies at the base of the *Erzberg*, which yields a large proportion of the iron of Carinthia. A visit to the mines, which pierce the hill on three sides, is interesting. We take the road by *Heft* and *Gossen* to (3 M.) *Knappenberg* (Kutzmann), where the miners and miners' houses are situated. (The traveller may go through the principal shaft, attended by a miner, to the Lölling side of the hill in 25 min.) From **Knappenberg** a road with fine views leads round the hill to *Ober-Semlach* and (3 M.) *Unter-Semlach* (3300'; Inn), where we enjoy a splendid panorama (the whole of the Karawanken chain to the S.); it then descends to (1½ M.) *Lölling* (see above), or past the *Preisenhof* to (3 M.) *Hüttenberg*. — A good path leads from Hüttenberg to the S.W. to the (1¼ hr.) large pilgrimage-church of *Maria-Weitschach* (3780'), a fine point of view.

The train now turns to the W. and enters the valley of the **Glan**. — 95½ M. **Glandorf** (1530'; *Rail. Restaurant*).

FROM GLANDORF TO KLAGENFURT (11 M.), railway in ¾ hr., traversing the Zollfeld, an extensive and at places marshy plain, where many Roman coins and other antiquities have been found. To the left of (3½ M.) *Zollfeld* is the château of *Töltschach*, probably erected on the site of the Roman station, *Virunum*; to the right, on the hill, on the opposite bank of the Glan, rises the castle of *Tanzenberg*. 5½ M. *Maria Saal*, with a pilgrimage-church. Beyond Maria-Saal we soon obtain a view of the long chain of the Karawanken. — 11 M. *Klagenfurt*, see p. 418.

97 M. **St. Veit** (1560'; *Stern*; *Rössl*), an ancient town with 3000 inhab., was the capital of Carinthia and the residence of the dukes down to 1519. A fountain-basin of white marble in the market-place, 30' in diameter, excavated in the Zollfeld, is said to be Roman. Pretty promenades to the *Vitusquelle*, the *Calvarienberg*, and the *Maraunberg*.

Interesting excursion to the N.W., viâ *Ober-Mühlbach*, to (1 hr.) *Schloss Frauenstein* and the (½ hr.) **Kreugerschlösser**, consisting of the picturesque ruins of *Alt-* and *Neu-Kreug*. We may return past the little *Kreuger See* and *Hungerbrunn* to (1½ hr.) St. Veit. — The Schneebauerberg (4405'), to the W., easily ascended viâ *Sörg* in 3½ hrs., commands a wide prospect.

The line follows the marshy valley of the Glan. 100 M. *Lebmach*; 101½ M. *Feistritz-Pulst* (1590'). Pulst, with an old commandery of the Teutonic Order, lies 1¼ M. to the N., at the foot of the ruin of *Liebenfels* (2360'), a fine point of view. To the left rises the ruined castle of *Karlsberg*, with its huge tower; then that of *Hardegg*. — 105 M. *Glanegg*, with another old castle. The train winds through a narrow wooded valley, quits the Glan, which rises a little to the S., crosses a low hill, and enters the broad valley of the *Tiebel*. — 112 M. **Feldkirchen** (1800'; *Rauter*; *Lackenwirth*), a considerable village (10 M. to the N.W. of which are the baths of St. Leonhard, p. 426). On the left are the iron-works of *Buchscheiden*; on the right the loftily situated church of *Tiffen*, near a station of the same name. The line traverses an extensive moor, with numerous hay-sheds, and then at (117½ M.) *Steindorf* approaches the **Ossiacher See** (1600'), a lake 6½ M. in length, on the N. bank of which it skirts the base of the *Gerlitzen-Alp* (p. 422).

Opposite (119 M.) *Ossiach* is the monastery of that name. 123 M. *Sattendorf*, the station for the *Kur-Hôtel Annenheim* (pens. 3 fl.; steamboat in connection with the train; diligence twice daily to

Villach), on the S. bank of the lake, with shady grounds, milk-cure, lake-baths, etc. On a buttress of the *Hunberg*, at the S.W. end of the lake, stands the large ruin of *Landskron* (p. 422). The train crosses the *Treffner Bach* near (125 M.) *St. Ruprecht*, then turns to the S. and describes a wide curve to the S. Station (on the N. side of the town, left bank of the Drave) of —
127½ M. *Villach*, see p. 422.

77. From Laibach to Villach.
Comp. Maps, pp. 408, 334.

81 M. RAILWAY (*Kronprinz-Rudolfbahn*) in 5½-7½ hrs. Provisions should be taken. Views generally to the left.

Laibach, see p. 410. The line traverses the broad plain of the *Sau*, or *Save*, towards the N., and beyond (3½ M.) *Vizmarje* approaches the river, which here forces a passage through a chain of green hills. (Ascent of the *Grosse Gallenberg*, see p. 410.) At (7½ M.) *Zwischenwässern* we cross the *Zeier*, beyond which opens the broad basin of Krainburg, with the Grintouz and other Saunthal Alps on the right and the triple-peaked Terglou on the left. — 12½ M. *Laak*. The little town of **Bischofslaak** (1150′; *Krone*) lies 1½ M. to the W., at the confluence of the Zeier and the Soura.

To TOLMEIN in the Isonzo Valley, to the W., an easy route. Diligence from Bischoflaak daily in 2½ hrs. viâ *Selzach* to (10 M.) *Eisnern* (1500′); walk by (1¼ hr.) *Sattlog* to (1½ hr.) *Zarz* (2680′), and cross the low saddle of *Na Kotscha* to (1¾ hr.) *Podberdo* (1710′; Valentintschitsch, tolerable), in the parish of *Deutschruth*; then descend the picturesque *Bara Valley* (road most of the way) to (15 M.) *Tolmein* (p. 441). — To the N. of ZARZ (see above) an easy route crosses the plateau of the *Jelover Wald* (3970′) to (5 hrs.) *Feistritz* in the Wochein (see p. 430).

18 M. **Krainburg** (1165′; *Elephant*; *Post*), a small town on a hill, at the influx of the *Kanker* into the Sau.

Route hence over the *Loibl* to *Klagenfurt*, see p. 420; over the *Seeberg* to *Kühnsdorf*, see p. 418; the *Saunthal Alps*, see p. 408. — The *St. Margarethenberg* (2145; 1 hr.) and the *Jodociberg* (2760′; 1½ hr.) afford a fine view of the Terglou, the Saunthal Alps, etc.

The valley contracts. 24½ M. *Podnart-Kropp*. The train crosses the Save and enters a tunnel. 30 M. *Radmannsdorf* (1610′), at the union of the *Wurzener* and the *Wocheiner Save*. — 31½ M. **Lees-Veldes** (*Wucherer; Zum Triglav*, outside the village), the station for Veldes and the Wochein.

About 2 M. to the N.E., at the foot of the mountains, lies **Politsch** (1785; *Sturm's Inn*), a favourite summer-resort. Adjoining it, to the E., on the Bogunschitza, is *Vigaun*, with a large prison, whence a picturesque road leads along the hillside to (6 M.) *Neumarktl*, comp. p. 420. The ascent of the **Bogunschitza** (6770′; 4½ hrs., with guide), from Politsch, is recommended to geologists.

From stat. Radmannsdorf a road (diligence from every train in ½ hr., 50 kr.; one-horse carr. 1 fl.) leads to the W., crossing the Save, to (3 M.) **Veldes** (1640′; *Hôtel Mallner; °Louisenbad*, both on the lake; *Erzherzog Sigismund*, or *Petran*, ¾ M. farther on, on the S. bank; *Dane, Poschnik, Jekler*, in the village, ¼ M. from the lake; furnished rooms at *Moschnik's*), a favourite watering-place, charmingly situated on the *Veldeser See* (1570′). On an islet in the lake rises the pilgrimage-church of *St. Ma-*

ria im See. On a precipitous rock on the N. side stands the picturesque
Schloss Veldes (1980'; Restaurant; fine view). At the foot of the castle
is a new bath. Swimming-bath in the lake, adjoining the garden of the
Louisenbad; also two warm swimming-baths. Rikli's 'Naturheilanstalt' is
also much frequented. — A road leads from Veldes to the N., viâ *Unter-
Göriach* to (6 M.) stat. *Jauerburg* (p. 431); but walkers will find it better
to go viâ *Asp* and the little church of *St. Katharina* to the (1½ hr) *Roth-
weiner Waterfall*, and thence viâ *Dobrava* to (1 hr.) Jauerburg.

The VALLEY OF THE WOCHEINER SAVE (or '*Savitza*', little Save) affords
a favourite excursion from Veldes (one-horse carr. to the Wocheiner See
and back 5 fl.; light post-conveyance to Feistritz daily at 10.30 a.m. in
3 hrs., 1 fl.). The road skirts the S. bank of the lake of Veldes, crosses
a low ridge, and near (4¼ M.) the *Wocheiner Vellach* (Slavonic *Bohinska Beta*)
enters the smiling green valley of the Wocheiner Save. On the opposite
bank of the Save rise the cliffs of *Babji Zob* ('woman's tooth', 3704'), with
a fine *Stalactite Cavern* (3 hrs. from Veldes), rendered accessible by the
Austrian Tourist Club. The road continues, viâ *Vellach*, *Neuming*, and
Witnach, to (13 M.) **Feistritz** (1660'; *Post*; *Schoytitz*: *Triglav*), the chief
village in the Wochein, situated in a basin at the junction of the *Feist-
ritzbach* with the Save, with extensive iron-works. The *Fall of the Feistritz*,
3 M. to the S.W., is worth a visit. — The Wocheiner See is 3½ M. from
Feistritz. Beyond *Savitza* the huge Terglou (see below) rises to the right.
On the lake are the church of *St. Johann*, and a *Touristenhaus* (Inn, R. 70 kr.-
1 fl.). The sequestered **Wocheiner See** (1730'; 2¾ M. long, ½ M. broad), resembling the Lake of Hallstatt (p. 98), is enclosed partly by wooded hills and
partly by lofty walls of rock (on the S.W. the jagged *Skerbinja*). Boat to
the chalets at the upper end of the lake (1 hr.), 1-2 pers., there and back
2 fl., each additional person 50 kr. — From the chalets a footpath (the
boatman acts as guide; fee ½ fl.) ascends gradually through meadows to
a bridge over the Savitza, and then more steeply through wood, and
finally by a dilapidated flight of steps to the (1¼ hr.) *Savitza Fall* (2745'),
the picturesque source of the Save. The infant river is precipitated from
an aperture in the rock, 200' in height, into a dark green pool at the
bottom of a narrow ravine enclosed by huge perpendicular cliffs. — PASSES
(guides, Peter Logar, Jak. Preitner, and Urb. Mencinger). From Feistritz
viâ the *Tschernagora Alp* to the (2½ hrs.) *Mallner Refuge Hut* (4755'), and
thence to (1¼ hr.) the top of the **Schwarzenberg** (*Cerna Prst*, 6050'), an
admirable point of view (panorama by Siegl), descending through the
German oasis of (2 hrs.) *Deutschruth* (Inn), to (4 hrs.) *Tolmein* (p. 441), a
tolerably easy route. — An easier route (bridle-path), also attractive,
crosses the **Baza** (pron. Badja) **Pass** (guide convenient, to Podbordo 2½ fl.):
from Feistritz through the *Jelower Wald* to the pass 2½ hrs., *Podbordo*
(p. 429) 1¼ hr., *Grahovo* 2½ hrs.; thence a road to (9 M.; carr. with one
horse 3 fl.) Tolmein. — From the W. end of the Wocheiner See over the
Skerbinja-Joch (6240') to Tolmein 8-9 hrs., fatiguing but interesting. The
Kuk (6844'), to the W. of the pass, may be ascended thence without trouble
in ¾ hr.; view similar to that from the Schwarzenberg.

The ascent of the *Terglou or *Triglav*, the highest peak of the Julian
Alps, is fit for experts only, with trustworthy guides. The usual starting-
point is *Mitterdorf* (2040'; Inn, poor; Lor. Schest, Jak. Jeller, good guides),
a village 3½ M. to the N. of Feistritz, or from *Althammer* (1790'; quarters
at the manager's), 4½ M. to the W. From both of these points a good
path, steep only at places, ascends in 4½ hrs. to the *Belopolje Alp* (5130')
where good drinking-water is to be had, and in 2 hrs. more to the *Maria-
Theresien-Schutzhaus* (7890'), built by the Austrian Tourist Club at the
foot of the Little Terglou, where the night is spent. From this point
the ascent leads over loose stones and debris and through a narrow fissure
('*Gate of the Terglou*') to the (1 hr.) summit of the *Little Terglou* (8990').
Hence a narrow ridge, about 80 yds. long (suitable only for those with
steady heads) leads to the foot of the *Great Terglou*, beyond which we
ascend the arête to the E., and scale the (¾ hr.) highest summit by a steep
but of late much improved path (iron stanchions, steps, etc.). The view,
one of the most sublime among the Alps, embraces a large portion

of the Adriatic (panorama by Fernhart). — The ascent of the Terglou from the N. is shorter. A new path ascends from *Moistrana* (see below) through the *Kothhal*, to (4½-5 hrs.) the *Deschmannhütte* (7220'), which is attractively situated on the verge of the large 'Doline' (funnel) of *Pokel*. Thence the summit is reached (by those free from giddiness) in 1½-2 hrs. — The *Urbanova* (7525'; ½ hr.), *Krederca* (8065'; 1 hr.), *Rjovina* (8315'; 1½ hr.), and *Cmir* (7845'; 1½ hr.) may also be conveniently ascended from the Deschmannhütte. — Mountaineers are recommended to descend past the **Terglou Lakes** to the *Wocheiner See* (able guide necessary). After a weary walk of 4 hrs. from the Maria-Theresia Hut, over the grand plateau of *Hribarze* (to the right the *Kanianz*, 8430'), we reach the *Gross-See*, the largest and finest of these lakes. We then descend by a somewhat better path to the (1½ hr.) *Doppelsee*, where another refuge has been built by the Austrian Tourists' Club (*Erzherzog Franz-Ferdinand-Schutzhaus*, 5750'), and the (1 hr.) sombre *²Schwarzsee* (3940'), embosomed in wood; then through wood to the (1 hr.) brink of the *Komarza*, an almost perpendicular precipice, about 2000' high (grand view), which we descend by a good path, recently widened (to the left is a wire-rope tramway, 850 yds long, used for transporting timber). In 1½ hr. we reach the path leading from the Wocheiner See to the Savitza Fall (see above). — Those who wish to visit the lakes without ascending the Terglou should start from the *Batopolje Alp* (p. 430), the ascent from the Wocheiner See being long and wearisome.

MOISTRANA (see below) is reached from the Wochein in 10-11 hrs., by a rugged path crossing the **Kerma Sattel** (6645'), between the Terglou and Drassberg, and traversing the *Kerma-Thal*, which opens into the Rothwein Valley (see p. 430) about 1 hr. to the S. of Moistrana. This route is also recommended for the descent of the Terglou; there is a spring of good water on the left slope, a little beyond the head of the pass.

The train approaches the S. base of the *Karawanken Mts.*, of which the *Stou* is the most conspicuous. To the left is the mouth of the *Radovna*, or *Rothweinbach*. The valley contracts. —
38½ M. **Jauerburg** (1855'; *Kolb*), at the mouth of the *Jauornik*.

The shortest ascent of the **Stou** (7346') is made from Jauerburg (5 hrs., with guide, comp. p. 420).⁴ We follow the road by *Karnervellach* to the (7½ M.) *Valvasor-Hütte* (4265'), formerly a miners' house, fitted up by the Austrian Tourist Club, and thence ascend viâ the *Schäferhütte* and the *Kleine Stou* to the (3 hrs.) summit. The descent may be made to the *Bodenthal* or to the *Bärenthal*, see p. 420. A road leads to the S. from Jauerburg viâ *Unter-Göriach* to (6 M.) *Veldes*. Viâ *Dobrava* to the *²Rothweiner Fall*, see p. 430.

40½ M. *Assling* (Post); 46 M. **Lengenfeld** (2090'; *Jansa*), at the foot of the *Mittagskogel* (p. 422). On the opposite bank of the Save lies *Moistrana* (Schmerz), at the mouth of the *Urata Valley*, which stretches hence to the Terglou.

The '**Urata Valley**, or valley of the *Feistritz* (*Bistritza*), is worthy of a visit. A good road (suitable for driving) leads from Moistrana on the left bank of the brook to the (3½ M.) *²Peristchnik Fall*, a picturesquely-situated cascade, behind which the visitor can pass. In 2 hrs. more we reach the imposing head of the valley, on the S.E. side of which the huge Terglou rises precipitously. A rugged route leads from the head of the valley over the **Luknia Pass** (5835') into the valleys of the *Sadenza* and *Isonzo* (to *Flitsch* 9-10 hrs.; guide 6 fl.). — Through the wide opening to the S. of Moistrana a cart-track leads to (2½ M.) *Ober-Rothwein*, at the mouth of the *Kerma-Thal* (see above), and then through the *Radoina* or *Rothwein Valley* to *Göriach* and (8 M.) *Veldes* (p. 430). — For travellers from the N., Moistrana (where several of the guides speak German) is the best starting-point for the ascent of the **Terglou** (see above): through the *Kermathal* and over the *Kerma Pass* to the *Terglou Hut* 6 hrs., and to the top 1¾ hr. more. Guides. Gregor Legat of Lengenfeld, Joh. Klauenik, nicknamed 'Simenz', Simon Pinter, and F. Skumauc of Moistrana.

54 M. **Kronau** (2665'; *Urbani*), at the mouth of the picturesque *Pischenza Valley*; in the background rise the *Prisanig* and *Razor*.

OVER THE VERSCHITZ-SATTEL TO FLITSCH (to the Baumbachhütte 4½-5 hrs., to Flitsch 9-10 hrs.; guide 5 fl.), the easiest and most picturesque approach to the Valley of the Isonzo. A tolerable path ascends the pastures of the Pischenza Valley to its (1½ hr.) grand termination, and then mounts rapidly to the (1½ hr.) **Verschitz-Sattel** (*Moistroka Pass*, 5300'), between the *Moistroka* (7705'; ascended from the pass in 2½ hrs., easy and attractive) on the right and the *Prisanig* on the left (6382'; a good point of view, ascended from the pass in 3 hrs., somewhat fatiguing). Descent to (1 hr.) the *Trenta Valley* (interesting excursion from the first houses to the *Source of the Isonzo*, in a rocky cleft at the foot of the *Travnik*, ¾ M. to the W.) and (½ hr.) the church of *St. Maria* or *Trenta* (2455'; primitive inn; quarters at the curé's or at the huntsman's; guide, Anton Tozbar). We next descend to (½ hr.) *Loog*, at the influx of the *Sadenza* into the Isonzo (near the *Baumbachhütte*, p. 442) and through a rocky gorge of the Isonzo to (2½ hrs.) *Sotscha* (1560'; poor inn), whence the *Åern* (p. 441) may be ascended (6 hrs.) viâ the *Lepenja-Thal*. Thence through a desolate but imposing valley, with the Grintouz and Saurüssel on the N., to (2 hrs.) *Flitsch* (p. 442).

From *Wurzen* (*Post), 2 M. above Kronau, a road crosses the *Wurzen-Sattel* (3515') to (15 M.) *Villach* (p. 422).

About halfway between Wurzen and Ratschach the *Save* (*Wurzener Sau*) flows out of a morass. The source of the river (3945') is in the wild *Planitza Valley*, which opens opposite; it emerges from an aperture in the rock, and falls from a height of 390' in considerable volume. It then pursues a subterranean course for some distance, and re-appears at Ratschach. Interesting excursion from Ratschach station, there and back in 5 hrs.

59 M. **Ratschach-Weissenfels** (2850'), on the watershed between the Save and the Drave. The village of *Ratschach* (Kirchmaier) lies 1½ M. to the E., and *Weissenfels* (2590'; *Post; Tourists' Inn, near the Schloss-Park), 2 M. to the W.

The *Schlossberg* (4010'; 1 hr.) at Weissenfels, on which is a ruined castle, commands a fine view of the Carinthian and Carnian Alps, the Gailthal, Kanalthal, etc.

Charming excursion to the two picturesque ***Weissenfels Lakes** (3060'; ¾ hr. from the station or from the village of Weissenfels; guide 60 kr.). Leaving the Post Inn at Weissenfels, we ascend the valley to the (¼ M.) smelting-works of Hr. Neiss (Restaurant) turn to the right and follow the road which passes below the railway and mounts to the left along the stream. The best view of the magnificent head of the valley, with the towering Manhart and the rocky spurs diverging from it, is obtained from the *Rudolfsfelsen*, between the two lakes. Close to the base of the Manhart, ¾ hr. farther up the valley, lies the *See-Alpe* (Dairy, whey). — The ascent of the *Manhart* (8786') from this side, across the *Lahnscharte* is laborious (5-6 hrs.; guide, Kirchmaier of Ratschach); it is easier from *Raibl* (p. 443).

Beyond the industrial village of *Weissenfels*, which it passes on the right, the train crosses the *Schwarzenbach*, the *Weissenbach*, the frontier of Carniola and Carinthia (lofty viaduct), and the deep ravine of the *Schlitza* (bridge 160' high). 64 M. *Tarvis*, and thence to (81 M.) *Villach*, see p. 433.

78. From Villach to Udine. Pontebba Railway.
Comp. Map., p. 334.

81 M. RAILWAY. Express in 4 hrs.; ordinary trains in 6 hrs. The *Pontebba Line*, forming the continuation of the Rudolfbahn from Villach to Pontafel, affords a shorter route (by 91 M.) between Vienna and Venice than the line viâ Nabresina and Cormons (express from Vienna to Venice in 16½ hrs.; fares 84 fr. 45, 61 fr. 95 c.). In the wild grandeur of the scenery traversed and in boldness of engineering, particularly between Pontebba and Resiutta, this line surpasses all the other Alpine railways.

Villach, see p. 422. Skirting the town, the train runs towards the S. and crosses the *Drave* by a handsome iron bridge. On the right bank lies the goods-station of the Rudolfbahn. 2½ M. *Bad-Villach* (p. 422). Crossing the *Gail*, we next reach (5½ M.) *Firnitz* (1660′), opposite *Federaun*, with its lofty shot-tower (p. 422). On the left diverges the road over the *Wurzen* (p. 432). 10½ M. *Arnoldstein* (Post). To the right rises the long Dobratsch, on which marks of the great landslip of 1348 are still traceable. The train crosses the *Gailitz (Schlitza)*. 14 M. *Thörl-Maglern* (Strasshof; Lufthof), the station for the *Gailthal* (p. 423). The train runs high up on the left side of the deep valley of the Gailitz, passes through two tunnels, and crosses the *Wagenbach* to (17½ M.) *Tarvis*, the junction of the Laibach Railway (see R. 77).

Tarvis (2410′; *Railway Hotel & Restaurant*, with fine view, R. 1½ fl.; *Filafer*, unpretending), a large and finely-situated village, and a summer-resort, consists of *Unter-Tarvis* (Teppan), in the valley, ½ M. from the station, and *Ober-Tarvis* (2465′; *Hôtel Schnablegger*; *Gelbfus*, with garden and fine view), on the hillside, ¾ M. farther distant, where the ordinary passenger-trains also stop (see p. 434).

EXCURSIONS. To the *Graf-Carl-Steig* (there and back ¾-1 hr.). Above the railway-bridge (5 min. from the station) a path descends to a wooden bridge over the *Schlitza*, and ascends on the left bank of the wild and picturesque gorge, rendered accessible by wooden bridges and steps in the rock. It then passes under the imposing railway-bridge, where a stone bears an inscription to Count Carl Arco-Zinneberg, in memory of whom the path was constructed to the 'Arco Ruhe'. From this point we return by the same route (the more convenient) or through wood to the *Greutersteg* over the Schlitza, and on the left bank by a steep ascent to the road (fine view) and station (to the left).

A picturesque walk leads to the *Bartolograben* (2½ hrs. from Ober-Tarvis and back); from the farther end an attractive pass crosses the *Bartolo Wiesen* (highest point, 3894′) to *Feistritz* in the Gailthal (interesting gorge and cliffs), whence we may return to (5-6 hrs.; guide 2 fl.) Tarvis viâ Thörl (p. 423). — The **Göriacher Alm** (5500′), which affords a remarkably picturesque view, is easily reached from Tarvis in 3½ hrs. (guide, 2 fl., unnecessary), viâ *Goggau*, by a path running mostly through wood. — A beautiful excursion may be taken in the **Römerthal**, over the *Grenter Plateau* to the *Karnitza*, at the striking head of the valley (5 hrs. there and back; guide 1 fl. 20 kr.). The route over the *Schutzhaus-Scharte* to the (5-6 hrs.) *Mankart-Schutzhaus*, is fit only for adepts (p. 443). — To the *Kaltwasserthal* and across the *Braschnik-Sattel* or *Karnitza-Sattel* to the *Seisera*, see p. 434.

The *Luschariberg* (see below) is frequently ascended from Tarvis: take the Saifnitz road to the W. to the (1½ M.) stone angel (p. 434); then ascend to the left.

From Tarvis to *Raibl* (one-horse carr. 2 fl., to the lake 3 fl., two-horse 4 and 6 fl.; to Predil one-horse carr. 4, two-horse 6 fl.), see p. 443; to the *Weissenfels Lakes* (one-horse carr. 2, two-horse 5 fl.), see p. 432; to *Pontebba* and *Chiusaforte* (one-horse carr. 8, two-horse 12 fl.), see p. 435. Carriages at Tarvis station.

The train runs to the W., passing Unter-Tarvis, to (19½ M.) *Ober-Tarvis*, and ascends (with the *Luschariberg* on the left, and the Mangart behind) to (22½ M.) **Saifnitz** (2615'; *Ehrlich*), on the watershed between the Black Sea and the Adriatic.

The *Luschariberg or Heilige Berg* (5880'), the most frequented pilgrimage-resort in Carinthia, is generally ascended from Saifnitz (2½ hrs.; guide, 1 fl. 60 kr., unnecessary; horse 4 fl.). We follow the Tarvis road to a (½ M.) stone angel, ascend the pilgrims' path to the right, through the *Luscharigraben*, to the (1 hr.) *Annabründl*, and mount to the (¾ hr.) *Luschariatpe* and the (½ hr.) pilgrimage-church (*Inn*, adjacent). Extensive *View a little to the S. of the summit (panorama to be had at Tarvis, 30 kr.). — A shorter and pleasanter ascent is by the so-called *Steinweg*, on the wooded N.W. slope (to the church 2 hrs.). Descent on a grass-sledge in 20 min. (1 fl.; safe enough, but not pleasant). Descent to *Kaltwasser* and *Raibl*, see p. 443.

The *Seisera is a most interesting valley, one of the grandest among the Dolomites. Road to (3 M.) *Wolfsbach* (two inns; guides Jos. Kandutsch and Jos. Keil); then an Alpine track to the (1½ hr.) *Seisera* or *Wolfsbach Alpe* (3340'), grandly situated (Wischberg, Bulitzen, Bramkofel, Köpfach, Mittagskofel). From the *Spranja*, the head of the Seisera Valley, a fatiguing route crosses the *Bärenlahnscharte* (called *Moserscharte* on the Austrian Ordnance Map; 6962'), between the *Cregnedul* and the *Kastreinspitze*, to the *Wischberghütte* and (3 hrs.) *Raibl* (see p. 443; guide 5 fl.; including ascent of the Wischberg, 6 fl.). On the W. side of the pass is a steep slope of snow (35-50°), where steps must be cut. — From Wolfsbach through the *Saitelgraben* and across the *Braschnik-Sattel*, or through the *Zapraha-Thal* and across the *Karnitza-Sattel* to *Kaltwasser* and *Raibl* or *Tarvis* (6-7 hrs.; guide 3 fl.), see p. 443. We then descend by the *Fischbach-Alpe* (p. 443) to Raibl. Ascent of the *Wischberg*, see p. 443. — From the Seisera, to the W., an easy route crosses the *Somdegna Pass* (4920'), between the Köpfach and the Mittagskofel, to the *Dognagraben* (with the huge precipices of the Bramkofel and the Cimone on the left) and (7 hrs. from Wolfsbach) stat. *Dogna* in the Fella Valley (see p. 435).

The train gradually descends on the bank of the *Fella*, which rises a little to the N., past the rock-strewn mouth of the *Wolfsbach-Graben* (splendid view, with the jagged Wischberg in the background), to (26 M.) **Uggowitz** (2580'; *Ehrlich; Kandutsch*).

Excursions (guide, *Blasius Errath*). A path, steep at first, ascends to the N. through the *Uggwea-Thal* to the extensive **Uggowitzer Alpe**, with its numerous chalets. (To the *Hintere Alpe*, 3060', 2½ hrs.) The **Osternig** (6078'), a very fine point of view, may easily be ascended thence, via the *Feistritzer Alpe* (4860'; with ten beds), in 3 hrs. (guide from Uggowitz 3 fl.). Descent from the inn to *Feistritz* or *Vorderberg* in the Gailthal, 3 hrs.

The train crosses the Uggowitz brook, passes the picturesque *Fort Malborget*, situated on a rocky barrier which intersects nearly the whole valley (with a monument at its base, in memory of the heroic defence of the fort by Capt. Hensel in 1809), and then crosses the Fella to (28 M.) **Malborget** (2365'). The large village of that name (*"Schnablegger; Holaky; Rumpler*) lies on the opposite bank.

Excursions (guide, *Franz Moschik*). The **Mittagskofel** (*Jos di Mezzanotte*, 6800'), a fine point of view, is ascended without difficulty through the *Rankgraben* in 4½ hrs. (guide 3 fl.). — Over the Lussnitzer Alp to

Dogna (9 hrs.; guide 4 fl.), a very attractive tour. We proceed through the *Granuda Graben* to the *Granuda-Alp*, *Lusnitzer Alp*, and (5 hrs.) *Dantsche Alp* (4850') to the E. of the *Lipnik* (6405'); and then descend via the chalets of *Bieliga* and *Chiout* to (4 hrs.) *Dogna* (see below). — The ascent of the **Poludnig** (6568'; 4½ hrs.; guide 3 fl.) is easy and attractive. The route leads through the *Malborgetgraben* to the (1½ hr.) *Tschurtschele-Alp* (3620'), then either to the left across the *Gaisrücken* (5780') or to the right through the *Kesselwald*, to the (3 hrs.) summit, which commands an extensive view. Descent on the N.W. side to the *Eggeralpe* (4590'), with its little lake, thence to the N. to *Möderndorf* and *Hermagor* (p. 423), or to the S., through the Malborgetgraben back to Malborget.

The train threads its way through a narrow rocky valley. On the right rise the precipices of the *Guggberg* and the *Schinoutz*, on the left those of the *Lipnik*. 32½ M. *Lusnitz* (2070'), with a small sulphur-bath. The train crosses the Fella and is carried along its right bank by means of cuttings in the rock and embankments of masonry. Before passing *Leopoldskirchen* (on the left) the line crosses the wild *Planja-Graben* by means of a vaulted cutting. It then crosses the *Fickergraben*, which descends from the Schinoutz, and the rapid *Vogetbach*, and reaches —

38 M. **Pontafel** (1875'; *Rail. Restaurant;* in the village, *Hôtel Bahnhof*, *Post*), the Austrian frontier-station, splendidly situated (custom-house examination for travellers leaving Italy).

A tolerable track leads to the N. through the *Bombaschgraben* to the (3¼ hrs.) *Nassfeld* (5000'; refuge-hut), whence the **Rosskofel** (7330'; 4 hrs.; guide 5 fl.) may be ascended by the *Tresdorfer Alm* and the *Rudniker Sattel* (splendid view). Descent from the Rudniker Sattel on the W. past the *Troghütte* and *Casarotta* to the *Confingraben*, and along the Pontebbana to Pontafel, 4½-5 hrs. — The *Gartnerkofel* (7210'; comp. p. 423) is ascended either from the Nassfeld via the *Watschiger Alm* in 2½ hrs.; or from the Bombaschgraben via the *Kronalp* and the *Garnitzen-Alp* (5½ hrs. from Pontafel to the top). Guides, Ant. Gitschthaler and Martin Troier of Pontafel.

The train crosses the *Pontebbana*, the frontier between Austria and Italy, and reaches —

38½ M. **Pontebba** (*Rail. Restaurant;* Ital. custom-house), a village of quite Italian character. Interesting carved altar in the old church.

The construction of the line from Pontebba through the wild, rocky ravine of the Fella (*Valle del Ferro*) to Chiusaforte was attended with extraordinary difficulties, necessitating an almost uninterrupted series of rock-cuttings, tunnels, huge bridges, and imposing viaducts. (Between Pontebba and stat. La Carnia, a distance of 17½ M., there are 24 tunnels.) The traveller who takes an interest in the structural features of the line should walk (2¼ hrs.) or drive to Chiusaforte (one-horse carr. in 1¼ hr.; there and back 3 fl.), or, if time be limited, descend the valley from Pontebba to (1 hr.) the picturesquely situated hamlet of *Pietra Tagliata*. The train now descends rapidly on the right bank of the Fella, and crosses it at *Ponte di Muro* by means of an iron bridge, 158 yds. long, 131' high, borne by four huge buttresses. 43 M. *Dogna* (1520';

the village lies on the opposite bank), at the mouth of the *Canale di Dogna* or valley of the Dogna, at the head of which, towards the E., rises the grand pyramid of the *Bramkofel* (p. 443). The train crosses the boisterous Dogna by a lofty bridge of four arches, skirts the slopes of the *Col della Baita* by means of rock-cuttings and galleries, traverses several viaducts, and again crosses the Fella.

46 M. **Chiusaforte** (1280'; **Albergo alla Stazione*, with garden and staircase to the station; *Fratelli Martino*), below which, on the left, opens the wild *Raccolana Valley* (p. 443), with the peaks of the Mte. Kaniu in the background (p. 442). The floor of the valley of the Fella is bestrewn with rocky debris for a long distance. The train skirts the slopes of the right bank, above the high-road, and at *Peraria* crosses the Fella for the last time, by a bridge 184 yds. in length. We next cross the *Resia* to —

51 M. **Resiutta** (1035'). The village (Bräuhaus; Alb. Morandini), with its two churches, lies on the opposite bank, at the mouth of the *Resia Valley*, which ascends towards the E. to the Mte. Kaniu. 53 M. **Moggio** (970'). The village lies opposite, on the N. side of the Fella valley, at the mouth of the *Val di Moggio*.

The valley of the Fella expands, and its rock-strewn floor is intersected with numerous water-courses. — 56 M. **Stazione per la Carnia** (850'; *Inn* at the station).

From this station (diligence to Tolmezzo from each train, 1 fr.) a post-road leads to the W., through the broad *Val Tagliamento*, viâ *Amaro*, to (7 M.) **Tolmezzo** (1085'; *Leone Bianco*, indifferent), near the influx of the *But* into the Tagliamento. (Route through the valley of the But or *Valle di S. Pietro* to *Paluzza*, and over the *Plöken* to *Kötschach*, see p. 335.) About 3½ M. above Tolmezzo lies *Villa Santina* (1195'; Inn), where the valley of the Tagliamento divides. Through the N. arm, the *Canal di Gorto*, watered by the *Degano*, a carriage-road (diligence from Tolmezzo, daily at 1 p.m., 1½ fr.) leads viâ *Ovaro* to (9 M.) *Comeglians*, whence it is continued by a cart-track to (4 M.) *Rigolato* and (1½ M.) **Forni Avoltri** (2880'; tolerable inn), beautifully situated at the N. base of *Mte. Tuglia*. Thence to *Sappada*, see p. 352. A fine route towards the N. crosses the *Veranisjoch* and *Hochalpeljoch* (7210') to (7 hrs.) *St. Lorenzen* in the *Gailthal* (comp. p. 334; ascent of the *Paralba* from the pass, 1½ hr., easy and very attractive). Another fine route leads to the N.E. over the *Wolayer Joch* (6550'), and past the *Wolayer-See*, to the (6 hrs.) *Plöken* (p. 335).

The prolongation of the valley of the Tagliamento towards the W., above Villa Santina, is called the *Canal di Socchieve*. A road leads by *Socchieve* to (7½ M.) **Ampezzo di Carnia** (1866'; *Colomba*), the capital of the valley, on the *Lumiei*. (Post-conveyance from Tolmezzo to Ampezzo daily, 1½ fr.) The road next leads viâ (9 M.) *Forno di Sotto* to (6 M.) *Forno di Sopra* or *Vico* (3265'; Inn), and crosses the Mauria Pass (4305'), between *Mte. Mieron* and *Mte. Stinzoi*, to (9 M.) *Lorenzago*. It then descends the *Val Cadore*, crosses the Piave at (2 M.) *Pelos*, and leads to the left viâ *Lozzo* to (9 M.) *Pieve di Cadore* (p. 351). — To the N.W. of Ampezzo, in the upper part of the *Val Lumiei*, lie the sequestered villages of **Sauris** (*Sauris di Sotto*, 3955'; *Sauris di Sopra*, 4140'), which, like Sappada (p. 352), are inhabited by Germans. From Ampezzo over the *Mte. Pura* (4730') to Sauris di Sopra 5 hrs.; thence a bridle-path across the *Col di Razzo* (5745') to (2 hrs.) *Campo* in the upper part of the *Val Frisone*. From Campo we may either descend the valley northwards to (2½ hrs.) *S. Stefano* in the *Val Comelico* (p. 352) or proceed to the W. viâ *Mte. Doranu* to *Vigo* and (3½ hrs.) *Pelos*.

A little lower down, in the midst of an extensive plain, the Fella falls into the *Tagliamento*. We then cross the *Venzonazza* to —
59 M. **Venzone** (755'), an old walled town on the Tagliamento. The train crosses the marshy *Rughi Bianchi* by an imposing viaduct of 55 arches, 860 yds. in length, and quits the Tagliamento, which descends towards the S.W. to the Adriatic. (A direct line through the Tagliamento Valley to *Portogruaro* and Venice is being built.) 62½ M. *Gemona-Ospedaletto*; 66 M. *Magnano-Arteyna*; 69 M. *Tarcento*; 71½ M. *Tricesimo*; 75 M. *Reana del Rojale*.

81 M. **Udine** (*Italia; Croce di Malta, etc.), see *Baedeker's N. Italy*.

79. Trieste and Environs.

Railway Station (Pl. a, B, 2), a handsome edifice about 1 M. to the N. of the centre of the town. *Hotel Omnibuses* 30-40 kr.; *Cab* 50, with two horses 1 fl. 20 kr. (from midnight to 6 a.m. 80 or 1 fl. 60 kr.). Each box 10-15 kr.; small packages free. — The new '*Rivabahn*', 1½ M. in length, connects the principal station with the *Stazione S. Andrea* (Pl. B. 7), the terminus of the line Trieste-Herpelje-Pola (p. 444).

Hotels. *HÔTEL DE LA VILLE (Pl. a; C, 4), Riva Carciotti 3, on the quay, R. 1½-5 fl., L. & A. 70 kr., D. 2 fl.; *HÔTEL DELORME (Pl. b; C, 4), Via al Teatro 2, opposite the Exchange, R. 1½-2 fl., L. & A. 60 kr.; EUROPA (Pl. c; C, 3), Piazza della Caserma, ¼ M. from the station, R. 1 fl. 70, L. & A. 40 kr., with café; AQUILA NERA (Pl. d; C, 4), Via S. Spiridione 2, R. & L. 1 fl. 20 kr., with good restaurant; STADT WIEN (*Villa di Vienna*), Via S. Nicolo 11. — *Hôtel Garni*, Piazza Grande 5, with baths, R. 1-3 fl. — The *Sardine, Branzino, Tonina*, and *Barbone* are good sea-fish. *Prosecco* is a half-effervescing wine of the country, *Refosco*, a very dark sweet wine; the ordinary wines are *Terrano* and *Istriano*, both dark red, usually drunk mixed with water.

Cafés. *Litke and *Degli Specchi*, Piazza Grande; *Oriental*, in the Lloyd buildings, opposite the Tergesteum; *Vecchio Tommaso*, near the Hôtel de la Ville; *Tergesteo* and *Teatro*, in the Tergesteum, Piazza del Teatro; *Stella Polare*, *Caffè Adriatico*, near the post-office. — **Restaurants.** *Puntigamer Bierhalle*, Via S. Nicolo 5 (better restaurant on the first floor); *Steinfelder Bierhalle*, Piazza della Borsa 12; *Pilsener Bierhalle*, opposite the post-office; *Berger*, Via S. Nicolo 15; *Belvedere*, in the old town, at the foot of the castle (approached by the Vicolo S. Chiara), with fine view from the garden. — **Osterie** in the Italian style: *All' Adriatico*, Via di Vienna; *Bissaldi*, Canal Grande, etc.

Cabs ('*Broughams*'). From the station to the town, see above; from the town to the station 40 or 80 kr. — Per ¼ hr., one-horse 30, two-horse 45 kr., ½ hr. 50 or 80 kr., ¾ hr. 75 kr. or 1 fl. 10 kr., 1 hr. 1 fl. or 1 fl. 10 kr., each additional ¼ hr. 20 or 30 kr., luggage 15 kr. Between 9 p.m. and 6 p.m. 10 kr. extra per ¼ hr.

Tramway from the station, along the harbour, past the Tergesteum, and through the Corso and the Corsia Stadion to the Giardino Pubblico, the Boschetto, and the Campo Marzo (fare 5-10 kr.).

Porters. Luggage not exceeding 110 lbs., within the city, 20 kr.

Steamboats. To Muggia, and to Capo d'Istria and Pirano several times daily; local steamers to Parenzo, Rovigno, and Pola daily. Steamers of the 'Austrian Lloyd' to Venice thrice, to Dalmatia via Istria thrice, to Fiume twice weekly; to Greece, Constantinople, and the Levant once weekly; direct to Alexandria every Friday; to Bombay monthly.

Post Office (Pl. 12; C, D, 3), in the Via Caserma. — **Telegraph Office** (Pl. 13; C, 3), Via della Dogana.

Baths. Warm at *Oesterreicher's*, Via Lazzaretto Vecchio 7, near the artillery arsenal, and at the *Hôtel de la Ville*, the *Hôtel Garni*, etc. — Vapour Baths at *Rikli's*, in the street leading to the Boschetto. — Sea-baths at the *Bagno Maria*, opposite the Hôtel de la Ville (reserved for ladies in the afternoon); *Bagno Excelsior*, in *Barcola*. Ferry to or from the military-baths 3 kr. each (a single person 6 kr.); small steamer to Barcola, every hour from the Lloyd Buildings; omnibus from the station every 5 minutes. Boats 1-1½ fl. '*per ora*'.

Theatres. *Teatro Comunale* (Pl. C, 4), opposite the Tergesteum; *Teatro Filodrammatico* (Pl. D, 4), French and German plays sometimes performed; *Armonia* (Pl D, 4), dramas and operas; *Politeama Rossetti*, on the Acquedotto (Pl. E, 3).

British Consul, *Sir Richard Burton*, Via Nuova 8 (office-hours 10 a.m.-1 p.m.). — **American Consul,** *H. W. Gilbert, Esq.*

English Church Service in the Via S. Michele at 11 a.m. and 6 p.m.

Trieste, the *Tergeste* of the Romans, and the principal seaport of Austria, with 72,000 (including the suburbs 133,000, including the commune and garrison 144,500)inhab., lies at the N.E. end of the Adriatic. It was constituted a free harbour in the reign of Emp. Charles VI. in 1719, and may be termed the Hamburg of S. Germany. About 14,000 vessels, including 5000 steamers, of an aggregate burden of 2¼ million tons, enter and quit the harbour annually. The annual value of the imports is about 170 million florins, that of the exports about 165 million florins. The inhabitants are natives of many different countries, but the Italian element predominates. About one-sixth are Slavonians, and there are only 5000 Germans.

The business of the town centres in the **Harbour**, which has been extensively enlarged and improved during recent years at a cost of 14,600,000 fl. From the *New Harbour* near the railway-station, which is sheltered by a breakwater, the *Old Roads*, with several moles, stretch southwards to the *Molò S. Teresa* (Pl. A, 5, 6), on which stands a *Lighthouse (Fanale Marittimo)*, 108 ft. high. On the *Riva dei Pescatori*, to the N., is the *Health Office (Sanità* ; Pl. B, 5). Adjacent, on the Piazza Grande (p. 439), are the handsome new offices (by Fersted) of the '*Austrian Lloyd*' (Pl. B, 4), a steamboat-company established in 1833, which carries on the postal service and passenger-traffic between Austria and the E. Mediterranean and India. Farther to the N., between the Molo del Sale and the busy *Molo S. Carlo* (begun in 1751 on the site of an ancient Roman mole), is the mouth of the *Canal Grande* (Pl. C, 3, 4), completed in 1756, which penetrates into the new town or Theresienstadt (358 yds. long, 16 yds. wide), and is always filled with shipping. At the E. end of the canal is the church of *St. Antonio Nuovo* (Pl. 4), built in 1830 in the Greek style.

On the Riva Carciotti, to the S. of the Hôtel de la Ville, is the *Greek Church (*S. Niccolò dei Greci*, Pl. 6; C, 4; divine service 6-8.30 a.m. and 5-7 p.m.), sumptuously fitted up in the interior. To the left of the Hôtel de la Ville is the handsome *Palazzo Carciotti*, with columns on the façade and a green dome. — Near the Molo S. Carlo and the Riva Carciotti rises the *Teatro Communale*. Opposite, in an open piazza, is the **Tergesteum** (Pl. C, 4), an extensive block of buildings, with shops and offices on the outside, and intersected in the interior by a cruciform arcade roofed with glass. This arcade with the adjoining rooms on the ground-floor is used as an *Exchange* (principal business-hours 12-2 o'clock). Visitors are admitted to the well-stocked *Reading Room* of the Exchange.

Near the Tergesteum lie the two busiest piazzas in the city: the *Piazza della Borsa* (Pl. C, 4) with the old Exchange, adorned with a *Group of Neptune* in marble, and a *Statue of Emp. Leopold I.*, erected in 1660; and the *Piazza Grande* (Pl. C, 4), with the new **Municipio**, containing the handsome hall of the provincial diet. In front of the Municipio are the *Maria Theresa Fountain*, erected in 1751, and a Statue of Emp. Charles VI.

The *Via del Corso* (Pl. C, D, 4), the principal street of Trieste, which leads inland from these piazzas, separates the New Town, with its broad streets and handsome houses, from the Old Town. The streets of the latter, nestling round the castle-hill, are narrow and steep, and in some cases inaccessible to carriages.

On the way from the Piazza Grande to the cathedral, to the left, is the **Jesuits' Church** (*S. Maria Maggiore*, Pl. 5; C, 4), containing a large modern fresco by *Sante*. A few paces to the W., higher up, lies the small *Piazzetta di Riccardo*, which is said to have been named after Richard Cœur de Lion, with the *Arco di Riccardo* (Pl. C, 5), supposed by some to have been a Roman gateway, but probably part of an old viaduct.

Ascending the Via della Cattedrale, we soon reach on the right the entrance to the **Musco Lapidario** (Pl. 9; B, 5; custodian opposite, No. 16; fee 30 kr.), a collection of Roman antiquities, exhibited in the open air in an old burial-ground. A small temple here contains the monument of *Winckelmann*, the famous German archæologist, who was murdered at Trieste in 1768.

The loftily-situated **Cathedral of S. Giusto** (Pl. 3; D, 5) occupies the site of an ancient Roman temple, of which, by the tower, portions of the foundations and columns have been brought to light. The present building was formed in the 14th cent. by uniting three contiguous edifices of the 6th cent., an early-Christian basilica, a baptistery, and a small Byzantine church with a dome. The façade is adorned with three busts of bishops in bronze. To the right and left of the portal are six busts in relief from Roman tombs. The interior has been whitewashed. In the altar-recess on the right is Christ between SS. Justus and Servatius; in that on the left is Mary between Gabriel and Michael, with the Apostles below (7th cent.). The capitals are partly antique, partly Romanesque.

Beneath a stone slab in front of the church is interred *Fouché*, Duke of Otranto (d. at Trieste in 1820), once the powerful minister of police of Napoleon I. The projecting terrace commands a view of part of the town and the sea.

In the *Piazza Lipsia* (Pl. B, 5), which is laid out in promenades, is the **Nautical Academy** (Pl. 8). On the second floor of this building is the *Ferdinand-Maximilian Museum* (Wed. and Sat. 10-1; Sun. 11-1), which contains a complete collection of the fauna of the Adriatic. Crossing the court in a straight direction and ascending to the second floor, we enter the *Municipal Museum* (daily 9-1; fee 30 kr.), which contains terracottas, vases, bronzes, and other small antiquities, ancient and modern coins, a collection of weapons, and various objects relating to the town of Trieste.

At the corner of the Via della Sanità and the Piazza Giuseppina is the **Palazzo Revoltella** (Pl. 10; B, 5), handsomely fitted up, and embellished with pictures and sculptures, which was bequeathed to the town by its late proprietor Baron Revoltella, together with a sum of money for its maintenance. (Admission daily, 11-2.) The principal façade of the building, which was erected in 1857 from designs by Hitzig, looks towards the Josefs-Platz, where a *Statue of Emperor Maximilian of Mexico* (d. 1867), in bronze, designed by Schilling, was erected in 1875.

An avenue *(Passeggio di S. Andrea)*, 2½ M. in length, skirting the coast, and commanding a variety of views, leads along the shore, on the S. side of the town, past the *Villa Murat*, the *Lloyd Depôt*, and the *Gas-Works*, to *Servola*. The extensive docks of the *Austrian Lloyd Co.*, opposite Servola, are shown daily (except Sun. and Sat.), 9-11 and 2-4, on application at the office in the Lloyd Palace (guide ½ fl.).

On the road to *Zaule*, which is noted for its oyster-parks, lie the handsome *Cemeteries*. — A favourite walk on the E. side of the town is afforded by the *Boschetto*, which is reached by the tramway (10 kr.) through the Corso, the Piazza della Legna, the Corsia Stadion, and past the shady *Giardino Pubblico* (Pl. E, 2, 3). Shady walks ascend hence in 30-40 min. to the *Villa Ferdinandea* (Restaurant al Cacciatore), situated on a plateau 755' in height. Here, too, stands the *Villa Revoltella*, with its park and chapel, now the property of the town (splendid view of the town, the sea, and the coast).

EXCURSIONS. The château of *Miramar, formerly the property of Emp. Maximilian of Mexico (d. 1867), charmingly situated near Grignano, 5½ M. to the N.W. of Trieste, affords a pleasant excursion from Trieste. (The château is ¾ M. from stat. Grignano, p. 414; boat from Trieste 3 fl., one-horse carr. 2, carr.-and-pair 3 fl.) The beautiful park, with its palms and groves of camellias and laurels, and splendid views of the sea and the town of Trieste, is always open to the public. The handsome rooms of the château are shown (Sundays excepted) on application to the major-domo. To the right of the entrance to the garden is a *Museum*, containing Egyptian and Greek antiquities. Halfway to Miramar is *Barcola* (Restaurant), frequently visited from Trieste.

To '**Obcina** (1130'; *Hôtel-Pension all' Obelisco*), 3½ M. to the N., with a fine survey of the town and the sea, particularly from the trigonometrical signal beyond the road, 5 min. from the inn. Also to *Servola* (see above); to *St. Canzian* (by carriage viâ *Corgnale*, 2½ hrs., see p. 414), etc.

From Trieste to *Herpelje* and *Pola*, see p. 414.

441

80. From Trieste to Villach viâ the Predil.

Comp. Map, p. 394.

120 M. RAILWAY to (35½ M.) Gorizia (Görz) in 2-2½ hrs. DILIGENCE from Gorizia to (67 M.) Tarvis daily in 16 hrs. (5 fl. 94 kr.). RAILWAY from Tarvis to (17½ M.) Villach in 1½ hr.

From Trieste to (12 M.) *Nabresina*, see p. 414. The railway diverges to the right, at the station of *Bivio Duino*, and runs in wide curves towards the N.W., near the coast. At *Duino* a tunnel 300 yds. long is traversed; the little town lies on the sea, to the left, with a château of Princess Hohenlohe. At *S. Giovanni* the *Timavo* (Roman *Timavus; Virg. Aen. I. 244-46*), which under the name of *Reka* disappears near St. Canzian (p. 414) in the grottoes of the Carso, emerges from a rock after a subterranean course of 18 M., and falls into the Adriatic 1½ M. lower down. Near (22 M.) *Monfalcone* the train quits the coast, and then turns to the N., skirting the W. spurs of the Carso. 23 M. *Ronchi;* 26 M. *Sagrado*, beyond which we follow the valley of the *Isonzo*. 28½ M. *Gradisca;* 31 M. *Rubbia-Savogna*.

35½ M. **Gorizia**, Ger. *Görz* (280'; *Posta; *Hôtel-Pension Formentini*, with a pleasant garden; *Cur-Pension Hausner*, 3-4½ fl. per day; *Corona d'Ungheria; Leone; Angelo d'Oro*), the capital of an archiepiscopal see, with 20,912 inhab., charmingly situated on the *Isonzo*, is now a favourite resort of lung-patients owing to the mildness and dryness of the climate. (Pleasant walks and excursions; theatre; military music in the Giardino Pubblico and in the Piazza several times weekly.) The cathedral merits inspection. In the upper and older part of the town is the ancient castle of the Counts of Gorizia, now in a ruinous condition, and partly used as a prison. Charles X. of France, who died here in 1836, and his grandson the Count of Chambord (d. 1883), are interred in the chapel of the monastery of *Castagnavizza*, on a height above the town (20 min.). The *Monte Santo* (2244'), 2½ hrs. to the N., crowned with a pilgrimage-church, commands a fine view.

The HIGH ROAD leads from Gorizia on the left bank of the *Isonzo*, viâ *Salcano*, to (13½ M.) —

49 M. *Canale*, where it crosses the river. It then leads viâ *Ronzina* to (10 M.) *Volzano*, Ger. *Wolltschach* (Koffou), and crosses the Isonzo to (1¼ M.) **Tolmino**, or *Tolmein* (660'; Posta, dirty), in the château of which Dante, when a guest of the Patriarch of Aquileia, wrote several cantos of his Divine Comedy.

EXCURSIONS (guides, *Ant. Benedejcio, Joh. Carli, Franz Tutta*). To the *Dante Grotto* in the gorge of the *Tolmeiner Bach (Tominska Dolina)*, 3 M. to the N.E. (guide 1 fl.). — The ascent of the **Kern** (7370'; 8 hrs.; guide 4 fl., with descent to Flitsch or Sotscha 6 fl.) is highly attractive and especially interesting for botanists. Passing the castle-hill we follow the left bank of the Isonzo to the hamlet of *Gabrie*, where we turn to the right, and ascend to the (3½ hrs.) village of *Kern* (quarters at the Iwantsch farm). Thence we reach the summit viâ the *Kasina-Alp* and *Zaslap-Alp* in 4-5 hrs. [The Kern may also be ascended from Caporetto viâ *Dreschenza* in 6 hrs., or from Flitsch viâ the *Spredolina Alp* in 9 hrs., or from Sotscha

(p. 432) viâ the *Planina Alp*, in 6 hrs.) — From Tolmino over the *Sker-binja-Joch* or the *Schwarzenberg* to *Faistritz* (guide 4 fl.), see p. 430; viâ *Deutschruth* to *Laak*, see p. 429.

70½ M. **Caporetto**, Ger. *Karfreit* (1015'; Deutschwirth). To the right are the precipices of the *Kern* (see above); to the left rises the *Matajur* (5390'; easily ascended in 4 hrs.; interesting). The next places are *Ternova*, *Serpenizza*, and —

84 M. **Flitsch** (1470'; *Post; Huber*), a poor village in a sequestered basin. On the W. rises the huge *Mte. Kanin* group.

ASCENTS (guides; Jos. and Andr. *Makritsch*, and Andr. *Sortsch* of Flitsch, Andr. *Komaz*, Joh. *Sortsch*, and Ant. *Tozbar* of Trenta). The ascent of the **Prestrelenik** (8220'; guide 5 fl.), viâ the *Karnitza Alp* in 7½ hrs., is fatiguing, but repaying; the descent may be made by the *Nevea Alp* to (6 hrs.) *Raibl* (see p. 443). — The **Kanin** (8470'; guide 6 fl.), viâ the *Gos-ditsch Alp*, in 8½-9 hrs., is also fatiguing (from the Kanin to the Prestrelenik 3 hrs.). — The **Romben** (or *Veliki Vrh*; 7250'), viâ the *Goriciza Alp* in 5 hrs. (guide 5 fl.), offers less difficulty. — From Flitsch to the *Valley of the Trenta* (passes to the *Pischenza* and *Urata* valleys), see p. 432. Near *Loog* in the upper Trenta valley, 4½ hrs. from Flitsch, is the **Baum-bachhütte** (1970'), erected by the German Alpine Club. The ascent of the *Terglou* (6 hrs.; guide 5 fl; p. 430) from this point, by the '*Kugy Path*', viâ the rocky *Skok* and the *Dolez-Sattel*, is fit only for adepts with steady heads. The ascent of the *Prisanig* hence (8390'; 4½ hrs., 4 fl.), viâ the *Kronauer Chalet*, is easier than from the N. side (p. 432). — The *Razor* (8530'; 5½ hrs.; with guide), ascended viâ the Kronauer Alp and the saddle between the Prisanig and the Razor, is difficult. — The *Flitscher Grintouz* (7710'; 6 hrs.; 3 fl.), ascended viâ the *Zepotocco-Alp* (4285') from the inner Trenta, is difficult. — The *Jalouz* (8710'; 6-7 hrs.; 7 fl.), ascended by the *Trenta-Alp* (4480'), is also a difficult peak and not without danger. — Another arduous ascent is that of the *Kaniauz* (*Kanjavec*, 8432'), accomplished viâ the *Trebischnja-Alp* in 6 hrs., or viâ the *Dolez-Sattel* in 4½-5 hrs. (guide 4 fl.). Fine view. The descent may be made if preferred to the *Terglou Lakes* (p. 431).

The road now quits the Isonzo valley, which ascends to the E. towards the Terglou (p. 430), and follows the course of the *Koritenza* towards the N., into a defile called the *Flitscher Klause* (1745'), guarded by a new fort. Beyond this pass, near (5 M.) *Unterbreth*, a view of the imposing *Mangart* (p. 443) is disclosed; to the E. rises the abrupt *Jalouz* (8710'). The road ascends in long windings past *Mittelbreth* (Inn) to *Oberbreth*, grandly situated, passes the mouth of the *Mangart Valley*, and a small fort, where a handsome monument commemorates the death of a Capt. Hermann, who fell in a skirmish here in 1809, and reaches (4 M.) the highest point of the **Predil** (3810'; *Baumgartner's Inn*, to the right, unpretending). We now descend (choosing the 'Sommerstrasse' or upper of the two roads), enjoying fine views of the lightgreen *Raibler See*, and of the *Seethal* with the *Seekopf* and *Wischberg*, to (2½ M.) —

95½ M. **Raibl** (2925'; *Schnablegger's Touristenhäuser*, R., L., & A. 1 fl. 30 kr.; *Post*), a picturesquely-situated village on the *Schlitza* (the outlet of the Raibler See), with extensive lead-foundries, and a summer-resort. To the W. rises the dolomitic *Königsberg* (6292'), and opposite to it is the *Fünfspitz* (6240'), with its five huge pinnacles.

to *Villach*.   RAIBL.   *VIII. Route 80.* 443

EXCURSIONS (guides, *Rud. Baumgartner* and *Jakob Pinter* of Raibl). Pleasant walk by the 'Winterstrasse' to the (1 M.) *Lake of Raibl* (3250'; baths in summer; boats for hire), at the upper end of which is a new fort. — Ascent of the *Luschariberg* (5880'), viâ *Kaltwasser* in 4 hrs. (guide, 2 fl. 60 kr.), not difficult (descent to Saifnitz, p. 434). — Pleasant excursion of 1/2 day to the **Kaltwasserthal**, with the grand scenery at its head. Interesting day's excursion (7 hrs.; guide, 3 fl. 80 kr.) across the *Raibler Scharte* (4345') to the Kaltwasserthal; then over the *Braschnik-Sattel* (4885'), between the *Steinerne Jäger* and the *Schwalbenspitzen*, or (steeper but more interesting) across the *Karnitza-Sattel* (4920'), between the *Schwalbenspitze* and the *Gamsmutter*, to the *Seisera Valley* and to Wolfsbach and Tarvis (p. 434). — The **Königsberg** (6292'; 3½ hrs.; guide 2½ fl.) is ascended without difficulty and commands a fine view. — The **Fünfspitz** (6240'; 3½-4 hrs.; guide 3½ fl.) is a difficult peak, fit only for those who are free from giddiness. — Ascent of the *°Manhart* or **Mangart** (8786'; 6-7 hrs.; guide, 5 fl., with descent to Weissenfels 6 fl.), not difficult, and very interesting. Beyond the (1 hr.) Predil we turn to the left and ascend the *Manharithal* to the *Manharl-Alp* and to the (3 hrs.) *Manhart Hut* (6560'; refreshments and night-quarters). Thence to the top by a good path in 2½ hrs. more, past the *Kleine Manhart* (imposing view). Descent over the *Lahnscharte* to *Weissenfels* (p. 432), steep and trying; across the *Schutzhaus-Scharte* to the *Karnitza* (steep, fit only for experienced mountaineers) and through the *Römerthal* to *Tarvis* (p. 433), interesting and attractive. — The **°Wischberg** (8756'; 7 hrs.; guide 5 fl.), a very striking point of view, also ascended from Raibl, is fatiguing but free from danger. We pass the Raibler See and ascend the Seethal to the (2½ hrs.) *Fischbachalpe* and the (1 hr.) *Wischberg Hut* (5930') in the *Untere Karnitza*, erected by the German Alpine Club. Thence to the summit through the *Obere Karnitza* and over the *Gamsmutterscharte* in 2½ hrs.; superb view. Descent across the *Bärenlahn-Scharte* (6060') into the Seisera valley and to (6 hrs.) *Wolfsbach*, toilsome (steep snow-field in the Bärenlahn, see p. 434). — An interesting excursion, which may be especially recommended to botanists, leads from the *Wischbergbütte* across the *Stiege* to the *Crognedul-Alp* and *Pecollo-Alp*, returning by the *Nevea-Alp* (from Raibl and back 10 hrs.; guide 4½ fl.). — The **Bramkofel** (*Jof del Montasio, Montasch*; 9030') is difficult, and fit for experts only (guide 7 fl.). The previous night should be spent at the *Pecollo Alp* (6330'), 5 hrs. from Raibl (6 hrs. from Chiusaforte). To the summit, a magnificent point of view, 4-5 hrs. more. — The Mte. **Cimone** (7812'), between the Dogna and Raccolana valleys, 3½-4 hrs. from the Pecollo Alp, is also repaying. — The **Kanin** (8470'; guide 7 fl.) and the *Prestrelenik* (8220'; 6 fl.), difficult, may each be ascended in about 8 hrs., the night being spent in the *Kanin-Hütte* (6500'), 2½ hrs. above the *Nevea Alp* (see below), where the keys should be ordered by telegraph from Chiusaforte. From the hut to the top 2½-3 hrs. These peaks, however, are better ascended from Flitsch (see above).

To CHIUSAFORTE, an interesting route (7 hrs.; guide 5 fl.). We pass the Raibler See and ascend the Seethal to the (3 hrs.) finely-situated *Alp Nevea* (3950'), at the N. base of the Prestrelenik; and then descend through the grand, but shadeless **Raccolana Valley** (with the *Bramkofel* and the *Mte. Cimone* on the N.) to (1½ hr.) *Stretti*, (1½ hr.) *Satetto* (inn, primitive), and (1½ hr.) *Raccolana*, at the influx of the Roccolana into the Fella, ¾ M. to the S. of *Chiusaforte* (p. 436). We may then return to Raibl by the Pontebba line and Tarvis.

From Raibl (one-horse carr. 2, two-horse 4 fl.) the road leads through the smiling valley of the *Schlitza*, viâ *Kaltwasser* (lead stamping-mill) and *Flitschl*, to (6½ M.) *Unter-Tarvis*, ½ M. from the railway-station —

102½ M. **Tarvis** (p. 433). Thence to (120 M.) **Villach**, see p. 433.

81. From Trieste to Pola and Fiume.

STEAMBOAT to Pola daily in 8½ hrs. (first-class fare 3 fl.); from Pola to Fiume twice weekly in 11 hrs. (fares from Trieste 6 fl. 50, 4 fl. 70 kr.). Good restaurant on board, D. 2½, S. 1 fl. — RAILWAY viâ *Herpelje-Kozina* (junction of the line from Divača, p. 414) to Pola in 4 hrs.; viâ St. Peter to Fiume in 7½ hrs., see p. 413.

The steamer skirts the undulating, olive-clad coast of Istria. In a distant bay to the S.E. lies *Capo d'Istria*, with its large prison. On an eminence rises the church of *Pirano*. The town (7400 inhab.), with its salt-pans, is picturesquely situated in a bay; the pinnacles and towers of the old fortress peep from amidst olive-groves. The lighthouse of *Salvore* is next passed, then *Umāgo*, the castle of *Daila*, *Cittanuova* (on the site of the ancient *Noventium*), *Parenzo* (once a usual halting-place of the crusaders, with a remarkable cathedral, a basilica of 961), *S. Niccolò* (on an island with a watch-tower and deserted monastery), *Orsēra*, and the *Canat di Leme*, an inlet 28 M. long. In the distance to the E. rises *Monte Maggiore* (4560'). The vessel now stops at **Rovigno** (the ancient *Arupenum* or *Rubinum*), a prosperous town with 9,600 inhabitants. The staple commodities: are wine (the best in Istria), oil, and sardines. Baptistery of the 11th century. Railway to *Canfanaro (Pola, Trieste)*, see p. 414.

To the right near *Fasāna* rise the *Brionian Islands*, separated by a narrow strait from the mainland, where the Venetian fleet was defeated by the Genoese in 1379. The Venetians once quarried the stone for their palaces here. The grand amphitheatre of Pola now comes in sight. The excellent harbour, the principal station of the Austrian fleet since its withdrawal from Venice, and now of considerable commercial importance, is defended by two towers.

Pola (*Hotel Ribotti*, near the harbour; **Schreiner*; **Restaurant Lloyd*; *Café* in the market-place; beer at *Dreher's;* wine at the *Al Tempio di Augusto; Trattoria al Buon Pesce*, on the way to the Arena), a thriving seaport with 16,324 inhab., is of very ancient origin, having probably been founded by Thracians. According to tradition it was founded B. C. 1350 by the Colchians who were in pursuit of Jason in order to recover the golden fleece. It was conquered B. C. 178 by the Romans, who established a colony here, afterwards known as *Pietas Julia*. Under Augustus and his successors it attained its highest prosperity (35,000 inhab.) and was an important war-harbour. In 550 Belisarius, the general of Justinian, assembled an army here for the purpose of chastising the piratical inhabitants of the coast. In 1148 Pola was taken by the Republic of Venice, and during the subsequent contests for supremacy between the Venetians and Genoese the town was frequently destroyed. From the last of these disasters in 1379 it never recovered, and has since been little more than a ruin.

Its magnificent and highly-interesting antiquities, which date from the Roman period, may be visited in the following order. (The

Temple of Augustus and the Arena are surrounded by an iron railing, the key to the gate of which is kept at the *Palazzo Pubblico*, where a guide may also be obtained if desired.)

The *Temple of Augustus and Roma (B. C. 19), 26' in height and 50' in width, with a colonnade of six Corinthian columns 23' in height, and with admirably-executed enrichments on the frieze, is in almost perfect preservation. The inscription can be traced only by the holes of the nails by which the letters were once attached to the wall *(Romae et Augusto Caesari Divi F(ilio) Patri Patriae)*. The collection of antiquities in the interior is insignificant.

In the vicinity stood a temple of *Diana*, or more probably of *Roma*, of which the posterior wall only is preserved. This fragment was employed about the year 1300 in the construction of the *Palazzo Pubblico*, which is incorporated with it with considerable skill. A monument has been erected here to *Signor L. Carrara* (d. 1854), in memory of his praiseworthy exertions in securing the preservation of the antiquities.

We now cross the market-place towards the S., and at the end of a long street reach the *Porta Aurea*, an elegant isolated arch in the Corinthian style, 20' in height, erected by the Sergii, a distinguished family of the place. At some distance to the right stood the ancient *Theatre*, the site of which only is now recognisable by a semicircular depression in the hill. The whole neighbourhood is now covered with modern houses. Farther to the right is a hill with the *Meteorological Station*, the grounds in front of which, embellished with a statue of *Adm. Tegetthoff*, command an admirable view of the town and harbour.

Excavations, which are still prosecuted, have brought to light the two ancient E. gates, the *Porta Erculea* (so called from the head and club beside the key-stone) and the double *Porta Gemina*, probably erected about A. D. 150. These were the entrances to the Roman capitol, the site of which is now occupied by the *Castle*, erected by the Venetians in the 17th cent., and restored under Emp. Francis I. Passing round the latter on the N. side, the traveller reaches the *Franciscan Monastery*, erected in the 13th cent., now a military magazine. It possesses fine cloisters, and a Romanesque portal on the W. side quaintly adorned with shells.

Beyond the monastery we reach the *Arena, which presents an imposing appearance when seen from the sea. It was erected, as the style indicates, about the period of the Antonines (A. D. 150) and could accommodate 15,000 spectators. Height 78', diameter 344'. The lower stories consist of two series of arches (72 in number) 18' in height, one above the other; the upper story is a wall with square openings for windows.

The exterior is in admirable preservation, but the interior presents a desolate scene; the arrangements for the *Naumachia* in the centre can alone now be traced. Four gates, with projections of which the object is unknown, form the entrances. The ground is meagrely covered with creeping plants, thistles, and herbage. Most of the stones of the tiers of seats have been removed in previous centuries and used for building purposes in Venice. The view from the hill (where an echo may be awakened), through the lofty arches, of the sea and the small islands *(Scoglte)* and promontories, and of the olive-clad hills of this remote coast-district, is very striking.

The steamer now skirts the S. extremity of the promontory of Istria, passes the islands of *Cherso* and *Veglia* on the right, and reaches the broad *Bay of Quarnero*. To the left rises the *Mte. Maggiore* (4560'), with *Abbazia* (p. 413) nestling at its foot; to the right in the distance are the Croatian Mts., conspicuous among which is the *Capella* range.

Fiume, Illyr. *Rieka* (*Europa*, on the quay; *Hôtel de la Ville*, near the station; *Goldner Stern*; *Jägerhorn*), the only seaport of Hungary, is picturesquely situated at the head of the Bay of Quarnero. Under the name of *Vitopolis* it was a flourishing town in antiquity; subsequently it passed under the rule of the patriarchs of Aquileia and then under that of the counts of Duino and barons of Gorizia, but in 1471 the emperor Frederick III. added it to the possessions of the house of Hapsburg. Since 1870 Fiume has been recognized as belonging to Hungary. The town (16,300 inhab.; including suburbs, 20,981) has three harbours: the *Porto Canale Fiumara*, the *Porto Nuovo*, with large warehouses on the piers, and the *Petroleum Harbour*. The trade and manufactures of Fiume have recently been much extended; Mr. Whitehead's large torpedo-factory and Messrs. Smith and Meynier's paper-mill deserve mention. The town is the seat of an *Imperial Marine Academy*, founded in 1856, and now housed in a handsome building. Among the other chief edifices are the *Cathedral*, with a new front in the style of the Pantheon at Rome; the *Church of St. Veit*, built in imitation of S. Maria della Salute in Venice; the *Government Buildings*; the *Theatre*; and the royal *Tobacco Factory*. Few relics of antiquity are now extant at Fiume; the chief is a Roman *Triumphal Arch*, said to have been erected in honour of the emperor Claudius II. Gothicus (268-270 A. D.). Pleasant new Giardino Pubblico.

In the vicinity is a much-frequented Pilgrimage Church, reached by a path with 400 steps, with a picture of the Madonna of Loretto, painted according to tradition by St. Luke himself. Numerous votive offerings from grateful mariners are suspended on the pillars. View of the apparently land-locked Bay of Quarnero, with the islands of *Veglia* and *Cherso*.

Near the church rises the château of Tersato, once the property of the Hungarian Count Frangipani, who was executed in 1671, and lately that of Count Nugent, an Austrian marshal (d. 1862), by whom the ruin was restored, and who is interred in one of the vaults which was formerly a dungeon. A small temple here contains a collection of reliefs, busts, mosaics, statues, and other antiquities, including an admirably-draped Venus. A column, eagle, and marble tablet erected by the French on the field of Marengo, are also preserved here. *View of the extensive Bay of Quarnero, with its islands, of Fiume, and the coast.

Excursion to *Abbazia*, see p. 413.

INDEX.

Abbazia 413.
Aber-See, the 107.
Aberstöckl 260.
Abfaltersbach 334.
Ableithen-Alp, the 46.
Absam 160.
Abtenau 101.
Abtei 342.
Abwinkel 45.
Ach, the Bregenzer 196.
—, the Dornbirner 197.
Ache, the Aschauer 174.
—, the Bischofswieser 70.
—, the Brandenberger 49. 159.
—, the Brixenthaler 158. 171. 175.
—, the Deferegger 139.
—, the Fuscher 116.
—, the Gasteiner 115.
—, the Grossarler 114.
—, the Grosse 55. 120. 175.
—, the Gurgler 249. 254.
—, the Kapruner 132.
—, the Kitzbühler 120. 174.
—, the Königseer 71.
—, the Krimmler 137.
—, the Niederthaler 240.
—, the Oetzthaler 233. 236.
—, the Pillerseer 119.
—, the Plansee 23.
—, the Pramauer 119. 120.
—, the Rainsamer 71.
—, the Kauriser 116.
—, the Reitner 120. 174. 175.
—, the Strub 176.
—, the Urschlauer 57. 118.
Achen, defile 47.
Achenkirch 47.
Achenkogl, the 236.
Achenrain 150.
Achensee, the 47.
Achenwald 47.
Achleiten 306.
Ackerlspitze 175.
Ackernalp 52.
Acqualunona 354.
Adamello 307.

Adda, the 314. 283.
Adelheidsquelle 41.
Adelholzen 55.
Adelsberg 411.
Adige, the 250. 293.
Adlerhöhle 107.
Adlersruhe 147. 153.
Adlerwand 11.
Adlitzgraben 367.
Admont 387. 384.
Adnet 83.
St Adolart 176.
Adriatic, the 438.
St. Aegyd 374.
Aeschach 7.
Aforser Thal 225.
Affenthal 159. 340.
Aflenz 375.
Afritz 422.
Agaro, Mte. 318.
St. Agatha 96.
Agatharied 50.
Ager, the 86. 87. 88.
Aggenstein 22.
Agls-Alpe 222.
Agls-Joch 222.
Agner Kopf 144.
Agnerola, Alp 327.
St. Agnes 409.
Agola, Val 304.
Agordo 358.
—, Canal di 358.
Agram 409.
Ahornach, near Bregenz 196.
—, near Taufers 337. 338.
Ahornboden, the 43.
Ahornbüchsen 85.
Ahornkar 394.
Ahornspitze 182.
Abrenthal, the 188. 138.
Aibling 53.
Aich 394.
Aicha 328.
Aichgraben 379.
Aidling 37.
Aidlinger Höhe 37.
Aigen, near Ischl 108.
—, near Salzburg 65. 83.
Aigner 394.

Ainet 138.
Aitrang 3.
Ala 295.
Alba 323.
St. Alban, baths 26.
Albeins 295.
Alberfeldkogel 91.
Alberschwende 206.
Albrechtsberg 380.
Aldein 261.
Aldeno 295.
Aldrans 170.
Alexiaklamm 150.
Alfnchjoch 228.
Alfenabach, the 202. 213.
Alfreid 275.
Algäu, the 4.
Algone, Val d' 304.
Algund 274.
Alla Nave 293.
Alleghe 357.
—, Lake of 357.
Allerheiligen 378.
Almannshausen 25.
Alttrissjoch, the 222.
Alm, the 68. 83. 84.
— (Urschlau) 119.
Almagmach 5.
Almbach-Klamm 71. 72.
Almbachstrub 84.
Almberg Alpe 177.
Almejurbach 211.
Almejurjoch 204.
Almsee, the 90.
Alpbach, the 159.
Alpbach-Thal 159.
Alpeiner Alp 228.
Alpeiner Glacier 228.
Alpeiner Scharte 186.
Alpeleck 365.
Alpel-Scharte, the 78.
Alpel-Thal 73.
Aelpele (near Feldkirch) 10. 199.
Alperschonthal, the 211.
Alpgarten, the 81.
Alpilla 242.
—, Alp 214.
Alpsee, the (near Hohenschwangau) 17.
—, (near Immenstadt) 5

Alpspitze, the 32.
Alp-Vera-Jöchl 214.
Alpwen, Alp 198.
Alt-Aussee 97.
Altenberg 259. 366. 415.
Altenburg 266.
Altenmarkt 380. 384. 397.
Altenstein-Thal 333.
Altenzoll 247.
Alte Schanze 118.
Alt-Finstermünz 249.
Althammer 430.
Althausschneid 144.
Althofen 426.
Alt-Hohenems 197.
Altlach 39.
Altmühle 88.
Altmünster 88. 90.
Alto, Monte 357.
Alt-Prags 330.
Altstetten 8.
Alvierbach, the 201.
Alwind 7.
Alzing 55.
Amaro 436.
Ambach 25. 44.
Amblar 268. 311.
Ambras, château 168.
Ambriz, Forcella d' 353.
Ameishühel 371.
Amerlügen 199.
Ameten 329.
Amlach 334.
Ammer, the 26. 27. etc.
Ammergau, the 28.
Ammerland 25.
Ammersee, the 26.
Ammerthaler Oed 141.
Ammerwaldalp 29.
Ampass 170.
Ampelsbachthal, the 47.
Amper, the 3. 27.
Ampezzo di Carnia 436.
—, Cortine di 349.
Ampezzo, Val 340.
Ampola, Val 300.
Amras, château 168.
Amstetten 381.
Amthorspitze 222.
Andalo 303.
Andechs 27.
Andelsbuch 207.
Anderl Alp 176.
St. Andrä 225. 415. 418.
Andraz 355.
Andria 357.
Andrian 299.
Andritz-Ursprung 404.
Anfo 309.
S. Angelo, Col 351.
Angeluspitze 289.
Anger 38. 42. 83.
Angerhöhe 392.

Angerhütte (Rainthal) 32.
Angerhütte (Karwendel-
   thal) 36.
Angerthal, the 121.
Angoraz, Val d' 327.
Anichen 222.
Anif, château 66.
Ankogel 400. 124. 126.
Anlaufthal, the 124.
St. Anna 294. 420.
Annaberg 102. 374.
Annabründl 434.
Annenberg 252.
Annenthal 404.
Anninger 364.
Anrauth 210.
Ansiei, the 352.
Antelao, Monte 354.
Antengraben 377. 376.
Antermoja Lake 322.
   262.
— Pass 322.
— Kogel 262.
— Valley 322.
Antholz 329.
Antholzer See 330.
— Scharte 340.
— Thal 329.
St. Anton (Arlberg) 203.
— (near Botzen) 216. 260.
— (near Meran) 273.
— (Montavon) 213.
—, chapel 29. 283.
St. Antonierjoch 215.
St. Antonikapelle 78.
S. Antonio 282. 283.
S. Antonio di Mavignolo
   305.
Antorf 37.
Antruilles, Croda d' 348.
Anzenau 95.
Aorine Pass 358.
Apere Freiger 230.
Apere Pfaff 230.
St. Apollonia 283.
Apothekerhöfe 66.
Apriach 151.
Aprica 314.
St. Arbogast 198.
Archenköpfe 73.
Arco 297.
Ardenno-Masino 284.
Ardetzenberg 198.
Ardning 388.
Ardo 354.
Arlberg, the 208.
Arlberg Tunnel 203.
Arlscharte 115. 399.
Arlthörl 114.
Armentara 341.
Armkaar, the 101.
Arno, the 304. 308.
—, Lago d' 308.

Arnoldstein 433.
Arriach 422.
Arsic 355.
Arsiero 319.
Arso, Val' 295.
Arta 336.
Artegna 437.
Arten 327. 355.
Artilone, Alp 299. 300.
Artstetten 380.
Arzberg 113.
Arzberghöhle 377.
Arzl near Innsbruck 161.
— in the Pitzthal 245.
Arzlerscharte 87.
Arzon, Cima d' 327.
Aschach 384.
Aschmalp 136.
Aschau, on the Lech 240.
—, in the Zillerthal 179.
—, in the Spertenthal 172.
Aschauer Weiher 70.
Aschbach 237. 340. 382.
Aschbach-Thal 371.
Aschenau 67.
Aschenthaler Wände 56.
Aschlerbach, the 269.
Asiago 319.
Asinella, Valle 305.
Asinozza, Val 327.
Asp 430.
Aspang 363.
Assenza 301.
Assling 53. 431.
Asta, Cima d' 326.
Aston 125. 382.
Astenthal, the 150.
Astfeld 260.
Astico, Val d' 317.
Attel, the 53.
Attersee 109.
Attersee, the 109.
Attmang 87.
Atzgersdorf 361.
Atzwang 226.
Au in the Vorarlberg 208.
— near Berchtesgaden 71.
— near Immenstadt 8.
— on the Mondsee 109.
— in the Oetzthal 232.
   237.
— near Schliersee 50.
— near Tegernsee 45.
Aua da Pisch 254.
Aubach, the 156. 52.
Aubach-Fall 86. 103.
Aubing 3.
Aueleswände, the 21.
Auen 12.
Auenalp, the 12.
Auenfeldalp, the 209.
Auenfeldjöchl, the 209.
Auen-Joch 260.

INDEX. 449

Auer 203.
—, château 273.
Auerberg 14.
Auerspitze, the 51.
Aufacker, the 28.
Auf der Lend 378.
Aufhausen 135.
Aufhofen 320.
Aufkirchen (Pusterthal) 331.
— (Lake of Starnberg) 25.
Augsburgerhütte, the 235.
Augstbachthal, the 94.
Augstenberg, the 217.
Auland 37.
Aurach (Achenthal) 174.
— (near Bair. Zell) 51.
—, the 88.
Aurachkar, the 100.
Aurachkirchen 88.
Auraehthal, the 88.
Auronzo 352.
Auronzo, Val d' 352.
Aussee 96.
Ausseer Salzberg 96.
Ausser-Fragant 150.
Ausser-Gschlöss 140.
Ausserhof 275.
Aussermühlwalder Klamm, the 188.
Ausser-Pens 260.
Ausser-Prags 330.
Ausserwald-Thal, the 176.
Austria Hütte 395.
Averau 349. 355.
Avio 295.
—, Val d' 307.
Avisio, Mte. 312.
Avisio, the 203. 317. 320.
Axljoch 18.

Baad, near Mittelberg 10.
Bahn, the 408.
Babji Zob 430.
Bacher Mts. 407.
Bacher Loch, the 11.
Bacherspitze, the 333.
Bacherthal (Reinthal) 330.
— (Sexten) 333.
Bachgart 328.
Bachlenke, the 143.
Bäckeralp, the 52.
Badbruck 124.
Baden 362.
Badersee, the 30.
Badia 342.
Badile 285.
Badl (St. Isidor) 258.
Bädle 213.
Badlwand 369.
Baghella, Mte. 313.
Baierbach-Alp, the 47.

Baierdiessen 26.
Bairisch-Zell 51.
Baita, Col della 486.
Balderschwang 14.
Baldo, Monte 299. 295
Balken, the 21.
Ball, Cima di 326.
—, Passo di 326.
Ballino 301.
Ballunspitze, the 216.
Balzers 199.
Banale, Villa di 304.
Bannwaldsee, the 14.
Barbarana Ravine 302.
Barbian 226. 250.
Barcola 440.
Bardolino 301.
Bärenbach, the 320.
Bärenbad (Stubai) 228.
Bärenbadalp 48. 158.
Bärenbart-Ferner 250.
— Joch 250.
— Kogl 250.
Bärenfall, the 125. 265.
Bärenkopf (Achensee) 48.
Bärenköpfe (Heiligenblut) 153.
Bärenlahnscharte 434. 443.
Bärenloch, the 262.
Bärenschütz 369.
Bärenthal 420.
Barghe 309.
Barmsee, the 40.
Barmstein, the Kleine and Grosse 83. 84.
Bärndorf 388.
Börnstatt 175.
St. Bartholomä 74.
Bartholomäberg Ausser and Inner 202. 213.
St. Bartholomew, Lake of 73.
Barthümmeljoch, 200.
Bartolograben 433.
S. Bartolommeo, Monte 301.
Baschl-Sattel 418.
Baselga 317.
Bassano 320.
Bastianshütte 353.
Batschuns 198.
Bauernalpe, the 133.
Bauernkollern 258.
Baumbach Hütte 442.
Baumgarten-Alp 56.
Baumgartenjoch 42.
Baumgartenschneid 45.
Bäumle 198.
Bäunalp 41.
Baura 86.
Bayen 207.
Bayersoyen 26.

Baza Pass 430.
— Valley 429.
Becchei di Sotto, Col 341.
Beckstetten 3.
Bedole, 307.
Bedross 250.
Beidewasser 277.
Bellamonte 324.
Bellano 354.
Belvedere (Cortina) 349.
St. Benedikt 149.
Benediktbeuern 38.
Benediktenwand 38. 41.
Berchtesgaden 60.
Berchtesgadener Hochthron, the 67.
Berg (Lake of Starnberg) 25.
Bergen 55.
Bergerkogl (Fusch) 130.
— (Virgenthal) 142.
Berger Thörl 148.
Berggündele-Thal 21.
Berglerkogl 287.
Berglerkopf 218.
Berliner Hütte 185.
Bernardin-Alp, the 32.
Bernau 55.
Berndorf 380.
Bernerau 390.
Bernhardsthal, the 210.
Bernhaupten 55.
Bernina, the 284.
Bernkogl, the 126.
Bernried 25. 37.
Bersbach 207.
Bertiaga, Mte. 310.
Berwang 18. 210.
Besenbach 38.
Beseno, château 295.
Betzgau 4.
Beuerberg 25.
Bezau 207.
Bezecca 300.
Bezegg, the 208.
Biacesa 308.
S. Biagio, Isola di 307.
Bianco, Corno 307.
—, Lago 347.
—, Sasso 324.
—, Vallon 341.
Biberkopf, the 12. 211.
Bichl 38. 41.
Bichlbach 18.
Bicheneck 247.
Bicherwier 19.
Biclerhöhe, the 216.
Bierbaum 334.
Biessenhofen 3.
Bigontina, Plan della 349.
Bildstein 196.
Bildstöckl-Joch 230. 252.
Bilkengrat, the 214.

Bnsalp 40.
Binswang 20.
Biois, Val B25. 357.
Birchabruck 261.
Birchkogl 231.
Birgsau 11.
Birkenberg 23.
Birkenkofl 347.
Birkenstein 50.
Birkenthal, the 22.
Birnbach 57.
Birnhorn, the 119.
Birnlucke, the 192.
Bischoffeld 424.
Bischoflaak 429.
Bischofshofen 188. 307.
Bischofsmütze 101. 397.
Bischofswies 76.
Bistriza, the 411.
Bivio Duino 441.
Bivio di Prad, see Prad.
Bizau 208.
Binichach 7.
Blankahorn, the 205.
Blankajoch 205. 218.
Blaser, the 220.
Blassenstein 380.
Blassstein 371.
Blaue Gumpen, the 32.
— Tumpf, the 399.
— Wand, the 176.
Blaueis Glacier, the 78.
Bleiberg 422.
Bleiburg 416.
Bletschenthal, the 265.
Blickspitze, the 240.
Blindau 57.
Blindenmarkt 381.
Blindsee, the 19.
Blomberg 41. 109.
Blons 200.
Bludenz 200.
Blühnbachthal 113. 75.
Blühnbachthörl 113. 75.
Bluntau 226.
Bluntauthal, the 75.
Böbing 26.
Bobingen 3.
Bocche, Cima di 325.
Bockfeld-Alpe, the 121.
Bockhart-Scharte, the 125.
— Seen, the 125.
— Thal, the 125.
Bockhütte, the 82.
Bockkar, the 12.
Bockkarkees, the 132. 153.
Bockkarkopf, the 12.
Bockkarscharte, the 132. 152.
Bockkogl, the 229.
Bockstein 124. 427.
Bocksteinkogl, the 121.

Boden (Lechthal) 210.
— (Pflersch) 222.
Bodenbach, the 420.
Bodenhauer 375.
Bodenbühl, the 178.
Bodenlahne, the 32.
Bodenschneid, the 51.
Bodensee, see Lake of Constance.
Bödensee 333. 346.
Bodenthal 420.
Bödmen 209.
Bodner 420.
Boe, the 275.
Boghiaeo 392.
Bogunschitza, the 429.
Böheimkirchen 379.
Boimont 266
Boite, the 355.
Bojen 388.
Bojerbach 189
Bolbeno 304.
Bolladore 283.
Bombaschgraben 435.
Bondo 308.
Bondone 301.
—, Monte 292.
Borea 351.
Borgo di Val Sugana 318.
Bormina, Val 283.
Bormio 282.
—, Bagni di 281.
Boruniza, the 411.
Borzago 304. 305.
Bos, Col dai 350.
Bosco, Cant. al 279.
Böse Weibl, the 335.
Bösenstein 424. 389.
Bosruck, the 388.
Botzen 256.
Botzener Leitach 226.
Botzer, the 223.
Botzer-Scharte 299.
Bowojach 141.
Brad, see Prad.
Bramberg 136.
Bramkofel 443.
Brana 408.
Brand near Bludenz 201.
— (Urschlau) 57.
Brand, the 237.
Brand-Alp, the 57.
Brandberg 182.
Brandberger Kolm 180.
Brandenberger Joch 159.
Brandenberger Thal 50.
Brandenthal, the 261.
Brandhof 374.
Brandis, Alt- and Neu-208.
Brandjoch, the 235.
Brandkogl, the 157.
Brandner Glacier 201.
Brandner Thal 201.

Brandriedel, the 395.
Brandstätt 300.
Brandstein 375.
Brandstädter Thörl 424.
Brandtner Alpe 388.
Brandwieshütten, the 94.
Brannenburg 156.
Branzoll 208.
Braschnik-Sattel 433. 434.
Bratschenkopf 113. 153.
Bratz 202.
Braulio, the 281.
—, Monte 281.
Braunarlenspitze 209.
Braunau 87.
Brauneck, the 41.
Bräuningzinken 97.
Braunsberg 268.
Brecherspitze 50. 51.
Bregenz 6. 7. 195.
Bregenzer Wald 206.
Breguzzo, Val 308.
Breitach, the 8. 9. 209.
Breitenau 369.
Breitenbach, the 50.
Breitenberg, the 109.
Breitenbrunn 27.
Breitenschützing 87.
Breitenstein 307.
Breitenstein, the 68.
Breitenwang 18. 22.
Breithorn, the (Steinernes Meer) 119.
— (Loferer Steinberge) 176.
Breitkopf, the 132. 153.
Breitlahner Alp 185.
Breitlehn-Alp 245.
Breitlehner Jöchl 237. 246.
Breitnock, the 187.
Breitriedel 73.
Brannbichl 234.
Brenner 219. 221.
Brennerbad 221.
Brennersee, the 221.
Brennkogl, the 130. 131. 154.
Breunsee 422.
Breno 313.
Brenta, the 317.
Brenta Mts. 306.
Brenta, Val 305.
—, Bocca di 306.
—, Canale di 319.
—, Cima di 306.
Brentenjoch, the 157.
Brentonico 299.
Brescenti-Klause 377.
Brescia 301. 309.
Breslauer Hütte, the 238.
Brettboden, the 152.
Brettfall, chapel 178.

INDEX. 451

Brettklammi, the 73.
Brez 311.
Bribano 354. 358.
Bricciuskapelle, the 151.
Brione, Monte 299.
Brionian Islands 444.
Brixen (Brixenthal) 172.
— (on the Eisak) 294.
Brixener Klause 171. 224.
Brixenthal, the 171. 172.
Brixlegg 159.
Brizzihütte, the 239.
Brochkogl, the Hintere 246.
Brogon Pass 319.
Brod 410.
Bruanago, see Brugnach.
Bruck on the Mur 368.
— on the Amper 3.
— near Hindelang 21.
— in the Pinzgau 116.
—, chât., near Lienz 334.
Bruckerklamm 395.
Bruckgraben, the 386.
Brückl 427.
Bruckmühl 53.
Brucksattel, the 387.
Bruckstein 387.
Bruggen 206.
Brugnach 358.
Bründlingalpe 55.
Bruneck 328.
Brunn 361.
Brunnau 236.
Bruundorf 410.
Brunnenburg 272.
Brunnenfeld 213.
Brunnenkogl, the Hintere and Vordere 228. 237. 246.
Brunnenkogeljoch 228.
Brunnsee 406.
Brunnstein 156. 392.
Brunnthal 377.
Bschlabs 210.
Buch 404.
Buchau 47.
Buchau, the 384.
Buchauer Scharte, the 119.
Buchauer Saddle 388.
Buchberg 109. 362. 365. 375. 379.
Buchboden 200.
Buchehen 127.
Buchen 35. 233.
Buchenstein 342. 356.
Buching 14.
Buchkogl 404.
Büchl 207.
Buchloe 3.
Buchrainer Alp 13.
Buchs 199.

Buchscheiden 428.
Buchsenhausen 170.
Buchstein, Grosse 368. 386. 387.
Buco di Vela 296.
Budweis 382.
Buhel (near Immenstadt) 5.
— (Zillerthal) 181.
Buin, Piz 277.
Büllele, Joch 333.
Bullköpfe, the 332.
Buon-Consiglio, château 294.
Buona, Val (Auronzo) 352.
— (Giudicaria) 308.
Burgau 109.
Burgherg 8.
Burgeis 250.
Bürgeralp (Mariazell) 373.
— (Aflenz) 375.
Bürgerbach, the 139. 145.
Bürgermeisteralp, the 82.
Burggraben, the 109.
Burghalde, the 4.
Bürglhütte, the 135.
Burgstall (Brixen) 225.
— near Oberstdorf 9.
— near Schönberg 219.
— (Pitzthal) 245.
— (Zillerthal) 181.
—, the Hohe (Stubai) 228.
— (near Heiligenblut) 153.
Burgum 187.
Burgwies 135.
Burs 201.
Bürserberg 201.
Bürsegg 201.
Burtschakopf, the 202.
Bus dal Lega 341.
Buso 319.
But, the 336.

Caderzone 305.
Cadin del Laudo 349.
Cadino 296.
Cadini, Mti. 345. 347.
Cadore, Val di 352. 436.
Caffaro 308.
Cagno 311.
Calaita Lake, the 327.
Calamento, Val 318.
Caleeranica 317.
Caldes 311.
Caldonazzo 317.
—, Lake of 317.
Calliano 295.
Callongehe 357.
Camonica, Val 313.
Campedie, Mte. 322.

Campelli Pass 313.
Campese 319.
Campiglio 305.
Campill 342.
— Valley, the 342.
Campitello 323. 260.
Campo 305. 308. 436.
Campo, Lago di 308.
Campo Croce, Val 341.
Campo di Sotto 349.
Campolongo 319. 362.
Campolungo 343.
Campo Moro, Val 284.
Canale 357. 441.
Canale S. Bovo 326.
Canali, Cima di 326. 327.
—, Passo di 327.
Canazei 323.
Cancia 351.
Canciano, Passo di 284.
Candide 352.
Canezza 317.
Canfanaro 414.
Canin see Kanin.
Canisflub, the 208.
Canove 319.
S. Canzian 413.
Capella Mts., the 446.
Capo d'Istria 444.
Capo di Ponte (Val Camonica) 313.
— (near Belluno) 354.
Caporetto 442.
Caprile 356.
Caprino 299.
Capuzinachköpfl 142.
Capuzinerberg, the 65.
Carano 321.
Carè Alto 304.
Careser Glacier, the 286.
Caressa Pass, the 262.
Carct, Alp 307.
Carl August Steig 384.
Carlinbach, the 250.
Carnia, Stazione per la 436.
Carniola 410.
Carpano 319.
Carthaus 242.
Casadio, Mte. 349.
Casale, Mte. 340.
Casotto 317.
St. Cassian 311. 342.
Casone 301.
Caslagnavizza 441.
Castelbell 253.
Castelfondo 310. 311.
Castellazzo, Monte 325.
Castelletto 319. 301.
Castello (Val di Sole) 311.
—, Monte 321.
— Passo 312.

29*

452 INDEX.

Castelnuovo 318.
Castel Tesino 318.
Castione 284.
Catacggio 284. 285.
S. Caterina (Val Furva) 282.
St. Catharina (Schnalser Thal) 242.
Cauria 326.
Cavalazza 325.
Cavalese 321.
Cavareno 268. 310.
Cavallina, Val 313.
Cavedine, Val 296.
Cavelljoch, the 214.
Cavrasto 304.
Cecina 302.
Cedegolo 313.
Cedeh, Val di 262. 292.
—, Vedretta di 291. 292.
Ceggio, the 318.
Cembra 317.
—, Val 320.
Cencenighe 357.
Ceneda 354.
Cengia 333.
Ceniga 297.
Cenia, Val 317.
Ceppina 283.
Ceraino 295.
Cereena Pass, the 311.
Cereda Pass, the 358.
Cerna 409.
Ces, Alp 325.
Cesio-Busche 354.
Cespede Alp 276.
Cesta 349.
Cevedale, Monte 286. 289.
—, Passo 287. 292.
— Hut 312.
Cherso 446.
Cherz 343.
Chiapuzza 350. 351.
Chiarano 297.
S. Chiatar 311.
Chieming 54.
Chiemsee, the 53.
Chiepina, Val 318.
Chiesa 284.
Chiese, the 308.
Chiusa di Verona 295.
Chiusaforte 436.
Chorinsky Klause 95.
Christberg, the 202.
St. Christina 248. 263.
Christles-See, the 10.
Christlieger 73.
St. Christoph 204. 208. 268.
Churburg, the 251.
Ciavalatsch, Piz 251.
Cibiana, Forcella 358.
—, Val 351.

Cilli 407.
Cima 352.
Cimego 308.
Cimirlo 317.
Cimon della Pala 325.
Cimone, the 317. 345.
Cinque Torri 355
Cislon 321.
Cismone 310.
—, the 319. 325.
Cittadella 320.
Cittanova 444.
Civetta, Monte 354. 357.
Civezzano 316.
Cividate 313.
Civita,Monte,seeCivetta.
Clarahütte, the 144.
Clegna, Val 313.
Cles 310.
Clez 311.
Cmir 431.
Cocadain 330.
Codalonga 356.
Cogolo 311.
Colbricon, Cima 325.
—, Passo di 325.
Coldai, Passo 357.
Col de Rü 341.
Colfosco 343.
Col Freddo 347.
Colico 285.
Colle di S. Lucia 357.
Collesei 333.
Cologna 297.
S. Colombano, Corno 282.
Comano 296. 303.
Comedon Pass 358.
Comeglians 436.
Comelico 352.
Comelle Pass 326.
Como, Lake of 285.
Comparsa, Val 357.
Compatsch 218.
Concei, Val 300.
Concordiahütte 112.
Condino 308.
Conegliano 354.
Confinale, Monte 282.
Constanze 7.
—, Lake of 7. 195.
St. Constantin 264.
Contrinjoch, the 324.
Contrinthal, the 324.
Conturinspitze 343.
Cordevole, the 352. 354. 355.
Corgnale 414.
Corna Rossa Pass 281.
St. Cornua 380.
Corte 343.
Cortenedolo 314.
Coriceno, Val di 313.
Cortina di Ampezzo 349.

Cortina, near St. Vigil 341.
Corvara 343.
Corvo, Lake 276.
Cosio 285.
Costalunga Alp & Valley 262. 261.
Costeana 355.
Costonzella Pass 325.
Covolo 319.
Cregnedul, the 434.
Creps, Mte. 340.
Crepedel 349.
Crespano 320.
Crespena 343.
Cresperspitze, the 216.
Creto 308.
Cridola, Mte. 352.
Cristallino, the 345. 346.
Cristallo, Monte (Ampezzo) 346. 350.
— (Ortler) 279.
Cristall Pass 346. 350.
Crna Prst 430.
Croatenloch, the 85.
S. Croce 354.
—, Lago di 354.
Croce, Mte. 333. 335.
Croda Grande 358.
Croda Rossa 345.
Cromerthal, the 216.
Cusiano 311.
St. Cyprian 262.

Daberspitze, the 144.
Daberthal, the 144.
Dachauer Moos, the 3.
Dachstein, the 100. 101. 395.
Dai, Col 357.
Daila, castle 444.
Daimerhütte 190.
Dalaas 202.
Dalanser Staffel, the 212.
Dalfaz-Alp, the 49.
Dalsen 177.
Dam, Sasso di 322.
Dambel 311.
Damberg 388.
Dambóckhaus, the 365.
Damüla 208.
Daniel, the 19.
St. Daniel 423.
Danöfen 202.
Dante Grotto 444.
Daube, the 382. etc.
Daunchell, the 250.
Daone, Val 308.
Darching 49.
Darè 301.
Darfo 313.
Darzo 308.
Daumen, the 20.

INDEX. 453

Daunkoglferner, the 237.
Daunkopf, the 200.
Davennakopf, the 213.
Dazio 308.
Debant 149.
Defregger-Thal, the 138.
Defregger Hut 142.
Degano 436.
Deisenhofen 40.
Deleblo 285.
Dellach 336, 423.
Dellacher Keesflecken, the 143.
Delnice 410.
Denno 310.
Dermulo 310.
Desenzano 307.
Deutschenthal 407.
Deutsch-Landsberg 404.
Deutsch-Metz, see Mezzo-Tedesco.
Deutschnofen 261.
Deutschruth 429.
Dexelbach 109.
Dezzo 313.
Dichtenkopf 136.
Dichtlmühle, the 88.
Dieci, Cima 318.
Dielau-Alpe, the 92.
Diemendorf 25.
Diemjoch, the 241.
Diemkogl, the 241.
Diemthal 244.
Dienten 119.
Dientenbach, the 115.
Dientner Schneeberg, the 113.
Diesbach 78.
Diesbach-Scharte, the 75, 119.
Diessen 26.
Dietenhelm 320.
Dieterubachthal, the 10.
Dietfeldkaser 70.
Diethülle 391.
Dietmannsdorf 388.
Digonera 356.
Dimaro 311.
S. Dionigi, Chapel 352.
Dirabach 391.
Dirndln, the 396.
Dirschentrittjoch 210.
Disgrazia, Mte. della 284.
Divača 413.
Dobratsch, the 422.
Dobrava 422, 430.
Dobrein-Thal 371.
Dobriach 422.
Dodici, Cima 318.
Dogna 435.
Dognagraben 434, 436.
Döllach 150.

Döllerhof 102.
Dollinger 20.
Dolomites 344, 320. etc.
Dölsach 149, 335.
Domegge 352.
Domegliara 295.
Dominicushütte 186.
Don 311.
Donatiberg 407.
Donawitz 395.
Donnajoch 322.
Donnerkogln, the 100.102.
Donnersbach-Thal 393.
Dont 353, 358.
Dopplersteig, the 67.
Dorf (Oetzthal) 120, 237.
Dorfer Glacier 142.
— Oed, the 146.
— See, the 146.
— Thal, the 146.
Dorfheim, château 118.
Dormitz 20.
Dornauberg 184.
Dornbirn 197.
Dornegg-Feistritz 413.
Dorner Alp, the 106.
Dornsberg 253.
Dorsino 304.
Dosoledo 352.
Dos-Pez 310.
Dossaccio 325.
Dos-Trento 294.
Doss Negro 296.
Dössner Scharte, the 399.
Dössner Thal, the 126.
Dostberg 407.
Douglashütte, the 201.
Dovana, Mte. 436.
Drachenhöhle 369.
Drachenloch, the 68.
Drachensees, the 19.
Drachenstein, the 110.
Drahtkogel 368.
Drauburg 416.
Drave, the 327, 438. etc.
Drei Brunnen, see Three Holy Springs.
Dreiergraben 35.
Dreifingerspitze, the 331.
Dreiherrnspitze 144, 191.
Dreikirchen 226.
Dreiländerspitze, the 217.
Dreischusterspitze, the 383.
Drei Schwestern, the 199.
Dreisprachenspitze 280.
Dreithorspitze, the 83.
Drei Zinnen 333, 347, 352.
Drenn, Castello di 297.
Dres 311.
Dresdner Hütte, the 230.
Dro 297.
Drusenfluh, the 214.

Drusenthor, the 214.
Dugon 353.
Duino 303, 441.
Durach 14.
Duram Pass 358.
Durcheckalp, the 129.
Durchgang-Alpe, the 125.
Durchholzen 58.
Durchlass 381.
Durlassboden, the 180.
Dürnbachgraben 137.
Dürnbachthal 362.
Dürnberg 83.
Dürnholz 260.
Durnstein, château 272.
Dürnstein 420.
Durona, Alp 353.
Durone, Passo 304.
Duroner Alp, the 323.
Duron Valley 322, 323.
Dürrach, the 42.
Dürrachklamm, the 42.
Dürreberg, the 18.
Dürrenbach 49.
Dürrenschöberl 388.
Dürrensee, the (Styria) 375.
— (Ampezzo) 344.
Dürronstein 330, 346, 384.
Dürrfeichtenalp, the 85.
Duxerköpfl, the 157.
Duxer Thal, the 182.

Ebbs 58.
Eben 49, 397.
Ebenalpe 180.
Ebenberg-Alp 117.
Ebene 232, 236.
Ebene Reichenau 398.
Eben Glacier 280.
Ebensee 91.
Ebenstein 375, 377.
Ebenthal 418.
Ebenwald 133.
Ebenwand, the 280.
Ebenwand Glacier 287.
Eienzweier 88, 90.
Eberndorf 417.
Ebersberg 38.
Eberstein 427.
Ebnerkapelle, the 174.
Ebnit 197.
Ebriachbach, the 417.
Echerntbal, the 99.
Eckartau 181.
Eckhauer, the 30.
Eckenalp, the 57, 176.
Eckenberg 29.
Ecker-Alpe, the 73.
Eckerastel, the 85.
Eckerfirst, the 73, 85.
Eckkapelle, the 56.
Ed-Alp the 102, 157.

Edelboden 376.
Edelgrieshöhe, the 335.
Edelweisslahnerkopf 78.
Edelweisswand, the 237.
Ederbauer 87.
Ederplan 149. 335.
Edlitz 363.
Edolo 312.
Egard 253.
Egelsee, the 106.
Egerdach 170.
Egern 45. 46.
Egg 206. 12.
Eggenberg, château 404.
Eggenthal, the 260.
Egger Alpe, the 435.
Egger Bach, the 224.
Eggerbauer, the 274.
Eggerberg 331.
Eggessen-Grat 230.
Eglsee 106.
Egna, see Neumarkt.
St. Egyden 364.
Ehbach Valley 37. 232.
Ehmatbach, the 133.
Ehrenberg, castle 18. 332.
Ehrenberger Klause 18.
Ehrenburg 328.
Ehrenfels 389.
Ehrenhausen, château 406.
Ehrenschwang Alp, the 5.
Ehrwald 19. 33. 31.
Ehrwalder Köpfe 33.
Eibelklamm, the 177.
Eiberg 158.
Eibiswald 405.
Eibsee, the 31.
Eichberg 87. 276.
Eichelau 387.
Eichleit 317.
Eichgraben, the 379.
Eidechsspitze, the 328.
Eierkopf, the 144.
Einöd 426.
Einöde 422.
Einödsbach 11.
Einstein, the 22.
Eisak, the 221. 257. 293. etc.
Eisbruck Joch 189.
Eiseler, see Iseler.
Eisenärzt 57.
Eisenauer Alpe, the 107.
Eisenbrechc, the 21.
Eisenerz 385.
Eisenerzer Höhe 378.
Eisengabel, the 341.
Eisenhut 426.
Eisenkappel 417.
Eisenkopf, the 204.
Eisenstein, Bad 159.
Eisenstrasse, the 384.

Eisenzieher 388.
Eiser, the Kleine 134.
Eiserne Thor 362.
Eishof 242.
Eisjoch 242. 244.
Eisjöchl am Bild 242.
Eiskapelle, the 74.
Eiskögele, the 153.
Eiskogl (Trafoi) 279.
Eisnern 429.
Eisrinne Hohe 278. 292.
Eissee Pass, the 287. 292.
Eiswandbühel 132. 153.
Eibigenalp 210.
Elendalp, the 51.
Elendhütte, the 399.
Elferscharte 337. 399.
Elferkofel, the 333.
Elisabethruhe, the 152.
Elixhausen 88.
Ellbach 50.
Ellenbogen 207. 211.
Elmau near Mittenwald 30.
— near Tegernsee 45.
— (Achenthal) 175.
Elmauer Gries, the 23.
Elmen 18. 210.
Elmsee, the 96. 391.
Elsbethen 65. 83.
Embach 116. 129.
Embacher Plaike, the 115.
Emmersdorf 423.
Empfing 55.
Emser-Reute 197.
End der Welt, Glacier 289.
Endorf 53.
Endsthal, the 72.
Enego 319.
Eng, the (Riss) 42. 49.
— (Höllenthal) 365.
Engadinerjoch, the 218.
Enge, the 22.
Engelsberg, ruin 172.
Engelswand, the 236.
Enguiso 300.
Enn, château 321.
Enneberg, valley of 340.
Enns 382.
—, the 378 etc.
Ennsbrand 386.
Ennsdorf 383.
Ennseck, château 382.
Ennsleithen 383.
Enter-Rotlach 45.
Entschenkopf, the 10.
Enzenau 41.
Enzengraben, the 52.
Enzesfeld 380.
Enzinger Boden, the 146.
Enzisweiler 7.
Epfenhausen 3.

Eppan 266.
S. Eremo 301.
Erl-Alp 36. 222.
Erlach 363.
Erlakogel, the 92.
Erlauf 380.
Erlaufsee 373.
Erling 27
Erlsattel 36. 292.
Erlsbach 139. 330.
Ernsthofen 383.
Erpfendorf 175. 58.
Erzbach 385.
Erzberg, the 428. 385.
Erzboden 378.
Erzgunder See, the 21.
Erzh. Johannshütte 147.
Erzh. Johanns-Klause 50.
Eschenauer Plaike, the 115.
Eschenklamm 28.
Eschenkogel 301.
Eschenlahne, the 28.
Eschenloh (Ulten) 276.
— (Loisach) 28.
Eschenthal, the 28.
Eselstein, the 396.
Esselthalgraben, the 84.
Esterbergsee 31.
Etsch, see Adige.
Eutal 28.
Etzlaler Mandl, the 28.
Ettenberg 71.
Ettendorf 415.
Etzerschlössl, the 71.
Eugendorf 88.
Eurasburg 25.
Ewiger Schnee, the 113.
Exkopf, the 200.
Eyrs 262.

Faak 422.
Faaker See 422.
Faal 415.
Fadalto 354.
Fadnerspitze, the 216.
Faè 357.
Faggen 247.
Faggenboden, the 247.
Fahnengrat, the 207.
Fahrnau, the 89.
Fai 303.
Faistenau 11. 12. 84.
Faistenauer Schafberg, the 84. 108.
Falcade 325. 357.
Falepp 50.
—, the Rothe 50.
—, the Weisse 50.
Falginjoch, the 248.
Falken, the 43.
Falkenstein, ruin, near Kufstein 156.

INDEX.   455

Falkenstein, on the Königssee 74.
—, near Inzell 55.
—, the in the Möllthal 149.
—, — (Wolfgangsee) 107.
—, —, near Krimml 137.
Falknis, the 199.
Fall 42.
Fallbach 9. 197. 202. etc.
Fallenstein 372.
Fallwand 322.
Faloria, Tondi di 349.
Falschauer Bach 208.
Falschungspitze 244.
Faltenbacher Wasserfall, the 9.
Falzalp, the 77.
Falzarego Pass 355. 350.
Falzthurn-Alp, the 48.
Fanatjoch, the 241.
Fanes, Gross- and Klein 341.
Fanesthal, the 341.
—, the Ampezzaner 341.
Farchant 29.
Fargorida Fall 307.
Farmach, château 118.
Fasana 444.
FaschaunerThörl. the 399.
Faschinajoch, the 208.
Faselfadspitze 203.
Faselsberg, the 72.
Fassa. Val 323.
Fassa Pass 323.
Fastenberg 395.
Fasulthal, the 204.
Fatschalv Piz 217.
Faukenschlucht 29.
Faver 317.
Fechtehenkopf, the 136.
Fedaja Pass, the 323.
Feder, Castel 321.
Federa, Alp 349.
Federaun 422.
Federbett 188.
Feeberg 425.
Feigenbach, the 18.
Feistagraben (Sölk) 394.
Feistergraben 369.
Feisterscharte, the 396.
Feistritz on the Drave 415. 416.
— on the Mur 369.
— on the Gail 423.
— near Aspang 364.
—. Windisch 407.
— Pulst 428.
— in the Wochein 430.
Feistritz, the 409. 413. 431.
— Graben, the 408.
Feld 75. 422.
Feldafing 24.

Feldalpe, the 158. 58.
Feldernkopf, the 36.
Feldkirch 198.
Feldkirchen 428.
Feldkögele, the 238.
Feldkopf 185. 186.
Feldthurns 226.
Feldwaiblalp 333.
St. Felix (Val di Non) 310.
— near Meran 274.
— (Val Fierozza) 317.
Felixdorf 363.
Felizon 347. 348.
Fella 434.
Fellhorn, the (near Oberstdorf) 12.
— (near Waidring) 57. 176.
Felsegger Schwaige, the 262.
Felsenstein, ruin 269.
Felsenweissachthal 46.
Feltre 354.
—, Vette di 325.
Fend, see Vent.
Fensterlekofel, the 337.
Ferara-Alp 264. 343.
Ferchenbach, the 32.
Ferchensee, the 30. 31.
Ferchenthal, the 30.
Ferdinand Falls 291.
Ferdinandshöhe 280.
Ferleiten 129.
Fermersbachthal 35. 42.
Fermunt, see Vermunt.
Fernazza, Mte. 356.
Fernau-Joch, the 231.
Fernerkogl (Selrain) 228.
— (Oetzthal) 240.
Fernpass, the 19.
Fernstein, château 19.
Ferro, Mte. 352.
—, Val del 435.
Fersenthal 317.
Fersina, the 316.
Fervallthal, the 203.
Festenbach 49.
Fenchtau Lakes 384.
Feuchten 247.
Feuerkogl, the 91.
Feuerpalfen, the 75.
Feuersang, the 121.
Feuerstein 220.
Fiammes 349.
Fiave 304.
Fickergraben 435.
Fieberbrunn 118. 119.
Fiemme, Val 320. 321.
Fiera di Primiero 326.
Fierozza, Val 317.
Filzen-Alpe, the 125.
Filzensattel, the (Urschlauthal) 119.

Filzensattel (Windau) 172.
Filzmoos 396.
Fimberpass, the 218.
Fimberthal, the 218.
Finailjoch, the 242.
Finailspitze, the 239.
Finelebach, the 253. 278.
Fincleloch, the 253.
Finestra, Passo della 327.
Finkenberg 182.
Finkenstein 422.
Finsingbach, the 179.
Finsterbach, the 259.
Finstermünz 249.
Finsterthal Joch 231. 232.
Fiorentina, Alp 353. 357.
Fiori, Malga 308.
Firmianalp, the 67.
Firmisanschneide 243.
Firuitz 433.
Fischach, the 88.
Fischbach 156.
—, the 57.
Fischbachalpe, the 35. 40.
Fischbachau 50.
Fischbachthal, the 35. 40. 57.
Fischburg, château 263.
Fischeleinboden, the 333.
Fischen 8. 26.
Fischerndorf 97.
Fischhausen 50.
Fischhorn, château 116.
Fischsee 425.
Fischankhalp, the 74.
Fitscherbach, the 245.
Fiume 446.
Flaas 258.
Flachau 397.
Fladung 417.
Flammspitze, the 216.
Fläscherberg, the 199.
Flaithal, the 219.
Flattach 150.
Flattnitz 426.
Flanrling 233.
Flavon 310.
Fleck 42.
Flecken 119.
Fleimserthal, see Fiemme.
Fleischbachspitze 310.
Fleiss, the Grosse and Kleine 154.
Flelsa, the Obere 151.
Flexensattel, the 13. 212.
Fliess 285. 245. 247
Flimbach, the 285.
Flimjoch, the 287
Flirsch 205.
Flitsch 442.
Flitscher Klause 442.
Flitschl 443.
Flitzen-Alpe 388.

Flitzthal, the 225.
Flodige 346.
Floiten Glacier, 190. 191.
Floitenspitze, the 191.
Floitenthal, the 184. 190.
Floning 376.
Floruz 317.
Fluchgraben 371.
Fluchthorn, the 217.
Fluchtkogl, the 240.
Fludergraben, the 94.
Fluh, near Bregenz 6. 196.
Fluhenstein 20.
Fluhspitze, 216.
Fobesthörl 377. 378.
Fochezkopf, the 134.
Fockenstein, the 42.
Fodara Vedla, Alp 341.
Föderlach 421.
Fobnsdorf 425.
Folgaria 318.
Föllbaumhöhe 381.
Fölzstein, the 375.
Fonda, Val (Primiero) 327.
— (Ampezzo) 345.
Fondo 268. 310.
Fontana Fredda 321.
Fontanella 208.
Fonteklaus 226.
Fonzaso 327. 355.
Forada, Forcella 353. 357.
Forame, Punta 347.
Forca, the 347.
—, Mte. 357.
Forcella Alta, the 345.
— Bassa 351.
— Grande 356.
— Piccola 351.
Forchach 210.
Förchensee, the 57.
Forchtenstein 363. 426.
Fornarinsee, the 212.
Formin, Croda di 356.
Forni Avoltri 436.
Forno 322.
Forno di Canale 357.
— di Zoldo 358.
— di Sopra and di Sotto 436.
Forno, Val 282.
— Glacier 282.
Förolach 423.
Forscher Alp, the 333.
Forst 253. 274. 416.
Fortogna 354.
Fosses 347.
Fradusta, Cima della 325.
Fraele, Val 281.
Fragant 150.
Fraganter Tauern, the 128.

Fragenstein, ruin 37. 282.
Fragsburg 274.
Framont, Cima di 357.
Frangart 266.
Frankbachjoch 191. 182.
Frankbachthal, the 191.
Frankenmarkt 87.
Franzdorf 411.
Franzensfeste 224.
Franzenshöhe, the 279.
St. Franziskus 317.
Franz-Josefsbad 409.
Franz-Josefs-Höhe, the 131. 152.
Franzl im Holz 90.
Franzosensteig, the 34.
Franz-Senn-Hütte 228.
Frasch-Alp 215.
Fräschenlücke 215.
Frasen, the Hohe 201.
Frassene 358.
Frassilongo 317.
Frastanz 199.
Frastanzer Sand, the 199.
Fratte, the 215.
Frauenalpe, the 32.
Frauenberg 198. 369. 388.
Frauenburg, ruin 425.
Frauenchiemsee 54.
Frauenmauer Cavern 377. 386.
Frauenstein 107. 428.
Frauenwand, the 183.
Frauenwörth 54.
Frauhütt, the 162.
Frauhütt-Sattel 37.
Fraxern 197.
Freibach 420.
Freddo, Col 347.
Freibergsee, the 9.
Freibrunnerspitze, the 250. 251.
Freienfeld 224.
Freiger, the Wilde 229.
Freigerscharte 229.
Freihof, the Wilde 45.
Freiland 374.
Freilassing 56.
Freilchen 72.
Freimannbrücke, the 69.
Frein 372.
Freinberg, the 382.
Freinsattel 372.
Freithof, Wilde 183.
Freiwand, the (Ködnitz-thal) 146.
— (Pasterze) 152.
— (Velber Thal) 141.
Freiwand-Glacier 153.
Frenzela, Val 319.
Frerone, Mte. 313.
Freschen, the Hohe 197.
Fresen 415.

Freundsberg 160.
Fricken, the Hohe 29.
Friedanwerk 385.
Friedrichshafen 7.
Friedstein 392.
Friesach 426.
Frillensee, the 31.
Frischauflaus 418.
Frisolet, Mte. 356.
Frisone, Val 436.
Fritz 57.
Fritzbach, the 397.
Fritzthal, the 397.
Fritzens 160.
Frodolfo, the 283.
Fröhnleiten 309.
Fröhnthal, the 334.
Frohnwies 78.
Froi 225.
Frölichsburg 251.
Fröllspitze, the 225.
Fronau 77.
Fronebon Alpe 228.
Fröschnitz 368.
Froschsee, the 57.
Frosnitzthal, the 130.
Frötschbach, the 265.
Frusnitz Glacier 146.
Frutzbach, the 198.
Fuchsau 57.
Fuchskarspitze, the 21.
Fucine 311.
Fugazze, Passo delle 295.
Fügen 179. 159.
Fulpmes, see Vulpmes.
Fumo, Val di 308.
Fundelkopf, the 200.
Fünfspitz, the 443.
Funtensee, the 75. 118.
Funtensee-Alpe, the 75.
— Tauern, the 74. 75.
Fürberg 108.
Furgler Joch 219. 248.
Furka, the Grosse 200.
—, the Kleine 200.
—, the Laternser S. 156.
—, the Rothe 217.
Furkel, the 208. 341.
Fürkele 291.
Fürkele-Ferner, the 286.
Fürkele-Scharte 286.
Fürstenbrunnen 67.
Furstenburg, château 250.
Fürstenfeld 3.
Fürstenstein 70.
Fürt, Alp 222.
Furth 135.
Further Thal 380.
Furva, Val 282.
Furx, Alp 198.
Fusch 128.
Fuscher Bad, the 129.
— Thal, the 116. 128.

INDEX. 457

Fuscher Thörl, the 130.
Fuscherkarkopf 182. 152.
Fuscherkerscharte 132.
Fuschl 108.
Fuschlsee, the 108.
Fusine 353.
Füssen 15.
Futschölpass, the 217.

Gabraun 369.
Gache Blick 245.
Gacht 22.
—, Pass 22.
Gachtspitze 22.
Gader, the 328.
— Thal, the 340.
Gafalljoch, the 214.
Gaflenz 382.
Gafluna Thal 215.
Gagenmühle 6.
Gagering 179.
Gail, the 423. 433.
Gailbach 223.
Gailberg, the 335.
Gailitz, the 433.
Gailthal, the 423.
Gainfarn 362.
Gaino 302.
Gais 337.
Gaisalp, the 46.
Gaisbach 126.
—, the 158.
Gaisberg 65.
—, the 66.
Gaisberg Glacier 243.
Giselsberg 329.
Gaishorn 389.
Gaislach 238.
Gaislachkogel 238.
Gaisloch 366.
Gaisrucken 435.
Gaisstein, the (near Radstadt) 397.
— (near Kitzbühel) 148. 135. 174.
Gaisthal, the 35.
Galgentobel, the 201.
Galgennel 215.
Galizenklamm 335.
Galizien 418.
Gall, the 268. 269.
St. Gallen 384.
Gallenberg Grosse 410.
St. Gallenkirch 215.
Galluno 314.
Gallenstein, château 384.
Gallinkopf, the 199.
Gallinathal, the 199.
Gallio 319.
Galtür 217.
Galzig 204.
Gaming 380.
Gamlitz 406.

Gamp 199.
Gampadel-Alp, the 214.
Gampadelthal, the 214.
Gampen-Alp, the 310.
Gampenhöfe, the 268.
Gampenpass, the 310.
Gampern 87.
Gamperton-Thal, the 200.
Gamplaschg 214.
Gampretz 214.
Gams 379. 415.
Gamsecksteig 365.
Gamsfeld, the 95. 101.
Gamsgraben 369. 379.
Gamsgrube, the 152.
Gamsjöchl, the 43.
Gamskarkogl, the 121. 124.
Gamskarl, the 158.
Gamskogl, the 157. 237.
Gamslanernock, the 190.
Gamsleeher, the 67.
Gamsspitze, the 49. 229.
Gamsthal, the 334.
Gand 285.
Gandberg 267. 266.
Gandegg 266.
Ganeu, Alp 215.
Ganiskopf, the 176.
Ganerajoch, the 215.
Ganerathal, the 215.
Gänsebiehljoch 340.
Gansriese 365.
Gantkofel, the 266. 269.
Garatshausen 25
Gärberbach 227.
Garda 301.
—, Isola di 301.
—, Lago di 300. 298.
Gardellon 358.
Gardena Pass 343.
Gardenazza, the 342.
Gardeno, Val 261.
Gardone-Rivera 302.
Gares 326.
Garfulla 212.
Gargazon 269.
Gargellen 215.
Gargellenthal, the 215.
Gargnano 302.
Garmisch 29.
Garnstein 226.
Garsella 199.
Garrella-Tobel, the 250.
Garsten 393.
Gartenau, château 68.
Gartnerkofel 423. 435.
Garza, Val 302.
Gasehurn 215.
Gassen 329.
Gösteig (Stubai) 228.
— (Ridnaun) 233.
— (Achenthal) 158.

Gastein, the 125.
—, Dorf 120.
—, Hof 120.
—, Wildbad 121.
Gatschach 336.
Gatschkopf, the 235.
Gatterl, the 19. 33.
Gatternock 339.
Gaudenz, Alp 199.
Gauenstein 213.
Gauerthal, the 214.
Gaul, the 268.
Gauting 24.
Gaverdina, Val 308.
Gavia-Pass, the 283.
Gavia, Monte 283.
Gayenhofen 201.
Gazza, Monte 290.
Gebhardsberg, the 196.
Gefrorne Wand, the 183.
Gefrorne Wandspitzen 183. 186.
Gehackte 375.
Geiereck, the 67.
Geierkogel, the 416. 427.
Geiersbühl 149.
Geiersburg 426.
Geige, the 172.
Geigelstein, the 55. 56.
Geiger, the Grosse 143.
Geigerstein, the 42.
Geinfeld 113.
Geinfeldbach 113.
Geisach 41.
Geisalphorn, the 10.
Geisalpsee, the 10.
Geiseck, the 21.
Geiselkopf, the 125.
Geiselsberg 329. 344.
Geiselsberger Thal 329.
Geisfuss 10.
Geishorn, the 21.
Geislerspitzen, the 264. 225.
Geisspitz, the 214.
Geisterspitze, the (Ortler) 277. 280.
Geitau 51.
Geltthal, the 337. 339.
Gemärk 347.
Gemersdorf 415.
Gemona 437.
Gennach, the 3.
Genova, Val di 306.
Gentschoijoch, the 266.
St. Georg (Gailthal) 423.
St. Georgen, in Bavaria 26.
— in Carinthia 425.
— am Längsee 427.
— am Reith 381.
— in the Pinzgau 116.
— in Styria 407.

458   INDEX.

St. Georgen near Taufers 337.
St. Georgenberg 159.
Gepatschalp, the 247.
Gepatsch Glacier, the 247. 240.
Gepatschhaus, the 247.
Gepatschjoch 240. 248.
Geralscharte, the 134.
Gercut 317.
Gerlitzen-Alp 422.
Gerlos 137. 179.
—, the 179.
—, the Hohe 181.
—, the Wilde 180.
Gerloswand, the 179.
Gerlouz 420.
Gern 67. 71.
Gernalp, the 43.
Gernspitz, the 18.
Gerold (near Mittenwald) 34.
St. Gerold (Walserthal) 200.
Gersberg-Alpe, the 66.
Gerstruben 10.
St. Gertraud on the Inn 159.
St. Gertrud (Sulden) 288.
— (Ultenthal) 276.
— (Lavantthal) 416.
Gertrusk 416.
Gesäuse, defile of 380. 387.
Geschelbte Thurm 259.
Geserberg 196.
Gesuretta, Forcella 326.
Gewellkopf, the 215.
Gfäll 219.
Gfaller Mühle, the 156.
Gfallwand, the 275.
Gfiederberg 304.
Gfrill 310.
Ghedina, Lago 349.
S. Giacomo 299. 413.
Giatel, Col 356.
Giau, Mte. 356.
Gichel 21.
Giebeln, Ober and Unter 211.
Giglachscharte 396.
St. Gilgen 108.
Gimbach-Alpe, the 92.
Gimpelspitze, the 22.
Gindelalp, the 50.
Ginzling 184.
S. Giovanni, in the Friuli 441.
—, in the Val di Fassa 322.
Giralba 352.
Giralba-Joch 333.
Girlan 266.
Giselawarte 383.

Gitsch, the 328.
Gitschthal 33. 336.
Gindicaria 303.
S. Giuliano 306.
Giumella, Mte. 298.
S. Giustina 354.
Giustino 305.
Gjaidalpe, the 100.
Gjaidköpfe, the 75.
Gjaidstein, the 100.
Gjaidtroghöhe 154.
Glammergrube, the 230.
Glan, the 67. 418. 438.
Glandorf 428.
Glanegg 67. 3.
Glanegg 428.
Glanfurtbrücke 420.
Glaning 258.
Glanzsee 336.
Glashütte (Bavaria) 47.
— (Styria) 405.
Gleichenberg-Alpe 55.
Gleif, chapel 266.
Glein 424.
Gleinalpe 370. 424.
Gleink 383.
Gleinker See 391.
Gleinser Jöchl, the 220.
Gleinthal, the 424.
Gleirscher Jöchl, the 231.
— Thal, the 36. 161. 231.
Glemmthal, the 118.
Gliederferner 187.
Gliesshof, the 251.
Glimmspitze, the 210.
Glockenjoch, the 279.
Gloekerin, the 153.
Glockner, see Gross-Glockner.
Glocknerhaus, the 152.
Glocknerkarkweg 154.
Glocknerscharte, the Obere and Untere 147.
Glocknerwand, the 153.
Glockthurm 247. 248.
Gloggnitz 364.
Glopper, the 197.
Glozza, Val 217.
Glungetzer, the 161.
Glurns 251.
Glurnser Köpfl, the 251.
Gmund (Adige) 207. 293.
— (Tegernsee) 44.
Gmünd (Carinthia) 398. 397.
— (Gerlos) 180.
Gmunden 85.
Gmundener Berg, the 88.
Gmadenwald 161.
Gobbera 318.
Gobernitz 424.
Göflan 252.
Gogau 439.

Gogna 352.
Göhlstein 73.
Göhrenspitze, the 35.
Going 175.
Goisern 95.
Goldberg Glacier, the (Rauris) 127.
Goldberg-Tauern 128.
Goldeck 385.
Goldegg 115.
Goldenbachbrücke 69.
Goldenstein 83.
Goldrain 252.
Goldzechscharte 154.
Göll, see Hohe-Göll.
Golling 84.
Golling-Scharte 96.
Göllheiten, the 73.
Gollrad 374.
Gölsen 379.
Gölser Berg 230.
Gomagoi 277.
Gond 285.
Gonobitz 407.
Gopfberg, the 208.
Göpfing 384.
Gorfen 217.
Göriach 431.
Göriacher Alm 433.
Göriachwinkel, the 396.
Goriciza, Alp 442.
Gorizia 441.
Gorratschamp 147.
Gorto, Canal di 436.
Görtschitzthal 427.
Görz, see Gorizia.
Gosaldo 358.
Gosau 100.
Gosau-Bach, the 100.
— Glacier, the 101.
— Mill 96. 100.
— Schmied 100.
— Seen, the 100.
— Zwang, the 100.
Gosaubals 96.
Gosditsch Alp 442.
Gosdorf 406.
Goss 379.
Göss 424.
Gösseck 389.
Gösselsdorf 417.
Gossau 428.
Gösensauss 222.
Göss Fall 399.
Gössgraben 399.
Gosshwk 6.
Gössl 97.
Gössnitz Fall, the 148.
Gosting 404. 370.
Göstling 381. 378.
Gästritz 367.
Gotschakogel, the 367.
Gotteres 347.

Gottesackerwände 12.
Gottschee 410.
Gotzenalp, the 74.
Gotzentauern, the 75.
Gotzenthal 74.
Götzis 197.
Goubachspitze, the 143.
Goyen, château 273.
Graba 230.
Grabagrubennieder 229.
Grabanock, Alp 229.
Grabnerthörl, the 388.
Grabspitz, the 187.
Gradau 391.
Gradenthal, the 150.
Grades 426.
Gradisca 441.
Graf-Carl-Steig 433.
Grafeil 254.
Grafenbrunn 411.
Grafendorf 369. 423.
Grafenegg 392.
Grafenherbergalp, the 52.
Grafenstein 418.
Grafing 53.
Grafraith 3. 27.
Grähn 22.
Grahovo 430.
Grainau 31.
Gramaisalp, the Upper and Lower 48.
Gramaisthal, the 210.
Gramaiser Joch 49.
Gramsenspitze 147. 286.
Granatscharte, the 146.
Granatspitze, the 146.
Grande, Val (Oglio) 312.
Grande, Val (Ampezzo) 336.
Granuda 435.
Granvilla 352.
Graseck 30.
Grasleiten 262.
Grassnitz 375.
Grasstein 224.
Graswang 23.
Graswang Thal, the 23.
Grailspitze, the 150.
Gratsch 272. 331.
Gratwein 370.
Gratz 400.
Graue Glacier, the 147.
Graukogl, the 124.
Graun 250.
Grauspitze, the 199.
Grawander Schinder 185.
Grebenzen 424.
Greifenberg 27. 396.
Greifenburg 336.
Greifenstein, château 259.
Greimberg, the 426.
Greiner, the Grosse 186.
Greith 371. 376. 380.

Greuzeckkopf, the 217.
Greut 37.
Gribele-Thal, the 218.
Gries near Botzen 258.
— (Ischl) 95.
— on the Brenner 221.
— in the Val Fassa 323.
— in the Pinzgau 116.
— in the Sulzthal 230. 232. 237.
— in the Selrain 231.
Griesalp, the 76.
Griesen 23. 34.
Griesenau 158.
Grieser Thal, the 231.
Griesjoch, the 232.
Grieskareck 397.
Grieskogel 233.
Grieskopf 205. 238.
Griesmauer, the 386.
Griessen, Pass 119.
Griessenbach, the 119.
Griesstein 377.
Grieswies-Alp, the 127.
Griffeltobel, the 202.
Griffen 426.
Grignano 414.
Grigno 348.
Grillitschhütte, the 405.
Grimming, the 393.
Grimmingbach, the 393.
Grimmjoch 261.
Grintouc or Grintonz, the (Sannthal Alps) 418.
— (Isonzo valley) 442.
Grins 235.
Gröbming 394.
Groder 148.
Grödener Bach, the 263.
— Joch, the 264. 343.
— Thal, the 263.
Grödig 67. 68.
Grödiger Thörl, the 67.
Grohmannspitze, the 263.
Groppenstein Fall 149.
Grosina, Val 284.
Grosio 283.
Grossaitingen 3.
Grossarl 114.
Grossarl-Thal 114.399.
Grossarler Klammen 114.
Grossbachthal, the 143.
Grossbergthal, the 188.
Grossdorf (Bregenzer Wald) 207.
— (Kals) 145.
Grosselitchstein, the 388.
Gross-Elendthal 400.
Gross-Florian 404.
Grosser Geiger 142.
Grossglockner 146. 153.
Gross-Gmain 81.

Grosse Gries 307.
Grosshesselohe 40.
Gross-Ingent, the 184.
Gross-Karolinenfeld 53.
Grosse-Kirchheim 150.
Grosse Knallstein 394.
Gross-Laschitsch 410.
Grosse Priel, the 391.
Grosse Pyhrgass 388. 392.
Grossotto 284.
Gross-Ramming 384.
Gross-Reifling 378. 384.
Gross-Sierning 389.
Grosse Steinscharte 13.
Grosstiefenthal 51.
Gross-Venediger, the 140. 142.
Gross-Vermunt 216.
Grossweitalp 136.
Grosse Wilde 11.
Grotta, la 299.
Grub (Langtaufers) 121. 250.
Grub, château 96.
Grubalm, the 134.
Grubbachfall, the 134.
Grubberg 384.
Grubeck 393.
Gruben 10. 140. 214.
Gruben-Alp, the 77.
Grubereck, the 46. 126.
Gruberalm, the 119. 366.
Grüblglacier, the 229.
Grubschartl 387.
Grünau (Almthal) 90.
Grünau, the (near Mariazell) 373.
Grünberg, the 90.
Grundlsee, the 97.
Grundschartner, the 182.
Grün-Habachkopf 136.
Grünkopf, the 35.
Grünschacher 365. 366.
Grünsee (Ultenthal) 286.
— (Schafberg) 107.
— (Spronserthal) 275.
— (Steinernes Meer) 75.
— (Stubachthal) 146.
— (Tragöss) 380.
Grünsee-Alp, the 75.
Grünsee-Tauern 74.
Grünspitz, the 22.
Grünstein, the 19.
Grünsteinscharte, the 19.
Grünten, the 8.
Grünwaldthal, the 337.
Gruttenstein 80.
Gsallbach, the 247.
Gscheid 316.
Gschiser Tobel, the 201.
Gschliess, Inner 140.
Gschnitz 220.
Gschnitzthal, the 220.

INDEX.

Gschlöder 377.
Gschlöderkar, the 377.
Gschütt, Pass 101.
Gschwand 372.
Gschwandalp 94.
Gschwendmühle, the 5.
Gschwendt 389.
Gsollknoten, the 333.
Gsieser Thörl 139.
— Thal 139. 330.
Gsengschneide, the 388.
Gsoll 91.
Gsollgraben, the 386.
Gstatterboden 386.
Gstattmeier Niederalpe, the 388.
Gsteig, the 236.
Gsteirhof 275.
Guarda 217.
Guffert, the 47.
Guildaun 225. 226.
Guggenthal 108.
Guggberg 435.
Guglalp, the 77.
Guglschneide, the 77.
Gummern 337.
Gumpach-Kreuz, the 142.
Gumpeneck 393. 394.
Gumpoldskirchen 362.
Gundlalp, the 8.
Gunkel, the 185.
Gunskirchen 86.
Guntenhang, the 208.
Guntramsdorf 362.
Guntschnaberg, the 258.
Günzach 3.
Gupfsattel 366.
Gurgl 238.
Gurgler Thal (nearlmst) 20. 234.
— (Oetzthal) 243.
Gurgler Ferner, the 243.
Gurgler Joch, the 244.
Gurk 427.
Gurk, the 418. 426.
Gürtelscharte 228.
Gurtepohl 215.
Gurtis 199.
Gurlisspitze, the 199.
Guschghel Alpe 199.
Guslar Glacier, the 240.
Guslarjoch, the 240.
Gusswerk 374.
Gutenstein 363. 415.
Gütle 197.
Gutthal, the 131. 151.

Haag 382.
Haagen 373.
Haar 53.
Habach 87. 130.
Habachkees, the 130.
Habachthal, the 130.
Habberg, the 58.
Habernau 390.
Habersauer Thal 158.
Habichen 236.
Habicht, the 220. 228.
Hachau 55.
Hackhoferkaser 232.
Hacking 379.
Hadersdorf 379.
Hafelekar 171.
Hafling 275.
Hafnereck, the 400. 398.
Hagelhütte, the 42.
Hagenegg 417.
Hagengebirge, the 86. 112.
Hägerau 211.
Haggen 231.
Hahnenberg, the 198.
Haindlmauer 387.
Haidbausen 53.
Haidnerhöhe, the 426.
Haiming 233.
Hainbach 54.
Hainfeld 379.
Hainzen, the 94.
Hainzenberg, the 179.
Hairlach 245.
Hairlachbach 232. 236.
Halbenrein 406.
Haldensee, the 22.
Haldenwangereck, the 13.
Hall near Steyr 390.
— near Admont 388.
— in the Tyrol 100.
Hall Salt-mine, the 164. 30.
Hallbachthal 380.
Hallbauer 274.
Hallein 83.
Haller Anger, the 36. 164.
Haller Mauern, the 386.
Hallkogl, the 237.
Hallstatt 96. 98.
—, Lake of 96. 98.
— Glacier 100.
Hallthal 101. 372.
Hallthurm, Pass 76.
Hallwang 88.
Hals, the 376.
Haltspitze, the 158. 175.
Hammerau 79.
Hammersbach 31.
Handlhof, the 102.
Hangende Ferner, the 229.
Hangende Stein, the 68.
Hangerer 243.
Happ, the Grosse and Kleine 148.
Harbatzhofen 6.
Hardegg 428.
Hartelsgraben, the 385.

Hartlalpe, the 426.
Haseck, the 121.
Haselberg, the 332.
Haselburg 258.
Häselgehr 210.
Haselstauden 197.
Hasenohr 287.
Haslach (Eisak valley) 258.
— (Kaiser Thal) 145.
— (Rhine valley) 197.
— (Traunthal) 58.
Haslau 172. 390.
Hatlerdorf 197
Hätten 14.
Hatting 233.
Hauenstein, ruin 264.
Hauensteiner Wald 264.
Hauerkogl, the 287.
Haunold, the 393.
Haus (Ennsthal) 394.
— (Stillup) 182. 184.
Haus am Bacher 407.
Hausham 50.
Häuslhütte, the 134.
Häusling 182.
Hausruck. the 87.
Hebung, the 208.
Hechtsee. the 157.
Heckbachthal, the 12. 211.
Heft 425.
Heidersee, the 250.
Heilbrunn, baths 41.
Heilige Berg, see Luschariberg.
Heiligenblut 150.
Heiligenbluter Tauern, the 131
Heiligengeist (Kasern) 144.
— (near W.-Kappel) 408.
— (near Villach) 423.
Heiligengeist-Jöchl 182. 191.
Heilig-Kreuz 238. 342.
Heiligkreuz-Kofel 341. 312.
Heiligkreuz-Kirche 341.
Heiligwasser 171.
Heimgarten, the 28. 39.
Heimspitze, the 215.
Heimwaldkofel, the 330.
St. Heinrich 25.
Heinzelkogel 371.
Heiterwand 210.
Heiterwang 18.
Helenenthal 362.
Hellbrunn, château 66.
Helm, the 332. 333.
Hengst, the 391.
Hengatthal 366.
Herpatz 6.

INDEX. 461

Hermagor 423.
Hermannshöhle 364.
Herndl 384.
Herndlschmied 390.
Herpelje 414.
Herrenchiemsee 53.
Herrstein, the 331.
Hersching 27.
Herzog Ernst, the 127.
Herzogstand, the 38.
Hetzendorf 361.
Heuberg 58. 156. 363.
Heufeld 53.
Heukaareck, the 115.
Heukuppe 366.
Heunfels 333.
Heuthal, the 57. 177.
Hexenthurm, the 387.
Hieburg 137.
Hieflau 385. 378.
Hierlatz, the 99.
Hiesel Alpe, the 388.
Hietzing 379.
Hilgerberg 70.
Hilm-Kematen 381.
Hilmteich 404.
Himberstein 387.
Himmeleck, the 21.
Himmelmoos - Alp, the 156.
Himmelreichwiese 90.
Himmelschroffen, the 9.
Himmelwand, the 124.
Hindelang 20.
Hinteralpe, the 55.
Hinteranthal, the 33. 161.
Hinterbad, the 198.
Hinterberg, the Wilde 228.
Hinter - Brandkopf, the 72.
Hinterbühl 142. 143.
Hinter-Dux 183.
Hintereck 72.
Hintereis Glacier 239. 240.
Hintergasse 202.
Hintereisjoch, the 240.
Hintergern 71.
Hinter-Gosau 100.
Hintere Grat, the 289.
Hinterhorn, the 176.
Hinterhornalp, the 161.
Hinter-Hornbach 13.
Hinterjoch 22.
Hinterkirch 248. 250.
Hintermoos 196.
Hinterreute 208.
Hinterriss 43.
Hintere Schwärze 239.
Hintersee (Ramsau) 78.
— (Velber Thal) 141.
Hinterstein 21.

Hintersteiner See 158. 175.
Hintersteiner Thal 21.
Hinter-Stoder 391.
Hintertambergau 390.
Hinterthal 113. 119.
Hinter-Tuf 183.
Hinterwaldhof 133.
Hintere Wandln. the 286.
Hinter-Wildalpen 378.
Hippach 181.
St. Hippolyt 268.
Hirlatz, the 99.
Hirschau 208.
Hirschbachthal, the 42.
Hirschberg, the (near Bregenz) 196.
— (near Tegernsee) 45. 47.
— (near Hindelang) 20.
Hirschbichlkopf 31.
Hirschbühl 78.
Hirschegg 10.
Hirschelau 75.
Hirschenspitze, the 212.
Hirschgunder Thal, the 13.
Hirschkaar, the 124.
Hirschsprung, the 8.
Hirschthal Alpe 42.
Hirschwaldstein 390.
Hirschwang 365.
Hirschwiese, the 76.
Hirt 427.
Hirzbachfall, the 128.
Hirzbachthal, the 128.
Hirzbachthörl, the 129.
Hirzer, the 275.
Hittisau 5. 206.
Hittisberg, the 206.
Hochalpe, the Brucker 369.
— (Kaisergebirge) 58. 158.
— (Karwendelthal) 36.
— (Hochschwab) 375. 377.
— (near Olang) 329.
— (Partenkirchen) 32.
— (Praga) 331.
— (near Unken) 177.
Hochalpeljoch 334. 436.
Hochalpenspitze 400.
Hochalpenthal 13.
Hochälple, the 207.
Höchbauer 363.
Hochberg, the 55.
Hochbrett, the 72. 73.
Hochbrunnerschneide 333.
Hochebenkofel 332. 347.
Hocheck 77. 380.
Hochederspitze, the 233.
Hocheiser, the 134.

Hocheisspitze, the 78.
Hoch-Eppan, ruin 266.
Hochfeller 187. 189.
Hochfellen, the 55. 57.
Hochfilzen 119.
Hoch-Finstermünz 249.
Hochfrottspitze, the 12.
Hochgall, the 139. 339.
Hochgallmig 247.
Hochgern, the 55. 56.
Hochgeschirr, the 90.
Hochgolling 396.
Hochgrat, the 5.
Hochgrindl, the 229.
Hochgruber Glacier, the 153.
Hoch-Gründeck 113. 114.
Hochhädrich, the 206.
Hochhaide 388.
Hochhorn, the 55.
Hochiss 49.
Hochjoch (Oetzthal) 212.
— (Ortler) 291.
— (Silberthal) 214.
— (Pflersch) 229.
— Glacier 242.
Hochkaar 381.
Hochkail, the 113.
Hochkaiser, the 158.
Hochkalter, the 78.
Hochkogel, the 88.
Hochkönig, the 113. 119.
Hochkopf, the 39. 43.
Hochkrumbach 10. 209.
Hochlantsch 360.
Hochleitenjoch, the 278.
Hochleitenspitze, the 278. 289.
Hochlekengebirge 109.
Hochnaderer 246.
Hochmölbing, the 392.
Hochmoos 176.
Hochmuth, the 95.
Hochnarr, see Hohenaar.
Hochnörderer, the 217.
Hochobir 417. 418.
Hoch-Osterwitz 427.
Hochplatte, the 56.
Hochplatter Bauer 275.
Hochreichart 424. 389.
Hochriss, the 54.
Hochscheibe 388.
Hochschloss 26. 368.
Hochschober 138. 147.
Hochschwab 375. 376. 377.
Hochstadt, the (Pusterthal) 335.
— (Styria) 377.
Hochstauffen, the 82.
Hochsteig, the 184. 399.
Hochsteigfeld, the 133.
Hochstein 394. 396.
Hochsteinscharte 394.

462 INDEX.

Hochtauern, the 124.
Hochtenn 129. 130. 210.
Hochthor 387.
Hochthron, the Salzburger 67.
—, the Berchtesgadener 67.
Hochthurm 385.
Hoch-Vernagt Glacier, 240. 241.
Hochvernagtspitze 239.
Hochvogel, the 12. 21.
Hochwanner, the 33.
Hochwart (Grünten) 8.
— (near Meran) 275.
— (near Gschöder) 377.
Hochwilde 244.
Hochwildstelle 396.
Hochzink, the 119.
Hoch-Zinödl, the 387.
Hof (Salzburg) 108.
— (Bregenzer Wald) 207.
Hofalpe, the 54.
Höfatsspitze, the 10.
Hofbauerngschloss 395.
Höfen 210. 218.
Höflein 418.
Hofmannshütte, the 152.
Hofmannsruhe, the 9.
Hofmannsweg, the 158.
Hofstatt (Prags) 330.
Högelberg, the 79.
Höhhauer 363.
Hohe Aderl, the 141. 142.
Hohe Brücke, the 128.
Hohe Burgstall 153. 228.
Hohe Docke, the 132.
Hohenferner 286.
Hohe Frassen, the 201.
Hohe Freschen 198. 208.
Hohe Fricken, the 29.
Hohe Fürleg, the 136.
Hohe Fürst 243.
Hohe Gaisl 330. 347.
Hohe Gang, the 19. 132.
Hohe Geige 237. 245. 246.
Hohe Gerlos, the 181.
Hohe Gjaidstein, the 100.
Hohe Göll, the 68. 73. 84. 85.
Hohe Ifen, the 12.
Hohe Joch, the 251.
Hohe Kalmberg, the 94. 95.
Hohe Koien, the 208.
Hohe Kranzberg, the 34.
Hohe Kugel, the 197.
Hohe Licht 12.
Hohe Moos Alp 229.
Hohe Munde, the 35. 233.
Hohenaar, the 128. 154.
Hohenaschau 54.
Höhenau Alpe 182.

Hohenberg 374.
Höhenburg (Kaprun) 134.
Hohenburg, château 41.
Höhendorf 28.
Hoheneck 407.
Hohenegg 389. 407. 415.
Hohenems 197.
Höhenfeld 394.
Hohenferner 286.
Hohenfernerjoch 286.
Hohenmauthen 415.
Hoheneck 384. 391.
Hohen-Osterwitz, château 427.
Hohen-Salzburg, castle 63.
Hohe Sandling 97.
Hohe Schrott, the 94.
Hohenschwangau, château 15.
Hohentauern 389. 425.
Hohenwang 368.
Hohenwart 426.
Hohenwartscharte 153.
Hohenwerfen, castle 113.
Hohe Peissenberg, the 26.
Hohe Rad, the 216.
Hohe Riffel, the 158.
Hohe Salve 158. 171.
Hohe Säule, the 144.
Hohe Schneide, the 279.
Hohe Schrott, the 92.
Hohe Stellen-Scharte 230.
Hohe Veitsch 368. 371.
Hohe Wand, the (Oetzthal) 239.
— (Piesting Valley) 362.
Hohe Wilde 243.
Hohe Wildstelle, the 396.
Hohe Zieten, the 335.
Hohe Zinken, the (Wolfgang-See) 107.
— (near Sekkau) 389. 424.
Hohlenbach, the 321.
Hohlenstein 46. 373.
Möhlenstein 344.
Hoierberg, the 6. 7.
Hoiren 7.
Hoisengut, the 90.
Hojer 370.
Hölle, the, in Styria 376.
— (Pilerschthal) 222.
Höllenbachthal, the 82.
Hollenburg 420.
Hollenegg 405.
Hüllengebirge, the 91.
Höllenhörner, the 11.
Hollenstein 381.
Hollenstein 361.
Höllenthal, the (Semmering) 365.

Höllenthal (Partenkirchen) 31.
Höllentbalklamm, the 31.
Höllentobel, the 202.
Hollenzen 180.
Hollenzenbach, the 180.
Hollersbach 135.
Hollersbachthal, the 135.
Höllkar, the 110.
Hölltobel, the 10.
Holzalpl, the 159.
Holzgau 211.
Holzhausen 215.
Holzkirchen 40.
Holzleiten, the 20. 87.
Holzpointalp, the 45.
Holzstuben 105.
Hönigkogl, the 118.
Hopfgarten (Brixenthal) 171.
— (Defereggenthal) 239.
Hopfreben 209.
Horlachbach, the 232. 236.
Horn Glacier 190.
Hornbach, Vorder and Hinter 13. 210.
Hornbachjoch, the 13.
Hornbachthal, the 13.
Hörndlalpe, the 376.
Hörndljoch, the 182.
Hörndlmauer 377
Hörnle, the 28.
Hornspitzen (Zillerthal) 186. 190.
— (Rhäticon) 200.
Horastein 362.
Hornthalerjoch, the 232.
Hörsching 86.
Hörtenberg 233.
Hötting 160.
Hrastnigg 409.
Hribarze 431.
Huben (Oetzthal) 237.
— (Iselthal) 138.
— (Salzburg) 55.
Hugling 27.
Hühnereuit-Sattel 372.
Höhnerspiel, the 222.
Humberg, the 429.
Hundham 50.
Hundsbacher Jöchl 237.
Hundschupfen, the 368.
Hundsdorfer Alp, the 130.
Hundskehlgrund 182.
Hundskehljoch 182. 191.
Hundskögel, the 93.
Hundstein, the 118.
Hundsthal 232.
Hundstod, the 76.
Hunerkogl Scharte 395.
Hungerbach, the 27.
Hungerbrunn 428.

INDEX. 463

Hungerburg, the 170.
Husselmühle, the 35.
Hüttau 397.
Hutteldorf 379.
Hüttenberg 427.
Hütteneckalp, the 94.
Hüttenstein 108.
Huttler Thal, the 200. 212.
Hüttschlag 114.
Hüttwinkel-Thal 127.
Ilutweiden-Thal, the 286.

Ichsichi 413.
Idria 411.
Idro 309.
—, Lago d' 309.
Ifenwand, the 12.
Iffeldorf 87.
Iffinger, the 275.
Igendorf 411.
Iggdorf 410.
Igla ('Sulzbach needle') 408.
Igling 3.
Igls 169. 170.
Ika 413.
St. Ilgen 375.
Ilkahöhe, the 25.
Ill, the 199.
Iller, the 4. 8. etc.
Illklamm, the 198. 199.
Illstern 238.
Ilsankimühle, the 76.
Imbachhorn, the 128. 134.
Imberger Horn, the 20.
Imer 327.
Imlauer Gebirge, the 113.
Immenstadt 4.
Immenstadter Horn, the 4.
Imst 20. 234.
Innsterberg 234.
Incansle 295.
Incisa Saddle 343.
Ineudine 312.
Ingent, the 184. 185.
Ingering-Thal 424.
Inn, the 53. 156. 162 etc.
Innerbad 276.
Innerberg 262.
Innerfeld 332.
Inner-Ganifer 204.
Inner-Gschlöss 140.
Inner-Kreuss 366.
Inner-Pflersch 222.
Inner-Prags 330.
Inner-Schmirn 183.
Innerst, in der 333.
Inner-Wallgau 200.
Innichen 332.
Innicher Wildbad 332.
Inning 27.

Inningen 3.
Innsbruck 161.
Inzell 55.
Inzing 232.
Ippelcskogl 223.
Irdning 393.
Irrsdorf 110.
Irrsee 3. 110.
Isar, the 34. 86. 39. etc.
Ischgl 218.
Ischia 317.
Ischl 92.
— brook, the 92. 103.
Ischl Salt-mine, the 94.
Iscl, the 142. 334.
—, hill, near Bregenz 196.
—, —, near Innsbruck 168.
Iseler, the 20.
Iselsberg, the 149.
Iselthal, the 138.
Iseo 313.
—, Lago d' 313.
Isera 295.
St. Isidor 258.
Islitzbach 142.
Isoletto, rock 301.
Isonzo, the 431. 432. 441.
Iss-Alpe (Stubai) 228.
— (Gerlos) 180.
Issenanger 36. 161.
Istalanz-Thal, the 219.
Itschgerney, Alp 200.
Itter, château 171.
Ivano, château 318.
Ixenbach 332.
Jachen, the 42.
Jachenau 42.
—, the 42.
St. Jacob (Arlberg) 204.
— (Defereggen) 139. 143.
— (Gailthal) 334.
— (Gardena) 263.
— im Haus 119. 175.
— (Lavantthal) 416.
— (Pfitsch) 187.
— (Prettau) 191.
— (Rosenthal) 421.
— am Thurn 65.
— (Villnöss) 225.
Jacobskogl, the 366.
Jaggerreith 381.
Jägerkamp, the 40. 51.
Jägermayr 383.
Jäger-See, the 115.
Jainzen-Thal, the 93.
Jalouz, the 442.
Jamjoch 217.
Jamspitze, the 217.
Jamthal, the 217.
Jamthalhütte, the 217.
Jassinggraben, the 386.

Jauerburg 431.
Jauernik, the 431.
Jaufen, the 254.
Jaufenburg, ruin 254.
Jaufenthal, the 260.
Jauken 423.
Jaunthal, the 416.
Javornik, the 441.
Javré 304.
Jelover Wald, the 429.
Jenbach 49. 150.
Jenbach, the 58.
Jenesien 258.
Jenner, the 72.
Jepitza Alp 422.
Jerischach 417.
Jerzens 245.
Jeserlathal, the 408.
Jes-Fürkele, the 199.
Jessnitz 380.
Jettenberg 77. 82.
Jochalp, the 13. 75.
Jochberg 174.
—, the 30.
Jochberg-Wald 174.
Jocher Alpe 39.
Jocherbauer, the 274.
Joch-Grimm, the 264.
Jöchlalp, the 58. 310. 341.
Jodoeiberg, the 429.
St. Jodok 220. 182.
St. Johann in the Ahrenthal 190.
—, in the Görtschitzthal 427.
— im Steinfelde 364.
— (Lavantthal) 416.
—, in the Leukenthal 120. 175.
—, in the Pongau 114.
— am Tauern 425.
— in Tyrol 120. 175.
— im Wald 188.
—, in the Wochein 430.
—, island, in the Königssee 73.
Johannesjoch, the 212.
Johanneskopf, the 212.
Johannesthal, the 43.
Johannisberg, the, near Heiligenblut 134. 153.
St. Johanneshügel, the 79.
Johannshütte, the (Grossglockner) 152.
— (Venediger) 142.
Johannskofel, the 260.
Johnsbach 387.
Johnsbachthal, the 387.
Jörgenhütte, the 146.
Jos di Montasio 443.
St. Josef (Sexten) 333.
— (Villnöss) 225.

Josefsberg, 274. 373. 407. 415.
Judenalp, the 130.
Judenberg-Alpe 66.
Judenburg 425.
Judendorf 370.
Judenkirche, the 9.
Judicaria, see Giudicaria.
Juifen, the 47.
Julian Alps, the 410. 411.
Jungbrunn 334.
Jungbrunnenthal 265.
Jungfernsprung, the (Mölltlial) 150.
— (near Gratz) 404.
Juppenspitze, the 209.
Jurdani 413.
Jürgbauer, the 424.
Jürgenhütte, the 357.
Juribell, Alp 325.
Juribruit, Alp 325.
Juval, castle 253.

Käferthal, the 129.
Kahlersberg, the 73.
Kainach, the 404. 405.
Kaindlgrat, the 134.
Kaindlhütte, the 134.
Kaindl 223.
Kainisch 393.
Kainzen Bad, the 34.
Kaiser, the Hintere 58. 178.
—, the Scheffauer 175.
—, the Treffauer 175.
—, the Vordere 175.
—, the Wilde 175.
Kaiserau 388.
Kaiserbrunn 365.
Kaiserbrunnen, the 365.
Kaisergebirge, the 158. 175.
Kaiserhochalpe, the 175.
Kaiserhöfe, the 158.
Kaiserjoch, the (Lechthal) 204.
— (Kaunserthal) 248.
Kaiserklause, the 50.
Kaisers 211.
Kaisersberg 424.
Kaiserscharte, the 394.
Kaiserschild, the 385.
Kaiserstein, the 365.
Kaiserstrasse, the 175.
Kaiserthal, the (Lechthal) 211.
— (Kaisergebirge) 157.
Kaiserwacht, the 47.
Kaiserwald, the 363.
Kaid 82.
Kälberstein, the 70. 71.
Kälberthal, the 212.
Kalbling, the 388.

Kalditsch 321.
Kalkspitze 396.
Kallwang 389.
Kalmberg 94. 96.
Kals 146.
Kalsdorf 405.
Kaiser Tauern 145. 146.
Kalser Thal, the 145.
Kals-Matreier Thörl 139. 145. 147.
Kalteberg, the 202. 204.
Kalte Keller, the 71.
Kaltenbach 179.
Kaltenbrunn (Tegernsee) 44.
— (Partenkirchen) 34.
— (near Neumarkt) 321.
— (Kaunserthal) 247.
Kaltenhausen 83.
Kaltenleutgeben 364.
Kalte Rinne, the 367.
Kalterer See, the 267.
Kaltern 267.
Kaltherberg-Alpe 394.
Kaltwasser 434. 443.
Kaltwasserspitze, the 43.
Kammer 108.
Kammergebirge, the 394.
Kammerköhr-Alp, the 176. 177.
— Platte, the 176.
Kammerl Alpe 389.
Kammerlinghorn, the 78.
Kammern 389.
Kammersberg 426.
Kammersee, the, near Aussee 97.
— (Upper Austria) 109.
Kammspitze, the 394.
Kampel, the 371.
Kampen, the 42.
Kampenhöhe, the 54.
Kampenn 258.
Kampenwand, the 54.
Kampil 258.
Kandellen 382.
Kanin 442. 443.
Kanker 409. 418.
Kapell 58.
Kapellen 406. 370.
Kapf ob Wasach 9.
Kapfenberg 368.
Kapflag 179.
Kappel (Bavaria) 14.
Kappl (Patznaun) 218.
Kappler Alpe, the 329.
Kapron 250.
Kapran 132.
Kapruner Thal, the 132.
— Thörl, the 134.
Kar-Alp 405.
Karawanken, the 420. 431.
Kardaun 226. 260.

Kardeis 114.
Karer Pass 262.
Karfreit 442.
Karlalpe, the Lower 377.
Karlbad 399.
Karles Glacier 239.
Karlesspitze 248.
Karl-Hochkogel, the 375.
Karlinger Glacier 133.
Karl-Ludwigshaus 366.
Karlsbach 381.
Karlsberg 428.
Karlsbader Hütte 251.
Karlsberg 179.
Karls-Eisfeld 100. 396.
Karlssteg, the 184.
Karlstein 82. 178.
Karneid 261. 226.
Karnervellach 431.
Karnitza Alp 433. 443.
Karolinenfeld 53.
Karpfenwinkel, the 25.
Karrer Alm 366.
Karrerseen, the 261.
Karres 234.
Karrösten 234.
Karröstner Alp 234.
Karst 413.
Kartell Glacier, the 208.
Karlitsch 333.
Kartnerkogel, the 367.
Karwendelgebirge, the 34. 35.
Karwendelspitze, the 35.
Karwendelthal, the 36.
Kasbach, the 49.
Käseralpe, the 11.
Kasereck (near Bad Fusch) 129.
— (near Heiligenblut) 131.
Kasern (Schnirn) 183.
— (Prettau) 136. 191.
Kasparstein 415.
Kassberg, the 90.
Kassianspitze, the 226.
Kastelruth 265.
Kasten-Alp 223. 86.
Kastenreith 382. 384.
Kastenriegel, the 374.
Kastreinspitze, the 434.
Katergebirge, the 94.
St. Katharina in der Scharte 275.
— (Navisthal) 220.
Katharinaberg, the 410.
St. Kathrein 386.
Katsch 426.
Katschberg, the 426.
Katschberg, the 338.
Katzenkopf, the 39.
Katzenloiter 266. 345.
Katzensteig, the 148.
Katzenstein, château 269. 278.

INDEX. 465

Kaufbeuren 3.
Kaufering 3.
Kaumberg 380.
Kaunerwand, the 74.
Kauns 247.
Kaunserthal, the 247.
Kecsau, the 136.
Kceskogel. the 115.
Kehlburg 337.
Kehlegg 197.
Kehlstein 73.
Keilbach-Joch 182. 191.
Keilbachspitze 191.
Keilscharte, the 153.
Kelchsau-Thal, the 172.
Kellerjoch, the 160. 179.
Kellerlahn, the 254.
Kellersberg 152.
Kellerwand, the 335.
Kelmen 210.
Kematen (Pütsch) 187.
— (Innthal) 231.
— (Kremsthal) 389.
— (Taufers) 388.
Kemmelbach 381.
Kempten 4.
Kennelbach 196.
Kerma-Pass and Valley 431.
Kern, the 441.
Kerngraben, the 366.
Kerschbaumer Alp 335.
Kerschbuchhof 170.
Kerschdorf 423.
Kesselalpe 106.
Kesselbach, the 13. 38. 74.
Kesselberg, the 38.
Kesselbühl, the 132.
Kesselfall, on the Königsee 74.
— (Nassfeld) 125.
— near Heiligenblut 151.
Kesselklamm, the 133.
Kesselkogel, the 262. 322.
Kesselkopf, the 140.
Kesselwand Glacier 240.
Kesselwandjoch, the 240.
Kesselwandspitze,the 240.
Kicfersfelden 156.
Kienberg 55. 380.
—, the 416. 427.
—, the Seehauser 57.
Kienbergklamm 157.
Kienburg 138.
Kiens 328.
Kienthal, the 27.
Kilfebon 241.
Kimpflalpe 51.
Kindberg 368.
Kinzelspitze, the 209.
Kirchbach 423.
Kirchberg (Brixenthal) 172.

Kirchberg on the Wechsel 364.
Kirchberg, baths 81. 173.
Kirchberger Joch, the 276.
Kirchbichl 158.
Kirchbüchl, Schloss 416.
Kirchdachspitze, the 220.
Kirchdorf (Austria) 392.
— (Bavaria) 14.
Kirchfeld, the 392.
Kirchseeon 53.
Kirchstein, the 42.
Kirchstetten 379.
Kirschenthener 420.
Kistenkopf, the 28.
Kitzbühel 120. 174.
Kitzbühlerhorn, the 174.
Kitzlochklamm, the 116.
Kitzsteinhorn, the 134.
Klachau 393.
Klafferkessel, the 396.
Klagenfurt 418.
—, Lake of 421.
Klais 31.
Klamm, ruin, near Obersteig 20.
— (Olsnthal) 426.
— (Semmering) 367.
Klamm-Alpe, the 377.
Klamm-Pass, the 120.
Klammbachfall, the 47.
Klamml-Joch 340.
Klammstein, ruin 120.
Klapfalp, the 57.
Klaus (near Mellau) 208.
— (near Götzis) 198.
— (Steyrthal) 390.
Klausbrücke, the 208.
Klause, the Bregenzer 196.
— near Kufstein 157.
Klausen 225.
Klausenbach 174.
Klauswald, the 233.
Kiebenstein 260.
Kleblach-Lind 336.
Kleinarl-Thal, the 115.
Kleinbachthal, the 142.
Kleinboden 278.
Kleine Eiser, the 134.
Klein-Elend-Scharte, the 400.
Klein-Fanes 341.
Kleinglockner 147.
Kleine Göll, the 75.
Klein-Hollenstein 381.
Klein-Ischthal, the 142.
Klein-Kirchheim 398.
Kleinleitenspitze 241.
Klein-Mariazell 380.
Kleinmünchen 382.
Klein-St. Paul 427.

Kleine Ramsau 90.
Klein-Reifling 384.
Kleinsee, the 5.
Kleinspitze, the 209.
Klein-Sölk 394.
Klein-Sölkthal, the 394.
Klcinstein 259.
Kleintiefenthal 51.
Klein-Venediger, the 140.
Klein-Vermuntthal 217.
Klein-Wolkersdorf 363.
Klein-Zell 380.
Klemenschek, Alp 408.
Klesenza, Alp 212.
Klesheim 56.
Klinserscharte, the 391.
Klippitzthörl 427.
Klonscherthal, the 52.
Klobenstein 230. 259.
—, Pass 56.
Klopeiner See, the 417.
Klöpfelstaudach 179.
Kloster Pass, the 217.
Klösterl 39.
Klösterle in the Vorarlberg 202.
Klosters 215.
Klosterthal, the 202. 217. 363.
Klosterwappen, the 365.
Klotzhütte 240.
Knallstein, Grosse 394.
Knappenbach 347.
Knappenberg 428.
Knappendorf 366. 374.
Kneifelspitze, the 72.
Knie, the Obere and Untere 12.
Kniepass, near Reutte 17.
—, near Unken 177.
Knieps, the 416.
Knittelfeld 424.
Knollkopf, the 390.
Knorrhütte, the 33.
Knutten 340.
Knuttenthal 339.
Kobenz-Thal, the 424.
Koblach 197.
Kochel 38. 41.
Kochelsee, the 38.
Kochenmoos, baths 253.
Koder-Alpe 387.
Ködnitz Glacier 146.
Ködnitzthal 146. 148.
Kofel 335.
Kofel Pass 335.
Köflach 404.
Kögelalp, the 48.
Kögeljoch, the 47.
Kögelrücken, cavern 360.
Köglergraben, the 174.
Kohler Alp 36.

BAEDEKER's Eastern Alps. 6th Edit. 30

Kohlgrub 28. 87.
Kohlhäusl 83.
Kohlmauer, the 365.
Kohlnthal, the 58.
Kolben, lm 127.
Kolbermoor 53.
Kolbnitz 149.
Kolfuschg 343.
Kollern 253.
Köllespitze 22.
Kollinkofel, the 335.
Kollmann 226.
Kollmannsberg 110.
Kolm Saigurn 127.
Kolowratshöhle, the 67.
Komarza, the 431.
Königsalp, the 46.
Königsbach, the 74.
—, Alp 75.
Königsberg-Alp 75.
Königsberg, the 442, 443.
Königsberghorn, the 102.
Königsdorf 41.
Königshof 229.
Königsjoch, the 291.
Königssee, the 73.
Königsspitze 282, 291.
Königstuhl, the 390.
Königsthal-Joch 244.
Konstanzer Ach, the 4.
Konstanzer Hütte 204.
Konstanzer Thal, the 5.
Köpfle 244.
Koppen, the 96.
Koppenbrüller Cavern 96.
Koppenkarstein 396.
Kopreinsattel, the 408.
Kor-Alpe, the 409. 416.
Korb 266.
Koritenza 411. 442.
Kornau 9.
Korn-Tauern, the 124.
Koroschitza-Alp 408.
Korspitze, the 278.
Kortsch 252.
Koschach 399.
Koschuta, the 417.
Küssen 58.
Küstendorf 87.
Köstland 225.
Koth-Alpe, the 48.
Kötschach 124. 423.
Kötschachthal, the 124. 400.
Kotschna, the Seekauder 418.
Köttelach 415.
Krüh-Alps 115.
Krainburg 429.
Krainer Hütten, the 362.
Krainer-Schneeberg, the 411.

Krainsky-Rak Saddle, the 409.
Krainer Storschitz 418.
Krakaudorf 394.
Krakofel 225.
Kramer, the 31.
Kramerspitze, the 188.
Kramets-Au 42.
Krametseck 42.
Krampen 371.
Kramsach 159.
Kramul, the 147.
Kranabetsattel, the 91.
Kranewitten 170.
Kranewitter Klamm 170.
Kraniehberg 364.
Kranichsfeld 407.
Krankenheil, baths 41.
Kranzberg, the Hohe 34.
Kränzelstein 260.
Kranzhorn, the 156.
Krapfenkarspitze, the 43.
Krapina Töplitz 406.
Krappfeld 427.
Kraspesspitze, the 232.
Kratzenberg, the 135.
Kratzer, the 12.
Krausgrotte, the 379.
Krautinsel, the 54.
Krautkaser-Alpe, the 72.
Krautschneiderbrücke, the 71.
Krautwaschl 370.
Kraxentrag, the 221.
Kreckelmoos, baths 22.
Krederes, the 431.
Kreh, the 91.
Kreidensee, the 341.
Kreilspitze, the 288.
Krekelmoos 22.
Kremsbruck 398.
Kremsmünster 390.
Kremsthal, the 389.
Kressbach 228.
Kressnitz 410.
Kresswasserl 329.
Kreugerschlösser 428.
Kreuth, Wildbad 46.
—, village (Bavaria) 46.
Kreuz Glacier 238.
Kreuzalpe, the 32.
Kreuzberg (Carinthia) 336. 372.
— (Salzach valley) 397.
— (near Schliersee) 50.
— (Sexten) 333.
Kreuzeck, the 12. 336.
Kreuzecksspitze 336.
Kreuzgarse 215.
Kreuzhütte, the 233.
Kreuz-Joch, the (Gerlos) 179.
— (Praga) 331.

Kreuz-Joch (Selrain) 231. 233.
Kreuzjöchl 260.
Kreuzkofel, the 334. 335.
Kreuzkogl, the 124.
Kreuzspitze, the (Oetzthal) 238.
—, the Wilde 187. 221.
Krieglach 368.
Krimberg, the 410.
Krimml 137.
—, the Wilde 179.
Krimmler Glacier 138. 142.
— Tauern, the 138. 191.
— Thörl, the 142.
— Waterfalls 137.
Krippeneck 100. 396.
Krippenstein, the 100.
Krippes 341.
Kristallspitzen, the 277. 279.
Kristberg, the 202.
Kristanalp 86.
Kristenbach, the 36.
Krn, the 441.
Krostenloch, the 85.
Kron-Alp 435.
Kronau 432.
Kronburg, ruin 234.
Kron-Metz 309.
Kronplatz, the 329.
Kropfleiten 72.
Kropfsberg, ruin 159.
Krotensee, the 108.
Krotienkopf (Algäu) 12.
— (Partenkirchen) 31.
Krumbach, the 180. 211.
Krumbach ob Holz 209.
Krumbachthal 13. 180.
Krumelbach, the 127.
Krummbachsattel, the 365.
Krumme Steyerling 384.
Krummgampenthal 247.
Krummnussbaum 381.
Krumpendorf 421.
Krumpensee 246.
Krün 33. 40.
Kublia 214.
Küchelberg 270.
Kuchelmoosalp, the 182.
Küchelspitze, the 204.
Kuchenjoch 204.
Kuchenspitzen, the 204.
Kuchl 84.
Kuchler Loch, the 74.
Kuens 253.
Kufstein 52. 157.
Kugelbachbauer, the 82.
Kugelhorn, the 21.
Kühbach, château 258.

INDEX. 467

Kühbergl 329.
Kühbühel, the 118.
Kuhflucht, the 30.
Kühkarköpfl, the 129.
Kühkarspitze, the 43.
Kühnsdorf 417.
Kuhroint-Alp, the 77.
Kuhschneeberg 366.
Kühtni 231.
Kühthal, the 250.
Kühtreien, ravine 238.
Kühzacklalp, the 51.
Kuk, the 430.
Küllenberg 413.
Kulm (Grimming) 393.
— (Samina) 199.
— (Ramsau) 395.
Kulmalpe, the 377.
Kulmspitz, the 110.
Kulpa, the 410.
Kumberg, the 409.
Kummenberg, the 197.
Kummersee, the 254.
Kundl 159.
Kuntersweg, the 226.
Künzel-Spitze, the 209.
Kuppelwies 276.
Kürsinger Hütte 137.
Kurlatsch 267.
Kurze Grund, the 172.
Kurzenhof, the 242.
Kurzras 242.

Laafeld, the 73.
Laak 429.
Laakirchen 87.
Laas (Carnia) 411.
— (Vintschgau) 252.
Laase 410.
Laaser Ferner, the 293.
Laaser Spitze 252. 286.
Laaser Thal, the 252.
Laatsch 253.
Labau 57.
Labauner Joch 249.
Labauner Kopf 249.
Lachalpe, the 276. 371.
Lachenspitze, the 22.
Lackenhof 366. 374. 381.
Lackerhoden, the 365.
Lading 416.
Ladis 247.
Ladlz 43.
Ladritsch Bridge 224. 328.
Lafraun 317.
Lagant Alp 201.
Lagarina, Val 295.
Lagazuoi 342. 343.
Lägerthal, see Lagarina.
Lago Bianco (Ampezzo) 347.
— — (Val Cavia) 283.

Lago Ghiacciato, Passo del 308.
— Morto 354.
— Nero (Val Mazza) 283.
—, Croda da 349. 355.
—, Lago da 349.
Lagoscuro, Passo 308.
Lagutz, Alp 212.
Lähn 18. 99.
Lahngangseen, the 98. 391.
Laibach 410.
—, the 410.
Laibacher Moos, the 410.
Laimach 181.
Lainach 150.
Lainaustiege, the 90.
Lainbach 370.
Lainkarscharte 125.
Lainthal, the 34.
Lajen 263.
Laliders 43.
Lambach 86.
St. Lambrecht 426.
Laningbach, the 386.
Lammer, the 102. 112.
Lammeröfen, the 86.
Lammersberg 97.
Lamprechts-Ofenloch 78.
Lamprechtsburg, the 329.
Lamsenjoch, the 160.
Lana 260.
—, Col di 356.
Land 381.
Landauer See, the 398.
Landeck 234.
Landeckkopf 146.
Landecksäge, the 140.
Landeckthal 140.
Lander, Val 357.
Landl (near Kufstein) 52.
— (Ennsthal) 384.
Landol 412.
Landro 344.
Landsberg on the Lech 3.
Landschau 213.
Landschitz-Scharte, the 394.
Landskron, chât. 368.
—, ruin 422. 429.
Landsteg, the 116. 126.
Landthal, the 75.
Landthal-Alp, the 75.
Landthal-Wand, the 73.
Lauersbach 183.
Langacker 82.
Langau 374.
Langbath 91.
Langbath Lakes, the 91.
Langeck 260.
Lange Grund, the 172.
Langen 6. 202.
Langenauthal, the 46.

Langenberg 42.
Langenfeld, the 32.
Längenfeld 237.
Langenferner 286. 287. 292.
Langenthal-Alp 41.
Längenthaler Alp 232.
Langenwang 8. 368.
Langostei 219.
Langethal (Stubai) 229.
— (Gardena) 264.
Langfall 275.
Langgrub 260.
Langgries 41.
Langgrub-Joch, the 250. 252.
Langkampfen 158.
Langkofl, the 263. 323.
Langpoltner Graben 392.
Langsee, the 115. 275.
Längsee, the 52. 427.
Langsteg-Thal, the 416.
Langtauferer Joch 240.
— Ferner, the 240.
— Spitze, the 240.
— Thal, the 250.
Langthal (Oetzthal) 243.
Langthaler Eissee 243.
— Joch 244.
Langwies 92.
Lannach 404.
Lans 170.
Lanser Köpfe, the 169.
Lanterna, Val 284.
Lanza 149.
Lanzada 284.
Laperwitz Glacier 146. 153.
Lapones, Alp 220.
Lappach 189.
Lappacher Joch 189.
Lappacher Thal 188.
Larchbühel, the 275.
Larchet-Alp, the 36.
Lardaro 308.
Lareinthal, the 218.
Lares, Vedretta di 304. 307.
—, Cima di 307.
— Falls 307.
— Hut 307.
Larosbach, the 69.
Laroswacht, the 77.
Larsenbach, the 234.
Lasaberg Alpe 398.
Lasankaiobui, the 201.
Laserz Lake, the 335.
Lasnitzthal, the 142.
Lassbring, the 141. 142.
Lassach 126.
Lassing 381.
Lassing, the 373. 378.
Lassnitz, the 405.

30*

INDEX.

Lasta, Cima 313.
Latemar, the 262.
Laterns 198.
Laternser Thal 198. 208.
Latsch 253.
Latschach 422.
Lattengebirge, the 72. 76.
Latz 200.
Latzfons 226.
Latzfonser Joch, the 226.
Laudachsee, the 90.
Laudeck, ruin 247.
Laufbühler See, the 21.
Laufen 95. 94. 408.
Laugenspitze, the 275. 276.
Launsdorf 427.
Laurein 310.
Laurengo, Malga di 310.
Lausberg-Lahne, the 85.
Laussa, the 384. 391.
Lauter 56.
Lauterbach, the 172.
Lautersee, the 30. 34.
Lautrach 196.
Lavamünd 415.
Lavant, the 415.
Lavant, château 426.
Lavant-Thal, the 415.
Lavarda 317.
Lavaredo, Cime di 352.
Lavarone 317.
Lavatsch-Thal, the 36.
Lavatscher Joch, the 36. 161.
Lavazzo, Castel 353.
Lavenone 309.
Lavinores, the 341. 348.
Lavis 293.
Lawinenstein, the 393.
Laxenburg 361.
Lazins 242. 244. 254.
Lazinser-Thal, the 244.
Lazise 301.
Lazzacher Thal 223.
Lebenberg, château (near Meran) 273.
— (near Kitzbühel) 174.
Lebenberger Alp 275.
Lebmach 428.
Lebring 405.
Lech, village 13. 211.
Lech, the 3. 209. 210. etc.
Lechfeld, the 3.
Lechleiten 13. 211.
Lechler Kanz, the 13.
Lechthal, the Upper 210. 211.
Leckneraee, the 206.
Ledro, Lago di 300.
—, Val di 300.
Lees 429.
Legerwand, the 288.

Lehberger, the 44.
Lehngriesalp, the 86.
Leibnigthal, the 138.
Leibnitz 405.
Leibnitzer Feld, the 405.
Leifers 261.
Leilachspitze, the 22.
Leipsic Hut 307.
Leisach 395.
Leiseralm, the 275.
Leitach 225.
Leiten 37. 47.
Leiterbach, the 148.
Leiter Fall, the 151.
Leiterhütte, the 148.
Leiterköpfe, the 154.
Leiterthal, the 148.
Leitha Mts., the 362.
Leitnoralp, the 136.
Leitstuben 57.
Leitzach 50. 51.
Leklebach 245.
Lend, on the Lech 211.
—, on the Salzach 115. 120.
Lend-Canal, the 421.
Lendorf 336.
Lengdorf 135.
Lengenfeld 431.
Lenggries 41.
Lengmoos 259.
Lengstein 259.
Lengstein, the Grosse 339.
Lenkjöchl 191.
Lenkjöchl-Hütte 191.
Leno 295.
Lenzumo 300.
Leoben 424. 308.
Leobersdorf 362.
Leogang 119.
Leogang-Thal, the 110.
Leogra, the 295.
Leonburg 268.
St. Leonhard (Defereggerthal) 139.
— (Enneberg) 342.
— (Karfitschthal) 333.
— (Carinthia) 408. 426.
— (Lavantthal) 416.
— (Lungau) 398.
— (Passeir) 251.
— (Pitzthal) 245.
— (Untersberg) 68.
St. Leonhards-Sattel 408.
Leonhardstein, the 46.
Leoni 25.
Leonsberg-Zinken, the 91.
Leonstein (Styria) 384.
— (Carinthia) 421.
Leopoldskirchen 435.
Leopoldskron, château 67.
Leopoldskroner Moos 67.
Leopoldsruh, baths 334.
Leopoldstein, château 385.

Leopoldstein, Lake of 385. 378.
Leppengraben, the 416.
Lercheck 388.
Lermoos 18.
Lesach 145.
Lesachthal 147.
Lescee 413.
Leska Dolina 411.
Lessachgraben 394.
Lessachthal, the 333.
Leuchtenburg 267.
Leukenthal, the 120. 171.
Leutaschklamm 34.
Leutaschmuhl 35.
Leutasch Valley, the 35.
Leutasch-Platzl 35.
Leutasch-Widum 35.
Leutascher Mähder 35.
Leutsch 408.
Leutschthal 408.
Levico 317. 318.
Leytha, see Leitha.
Libuska 416.
Lichtenbachgraben 371.
Lichtenberg (Pinzgau) 118.
— (Vintschgau) 251.
Lichtenegg 368.
Lichtmessberg, the 388.
Lichtwohr, ruin 159.
Liebener Spitze 243.
Liebenfels 428.
Lieboch 404.
Lieburg, the 334.
Liechlkopf, the 13.
Liechtenstein, castle 199. 425.
Liechtenstein-Klammen, the 114.
Liechtensteru Hütten 366.
Lienz 334.
Lienzer Klause 334.
Lieuzinger 135.
Liera 326.
Lieser, the 337.
Lieseregg 400.
Lieser-Thal, the 336.
Liesing 334. 361.
Liesing-Thal, the 424.
Lietzen 392.
Lilienfeld 374.
Limbergalpe, the 133.
Limo, Joch 311.
Limone 302.
Lind 421.
Lindau 6. 7.
Lindenberg 6.
Lindenhof, the 7.
Linderhütte 335.
Linderhof 23.
Lindthal 184.

INDEX.   469

Lingenau 206.
Linkerskopf, the 12.
Linning 380.
Linz 86. 382.
Lipnik, the 435.
Lisenzer Glacier, the 232.
Lisenser Thal, the 232.
Listolade 358.
Lisisee, the 81.
Liststeig, the 366.
Littai 410.
Litzbach, the 213.
Litzner, the Grosse and Kleine 217.
Livinalongo, Val 356.
Livo 310.
Livrio, Monte 277. 280.
Lizzana 295.
Lobbia Glacier 307.
Lohnitz, the 415.
Lobspitze, the 215. 216.
Loch 207.
Lochau 7.
Lochbachthal 14.
Lockstein, the 70.
Lödensee, the 57.
Lodrone 308.
Lodschia, Col di 343.
Lofer 176.
Loferer Alpe, the 176.
Loferer Hochthal, the 176.
Loferer Steinberge 176.
Löffelspitze, or
Löffler 184. 191.
Logarthal, the 408.
Loibachfall, the 45.
Loibiser Joch 245.
Loibl, the 420.
Loibl, the Kleine 420.
Loisach, the 18. 24. 28. 38.
Loilsch 411.
Lokva, the 412.
Lölling 427.
Longarone 353.
Loog 432. 442.
Loosdorf 380.
Loose, the 207. 197.
Loppio 298.
Lorena, the 206.
Lorenzago 436.
St. Lorenzen (Pusterthal) 328. 334.
— (Carinthia) 415.
— (Styria) 424.
Loreth 218.
St. Loretto 9.
Lorina, Val 300.
Loruns 213.
Losbühel 365.
Lose 207. 197.
Lösenstein 384.
Loser, the 97.
Loswand 365.

Lotterbad 276.
Lötz 235. 211.
Lötzenbach, the 235.
Lotzer Klamm 235.
Lötzer Thal, the 235.
Lovere 313.
Lovero 284.
Lovitz-Alpe 187.
Lovrano 413.
Lozzo 352. 436.
S. Lucano, Val 326. 358.
—, Pala di 357.
Luchsboden 365.
S. Lucia (near Verona) 296.
— (Valtellina) 283.
— (near Caprile) 357.
Luckel, the 392.
Lucknerhütte, the 146.
Ludergrube 33.
Ludesch 200.
Ludescherberg 200.
Ludwigshafen 7.
Lueg 413.
Lueg, Pass 86. 112.
Luftenstein, Pass 176.
S. Lugano 321.
Luganer, the 385.
Lugen 208.
Lukashanslaip, the 131.
Lukaskreuz, the 139.
Luknia Pass, the 431.
Lumiei, the 436.
Luna, Mte. 358.
Lünersee, the 214.
Lüner Krine, the 214.
Lünersee, the 201. 214.
Lungau, the 114. 308.
Lunghiega 310.
Lunz 381.
Lursfeld, the 336.
Luscharlberg 433. 431.
Luserna 317.
Lusia Pass 322.
Lusnitz 435.
Lustbühel 404.
Lustheim, château 73.
Luttach 189. 338.
Luttenberg 406.
Lutzbach, the 200.
St. Luziensteig, the 199.
Lyliapitze, the 252.

Macchietto 353.
Machtling 27.
Mackner Kessel, the 260.
Madatsch, the 277.
Madatsch Glacier, the 277.
Madatschjoch, the (Ortler) 279.
— (Pitzthal) 246.
Madau 211.
Mädele-Gabel, the 12.

Mädelejoch, the 12.
Maderer, the 216.
Maderno 302.
Madleiner Thal, the 218.
Madlenerhaus, the 216.
Madonna di Campiglio 305.
Madonna di Neve 324.
Madriol-Thal 235.
Madonna di Tirano 284.
Madritschbach, the 286.
Madritschjoch 286. 289.
Madritschspitze, the 289.
Madriser Spitze, the 215.
Maè 353.
Magasa 300.
St. Magdalena (Gsies) 139.
— (Ridnaun) 223.
— (Villnöss) 225.
— (Schrain) 232.
— (near Linz) 383.
Magdalenaberg, the 427.
Magdeburger Hütte 222.
Maggiore, Monte (Mte. Baldo) 299.
— (Istria) 413.
Maglern 423. 433.
Magnano 437.
Mahlknecht 262.
Mahlknecht-Joch 265. 323.
Mahr-Alpe, the 400.
Mahrenberg 404. 405. 415.
Mahrhof 423.
Maienburg 268.
Maiereck 384.
Maierhof 55.
Maiernigg 421.
Maipitsch, Piz 251.
Mairalm, the 38.
Mairhofen 190. 181.
Maiselstein 8.
Maishofen 118.
Malstatt 331.
Maitschern 302.
Majano 310.
Majenwand 205.
Matag 248. 250.
Malborget 434.
Malhun-Thal, the 199.
Maleesine 301.
Melchbach, the 234.
Malè 311.
Malenco, Val 284.
Malero, the 284.
Malfonthal, the 205.
Malhamspitze, the 144.
Mallnitz 126.
Mallnitzer Tauern 126.
Mallnitz-Thal, the 149.
Malonno 313.
Malosco 268. 310.
Mals 250.
Malser Heide, the 250.

470 INDEX.

Maltathal, the 124. 399.
Maltein 399.
Mandling 396.
—, the 362. 378.
Mandlscharte 37
Mandriola, Cima 318.
Mandron Glacier 307.
Manerba 302.
Mangart, the 443. 432.
Mangart Lakes, the 432.
Mangart Valley, the 442.
Mangfall, the 17. 49.
Mänkbach, the 200.
Manndlwand 113.
Mannhart, see Mangart.
Mannhartalp, the 126.
Manning 87.
Marauner Thal 275.
Marbach 381.
Marburg 405.
Marceana 351.
Marchkareck, the 308.
Marchkopf, the 179.
Marchtrenk 86.
S. Marco 295. 352.
Mare, Pallon della 311.
—, Valle della 311.
Marein 368. 416.
Mareit 223.
Mareson 358.
Maretsch 260.
St. Margarethen 156. 196. 416.
St. Margarethenkapf 108.
Margreid 267.
St. Maria (Gardena Valley) 264.
— (Münsterthal) 251.
— della Salute 353.
— (Steivio) 280.
— (Val Trenta) 432.
— (Glashütten) 405.
Maria-Brunn 170. 379.
Maria-Brunneck 86.
Maria-Eck 58.
Maria-Gail 422.
Maria-Grün (near Feldkirch) 109.
— (near Gratz) 404.
Maria-Kumnitz 393.
Maria-Kuntersweg 77.
Maria-Loretto 421.
Maria-Luggau 333.
S. Maria dei Poveri 300.
St. Maria Magdalena 232.
Maria-Pfarr 308.
Maria-Plain, pilgr.-church 67.
Mariarast 415.
—, chapel 179.
Maria-Rehkogl 369.
Maria-Saal 428.

Maria-Schmelz 285.
Maria-Schnee 259.
Maria-Schutz 367.
Maria-Strassengel 370.
Maria im See 429.
Maria-Taferl 381.
Maria-Trost 404.
Maria-Waldrast 220.
Maria-Weitschach 428.
Maria-Wörth 421.
Maria di Zanin 340.
Mariazell 372.
Marienberg, abbey 250.
—, the, near Kempten 4.
Marienbergjoch, the 19.
Marienbrücke, the 17.
Mariensee 363.
Markersdorf 380.
Markt-Rohitsch 407.
Markt-Tüffer 409.
Marling 273.
Marlinger Berg 269. 274.
Marlt Glacier 291.
Marltschneid, the 291.
Marmarole, the 352.
Marmolada, the 324.
Marone 313.
Marquartstein 56.
Marteck 180.
Martell 285.
Marteller Alp 286.
Martellthal, the 285.
St. Martin (Ahrenthal) 338.
— (Gratz) 404.
— (Ennsthal) 422. 394
— (Gaderthal) 340. 342.
— (near Hall) 161.
— auf dem Kofel 252.
— (Passeir) 254.
— (on the Saalach) 176.
— (Salzkammergut) 102.
— (Schneeberg) 223.
S. Martino (Val Masino) 285.
S. Martino di Castrozza 325.
Martinswand, the 232.
Marul-Thal, the 201.
Marul 212.
Marulthal, the 200.
Marzen 72.
Marxwiesen, the 154.
Marzell Glacier 241.
Marzellspitzen, the 241.
Märzle, the 10.
Marzon, 333. 352
Mas 358.
Maschelalp, the 127.
Maschun 411.
Masino, Bagni di 285.
—, Val 284. 285.
Maso, the 318.

Maso Bariscili 316.
Masuccio, Piz 284.
Masul Gorge, the 275.
Matajur 442.
Matavun 414.
Materott, Malga 307.
Mathon 204. 218.
Matler Alpe, the 199.
Matrei 220.
—, Windisch 139.
Matreier Tauern, the 141.
— Kalser Thörl, the 139.
Matschatsch 267.
Matscher Glacier, the 251.
— Joch, the 250.
— Thal, the 251.
Matschon-Joch, the 200.
Matschonspitze, the 200.
Mattarello 205.
S Matteo, Punta di 283. 312.
Mattersberg 140.
Mattersdorf 363.
Mattsee 88.
Matuglie 413.
Matzen, château 150.
Matzendorf 382.
Mauer 382.
Mauerscharte, the 75. 113.
Mauls 224.
Maulasch, ruin 269.
Maurach 49. 177.
—, the (Oetzthal) 236.
Maurer Alp 143.
Maurerkeesköpfe 142. 138.
Maurerthal, the 142.
Maurerthörl, the 143.
Mauria Pass, the 436.
Mauritz-Alpe, the 49.
Mautern 380.
Mauterndorf 397.
Mauthen 335.
Mauthhäusel, the 55. 82.
Mauthhausen 83.
Maxhütte, the 55.
Max-Josephsthal, the 50.
Mayenburg 268.
Mayenfeld 109.
Mayeralp 136.
Mayrhofen (Gastein) 120.
— (Zillerthal) 184.
Mazzin 323.
Mazzo 284.
Medjidoh Saddle 420.
Medraz 228.
Meersburg 7.
Mehlweg 83.
Mehrn 150.
Meidling 361.
Meiselberg 427.

INDEX.   471

Melach, the 231. 232.
Melcherloch, the 119.
Meledrio, the 305.
Melk 380.
Melkerscharte, the 185.
Mellau 208.
Melleck 178.
Mellenbachthal, the 208.
Melnik Fall 399.
Memmingen 4.
Memminger Hütte 211.
Mendel Pass 267.
Mendola, see Mendel.
Menicigolo, Monte 307.
Mentelberg 170.
Meran 269.
Meranson 328.
Merbjöchl, the 191.
Mererau 196.
Merkenstein 362.
Merzlagora, the 408.
Messnerin, the 375.
Mesules 263.
Metnitz 426.
Mettenham 56.
Metzenleiten 71.
Mezzana 311.
Mezzano 327.
Mezzavia, Campo di 319.
Mezzo, Colle di 304.
Mezzo-Lago 300.
Mezzo-Lombardo 309.
— Tedesco 309.
Mezzodi, Becco di (Ampezzo) 349.
Miana 358.
St. Michael (Lungau) 398.
— (near Hall) 161.
— (near Leoben) 424.
— (Uebertsch) 266.
Michaelsburg, the 328.
Michelbach-Alpe, the 188.
Michelbauer, the 371.
Micheldorf 300.
S. Michele 293. 302.
Michelreiss 338.
Mieders 227.
Mieminger Mts. 19. 233.
Mies 408. 415. 416.
Miesbach 49. 415.
Miesenbach 362.
Miesing, the 51.
Mietenkam 56.
Migion, Mte. 366.
Miklauzhof 417.
Milan Hut 282.
Milders 228.
Milcins 225.
Millstatt 336.
Millstatter See 336.
Mils 234.
Mincio, the 301.
Mirafall, the 362.

Miramar, château 404.
Mirnock 336. 422.
Mis 358.
Missenstein Pass 275.
Missian 266.
Misslingthal, the 415.
Misurina, Lago 351.
Mitting, the 4.
Mittagskofel, the 434.
Mittagskogl, the (Pitzthal) 246.
— (Carintia) 422.
Mittagspitze (Bregenzer Wald) 207.
— (near Hinterstein) 21.
— (Montavon) 214.
Mittagsscharte, the 68.
Mittelberg (near Immenstadt) 3.
— (Walserthal) 10. 209.
— (Pitzthal) 245.
— (Bätten) 260.
Mittelberg Glacier 239. 245.
Mittelbreth 442.
Mitteldorf 141.
Mitten 7. 151.
Mittenwald 34.
Mittercralpe, the 156. 375.
Mitterbach 373.
—, the 189.
Mitterbachjoch 190.
Mitterbad 278.
Mitterberg 113.
Mitterdorf (Carnia) 430.
—, château, on the Semmering 368.
Mitteregg 210.
Mitterfeld-Alp, the 113.
Mitterhorn, the 176.
Mitterkar Glacier 239.
Mitter-Kleinarl 115.
Mitterkopf, the 136.
Mitterndorf 393.
Mitter-Olang 329.
Mittersee, the (Bavaria) 57.
— (Reschen) 250.
Mittersendling 40.
Mittersill 135.
Mitterthal 329.
Mitterthörl, the 131.
Mittewald (Brenner) 224.
— (Pusterthal) 334.
— (near Villach) 422.
Mixnitz 369.
Monr-Thal 261.
Monceniyo 320.
Moderndorf 495.
Mocheni, Val dei 317.
Möders 224.
Mödling 361.
Modring 426.

Moena 322.
Möggers 6.
Moggio 436.
Mohnenfluh, the 209.
Moistrana 431.
Moistroka, the 432.
Mojazza, Mte. 358.
Molberding 55.
Mollignon 262.
Molina 300.
Moline 327.
Mölk 380.
Molkenbauer, the 82.
Möll, the 149. 150. 151. 336.
Möllbegg, the 393.
Möllbrücken 149.
Molln 384.
Möllthal, the 149.
Mölten 258.
Möltener Bach 269.
Molveno 304.
—, Lago di 304.
Mönchsberg, the 63.
Mondadizza 283.
Mondatsch, see Madatsch.
Mondin, Piz 243. 248.
Mondsee 110.
—. the 109.
Monfalcone 441.
Monfenera 320.
Mönichberg, the 154.
Mönichkirchen 363.
Monno 313.
Montagna (Valtellina) 284.
Montan (Martell) 252. 285.
— (near Neumarkt) 321.
Montasio 443.
Montavon 213.
Monte, Val del 312. 283.
Montecroce 327.
Monte Croce-Pass 333.
Monteneu 214.
Montiggel 207.
Montiggl Lakes, the 267.
Montina, Val 353.
Montozzo, Passo di 312.
Monzon 323.
Monzoni, Val 322.
Moos (Passeir) 254.
— (Sexten) 333.
Monsalpe, the 35.
Morserboden 133.
Moosthal, the 203. 254.
Morbegno 286.
Mörchenscharte 184.
Mörchenspitze (Mörchner), the 186.
Morgenkofel, the 337.
Mori 295. 298.
Morignone 283.

INDEX.

81. Moritzen (Ahrnthal) 338.
Moritzenthal 398.
Moritzing 269.
Moriclithal 285.
Mortenau 13. 210.
Morter 285.
Mortirolo Pass 283. 313.
Mörischach 150.
Mörzelspitze 208.
Moschesin Pass, the 356.
Möschitzgraben, the 425.
Moschkogel, the 405.
Mösel 427.
Möselbad 331.
Mösele 86. 190.
Mosenalp, the 42.
Möseralpe, the 57.
Mösle-Alp, the 21.
Moserhütte, the 125.
Mosern 97.
Mösern 37. 233.
Mössna 394.
Mostnock, Grosse 337. 339.
Moszenik, the 420.
Motta, la 314.
Mottenkopf, the 201.
Mötz 233.
Muckendorf 362.
Mugoni 322.
Muhl 18.
Mühlau 170. 388.
Mühlauer Klamm, the 170.
Mühlbach (Hallstatt) 98.
— (Pinzgau) 136.
— (Pongau) 113.
— (Pusterthal) 328.
— (near Taufers) 337.
—, the 98. 226.
Mühlbacher Joch, the 337.
Mühlbacher Klause 328.
Mühlbachthal (near Bischofshofen) 113.
— (uear Niedernsill) 135.
— (near Taufers) 337.
Mühldorf 90. 149.
Mühlen 337.
Mühlfeld 27.
Mühlhorn, the 54.
Mühlrain 108.
Mühlsturzhorn, the 78. 176.
Mühlthal 24.
—, the 118. 135.
Mühlwald 189.
Mühlwalder Joch 190.
Mühlvald-Thal 188. 337.
Mullitzthal, the 141.
Mullitzthörl, the 143.
Mülleralp 92.
Mülln 64.
Mullnerhorn, the 178.

Mullwitz-Aderl 142.
Mullwitz Glacier 142.
Münster (Grisons) 251.
Muntaniv, the 147.
Muntlix 198.
Mur 398.
Mur, the 368. 369. 401. 424.
Mur, Sasso di 327. 358.
Muranza, Val 251. 280.
Murau 398.
Murauer Kopf, the 125.
Mureck 406.
Muretto Pass, the 284.
Murnau 27.
Murnauer Scharte, the 118.
Murthörl, the 115.
Murwinkel, the 398.
Mürz, the 368. 371.
Mürzsteg 371.
Mürzzuschlag 368.
Müselbach 206.
Muslone 302.
Mustarin, Alp 212.
Mutberg, the 243.
Muteck, the 238.
Muthspitze, the 275.
Mutmalspitze, the 240.
Mutnock, the 187.
Mutspitze 286.
Muttekopf, the 234.
Mutterberg, Alp 230.
Mutterberger Joch 230.
Mutterberger See 230.
— Thal 229.
Mutters 171.
Muttersberg 201.

Naafkopf, the 199. 200.
Nabresina 414.
Nadel, the (Sanntbal) 408.
Naeswand, the 9.
Naglerspitze, the 277. 279.
Nago 298.
—, Altissimo di 299.
Naiderach-Thal, the 23.
Naif, the 272.
Nals 268.
Nambino, Val 304. 305.
Nambron, Val 305.
Namlos 210.
Namloser Thal 210.
Nanos, the 412.
Napfspitze, the 191.
Naraun 268.
Narcaue, Val 308.
Nardis, Pizs di 306.
Nashornspitze, the 277.
Nasbauer, the 365.
Nassereit 29.
Nasse Wand, the 248.
Nassfeld, the (Fusch) 130.

Nassfeld (Gastein) 125.
— (Pfandlthal) 132. 141.
— (Pontafel) 435.
Nassfelder Tauern, the 126.
Nasskamm, the 365.
Nasskhör, the 371.
Nassthal, the 365.
Nasswald 365.
Natterriegel, the 388.
Naturns 243. 253.
Nauderer Tscheythal 249.
Nauders 249.
Naudersberg 249.
Naunspitze, the 158.
Nave S. Rocco 293.
Navis 161.
Navisjoch, the 161.
Navisthal, the 220.
Nebelhorn, the 11.
Neder 228.
Nembia, Lago di 304.
Nendeln 199.
Nenzigast-Thal, the 202.
Nenzing 200.
Nenzinger Himmel 200.
Nesselgraben, the Upper and Lower 82. 178.
Nesselwang 14.
Nesselwängle 22.
Nettingsdorf 380.
Neuberg 159. 370.
Neubeuern 156.
Neubruck 380.
Neudenstein 418.
Neue Welt 286.
Neuhaus, baths in Styria 407.
Neubaus, Ahrenthal 191.
—, Styria 407.
—, near Salzburg 108.
—, in Bavaria 50.
—, in Tyrol 269.
—, near Mariazell 371.
Neuhäusl 84.
Neuhofen 389.
Neu-Hoheuëms 197.
Neu-Kematen 889.
Neukirch 87.
Neukirchen (Pinzgau) 136.
— (Styria) 407.
— (near Traunstein) 58.
Neulongbach 379.
Neumarkt on the Adige 293. 321.
Neumarkt in Salzburg 87.
— in Styria 326.
— in Austria 381.
Neumarktl 420.
Neuming 430.
Neu-Montfort 197.
Nennerkofel, the 341.

INDEX.

Neunkirchen 364.
Neu-Prags 330.
Neurateis 242.
Neureut, the 45.
Neu-Schwanstein 16.
Neu Spondinig 252.
Neustadt, Wienerisch 363.
Neu-Starkenberg 20.
Neustatt-Alpe, the 395.
Neustift, near Brixen 224.
—, in the Stubaithal 228.
Neuwaldegg 377.
Neu-Weg, the 82.
Neves, Alp 448.
Neves-Alp 189.
Neves-Sattel, the 189.
Neves-Thal, the 189.
Neveser Glacier, the 190.
Neveser Joch, the 189.
S. Niccolo, near Riva 298.
—, in Istria 444.
—, near Bormio 282.
—, in Cornelieu 352.
St. Nicolai 394.
Nickenalp 21.
St. Nicolaus (Ultenthal) 276.
Niederalpl, the 371.
Niederschau 54.
Niederdorf 331. 398.
Niederhofen 392.
Niederhütte, the 392.
Niederjoch, the 241.
Niederjoch Glacier 211.
Niederjöchl, the 246.
Niederlana 268.
Niedernach 42.
Niederndorf on the Inn 55. 58.
Niedernsill 135.
Nieder-Oeblarn 303.
Niederpöcking 24.
Niedersonthofer See 4.
Niedertai 282.
Niederthal (Oetzthal) 244.
— (Ambolz) 329.
Nieder-Vachenau 57.
Niklasdorf 424.
Niklaskopf, the 142.
St. Nikolaus 98.
Nikolsdorf 335.
Nomna, Val della 327.
Nose, the 311.
Nockspitz, see Saile.
Nockstein 66. 108.
Nöderberg, the 248.
Nöderkogl, the 237. 238.
Nofels 199.
Noggls 218.
Non 81.
—, Val di 309. 310.
Nonnberg, convent 64.

Nounthal 60.
Nonsberg, see Val di Non.
Norkenspitze, the 251.
Nöstelbach 389.
Noth, the 381.
Nötsch 423.
Novaledo 318.
Novella, the 310. 311.
Nufels 247.
Nürnbergerhütte 229.
Nussdorf 109. 140.
Nussensee, the 94.
Nussingkogel, the 140.
Nuvolau, Monte 349.
Nüziders 200.
Nymphenburg 3.

Občina 440.
Obdach 416.
Obdorf 201.
Oberaich 337.
Oberalm 83.
Ober-Ammergau 28.
Oberau (Bavaria) 28.
— (Tyrol) 224.
Oberaudorf 58. 156.
Oberbacherjoch 333.
Oberberg (Stubai) 228.
Oberbergthal, the (Schnals) 242.
Oberbotzen 259.
Oberbreth 442.
Oberbuch 399.
Oberburg 409.
Obercilli 467.
Oberdorf (Bavaria) 4.
— (Tragös) 386.
— (near Füssen) 14.
—, baths 20.
Oberdrauburg 335.
Oberdrum 335.
Obereck 94.
Oberetten Ferner 240.
Oberettenjöchl, the 252.
Oberferlach 420.
Obergiebeln 211.
Ober-Görlach 430.
Obergrainau 31.
Obergünzburg 3.
Ober-Gurgl 243.
Oberhof (Nassthal) 365.
— (Metnitz) 426.
Oberhofen 87. 110.
Oberhofer Alp 46.
Oberigg 410.
Ober-Iss, Alp 228.
Oberjoch 21.
Oberkindberg 368.
Oberlahner-Alp 75.
Oberlaibach 440.
Oberlana 268.
Oberland 382.

Ober-Leibnig 189.
Oberleiten 317.
Ober-Leulasch 35.
Ober-Lienz 188.
Oberluttach 190.
Obermädele, Alp 12.
Obermais 270.
Obermauer 141.
Obermiemingen 20.
Ober-Mühlbach 428.
Obernach 28. 39.
Obernbergthal, the 221.
Oberndorf (on the Inn) 58.
— (near Kitzbühel) 120.
Oberort 396.
Ober-Peischlach 145.
Ober-Perfuss 231.
Ober-Piesting 362.
Ober-Planitzing 267.
Oberpolzberg 381.
Ober-Purstein 338.
Oberrain, baths 177.
Oberreiinau 6.
Oberreutte 5.
Ober-Rothwein 431.
Ober-Schladmingthal,the 396.
Ober-Schönberg 227.
Obersee, the 74. 330.
Ober-Seeland 418.
Ober-Siegsdorf 57.
Oberstanfen 5.
Oberstdorf 7.
Obersulzbach-Glacier 137. 142.
Obersulzbach-Thal 136.
Obersulzbach-Thörl 142.
Ober-Turvis 433.
Oberthal 21.
—, the 394.
Ober-Tilliach 333.
Obertraun 96.
Ober St. Veit 379.
Ober-Vellach 149.
Ober-Vernagt 241.
Obervintl 328.
Ober-Warngau 40.
Oberweis 87.
Oberweissbach 78. 177.
Oberweissenbach 95.
Oberwielenbach 329.
Ober-Wildon 405.
Ober-Wölz 426.
Oberzeisenering 25.
Oberzwain 375.
Obir, the 417.
Obladis 247.
Obsteig 20.
Obtschenu 422.
Ochsenberg 379.
Ochsenberglerkopf, the 203.

474   INDEX.

Ochsenboden 365.
Ochsengarten 231.
Ochsenhorn, the 176.
Ochsenkarkees, the 127.
Ochsenlenke 191.
Ochsenkopf, the 186.
Ochsenplatten, the 152.
Ochsenreichkar, the 376.
Ochsenthal, the 211.
Ochsenwiesalpe, the 100.
Ochsner, the 186.
Oeblarn 393.
Oed 362.
Oedbauer 25.
Oedensee, the 393.
Oedenseer Traun, the 393.
Oedenwinkel Glacier 146.
Oedenwinkelscharte, the Upper and Lower 151.
Oedernalm, the 98.
Oedernthörl, the 98.
Oedstein, the 387.
Oefen (Salzach) 85.
— (Waidring) 176.
Oehling 382.
Oelgrubenjoch 246. 248.
Oelgruben Glacier 246.
Oelgrubenspitze, the Innere and Aeussere 246. 247.
Oelrain, the 196.
Oelschen-Inn 181.
Oelscher, the 381.
Oetschergraben, the 373.
Oetz 236.
Oetzthal, the 236.
Oetzthal (station) 236.
Oetzthaler Glacier 243.
Ofenauer Berg, the 112.
Ofenloch, the 78.
Offensee, the 92.
Oglio, the 312.
Ohlstadt 28.
Ohlstädter Alpe 39.
Ohlstorf 88.
Ohrenspitzen, the 380.
Oib 10.
Oisthal, the 374. 381.
Oistritza, the 408.
Oken 311.
Okresel 408.
Olang 329.
Oldese 302.
Olicro 319.
Olle 318.
Olperer, the 186.
Olperer Hütte 186.
Olsa-Thal, the 426.
Oltro, Cima d' 327. 358.
Ombretta, Forcella di 324.
—, Val 324.
Omishorn, the 211.

Opponitz 382.
Oregione, Forcella dell' 334.
Orsera 444.
Ort, château 89.
Ortenburg, ruin 336.
Ortler, the 277. 278. 287. 291.
Ortler Glacier, the Upper and Lower 277.
Ortler Pass, the 279.
Ortmann 362.
Osol 311.
Ospedaletto 437.
Ospitale 347. 353.
Ossana 311.
Ossiach 428.
Ossiachberg 422.
Ossiacher See, the 428.
Osterburg 380.
Osterhofen 51.
Ostermünchen 53.
Osternig, the 434.
Ostersee, the 37.
Ostrach, the 7. 20.
St. Oswald 404. 425.
Oswaldhütte, the 42. 35.
Oswaldiberg, the 422.
Oten, Val 351.
Otterberg, the 364.
Otto Chapel, the 157.
Ova, Pian dell' 350.
Ovaro 436.
Oy 14.
Oythal, the 11.

Paalgraben, the 308.
Padaunerkogl, the 221.
Padeon 347.
Padergnone 296.
Padinger Alp 81.
Padola 352.
Padon, Forcella di 324. 336.
Padou, Monte 324.
Padrio, Monte 314.
Paganella, Mte. 296.
Pahl 26.
Pala, Cimon della 325.
Pala di S. Martino 326.
Palatsch Pass 323.
Palau, see Palü.
Palazzolo 313.
Palfau 378.
Palfelhorn, the 76.
Palfner See, the 124.
Palfrad 340.
Pallafavera, Val 353.
Pallaus 225.
Pallon della Mare 283. 312.
Palten, the 388. 392.
Palü 317.

Palü Lake 284.
Palüd-Alp, the 200.
Paluzza 336.
Panargenspitze, the 143.
Panchia 321.
St. Panckraz (Ulten) 276.
— (near Reichenhall) 82.
— near Windischgarsten 391.
Paneveggio 325.
Panülerschroffen, the 200.
Pape, Cima di 357.
Paralba 334. 436.
Paratico 313.
Paratsch, the 341. 331.
Parenzo 444.
Paresberg, the 341.
Parona 205.
Parsberg 50.
Parsch 83.
Parseier Spitze, the 271. 285.
Partenkirchen 29.
Partnach, the 30. 33.
— Ursprung 33.
Partnachklamm, the 30.
Partnun-Joch, the 214.
Partnuner Staffel 214.
Partschins 274. 253.
Paschberg, the 169.
Pasing 3. 24.
Passenjoch 189.
Passer, the 253. 270.
Passeierthal 253.
Pasterze Glacier, the 132. 152.
Pastore, Alp 282.
Patenen 216.
Paternion 337.
Paterkofel 346.
Paternsattel 346.
Patroithal, the 235.
Patsch 219.
Patsch-Thal, the 139.
Patscher Kofel, the 170.
Patschger, the 124.
Patteriolspitze, the 201.
Patznaun 213. 218.
Patznaunthal 217.
St. Paul 415.
Pauliner Kopf, the 218.
Paulitsch Sattel, the 409.
St. Pauls 266.
Pavione, Mte. 326. 327.
Pawigl 275.
Payerbach 361.
Payerhütte, the 277. 279. 289. 291.
Payerjoch, the 291.
Payerspitze, the 279.
Pazzone 299.
Peajo 351.
Pebell-Alp 143.

INDEX. 475

Pechgraben, the 384.
Pecol 353.
Pederbach, the 286.
Pederoa 342.
Pederspitzen 252. 286. 289.
Pederū 341.
Pedescala 317.
Pedraisches 342.
Peggau 369.
Peintl-Alp 35.
Peischelkopf, the 204.
Peischlach 145.
Peischlag-Thörl, the 148.
Peissenberg 26.
Peissenberg, the Hohe 26.
Peisting 362.
Peiting 14.
Peitlerkofel, the 342.
Pejo 311. 312.
Poekel 431.
S. Pellegrino 322.
—, Passo di 322.
Pellinkopf, the 218.
Pelmo, Monte 351. 353.
Pelos 352. 436.
Pelsa, Mte. Alto di 357.
Pelugo 304.
Pemmern 259.
Pendelstein 220.
Pendling, the 157.
Pendolasco 284.
Penoda 298.
Penegal, the 268.
Penia 323.
Penkenberg, the 182.
Pens 260.
Penser-Joch, the 260.
Penser-Thal 260.
Penzberg 37.
Penzing 379.
Peraria 436.
Perarolo 358.
Percha 320.
Perchtholdsdorf 361.
Perchting 27.
Perfall 344.
Perfuchs 206.
Pergine 317.
Peri 295.
Perischnik-Fall, the 431.
Perjen 235.
Pernegg (near Ischl) 94.
— (Styria) 369.
Pernitz 362.
Peron 358.
Perra 262. 322.
Persailhorn, the 118.
Perschlingbach, the 379.
Pertisau 48.
Pescantina 295.
Pescara, the 310.
Peschiera 301.

Peschiera d'Isco 343.
Pescul 353.
Pestcapelle near Ehrwald 19. 41.
St. Peter (Ahrenthal) 191.
— (near Botzen) 259.
— (near Enns) 382.
— Freienstein 385.
— (Gardena) 263.
— im Holz 386.
— (on the Ill) 202.
— (on the Carso) 412.
— (on the Katschbach) 426.
— (near Meran) 272.
— (Villnöss) 225.
Peter-Anich Refuge Hut 283.
Petersberg on the Inn 156.
Petersberg in Carinthia 426.
Petersbrunnen, the 130.
Petteneu 204.
Pettorina, Val 324.
Petzeck 150.
Petzen, the 416. 417.
Petzes-Alp 225.
Petziner Spitze 218.
Peuschelkopf, the 246.
Peutelstein 348.
Pezziè di Parù 356.
Pezzo 283.
Pfaffen Glacier 231.
Pfaffenhofen 233.
Pfaffennieder, the 230.
Pfaffensattel 231.
Pfaffenstein, the 385.
Pfaffar 240.
Pfaffnock, the 190.
Pfalzau 379.
Pfandelscharte, the 131.
Pfandelschartenbach 132.
Pfänder, the 6. 196.
Pfandl 103.
Pfandlbach, the 131.
Pfandler Alp, the 158.229.
Pfandlerhof, the 254.
Pfandlgraben 51.
Pfannberg, château 369.
Pfannenknecht, the 201.
Pfannensee, the 215.
Pfannhorn, the 332.
Pfannspitz 225.
Pfeiferin, the 98.
Pfeisthal 37.
Pfelders 254.
Pfeldersthal, the 242. 251.
Pfitscher Bach, the 188. 223.

Pfitscherjoch, the 187.
Pfitschsee, the 275.
Pfitsch-Thal, the 187.
Pflach 17.
Pflaum 310.
Pflersch 222.
Pflerscher Hochjoch, the 229.
Pflerscher Pinkl, the 220.
Pflerschthal 222.
Pfliegelhof 44.
Pflintsberg, ruin 97.
Pflügelhof, the (Maltathal) 399.
Pflunspitzen 204.
Pfons 220.
Pförneralp 46.
Pforzen 3.
Pfossenthal, the 242.
Pfronten 14.
Pfunders 328.
Pfunders-Joch, the 188. 328.
Pfunders-Thal, the 328.
Pfunds 248.
Pfundser Thal, the 248.
Pfundser Tschoythal 249.
Pfarrsee, the 222.
Pian, Monte 345. 351
Pians 205.
Piatta Martina 281.
Piave, the 352.
Piazza, Cima di 281. 282.
Piburger See 236.
Piccolein 341.
Pichelu 136.
Pichl 103. 109. 396.
Pichlwang 108.
Piding 79.
Pielach, the 380.
Piesendorf 135.
Piesling-Ursprung 391.
Piesling 362.
Pietra, Castel in 327. 358.
Pietra Murata 297.
Pietra Rossa. Val di 284.
S. Pietro 314. 317. 318.
—, Val di 336.
— Berbenno 284.
Pieve di Cadore 351.
— di Ledro 300. 308.
— di Livinalongo 356.
— di Val Rendena 305.
— Tesino 318.
Pihapper Spitze, the 135.
Piller 245.
Pillerhöhe, the 216.
Piller Saddle, the 245.
Pillersee 119.
—, the 176.
Pillsteiner Alp 375.
Pilthal, the 217.

476 INDEX.

Pilsen-See, the 27.
Pine, Val 317.
Pinguente 414.
Pinniser Joch 220. 228.
Pinnisthal, the 228.
Pinsdorf 88.
Pinswang 18.
Pinzgau, the 102. 118.
Pinzgauer Höhe, the 181.
Pinzgauer Spazierweg, the 117.
Pinzolo 305.
Pioda 285.
Piösmös 245.
Piovere 302.
Pirano 444.
Pirlo Lakes, the 284.
Pischenza, Val 482.
Pisgana, Punta di 308.
Pisino 414.
Pisogne 313.
Pissa, la 253.
Pitschiköpfe, the 212.
Pitten 363.
Pitzbach, the 263.
Pitzenbach, the 254.
Pitzerbach, the 185.
Pitzhütte, the 388.
Pitzthal, the 245.
Pitzthaler Jöchl, the 246.
Piz, il 358.
Pizlai 249.
Pizzano 312.
Pizzocco, Mte. 351.
Pizzocolo, Mte. 302.
Plabutsch 401.
Plaiken 175.
Plain 81.
Plan (Gardena) 264.
— (Pfelderthal) 254.
— (Sannaun) 218.
Planailthal, the 250.
Planegg 24.
Plang de Corones 329.
Plangeross 245.
Planina 411.
Planinschek 408.
Planitza, Val 432.
Planitzing 267.
Planja-Graben 435.
Plankenau 414.
Plankenstein, the 45.
Plankenwart 404.
Plansee, the 23.
Planspitz, the 336.
Planta, château 272.
Plars 274.
Plassegen-Joch 214.
Plassen, the 99.
Platt 218. 247. 254.
Plattach Glacier, the 31.
Platte, the 404.
Plattei, the 240.

Plattenalpe 385.
Plattenkogl, the 138. 181.
Plattenspitze 216. 286. 289.
Plattkofel 263. 323.
Plattsee 141.
Platzers 275.
Plätz-Wiesen, the 330.
Plazera 200.
Pleiss, the Stickle 278.
Pleisshorn, the 277.
Plenitzscharte 136.
Pleschberg, the 387.
Pleschkogel, the 370.
Plesnikbauer, the 408.
Plesnitzscharte 400.
Pletzerer Alp 46.
Plima, the 252. 285.
Plöken, the 335. 423.
Ploner 259.
Plose, the 225.
Plotscherboden, the 377.
Plumser Joch, the 43.
Pöchlarn 380.
Pocci 350. 355.
Podberto 429.
Poddestagno 348.
Podkraj 411.
Podlog 418.
Podnart 420.
Podwolloulcg 409.
Poganeck 460.
Poik, the 410.
Pokhorn 150.
Pola 444.
Pölfing 405.
Polinigg 335. 423.
Polinik 149.
Politsch 429.
Pöllat, the 16. 17.
Polles Glacier 240.
Polling 27.
Polpet 354.
Polster, the 385.
Polsterlucke, the 391.
Polsterthal, the 391.
Pölstthal, the 389.
St. Pölten 379.
Poltschach 407.
Poludnigg 435.
Pomagagnon 347.
Pomagraben 405.
Pounle Fall, the 299.
Pongau, the 115.
Ponigl 407.
Pontafel 435.
Pontagna 312.
Ponte Alto 350.
Ponte del Diavolo 283.
— della Lasta 362.
— di Muro 435.
— di Legno 283. 312.

Ponte delle Vacche 283.
— di Pietra 283.
— nelle Alpi 354.
Pontebba 435.
Pontebbana, the 455.
Pontet 327.
Pontives 263.
Pontlatzer Brücke 247.
Popena, Piz 345.
—, Val 345. 351.
Poppenalm, the 301.
Porcellizza, Val 285.
Pordoi, Mte. 323.
Pordoi-Joch 323.
Portogruaro 437.
Pörtschach 421.
Poschenmühle 81.
Poschiavino, the 281.
Poschner Inn 418.
Posruck, the 406.
Possagno 320.
Possenhofen 24. 25.
Possnitz 406.
Pöstlingberg, the 383.
Potei, Col 353.
Potorce, Col 350.
Pötschen, the 96.
Potschula Sattel 417.
Pottenbrunn 379.
Pottenstein 380.
Pottschach 364.
Pozza 322.
Prad 251. 277.
Pradidali, Val and Passo di 326. 327.
Pradl 168.
Pragerhof 407.
Prager Hütte 140.
Prägraten 141.
Prägratner-Thörl 143.
Prags, Alt and Neu 330.
Pragser See, the 331.
Pragser Thal, the 330.
Pranau-Thal, the 119.
Pramper, Val 353.
Pramper Mta., the 358.
Prantl-Alp, the 35.
Pranzo 301.
Prassberg 408.
Pratigau, the 213.
Prävali 416.
Präwald 412.
Praxmar 232.
Preber-See, the 398.
Preber-Spitze, the 398.
Preberthörl, the 394.
Prebl 416.
Prebühl, the 385. 424.
Predasel 406.
Predazzo 324.
Predigstuhl 394.
Predigtstuhl, the 94.
Predil Pass, the 442.

Preding 404.
Predlitz 398.
Predlitzgraben, the 398.
Predore 313.
Pregasina 299.
Prograten 141.
Preimel Fall 399.
Preimelspitze 399.
Prein 366.
Preinthal, the 366.
Preisenhof 428.
Prolongei 343.
Premstetten 404.
—, château 405.
Prenn 275.
Prennspitze, the 275.
Preore 304.
Preroman 342.
Presanella, the 308.
Prese, Le 283.
Presena, Passo di 308.
Preseker See, the 423.
Presenajo 352.
Preseglie 309.
Pressbaum 379.
Pressura, Monte 280.
Prestranek 412.
Prestrelenik, the 442.
Prettau 188, 191.
Preuneggthal 396.
Prevali 446.
Priel, the Grosse 391. 98.
—, the Kleine 391.
Prielau, château 118.
Prien 53.
Prienthal, the 53. 54.
Priesberg-Alpe, the 73. 75.
Prillinger 90.
Primau 58.
Primiero 326.
Primolano 319.
Prinzersdorf 380.
Prisanig 432. 442.
Prissian 268.
Prissianer-Thal 268.
Pritschitz 421.
Probst-Alp 41.
Prodinger Hütte 398.
Proleswand, the 372.
Pröller, the 390.
Proschowitz 422.
Prosecco 414.
Prosek 140.
Prossau 124.
Prössels, château 226.
Proveis 310.
Pruggern 391.
Pruller Alpe 391.
Prutz 247.
Puch 83.
Puchheim, château 87.
Püchel 386.
Püchl, château 368.

Pucz Alp 343.
Pufels 263.
Puflatsch, the 263. 265.
Puikogl 245. 246.
Pulst 428.
Punta Nera 349.
Puntigam 405.
Pura, Mte. 436.
Purgametsch-Thal 262.
Purglstein 103.
Purgstall 380.
Purkersdorf 379.
Purstein 338.
Pusterthal, the 327.
Putschall 150.
Putzernoek 339.
Pyhrgass, the Grosse 388. 392.
Pyhrgassgatterl, the 388.
Pyhrnbach, the 392.
Pyhrn-Pass, the 392.
Pyramidenspitze, the 158.
Pyrkerhöhe, the 123.

Quadrathöfe, the 274.
Quarnero, bay 446.
Quellspitze, Innere and Aussere 251.
St. Quirin 44.

Rabbi, Baths of 311.
Rabbi, Val di 311.
Rabenmühle 89.
Rabenspitze, the 43.
Rabenstein (Passeir) 254.
— (Penser Thal) 260.
—, château 141. 369.
Rabenschwand 87.
Rabland 253.
Raccolana Valley 443.
Radeck, Alp 124.
Radegund, Bad 404.
Radein 406.
Radelberg, the 405.
Radenthein 398. 422.
Radbansberg, the 125.
Radkersburg 406.
Radlbach, the 415.
Radlgraben 399.
Radmannsdorf 429.
Radmer 385.
Radmer an der Hasel 387.
— an der Stuben 385.
Radmerbach, the 376.
Radmerhals 385.
Radmer-Thal, the 385.
Radoina, the 431.
Radoua Gorge, the 202.
Radstadt 397.
Radstadter Tauern, the 397.
Radueha, the 408.

Radurschel-Thal 243.
Rafenstein, ruin 260.
Raffein 241.
Raggal 200.
Raggaschlucht 149.
Ragoli 304.
Rai, the 354.
Raibl 442. 431.
Raiblerscharte 443.
Raibler See 442. 443.
Rain, see Rein.
Rainoralp, the 140.
Rainer Glacier 141. 142.
Rainerhorn 141. 142.
Rainerhütte, the 134.
Rainerkogl, the 404.
Rainthal (Bavaria) 32.
— (Taufers) 337. 339.
Rainthaler Bauer 32.
— See, the 159.
Rak-Sattel, the 408.
Rakek 411.
Ralf Glacier 147.
Rambach, the 251.
Ramboldplatte, the 156.
Rametz, château 274.
Raminges 222.
Ramingstein 398.
Rammelstein 329.
Rammerthal, the 374.
Ramminghach, the 384.
Rammingdorf 383.
Ramoljoch 239. 244.
Ramolkogl, the 239.
Rams, the 364.
Ramsau, near Berchtesgaden 76. 77.
—, near Goisern 95.
— on the Gölsen 379.
— (Ennsthal) 395.
—, the (river) 28. 379.
Ramsauer Gebirge, the 94.
Rauseider-Scharte, the 75. 113.
Ranalt 228.
Rangersdorf 150.
Rankweil 198.
Rappenalpenthal, the 13.
Rappenloch Gorge 197.
Rasberg-See, the 136.
Raschenberg, ruin 56.
Raschötzer Alp 225. 263.
Rasen 329.
Rastezen-Alp 124.
Rathhausberg, see Radhansberg.
Räticon chain, the 213.
Ratschach 432.
Ratschinges Thal 223.
Ratteis 242.
Rattenberg 150.
Ratzes 265.

INDEX.

Raubling 156.
Raucheck, the 113.
Rauchengraben 368.
Rauchespitze, the 212.
Rauchkofl, the (Pusterthal) 337.
— (Ahrenthal) 191.
Rauhe Bühel, the 275.
Raubeck 12.
Rauhe Kopf, the 240.
Rauhenberg Lake 396.
Rauheneck, ruin 362.
Rauhenstein, ruin 362.
Rauhenzell 8.
Rauhhorn, the 21.
Rauhkofl (Ampezzo) 345.
Rauhthal, the 340. 341.
Rauris 116. 126.
Rauris, the 126.
Rauris Goldmines 127.
Rauriser Tauern 127.
Rauschberg, the 55. 57.
Raut 22.
Rautekopf, the 203.
Ravazzone 298.
Raveisch 218.
Ravina 294.
Ravni, the Obere 418.
Raxalp, the 366.
Raxenmauer 366.
Razoibach, the 288.
Razor 432. 442.
Razzo, Col di 436.
Realspitze 183. 185.
Reana del Rojale 437.
Rechberg 417.
Rechenau 52.
Redasco, Piz 281.
Redenbachthal, the 382.
Redl 87.
Reedsee, the 124.
Regana, Val 326.
Regenalp, the 75.
Reggenthörl, the 143.
Regnana 317.
Reichartkogel, the 389.
Reichenau 304. 398.
Reichenbach S. 14.
Reichenfels 416.
Reichenhall 79.
Reichenspitze, the 180.
Reichenstein, the 385. 386.
Reich-Ramning 384.
Reichstein, Alp 52.
Reifenstein 222. 224.
Reifling 384. 382.
Reifnig 415.
Reifnitz 410.
Reigersbeuern 40. 42.
Reihüben-Alp 124.
Rein 339.
—, monastery 370.

Reinbach Falls, the 338.
Reinberg, the 64.
Reindleralpe, the 156.
Reindlerthal, the 156.
Reindlmühle 88.
Reinswald 260. 339.
Reintbal, the 337. 339.
Reisalpe, the 379.
Reischach 329.
Reischlklamm, the 82.
Reiserkogl, the 245.
Reissach 423.
Reissacher Bad 423.
Reisseck, the 399.
Reissende Lahne, the 36.
Reisskofl, the 336. 423.
Reissthal, the 366.
Reit im Winkel 56.
Reitalpgebirge, the 176. 177.
Reiterboden, the 139.
Reiterjoch, the 261.
Reiterndorf 94. 170.
Reith 37. 159.
Reitherkogl, the 159. 178.
Reitherspitze, the 37.
Reithof, the 365.
Reiting, the 380.
Reka 413.
— Caverns 413.
Rekawinkel 379.
Rellsereck, the 213.
Rellsthal, the 214.
Remschenigggraben 408.
Remsköpfl, the 132.
Remsspitze, the 251.
Remüs 218.
Ren 358.
Rendelspitze, the 203.
Rendena, Val 304.
Rennfeld, the 369.
Rennweg 398.
Rentsch 259.
Reschen 249.
Reschen-Scheideck 249.
Reschen-See 249.
Resia Valley 436.
Resiutta 436.
Rester Höhe, the 174.
Reth-Thal, the 211.
Rettenbach 175.
Rettenbachthal (near Ischl) 93.
— (Oetzthal) 246.
Rettenbach Glacier, the 246.
Rettenberg 8.
Rettenstein (Ramsau) 397.
Rettenstein, Grosse 172.
Retterschwangthal 20.
Reut im Winkel, see Reit.

Reute, baths 208.
Reuten 56.
Reutte 18.
Revo 311.
Rezzo, Val di 283.
Rheinberg 198.
Rhonspitze, the 203.
Riccobetta, the 322.
Ricegon, the 331
Rickenbach 196.
Ridnaun 222. 223.
Ridnaun-Thal 223. 224.
Ried on the Ammersee 27.
— on the Eisak 222.
— on the Inn 248.
— on the Loisach 38.
— (Sarnthal) 260.
— (Zillerthal) 179.
Rieden 27. 196.
Riederbach, the 180.
Riedererstein, the 45.
Riefenhof 247.
Riegeralpe, the 129.
Riegerin 377.
Rieglerjoch, the 189.
Rienz, the 327. 344. 345.
—, the Schwarze 344.
Riepen-Sattel, the 186.
Riesachsee 396.
Riese 196.
Riesenalp, the 54.
Rieselsberg-Alp, the 47.
Riesenkopf, the 54.
Rieserferner 330. 339.
Rieserferner Hut 339.
Riesernock, the 339.
Riess 404.
Riesserbauer, the 30.
Rietz 233.
Riezlern 10.
Rif 358.
Riffeljoch, the 248.
Riffelsattel, the 373. 381.
Riffelscharte, (Gastein) 125.
— (Partenkirchen) 31.
— (Zillerthal) 173. 185.
Riffelsee, the 246.
Riffelthor, the 134. 151.
Riffenkopf, the 11.
Riffian 253.
Riffl Glacier, the 134.
Riffler 185. 188. 206. 218.
Riffler-Hütte 185.
Rigolato 436.
Rimbinuco 345. 346.
Rindalphorn, the 5.
Ring, the 374. 376.
Ringberg 45.
Ringelstein 199.
Rinka 408.
Rinka-Fall, the 408.

INDEX. 479

Rinn 161.
Rinnbachfall, the 91.
Rinnen 210.
Riss, the 35. 42.
Rissalpe, the 46.
Risshach, the 35.
Risserkogl, the 45.
Ristfeicht 178.
Ristfeichthorn 82. 178.
Ritorto, Mte. 305.
Ritschergraben 386.
Ritten, the 259.
Rittnerhorn 259.
Ritzenried 245.
Riva 298. 302.
— (Lago d'Iseo) 313.
Rjovina 431.
Riviera (Lake of Garda) 301.
Rivalgo 353.
Rivoli 295.
Roana 319.
Roasco 284.
Rocca 301. 328.
Rocca, La 299.
Rochetta, the 293.
Rocchetta Pass 309.
Roccolo, Monte 302.
St. Rochus 200.
Rodella, Col di 264.
Rodeneck 328.
Rödtspitze, the 144. 340.
Roën, Monte 267.
Rofan 49.
Rofelewand, the 245.
Rofen 241.
Rofensee, the 241.
Rofen-Thal, the 241.
Rogelskopf, the 202.
Robitsch, Baths of 407.
Rohnberg, the 50.
Rohnthal, the 43.
Rohr 389.
Rohrmoos 13.
Rohrmoosberg 395.
Rohrsee, the 38.
Roithain 86.
Rojaberg, the 199.
Rojach 415.
Rolle Pass 325.
Romagnano 295.
Romano 320.
Romanshorn, 7.
Romariswandkopf 147.
Rombon 442.
S. Romedio 311.
Romeno 310.
Römerbad 409.
Römerquelle 415.
Römerthal 438. 448.
Ronach 137. 172. 181.
Roncegno 318.
Ronch, Sasso di 356.

Ronchi 441.
Ronco 318.
Roncone 308.
Ronzano 208.
Ronzina 441.
Roppen 233.
Rorschach, 7.
Rosa, La 347.
Rosà, Col 350.
Rosalien-Capelle, the 363.
Rosank 415.
Rosanna, the 203.
Roschizza Saddle 421.
Rosegg 421.
Rosenau 331.
Rosenbach 410. 421.
Rosenberg (Gratz) 403.
Rosenberg, château 119.
Rosengarul-Schlucht, the 234.
Rosengarten, the 262. 322.
Rosenheim 53.
Rosenkogel, the 425.
Rosenthal (Carinthia) 421.
Rosetta 325.
Rosin-Boden 288.
— Glacier 289.
Rosimjoch, the 252. 293.
Rositlenalp, the Upper and Lower 67.
Rossberg, the 136.
Rossbergjoch, the 241.
Rossbrand, the 397.
Rossfeld, the 83. 85.
Rossgrub-Alp 135.
Rosshag 185.
Rosshaupten 14.
Rossi, Cima di 323.
Rosskar, the 177.
Rosskofel, the 380. 435.
Rosskogl, the 231. 372.
Rosskopf, the 222.
Rossleithen 391.
Rossruck, the 185.
Rossrücken, the 22.
Rossrückjoch, the 190.
Rossstein, the 42.
Rosszähne, the 323.
Rostitzalpe 247.
Rothach 45. 46.
Rothachfälle, the 45.
Rothachthal, the 46.
Rothbach, the 190.
Rothbleiskopf, the 235.
Rothebenferner, the 250.
Rothe Karle, the 239.
Röthelmoos-Alp 57.
Röthelsee, the 91.
Röthelspitze 275.
Röthelstein 369.
—, château 387.

Röthenbach 6.
Rothenbrunn, baths (Selrain) 281.
— (Walserthal) 200.
Rothenfels 5. 426.
Rothenmannsjoch 191.
Röthenspitze, the 229.
Röthenstein 393.
Röthenstein Lakes,the 46.
Rothenthurm 337.
Rothe Rinne, the 395.
Rothe Säule, the 291.
Rothe Wand (Formarinsee) 212.
— (Val Fassa) 322.
— (Samina) 199.
Röthferner, the 144.
Rothgratscharte, the 229.
Rothgülden 398.
Rothhaide 425.
Rothholz 178.
Rothhorn, the (Bregenzer Wald) 200.
Rothkopf, the 185.
Rothlechthal, the 210.
Rothmoos-Glacier 243.
Rothmoosferner-Joch 244.
Rothsoolhütten, the 371.
Rothspitze 191. 286.
Rötlspitze 144. 340.
Rothsteinkogl, the 275.
Röththal 491.
Rothwand, the 74.
Rothwand (Ampezzo) 330.
— (Bavaria) 26.
— (Fassa) 322.
— (near Meran) 258.
— (Pfitscher Joch) 187.
— (Sexten) 333.
— (Vorarlberg) 212.
Rothwein 414. 431.
Rothwein Fall 430.
Rötis 198.
Rottach, see Rothach.
Rottenbuch 26.
Rottenkogl 139. 147.
Rottenmann 388.
Rottenstein 272.
Rottmannshöhe 26.
Rover, Mte. 317.
Rovereto 295.
Rovigno 444.
Rù, Col de 341.
Rubbia 441.
Rubein 272.
Rubi S. 10.
Rubihorn, the 10.
Rucerva 353.
Ruderatshofen 3.
Ruderhofspitze 228. 229.
Rudniker Sattel 435.
Ronlo di sora 341.
— di sotto 341.

Rudo, Vallon di 341.
Rudolfshütte, the 146.
Rucfenberg 225.
Ruffrè 268.
Rufreddo 347.
Ruhpolding 57.
Rum 161.
Rumaschlung 342.
Rumo 310.
Rungelin 201.
Runkelstein, château 260.
St. Rupert am Kulm 395.
Russbachsag 101. 103.
Rust 222.
Ruthnerhorn, see Schnebige Nock.
Rutorto Alp 353.
Rutzbach, the 227.

Saalach, the 56. 79. 80. 118. 176.
Saalbach 118.
Saalfelden 118.
Saalhof 118.
Säben 225.
Sabbia, Val 309.
Sabbio 308.
Sabbione, Hog del 304. 305.
Sachenbach 42.
Sachrang 55.
Sachsenburg 336.
Sachsenfeld 408.
Sachsenklemme, the 224.
Sack 423.
Sackwiesen-See 375. 377.
Sadenza, the 432.
Saderer Joch, the 249.
Sadererthal 249.
Sagereckalp, the 75.
Sagereckwand, the 74. 75.
Sagor 409.
Sagrado 441.
Sagritz 150.
Sagron 327. 358.
—, Piz di 358.
Saifnitz 434.
Sailespitze, the 171.
Salaberg 382.
Sakdinnspitze, the 202.
Salarno 313.
Salarnel-Joch 200.
Salcano 442.
Saldenhofen 415.
Sale Marasino 313.
Salegg 261.
Salern 225.
Salvei 355.
Saletto 443.
Sallilog 429.
Sällentjoch 286.
Salletalp, the 74.
Salloch 410.

Salmshütte, the 153.
Salò 304. 309.
Salomonsbrunnen 329.
Salt, baths 285.
Sattaus 253.
Sattric Gorge 323.
Salurn 293.
Salurnferner 251.
Salurn-Spitze, the 251.
Salve, the Hohe 171.
Salvore 444.
Salza, the Styrian 98. 372. 374. 376. 393. etc.
— (Pinzgau) 137.
Salzach, the 56. 61. 88. 112. 137. etc.
Salzach-Joch, the 172.
Salzberg, the, near Berchtesgaden 71.
—, near Ischl 94.
—, near Aussee 97.
—, near Hall 161.
—, near Hallstatt 99.
Salzbüchsel 81.
Salzburg 60.
Salzburger Hochthron, the 67.
Salzkammergut 88.
Salzsteig, the 98. 391.
Samerhütte, the 399.
Samerthal 37.
Samina-Joch, the 199.
Samina-Thal, the 199.
Samnaun 218.
Samspitze, the 203.
Sandesjoch 220.
Sandesthal 220.
Sandhof 254.
Sandkogl, the 426.
Sandkopf, the 154.
Sandling, the 97.
Sannoarhütte 241.
Sann, the 407. 408.
Sauna, the 205.
Sannbrücken 408.
Sannthal, the 407.
Sannthal Alps 407.
Saunthaler Sattel 417.
Sante Bühel 333.
Santicolo 314.
Santner Pass 262.
Santo, Monte 441.
Sanzeno 310.
Saone 304.
Sapiane 443.
Sappada 352.
Sarnuta, the 324.
Sarca, the 296. 303.
Sarca, Val 296. 303.
—, Falls 307.
Sarche, Alle 296.
Sardagna 294.

Sarcisor Joch 199.
Sareuen, Alp 199.
Sarl 346.
Sarlkofel, the 346.
Sarner Schloss 260.
Sarnico 313.
Sarnkofel 330. 332.
Sarnonico 268.
Sarnthal, the 260. 257.
Sarnthein 260.
Sarotlathal, the 214.
Sarstein, the 98. 99.
Sass Maor, the 326.
Sassella 284.
Sasso Bianco, the 324.
Sasso Bissolo, Val di 284.
— di Dam 322.
— di Mur 327
— di Ronch 356.
— di Stria 355.
— Maggiore 326.
— Vernale 324.
Sattelgraben 434.
Satteljoch 251.
Sattelsteig, the 97.
Sattendorf 422. 428.
Sattnitz, the 420.
Sau, see Save.
Sau-Alpe, the 427.
Sauerbrunn 363.
Sauerlach 40.
Sauersberg 47.
Saugasse, the 75.
Säuleck, the 399.
Saulgrub 28. 29.
Säuling, the 17.
Säumerbrunnen, the 131.
Saurüssel 381.
Sauris 436.
Sausal Mts. 405.
Sauschloss, the 259.
Säusenstein 381.
Sautens 286.
Sauthal 418.
Sava 409.
Save, the 429. etc.
—, the Wocheiner 429.
—, Wurzener 429.
Savitza 430.
Savogna 441.
Scaliereitt 322.
Scale, Monte delle 281.
Scans 311.
Scanupia, Mte 317. 318.
Scesaplana, the 201.
Schaan 199.
Schaanerfürkele, the 199.
Schals 328.
Schachen 7.
Schachenalp, the 32.
Schachenbad 7.
Schachenplatte, the 32.
Schuchensee, the 32.

INDEX. 481

Schachenstein, ruin 375.
Schadona-Sattel 200.
Schafberg (Salzkammergut) 105. 103.
— (Vorarlberg) 212.
Schafboden, the 216.
Schafbuchjoch, the 204.
Schafbühel, the 146.
Schafeck-Alpe, the 100.
Schäffler-Alpe, the 417.
Schafgafall, the 214.
Schafhals-Sattel 378. 376.
Schafkogl 425.
Schafkopf, the 250.
Schaflanernock, the 190.
Schafloch, the 107.
Schaftlach 40. 44.
Schaida 417.
Schalderjoch, the 225.
Schalderer Thal 225.
Schalf Glacier, the 241.
Schalfkogl 241. 243.
Schallaburg 380.
Schaller Alpe 228.
Schaller Alpe 368.
Schanzbichl, the 108.
Schanzriegel 418.
Schappach 75.
Schärding 87.
Schareck, the 124. 127.
Scharfeneck 362.
Scharfling 108. 109.
Scharfreiter, the 42.
Scharitzkehlalp, the 72.
Scharl-Alp 395.
Scharling 46.
Scharlinz 380.
Scharnitz 36.
—, defile of 36.
Scharti 329.
Scharwandalp, the 101.
Schattenberg, the 11.
Schattenburg, chât. 198.
Schuttwald 22.
Schaubachhütte, the 288.
Schaufelspitze, the 230.
Scheffau (Lammerthal) 103.
— (near Söll) 175.
Scheffauer Kaiser 175.
Scheibbs 380.
Scheibelstein 387.
Scheiblalpe 389.
Scheiblerkopf 204.
Scheiblingkirchen 363.
Scheiblingsee, the 115.
Scheibmühl-Traisen 374. 379.
Scheibwaldhöhe, the 366.
Scheibwaldmauer 365.
Scheichenspitze, the 396.
Scheidegg, 6.
Scheidsee 204.

Scheißling 338. 425.
Scheiterboden 372.
Schelleberg 218.
Schellegrübl 220.
Schellenberg 69.
Schellenberger Sattel, the 67.
Schellgaden 398.
Schergenbach, the 218.
Schesa-Tobel, the 201.
Scheuchegg-Alp 385.
Scheyrer Alp, the 46.
Schgaguler Schwaige, the 263.
Schgums 251.
Schiboutbauer 409.
Schiers 214.
Schiesseck, the 426.
Schiesswald, the 388.
Schiesswaldrücken 388.
Schiffwald-Sattel 378.
Schilcherhöhe, the 398.
Schildenstein, the 46.
Schildspitze, the 286.
Schilpario 313.
Schinder, the 46. 50.
Schindlerspitz 177.
Schinoutz, the 435.
Schio 295.
Schittdach 177.
Schlachters 6.
Schladming 394.
Schladming Glacier 395.
Schladmingthal, the 396.
Schlainer Keesflecken, the 144.
Schlandermann-Thal, the 242. 252.
Schlanders 252.
Schlangenburg 407.
Schlapinajoch, the 215.
Schlappereben Glacier 126.
Schlappolt 11.
Schlaten Glacier 140. 142.
Schlattanbauer, the 30.
Schlautwirth 416.
Schleching 56.
Schlegeis-Scharte 18. 9.
Schlegeis-Thal 186.
Schlehdorf 38.
Schlierfall near Hallstatt 99.
—, near Kitzbühel 174.
—, Maltathal 399.
—, Gastein 125.
Schleinitz, the 335.
Schleis 250.
Schlenken 84.
Schliern, the 226. 265.
Schliernalp, the Upper and lower 265.
Schliernklamm, the 266.

Schlickerbach, the 228.
Schlieferspitze, the 137.
Schlieræhithal, the 49.
Schlierbach 390.
Schliersee 45. 50.
—, the 50.
Schlinigthal, the 250.
Schlitters 178.
Schlittersberg, the 178.
Schlitza, the 443.
Schlöglmühl 364.
Schlossberg, the, near Gratz 401.
—, near Reutte 18.
—, near Weissenfels 432.
Schluderbach 345.
Schluderhorn 285.
Schluderns 251.
Schluderapitze, the 252.
Schlusseljoch 188. 221.
Schlüsselspitze, the 142.
Schmalsee, the 34.
Schmalzkopf 249.
Schmelz, the 24. 225. 277. 425.
Schmidlebach, the 206.
Schmidtenstein, the 68.
Schmieden 380.
Schmiedinger Glacier 134.
Schmiedtobel, the 202.
Schmirn 183.
Schmirner Joch, the 183.
Schmirner Thal 183. 220.
Schmitten 147.
Schnittenhöhe, the 147.
Schnittenstein, the 84.
Schnabelalpe, the 390.
Schnaizkreut 178.
Schnalserbach, the 242.
Schnalser Thal 242. 252.
Schmann 205.
Schnanner-Klamm 205.
Schnappen, the 56.
Schneebig Nock, the 339.
Schneealp, the 371.
Schneeberg (Austria) 365.
— (Carnia) 411.
— (Passeir) 229.
— (Pongau) 113.
Schneeberg, château 220. 411.
Schneedörfel, the 365.
Schneeferner, the 33. 12.
Schneefernerkopf 19. 33.
Schneeglocke, the 279.
Schneespitze, the 220. 222.
Schnee-Wiese, the 90.
Schneewinkelkopf, the 135. 153.
Schnürlstein, the 73.
Schneidjöchl, the 208. 218.
Schnepfau 208.
Schnepfegg, the 208.

BAEDEKER's Eastern Alps. 6th Edit. 31

Schober (Carinthia) 138. 147.
— (Mondsee) 110.
Schoberkogl 416.
Schober Pass, the 389.
Schoberstein 384.
Schober-Thörl 150.
Schöckel, the 404.
Schockhütten 127.
Schöder-Thal, the 115.
Scholastika, Inn 47.
Schöllang 8.
Schönachttal 180.
Schönalpelkopf, the 43.
Schönau (Passeir) 254.
— (near the Königssee) 71.
— (in Austria) 362.
— (Maltathal) 399.
Schönbach 180. 204.
Schönberg (Brenner) 219. 227.
— (Samina) 199.
Schönbichl, the 395.
Schönbichler Horn 187.
Schönbrunn 379.
Schönbüchele, the 335.
Schondorf 27.
Schöndorf 87.
Schöneben 368. 272.
Schöneck, the 119. 269.
Schönfeldspitz 74. 77. 119.
Schönfervall 204.
Schongau 8.
Schöngeisinger Wald 3.
Schöngelair 229. 230.
Schönjöchl 229. 247.
Schönleitenhütte 289.
Schönleitenthal 345.
Schönna, château 273.
Schönlaufspitze 287. 289.
Schönwies 234.
Schöpfl, the 380.
Schoppernau 209.
Schösswend 141.
Schöttlgraben, the 426.
Schöttlkarspitze 36. 43.
Schottwien 367.
Schrainbach, the 74. 75.
Schrainbach-Alp, the 75.
Schrambach 374.
Schrammacher, the 186.
Schrankogel, the 228. 237.
Schranspitze 286.
Schrattenberg 426.
Schreckbrücke, the 123.
Schreckbühel 267.
Schrecken, the 209.
Schrecksee, the 52.
Schreiende-Bach, the 392.
Schrine, the 12.
Schrofenpass, the 13.

Schrötterhorn, the 288.
Schruns 213.
Schupfenboden, the 338.
Schupfen Inn, the 227.
Schuss, the 353.
Schüsserlbrunn 369.
Schüttachgraben, the 177.
Schüttalp, the 94.
Schüttbach, the 337.
Schützensteig, the 17.
Schwalbenalpenkopf 332.
Schwalbenkopf, the 246.
Schwalbhausen 3.
Schwalbthal, the 384.
Schwalmünchen 3.
Schwadering, the 395.
Schwaigbauer 360.
Schwaigmühl Alp 67.
Schwalbenkofel, the 332.
Schwalpenspitzen 443.
Schwanberg 404. 405.
Schwanberg Alps, the 405.
Schwangau 14.
Schwanenstadt 87.
Schwansee, the 15.
Schwarzach (Pongau) 115.
— (Vorarlberg 196. 207.
— (Gerlos) 180.
— (Defereggen) 139.
Schwarzachenthal, the 55.
Schwarzachthal, the 139.
Schwarzachtobel 206.
Schwarzau, the 364.
Schwarzbach 77.
—, the (Schafberg) 108.
— (near Golling) 84.
Schwarzbach Falls 84.
Schwarzbachthal, the (Salzburg) 108.
— (Defereggen) 139.
Schwarzbachwacht 76.77.
Schwarzberg, the 86. 331.
Schwarzbergklamm 177.
Schwärze, Hintere 239.
Schwarze Gupf 420.
Schwarzenbach (near Ischl) 103.
— (Carinthia) 432.
— (Carnia) 408.
—, the (Ahrenthal) 190.
Schwarzenbachjoch 190.
Schwarzenberg 207. 206.
—, the 50.
— (Pass) 180.
Schwarzenberghütte 163.
Schwarzenbergjoch 228.
Schwarzensee 185.
Schwarzenstein 186. 190.
Schwarzenstein Glacier, the 186.
Schwarzenstein-Grund, the 185.
Schwarzentenn-Alp 45.

Schwarze Schneide, the Aeussere and Innere 240.
Schwarze See, the 105.
Schwarze Thörl, the 144.
Schwarze Wand 268. 337
Schwarzhanskarkopf 22.
Schwarzhorn, the (Montavon) 214.
— (Fassa) 261. 321.
Schwarzhörnsee 400.
Schwarzkopf, the 129.
Schwarzlakcapelle 150.
Schwarzort, the 70.
Schwarzschädel, the 129.
Schwarzsee, the (near Kitzbühel) 174.
— (Zemmgrund) 185.
— (Moritzenthal) 308.
— (Schafberg) 105.
— (Sölk) 394.
— (Terglou) 431.
Schwarzsee-Scharte 229.
Schwarzseespitze 223.
Schwarzwandscharte 230.
Schwarzwasserthal 12. 210.
Schwaz 159.
Schwefel 197
Schweighof 46.
Schweinthal 49.
Schweizerhütte, the (Nassfeld) 125.
Schweizersberg, the 391
Schweizer-Thor, the 214.
Schwemm-Alp, the 185.
Schwemser Spitze 251.
Schwendt 58. 158.
Schwerteck, the 153.
Schwöb 73.
St. Sebastian 318.
S. Sebastiano, Mte. 358.
Sebi 55. 58.
Seblasjoch, the 218.
Sechsegerten Glacier 240. 246.
Seckau 424.
—, château 405.
Seckan Alp 424.
Sedlec 354. 358.
See (Mondsee) 109.
Seealp, the 11. 417.
Seeau, the, near Eisenerz 378.
— on the Königssee 74.
Seebach 82. 336. 400.
Seebach, Alp 139.
Seebachhof 394.
Seebachthal 126. 221. 381.
Seehen-See, the 19.
Seehenbachfall, the 19.
Seebenstein 363.
Seeberg, the 374. 382. 418.
Seebertbal 244. 254.

INDEX. 483

Seebichl 154.
Seeboden 386.
Seebruck 54.
Seefeld 27. 37.
Seegatterl, the 57.
Seegraben, the 375.
Seehaus 57. 254.
Seehausen 27.
Seehäusl 117.
Seehof, the 381.
Seehorn, the 216.
Seekarspitze, the (Achensee) 43.
— (near Radstadt) 397.
Seekirchen 88.
Seekofel 331. 341. 350.
Seekopf (Rhäticon) 201.
— (Patznaun) 218.
— (Raibl) 442.
— (Carinthia) 443.
Seelandbach 347.
Seeländer Kotschna 418.
Seelandthal, the 330.
Seelein-Alpe 73.
Seemauer 377. 381.
Secon 54.
Seeshaupt 25. 37.
Seespitz, the 49. 228.
Seesvenna, Piz 251.
Seethal, the (Styria) 375.
— (Raibl) 442.
Seethal Alps, the 425.
Seetraun, the 57.
Seewalchen 109.
Seewände, the 11.
Seewiesen 375.
Seewigthal 394.
Seewis 199.
Seghe, Val delle 306.
Segonzano 317.
Seidlwinkel 127.
Seinsbach, the 35.
Seinsgraben 35.
Seis 264.
Seisenbach, the 378.
Seisenbergklamm, the 78.
Seisera, the 434.
Seiser Alp, the 264.
Seit 258.
Seitenstetten 382.
Seitenwinkelthal, the 127.
Seiterjöchl, the 240.
Seitz 389.
Sekkau 421.
Sulelta, the 349.
Sella (Fassa) 343.
—, Val di 318.
— di Senes, Mte. 331.
Sellajoch (Fassa) 264. 343.
Sellero 313.
Selrain Valley 231.
Selva, château 318.
Selva (near Caprile) 358.

Selva (Val Zoldo) 353.
Selva, Val 305.
Selzach 429.
Selzthal 388.
Semlach 428.
Semmering 367.
—, the 367.
Semmering Railway 364.
Semslach 150.
Senale 310.
Senes, Alp 341.
Sengesthal 224.
Sengsengebirge, the 390.
Senkstein, am 371.
Seuneregertenthal 223.
Serfaus 219. 248.
Serlesspitze, the 227.
Sernioue, peninsula 301.
Sernio 284.
Serpenizza 442.
Serra di Morignone 283.
Serraja, Lago 317.
Serravalle 295. 354.
Servola 440.
Sesis, Val 352.
Sessana 414.
Sett Sass 343.
Sette Comuni, the 319.
Setzberg, the 46.
Sexten 332.
Sextenjoch, the 240.
Sextenthal, the 332.
Sextner Bad, the 333.
— Böden, the 333.
Sforzellina-Pass 283.
Sibratsgfäll 13.
Siebenbrunnenthal 360.
Siebeneich 259. 269.
Siebenmühlen 108.
Siebensee 376. 378.
Sieben Sprünge, the 32.
Sieglhof 398.
Siegsdorf 57.
Sielva 251.
Sierning 380.
Sierningbach 364.
Sierninghofen 390.
Sigishofen 8.
Siglitzthal, the 125.
St. Sigmund 281. 328.
Sigmundsburg, ruin 20.
Sigmundscapelle 374.
Sigmundskron 268.
—, castle 266.
Sigmundsried, chât. 248.
Sigmundsruhe 41.
Silberpfennig, the 125.
Silberspitze, the 285.
Silberthal 213. 215.
Sillbach, the 52.
Sill, the 162. 219. 221.
Silla, the 317.
Sillian 333. 423.

Silvester Thal 331.
Silvretta, the 217.
Silz 233.
Similaun, the 241.
Similaunjoch, the 241.
Simm-See, the 53.
Simming-Glacier 220.
Simmingjöchl 229.
Simony Glacier 143.
— Spitze 144.
Simonyhütte, the 100.
Sinabell, the 396.
Sinachbach, the 274.
Singerin, the 365.
Sinseu 218.
Sintersbach Alpe 118. 174.
Siriuskogel 93.
Siror 326.
Sitzenthal 380.
Siviano 313.
Skarbin, the 418.
Skarje-Sattel, the 408.
Skerbinja 430.
Skuta 418.
Slivenza, the 411.
Sobatsch 225.
Socchieve 436.
Soiern, Am 40.
Soiern Lakes 40.
Soiernspitzen, the 40.
Soinsee, the 51.
Sojat, the 262. 323.
Solagna 320.
Sölden 287.
Söldener Jöchl, the 246.
Söldenköpfl, the 76.
Sole, Val di 309. 311.
Solk 394.
Solkerscharte, the 394.
Sölkthal, the 394.
Söll 175.
Söllland, the 175.
Söllbach, the 45.
Solstein, the Grosse and Kleine 232. 36.
Somdogna Pass 434.
Sommerermühle, the 332.
Sommerscharte, the 118.
Sommerstein, the 118.
Sommerthörl 425.
Sondalo 283.
Sondrio 284.
Sondergrund, the 182.
Senger, Sass 341.
Sonico 313.
Sonklarhütte, the 339.
Sonklarspitze 280. 223.
Sonnblick, the 146. 400.
Sonnblick Glacier 128. 146.
Sonnenburg, monast. 328.
Sonneneck, the 158.

31*

484 INDEX.

Sonnenjoch, the 48.
Sonnenkogl, the 246.
Sonnenspitze, the 19.
Sonnenwelleck 153.
Sonnschienalpe 375. 376.
Sonnstein, the 90.
Sonntag 200.
Sonntagberg, the 281.
Sonntagshorn 177.
Sonntagskopf, the 137.
Sonnwendgebirge 49.
Sonnwendjoch, the Vordere 49. 179.
—, the Hintere 52.
Sonnwendstein 367.
Sonthofen 7.
Sopiane 302.
Sopramonte 294.
Soraga 321.
Surapiss, the 350. 351.
—, Lago 349. 353.
—, Val 349.
Sorda, Val 320.
Soré, the 343.
Sotscha, the 432.
Sottla, the 407.
Sotto, Campo di 340.
Sotto, Valle di 283.
Sottogude, Gorge of 324.
Soyjoch, the 286.
Sparnfeld, the 387.
Sparanger Kopf, the 125.
Sparchen 58. 157.
Sparchenbach, the 157.
Speiereck, the 398.
Speikboden 189. 338. 376.
Speikkogel, the 370.
Sperrbachsteg 10.
Sperrbachtobel, the 12.
Spertenthal, the 172.
Spessa, Cima 308.
Spiazzi 209.
Spiegel Glacier 244.
Spiegelkogl 244.
Spielberg 100. 118. 119.
Spielbichler 373.
Spielfeld, château 406.
Spielistjoch, the 43.
Spieljoch, the 48.
Spielmann 131.
Spielmannsau, the 10.
Spinale, Monte 305.
Spindeleben 382.
Spinges 328.
Spitzer Mühle 218.
Spital (Semmering) 368.
— (Pusterthal) 386.
— am Pyhrn 392.
Spitzenbachgraben 384.
Spitzhörndl, the 329.
Spitzing-See, the 15. 50.
Spitzkofl, the 335. 343.
Spitzmauer, the 391.

Spitzstein, the 55.
Spitzstein-Alp 92.
Spondalonga 281.
Spondinig 277.
Sporeralp, the 214.
Sporer Pass 214.
Spranja, the 434.
Sprechenstein 222. 223.
Spredolina 442.
Spreubach, the 212.
Springen 207.
Spritzbachfall, the 127.
Spronser Joch 244.
Spronser Thal 275.
Spullersee, the 212.
Staben 263.
Stabiziane 352.
Stablein 268.
Stadel Alp 387
Stadl 308.
Stadolina 312.
Staffelsee, the 27.
Stafflach 220.
Staig 398.
Staininger 90.
Stall 150.
Stallanzer Bach 248.
Stallau 41.
Stallen-Alpe, the 160.
Stallenthal, the 160.
Staller Sattel 330.
Staller Thal, the 139. 330.
Stallhofen 149.
Staltach 37.
Stambach 95.
Stampfanger Graben 172.
Stampfen 150.
Stampfl Glacier, the 187.
Stams 233.
Stamser Alpe, the 233.
Stanagalpe, the 426.
Stange, the 172.
Stangenach 206.
Stangenwald, the 31.
Staniska 145.
Stanser Joch, the 160.
Stanskogel 204.
Stanz 205. 235.
Stanz, the 127.
Stanzach 210.
Stanzerthal, the 203.
Stanzerwand, the 235.
Stanziwurten 150.
Starhemberg 362.
Staritzen 374.
Starkenberg 234.
Starnberg 24.
Starnberg, Lake of 24.
Staractjoch, the 10.
Starnlach, the 13.
Staubfall (near Jettenberg) 77.
(near Unken) 57. 177.

Staudach 56.
Stauffen, the 82.
Staufencek 79.
Stauffenwand, the 55.
Staulanza, Forcella di 353.
Stazione per la Carnia 436.
Stazzona 314.
Stebüsi, the 213.
Stechwand 189.
St. Stefan 423.
Stefanie-Schutzhütte 413.
Stefanie-Warte 414.
S. Stefano 423. 306. 352.
Stefansbrücke 219. 227.
Steg (Lechthal) 204.
— (near Hallstadt 96.100.
— (Eisakthal) 226.
—, Alp (Samina) 199.
Stegen 27. 329.
Stegenwacht 114.
Stegfeld bridge, the 133.
Steibis 5.
Steiglbachthal, the 5.
Steigl, the 101.
Steigwand, the 97.
Steilenfälle, the 32.
Steilererhütte 426.
Stein (Chiemsee) 64
— (Ennsthal) 394.
— (Iselthal) 140.
— (Carnia) 409.
— (Pfitsch-Thal) 187.
— (Pilerschthal) 222.
— (Pusterthal) 336.
— (Schladming) 100. 306.
Steinabrückl 362.
Steinach (Brenner) 220.
— (Ennsthal) 392.
— (on the Vils) 14.
Steinapiesting 362.
Steinbach 14. 109. 140.
Steinbachthal, the 177. 374.
Steinbauer, the 368.
Steinberg 47.
Steinbergalm, the 176.
Steinberge, the Loferer 78. 176.
Steinbergerspitze, the 47.
—, Alp, the 51.
Steinbrück 409.
Steindorf 87. 135. 428.
Steineberg, the 5.
Steiner Sattel, the 408.
Steinerhof 368.
Steinerne Jäger 443.
— Meer, the 76. 348.
— Stiege, the 67. 175.
— Tisch, the 243.
Steinfeld 379.
Steingaden 14. 336.
Steingrabenschneid 99.

Steinhaus 71. 191. 367.
Steinhof 245
Steinkogl 92.
Steinmüller-Graben 424.
Steinpass 55. 178. 394.
Steinriesen-Thal, the 396.
Steinschlag Joch and Glacier, the 240.
Steinwald 198.
Steinwandklamm 380.
Stellkopf 150.
Stelvio 277.
—, Passo di 280. 277.
Stelvio Glacier 280.
Stelzing 427.
Stempeljoch, the 37. 161.
Stenico 308.
Stephanskirchen 53.
Steppberg-Alp, the 81.
Stern 343.
Sternberg 421.
Sternstein 407.
Sterzing 222.
Sterzinger Moos 224.
Stetten 14.
Steyr 383.
Steyrbruck 390.
Steyrdorf 383.
Steyrer See, the 98.
Steyrermühle 87.
Steyrling 390.
Steyrlingthal 390.
Steyrreith 390.
Steyrthal 384.
Stickle Pleiss, the 278.
Stiege, the 385.
Stiegenwand, the 146.
Stierlahnerwand 137.
Stilfes 224.
Stilfs 277.
Stilfser Joch, see Stelvio.
Stillach, the 8.
Stille Bach, the 249.
Stillupbach 182. 181.
Stipler Alp 161.
Stivo, Monte 295. 296.
Stixenstein 306.
Stock 53. 198.
Stockach 211.
Stockach-Alpe 231.
Stöck 198.
Stockenboi 336.
Stockeralp, the 50.
Stockerseen, the 52.
Stockham 115.
Stöcklen Alp 238.
Stoder 390.
Stoder-Zinken, the 394.
Stoffelsberg, the 4.
Stoisser-Alpe, the 58. 82.
Storé 407.
Storo 300.
Storschitz, the 418.

Stötten 14.
Stou, the 420. 431.
Stouhütte 420.
Strahelebenkopf, the 125.
Strada 308.
Strancekthal 390.
Straneralm 400.
Strass 159. 178. 184.
Strassberg, ruin 222.
Strassburg 427.
Strassengel 370.
Strassenhaus 200.
Strasser 264.
Strassgang 404.
Strasswalchen 87.
Straubinger Alp 125.
Strechau, château 388.
Strechengraben, the 388.
Streden 143.
Streichen 56.
Streitbühl, the 81.
Strembo 305.
Strengen 205.
Stretti 443.
Stria, Sasso di 355.
Strigno 318.
Strino 312.
Stripsenjoch 158.
Stritkopf, the 201. 216.
Strobl 103.
Strombodingfall, the 390.
Stronachkopf 149.
Strub, the 76.
Strubache, the 176.
Strubbach, the 84.
Strubberg, the 103.
Strubpass, the 176.
Stubachthal, the 135. 145.
Stubacher Tauern 146.
Stubaithal, the 227.
Stubalpe 401. 425.
Stuben on the Arlberg 13. 203.
— in Bavaria 47.
— on the Inn 248.
Stubennlp, the 47.
Stubenbach, the 212.
Stüberfall, the 216.
Stübing 370.
Stübinggraben, the 370.
Stübmingthal, the 375.
Student, the 372.
Studlhütte, the 146.
Studlweg, the 147.
Stuhlalp, the 102.
Stuhleck, the 368.
Stuhlfelden 135.
Stuiben, the 5.
Stuiben Fall (Plansee) 23.
— (Oetzthal) 232. 236.
— (Oythal) 11.
— (Pitzthal) 245.
Stuibensee, the 32.

Stuttennock 339.
Stuvu Alp, La 344.
Säcka, Alp 199.
Sogana, Val 318.
Suggadinbach, the 215.
Suhadolnik 418.
Sulden 288. 254.
Suldenbach, the 287.
Sulden Glacier 287. 288.
Suldenspitze 287. 291.
Suldenthal 277. 287.
Sulm, the (Styria) 405.
Sulz (Rankweil) 198.
— (Weilheim) 26.
Sulz, Bad 26.
Sulzano 313.
Sulzau 112.
—, the 136.
Sulzbach 389. 408.
Sulzbach Alps 408.
Sulzbachthal, Ober and Unter 136. 390.
Sulzbachthörl 141.
Sulzberg 5. 14.
Sulzberg, the 311.
Sulzbrunn 14.
Sulzenau 280.
Sulzenhals, the 395.
Sulzhöh, the 214.
Sulzkaar Alp 387.
Sulzkaarhund-Sattel 387.
Sulzköpfe, the 208.
Sulzthal, the (Ischl) 94.
— (Oetzthal) 237.
Sulzthal Glacier 237.
Sunk, the 349.
Surberg 55.

Tabaretta Glacier, the 289. 291.
Tabarettascharte, the 291.
Tabarettaspitze 289.
Tabarettawände, the 291.
Tabland 253.
Tabor, the 383.
Taé 348.
Taferl-Klause 109.
Tagenbrunn 427.
Tagliamento, the 437.
Tai di Cadore 354.
Taibon 326. 358.
Taisnach 418.
Tajakopf, the 19.
Tajo 319.
Talamona 285.
Talfer 257. 260. etc.
Talgenkopf 187.
Tall 275.
Taller-Alp, the 275.
Tamberg 390.
Tamers, Alp 341.
Tamischbachthurm, the 385. 386.

Tamaweg 398. 425.
Tangern 400.
Tannberg, the 87. 211.
Tannenalp, the 52.
Tannenburg 197.
Tannheim 22.
Tannleger, Alp 212.
Tanzbachthal 259.
Tanzboden, the 384.
Tanzenberg, château 428.
Tanzkopf, the 214.
Tappenkarsee, the 115.
Turcento 437.
Tarrenz 20.
Tartsch 251.
Tartscher Alm 278.
Tarvis 433.
Taschach Glacier 239. 245.
Taschachhütte, the 246.
Taschachjoch, the 240.
Taschachthal, the 246.
Taschl-Joch, the 242.
Tasna, Val 218.
Tatzelwurm 52. 156.
Taubenberg, the 49.
Taubensee, the 77.
Tauern, the 18. 22.
Tauernache, the 397.
Tauernfall, the 124.
Tauernkogl, the 135. 141.
Tauernthal, the 140.
Taufers (Ahrnthal) 188. 338.
— (Münsterthal) 251.
Tauferer Boden 337.
Tauferer Thal 188.
Taufkar Glacier 239.
Taufkarjoch, the 239.
Taufkarkogl, the 239.
Taugelbach, the 84.
Taulen 351.
Tauplitz 391. 393.
Taurachthal, the 397.
Tauron, the 56.
Tavernola 313.
Taviela, Mte. 311.
Tavodo 304.
Tawinferner, the 235.
Taxacher Alp 182.
Taxenbach 146.
Tayathal, the 426.
Techendorf 396.
Tedesca, Malga 307.
Tegelberg, the 15.
Tegelstein 7.
Tegernsee 44.
—, the 44.
Teglachthal, the 143.
Teglio 281.
Teichalp, the 369.
Teichlbach, the 390.
Teichlbruck 391.

Teischnitz Glacier 147.
Teisenberg, the 58. 82.
Teisendorf 56.
Telfes 227.
Telfs 20. 263.
Tellina, Val 283.
Telvana, château 318.
Tenera, Mte. 300. 298.
Tenn-Inn 171.
Tenna 317.
Tenneberg 380.
Tennengebirge 113.
Tenno 299. 304.
—, Lago di 304.
Teplitzerhütte 223. 229.
Terenten 328.
Terfens 160. 161.
Terglou, the 430.
— Lakes 431.
Terkl-Wirth 417.
Terlago 296.
Terlan 269.
Termine 318. 353.
Ternberg 384.
Ternitz 364.
Ternova 442.
Terrarossa, Mt. 317.
Terres 310.
Tersato, castle 446.
Tesero 261. 321.
Tesino, Val 318.
Tessino, the 301.
Teufelsbadstube, the 366.
Teufelsbrücke 420.
Teufelsgesass, the 32.
Teufelsgraben, the 40.
Teufelsbörner, the 74.
Teufelsmühle, the 146.
Teufenbach 426.
Tezze, le 319.
Thal (Martell) 285.
— (near Gratz) 404.
— (Pusterthal) 334. 331.
Thalgau 110.
Thalham 49.
Thalheim 425.
Thalhof 365.
Thulkirchdorf 5.
Thalkirchen 53.
Thalleitspitze, the 238.
Thalschnalp, the 55.
Thanaller, the 18. 210.
Thaur 161.
Theiss 225.
Theresienfeld 363.
Theresicuklause 71.
Thialspitze, the 235.
Thierberg, the 157.
Thiersee, the 52.
—, Hinter and Vorder 52.
Thomasroith 87.
Thoran-Alp 57.
Thorhelm, the 180.

Thorkopf, the 134.
Thörl (Thörlthal 375.
— (Gailitzthal) 433.
— (Grünsteinscharte) 19.
Thörlbach, the 375.
Thörl Glacier 134.
Thörlen, the 19.
Thörlsteig 366.
Thörlthal, the 376.
Thorsäule 113.
Thorscharte, the 113.
Thorstein, the 101. 396.
Thorsteinhöhle 377.
Three Holy Springs 277.
Thumburg, ruin 224.
Thumersbach 117.
Thumsee, the 82. 178.
Thun, château 310.
Thüringen 200.
Thurn, Pass 174.
—, château 390. 342.
Thurnerkamp 193. 186.
Thurnfeld 394.
Thurwieserspitze 279. 282.
Tiarno 300.
Tiebel, the 428.
Tiefbrunau 84. 108.
Tiefenbach, baths 8. 9.
Tiefenbach-Joch 240.
Tiefenthal-Jöchl, the 246.
Tiers 262.
Tierser Alpel 262. 323.
Tierser Thal, the 262.
Ticsens 265.
Tiffen 428.
Tiguale 302.
Tilisuna 214.
Tillfuss-Alpe 35.
Timau 330.
Timavo 441.
Timbler Bach, the 251.
— Ferner 229.
— Joch 244. 254.
Timelkam 87.
Timmersdorf 389.
Tiolo 283. 313.
Tione 304.
Tirano 284.
Tirol, Dorf 272.
—, Schloss 272.
Tisch, the 124.
Tischlkar Glacier 121.
Tisens 241.
Tisenthal, the 241.
Tisens 268.
Tiser 358.
Titschen, the 258.
S. Tiziano di Gofusa 358.
Tobelbach 404.
Tobel Fall, the 339.
Toblach 331.
Toblacher Feld, the 331.

INDEX. 487

Toblacher See, the 344.
Toblinger Riedel 333. 346.
Toblino 296.
TodteGebirge, the 98. 390.
Todtenalp, the 201.
Todte Klammen, the 83.
Todtenfeld Glacier 217.
Todtenkorspitze, the 144.
Todten Weib, Zum 372.
Todte Mann, the 72.
Tofana, Monte 350. 355.
Tognazza 325.
Tognola Alp & Pass 325.
Toinig, the 142.
Töll, the 253. 274.
Tolmezzo 436.
Tolmino 441.
Töltschach, chât. 428.
Tölz 40.
Tonadico 327.
Tonale Pass, the 312.
Toplitz-See, the 97.
Torbole 298. 299.
Tormini 309.
Torra, Val 317.
Torre 284.
Torrener-Joch 75.
Torri 301.
Tosa, Cima 306.
Toscolano 300.
Tosens 248.
Tovo 284.
Traboch 389.
Trafoi 277.
Trafoi-Bach 277. 287.
Trafoier Eiswand, the 277. 279.
Trafoier Ferner, the 277.
Trafoier Joch, the 279.
Tragössthal, the 386.
Trahütten 405.
Traisen, The 374. 379.
Tra i Sassi, Passo 342. 355.
Traithen 52. 156.
Tramer Scharte 128.
Tramin 267.
Traona 185.
Trattalpe, the 174.
Tratten 423.
Trattenbach 384.
Tratterjoch, the 190.
Tratzberg, chât. 159.
Traubing 27.
Trauchbach, the 10.
Trauchberg, the 15.
Tranchgau 14.
Trautjoch, the 229.
Traun 380.
Traun, the 55. 86. 91. 92. 96. 382.
— (Altaussee) 97.

Traun (Grundlsee) 97.
— (Oedensee) 393.
— (Rothe) 55. 58.
— (Weisse) 55. 58.
Trauueralpe, the 131.
Traun, Falls of the 86. 10.
Traunkirchen 91.
Traunkirchensee 91.
Traunsee 91.
—, the 90.
Traunstein 55.
—, the 90.
Traunweissenbach 92.
Trautenfels 393.
Trautmannsdorf 272.
Trantson, château 220.
Travernanzes, Val 350.
Travignolo, Val 321. 324.
Travnik-Sattel 432.
Trawies-Sattel 375.
Trawiesen-Alpe 375.
Traxhütte 399.
Tre Croci, Passo 345. 350.
Treffauer Kaiser 175.
Treffen 422.
Treffner Alp 387.
Treffner Bach 429.
Trefling 400.
Trollbach 427.
Tremosine 302.
Trenkelbach 93.
Trenkwald 245.
Trens 224.
Trent 293.
Trenta 432.
Trento 293.
Tre Ponti 352.
Tre Sassi, see Trai Sassi.
Tresenda 284.
Tresenga, the 310.
Tresoro, Piz 281. 283.
Tre Signori, Corno dei 283
Tresenstein 98.
Tret 316.
Tretschach 416.
Trettach, the 8.
Trettachspitze, the 12.
Tribulaun, the 220.
Tricesimo 437.
Trieben 389. 425.
Trient, see Trento.
Triesen 199.
Triesnerberg, the 199.
Triest 487.
Triesting, the 380.
Triestinghof 380.
Trifail 409.
Triglav, see Terglou.
Trinclono, Isola 301.
Trinkstein Sattel 366.
Trins 230.

Trippach, the 190.
Trippachferner 191.
Trippach Saddle 184. 190.
Trisauna 205. 213.
Trischübl 75. 76.
Trisselwand 98.
Tristach 334.
Tristenbach, the 189.
Tristensee, the 190.
Tristenspitze, or Tristner 184. 189.
Tristkopf, the 246.
Trodena, see Truden.
Trofajach 385.
Trofeng 385.
Trogalp, the 148.
Trögen 6.
Trojenstein 258.
Trojer-Thal, the 139. 143.
— Thörl, the 143.
Trostberg 215.
Trostburg 226.
Trubinasca, Piz 285.
Truden 58.
Trudering 58.
Trumersee, Ober and Nieder 88.
Tschafein 213.
Tschagerjoch, the 263.
Tschaggans 213.
Tschamintbal, the 262.
Tschamipatsch 343.
Tschapitbach, the 265.
Tschars 253.
Tschengels 252.
Tschengelser Hochwand, the 252. 289.
Tscherms 268.
Tschey-Joch, the 249.
Tscheyer Schartl, the 249.
Tschiefock, the 292.
Tschigatspitze 253. 275.
Tschirueck, the 399.
Tschislerbach, the 264.
Tschötsch 225.
Tschuggen, Alp 198.
Tschurgant, the 234.
Tuckettjoch, the 279.
Tuckettspitze, the 279.
Tuenno 310.
Tuffer 188.
Tuimino, see Tolmein.
Tümmeljoch, the 254.
Tumpen 236.
Tuoi, Val 217.
Tupalitsch 418.
Turchwand, the 124.
Türkenfeld 3.
Türkensturz 363.
Turnauer Graben 369.
Türnitz 374.
Turrach 398. 426.
Tutzing 25.

Tux 183.
Tuxer Joch 183.
Tuxerthal, the 182.
Tweng 397.
Twimberger Graben 416.
Tyrol, see Tirol.

Uderns 179.
Udine 437.
Uebelbach 369.
Uebelhorn, the 8.
Uebertsch 266.
Uebergossene Alp, the 113.
Ueberlingen 7.
Uebersaxen 199.
Ueberschall, the 160.
Uebersee 55.
Ueblenthal Glacier 222. 223.
Uenschellerspitze 209.
Uffing 27.
Uggowitz 434.
Uggwa Valley 434.
Ulmerfeld 381.
Ulmich 218.
St. Ulrich on the Piller-see 176.
— in Gardena 263.
— near Steyr 383.
Ulrichsbrücke, the 17.
Ultenthal, the 276.
Umago 444.
Umbal Glacier 144.
Umbal-Thal, the 143.
Umbalthörl, the Vordere and Hintere 144. 192.
Umbrail Pass 280.
Umbrail, Piz 280.
Umhausen 231. 236.
Ummelberg 161.
Unken 177.
Unkener Klamm 177.
Unlass-Alp 138.
Unnutz 48.
Unser Frau in the Schnalser Thal 242.
— — im Walde 310.
Unterach 109.
Unter-Ammergau 28.
Unterau (Eisak Valley) 224.
— (Stubai) 219. 228.
— (Achenthal) 58.
— (Pfitschthal) 187.
— (Gutenstein) 362. 379.
Unterbergen 420.
Unterbreth 442.
Unter-Bergau 105.
Unter-Drauburg 415.
Untereggen 261.
Unterfeicht 109.
Unterfurinch 430.
Untergicheln 211.

Unter-Grainau 81.
Unter-Grimming 393.
Unterhöfen 210.
Unterinn 259.
Unterjoch 21.
Unter-Kainisch 96.
Unterlana 268.
Unterlaner, Alp 75.
Unter-Lescee 414.
Unter-Leutasch 35.
Unter-Loibl 420.
Untermais 269. 270.
Untermof 341.
Unter-Peissenberg 26.
Unter-Perfuss 232.
Unter-Piesting 362.
Unter-Planitzing 267
Unter-Rohr 389.
Untersberg, the 67.
Unter-Schönau 210.
Unter-Schönberg 227.
Unter-Seeland 418.
Unterstein, château 73.
Unterstein (Lend) 115.
Unter-Steinbach 41.
Unter-Sulzbach Glacier 136.
Unter-Sulzbachfall 136.
Unter-Sulzbachthal 136.
Unter-Sulzbachthörl 136.
Unter-Tarvis 448.
Untertauern 397.
Unter-Vintl 326.
Unter-Wessen 50.
Unzmarkt 425.
Upsberg, the 19.
Urata, Val 431.
St. Urban 406.
Urbanova 431.
Urbeleskarspitze 13.
Urfeld 25.
Urgbach, the 247.
Uri-See, the 18.
Urkund, Oetzthaler 238.
Urschlau (Achenthal) 57.
Ursitsch-Bauer 409.
Urslau (Pinzgau) 119.
Urslauer Scharte 117.
Uspring 52. 390.
Ussprinj, the 415.
Ustelstein, the 362.
Uttendorf 135.
Uttenheim 337.
Utting 27.

Vadret, Piz 218.
Vaduz 199.
Vahrn 225. 221.
Vajolett 262. 322.
Vajolon 263.
Valaccotta 281. 282.
Valencia 322.
Valnlin 358.

Valbeson 228.
— Valley, the 229.
Valbonkogel, the 262.
St. Valentin auf der Heide 250.
— on the Enns 382.
— (Prettau) 191.
— (Seisser Alp) 265.
— (Villnöss) 225.
Valentin valley, the 335.
S. Valentino, Val 304.
Valentinthörl 385.
Valina, Alp 199.
Valle 342. 351.
Valles Pass 325.
Vallesina, the 351.
Vallon Bianco, the 348.
Vallonga 202.
Vallorsch-Thal, the 199.
Vallüla-Spitze, the 210.
Valpera 349.
Valparola, Alp 342.
Vals 328.
Valschaviel 215.
Valschavielkopf 215.
Valserthal (Brenner) 221.
— (Pusterthal) 328.
Valsorda 317.
Valstagna 319.
Valtellina, the 283.
Valvasor Hütte 420.
Valzarego see Falzarego.
Valzerfenz-Thal 215.
Vandans 213.
Vanitscharte, the 146.
Vanoi 326.
Varda 328. 343.
Varignano 297.
Varone 297. 299.
Vattaro 317.
Vedorchia, Mte. 352.
Veglia 446.
St. Veit (Carinthia) 428.
— (Defereggen) 139.
— an der Gölsen 379.
— (Prags) 331.
— (Pongau) 115.
— (Sexten) 332.
— an der Triesting 380.
St. Veit-Bruckl 103.
Veitlbauern-Alm 399.
Veitsberg, the 52.
Veitsch 368.
Veitschalp, the 368. 371.
Veitschbachthörl 371.
Veitschtlul 368.
St. Veitskapf, the 199.
Veitschtlul, the 368.
Veitsbach, the 141.
Velber Tauern, the 141.
— Thal, the 135.
Velden am See 424.
Veldes 429.

INDEX. 489

Veliki Vrh, the 442.
Velka Kappa 415.
Vellach, Bad 417.
— (near Villach) 422.
— (Wochein) 430.
Vellacher Kotschna 417.
Vellern 146.
Veltlin, see Valtellina.
Venaders 221.
Venas 351. 353.
Venediger, see Gross-Venediger.
Veneggie Alp 357.
Veneggie, Val 325.
Venerocolo, Mte. 307.
Venetberg, the 235. 247.
Veneziaspitze, the 286.
Venexia, Val 312.
Vennabach, the 221.
Venosta 284.
Vens 213.
Vent 238.
Venter Thal, the 238.
Venzonazza, the 437.
Venzone 437.
Veranisjoch 436.
Verbeila-Bach 204. 216.
Verda 343.
Verdins 275.
Vereinsalpe, the 35.
Verona, Mte. 318.
Vergalden 216.
Vergaldner Jöchl 215.
Vergetschen 247.
Vergrösskar, the 203.
Vermaies Alp 199.
Vermiglio, Val 312.
Vermuhlbach 215.
Vermunt, Gross and Klein 216.
Vermuntbach, the 216.
Vermunt Pass, the 216.
Vermunt Glacier 217.
Vermunt Thal 216.
Vernagelwand, the 240.
Vernale, Sasso 324.
Vernel, Monte 323.
Verona 296.
—, Chiusa di 295.
Verpailjoch, the 246.
Versailspitze, the 216.
Verschitz-Sattel 432.
Vertainspitze 289. 293.
Vesena 318.
Vesilspitze, the 216.
Vesilthal, the 218.
Vestino, Val 300.
Vestone 309.
Vette di Feltre 326.
Vezza 312.
Vezzana, Cima 326.
Vezzano 296.
Vico 436.

Victorsberg 198.
Videgg 275.
Viechl 160.
Viechter Kanzl 160.
Vichofen 118.
Vierhöfer Thal, see Fierozza.
Viehkogl, the 75.
Vigaun 420. 429.
St. Vigil 340. 337.
Vigiljoch, the 274.
Vigilthal, the 340.
S. Vigilio, promont. 304.
—, chapel 305.
Vignole 298.
Vigo (Giudicaria) 304.
— (Val di Non) 310.
— di Fassa 322.
Vigolo 296. 317.
Viktring 421.
Vill 170.
Villa (Rendena) 304.
— Grande (Auronzo) 352.
— Piccola 352.
— Lagarina 295.
Villach 422.
—, baths 422.
Villacher Alp 422.
Villacher Hütte 400.
Villanders 226. 259.
Villgratten 139. 333.
Villgratinerjoch, the 139.
Villgraitenthal, the 333.
Villnöss 225.
Villnössthal, the 225.
Vilminore 313.
Vilpian 269.
Vils 14. 22.
—, the 14. 22.
Vilsalper See, the 22.
Vilsrein 22.
Vilsthal, the 22.
Viltragen Glacier 136.140.
Vinil 328.
Vintschgau, the 250.
Viola, Val 282.
Vios, Cima 312.
—, Monte 312.
Virgen 141.
Virgenthal, the 139.
Virgllenberg 426.
Virgl 258.
Visdende, Val 352.
Vismöy-Thal, the 248.
Vitelli, Val 281.
S. Vito 351.
Vittorio 354.
Viznarje 429.
Vobarno 309.
Vöckla, the 87.
Vöcklabruck 87.
Vöcklamarkt 87.
Voda 351.

Vogedura Valley 337.
Vogelbach, the 435.
Vogelweiderhof 283.
Vois-Thal, the 365.
Volderau 228.
Volderer Bad 161.
Volders 160.
Volder-Thal, the 161.
Völkermarkt 417.
Völlan 268.
Voloska 413.
Völs near Bolzen 265.
— near Innsbruck 231.
Voltago 358.
Volxano 441.
Vomp 160.
Vomper Bach, the 160.
Vomper Thal, the 160.
Voralpe 381. 384.
Vöran 275.
Vorarlberg 195.
Vorberg 167.
Vorderbrand 72.
Vorder-Dux 183.
Vorderock 71.
Vorder-Capelljoch 214.
Vorder-Gusau 100.
Vorder-Graseck 30.
Vorder-Hindelang 20.
Vorder-Hornbach 13.
Vorderjoch, the 21.
Vorderkaser-Klamm 177.
Vorderlochberg-Alp 40.
Vordernberg 385.
Vorderriss 35. 42.
Vorder-Stoder 391.
Vorberg, the 423.
Vorkloster 196.
Vösslau 302.
Vulpmes 228.

Waasen 424.
Wacht 111.
Wackersberg 11.
Wagenau 56.
Wagenbach, the 433.
Wagenbrech-See, the 34.
Waggraben 385.
Wagrein 115. 397.
Wahlen 332.
Waidbrück 226.
Waidhofen 351.
Waidisch 420.
Waidring 176.
Waisach 336.
Waizinger Alp 50.
Walchen 135.
Walchen, the 42.
Walchensee 35. 39.
—, the 33. 38.
Walcheralpe, the 130. 131.
Walchern Thal 323.
Walchsee 58.

490   INDEX.

Wald (Arlberg) 202.
— (Liesingthal) 389.
— (Nassereit) 20.
Wald (Pinzgau) 137.
Waldbachstrub, the 99.
Waldberg 181.
Waldbrunn 330.
Waldegg 362.
Walder Alpe 161.
Waldhornalpe 396.
Wählilitobel Bridge 202.
Waldrastersptiz, the 227.
Waldstein 370.
Walgau, Inner 200.
Wallberger Alp, the 46.
Wallenburger Alp 51.
Waller Alp, the 157.
Waller Bach, the 303.
Wallersee, the 87.
Wallfahrts-Jöchl, the 246.
Wallgau 30.
Wallnerhütte, the 152.
Wallnerinsel, the 74.
Walnberg, the 56.
Walser Alp, the 214.
Walser Schanzle 9, 10.
Walser Thal, the Grosse 200, 208.
—, the Kleine 9.
Walten 254.
Waltenbergerhaus 12.
Waltenhofen 4.
Walten-Thal, the 254.
Wang 29.
Waugenitzthal, the 150.
Wanneck, the 19.
Wanner 426.
Warschegg 416.
Warscheneck, the 391.
Wart 266.
Wartberg 368, 390.
Wartberg-Kogel, the 368.
Wartenfels 110.
Wartenstein 364.
Warth 13, 271.
Warthorn, the 211.
Wasach 9.
Wasenspitze, the 201.
Wasserburg 7.
Wasserfall-Alp, the 133.
Wasserfallboden 133.
Wasserfallspitze 339.
Wasserklamm, the 382.
Wasserstubentafel 215.
Wastelbauer 399.
Waltens 100.
Watzekopf, the 246.
Watzmann, the 69, 76.
Waxeck 185.
Waxenstein, the 31.
Waxriegel, the 365.
Wechsel, the 363.
Wechselalp, the 45.

Wegscheid (Bavaria) 42.
—, (Styria) 371, 374.
Wehrgrube, the Grosse and Kleine 176.
Weichselbachhöhe 129.
Weichselbacher Thal 129.
Weichselboden 376.
Weichselthal 362.
Weidberg Alp 47.
Weidenkamp 25.
Weidenthal, the 183.
Weidlingau 379.
Weierhof 136.
Weiherbad 331.
Weiherburg 170.
Weilburg 362.
Weiler 6, 8, 198.
Weilheim 26.
Weinasch 420.
Weinbach, the 103.
Weinebene 405.
Weinleite, the 56.
Weinzetielwand, the 367.
Weiskirchen 404.
Weissach (Algan) 207.
— (Weissensee-Thal) 336.
—, — (Tegernsee) 46.
Weissachthal, near Kufstein 158.
— (Bregenzer Wald) 7.
—, near Adelholzen 55.
Weissbach (Pfronten) 14.
— (near Inzell) 55.
— (near Reichenhall) 78.
—, the (near Inzell) 55.
— (Saalachthal) 81, 82, 119.
—, — (Görlos) 180.
Weisslachelscharte 119.
Weissbriach 336.
Weissbriachthal, the 368.
Weisskirchen 416, 425.
Weisse Knott, the 278.
Weisse Kogl, the 239.
Weissenbach on the Lech 22, 210.
— (Ahrnthal) 189.
— (Attersee) 109, 92.
— (Ennsthal) 392.
—, the (near Ischl) 95.
—, the (Ahrnthal) 189.
— (near Kössen) 58.
— on the Enus 392.
— on the Triesting 380.
Weissenbach - St. Gallen 391, 384.
Weissenbachthal 58, 85, 109, 189.
Weissenberg, chât. 389.
Weissenegg, chât. 405.
Weissenecker Scharte, the 136.
Weissenfels 432.

Weissenfels lake 432.
Weissenreute 196.
Weissensee (near Lermoos) 19.
— — (near Füssen) 14.
— — (Carinthin) 336.
Weissensee-Thal 336.
Weissenstein, chât. 139.
—, monastery 261.
Weisse Wand 188.
Weisshorn 261.
Weisskirchen 425.
Weisskugel 239, 242, 250, 251.
Weisskngeljoch, the 250.
Weisslahnbad 262.
Weisslofer Thal 57, 58.
Weissplatter, the 274.
Weissaee, the (Kauuserthal) 245.
— (Stubachthal) 146.
Weisseeejoch, the 248.
Weisseeespitze 248.
Weisszint, the 187, 189.
Weisszintscharte 189.
Weitenberg Alpe 323.
Weitenegg 380.
Weitensfeld 427.
Weitenstein 407.
Weitenthal, the 323.
Weitlahnbrunn 333.
Weitsee, the 57.
Welitz Glacier 144.
Welka Kappa 416.
Wellenburg 3.
Wels 86.
Welsberg 330.
Welschellen 311.
Welschnofen 261.
Welskogel 205.
Welzelach 141.
Welzenegg 418.
Wendelstein 50, 51, 156.
Weng 87, 388.
Wengen 342.
Wengenalp, the 11, 21.
Wengenthal, the 342.
Wenns 245.
Werdenfels 29.
Werfen 113.
Wernberg 421.
Werlach 21.
Wertach, the 3, 14.
Wertatscha Sattel 420.
Wery Hütte 183.
Wessen, Ober and Unter 56.
Westendorf 172.
Westerreingen 3.
Westerham 53.
Westerhof 45.
Wetterkogel, the 375.
Wetterkreuz, the 83.

INDEX. 491

Wetterschroffen, the 18.
Wetterspitze, the Innere and Aeussere 229.
Wetterstein Alp 32.
Wettersteingebirge 18. 32.
Wetterwand, the 113.
Weyarn 49.
Weyer 369. 382.
Weyerburg 138.
Weyregg 109.
Weyrer Lindl, the 49.
Widderstein, the 209.
Wieden 206. 187.
Wiedersberger Horn 179.
Wiedhof, château 368.
Wielinger Glacier 134.
— Scharte, the 134.
Wien, the 379.
Wienerbrückl 373.
Wiener Hütte 187.
Wiener-Neustadt 368.
Wiener-Neustädter Hütte 33.
Wiener Wald, the 379.
Wies 401.
Wiesalp, the 42. 100.
Wiesbachhorn 130. 134. 153.
Wiesbach-Thörl 134.
Wiesberg, the 157.
Wiesberg, châl. 205. 219.
Wieselburg 880.
Wieselsdorf 104.
Wiesen 188. 218. 245. 363.
Wiesenschwang 120.
Wiesensee, the 119.
Wieserhütte 396.
Wieshäusle 62.
Wiessee 44.
Wiessneck 174.
Wiesthal 81. 108.
Wildalpen 377. 376.
Wildbad Gastein 121.
Wildbichl 55.
Wildebene Glacier 202.
Wildegg 150.
Wilde Freiger, the 223.
Wilde Gerlos, the 180.
Wilde Kogel, the 89.
Wilde Kreuzspitze 187. 224.
Wilde Krimml, the 179.
Wilde Manul, the (Algau) 11.
— (Oetzthal) 238.
Wilde Pfaff 228.
Wildensee, the 411.
Wildenstein, ruin 94.
Wildenstein Waterfall 417.
Wildenthal 78. 176.
Wilde See 92. 187. 221.
Wildgall 339.

Wildgerlosspitze 180.
Wildgraben, the Innicher 332.
Wildgraben-Joch 332. 345.
Wildgrat 234.
Wildgrub 156.
Wildhaus 415.
Wildkar, the 100.
Wildkogel, the 136.
Wildlahnerthal, the 183.
Wildlochscharte 396.
Wildon 405.
Wildpoldsried 4.
Wildsee, the 37.
Wildspitze, the Venter 239. 246.
Wildstelle, the Hohe 396.
Wilhelmsburg 379.
Willeck 177.
Willersalp, the 21.
Wilten, Abbey 167.
Wilzhofen 26.
Wimbach-Klamm, the 76.
Wimbachthal, the 76.
Wimmerbach, the 180.
Windach Glacier 230.
— Thal 230.
Windauer Thal, the 172.
Windbachthal 138. 192.
Windegg 267.
Windische Bühel 406.
Windisch-Bleiberg 420.
Windisch-Feistritz 407.
Windisch-Garsten 391.
Windischgratz 415.
Windischgrätzhöhe 128.
Windisch-Matrei 130.
Windisch-Scharte 128.
Windleger Scharte 396.
Windlucke, the 191. 396.
Windschar 329. 337.
Windthal, the 144.
Winkel (Isarthal) 42.
— (Wolfgangsee) 108.
— (Mollthal) 151.
—, baths 338.
Winkelmoosalp, the 57.
Winkelthal, the 139.
Winklern 149.
Winnebach Ferner 232.
Winterjöchl, the Gallauer 204. 245.
—, the Gaschurner 216.
—, the Silberthaler 215.
—, the Verbellner 204.
Winterleitseen, the 425.
Winterstall 238.
Wird 216.
Wirtatobel, the 6.
Wischberg, the 443.
Wischberg Hütte 413.
Wistra-Sattel 408.
Witnach 439.

Wittmannsdorf 362. 380.
Wochein, the 430.
Wocheiner Save, the 430.
— See, the 430.
Wolayer Pass 436. 335.
— See 335.
Wolfbauer 387.
Wolfendornspitze 221.
St. Wolfgang (Rein) 389.
— (Salzburg) 105.
— (Styria) 406.
Wolfganghütte 399.
St. Wolfgangs-Bad 129.
St. Wolfgangs-See 107.
Wolfkehr 247.
Wolfrathshausen 41.
Wolfsbach 434. 443.
Wolfsbachgraben 434.
Wolfsberg 224. 415. 427.
Wolfsbergkogel 367.
Wolfsegg 87.
Wolfsgraben 380. 379.
Wolfsgruben 259.
Wolfsschlucht 46.
Wolfsthurn 223.
Wolfurt 106.
Wolkenstein (Gardena) 264.
— (Ennsthal) 392.
Wöllaner-Nock 422.
Wöllatlhal 150. 336.
Wöllatration 150. 336.
Wöllersdorf 362.
Woltschach 441.
Wölzer Thal, the 425.
Wommelberg 247.
Wöping 362.
Wörgl 158.
Worms 282.
Wormser Joch 280.
— Loch 281.
Wörner, the 85.
Wornsmühl 50.
Wörsebach 392.
Wörth (Rauris) 127.
Wörther See, the 419.
Wörtlsee, the 27.
Wotsch, the 407.
Wuchern 415.
Wurbauer-Kogl 391.
Wurm, the 3.
Wurmsau 28.
Wurmsee, the 21.
Wurten Glacier, the 128.
Wurzen 432.
Wurzener Save, the 432.
Wurzen Pass 225.
Wüstlau 133.

Ybbs 373.
Ybbs, the 373. 381.
Ybbsitz 382.

INDEX

Zaberbach, the 180.
Zagurie 411.
Zaibach, the 288.
Zaithal, the 289.
Zallinger Alp, the 263.
Zamangspitze, the 215.
Zamaugtobel, the 215.
Zams 234.
Zamser Alp, the 186.
Zamsorbach, the 186.
Zamsergrund, the 186.
Zangenberg 197.
Zanzenberg, the 261.
Zaprahalhal 434.
Zargenmauer 378.
Zarkenboden 375. 377.
Zarz 429.
Zauchen 393.
Zauchengraben 417.
Zaule 440.
Zaunhof 245.
Zavnikbauer 409.
Zeblesjoch, the 218.
Zebru, the 291. 282.
—, Val 282.
—, Passo 282.
Zederhausthal 308.
Zehnkaser Alp 67.
Zeier, the 429.
Zeiger, the 11. 21.
Zeilbach 27.
Zeinis-Joch, the 216.
Zeiritzkampel 389.
Zeisberg-Alp, the 66.
Zeiselbach, the 45.
Zeitschach 426.
Zell, Bairisch 51.
— on the Inn 57.
— am Moos 110.
— near Ruhpolding 57.
— am See 116.
— in the Zillerthal 179.
Zell-Freibach 420.
Zell-Pfarr 420.
Zellerburg 157.
Zeller Moos 116.
Zellerrain 157 373.

Zeller See (Pinzgau) 116.
— (Salzburg) 110.
Zeltweg 424
Zemmbach, the 182. 184.
Zemmgrund 185.
Zemmthal, the 183.
St. Zeno (Val di Non) 310.
— (near Reichenhall) 81.
Zenoburg, the 272.
Zephirau, the 174.
Zerbenriegel 367.
Zesenthal, the 189.
Zettenkaiser, the 175.
Ziano 321.
Ziegerberg 213.
Zieler-Alpe 275.
Zielspitze, the 272.
Zielthal, the 274.
Zigolon 308.
Zikafahnler Alp 366.
Zill 84.
Ziller, the 179. 182.
Zillergrund, the 182.
Zillerkopf, the 180.
Zillerthal, the 178.
Zimbaspitze, the 214.
Zimitz, the 94.
Zimmers, see Cembra.
Zinken, the 98.
Zinken, Seckauer 389.
—, Stoder 304.
Zinscler, the 222.
Zipf 87.
Zipfelsalp, the 21.
Zirbitzkogl, the 425. 426.
Zirknitz 411.
Zirknitz, the Kleine 128.
Zirknitz, the Grosse 128.
Zirknitzfall, the 150.
Zirknitzer See, the 411.
Zirknitzscharte, the 128.
Zirknitzthal 128. 150.
Zirl 37. 232.
Zirmenkopf, the 201.
Zirm-See, the 151.
Zistelalp, the 66.

Zitterauer Alp, the 124.
Zlacken-Sattel 375.
Zlainitzbach 150.
Zlappfall, the 150.
Znachsattel 396. 398.
Znachthal 398.
Zochenpass, the 335.
Zoderalpe 416.
Zoldo, Val di 353.
Zollfeld, the 427.
Zopetnitz Thal, the 142.
Zoppè 353.
Zorneding 53.
Zovo, Mte. 352.
Zsigmondy Hütte 383.
Zsigmondispitze 185.
Zucco, Mte. 352.
Zuckerhutl 231. 223.
Zuelò 304.
Zuel 354.
Zufall, see Covedale
Zufall Glacier, the 286.
Zufall-Hütte 286.
Zufritterner, the 286.
Zufrittjoch, the 286
Zufrittspitze, the 286
Zug 212.
Zuglio 336.
Zugspitze, the 33.
Zumeles 347. 349.
Zunderköpfe, the 161.
Zunigkopf, the 140.
Zürs 212.
Zürsbach, the 211.
Zwenewald-Thal 139.
Zwerger 39.
Zwiesel, the 41. 82.
Zwieselalp, the 82. 101.
Zwieselstein 238. 254.
Zwillings Fall 399.
Zwingsteg, the 9.
Zwischenwässern 420
Zwischenwasser 340.
Zwölfferkofel, the 333.
Zwölferkogl, the 99.
Zwölferkopf, the 209.

www.ingramcontent.com/pod-product-compliance
Lightning Source LLC
Chambersburg PA
CBHW031947290426
44108CB00011B/711